Hoover's Handbook of

Edited by
Gary Hoover,
Alta Campbell, Alan Chai,
and Patrick J. Spain

Hoover's Handbooks are intended to provide their readers with accurate and authoritative information about the enterprises profiled in them. The Reference Press asked all profiled companies and organizations to provide information for its books. Many did so; a number did not. The information contained herein is as accurate as we could reasonably make it. In many cases we have relied on third-party material that we believe to be trustworthy but were unable to independently verify. We do not warrant that the book is absolutely accurate or without any errors. Readers should not rely on any information contained herein in instances where such reliance might cause loss or damage. The editors and publishers specifically disclaim all warranties, including the implied warranties of merchantability and fitness for a specific purpose. This book is sold with the understanding that neither the editors nor the publisher is engaged in providing investment, financial, accounting, legal, or other professional advice.

The financial data (How Much section and Where and What tables) in this book are from a variety of sources. For US publicly traded companies with American Depository Receipts and companies that trade directly on US exchanges, when data are shown in US dollars, Standard & Poor's Compustat, Inc., provided the data (except for Mexican companies, for which The Reference Press calculated US dollar amounts). For country profiles, the Economist Intelligence Unit provided the data for the How Much section and for the Export/Import and Origins of GDP tables. All other financial and economic data were prepared by The Reference Press from publicly available documents and reports and from information provided directly from the enterprises profiled. The Reference Press, Inc., is solely responsible for the presentation of all data.

Many of the names of products and services mentioned in this book are the trademarks or service marks of the companies manufacturing or selling them and are subject to protection under US law. Space has not permitted us to indicate which names are subject to such protection, and readers are advised to consult with the owners of such marks regarding their use.

Copyright © 1991 by The Reference Press, Inc. All rights reserved. No part of this book may be reproduced or transmitted in any form or by any means, electronic or mechanical, including by photocopying, recording, or using any information storage and retrieval system, without permission in writing from The Reference Press, Inc., except that brief passages may be quoted by a reviewer in a magazine, newspaper, or broadcast review.

10 9 8 7 6 5 4 3 2 1

Publisher Cataloging-In-Publication Data

Hoover's Handbook of World Business 1992. Edited by Gary Hoover, Alta Campbell, Alan Chai, and Patrick J. Spain

Includes indexes.
1. Business enterprises — Directories. 2. Corporations — Directories.
HF3010 338.7

Hoover's Handbooks are available on-line on Mead Data Central, Inc.'s Lexis/Nexis service and in Sony Data Discman Electronic Book format.

ISBN 1-878753-02-9
ISSN 1055-7199

This book was produced by The Reference Press on Apple Macintosh computers using Aldus Corporation's PageMaker 4.01 software and Adobe Systems, Inc.'s fonts from the Clearface and Futura families. Maps were created using Adobe Illustrator and MapArt software, a product of MicroMaps Software, Inc. Graphs were created using DeltaGraph, a product of DeltaPoint, Inc. Cover design is by Hixo, Inc., of Austin, Texas. Electronic prepress was done by The Courier Connection at Westford, Massachusetts, and the book was printed by the Courier Corporation at Kendallville, Indiana. Text paper is 60# Windsor offset (manufactured by Domtar) and cover paper is 10 point, coated one side, film laminated.

This book is distributed to the North American book trade exclusively by

PUBLISHERS GROUP WEST

4065 Hollis, Emeryville, California 94608 415-658-3453

Hoover's Handbooks are available at special discounts for bulk purchases for sales promotions, premiums, fund-raising, or educational use. Special editions or book excerpts can also be created to specification. For details, contact Patrick Spain at **The Reference Press, Inc.**, 6448 Highway 290 East, Suite E-104, Austin, Texas 78723 Phone: 512-454-7778 Fax: 512-454-9401

Contents

Countries Profiled

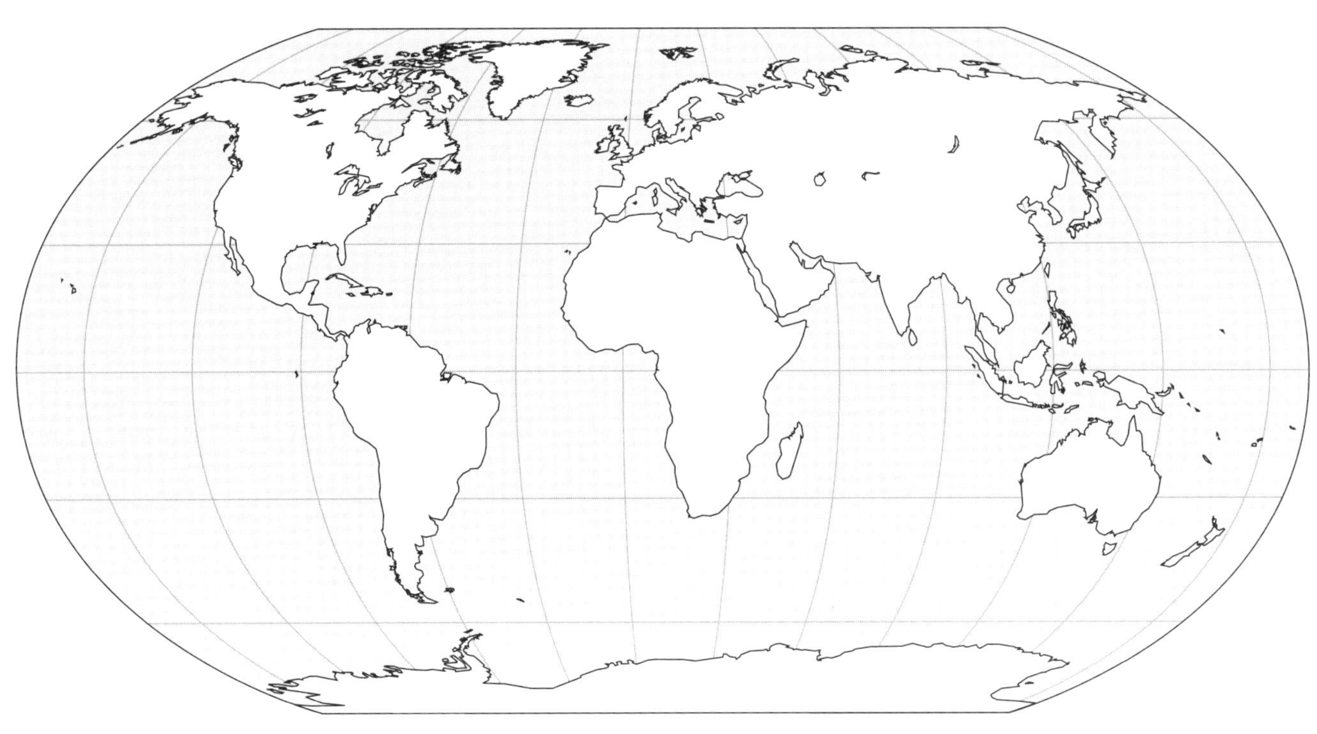

Companies Profiled

ACKNOWLEDGMENTS

Publisher and Senior Editor: Gary Hoover
Editor-in-Chief: Alta Campbell (AMC)
Senior Editor: Patrick J. Spain (PJS)
Senior Writer and Editor: Alan Chai (AC)
Production Director: Holly Whitten (HW)
Desktop Publishing/Art Director: Marcia Jenkins
Senior Writers: Cliff Avery (CA), Dale Ann Bean Underwood (DABU), John Mark Haney (JMH)
Office Manager: Tammy Fisher
Director of Special Markets: Lawrence A. Hagemann (LAH)
Editorial Board: Ray Bard, Steve Mathews

Contributing Writer
Barbara M. Spain (BMS)

Financial Editors
Cynthia G. Dooley, Bram Goodwin, Maryellen Maurer, Wendy Weigant

Senior Editors
Jeff Morris, Deborah Stratton

Senior Proofreaders and Fact Checkers
Peter A. Balderas, Britton E. Jackson, Jeanne Minnich, Jim Patterson

Proofreaders and Fact Checkers
Kathryn A. Baker, Sara Barker, Paul Beutelman, Tara Ellis, Kim L. Emery, Nick Evans, K. C. Francis, Linda Gittins, Diane Lee, Liz Taute, Lori Vermaas, Barbara E. Wand

Senior Desktop Publishers
Scott T. Allen, Kristin M. Jackson, Mercedes Newman

Desktop Publisher
Monica Shomos

Indexers
Alana Cash, Linda Webster

Marketing Assistant
Lisa Treviño

Other Contributors
Scott A. Blech (SAB), Cheryl E. Branch, David Henry Sanders (DHS)

Note: At the bottom of each profile, we have placed the initials of the writer(s) responsible for that page.

We lovingly dedicate this book to our parents:

Eva B. Campbell, Chi-Hui Chai, Feng-Yang Chai, Judith E. Hoover, Wilbur C. Hoover, James W. Spain

and in memory of:

Ronda J. Campbell, Edith J. Spain

The Reference Press Mission Statement

1. To produce business and economic reference books of the highest quality, accuracy, and readability
2. To make those books widely available through mass distribution at an affordable price
3. To make sure people are aware of our product through publicity, advertising, and shelf exposure
4. To create interesting, worthwhile jobs
5. To reward our employees creatively and fairly, without prejudice
6. To allow our key people to participate in the fruits of their labor through an incentive stock option program
7. To hold to the highest ethical business standards, including complete honesty and openness in all our dealings, erring on the side of generosity when in doubt
8. To enhance the wealth of our suppliers, from distributors and printers to landlords
9. To continually expand our product line
10. To enhance the wealth of our shareholders by creating an enterprise of lasting value

Navigating the
New World Order

Last year we at The Reference Press broke new ground with the first annual publication of *Hoover's Handbook*. This book, the first reasonably priced, widely distributed, easy-to-use corporate reference annual, was an immediate hit. Since its publication we have received numerous cards, letters, and phone calls, and we have continued to study the world of business.

From all this input we have concluded that the world of business really does involve the whole world. In the 1950s, giant corporations were largely an American and European phenomenon. Today the idea of the large profit-driven business enterprise is accepted globally. While it is obvious to anyone with open eyes that world politics are changing, it may be less obvious that world economics are changing just as fast.

If you're looking for a job, you may be missing great opportunities if you are unwilling to talk to foreign-owned firms such as Doubleday Publishing, Universal Studios, and Lever Brothers. If you are selling products but don't call on Toyota, Honda, and Panasonic, you're missing the boat. If you're buying stocks but not considering foreign companies, you may be cheating yourself out of opportunities at Sony, Shell, Nestlé, and Reuters.

To fully describe this new world order of business, we have substantially expanded our coverage of business outside the United States, resulting in the publication of this book, companion volume to *Hoover's Handbook of American Business 1992* (to be published in late 1991). This book consists of the following 4 components:

1. This section, "Navigating the New World Order," describes the nature of international business, describes the trends at work, and looks at the futures of several specific countries ("Winners and Losers for the '90s"). We then go on to look briefly at investing abroad, review our list of the top ten companies for the '90s, and conclude with information on how to understand the profiles and where to look for further information.

   Last year the front section of the book contained a brief summary of business: how it works, how it's measured, and what all the statistics mean. Many of our readers found this section useful: it appears again in *Hoover's Handbook of American Business 1992*.

2. The next section, "A List-Lover's Compendium," contains numerous lists of the largest companies in the book, the largest companies in key industries, and major stock indexes.

3. The 2 main sections of the book contain concise one-page profiles of key economic entities: first, 66 significant regions and nations, and the United Nations; second, 165 corporations of global importance. Virtually all of these companies are based outside the United States, and most are public companies.

4. The book concludes with 3 indexes: first, an index of profiles by headquarters location; second, an index of companies by industry; and, finally, a complete index of all the names (brands, companies, people, and places) used in the profiles.

We hope you continue to find our books useful and have again included a postage-paid postcard at the back of the book on which you may send us your comments, questions, and orders.

The Editors
Austin, Texas, September 18, 1991

THE ROLE OF THE UNITED STATES IN A CHANGING WORLD

"Most of us were born into a world where 'the Big Three' meant GM, Ford, and Chrysler; we may leave a world where the Big Three are Toyota, Nissan, and Daimler-Benz."

We believe that it is more important than ever for Americans to understand the "rest of the world." As we have said before, most of us were born into a world where "the Big Three" meant GM, Ford, and Chrysler; we may leave a world where the Big Three are Toyota, Nissan, and Daimler-Benz. Where does America fit into this changing world?

We've all seen the same headlines: America bought out by Japanese; America losing market share; America needs to learn the lessons of Japanese management; "fortress Europe" will be tough to compete with. Along with these economic statements, much has been written about the changing role of America in terms of diplomacy and defense. Many of these headlines are pretty pessimistic or, at best, worried.

Our travels around the world, and our investigations of the major companies of the world, have led us to some different conclusions. They don't make such stunning headlines, but we think our conclusions will be more helpful in understanding an admittedly changing world.

One hundred years ago, America itself was very fractured: South hated North, North hated South, and every young man headed West. "Yankees" preferred beer from Milwaukee, pianos from New York, and horses from Kentucky. Today, we are a more unified and less regional society: we have matured. We don't mind that our biggest retailer is from Arkansas, our leading shoemaker is in Oregon.

We believe that the next 20 to 50 years will see the world go through a similar change; at least, we hope so. Already, airlines from Frankfurt to Singapore prefer planes from Seattle (Boeing); viewers from Stockholm to Sydney prefer TVs from Tokyo; women from Buenos Aires to Boca Raton prefer their perfume from Paris (L'Oréal).

As labor and other costs (e.g., the US has some of the cheapest real estate in the developed world) become more equal, actual production of products spreads out. Just as Milwaukee-based Miller now makes its beer in Texas and California, Matsushita is making its famed Panasonic products everywhere from the US to Europe. America's ability to overcome its own regional differences should serve as a model for the world as a whole.

The world seems topsy-turvy. America's high-end stereo makers ship 60% of their product to Japan. GE TVs and RCA camcorders are made by a French company. The latest hardware-store gadget, which uses radar to measure room sizes, is made in China. CBS Records and Columbia Pictures are parts of a Japanese company. Jaguar and Lotus are part of Ford and GM. But this is not a topsy-turvy world; it is one that is beginning to make sense, and one that is above all else inevitable.

People are writing books, telling us to be afraid of all the purchases of American companies and real estate by the Japanese. These are the same type of people who told us to be afraid of being owned by the "Arabs" 20 years ago, the same type of people who told the Europeans to be afraid of us 30 years ago when we were "buying them up." Thank heavens these people weren't around 150 years ago when the British financed our American railroad system.

What could be more American than the movie *E. T.* and Tom Clancy novels, both from MCA Inc.? Should we have been petrified when Matsushita, the Panasonic people, bought MCA for $6.6 billion? Our Secretary of the Interior was publicly petrified at the thought that the Japanese would sell us our snacks at Yosemite Park, the concession being held by another part of MCA.

As business analysts we see the following: if Matsushita wants to rape MCA, they will have to take every cent of MCA's profits out of the US for about 20 years just to break even — to get back the money they just put into American pockets when they bought the company. If, on the other hand, Matsushita really wants to profit from their new (and largest ever) acquisition, it is more likely they will pour more and more money into MCA, and they will take advantage of what they really bought: the demonstrated superiority of American creativity when it comes to entertaining people. We find Matsushita's purchase of MCA no more alarming than General Electric's effort to become Europe's light-bulb maker, including their investment in a large Hungarian firm.

As we enter this new era of "globalization," where does America stand? Do we make shoddy, uncompetitive products? In some areas the answer is certainly yes. In many areas, such as cameras and TVs, we barely try. But look around you. Travel to Europe and look around you; travel to Asia and look around you. Who makes the airliners, the shampoo, the records, the soft drinks, the movies, the novels, the computer programs?

America is far from dead. We believe that America will play a more important role in this new world economy than any other single nation. No one, from Moscow to Beijing, can argue with the fact that America is the "world headquarters" of higher education, of science, of innovation, and of entrepreneurship. It is a leadership role we will increasingly share, but only because others will learn from us. They aren't stupid. ▲

"We believe that America will play a more important role in this new world economy than any other single nation."

WORLD TRADE IN THE GLOBAL ECONOMY

"The total world economy is somewhere around $20 trillion."

The Size of the Global Economy

Anyone who studies international economics knows that the underlying statistics are in rough shape. Throughout this book we have tried to use uniform sources for such numbers as annual Gross Domestic Product (GDP), an indicator of the size of each country's economy. However, no one can honestly claim that we really know the GDP of the Soviet Union. Converting those estimates into a common currency is another challenge, especially in areas like Latin America, where national currencies inflate rapidly and continuously.

Nevertheless, it appears that the total world economy is somewhere around $20 trillion. That's a lot. A trillion is a million million. A trillion seconds is just over 31,000 years.

Of this, the United States represents $5½ trillion, or about ¼ of the world's economic activity. By definition, this is ¼ of the world's production as well as ¼ of the consumption.

The next biggest factor in the world, with a $3 trillion economy, is Japan. In other words, it is about half as important as the United States. The Japanese economy is followed by five others that are each in the $1.0–1.5 trillion range: Germany (the biggest), France, Italy, the United Kingdom, and probably the Soviet Union.

These seven nations together represent over 75% of world economic activity. If you drop out the Soviet Union and add back in the other members of the Organization for Economic Cooperation and Development (OECD; see box at right), the percentage is even higher, with less than 20% of the world's 5 billion people.

The 25 Largest Free-Market Economies

Rank	Country	1990 Gross Domestic Product ($ bil.)
1	United States	5,423
2	Japan	2,932
3	Germany	1,493
4	France	1,190
5	Italy	1,072
6	United Kingdom	971
7	Canada	579
8	Spain	492
9	Brazil	355
10	Australia	295
11	Netherlands	276
12	Mexico	238
13	India	231
14	Korea	228
15	Sweden	228
16	Switzerland	228
17	Belgium	198
18	Taiwan	157
19	Denmark	128
20	Turkey	109
21	Indonesia	104
22	South Africa	101
23	Saudi Arabia	95
24	Thailand	83
25	Greece	68

OECD: The Developed World

Australia	Japan
Austria	Luxembourg
Belgium	The Netherlands
Canada	New Zealand
Denmark	Norway
Finland	Portugal
France	Spain
Germany	Sweden
Greece	Switzerland
Iceland	Turkey
Ireland	United Kingdom
Italy	United States

The Scope of International Business

Within this context "foreign trade" is of major importance: broadly defined, we estimate it at over $7 trillion, or more than ⅓ of all economic activity. This proportion has grown substantially since World War II and can be expected to continue to grow as the world economy becomes more unified.

In "trading states" like the Netherlands, Singapore, or Hong Kong, foreign trade is much more important as a percentage of economic activity than it is in large, self-sufficient nations like the United States. In other words, Hong Kong would not survive without trade, whereas it is merely a nice plus to the giant American economy.

Nevertheless, because of the huge size of America, we are the most important force in world trade, representing perhaps ⅐ of world trade and 20% more international economic activity than either #2 Germany or #3 Japan. The developed nations together represent ⅔ or more of all this trade.

The Changing Nature of World Trade

When we think of "foreign trade," we may hark back to '30s movie scenes of Humphrey Bogart awaiting the tramp steamer from Shanghai or life on the far-away plantation. The reality of international activity is increasingly likely to be the McDonald's in Moscow, the Japanese purchase of CBS Records, the Toyota plant down the street, or the RCA camcorder made in Japan and sold in the US by a company owned by the French government (Thomson). The diverse types of international business, and the ways in which they are changing, are summarized in the following paragraphs.

Exports and Imports

Today, world exports total around $3 trillion. As might be expected, so do world imports. These goods and (increasingly) services therefore represent less than ½ of total world trade. While about ⅓ of the trade in goods represents raw materials — oil, minerals, wheat, other agricultural products — that proportion is likely to fall over time. Although in any given year the dollar value of trade in commodities can rise and fall dramatically, the long-term trends are for nations to spend less on these basics as they become richer, as they develop their own resources, and as they move to substitutes that can be made at home (as we have done with synthetic rubber and synthetic textiles). Manufactured products — already far and away the biggest category — can be expected to grow in importance over time.

Even more important will be the continued increase in the importance of services relative to goods. In other words, the trade in goods will not grow as fast as the

"Because of the huge size of America, we are the most important force in world trade."

"Information is faster, easier, and cheaper to move around the globe than are goods or people."

trade in services. Whether one looks at consulting, financing, communications, travel, education, or information services, they are all booming in world trade, much as they are booming in the individual domestic economies of the developed countries. Ireland has, for example, become a data-entry center for companies from all over the world.

It is important to note that information is faster, easier, and cheaper to move around the globe than are goods or people. This fact is also a reason that "foreign production" is growing faster than imports and exports.

Foreign Production

This quaint term is the one used for the Toyota plant down the street, or Sony's ownership of Columbia Pictures. It is extremely hard to get your hands around, because nobody keeps good numbers: we have to look at how much money companies invest in foreign countries (foreign direct investment) and make assumptions about how much revenue is generated by these offshore enterprises. At least since the early '80s, foreign production (the revenues of such offshore enterprises) has been a bigger factor in international business than exports and imports. From 1984 to 1989 global foreign direct investment grew at over 29% per year. We estimate the present foreign production total to be over $4 trillion a year.

It is expected that foreign production will continue to grow faster than exports and imports (and therefore much faster than the economy as a whole) for 6 reasons:

1. **The increasing ease of moving information.** Cheaper, better, faster computers and communication systems make it easier for Tokyo to oversee a Tennessee car plant than it would have been 20 years ago. It may be easier for Hewlett-Packard to train managers of a Singapore plant in California than to keep the whole plant in California.
2. **Concerns about protectionism.** The great rise of Japanese car plants in the US was largely in response to fears that the US would limit imports of cars from Japan.
3. **Economies of scale.** When Toyota first exported cars to the US, they didn't sell many; once their US demand was larger, it was worth putting a plant here. If new manufacturing and design technologies reduce the required scale of manufacturing plants (as in steel minimills), this transition can happen earlier.
4. **Changing cost relationships.** Twenty years ago Japanese labor was much cheaper than US labor. As Japan has become wealthy (and expensive to live in), that gap has evaporated. Over the same period computers have come down in price but oil has not, so shipping costs from Asia to the US have risen as a percent of the total cost. Increasingly, in response to cost and skill gaps, parts are made in one place, assembled in another, and packaged in yet another.
5. **The rise of services relative to goods.** Certain services are delivered almost entirely by foreign, on-site offices of companies. The Big Six accounting firms dominate world accounting, but they deliver their services by opening offices locally, often staffed with locals, rather than via exports. International retailing, advertising, and insurance are other industries where imports and exports are of minimal importance.
6. **The increasing ease of international investments.** As discussed under "Trade Barriers" later in this section,

many nations restrict investments by foreigners in some or all industries; some require that locals maintain large or even controlling interests. Such restrictions can make it difficult to make the foreign direct investments that allow foreign production. However, these and other barriers are gradually coming down, and we expect this to continue, further encouraging the rise of foreign production.

Trends in Foreign Production

At the turn of the century, the rubber or banana plantation, owned by the Americans or the Brits, was the standard form of foreign production. After World War II these two nations continued to dominate offshore factories: in 1960, 55% of global foreign direct investment was by US multinationals and another 20% by British giants. As far as the US was concerned, this role was encouraged by the US government, which wanted to help rebuild Europe and Japan.

As the rest of the world has begun to catch up (when you put them all together) with the US in wealth and global influence, the American share of foreign direct investment has declined, to ⅓ or less today. Japan has come on especially strong in the late '80s, and other Asian nations can be expected to rise in the future (see "Winners and Losers for the '90s" later in this section).

At the same time, the old model of the plantation has about disappeared. Today, about 50% of foreign direct investment is in manufacturing, 20% in mining and oil, and 30% in trade, finance, and services, the growth areas.

Interestingly, the US has become the leading host country for foreign investment — in other words, here's where the other countries are putting their money. This reflects the fact that, once the foreign companies have grown rich enough and large enough to invest overseas, they invest first and foremost in the US because:

1. The US is one of the most open and free of all world markets; we have fewer barriers than most.
2. We have by far the largest market in the world.
3. We continue to have the most stable and sound economy in the world.

In general, foreign production tends to follow 5 geographical patterns:

1. **Invest in neighbors:** the US in Mexico; Japan in Southeast Asia; the US and Canada in each other.
2. **Invest in former colonies:** the UK in US, Canada, Australia; France in Africa; the Netherlands in Indonesia.
3. **Invest where there are valuable resources:** the presence of oil has brought capital to Algeria, Nigeria, Indonesia, and others.
4. **Invest where there is a big domestic market:** Argentina, Brazil, Mexico, Philippines, Thailand.
5. **Invest where there is a good, well-educated work force:** Thailand, Mexico, Malaysia, Singapore.

Note that the US qualifies as a magnet for foreign investment on all 5 counts.

Other Types of International Transactions

As discussed above, traditional foreign trade — imports and exports — is growing faster than the world economy as a whole. Foreign production — the operation of plants or

"Once the foreign companies have grown rich enough and large enough to invest overseas, they invest first and foremost in the US."

"The international flow of royalties, franchise fees, TV rerun fees, and licensing agreements is huge and growing."

offices in other countries, including buying up whole companies — is growing even faster. There are yet other ways that the economy is increasingly becoming "globalized," other ways we trade with each other. These parts of international business are probably the fastest-growing of all, and include:

1. **International trade in rights and other intangibles.** The international flow of royalties, franchise fees, TV rerun fees, and licensing agreements is huge and growing. While good numbers are virtually impossible to come by, in the early '80s US businesses alone were already taking in over $5 billion a year on these items — in agreements with over 10,000 foreign enterprises.
2. **Joint ventures and alliances.** Corporations (and governments) from around the world are becoming increasingly creative in the ways they work together. "Strategic alliance" has become the buzzword of the day. As an example, Swissair, Singapore Airlines, and Delta are each buying up to 5% of each other; more importantly, they're getting together on ticketing, reservations, and marketing.
3. **Portfolio investments.** In previous paragraphs, we talked about the role of foreign production — where a "foreigner" owns or controls a business. But people and institutions from other countries can also make smaller investments, buying corporate stocks, corporate bonds, and government securities. They make these investments to diversify their portfolios and to take advantage of booming local economies. While US Government securities have long been regarded as "the safest you can buy" by investors around the world, American individuals are also increasingly buying foreign stocks and mutual funds. See "Investing Abroad," a later section.
4. **International lending.** Banking was one of the first major industries to cross national borders. Despite some overlending, particularly to Latin America, we expect continued growth here. For example, the big European banks would like to be truly European, and the Japanese would like to serve all of Asia.
5. **Citizens living abroad.** Whether Pakistani workers in Kuwait or American soldiers in Germany, these people are spending money where they are "stationed" as well as probably sending money "home."
6. **Transactions between governments and international organizations.** Foreign aid, the United Nations, the World Bank, and many other organizations and their people also add to the list of international transactions.

Why World Trade?

Trade between peoples is probably as old as mankind itself. It continues to grow faster than productive activity as a whole, becoming more important to all of us. All this is not without reason. The reasons include:

1. **Desire to have things from elsewhere:** it is easier to buy bananas from Central America than to build hothouses in the US.
2. **Desire to sell our stuff elsewhere:** likewise, since we're confident we make the best airliners, we'd like to sell Boeings abroad.
3. **The fact that you sometimes get more for your money elsewhere:** toys made in Hong Kong.

4. **The fact that some people seem to be better at some things than at others:** American movie makers, German car designers, Swiss watchmakers, Japanese TV makers.
5. **The desire for world peace:** we are less likely to attack each other if we all know each other and depend on each other.

Trade Barriers

We believe that the world is coming around to seeing the benefits of free, openly flowing markets, both within countries and between countries. Locked out of the greater world economy, much of the Communist world remained at least 50 years behind the developed countries in most aspects of everyday life.

India, intent on going it alone in its 45 years of independence, has a per capita income 1/10 that of Mexico. This, while most of Southeast Asia has charged ahead, leaving Third World status behind.

Throughout the world, trade barriers are coming down: the US and Canada, the US and Mexico, within Europe. Nevertheless, there are still vestiges of the barriers that can make trade difficult. There is even an occasional outbreak of protectionism, trying to introduce new barriers or heighten old ones in the US, the nation most historically predisposed toward free markets.

It is odd that we try to protect the textile industry because protection seems simple and painless — just limit the less expensive imports. And yet no one said "Let's not have airlines so railroaders can keep their jobs." Economic change is real and happens, and putting up artificial barriers is just fooling (and cheating) ourselves.

Here's a checklist of challenges you may encounter when doing international business:

1. **Tariffs on imports**
2. **Quotas on imports**
3. **Restrictions on moving money** (profits, currency)
4. **Taxation differences**
5. **Accounting differences**
6. **Foreign ownership limits**
7. **Local content requirements**
8. **Unavailability of talented labor and management**
9. **Varying power of trade unions**
10. **Real and perceived risk of political and economic instability** (currency exchange rates, inflation)
11. **Immigration/visa/work permit limitations**
12. **Censorship of information**
13. **Lack of patent/trademark/copyright protection**
14. **Lack of adequate legal system** (enforcement of contracts, resolution of disputes)
15. **Local rules** (environmental, product safety, employee benefits, labeling, store size limits, banned contents, etc.)
16. **Cultural differences** (attitudes toward authority, work, and achievement; expression of disagreement and resolution of conflict; patterns of decision-making; social mobility; taste and flavor preferences; etc.)
17. **Language differences**
18. **Technical differences** (metric system, voltage, etc.) ▲

"Throughout the world, trade barriers are coming down: the US and Canada, the US and Mexico, within Europe."

TRENDS IN A CHANGING WORLD

"When Pasteur and Edison invented things, it took years for the discoveries to spread around the world. Today, new ideas can be faxed in minutes at very little cost."

A number of trends in the world seem pretty reliable; most have been going on for some time and can be expected to continue. The ones we'd place our bets on include:

1. **Slowing population growth.** The developed countries have already slowed; Hungary and Germany have about stopped growing, aside from in-migration. This trend is expected to spread to other countries, ending in Africa late in the first half of the 21st century. This trend is linked to:
2. **Aging population.** Again led by the developed world, we're getting older, and the number of senior citizens will continue to grow rapidly.
3. **Continued urbanization, especially in the Third World.** The world's giant cities will increasingly be in Asia and Latin America; Mexico City will continue to be #1.
4. **Accelerating and compounding technological gains.** When Pasteur and Edison invented things, it took years for the discoveries to spread around the world. Today, new ideas can be faxed in minutes at very little cost. The revolution in communications accelerates the revolutions in other areas of technology. Not only will scientific advancements in new materials, biotech, computers, and communications continue unabated, but they will affect each other as well. Technological gains in areas not always thought of as high-tech will also continue: chicken-raising, hybrid seeds, discount retailing, toothpaste, commercial airliners.
5. **Growing global interdependence.** Largely as a result of all the foreign production noted previously, we will all become more economically dependent on each other. If we get into a fight, it is easy to cut off imports and exports of manufactured goods. It is more complex to seize that Ohio Honda plant because we're mad at the Japanese. All forms of global trade and communication increase our closeness. CNN and even Rambo are, in their own ways, unifying forces.
6. **The generally southward movement of manufacturing in pursuit of low wages.** Not unlike what has happened in the United States east of the Mississippi, manufacturing around the world will tend to move from north (Europe, Japan, US) to south (Latin America, Southeast Asia, South Asia).
7. **The collapse of economic borders.** Examples include "unified" Europe, US deals with both neighbors, Latin American alliances, and the Association of South East Asian Nations (ASEAN).
8. **Privatization.** This trend is the global tendency for governments to "get out of business." While it may not happen in postal services or railroads, it is happening in airlines, banking, telecommunications, steel, and other areas. Privatization opens many large opportunities for native entrepreneurs and global corporations in Europe, Asia, and Latin America.
9. **Creative ways of doing business abroad.** Examples include strategic alliances, joint ventures, corporations with headquarters (and management and ownership) in 2 or more countries (Royal Dutch/Shell, Unilever, ABB Asea Brown Boveri).
10. **Ever-increasing role of information and education at all levels.** From technical training to PhDs, from CNN to this book, information is the one product you can share and still have.

In addition to these trends that we see, we have included in the box below the "14-part multifold trend" developed by the late futurist Herman Kahn and his staff at the Hudson Institute. Mr. Kahn's ideas have generally been borne out by events; we think these trends that he identified prior to 1979 are certainly thought provoking.

The Basic Long-Term Trend

(Most components have been at work for centuries.)

1. **Increasingly sensate culture** (secular, humanistic, rational, as opposed to sacred, superstitious; perhaps some "backsliding" with rise of religious fundamentalism and new age philosophies)
2. **Accumulation of scientific and technological knowledge** (development of cohesive theories)
3. **Institutionalization of technological change** (research, development, and innovation are shared, spread, and managed)
4. **Increasing role of bureaucratic and meritocratic elites** (thinkers, communicators, innovators gaining power; the rise of the knowledge industry)
5. **Increasing military capability of western cultures** (maybe this one has peaked)
6. **Increasing area of world dominated by western culture**
7. **Increasing affluence**
8. **Decreasing rate of population growth**
9. **Urbanization** (rise of "megalopolis" — like Boston–New York–Philadelphia–Washington)
10. **Increasing attention to the environment**
11. **Decreasing importance of primary and secondary occupations** (decline of mining, agriculture, manufacturing; rise of thinking, teaching, programming, serving, consulting, etc.)
12. **Emphasis on progress and future-oriented thinking**
13. **The spread of all these trends to more people in more places**
14. **Increasing speed of change in all these trends**

Adapted from *World Economic Development: 1979 and Beyond*, by Herman Kahn with the Hudson Institute.

Winners and Losers for the '90s

In this book you will find business-oriented profiles of the world's most important countries and regions. These precede the profiles of the most important companies based outside the US. In the country profiles we have included a general description of each country (Overview) and the story of how they got to where they are today (When). Combined with the other data on each page, these will give you a good feeling for the economic nature and position of each country.

Making predictions about the course of individual nations is difficult. As we write this, the Soviet Union has had two, or maybe three or more, rulers in the last ten days; now it is unclear whether it will continue to exist as a sovereign nation. Nevertheless, we will go a little way out on a limb and place these bets:

1. Southeast Asia will continue to be the strongest region of the world in economic growth. Thailand, Indonesia, Malaysia, and the Philippines will, to varying degrees, benefit from this. Singapore, by serving as the "regional capital," may benefit the most. This part of the world will continue to boom because of such things as:
   - Increasingly stable politics
   - A huge population (about 300 million)

"Southeast Asia will continue to be the strongest region of the world in economic growth."

"*The heralded opportunities of Eastern Europe will take a great deal of patience on the part of Western investors.*"

- A well-educated and well-fed population
- Low labor costs
- Japanese investments
- Acceptance of free-market principles

2. Korea and Taiwan will continue to boom over the long term. While political and other issues may give these two nations some ups and downs, the sheer energy that has propelled them in the '70s and '80s will not dry up and go away. Industry will continue to move from Japan to these nations, then on to Southeast Asia.
3. Hong Kong and China present a tremendous opportunity — for themselves and the rest of the world. If China learns about the free market from Hong Kong and intelligently uses the business infrastructure that Hong Kong has built, then China could develop into a major world economic power. Note that Taiwan and the economies of Southeast Asia are largely driven by people of Chinese ancestry. We hope that China will fully join the world community, but Tiananmen Square is the symbol of another possible outcome. The real path is likely to be a convoluted one, not unlike the fall of Soviet Communism.
4. The United States will remain the most important country in the world economy; Japan will remain a strong number two. Increased world cohesion will only profit these two countries and their people.
5. The major industrial powers of northern Europe should benefit from the increasingly unified common market of Europe, West and East. While these powers will continue having difficulty competing with American and Japanese products and services, Germany should maintain its strength, followed by the United Kingdom, Switzerland, the Netherlands, and Sweden. They have great opportunities in their own backyard.
6. France and Italy will participate in this opportunity as well if they open up their markets and reduce the role of government in running businesses. It is not clear to us whether or not they will do this.
7. The European sunbelt will grow quickly, especially relative latecomers Spain and Turkey.
8. Eastern Europe and the Soviet Union will have a real rough time. While some of these countries are farther along in joining the West (Hungary) and others are not even close (Albania), most do not have the grasp of entrepreneurialism or the infrastructure (e.g., legal, banking, and accounting systems) that will be required to join the free-market world. It isn't just that they're broke; they don't know where to start. The heralded opportunities of Eastern Europe will take a great deal of patience on the part of Western investors.
9. Latin America may be finally getting their act together. Long blessed by population, land, minerals, and pockets of oil, these nations have too often allowed corrupt dictators and silly economics to overcome these strengths. The leading Latin American nations may be changing all this. Mexico, Chile, and Brazil appear to be on the rise. While past history makes us hesitant to predict that any Latin trends will continue for long, we certainly hope that the rise of the free market will continue and spread on that continent.

10. Most of Africa is in bad shape, with little hope of improvement. If Asia is booming, if Eastern Europe and Latin America seem to want to join the developed world, most of sub-Saharan Africa is not even knocking at the door. In many countries education levels are worse than they were during colonial times 40 years ago. Highways are gone and communications slower. Despite vast mineral resources and potentially arable land, the countries lack the money and skills to put these assets to work. Can there be …

Any Hope?

Forty years ago, you could travel around the world and see that there was a First World and a Third World. People from Western Europe, Canada, the US, and Australia could arrogantly presume that this world order would not change. The Third World stretched from Korea to India to Chile. Even standards of living in Western Europe were not up to those in North America.

This has all changed. Tokyo makes many American cities look tired and dirty (and inexpensive); excitement is in the air in Singapore and Budapest. Country after country has proven that you can develop out of poverty. At the same time they all have neighboring countries that haven't budged; some, as in Africa, have gotten worse. Why the difference?

The best analysis of this that we have seen is by Lloyd Reynolds in *Economic Growth in the Third World, 1850–1980*. This scholar studied 37 nations in Asia, Latin America, and Africa and found 8 factors that caused or allowed people in a Third World country to grow and prosper:

1. **Growth in agricultural production**
2. **Growth in exports**
3. **Growth in investment relative to production**
4. **Sense of being a nation** (as opposed to a tribe or ethnic minority, etc.)
5. **Continuity of political leadership**
6. **Orientation of leadership.** To quote Reynolds, "Historically, most governments have concentrated on staying in power, putting down dissenters, and perhaps making war on neighboring nations. Attaching high priority to economic progress might be regarded as unusual, even eccentric."
7. **Administrative competence**
8. **Policy stance.** In essence, central planning has been a disappointment virtually everywhere it's been tried; individual decisions, perhaps encouraged with government incentives, work much better. ▲

"Forty years ago… the Third World stretched from Korea to India to Chile."

INVESTING ABROAD

"The Templeton Funds, founded by renowned investor John Templeton, have long focused on investing around the world."

Just as corporations from around the world are making major investments in "foreign" countries, individual investors have begun to do the same. Much as investors buy stock in biotech companies because of future growth prospects, they are now buying into the futures of Thailand, Germany, and other countries. For the American investor there are 4 major ways to invest in non-US companies:

1. **US-traded foreign company shares.** Some large foreign companies issue shares that are actively traded in the US; they include Seagram and other Canadian companies and Royal Dutch/Shell. Some of these stocks have been traded in the US for a long time. American individuals and institutions may own large pieces of these companies.
2. **American Depository Receipts, or ADRs.** These securities represent shares in foreign companies and may be traded on the New York Stock Exchange (NYSE), American Stock Exchange (ASE), or Over-the-Counter (NASDAQ or OTC). ADRs can each represent a portion of a foreign share or a group of foreign shares. For example, some Asian company stocks trade under a dollar, so an ADR might represent 10 shares. On the other hand, some Swiss stocks trade for thousands of dollars, so an ADR might represent 1/200 of a "native" share.

   Most of the large foreign companies profiled in this book have shares traded in the US under one of these two methods. We have listed many of the shares available here, by country, starting on page 62.
3. **Mutual funds.** Long popular as a way for small investors to use the services of expert stock pickers, mutual funds have entered the international arena. There are global and international funds that invest around the world, regional funds (e.g., Asia/Pacific), and country funds (Brazil Fund, Turkish Investment Fund, Singapore Fund, etc.). The Templeton Funds, founded by renowned investor John Templeton, have long focused on investing around the world.
4. **Direct investment overseas.** Your stockbroker can help you invest abroad, via various trading mechanisms. While some stock markets do not let foreigners buy stock directly, most of these barriers are coming down. Some markets, such as the Toronto exchange, are very open.

   Note that most non-US stock markets have a stock market index, parallel to the Dow Jones averages in the US. We have noted several of these, and their component stocks, starting on page 59.

Risks of Foreign Investment

Of course, investing in foreign companies bears the same fundamental risks and rewards as investing in US companies (see *Hoover's Handbook of American Business* for basic stock market principles). But there are also these factors to be aware of:

1. Most non-US markets are not as heavily regulated as American exchanges. For example, many Asian stock markets have no bans on insider trading. Even in much of Europe, it is considered unethical but not illegal. While economists may argue about the importance of banning insider trading, most Americans have come to expect such "protection."

2. Accounting rules vary substantially around the world. Even UK and US rules have big differences. In Japan and Switzerland, companies can maintain virtual "hidden reserves," money set aside for a rainy day. In the US, companies generally have to show their hard times and their good times, not blend the two. Some of the measures most heavily used by American investors, such as Return on Equity (see *Hoover's Handbook of American Business*), begin to lose their comparability when you look abroad.

3. Many times governments tax dividends paid to foreigners. While these tax rates are not usually onerous, they do mean you may get less than "natives" at dividend time.

4. Your broker may charge unusually high commissions if you buy stocks on foreign exchanges. These charges often reflect the actual costs of dealing with foreign brokers.

5. Fluctuations in currency exchange rates can affect foreign investments. Say you buy a Japanese stock when it's trading at 150 yen and sell it at 300 yen. If the exchange rate goes from 150 yen per dollar to 300 yen per dollar, you make no money after converting to US dollars. This effect can work the opposite way — in your favor — and often has in the case of Japanese stocks.

Despite these risks we believe that investing in non-US companies will become an important part of any balanced long-term investment (savings) plan. The US is only 1/7 of the world economy: a good portfolio should take advantage of some of the other opportunities around the world. Investors concerned with safety may want to focus on stocks listed on the NYSE and on mutual funds run by professionals. ▲

"Despite these risks we believe that investing in non-US companies will become an important part of any balanced long-term investment (savings) plan."

TOP TEN WORLD COMPANIES FOR THE '90s

"Bertelsmann stayed out of the limelight, quietly building itself into the world's largest and richest media company."

We have profiled 165 corporate giants from around the world in this book. All have been included for their large and increasing role in the world economy. On the following pages we focus on ten that we think are particularly exciting. These are companies that are well positioned to take maximum advantage of the opportunities brought about by the new world order. If their managers continue to make the right moves, they should emerge stronger at the end of the decade than they were at the start. They are presented in alphabetical order.

Note that these top ten may not match the highest-scoring companies in "Hoover's Ratings," described later. The ratings were based on past and present performance; the following comments look to the future.

Bertelsmann

These days the words *media, merger,* and *massive debt* seem to go hand in hand — except in the solid, wood-paneled offices of Bertelsmann. While media moguls Robert Maxwell and Rupert Murdoch spent the late '80s building mountains of debt to buy high-profile properties like Macmillan and Twentieth Century Fox, Bertelsmann stayed out of the limelight, quietly building itself into the world's largest and richest media company. Not even the combined strength of Time and Warner can touch the German media giant: Bertelsmann is a major worldwide publisher and book club operator; it is Europe's leading magazine publisher; it owns record labels in the US, Europe, and Japan; and, with the industry's strongest balance sheet and about $4 billion of cash in hand, it is poised to extend its influence in publishing, printing, recording, and TV broadcasting around the world.

Bertelsmann owns Bantam Books, Dell paperbacks, and Doubleday Publishing, which together make up one of the world's largest English-language publishing groups. Since buying Doubleday in 1986, Bertelsmann has returned the once-great American publishing house to respectability after Doubleday had endured years of a bad reputation for the poor physical quality of its books. Bantam Doubleday Dell boasts an impressive list of best-selling authors, including Stephen King, John Jakes, and Danielle Steele.

Gruner + Jahr, Bertelsmann's newspaper and magazine division, invented the concept of a Pan-European magazine — *Prima* — sold in Germany, France, Spain, and the UK. The division is especially suited to take advantage of new opportunities in Eastern Europe. It now owns four eastern German newspapers (including *Berliner Zeitung*), and Bertelsmann has earmarked some $650 million to finance further regional expansion.

Bertelsmann's record labels include Arista, RCA, BMG Ariola, and BMG Victor; its roster of stars includes Whitney Houston, K. T. Oslin, Kenny G, and Stevie Wonder. Bertelsmann operates RTL Plus, Germany's most popular TV station, and owns a stake in the pay TV channel Premiere. It is building leadership as a sports broadcaster and recently won exclusive rights to televise Wimbledon and the German national soccer matches.

Since it is mostly owned by the Bertelsmann Foundation and the heirs of the company's founding family, Bertelsmann's stock is not for sale. But in terms of sheer size and vision, Bertelsmann is the media company to watch in the '90s.

Hutchison Whampoa

Hutchison Whampoa represents Hong Kong's past and its future. Originally a *hong* (British trading company) and now controlled by Hong Kong Chinese billionaire Li Ka-shing, it has interests in shipping and terminal services, real estate, telecommunications, and retailing — perhaps the four businesses most associated with Hong Kong's rise as a regional business center. Unlike other Hong Kong businesses still controlled by UK interests that are moving their headquarters out of Hong Kong (e.g., HSBC and Jardine Matheson), Hutchison Whampoa remains headquartered in Hong Kong and continues to invest there.

The company has not, however, ignored opportunities outside Hong Kong, investing in a UK container port, an Australian paging company, supermarkets in China, retail operations in Taiwan, and Canada's Husky Oil. Li's son even bid on the junk-bond portfolio of the failed Columbia Savings & Loan in California.

Through its HutchVision unit, Hutchison Whampoa hopes to become the dominant Pan-Asian television service provider. Its satellites will be able to reach 2.7 billion people, over half the world's population, in the region of the world that is growing faster economically than any other.

With sales and profits increasing almost 20% each year since Li took over in 1979, Hutchison Whampoa's star is rising over Asia.

When you visit Hong Kong, it won't matter to Li whether you stay at the Sheraton or the Hilton because Hutchison Whampoa owns big pieces of both.

L'Oréal

Controlling such well-known brands as Cacharel, Guy Laroche, Helena Rubenstein, Lanvin, and Lancôme, L'Oréal is the world leader in cosmetics and perfumes. L'Oréal was propelled to the top by 20 years of acquisitions but, unlike many other big acquirers, the company entered the '90s with a strong balance sheet and record earnings.

L'Oréal's ability to continuously develop acquired and existing brands has been critical to the company's progress. Particularly important has been L'Oréal's success in gaining international acceptance for many of its lines (i.e., Biotherm, Vichy, Guy Laroche). The company has developed extensive worldwide distribution channels and is expanding in Asia, where economic growth augurs well for sales of beauty products. Demand for L'Oréal's products will rise in most industrialized countries as more women enter the work force and populations age.

Marketing and distribution are backed up by a strong commitment to research and quality. L'Oréal's product-development spending, 4.9% of sales in 1990, is high by industry standards.

Any investor hopes for a hostile takeover of L'Oréal will not materialize over the near term, since Liliane Bettencourt and Swiss food giant Nestlé each effectively own about 28% of the company. However, under the terms of an agreement signed in 1974, Nestlé has the right to acquire Bettencourt's stake in 1994. Hitched to Nestlé or unattached, L'Oréal will be looking good in the '90s.

Reuters

Technological change has swept over the financial services industry, accommodating ever-increasing demand for faster access to information and for the ability to transact with anyone, anywhere, any time. To be sure, many major institutions overseeing stock and commodity markets cling to the traditions of manned trading windows or frenzied trading pits in which hand signals communicate buying or selling intentions.

"With sales and profits increasing almost 20% each year since Li took over in 1979, Hutchison Whampoa's star is rising over Asia."

"Pure Premium not-from-concentrate orange juice led Tropicana's jump to the #1 position in the US in 1990, just 2 years after Seagram acquired the juice maker."

But these institutions look increasingly anachronistic when compared to the newer, less tradition-bound markets such as the one for foreign exchange. Linked to their counterparts by a global network of computer terminals, foreign exchange traders transact with each other in an electronic marketplace that knows no national boundaries and is open around the clock. The undisputed technological leader in these kinds of marketplaces is Reuters.

With over 200,000 terminals installed, Reuters is clearly the dominant electronic distributor of financial information. Real-time stock, bond, option, and commodity prices are available through Reuters, and these information services provide the company with the bulk of its revenue. But even more promising are Reuters's transaction products, those similar to the foreign-exchange service described above. The volume of shares traded over Reuters's Instinet stock-trading service for institutions increased 300% between 1986 and 1990. The company's transaction-oriented terminals currently installed number 15,200, up from 10,700 at the end of 1988. The growth in trading terminals has occurred despite the absence of automatic order matching — a key feature in fully automated trading — in all but Reuters's Instinet system. The company is working on adding an order matching feature to its foreign-exchange service and is developing after-hours futures and options trading systems with the Chicago Mercantile Exchange and the Chicago Board of Trade, among others.

It appears inevitable that, as technical challenges are overcome, electronic trading will render physical exchanges obsolete. Opportunities for Reuters will be numerous and tantalizing in all markets for financial instruments and commodities. As Peter Schwartz of Global Business Network said to *Business Week*, "The new global market will be a Reuters market."

Seagram

Seagram is a world leader in wine and liquor. In the US, where the company's liquor strategy calls for emphasis on premium brands, Seagram's 7 Crown is the #1 whiskey and Seagram's Extra Dry is the #1 gin. Seagram also owns Tropicana, the new US orange juice leader, and Seagram's wine coolers share the US lead with Gallo's Bartles & James. In fact, Seagram is so well entrenched in the US that most of the Canadian company's growth potential lies outside of North America.

After decades of opening new branches, establishing joint ventures, and acquiring local distillers, Seagram controls a vast, worldwide distribution system that the company believes is unmatched in the industry. In Europe Seagram even acts as an agent for competitors' products. Assembly of the distribution network has been part of the company's successfully executed scheme to build and globalize many of its brands. Today, Seagram products that are internationally known include Chivas and Glenlivet scotch, Mumm champagne, Martel cognac, and Sandeman ports and sherries.

Tropicana is Seagram's most recent example of brand-building success. Pure Premium not-from-concentrate orange juice led Tropicana's jump to the #1 position in the US in 1990, just 2 years after Seagram acquired the juice maker. Brands of well-respected marketers Coca-Cola (Minute Maid) and Procter & Gamble (Citrus Hill) were left behind. Seagram wants to leverage Tropicana's success by extending the brand into frozen, bottled, and carbonated juice categories, and the company is now launching the Tropicana brand in Canada, Asia, and Europe.

Investors should note that Seagram owns 24.5% of US blue-chip chemical and oil company Du Pont. Although the way

Seagram accounts for the investment adds cyclicality to its earnings, Du Pont dividend income is likely to continue to increase steadily through the decade. For investors, employees, and consumers alike, Seagram looks like a refreshing choice for the '90s.

Sharp

In the '60s researchers at RCA began working with liquid crystals, hoping to make a flat TV that could hang on a wall like a painting. RCA abandoned the technology, as did most other US electronics manufacturers. In 1970 Japan's Sharp Corporation began investigating liquid crystal display (LCD) technology and three years later introduced the world's first electronic calculator with an LCD. Since then Sharp has become the world leader in sales of optoelectronic devices. The company is #1 in the rapidly growing markets for active-matrix LCDs (fast, lightweight, flat screens for laptop computers and miniature televisions) and laser diodes (used in compact disc and videodisc players and laser printers). In the US, Sharp is first in sales of fax machines. In Japan the company leads in electronic diaries and projection TVs.

Sharp has forged its way to the top in optoelectronics in Japan, the land of electronics giants, by placing winning bets on unproven technologies. The company says it "is going all out" in optoelectronics R&D. Such devotion to innovation has enabled Sharp to seize the lead, in both technology and sales, in its new markets. The reward for market leadership in active-matrix LCDs is expected to be enormous as production costs decline and flat screens supplant conventional tubes in computers and televisions. Other promising areas of research include photovoltaics (solar cells) and high-speed optical memory for computers.

Sharp's plan for the '90s calls for a quadrupling of sales and entry into the ranks of Japan's electronics heavyweights. Expect a proliferation of new Sharp products based on its advanced technology. Seat-back movie screens on aircraft and video telephones are possibilities. You will not have to wait for a wall-hanging TV — Sharp introduced a home model in 1991.

Singapore Airlines

"Airline heaven" is the way one passenger described Singapore Airlines in the 1990 *Zagat Airline Survey* of frequent fliers. The company was named "airline of the year" in 1990 by *Air Transport World* and the "best international airline" by *Business Traveller International*.

The key to Singapore Airlines' stellar reputation is the high level of service it provides on the ground and in the air and represents in advertisements with young, attractive "Singapore Girls." Taking advantage of relatively low wage rates in its home country, the airline employs three more cabin attendants than US carriers on long-haul flights. In the first-class cabin, flight attendants memorize passengers' names and pour Dom Pérignon. To maintain its employees' service orientation, the airline is building a $50 million training facility. The newness of Singapore Airlines aircraft (the youngest commercial fleet in the world) further enhances the airline's appeal to passengers.

Although Singapore Airlines is 54% government-owned and employs 1 of every 79 workers in Singapore, it receives no subsidies and operates on a for-profit basis. But the airline benefits from its status as the city-state's flag-carrier. The government has given the airline the most profitable, protected routes by selectively negotiating reciprocal landing rights with other national airlines eager to serve Singapore.

" 'Airline heaven' is the way one passenger described Singapore Airlines in the 1990* Zagat Airline Survey *of frequent fliers."

"Michael Jackson, the Rolling Stones, **Ghostbusters,** *'Wheel of Fortune,' and 'Jeopardy!' are all a part of Sony's repertoire."*

Protected routes, low labor costs, a base in a major hub of the fastest growing region in the world, and a great reputation for service — no wonder Singapore Airlines was the world's most profitable airline in 1990. For international travelers and investors of the '90s, Singapore Airlines is a great way to fly.

Sony

Sony is a media powerhouse. Not only does it make top-quality TVs, VCRs, audio equipment, camcorders, and CD players, but it also creates the music, movies, and television programs to run on these products through its ownership of Sony Music (formerly CBS Records) and Sony Pictures Entertainment (formerly Columbia Pictures), both purchased in the last several years at a cost of some $7 billion. Michael Jackson, the Rolling Stones, *Ghostbusters*, "Wheel of Fortune," and "Jeopardy!" are all a part of Sony's repertoire. Sony is also a pioneer in such new technologies as DAT, interactive CD-ROM, and 8mm video.

If all this weren't enough, Sony is developing new outlets for its entertainment products, including its Loew's Theatre chain and an amusement park in California to be called Sonyland.

Sony is also heading into electronic publishing in a big way. With a dominant position in the US market for CD-ROM players and its soon-to-be-introduced CD-ROM–based Data Discman Electronic Book (which will give its users access to the equivalent of an entire bookshelf of books on a 3" optical disc, played on a portable device weighing under 2 pounds), Sony is well positioned to drive this emerging market.

The company, perhaps more than any of its Japanese competitors, has always looked to the US market for ideas and then focused its efforts on selling to that market. One of Sony's strengths is its willingness to partner with other companies. It worked with Dutch electronics giant Philips on the standard for interactive CDs and may do so again on DAT standards. It has also partnered with such smaller companies as Compression Labs and The Reference Press (publisher of *Hoover's Handbook*, which will be available on the Data Discman in late 1991).

Its reputation for innovation and leadership has given Sony one of the best-known brand names in the world and has made it one of the top choices of Japanese university graduates for employment. Sony is no faceless conservative Japanese trading company. Its US software operations are headed by a 48-year-old US physicist who rose through Sony's ranks. His protege is a 29-year-old native of Iceland who writes short stories and novels in his spare time.

Sony's willingness to take chances has brought it annualized sales growth of almost 18% (compared to 12% for archrival Matsushita) over the past decade. That's more than a walk, man.

Teléfonos de México

In the last two years US investors have discovered Teléfonos de México (Telmex), bidding up the share price, then soaking up a $1.1 billion ADR offering in 1991. As a high-growth monopoly, Telmex has special appeal to the investment community. Because its shares represent 20% of the total value of the Mexican stock market, they are considered to be an excellent way to participate in the economic growth of Mexico.

Today the Mexican telephone system is unreliable at best, and one million would-be customers await installation. But the Salinas government, understanding the economic importance of communications, has set the stage for a dramatic upgrading of telephone service by selling a 51% voting interest in Telmex to a group that includes two telecommunications experts: Southwestern Bell and France Telecom. By meeting targets for telephone line capacity expansion, Telmex will retain its monopoly on long-distance service until 1996 and receive tax credits. Telmex plans to spend $2.5 billion annually to add lines. Rapid expansion could continue for many years — as of 1990, Mexico had under 10 telephone lines per 100 people compared to 52.7 per 100 in the US.

Recent liberalization of rules governing foreign investment and the shift toward free trade with the US, the biggest market in the world, are expected to lead to a new era of growth in Mexico. By helping Mexico reach its economic potential, Telmex should become the telecommunications growth story of the '90s.

Toyota

Number one in Japanese vehicle production since 1952, Toyota sold more cars in Japan last year than Nissan, Honda, and Mazda combined. Toyota has risen to fifth place in US car sales since entering the US market in 1957 and is likely to move ahead of Chrysler in the early '90s. Measured in units, Toyota's Lexus line is already outselling BMW and closing in on Mercedes-Benz. The EC is limiting European sales of Japanese autos until the year 2000 because Toyota and its Japanese brethren have demonstrated an ability to batter well-entrenched rivals on their home turf.

Toyota has continued to gain ground because its products have been reliable and reasonably priced. A 1990 J. D. Power & Associates study showed Lexus and Toyota lines to have the fewest problems among all makes of cars sold in the US. BMW CEO Eberhard von Kuenheim complains that Toyota does not have the "courage" to charge luxury-class prices for its Lexus cars, but US car buyers seem to like the wimpy pricing.

How does Toyota do it? Toyota pumps its profits into long-term R&D and capital investments — even during recessions — to stay a step ahead of its competitors. The company's *kaizen* (continuous improvement) culture and vigilance against "big company disease" (success-bred complacency) have created a steady stream of quality and productivity improvements. In *The Machine That Changed The World*, a book based on a five-year MIT study, Toyota is cited as the leader in "lean production," a low-cost system characterized by just-in-time inventory deliveries and flexible production lines that manufacture exactly what is needed when it is needed — in Japan Toyota can build a car against a customer order and deliver it in less than ten days.

Because of its long-term view, its lead in low-cost production, its ample opportunity to expand geographically and broaden its product lines, and the great reputation of its products, Toyota is our pick for auto maker of the '90s.

"Runners-Up"

There are of course many other fine companies in the book. Some that appear to have especially exciting futures are:

Cable and Wireless
Fuji Photo Film
Glaxo
Ito-Yokado
Royal Dutch/Shell
SmithKline Beecham. ▲

"BMW CEO Eberhard von Kuenheim complains that Toyota does not have the 'courage' to charge luxury-class prices for its Lexus cars, but US car buyers seem to like the wimpy pricing."

USING THE PROFILES

REGIONAL AND COUNTRY PROFILES

The profiles of 165 corporations based outside the United States are preceded by 5 regional profiles (Asia/Pacific, Eastern Europe, etc.), a profile of the United Nations, and then 61 one-page profiles of individual countries, presented alphabetically.

We selected these 61 countries based on three criteria:

1. **The economic importance of each country in world trade.** We have included most of the developed countries.
2. **Newsworthiness.** For example, we have included Poland and Iraq.
3. **Finally, we wanted to sample "the rest of the world."** For example, under the first two criteria, we might not have included sub-Saharan African nations, a Pacific Island nation, or Cuba.

Picking which countries to include, like picking the companies, was not easy. We hope we've chosen the ones most useful to you and invite your suggestions. We hope to expand our coverage in future editions.

Our profiles are aimed specifically at people who are interested in international business or investments. While we have touched on political and cultural issues to the extent they bear on commercial activity, our focus is clearly economic.

Last year, in *Hoover's Handbook 1991*, we established a standard profile format that has been generally praised for its ease of use. Therefore, we have applied this basic format to the country profiles. The sections of each profile and selected sources of information are described in the following paragraphs.

Overview

Each profile begins with a thumbnail sketch of the country. We have tried to touch on key imports and exports and other significant business factors.

When

As in the When sections of the company profiles, we have given significant emphasis to the historical development of each country and its economy. Because most of the modern world economy has developed since World War II, our emphasis is on that period, although we have not ignored the foundations laid and traditions formed in previous eras.

In both the When and the Overview sections, we relied on many sources, from daily newspapers to history texts to US Department of State publications. We have tried to distill this information for your easy consumption.

At the top right of each page, we have given you the "basics":

- The official name of the country
- The official language
- The currency
- The end of the government's fiscal year

Who

Here we have listed the key officers of the government, the country's ambassador to the US, and the American ambassador to the country.

Where

In this section we have included the address of the country's government ("headquarters"), its embassy in the US, the US embassy over there, and the national chamber of commerce. In each case we have included telephone and fax numbers, when available.

Many sources were used for this information. One source, a personal computer software program called "Speak Out," published by Speak Out Software, contains the names, addresses, and telephone numbers of 3,000 key world leaders. Copies of the program may be purchased from The Reference Press at 800-486-8666.

The Where section also lists the capital city, its time zone, and the average temperatures there. We go on to touch on the level of urbanization (what percent of the population lives in cities and their suburbs) and population density. This section concludes with tables showing which countries are exported to and which countries are imported from. This data was provided to us by The Economist Intelligence Unit/Business International (EIU), the international information arm of the *Economist* magazine. More information about EIU services is given on page 335.

What

This section begins with a table showing the origins of Gross Domestic Product (GDP), a key measure of the size of a country's economy. The economy is broken out into categories such as agriculture, manufacturing, etc. This data, also supplied by EIU, varies by country (see comments on How Much section, below).

The What section then proceeds to list, when available:

1. **GDP per capita**, a measure of the prosperity of the people.
2. **Level of indebtedness to "foreigners."**
3. **The country's literacy rate, as reported to international organizations.** Note that these generally high literacy rates do not always reflect the literacy skill level. While we say 99% of Americans are literate, that does not mean that 99% of Americans are fully functioning readers.
4. **The UN Human Development Index.** This interesting statistic, which we have converted to a scale of 100%, combines measures of longevity, knowledge, and living standards.
5. **Human Freedom Index.** *The World Human Rights Guide*, by Charles Humana, provides this index, on a 40-point scale, of the level of political freedom and human rights in each country.
6. **Purchasing power as a % of US.** While GDP per capita (above) is often used as a measure of wealth, it does not take into account relative living costs. The UN and other international organizations are trying to develop more accurate measures of relative well-being, and this one is a start. For example, while Mexico's GDP per capita is less than 1/7 that of the US, Mexico's low cost of living allows the average person to live 1/4 as well as the average American, by this measure.
7. **Capital city cost of living as a % of the cost of living in Washington, DC.** This information was generated by The Reference Press based on data provided by EIU.
8. **Defense spending as a % of GNP.**
9. **Education spending as a % of GNP.**
10. **Principal airlines.**
11. **Principal stock exchanges.**

How Much

Most of the data in this section were provided to us by EIU, The Economist Intelligence Unit. Data in italics are estimates generated by The Reference Press. We have tried to show 5 years of data, when available. The line entries are:

1. **Population**, usually estimated since the last census.
2. **Some measure of the total size of the economy, converted to US dollars.** Most often, this measure is Gross Domestic Product (GDP). Sometimes it is Gross National Product (GNP), which is normally slightly larger because it adds in money sent home by citizens working abroad. Sometimes it is Net Material Product (NMP) or some other Communist concept. NMP excludes certain key "services," such as defense and education, and is therefore not directly comparable to GDP or GNP. Note also that the process of converting to US dollars, for comparability, can distort year-to-year changes in the size of the economy. For example, if the nation's currency falls relative to the dollar (devalues), our table may make it look as if the country's economy shrank, when locals think it grew. For this reason, to compare economic growth, it is better to look at:
3. **Real GDP (or GNP or NMP) growth rate.** By taking out inflation and ignoring currency exchange rates, you can get a pretty good idea of whether the economy really grew or not in any given year.
4. **Exports of merchandise in US dollars.**
5. **Imports of merchandise in US dollars.**
6. **Trade balance in US dollars.** This is the amount by which merchandise exports exceed imports; a negative number means that imports exceeded exports in that year.
7. **Current account in US dollars.** This figure is calculated by starting with the trade balance, then adding in such nonmerchandise transactions as:
   - Freight and transportation charges received (paid would be a negative).
   - Tourism by foreigners (tourism by citizens in foreign countries would be a negative).
   - Exports (imports) of services.
   - Investment income (expense): dividends, interest, etc.
   - Royalties and fees in (out).
   - Personal spending of foreigners living in the country (minus spending of its citizens living abroad).
   - Receipts (expenditures) of foreign aid, whether between governments or family members.

   In short, the current account tries to show whether money is flowing into or out of a country; it is much like the profit-and-loss statement of a corporation. It does not, however, include investments, in which people or companies are buying and selling stocks, companies, factories, etc., or building foreign facilities.
8. **Government budget balance**. Positive is a surplus, negative a deficit.
9. **Annual consumer inflation rate.**
10. **Annual unemployment rate.**

Reader Beware!

It is easy to lull oneself into regarding national economic statistics as hard and fast. In the United States and many other developed countries, we have been calculating our GNP and tracking our imports and exports for a long time. This does not mean that anyone really knows what the actual figures are. It just means that we have been using consistent methods over the years, and that we are doing the best we can. If our estimate of our country's GNP is a little high, it was probably a little high last year; the rate of change is much more important than the absolute level.

If national economic statistics in the developed world are less than perfect, the situation is worse when you look beyond the leading nations. At the extreme the numbers from the old Communist world are very suspect. Who really knows the inflation rate or the unemployment rate in most Third World countries? While we tend to take the accuracy of population data for granted, some nations have not even tried to take a census in the last 30 years.

As reference publishers, we are always desirous of accurate, comparable data. But such data are rarely available, and you should be aware of this when using the information contained in our country profiles.

Further Reading and Resources on the Nations of the World

For those wanting to keep up with economic developments around the world, we recommend the following periodicals:

The Economist
The Far Eastern Economic Review
The New York Times
Financial Times
The Wall Street Journal

Books we have found useful in understanding the world about us include:

Area Handbook Series (one on each country, various dates), US Government Printing Office for the Army and the Library of Congress
Asian Power and Politics (1985), Pye
Cambridge World Gazetteer (1988), edited by Munro
The CIA World Factbook (annual)
Columbia Dictionary of Political Biography (1991), *The Economist*
Department of State Background Notes (one on each country, periodic)
Economic Growth of the Third World, 1850–1980 (1985), Reynolds
The Economist Book of Vital World Statistics (1990)
The Economist World Atlas and Almanac (1989)
Exportise (1990), Small Business Foundation of America
The Four Little Dragons (1989), Kelly and London
Human Development Report (1991), United Nations
International Business and Multinational Enterprise (4th edition, 1989), Robock and Simmonds
International Financial Statistics (monthly), International Monetary Fund
The New International Atlas, Rand McNally
The Pacific Rim Almanac (1991), Besher
The Statesman's Yearbook (annual), edited by Paxton
The Universal Almanac (annual)
Video Night in Kathmandu (1988), Iyer
The Wealth of Nations, Smith
The World Almanac (annual)
World Economic Development: 1979 & Beyond (1979), Kahn
World of Information series of books (one on each continent, annual)
World Outlook (annual), The Economist Intelligence Unit
World Tables (annual), The World Bank
World Today Series (one on each continent, annual)
World Weather Guide (1990), Times Books

In addition to these periodicals and books, there are a number of information services and sources that can be helpful. In addition to the EIU, described on page 29, the United Nations (New York), World Bank (International Bank for Reconstruction and Development, Washington), and International Monetary Fund (IMF, Washington) generate copious data on the countries of the world. The major international banking organizations, such as the Bank of America (San Francisco), also produce statistical summaries and forecasts. The Bank of America's *Country Outlooks*, *Country Data Forecasts*, and *Country Risk Monitor* are very helpful; you can get more information about them at 714-545-7118. The IMF can be reached at 202-623-7430 and the World Bank at 202-477-1234.

COMPANY PROFILES

Selection of the Companies Profiled

The 165 corporations profiled here include several private and government-owned entities and one nonprofit entity (The Red Cross). These were included because they are economic entities that employ people, that have global economic importance, and that often compete with public and private companies. Their histories and dynamics are just as fascinating as those of other economic entities.

Because this book focuses on the needs of buyers, sellers, investors, and managers, the majority of the companies included are large, publicly traded companies, much like those in *Hoover's Handbook of American Business*, our companion volume. Selecting these companies was not easy, especially given the dearth of information available on some non-US companies. We tried to imagine what companies would be of most interest to our readers, resulting in our selection of these 5 types of companies:

1. Companies with substantial activity in the United States, either exporting their products to the states, or making products (or services) here.
2. Truly global enterprises. For example, we included all 6 of the Big Six accounting firms, no matter where headquartered, because they serve the world. These include the only US-headquartered firms contained in this book.
3. Businesses that either dominate big industries or lead the industry in their country (e.g., Rhône-Poulenc, France's biggest chemical company).
4. Representative companies from around the world (one Indian company, Tata; one Taiwanese company, Formosa Plastics; etc.).
5. Companies representing virtually every major industry, from steel to hotels, from brewing to publishing.

Once we had covered these bases, we had a bias toward the more advanced economies where there are more major companies (Western Europe, Canada, Japan). We also have a slight bias toward consumer and growth industries, because we believe our readers are more likely to deal with, or hear of, such companies.

Organization of the Profiles

The 165 company profiles are presented in alphabetical order. We have shown the full name of the enterprise at the top of each page, unless it is too long, in which case you will find it above the address in the Where section of the profile. If a company name starts with a person's first name, like

Arthur Andersen, it will be alphabetized under the first name. We've generally tried to alphabetize companies where you'd expect to find them — for example, Deutsche Lufthansa is in the L's. All company names (past and present) used in the profiles are indexed in the main (last) index of the book.

Certain pieces of basic data are listed at the top right of each profile: where the company's stock is traded if it is public, what the stock ticker symbol is if the stock is available in the US, and when the company's fiscal year ends.

In this area of the page we have also shown "Hoover's Rating" for each company. The ratings for all companies, from A+ through F, are shown on pages 38–39. Each company's rating is intended to measure the overall strength of the company, primarily based on performance in the '80s and position at the end of 1990. The ratings combine specific statistical measures and our subjective conclusions based on our studies. There are 4 major determinants:

- Financial performance — sales and earnings growth, return on equity
- Financial strength — relative indebtedness
- Innovation within their industry
- Dominance/market share in their industry

Note that these measures are based on those used in America — return on equity, for example — and may not be as important elsewhere (e.g., Japan). Also note that, while past performance is often the best indicator of future performance, this is not always the case.

The annual information contained in the profiles was current through fiscal year-end 1990 (including companies whose years ended as late as March 31, 1991). To the extent possible, we have also noted significant, more recent developments through August 1991.

Overview

In this section we have tried to give a thumbnail description of the company and what it does. We recommend that you read this section first.

When

This longer section reflects our belief that every enterprise is the sum of its history, and that you have to know where you came from in order to know where you are going. While some companies have very little historical awareness and were unable to help us much and other companies are just plain boring, we think the vast majority of the enterprises in the book have colorful backgrounds. When we could find information, we tried to focus on the people who made the enterprise what it is today. We have found these histories to be full of twists and ironies; they can make for some fascinating reading.

Who

Here we list the names of the people who run the company, insofar as space allows. We have shown age and pay information when available, although most non-US companies are not required to report the level of detail revealed in the US.

While companies are free to structure their management titles any way they please, most modern corporations follow standard practices. The ultimate power in any corporation lies with the shareholders, who elect a board of directors, usually including officers or "insiders" as well as individuals from outside the company. The chief officer, the person on whose desk the buck stops, is usually called the chief executive officer (CEO) in the US. In other countries, practices vary widely. We have tried to list the most senior officers first.

A multitude of other titles exist, including managing director and vice chairman (VC). We have tried to list the most important officers, including the Chief Financial Officer (CFO) and chief personnel (human resources) person.

The people named in the profiles are indexed at the back of the book by their last names.

The Who section also includes the name of the company's auditing (accounting) firm and the number of employees. This last statistic can be viewed as a measure of the complexity of managing the enterprise, since most managing is managing people.

Where

Here we include the company's headquarters address and phone and fax numbers as available. We also list the same information for the main US office of each company. Telephone numbers of foreign companies are shown as they would be dialed from the US.

We have also included as much information as we could gather and fit on the geographical distribution of the company's business, including sales and profit data. Note that these profit numbers, like those in the What section below, are usually operating profits rather than net profits. Operating profits are generally those before financing costs (interest payments) and taxes, which are considered costs attributable to the whole company rather than to one division or part of the world. For this reason the net income figures (in the How Much section) are usually much lower, since they are after interest and taxes. Pretax profits are after interest but before taxes.

What

This section lists as many of the company's products, services, brand names, divisions, subsidiaries, and joint ventures as we could fit. We have tried to include all its major lines and all familiar brand names. The nature of this section varies by industry, company, and the amount of information available. If the company publishes sales and profit information by type of business, we have included it. The brand and division names are listed in the last index in the book, with past and present company names.

Key Competitors

In this section we have listed those other companies in the book and its companion volume, *Hoover's Handbook of American Business*, that compete with the profiled company. This feature is included as a quick way to turn to similar companies and compare them. In the case of some highly diversified or always-changing companies, we didn't have enough room to list everybody and have referred you to broad industry groupings. All the companies in the book are listed by broad industry groups in the first index at the back of the book.

How Much

Here we have tried to present as much data about each enterprise's financial performance as we could compile in the allocated space. While the information varies somewhat from industry to industry, and is less complete in the case of private companies that do not release this data, the following 2 types of information are generally present:

1. A ten-year table, with relevant nine-year (1981 through 1990) compound growth rates, covering:

- Fiscal year sales (year-end assets for most financial companies)
- Fiscal year net income (before extraordinary items)
- Fiscal year income as a percent of sales (Return on Sales or ROS)
- Fiscal year Earnings Per Share (EPS) (fully diluted unless italicized)
- Calendar year stock price high, low, and close
- Calendar year high and low Price/Earnings ratio (P/E)
- Fiscal year dividends per share for companies where data are converted to US dollars; calendar year dividends if data are shown in local currency
- Fiscal year-end book value (shareholders' equity per share)

For fiscal years ending between April 1, 1990, and March 31, 1991, we have called the year 1990.

2. Key year-end 1990 statistics that generally show the financial strength of the enterprise, including:

- Debt ratio (long-term debt as a percent of combined long-term debt and shareholders' equity)
- Return on average equity (average of beginning shareholders' equity and ending shareholders' equity) for the fiscal year
- Cash and marketable securities on hand at the end of fiscal 1990
- Current ratio at year-end fiscal 1990 (ratio of current assets to current liabilities)
- Total long-term debt at year-end fiscal 1990
- Number of shares of common stock outstanding at year-end fiscal 1990
- Dividend yield (fiscal or calendar year 1990 dividends per share divided by the year-end closing stock price)
- Dividend payout (fiscal or calendar year dividends divided by fiscal year Earnings Per Share for 1990)
- Market value at the end of 1990 (calendar year-end closing stock price multiplied by fiscal year-end number of shares outstanding)

Major Currency Symbols

Country	Currency	Symbol
Australia	dollar	$A
Belgium	franc	BF
Brazil	cruzeiro	Cr$
Canada	dollar	C$
Denmark	krone	DK
France	franc	FF
Germany	deutsche mark	DM
Hong Kong	dollar	HK$
India	rupee	Rs
Italy	lira	L
Japan	yen	¥
Mexico	peso	peso
Netherlands	florin	Fl
New Zealand	dollar	NZ$
Philippines	peso	P
Singapore	dollar	S$
South Africa	rand	R
South Korea	won	Won
Sweden	krona	SEK
Switzerland	franc	SF
Taiwan	dollar	NT$
UK	pound, pence (p = 1/100 £)	£, p
US	dollar	$
Venezuela	bolivar	B

The lower left-hand corner of each page contains key data in US dollars, even if the ten-year table is in local currency (see foreign currency symbol table on page 35). Such key data include market value and sales or assets if not shown in the larger table.

Note that, throughout the How Much section, per-share data are based on fully diluted common shares of stock unless otherwise noted. Historical per-share data are adjusted for stock splits. Much of the data for public companies (and selected others) have been provided to us by Standard & Poor's Compustat, a unit of McGraw-Hill and the nation's leading compiler of corporate share data. Compustat has gone to great lengths to make the data comparable between companies, sometimes producing numbers that will disagree with the numbers you may find in other sources. In cases in which Compustat did not provide data, primarily those tables shown in local currency, data were generated by The Reference Press based on information provided by the company.

In the case of private companies, we usually relied on data from the companies themselves.

We have shown data in US dollars if available and unless otherwise noted. Note that this conversion process can indicate trends different from those that might be seen in the domestic currency. For example, if a country posted hyperinflation (100%, 1000%, or even more per year) in the '80s, a company's sales and earnings could have likewise skyrocketed in the same time frame. However, when the currency is converted to a more stable currency like the US dollar, the trend could be flat or even down, depending on how much the foreign currency was devalued.

In addition, as mentioned before, accounting rules differ dramatically from one country to another.

In the case of certain industries, we have substituted more relevant statistics for the above data. For example, the current ratio is not meaningful for financial service businesses, so for most of these we have shown total assets instead.

Throughout the profiles we have tried our best to present data that are accurate and comparable. However, the new world order must become much more standardized before we can confidently promise accurate comparability.

Further Reading and Resources on Non-US Companies

The general world information periodicals listed on page 31 contain news about the specific companies in this book. The *Economist* and *Financial Times* are particularly good. If you would like present or past annual reports on these or other non-US companies, we recommend you contact Global Research Company at 314-647-0081. Books we found helpful include:

Asian Company Handbook (annual), Toyo Keizai Inc.
French Company Handbook (annual)
The Global Marketplace (1987), Moskowitz
International Directory of Company Histories (1988, multi-volume set), Derdak, St. James Press
Japan Company Handbook (quarterly), Toyo Keizai Inc.
Spanish Company Handbook (annual)

Many of the companies are also represented in traditional sources like *Moody's* and *Value Line*; see *Hoover's Handbook of American Business* for a complete list of these sources. ▲

A List-Lover's Compendium

Hoover's Ratings of the Companies Profiled in this Book

Company	Rating
Reuters Holdings PLC	A+
Glaxo Holdings PLC	A+
Nintendo Co., Ltd.	A+
Singapore Airlines Ltd.	A+
Bertelsmann AG	A+
L'Oréal SA	A+
LM Ericsson Telephone Company	A+
Cable and Wireless PLC	A
SmithKline Beecham PLC	A
Teléfonos de México, SA de CV	A
Ito-Yokado Co., Ltd.	A
Fuji Photo Film Co., Ltd.	A
Toyota Motor Corporation	A-
Dentsu Inc.	A-
Marks and Spencer PLC	A-
British Telecommunications PLC	A-
Formosa Plastics Group	A-
Sandoz Ltd.	A-
Pioneer Electronic Corporation	A-
The Seagram Company Ltd.	A-
Canon Inc.	A-
Guinness PLC	A-
The General Electric Company PLC	A-
Sony Corporation	A-
Samsung Co., Ltd.	B+
Siemens AG	B+
Royal Dutch/Shell Group of Companies	B+
Heineken NV	B+
Daimler-Benz AG	B+
Thorn EMI PLC	B+
Sharp Corporation	B+
Lucky, Ltd.	B+
Roche Group	B+
NEC Corporation	B+
Hutchison Whampoa Ltd.	B+
Anglo American Corporation	B+
Carlsberg AS	B+
Yamaha Corporation	B+
Unilever	B+
Rolls-Royce PLC	B+
Matsushita Electric Industrial Co., Ltd.	B+
LVMH Moët Hennessy Louis Vuitton	B+
Fujitsu Ltd.	B+
Robert Bosch GmbH	B+
The Red Cross	B+
Kirin Brewery Company, Ltd.	B+
ABB Asea Brown Boveri Ltd.	B+
British Airways PLC	B+
Source Perrier, SA	B
Peugeot SA	B
Moore Corporation Ltd.	B
Ciba-Geigy Ltd.	B
Grand Metropolitan PLC	B
BSN Groupe	B
Alcatel Alsthom	B
Cadbury Schweppes PLC	B
Allianz AG Holding	B
The Dai-Ichi Kangyo Bank, Ltd.	B
Nestlé SA	B
Reed International PLC	B
Tata Group	B
Petróleos Mexicanos	B
Arthur Andersen & Co.	B
Thyssen AG	B
Imperial Chemical Industries PLC	B
Hitachi, Ltd.	B
The Nomura Securities Company, Ltd.	B
The Industrial Bank of Japan, Ltd.	B
The RTZ Corporation PLC	B
Minolta Camera Co., Ltd.	B
Hoechst AG	B
San Miguel Corporation	B
Volkswagen AG	B
KPMG	B
Telefónica de España, SA	B
Bayer AG	B
Casio Computer Co., Ltd.	B-
Deutsche Bank AG	B-
Toshiba Corporation	B-
Norsk Hydro AS	B-
Inco Ltd.	B-
The British Petroleum Company PLC	B-
Bass PLC	B-
Fiat SpA	B-
The Rank Organisation PLC	B-
Hyundai Corporation	B-
Tokio Marine and Fire	B-
Jardine Matheson Holdings Ltd.	B-
Honda Motor Co., Ltd.	B-
Royal Bank of Canada	B-
Accor SA	B-
Swire Pacific Ltd.	B-
Ernst & Young	B-
Petróleos de Venezuela, SA	B-
Nippon Telegraph and Telephone Corp.	B-
Pearson PLC	B-
BASF AG	B-
AB Volvo	B-
The Thomson Corporation	B-
The Broken Hill Proprietary Company Ltd.	B-
HSBC Holdings PLC	B-
Société Nationale Elf Aquitaine	B-
Hanson PLC	B-
Bayerische Motoren Werke AG	C+
Union Bank of Switzerland	C+
Price Waterhouse	C+
Deloitte & Touche	C+
Saab-Scania AB	C+
Fletcher Challenge Ltd.	C+
Maxwell Communication Corporation PLC	C+

Hoover's Ratings of the Companies Profiled in this Book (continued)

Company	Rating	Company	Rating
John Labatt Ltd.	C+	Qantas Airways Ltd.	C
BCE Inc.	C+	Philips Electronics NV	C
Coopers & Lybrand	C+	Suzuki Motor Corporation	C
Mazda Motor Corporation	C+		
Nippon Steel Corporation	C+	Mitsui & Co., Ltd.	C
		Saatchi & Saatchi Company PLC	C-
Imperial Oil Ltd.	C+	Rhône-Poulenc SA	C-
Crédit Lyonnais	C+	Petróleo Brasileiro SA	C-
Canadian Imperial Bank of Commerce	C+	Foster's Brewing Group Ltd.	C-
Allied-Lyons PLC	C+		
The Tokyo Electric Power Company, Inc.	C+	Alcan Aluminium Ltd.	C-
		CS Holding	C-
Oki Electric Industry Co., Ltd.	C+	IRI Holding	C-
KLM Royal Dutch Airlines	C+	Michelin	C-
The News Corporation Ltd.	C	Vendex International NV	C-
Petrofina SA	C		
Imasco Ltd.	C	Bridgestone Corporation	C-
		Daewoo Corporation	C-
AB Electrolux	C	Airbus Industrie	C-
Sumitomo Corporation	C	Canadian Pacific Ltd.	C-
Japan Airlines Company, Ltd.	C	Isuzu Motors Ltd.	D
Nobel Industries Sweden AB	C		
Hachette SA	C	Renault	D
		Friedrich Krupp GmbH	D
Nissan Motor Co., Ltd.	C	Pirelli SpA	D
Hudson's Bay Company	C	Thomson SA	D
Mitsubishi Corporation	C	Lloyd's of London	D
Barclays PLC	C		
Scandinavian Airlines System	C	Compagnie des Machines Bull	F
		Ing. C. Olivetti & C., SpA	F
B.A.T Industries PLC	C	Koor Industries Ltd.	F
Deutsche Lufthansa AG	C	Bond Corporation Holdings Ltd.	F
		Campeau Corporation	F

Companies in *Hoover's Handbook of World Business 1992* Ranked by Sales

Rank	Company	1990 Sales ($ mil.)
1	Sumitomo Corporation	167,393
2	Mitsubishi Corporation	137,207
3	Mitsui & Co., Ltd.	123,537
4	Royal Dutch/Shell Group of Companies	106,479
5	Toyota Motor Corporation	68,096
6	IRI Holding	59,331
7	The British Petroleum Company PLC	59,140
8	Daimler-Benz AG	57,383
9	Fiat SpA	50,852
10	Volkswagen AG	45,679
11	Hitachi, Ltd.	44,797
12	Nippon Telegraph and Telephone Corp.	44,459
13	Siemens AG	42,406
14	Nissan Motor Co., Ltd.	41,815
15	Unilever	39,620
16	Matsushita Electric Industrial Co., Ltd.	37,753
17	Société Nationale Elf Aquitaine	37,218
18	Nestlé SA	36,511
19	Philips Electronics NV	33,018
20	Renault	32,209
21	Toshiba Corporation	31,496
22	Peugeot SA	31,491
23	The Dai-Ichi Kangyo Bank, Ltd.	31,380
24	Barclays PLC	31,327
25	BASF AG	31,291
26	The Tokyo Electric Power Company, Inc.	30,274
27	Hoechst AG	30,109
28	Alcatel Alsthom	28,346
29	Bayer AG	27,948
30	ABB Asea Brown Boveri Ltd.	26,688
31	Imperial Chemical Industries PLC	24,909
32	Honda Motor Co., Ltd.	24,385
33	Thyssen AG	24,285
34	Petróleos de Venezuela, SA	23,469
35	British Telecommunications PLC	23,399
36	NEC Corporation	21,799
37	The Industrial Bank of Japan, Ltd.	21,453
38	Robert Bosch GmbH	21,358
39	B.A.T Industries PLC	20,552
40	Petróleos Mexicanos	19,330
41	Nippon Steel Corporation	19,059
42	Fujitsu Ltd.	18,889
43	Sony Corporation	18,760
44	Bayerische Motoren Werke AG	18,240
45	Grand Metropolitan PLC	18,130
46	Mazda Motor Corporation	17,793
47	The General Electric Company PLC	16,957
48	BCE Inc.	15,832
49	Ciba-Geigy Ltd.	15,514
50	Rhône-Poulenc SA	15,514
51	Thomson SA	14,809
52	AB Volvo	14,765
53	AB Electrolux	14,642
54	Royal Bank of Canada	14,628
55	Petrofina SA	14,078
56	Ito-Yokado Co., Ltd.	13,867
57	Hanson PLC	13,401
58	Bridgestone Corporation	13,215
59	Imasco Ltd.	13,043
60	Canon Inc.	12,800
61	Michelin	12,350
62	Foster's Brewing Group Ltd.	11,943
63	Isuzu Motors Ltd.	11,259
64	Canadian Imperial Bank of Commerce	11,211
65	Samsung Co., Ltd.	11,137
66	Vendex International NV	10,952
67	Marks and Spencer PLC	10,823
68	Kirin Brewery Company, Ltd.	10,578
69	Sandoz Ltd.	10,525
70	Friedrich Krupp GmbH	10,450
71	BSN Groupe	10,413
72	Norsk Hydro AS	10,390
73	The Broken Hill Proprietary Company Ltd.	10,304
74	Sharp Corporation	9,963
75	Allied-Lyons PLC	9,907
76	The RTZ Corporation PLC	9,801
77	Deutsche Lufthansa AG	9,696
78	Imperial Oil Ltd.	9,673
79	Japan Airlines Company, Ltd.	9,296
80	SmithKline Beecham PLC	9,195
81	Canadian Pacific Ltd.	9,048
82	Pirelli SpA	9,012
83	Bertelsmann AG	8,935
84	Telefónica de España, SA	8,904
85	The Nomura Securities Company, Ltd.	8,896
86	Hyundai Corporation	8,863
87	Alcan Aluminium Ltd.	8,757
88	Bass PLC	8,610
89	Fuji Photo Film Co., Ltd.	8,588
90	Deutsche Bank AG	8,520
91	LM Ericsson Telephone Company	8,182
92	Crédit Lyonnais	8,037
93	Ing. C. Olivetti & C., SpA	8,033
94	British Airways PLC	7,973
95	Roche Group	7,614
96	Bond Corporation Holdings Ltd.	7,349
97	Daewoo Corporation	7,347
98	Suzuki Motor Corporation	7,281
99	Fletcher Challenge Ltd.	7,179
100	Thorn EMI PLC	7,172
101	Tokio Marine and Fire	7,165
102	Rolls-Royce PLC	7,083
103	Compagnie des Machines Bull	6,807
104	Guinness PLC	6,776
105	The News Corporation Ltd.	6,720
106	Cadbury Schweppes PLC	6,069
107	Jardine Matheson Holdings Ltd.	6,034
108	L'Oréal SA	5,976
109	Hachette SA	5,915
110	Scandinavian Airlines System	5,663

Companies in *Hoover's Handbook of World Business 1992* Ranked by Sales (continued)

Rank	Company	1990 Sales ($ mil.)
111	The Thomson Corporation	5,364
112	Saab-Scania AB	5,157
113	The Seagram Company Ltd.	5,031
114	Glaxo Holdings PLC	4,966
115	Heineken NV	4,887
116	Nobel Industries Sweden AB	4,689
117	Oki Electric Industry Co., Ltd.	4,667
118	Airbus Industrie	4,600
119	John Labatt Ltd.	4,547
120	Cable and Wireless PLC	4,470
121	Tata Group	4,374
122	Hudson's Bay Company	4,284
123	Arthur Andersen & Co.	4,160
124	Swire Pacific Ltd.	3,997
125	LVMH Moët Hennessy Louis Vuitton	3,904
126	Teléfonos de México, SA de CV	3,838
127	Yamaha Corporation	3,694
128	Union Bank of Switzerland	3,677
129	KLM Royal Dutch Airlines	3,395
130	Pioneer Electronic Corporation	3,239
131	Inco Ltd.	3,108
132	Reed International PLC	3,046
133	Pearson PLC	2,963
134	Singapore Airlines Ltd.	2,927
135	Qantas Airways Ltd.	2,795

Rank	Company	1990 Sales ($ mil.)
136	Moore Corporation Ltd.	2,770
137	Accor SA	2,712
138	Source Perrier, SA	2,683
139	Reuters Holdings PLC	2,640
140	Minolta Camera Co., Ltd.	2,573
141	The Rank Organisation PLC	2,573
142	Koor Industries Ltd.	2,507
143	Maxwell Communication Corporation PLC	2,397
144	Casio Computer Co., Ltd.	2,259
145	Lucky, Ltd.	2,220
146	Hutchison Whampoa Ltd.	2,048
147	Carlsberg AS	1,813
148	Nintendo Co., Ltd.	1,778
149	San Miguel Corporation	1,611
150	Saatchi & Saatchi Company PLC	1,514
151	Dentsu Inc.	1,166
152	Formosa Plastics Group	1,112
153	Campeau Corporation	220

Companies in *Hoover's Handbook of World Business 1992* Ranked by Profits

Rank	Company	1990 Net Income ($ mil.)
1	Royal Dutch/Shell Group of Companies	6,533
2	Toyota Motor Corporation	3,267
3	The British Petroleum Company PLC	3,000
4	British Telecommunications PLC	2,867
5	Petróleos de Venezuela, SA	2,414
6	Société Nationale Elf Aquitaine	2,092
7	Grand Metropolitan PLC	2,063
8	The Nomura Securities Company, Ltd.	2,044
9	Unilever	1,980
10	Nippon Telegraph and Telephone Corp.	1,933
11	Peugeot SA	1,822
12	Hanson PLC	1,819
13	Nestlé SA	1,789
14	Petróleos Mexicanos	1,486
15	Matsushita Electric Industrial Co., Ltd.	1,482
16	Fiat SpA	1,434
17	Alcatel Alsthom	1,423
18	Glaxo Holdings PLC	1,380
19	Hitachi, Ltd.	1,335
20	Bayer AG	1,262
21	Imperial Chemical Industries PLC	1,191
22	Daimler-Benz AG	1,130
23	Teléfonos de México, SA de CV	1,122
24	The Dai-Ichi Kangyo Bank, Ltd.	1,074
25	Hoechst AG	1,056
26	SmithKline Beecham PLC	1,050
27	The General Electric Company PLC	1,048
28	Guinness PLC	1,044
29	Siemens AG	1,038
30	BCE Inc.	988
31	The RTZ Corporation PLC	979
32	IRI Holding	978
32	Toshiba Corporation	978
34	Bass PLC	907
35	Nissan Motor Co., Ltd.	859
36	The Broken Hill Proprietary Company Ltd.	847
37	Royal Bank of Canada	832
38	Ciba-Geigy Ltd.	813
39	Telefónica de España, SA	792
40	Crédit Lyonnais	787
41	Sandoz Ltd.	761
42	The Seagram Company Ltd.	756
43	Barclays PLC	754
44	Marks and Spencer PLC	753
45	Roche Group	746
46	BASF AG	743
47	Fuji Photo Film Co., Ltd.	728
48	Nippon Steel Corporation	719
49	Petrofina SA	712
50	Volkswagen AG	707
51	Union Bank of Switzerland	706
52	Canadian Imperial Bank of Commerce	691
53	Singapore Airlines Ltd.	690
54	Deutsche Bank AG	688
55	B.A.T Industries PLC	685

Rank	Company	1990 Net Income ($ mil.)
56	LVMH Moët Hennessy Louis Vuitton	664
57	Sony Corporation	655
58	Fujitsu Ltd.	644
59	Cable and Wireless PLC	633
60	The Industrial Bank of Japan, Ltd.	615
61	Tokio Marine and Fire	615
62	BSN Groupe	608
63	The Tokyo Electric Power Company, Inc.	607
64	LM Ericsson Telephone Company	605
65	Allied-Lyons PLC	604
66	ABB Asea Brown Boveri Ltd.	590
67	Anglo American Corporation	589
68	Alcan Aluminium Ltd.	543
69	Ito-Yokado Co., Ltd.	524
70	Honda Motor Co., Ltd.	517
71	Petróleo Brasileiro SA	511
72	NEC Corporation	497
73	Bayerische Motoren Werke AG	464
74	Thyssen AG	463
75	Canon Inc.	455
76	Hutchison Whampoa Ltd.	451
77	Mitsubishi Corporation	444
78	Inco Ltd.	441
79	Imperial Oil Ltd.	425
80	Reed International PLC	407
81	British Airways PLC	405
82	Reuters Holdings PLC	399
83	Thorn EMI PLC	394
84	Fletcher Challenge Ltd.	389
85	HSBC Holdings PLC	385
86	The Thomson Corporation	385
87	The Rank Organisation PLC	382
88	Robert Bosch GmbH	376
89	Sumitomo Corporation	370
90	L'Oréal SA	360
91	Rolls-Royce PLC	355
92	Norsk Hydro AS	348
93	Cadbury Schweppes PLC	346
94	Bertelsmann AG	342
95	Swire Pacific Ltd.	314
96	Kirin Brewery Company, Ltd.	311
97	Sharp Corporation	311
98	Canadian Pacific Ltd.	306
99	The Red Cross	306
100	Pearson PLC	303
101	Oki Electric Industry Co., Ltd.	281
102	Imasco Ltd.	254
103	Nintendo Co., Ltd.	244
104	Renault	238
105	Jardine Matheson Holdings Ltd.	230
106	Mitsui & Co., Ltd.	230
107	Heineken NV	218
108	The News Corporation Ltd.	216
109	Rhône-Poulenc SA	216
110	Maxwell Communication Corporation PLC	195

Companies in *Hoover's Handbook of World Business 1992* Ranked by Profits (continued)

Rank	Company	1990 Net Income ($ mil.)
111	Pioneer Electronic Corporation	186
112	Nobel Industries Sweden AB	184
113	Friedrich Krupp GmbH	183
114	Mazda Motor Corporation	170
115	Accor SA	157
116	CS Holding	151
117	John Labatt Ltd.	146
118	Formosa Plastics Group	136
119	Hudson's Bay Company	136
120	Carlsberg AS	133
121	Japan Airlines Company, Ltd.	133
122	AB Electrolux	132
123	Pirelli SpA	124
124	Moore Corporation Ltd.	121
125	Foster's Brewing Group Ltd.	105
126	Dentsu Inc.	96
127	Lucky, Ltd.	87
128	KLM Royal Dutch Airlines	82
129	Daewoo Corporation	74
130	Source Perrier, SA	71
131	San Miguel Corporation	66
132	Saab-Scania AB	63
133	Casio Computer Co., Ltd.	59
134	Vendex International NV	54
135	Ing. C. Olivetti & C., SpA	53
136	Hachette SA	45
137	Suzuki Motor Corporation	44
138	Yamaha Corporation	44
139	Bridgestone Corporation	37
140	Minolta Camera Co., Ltd.	30
141	Samsung Co., Ltd.	18
142	Saatchi & Saatchi Company PLC	13
143	Hyundai Corporation	9
144	Qantas Airways Ltd.	9
145	Deutsche Lufthansa AG	7
146	Scandinavian Airlines System	(12)
147	Koor Industries Ltd.	(49)
148	Isuzu Motors Ltd.	(59)
149	AB Volvo	(181)
150	Campeau Corporation	(428)
151	Thomson SA	(487)
152	Bond Corporation Holdings Ltd.	(826)
153	Michelin	(947)
154	Compagnie des Machines Bull	(1,337)
155	Philips Electronics NV	(2,680)

Companies in *Hoover's Handbook of World Business 1992* Ranked by Market Value

Rank	Company	1990 Market Value ($ mil.)
1	Nippon Telegraph and Telephone Corp.	113,822
2	The Industrial Bank of Japan, Ltd.	57,469
3	Toyota Motor Corporation	43,648
4	Royal Dutch/Shell Group of Companies	42,149
5	The Dai-Ichi Kangyo Bank, Ltd.	42,120
6	The Tokyo Electric Power Company, Inc.	35,500
7	British Telecommunications PLC	34,789
8	IRI Holding (public companies only)	34,445
9	The British Petroleum Company PLC	34,367
10	Allianz AG Holding	28,893
11	Hitachi, Ltd.	26,457
12	The Nomura Securities Company, Ltd.	25,685
13	Unilever	25,184
14	Matsushita Electric Industrial Co., Ltd.	24,547
15	Glaxo Holdings PLC	24,468
16	Nippon Steel Corporation	22,858
17	Nestlé SA	21,471
18	Siemens AG	20,023
19	Hanson PLC	17,871
20	Deutsche Bank AG	17,630
21	Daimler-Benz AG	17,475
22	Toshiba Corporation	16,594
23	B.A.T Industries PLC	16,113
24	Mitsubishi Corporation	15,841
25	Nintendo Co., Ltd.	14,700
26	NEC Corporation	14,436
27	Tokio Marine and Fire	14,383
28	Sony Corporation	14,273
29	SmithKline Beecham PLC	13,992
30	Société Nationale Elf Aquitaine	13,697
31	Japan Airlines Company, Ltd.	13,552
32	Guinness PLC	13,268
33	Fujitsu Ltd.	13,081
34	Nissan Motor Co., Ltd.	13,010
35	Grand Metropolitan PLC	12,923
36	Roche Group	12,292
37	Union Bank of Switzerland	11,995
38	Imperial Chemical Industries PLC	11,682
39	Marks and Spencer PLC	11,599
40	The Broken Hill Proprietary Company Ltd.	11,575
41	Alcatel Alsthom	11,502
42	Barclays PLC	11,209
43	Fuji Photo Film Co., Ltd.	10,889
44	Fiat SpA	10,779
45	Kirin Brewery Company, Ltd.	10,688
46	Ito-Yokado Co., Ltd.	10,445
47	BCE Inc.	10,422
48	Ciba-Geigy Ltd.	10,288
49	Sandoz Ltd.	9,822
50	Imperial Oil Ltd.	9,708
51	Honda Motor Co., Ltd.	9,364
52	Bayer AG	9,263
53	LVMH Moët Hennessy Louis Vuitton	9,199
54	Cable and Wireless PLC	9,185
55	Sharp Corporation	9,057
56	The General Electric Company PLC	9,018
57	Mitsui & Co., Ltd.	8,799
58	The RTZ Corporation PLC	8,591
59	Anglo American Corporation	8,572
60	The Seagram Company Ltd.	8,249
61	Hoechst AG	8,174
62	Telefónica de España, SA	8,151
63	Sumitomo Corporation	8,009
64	The Thomson Corporation	8,000
65	Allied-Lyons PLC	7,963
66	BASF AG	7,919
67	BSN Groupe	7,687
68	Volkswagen AG	7,464
69	Teléfonos de México, SA de CV	7,181
70	Bass PLC	7,133
71	Canon Inc.	7,019
72	Petrofina SA	6,992
73	LM Ericsson Telephone Company	6,635
74	Norsk Hydro AS	6,316
75	Royal Bank of Canada	6,080
76	Reuters Holdings PLC	5,656
77	Bridgestone Corporation	5,654
78	Canadian Pacific Ltd.	5,409
79	L'Oréal SA	5,378
80	Pioneer Electronic Corporation	5,252
81	Peugeot SA	4,852
82	Singapore Airlines Ltd.	4,796
83	Hutchison Whampoa Ltd.	4,725
84	CS Holding	4,693
85	Mazda Motor Corporation	4,510
86	Alcan Aluminium Ltd.	4,342
87	Cadbury Schweppes PLC	4,272
88	Reed International PLC	4,034
89	Canadian Imperial Bank of Commerce	3,983
90	Bayerische Motoren Werke AG	3,956
91	HSBC Holdings PLC	3,912
92	Crédit Lyonnais	3,865
93	Isuzu Motors Ltd.	3,864
94	Thyssen AG	3,849
95	Thorn EMI PLC	3,789
96	The Rank Organisation PLC	3,584
97	Philips Electronics NV	3,492
98	Pearson PLC	3,431
99	Swire Pacific Ltd.	3,013
100	Rolls-Royce PLC	2,983
101	AB Volvo	2,891
102	Oki Electric Industry Co., Ltd.	2,883
103	Accor SA	2,807
104	Imasco Ltd.	2,783
105	Inco Ltd.	2,650
106	Carlsberg AS	2,595
107	Heineken NV	2,590
108	Foster's Brewing Group Ltd.	2,579
109	Rhône-Poulenc SA	2,416
110	Yamaha Corporation	2,410

Companies in *Hoover's Handbook of World Business 1992* Ranked by Market Value (continued)

Rank	Company	1990 Market Value ($ mil.)
111	Jardine Matheson Holdings Ltd.	2,328
112	Moore Corporation Ltd.	2,180
113	Fletcher Challenge Ltd.	2,141
114	Deutsche Lufthansa AG	2,105
115	AB Electrolux	2,101
116	British Airways PLC	1,982
117	Source Perrier, SA	1,940
118	Formosa Plastics Group	1,937
119	Casio Computer Co., Ltd.	1,901
120	Daewoo Corporation	1,848
121	Maxwell Communication Corporation PLC	1,845
122	Suzuki Motor Corporation	1,828
123	Saab-Scania AB	1,691
124	Pirelli SpA	1,539
125	Lucky, Ltd.	1,460
126	Ing. C. Olivetti & C., SpA	1,437
127	John Labatt Ltd.	1,376
128	Michelin	1,327
129	Minolta Camera Co., Ltd.	1,257
130	The News Corporation Ltd.	1,057
131	Nobel Industries Sweden AB	948
132	Hudson's Bay Company	776
133	San Miguel Corporation	624
134	KLM Royal Dutch Airlines	607
135	Hachette SA	591
136	Samsung Co., Ltd.	403
137	Compagnie des Machines Bull	302
138	Koor Industries Ltd.	301
139	Hyundai Corporation	179
140	Saatchi & Saatchi Company PLC	107
141	Campeau Corporation	77

Companies in *Hoover's Handbook of World Business 1992* Ranked by No. of Employees

Rank	Company	1990 Employees
1	IRI Holding	416,193
2	Daimler-Benz AG	376,785
3	Siemens AG	373,000
4	Unilever	304,000
5	Fiat SpA	303,238
6	Hitachi, Ltd.	290,811
7	Nippon Telegraph and Telephone Corp.	272,903
8	Philips Electronics NV	272,800
9	Volkswagen AG	268,744
10	Tata Group	248,000
11	British Telecommunications PLC	245,665
12	B.A.T Industries PLC	217,373
13	ABB Asea Brown Boveri Ltd.	215,154
14	Alcatel Alsthom	205,500
15	Nestlé SA	199,021
16	Matsushita Electric Industrial Co., Ltd.	198,299
17	Imasco Ltd.	190,000
18	Samsung Co., Ltd.	180,000
19	Robert Bosch GmbH	179,636
20	Hoechst AG	172,890
21	Bayer AG	171,000
22	Petróleos Mexicanos	167,952
23	Peugeot SA	159,100
24	Renault	157,378
25	Thyssen AG	152,078
26	AB Electrolux	150,892
27	Toshiba Corporation	142,000
28	Michelin	140,826
29	Grand Metropolitan PLC	138,149
30	Royal Dutch/Shell Group of Companies	137,000
31	BASF AG	134,647
32	Imperial Chemical Industries PLC	132,100
33	Nissan Motor Co., Ltd.	129,546
34	Jardine Matheson Holdings Ltd.	120,000
35	BCE Inc.	119,000
36	The British Petroleum Company PLC	118,050
37	Barclays PLC	115,300
38	Fujitsu Ltd.	115,012
39	NEC Corporation	114,599
40	The General Electric Company PLC	107,435
41	Thomson SA	105,500
42	Lucky, Ltd.	100,000
43	Bass PLC	98,345
44	Toyota Motor Corporation	96,849
45	Sony Corporation	95,600
46	Bridgestone Corporation	95,276
47	Ciba-Geigy Ltd.	94,141
48	Rhône-Poulenc SA	91,571
49	Société Nationale Elf Aquitaine	90,000
50	Vendex International NV	89,100
51	Allied-Lyons PLC	83,000
52	Accor SA	81,686
53	Hanson PLC	80,000
54	Honda Motor Co., Ltd.	79,000
55	KPMG	77,300

Rank	Company	1990 Employees
56	Marks and Spencer PLC	75,000
57	Telefónica de España, SA	74,827
58	The RTZ Corporation PLC	73,612
59	Canadian Pacific Ltd.	72,200
60	Bayerische Motoren Werke AG	70,948
61	LM Ericsson Telephone Company	70,238
62	AB Volvo	68,797
63	Pirelli SpA	68,703
64	Deutsche Bank AG	68,552
65	Crédit Lyonnais	68,486
66	Teléfonos de México, SA de CV	65,195
67	Ernst & Young	65,000
68	Rolls-Royce PLC	64,200
69	Friedrich Krupp GmbH	59,044
70	Thorn EMI PLC	57,932
71	Deutsche Lufthansa AG	57,567
72	Royal Bank of Canada	56,889
73	Arthur Andersen & Co.	56,801
74	Petróleo Brasileiro SA	55,569
75	Alcan Aluminium Ltd.	55,000
76	Hudson's Bay Company	55,000
77	HSBC Holdings PLC	54,408
78	Canon Inc.	54,381
79	SmithKline Beecham PLC	54,100
80	Ing. C. Olivetti & C., SpA	53,679
81	Roche Group	52,685
82	Sandoz Ltd.	52,640
83	British Airways PLC	52,054
84	The Broken Hill Proprietary Company Ltd.	52,000
85	Canadian Imperial Bank of Commerce	48,500
86	The Rank Organisation PLC	47,816
87	Petróleos de Venezuela, SA	46,940
88	Price Waterhouse	46,406
89	BSN Groupe	45,932
90	The Thomson Corporation	44,800
91	Compagnie des Machines Bull	44,476
92	CS Holding	44,153
93	Bertelsmann AG	43,509
94	Allianz AG Holding	43,117
95	Formosa Plastics Group	43,065
96	Nippon Steel Corporation	41,257
97	Scandinavian Airlines System	40,830
98	Fletcher Challenge Ltd.	40,000
99	The Tokyo Electric Power Company, Inc.	39,404
100	The News Corporation Ltd.	38,400
101	Cable and Wireless PLC	37,680
102	San Miguel Corporation	35,694
103	Cadbury Schweppes PLC	35,653
104	Sharp Corporation	34,017
105	Foster's Brewing Group Ltd.	33,702
106	Norsk Hydro AS	33,042
107	Glaxo Holdings PLC	31,327
108	Ito-Yokado Co., Ltd.	31,110
109	Hachette SA	30,000
110	Pearson PLC	29,410

Companies in *Hoover's Handbook of World Business 1992* Ranked by No. of Employees (cont.)

Rank	Company	1990 Employees
111	Saab-Scania AB	29,388
112	L'Oréal SA	29,286
113	Heineken NV	28,908
114	Mazda Motor Corporation	28,573
115	Swire Pacific Ltd.	28,000
116	Union Bank of Switzerland	27,470
117	Nobel Industries Sweden AB	26,654
118	KLM Royal Dutch Airlines	25,195
119	Moore Corporation Ltd.	25,021
120	Petrofina SA	23,800
121	Bond Corporation Holdings Ltd.	23,000
121	Guinness PLC	23,000
123	Fuji Photo Film Co., Ltd.	21,946
124	Japan Airlines Company, Ltd.	21,047
125	Maxwell Communication Corporation PLC	20,652
126	Singapore Airlines Ltd.	19,867
127	Inco Ltd.	19,387
128	Oki Electric Industry Co., Ltd.	19,331
129	Reed International PLC	19,000
130	Deloitte & Touche	18,800
131	The Dai-Ichi Kangyo Bank, Ltd.	18,466
132	Koor Industries Ltd.	18,450
133	Qantas Airways Ltd.	17,997
134	The Seagram Company Ltd.	17,700
135	Source Perrier, SA	16,781
136	John Labatt Ltd.	16,500
137	Coopers & Lybrand	16,145
138	Imperial Oil Ltd.	15,200
139	The Nomura Securities Company, Ltd.	15,000
140	Daewoo Corporation	14,286
141	Pioneer Electronic Corporation	13,898
142	LVMH Moët Hennessy Louis Vuitton	13,732
143	Mitsubishi Corporation	13,623
144	Suzuki Motor Corporation	13,561
145	Isuzu Motors Ltd.	13,427
146	Saatchi & Saatchi Company PLC	13,300
147	Yamaha Corporation	12,423
148	Carlsberg AS	12,192
149	Tokio Marine and Fire	12,000
150	Mitsui Co., Ltd.	11,656
151	Reuters Holdings PLC	10,810
152	Sumitomo Corporation	8,630
153	Kirin Brewery Company, Ltd.	7,673
154	Minolta Camera Co., Ltd.	6,537
155	The Red Cross	5,940
156	Dentsu Inc.	5,893
157	The Industrial Bank of Japan, Ltd.	5,500
158	Casio Computer Co., Ltd.	3,757
159	Lloyd's of London	2,147
160	Anglo American Corporation	2,000
161	Airbus Industrie	1,400
162	Hyundai Group (Corporate staff only)	845
163	Nintendo Co., Ltd.	730
164	Campeau Corporation	540

The World's Largest Companies

Rank	Company	Headquarters	Sales ($ bil.)
1	General Motors	US	125.1
2	Royal Dutch/Shell Group	Britain/Netherlands	107.2
3	Exxon	US	105.9
4	Ford Motor	US	98.3
5	Int'l Business Machines	US	69.0
6	Toyota Motor	Japan	64.5
7	IRI	Italy	61.4
8	British Petroleum	Britain	59.5
9	Mobil	US	58.8
10	General Electric	US	58.4
11	Daimler-Benz	Germany	54.3
12	Hitachi	Japan	50.7
13	Fiat	Italy	47.8
14	Samsung	South Korea	45.0
15	Philip Morris	US	44.3
16	Volkswagen	Germany	43.7
17	Matsushita Electric Industrial	Japan	43.5
18	ENI	Italy	41.8
19	Texaco	US	41.2
20	Nissan Motor	Japan	40.2
21	Unilever	Britain/Netherlands	40.0
22	E.I. Du Pont de Nemours	US	40.0
23	Chevron	US	39.2
24	Siemens	Germany	39.2
25	Nestlé	Switzerland	27.7
26	Elf Aquitaine	France	32.9
27	Chrysler	US	30.9
28	Philips' Gloeilampenfabrieken	Netherlands	30.9
39	Toshiba	Japan	30.2
30	Renault	France	30.0
31	Peugeot	France	29.3
32	BASF	Germany	29.2
33	Amoco	US	28.3
34	Hoechst	Germany	27.7
35	Asea Brown Boveri	Switzerland	27.7
36	Boeing	US	27.6
37	Honda Motor	Japan	27.1
38	Alcatel Alsthom	France	26.5
39	Bayer	Germany	26.1
40	NEC	Japan	24.4
41	Procter & Gamble	US	24.4
42	Total	France	23.6
43	Petróleos de Venezuela	Venezuela	23.5
44	Imperial Chemical Industries	Britain	23.3
45	Daewoo	South Korea	22.3
46	Occidental Petroleum	US	21.9
47	United Technologies	US	21.8
48	Thyssen	Germany	21.5
49	Mitsubishi Electric	Japan	21.2
50	Nippon Steel	Japan	21.2

Source: *Fortune*, July 29, 1991

The World's Wealthiest People

Rank	Who	Where	What	How Much 1990 ($ bil.)
1	Sultan Sir Hassanal Bolkiah	Brunei	Oil & Gas	31.0
2	Walton family	Arkansas	Wal-Mart	21.1
3	King Fahd and family	Saudi Arabia	Oil & Gas	18.0
4	Reichmann brothers	Canada	Real Estate	12.8
5	Mars family	US	Candy	12.5
6	Newhouse family	New York	Publishing	12.1
7	Queen Elizabeth II	UK	Inheritance	10.7
8	Taikichiro Mori	Japan	Real Estate	10.0
9	John Kluge	Virginia	Metromedia	7.1
10	Kenneth Thomson	Canada	Publishing, Retail	6.7
11	Grosvenor family	UK	Real Estate	6.6
12	Chung family	Korea	Hyundai	6.5
13	Rausing brothers	UK	Tetra Pak	6.3
14	Nakajima family	Japan	Pachinko Machines	5.6
15	Lauder family	New York	Cosmetics	5.2
16	Maktoum family	Dubai	Oil	5.0
17	Cox sisters	US	Publishing	4.8
18	Koch brothers	US	Oil	4.7
19	Warren Buffett	Nebraska	Investments	4.4
20	Pritzker family	Illinois	Hyatt, Marmon	4.2
21	Tsai family	Taiwan	Insurance	4.2
22	Bronfman family	North America	Seagram	4.1
23	Bass family	Texas	Investments	4.0
24	Erivan Haub	Germany	Supermarket	4.0
25	Nahayan family	Abu Dhabi	Oil	4.0

Source: *Fortune*, Sept. 9, 1991

10 Best Airlines and Airports

Rank	10 Best Airlines (1991)	Rank	10 Best Airports (1991)
1	British Airways	1	Singapore Changi
2	Singapore Airlines	2	London Heathrow (Term. 4)
3	Swissair	3	Amsterdam Schipol
4	American Airlines	4	Zurich Kloten
5	Lufthansa	5	Frankfurt
6	Cathay Pacific	6	London Gatwich
7	Virgin Atlantic	7	Copenhagen
8	KLM	8	Chicago O'Hare
9	SAS	9	Paris Charles de Gaulle
10	Canadian International	10	Geneva Cointrin

Source: Consumer Survey, *Euromoney*, April 1991

10 Worst Airlines and Airports

Rank	10 Worst Airlines (1991)	Rank	10 Worst Airports (1991)
1	Pan Am	1	New York JFK
2	TWA	2	London Heathrow (Terms. 1-3)
3	Aeroflot	3	Paris Charles de Gaulle
4	United	4	Tokyo Narita
5	Continental	5	Toronto
6	Northwest	6	Hong Kong
7	Alitalia	7	New York La Guardia
8	Garuda	8	Milan
9	Air India	9	Athens
10	Air France	10	Sydney
		10	Los Angeles LAX

Source: Consumer Survey, *Euromoney*, April 1991

Top 10 Tourist Destinations

Rank	Country	1988 Tourists (thou.)
1	France	38,000
2	Spain	35,000
3	United States	33,860
4	Italy	28,000[1]
5	United Kingdom	16,756
6	West Germany	16,571
7	Canada	15,493
8	Austria	13,113
9	China	12,367[1]
10	Switzerland	11,700

Source: World Tourism Organization; *Travel Industry World Yearbook*, 1990

[1] Estimates

10 Highest Revenue Tourist Destinations

Rank	Country	1988 Tourism Receipts ($ mil.)
1	United States	29,202
2	Spain	16,686
3	France	13,744
4	Italy	12,399
5	United Kingdom	11,051
6	West Germany	8,572
7	Austria	8,521
8	Switzerland	5,615
9	Canada	5,601
10	Hong Kong	4,273

Source: World Tourism Organization; *Travel Industry World Yearbook*, 1990

Foreign Country Travel Advertising Expenditures in the US

Rank	Country	1988 Expenditures ($ thou.)
1	Canada	11,193
2	Mexico	10,560
3	Jamaica	9,972
4	Bermuda	9,714
5	Bahamas	4,235
6	France	3,500
7	Australia	3,318
8	Spain	3,011
9	Barbados	2,766
10	Singapore	2,393

Source: Ogilvy & Mather, *Travel Industry World Yearbook*, 1990

Top 10 Spenders for Tourism

Rank	Country	1988 Tourism Expenditures ($ mil.)
1	United States	32,112
2	West Germany	24,938
3	Japan	18,682
4	United Kingdom	14,555
5	France	9,677
6	Netherlands	6,717
7	Canada	6,316
8	Italy	6,053
9	Switzerland	5,019
10	Austria	4,829

Note: Expenditures are monies spent abroad by citizens of the country listed.

Source: World Tourism Organization; *Travel Industry World Yearbook*, 1990

Top 20 Airports

Rank	Airport	1988 Passengers
1	O'Hare, Chicago	56,678,991
2	Hartsfield, Atlanta	45,900,098
3	Los Angeles	44,398,611
4	Dallas/Ft. Worth	44,271,038
5	Heathrow, London	37,525,300
6	Tokyo-Haneda, Japan	32,177,040
7	Stapleton, Denver	31,797,747
8	Kennedy, New York	31,165,676
9	San Francisco	30,506,794
10	Miami	24,525,302
11	Frankfurt/Main, Germany	24,442,996
12	La Guardia, New York	24,158,780
13	Logan, Boston	23,369,002
14	Newark, NJ	22,495,568
15	Orly, Paris	22,205,823
16	Gatwick, London	20,761,200
17	Lambert, St. Louis	20,170,060
18	Honolulu	20,155,834
19	Osaka, Japan	20,060,795
20	Detroit Metropolitan	19,708,029

Source: Airport Operators Council International; *Travel Industry World Yearbook*, 1990

Top 10 Airlines — No. of Passengers

Rank	Airline	1990 Passengers (thou.)
1	Aeroflot	137,742
2	American	73,251
3	Delta	65,789
4	US Air	60,059
5	United	57,612
6	Northwest	41,046
7	Continental	35,496
8	All Nippon	33,048
9	British Airways	25,172
10	TWA	24,416

Source: *Air Transport World*, June 1991

Top 10 Airlines — No. of Aircraft

Rank	Airline	1990 Aircraft
1	Aeroflot	1,379
2	American	552
3	United	462
4	US Air	452
5	Delta	444
6	Continental	339
7	Northwest	332
8	Federal Express	259
9	British Airways	227
10	TWA	210

Source: *Air Transport World*, June 1991

World Airliner Fleet

	Aircraft in Service 1990	On Order Year-end 1990
Jets		
Boeing	4,787	1,536
McDonnell Douglas	2,133	464
Lockheed	226	1
Other US	36	0
Canadian	0	20
Airbus	585	638
Other European	504	89
Soviet	1,396	NA
Total jets	**9,667**	**2,748**
Turboprops	3,639	375
Piston-engines	879	1
Helicopters	104	2
Miscellaneous	33	0
All aircraft	**14,322**	**3,126**

Source: *Air Transport World*, June 1991

US Airlines in World Markets

Airline	1990 Passengers (thou.)			
	Atlantic	Latin America	Pacific	Total
American	1,764	4,905	187	**6,856**
Continental	637	2,168	2,457	**5,262**
Delta	1,168	1,548	350	**3,066**
Eastern	0	881	0	**881**
Northwest	1,053	0	4,724	**5,777**
Pan Am	6,568	3,515	0	**10,083**
TWA	3,991	0	0	**3,991**
United	158	0	4,849	**5,007**
US Air	171	370	0	**541**
Total	**15,510**	**13,387**	**12,567**	**41,464**

Source: *Air Transport World*, June 1991

Largest Acquisitions of Foreign Businesses by US Companies

Rank	Acquirer	1990 Acquisition	Industry	Price ($ mil.)
1	Philip Morris Cos. Inc.	Jacobs Suchard Ltd. (Switzerland)	Chocolate, coffee	$3,800.0
2	Ford Motor Co.	Jaguar PLC (UK)	Autos	2,643.6
3	Ameritech Corp. and Bell Atlantic Corp.	Telecom Corp. (New Zealand)	Telephone service	2,460.0
4	Southwestern Bell Corp., France Telecom, and Grupo Carso (Mexico)	20.4% of Teléfonos de México SA (Mexico)	Telephone service	1,757.0
5	Tyco Laboratories Inc.	Wormald International Ltd. (Australia)	Fire protection	642.5
6	Emerson Electric Co.	Leroy-Somer (France)	Electric motors	460.0
7	Goldman, Sachs & Co.	28% of Wolters Kluwer NV (Netherlands)	Publishing	444.2
8	General Electric Co.	Burton Group Financial Services PLC (UK)	Credit cards	329.0
9	PepsiCo Inc.	Empresas Gamesa SA de CV (Mexico)	Snack foods	320.7
10	American Brands Inc.	Whyte & Mackay Distillers Ltd. (UK)	Liquor	237.8

Source: *Mergers & Acquisitions*, May/June 1991

Largest Acquisitions of US Businesses by Foreign Companies

Rank	Acquirer	1990 Acquisition	Industry	Price ($ mil.)
1	Rhône-Poulenc SA (France)	68% of Rorer Group Inc.	Pharmaceuticals	$3,297.7
2	Roche Holding Ltd. (Switzerland)	50% of Genentech Inc.	Genetic engineering	2,013.0
3	Bass PLC (UK)	Holiday Inn division of Holiday Corp.	Hotels	1,980.0
4	Compagnie de Saint-Gobain SA (France)	Norton Co.	Industrial products	1,833.0
5	Investcorp International Inc. (Bahrain)	Saks Fifth Ave. unit of B.A.T Industries PLC	Retailing	1,600.0
6	ABB Asea Brown Boveri (Holding) Ltd. (Sweden/Switzerland)	Combustion Engineering Inc.	Power generation equipment	1,565.4
7	Group led by Sir James Goldsmith (UK)	49% of Newmont Mining Corp.	Gold and minerals	1,299.0
8	Reckitt & Colman PLC (UK)	Boyle-Midway unit of American Home Products Corp.	Household products	1,250.0
9	Accor SA (France)	Motel 6 LP	Motels	1,202.7
10	ACC Acquisition Corp. (controlled by Mitsubishi Corp., Japan)	Aristech Chemical Corp.	Chemicals	898.2

Source: *Mergers & Acquisitions*, May/June 1991

50 Largest Advertising Organizations

Rank	Organization	HQ	1990 Worldwide Sales ($ mil.)
1	WPP Group	UK	2,715.0
2	Saatchi & Saatchi Co.	UK	1,729.3
3	Interpublic Group of Cos.	US	1,649.8
4	Omnicom Group	US	1,335.5
5	Dentsu Inc.	Japan	1,254.8
6	Young & Rubicam	US	1,073.6
7	Eurocom Group	France	748.5
8	Hakuhodo Inc.	Japan	586.3
9	Grey Advertising	US	583.3
10	Foote, Cone & Belding Comm.	US	536.2
11	D'Arcy Masius Benton & Bowles	US	532.5
12	Leo Burnett Co.	US	531.8
13	Publicis-FCB Comm.	France	430.0
14	Roux, Seguela Cayzac & Goudard	France	346.2
15	BDDP Worldwide	France	236.0
16	Bozell, Jacobs, Kenyon & Eckhardt	US	214.0
17	N W Ayer	US	185.9
18	Tokyu Agency	Japan	170.3
19	Daiko Advertising	Japan	159.5
20	Alliance International Advertising Group	UK	141.8
21	TBWA Advertising	US	138.3
22	Chiat/Day/Mojo	US	136.8
23	Ketchum Communications	US	134.2
24	Dai-Ichi Kikaku Co.	Japan	133.8
25	Dentsu, Young & Rubicam Part.	US/Japan	126.8
26	Asatsu Inc.	Japan	125.0
27	Ross Roy Group	US	110.0
28	Wells, Rich, Greene	US	105.0
29	I&S Corp.	Japan	104.2
30	Yomiko Advertising	Japan	102.9
31	GGT PLC	UK	95.0
32	Asahi Advertising	Japan	88.9
33	Man Nen Sha	Japan	87.0
34	FCAB	France	83.1
35	GGK International	Switzerland	79.3
36	Cheil Communications	Korea	73.1
37	MPM Propaganda	Brazil	65.2
38	Armando Testa Group Worldwide	Italy	63.3
39	Nihon Keizaisha Advertising	Japan	62.5
40	Sogei Inc.	Japan	57.8
41	Orikomi Advertising	US	57.5
42	Telephone Marketing Programs	US	55.8
43	W.B. Doner & Co.	US	51.4
44	Clemenger/BBDO	Australia	50.7
45	CDP Europe	UK	50.5
46	Hill, Holliday, Connors, Cosmopulos	US	50.1
47	Admarketing Inc.	US	49.7
48	Chuo Senko Advertising Co.	Japan	49.1
49	Earle Palmer Brown Cos.	US	48.5
50	Oricom Inc.	Korea	46.2

Source: *Advertising Age*, March 25, 1991, Crain Communications, Inc.

Largest Advertising Agency in Each Country

Country	Agency	1990 Sales ($ mil.)
Argentina	Lautrec/SSA	5.3
Australia	George Patterson Pty.	78.1
Austria	GGK Vienna/Salzburg	10.6
Bahrain	Fortune Promoseven	11.4
Barbados	Lonsdale/SSA	0.6
Belgium	McCann-Erickson Belgium	19.8
Bermuda	Advertising Assoc. Compton	1.5
Botswana	Horizon Advertising	0.2
Brazil	MPM Propaganda	63.7
Cameroon	Lintas:Cameroon	0.3
Canada	McCann-Erickson Canada	29.4
Chile	J. Walter Thompson Chilena	3.7
China	McCann-Erickson Jardine China	0.8
Costa Rica	McCann-Erickson Centroamericana	1.1
Cyprus	Impact/BBDO	3.7
Denmark	Grey Communications Group	20.2
Ecuador	Norlop Thompson Asociados	2.2
Egypt	Saatchi & Saatchi Advertising	0.2
El Salvador	McCann-Erickson Centroamericana	0.9
Finland	AS & Grey	19.3
France	RSCG France	180.0
Germany	Lintas:Deutschland	70.4
Greece	Spot/Thompson Advertising	7.8
Guatemala	Publicidad McCann-Erickson	1.0
Honduras	McCann-Erickson Centroamericana	0.4
Hong Kong	Ogilvy & Mather	14.1
Hungary	Young & Rubicam Hungary	1.5
India	Hindustan Thompson Assoc.	10.9
Indonesia	Lintas:Indonesia	4.5
Ireland	Wilson Hartnell Group	8.2
Israel	Ariely Communication Group	6.0
Italy	Gruppo Armando Testa	61.9
Ivory Coast	Lintas:Abidjan	1.2
Jamaica	McCann-Erickson Jamaica	1.1
Japan	Dentsu Inc.	1,142.5
Kenya	McCann-Erickson Kenya	1.0
Malawi	Graphic:Lintas Malawi	0.4
Malaysia	Ogilvy & Mather	4.6
Mexico	McCann-Erickson	12.7
Morocco	Klem RSCG	1.0
Namibia	Lintas:Namibia	0.2
Netherlands	BBDO/Nederland	41.0
New Zealand	Clemenger/BBDO NZ	16.3
Nigeria	Insight Communications	8.7
Norway	BSB Batesgruppen	21.8
Pakistan	R:Lintas	1.2
Panama	Campagnani, Aleman Publicidad	1.1
Peru	J. Walter Thompson Peruana	10.6
Philippines	McCann-Erickson Philippines	4.1
Portugal	McCann-Erickson/Hora	13.1
Saudi Arabia	Saatchi & Saatchi Advertising	1.7
Singapore	Batey Communications Group	11.3
South Africa	Ogilvy & Mather Rightford	14.7
South Korea	Cheil Communications	73.1
Spain	Grupo BSB	52.4
Sri Lanka	Grant Bozell Sri Lanka	0.6
Sweden	Hall & Cederquist/Young & Rubicam	21.0
Switzerland	Advico Young & Rubicam	23.6
Taiwan	Ogilvy & Mather	8.1
Thailand	Lintas:Thailand	9.4
Trinidad	McCann-Erickson Trinidad	2.2
Turkey	Cenajans Grey	7.7
UK	Saatchi & Saatchi Advertising	187.5
US	Young & Rubicam	1,073.6
Uruguay	Corporacion/Thompson	0.8
USSR	Young & Rubicam/Sovero	0.2
Venezuela	Corpa	8.2

Source: *Advertising Age*, March 25, 1991, Crain Communications, Inc.

Top 20 International Loan Providers

Rank	Bank	1990 Amount ($ mil.)	No. of Issues
1	NatWest	10,819.60	409
2	Barclays Bank Group	8,948.39	355
3	Citicorp	8,667.47	245
4	Fuji	8,654.11	320
5	Sumitomo	7,787.58	309
6	Dai-Ichi Kangyo	6,898.08	224
7	Industrial Bank of Japan	6,733.87	213
8	Chemical	6,299.89	153
9	Chase Manhattan	6,239.43	250
10	Manufacturers Hanover	6,190.99	225
11	ABN Amro	6,141.86	247
12	Bank of America	6,092.54	234
13	Banque Nationale de Paris	5,829.76	240
14	Crédit Lyonnais	5,772.53	274
15	First National Bank of Chicago	5,669.58	191
16	Union Bank of Switzerland	5,563.07	236
17	CSFB/Crédit Suisse	5,557.07	171
18	J.P. Morgan	5,430.37	165
19	Deutsche	5,285.05	165
20	Swiss Bank Corporation	5,203.36	175

Source: Euromoney Loanware; Special Supplement, *Euromoney*, March 1991

Top 20 Managers — International Equity Issues

Rank	Manager	1990 Amount ($ mil.)	No. of Issues
1	Goldman Sachs	1,286.45	50
2	Banque Indosuez	906.83	41
3	Nomura Securities	900.91	62
4	Merrill Lynch	843.70	47
5	Deutsche	726.53	40
6	CSFB/Crédit Suisse	620.30	60
7	Barclays Bank Group	537.48	23
8	SG Warburg	513.75	50
9	Salomon Brothers	511.43	53
10	Morgan Stanley	446.11	40
11	Daiwa Securities	409.01	45
12	Baring Brothers	356.63	28
13	Banque Paribas	352.85	53
14	Yamaichi Securities	316.44	35
15	ABN Amro	307.77	45
16	Lehman Brothers	306.75	30
17	Swiss Bank Corporation	267.22	60
18	Banque Nationale de Paris	267.17	23
19	Robert Fleming	247.42	16
20	Se Banken	238.52	20

Source: Euromoney Bondware; Special Supplement, *Euromoney*, March 1991

20 Largest African Banks

Rank	Bank	HQ Location	Assets ($ bil.)
1	Stanbic	South Africa	13.9
2	First National Bank of Southern Africa	South Africa	11.3
3	Nedcor	South Africa	10.5
4	Bankorp	South Africa	9.1
5	Volkskas Bank	South Africa	7.3
6	Commercial Bank of Ethiopia	Ethiopia	2.1
7	National Bank of Commerce	Tanzania	1.6
8	Société Générale de Banques en Côte d'Ivoire	Ivory Coast	1.4
9	United Bank for Africa	Nigeria	1.4
10	Banque Int pour le Commerce & l'Industrie	Cameroon	1.2
11	Boland Bank	South Africa	1.2
12	First Bank of Nigeria	Nigeria	1.1
13	Union Bank of Nigeria	Nigeria	1.1
14	Bank of Khartoum	Sudan	0.9
15	Banque Int pour le Commerce & l'Industrie	Ivory Coast	0.8
16	Kenya Commercial Bank	Kenya	0.7
17	Société Ivoirienne de Banque	Ivory Coast	0.7
18	Société Générale de Banques au Cameroon	Cameroon	0.6
19	Mauritius Commercial Bank	Mauritius	0.6
20	Zimbabwe Banking Corp.	Zimbabwe	0.5

Source: *The Banker*, September 1990

20 Largest Arabian Financial Institutions

Rank	Institution	HQ Location	Assets at 12/31/89 ($ bil.)
1	Rafidain Bank	Iraq	46.8
2	Bank of Credit & Commerce International	Luxembourg	23.5
3	National Commercial Bank	Saudi Arabia	23.1
4	Arab Banking Corporation	Bahrain	21.7
5	Banque Extérieure d'Algérie	Algeria	13.4*
6	National Bank of Kuwait	Kuwait	13.2
7	Arab Bank	Jordan	13.0
8	Banque de l'Agriculture & du Dévelop. Rural	Algeria	12.2
9	Riyad Bank	Saudi Arabia	11.9
10	Gulf International Bank	Bahrain	9.9
11	Crédit Populaire d'Algérie	Algeria	8.8
12	Banque Nationale d'Algérie	Algeria	8.2
13	UBAF - Union de Banques Arabes et Françaises	France	7.8
14	National Bank of Egypt	Egypt	7.5
15	Saudi American Bank	Saudi Arabia	7.1
16	Commercial Bank of Kuwait	Kuwait	6.9
17	Gulf Bank	Kuwait	6.6
18	Al Rajhi Banking & Investment Corporation	Saudi Arabia	6.6
19	Banque Misr	Egypt	6.5
20	National Bank of Dubai	United Arab Emirates	6.3

* At 12/31/88

Source: *The Banker*, November 1990

20 Largest European Banks

Rank	Bank	HQ Location	Assets at 12/31/89 ($ bil.)
1	Crédit Agricole	France	242.0
2	Banque Nationale de Paris	France	231.5
3	Crédit Lyonnais	France	210.7
4	Barclays Bank	UK	204.9
5	Deutsche Bank	Germany	202.3
6	National Westminster Bank	UK	186.6
7	Société Générale	France	164.7
8	Groupe des Caisses d'Epargne Ecureuil	France	152.7
9	Dresdner	Germany	147.0
10	Compagnie Financière de Paribas	France	138.7
11	Union Bank of Switzerland	Switzerland	113.9
12	Commerzbank	Germany	112.8
13	DG Bank	Germany	109.2
14	Istituto Bancario San Paolo de Torino	Italy	107.4
15	Swiss Bank Corp.	Switzerland	105.0
16	Westdeutsche Landesbank Girozentrale	Germany	104.5
17	Bayerische Vereinsbank	Germany	102.2
18	Banca Nazionale del Lavoro	Italy	101.0
19	Midland Bank	UK	100.3
20	Amro Bank	Netherlands	93.8

Source: *The Banker*, October 1990

20 Largest Japanese Banks

Rank	Bank	HQ Location	Assets at 3/31/90 ($ bil.)
1	Dai-Ichi Kangyo Bank	Tokyo	408.0
2	Sumitomo Bank	Osaka	372.4
3	Fuji Bank	Tokyo	366.7
4	Sanwa Bank	Osaka	357.8
5	Mitsubishi Bank	Tokyo	355.0
6	Industrial Bank of Japan	Tokyo	260.0
7	Tokai Bank	Nagoya	230.4
8	Norinchukin Bank	Tokyo	222.3
9	Mitsui Bank	Tokyo	205.6
10	Bank of Tokyo	Tokyo	202.9
11	Long-Term Credit Bank of Japan	Tokyo	176.2
12	Taiyo Kobe Bank	Kobe	175.0
13	Mitsubishi Trust & Banking Corporation	Tokyo	130.9
14	Nippon Credit Bank	Tokyo	115.2
15	Daiwa Bank	Osaka	112.2
16	Sumitomo Trust & Banking	Osaka	109.9
17	Saitama Bank	Urawa, Saitama	99.8
18	Kyowa Bank	Tokyo	99.0
19	Mitsui Trust & Banking	Tokyo	98.2
20	Yasuda Trust & Banking	Tokyo	87.5

Source: *The Banker*, January 1991

20 Largest Latin American Banks

Rank	Bank	HQ Location	Assets at 12/31/89 ($ bil.)
1	Banco da Brasil	Brazil	82.7
2	Banco Bradesco	Brazil	19.5
3	Banamex	Mexico	18.4
4	Nacional Financiera	Mexico	16.8
5	Bancomer	Mexico	15.9
6	Banco Itaú	Brazil	13.7
7	Banco do Estado de Sâo Paulo	Brazil	13.2
8	Banca Serfin	Mexico	8.6
9	Banco de la Nacion Argentina	Argentina	7.3
10	Banco Nacional de Comercio Exterior	Mexico	7.2
11	Unibanco	Brazil	5.8
12	Banco Reál	Brazil	5.0
13	Banco Nacional de Desarrollo	Argentina	4.9*
14	Banco del Estado de Chile	Chile	4.4
15	Banco de Chile	Chile	4.2
16	Banco Nacional	Brazil	4.0
17	Banco de Crédito Nacional	Brazil	3.7
18	Banco de la Provincia de Buenos Aires	Argentina	3.6
19	Multibanco Comermex	Mexico	3.5
20	Banco de la Republica Oriental del Uruguay	Uruguay	3.0

* At 12/31/87

Source: *The Banker*, August 1990

Where the Japanese Electronics Companies Compete

	Calculators	Cameras (35 mm)	CD/CD-Rom	Computers (PCs)	Computers (other)	Consumer Audio	Consumer Video	Copiers	Fax Machines	Major Appliances	Musical Instruments	Printers	Telephones	Typewriters	Watches
Canon	•	•		•			•	•	•			•		•	
Casio	•			•			•				•	•			•
Fuji		•					•	•							
Fujitsu			•	•	•	•			•			•	•		
Hitachi			•	•	•	•	•		•	•		•	•		
Matsushita			•	•	•	•	•	•	•	•	•	•	•	•	
Minolta		•					•	•	•			•			
NEC			•	•	•		•			•		•	•		
Oki				•	•				•			•	•	•	
Pioneer			•			•	•						•		
Sharp	•			•		•	•	•	•	•		•	•	•	•
Sony			•	•	•	•	•						•	•	
Toshiba			•	•	•	•	•	•	•	•		•	•		
Yamaha			•			•					•				

Source: The Reference Press

World's Top Information Science Companies

Rank	Company	1990 Revenue ($ mil.)
1	IBM	67,090.0
2	Digital	13,072.3
3	Fujitsu	12,361.5
4	NEC	12,350.3
5	Hitachi	9,590.9
6	Unisys	9,302.0
7	Hewlett-Packard	9,300.0
8	Siemens/Nixdorf	7,735.1
9	Olivetti	6,414.5
10	Groupe Bull	6,349.6
11	Apple	5,740.0
12	NCR	5,617.0
13	Toshiba	4,764.5
14	Canon	4,669.2
15	Matsushita	3,731.0

Note: Revenues include hardware, software, peripherals, services, etc.

Source: *Datamation*, June 15, 1991

World's Top Computer Makers

Rank	Company	Manufacturing Revenues ($ bil.)
1	IBM	31.7
2	NEC	6.4
3	Digital Equipment	5.8
4	Apple	4.3
5	Hewlett-Packard	4.2
6	Fujitsu	3.6
7	Groupe Bull	3.3
8	Unisys	3.3
9	Compaq	3.0

Source: *Dataquest, New York Times*, September 5, 1991

World's Top Semiconductor Makers

Rank	Company	Market Share
1	NEC	8.4%
2	Toshiba	8.3%
3	Hitachi	6.7%
4	Motorola	6.3%
5	Intel	5.4%
6	Fujitsu	4.9%
7	Texas Instruments	4.4%
8	Mitsubishi	4.0%
9	Phillips	3.5%

Source: *Dataquest, New York Times*, September 5, 1991

Top European Large Computer Makers

Company	1989 Market Share
IBM	32%
Digital	10%
Siemens-Nixdorf*	9%
Groupe Bull	7%
Hewlett Packard	6%
Unisys	4%
International Computers (Fujitsu)	3%
Other companies	29%

*Siemens and Nixdorf merged in early 1990.

Source: *Dataquest, New York Times*, April 22, 1991

Top European Personal Computer Makers

Company	1990 Market Share
IBM	14%
Commodore	12%
Atari	6%
Apple	6%
Compaq	6%
Olivetti	6%
Amstrad	4%
Other companies	46%

Source: *Dataquest, New York Times*, April 22, 1991

Top European Car Makers

Rank	Company	1990 Cars Made (thou.)
1	Volkswagen	2,397
2	Peugeot	1,978
3	Fiat	1,876
4	General Motors	1,717
5	Ford	1,604
6	Renault	1,514
7	Daimler-Benz	574
8	BMW	500
9	Rover	465
10	Volvo	373
11	Nissan	76
12	Porsche	32

Source: *Automotive News*, 1991 Market Data Book Issue

World's Top Automotive Producers

Rank	Company	1990 Units Produced (thou.)
1	General Motors	7,451
2	Ford Motor Co.	5,872
3	Toyota Motor Corp.	4,889
4	Nissan Motor Co.	3,063
5	Volkswagen AS	3,058
6	Peugeot-Citroen PSA	2,194
7	Fiat Group	2,163
8	Honda Motor Co.	1,993
9	Chrysler Corp.	1,984
10	Renault SA	1,843
11	Mazda Motor Corp.	1,607
12	Mitsubishi Motor Corp.	1,333

Note: Includes cars, trucks, and buses.

Source: Automotive News Data Center

Top Japanese Car Makers

Rank	Company	1990 Cars Made (thou.)
1	Toyota	3,346
2	Nissan	2,021
3	Honda	1,223
4	Mazda	1,118
5	Mitsubishi	833
6	Suzuki	511
7	Daihatsu	373
8	Fuji	320
9	Isuzu	202

Source: *Automotive News*, 1991 Market Data Book Issue

Top Imported Cars into the US

Rank	Company	1990 Cars (thou.)
1	Toyota	367
2	Nissan	312
3	Honda	252
4	Mazda	153
5	Acura	138
6	Hyundai	137
7	Volkswagen	130
8	Mitsubishi	100
9	Subaru	93
10	Volvo	90

Source: *Automotive News Insight*, March 11, 1991

World Vehicle Production

Year	World Total (thou.)	US (thou.)	Japan (thou.)
1950	10,579	8,006	32
1960	16,383	7,902	482
1970	29,708	8,267	5,289
1980	38,838	8,010	11,043
1990	44,165	9,888	13,487

Source: *Automotive News*, 1991 Market Data Book Issue

The 225 Japanese Companies in the Nikkei Index

All Nippon Airways
Anjinomoto
Asahi Breweries
Asahi Chemical Industry
Asahi Denka Kogyo
Asahi Glass
Bank of Tokyo
Bridgestone
C. Itoh
Canon
Chiyoda
Citizen Watch
Dai Nippon Pharmaceutical
Dai Nippon Printing
Dai-Ichi Kangyo Bank
Daito Woolen Spinning & Weaving
Daiwa House Industry
Denki Kagaku Kogyo
Dowa Mining
Ebara
Fuji Bank
Fuji Electric
Fuji Photo Film
Fuji Spinning
Fujikura
Fujita
Fujitsu
Furukawa
Furukawa Electric
Godo Shusei
Heiwa Real Estate
Hino Motors
Hitachi
Hitachi Zosen
Hohnen Oil
Hokuetsu Paper Mills
Honda Motor
Honsu Paper
Ishikawajima-Harima Heavy Industry
Isuzu Motors
Iwantani International
Japan Securities Finance
The Japan Steelworks
Japan Synthetic Chemical Industry
Japan Wool Textile
Jujo Paper
Kajima Corporation
Kanebo
Kansai Electric Power
Katakura Industries
Kawasaki Heavy Industries
Kawasaki Kisen
Kawasaki Steel Corporation
Keihin Electric Express Railway
Keio Electric Railway
Keisei Electric Railway
Kikkoman
Kirin Brewery
Kobe Steel
Komatsu
Konica
Korakuen
Koyo Seiko
Kubota
Kuraray
Kyokuyo
Kyowa Hakko Kogyo
Marubeni
Maruzen
Matsushita Electrical Industrial
Matsuzakaya
Mazda Motor
Meidensha
Meiji Milk Products
Meiji Seika
Mitsubishi
Mitsubishi Bank
Mitsubishi Chemical Industry
Mitsubishi Electric
Mitsubishi Estate
Mitsubishi Heavy Industries
Mitsubishi Metal Corporation
Mitsubishi Mining & Cement
Mitsubishi Oil
Mitsubishi Paper
Mitsubishi Rayon
Mitsubishi Steel Manufacturing
Mitsubishi Trust & Banking
Mitsubishi Warehouse & Trans.
Mitsui
Mitsui Taivo Kobe Bank
Mitsui Engineering & Shipbuilding
Mitsui Mining
Mitsui Mining & Smelting
Mitsui O.S.K. Lines
Mitsui Real Estate
Mitsui Toatsu Chemicals
Mitsui Trust & Banking
Mitsui Warehouse
Mitsukoshi
Morianga
Nachi-Fujikoshi
Navix Line
NGK Insulators
Nichirei
Nichiro Gyogyo
Nihon Cement
Niigata Engineering
Nikkatsu
Nikko Securities
Nikon
Nippon Beet Sugar
Nippon Carbide Industries
Nippon Carbon
Nippon Chemical Industrial
Nippon Denko
Nippon Electric Corporation
Nippon Express
Nippon Flour Mills
Nippon Kokan
Nippon Kyaku
Nippon Light Metal
Nippon Metal Industry
Nippon Mining
Nippon Oil
Nippon Oil & Fats
Nippon Piston Ring
Nippon Seiko
Nippon Sharyo
Nippon Sheet Glass
Nippon Shinpan
Nippon Soda
Nippon Stainless Steel
Nippon Steel Corporation
Nippon Suisan
Nippon Telegraph & Telephone
Nippon Yankin Kogyo
Nippon Yusen
Nippondenso
Nissan Chemical Industrial
Nissan Motor
The Nisshin Oil Mills
Nisshinbo Industries
Nitto Boseki
Nomura Securities
Noritake
NTN Toyo Bearing
NTT
Odakyu Electric
Ohbayashi
Oji Paper
Oki Electric Industry
Okuma Machinery Works
Onoda Cement
Osaka Gas
Rasa Industries
Ricoh
Sankyo
Sanraku
Sanyo Electric
Sanyo-Kokusaku Pulp
Sapporo Breweries
Sato Kogyo
Sharp Corporation
Shimizu
Shimura Kako
Shin-Etsu Chemical
Shinagawa Refractories
Shochiku
Showa Denko
Showa Electric Wire & Cable
Showa Line
Showa Shell Sekiyu
Somitumo
Sony
Sumitomo Bank
Sumitomo Cement
Sumitomo Chemical
Sumitomo Coal Mining
Sumitomo Electric Industries
Sumitomo Metal Industries
Sumitomo Metal Mining
Suzuki Motor
Taisei
Taisho Marine & Fire Insurance
Taito
Takara Shuzo
Takashimaya
Takeda Chemical Industries
Teijin
Teikoku Oil
Teikoku Sen-i
Tekken
Toa
Toa Nenryo Kogyo
Toagosei Chemical Industry
Toboshima
Tobu Railway
Toei
Toho
Toho Rayon
Toho Zinc
Tokai Carbon
Tokio Marine & Fire
Tokyo Electric
Tokyo Gas
Tokyo Rope Manufacturing
Tokyu
Tokyu Department Store
Toppan Printing
Toray Industries
Toshiba
Tosoh Corporation
Toto
Toyo Seikan
Toyobo
Toyota Motor
Ube Industries
Unitika
Yamaha
Yamanouchi Pharmaceutical
Yasuda Fire & Marine Insurance
Yokogawa Electric
Yokohama Rubber
Yusasa Battery

Source: Osaka Securities Exchange; *The Handbook of Financial Market Indexes, Averages, and Indicators*; Dow Jones; Tokyo Stock Exchange
List current as of August 8, 1991

UK Companies in the FT-SE 100 Index

Abbey National
Allied-Lyons
Anglian Water
Argyll Group
Asda Group
Associated British Foods
BAA
Bank of Scotland
Barclays
Bass
B.A.T
BET
BICC
Blue Circle Industries
BOC Group
Boots
British Aerospace
British Airways
British Gas
British Petroleum
British Steel
British Telecommunications
BTR
Burmah Castrol
Cable & Wireless
Cadbury Schweppes
Commercial Union
Courtaulds
Dalgety
Enterprise Oil
Eurotunnel
Fisons
General Accident
GEC
G K N
Glaxo Holdings
Grand Metropolitan
Great Universal Stores
Guardian Royal Exchange
Guinness
Hammerson Prop. Inv. & Dev.
Hanson
Harrisons & Crosfield
Hawker Siddeley Group
Hillsdown Holdings
Imperial Chemical Industries
Kingfisher
Ladbroke Group
Land Securities
LASMO
Legal & General Group
Lloyds Bank
Lonrho
Lucas Industries
Marks and Spencer
Maxwell Communication
MEPC
Midland Bank
National Westminster Bank
North West Water Group
Pearson
Peninsular & Oriental Steam Navigation
Pilkington
Prudential Corporation
Racal Electronics
The Rank Organisation
Ranks Hovis McDougall
Reckitt & Colman
Redland
Reed International
Reuters Holdings
RMC Group
Rolls-Royce
Rothmans International
The Royal Bank of Scotland Group
Royal Insurance Holdings
RTZ
J. Sainsbury
Scottish & Newcastle Breweries
Sears
Severn Trent
Shell Transport and Trading
Smith & Nephew
SmithKline Beecham
STC
Sun Alliance Group
Tarmac
Tesco
Thames Water
Thorn EMI
Trafalgar House
Trusthouse Forte
TSB Group
Ultramar
Unilever
United Biscuits Holdings
Wellcome
Whitbread
Wiggins Teape Appleton
Willis Corroon

Source: *The Hambro Company Guide*, Feb.–April 1991
List current as of December 31, 1990

French Companies in the CAC-40 Index

Accor
Air Liquide
Alcatel Alsthom
Arjomari
Axa-Midi
Bouygues
BSN
Canal+
Cap Gemini Sogeti
Carrefour
CGIP
Chargeurs
Cie. Bancaire
Club Méditerranée
Crédit Commercial
Crédit Foncier
Elf Aquitaine
Economiques du Casino
Générale des Eaux
Hachette
Havas
Lafarge Coppée
Legrand
L'Oréal
LVMH Moet-Hennessy
Lyonnaise-Dumez
Matra
Michelin
Paribas
Pernod Ricard
Peugeot
Saint-Gobain
Saint Louis
Sanofi
Schneider
Société Générale
Source Perrier
Suez
Thomson-CSF
UAP

Source: Dow Jones; French Trade Office, Société de Bourses Francaises
List current as of August 6, 1991

The 33 Hong Kong Companies in the Hang Seng Index

Bank of East Asia
Cathay Pacific Airways
Cavendish International Holdings
Cheung Kong (Holdings)
China Light & Power
Dairy Farm International Holdings
Green Island Cement (Holdings)
Hang Lung Development
Hang Seng Bank
Henderson Land Development
Hong Kong & China Gas
Hongkong & Shanghai Hotels
Hongkong Electric Holdings
Hongkong Land Holdings
Hong Kong Telecommunications
Hopewell Holdings
HSBC Holdings
Hutchison Whampoa
Hysan Development
Jardine Matheson Holdings
Jardine Strategic Holdings
Kowloon Motor Bus
Lai Sun Garment (International)
Mandarin Oriental International
Miramar Hotel & Investment
New World Development
Sun Hung Kai Properties
Swire Pacific
Television Broadcasts
The Wharf (Holdings)
Winsor Industrial
World International (Holdings)

Source: The Stock Exchange of Hong Kong Ltd.
List current as of August 2, 1991

The 30 German Companies in the DAX

Allianz
BASF
Bayer
Bayerische Hypotheken und Wechselbank
Bayerische Vereinsbank
BMW
Commerzbank
Continental Gummiwerke
Daimler-Benz
Degussa
Deutsche Babcock & Wilcox
Deutsche Bank
Dresdner Bank
Henkel KGaA
Hoechst
Karstadt Group
Kaufhof
Linde
Lufthansa
MAN (GHH)
Mannesmann
Metallgesellschaft
Preussag
RWE
Schering
Siemens
Thyssen
VEBA
VIAG
Volkswagen

Source: Dow Jones; Frankfurt Stock Exchange
List current as of August 6, 1991

Australian Companies in the Australian Stock Exchange All Ordinaries Index

Aberfoyle
ACM Gold
Action Holdings
Adelaide Brighton Cement Holdings
Advance Bank Australia
AFP Group
Agen
Alcan Australia
Altrack
Amcor
Ampol Exploration
Argo Investments
Ariadne Australia
Arimco
Armstrong Jones Prime Investment Fund
Arnotts
Arrowfield Group
Asarco Australia
Ashton Mining
Atkins Carlyle
Atlas Steels
Australia & New Zealand Banking Group
Australian Agricultural Company
Australian Chemical Holdings
Australian Consolidated Investments
Australian Consolidated Minerals
Australian Foundation Investment
Australian Gas Light
Australian National Industries
Australian Oil and Gas
AWA
Aztec Mining
Ballarat Brewing
Bank of Melbourne
Bank of Queensland
Boral
Bougainville Copper
Brambles Industries
Brash Holdings
Brickworks
Bridge Oil
Brierley Investments
Broken Hill Proprietary
BT Australian Equity Management
BT Global Asset Management
BTR Nylex
Bundaberg Sugar
Bunnings
Burns, Philp & Company
Burswood Property Trust
Caltex Australia
Capcount Property Trust
Capital Property Trust
Carlton Investments
Central Norseman Gold
Central Pacific Minerals
Challenge Bank
Charles Davis
Clyde Industries
Coal & Allied Industries
Coca-Cola Amatil
Coles Myer
Colonial Mutual Australian Property Fund
Comada Energy
Comalco
Command Petroleum Holdings
Compass Holdings
Computer Power Group
Consolidated Rutile
Country Road
Coventry Group
C R A
G.E. Crane Holdings
Crusader
C S R
Cudgen RZ
Darrell James
Defiance Mills
Delta Gold
Denehurst
Devex
Dominion Mining
Email
Emperor Mines
Energy Resources of Australia
ENT
Equitilink
Evans Deakin Industries
Exicom
FAI Insurances
F.H. Faulding & Company
First National Resource Trust
Fletcher Challenge
Foodland Associated
Forrestania Gold
Foster's Brewing Group
Franked Income Fund
Futuris
Galore Group
Gazal Corporation
General Property Trust
George Weston Foods
Gibson Chemical Industries
Gold Mines of Kalgoorlie
Goodman Fielder Wattie
Gowing Bros.
G.U.D. Holdings
Gwalia Consolidated
Harvey Norman Holdings
Hastings Deering
Hawker de Havilland
Helm Corporation
Highlands Gold
Hills Industries
Homestake Gold of Australia
Howard Smith
Hudson Conway
I C I Australia
Incitec
Independent Holdings
James Hardie Industries
Jennings Group
Jennings Properties
Jupiters Development
Jupiters Trust
Kalamazoo Holdings
Kern Corporation
Kern Property Fund
Kidston Gold Mines
Leighton Holdings
Lend Lease
MacMahon Holdings
Macquarie Property Trust
Macraes Mining
Magellan Petroleum Australia
Markalinga Trust
Mayne Nickless
McIntosh Securities
McPherson's
Meekatharra Minerals
Memtec
Metal Manufactures
Metway Bank
Mildara Wines
Milton
M.I.M. Holdings
Minora Resources
Minproc Holdings
Mirvac
Mount Edon Gold Mines (Aust)
National Australia Bank
National Can Industries
National Consolidated
National Mutual Property Trust
Newcrest Mining
News Corporation
Nine Network Australia
Niugini Mining
Normandy Poseidon
North Broken Hill Peko
North Flinders Mines
O P S M Industries
Oakbridge
Oil Search
Orbital Engine
Pacific BBA
Pacific Dunlop
Pacific Mutual Australia
Palmer Tube Mills
Pan Australia Mining
Pancontinental Mining
Paragon Resources
Parbury Henty Holdings
Pasminco
Peptide Technology
Permanent Trustee
Perpetual Trustees Australia
Peter Kurts Properties
Petersville Sleigh
Pioneer International
Placer Pacific
Plutonic Resources
Poseidon Gold
Power Brewing
Premier Investments
Q B E Insurance Group
QCT Resources
QDL
QIW Retailers
Queensland Metals
Q.U.F. Industries
Ramtron Holdings
Reece Australia
Renison Goldfields Consolidated
Rothmans Holdings
Rural Press
S.A. Brewing Holdings
Sagasco Holdings
Santos
Schroders International Property Fund
Schroders Property Fund
Sea World Property Trust
Siddons Ramset
Sons of Gwalia
Southern Pacific Petroleum
Spicers Paper
Spotless Group
Spotless Services
Steamships Trading
Stockland Trust Group
Stroika
T N T
Templeton Global Growth Fund
Tubemakers of Australia
Tyco Investments (Australia)
Vamgas
Village Roadshow
Waco International
Washington H. Soul Pattinson & Co.
Wattyl
Wesfarmers
Western Capital
Western Mining Corporation Holdings
Westfield Holdings
Westfield Trust
Westpac Banking
Westralian Forest Industries
Westralian Sands
W.D. & H.O. Wills Holdings
Wolf Blass Wines
Woodside Petroleum
Zapopan

Source: Australian Stock Exchange

List current as of June 30, 1991

Non-US Company Stocks Available Through US Stock Markets (Listed by Country)

Company	Exchange	Symbol
AFRICA		
Botswana		
Botswana RST Limited	OTC	
South Africa		
Abercom Group Limited	OTC	
AE and CI Limited	OTC	
AFMIN Holdings Limited	OTC	
Afrikander Lease Limited	OTC	
Anglo American Coal Corporation	OTC	
Anglo American Corporation of SA Ltd.	NASDAQ	ANGLY
Anglo American Gold Investment	NASDAQ	AAGIY
Anglo American Investment Trust Ltd.	OTC	
Anglo-Alpha Cement Limited	OTC	
Anglovaal Holdings Limited	OTC	
Barlow Rand Limited	OTC	
Beatrix Mines	OTC	
Blue Circle Cement Limited	OTC	
Blyvooruitzicht Gold Mining Co., Ltd.	NASDAQ	BLYVY
Bracken Mines Limited	OTC	
Buffelsfontein Gold Mining Ltd.	NASDAQ	BFELY
Consolidated Modderfontein	OTC	
Consolidated Murchison Limited	OTC	
DAB Investments Ltd.	OTC	
Daggafontein Mines Limited	OTC	
De Beers Consolidated Mines	NASDAQ	DBRSY
Deelkraal Gold Mining Company Ltd.	OTC	
Doornfontein Gold Mining Company	OTC	
Driefontein Consolidated Limited	NASDAQ	DRFNY
Duiker Exploration Limited	OTC	
Durban Roodeport Deep Limited	OTC	
East Daggafontein Mines Limited	OTC	
East Rand Gold and Uranium Co. Ltd.	OTC	
East Rand Proprietary Mines Limited	OTC	
Eastern Transvaal Consolidated Mines Ltd.	OTC	
Egoli Consolidated Mines Limited	OTC	
Elandsrand Gold Mining Co.	OTC	
Elsburg Gold Mining Company Limited	OTC	
Federale Mynbou Beperk	OTC	
Free State Consolidated Gold Mines Ltd.	NASDAQ	FSCNY
Free State Development & Invest Corp.	OTC	
Genbel Investments Limited	OTC	
Gencor Ltd.	OTC	
Gold Fields of South Africa	NASDAQ	GLDF
Gold Fields Property Company Limited	OTC	
Grootvlei Proprietary Mines	OTC	
Harmony Gold Mining Company	OTC	
Hartebeestfontein Gold Mining	OTC	
Highveld Steel and Vanadium Corp.	NASDAQ	HSVLY
Impala Platinum Holdings Limited	OTC	
Johannesburg Consolidated Invest Company	OTC	
Kinross Mines Limited	OTC	
Kloof Gold Mining Company Limited	NASDAQ	KLOFY
Leslie Gold Mines Limited	OTC	
Libanon Gold Mining Company	OTC	
Loraine Gold Mines Limited	OTC	
Lydenburg Platinum Limited	NASDAQ	LYDPY
Messina Limited	OTC	
Middle Witwatersrand (Western Areas) Ltd.	OTC	
Modder B Gold Holdings Ltd.	OTC	
New Wits Limited	OTC	
O'Okiep Copper Company Limited	ASE	OKP
Orange Free State Investments Ltd.	NASDAQ	OESLY
Palabora Mining Company Limited	OTC	
Rand Mines Limited	OTC	
Rand Mines Properties Limited	OTC	
Randex Limited	OTC	
Randfontein Estates Gold Mining Co. WITW	OTC	
Rembrandt Group Limited	OTC	
Rustenberg Platinum Holdings	OTC	
Samancor Limited	OTC	
Sasol Limited	NASDAQ	SASOY
Simmer and Jack Mines Limited	OTC	
South African Breweries Ltd.	OTC	
South African Land & Exploration Co., Ltd.	OTC	
South Roodeport Main Reef Areas	OTC	
Southvaal Holdings Limited	OTC	
St. Helena Gold Mines Limited	NASDAQ	SGOLY
Stilfontein Gold Mining Company	OTC	
Sub Nigel Gold Mining Co., Ltd.	OTC	
Theron Holdings Limited	OTC	
Transnatal Coal	OTC	
Unisel Gold Mines Limited	OTC	
VAAL Reefs Exploration & Mining Company	NASDAQ	VAAL
Venterspost Gold Mining Co. Ltd.	OTC	
Vereeniging Estates Limited	OTC	
Vlakfontein Gold Mining Co. Ltd.	OTC	
Welkom Gold Holdings Limited	NASDAQ	WLKMY
West Rand Consolidated Mines Ltd.	OTC	
Western Areas Gold Mining Co. Ltd.	OTC	
Western Deep Levels Limited	NASDAQ	WDEPY
Winkelhaak Mines Limited	OTC	
Witwatersrand Nigel Limited	OTC	
Zandpan Gold Mining Company Ltd.	OTC	
Zambia		
Zambia Consolidated Copper Mines Limited	OTC	
Zimbabwe		
Mhangura Copper Mines Limited	OTC	
ASIA/PACIFIC		
Australia		
Agen Limited	OTC	
Altrack Limited	OTC	
Amadeus Oil NL	OTC	
Amcor Ltd.	OTC	AMRLF
Ampol Exploration Limited	OTC	
Anglo Gold Mines Limited	OTC	
Ashton Mining	OTC	
Asia Oil and Minerals Limited	OTC	
Astro Mining NL	OTC	
Australia & New Zealand Banking Group	OTC	ANEWY
Australia Wide Industries	OTC	
Australian Consolidated Investments Ltd.	OTC	
Australian Hydrocarbons NL	OTC	
Australian National Industries	OTC	
Australian Oil and Gas Corp. Ltd.	OTC	
Barrack Energy Limited	OTC	
Barrack Mines Limited	OTC	
Barrack Technology Limited	OTC	
Barrier Exploration NL	OTC	
Black Hill Minerals	OTC	
Bond Corporation Holdings Ltd.	OTC	
Boral Limited	NASDAQ	BORAY
Boulder Gold	OTC	
Bridge Oil Limited	OTC	
Brierly Investment Ltd.	OTC	
Broken Hill Proprietary Company Ltd.	NYSE	BHP
Browns Creek Gold NL	OTC	
Brunswick NL	OTC	
Burns, Philip and Company Ltd.	OTC	
Cape Range Oil NL	OTC	

Non-US Company Stocks Available Through US Stock Markets (continued)

Company	Exchange	Symbol
Australia (continued)		
Centaur Mining and Exploration Ltd.	OTC	
Central Norseman Corporation	OTC	
Central Pacific Minerals NL	NASDAQ	CPMNY
Charter Mining NL	OTC	
City Resources Ltd.	OTC	
Claremont Petroleum NL	OTC	
Clyde Industries Limited	OTC	
Coca Cola Amatil Limited	OTC	
Coles Myer Limited	NYSE	CM
Comalco Ltd., "A" Shares	OTC	
Consolidated Gold Mining Areas	OTC	
Coopers Resources NL	OTC	
Cord Holdings Limited	OTC	
CRA Limited	OTC	CRADY
Cracow Gold Limited	OTC	
Crystal Mining NL	OTC	
CSR Limited	OTC	
Delta Gold NL	OTC	
Denehurst Limited	OTC	
Dominion Mining Limited	OTC	
E.R.G. Australia Limited	OTC	
East West Minerals NL	OTC	
Eastern Group Limited	OTC	
Email Limited	OTC	
Emperor Mines Limited	OTC	
Energy Oil and Gas NL	OTC	
Enterprise Gold Mines NL	OTC	
Euralba Mining Limited	OTC	
Expo Limited	OTC	
F.H. Faulding & Co. Limited	OTC	
FAI Insurances Limited	NYSE	FAI
Federation Resources NL	OTC	
Firstpac Limited	OTC	
Forsayth NL	OTC	
Foster's Brewing Group Ltd.	OTC	
Giant Resources Limited	OTC	
Golconda Minerals NL	OTC	
Gold & Minerals Exploration NL	OTC	
Gold Mines of Kalgoorlie Ltd.	OTC	
Golden Valley Mines NL	OTC	
Goodman Fielder Wattie Limited	OTC	
Grants Patch Mining	OTC	
Great Eastern Mines Limited	NASDAQ	GOLDY
Great Fingall Mining Co. NL	OTC	
Greenbushes Tin Ltd.	OTC	
Greenvale Mining NL	OTC	
Gwalia International Limited	OTC	
Gwalia Resources Ltd.	OTC	
Haoma Northwest NL	OTC	
Hartogen Energy Limited	OTC	
HMC Australasia	OTC	
Hooker Corporation	OTC	
Hoyts Entertainment Limited	OTC	
Independent Resources Limited	OTC	
Indonesian Diamond Corporation Ltd.	OTC	
International Mining Corporation	OTC	
James Hardie Industries Limited	OTC	
Jason Mining Limited	OTC	
Jimberlana Minerals NL	OTC	
Jingellic Minerals NL	OTC	
Jones David, Limited	OTC	
Julia Mines NL	OTC	
Kalbara Mining NL	OTC	
Kern Corporation	OTC	
Kidston Gold Mines Ltd.	OTC	
Kitchener Mining NL	OTC	
Leisureland Corp. Ltd.	OTC	
Lenward Oil NL	OTC	

Company	Exchange	Symbol
M.I.M. Holdings Limited	OTC	MIMAY
Magellan Petroleum Australia Ltd.	OTC	
Magnet Group Limited	OTC	
Matrix Telecommunications Limited	OTC	
Mawson Pacific Limited	OTC	
Mayne Wickless Ltd.	OTC	MAYNF
McPherson's Limited	OTC	
Memtec Limited	OTC	
Meridian Oil NL	NASDAQ	MEDLY
Merlin Mining NL	OTC	
Metana Minerals NL	OTC	
Mid-East Minerals NL	OTC	
Mincorp Petroleum NL	OTC	
Minefields Exploration NL	OTC	
Mintaro Slate & Flagstone Co., Ltd.	OTC	
Monarch NL	OTC	
Mount Burgess Gold Mines NL	OTC	
Mount Leyshon Gold Mines Limited	OTC	
National Australia Bank Ltd.	NYSE	NAB
Network Media Limited	OTC	
New Australia Resources	OTC	
News Corporation Ltd.	NYSE	NWS
Normandy Poseidon Limited	OTC	
North Broken Hill-Peko Limited	OTC	
North Queensland Resources NL	OTC	
Oil Search Limited	OTC	
Orbital Engine Corp. Ltd.	OTC	
Pacific Dunlop Limited	NASDAQ	PDLPY
Pact Resources, NL	OTC	
Palmer Tube Mills	OTC	
Pancontinental Mining Ltd.	OTC	
Paragon Resources NL	OTC	
Pelsart Resources NL	NASDAQ	PELR
Petrogulf Resources Limited	OTC	
Petroz NL	OTC	
Pioneer International Limited	OTC	PONNF
Placer Pacific Limited	OTC	
Poseidon Gold Limited	OTC	
Ramtron Holdings Limited	NASDAQ	MEMR
Range Resources Ltd.	OTC	
Regent Mining Ltd.	OTC	
Rowlands Corporation Limited	OTC	
Roycol Limited	OTC	
S.A. Brewing Holdings Limited	OTC	
Samantha Gold NL	OTC	
Samson Exploration NL	OTC	
Santos Ltd.	NASDAQ	STOSY
Sapphire Mines NL	OTC	
Sirius Corporation NL	OTC	
Smith (Howard) Limited	OTC	
Sons of Gwalia NL	OTC	
Southern Goldfields Limited	OTC	
Southern Pacific Petroleum	NASDAQ	SPPTY
Southern Resources Limited	OTC	
Southern Ventures NL	OTC	
Southwest Gold Mines	OTC	
Sovereign Oil Australia Limited	OTC	
Spargos Mining NL	OTC	
Swan Resources Limited	NASDAQ	SWANY
Tennyson Holdings Ltd.	OTC	
Terrex Resources NL	OTC	
TNT Limited	OTC	TNTLF
Total Assets Protection Ltd.	OTC	
Trans Global Resources NL	OTC	
Transcontinental Holdings	OTC	
Triad Minerals NL	OTC	
Trust Company of Australia Ltd.	OTC	
Vam Limited	OTC	
Vamgas Limited	OTC	

Non-US Company Stocks Available Through US Stock Markets (continued)

Company	Exchange	Symbol
Australia (continued)		
Victoria Petroleum NL	OTC	
Walhalla Mining Co. NL	OTC	
Wattle Gully Gold Mines NL	OTC	
Western Capital Limited	OTC	
Western Mining Corporation Holdings Ltd.	NYSE	WMC
Westpac Banking Corporation	NYSE	WBK
Woodside Petroleum Limited	OTC	
Zanex Limited	OTC	
Hong Kong		
Applied International Holdings	OTC	
Carrian Investments	OTC	
Cathay Pacific Airways Limited	OTC	
Cheung Kong (Holdings) Limited	OTC	
China Light and Power	OTC	
Chuangs Holdings Limited	OTC	
Conic Investment Company Limited	OTC	
Evergo Holdings Company Ltd.	OTC	
F.P. Special Assets Ltd.	OTC	
Hang Lung Development Company	OTC	
Hang Seng Bank	OTC	
Henderson Land Development Co., Ltd.	OTC	
Hong Kong and China Gas Co., Ltd.	OTC	
Hong Kong Electric Holdings	OTC	
Hong Kong Telecommunications	NYSE	HKT
Hopewell Holdings Limited	OTC	
Hutchison Whampoa Ltd.	OTC	
Hysan Development	OTC	
Industrial Equity (Pacific) Ltd.	OTC	
New World Development Co., Ltd.	OTC	
Playmates International Holdings Ltd.	OTC	
Sino Land Company Ltd.	OTC	
Sun Hung Kai & Co., Limited	OTC	
Sun Hung Kai Properties Ltd.	OTC	
Swire Pacific Ltd. "A"	OTC	
Television Broadcasts Limited	OTC	
TVE (Holdings) Ltd.	OTC	
Wah Kwong Shipping and Invest Co. Ltd.	OTC	
Wharf Holdings Ltd.	OTC	
Winsor Industrial Corporation Ltd.	OTC	
Indonesia		
P.T. Inti Indorayon Utama	OTC	
Japan		
Aida Engineering	OTC	
Ajinomoto Company	OTC	
Akai Electric	OTC	
All Nippon Airways Co. Ltd.	OTC	ALNPY
ALPS Electric Co., Ltd.	OTC	AECJY
Amada Co., Ltd.	OTC	AMCJY
Asahi Chemical Industry	OTC	
Asahi Glass Company, Limited	OTC	ASGLY
Ashikaga Bank Ltd.	OTC	
Bank of Fukuoka	OTC	
Bank of Tokyo	OTC	
Bank of Yokohama	OTC	
Banyu Pharmaceutical Co., Ltd.	OTC	BYPJY
Bridgestone Corporation	OTC	
Brother Industries	OTC	
C. Itoh & Co., Ltd.	OTC	
Calpis Food Industry Co., Ltd.	OTC	
Canon Inc.	NASDAQ	CANNY
Casio Computer Co., Ltd.	OTC	
CSK Corporation	NASDAQ	CSKKY
Dai Nippon Printing Co., Ltd.	OTC	DNPPY
Dai'el, Inc.	NASDAQ	DAIEY
Dai-Ichi Kangyo Bank, Ltd.	OTC	DKBJY

Company	Exchange	Symbol
Daiwa Danchi Co., Ltd.	OTC	
Daiwa House Industry Co., Ltd.	OTC	DHIJY
Daiwa Securities Co., Ltd.	OTC	
Daiwa Seiko, Inc.	OTC	
Ebara Corporation	OTC	
Eisai Company	OTC	ESAJY
Fuji Bank, Ltd.	OTC	FUJPY
Fuji Heavy Industries Ltd.	OTC	FUJHY
Fuji Photo Film Co., Ltd.	OTC	FUJIY
Fujita Corporation	OTC	
Fujitsu Ltd.	OTC	FJTSY
Furukawa Electric Co., Ltd.	OTC	
Hachijuni Bank, Ltd.	OTC	
Hino Motors, Ltd.	OTC	
Hitachi Cable, Ltd.	OTC	
Hitachi Koki Co., Ltd.	OTC	
Hitachi Ltd.	NYSE	HIT
Hitachi Metals, Ltd.	OTC	
Hochiki Corporation	OTC	
Hokuriku Bank, Ltd.	OTC	
Honda Motor Co., Ltd.	NYSE	HMC
Industrial Bank of Japan, Ltd.	OTC	
Isuzu Motors Ltd.	OTC	ISUZY
Ito-Yokado Co., Ltd.	NASDAQ	IYCOY
Japan Airlines Company, Ltd.	OTC	JAPNY
Japan Steel Works	OTC	
JUSCO Co., Ltd.	OTC	
Kajima Corporation	OTC	KAJMY
Kanebo, Ltd.	OTC	
Kao Corporation	OTC	
Kawasaki Steel Corporation	OTC	
Kirin Brewery Company, Ltd.	NASDAQ	KNBWY
Komatsu Limited	OTC	KMATY
Konica Corporation	OTC	
Kubota Corporation	NYSE	KUB
Kumagai Gumi Co., Ltd.	OTC	
Kyocera Corporation	NYSE	KYO
Kyowa Bank, Ltd.	OTC	KYBJY
Makita Corporation	NASDAQ	MKTAY
Marubeni Corporation	OTC	
Marui Co., Ltd.	OTC	
Matsushita Electric Industrial Co., Ltd.	NYSE	MC
Matsushita Electric Works	OTC	MSEWY
Meiji Seika Kaisha Limited	OTC	
Minebea Co., Ltd.	OTC	
Mitsubishi Bank, Ltd.	NYSE	MBK
Mitsubishi Chemical Machinery Mfg., Co.	OTC	
Mitsubishi Corporation	OTC	
Mitsubishi Electric Corp.	OTC	MIELY
Mitsubishi Estate Company, Ltd.	OTC	MITEY
Mitsubishi Kasei Corporation	OTC	
Mitsubishi Trust & Banking Corp.	OTC	
Mitsui & Company Limited	NASDAQ	MITSY
Mitsui Marine and Fire Insurance Co.	OTC	
Mitsui Taiyo Kobe Bank, Ltd.	OTC	MTKBY
Mitsukoshi, Ltd.	OTC	
Nagoya Railroad Co., Ltd.	OTC	
NEC Corporation	NASDAQ	NIPNY
New Japan Securities Co., Ltd.	OTC	
Nifco Inc.	OTC	
Nikko Securities Co., Ltd.	OTC	
Nikon Corp.	OTC	NINOY
Nintendo Co., Ltd.	OTC	NINTY
Nippon Kangyo Kakumaru Securities Co.	OTC	
Nippon Seiko K.K.	OTC	NSKKY
Nippon Shinpan Co., Ltd.	OTC	
Nippon Shokubai Kagaku Kogyo	OTC	
Nippon Suisan Kaisha, Ltd.	OTC	

Non-US Company Stocks Available Through US Stock Markets (continued)

Company	Exchange	Symbol
Japan (continued)		
Nippon Yusen Kabushiki Kaisha	OTC	
Nippondenso Co., Ltd.	OTC	
Nissan Motor Co., Ltd.	OTC	NSANY
Nisshin Steel Co., Ltd.	OTC	
Nitto Denko Corp.	OTC	
NKK Corporation	OTC	
Nomura Securities Company, Ltd.	OTC	NMRJY
Oji Paper Company Limited	OTC	
Omron Corporation	OTC	OMTJY
Onoda Cement Company Ltd.	OTC	
Onward Kashiyama & Co. Ltd.	OTC	
Osaka Building Co., Ltd.	OTC	
Pioneer Electronic Corporation	NYSE	PIO
Ricoh Company, Ltd.	OTC	RICOY
Saitama Bank, Ltd.	OTC	SATMY
Sanko Steamship Co., Ltd.	OTC	
Sanwa Bank Limited	OTC	SNBJY
Sanyo Electric Co., Ltd.	NASDAQ	SANYY
Secom Co., Ltd.	OTC	
Sekisui House, Ltd.	OTC	SKHJY
Seven-Eleven Japan Co., Ltd.	OTC	
Sharp Corporation	OTC	SHCAY
Shiseido Co., Ltd.	OTC	
Shizuoka Bank, Ltd.	OTC	
Showa Sangyo Co., Ltd.	OTC	
Sony Corporation	NYSE	SNE
Sumitomo Bank, Limited	OTC	SUBJY
Sumitomo Electric Industries	OTC	
Sumitomo Metal Industries, Ltd.	OTC	SUMEY
Suruga Bank Limited	OTC	
Taisei Corporation Ltd.	OTC	TASJY
Taiyo Yuden Co., Ltd.	OTC	
TDK Corporation	NYSE	TDK
Teijin Limited	OTC	
Teijin Seiki Co. Ltd.	OTC	
Toa Harbor Works Company Limited	OTC	
Tokai Bank Limited	OTC	
Tokio Marine & Fire Insurance Company	OTC	TKIOY
Tokyo Dome Corporation	OTC	
Tokyu Land Corporation	OTC	
Toppan Printing Co., Ltd.	OTC	TONPY
Toray Industries, Inc.	OTC	
Toto Ltd.	OTC	
Toyo Suisan Kaisha Ltd.	OTC	
Toyobo Co., Ltd.	OTC	
Toyota Motor Corporation	OTC	TOYOY
Tsubakimoto Precision Products Co., Ltd.	OTC	
Tsugami Corporation	OTC	
Victor Company of Japan	OTC	VJAPY
Wacoal Corporation	OTC	
Yamaichi Securities Co. Ltd.	OTC	
Yamazaki Baking Co., Ltd.	OTC	
Yasuda Trust and Banking Co. Ltd.	OTC	
Malaysia		
Bandar Raya Developments Berhad	OTC	
Berjaya Corp. Berhad	OTC	
Boustead Holdings Berhad	OTC	
Genting Berhad	OTC	GEBEY
Kesang Corporation Berhad	OTC	
Kuala Lumpur Kepong Berhad	OTC	KLKBY
Malayan United Industries Berhad	OTC	
Perlis Plantations Berhad	OTC	
Selangor Properties Berhad	OTC	
Supreme Corporation Berhad	OTC	
Sime Darby Berhad	OTC	SIDBY
New Zealand		
Fletcher Challenge Ltd.	OTC	FLCAY
New Zealand Petroleum Company	NASDAQ	NZPCY
Telecom Corporation of New Zealand Ltd.	NYSE	NZT
Papua New Guinea		
Bougainville Copper Limited	OTC	
Niugini Mining Limited	OTC	
Philippines		
Philodrill Corporation	OTC	
Singapore		
City Developments Limited	OTC	CDEVY
Cycle and Carriage Limited	OTC	
Development Bank of Singapore Ltd.	OTC	
GB Holdings	OTC	
Inchcape Berhad	OTC	
Keppel Corporation Ltd.	OTC	KPELY
Malayan Credit Limited	OTC	
Neptune Orient Lines Ltd.	OTC	NEPSY
Overseas Union Bank, Limited	OTC	
Sembawang Shipyards Limited	OTC	SSYSY
Singapore Land Limited	OTC	SINPY
United Overseas Bank Limited	OTC	UOBSY
United Overseas Land Limited	OTC	
Thailand		
Asia Fiber Company Limited	OTC	
BERMUDA		
BT Shipping	NASDAQ	BTBTY
Dairy Farm International Holdings Ltd.	OTC	
Fairhaven International Ltd.	NASDAQ	NIMSY
First Pacific Company Ltd.	OTC	
HongKong Land Holdings Ltd.	OTC	
Jardine Matheson Holdings Ltd.	OTC	
Jardine Strategic Holdings Ltd.	OTC	
Mandarin Oriental International Ltd.	OTC	
Zambia Copper Investments Limited	OTC	
CANADA		
Alcan Aluminium Ltd.	NYSE	AL
BCE Inc.	NYSE	BCE
Canadian Pacific Ltd.	NYSE	CP
Imperial Oil Ltd.	ASE	IMOA
Inco Ltd.	NYSE	N
Moore Corporation Ltd.	NYSE	MCL
Seagram Company Ltd.	NYSE	VO
EUROPE		
Austria		
Veitscher Magnesitwerke AG	OTC	
Belgium		
Gevaert Photo-Production NV	OTC	
Petrofina SA	OTC	PTRFY
Denmark		
Den Danske Bank	OTC	
Novo Nordisk AS	NYSE	NVO
Finland		
Amer Group Ltd.	OTC	
Cultor Ltd.	OTC	
Instrumentarium Corporation	NASDAQ	INMRY
Nokia Corporation	OTC	

Non-US Company Stocks Available Through US Stock Markets (continued)

Company	Exchange	Symbol
France		
Alcatel Alsthom	OTC	ACALY
BSN Groupe	OTC	BSNOY
Canal Plus	OTC	CNPLY
Clarins	OTC	
Club Mediterranee	OTC	
Compagnie Generale Maritime	OTC	
Elf Aquitaine	NYSE	ELF
Fiat France SA (FFSA)	OTC	
Havas	OTC	
L'Air Liquide	OTC	
L'Oréal Company	OTC	LORLY
LVMH Moët Hennessy Louis Vuitton	NASDAQ	LVMHY
Machines Bull	OTC	
Peugeot SA	OTC	PGTRY
Rhône-Poulenc SA (CIPS)	NYSE	RPU
Schneider et Cie	OTC	
Source Perrier SA	OTC	
Thomson-CSF	NASDAQ	TCSFY
Valeo	OTC	
Germany		
AEG AG	OTC	
BASF AG	OTC	BASFY
Bayer AG	OTC	BAYRY
Bayerische Vereinsbank AG	OTC	
Commerzbank AG	OTC	DBKAY
Continental AG	OTC	
Daimler-Benz AG	OTC	
Deutsche Bank AG	OTC	DBKAY
Dresdner Bank AG	NASDAQ	DRSDY
Gelsenskirch Bergwerks AG	OTC	
Hoechst AG	OTC	HOEHY
Hoesch, AG	OTC	
Kloeckner Werke, AG	OTC	
Lufthansa AG	OTC	
Mannesman AG	OTC	
Rosenthal, AG	OTC	
Rudolf Karstadt AG	OTC	
RWE AG	OTC	
Siemens AG	OTC	SMAWY
Stahlwerke Peine Salzgitter, AG	OTC	
Thyssen Huette, AG	OTC	
Thyssen Industrie AG	OTC	
Volkswagen AG	OTC	VLKAY
Greece		
John Boutari & Son, SA	OTC	
Ireland		
Allied Irish Banks, PLC	NYSE	AIB
CRH PLC	NASDAQ	CRHCY
Elan Corp/Drug Research Corp. Unit	ASE	
Elan Corporation, PLC	ASE	ELANY
Glencar Exploration PLC	OTC	
Power Corporation PLC	OTC	
Waterford Wedgewood PLC	NASDAQ	WATFZ
Italy		
Bastogi I.R.B.S.	OTC	
Benetton Group SpA	NYSE	BNG
Eridania Z.N. SpA	OTC	
Fiat SpA (ordinary)	NYSE	FIA
Italcementi Fabriche Riunite Cemento SpA	OTC	
La Rinascente SpA	OTC	
Ledoga "Pref" SpA	OTC	
Luxottica Group SpA	NYSE	LUX
Montedison SpA	NYSE	MNT
Olivetti & C., SpA (ordinary shares)	OTC	OLIVY
Pirelli SpA	OTC	
SNIA Viscosa	OTC	
Soc. Fin. Siderugica "A"	OTC	
STET (Societa Finanziara Telefonica SpA)	OTC	
Luxembourg		
Anangel American Shipholdings	NASDAQ	ASIPY
Minorco SA	NASDAQ	MNRCY
Netherlands		
Aegon NV	NASDAQ	AEGNY
Ahold NV	NASDAQ	KAHLY
Akzo NV	NASDAQ	AKZOY
Buhrmann-Tetterode	OTC	
DSM NV	OTC	
Elsevier NV	OTC	
Fokker NV	OTC	
Heineken NV	OTC	HINKY
KLM Royal Dutch Airlines	NYSE	KLM
Koninklijke BI Jenkorf Beheer KBB NV	OTC	
Koninklijke Nederlandsche Hoogovens EN	OTC	
Koninklijke Wessanen NV	OTC	
NV Verenigo Bezit	OTC	
OCE van der Grinten NV	NASDAQ	OCENY
Philips Electronics NV	NYSE	PHG
Polygram NV "New York Shares"	NYSE	PLG
Royal Dutch Petroleum Co.	NYSE	RD
Royal Nedlloyd Group NV	OTC	
Unilever NV	NYSE	UN
Van Ommeren Ceteco NV	OTC	
Wolters Kluwer NV	OTC	
Norway		
Bergesen D.Y. AS (A Shares)	OTC	
Hafslund Nycomed AS "A" Shares	OTC	HAFAY
Nora Industries AS	OTC	
Norsk Data AS	NASDAQ	NORKZ
Norsk Hydro AS	NYSE	NHY
Saga Petroleum "A"	OTC	
Unitor Ships Services AS	OTC	
Vard AS Class "A"	OTC	
VIP Scandanavia	OTC	
Portugal		
Banco Comercial Portugues	OTC	
Spain		
Banco Bilbao Vizcaya, SA	NYSE	BBV
Banco Central, SA	NYSE	BCM
Banco de Santander	NYSE	STD
Banco Espanol de Credito (Banesto)	OTC	
Corporacion Mapfre	OTC	CRFEY
Empresa Nacional de Electricidad, SA	NYSE	ELE
Repsol SA	NYSE	REP
Telefónica de España, SA	NYSE	TEF
Sweden		
AGA AB "B" Shares	OTC	
Asea AB "B" Shares	NASDAQ	ASEAY
Atlas Copco AB "A" Shares	OTC	ATLSY
Electrolux AB	NASDAQ	ELUXY
LM Ericsson Telephone Co. "B" Shares	NASDAQ	ERICY
Esselte AB "B" Shares	OTC	
Gambro AB	NASDAQ	GAMBY
Pharmacia AB	NASDAQ	PHABY
PLM AB "A" Shares	OTC	
PLM AB "B" Shares	OTC	
Sandvik AB	OTC	SAVKY
SKF AB	NASDAQ	SKFRY

Non-US Company Stocks Available Through US Stock Markets (continued)

Company	Exchange	Symbol
Sweden (continued)		
Svenska Cellulosa AB	NASDAQ	SCAPY
Volvo AB "B" Shares	NASDAQ	VOLVY
Switzerland		
BBC Brown Boveri Limited	NASDAQ	BBCZ
Ciba-Geigy AG	OTC	CBGXY
Nestlé SA Participation Certificate	OTC	NESAY
United Kingdom		
ADT Limited	NASDAQ	ADTL
AEGIS Group PLC	NASDAQ	WCRSY
Airship Industry	NASDAQ	AIRSY
Albert Fisher Group	OTC	
Allied-Lyons PLC	OTC	ALLY
Associated British Foods	OTC	
Astec (BSR) PLC	OTC	
Attwoods PLC	NYSE	A
Automated Security Holdings PLC	NASDAQ	ASHBY
B.A.T Industries PLC	ASE	BTI
Barclays Bank PLC	NYSE	BCS
Bass PLC	NYSE	BAS
Beazer PLC	NYSE	BEZRY
BET Public Limited Company	NYSE	BEP
BIO-Isolates (Holdings) PLC	OTC	
Blenheim Exhibitions Group PLC	OTC	
Blue Circle Industries PLC	OTC	
BOC Group PLC	OTC	BOCNY
Booker PLC	OTC	
Boots Company PLC	OTC	
Bowater Industries PLC	NASDAQ	BWTRY
Brent Walker Group PLC	OTC	
Bristol Oil and Minerals PLC (BOM)	OTC	
British Airways PLC	NYSE	BAB
British Gas Public Limited Company	NYSE	BRG
British Petroleum Company PLC	NYSE	BP
British Steel PLC	NYSE	BST
British Telecommunications PLC	NYSE	BTY
BTR PLC	OTC	
Burmah Castrol PLC	NASDAQ	BURMY
Burton Group PLC	OTC	
Cable and Wireless PLC	NYSE	CWP
Cadbury Schweppes PLC	NASDAQ	CADBY
Carlton Communications PLC	NASDAQ	CCTVY
Charter Consolidated PLC	OTC	
Charterhall PLC	OTC	
Chloride Group Limited	OTC	
Christian Salvesen PLC	OTC	
Christies International PLC	OTC	
Coats Viyella PLC	OTC	
Condor Minerals and Energy Limited	OTC	
Courtaulds, PLC	ASE	COU
Davy Corporation PLC	OTC	
De La Rue Company PLC	OTC	
Dixons Group PLC	OTC	DXN
Dowty Group PLC	OTC	
East Midlands Electricity PLC	OTC	
Eastern Electricity PLC	OTC	
ECC Group PLC	NASDAQ	ECLAY
Egerton Trust PLC	OTC	
Eurotunnell PLC/Eurotunnel SA	OTC	
Fisons PLC	NASDAQ	FISNY
GB & NI Treasury Loan Stock 3.50%	OTC	
General Electric Company PLC	OTC	GNELY
Gestetner Holdings PLC (ordinary)	OTC	
GKN PLC	OTC	GUKEY
Glaxo Holdings PLC	NYSE	GLX
Gold Greenlees Trott PLC	OTC	
Govett Strategic Investment Trust PLC	OTC	
Grand Metropolitan PLC	NYSE	GRM
Great Universal Stores PLC	OTC	
Great Universal Stores PLC "A"	OTC	
Guinness PLC	OTC	GURSY
Hanson PLC	NYSE	HAN
Hartstone Group PLC	OTC	
Harvard Group PLC	OTC	HARVY
Hawker Siddeley Group Public Limited	OTC	GNELY
Hillsdown Holdings PLC	OTC	
HSBC Holdings PLC	OTC	
Huntingdon International Holdings	NYSE	HRCLY
ICI Public Limited Company	OTC	ICI
Imperial Chemical Industries PLC	NYSE	ICI
Kingfisher PLC	OTC	
Ladbroke Group PLC	OTC	
Lasmo PLC	OTC	LSMOY
Laura Ashley Holdings PLC	OTC	
Leica PLC	OTC	
LEP Group PLC	NASDAQ	LEPY
London & Scottish Marine Oil PLC	OTC	
London and Overseas Freighter PLC	OTC	
London Electricity PLC	OTC	
London Finance and Investment	OTC	
London International Group	NASDAQ	LONDY
Lonrho PLC	OTC	
Manweb PLC	OTC	
Marks and Spencer PLC	OTC	
Maxwell Communication Corporation PLC	OTC	MWCL
MB-Caradon PLC	OTC	
Medeva PLC	OTC	
Micro Focus Group PLC	OTC	
Midlands Electricity PLC	OTC	
National Power PLC	OTC	
National Westminster Bank PLC	NYSE	NW
NFC PLC	ASE	NFC
NMC Group PLC	OTC	
Northern Electric PLC	OTC	
Norweb PLC	OTC	
Peninsular and Oriental Steam Navigation	OTC	
Pentos PLC	OTC	
Polly Peck International PLC	OTC	
Powergen PLC	OTC	
Premier Consolidated Oilfields PLC	OTC	PCONY
Prudential Corporation PLC	OTC	
Racal Electronics PLC	OTC	RACLY
Racal Telecom Public Limited	NYSE	RTG
Rank Organisation PLC	OTC	RANKY
Ratners Group PLC	NASDAQ	RATNY
Redland PLC	OTC	
Reed International PLC	OTC	RENEY
Regional Elec Co.'s Unit	OTC	
Reuters Holdings PLC	NASDAQ	RTRSY
Rodime PLC	OTC	RODMY
Rolls-Royce PLC	OTC	
Rothmans International PLC	OTC	
Royal Bank of Scotland - Pref.	NYSE	
RTZ Corporation PLC	NYSE	RTZ
Ryan Hotels PLC	OTC	
Saatchi & Saatchi Company PLC	NYSE	SAA
Sainsbury PLC	OTC	
Scantronic Holdings PLC	OTC	
Scottish and Universal Investments PLC	OTC	
Scottish Heritable Trust PLC	OTC	
SD-Scicon PLC	OTC	
Sears PLC	OTC	
Sedgwick Group PLC	OTC	
Seeboard PLC	OTC	
Senetek PLC	NASDAQ	SNTKY
Shell Transport & Trading Company Ltd.	NYSE	SC

Non-US Company Stocks Available Through US Stock Markets (continued)

Company	Exchange	Symbol
United Kingdom (continued)		
Siebe PLC	OTC	
SmithKline Beecham PLC	NYSE	SBH
SmithKline Beecham PLC (equity)	NYSE	SBE
South Wales Electricity PLC	OTC	
South Western Electricity PLC	OTC	
Southern Electric PLC	OTC	
Southwest Resources PLC	OTC	
Summer International PLC	OTC	
Systems Connection Group PLC	OTC	
T & N PLC	OTC	
Tarmac PLC (Amps) Series "A"	OTC	
Tate and Lyle PLC	OTC	
Tesco PLC	OTC	
Thorn EMI PLC	OTC	THOEY
TI Group PLC	OTC	
Tiphook PLC	OTC	
F.H. Tomkins PLC	NASDAQ	TOMK
Trafalgar House Public Limited Co.	OTC	
Transco Exploration Partners Ltd.	OTC	
Transport Development Group Ltd.	OTC	
UK of GB and N. Ireland 3.5% War Loan St	OTC	
Ultramar PLC	OTC	
Unigate PLC	OTC	
Unilever PLC	NYSE	UL
Unitech PLC	OTC	
United Newspapers Public Limited Company	NASDAQ	UNEWY
Vickers Public Limited Company	OTC	
Wace Group PLC	OTC	
Wellcome PLC	OTC	WLLCY
Wembley PLC	OTC	
Whitbread and Co. Limited "A" Shares	OTC	WHITY
Williams Holdings	OTC	
Willis Corroon PLC	NYSE	WCG
WPP Group PLC	NASDAQ	WPPGY
Yorkshire Electricity Group PLC	OTC	
LATIN AMERICA		
Chile		
Compania de Telefonos de Chile (CTC)	NYSE	TCH
El Salvador		
Compania de Alumbrado Electrico de SS	OTC	ELSA
Mexico		
Cifra, SA de CV	OTC	
Corporacion Industrial Sanluis Ser A	OTC	
E.P.N., SA de CV	OTC	
Grupo Sidek, SA de CV	OTC	
Grupo Synkro, SA de CV	OTC	
IEM SA (Industria Electrica de Mexico)	OTC	
Internacional de Ceramica, SA de CV	OTC	
Ponderosa Industrial, SA de CV	OTC	
Teléfonos de México SA de CV Ser A	NASDAQ	TFONY
Teléfonos de México SA de CV Ser L	NYSE	TMX
Tolmex, SA de CV "B" Shares	OTC	
Tubos de Acero de Mexico, SA	ASE	TAM
MIDDLE EAST		
Israel		
Bank Leumi Le-Israel	NASDAQ	BKLNY
Elite Industries Limited NIS 1	OTC	
IDB Bankholding Corporation	NASDAQ	IDBBY
Israel Land Development Co., Ltd.	NASDAQ	ILDCY
Teva Pharmaceutical Industries Ltd.	NASDAQ	TEVIY
Turkey		
NET Holding Inc.	OTC	

Source: List provided by The Bank of New York; ticker symbols obtained by The Reference Press

List current as of July 30, 1991

The Country Profiles

ASIA/PACIFIC

Major languages: Bahasa Indonesian, Chinese, English, Hindi, Japanese
Major regional organizations:
Association of South East Asian Nations (ASEAN)
Colombo Plan
South Pacific Forum

Countries in Asia/Pacific:

Afghanistan
Australia
Bangladesh
Bhutan
Brunei
Cambodia
China
Fiji
Hong Kong
India
Indonesia
Japan
Kiribati
Republic of Korea
Laos
Macao
Malaysia
Maldives
Mongolia
Myanmar
Nauru
Nepal
New Zealand
North Korea
Pakistan
Papua New Guinea
Philippines
Singapore
Solomon Islands
Sri Lanka
Taiwan
Thailand
Tonga
Tuvalu
Vanuatu
Vietnam
Western Samoa

Regional Population (%)

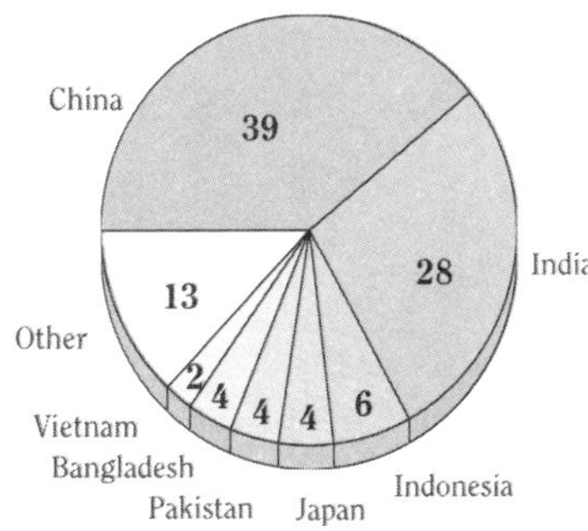

Regional Area (%)

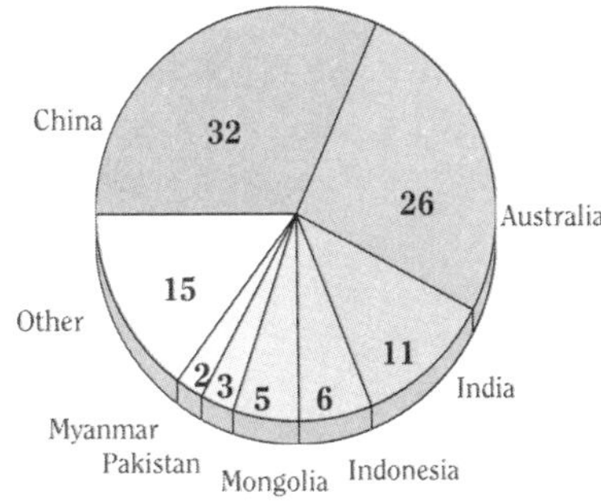

Regional GDP (%)

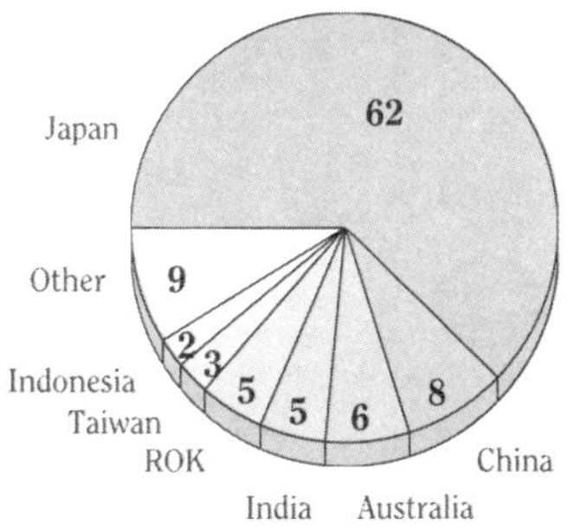

OVERVIEW

The economies of the most prosperous Pacific Rim countries (Japan, Hong Kong, Singapore, Taiwan, and the Republic of Korea) each grew nearly tenfold or more between 1970 and 1988, driven by aggressive export strategies. All 5 depend on imports to supply their industries, and most are not self-sufficient in food. Yet they prosper because of a dedication to education, good communications and transport systems, strong work ethics, free-market philosophies, and global-trade orientations.

A 2nd tier of states on the way up includes Malaysia, Indonesia, and Thailand. They have grown three- to fivefold since 1970 on the strength of increasing exports, commercialization, and exploitation of resources. Malaysia, in particular, is well endowed with natural resources, including oil and gas.

Most of the other nations (including China, India, Pakistan, the Philippines, and Sri Lanka) are troubled by large, poverty-stricken populations; low educational levels; political instability; and lack of food and resources, which necessitates spending large portions of scarce foreign exchange that cannot then be used for long-term investment.

Australia and New Zealand traditionally considered themselves part of the European world. But as the realities of geography and the implications of their exclusion from the EC set in, they are reorienting trade toward Asia.

The Pacific island countries have niche economies based on such industries as sugar and tourism (Fiji), financial services (Vanuatu), and bird guano (Nauru).

WHEN

Indian culture dates from the Indus civilization of 3000 BC, whose archeological remains include stone, copper, and bronze tools; elaborate irrigation systems; and seals indicating trade with Mesopotamia as early as 2300 BC.

Chinese civilization dates from the 17th century BC Shang dynasty, which already had wheeled carts, writing, and bronze work.

Though the world populations remained small and sparse, technical innovations tended to cluster in distinct periods. Coinage appeared in both Greece and China in the 7th century BC. Alexander the Great's conquest of Central Asia and northern India (325 BC) brought India, China, and the Mediterranean into closer contact, stimulating trade that eventually included gold from Europe, silk from China, and gems from India.

From the 3rd century BC to the 2nd century, China expanded into Korea and Vietnam, while increasing trade with the West. At the same time, Indian civilization (with Buddhism) spread through the subcontinent into Ceylon, Indochina, and Malaya.

By the first century, trade between Asia and the West had increased, with Roman coinage finding its way to Vietnam. Also about this time the Polynesians began their epic voyages to Hawaii, Australia, and New Zealand.

From the 2nd through the 8th centuries, Southeast Asian societies became trade links between India and China and contributed spices and gold to regional trade. Trade routes ran from China to the coasts of Vietnam, Siam (Thailand), and Malaya, through the Strait of Malacca (now the site of Singapore) to India. Agriculture followed trade, and many settlements developed elaborate irrigation systems.

Japan kept to itself, developing a sophisticated but xenophobic society.

Islam arrived in northern India in the 8th century and by the 15th century was established in India, Malaya, Indonesia, and parts of the Philippines.

The Europeans broke Islam's monopoly over Asian trade by finding new sea routes. For 4 centuries Asia came increasingly under European dominance, until the 19th century, by which time only Japan and Siam had escaped the European yoke. Portugal, Holland, Spain, and Britain colonized most of Asia and the Pacific, using the colonies as captive markets. Though China was never colonized, its territories were divided into spheres of influence by the Europeans and Japanese. Australia and New Zealand, whose natives had a less organized culture, were colonized, with whites becoming the majority.

The arrival of the US fleet in 1854 roused Japan from isolation and stimulated modernization that allowed it to win a war against Russia in 1905. The Japanese then expanded into Korea (annexed 1910) and China (1931), envisioning a united Asia led by Japan.

WWII spoiled both Japan's vision and Europe's colonialism. Between 1948 and 1960 most of Asia became independent.

Japan, with an established industrial base, recovered quickly from the war. Starting with unsophisticated, mass-produced copies of US goods, the Japanese redeveloped their heavy industries, improved their auto and consumer goods sectors, and finally moved on to high-tech electronics.

Other Asian nations followed the same pattern. As Japanese labor costs increased, South Korea (the Republic of Korea) became the premier producer of low-cost, low-tech goods and then of heavy industry and automotive goods. It is now turning to high-quality, high-tech products. Increasing labor costs have driven many of the elementary industries to still poorer developing nations, such as Indonesia, the Philippines, and Malaysia.

Meanwhile, the city-states of Hong Kong and Singapore, without many heavy industrial facilities, have concentrated on light industry, international shipping, and regional finance.

New Zealand and Australia, with their large land areas and sparse European-dominated populations, have older industrial facilities and economies dominated by pastoral, mineral, and agricultural products, which are in demand by the densely populated nations of the area.

China and India are burdened with vast populations. Both nations play a smaller role in the economic life of the region than they used to because of their large internal markets, Socialist economic controls, and relative poverty.

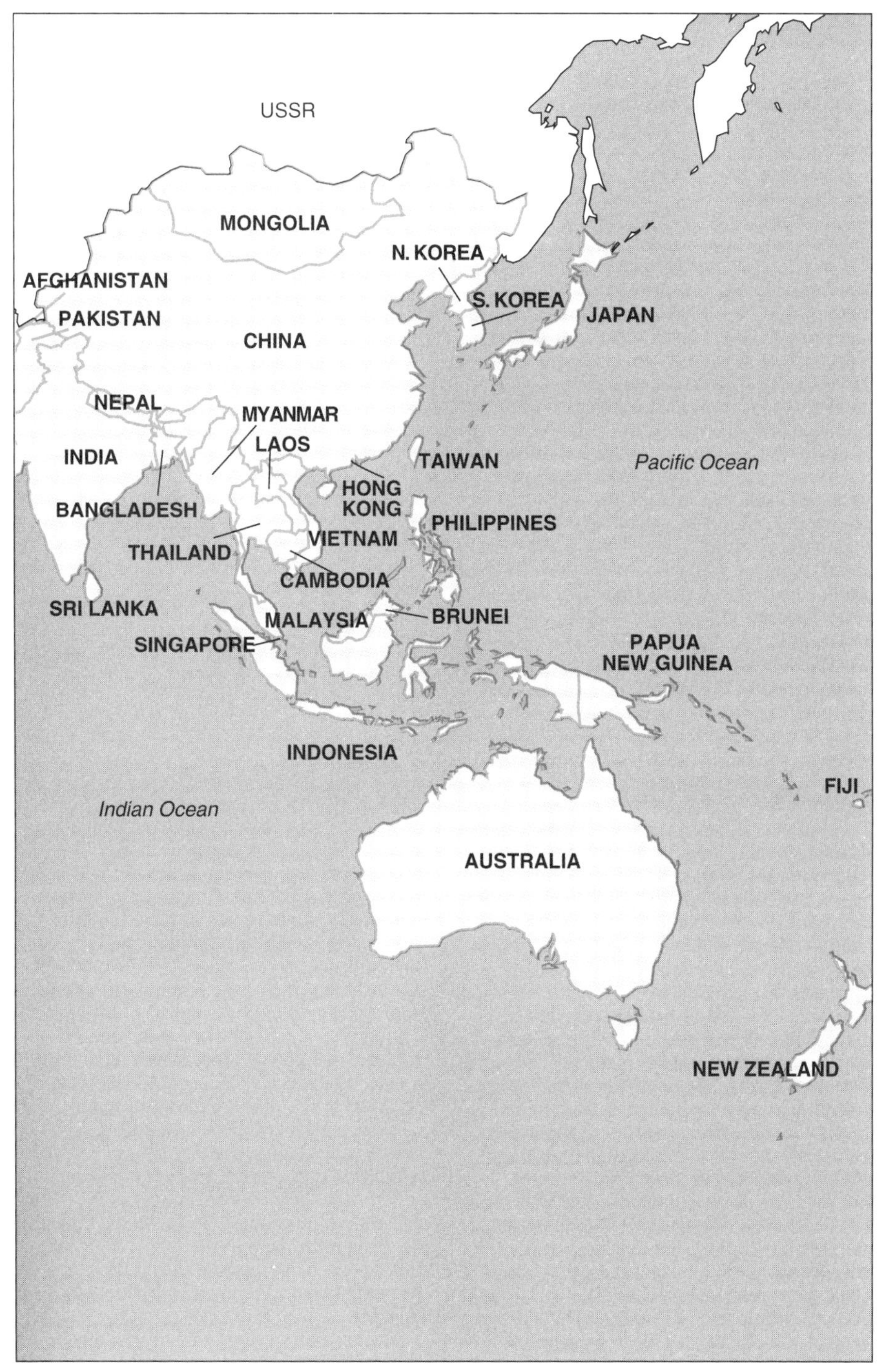

HOW MUCH

	1980	1981	1982	1983	1984	1985	1986	1987	1988	1989
Population (mil.)	2,460	2,506	2,549	2,596	2,640	2,685	2,730	2,780	2,831	2,882
GDP ($ bil.)	2,078	2,248	2,194	2,317	2,441	2,529	3,191	3,754	4,484	4,650
GDP per capita	845	897	861	893	925	942	1,169	1,350	1,584	1,614
Trade balance ($ mil.)	—	—	—	—	—	17,328	67,049	88,306	67,151	47,571
Current acct. ($ mil.)	—	—	—	—	—	(69,530)	(52,624)	(22,882)	912	(10,145)

ASSOCIATION OF SOUTH EAST ASIAN NATIONS

In 1967, during the Vietnam War, Malaysia, the Philippines, Indonesia, Singapore, and Thailand (Brunei joined in 1984) formed the Association of South East Asian Nations (ASEAN) to promote economic, social, and educational progress and stability. The aim was to coordinate intra- and extraregional trade, reduce trade barriers, and eventually establish a single EC-like market. But the war and its aftermath — the victory of communism in Vietnam, the near-destruction of Cambodia by the Khmer Rouge, border clashes between Cambodia (Kampuchea) and Thailand, and massive waves of refugees through the area — prevented achievement of this goal and created a new set of problems as well.

ASEAN's efforts have been mostly aimed at ameliorating the effects of the Vietnam War and attempting to keep peace in the region. This is complicated by the nondefensive nature of the alliance, as well as by numerous bilateral territorial disputes, such as that between Malaysia and the Philippines over Sabah, on Borneo. There are also long-standing tensions between Singapore and Malaysia and between Malaysia and Indonesia.

ASEAN has not been very successful in one of its proposed roles, as a sponsor of joint ventures between members, but the association has served as a reasonably successful vehicle for resolution of tax and customs difficulties between members. In 1988 ASEAN established a fund to promote the establishment of small- and medium-sized businesses.

In the 1980s, as the world economy boomed, ASEAN made an agreement with the EC for technical and scientific assistance and encouraged European investment. It also concluded agricultural and development assistance agreements with Australia and New Zealand.

The single market, however, remains a distant goal at best. Though ASEAN is attempting to develop complementary industries in member countries, most of its members' economies are in competition. At least one member, Indonesia, believes its economy would suffer from free trade, so members desiring a reduction of trade barriers deal with each other directly rather than through the association.

With the sweeping changes in world alignments produced by the fall of Soviet and European communism and the increasing strength of China in the world market, ASEAN will be forced to redefine itself and its goals. Items on the agenda for consideration in the 1990s include admitting other nations to the association, coming to terms with Japan's dominance of area trade, helping members remain competitive, and reorganizing the association into a body that works by majority rather than by unanimous agreement and that provides for both national and regional defense.

EASTERN EUROPE

Major languages: Albanian, Bulgarian, Czech, Hungarian, Polish, Romanian, Russian, Serbo-Croatian, Slovak

Major regional organizations:
- Council for Mutual Economic Assistance (CMEA/COMECON) (dissolved in 1991)
- Danube Commission
- Visegrad
- Warsaw Treaty Organization (WTO, the Warsaw Pact) (dissolved in 1991)

Countries in Eastern Europe:

Albania	Poland
Bulgaria	Romania
Czechoslovakia	USSR
Hungary	Yugoslavia

Regional Population (%)

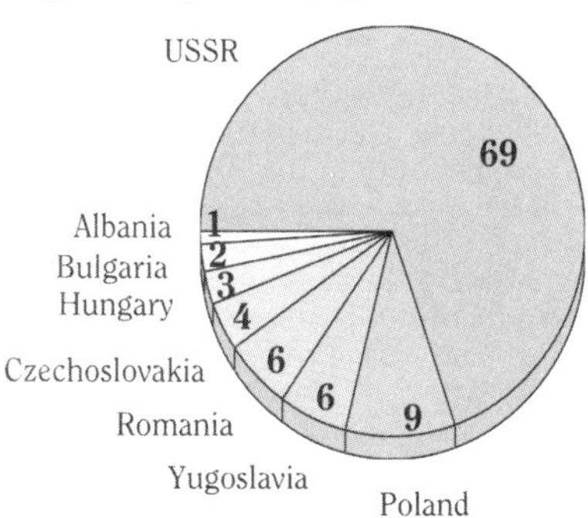

Regional Area (%)

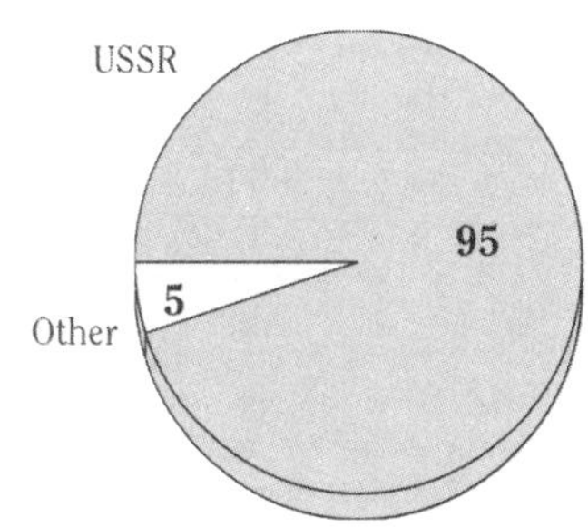

Regional GDP (%)

USSR 62
Hungary 2
Czechoslovakia 2
Poland 3
Bulgaria 4
Romania 8
Yugoslavia 19

OVERVIEW

Most of Eastern Europe is now becoming truly politically and economically independent for the first time, as Soviet political and economic domination of the region disintegrates.

Since the 1950s most of Eastern Europe has been united under 2 USSR-sponsored organizations, the Warsaw Pact and COMECON. The Warsaw Pact was formed in 1955, ostensibly to defend against Western aggression but in practice to enforce Eastern bloc "discipline." It used membership as a pretext to intervene militarily in Hungary in 1956 and Czechoslovakia in 1968 and to threaten Poland in 1981. With the end of the Cold War in 1989, the Warsaw Pact became unnecessary and members dissolved it in 1991.

COMECON (Council for Mutual Economic Assistance) was formed in 1949 to promote "socialist economic integration" among Soviet client states. It was an extension of the USSR's economic planning, functioning as a central coordinator for production of goods within the group. Member countries traded for each other's nonconvertible currency or, more often, bartered.

The fiction under which COMECON labored — that the Communist world had one economy — caused the organization to fail in the 1980s, and it, too, was dissolved in 1991. Members now trade with each other and with outsiders for hard currency. Most members are committed to instituting free-market economies, though on varying timetables. East Germany has gone the farthest — reuniting with West Germany. Czechoslovakia and Poland have started to sell off state properties and adapt to a market economy, while Hungary and Yugoslavia, more market oriented to begin with, have made fewer changes. Romania, Bulgaria, and Albania have liberalized their economies the least.

Resurgent regionalism plagues Eastern Europe, leaving its nations' economies vulnerable to political upheaval. The Slovaks are a discontented minority within Czechoslovakia. In Yugoslavia, violence has erupted as the central government seeks to prevent secession by Croatia and Slovenia. Poor treatment of Eastern European ethnic minorities within other Eastern European nations has soured relations (e.g., between Yugoslavia and Bulgaria and between Hungary and Romania).

The outlook for the former East Germany, Poland, Czechoslovakia, and Hungary is reasonably good, but the Balkan states (Yugoslavia, Albania, Bulgaria, and Romania) may subside into their traditional anarchy. What will happen in the USSR is anyone's guess.

WHEN

From prehistory until the fall of Rome, waves of nomads spilled out of central Asia into Asia Minor and southern and western Europe, displacing existing populations and driving them westward toward other populations. The migrations slowed and the migrants settled down to agriculture, with Poland, Bohemia, and Hungary emerging in the late Middle Ages and Renaissance. They lay on ancient overland trade routes between Asia and Europe (silks, spices, and jewels) and between the Baltic and Southern Europe (amber, timber, and furs).

Hungary and the Balkans fell to the Turks in the 15th and 16th centuries; Bohemia was absorbed by Austria, and Poland disappeared into its neighbors in 1795.

Though Poland and Bohemia (part of modern Czechoslovakia) claimed to be outposts of Western civilization, and Russia claimed successorship to Rome and Byzantium, Eastern Europe remained rural, unindustrialized, and uninvolved in trade. In the 17th and 18th centuries, while Western Europe explored the world, Eastern Europe remained preoccupied with repelling the Turks. Economic development was also hampered by Eastern Europe's tradition of subsistence-level agriculture, which required fewer manufactured and consumer goods. This situation persisted until WWI.

The demise of the Russian, Austrian, and Prussian monarchies following WWI allowed Poland, Czechoslovakia, Yugoslavia, and Hungary to arise as modern nation-states, though ethnic rivalries continued, exacerbated by discontent with newly created national borders.

These lands were seized by the USSR after WWII, as much to be used as a buffer against the West as to fulfill communism's imperial aspirations. The USSR imposed Communist governments on Poland, Bulgaria, Czechoslovakia, Romania, East Germany, and, to a lesser extent, Hungary. Yugoslavia defied the USSR's edicts and turned westward. Albania, already Communist under Enver Hoxha, maintained close ties to the USSR but later sank into isolationism.

Most countries in the region began a crash program of heavy industrialization (shipbuilding and steel and machinery manufacture). Outdated technology caused horrendous pollution and inefficiency, while central management was unresponsive and self-protective. East Germany and Czechoslovakia, reasonably industrialized before the war, became the showplaces of Eastern Europe.

Through the 1970s dissent grew. In 1980 a series of strikes brought down Poland's government and set in motion the events that would lead, 9 years later, to all countries throughout the region gaining effective independence from the USSR.

The collapse of communism stemmed from a steady decline in regional economic conditions and from the USSR's lack of will to maintain power. In 1989 Hungary's government invited participation by non-Communists, while East German economic conditions deteriorated. Thousands left for Hungary in hopes of easy escape. Hungary made it easier by opening its borders with Austria. East Germany relaxed border control and the resultant flood forced it to open its borders with the West, which quickly led to an astoundingly rapid reunification with West Germany in 1990.

Czechoslovakia's Communist government fell, Romania's was overthrown, and Bulgaria and Hungary moved to liberalize their economies. Albania has just begun taking its first tentative steps toward a more open society.

TREUHANDANSTALT

After communism collapsed, all the nations of Eastern Europe were faced with the problem of divesting unprofitable state-owned businesses and involving their sometimes unenthusiastic citizens in capitalism.

Though in eastern Germany this task is seemingly simplified by the presence of a wealthier partner, eastern Germany must go even further and somehow bring its standard of living up to the high level of western Germany's in order to help keep economic reunification from crumbling.

The Treuhandanstalt (trust administration) was created by the last East German government in 1990 to preserve the people's property and the bureaucracy's jobs. When the West German government took over at economic unification in July 1990, the trust owned 8,000 businesses employing 1/2 of eastern Germany's work force (10 million workers, making the trust the world's largest employer) and controlled 40% of the land, including former collective farms, forests, and secret police buildings.

The trust was charged with restructuring eastern Germany's economy, closing the most unprofitable companies, determining and maintaining the value of potentially profitable businesses until sale, and selling the most profitable ones. This task was complicated by eastern Germany's nonadherence to generally accepted accounting principles and by the government's commitment to finding and compensating the owners of previously confiscated property.

Treuhand's first western administrator lasted 5 weeks; the second, Detlev Rohwedder, reorganized the administration and liquidated some of the most unprofitable businesses, including both car makers and Interflug, eastern Germany's airline. The resulting loss of jobs made the trust deeply unpopular. Rohwedder was murdered on April 1, 1991, by the Red Army Faction, which had links with East Germany's secret police.

The trust's new administrator, Birgit Breuel, continued Rohwedder's policies. One of the greatest obstacles to sales had been the claims filed by former property owners. By March 1991, when the government ruled that job-creating investments should take precedence over past ownership, there were 1.2 million claims, and only 700 businesses had been sold. By July 1991, over 2,500 businesses had been sold, primarily to Germans, for about $5.3 billion.

In addition to the costs of its own bureaucracy (1,500 people in 15 regional offices), Treuhand is responsible for the operating costs of its businesses (already nearly $17 billion in short-term loans) as well as for their debt. The decision to convert eastern Germany's currency one-to-one with western Germany's raised eastern companies' debts to $67 billion as of June 1990 and devalued their inventories. The difference between the sales value of the businesses and their debt and operating expenses will throw Treuhand into the red by over $10 billion in 1991.

HOW MUCH

	1980	1981	1982	1983	1984	1985	1986	1987	1988	1989
Population (mil.)	379	383	385	389	395	397	400	404	406	409
GDP ($ bil.)	—	—	—	—	—	922	1,050	1,214	1,299	1,314
GDP per capita	—	—	—	—	—	2,324	2,621	3,006	3,196	3,214
Trade balance ($ mil.)	—	—	—	—	—	(3,569)	(9,321)	(2,743)	(5,624)	(11,982)
Current acct. ($ mil.)	—	—	—	—	—	596	(1,252)	3,049	1,899	(1,887)

LATIN AMERICA AND THE CARIBBEAN

Major languages: English, French, Portuguese, Spanish

Major regional organizations:

- The Andean Group
- Caribbean Community (CARICOM)
- Central American Common Market (CACM)
- Latin American Integration Association (LAIA)
- Mercosur
- Organization of American States (OAS)

Countries in Latin America and the Caribbean:

Anguilla	Cuba	Nicaragua
Antigua	Dominica	Panama
Argentina	Dominican Republic	Paraguay
Aruba	Ecuador	Peru
Bahamas	El Salvador	St. Kitts and Nevis
Barbados	French Guiana	St. Lucia
Belize	Grenada	St. Vincent
Bermuda	Guadeloupe	Suriname
Bolivia	Guatemala	Trinidad and Tobago
Brazil	Guyana	Turks and Caicos Islands
British Virgin Islands	Haiti	Uruguay
Cayman Islands	Honduras	Venezuela
Chile	Jamaica	
Colombia	Mexico	
Costa Rica	Montserrat	

Regional Population (%)

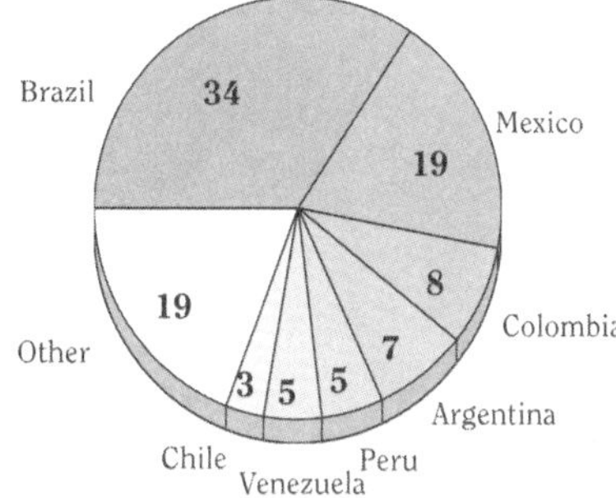

Regional Area (%)

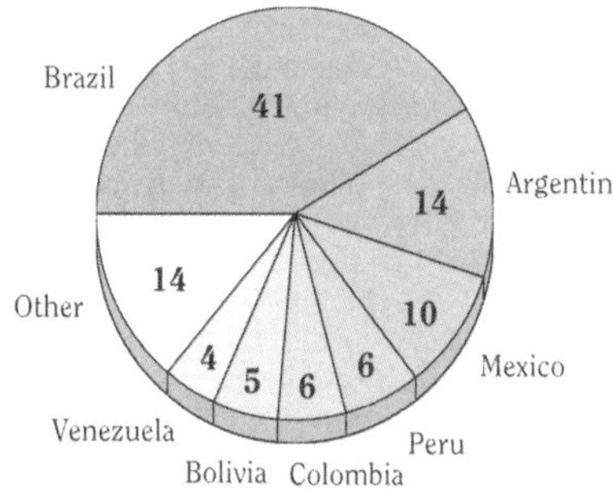

Regional GDP (%)

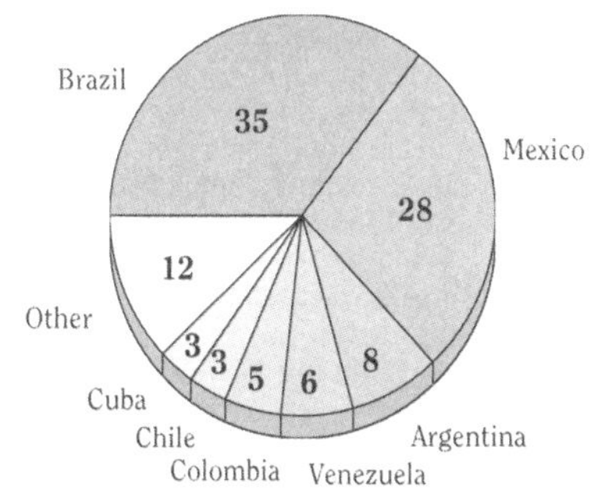

OVERVIEW

The Latin American and Caribbean nations represent 1/6 of the total world landmass. The countries share a common colonial lineage (largely Spanish, with Portuguese, British, French, and Dutch influences) but have a diverse ancestry. The region is blessed with rich mineral resources, fertile soil, and extensive forests. Wealth is unevenly distributed, and many current difficulties can be traced to poverty — a result of decades of rule by traditional elites of the countries.

Staggering debt ($430 billion for the region) has resulted from years of borrowing. Servicing this debt has required almost every country to establish austerity programs and to curtail much-needed development programs.

Compounding the problem are declining prices for the region's primary exports — sugar, coffee, and copper. Export diversification has been slow, as foreign investors lack confidence in the stability of the region's economies. Chile stands out as an exception. It has successfully diversified its economy and grown in the face of declining copper prices.

Inflation is a chronic problem in the region; recently, Bolivia, Brazil, and Argentina have had annual rates of over 1,000%.

Dictators have given way to the ballot box in many cases (Argentina, 1983; Brazil, 1985; Chile, 1990; and Nicaragua, 1990), but the trend toward democracy is threatened by endemic social and political problems. The influence of the military remains strong in some countries (e.g., Peru and Colombia) that are combating leftist guerrilla movements. The civilian leaderships face the problem of redefining the role of the military in the newly democratic societies.

Many countries have been touched by drug trafficking, especially in cocaine — coca leaves are grown and harvested in Bolivia, Peru, and Ecuador and processed in Colombia and Venezuela. Coca plantings can return profits 18 times higher than other crops; high profits attract corrupt and violent drug cartels.

Natural resources are under attack. Toxic by-products from drug processing are dumped in rivers; rain forests are cut for timber and cattle grazing. Industrialization has polluted the air and water, particularly in Mexico.

Yet not all the news is bad. Brazil has again begun making payments on long-defaulted debt, and Chile just qualified for regular commercial bank loans for the first time in nearly a decade. Democracy continues to replace totalitarian regimes. Efforts to control the drug cartels have had sporadic success in Colombia, and "debt-for-nature swaps" (e.g., in Costa Rica) have allowed environmental groups to buy up debt and forgive it in exchange for government agreements to preserve natural areas.

WHEN

Italian and Levantine middlemen who controlled the overland trade routes to the Orient drove traders to seek sea routes. Italian sea captain Christopher Columbus, convinced that a westerly sea route to China existed, solicited funding from Ferdinand and Isabella of Spain and set sail. Columbus did not reach China, but he did reach Costa Rica, the Bahamas, Cuba, Jamaica, Hispaniola, Panama, and Venezuela. Colonial rivalry in the 15th century led to a 1494 treaty that divided the New World between Spain and Portugal.

Spain and Portugal turned to the exploitation of their New World territories. The French, Dutch, and English soon followed and claimed their own territories. Early explorers, driven by their quest for gold and silver, enslaved the natives and brought disease.

Gold and silver mining flourished in Peru, Mexico, Chile, and Colombia. Agriculture arose to support the mining, and, where precious metals proved elusive, became a primary activity, with settlers growing wheat, tobacco, cacao, and indigo. Sugar cane was planted in Hispaniola, Mexico, and Peru. African slaves provided the labor. The import of domestic animals created secondary markets for hides, wools, and textiles.

Resenting the Spanish monopoly, English, Dutch, and French pirates relieved the Spanish of their gold but also established ports in Barbados, Jamaica, Curaçao, and Martinique.

Catholic missionaries educated and converted the natives. Although the Jesuits were expelled from the Indies in 1767, Catholicism remained influential.

The American and French revolutions inspired Latin American countries to begin declaring independence in the early 1800s, and by 1825 only Cuba and Puerto Rico remained under the Spanish flag. In 1822 Brazil became an independent monarchy, and in 1891 a republic. After a period of political struggles and economic deterioration, stability returned to the region in the late 1800s. The economies started to grow as the European market for Latin American commodities expanded. European immigration fueled the growth of Argentina, Brazil, and Chile.

By 1900 most economies were still dependent on price-sensitive commodities such as coffee. The Depression destroyed commodity markets. The prosperity hoped for after WWII proved elusive, as commodities competition increased from other emerging nations.

Castro's Marxist regime (1961) in Cuba marked the first and only Soviet-style Communist government in the Western Hemisphere. Elsewhere in the region, right-wing dictators arose to quell leftist guerrillas. Human rights suffered.

Government payrolls swelled and trade deficits increased, leading to substantial foreign debt. The oil price increases of the 1970s worsened economic conditions, except in oil-rich Mexico and Venezuela. Commodity prices and export revenue fell. High interest rates in the early 1980s hampered economic progress. The collapse of oil prices after 1986 left Mexico and Venezuela deeply in debt, with decreased revenues, while benefiting those dependent on imported oil.

In the early 1990s, with political turmoil at an ebb and the economies of the region beginning to recover, there is more hope for the region's future than there has been in decades.

HOW MUCH

	1980	1981	1982	1983	1984	1985	1986	1987	1988	1989
Population (mil.)	348	357	365	373	381	389	397	405	414	422
GDP ($ bil.)	1,080	1,219	1,111	1,025	1,092	1,139	1,220	1,324	1,506	1,686
GDP per capita	3,103	3,415	3,046	2,746	2,867	2,927	3,075	3,268	3,642	3,994
Trade balance ($ mil.)	(31,997)	(44,577)	(43,358)	(11,143)	(3,570)	(6,131)	(20,354)	(14,177)	(14,388)	(11,473)
Current acct. ($ mil.)	(31,032)	(43,025)	(42,229)	(9,283)	(1,144)	(2,572)	(17,054)	(9,865)	(8,635)	(6,866)

ORGANIZATION OF AMERICAN STATES

The predecessor to the Organization of American States, the International Union of American Republics, was founded in 1890 at the First International Conference of American States, held in Washington, DC; the US was a member. This conference had been called by the US during the 1880s, when political stability in the Latin states and improved transportation made trade more profitable between the US and its southern neighbors. The organization was to facilitate trade and promote peace and understanding among the states.

The 1890s, however, marked the start of a period of aggressive US involvement in Latin America, which impeded Pan American unity and stunted the Union's growth as a mechanism for equalizing relations among its members. The US fought the Spanish-American War (1898, whose peace treaty included a provision for at-will intervention in Cuba) and intervened in Colombia, helping Panama break away in 1903 in order to gain the right to dig the canal. It also invaded Mexico (1913) and Nicaragua (1912, 1927) and insisted on unilateral enforcement of the Monroe Doctrine (the 1823 US policy prohibiting European, but not US, interference in the Americas). These actions caused resentment in Latin America.

Franklin Roosevelt's Good Neighbor policy renounced military intervention in Latin America. After WWII the members of the Union were instrumental in shaping the UN charter's provisions which obligate the UN to resort to locally established procedures and to foster regional defensive organizations. In 1948 the Union was reborn as the Organization of American States under the aegis of the UN.

During the 1950s and 1960s, the OAS developed procedures for settling territorial, political, and economic disputes and for promoting joint defense and freer trade among the members. Among other things, the OAS established the Inter-American Development Bank, took action to contain the spread of communism, mediated a dispute between the US and Panama, imposed sanctions against Cuba (including suspension from participation in, but not ejection from, the OAS), and took joint military action with the US in the Dominican Republic in 1965.

In the 1970s and 1980s, the organization became still more active, establishing a General Assembly with regularly scheduled meetings (replacing periodic conferences) and tackling the difficult question of human rights in Latin America. It also continued to mediate conflicts, establishing cease fires in actions between El Salvador and Honduras (1976), Ecuador and Peru (1981), and the Sandinistas and contras in Nicaragua (1986).

Relations between the US and other OAS members remain ticklish since the US still regards the rest of the Americas (except Canada, which is not a member) as its special territory and continues to try to influence area politics and events. In 1978 the US reduced its payments to the OAS, and in the 1980s the US supported the contras, did not support the Nicaraguan peace plan, and took military action in Grenada.

MIDDLE EAST

Major languages: Arabic, English, Farsi, French, Turkish
Major regional organizations:
The League of Arab States
Organization of the Petroleum Exporting Countries (OPEC)

Countries in the Middle East:

Algeria	Kuwait	Sudan
Bahrain	Lebanon	Syria
Cyprus	Libya	Tunisia
Djibouti	Mauritania	Turkey
Egypt	Morocco	United Arab Emirates
Iran	Oman	Yemen
Iraq	Qatar	
Israel	Saudi Arabia	
Jordan	Somalia	

Regional Population (%)

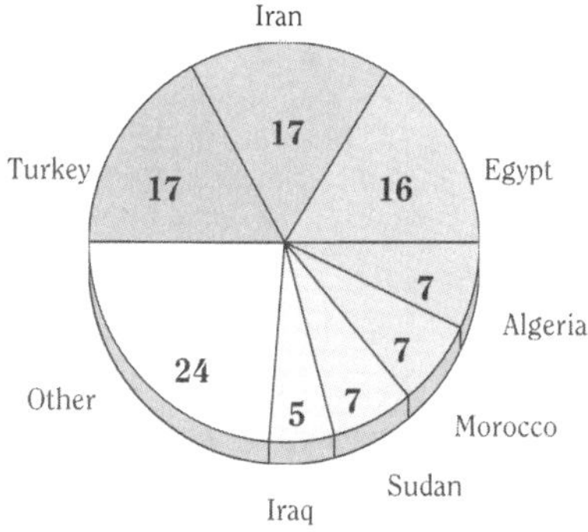

Regional Area (%)

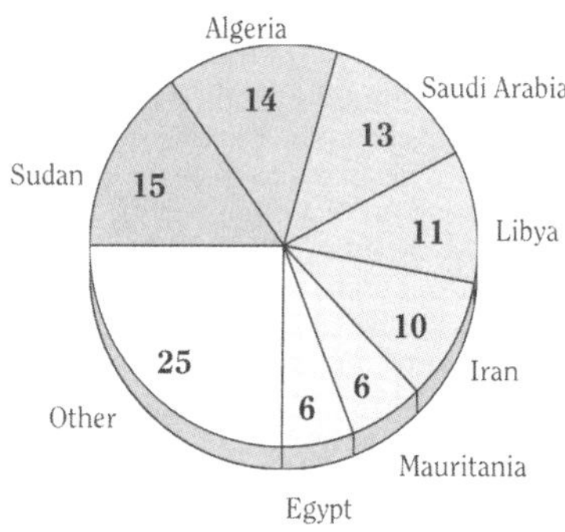

Regional GDP (%)

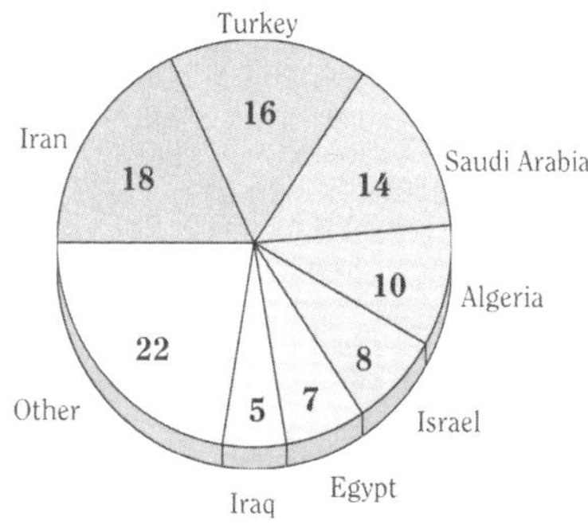

OVERVIEW

The tension between national interests and the desire for Islamic unity, plus the presence of Israel, make the Middle East a volatile place.

Though the Middle East has the world's largest concentration of oil, many of its nations (Syria, Jordan, Turkey) have little or no oil. Wealth from oil is unearned, and the wealthiest nations are those in which revenues are divided among the fewest people (Kuwait, Saudi Arabia) while other nations with large populations are proportionately poorer (Iran, Iraq). The disparity between ease and effort, as much as between rich and poor, inspires resentment and division and contributed to Iraq's invasion of Kuwait.

The artificiality of national borders is another problem. Only in Turkey, Iran, Egypt, and (to some extent) Saudi Arabia do national identities coincide with natural borders. The other nations of the Middle East were created to suit Europeans (e.g., Jordan's shape reflected Britain's need to maintain a pipeline from Iraq to Haifa). The result has been civil war (e.g., in Lebanon) and a series of wars involving Israel, which has the region's most advanced, integrated economy. Even making peace can be divisive, as Egypt found when it became a regional pariah by making peace with Israel.

Islamic unity is hampered by the schism between Sunni Islam (practiced by the majority) and Shi'a Islam (practiced primarily in non-Arab Iran). After the 1979 Islamic revolution that overthrew the shah, Iran tried to export its revolution to such "enemy" states as Saudi Arabia and Kuwait.

WHEN

The Middle East is the site of the earliest advances (agriculture, trade, writing), of many great empires (Chaldean, Egyptian, Persian, Roman, Ottoman), and of the birthplaces of Judaism, Christianity, and Islam.

In 325 Christianity became the official religion of the Roman Empire, which reached from Spain and Morocco to Iraq. The empire had a rich and varied trade, not only internally, but with Central Asia, Northern India, and China. In the 5th century the empire split and the eastern part, containing the richest commercial areas, became the Byzantine Empire.

In the 7th century Mohammed the Prophet established a new religion called Islam, which means "submission to God." Within 100 years Palestine, Persia, Arabia, North Africa, and Spain had submitted to Islam. Within 1,000 years Islam had spread to Byzantium, India, Malaysia, Greece, and Central Europe.

Islamic teachings contain specific strictures on economic dealings, including prohibition of interest. Islam's trade linked western sub-Saharan and eastern coastal Africa (metal goods, ivory, gold, and slaves), Arabia (pearls), India (gems, cloth), the East Indies (spices), and China (silks, porcelain).

The Osmanli (Ottoman) Turks had the largest Islamic empire, which declined after the 17th century. To the east another Islamic realm, Persia, remained independent but declined in the 18th century.

The Ottoman empire shrank in the 19th century, losing Greece (1829), Egypt (1832), and the Balkans (1878–1912), thus becoming known as "the sick man of Europe." In WWI the Ottomans sided with Germany. Britain created a 2-front war for the Turks by fomenting Arab revolts with promises of future independence. After the Turkish defeat in 1918, the Europeans, instead of sponsoring Arab independence, divided Palestine, Egypt, and North Africa into protectorates and set up local governments. Only strong internal resistance prevented dismemberment of Turkey itself.

European interest in the area was based on the discovery of oil in Iran in 1908 and in Iraq in 1914 and the desire to control its production. Additional oil reserves were discovered in Kuwait and Arabia between the wars.

The Middle East was unsettled in the interwar years. An army officer overthrew the Persian government and installed himself as shah; Iraq and Egypt experienced political turmoil. But Palestine had the worst problem. The British Balfour Declaration of 1917 had promised a Jewish homeland in Palestine. Jewish immigration increased, becoming a deluge with WWII, disrupting Arab communities.

The 1947 UN vote to divide Palestine into Jewish and Palestinian states led to the Israeli War of Independence. The Palestinian state never emerged, and the Arab world refused to recognize Israel. The resulting warfare and terrorism have continued for decades. Displaced Palestinians crowded into refugee camps or migrated through the region.

Though Iraq and Iran began oil production before WWI, most of the area's oil was unexploited until the 1950s. From 1945 to 1972 Western oil companies controlled production, resulting in high company profits, low consumer prices, and low revenues for the oil's owners.

In 1972 OPEC (formed in 1960) states began nationalizing production and raising prices in recognition of their power. Money flooded into the oil states and overflowed as aid for nonproducing states such as Jordan. In the 1980s better conservation and new production from areas such as the North Sea led to a decline in oil demand and prices.

The 1980s was a decade of disunity in the Middle East. Egypt broke the Arab world's united front by making peace with Israel. Ethnic strife, particularly in Lebanon, threatened stability as did a long, indecisive war between Iran and Iraq. Declining oil prices broke OPEC as members produced above their quotas; Kuwait's overproduction plus a long-simmering border dispute led Iraq to invade Kuwait in 1990.

US/UN troops drove Iraq's armies out of Kuwait in February 1991, but the war damaged Kuwait's production capacity and the burning of Kuwait's oil fields caused horrendous pollution. The war also weakened the region's economy, forcing even the Saudis to borrow money from abroad. In the wake of the war it was hoped that US diplomacy would bring a lasting settlement.

ORGANIZATION OF PETROLEUM EXPORTING COUNTRIES

In 1960 Iran, Iraq, Kuwait, Saudi Arabia, and Venezuela formed the Organization of Petroleum Exporting Countries (OPEC) to combat the dominance of western oil companies, which for decades had negotiated advantageous concessions from the oil-producing countries. OPEC's efforts in the 1960s to improve concession terms and coordinate members' production had little effect on the oil market because the US (then the world's greatest user) produced almost as much as it consumed and the output from new reserves kept pace with growth in demand.

In the early 1970s OPEC members took control of the emerging seller's market away from the oil companies. Libya led by threatening to nationalize oil company assets in Libya and requiring the companies to negotiate individually rather than as a bloc. OPEC members began requiring oil companies to sell local governments interests in the oil companies (most governments have since bought all of their countries' oil companies).

In the 1973 Arab-Israeli war, OPEC's Arab members raised prices 170% and declared an embargo on oil to the US and the Netherlands in retaliation for their support of Israel.

OPEC seemed to control the market as prices rose, and the US, Europe, and Japan struggled to adapt. Because the value of the money (the US dollars) raised by these high prices depended on the economic health of the West, Saudi Arabia moved to avert wild price hikes by adjusting its output to compensate for over- or underproduction by other members.

By the late 1970s conservation by oil-consuming nations and overproduction (despite OPEC discipline) brought on an oil glut, only partially dissipated by the cessation of exports by Iran and Iraq during the Iranian revolution and the subsequent Iran-Iraq war.

Because of soft demand, the loss of oil from Iran and Iraq in 1981 and 1982 did not push up prices. OPEC had admitted other, poorer nations, such as Nigeria, which desperately needed money and could not afford to abide by production quotas and price guidelines. By the mid-1980s OPEC was again at the mercy of market forces. Conservation measures, oil and gas production from the North Sea and Mexico, and the use of alternate energy sources (nuclear power, coal) reduced demand; the members' national interests triumphed over OPEC solidarity; and a deteriorating economy forced the USSR to begin selling its oil on the world market. Oil prices collapsed in 1986. In that year the price of a barrel of oil stood at about $13, down from about $35 in 1981. Members broke their quotas and undersold price guidelines to meet expenses.

Oil stayed under $20 per barrel until 1990. In that year, with OPEC in disarray, Iraq invaded Kuwait, partly because of outstanding territorial disputes and partly because of Kuwait's quota overproduction. After an initial rise, oil prices fell as Saudi Arabia increased production to compensate for loss of Kuwait's oil and to help pay for the multinational force that drove Iraq out of Kuwait. Even with Iraq prohibited by the UN from selling oil, and Kuwait's wells burning, prices following the Gulf War remained in the $20-per-barrel range. Barring a cataclysmic event in the Middle East, OPEC is unlikely to regain the upper hand over oil-consuming nations in the forseeable future.

HOW MUCH

	1980	1981	1982	1983	1984	1985	1986	1987	1988	1989
Population (mil.)	239	246	253	261	269	276	285	293	301	310
GDP ($ bil.)	492	540	543	557	558	577	627	566	581	588
GDP per capita	2,059	2,192	2,146	2,136	2,076	2,088	2,204	1,936	1,928	1,897
Trade balance ($ mil.)	54,529	37,783	6,539	(22,598)	(25,775)	(17,829)	(28,489)	(19,927)	(15,278)	2,365
Current acct. ($ mil.)	66,423	48,182	13,541	(16,245)	(14,530)	(5,242)	(18,650)	(9,781)	(8,311)	3,862

WESTERN EUROPE

Major languages: Dutch, English, French, German, Italian, Spanish

Major regional organizations:
- BENELUX
- Council of Europe
- European Community (EC)
- European Free Trade Association (EFTA)
- Nordic Council
- North Atlantic Treaty Organization (NATO)
- Organisation for Economic Co-operation and Development (OECD)
- Western European Union

Countries in Western Europe:

Andorra	Greece	Norway
Austria	Iceland	Portugal
Belgium	Ireland	San Marino
Cyprus	Italy	Spain
Denmark	Liechtenstein	Sweden
Finland	Luxembourg	Switzerland
France	Malta	United Kingdom
Germany	Monaco	Vatican City
Gibraltar	The Netherlands	

Regional Population (%)

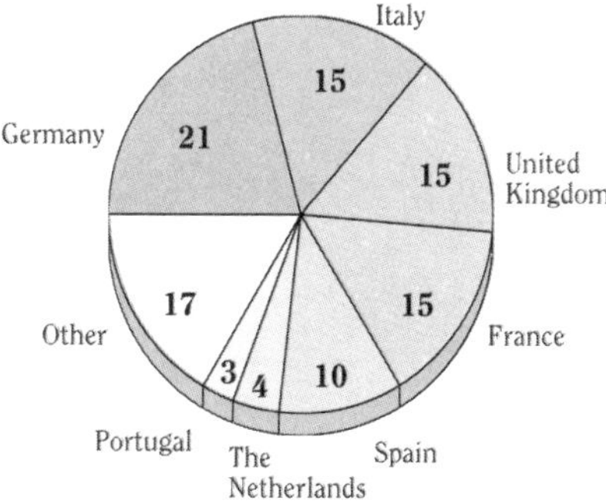

Regional Area (%)

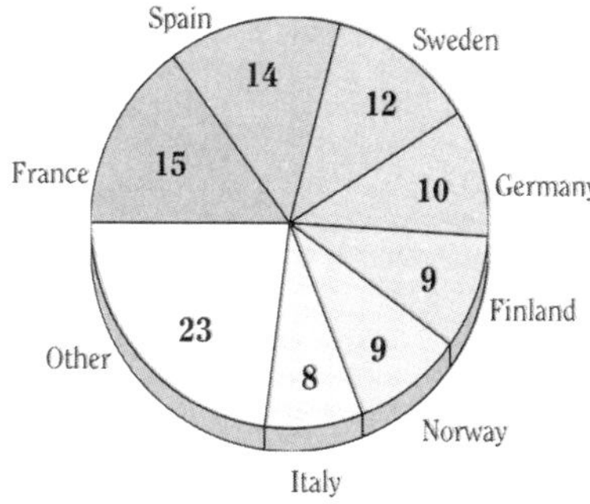

Regional GDP (%)

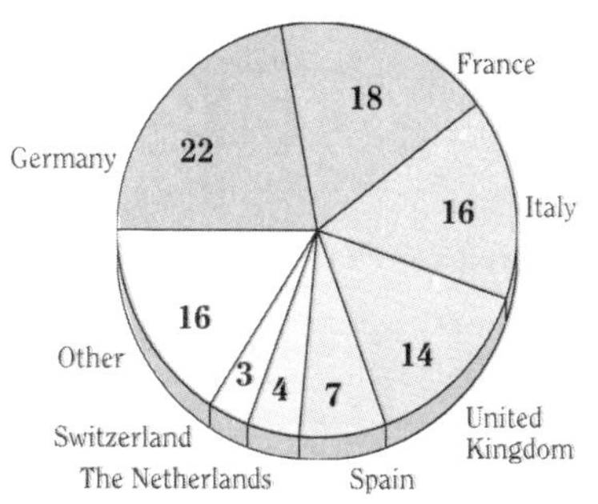

OVERVIEW

With less than 3% of the world's land and less than 10% of its population, Western Europe plays a disproportionately large role in the world's economy. In the last 40 years, it has recovered from crippling war and continental division and has begun to transform itself into the mightiest trading entity in the world.

Western Europe has a wide variety of natural resources, but distribution among its countries is not proportional to national industrial outputs. The region is a net importer of raw materials used to produce finished products of all types. It is self-sufficient in food, but distribution of agricultural bounty is uneven; France is a net exporter, while a mountainous terrain forces Switzerland to import much of its food.

Western Europe's living standard ranks among the highest in the world and is supported by a wide array of social welfare programs, which are most advanced in the Scandinavian countries. However, in many countries, the social programs have proven a heavy burden on the economy, forcing some nations, such as Denmark, deeply into debt. Other nations, including the UK, have attempted to cut back on such programs.

Though culturally diverse, with more than 12 national languages, Western Europe is becoming Americanized in architecture and lifestyle (the US is the EC's largest trading partner). Some find this influence disturbing; France is particularly averse to cultural and linguistic dilution.

Following WWII the nations of Western Europe put aside their traditional enmity and united against the larger threat of an expansionist USSR. International economic and defensive organizations (including EFTA, the BENELUX pact, the EC, and NATO) sprang up.

Future challenges include establishing a single EC market, planned for 1992; addressing a social malaise caused by affluence and lack of national goals; handling Eastern Europe's deluge of immigrants and the new governments' demands for financial assistance; and maintaining a supply of oil from the war-torn Middle East.

WHEN

All roads led to Rome. Roman roads united the Mediterranean area into a single world of peace and free trade from the 3rd century BC to the 5th century. As Rome declined, migrants from the East overran Europe. Order vanished, trade diminished, and the weak became indentured under feudalism. Workers were not free, but they were not slaves; they were tied to land, serving lords who, though absolute rulers on their own lands, were subject to other lords. There was no government, no money economy, no alternative.

By the 12th century the Christian West was confident enough to strike back at the last of the invaders — Muslim Arabs and Turks. The Crusaders' contact with Islam revived trade; brought in new goods, textiles, and foods; and invigorated the intellectual climate by introducing science and reviving interest in forgotten Greek and Roman knowledge.

Mobility, the spread of a money economy, and increased trade ended feudalism. Impoverished lords gave civil and political rights to towns in exchange for rents and other revenues. The growth of towns and trade spurred development of central government.

Plague struck for the first time in 1347, eventually killing 1/3 of the population. When it was all over, Europe rebounded, as the dead had left property and opportunity to the survivors. Population growth rate exploded, and economic activity grew along with centralized government. Culture and commerce blossomed; merchant princes, especially in Italy, patronized artists and scholars in a renaissance of art and learning. The invention of printing permitted dissemination of new knowledge and ideas.

By 1500 Christians had driven the Moors out of Spain, America had been discovered, and Constantinople had fallen. Western Europe turned its attention toward exploring the world and establishing new trade. The Reformation (1517) divided Europe, leading to 200 years of intermittent warfare in which religious and national interests merged, while trade and commerce grew and Western European countries established colonies abroad.

From the 17th to the early 18th century new ideas about the relation of government and people arose, leading to independence in the New World (1776, the US) and revolution in France (1789). In 1815 the nations victorious over Napoleon fixed Europe's boundaries, sowing the seeds of future wars.

In the 19th century much of Europe followed England into industrialization. Freedom from war on its own soil, generous deposits of coal and iron, and colonies were Britain's advantages; its lead in trade and industry was not challenged until the 1880s, by Germany. European nations moved into Africa in the late 19th century, seeking raw materials and, to a lesser extent, new markets.

By 1910 England was past its industrial prime, Germany was ascendant, and the US was about to become the world's dominant industrial power. European nations fell into war in 1914; though materially destructive, the war's main cost was human. Again the map was redrawn and new nations such as the Baltic republics emerged. But it was a sour peace, with arbitrary national borders and vindictive reparations imposed upon Germany. The resulting war was the worst ever.

After WWII the US, the sole untouched industrial power, initiated a better peace, which included democratic governments for West Germany and Italy and enormous amounts of aid for rebuilding under the Marshall Plan. The result was 20 years of sustained economic growth in Europe and unprecedented prosperity.

This led to the formation of the European Economic Community (now the European Community [EC]), a voluntary union in which Europeans could move and trade freely. The EC has provided a steadily expanding framework for trade since 1958 and is now preparing for a unified European market in 1992.

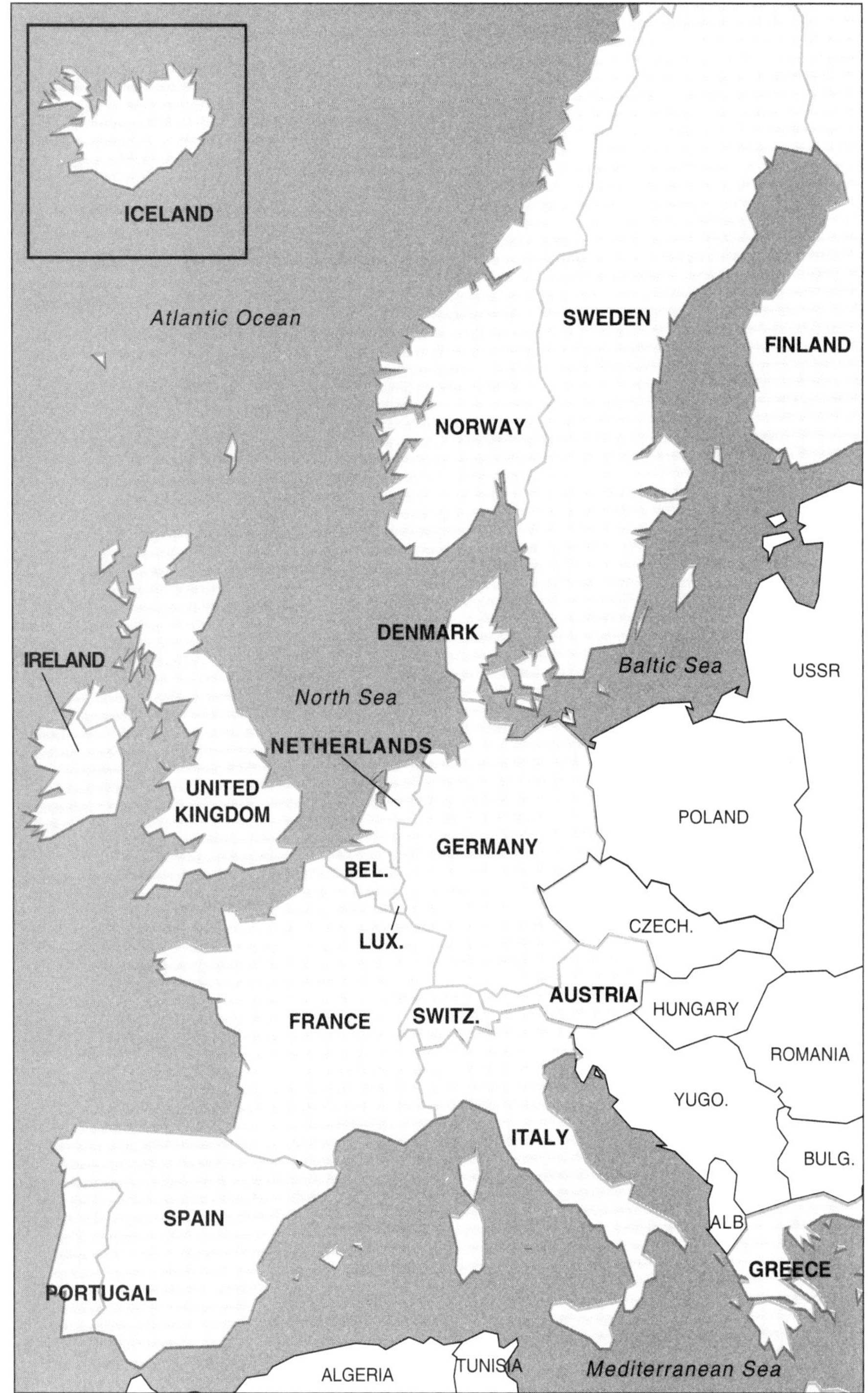

HOW MUCH

	1980	1981	1982	1983	1984	1985	1986	1987	1988	1989
Population (mil.)	350	351	352	352	353	354	355	356	357	358
GDP ($ bil.)	3,541	3,133	3,020	2,929	2,811	2,907	3,986	4,935	5,477	5,667
GDP per capita	10,129	8,929	8,588	8,311	7,960	8,214	11,232	13,866	15,343	15,832
Trade balance ($ mil.)	(30,491)	(3,037)	(211)	18,916	33,639	39,522	70,890	59,959	42,761	39,625
Current acct. ($ mil.)	(46,577)	(23,052)	(15,631)	340	14,552	21,736	46,455	30,488	(4,105)	(235)

THE EUROPEAN COMMUNITY

The European Community (EC), based in Belgium, is an outgrowth of the US Marshall Plan, the 1947 blueprint for rebuilding Europe after WWII. The plan required all recipients to agree on expenditures; the Organization for European Economic Cooperation decided how to spend the money, and the European Payments Union administered payment.

The confidence in joint action that European nations gained from this experience led to the formation of the 1951 European Coal and Steel Community (West Germany, Italy, France, the Netherlands, Belgium, and Luxembourg). In 1957 these nations agreed in the Treaty of Rome to create the European Economic Community (EEC). The treaty provided for elimination of tariffs and customs barriers, free movement of workers and money, and equalization of agricultural prices among members. As the organization's political side developed in response to increasing need for legal unity, "Economic" was dropped from the name and the EEC became the EC.

These initial measures were successful, but nontariff barriers, such as passport and border controls, plant and animal inspection, differences in product standards, and protectionist tax systems, remained a problem. Also, many key nations were not members (including the UK, Norway, Sweden, Denmark, and Switzerland). In 1973 the UK, Denmark, and Ireland joined. Switzerland and Sweden did not join because EC defense provisions violated their neutrality (they are reconsidering). Spain, Portugal, and Greece joined later. Turkey wants to join but has not been accepted, partly because of Greek opposition and partly because members fear a flood of Turkish workers.

European business in the 1970s and early 1980s was undynamic, afflicted with so-called Eurosclerosis. It seemed unable to compete with the US, Japan, and the developing industrial nations in Asia. Then Europeans began to realize that, though they were unable to compete individually with the economic superpowers, a united Western Europe would be an economic superpower itself.

In 1985 proposals to make Europe a single market were made and in 1987 the European parliament adopted the Single European Act, which allowed a majority vote of the council to determine EC action, rather than a unanimous vote. This made the EC more powerful as a legislative and administrative entity. The single market entails removal of nontariff barriers and harmonization of national laws relating to business, patents, taxes, and industrial ownership restrictions. Product and technological standards must be made uniform. But many nations find it difficult to reconcile national sovereignty with EC-wide regulations, especially on monetary policy (the UK, under Mrs. Thatcher, found this especially hard).

There is doubt that these issues can be resolved by December 31, 1992, the deadline for unification. In addition, the former Communist nations are clamoring for admittance. Cracks in EC unity are appearing as Spain, Portugal, and Greece, the EC's poorest members, seek preferential treatment. Many nonmember states fear they will be locked out of Europe and that world trade may degenerate into competition between trading blocks.

THE UNITED NATIONS

OVERVIEW

The United Nations is the largest representative organization in the world. It has 159 member nations and 18 nonmember observer entities, representing virtually the entire world's population. The UN's 4 purposes are to maintain international peace, develop friendly relations among countries, resolve international problems, and harmonize the actions of nations.

To improve the social, medical, and educational welfare of the world's people, the UN operates 13 programs, probably the best known of which is the UN children's fund (UNICEF), and coordinates its activities with 16 specialized agencies.

The US has worked hard to support the UN. John D. Rockefeller, Jr., provided the land for its New York City headquarters; the US contributes the largest share of the UN's annual budget; and the US has appointed some of its most distinguished citizens to represent it in the UN, including Henry Cabot Lodge, Adlai Stevenson, and George Bush.

Since WWII the UN has tackled major political and economic concerns, playing a vital role in reducing world tensions, improving the health and welfare of the disadvantaged, protecting the common heritage of mankind, developing international law, and encouraging respect for basic human rights.

Founded: 1945
Fiscal year ends: December 31

WHO

Secretary-General: Javier Pérez de Cuéllar, age 70
Under-Secretary-General, Chef de Cabinet: Virendra Dayal
Under-Secretary-General, The Legal Counsel: Carl-August Fleischhauer
Assistant Secretary-General, Controller: Kofi Annan
Assistant Secretary-General, Office of Human Resources Management: Abdou Ciss
US Ambassador to the UN: Thomas R. Pickering
Auditors: UN Board of Auditors
Employees: 23,000

WHEN

Franklin Roosevelt described the nations allied against the Axis powers in WWII as the "United Nations." The structure of the UN was fixed by the US, the UK, the USSR, and China in a series of meetings at Dumbarton Oaks in Washington, DC, between August and October 1944. Issues of Security Council membership and voting procedures and membership eligibility were settled at the Yalta Conference in 1945. At the end of WWII, the 26 original members, Poland (retroactively made an original member), and 24 other states signed the Charter of the United Nations in San Francisco on June 26, 1945. It went into effect on October 24, 1945.

The effects of one of the UN's early decisions, the partition of Palestine in 1947, continue today, resulting in instability and repeated UN military action in the region. During the 1950s the UN took armed action in Korea (an operation approved only because of Soviet absence from the Security Council when it voted to intervene) and in Egypt (1956), when Israel, France, and the UK tried to seize the Suez Canal.

Also during the 1950s and early 1960s, under the leadership of Secretary-General U Thant, the UN was an advocate for the end of colonialism, assisting in the movement to independence of many African nations. One of these, the Congo, erupted into tribal warfare, requiring military intervention (1960–64).

During the 1960s, in addition to peacekeeping activities in Cyprus and the Middle East, the UN turned its attention to population control and prevention of the spread of nuclear weapons.

During the 1970s and 1980s, focus shifted to differences between developed nations and the Third World. Some UN agencies became politicized, resulting in withdrawal of US financial support to the UN Educational, Scientific and Cultural Organization (UNESCO; since resumed). Also during this time attention turned to the conservation and apportionment of natural resources in extraterritorial areas (e.g., sea floors).

Though for many years the world body seemed paralyzed by politics, it began to display some of its promise under the leadership of Javier Pérez de Cuéllar (Secretary-General until September 1991). Under Pérez de Cuéllar the UN oversaw the withdrawal of Soviet troops from Afghanistan and the elections in Nicaragua and was effective in mobilizing international action in the wake of the Iraqi invasion of Kuwait (though it was somewhat less successful in dealing with the war's aftermath). In 1991 two of the last nations kept from membership by Cold War politics — North Korea and South Korea — agreed they would apply for separate membership.

The UN's greatest challenges in the 1990s will be cutting through its own inefficient bureaucracy, which has kept the UN from achieving its full potential in the new world order, and dealing with the consequences of monumental changes in Eastern Europe.

WHERE

HQ: United Nations, New York, NY 10017
Phone: 212-963-1234
Fax: 212-758-2718

The UN has offices in Geneva and Vienna.

	1989 Contributors
Country	% of total
US	25.0
Japan	10.8
USSR	10.2
Germany	9.6
France	6.4
UK	4.9
Italy	3.8
Canada	3.1
Spain	2.0
The Netherlands	1.7
Australia	1.7
Brazil	1.4
Ukrainian Soviet Socialist Republic	1.3
Sweden	1.3
Belgium	1.2
Others	15.6
Total	**100.0**

WHAT

Functions
- Children's welfare
- Coordination of specialized agencies
- Development of international law
- Disaster relief
- Dispute resolution
- Economic and social development
- Food production and distribution
- Peacekeeping
- Public health
- Refugee assistance
- Trade agreements
- Trusteeship of non–self-governing areas

Principal Organs
- Economic and Social Council
- General Assembly
- International Court of Justice
- Secretariat
- Security Council
- Trusteeship Council

Specialized Agencies
- Food and Agriculture Organization (FAO)
- General Agreement on Tariffs and Trade (GATT)
- International Atomic Energy Agency (IAEA)
- International Civil Aviation Organization (ICAO)
- International Fund for Agricultural Development (IFAD)
- International Labor Organization (ILO)
- International Maritime Organization (IMO)
- International Monetary Fund (IMF)
- International Telecommunication Union (ITU)
- United Nations Educational, Scientific and Cultural Organization (UNESCO)
- United Nations Industrial Development Organization (UNIDO)
- Universal Postal Union (UPU)
- World Bank
- World Health Organization (WHO)
- World Intellectual Property Organization (WIPO)
- World Meteorological Organization (WMO)

HOW MUCH

	7-Year Growth	1984 –85	1986 –87	1988 –89	1990 –91
Total budget[1] ($ mil.)	5.0%	1,611	1,712	1,769	2,134
Policy-making ($ mil.)	(3.6%)	40	46	45	31
Political affairs ($ mil.)	3.1%	120	125	121	149
Int'l justice & law ($ mil.)	8.7%	24	28	29	43
Human rights ($ mil.)	2.9%	505	477	496	618
Public info. ($ mil.)	4.0%	70	76	77	92
Support services ($ mil.)	4.5%	570	650	711	777
Special expenses ($ mil.)	13.4%	17	17	4	41
Cap. expend. ($ mil.)	20.3%	20	31	19	73
Staff assessment ($ mil.)	3.4%	245	262	267	310

[1]UN budgets are for 2 years.

ARGENTINA

OVERVIEW

Argentina is South America's 2nd largest country (after Brazil). The breadbasket of Argentina — the central plains known as the *pampas* — extends nearly 500 miles westward from Buenos Aires. This area is one of the world's most productive in wheat, corn, and major oil seeds and supports the world-famous Argentine beef industry, which was the world's 3rd largest producer in 1988 (2.6 million tons of beef). Argentina also has deposits of coal, lead, zinc, tin, and uranium.

Although representing only 15% of GDP, agriculture accounts for nearly 70% of the country's foreign exchange earnings. The adult literacy rate is 94% — one of the highest in Latin America. Over 85% of the population lives in urban areas.

Despite its excellent material and human resources, Argentina remains in economic chaos because of its history of political instability and deficit spending. Hyperinflation of nearly 5,000% in 1989 was reduced to under 2,000% in 1990 by President Carlos Menem, who has attempted to downsize the inefficient public sector. The Menem government faces many challenges in 1991, as unemployment and underemployment have risen to nearly 20%. Labor unrest has resulted from the fall of real wages and concern over massive state-led economic reforms. But Argentina is improving. In 1991 the currency was linked to the dollar, privatization of state companies proceeded, and inflation and interest rates dropped.

WHEN

By the time Spaniard Juan de Solis discovered Argentina in 1516 the Incas had already built roads halfway into the modern-day country. European settlement proceeded slowly and was primarily agrarian in nature. For nearly 200 years the region was governed by the Viceroyalty of Peru and then became part of the Viceroyalty of the Río de la Plata (1776), which included what is now Argentina, Paraguay, Bolivia, and Uruguay.

General José de San Martín led a 6-year struggle for independence that succeeded in 1816 but was followed by almost 40 years of internal struggle between the Spanish-Indian *gauchos* of the interior, the coastal ranchers, and the European mercantilists and intellectuals in Buenos Aires. The countries of Paraguay, Bolivia, and Uruguay broke away during these unsettled times.

Buenos Aires, long a destination of European immigrants, experienced a massive influx of them in the late 19th century. Rapid rail expansion, increased agricultural exports, and improved education soon made Argentina the most advanced of all Latin American countries. Industrialization, largely capitalized by the British, began in the late 19th century and provided jobs to these immigrants. With industrialization came unionism and demands for democratic government.

In 1916 the first democratically elected government took power, ruling until a 1930 military coup. The populist leader Colonel Juan Perón, supported by his famous wife, Eva Duarte, won the 1946 presidential election. By creating jobs in government, establishing ill-conceived new industries, and heavily taxing agriculture, he created economic chaos, causing real income to fall, inflation to rise, and foreign debt to increase. Perón fled Argentina in 1955, but economic conditions failed to improve.

Perón returned in 1973, was reelected president, died in 1974, and was succeeded by his vice-president (and wife), Isabel Martinez, who did little to curb rising violence and inflation. A military junta deposed her in 1976, imposing economic austerity measures that cut inflation and increased agricultural production. However, Argentina paid a high price for economic success, as the military, seeking to suppress left-wing terrorism, imprisoned or killed nearly 10,000 people.

In 1982 junta leader Leopoldo Galtieri invaded the long-disputed (149 years) British-ruled Falkland Islands in an effort to restore the government's popularity, which had declined precipitously in the face of inflation and high unemployment in the early 1980s. Britain won the ensuing war.

With the junta in disgrace, military rule gave way to civilian rule. Raúl Alfonsín, elected president in 1983, negotiated new terms on Argentina's $48 billion public debt, issued new currency, and froze wages and prices. President Carlos Menem (elected 1989) is determined to take strong steps to bring the economy under control. In 1991 Menem actively encouraged foreign investment (particularly from the US), cut government spending, and cracked down on tax evaders in an effort to improve economic conditions.

HOW MUCH

	4-Year Growth	1986	1987	1988	1989	1990
Population (mil.)	*1.3%*	30.7	31.1	31.5	31.9	32.3
GDP ($ bil.)	*(1.6%)*	*69*	*71*	*69*	*66*	*65*
Real GDP growth rate	—	5.6%	2.2%	(2.7%)	(4.6%)	(1.0%)
Exports ($ mil.)	*14.8%*	6,852	6,360	9,134	9,573	11,911
Imports ($ mil.)	*(4.3%)*	4,406	5,392	4,900	3,864	3,700
Trade balance ($ mil.)	—	2,446	968	4,234	5,709	8,211
Current account ($ mil.)	—	(2,859)	(4,239)	(1,615)	(1,305)	2,100
Govt. budget bal. ($ mil.)	—	*(2,500)*	*(5,109)*	—	*(14,520)*	*(3,250)*
Consumer inflation	—	90%	131%	343%	3,079%	2,314%
Unemployment rate	—	5.2%	5.7%	6.1%	*8.0%*	*9.0%*
Exchange rate with US$	—	0.943	2.144	8.753	423	4,876

Source: Economist Intelligence Unit and *The Reference Press*

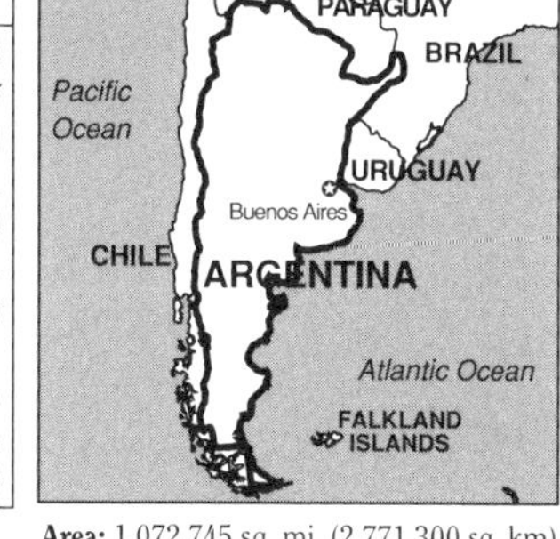

Area: 1,072,745 sq. mi. (2,771,300 sq. km)

Official name:
Republic of Argentina
República Argentina
Official language: Spanish
Currency: 1 austral (A) = 100 centavos
Fiscal year ends: December 31

WHO

President of the Republic: Carlos Saúl Menem, age 56
Vice-President: Eduardo Duhalde
Minister of Economy: Domingo Cavallo
Minister of Foreign Affairs: Guido Jose Maria Di Tella
Ambassador to US: Carlos Ortiz de Rozas
US Ambassador to Argentina: Terence A. Todman

WHERE

Executive HQ: Casa De Gobierno Balcarce 50, 1064 Buenos Aires, Argentina
Embassy in US: 1600 New Hampshire Ave. NW, Washington, DC 20009
Phone: 202-939-6400
Fax: 202-332-3171
US Embassy in Argentina: 4300 Colombia, 1425 Buenos Aires, Argentina
Phone: 011-54-1-774-7611
Chamber of Commerce: Cámara Argentina de Comercio, Avenida Leandro N. Alem. 36, 1003 Buenos Aires, Argentina
Phone: 011-54-1-331-8051

Argentina has 23 provinces and 1 district and has diplomatic representatives in 69 countries.

Capital city: Buenos Aires
Time change from EST: +1 hour
Avg. high/low temp: Jan. 85°F (29°C)/63°F (17°C)
July 57°F (14°C)/42°F (6°C)

Urbanization: 86%
Population density: 30/sq. mi. (12/sq. km)

Exports as % of Total		Imports as % of Total	
US	13	US	22
Netherlands	11	Brazil	17
Brazil	11	Germany	10
Germany	5	Italy	6
Other countries	60	Other countries	45
Total	**100**	**Total**	**100**

WHAT

Origins of GDP	% of Total
Manufacturing	22
Agriculture, forestry & fishing	15
Electricity & water	6
Mining	3
Construction	2
Other	52
Total	**100**

1990 GDP per capita: $2,019
1990 year-end external debt: $60 billion
Literacy rate: 94%
UN Human Development Index: 85%
Human Freedom Index (0-40 scale): 25
Purchasing power as % of US: 26%
Capital city cost of living as % of DC: 88%
Defense as % of GNP: 1%
Education as % of GNP: 1%
Principal airline: Aerolíneas Argentinas
Principal exchange: Bolsa de Comercio de Buenos Aires

AUSTRALIA

OVERVIEW

Australia is the world's smallest continent, the 6th largest country in land area, and one of the most sparsely inhabited nations on earth, with only 2 people per square kilometer (only Mauritania and Mongolia are less dense). Its location far from the world's trade corridors has shaped its history, culture, and economy.

Australia's free-market economy is sprinkled with ample doses of government intervention, including a generous social welfare system, a centrally determined wage structure, government ownership of industry (particularly telecommunications and transportation), and a tradition of protecting local business through trade and investment barriers. Recently the economy has been liberalized, but strong union opposition has delayed efforts to privatize public enterprises and has made industry less flexible and efficient than in other industrialized countries.

Australia's largest trading partner is Japan, which accounts for 25% of its foreign trade; the US is 2nd. Australia's diverse manufacturing sector, developed to serve its domestic market, is protected from foreign competition by trade barriers. Three-quarters of the country's exports come from agriculture, livestock, and mineral products. Australia is the world's largest wool producer, the largest beef exporter, and a leading wheat producer and exporter. The country is also a leading exporter of minerals, from aluminum to zinc. Abundant coal, gas, uranium, and petroleum resources make it a net energy exporter.

Australia's dependence on primary products, which are subject to the vicissitudes of weather (there are periodic droughts) and world commodity prices, has caused prosperity to fluctuate drastically. Low demand for these products led to economic problems in 1990 and 1991.

WHEN

First settled by hunter-gatherer aboriginal tribes some 40,000 years ago, Australia remained largely undisturbed until 1770, when Captain James Cook claimed it for Great Britain. In 1788 the first of many British penal colonies was established. Freed prisoners grew grain successfully as early as 1791. Soldiers created the first mercantile enterprise (and Australia's first monopoly) in 1793 when they pledged their future pay to buy for resale the entire rum stock (7,500 gallons) of an American trader.

In the early 19th century, free settlers (mostly sheep herders) trickled into Australia. The trickle became a torrent in 1851 when gold was found. By 1868, when transport of convicts to Australia ceased, 160,000 prisoners had arrived. Mining (mostly gold and copper), livestock raising (sheep and cattle), and agriculture (wheat) became the 3 legs of the Australian economy.

In the early 20th century, Australia implemented a wide-ranging social welfare system. WWI boosted the economy, and prosperity continued for the next decade, during which a strong labor movement developed. The Great Depression stopped all economic growth in 1931.

WWII led Australia to develop close military and economic ties with the US. Australia shared in the postwar boom, during which it developed most of its industrial sector. It also experienced another wave of immigrants.

During the 1960s large deposits of minerals and the first petroleum were discovered.

In 1972 newly elected Prime Minister E. Gough Whitlam redirected Australia's strategic alliances and economy to reflect its geographic location and current needs. He liberalized immigration laws (resulting in an influx of Asian immigrants); reduced defense spending; restricted foreign investment; and began looking to Asia (particularly Japan), rather than the UK and the US, for new markets.

The 1973 oil price increases created unemployment and a persistent inflation that the government has yet to control. Australia was again hard hit by the worldwide 1979 recession and a long drought that did not end until 1983. In 1984 the economy experienced explosive growth of 10%, increasing inflation again and adversely affecting Australia's chronic trade imbalance, as Australian consumers spent heavily for imported goods.

To address these problems and the increasingly large foreign debt, Prime Minister Robert Hawke began in 1984 to deregulate financial markets, let the Australian dollar float, decrease government spending, liberalize trade, and obtain wage concessions from the unions. As a result, in 1988 and 1989 the economy experienced strong GDP growth of 3.8% and 4.9%, respectively. The global economic slowdown of 1990 and 1991 slowed growth, increased unemployment, and weakened export growth, but decreased inflation.

HOW MUCH

	4-Year Growth	1986	1987	1988	1989	1990
Population (mil.)	*1.5%*	16.1	16.4	16.7	17.0	17.1
GDP ($ bil.)	*15.3%*	*167*	*198*	*250*	*285*	*295*
Real GDP growth rate	—	1.9%	4.1%	3.8%	4.9%	1.3%
Exports ($ mil.)	*15.0%*	22,200	26,300	32,800	36,400	38,900
Imports ($ mil.)	*12.6%*	24,300	26,800	33,900	40,400	39,000
Trade balance ($ mil.)	—	(2,100)	(500)	(1,100)	(4,000)	(100)
Current account ($ mil.)	—	(9,500)	(8,100)	(10,600)	(16,900)	(14,500)
Govt. budget bal. ($ mil.)	—	*(3,826)*	*(1,888)*	*1,563*	*4,683*	*7,109*
Consumer inflation	—	9.1%	8.5%	7.2%	7.6%	7.3%
Unemployment rate	—	8.0%	8.3%	7.8%	6.6%	*8.4%*
Exchange rate with US$	—	1.50	1.43	1.28	1.26	1.28

Source: Economist Intelligence Unit and *The Reference Press*

Area: 2,966,151 sq. mi. (7,682,300 sq. km)

Official name:
Commonwealth of Australia
Official language: English
Currency: 1 dollar = 100 cents
Fiscal year ends: June 30

WHO

Governor General: William George Hayden, age 58
Prime Minister: Robert James Lee Hawke, age 62
Deputy Prime Minister: Brian Howe, age 55
Federal Treasurer: John Charles Kerin, age 54
Minister for Foreign Affairs and Trade: Gareth J. Evans, age 47
Ambassador to US: Michael John Cook, age 60
US Ambassador to Australia: Melvin F. Sembler

WHERE

Executive HQ: Government House, Canberra, ACT 2600, Australia
Embassy in US: 1601 Massachusetts Ave. NW, Washington, DC 20036
Phone: 202-797-3000
Fax: 202-797-3168
US Embassy in Australia: Moonah Pl., Canberra, ACT 2600, Australia
Phone: 011-61-6-270-5000
Fax: 011-61-6-270-5970
Chamber of Commerce: Australian Chamber of Commerce, PO Box E139, Queen Victoria Terrace, ACT 2600, Australia
Phone: 011-61-6-285-3523
Fax: 011-61-6-285-3590

Australia has 6 states and 2 territories and has diplomatic representatives in 72 countries.

Capital city: Canberra
Time change from EST: +16 hours
Avg. high/low temp: Jan. 82°F (28°C)/55°F (13°C)
July 52°F (11°C)/33°F (1°C)

Urbanization: 86%
Population density: 6/sq. mi. (2/sq. km)

Exports as % of Total		Imports as % of Total	
Japan	26	US	24
US	11	Japan	19
New Zealand	5	UK	7
Other countries	58	Other countries	50
Total	**100**	**Total**	**100**

WHAT

Origins of GDP	% of Total
Manufacturing	17
Commerce	15
Other services	15
Primary production & mining	11
Finance & business services	11
Ownership of dwellings	8
Transport & communications	8
Other	15
Total	**100**

1989 GDP per capita: $16,788
1990 year-end external debt: $120 billion
Literacy rate: 99%
UN Human Development Index: 97%
Human Freedom Index (0-40 scale): 33
Purchasing power as % of US: 71%
Sydney cost of living as % of DC: 114%
Defense as % of GDP: 3%
Education as % of GNP: 6%
Principal airline: Qantas Airways Ltd.
Principal exchange: Australian Stock Exchange Ltd

BELGIUM

OVERVIEW

Though one of the smallest and youngest nations of Europe, Belgium today plays an integral part in the military and economic life of a Europe on the brink of unification.

Belgium is the home of the European Parliament, NATO, and many multinational companies. This concentration of international organizations' offices has made Brussels the unofficial capital of Europe.

Belgium is the 2nd most densely populated nation in Europe (after the Netherlands) and is highly urbanized (agriculture employs only 2% of the work force). It is the most heavily unionized nation in Western Europe.

There is tension between its various ethnic/linguistic groups, which, in addition to the Flemish population and the French-speaking Walloons, include German speakers and a large foreign population (30% of Brussels's population) because of its status as a hub of international government and business.

Belgium has the densest concentration of railroads in the world. Its main port, Antwerp, is one of the largest, most efficient ports in Europe. Major exports include iron and steel, transportation equipment, and petroleum products. Antwerp is also one of the world's great gem-cutting and -trading cities; about 60% of the world's jewel-grade diamonds pass through Antwerp.

Belgian agriculture is among the more efficient in Europe, and the nation is nearly self-sufficient in food.

With 2/3 of its energy needs met by imported oil (90% of it from the Middle East) and with its energy-hungry steel mills, Belgium is particularly vulnerable to fluctuations in the price of oil.

WHEN

Belgium's famed cities of Liege and Antwerp developed in the Middle Ages as commercial cities. Beginning in the 15th century, the area that became Belgium passed to Spain, to the Austrian Empire, and to France under Napoleon. In 1815 it was included in the Kingdom of the Netherlands.

In 1830 the Belgians declared independence, establishing a monarchy under Leopold I. Belgium escaped the European turmoil of the 1830s and 1840s, allowing it to concentrate on developing trade and industry. It was the first nation in Europe to establish a commercial railway system (1835).

Though not particularly well endowed with natural resources, Belgium had considerable coal and some iron reserves in the south, which fostered a thriving steel industry beginning in the early 19th century. The north remained largely agricultural. The 2 main ethnic groups, the Dutch-speaking Flemings and the French-speaking Walloons, were similarly divided, with Walloons in the south and the Flemings in the north.

After 1860 European nations scrambled to divide Africa. King Leopold II claimed a vast territory, the Congo (now Zaire). The subsequent harsh exploitation of the area enriched the crown and resulted in the transfer of the Congo's administration to parliament in 1908.

In WWI Germany ignored Belgium's neutrality, and the nation became a battlefield; the war destroyed much of the country's industrial infrastructure. In WWII its neutrality was again ignored, and Belgium was occupied. Not badly damaged, it recovered rapidly with Marshall Plan aid and heavy taxation of profits earned by businessmen who had collaborated with the Nazis.

After WWII Belgium instituted generous welfare programs, including unemployment benefits and medical insurance. Program costs increased 12-fold between 1960 and 1980, exhausting the government's ability to fund the programs and forcing it to borrow heavily.

Since WWII Belgium has developed its light industry, chemical, and service sectors (mostly in the north), while its aging heavy industries in the south have declined. In 1960 Belgium granted the Congo independence, losing its source of copper, cobalt, and uranium.

In the early 1980s Belgium's government budget deficit ran as high as 13% of GDP. Reductions in public spending and welfare benefits halved this by the end of the decade but drove unemployment up to 11.3% in 1987 (by 1990 it was down to 8.8%). Public debt is 135% of GDP.

The devolution of certain responsibilities (e.g., export promotion and public works) to the regional level is likely to remain the dominant political issue of the early 1990s, with significant economic ramifications as the regions face the costs of their new responsibilities. In 1991 the economy remained hampered by slow growth and high unemployment, due to a shortage of skilled labor.

HOW MUCH

	4-Year Growth	1986	1987	1988	1989	1990
Population (mil.)	*0.2%*	9.86	9.87	9.87	9.93	9.93
GDP ($ bil.)	*14.7%*	*114*	*143*	*154*	*157*	*198*
Real GDP growth rate	—	1.6%	2.3%	4.6%	4.1%	3.7%
Exports ($ mil.)	*14.5%*	68,600	82,900	91,900	100,000	118,100
Imports ($ mil.)	*15.0%*	68,500	83,100	92,000	98,500	119,800
Trade balance ($ mil.)	—	100	(200)	(100)	1,500	(1,700)
Current account ($ mil.)	—	3,105	2,866	3,124	3,756	4,970
Govt. budget bal. ($ mil.)	—	*(12,327)*	*(11,716)*	*(11,250)*	*(10,812)*	*(13,054)*
Consumer inflation	—	1.3%	1.6%	1.2%	3.1%	3.4%
Unemployment rate	—	11.6%	11.3%	10.3%	9.3%	8.8%
Exchange rate with US$	—	44.7	37.3	36.8	39.4	33.4

Source: Economist Intelligence Unit and *The Reference Press*

Area: 11,799 sq. mi. (30,519 sq. km)

Official name:
Kingdom of Belgium
Royaume de Belgique-Koninkrijk België
Official languages: Dutch, French, German
Currency: 1 franc (BF) = 100 centimes
Fiscal year ends: December 31

WHO

Monarch: HM King Baudouin I, age 61
Heir Apparent: Prince Albert of Liége (brother of the King), age 57
Prime Minister: Wilfried Martens, age 55
Deputy Prime Minister: Philippe Moureaux, age 52
Minister of Finance: Philippe Maystadt, age 43
Minister of Foreign Affairs: Mark Eyskens, age 58
Ambassador to US: Juan Cassiers, age 60
US Ambassador to Belgium: Bruce Gelb, age 64

WHERE

Executive HQ: Prime Minister, 15 Rue De La Loi, 1000 Brussels, Belgium
Embassy in US: 3330 Garfield St. NW, Washington, DC 20008
Phone: 202-333-6900
Fax: 202-333-3079
US Embassy in Belgium: 27 Boulevard du Regent, B-1000 Brussels, Belgium
Phone: 011-32-2-513-3830
Fax: 011-32-2-511-2725
Chamber of Commerce: International Chamber of Commerce, 8 Rue des Sois, B-1000 Brussels, Belgium
Phone: 011-32-2-512-6541

Belgium has 3 regions, 3 cultural communities, 9 provinces, and 589 communes.

Capital city: Brussels
Time change from EST: +6 hours
Avg. high/low temp: Jan. 40°F (4°C)/30°F (-1°C)
July 73°F (23°C)/54°F (12°C)

Urbanization: 97%
Population density: 842/sq. mi. (325/sq. km)

Exports * as % of Total		Imports * as % of Total	
Germany	21	Germany	24
France	19	Netherlands	18
Netherlands	15	France	16
UK	9	UK	8
Other countries	36	Other countries	34
Total	**100**	**Total**	**100**

* Includes Luxembourg

WHAT

Origins of GNP	% of Total
Commerce & finance	32
Other services	28
Manufacturing	22
Transport & communications	7
Other	11
Total	**100**

1990 GDP per capita: $19,927
1990 year-end external debt: $33 billion
Literacy rate: 98%
UN Human Development Index: 96%
Human Freedom Index (0-40 scale): 35
Purchasing power as % of US: 65%
Capital city cost of living as % of DC: 124%
Defense as % of GNP: 3%
Education as % of GDP: 7%
Principal airline: Belgium World (SABENA)
Principal exchange: La Bourse de Bruxelles

BRAZIL

OVERVIEW

Brazil boasts one of the world's 10 largest economies (larger than the rest of South America combined), the world's 5th largest land area, and Latin America's largest population, as well as the world's largest rain forest, out of which flows the world's 2nd longest river, the Amazon. Leading the world in production and export of coffee and orange juice concentrate, it is also a major exporter of cotton, meat, and soybeans. Brazil is rich in iron and manganese and may have the world's largest gold deposits. Chemical, pharmaceutical, computer, and armament industries exemplify Brazil's well-developed industrial base.

Brazil is also an economic disaster of gargantuan proportions. Because of its vast debt ($110 billion), debt service eats up most of its large trade surplus. Inflation in 1990 neared 3,000%. Wealth is distributed unevenly, with 1% of the population owning almost 1/2 the agricultural land and 10% of the people spending 51% of the national income.

Brazil has a mixture of private and state enterprise; executives are highly compensated (20% more than US counterparts) and workers struggle to keep up with endemic hyperinflation. Business is supported by an array of costly state-sponsored subsidies; protective tariffs; and extensive controls of prices, wages, and interest and exchange rates.

In 1990 newly elected president Fernando Collor attempted unsuccessfully to control the chaotic economy by implementing his "shock" stabilization program, which included freezing bank accounts and issuing a new currency to control inflation and liberalize the economy. In early 1991 Collor tried again, closing banks and freezing wages and prices.

WHEN

Portuguese explorer Pedro Cabral discovered Brazil in 1500. With European settlement in the 1540s came cattle, sugar-cane plantations, and slavery of both natives and imported Africans. Ranching, plantation agriculture, and forest products remain the economic base for 2 centuries. Jesuits tried to protect the natives from exploitation by teaching them farming but were expelled from the colony in 1759.

In 1808 Brazil became the seat of Portuguese government when the Napoleonic Wars drove the court from Portugal. Upon the court's departure Brazil resisted recolonization, declaring independence in 1822. Brazil established a monarchy; the first king (Dom Pedro) was, in 1831, the first of many rulers to be removed by the military. In the 1850s and 1860s, conflicts with neighbors enhanced the military's position. This period also saw the first industry and railroads, which attracted foreign capital and immigrants. From the 1870s to the mid-20th century, 5 million people immigrated, fueling Brazil's growth.

Despite prosperity in the early 20th century, high foreign debts and excessive government spending (recurrent Brazilian themes) and competition from other developing countries in commodity markets combined with the Great Depression to devastate the Brazilian economy by 1930. Military intervention ensued.

The return of democratic government in 1946 brought political and economic problems, including the rise of left-wing radicals and chronic inflation. In 1964 the military intervened, taking measures that reduced inflation from 100% to 25% in 1967. They then revved up the economy by borrowing heavily and developing local industry. The resultant "economic miracle" caused the economy to grow 11% annually between 1968 and 1973, slowing to a still impressive 6% annually between 1974 and 1980. Oil price increases of the 1970s and the 1979–81 worldwide recession halted growth.

Brazil made a remarkable effort to wean itself from imported oil (its single largest import) by commercializing ethanol substitutes made from local sugar cane. By 1986, 90% of all cars ran on ethanol. Laws like the 1984 Law of Informatics, which reserved the burgeoning electronic and computer (except mainframes) industries for local manufacturers, revived economic growth. However, ethanol production had to be heavily subsidized, and protected manufacturers charged high prices. Inflation became uncontrollable.

In 1990 President Collor reversed course, creating a more open economy by privatizing government industry, reducing tariffs, and making exchange rates more realistic. Despite his efforts, economic chaos has forced some foreign investors, such as Black & Decker, to close some of their operations and others, such as Vendex, to close all of them.

HOW MUCH

	4-Year Growth	1986	1987	1988	1989	1990
Population (mil.)	*2.2%*	137.3	141.0	144.0	147.0	150.0
GDP ($ bil.)	—	*282*	*325*	*315*	*293*	*355*
Real GDP growth rate	—	7.5%	3.6%	—	3.6%	(4.6%)
Exports ($ mil.)	*8.9%*	22,300	26,200	33,800	34,400	31,400
Imports ($ mil.)	*9.9%*	14,000	15,100	14,700	18,300	20,400
Trade balance ($ mil.)	—	8,300	11,100	19,100	16,100	11,000
Current account ($ mil.)	—	(5,300)	(1,500)	4,200	1,600	(1,600)
Govt. budget bal. ($ mil.)	—	*(8)*	*(5)*	*(28)*	*(37)*	—
Consumer inflation	—	145.0%	230.0%	683.0%	1,287%	2,938%
Unemployment rate	—	—	—	—	—	*5%*
Exchange rate with US$*	—	*13*	*39*	*262*	*2,833*	*68*

Source: Economist Intelligence Unit and *The Reference Press*
* In 1989 the new cruzado (Ncz) replaced the cruzado at the rate of 1=1,000. In 1990 the currency was renamed the cruzeiro.

Area: 3,286,487 sq. mi. (8,511,965 sq. km)

Official name:
Federative Republic of Brazil
República Federativa do Brasil
Official language: Portuguese
Currency: cruzeiro (Cr$)
Fiscal year ends: December 31

WHO

President of the Republic: Fernando Affonso Collor de Mello, age 40
Vice-President: Itamar Franco
Economy Minister: Marcílio Marques Moreira
Minister of Foreign Affairs: José Francisco Rezek, age 47
Ambassador to US: Rubens Ricupero
US Ambassador to Brazil: Richard H. Melton

WHERE

Executive HQ: President, Palácio do Planalto, Praça dos Três Poderes, 70150-Brasília, DF-Brazil
Embassy in US: 3006 Massachusetts Ave. NW, Washington, DC 20008
Phone: 202-745-2700
Fax: 202-745-2827
US Embassy in Brazil: Avenida das Nacoes, Lote 3, Brasília, Brazil
Phone: 011-55-61-321-7272
Fax: 011-55-61-225-9136
Chamber of Commerce: Brazil Chamber of Commerce, Avenida Rio Branco 91, 8 Andar S/10–12, 20040 Rio de Janeiro, Brazil
Phone: 011-55-21-221-1901

Brazil has 26 states and one federal district and has diplomatic representatives in 97 countries.

Capital city: Brasília
Time change from EST: +2 hours
Mean temperature: Jan. 72°F (22°C)
July 64°F (18°C)

Urbanization: 76%
Population density: 46/sq. mi. (18/sq. km)

Exports as % of Total		Imports as % of Total	
US	26	US	21
Netherlands	8	Germany	9
Japan	7	Japan	7
Germany	4	Argentina	5
Other countries	55	Other countries	58
Total	**100**	**Total**	**100**

WHAT

Origins of GDP	% of Total
Manufacturing	40
Commerce	9
Agriculture	8
Construction	7
Others	36
Total	**100**

1990 GDP per capita: $2,367
1990 year-end external debt: $110 billion
Literacy rate: 78%
UN Human Development Index: 76%
Human Freedom Index (0-40 scale): 18
Purchasing power as % of US: 25%
São Paulo cost of living as % of DC: 91%
Defense as % of GNP: 1%
Education as % of GNP: 5%
Principal airline: VARIG (Viação Aérea Rio Grandense)
Principal exchanges: Bolsa de Valores de Rio de Janeiro, Bolsa de Valores de São Paulo

CANADA

OVERVIEW

Canada has the world's 2nd largest land area (after the USSR). It is the largest exporter (and 3rd largest producer) of forest products; it is a net exporter of petroleum and the #1 exporter of minerals; and it exports more grain (mostly wheat) than any other country but the US. Although natural resource products generate less than 10% of employment and GNP, they constitute over 45% of Canada's exports.

Canada is also one of the world's most industrialized countries. Much of its industry is based in southeast Canada near Toronto and Montreal. Major industries include paper and motor vehicle manufacturing and food processing. While most industry in this free-market economy is private, over 300 companies (primarily in communications, transportation, and banking) are owned or controlled by the government. The government has privatized some of these companies recently, including Air Canada in 1989.

Canada and the US are each other's largest trading partners and have the world's largest bilateral trade relationship. Canada's trade with the US is 10 times greater than its trade with its 2nd largest trading partner, Japan. Nearly 75% of Canadian exports are to the US (Canada accounts for 20% of US exports). US companies, which have over $60 billion invested in Canada, represent 80% of all foreign investment and nearly 20% of Canadian nonfinancial business assets. Canadians have fretted over this special relationship for years, and much of Canadian economic policy has aimed either to encourage or discourage, at different times, US involvement in Canada.

Canada is now in a severe recession, in which unemployment went over 10% in early 1991 as the result of cutbacks from mergers, relocation of jobs to the US because of lower labor costs, and decreased demand for products, resulting from the US recession.

WHEN

French fur traders arrived in Canada in the 16th century. In 1670 Britain founded the Hudson's Bay Company to challenge French trade. Ninety years of rivalry and conflict ensued, ending with British victory in 1763.

In the 19th century Britain was Canada's primary source of capital. In 1846 Canada and the US entered into a free-trade pact, and trade burgeoned until the US cancelled the pact in 1866. During this period the economy grew, driven by the discovery of gold in British Columbia and the construction of a transcontinental railroad. During the 1870s Canada imposed substantial tariffs on imports in an effort to develop its own industries.

The early 20th century saw the growth of the mining industry. In 1911 the government advocated reinstating free trade with the US but was brought down over that issue.

WWI fostered close economic cooperation with the US, and in the postwar period US investors replaced the British as the primary foreign investors. During this period many US companies, partly to get around the high tariffs put in place 50 years earlier, began to open branches and subsidiaries in Canada.

The Great Depression destroyed Canada's export markets for natural resource products and brought economic intervention by the government, which formed the remains of bankrupt railroads into Canadian National. Many new enterprises were put into government hands, including airline and broadcasting companies.

WWII brought more cooperation with the US, and US investment helped fuel a postwar boom that further urbanized and industrialized Canada. During this time a substantial social welfare system was created.

By 1972 the Canadian government, concerned about US economic dominance, sought to enhance trade with Europe and Asia. While valuable new trade relationships were created, US presence did not decrease. In 1974 the Foreign Investment Review Act (FIRA) was passed to ensure that foreign investment benefited Canada, but it had the effect of discouraging investment, as did the National Energy Policy (NEP) legislation of 1980, which aimed to return Canada's oil industry to Canadian control. There followed a 3-year recession that paralleled the US recession but was more severe and longer lasting.

In 1985 the Conservative government began to undo FIRA and NEP. From 1983 to 1989 the Canadian economy experienced a sustained period of expansion. In 1989 a free-trade pact that will eventually eliminate tariffs between the US and Canada went into effect.

Canada has been troubled by economic alienation felt by the west and by persistent *Quebecois* separatism. These problems make future national unity uncertain.

HOW MUCH

	4-Year Growth	1986	1987	1988	1989	1990
Population (mil.)	*0.9%*	25.6	25.7	25.9	26.3	26.5
GDP ($ bil.)	*12.3%*	*364*	*415*	*491*	*552*	*579*
Real GDP growth rate	—	3.3%	4.0%	4.4%	3.0%	0.9%
Exports ($ mil.)	*9.4%*	89,000	97,900	115,800	123,200	127,500
Imports ($ mil.)	*9.8%*	81,300	89,100	106,600	116,400	118,000
Trade balance ($ mil.)	—	7,700	8,800	9,200	6,800	9,500
Current account ($ mil.)	—	(7,300)	(6,900)	(8,200)	(14,100)	(13,700)
Govt. budget bal. ($ mil.)	—	—	*(23,011)*	*(22,832)*	*(24,351)*	*(26,068)*
Consumer inflation	—	4.2%	4.4%	4.0%	5.0%	4.8%
Unemployment rate	—	9.6%	8.9%	7.8%	7.5%	8.1%
Exchange rate with US$	—	1.39	1.33	1.23	1.18	1.17

Source: Economist Intelligence Unit and *The Reference Press*

Area: 3,845,076 sq. mi. (9,970,610 sq. km)

Official name: Canada
Official languages: English, French
Currency: 1 dollar (C$) = 100 cents
Fiscal year ends: March 31

WHO

Governor General: H.E. The Rt. Hon. Ramon John Hnatyshyn, age 57, C$81,328 pay
Prime Minister: The Rt. Hon. Martin Brian Mulroney, age 52, C$73,600 pay
Deputy Prime Minister and Minister of Finance: The Hon. Donald Frank Mazankowski, age 56
Secretary of State for External Affairs: The Rt. Hon. Barbara Jean McDougall, age 54, C$49,100 pay
Ambassador to US: Derek H. Burney
US Ambassador to Canada: Edward N. Ney

WHERE

Executive HQ: Prime Minister, Langevin Block, Parliament Bldgs., Ottawa, Ontario K1A OA2, Canada
Embassy in US: 501 Pennsylvania Ave. NW, Washington, DC 20001
Phone: 202-682-1740
Fax: 202-682-7726
US Embassy in Canada: 100 Wellington St., Ottawa, Ontario K1P 5T1, Canada
Phone: 613-238-5335
Fax: 613-233-8511
Chamber of Commerce: Canadian Chamber of Commerce, 55 Metcalfe St., Suite 1160, Ottawa, Ontario K1P 6N4, Canada
Phone: 613-238-4000
Fax: 613-238-7643

Canada has 10 provinces and 2 territories.

Capital city: Ottawa
Time change from EST: 0 hours
Avg. high/low temp: Jan. 21°F (-6°C)/3°F (-16°C)
July 81°F (27°C)/58°F (14°C)

Urbanization: 76%
Population density: 7/sq. mi. (3/sq. km)

Exports as % of Total		Imports as % of Total	
US	74	US	65
Japan	6	Japan	7
UK	3	UK	3
Germany	1	Germany	3
Other countries	16	Other countries	22
Total	**100**	**Total**	**100**

WHAT

Origins of GDP	% of Total
Manufacturing & mining	25
Finance & insurance	15
Transport & communications	8
Construction	8
Agriculture, forestry & fishing	3
Other	41
Total	**100**

1990 GDP per capita: $21,864
1989 year-end external debt: $47 billion
Literacy rate: 99%
UN Human Development Index: 98%
Human Freedom Index (0-40 scale): 34
Purchasing power as % of US: 93%
Toronto cost of living as % of DC: 109%
Defense as % of GNP: 2%
Education as % of GNP: 7%
Principal airline: Air Canada
Principal exchange: The Toronto Stock Exchange

CHILE

OVERVIEW

Named by the indigenous Araucanian Indians, Chile means "place where the land ends." Uniquely shaped (2,600 miles long by no more than 250 miles wide), it comprises nearly 1/2 of the western coastline of South America. Chile also claims the mysterious Easter Island, which lies 2,000 miles offshore.

Chile's Codelco, the world's largest copper mining company, mines the world's largest copper deposits (accounting for nearly 40% of annual export revenue). Chile also has substantial nitrate, molybdenum, and lithium (nearly 33% of known world reserves) deposits. A net agricultural exporter, Chile sends much of its produce (especially apples and grapes) to the US. Its manufacturing sector has had excellent growth since 1984.

A turbulent economic climate that began during the Marxist Allende administration (1970–73) has substantially stabilized. Dictator General Augusto Pinochet (1973–89) and his democratically elected successor Patricio Aylwyn returned nationalized companies to their original owners, sold state-owned industries to the private sector, induced foreign investors to return, and generally promoted a free-market economy.

External debt, which was Latin America's highest per capita in 1982, remains the same today as it was then, but it is serviced by a substantially larger and more prosperous economy. Stable and pragmatic economic policies since 1986 have promoted an average annualized real GDP growth of 6%.

President Aylwyn has a number of challenges facing him, including improving the living conditions of the poor and redistributing wealth through tax reform.

WHEN

Enticed by Inca reports of silver and gold, Spanish fortune hunter Pedro de Valdiva ventured into Chile in 1541. Mineral wealth proved elusive, but early Spanish settlers, recognizing Chile's agricultural potential, enslaved the natives to exploit it. Throughout the colonial period Chile was governed by the Viceroyalty of Peru, its main trading partner, to which it exported wheat and cattle.

After an 8-year struggle Chile gained independence in 1818 with patriot Bernardo O'Higgins as dictator; he lasted only 5 years before wealthy land barons forced him out for attempting to redistribute wealth.

In the 1880s Chile captured areas from Peru and Bolivia that had valuable copper, nitrate, and guano deposits. Nitrate demand fueled growth of transportation and communication facilities, resulting in better seaport access for mineral and agricultural exports.

New-found affluence precipitated a civil war in 1891, when President José Balmaceda attempted major social reforms. Subsequent years saw ineffective governments aimed at protecting the ruling class, a decline in prices for Chile's nitrates (due to the invention of synthetics), and the unhappy effects of the Great Depression. In the 1930s and 1940s, the Radical Party undertook the expansion of educational and social welfare programs and initiated state-directed industrial development.

A surprise victory in the 1970 presidential election propelled Marxist Salvador Allende into office. He raised wages and fixed prices (bringing a short-lived consumer euphoria and spending spree), seized US-owned copper mines, and nationalized numerous banks and industries. A scarcity of food and consumer goods arose, domestic production dropped, and inflation ran to nearly 600% (1973). A junta led by General Pinochet overthrew Allende in a 1973 military coup, during which Allende supposedly committed suicide with a machine gun given him by Fidel Castro.

Pinochet launched a witch hunt for Marxists, which led to massive human rights violations. Influenced by University of Chicago economists advocating free-market economics, the regime returned property seized by Allende, cut government spending by nearly 20%, and allowed wages and prices to float. Inflation dropped to 10% in 1981.

The worldwide recession of the early 1980s caused unemployment to rise to over 20% and GDP to drop by 13% in 1982 alone. However, by the time of a plebiscite scheduled by Pinochet on his regime in 1988, economic prosperity had returned. Despite, or perhaps because of, the healthy state of the economy, Pinochet lost, and Patricio Aylwyn won the first free election in 19 years.

Things continue to improve in Chile. In 1990 Compañía de Teléfonos de Chile became the first Chilean company to be listed on the New York Stock Exchange. In 1991 Chile became the first Latin American country in 9 years to receive a regular commercial bank loan, an indication of its overall economic health.

HOW MUCH

	4-Year Growth	1986	1987	1988	1989	1990
Population (mil.)	*1.7%*	12.32	12.53	12.74	12.95	13.20
GDP ($ bil.)	*13.3%*	*17*	*19*	*22*	*25*	*28*
Real GDP growth rate	—	5.7%	5.7%	7.4%	10.0%	2.1%
Exports ($ mil.)	*18.7%*	4,199	5,224	7,052	8,080	8,328
Imports ($ mil.)	*22.9%*	3,099	3,994	4,833	6,502	7,068
Trade balance ($ mil.)	—	1,100	1,230	2,219	1,578	1,260
Current account ($ mil.)	—	(1,140)	(810)	(170)	(910)	(790)
Govt. budget bal. ($ mil.)	—	*(370)*	*(152)*	*(66)*	*127*	—
Consumer inflation	—	19.5%	19.8%	14.7%	17.0%	26.0%
Unemployment rate	—	13.9%	12.8%	11.8%	10.0%	10.0%
Exchange rate with US$	—	193.0	219.5	245.1	267.2	306.0

Source: Economist Intelligence Unit and *The Reference Press*

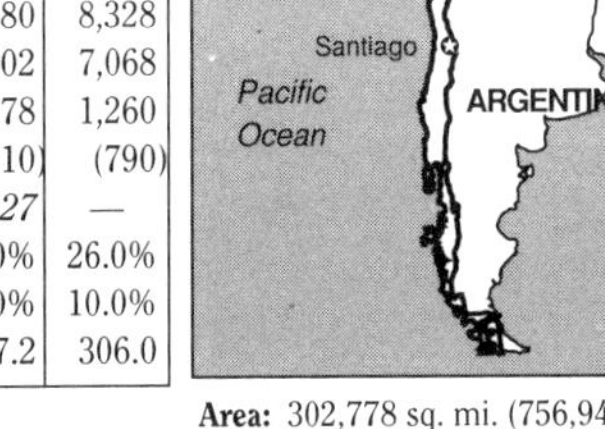

Area: 302,778 sq. mi. (756,945 sq. km)

Official name:
Republic of Chile
República de Chile
Official language: Spanish
Currency: 1 peso = 100 centésimos
Fiscal year ends: December 31

WHO

President of the Republic: Patricio Aylwyn Azócar, age 73
Minister of Finance: Carlos Ominami, age 40
Minister of Foreign Affairs: Enrique Cimma Silva, age 73
Ambassador to US: Patricio Silva, age 57
US Ambassador to Chile: Charles A. Gillespie, Jr.

WHERE

Executive HQ: President, Palacio De La Moneda, Santiago, Chile
Embassy in US: 1732 Massachusetts Ave. NW, Washington, DC 20036
Phone: 202-785-1746
Fax: 202-659-9624
US Embassy in Chile: Codina Bldg., 1343 Agustinas, Santiago, Chile
Phone: 011-56-2-710133
Fax: 011-56-2-697-2051
Chamber of Commerce: Cámara de Comercio de Chile, Santa Lucia 302, 4th fl., Casilla 1015 Correo Central, Santiago, Chile
Phone: 011-56-2-397694

Chile has 13 regions and has diplomatic representatives in 51 countries.

Capital city: Santiago
Time change from EST: +1 hour
Avg. high/low temp: Jan. 85°F (29°C)/53°F (12°C)
July 59°F (15°C)/37°F (3°C)

Urbanization: 85%
Population density: 44/sq. mi. (17/sq. km)

Exports as % of Total		Imports as % of Total	
US	17	US	19
Japan	16	Japan	8
Germany	11	Brazil	8
UK	7	Germany	7
Other countries	49	Other countries	58
Total	**100**	**Total**	**100**

WHAT

Origins of GDP	% of Total
Industry	21
Trade	18
Agriculture & forestry	8
Mining	7
Transport & communications	7
Construction	6
Electricity, gas & water	3
Fishing	1
Others	29
Total	**100**

1990 GDP per capita: $2,098
1990 year-end external debt: $19 billion
Literacy rate: 91%
UN Human Development Index: 88%
Human Freedom Index (0-40 scale): 8
Purchasing power as % of US: 28%
Capital city cost of living as % of DC: 67%
Defense as % of GNP: 5%
Education as % of GNP: 4%
Principal airlines: Lan-Chile and Ladeco
Principal exchange: Bolsa de Comercio de Santiago

CHINA

OVERVIEW

With 1.1 billion people (the most of any country), China has 25% of the world's population crowded into an area little larger than the US.

China's first priority is feeding its people. Only 11% of the land is arable; the rural population (70%) is faced with the task of feeding the country and producing for export from this minuscule portion. Vast areas have been deforested and some replanting is under way.

Mineral resources include oil, iron, coal, copper, tungsten, and titanium. Production of these commodities is inhibited by the lack of a transport and exploration infrastructure.

Almost all businesses are state-owned or collectives. Heavy industries are extensively developed, though antiquated. A decision to support light industry (and to add value to raw materials that would otherwise be exported at raw commodity prices) has brought about more emphasis on such consumer goods as bicycles, televisions, laundry equipment, refrigerators, and sewing machines.

Population is China's overriding problem. While the official rate of unemployment is 2.4%, the actual rate is probably much higher. Severe family planning regulations limit couples to one child, but this is widely flouted, especially in the country, where family-unit agriculture makes children an asset.

The government is afflicted with favoritism and corruption and lacks orderly succession procedures at its upper levels. Despite a crackdown on democratic forces, China is moving toward a more capitalist economy; it opened its first formal stock exchanges in Shanghai and Shenzhen.

WHEN

China is the oldest independent nation on earth. Its first recorded dynasty arose in the 2nd millennium BC. Merchants began selling their wares in the first millennium BC. The area came under centralized rule for the first time in the 2nd century, BC. China's civil service and land tenancy systems were in place by the end of the 2nd century, and it had developed paper, printing, porcelain, the marine compass, gunpowder and cannons, and silk manufacture by the 12th century. There were periodic invasions (which the Great Wall was built to prevent), but China absorbed its conquerors.

Though Chinese mariners reached East Africa in the 15th century and traded within Southeast Asia, they ceased exploration a few years later, just before the Portuguese penetrated Asia by sea. Despite Catholic missionaries and sea trade with the West (silk, tea, porcelain), China turned inward after 1500.

In the 19th century China's impotence was apparent in the Opium Wars with Britain and in territorial encroachments by Japan (Korea), Russia (Manchuria), Britain (Hong Kong), and France (Indochina). Numerous popular revolts led to imperial collapse.

Sun Yat-Sen established a republic that collapsed, leaving China to "war lord" rule. In 1931 the Japanese occupied Manchuria and in 1937 pushed southward militarily, slaughtering civilians as they went. Chiang Kai-shek's Kuomintang (Nationalists) and Mao Tse-Tung's Communists were enemies before WWII but struck a truce to fight the Japanese. In 1949, after a four-year civil war, the Communists drove the Nationalists to Taiwan.

The Communists reestablished order, relieved famine, and restored communications and transport. In the 1950s Mao began a series of 5-year plans. Following initial success he introduced the Great Leap Forward to alter society and increase industrial and agricultural output. Famine and stagnation resulted.

After others stabilized the economy, in 1966 Mao introduced the Cultural Revolution, to create a new Socialist society. Chaos ensued as teenaged Red Guards took over. Education and business ground to a halt. It was 10 years before the government repudiated the movement, after Mao's death.

In the 1980s the government returned agriculture to family farmers on leased land. Production rose. Restrictions on private enterprise were also relaxed. Increased prosperity resulted, along with economic disparities, destabilized prices, inflation, increased foreign trade, investment and tourism, and overseas schooling for Chinese students.

Economic liberalization and foreign contact brought popular aspirations for democratization in 1988 and 1989. Demonstrations in the spring of 1989 were crushed by the army. International reaction brought trade embargoes (since abated) and falling tourist revenues. GDP growth slowed from 10.8% in 1988 to 3.9% in 1989 but rebounded in 1991 to 10% annually by mid-year.

HOW MUCH

	4-Year Growth	1986	1987	1988	1989	1990
Population (mil.)	*1.9%*	1,061	1,080	1,096	1,126	1,143
GNP ($ bil.)	*7.4%*	*274*	*300*	*377*	*422*	*364*
Real GNP growth rate	—	8.3%	11.0%	10.8%	3.9%	5.0%
Exports ($ mil.)	*19.1%*	30,900	39,400	47,500	52,500	62,100
Imports ($ mil.)	*5.6%*	42,900	43,200	55,200	59,100	53,400
Trade balance ($ mil.)	—	(12,000)	(3,800)	(7,700)	(6,600)	8,700
Current account ($ mil.)	—	(7,000)	300	(3,800)	(4,300)	5,200
Govt. budget bal. ($ mil.)	—	*(2,027)*	*(2,149)*	*(2,149)*	*(2,523)*	*(1,862)*
Consumer inflation	—	6.0%	7.3%	18.5%	17.8%	2.0%
Unemployment rate	—	—	—	—	—	2.4%
Exchange rate with US$	—	3.45	3.72	3.72	3.77	4.78

Source: Economist Intelligence Unit and *The Reference Press*

Area: 3,682,131 sq. mi. (9,536,721 sq. km)

Official name:
People's Republic of China
Zhonghua Renmin Gonghe Guo
Official language: Modern Standard Chinese
Currency: 1 yuan (Y) = 100 fen
Fiscal year ends: December 31

WHO

State President: Yang Shangkun, age 84
Prime Minister, Chairman of the Commission for Economic Restructure: Li Peng, age 63
Vice-President: Wang Zhen, age 83
Deputy Prime Ministers: Tian Jiyun, Yao Yilin, Wu Xueqian
Minister of Finance: Wang Bingqian, age 66
Minister of Foreign Affairs: Qian Qichen, age 63
Ambassador to US: Zhu Qizhen
US Ambassador to China: James R. Lilley

WHERE

Executive HQ: President, c/o State Council Secretariat, Beijing, China
Embassy in US: 2300 Connecticut Ave. NW, Washington, DC 20008
Phone: 202-328-2500
Fax: 202-234-4055
US Embassy in China: PRC Box 50, Xiu Shui Bei Jie 3, 100600, Beijing, China
Phone: 011-86-1-532-3831
Fax: 011-86-1-532-3178

China has 21 provinces, 5 autonomous regions, and 3 government-controlled municipalities and has diplomatic representatives in 113 countries.

Capital city: Beijing
Time change from EST: +13 hours
Avg. high/low temp: Jan. 34°F (1°C)/14°F (-10°C)
July 88°F (31°C)/70°F (21°C)

Urbanization: 53%
Population density: 310/sq. mi. (120/sq. km)

Exports as % of Total		Imports as % of Total	
Hong Kong & Macau	43	Hong Kong & Macau	22
Japan	16	Japan	18
US	8	US	13
USSR	4	Germany	6
Other countries	29	Other countries	41
Total	**100**	**Total**	**100**

WHAT

Origins of GNP	% of Total
Industry	46
Agriculture	32
Commerce	11
Construction	7
Transport	4
Total	**100**

1990 GNP per capita: $318
1990 year-end external debt: $45 billion
Literacy rate: 75%
UN Human Development Index: 61%
Human Freedom Index (0-40 scale): 2
Purchasing power as % of US: 12%
Capital city cost of living as % of DC: 92%
Defense as % of GNP: 2%
Education as % of GNP: 3%
Principal airline: CAAC (Civil Aviation Administration of China)
Principal exchange: Shanghai Securities Exchange

COLOMBIA

OVERVIEW

Once famous only as the world's largest exporter of coffee, Colombia today is known more for its drug-related violence; drug production and trafficking account for nearly 30% of foreign exchange earnings. An estimated 80% of the world's cocaine originates in Colombia. The varied climate and soils also permit a variety of legitimate crops, including coffee, cotton, tobacco, and sugar cane.

The country is rich in oil, coal, gold, copper, and emeralds (90% of the world's output). The decline in coffee prices in recent years has been offset by the expansion of the cut flower, yarn, and cement businesses. Oil recently passed coffee as the #1 export.

Colombia is the oldest democracy in South America and has seen fewer than 5 years of military rule. Most (90%) of its people live in the mild valleys adjacent to the Andes.

The country has a reputation for conservative financial management. GDP grew in the 1980s as Colombia continued its policy of export diversification and trade liberalization. A rapidly growing export is books printed for US publishers. The long-term external debt ($17 billion in 1990) is well managed and considered low by regional standards. Inflation continues at annual rates of 25% to 30%.

Despite the recent violence that included the assassination of 3 presidential hopefuls, the current president, César Gaviria, remains committed to democracy. After Colombia announced that it would not extradite drug lords to the US, one of the most notorious, Pablo Escobar, surrendered and was jailed.

WHEN

When they arrived in South America in the early 1500s, the original Spanish explorers were searching for El Dorado, the legendary chief who covered himself with gold dust. Their landing point in what is now Colombia (named after Christopher Columbus) became the first European settlement in 1525 (Santa Marta). Natives were conscripted to serve as peasant labor on ranches, and African slaves worked the plantations and mines.

Gran Colombia (encompassing Colombia, Ecuador, Panama, and Venezuela) declared independence in 1819, but internal strife, including a 4-year dictatorship by Simón Bolívar, resulted in secession of Venezuela (1829) and Ecuador (1830) and a new name, New Granada. As steam power allowed penetration of the interior waterways, cotton, tobacco, and quinine became early exports.

Despite violent confrontations between liberals and conservatives lasting from 1839 to the late 1870s, the country flourished, its economy strengthened, and exports grew. It renamed itself Colombia in 1861. Coffee became the leading export in the late 1800s.

By 1890 a liberal/conservative war had broken out, coffee prices had fallen, and hyperinflation had begun. The war destroyed infrastructure and emptied the treasury, allowing Panama to secede (with US aid provided in exchange for rights to build a canal across its isthmus) in 1903.

The first 3 decades of the 20th century were prosperous. Colombia's credit was restored, railroads were built, and the coffee industry flourished; oil was also discovered. The 1930s brought the Great Depression but also saw the beginnings of industrial development. However, in 1949 a 10-year period of political violence (known as *La Violencia*) began, claiming tens of thousands of lives.

Alternate liberal and conservative governments over the next 20 years expanded various programs to diversify exports. By 1973 exports of coffee were eclipsed by manufactured goods. Inflation of 30% in 1974 was reduced to 20% only 2 years later as a result of effective economic reforms.

Falling coffee prices in the early 1980s led to the growth of the illicit cocaine industry and, with it, the rise of chieftains who, through bribery and violence, operated with impunity in Colombia. By 1982 the cocaine trade accounted for an estimated 9% of GNP. Both the Medellín and Cali cartels financed numerous guerrilla movements in Colombia. Drug-related violence greatly increased from 1987 to 1989, and President Virgilio Barco reinstated an extradition treaty with the US.

A temporary halt to cartel-supported terrorist activities took place in early 1990. In 1991 violence again broke out when the journalist daughter of an ex-president was kidnapped and murdered. Despite the enormous wealth cocaine has created, it is generally thought to have a negative effect on the economy. Drug barons buy mostly imported luxury goods and have not invested their capital in local job-creating enterprises.

HOW MUCH

	4-Year Growth	1986	1987	1988	1989	1990
Population (mil.)	*1.6%*	30.5	31.1	31.7	32.3	*32.9*
GDP ($ bil.)	*4.0%*	*35*	*36*	*39*	*39*	*41*
Real GDP growth rate	—	5.8%	5.4%	4.1%	3.2%	3.5%
Exports ($ mil.)	*6.0%*	5,331	5,661	5,343	6,029	6,740
Imports ($ mil.)	*10.1%*	3,409	3,793	4,516	4,548	5,015
Trade balance ($ mil.)	—	1,922	1,868	827	1,481	1,725
Current account ($ mil.)	—	383	336	(200)	42	230
Govt. budget bal. ($ mil.)	—	—	—	*378*	*269*	*(437)*
Consumer inflation	—	18.9%	23.3%	28.1%	25.8%	29.0%
Unemployment rate	—	12.3%	10.2%	10.2%	10.8%	—
Exchange rate with US$	—	194.3	242.6	299.2	382.6	502.2

Source: Economist Intelligence Unit and *The Reference Press*

Area: 440,829 sq. mi. (1,141,748 sq. km)

Official name:
Republic of Colombia
República de Colombia
Official language: Spanish
Currency: 1 peso = 100 centavos
Fiscal year ends: December 31

WHO

President: César Gaviria Trujillo, age 44
Minister of Finance and Public Credit: Rudolf Hollmes
Minister of Foreign Affairs: Luis Fernando Jaramillo
Ambassador to US: Jaime Garcia-Parra
US Ambassador to Colombia: Thomas E. McNamara

WHERE

Executive HQ: President, Casa De Narino, Carrera 8a, No. 7-26, Bogotá, Colombia
Embassy in US: 2118 Leroy Pl. NW, Washington, DC 20008
Phone: 202-387-8338
Fax: 202-232-8643
US Embassy in Colombia: PO Box A.A. 3831, Calle 38, No. 8-61, Bogotá, Colombia
Phone: 011-57-1-285-1300
Fax: 011-57-1-288-5687
Chamber of Commerce: Confederación Colombiana de Cámaras de Comercio, Carrera 9 No. 16-21, 10-piso, Apartado 29750, Bogotá, Colombia
Phone: 011-57-1-242-1678

Colombia has 23 departments, a Federal District, 4 intendancies, and 5 commissariats and has diplomatic representatives in 59 countries.

Capital city: Bogotá
Time change from EST: 0 hours
Avg. high/low temp: Jan. 67°F (19°C)/48°F (9°C)
July 64°F (18°C)/50°F (10°C)

Urbanization: 69%
Population density: 75/sq. mi. (29/sq. km)

Exports as % of Total		Imports as % of Total	
US	43	US	36
Latin America	10	Latin America	20
Germany	9	Japan	9
Netherlands	6	Germany	7
Other countries	32	Other countries	28
Total	**100**	**Total**	**100**

WHAT

Origins of GDP	% of Total
Manufacturing	20
Agriculture	17
Commerce	14
Government	8
Transport & communications	8
Other	33
Total	**100**

1990 GDP per capita: $1,241
1990 year-end external debt: $17 billion
Literacy rate: 85%
UN Human Development Index: 76%
Human Freedom Index (0-40 scale): 14
Purchasing power as % of US: 20%
Capital city cost of living as % of DC: 59%
Defense as % of GNP: 1%
Education as % of GNP: 3%
Principal airline: Avianca (Aerovías Nacionales de Colombia)
Principal exchange: Bolsa de Bogotá SA

COSTA RICA

OVERVIEW

Costa Rica is the 2nd smallest Central American country in area (El Salvador is smallest). It boasts one of the highest literacy rates in Central America (93%), owing to its active promotion of educational programs. The country has little mineral wealth, but its volcanic slopes and fertile valleys have promoted the development of a rich agricultural sector specializing in coffee (its #1 export), bananas, sugar cane, grain, and beef. Costa Rica has some hydroelectric capabilities; most other energy requirements are met by imported oil.

Costa Rica has since 1889 maintained strong democratic institutions and an orderly succession of governments — all without a standing army, which was constitutionally abolished in 1949. It is one of the region's strongest and most stable nations, both economically and politically.

Lower coffee prices and higher oil costs have led to a rapid expansion of long-term external debt. To reduce this debt, Costa Rica has agreed to preserve rain forests in exchange for debt forgiveness by conservation groups that have purchased its bank debt.

Real GDP growth averaged 4.5% in the late 1980s. Inflation ranges from 12% to 20%. Wealth is distributed unevenly. An influx of over 100,000 Nicaraguan immigrants has strained the economy, particularly in education and health care.

Newly elected (1990) President Calderón faces the challenge of shifting labor from the agricultural and import-substitution industries into more productive activities associated with tourism and light-industrial export programs. The government actively encourages foreign investment in the export sector.

WHEN

On his last voyage to the New World in 1502, Columbus landed on the shores of Costa Rica. Learning of rumored mineral deposits of gold, he named the country Costa Rica, meaning "rich coast." When the rumors proved false, the Spaniards developed an agricultural economy. The first permanent Spanish settlement was Cartago in 1564. Unlike other natives in the region, the Amerindians in Costa Rica escaped Spanish enslavement by fiercely fighting for their freedom.

The region remained very stable during the next 150 years, with only small-scale farming activities. Costa Rica remained a province of the Captaincy General of Guatemala under Spain. It declared independence from Spain in 1821, joining other alliances before becoming a republic in 1838.

Coffee was introduced from Cuba in 1808, and the government encouraged crop development by providing free land. Bananas soon became a basic product. New roads and railways were developed to take produce to market. Coffee and banana cultivation gave rise to new class distinctions, as wealth was unevenly accumulated.

Throughout the first half of the 20th century, Costa Rica's economy remained largely agricultural, its ups and downs dictated by commodity prices for coffee and bananas.

During the 1950s and 1960s, improvements were made in the social infrastructure; the minimum wage and funding of public schools were increased.

The 1970s and early 1980s were troubled times for Costa Rica. It refused to deport fugitive American investor Robert Vesco, who had invested some $60 million in local businesses and housing projects. Imported oil cost more by 1973, interest on foreign debt skyrocketed as rates rose in the early 1980s, and coffee prices fell. GDP fell by nearly 10% between 1981 and 1983, and the external debt reached $4.5 billion in 1986.

President Oscar Arias (elected in 1986) addressed the grim economic situation. Foreign debt was rescheduled over a period of 25 years. The IMF provided standby credit on condition that austerity measures be undertaken. Arias also tried to improve the lot of the poor by providing government jobs and housing. Arias wrote the 1987 peace plan that, it was hoped, would bring peace to the region, particularly the politically troubled country of Nicaragua. Although the parties involved never completely complied with it, this plan was viewed as a positive step in increasing democracy in Central America. Arias was awarded the Nobel Peace Prize in 1987.

President Rafael Angelo Calderón succeeded Arias in 1990. He will try to maintain economic growth while servicing the country's high debt (among the world's highest per capita). In 1991 Costa Rica imposed a 10% surcharge on all imports, resulting in retaliatory charges by other area governments.

HOW MUCH

	4-Year Growth	1986	1987	1988	1989	1990
Population (mil.)	*2.7%*	2.7	2.8	2.9	3.0	3.0
GDP ($ bil.)	*6.1%*	*4.4*	*4.5*	*4.6*	*5.2*	*5.6*
Real GDP growth rate	—	5.5%	4.8%	3.5%	5.5%	3.6%
Exports ($ mil.)	*6.0%*	1,085	1,107	1,181	1,323	1,368
Imports ($ mil.)	*16.3%*	1,045	1,245	1,279	1,577	1,909
Trade balance ($ mil.)	—	40	(138)	(98)	(254)	(541)
Current account ($ mil.)	—	(161)	(376)	(304)	(447)	(492)
Govt. budget bal. ($ mil.)	—	*(145)*	*(90)*	*(115)*	*(203)*	—
Consumer inflation	—	11.8%	16.9%	20.8%	16.5%	19.0%
Unemployment rate	—	6.0%	5.5%	5.5%	3.8%	5.4%
Exchange rate with US$	—	55.99	62.78	75.80	81.50	91.58

Source: Economist Intelligence Unit and *The Reference Press*

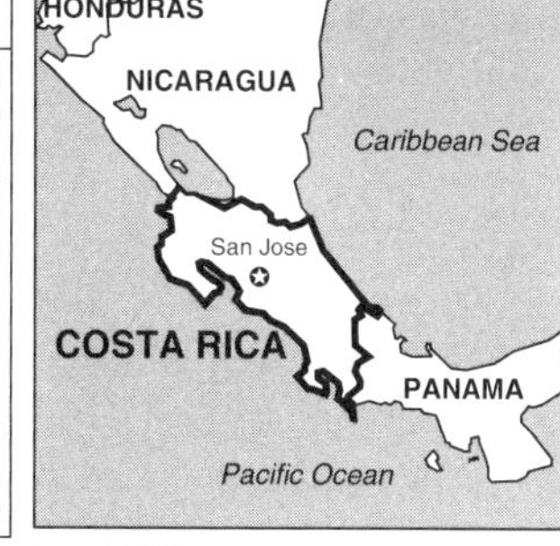

Area: 19,652 sq. mi. (51,032 sq. km)

Official name:
Republic of Costa Rica
República de Costa Rica
Official language: Spanish
Currency: 1 colon (¢)= 100 centimos
Fiscal year ends: December 31

WHO

President: Rafael Angel Calderón Fournier, age 42
Vice-Presidents: Herman Ferrano Pinto, Arnoldo Lopez Echndi
Minister of Finance: Thelmo Vargas
Minister of Foreign Relations: Verne Nifhaus
Ambassador to US: Gonzalo J. Facio
Chargé d'Affaires to Costa Rica: Robert Homme

WHERE

Executive HQ: President, Casa Presidencial Apartado 10089, San Jose 1000, Costa Rica
Embassy in US: 1125 Connecticut Ave. NW, Suite 211, Washington, DC 20009
Phone: 202-234-2945
Fax: 202-265-4795
US Embassy in Costa Rica: Pavas, San Jose, Costa Rica
Phone: 011-506-20-39-39
Fax: 011-506-20-2305
Chamber of Commerce: Cámara de Comercio de Costa Rica, Calle 1A y 3A Ave. Central, Apartado 1114, San Jose 1000, Costa Rica
Phone: 011-506-21-00-05

Costa Rica has 7 provinces and has diplomatic representatives in 37 countries.

Capital city: San Jose
Time change from EST: -1 hour
Avg. high/low temp: Jan. 75°F (24°C)/58°F (14°C)
July 77°F (25°C)/62°F (17°C)

Urbanization: 45%
Population density: 154/sq. mi. (59/sq. km)

Exports as % of Total		Imports as % of Total	
US	45	US	41
Germany	13	Venezuela	8
Italy	5	Japan	7
Guatemala	4	Mexico	6
Other countries	33	Other countries	38
Total	**100**	**Total**	**100**

WHAT

Origins of GDP	% of Total
Manufacturing & mining	22
Agriculture	19
Commerce	18
Government	9
Transport & communications	8
Other	24
Total	**100**

1990 GDP per capita: $1,847
1990 year-end external debt: $4 billion
Literacy rate: 93%
UN Human Development Index: 88%
Human Freedom Index (0-40 scale): 31
Purchasing power as % of US: 21%
Capital city cost of living as % of DC: 66%
Defense as % of GNP: 1%
Education as % of GNP: 5%
Principal airline: Lacsa (Líneas Aéreas Costarricenses)
Principal exchange: Bolsa Nacional de Valores SA

CUBA

OVERVIEW

Located 90 miles south of the US in the Caribbean, Cuba is the largest island in the West Indies. Sugar accounts for over 80% of export earnings. Tobacco ranks as the #2 export, followed by coffee, citrus products, and shellfish. Cuba is the world's 5th largest producer of nickel. Its literacy rate (99%) is by far the highest in Latin America.

Cuba has distanced itself economically, politically, and culturally from its neighbors through years of Communist revolutionary activity led by brothers Raúl and Fidel Castro. The government owns more than 70% of the farmland and all industries, banks, and small businesses. The US has enforced an economic embargo of Cuba for nearly 30 years (it formerly accounted for 50% of Cuba's trade). The embargo, along with poorly executed central economic control and changes in Eastern Europe, has devastated the Cuban economy.

Cuba's economy is dependent upon the USSR, which supplies 70% of Cuban imports, 90% of its fuel, and nearly 100% of all military goods. Soviet sugar purchases at above-market prices in 1988 accounted for $4.3 billion. With the changes in Eastern Europe, new trade rules prevail. All transactions are for hard currency at market prices rather than for barter or artificial prices, as had previously been the case. Cuba will have to pay market prices for Soviet oil (until 1987, resale of low-cost Soviet oil was Cuba's largest source of foreign exchange). Hard currency reserves are low; food and fuel are in short supply; and infrastructure is crumbling, as oxen replace tractors in the fields.

Hard times have led Cuba to renew ties with its neighbors. Jamaican businesses are helping develop Cuba's tourism, Chile and Paraguay have established diplomatic contact, and Cuba hosted the 1991 Pan Am games.

WHEN

On his first voyage to the New World in 1492, Columbus found Cuba. Thinking he had reached Asia, he sent scouts to present to the emperor of China letters from Ferdinand and Isabella. The disappointed scouts found only peaceful natives subsisting on maize and beans and smoking a native plant, *Nicotiana tabacum*. Colonization began in 1511.

During the 16th and 17th centuries, Havana became a supply point for Spanish fleets carrying bullion from Mexico and Peru to Spain. There was little other economic activity apart from small-scale cattle and tobacco operations. By the 18th century, as precious metal production declined, sugar and tobacco production soared with European demand.

A bloody 10-year war beginning in 1868 failed to win Cuba independence. Rebellion in 1895 and the subsequent sinking of the USS *Maine* in the Havana harbor in 1898 led to the Spanish-American War, ending in US victory and nominal Cuban independence in 1902 (the US got the right to intervene in Cuba at will).

A series of corrupt and repressive regimes ensued. In 1934 army sergeant Fulgencio Batista seized power. A special pricing agreement with the US revived a moribund sugar industry. From 1942 to 1947 the US purchased all Cuba's sugar exports. The people remained poor as the wealthy invested sugar revenues in urban tourist facilities.

During the 1950s sugar prices remained stable, foreign currency reserves rose, and industry grew. However, repression increased and the welfare of the masses declined, leading to a guerrilla campaign ending in Fidel Castro's assumption of power in 1959.

Within months Castro established a Communist state, and hundreds of thousands fled the country — mostly to the US. After the abortive, US-backed Bay of Pigs invasion in 1961, Castro publicly declared himself a Marxist-Leninist, and Cuba lapsed again into political repression. Cuba replaced GNP with GSP (Global Social Product) as a measurement of its economic activity. Use of GSP has led to double counting and changing data-collection methodologies, making economic growth difficult to measure.

The US trade embargo was imposed in 1963 and, with a few modest liberalizations (Americans may now legally purchase formerly contraband Havana cigars outside the US and import them), has been maintained to this day. The low point of US-Cuban relations occurred during 1962 when a Soviet attempt to install offensive nuclear missiles in Cuba nearly led to war. By 1983 Cuba's external debt to the Soviet Union was $8 billion, with an additional $3 billion owed to Western banks and governments. By 1986 Cuba owed $7 billion to Western banks; no interest has been paid on these loans since 1986. In 1991 Cuba agreed to repay Mexico $350 million of its debt through a series of joint ventures in industry and tourism.

HOW MUCH

	4-Year Growth	1986	1987	1988	1989	1990
Population (mil.)	*0.5%*	10.3	10.4	10.4	10.5	10.5
GSP ($ bil.)	*1.6%*	*32*	—	*33*	*34*	*34*
Real GSP growth rate	—	0.8%	(3.5%)	2.1%	2.0%	(1.5%)
Exports ($ mil.)	—	1,093	—	1,409	1,203	—
Imports ($ mil.)	—	1,290	—	1,327	1,215	—
Trade balance ($ mil.)	—	(198)	—	82	(13)	—
Current account ($ mil.)	—	(2,363)	—	(481)	(759)	—
Govt. budget bal. ($ mil.)	—	*(227)*	—	*(1,451)*	*(2,056)*	*(2,506)*
Consumer inflation	—	—	—	—	—	—
Unemployment rate	—	—	—	6.0%	—	—
Exchange rate with US$	—	0.83	—	0.79	0.79	0.79

Source: Economist Intelligence Unit and *The Reference Press*

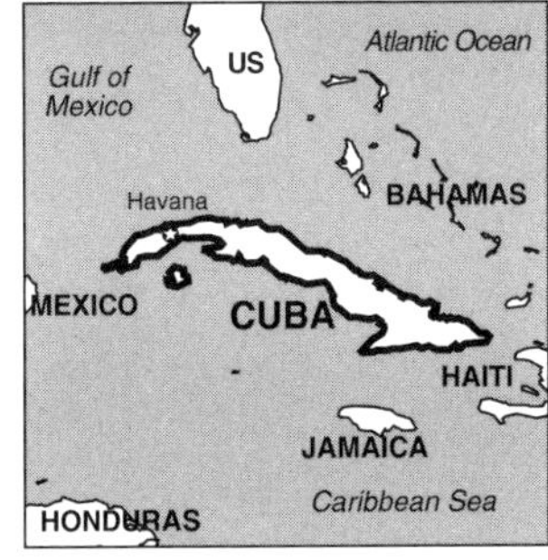

Area: 44,206 sq. mi. (114,524 sq. km)

Official name:
Republic of Cuba
República de Cuba
Official language: Spanish
Currency: 1 peso = 100 centavos
Fiscal year ends: December 31

WHO

President of the Councils of State and Ministers, First Secretary of the Communist Party, and Commander in Chief: Fidel Castro Ruz, age 64

First Vice-President of the Councils of State and Ministers, Second Secretary of the Communist Party, General of the Army, and Minister of Revolutionary Armed Forces: Raúl Castro Ruz, age 60

Minister of Foreign Relations: Isidoro Octavio Malmierca Peoli

Counselor to US: José Antonio Arbesu Fraga

Principal US Officer in Cuba: John J. Taylor

WHERE

Executive HQ: President, Ciudad De La Habana, Havana, Cuba

Representation of Cuba in US: Cuban Interests Section (under protection of Swiss Embassy), 2630 and 2639 16th St. NW, Washington, DC 20009

Phone: 202-797-8518

US Representation in Cuba: US Interests Section (under protection of Swiss Embassy), Calzada entre L y M, Vedado Seccion, Havana, Cuba

Phone: 011-7-329-700

Chamber of Commerce: Cámara de Comercio, Calle 21 No. 661, Apartado Postal 4237, Vedado, Havana 4, Cuba

Phone: 011-7-303-356

Cuba has 14 provinces and one special municipality (Havana) and has diplomatic representatives in 75 countries.

Capital city: Havana
Time change from EST: 0 hours
Avg. high/low temp: Jan. 79°F (26°C)/65°F (18°C)
July 89°F (32°C)/75°F (24°C)

Urbanization: 72%
Population density: 238/sq. mi. (92/sq. km)

Exports as % of Total		Imports as % of Total	
Socialist countries	86	Socialist countries	87
Japan	2	Spain	2
Spain	2	Argentina	2
Germany	1	Mexico	1
Other countries	9	Other countries	8
Total	**100**	**Total**	**100**

WHAT

Origins of GDP	% of Total
Industry	46
Commerce	20
Agriculture & forestry	16
Other	18
Total	**100**

1990 GSP per capita: $3,243
1989 year-end external debt: $8 billion
Literacy rate: 99%
UN Human Development Index: 75%
Human Freedom Index (0-40 scale): 5
Capital city cost of living as % of DC: —
Defense as % of GNP: 1%
Principal airline: Cubana (*Empresa Cubana de Aviación*)

CZECHOSLOVAKIA

OVERVIEW

Czechoslovakia is a federation of the Czech and Slovak Socialist Republics. As in the rest of Eastern Europe, democracy and capitalism have swept the nation. New president Václav Havel faces the problems of converting the socialist economy to a capitalist one and dealing with horrendous pollution, inefficient energy use, and resurgent Slovak separatism.

Mineral resources include coal (primarily sooty lignite), uranium, and magnesite. The landlocked nation has access to the sea via the Elbe, Oder, and Danube rivers.

Czechoslovakia's industry is antiquated. Under communism profits from successful light industries such as shoes, beer, and glassware subsidized such less-efficient heavy industries as iron, steel, and machinery. Timid management, central planning, worker apathy, and corruption blocked progress.

In 1990, as the Eastern bloc disintegrated, cash orders decreased, COMECON barter ceased, and import prices rose (especially for Soviet oil), pushing inflation briefly to 30%; industrial production decreased. In the first 3 weeks of 1991, the cost of living rose 40%.

Czechoslovakia's privatization program is the most drastic in Eastern Europe. It actively encourages foreign and domestic investment. In 1991 small businesses and shops sold at auction for an average of 11 times the expected prices. Czechoslovakia's relatively low foreign debt allows it to borrow from the IMF and World Bank.

Official name:
Czech and Slovak Federal Republic
Česká a Slovenská Federátivní Republika
Official languages: Czech, Slovak
Currency: 1 koruna (kčs) = 100 haler
Fiscal year ends: December 31

WHO

President of the Republic: Václav Havel, age 55
Prime Minister: Marián Čalfa, age 45
First Deputy Prime Minister and Minister of Foreign Affairs: Jiří Dienstbier, age 54
Minister of Finance: Václav Klaus, age 50
Ambassador to US: Rita Klimova
US Ambassador to Czechoslovakia: Shirley Temple Black

WHERE

Executive HQ: President of the Republic, 11908 Praha, 1 Hrad, Prague, Czechoslovakia
Embassy in US: 3900 Linnean Ave. NW, Washington, DC 20008
Phone: 202-363-6315
Fax: 202-966-8540
US Embassy in Czechoslovakia: Trziste 15, 125 48 Praha, Prague, Czechoslovakia
Phone: 011-42-2-53-6641
Fax: 011-42-2-53-2457
Chamber of Commerce: Chamber of Commerce & Industry of the CSFR, Argentinska 38, CS-17005, Prague 7, Czechoslovakia
Phone: 011-42-253-8736

Czechoslovakia has 12 administrative regions and has diplomatic representatives in over 90 countries.

Capital city: Prague
Time change from EST: +6 hours
Avg. high/low temp: Jan. 49°F (10°C)/7°F (-13°C)
July 91°F (33°C)/49°F (9°C)

Urbanization: 66%
Population density: 316/sq. mi. (122/sq. km)

Exports as % of Total		Imports as % of Total	
USSR	31	USSR	30
Germany	15	Germany	17
Poland	9	Poland	9
Austria	5	Austria	6
Other countries	40	Other countries	38
Total	**100**	**Total**	**100**

WHEN

Slavic tribes settled Czechoslovakia's Bohemia and Moravia regions. Bohemia was an independent kingdom (including Moravia and parts of Austria and Poland) until 1620, when it became part of the Hapsburg's Austrian empire. Bohemia became the most commercially and industrially advanced part of the empire. In the 19th century, inspired by Pan-Slavism and European nationalist ferment, the Czechs and Slovaks (then also part of the Austro-Hungarian empire) agitated for independence, but didn't achieve it.

In 1918 the Czechs and Slovaks joined in an independent state whose borders were unsatisfactory to many, particularly the new state's German and Hungarian minorities.

Czechoslovakia was prosperous between the wars, with a sophisticated light industrial base of crystal, china, textiles, beer, and light machinery manufacture. Throughout the 1930s Germany stirred unrest among the ethnic German population and in 1938, with the acquiescence of France and England, annexed part of Czechoslovakia — the Sudetenland. In 1939 Germany occupied the rest of the country.

Following WWII a coalition aiming to mix democratic government with a socialist economy took over, nationalizing industry and wholesale trade. The Communists seized full power in 1948. Nationalization of retail trade was completed by 1951. Agricultural collectivization, begun in 1949, eventually extended to over 90% of the land. Czechoslovakia became the most collectivized Eastern bloc nation.

It also remained the most Stalinist. Its first two 5-year plans stressed heavy industry, neglecting the consumer and agricultural sectors. But, shortages of meat, consumer goods, and housing arose, and in 1962 the 3rd 5-year plan was abandoned.

In early 1968 economic liberalization measures under First Secretary Alexander Dubcek led to some loosening of political control (a period known as the Prague Spring). In August Warsaw Pact troops invaded, installing Gustav Husak and clamping down on liberalization.

Soviet aid, though helpful in the short run, did not address the problems of aging infrastructure, inappropriate industrialization, and inefficient management. In 1981 the government tried combining several enterprises into less centrally planned conglomerates. The economy remained stagnant, and shortages appeared again. In the mid-1980s the government emphasized such industries as chemicals and electronics, resulting in the economy's respectable average annual growth of more than 3% from 1983 to 1985.

In 1989 political ferment increased. Demonstrations and calls for increased freedom initially received a repressive response; leaders of the movement for democracy were jailed. But, as the year wore on, the government's resolve crumbled in the face of nonviolent opposition (reinforced by the flow of East Germans on their way to Hungary), and the Husak government resigned in favor of a provisional coalition headed by Václav Havel and Alexander Dubcek.

WHAT

Origins of Net Material Product	% of Total
Industry	60
Productive services	22
Construction	11
Agriculture, forestry & water	7
Total	**100**

1990 NMP per capita: $2,307
1990 year-end external debt: $8 billion
Literacy rate: 99%
UN Human Development Index: 92%
Human Freedom Index (0-40 scale): 6
Purchasing power as % of US: —
Capital city cost of living as % of DC: 57%
Defense as % of GNP: 5%
Education as % of GNP: —
Principal airline: Ceskoslovenske Aerolinie

HOW MUCH

	4-Year Growth	1986	1987	1988	1989	1990
Population (mil.)	*0.2%*	15.5	15.6	15.6	15.6	15.6
NMP ($ bil.)	*3.2%*	*38*	*43*	*42*	*41*	*36*
Real NMP growth rate	—	2.6%	2.1%	2.3%	0.7%	(3.5%)
Exports to OECD ($ mil.)	*12.2%*	3,108	3,492	3,828	4,392	*4,929*
Imports from OECD ($ mil.)	*6.7%*	2,723	3,312	3,576	3,780	*3,535*
Trade balance ($ mil.)	—	385	180	252	612	*1,394*
Current account ($ mil.)	—	417	57	91	443	(550)
Govt. budget bal. (mil.)	—	*0*	*0*	*0*	—	—
Consumer inflation (%)	—	0.5%	0.1%	0.1%	1.4%	10.0%
Unemployment rate	—	0.0%	0.0%	0.0%	—	1.5%
Exchange with US$ rate	—	15.00	13.69	14.36	15.05	17.95

Source: Economist Intelligence Unit and *The Reference Press*

Area: 49,369 sq. mi. (127,899 sq. km)

DENMARK

OVERVIEW

Denmark consists of the Jutland Peninsula in northwestern Europe and 406 islands in the Kattegat and Baltic Seas. No place is more than 31 miles from its coast. Excluding flags of convenience, it has the world's 3rd largest shipping fleet (after Greece and Norway).

Though it is now a highly industrialized, or even post-industrial nation (over 2/3 of employment and GDP are provided by the service sector), 1/3 of its exports are generated by agriculture. It is the world's largest exporter of pork, with nearly 3 head of swine for every 2 of its people. It is also a major exporter of butter and cheese.

Denmark does not have a heavy industry sector but rather specializes in light, finished products, of which 35% to 40% are exported. It is the world's largest exporter of beer (Carlsberg-Tuborg) and insulin (Novo Nordisk produces 2/3 of Western Europe's needs). Other specialty businesses include hearing aids, radio telephones, and Lego toys. Nearly 1/2 of its industrial exports go to other members of the EC. Denmark has a free market economy of mostly small businesses; the government owns some public service companies, but no production industries.

Denmark is devoted to social engineering, providing a high living standard as a matter of right. Only around 1,000 people in the country have incomes in excess of $130,000 annually. The goal of full employment has led to a ballooning public sector. Social welfare benefits are largely paid for from the proceeds of high personal income taxes rather than directly by Danish businesses. High taxes are expected to cause problems in the 1992 EC market unification, and steps are being taken to bring Danish taxes more in line with the EC norm. High sales taxes on luxury items have caused Danes to shop abroad.

Denmark administers 2 overseas areas, Greenland (the world's largest island), where zinc, lead, iron, and coal are mined, and the Faroe Islands, the main industry of which is fishing.

WHEN

The Danes were part of the Viking hordes that devastated Europe in the 9th century. In addition to marauding, they settled in parts of the British Isles. From 1018 to 1042 the Danish king Canute ruled portions of England. After the 11th century, the invaders retreated to Scandinavia. By 1397 Denmark ruled all of Scandinavia and Iceland until the Swedes broke away in the 1520s. In 1849 Denmark became a constitutional monarchy.

In the 17th and 18th centuries, land reform laid the basis for Denmark's 19th century agricultural prosperity. The Danes exported meat, particularly pork, dairy products, and eggs to northern Europe and England. Other primary trades were fishing and shipping.

Significant industrialization did not begin until the early 20th century, taking the form of small shops and light industries. Agricultural products remained the main export (75%) until the 1930s.

Denmark was successfully neutral in WWI, but Germany occupied it in WWII, despite a 1939 nonaggression pact. Denmark's economy was forced to function for German benefit, and the nation submitted to German restrictions on political activity and to persecution of Jews. There was an active resistance.

Iceland dissolved its union with Denmark in 1944. In 1949 Denmark joined NATO and in 1953 joined Norway, Sweden, Finland, and Iceland to create a single labor market.

Following WWII Denmark developed an extensive web of social programs. When oil prices began to rise in the 1970s, the government had difficulty funding these programs. Despite revenues from the discovery of North Sea oil and gas, welfare programs were a drain on public coffers. Yet abandonment of such programs was politically risky, so public spending and debt rose rapidly in the 1970s and 1980s. The deficit rose 500% between 1975 and 1984, reaching 13% of GNP in 1983; by 1987 foreign debt had reached 40% of GNP, and Denmark's credit rating was lowered several times in the 1980s.

In the late 1980s Prime Minister Schluter abolished inflation-indexing of welfare payments, and imposed wage controls. Income tax rates were lowered from 73% to 68%. Investment and consumer consumption declined, causing flat to negative growth in GNP. By 1987 unemployment was down modestly (it has since gone back up, but not to the early 1980s level), inflation fell from about 10% in 1983 to under 3% in 1990, and GDP growth was again slightly positive in 1989 and 1990.

To better compete in Europe's coming unified market, Denmark's basic industries are merging to form larger entities.

HOW MUCH

	4-Year Growth	1986	1987	1988	1989	1990
Population (mil.)	*0.1%*	5.12	5.12	5.13	5.13	5.15
GDP ($ bil.)	*11.7%*	*82*	*102*	*108*	*105*	*128*
Real GDP growth rate	—	3.1%	(0.6%)	(0.2%)	1.3%	1.1%
Exports ($ mil.)	*9.2%*	21,300	25,700	27,500	28,100	30,300
Imports ($ mil.)	*4.9%*	22,800	25,400	25,900	26,700	27,600
Trade balance ($ mil.)	—	(1,500)	300	1,600	1,400	2,700
Current account ($ mil.)	—	(4,500)	(3,000)	(1,800)	(1,400)	1,500
Govt. budget bal. ($ mil.)	—	—	*(51)*	*(237)*	*(251)*	—
Consumer inflation	—	3.6%	4.0%	4.6%	4.8%	2.6%
Unemployment rate	—	7.8%	7.8%	8.6%	9.1%	—
Exchange rate with US$	—	8.09	6.84	6.73	7.31	6.19

Source: Economist Intelligence Unit and *The Reference Press*

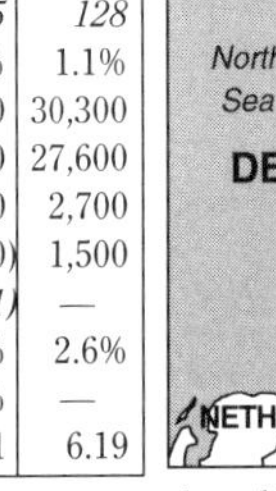

Area: 16,632 sq. mi. (43,076 sq. km)

Official name:
Kingdom of Denmark
Kongeriget Danmark
Official language: Danish
Currency: 1 krone (DK) = 100 øre
Fiscal year ends: December 31

WHO

Monarch: HM Queen Margrethe II, age 51
Heir Apparent: Crown Prince Frederik, age 23
Prime Minister: Poul Schlüter, age 62
Finance Minister: Henning Dyremose, age 46
Minister of Foreign Affairs: Uffe Ellemann-Jensen, age 50
Ambassador to US: Peter P. Dyvig, age 57
US Ambassador to Denmark: Keith L. Brown

WHERE

Executive HQ: Prime Minister, Christiansborg, Prins Jorgens Gard 11, Copenhagen K 1218, Denmark
Embassy in US: 3200 Whitehaven St. NW, Washington, DC 20008
Phone: 202-234-4300
Fax: 202-328-1470
US Embassy in Denmark: Dag Hammarskjolds Alle 24, 2100 Copenhagen O, Denmark
Phone: 011-45-31-42-31-44
Fax: 011-45-35-43-02-23
Chamber of Commerce: Danish Chamber of Commerce, Borsen, DK-1217 Copenhagen, Denmark
Phone: 011-45-33-91-23-23

Denmark has 14 counties and one borough and has diplomatic representatives in 150 countries.

Capital city: Copenhagen
Time change from EST: +6 hours
Avg. high/low temp: Jan. 36°F (2°C)/28°F (-2°C)
July 71°F (22°C)/57°F (14°C)

Urbanization: 86%
Population density: 310/sq. mi. (120/sq. km)

Exports as % of Total		Imports as % of Total	
Germany	18	Germany	22
UK	12	Sweden	12
Sweden	12	UK	7
Norway	6	US	7
Other countries	52	Other countries	52
Total	**100**	**Total**	**100**

WHAT

Origins of GDP	% of Total
Market sector services	39
Mining & manufacturing	20
Government services	18
Transport & communications	9
Building & construction	7
Other	7
Total	**100**

1990 GDP per capita: $24,876
1990 year-end external debt: $31 billion
Literacy rate: 99%
UN Human Development Index: 97%
Human Freedom Index (0-40 scale): 38
Purchasing power as % of US: 74%
Capital city cost of living as % of DC: 142%
Defense as % of GDP: 2%
Education as % of GDP: 7%
Principal airline: Scandinavian Airline System (SAS)
Principal exchange: Copenhagen Stock Exchange

EGYPT

OVERVIEW

Egypt, the most populous Arab country, is the political, educational, and cultural center of the Arab world. It is also one of the poorest Arab countries. Because opportunities are few at home, prior to the Gulf War 2.5 million of its citizens lived abroad, providing technical expertise and manual labor for their Arab neighbors.

Egypt gets most of its foreign exchange ($2 billion in 1990) from the tourists who come to view its Pharaonic legacy. It also exports oil and is an important cotton exporter.

Though only 6.5% of this arid land is arable, agriculture accounts for 34% of its work force and 20% of GDP, mostly because the riverbanks and delta of the Nile are so fertile. In recent years agricultural output has dropped because of lack of government emphasis on this sector. Egypt, once a net food exporter, is no longer self-sufficient in food.

The government is trying to reduce its 70% control of the economy. The government budget deficit has been lowered substantially in the last 2 years, and the trade deficit is dropping. Despite these advances Egypt's red tape, overvalued currency (which creates low-cost imports and high-cost exports), continued government involvement in business, and high population growth rate have stalled the economy. In repayment for Egypt's siding with the US and its allies in the Gulf War, the US forgave Egypt's entire military debt of $7 billion, Arab nations forgave an additional $6 billion, and other countries have agreed to forgive amounts totaling 1/2 Egypt's $49 billion debt. A 1991 IMF loan was conditional on institution of austerity measures, which will be made more painful by revenues lost from lack of overseas remittances, Suez Canal tolls, and tourism in the wake of the Gulf War.

Official name:
Arab Republic of Egypt
Jumhuriyat Misr al-Arabiya
Official language: Arabic
Currency: 1 pound (£E) = 100 piasters
Fiscal year ends: June 30

WHO

President of the Republic: Mohammad Hosni Mubarak, age 63
Prime Minister: Atef Sedky
Deputy Prime Minister for Foreign Relations and Minister of State for Emigration and Egyptian Abroad Affairs: Boutros Ghali
Finance Minister: Mohammed Ahmed al Razzaz
Minister of Foreign Affairs: Amr Moussa
Ambassador to US: El Sayed Abdel Raouf El Reedy
US Ambassador to Egypt: Robert Pelletreau, Jr.

WHEN

In 3200 BC King Menes united Upper and Lower Egypt into a single country that has retained its identity and borders continuously for over 5,000 years. By 1085 BC ancient Egypt had reached the height of its political and economic prosperity under the Pharaohs.

Egypt fell to the Persians and then the Greeks, from whom it got its name — Aiguptos, the Greek name for the ancient capital of Memphis. It passed to the Romans, the Byzantines, various Arab and Turkish leaders, and then the Ottomans.

Modern Egypt began under the rule of Pasha Muhammad Ali, who in 1806 took over leadership of the country for the Ottomans. Through internally generated funds, he made the first efforts at industrializing the country and improved agricultural productivity. However, his profligate grandnephew Ismail, during whose rule the Suez Canal was completed (1869), had no compunction about borrowing from foreigners to fund ill-advised development projects. He eventually lost Egypt's share of stock in the canal to Britain and bankrupted the country.

By 1882 the British were in effective control of Egypt. After decades of puppet rule, Egypt demanded independence, becoming a kingdom in 1922. Apart from the discovery of oil in 1909 (the first discovery of oil in an Arab country), few events of economic import occurred until 1952.

In that year Gamal Nasser seized power, implementing his plan of Arab socialism to redistribute land and nationalize major industries. In 1956 Nasser seized the Suez Canal, prompting the British, French, and Israelis to invade, only to be called off by the UN. Around this time Nasser began construction of the Aswan High Dam, which tamed the Nile River by providing water year-round rather than only in the flood season.

Nasser achieved some improvement in the Egyptian economy and, upon his death in 1970, was succeeded by Anwar Sadat, who allowed some liberalization of the economy. Sadat's administration, lacking the revolutionary fervor of his predecessor's, was plagued by charges of corruption. Egypt's appetite for arms and confrontation with Israel resulted in 2 more unsuccessful and economically devastating wars with Israel (1967 and 1973). From 1977 to 1979 Sadat negotiated peace with Israel; it has held since that time, allowing Egypt to focus on economic rather than military development.

When Sadat was assassinated in 1981, Egypt was experiencing strong economic growth of up to 10% annually. The dramatic fall of oil prices in 1986 put the brakes on the economy but did not cure the chronic inflation problem. Decreasing unemployment and inflation and improving the largely state-owned industrial sector remain challenges in the early 1990s.

WHERE

Executive HQ: President, Al-Etehadia Bldg., Heliopolis, Cairo, Egypt
Embassy in US: 2310 Decatur Pl. NW, Washington, DC 20008
Phone: 202-232-5400
Fax: 202-332-7894
US Embassy in Egypt: Lazougi St., Garden City, Cairo, Egypt
Phone: 011-20-2-355-7371
Fax: 011-20-2-355-7375
Chamber of Commerce: Federation of Egyptian Chambers of Commerce, 4 Midan El Falaki, Cairo, Egypt
Phone: 011-20-2-355-1164

Egypt has 26 governorates and has diplomatic representatives in 98 countries.

Capital city: Cairo
Time change from EST: +7 hours
Avg. high/low temp: Jan. 65°F (18°C)/47°F (8°C)
July 96°F (36°C)/70°F (21°C)

Urbanization: 48%
Population density: 141/sq. mi. (54/sq. km)

Exports as % of Total		Imports as % of Total	
Italy	14	US	15
Romania	12	Germany	10
Israel	10	Italy	7
USSR	6	France	7
Other countries	58	Other countries	61
Total	**100**	**Total**	**100**

WHAT

Origins of GDP	% of Total
Trade, finance & insurance	23
Agriculture	20
Industry & mining	18
Transport & communications	9
Construction	5
Petroleum & electricity	5
Other	20
Total	**100**

1990 GDP per capita: $805
1990 year-end external debt: $49 billion
Literacy rate: 45%
UN Human Development Index: 39%
Human Freedom Index (0-40 scale): 11
Purchasing power as % of US: 16%
Capital city cost of living as % of DC: 122%
Defense as % of GNP: 8%
Education as % of GDP: 6%
Principal airline: Egyptair

HOW MUCH

	4-Year Growth	1986	1987	1988	1989	1990
Population (mil.)	*2.4%*	49.6	50.7	51.9	53.1	54.5
GDP ($ bil.)	*(5.3%)*	*55*	*65*	*78*	*59*	*44*
Real GDP growth rate	—	9.1%	6.4%	6.2%	5.3%	2.1%
Exports ($ mil.)	*13.1%*	2,630	3,120	2,620	3,760	4,300
Imports ($ mil.)	*13.0%*	7,170	8,100	9,370	11,420	11,700
Trade balance ($ mil.)	—	(4,540)	(4,980)	(6,750)	(7,660)	(7,400)
Current account ($ mil.)	—	(1,810)	(250)	(1,190)	(1,690)	(2,150)
Govt. budget bal. ($ mil.)	—	*(11,761)*	*(12,483)*	*(19,070)*	*(7,023)*	*(3,726)*
Consumer inflation	—	23.9%	19.7%	17.6%	21.3%	16.8%
Unemployment rate	—	—	—	—	20.0%	*15.0%*
Exchange rate with US$	—	0.70	0.70	0.70	1.10	1.55

Source: Economist Intelligence Unit and *The Reference Press*

Area: 386,650 sq. mi. (1,001,450 sq. km)

FIJI

OVERVIEW

Fiji is a group of over 800 islands, atolls, and reefs located 1,300 miles north of New Zealand in the South Pacific. About 100 are inhabited, and 90% of the people reside on the 2 largest islands, Viti Levu and Vanua Levu. Fiji is the largest of the Pacific island states.

Natural resources include fertile farmland producing sugar cane, coconut palms, new pine groves for wood and pulp, and subsistence crops. Commercial fishing is gaining in importance, as Fiji's waters contain abundant food fish, including tuna. Mineral resources are limited but include gold, silver, limestone, and copper.

Industry is centered around processing and refining these resources and includes metals mining and smelting, sugar milling, palm oil production, and fish canning.

The population is generally well educated, with an 80% literacy rate, but is divided along ethnic lines. Ethnic Indians (49% of the population) are concentrated in the urban areas while native Fijians (46% of the population, although some now claim that Fijians outnumber Indians) are dispersed in rural areas.

Tourism remains an important part of the economy, and the government is trying to lure foreign investment to develop industry and mineral resources. To lessen its dependence on imported energy, Fiji is exploring for oil.

Fijian troops actively take part in UN peace-keeping missions.

WHEN

Fiji's original inhabitants were Melanesian and Polynesian voyagers who arrived in the 2nd century. The islands were sighted by Dutch navigator Abel Tasman in 1643 and visited by Captain James Cook in 1774. Much of Fiji was charted by Captain William Bligh, after he was cast adrift by mutineers on the HMS *Bounty*.

The first Western settlers were missionaries (mostly Methodists who were welcomed for the end they put to cannibalism), sailors, and sandalwood traders, who brought, respectively, the Gospel, Western diseases (especially measles and influenza), and commercial exploitation. These so disrupted society that, beginning in the 1850s, the Fijians appealed to Britain for protection.

In 1874 Britain agreed to take the islands under its wing and enacted laws to preserve Fijian rights to their own land and protect them from exploitation. Most of the land remained communally owned but was leased by government administrators to commercial farmers, who started large plantations, first to grow cotton and then, after the 1880s, sugar cane.

Indians were imported to work the plantations and the sugar mills. By the time Indian indentured labor was phased out in the 1910s and 1920s, Indians outnumbered native Fijians but had little voice in government. To protect the land of the Fijians, a minority in their own country, the British formed the Native Land Trust Board in 1940. All Fijian land was vested in the trust, which administers it for the good of the Fijian community.

When Fiji gained independence in 1970, Indians, though a majority of the population, remained largely excluded from government and the military, but they represented most of the professional and commercial community.

In 1987, however, Indians managed to gain a parliamentary majority for the first time. To prevent the Indians from taking control, Lt. Col. Sitiveni Rabuka seized power and appointed a new government. Racial violence ensued, leading to an exodus of educated Indians, including teachers, 2/3 of the lawyers, 1/2 of the doctors, and over 1/5 of the civil servants. In addition, sugar production (already in the doldrums because of low prices) was disrupted by a drought; tourists were scared off; and other nations, including the US, Australia, and New Zealand, began aid and trade embargoes. The Indian exodus allowed the Fijians to declare that they were again a majority of the population (a claim widely doubted).

Since the coup the government has encouraged timber production (commercial pine forests), tourism, vertical integration of sugar and alcohol production, coconut oil and copra production, and an increase in commercial fishing. Increased fishing has led to disputes with other nations over fishing rights.

Ethnic tensions collided with economic issues again in 1991. The renewals of many long-term leases granted by Fijian landowners to Indian sugar-cane plantation operators are in question, and Indian refusals to harvest cane make the economic future uncertain. The political future is similarly insecure. A new constitution ensures political power for ethnic Fijians but may not be workable, and General Rabuka seems likely to intervene again.

HOW MUCH

	4-Year Growth	1986	1987	1988	1989	1990
Population (mil.)	*1.0%*	0.71	0.71	0.73	0.74	0.74
GDP ($ bil.)	—	*1.3*	*1.1*	*1.1*	*1.2*	—
Real GDP growth rate	—	8.8%	(7.8%)	(2.5%)	12.1%	5.3%
Exports ($ mil.)	—	276	304	312	372	—
Imports ($ mil.)	—	438	375	454	617	—
Trade balance ($ mil.)	—	(162)	(71)	(142)	(245)	—
Current account ($ mil.)	—	(9)	(27)	40	32	—
Govt. budget bal. ($ mil.)	—	*(86)*	*(87)*	*(65)*	—	—
Consumer inflation	—	1.8%	5.7%	11.7%	6.2%	—
Unemployment rate	—	—	—	—	—	—
Exchange rate with US$	—	1.133	1.244	1.430	1.483	1.481

Source: Economist Intelligence Unit and *The Reference Press*

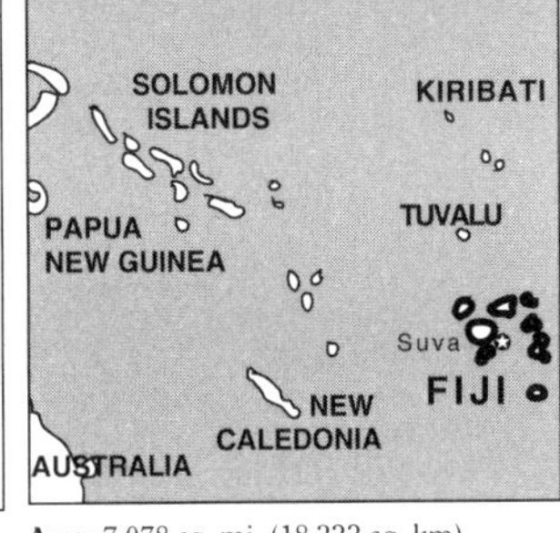

Area: 7,078 sq. mi. (18,333 sq. km)

Official name:
Republic of Fiji
Official language: English
Currency: 1 dollar (F$) = 100 cents
Fiscal year ends: December 31

WHO

President: Ratu Sir Penaia Ganilau, age 73
Army Commander: Major-General Sitiveni Rabuka, age 43
Prime Minister and Minister for Home and Foreign Affairs: Ratu Sir Kamisese Mara, age 71
Minister for Finance and Economic Planning: Josevata Kamikamica
Chargé d'Affaires: Ratu Finau Mara
US Ambassador to Fiji: Evelyn I. H. Teegan

WHERE

Executive HQ: President, Government House, Suva, Fiji
Embassy in US: 2233 Wisconsin Ave. NW, Suite 240, Washington, DC 20007
Phone: 202-337-8320
Fax: 202-337-1996
US Embassy in Fiji: PO Box 218, 31 Loftus St., Suva, Fiji
Phone: 011-679-314-466
Chamber of Commerce: Fiji Chamber of Commerce, Honson Arcade, 66 Thomson Street, Suva, Fiji
Phone: 011-679-313-505
Fax: 011-679-302-183

Fiji has 4 divisions and has diplomatic representatives in 8 countries.

Capital city: Suva
Time change from EST:+17 hours
Avg. high/low temp: Jan. 86°F (29°C)/74°F (23°C)
July 79°F (26°C)/68°F (20°C)

Urbanization: 43%
Population density: 105/sq. mi. (40/sq. km)

Exports as % of Total		Imports as % of Total	
UK	30	Australia	31
Australia	21	New Zealand	17
New Zealand	13	Japan	14
Other countries	36	Other countries	38
Total	**100**	**Total**	**100**

WHAT

Origins of GDP	% of Total
Services	31
Agriculture, forestry, fishing	23
Distribution (including tourism)	17
Transport & communications	13
Manufacturing	11
Utilities, building & construction	5
Total	**100**

1989 GDP per capita: $1,622
1989 year-end external debt: none
Literacy rate: 80%
UN Human Development Index: 69%
Human Freedom Index (0-40 scale): —
Purchasing power as % of US: —
Capital city cost of living as % of DC: —
Defense as % of GNP: 2%
Education as % of GNP: 7%
Principal airline: Air Pacific

BMS

FRANCE

OVERVIEW

Though renowned for fashions, fine wines, perfumes, tourism, and cinema, France has one of the world's most diverse and industrialized economies. It is the world's 4th largest industrial power; major exports include steel, machinery, textiles, and clothes.

France is Europe's top agricultural producer. The largest EC country in land area, it has a varied terrain and 1,200 miles of coastline, including the Riviera. Natural resources include iron ore, coal, bauxite, potash, salt, and fish.

Since WWII the economy has incorporated a free market; government ownership of much of industry, transportation, banking, and insurance; noncoercive central planning; comprehensive social programs; and small family businesses and farms. The stock market, the Paris Bourse, is one of Europe's most active.

Though independent in matters of national security, France has been a leader in the movement toward European economic cooperation and integration.

France emphasizes technological research, especially in nuclear energy, which generates about 70% of its electricity. After decades of subsidizing heavy industries (e.g., Renault), the government, under pressure from the EC, has recently begun withdrawing subsidies to heavy industry but continues to subsidize such high-tech companies as Bull and Thomson.

Concerns in France's future include unemployment (the rate for non–college-educated youth is about 30%), North African immigration, and the general economic slowdown that began in 1990 and continued into 1991.

Official name:
Republic of France
République Française
Official language: French
Currency: 1 franc (FF) = 100 centimes
Fiscal year ends: December 31

WHO

President of the Republic: François Mitterrand, age 75
Prime Minister: Edith Cresson, age 57
Minister of State for Economy, Finance and the Budget: Pierre Bérégovoy, age 66
Minister of State for Foreign Affairs: Roland Dumas, age 69
Ambassador to US: Jacques Andréani, age 62
US Ambassador to France: Walter J. P. Curley

WHERE

Executive HQ: Presidence de la République, Au Palais de l'Elysée, 55 et 57 rue du Faubourg-Saint-Honoré, 75008 Paris, France
Embassy in US: 4101 Reservoir Rd. NW, Washington, DC 20007
Phone: 202-944-6000
Fax: 202-944-6072
US Embassy in France: 2 Ave. Gabriel, 75382 Paris Cedex 08, Paris, France
Phone: 011-33-1-42-96-12-02
Fax: 011-33-1-42-66-97-83
Chamber of Commerce: Chambre de Commerce et d'Industrie International, 38 Cours Albert 1er, Paris, France
Phone: 011-33-1-49-53-28-28
Fax: 011-33-1-42-25-32-81

France has 22 metropolitan regions, 5 overseas departments, 5 overseas territories, and 2 special status territories.

Capital city: Paris
Time change from EST: +6 hours
Avg. high/low temp: Jan. 43°F (6°C)/34°F (1°C)
July 76°F (25°C)/58°F (15°C)

Urbanization: 74%
Population density: 256/sq. mi. (102/sq. km)

Exports	as % of Total	Imports	as % of Total
Germany	16	Germany	19
Italy	12	Italy	11
UK	10	Benelux	9
Benelux	9	US	8
Other countries	53	Other countries	53
Total	**100**	**Total**	**100**

WHEN

The Romans occupied France (then called Gaul) for centuries and introduced their laws, architecture, bureaucracy, and language (basis of French). When the Romans left, France sank into feudalism. In the 11th century trade and commerce began to revive; the Crusades spurred trade in spices and silk. France prospered in the 12th and 13th centuries.

The 14th through 16th centuries saw wars (mostly with England), the Black Plague, the Reformation, the growth of cities, and increased worker mobility. By 1660 over 120 guilds had been formed.

Louis XIV's court (1643–1715) at Versailles consumed vast quantities of luxury goods, creating markets for silks, tapestries, laces, porcelain, and furniture among the nobility and an imitative bourgeoisie. In the 17th century France also began to exploit the resources of the New World. In the 18th century, wars in North America (with England for territorial control) and Europe bankrupted the nation, leading to the French Revolution and the loss of Louis XVI's head. Twenty-six years of revolution and warfare saw the rise of Napoleon and left France at a disadvantage as the Industrial Revolution began.

In the mid-19th century, while England forged ahead, France was plagued by political unrest. Industry remained small-scale. Lack of colonial markets was one reason, and, from the 1860s to the 1890s, France colonized parts of Africa, the Middle East, and Indochina.

After WWI France's economy improved but then collapsed in the Great Depression. After WWII France's colonial empire broke apart, with wars in Indochina (1946–54) and Algeria (1954–62). Charles De Gaulle led post-WWII France from 1944 to 1946 and again from 1958 to 1969. France continues to have a strong influence on and economic relationships with many of its former colonies.

France benefited greatly from the Marshall Plan. From 1952 to 1957 GNP increased 10% per year and its growth averaged 5.5% annually from 1957 to 1973. This growth was achieved in a free market, though heavy industries (steel, autos, utilities) were primarily owned or controlled by the government through "le Plan," a series of advisory 5-year plans aimed at guiding economic growth.

The system worked until 1974, when high oil prices triggered inflation, low growth, and unemployment, which brought Socialists to power under François Mitterrand in 1981. Ironically, it was the Socialists who limited government spending, insisted that industry be run profitably or privatized, and encouraged investment. The 1980s generally saw strong growth and a reduction of inflation.

By mid-1991 GDP growth had declined to 2.5%, unemployment had risen to 9.4%, and the trade deficit was up sharply, leading French pundits to declare a state of "le malaise," an expression describing uneasiness about the future. That same year France's first woman prime minister, Edith Cresson, became known worldwide for her scathing attack on Japanese economic policies.

WHAT

Origins of GDP	% of Total
Services	64
Industry	26
Construction	6
Agriculture	4
Total	**100**

1990 GDP per capita: $21,081
1989 year-end external debt: none
Literacy rate: 99%
UN Human Development Index: 97%
Human Freedom Index (0-40 scale): 35
Purchasing power as % of US: 69%
Capital city cost of living as % of DC: 153%
Defense as % of GNP: 4%
Education as % of GDP: 7%
Principal airline: Air France
Principal exchange: Bourse de Paris

HOW MUCH

	4-Year Growth	1986	1987	1988	1989	1990
Population (mil.)	*0.4%*	55.4	55.6	55.9	56.1	56.4
GDP ($ bil.)	*12.9%*	*731*	*888*	*960*	*962*	*1,190*
Real GDP growth rate	—	2.5%	2.3%	4.2%	3.9%	2.8%
Exports ($ mil.)	*14.7%*	124,800	147,900	167,500	179,200	216,000
Imports ($ mil.)	*15.9%*	129,300	158,000	178,500	192,800	233,800
Trade balance ($ mil.)	—	(4,500)	(10,100)	(11,000)	(13,600)	(17,800)
Current account ($ mil.)	—	2,400	(4,400)	(3,500)	(3,800)	(7,500)
Govt. budget bal. ($ mil.)	—	*(21,255)*	*(22,945)*	*(16,762)*	*(15,674)*	*(16,514)*
Consumer inflation	—	2.7%	3.1%	2.7%	3.6%	3.4%
Unemployment rate	—	10.4%	10.5%	10.0%	9.5%	9.0%
Exchange rate with US$	—	6.93	6.01	5.96	6.38	5.45

Source: Economist Intelligence Unit and *The Reference Press*

Area: 220,668 sq. mi. (551,670 sq. km)

GERMANY

OVERVIEW

Germany is an uneasy mixture of 2 nations: one (formerly West Germany) among the most industrially advanced and wealthy on earth, the other (formerly East Germany) impoverished, environmentally polluted, and technologically retarded by decades of Soviet dominance and Communist government. Germany's task of becoming one people, *Ein Volk*, is complicated by differences in outlook arising from 45 years of separate ideologies.

Since economic unification in July 1990, demand for products from eastern Germany has fallen, owing to poor quality and the strength of the mark; obsolete factories have closed; unemployment and migration to western Germany have increased; and the government has imposed $30 billion worth of new taxes.

Reunited Germany passed the US to become the world's largest exporter in 1990, but the burden of carrying eastern Germany will mean higher inflation, government deficits (now up to $100 billion), and slower growth. Differences in pay and working conditions between the regions are a source of discontent.

International obligations, such as contributions to the Gulf War and the upcoming EC unification, will further complicate matters.

WHEN

Unlike most other Western European peoples, the Germanic tribes were never completely conquered by the Romans and were thus less affected by Rome's intellectual and administrative heritage. Unified briefly by Charlemagne, Germany became a crazy quilt of small principalities and city states (confederated loosely into the Holy Roman Empire with an elected king).

Overland trade routes from Italy passed through Ulm and Augsburg, which became banking centers. Cities on the Baltic and North Sea coasts formed the Hanseatic League to promote trade and mutual security, while settlement of the interior led to the discovery and mining of iron and silver.

In the 16th century silver and gold from Spain's New World conquests brought inflation and a decline in German silver mining. Europe's growing transatlantic orientation brought a decline in German banking, which was centered far from the coasts. Martin Luther's Reformation (begun in 1517) brought 150 years of warfare, divided Catholics and Protestants, and prevented the growth of central government.

After Napoleon's defeat 39 German entities united in the German League, whose largest member, Prussia, eventually united all of Germany into a single country in 1871. Germany dedicated itself to using its resources to catch up with and outdo the rest of Europe. By 1900 Germany led the world in chemical production and electrification, threatened Britain's naval dominion, and had entered the African colonial race.

Germany emerged from WWI largely intact, but reparations exacted by the victors devastated the economy, causing famine and spiraling inflation, leading to the rise of the Nazis. WWII brought war to German soil, and much of its infrastructure was destroyed in fighting or removed by the Russians. After WWII Germany was divided into 4 sectors; the 3 sectors controlled by the US, UK, and France became West Germany, and the one controlled by the Soviets became East Germany.

Sovietized East Germany was collectivized and centralized, becoming the most industrialized and prosperous member of the Eastern bloc, producing consumer goods, electronics, and transportation vehicles, in exchange for Soviet oil and gas. West Germany developed a free-market economy (tempered by social welfare programs), producing steel, machinery, cars, and electronics.

In the 1970s West Germany pursued a program (*Ost-politik*) to maintain and strengthen East Germany's economic ties to the West. Family ties and the proximity of western wealth helped undermine East German government claims about prosperity. In 1989 the end of travel restrictions within the Eastern bloc brought an avalanche of East German emigration (through Hungary to Austria and West Germany). The population hemorrhage caused East Germany to open its borders directly to West Germany. Within weeks, in January 1990, the East German government collapsed. A caretaker government oversaw economic reunification and, in December 1990, political reunification.

Germany's reunification aroused European fears of dominance by the most populous, wealthy nation in Western Europe. In 1991 the German parliament voted to return the seat of government to Berlin, a process expected to take a decade to complete.

HOW MUCH

1986–89 figures for West Germany only	4-Year Growth	1986	1987	1988	1989	1990
Population (mil.)	*6.6%*	61.0	61.1	61.4	62.0	78.8
GNP ($ bil.)	*13.7%*	*896*	*1,120*	*1,206*	*1,203*	*1,500*
Real GNP growth rate	—	2.3%	1.6%	3.7%	3.9%	4.6%
Exports ($ mil.)	*14.2%*	242,600	293,000	322,600	341,100	412,000
Imports ($ mil.)	*16.1%*	190,700	227,600	249,900	269,500	346,000
Trade balance ($ mil.)	—	51,900	65,400	72,700	71,600	66,000
Current account ($ mil.)	—	40,100	46,100	50,500	55,400	44,400
Govt. budget bal. ($ mil.)	—	—	—	—	*(8,000)*	*(61,700)*
Consumer inflation	—	(0.1%)	0.2%	1.3%	2.8%	2.7%
Unemployment rate	—	—	—	8.7%	7.9%	7.2%
Exchange rate with US$	—	2.17	1.80	1.76	1.88	1.62

Source: Economist Intelligence Unit and *The Reference Press*

Area: 137,427 sq. mi. (356,389 sq. km)

Official name:
Federal Republic of Germany
Bundesrepublik Deutschland
Official language: German
Currency: 1 deutsche mark (DM) = 100 pfennigs
Fiscal year ends: December 31

WHO

Federal Chancellor: Helmut Kohl, age 61
Federal President: Richard Von Weizsaecker
Vice-Chancellor and Foreign Minister: Hans-Dietrich Genscher, age 64
Finance Minister: Theodore Waigel, age 52
Ambassador to US: Juergen Ruhfus
US Ambassador to Germany: Vernon A. Walters

WHERE

Executive HQ: Federal Chancellor, Adenauerallee 141, 5300 Bonn 1, Bonn, Federal Republic of Germany
Embassy in US: 4645 Reservoir Rd. NW, Washington, DC 20007
Phone: 202-298-4000
Fax: The Embassy does not send or receive facsimile messages as a matter of official policy.
US Embassy in Germany: Deichmanns Aue, 5300 Bonn 2, Bonn, Federal Republic of Germany
Phone: 011-49-228-3391
Fax: 011-49-228-339-2663
Chamber of Commerce: Federation of German Chambers of Commerce (DIHT), Adenauerallee 148, 5300 Bonn 1, Bonn, Federal Republic of Germany
Phone: 011-49-228-1040
Fax: 011-49-228-104158

Germany has 16 federal states.

Capital city: Berlin
Time change from EST: +6 hours
Avg. high/low temp: Jan. 35°F (2°C)/26°F (-3°C)
July 75°F (24°C)/57°F (14°C)

Urbanization: —
Population density: 573/sq. mi. (221/sq. km)

Exports as % of Total		Imports as % of Total	
France	13	Benelux	17
UK	9	France	12
Italy	9	Italy	9
Netherlands	9	US	8
Other countries	60	Other countries	54
Total	**100**	**Total**	**100**

WHAT

Origins of GDP	% of Total
Services	41
Industry	39
Commerce & transport	15
Agriculture, forestry & fishing	2
Other	3
Total	**100**

1990 GNP per capita: $19,036
1989 year-end external debt: $97 billion
Literacy rate: 99%
UN Human Development Index: 96%
Human Freedom Index (0-40 scale): 35
Purchasing power as % of US: —
Capital city cost of living as % of DC: 127%
Defense as % of GNP: —
Education as % of GDP: 5%
Principal airline: Lufthansa
Principal exchange: Frankfurter Wertpapierbörse

GREECE

OVERVIEW

With over 9,000 miles of coastline and 2,000 islands in the eastern Mediterranean, Greece is a country whose fortunes have risen and fallen on the swells of maritime commerce. It has the largest merchant marine fleet in the world (though many of its vessels fly foreign flags of convenience), and shipping is the country's largest source of foreign exchange. Since the early 1980s shipping (heavily dependent on the depressed oil business) and, therefore, Greece's economy have been depressed.

Greece is closely aligned with the West in trade and defense. A strong Greek lobby in the US has ensured it a large (some would say disproportionate) share of US aid.

With a per capita GDP 1/3 that of other OECD members, Greece is classified by the OECD as a newly industrializing country. Its economic problems include overdependence on a single industry, inflation, and pollution.

While Greece's economy is market-oriented, 70% of the economy is still in government hands. Over 90% of Greek businesses employ fewer than 10 people, many of them family. A thriving underground economy may account for as much as 20% of GDP.

Greece runs a chronic trade deficit. Its traditional enmity with Turkey has delayed development of potential eastern Aegean oil fields that would reduce its imports of oil.

Many of the Socialist government's efforts during the 1980s to intervene in the economy are being undone by the New Democracy party, which came to power in 1990.

WHEN

Greece's first known civilization, that of the Minoans, arose on Crete around 3000 BC. The Minoans were highly developed artistically, socially, and commercially as a result of their control of the seas in the eastern Mediterranean. After the Minoans fell to Dorian invaders from the north around 1200 BC, Greece began its evolution into a series of politically disparate, yet commercially connected, city-states.

The cultural apex of ancient Greece occurred in 5th century BC Athens, where Western philosophy, politics, and drama were invented. The economic peak came with Alexander the Great's empire (336–323 BC), which stretched from Greece to present-day Pakistan. While his reign was short, Alexander introduced Western and Eastern culture to one another, establishing the foundation for the Western world's first international trading empire, under the Romans.

From the 2nd century BC, the Greeks were ruled by Rome, then Byzantium, and then by the Ottoman Turks, under whose rule they lived for 400 years. In 1821 the Greeks began a war of independence against the Ottomans, succeeding in establishing an independent kingdom in 1830. The country remained largely agrarian and concentrated on consolidating traditionally Greek lands until WWII, when it was occupied by the Germans. After the Axis defeat Greece was torn by civil war until 1949.

In the 1950s and 1960s, the economy boomed. During this time men such as Constantine Niarchos and Aristotle Onassis brought prosperity to their homeland by building large fleets of supertankers to carry oil. From 1970 to 1980, GDP grew almost 4.5% annually. In 1981, after 3 decades of strong economic growth, Greece was admitted to the EC as a full member. Since then, however, declining demand for oil (and the tankers to carry it) has wreaked havoc on the economy. GNP actually fell .5% in 1982.

In 1982 the newly elected Socialist government of Georges Papandreau tried to shore up failing industries and expanded public sector employment to make up for lost shipping industry jobs. Massive government budget deficits resulted, reaching 18% of GDP by 1989.

To bring the economy under control in 1990, the New Democracy government instituted austerity measures, including raising taxes, increasing fees for public services, liquidating or privatizing troubled state-owned industries, laying off 100,000 government employees, and discontinuing the inflation indexing of public-sector salaries. These measures are expected to cause unemployment to rise from its 1980s level of 7.5% and have already caused labor unrest.

The new government has targeted Greece's decrepit infrastructure (especially telecommunications) for improvement and hopes to lure foreign investment through economic liberalization and incentives. Remarkably, Greece's Sofokleous Street bourse showed strong gains (over 200%) during 1990, indicating investors' confidence that the government will succeed in turning the economy around.

HOW MUCH

	4-Year Growth	1986	1987	1988	1989	1990
Population (mil.)	*0.2%*	9.97	9.99	10.01	10.03	10.25
GDP ($ bil.)	*14.8%*	*39*	*46*	*53*	*54*	*68*
Real GDP growth rate	—	1.3%	(0.5%)	4.7%	3.4%	0.4%
Exports ($ mil.)	*9.2%*	4,500	5,600	5,900	6,000	6,400
Imports ($ mil.)	*16.4%*	10,200	12,600	13,600	15,100	18,700
Trade balance ($ mil.)	—	(5,700)	(7,000)	(7,700)	(9,100)	(12,300)
Current account ($ mil.)	—	(1,700)	(1,200)	(1,000)	(2,600)	(3,600)
Govt. budget bal. ($ mil.)	—	*(2,656)*	*(4,738)*	*(6,395)*	*(9,637)*	*(12,240)*
Consumer inflation	—	23.0%	16.4%	13.5%	13.7%	20.4%
Unemployment rate	—	7.4%	7.4%	7.7%	7.8%	*9.1%*
Exchange rate with US$	—	140.0	135.4	141.9	162.4	158.5

Source: Economist Intelligence Unit and *The Reference Press*

Area: 51,146 sq. mi. (131,957 sq. km)

Official name:
Hellenic Republic
Elliniki Dimokratia
Official language: Greek
Currency: 1 drachma (Dr) = 100 lepta
Fiscal year ends: December 31

WHO

President: Constantine Karamanlis, age 84
Prime Minister: Constantine Mitsotakis, age 73
Foreign Affairs Minister: Antonis Samaras, age 40
Minister of National Economy: Efthymios Christodoulou
Ambassador to US: Christos Zacharakis
US Ambassador to Greece: Michael G. Sotirhos

WHERE

Executive HQ: Ministry to the Prime Minister, 15 Vasilisis Sophias Ave., 10674 Athens, Greece
Embassy in US: 2221 Massachusetts Ave. NW, Washington, DC 20008
Phone: 202-939-5800
Fax: 202-939-5824
US Embassy in Greece: 91 Vasilisis Sophias Ave., 10160 Athens, Greece
Phone: 011-30-1-721-2951
Fax: 011-30-1-646-3450
Chamber of Commerce: International Chamber of Commerce, 27 Odos Caning St., Athens, Greece
Phone: 011-30-1-610-879

Greece has 51 prefectures and has diplomatic representatives in 60 countries.

Capital city: Athens
Time change from EST: +7 hours
Avg. high/low temp: Jan. 55°F (13°C)/44°F (6°C)
July 92°F (33°C)/73°F (23°C)

Urbanization: 62%
Population density: 200/sq. mi. (78/sq. km)

Exports as % of Total		Imports as % of Total	
Germany	22	Germany	20
Italy	18	Italy	14
France	8	France	8
UK	8	Netherlands	7
Other	44	Other	51
Total	**100**	**Total**	**100**

WHAT

Origins of GDP	% of Total
Manufacturing	17
Agriculture, forestry & fishing	17
Wholesale & retail trade	16
Transport & communications	8
Construction	6
Electricity, gas & water	3
Mining & quarrying	2
Other	31
Total	**100**

1990 GDP per capita: $6,611
1990 year-end external debt: $22 billion
Literacy rate: 90%
UN Human Development Index: 93%
Human Freedom Index (0-40 scale): 31
Purchasing power as % of US: 36%
Capital city cost of living as % of DC: 101%
Defense as % of GNP: 6%
Education as % of GDP: 3%
Principal airline: Olympic Airways
Principal exchange: Athens Stock Exchange

GUATEMALA

OVERVIEW

Guatemala is the most populous country in Central America. Nearly 50% of the population descends from the ancient Mayans. The economy is based on agriculture, which employs 60% of the labor force and provides 2/3 of export revenue. Coffee is the primary export product, followed by bananas, cotton, sugar, and cardamom. More than 1/2 of the country is forested with mahogany, cedar, and other hardwood trees. Guatemala is the 2nd largest supplier (after Mexico) of chicle gum to the US chewing gum industry.

Illiteracy (a very high 50%), internal guerrilla activity, and falling commodity prices are but some of the unfavorable influences on Guatemala's economy. High government spending has led to a rapid increase in inflation (over 40% in 1990, up from 11.4% in 1989). Debt service alone cost nearly 39% of earned export revenue in 1988, though external debt has remained stable for some years and is one of the region's lowest.

GDP grew 3.5% in 1990. Wealth is distributed unevenly, with 2% of the population owning 60% of the rich farmland. Average annual income per capita is $400, but there are more than 100 extremely wealthy families.

Guatemala's relatively backward economy is the result of over 3 decades of struggle between a right-wing military with its wealthy backers and left-wing guerrillas; this conflict has left 100,000 dead.

President Jorge Serrano, elected in 1991 in a clean and honest election, ran for office on a free-market platform. There is considerable disagreement as to whether he will be able to (or even wants to) distance himself from the military and other interests opposed to change. His biggest task will be to improve social services and the standard of living, and to reduce unemployment (which is estimated to be 40% to 45%) and inflation (the 1990 rate was the highest since WWII).

WHEN

The Mayan civilization thrived in Guatemala until 900. Spaniard Pedro de Alvarado arrived in 1523. As Guatemala had little mineral wealth, the Spaniards diverted much of their energy into developing neighboring Mexico.

The Spanish settlers who remained in Guatemala intermarried with the local population and introduced wheat, rice, and sugar cane to the already existing staples of maize and beans. For nearly 300 years the colony was governed from Mexico City by a local governor.

By 1823 Guatemala, El Salvador, Honduras, Nicaragua, and Costa Rica had all declared independence from Spain and had federated as the United Provinces of Central America, with a capital at Guatemala City. The federation collapsed in 1838. For the next century Guatemala was ruled by a series of leaders ranging from the dictatorial religious conservative Rafael Carrera (1838–65) to the dedicated Jorge Ubico (1931–44), during whose tenure the government took an active interest in developing manufacturing, finance, and transportation services.

Juan José Arévalo (1944–50) and Jacobo Arbenz Guzmán (1950–54) undertook major social reforms. Guzmán tried to break up and distribute the large estates to the peasant population, much to the annoyance of such large landowners as United Fruit Company (then known in Central America as the Octopus, now known as Chiquita Brands International). United was instrumental in Guzmán's overthrow, which began a string of right-wing governments that have steadfastly served the economic interests of the nearly feudal society dominated by large landowners.

In the 1960s economic growth was over 5%, the highest in Latin America, owing to exports of cotton, sugar, and coffee. Real GDP increased by an average of 5.7% annually in the 1970s, fueled by internal demand and large government projects (hydroelectric dams, housing, and road building).

The early 1980s saw the effects of declining coffee prices, high global interest rates, and higher prices for imported oil. GDP growth averaged only 1% annually from 1981 to 1983. Hard economic times brought a succession of military coups during the early 1980s. Democracy returned in 1985, but the military years had emptied the treasury, and the IMF had suspended all loans. Endemic corruption, open leftist insurgency, and saber-rattling from the military undercut President Vinizio Cerezo's (1985–90) ability to effect reform. Foreign investors continue to avoid the strife-torn country, but agricultural exports remain high. Newly elected President Serrano faces a formidable task in improving Guatemala's economy and the well-being of its people.

HOW MUCH

	4-Year Growth	1986	1987	1988	1989	1990
Population (mil.)	*3.2%*	8.2	8.4	8.7	8.9	9.3
GDP ($ bil.)	—	*8.4*	*7.0*	*7.8*	*8.5*	—
Real GDP growth rate	—	0.1%	3.1%	3.5%	4.6%	3.5%
Exports ($ mil.)	*4.9%*	1,044	978	1,073	1,126	1,265
Imports ($ mil.)	*16.3%*	876	1,333	1,413	1,485	1,605
Trade balance ($ mil.)	—	168	(355)	(340)	(359)	(340)
Current account ($ mil.)	—	(18)	(443)	(414)	(367)	(350)
Govt. budget bal. ($ mil.)	—	*(127)*	*(195)*	*(155)*	*(213)*	—
Consumer inflation	—	36.9%	12.3%	10.8%	11.4%	40.5%
Unemployment rate	—	—	—	—	—	—
Exchange rate with US$	—	1.88	2.50	2.62	2.82	4.51

Source: Economist Intelligence Unit and *The Reference Press*

Area: 42,042 sq. mi. (108,889 sq. km)

Official name:
Republic of Guatemala
República de Guatemala
Official language: Spanish
Currency: 1 quetzal (Q) = 100 centavos
Fiscal year ends: December 31

WHO

President: Jorge Antonio Serrano Elias, age 46
Vice-President: H. E. Gustavo Espina Salguero
Minister of Finance: Richard Aitkenhead Castillo
Minister of Foreign Affairs: Alvaro Arzú Irigoyen
Ambassador (designate) to US: Juan José Caso Fanjul
US Ambassador to Guatemala: Thomas F. Stroock

WHERE

Executive HQ: President, Palacio Nacional, Guatemala City, Guatemala
Embassy in US: 2220 R St. NW, Washington, DC 20008
Phone: 202-745-4952
Fax: 202-745-1908
US Embassy in Guatemala: 7-01 Avenida de la Reforma, Zone 10, Guatemala City, Guatemala
Phone: 011-502-2-31-15-41
Fax: 011-502-2-31-88-85
Chamber of Commerce: Cámara de Comercio de Guatemala, 10a Calle 3-80, Zone 1, Guatemala City, Guatemala
Phone: 011-502-2-82-68-15
Fax: 011-502-2-51-41-97

Guatemala has 22 departments and has diplomatic representatives in 28 countries.

Capital city: Guatemala City
Time change from EST: -1 hour
Avg. high/low temp: Jan. 73°F (23°C)/53°F (12°C)
July 78°F (26°C)/60°F (16°C)

Urbanization: 33%
Population density: 221/sq. mi. (85/sq. km)

Exports as % of Total		Imports as % of Total	
US	33	US	36
El Salvador	11	Venezuela	7
Germany	7	Japan	6
Costa Rica	6	Germany	6
Other countries	43	Other countries	45
Total	**100**	**Total**	**100**

WHAT

Origins of GDP	% of Total
Agriculture	26
Commerce	25
Manufacturing	15
Transport & utilities	10
Construction	2
Other	22
Total	**100**

1989 GDP per capita: $947
1990 year-end external debt: $3 billion
Literacy rate: 50%
UN Human Development Index: 49%
Human Freedom Index (0-40 scale): —
Purchasing power as % of US: 11%
Capital city cost of living as % of DC: 64%
Defense as % of GNP: 1%
Education as % of GNP: —
Principal airline: Aviateca (Empresa Guatemalteca de Aviación)

HONDURAS

OVERVIEW

The phrase "banana republic" was invented to describe Honduras. Though the 2nd largest in area (after Nicaragua) of the Central American countries, Honduras is the poorest and least developed. Bananas and coffee together account for more than 50% of export revenue. Agriculture accounts for over 20% of GDP and employs 2/3 of the labor force.

Honduras has zinc, silver, lead, coal, iron ore, and tin deposits, but extraction of these minerals provides only 2% of GDP.

Industry (only about 16% of GDP) is limited to textiles, cigar production, food processing, and wood products.

Wealth is unevenly distributed and there is almost no middle class. Most of the agricultural land is foreign owned (much of it by US banana growers), as is most of the industrial base. Per capita income hovers at a pathetic $130 annually. Malnutrition is widespread, as is underemployment. Over 40% of the population is illiterate.

Honduras has borrowed heavily (debt service is 30% of GDP) and failed to meet its payments. In the 1980s economic growth averaged 3.8% annually, barely ahead of Honduras's 3% population growth, a situation that impedes substantial economic progress.

One thing allows Honduras to keep functioning in the face of these grim economic numbers — massive US economic and military aid. Honduras served as the front line for US support of Nicaragua's contras. As a consequence it received and continues to receive a disproportionate share of US regional aid.

Honduras has lately become an assembly center for Hong Kong, Singapore, Taiwan, and South Korean firms seeking low-cost labor. Wisconsin clothes maker Oshkosh B'Gosh recently opened its first foreign plant there.

WHEN

Previously occupied by remnants of the Mayan civilization, Honduras was invaded in 1524 by rival Spanish factions from Guatemala seeking mineral wealth. In the 16th century economic activity consisted of gold and silver mining and subsistence farming; by 1600 ore deposits were played out. With the exception of a modest cattle ranching industry that arose in the early 1700s and a minor revival of mining activity in the 1730s, Honduras remained an undeveloped, sparsely colonized hinterland of the Spanish empire attached to the Captaincy General of Guatemala during the 18th century.

The British settled on the Honduran coastline beginning in the 1700s. Britain's economic interests lay in trade and lumber production, while its political interests lay in weakening Spain. Spain drove Britain from Honduras in the 1780s and was able to control Honduras until 1821 when Honduras declared independence. Dominated by small-scale cattle ranching and subsistence farming, Honduras's economy stagnated as a series of conflicts preoccupied the government.

Large-scale silver mining was resurrected in the late 1800s. Though the mining developed export revenues, Honduras derived little real benefit, as the mines were foreign owned and provided little employment. Several local farmers who began growing bananas were so successful that they attracted foreign interest. By 1910 over 80% of the banana acreage was controlled by such US companies as United Fruit (now Chiquita Brands) and Castle & Cooke (now Dole Food Company).

While the growth of the banana industry brought roads and railroads, this infrastructure served the foreign growers, only marginally benefiting the rest of the country. Bananas remained the dominant export product from 1910 until the late 1940s.

From 1932 to 1948 President Tiburcio Carias Andino tried to improve the lot of his people, building schools and undertaking reforms. In the early 1950s the government embarked on a program of export diversification and agricultural modernization. These efforts generated exports of beef, coffee, and cotton. During this period the first industrial efforts also began. Industry's rate of growth rapidly outpaced that of agriculture. In the 1960s economic growth accelerated but was brought up short by a series of man-made (oil price increases) and natural (Hurricane Fifi) disasters in the early 1970s. The late 1970s saw another period of prosperity as world commodity prices boomed and Honduras recovered.

Good times were short-lived. The global recession of the early 1980s, coupled with a nearly 50% decline in coffee prices, wreaked havoc on the economy. Economic growth was negative in 1982. Since then the drop in oil prices has improved economic matters somewhat. However, the country is still burdened with a massive debt, an essentially colonial economy, and political instability.

HOW MUCH

	4-Year Growth	1986	1987	1988	1989	1990
Population (mil.)	*3.1%*	4.51	4.66	4.80	4.95	5.10
GDP ($ bil.)	*11.2%*	*3.8*	*4.1*	*4.5*	*4.9*	*5.8*
Real GDP growth rate	—	2.8%	5.2%	4.8%	2.1%	(1.0%)
Exports ($ mil.)	*2.7%*	891	844	893	967	990
Imports ($ mil.)	*4.2%*	874	894	917	964	1,030
Trade balance ($ mil.)	—	17	(50)	(24)	3	(40)
Current account ($ mil.)	—	(255)	(306)	(319)	(302)	(350)
Govt. budget bal. ($ mil.)	—	*(246)*	*(149)*	*(137)*	—	—
Consumer inflation	—	4.4%	2.5%	4.5%	9.9%	28.0%
Unemployment rate	—	13.5%	—	—	—	—
Exchange rate with US$	—	2.00	2.00	2.00	2.00	2.00

Source: Economist Intelligence Unit and *The Reference Press*

Area: 43,277 sq. mi. (112,088 sq. km)

Official name:
Republic of Honduras
República de Honduras
Official language: Spanish
Currency: 1 lempira (L) = 100 centavos
Fiscal year ends: December 31

WHO

President: Rafael Leonardo Callejas, age 48
Minister of Finance and Public Credit: Benjamín Villanueva
Minister of Foreign Relations: Mario Carias-Zapata
Ambassador to US: Jorge Ramón Hernández-Alcerro
US Ambassador to Honduras: Cresencio S. Arcos

WHERE

Executive HQ: President, Casa Presidencial, Tegucigalpa DC, Honduras
Embassy in US: 3007 Tilden St. NW, Washington, DC 20008
Phone: 202-966-7702
Fax: 202-966-9751
US Embassy in Honduras: Avenida La Paz, Tegucigalpa, Honduras
Phone: 011-504-32-3120
Fax: 011-504-32-0027
Chamber of Commerce: Cámara de Comercio e Industrias de Tegucigalpa, Apartado No. 3444, Boulevard Centroamerica, Frente a Hondutel, Tegucigalpa DC, Honduras
Phone: 011-505-32-8210

Honduras has 18 departments and one federal district and has diplomatic representatives in 24 countries.

Capital city: Tegucigalpa
Time change from EST: -1 hour
Avg. high/low temp: Jan. 77°F (25°C)/57°F (14°C)
July 81°F (27°C)/64°F (18°C)

Urbanization: 43%
Population density: 118/sq. mi. (45/sq. km)

Exports as % of Total		Imports as % of Total	
US	50	US	52
Japan	10	Japan	9
Germany	8	Venezuela	5
Other countries	32	Other countries	34
Total	**100**	**Total**	**100**

WHAT

Origins of GDP	% of Total
Agriculture	21
Manufacturing	16
Commerce	13
Transport & utilities	10
Banking, finance & insurance	7
Other	33
Total	**100**

1990 GDP per capita: $1,137
1989 year-end external debt: $3 billion
Literacy rate: 56%
UN Human Development Index: 49%
Human Freedom Index (0-40 scale): —
Purchasing power as % of US: 6%
Capital city cost of living as % of DC: —
Defense as % of GNP: 2%
Education as % of GDP: 4%
Principal airlines: SAHSA (Servicios Aéreos de Honduras), TAN (Transportes Aéreos Nacionales)

HONG KONG

OVERVIEW

With nearly 6 million people in just over 400 square miles, Hong Kong is one of the most densely populated places in the world. It has the 2nd highest GDP per capita of any industrialized country in East Asia (after Japan). Hong Kong serves as a hub for many multinational companies' operations in Asia; 18,000 US citizens live there.

Facing a return to Chinese control in 1997, Hong Kong is uncertain about the future. When China agreed to make Hong Kong a Special Administrative Region, people hoped union with China would not be too disruptive. But recent Chinese attempts to discourage self-government and interfere with plans for a new airport, and the 1989 Tiananmen Square massacre, have caused disillusionment.

Emigration, already high, rose to 1,200 per week in 1990. Management talent is scarce and mobile; employment is near capacity, making expansion difficult; inflation is increasing as the remaining workers command higher salaries. Capital is also beginning to flee, as such companies as the Hongkong and Shanghai Bank (HSBC) and Jardine Matheson transfer their headquarters out. There has also been an increase in overseas investment: 50% of all foreign investment has been made since 1986. Though the majority goes to China, a great deal of money is also going into other Asian nations.

GDP growth has decreased dramatically since 1989, plunging from 13.9% in 1987 to 7.9% in 1988 and 2.4% in 1990.

WHEN

Britain received Hong Kong in 1842 when it won a war against China, thus allowing the British East India Company to continue importing opium into China. Renamed Victoria, the island became a base for protection of shipping from Shanghai. More clashes led to China's cession of part of Kowloon in 1860, and in 1898 the British leased a section of the mainland and several islands (the New Territories).

A good harbor and European control made Hong Kong a successful port and trading city for banks, insurance companies, and international trading companies. Port facilities and shipbuilding and servicing industries grew. The population grew from 500,000 in 1916 to over one million in 1939, as migrants entered freely from China to work for a while and then return home. Hong Kong grew peacefully until the Japanese arrived in 1941.

Japanese occupation lasted until 1945. Population fell during WWII but swelled again during the Chinese civil war, reaching 2 million in 1950 and forcing Britain to close the borders. The influx continued illegally.

With a large population and free trade, Hong Kong became a transportation, commercial services, and manufacturing center for East Asia. While China remained closed off from direct trade with most of the world, it used Hong Kong as a conduit for world trade.

Hong Kong's most important manufacturing sector is textiles. In the 1960s production of fabric predominated, but finished clothing later became more important. Initially the clothing was low-fashion, low-cost, and mass-produced, but it became more upscale in the 1980s. Assembly of electronics, watches, and cameras is also important for Hong Kong.

China claimed Hong Kong in 1933, 1948, and 1962. In 1982, with the end of the UK's lease on the New Territories nearing, negotiations on Hong Kong's future began. Though excluded from the lease, Kowloon and Hong Kong Island (both granted in perpetuity by China to the UK) depended on the New Territories for food and water and were part of China's claim. In 1984 Britain agreed to return all of Hong Kong to China in 1997 as a Special Administrative Region, whose commercial, civil, and political rights and laws will continue for 50 years.

Hong Kong's economy fluctuated during the 1980s. From 9.5% in 1984, GDP growth rates fell to -0.1% in 1985, then rose to 11.9% in 1987. Real estate values have been similarly variable, collapsing in the early 1980s following their 1980–81 peak, then rising in 1988 and 1989. Much of this was due to uncertainty about 1997. The departure of skilled laborers caused inflation; wages rose 44% between 1985 and 1988.

Hong Kong is buffeted by international events, too. Its dollar is linked to the US dollar and rises and falls with it. Hong Kong's stock market was so hard hit in 1987 that the government intervened for the first time.

A dispute with China during 1990 and 1991 about China's right to approve expenditures for a new airport, resolved in China's favor in 1991, suggests that the 1997 transition may not be smooth.

HOW MUCH

	4-Year Growth	1986	1987	1988	1989	1990
Population (mil.)	*1.4%*	5.53	5.61	5.68	5.76	5.84
GDP ($ bil.)	*6.5%*	*26*	*29*	*32*	*32*	*33*
Real GDP growth rate	—	11.9%	13.9%	7.9%	2.3%	2.4%
Exports ($ mil.)	*23.3%*	35,440	48,480	63,210	73,140	82,000
Imports ($ mil.)	*23.5%*	35,400	48,470	63,950	72,150	82,400
Trade balance ($ mil.)	—	40	10	(740)	990	(400)
Current account ($ mil.)	—	—	—	*3,000*	*5,600*	*5,500*
Govt. budget bal. ($ mil.)	—	—	*1,218*	*1,769*	*1,731*	*2,462*
Consumer inflation	—	2.3%	5.5%	7.4%	10.1%	9.8%
Unemployment rate	—	—	—	—	1.3%	*1.7%*
Exchange rate with US$	—	7.8	7.8	7.8	7.8	7.8

Source: Economist Intelligence Unit and *The Reference Press*

Area: 411 sq. mi. (1,064 sq. km)

Official name: British Dependent Territory of Hong Kong
Official languages: Cantonese, English
Currency: 1 dollar (HK$) = 100 cents
Fiscal year ends: March 31

WHO

Governor and Commander in Chief: Sir David Clive Wilson, age 56
Chief Secretary: Sir David Robert Ford
Financial Secretary: Sir Piers Jacobs
Attorney General: Michael Thomas
US Consul General to Hong Kong: Richard L. Williams

WHERE

Representation in US: Hong Kong Trade Development Council, 673 Fifth Ave., 4th Fl., New York, NY 10022
Phone: 212-838-8688
Fax: 212-838-8941
US Consulate General in Hong Kong: Box 30, 26 Garden Rd., Hong Kong
Phone: 011-852-5-239-011
Fax: 011-852-5-845-1598
Chamber of Commerce: Hong Kong General Chamber of Commerce, 22/F United Centre, 95 Queensway, Hong Kong
Phone: 011-852-5-299-229

Hong Kong consists of a main island, the peninsula of Kowloon, and the New Territories; has 19 administrative districts; and has representatives in 18 countries.

Capital city: Hong Kong
Time change from EST: +13 hours
Avg. high/low temp: Jan. 64°F (18°C)/56°F (13°C)
July 87°F (31°C)/78°F (26°C)

Urbanization: 93%
Population density: 14,209/sq. mi. (5,489/sq. km)

Exports as % of Total		Imports as % of Total	
China	25	China	37
US	24	Japan	16
Germany	7	Taiwan	9
Japan	6	US	8
Other countries	38	Other countries	30
Total	**100**	**Total**	**100**

WHAT

Origins of GDP	% of Total
Wholesale & retail import & export trade, hotels & restaurants	24
Finance, insurance, real estate & business services	20
Manufacturing	18
Construction	5
Other	33
Total	**100**

1990 GDP per capita: $5,695
1990 year-end external debt: none
Literacy rate: 90%
UN Human Development Index: 93%
Human Freedom Index (0-40 scale): 26
Purchasing power as % of US: 60%
Capital city cost of living as % of DC: 119%
Defense as % of GNP: 1%
Education as % of GDP: 4%
Principal airline: Cathay Pacific
Principal exchange: The Stock Exchange of Hong Kong Ltd.

HUNGARY

OVERVIEW

Hungary, a net exporter of food, has some of the most fertile land in central Europe and produces corn, wheat, potatoes, fruit, and excellent wines. Mineral resources include lignite, bauxite, and enough oil for 1/3 of the country's energy needs. Industries include steel, aluminum, and motor transport.

Although Hungary had a sizable head start among Eastern European nations that were reforming their economies, the transition to a market economy is proving difficult. In spite of considerable foreign investment, unemployment has risen to an estimated 200,000, and inflation rose to 30% in 1990. There are also balance-of-payment and deficit difficulties. Living standards have declined dramatically.

With 50% of GDP derived from exports, Hungary, to succeed in international markets, must hold the line on prices; this is becoming more difficult, as Hungary depends on Soviet oil and Eastern bloc imports for raw materials, which are no longer provided at below-market prices or for barter.

On the positive side, hard-currency exports rose 10% in 1990 and business formations have increased more than 80% since 1989. The state is committed to returning 5% to 8% of its industries to the private sector annually. Private ownership in services is growing quickly and in some fields, such as tourism, is replacing state-ownership. Banking regulations are being adapted to attract international investment.

Hungary has applied for Council of Europe membership and will likely eventually seek EC membership.

WHEN

The Magyars settled Hungary in the 9th century. Cattle breeding was the primary economic activity. A powerful kingdom by the 14th century, Hungary was overrun by Turks in 1526 and came under Austrian rule in 1699. In 1867 Hungary became part of a dual monarchy with Austria, under the Hapsburgs, and coal mining, steel mills, and engineering businesses sprang up. However, the economy remained primarily agrarian, with most people living in poverty.

Hungary became independent in 1918. Communists established the Hungarian Soviet Republic in 1919, nationalizing banks and industry and ending private land ownership, but they fell from power later that year.

Hungary lost 75% of its territory and 60% of its population in WWI. Deprived of raw materials from these territories, industry was severely disrupted. Hoping to regain the lost lands and isolated by hostile neighbors, Hungary sided with Germany in WWII. In 1945 the Soviet army occupied Budapest.

Hungary did not become Communist until 1949, after other parties were rendered impotent by underground attacks. A Stalinist economy emphasized heavy industry and collectivized agriculture. Between 1948 and 1953, living standards fell 20%. Dissatisfaction with economic conditions led to unrest, culminating in a 1956 anti-Soviet rebellion, and the USSR invaded.

By 1962 collectivization was 90% complete, and most businesses were government controlled. But in 1963 the government began to encourage small private businesses such as repair and mechanic shops. In 1968 government control of state businesses was relaxed, and industrial management was allowed to make its own decisions. The economy benefited, especially in agriculture, where artificially low prices had depressed production. In the mid-1960s Hungary was a food importer; by the 1980s it was an exporter. It also began to borrow in the West, accumulating an $8 billion hard-currency debt by 1981.

In 1982 Hungary joined the IMF and the World Bank and began privatizing state-owned businesses. To control debt, Hungary instituted austerity measures while receiving loans from the IMF and West German banks. A 1986 trade deficit triggered another round of austerity actions in 1987. Hard-currency debt was almost $18 billion by 1988.

In the mid-1980s Hungary eliminated subsidies and allowed incentive pay and employee discharge. The private sector was encouraged to grow. Concurrently, power struggles within the Communist party led to a voluntary erosion of power. By 1989 the government had called for a multiparty system and the Communist party had changed its name to the Hungarian Socialist party. In late 1989 thousands of East German refugees flooded Hungary, which opened its borders and allowed them into Austria, ending Eastern bloc cohesion and contributing to the fall of communism throughout most of Eastern Europe. Free elections in 1990 installed a non-Communist coalition government.

HOW MUCH

	4-Year Growth	1986	1987	1988	1989	1990
Population (mil.)	*(0.1%)*	10.62	10.60	10.59	10.38	10.57
GDP ($ bil.)	*4.2%*	*24*	*26*	*28*	*29*	*34*
Real GDP growth rate	—	1.5%	4.1%	(0.1%)	(0.2%)	(5.0%)
Exports ($ mil.)	*11.9%*	4,500	5,020	5,880	6,070	7,060
Imports ($ mil.)	*5.5%*	4,940	5,390	5,340	5,510	6,120
Trade balance ($ mil.)	—	(440)	(370)	540	560	940
Current account ($ mil.)	—	(1,490)	(880)	(800)	(1,440)	150
Govt. budget bal. ($ mil.)	—	*(988)*	*(732)*	*(202)*	*(824)*	—
Consumer inflation	—	5.3%	8.6%	15.7%	17.0%	30.0%
Unemployment rate	—	—	—	—	0.0%	1.0%
Exchange rate with US$	—	45.83	46.97	50.41	59.07	62.82

Source: Economist Intelligence Unit and *The Reference Press*

Area: 35,919 sq. mi. (93,030 sq. km)

Official name:
Republic of Hungary
Magyar Köztársaság
Official language: Magyar
Currency: 1 forint (Ft) = 100 fillér
Fiscal year ends: December 31

WHO

President of the Republic: Arpád Göncz, age 69
Prime Minister: József Antall, age 59
Minister of Finance: Milhály Kupa, age 50
Minister of Foreign Affairs: Géza Jeszensky, age 50
Chargé d'Affaires: Eniko Bolo Bas
Ambassador to Hungary: Charles H. Thomas

WHERE

Executive HQ: President of the Republic, Kossuth Liter tér 1-3, 1055 Budapest, Hungary
Embassy in US: 3910 Shoemaker St. NW, Washington, DC 20008
Phone: 202-362-6730
Fax: 202-966-8135
US Embassy in Hungary: V. Szabadsag tér 12, American Embassy, Budapest, Hungary
Phone: 011-36-1-112-6450
Fax: 011-36-1-132-8934
Chamber of Commerce: Magyar Gazdasagi Kamara, Hungarian Chamber of Commerce, PO Box 106, Kossuth Lajos tér 6/8, H-1055 Budapest, Hungary
Phone: 011-36-1-131-4155
Fax: 011-36-1-153-1285

Hungary has 19 counties.

Capital city: Budapest
Time change from EST: +6 hours
Avg. high/low temp: Jan. 34°F (1°C)/25°F (-4°C)
July 82°F (28°C)/62°F (16°C)

Urbanization: 60%
Population density: 294/sq. mi. (114/sq. km)

Exports as % of Total		Imports as % of Total	
Germany	20	USSR	20
USSR	18	Germany	18
Austria	7	Austria	9
Other	55	Other	53
Total	**100**	**Total**	**100**

WHAT

Origins of GDP	% of Total
Services	44
Manufacturing, mining & utilities	30
Agriculture & forestry	20
Construction	6
Total	**100**

1990 GDP per capita: $3,253
1990 year-end external debt: $22 billion
Literacy rate: 99%
UN Human Development Index: 91%
Human Freedom Index (0-40 scale): 7
Purchasing power as % of US: 31%
Capital city cost of living as % of DC: 59%
Defense as % of GNP: 3%
Education as % of GNP: 6%
Principal airline: MALÉV Hungarian
Principal exchange: Budapest Stock Exchange

INDIA

OVERVIEW

India, with the world's 2nd largest population (after China), occupies most of the South Asian sub-continent; it has a varied terrain, from mountains (the Himalayas) to tropical jungles. It has iron ore, coal, manganese, copper, nickel, and limited supplies of oil.

Agriculture accounts for 35% of GDP and over 70% of employment. India exports tea and sugar, but most crops, including rice, maize, and millet, are for domestic consumption. India is the largest exporter of gemstones.

Industry, divided between large-scale plants (generally government owned) and small privately owned operations, produces primarily for domestic consumption. Products include steel, heavy machinery, textiles, consumer goods, and chemicals. High-tech industries, particularly software design, are increasingly important. In the late 1980s the government began to repudiate its traditional policy of economic self-sufficiency in favor of increased trade and foreign investment. In 1991 new prime minister P. V. Rao oversaw the repeal of most of the restrictive laws on foreign trade.

Though India has an ample supply of educated workers, its school system emphasizes higher education over lower, so the overall literacy rate is low. Unemployment and underemployment combined run over 20%. This can be expected to increase as the economy slows in response to global recession and cessation of worker remittances in the wake of the Gulf War.

WHEN

Indian civilization began in 2500 BC, but it was politically fragmented until the 19th century. The Islamic Moguls conquered India in the 16th century, just after Europeans reached India by sea. In the 16th and 17th centuries, the Portuguese, Dutch, and French established coastal bases for trade.

Britain's East India Company, a private trading combine, arrived in 1619. Through conquest and treaties with local rulers, the company gradually came to rule the subcontinent. In 1857 a mutiny of Indian troops led the British government to take control.

Britain built roads and railways, united the country via telegraph, and organized an efficient national administration. When Britain opened government positions to Indians and British schools to their sons, Mohandas Gandhi used this opportunity to study law in England, eventually returning to lead the independence movement. During the 19th and early 20th centuries, India's economy was classically colonial — the British grew nonfood crops (e.g., jute) for export and made no effort to industrialize until the mid-1920s.

Agitation for independence grew during the 1920s and 1930s. At independence (1947), differences between Hindus and Muslims led to partition of British India into present-day India and Pakistan (from which Bangladesh broke away in 1971), to mass migrations between the 2 countries, and to mass murder. Tension over borders and territories (e.g., Kashmir) continues, sometimes causing war.

Prime Minister Jawaharlal Nehru attempted to eradicate India's caste system and to combat rural poverty by promoting steel, textiles, consumer goods, and machinery. India's import-substitution drive resulted in output increases of 50% between 1951 and 1959, raising industrial contribution to GDP to 22% by the early 1960s. In the 1960s government sought to control the direction and growth of industry with regulation designed to prevent monopolies. Limits were placed on expansion of production in some industries, especially luxury goods.

The 1960s green revolution made the country nearly self-sufficient in grain by the 1970s. Increasing prosperity in agriculture helped lead to the emergence of an entrepreneurial class opposing strict regulation (which led to formation of a large underground economy, from which the government derived no tax benefits).

Because of the size of the domestic market, the government has traditionally underemphasized exports and discouraged foreign investments. This changed in the late 1980s and early 1990s. In 1991, as oil prices rose, continuing political instability and religious intolerance complicated election-year politics. In May former prime minister and candidate Rajiv Gandhi was assassinated (as his mother Indira had been by Sikhs in 1984), by an alleged Sri Lankan Tamil separatist.

New prime minister Rao announced that he would seek closer trading ties with the US. In July 1991 India narrowly avoided defaulting on its debts, a situation brought on by its severe trade deficit.

HOW MUCH

	4-Year Growth	1986	1987	1988	1989	1990
Population (mil.)	*2.2%*	775	793	810	830	844
GDP ($ bil.)	*2.9%*	*207*	*227*	*251*	*223*	*231*
Real GDP growth rate	—	3.9%	3.8%	10.6%	4.5%	4.5%
Exports ($ mil.)	*17.5%*	9,700	11,600	14,000	16,500	18,500
Imports ($ mil.)	*12.1%*	15,500	17,000	19,500	21,500	24,500
Trade balance ($ mil.)	—	(5,800)	(5,400)	(5,500)	(5,000)	(6,000)
Current account ($ mil.)	—	(4,600)	(4,800)	(7,200)	(6,200)	(8,000)
Govt. budget bal. ($ mil.)	—	*(18,379)*	*(20,217)*	*(20,302)*	*(18,266)*	*(21,986)*
Consumer inflation	—	8.7%	9.2%	9.1%	7.5%	12.0%
Unemployment rate	—	—	—	—	—	9.9%
Exchange rate with US$	—	12.61	12.96	13.92	17.23	17.50

Source: Economist Intelligence Unit and *The Reference Press*

USSR
AFG.
CHINA
PAK.
NEPAL
BHUTAN
New Delhi
INDIA
Calcutta
MYAN.
Bombay
BANG.
Bangalore
Arabian Sea
Bay of Bengal
Madras
Indian Ocean
SRI LANKA

Area: 1,268,884 sq. mi. (3,287,263 sq. km)

Official name:
Republic of India
Bharat
Official language: Hindi in the Devanagari script
Currency: 1 rupee (Rs) = 100 paise
Fiscal year ends: March 31

WHO

President: Ramaswamy Venkataraman, age 81
Prime Minister: P. V. Narasimha Rao
Minister of Finance: Manmohan Singh
Minister of External Affairs: Madhavsinh Solanki
Ambassador to US: Abid Hussain
US Ambassador to India: William Clark, Jr.

WHERE

Executive HQ: President, Rashtrapti Bhavan, New Delhi 110004, India
Embassy in US: 2107 Massachusetts Ave. NW, Washington, DC 20008
Phone: 202-939-7000
Fax: 202-939-7027
US Embassy in India: Shanti Path, Chanakyapuri, New Delhi 110021, India
Phone: 011-91-11-600651
Fax: 011-91-11-6872028
Chamber of Commerce: Federation of Indian Chambers of Commerce and Industry, Federation House, Tansen Marg, New Delhi 110001, India
Phone: 011-91-11-344124
Fax: 011-91-11-3320714

India has 25 states and 7 union territories and has diplomatic representatives in 95 countries.

Capital city: New Delhi
Time change from EST: +10.5 hours
Avg. high/low temp: Jan. 70°F (21°C)/44°F (7°C)
July 96°F (36°C)/81°F (27°C)

Urbanization: 28%
Population density: 665/sq. mi. (257/sq. km)

Exports as % of Total		Imports as % of Total	
US	18	US	11
USSR	13	Japan	9
Japan	11	Germany	9
Germany	6	UK	9
Other countries	52	Other countries	62
Total	**100**	**Total**	**100**

WHAT

Origins of GDP	% of Total
Agriculture, forestry, mining & fisheries	35
Industry	27
Transport, communications & trade	17
Real estate & finance	10
Other services	11
Total	**100**

1990 GDP per capita: $274
1989 year-end external debt: $62 billion
Literacy rate: 36%
UN Human Development Index: 31%
Human Freedom Index (0-40 scale): 14
Purchasing power as % of US: 5%
Capital city cost of living as % of DC: 48%
Defense as % of GNP: 3%
Education as % of GNP: 1%
Principal airline: Air India
Principal exchange: The Stock Exchange, Bombay

INDONESIA

OVERVIEW

Indonesia has the world's 5th largest population and is the largest archipelago, with 13,500 islands. Though Indonesia is rich in mineral resources (petroleum [largest export earner], natural gas, coal, copper, tin, bauxite, and gold), agricultural commodities such as rubber, palm oil, tobacco, and timber are still the country's most important products.

The government develops mineral wealth through contracts with private, mostly foreign, companies. Other industries in which it takes an active interest are utilities, cement, glass, fertilizers, ceramics, machinery, and metal products. It encourages growth of private sector manufacturing enterprises to cushion the impact of world commodity price cycles, and courts foreign investment and joint ventures. Manufactured products include processed foods and beverages, tobacco products, clothes, automotive components, and electrical appliances. The government promotes handicraft cooperatives in rural areas.

Uneven population and wealth distribution are problems. The official unemployment rate is less than 3%, but underemployment is about 40%. In 1990 the government cut tariff and nontariff barriers to stimulate assembly industries. GDP grew 7.4% in 1989 and 8.5% in 1990, while inflation increased from 6.1% to 8.5%. After almost 25 years in power, President Suharto is now making plans for an orderly transfer of government.

WHEN

The islands of Indonesia were ruled by a succession of Asian empires until Portuguese explorers arrived in the 16th century. Dutch traders came to stay in the 17th century.

The Dutch East India Company, seeking valuable and exotic spices, began taking over Java in 1602 and gradually extended control over neighboring islands. After the company went bankrupt in 1799, the islands passed to direct Dutch control, which had extended throughout the archipelago by the 19th century. Dutch rule was characterized by extreme mercantilism, including forced labor in agriculture (rubber, palms) and mining (tin, coal). The Dutch made no attempt to educate Indonesians or prepare them for self-government. The exploitations of this regime led to Indonesian nationalist movements in the 1930s.

During WWII, nationalism was further stimulated because of severed communications with Holland and Japanese placement of Indonesians in administrative positions. Three days after Japan's surrender, a group led by Sukarno (his only name) declared independence. Four years of war ensued. US threats to discontinue Marshall Plan aid caused Holland to relent in 1949. In 1957 all Dutch property was expropriated.

Sukarno's government largely ignored day-to-day economic issues to pursue expansionist, destabilizing, and increasingly communistic policies in the region. He was toppled in 1967 and succeeded by General Suharto, who began a series of 5-year development plans. The first aim was to restore the colonial infrastructure neglected during war and civil turmoil; roads and irrigated fields had been allowed to deteriorate. The 2nd aim was to become self-sufficient in rice and to improve agricultural export production; this aim was achieved, but other vital food crops were neglected.

The economy grew about 7.5% a year through the 1970s, as development plans were financed by Indonesia's offshore oil wells. To try to create jobs for its expanding population (2.3% a year), the government encouraged foreign investors through tax and regulatory incentives.

The 1980s brought expansion in Indonesia's nascent manufacturing sector (cement, fertilizer, motorcycles, chemicals, paper pulp). Japanese and other multinational companies took advantage of the country's lower labor costs. The government also borrowed heavily against anticipated oil revenues to finance development. But oil prices fell in the 1980s. The Suharto government kept debt under control through austerity policies, and Indonesia remains a good credit risk.

Population growth is a problem; with 50% of the people under 20, education and job creation are priorities. Resources and income are poorly distributed among the far-flung islands. One of the brightest successes of the 1980s was the growth of the textile industry from $151 million in exports in 1983 to $1.9 billion in 1989, an annual growth of 38.8%.

The government is accelerating deregulation and technological investment. Greater prosperity may bring new problems, such as strains on infrastructure, labor unrest, and increased petroleum consumption. This could turn Indonesia into an oil importer.

HOW MUCH

	4-Year Growth	1986	1987	1988	1989	1990
Population (mil.)	*2.0%*	165.8	169.2	172.6	176.2	179.4
GDP ($ bil.)	*6.8%*	*80*	*76*	*85*	*94*	*104*
Real GDP growth rate	—	5.9%	4.8%	5.7%	7.4%	8.5%
Exports ($ mil.)	*16.8%*	14,800	17,100	19,200	22,200	27,500
Imports ($ mil.)	*19.1%*	10,700	12,400	13,200	16,400	21,500
Trade balance ($ mil.)	—	4,100	4,700	6,000	5,800	6,000
Current account ($ mil.)	—	(3,910)	(2,100)	(1,400)	(1,110)	250
Govt. budget bal. ($ mil.)	—	*1*	*1*	*2*	*3*	*0*
Consumer inflation	—	9.2%	9.3%	5.6%	6.1%	8.5%
Unemployment rate	—	—	—	—	*2.9%*	*2.5%*
Exchange rate with US$	—	1,283	1,644	1,686	1,770	1,841

Source: Economist Intelligence Unit and *The Reference Press*

Area: 741,098 sq. mi. (1,919,443 sq. km)

Official name:
Republic of Indonesia
Republik Indonesia
Official language: Bahasa Indonesia
Currency: 1 rupiah (Rp) = 100 sen
Fiscal year ends: March 31

WHO

President: Suharto, age 70
Vice-President: Sudharmono, age 64
Minister of Finance: J. B. Sumarlin, age 59
Minister of Foreign Affairs: Ali Alatas, age 59
Ambassador to US: Abdul Rachman Ramly, age 64
US Ambassador to Indonesia: John C. Monjo

WHERE

Executive HQ: President, Istana Merdeka, Jakarta, Indonesia
Embassy in US: 2020 Massachusetts Ave. NW, Washington, DC 20036
Phone: 202-775-5200
Fax: 202-775-5365
US Embassy in Indonesia: Medan Merdeka Selatan 5, Jakarta, Indonesia
Phone: 011-62-21-360-360
Chamber of Commerce: Dewan Perniagaan dan Perusahaan, Indonesian Chamber of Commerce, Jalan Medan Merdeka Timur 11, Jakarta, Indonesia
Phone: 011-62-21-377-459

Indonesia has 27 provinces divided into 246 districts and 55 municipalities and has diplomatic representatives in 96 countries.

Capital city: Jakarta
Time change from EST: +12 hours
Avg. high/low temp: Jan. 84°F (29°C)/74°F (23°C)
July 87°F (31°C)/73°F (23°C)

Urbanization: 28%
Population density: 242/sq. mi. (93/sq. km)

Exports	as % of Total	Imports	as % of Total
Japan	42	Japan	23
US	16	US	14
Singapore	8	Singapore	7
South Korea	4	Taiwan	6
Other countries	30	Other countries	50
Total	**100**	**Total**	**100**

WHAT

Origins of GDP	% of Total
Agriculture	23
Manufacturing	18
Wholesale & retail trade	17
Mining & quarrying	13
Transport & communications	6
Construction	5
Other	18
Total	**100**

1990 GDP per capita: $580
1990 year-end external debt: $46 billion
Literacy rate: 85%
UN Human Development Index: 50%
Human Freedom Index (0-40 scale): 5
Purchasing power as % of US: 9%
Capital city cost of living as % of DC: 101%
Defense as % of GNP: 2%
Education as % of GNP: 2%
Principal airline: Garuda Indonesia
Principal exchange: Jakarta Stock Exchange

IRAN

OVERVIEW

For 10 years after the overthrow of the shah in 1979, Iran tried to export its fundamentalist Shi'a Islamic Revolution to other Muslim countries. Since the death of the Ayatollah Khomeini (1989), the government has taken a more moderate course, to rejoin the world community and develop Iran's faltering economy along increasingly private, free-market lines.

Land reform, an important part of the revolution's agenda, has so far affected only 3% of land, but the threat of government confiscation makes owners reluctant to invest in new farming technologies or to maintain existing facilities. A once-abundant agricultural sector is now incapable of feeding the country.

The main industry is oil. Iran was one of the area's first producers and one of the first to diversify into refined products, and it is now one of the top 5 producers. Japan is one of Iran's most important trading partners, but it has in recent years reduced Iranian oil from 33% of its total oil imports to under 8%. Other important sectors are textiles (cotton, silk, and carpets), steel, cars, ceramics, and metalwork. Also important are fishing (the Caspian Sea is a source of caviar) and mining (lead, chrome, turquoise, coal, and iron ore).

WHEN

In the 15th century BC, the Aryans settled in the area that is now Iran. Aryan descendants, the Persians, founded an empire that stretched from India to Greece and boasted roads, a postal system, and codified laws.

Islam arrived in 641. Persia was conquered by the Seljuk Turks (11th century) and Mongols (13th century) before becoming independent again in the 16th century. In the 19th century, Britain and Russia vied for control of the area. In 1907, ignoring Persia's wishes, they divided Persia into spheres of Russian and British influence. The traditional base of the Persian economy was agriculture, herding, and textiles, especially silk and carpets.

Oil was discovered in 1908, leading to the founding of the Anglo-Persian Oil Company, the predecessor of British Petroleum. The government's inability to reduce foreign influence led to its overthrow by an army officer, Reza Khan, who became shah in 1925. He took the name Reza Pahlavi, regained central control of the country, and renegotiated early oil leases for more favorable terms. Oil revenues funded road, railway, and factory construction. Pahlavi introduced secularism, modern dress, and technical education, and in 1935 renamed the country Iran (Land of the Aryans).

In WWII, Britain occupied Iran; forced the shah to abdicate in favor of his son, Shah Mohammed Reza; and used Iran as a route to supply the Soviets. After the war Soviet troops briefly occupied the north. Iranian nationalism grew during this period, and in 1951 the elected premier nationalized oil, an action that caused the British to organize an international boycott of Iranian oil. The young shah fled as the country was plunged into political and economic instability, but with CIA backing he returned and came to terms with the oil companies. He then spent 10 years consolidating his power with the aid of his hated secret police, the SAVAK.

The shah's 1963 White Revolution included land redistribution (which, as religious foundations had many large holdings, alienated the Shi'a leaders, including Ayatollah Khomeini), educational improvements, and an increase in women's rights. Oil revenues funded factories, grand public works, and weapons.

Though enriching a few and creating a middle class, these measures brought social and economic disruption and popular resentment against corruption and secularization. Dissent grew in the 1970s, culminating in the return of the exiled Ayatollah and the Islamic Revolution in 1979, which drove the shah from power.

After the revolution, banking, oil, utilities, and mining were nationalized and the government began a self-sufficiency program, cutting imports and oil exports. Iraq declared war in 1980 over the Shatt-al-Arab waterway. Over the next 8 years, Iran's economy deteriorated because of defense costs, loss of manpower, and falling oil prices. By 1987 Iran was spending 1/3 of its oil revenues on food.

After the war ended in 1988, Iran's economic performance was poorer than it had been under the monarchy. By 1990 urban unemployment was high, and per capita income had fallen by 50%. Food, heating oil, and electrical shortages prompted the government to begin relaxing its control.

Iran remained neutral in the 1991 Gulf War and experienced an influx of refugees during the fighting. As its government moderated, it sought closer ties with the EC.

HOW MUCH

	4-Year Growth	1986	1987	1988	1989	1990
Population (mil.)	3.3%	49.4	51.1	52.5	54.2	56.2
GDP ($ bil.)	—	*236*	*147*	*133*	*121*	—
Real GDP growth rate	—	(8.4%)	(1.1%)	(4.8%)	4.0%	4.0%
Exports ($ mil.)	*24.1%*	7,170	10,640	9,800	13,600	17,000
Imports ($ mil.)	*10.9%*	10,590	9,000	11,800	14,750	16,000
Trade balance ($ mil.)	—	(3,420)	1,640	(2,000)	(1,150)	1,000
Current account ($ mil.)	—	(5,160)	(2,480)	(4,000)	(3,200)	(1,100)
Govt. budget bal. ($ mil.)	—	*(8,451)*	*(10,003)*	*(8,255)*	*(9,853)*	—
Consumer inflation	—	18.4%	28.6%	28.6%	22.4%	20.0%
Unemployment rate	—	—	—	28.7%	—	—
Exchange rate with US$	—	76.55	144.91	177.97	215.70	—

Source: Economist Intelligence Unit and *The Reference Press*

Area: 634,724 sq. mi. (1,648,000 sq. km)

Official name:
Islamic Republic of Iran
Jomhori-e-Islami-e-Irân
Official language: Farsi
Currency: 1 rial (IR) = 100 dinars
Fiscal year ends: March 20

WHO

Leader of the Islamic Revolution: Seyed Ali Khamenei, age 51
President: Hojatolislam Ali Akbar Hashemi Rafsanjani, age 57
First Vice-President: Hassan Ibrahim Habibi, age 54
Minister of Economic Affairs and Finance: Mohsen Nourbakhsh, age 43
Minister of Foreign Affairs: Ali Akbar Vellayati

WHERE

Executive HQ: President, Office of the President, Tehran, Iran
Representation of Iran in US: Iranian Interests Section (under protection of Algeria), 2209 Wisconsin Ave. NW, Washington, DC 20007
Phone: 202-965-4990
Representation of US in Iran: US Interest Section (under protection of Switzerland), Bucharest Ave., 17th St. No. 5, Tehran, Iran
Phone: 011-98-21-625223
Chamber of Commerce: Iranian Chamber of Commerce, Industries & Mines, 254 Ave. Ayatollah Taleghani, Tehran, Iran
Phone: 011-98-21-836031

Iran has 24 provinces and has diplomatic representatives in 26 countries.

Capital city: Tehran
Time change from EST: +8.5 hours
Avg. high/low temp: Jan. 45°F (7°C)/27°F (-3°C)
July 99°F (37°C)/72°F (22°C)

Urbanization: 54%
Population density: 88/sq. mi. (34/sq. km)

Exports as % of Total		Imports as % of Total	
India	17	Germany	15
Japan	12	Japan	11
Benelux	7	Turkey	7
Other countries	64	Other countries	67
Total	**100**	**Total**	**100**

WHAT

Origins of GDP	% of Total
Services	48
Agriculture	19
Industry	17
Oil	16
Total	**100**

1989 GDP per capita: $2,224
1990 year-end external debt: $6 billion
Literacy rate: 48%
UN Human Development Index: 58%
Purchasing power as % of US: 28%
Capital city cost of living as % of DC: 262%
Defense as % of GNP: 8%
Education as % of GDP: 3%
Principal airline: Iranair
Principal exchange: Tehran Stock Exchange

IRAQ

OVERVIEW

After nearly a decade of war in the past 12 years, Iraq finds itself a pariah among nations, virtually in ruins, with most of its civil and military infrastructure destroyed by the US and its allies during a brief, terrible war over the seizure of Kuwait.

From 1979 to 1990 Iraq's population grew from 13 million to just over 18 million, while per capita GDP dropped from $4,100 to under $1,200 in 1991 (about 70%) and defense spending grew to 27% of GDP, the highest in the world. Debt rose to $70 billion, much of it owed to former Arab allies, including Kuwait.

Iraq's oil reserves are among the 5 largest in the world, and oil accounts for 99% of exports. During the Gulf War the countries opposing Iraq closed its oil pipelines, and much of the country's refining capacity was crippled.

Iraq possesses an extensive irrigation system, allowing about 18% of the land to be cultivated. Crops include dates, wheat, barley, rice, and cotton. Iraq had traditionally been a food exporter, but, because of neglect and mismanagement, it had become a net importer by 1990, producing less than it had in 1961.

WHEN

The heart of Iraq is the Tigris-Euphrates valley — the cradle of civilization, site of the Garden of Eden — where writing arose in order to record commercial transactions.

The area, known as Mesopotamia, saw many rulers, including the Sumerians, Assyrians, Babylonians, and Persians; all were sophisticated administrative and trading cultures, with impressive architectural, agricultural, administrative, and military abilities.

Islam arrived in the 7th century, and Baghdad became a political and cultural center. Mongol invaders destroyed the city in the 13th century, and extensive irrigation systems fell into disuse (salting caused by lack of drainage still prevents farming in some areas).

From the 16th century to WWI, the Ottoman Empire controlled Iraq. In 1914 the Turks granted oil exploration rights to an Anglo-German company (Turkish Petroleum, predecessor to the largely US-owned Iraq Petroleum), whose activities were stopped by WWI. The British invaded during the war with the aid of Sharif Hussein of Mecca and others whose nationalist hopes were encouraged by T. E. Lawrence (Lawrence of Arabia).

Despite the discovery of oil, Iraq remained agricultural in the early 1900s, with dates, wool, barley, and opium as its major exports.

After WWI the Sykes-Picot Agreement, which divided much of the Middle East between Britain and France, dashed Arab hopes. As a conciliatory gesture Britain installed Hussein's son Faisal as king of Iraq in 1921 but continued to control Iraq's oil even after independence (1932). The new monarchy was subject to repeated coup attempts in the 1930s and 1940s. An extended regency period further weakened the regime, which was overthrown in 1958. Saddam Hussein took over in 1979.

The country's Kurdish minority (15–20%) has sought independence since WWII.

The initial oil concession provided for very low royalties (4 gold shillings per ton or 12 cents per barrel in 1931). Royalties were renegotiated, but the oil companies still controlled prices. To remedy this, Iraq became a founding member of OPEC in 1959.

The rises in oil prices of the early 1970s benefited Iraq less than other nations because of its large population and dependence on pipelines across other countries.

Disagreements with Iran over the Shatt al-Arab waterway (Iraq's main sea outlet) led Iraq to declare war in 1980. The war drained Iraq's $35 billion foreign exchange reserves and drove the country deeply into debt to other Arab nations. Exports and revenues plummeted. In July 1988, without winning anything, Iraq agreed to peace.

The military buildup continued. Iraq demanded that Kuwait (which it had claimed for years) write off Iraq's debt and pay revenues lost because of Kuwait's overproduction. On August 2, 1990, Iraq invaded Kuwait. The UN declared an embargo and boycott, Turkey and Saudi Arabia closed Iraq's export pipelines, and the US sent troops to Saudi Arabia.

On January 16, 1991, Allied forces began the most intensive air war in history and then invaded in a successful 4-day blitzkrieg in February. Iraq's forces surrendered or retreated, taking Kuwait's portable treasure and torching its oil fields. The war destroyed most of Iraq's civil and military infrastructure and left Iraq's people facing hunger and disease as sanctions continued in an effort to destroy Iraq's war-making capacity. As health conditions deteriorated, the UN considered allowing Iraq to resume oil exports to pay for food and medicine.

HOW MUCH

	4-Year Growth	1986	1987	1988	1989	1990
Population (mil.)	*3.0%*	16.1	16.3	17.3	18.1	18.1
GDP ($ bil.)	*(8.3%)*	49.42	59.86	57.36	66.19	35.00
Real GDP growth rate	—	(1.1%)	20.5%	(3.7%)	15.4%	5.0%
Exports ($ mil.)	*5.1%*	6,970	11,520	11,050	14,600	8,500
Imports ($ mil.)	*(5.4%)*	6,360	5,060	7,150	7,680	5,100
Trade balance ($ mil.)	—	610	6,460	3,900	6,920	3,400
Current account ($ mil.)	—	(3,040)	2,300	(140)	2,850	(900)
Govt. budget bal. ($ mil.)	—	—	—	—	*(21,222)*	*(23,151)*
Consumer inflation	—	35.0%	45.0%	40.0%	45.0%	45.0%
Unemployment rate	—	—	—	—	—	—
Exchange rate with US$	—	0.31	0.31	0.31	0.31	0.31

Source: Economist Intelligence Unit and *The Reference Press*

Area: 167,925 sq. mi. (434,934 sq. km)

Official name:
Republic of Iraq
al Jumhouriya al 'Iraqia
Official language: Arabic
Currency: 1 dinar (ID) = 1,000 fils
Fiscal year ends: December 31

WHO

President, RCC Chairman, Ba'ath Party Regional Command Secretary General: Saddam Hussein al-Takriti, age 54
RCC Vice-Chairman and Deputy Secretary General of Ba'ath Party Regional Command: Taha Muhyi al-Din Ma'ruf
Minister of Finance: Hisham Hasan Tawfiq
Deputy Prime Minister and Minister of Foreign Affairs: Tariq Mikhail Aziz, age 55
Minister Chargé d'Affaires ad interim to US: Khalid J. Shewayish
US Ambassador to Iraq: Vacant

WHERE

Executive HQ: President, Presidential Palace, Karradat Mariam, Baghdad, Iraq
Embassy in US: 1801 P St. NW, Washington, DC 20036
Phone: 202-483-7500
Fax: 202-462-5066
US Embassy in Iraq: Opposite Foreign Ministry Club (Masbah Quarter), PO Box 2447 Alwiyah, Baghdad, Iraq
Phone: 011-964-1-719-6138
Chamber of Commerce: Federation of Iraqi Chambers of Commerce, Baghdad Chamber of Commerce Bldg., Mustansir St., Baghdad, Iraq
Phone: 011-964-1-888-0091

Iraq has 18 provinces and has diplomatic representatives in 69 countries.

Capital city: Baghdad
Time change from EST: +8 hours
Avg. high/low temp: Jan. 60°F (16°C)/39°F (4°C)
July 110°F (43°C)/76°F (24°C)

Urbanization: 73%
Population density: 108/sq. mi. (42/sq. km)

Exports as % of Total		Imports as % of Total	
US	19	US	13
Japan	9	Germany	13
France	6	Turkey	9
Italy	5	UK	8
Other countries	61	Other countries	57
Total	**100**	**Total**	**100**

WHAT

Origins of GDP	% of Total
Oil	61
Services	22
Industry	12
Agriculture	5
Total	**100**

1990 GDP per capita: $1,934
1990 year-end external debt: $42 billion
Literacy rate: 65%
UN Human Development Index: 58%
Human Freedom Index (0-40 scale): 0
Purchasing power as % of US: —
Capital city cost of living as % of DC: —
Defense as % of GNP: 27%
Education as % of GNP: —
Principal airline: Iraqi Airways

IRELAND

OVERVIEW

Lacking in abundant natural resources, Ireland has as its primary economic resource its people. But for almost 150 years they have been leaving in droves. The population, which stood at 8.5 million in 1845, today numbers just over 3.5 million. Much of Ireland's national effort and economic policy since independence 70 years ago has been directed toward stemming emigration by creating economic opportunities at home.

Ireland is one of the youngest countries in Europe (1/2 the population is under age 25). It has the 2nd highest birthrate in the OECD (after Turkey) and remains one of the poorest countries in Europe, with per capita income barely 1/2 the OECD average.

However, its well-educated and abundant labor force, investment incentives, and unrestricted access to the European market have made it an attractive location for foreign industrial investment. Over 800 foreign firms have invested over $4 billion in chemical, high technology, machinery, and other industries. These companies are responsible for 80% of the country's industrial exports and employ 1/2 of all industrial workers.

Foreign trade is Ireland's lifeblood, accounting for over 60% of GNP. Because of this its economic health reflects that of its largest trading partners (the EC and US) and world economic conditions generally.

Inflation is less than 4% and GNP growth has risen to nearly the same level. Ireland's biggest economic challenges are to reduce its unemployment (over 15% and rising again after falling for several years) and to curtail government deficit spending, which has led to the highest public debt in Europe (110% of GNP). Since much of government spending goes to the unemployed and to industry incentives (programs not easily cut), this is a formidable task.

WHEN

Ireland's history starts in the 4th century BC with the invasion of Celtic people (the Gaels) from Europe. English-born St. Patrick brought Christianity and the Roman alphabet to the Celts in 432, and Ireland became a center of learning as the rest of Europe entered the Dark Ages. Ninth-century Viking raiders were defeated in 1014 by Brian Boru, a Celt who briefly unified Ireland. Wanting to rid Irish Christianity of its less-orthodox practices, Pope Adrian IV (the only English pope) issued a papal bull that gave Ireland to England in 1155, beginning 800 years of British political and economic domination of Ireland.

England, fearing a threat from its back while waging various wars in Europe, subjugated Ireland, prohibiting Catholicism, taking most of the land for feudal plantations, and wrecking Ireland's nascent wool trade. Irish peasants were reduced to tenant farmers dependent on potatoes for sustenance.

The potato famine (1845–48) starved a million people and drove more than another million to emigrate, mostly to the US. There followed an economic depression from which Ireland did not recover until the 20th century.

In the early 20th century, tenants were allowed to buy back agricultural land from absentee English landlords. Except for in the north, which remained a part of the UK after the south became independent (1921), there was no industry in Ireland. Its economy remained almost wholly agrarian until after WWII (during which it was neutral).

During the 1950s Ireland developed a welfare state and began to industrialize. Beginning in the 1960s, emigration dropped and population increased for the first time in 115 years, as economic conditions in Ireland improved when export markets developed for minerals, textiles, ceramics, and machinery. Ireland joined the EC in 1973. Its increased access to European markets (most of its trade prior to this had still been with the UK) and large-scale foreign investment (much of it from the US) in the industrial sector caused the economy to expand rapidly.

In 1981 the economy slumped because of increased oil prices and excessive government spending. Unemployment rose, trade deficits developed, and GNP growth slowed (turning negative in 1986). Reduced government spending and an improved balance of trade caused the economy to begin to improve in 1987.

With the global economic downturn of 1990–91, emigration declined, bringing higher rates of unemployment. Government austerity measures to reduce inflation succeeded but triggered public sector strikes. Nevertheless, Ireland's economy continued to grow at a faster rate than the EC average.

Official name:
Republic of Ireland
Éire
Official languages: English, Irish (Gaelic)
Currency: 1 pound (I£)= 100 pence
Fiscal year ends: December 31

WHO

President: Mary Robinson, age 47
Prime Minister and Minister for the Gaeltachi: Charles J. Haughey, age 66
Deputy Prime Minister: John Wilson Tanaiste
Minister of Finance: Albert Reynolds
Minister of Foreign Affairs: Gerard Collins, age 53
Ambassador to US: Padraic N. MacKernan
US Ambassador to Ireland: Richard A. Moore

WHERE

Executive HQ: Prime Minister, Taoiseach, Upper Merrion St., Dublin, Ireland
Embassy in US: 2234 Massachusetts Ave. NW, Washington, DC 20008
Phone: 202-462-3939
US Embassy in Ireland: 42 Elgin Rd., Ballsbridge, Dublin, Ireland
Phone: 011-353-1-688-777
Fax: 011-353-1-689-946
Chamber of Commerce: Association of Chambers of Commerce of Ireland, 7 Clare St., Dublin 2, Ireland
Phone: 011-353-1-764-291
Fax: 011-353-1-766-043

Ireland has 26 counties and has diplomatic representatives in 30 countries.

Capital city: Dublin
Time change from EST: +5 hours
Avg. high/low temp: Jan. 46°F (8°C)/34°F (1°C)
July 67°F (20°C)/52°F (11°C)

Urbanization: 59%
Population density: 129/sq. mi. (50/sq. km)

Exports as % of Total		Imports as % of Total	
UK	34	UK	41
Germany	11	US	16
Benelux	11	Germany	9
France	9	Japan	6
Other	35	Other	28
Total	**100**	**Total**	**100**

WHAT

Origins of GDP	% of Total
Industry including construction	37
Distribution, transport & communications	18
Agriculture, forestry & fishing	11
Public administration & defense	6
Other	28
Total	**100**

1990 GDP per capita: $12,000
1989 year-end external debt: $13 billion
Literacy rate: 99%
UN Human Development Index: 95%
Human Freedom Index (0-40 scale): 27
Purchasing power as % of US: 41%
Capital city cost of living as % of DC: 123%
Defense as % of GNP: 2%
Education as % of GDP: 4%
Principal airlines: Aer Lingus, Ryanair
Principal exchange: The Irish Stock Exchange

HOW MUCH

	4-Year Growth	1986	1987	1988	1989	1990
Population (mil.)	*0.0%*	3.5	3.5	3.5	3.5	3.5
GDP ($ bil.)	*2.1%*	*25*	*30*	*33*	*34*	*42*
Real GDP growth rate	—	(0.3%)	4.9%	3.4%	5.9%	3.6%
Exports ($ mil.)	*16.1%*	12,600	16,000	18,800	20,700	22,900
Imports ($ mil.)	*14.6%*	11,600	13,600	15,600	17,400	20,000
Trade balance ($ mil.)	—	1,000	2,400	3,200	3,300	2,900
Current account ($ mil.)	—	(700)	400	700	500	200
Govt. budget bal. ($ mil.)	—	*(1,860)*	*(1,761)*	*(488)*	*(376)*	—
Consumer inflation	—	3.9%	3.2%	2.1%	4.1%	3.3%
Unemployment rate	—	17.4%	17.7%	16.7%	15.7%	—
Exchange rate with US$	—	0.75	0.67	0.65	0.70	0.60

Source: Economist Intelligence Unit and *The Reference Press*

Area: 27,136 sq. mi. (70,282 sq. km)

PJS

ISRAEL

OVERVIEW

"Greater" Israel consists of the area declared independent in 1948 and territories occupied in subsequent wars, now settled by Israelis determined to stay. Because of these conquests and the higher Arab birthrate, only 60% of Israel's population is Jewish. A recent flood of Soviet immigrants has been welcomed as a corrective for this, though they also create short-term housing shortages and increased government spending and unemployment.

Israeli agriculture is among the most sophisticated in the world; the country is largely self-sufficient in food, producing fruits, vegetables, and grains and raising livestock.

Mineral reserves include copper, phosphates, and potash. Major industries include armaments (largest export sector; South Africa is a customer), tourism (hurt by the Arab revolt known as the *intifada*), diamond finishing, and electronics.

Government participates heavily in Israel's basically free-market economy. Some large companies are state controlled; they tend to be inefficient and unprofitable. A traditionally negative balance of trade has been mitigated by transfer payments and foreign loans (nearly 2/3 from the US). GNP growth fell from 5% in 1987 to 1% in 1989 but has recently rebounded. Israel is dependent on foreign oil, primarily from Egypt and Mexico.

The Arab boycott of Israel has kept many Japanese and European multinational companies from selling to or doing business in Israel. Recently, however, Honda began selling there.

WHEN

The Hebrews ruled Israel from about 1000 BC to 722 BC, when a series of foreign invasions began. Rome took control in 70 BC. Revolts beginning in 66 led to the destruction of all but the west wall of Solomon's Temple; in 70 Rome expelled the Jews, an exile known as the Diaspora. Those who remained in the area, by then called Palestine, were persecuted by the Byzantines and found Muslim rule (beginning in the 7th century) a relief.

In the late 1800s Russian and Polish pogroms created a flood of refugees that, along with the growth of socialism and Zionism, resulted in agitation for a Jewish homeland in Palestine based on communal principles. The British (who had taken control of Palestine from the Ottomans after WWI) endorsed this idea with the Balfour Declaration of 1917, which conflicted with earlier British promises of postwar Arab independence.

After WWI, Jewish immigration to Palestine increased. Superior education, organization, and funding enabled the Jews to start independent agricultural communities (*kibbutzim*). They bought land from absentee Arab landlords and worked it themselves, displacing tenants and causing resentment. They established schools, an aid agency, and a self-defense organization. Arabs protested violently. The British tried to limit immigration but failed, in part because of the number of Jewish refugees created by WWII.

In 1947 the UN partitioned Palestine, and in 1948 Israel defeated Arab armies to win independence and more land than intended by the UN, which had planned to create an Arab Palestinian state too. In the next 30 years, Israel fought 3 wars with its Arab neighbors.

Wars, embargoes, and boycotts by its natural local trading partners made foreign aid important to Israel's economy from the beginning. The US was a major source of funds, as were war reparations from West Germany.

Though Israel was socialist, its annual economic growth often exceeded 10% in the first 20 years. At first, agriculture was the strongest sector; later, industry and services surpassed it.

In the 1960s and early 1970s, rapid growth led to trade and budgetary deficits and high inflation. Israel was still heavily dependent upon US aid. Arab hostility meant defense costs of up to 25% of GNP.

Growth slowed in the mid-1970s and stagnated after 1982 because of high inflation (444% in 1984). A US-assisted stabilization program reduced inflation to under 20% by 1986. But the root cause — more imports than exports — remained. Attempts to privatize industry have recently proven fruitless.

In 1987 Palestinians began the *intifada*, a movement that includes violent demonstrations and a boycott of Israeli goods, to protest Israeli occupation. The economic damage of the *intifada* has been mitigated by the Soviet Jews, who enlarge the market for goods and take menial jobs usually left to Palestinians.

Israel has resisted international efforts since the Gulf War to instigate peace talks with Arab nations and the Palestinians. But, mindful of the need for $10 billion of US aid to build housing for immigrant Soviet Jews, Israel has not rejected peace talks outright.

HOW MUCH

	4-Year Growth	1986	1987	1988	1989	1990
Population (mil.)	*2.8%*	4.3	4.4	4.5	4.6	4.8
GDP ($ bil.)	*13.9%*	*30*	*35*	*43*	*47*	50
Real GDP growth rate	—	3.7%	5.5%	2.1%	1.3%	4.6%
Exports ($ mil.)	*13.1%*	7,154	8,454	9,752	10,738	11,704
Imports ($ mil.)	*13.0%*	9,645	11,921	12,960	13,197	15,700
Trade balance ($ mil.)	—	(2,491)	(3,467)	(3,208)	(2,459)	(3,996)
Current account ($ mil.)	—	1,620	(870)	(620)	1,150	100
Govt. budget bal. ($ mil.)	—	—	*27*	*(596)*	*(2,478)*	—
Consumer inflation	—	19.7%	16.1%	16.4%	20.8%	17.6%
Unemployment rate	—	—	—	6.4%	8.9%	8.8%
Exchange rate with US$	—	1.49	1.60	1.60	1.92	2.02

Source: Economist Intelligence Unit and *The Reference Press*

Area: 7,850 sq. mi. (20,325 sq. km)

Official name:
State of Israel
Medinat Israel
Official languages: Arabic, Hebrew
Currency: 1 shekel (NIS) = 100 agorot
Fiscal year ends: December 31

WHO

President: Chaim Herzog, age 73
Prime Minister and Labor Minister: Yitzhak Shamir, age 76
Deputy Prime Minister and Foreign Minister: David Levy, age 53
Vice–Prime Minister and Minister of Finance: Yitzhak Modaii, age 65
Ambassador to US: Zalman Shoval
US Ambassador to Israel: William A. Brown

WHERE

Executive HQ: Office of the Prime Minister, Hakirya, Kaplan St. 3, Jerusalem 91919, Israel
Embassy in US: 3514 International Dr. NW, Washington, DC 20008
Phone: 202-364-5500
Fax: 202-364-5610
US Embassy in Israel: 71 Hayarkon St., Tel Aviv, Israel
Phone: 011-972-3-654338
Fax: 011-972-3-663449
Chamber of Commerce: Federation of Israeli Chambers of Commerce, PO Box 501, 84 Hahashmonaim St., Tel Aviv 67011, Israel
Phone: 011-972-3-05612444
Fax: 011-972-3-5619025 or 7

Israel has 6 districts and 2 occupied areas and has diplomatic representatives in 93 countries.

Capital city: Jerusalem
Time change from EST: +7 hours
Avg. high/low temp: Jan. 55°F (13°C)/41°F (5°C)
July 87°F (31°C)/63°F (17°C)

Urbanization: 91%
Population density: 611/sq. mile (236/sq. km)

Exports as % of Total		Imports as % of Total	
US	29	US	18
Benelux	9	Benelux	17
Japan	7	Germany	12
UK	7	Switzerland	9
Other countries	48	Other countries	44
Total	**100**	**Total**	**100**

WHAT

Origins of GDP	% of Total
Commerce & services	34
Industry & construction	30
Transport, storage & communications	15
Construction	9
Agriculture	8
Electricity & water	4
Total	**100**

1990 GDP per capita: $10,458
1990 year-end external debt: $23 billion
Literacy rate: Jewish 88%, Arab 70%
UN Human Development Index: 95%
Human Freedom Index (0-40 scale): 19
Purchasing power as % of US: 52%
Tel Aviv cost of living as % of DC: 131%
Defense as % of GNP: 15%
Education as % of GDP: 6%
Principal airline: El Al Israel
Principal exchange: Tel Aviv Stock Exchange

ITALY

OVERVIEW

Italy is 2 countries, an industrialized and prosperous north and a less developed, agricultural south, where unemployment hovers at 20%. Together they form the 5th largest capitalist economy in the world (after the US, Japan, Germany, and France).

Italians are leaders in the machine tool and fashion industries and enjoy Europe's highest home ownership rate (67%). Strong demand for consumer goods causes a perennial trade deficit, usually balanced by tourist revenues and remittances from overseas workers. Italy imports 80% of its energy and raw materials, and has prospered in inverse proportion to the price of oil. Manufactured goods are 90% of exports. Tax-averse Italians have developed a thriving underground economy, which may be as much as 30% of GNP.

Industry is dominated by large public companies (3 state companies represent 10% of GNP) and large private enterprises (e.g., Fiat and Olivetti). State-owned companies dominate the banking (IMI) and energy (ENI) industries. The government has announced plans to privatize inefficient state-owned industry but has made little progress, as these companies are bastions of patronage for politicians in the ruling coalition. The private sector companies run by Italy's industrial moguls, known as *condottieri*, are better run and, frequently, leaders in their industries.

The government runs a huge budget deficit (10% of GNP) to fund chronic losses at state-owned companies and an extensive social services system, including massive aid to the impoverished south. As a result public debt equals Italy's GNP. While most money is borrowed internally (97%), deregulation of currency in preparation for European economic integration threatens to force the government to borrow abroad, as its citizens begin to invest their savings (Italians save 15% of their income) outside Italy. Despite its problems Italy's economy was relatively prosperous in 1990.

WHEN

According to tradition Rome was founded by Romulus in 753 BC. Only a small village at the time, encompassing 7 hills, it grew to become the most politically and economically powerful state in the world, first unifying the Italian peninsula in 265 BC and, by the first century, coming to rule all of the Western world from the British Isles to the Tigris and Euphrates Rivers. An essential precept of capitalism — private property — was first recognized in Western culture and legally protected by the Romans.

After the fall of Rome in 476, Italy disintegrated into small, quarrelsome city-states. One of these, Venice, rose to become a major trading state in the Middle Ages, and several others (most notably, Florence) became centers of wealth and trade in the 14th and 15th centuries. Modern banking arose in Italy to serve growing trade requirements and the needs of the papacy. From this wealth sprang the Renaissance, the patrons of which were wealthy merchants such as the Medicis. Italy was not united as a political and economic entity again until 1870.

Italy industrialized in the 19th and early 20th centuries. Most industry developed in the north, where transportation and hydroelectric power were available. Italy sided with the Allies in WWI but joined Hitler in WWII, turning against Germany following the overthrow of Mussolini. Italy emerged from WWII with high inflation and virtually no infrastructure with which to deliver social services. However, most of its factories in the north remained undamaged from the war.

Led by the steel, automobile, and machinery industries, Italy's economy began an unprecedented period of growth. Between 1953 and 1961 industrial production doubled and GNP growth was the highest in Europe, averaging 6% annually from the early 1950s to the early 1970s. During this same period employment in agriculture decreased from 38% to just over 15% of the work force.

In the early 1970s salaries and oil prices rose dramatically at the instigation of Italy's unions and OPEC, respectively, causing a massive trade deficit and inflation. As a result a short recession occurred in 1975, but economic growth took off again, continuing until 1980 when oil price increases again deflated the Italian economy for several years.

The Communist party lost seats in the parliament in the 1980s, and unions began losing some of their strength. In 1983 the framework for indexing salaries to inflation was modified. The result was 1/3 fewer hours lost to strikes and a decline in inflation. GDP again began to grow at about 3% per year, dropping to 2% in 1991 with the worldwide slowdown, high labor costs, and higher inflation rates.

HOW MUCH

	4-Year Growth	1986	1987	1988	1989	1990
Population (mil.)	*0.2%*	57.2	57.3	57.4	57.5	57.7
GDP ($ bil.)	*15.5%*	*602*	*755*	*832*	*866*	*1,072*
Real GDP growth rate	—	2.5%	3.0%	4.2%	3.2%	2.0%
Exports ($ mil.)	*16.6%*	98,000	116,000	129,000	149,000	181,000
Imports ($ mil.)	*17.3%*	100,000	125,000	139,000	162,000	189,000
Trade balance ($ mil.)	—	(2)	(9)	(10)	(13)	(8)
Current account ($ mil.)	—	2,500	(1,500)	(6,000)	(10,600)	(14,000)
Govt. budget bal. ($ mil.)	—	*(70,557)*	*(86,883)*	*(94,624)*	*(92,420)*	*(122,012)*
Consumer inflation	—	6.1%	4.6%	5.1%	6.6%	6.1%
Unemployment rate	—	11.1%	12.0%	12.0%	12.0%	10.6%
Exchange rate with US$	—	1,491	1,296	1,302	1,372	1,198

Source: Economist Intelligence Unit and *The Reference Press*

Area: 116,303 sq. mi. (301,225 sq. km)

Official name:
Republic of Italy
Repubblica Italiana
Official language: Italian
Currency: 1 lira (L) = 100 centesimos
Fiscal year ends: December 31

WHO

President: Francesco Cossiga, age 63
Prime Minister: Giulio Andreotti, age 72
Deputy Prime Minister: Claudio Martelli, age 48
Finance Minister: Rino Formica, age 64
Foreign Affairs Minister: Gianni De Michelis, age 51
Chargé d'Affaires to US: Minister Roberto Toscano
US Ambassador to Italy: Peter F. Secchia

WHERE

Executive HQ: Prime Minister, Palazzo Chigi, Piazza Colonna 370, 00100 Rome, Italy
Embassy in US: 1601 Fuller St. NW, Washington, DC 20009
Phone: 202-328-5500
Fax: 202-462-3605
US Embassy in Italy: Via Veneto 119/A, 00187 Rome, Italy
Phone: 011-39-6-46741
Fax: 011-39-6-4674-2356
Chamber of Commerce: International Chamber of Commerce, Via XX Settembre, Rome, Italy
Phone: 011-39-6-462438

Italy has 94 provinces and 20 regions.

Capital city: Rome
Time change from EST: +6 hours
Avg. high/low temp: Jan. 52°F (11°C)/40°F (5°C)
July 87°F (30°C)/67°F (20°C)

Urbanization: 68%
Population density: 496/sq. mi. (192/sq. km)

Exports as % of Total		Imports as % of Total	
Germany	17	Germany	21
France	16	France	15
US	9	Netherlands	6
UK	8	US	6
Other countries	50	Other countries	52
Total	**100**	**Total**	**100**

WHAT

Origins of GDP	% of Total
Services	57
Mining, manufacturing & utilities	32
Construction	6
Agriculture, forestry & fishing	5
Total	**100**

1990 GDP per capita: $18,255
1990 year-end external debt: $82 billion
Literacy rate: 97%
UN Human Development Index: 96%
Human Freedom Index (0-40 scale): 29
Purchasing power as % of US: 66%
Capital city cost of living as % of DC: 130%
Defense as % of GNP: 2%
Education as % of GNP: 4%
Principal airline: Alitalia
Principal exchange: Borsa Valori di Milano

IVORY COAST

OVERVIEW

Ivory Coast, now officially called by its French name — Côte d'Ivoire — is located on the south side of Africa's western bulge. It is home to over 60 ethnic groups bound together by a common language — French. Eighty-five percent of its people earn a living from agriculture, and only 11% earn wages.

The country is the world's largest cocoa producer and the 5th largest coffee producer. Other crops include bananas, pineapples, cotton, and sugar cane. Concentration on cash crops has left it not quite self-sufficient in food. It also exports tropical woods; however, heavy logging has deforested the land.

Natural resources include petroleum, iron ore, cobalt, and diamonds (the diamond industry is declining). Ivory Coast has become a regional oil refining center. Its oil and hydroelectric capacity make it largely energy self-sufficient.

Industries produce food and wood products, clothing, footwear, and electrical equipment for the domestic market.

Despite problems due to low commodity prices and relatively high foreign debt, Ivory Coast is the 11th most prosperous of Africa's 52 nations. It is politically stable and attracts immigrants from the rest of Africa.

Official name:
Republic of Côte d'Ivoire
République de la Côte d'Ivoire
Official language: French
Currency: 1 franc (Fr) = 100 centimes
Fiscal year ends: December 31

WHO

President: Félix Houphouët-Boigny, age 86
Prime Minister: Alassane D. Ouattara, age 49
Minister of Economy and Finance: Daniel Kablan Duncan
Minister of Foreign Affairs: Amara Essy
Ambassador to US: Charles Gomis
US Ambassador to Côte d'Ivoire: Kenneth L. Brown

WHEN

In the 1400s Portugal's Prince Henry the Navigator began sending explorers down Africa's west coast; they rounded the Cape of Good Hope in 1486. Europeans encountered 3 kingdoms and 50 tribal groups in the Ivory Coast. A forbidding coastline and the lack of a natural harbor discouraged early landings, but, with the spread of slavery in the 17th century, various nationalities set up trading forts.

After abolition of the slave trade in 1815, the French kept small trading posts, dealing in the commodity from which the country takes its name; they did not penetrate the interior.

In the mid–19th century, growing colonial competition among European nations led the French to acquire West African land despite stiff resistance from native tribes. In 1893 Ivory Coast became a colony that was incorporated with other French colonies in 1904 as French West Africa.

The French organized a plantation system, growing coffee and cocoa, among other crops. One of the features of the system was forced African labor. To facilitate trade the French built railways and roads. They tried to introduce schooling but failed, owing to the unwillingness of Europeans to move there. Yet French became the dominant language.

The Great Depression lowered already-marginal living standards. In WWII the Nazi-collaborationist Vichy government ran the colony.

After WWII France, exhausted and receiving US aid, was unable to suppress native nationalism. In the 1950s wars in Indochina and Algeria further sapped French resources and will to rule. In 1960 French West Africa was broken into several new nations, including Ivory Coast.

As in much of Africa, tribal loyalties did not always coincide with the new national boundaries, but the new (and so far only) leader of Ivory Coast, Félix Houphouët-Boigny, commanded loyalty across tribal lines because of his years as a leader of the independence movement.

For 20 years after independence, Ivory Coast was an African success story. It enjoyed close relations with France. Under a mixture of government- and private-industry ownership, it expanded its plantings of commodities, enjoying prosperity undreamt of elsewhere in Africa. In addition to coffee, cocoa, sugar cane, and palms, cash crops included tropical fruits, rice, and timber. The land also produced oil, natural gas, and modest amounts of diamonds. Manufacturing was encouraged to process commodities and supply domestic needs.

In the 1980s the trend reversed. The cocoa and coffee markets collapsed. Drought and fires destroyed a large portion of these crops. Fiscal austerity resulted in strikes in 1982 and 1983, during which schools were closed and striking professionals were threatened with military conscription. Diamond deposits were played out. Drought in the Sahel affected the northern parts of Ivory Coast, and overcutting timber left the country with one of the worst deforestation problems in West Africa.

Ethnic and racial rivalries arising from the concentration of commercial power in the hands of French and Lebanese residents are of increasing concern. President Houphouët-Boigny was reelected easily in 1990 elections held in response to public demonstrations. But with Houphouët-Boigny in his mid-80s, the question of succession must be addressed.

WHERE

Executive HQ: President, Blvd. Clozel BP1354, Abidjan, Côte d'Ivoire
Embassy in US: 2424 Massachusetts Ave. NW, Washington, DC 20008
Phone: 202-797-0300
Fax: 202-483-8482
US Embassy in Côte d'Ivoire: 01 BP1712, 5 Rue Jesse Owens, Abidjan, Côte d'Ivoire
Phone: 011-225-21-09-79
Fax: 011-225-22-32-59
Chamber of Commerce: Chambre de Commerce, 01 BP1399, 6 Ave. J. Anoma, Abidjan, Côte d'Ivoire
Phone: 011-225-32-46-79

Cote d'Ivoire has 34 departments and has diplomatic representatives in 32 countries.

Capital city: Abidjan
Time change from EST: +5 hours
Avg. high/low temp: Jan. 88°F (31°C)/73°F (23°C)
July 83°F (28°C)/73°F (23°C)

Urbanization: 46%
Population density: 101/sq. mi. (39/sq. km)

Exports as % of Total		Imports as % of Total	
France	16	France	31
Netherlands	16	Nigeria	10
US	7	Netherlands	6
Italy	7	Germany	6
Other countries	54	Other countries	47
Total	**100**	**Total**	**100**

WHAT

Origins of GDP	% of Total
Services	45
Agriculture	35
Industry	20
Total	**100**

1989 GDP per capita: $774
1989 year-end external debt: $15 billion
Literacy rate: 45%
UN Human Development Index: 31%
Human Freedom Index (0-40 scale): —
Purchasing power as % of US: 10%
Capital city cost of living as % of DC: 187%
Defense as % of GNP: 2%
Education as % of GNP: 3%
Principal airline: Air Afrique

HOW MUCH

	4-Year Growth	1986	1987	1988	1989	1990
Population (mil.)	*4.2%*	10.7	11.1	11.6	12.1	12.6
GDP ($ bil.)	—	*9.4*	*10.4*	*10.3*	*9.4*	—
Real GDP growth rate	—	3.4%	(1.6%)	(1.8%)	(1.0%)	(4.0%)
Exports ($ mil.)	*(8.3%)*	3,187	2,938	2,774	2,521	2,250
Imports ($ mil.)	*(5.6%)*	1,640	1,847	1,696	1,379	1,300
Trade balance ($ mil.)	—	1,547	1,091	1,078	1,142	950
Current account ($ mil.)	—	(300)	(951)	(1,102)	(858)	(800)
Govt. budget bal. ($ mil.)	—	*(283)*	*(346)*	*(866)*	*(1,392)*	*(1,047)*
Consumer inflation	—	7.3%	0.4%	7.1%	1.0%	(0.5%)
Unemployment rate	—	—	—	—	—	—
Exchange rate with US$	—	346.3	300.5	297.8	319.0	272.3

Source: Economist Intelligence Unit and *The Reference Press*

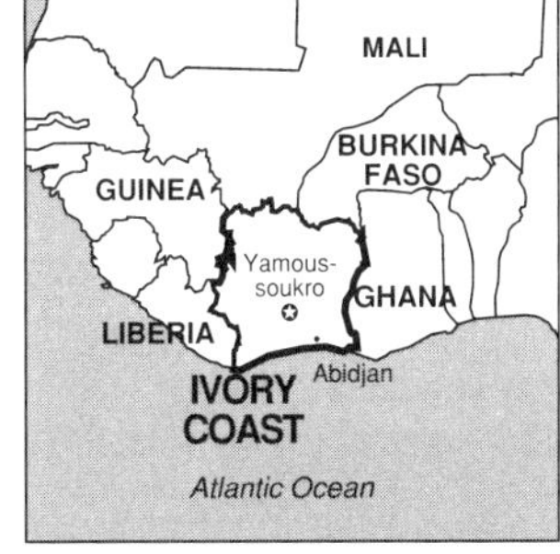

Area: 124,518 sq. mi. (322,362 sq. km)

JAMAICA

OVERVIEW

Nearly 80% mountainous, Jamaica is known for its pleasant climate and beautiful beaches. It has a diversified free-market economic base of agriculture (primarily sugar cane and bananas), industry (textiles), service (mostly tourism related), and mining (bauxite and alumina). Mining generates nearly 60% of export earnings. The US is Jamaica's largest trading partner, the destination for 37% of its exports and the source of 70% of its tourists.

The once-stable economy is still recovering from Hurricane Gilbert (1988), which damaged 1/2 the homes on the island and many of the tourist hotels, and destroyed nearly 20,000 acres of fruit. The storm forced Jamaica to use precious foreign exchange to pay for rebuilding the ravaged island.

Debt is high, with service on it accounting for more than 40% of the annual government budget. Unemployment has hovered between 18% and 28% recently. GDP has been growing at around 3%, while the population remains stable. Wealth is divided unevenly, with 5% of the population owning 90% of the wealth.

Prime Minister Michael Manley has promised to focus on the manufacturing sector to improve both domestic and export markets. Tax and duty-free incentives are expected to stimulate additional foreign investment. A prime target of the US's Caribbean Basin Initiative, Jamaica is home to over 150 US firms' operations. Divestiture of state-owned hotels continues. Tourism is Jamaica's #1 foreign exchange earner and will remain important to the economy, as it is forecasted to grow 30% by 1992. Jamaica is also looking to its burgeoning flower, data entry, and specialty food businesses for growth.

WHEN

Forced ashore in search of fresh water in 1494, Columbus claimed the island of Xamayca for Spain. As the island lacked precious metals, the Spanish used it as a supply base. In the 1500s and early 1600s, African slaves were imported to work the emerging sugar-cane plantations. The British invaded and took over in 1655.

Under British rule the slave trade flourished; within 45 years nearly 3 million slaves had arrived to work the cacao, indigo, and sugar-cane plantations. For the next 140 years, Jamaica was controlled by absentee English landlords.

Abolition of slavery in 1838 brought the demise of the plantation system. Production fell, the economy deteriorated, and poverty was widespread. A decline in sugar prices in the late 19th century aggravated the situation, and many workers emigrated to work on the Panama Canal.

Prosperity returned in the early 20th century when the introduction of refrigerated cargo vessels led to an expansion of banana exports through United Fruit. The discovery of bauxite in the 1940s ended Jamaica's dependence on agriculture and brought economic growth. Under the direction of American and Canadian companies (Alcoa, Alcan, Reynolds), Jamaica became the world's largest producer of bauxite. Both bauxite and alumina fueled economic expansion in the 1950s and 1960s. After Jamaica became independent in 1962, tourism developed into the 3rd source of foreign exchange and spurred a 6% annual average economic growth.

Socialist prime minister Michael Manley, elected in 1972, undertook agricultural "reforms" on the Cuban model. Economic growth slowed, as some banks and alumina companies were nationalized. Oil price increases in 1973 further damaged the economy. Closer relations with Cuba were dimly viewed by foreign investors, and bauxite production fell nearly 25% after the imposition of a production tax in 1974. Manley instituted massive increases in government spending. Relations with the IMF soured and exports declined, leaving Jamaica deeply in debt.

Prime Minister Edward Seaga (elected 1980) severed relations with Cuba and aligned Jamaica with the US. An economic turnaround proved elusive; growth averaged only 1% from 1981 to 1985. IMF relations were restored as the Jamaican dollar was devalued. Tourism increased and GDP grew 6% in 1987.

Michael Manley was reelected in 1989 but maintained US ties. In 1991 Jamaica's stock exchange (42 listed shares) agreed to cross-list stocks with other Caribbean exchanges as the first step toward a unified regional stock exchange. Jamaica and its fellow members of the Caribbean Common Market (formed 1973 by Trinidad and Tobago, Jamaica, Guyana, and Barbados, and soon joined by St. Kitts, Belize, and the Bahamas) took steps to form a single market on the EC model.

HOW MUCH

	4-Year Growth	1986	1987	1988	1989	1990
Population (mil.)	*2.1%*	2.3	2.4	2.5	2.4	2.5
GDP ($ bil.)	*12.5%*	*2*	*3*	*3*	*4*	*4*
Real GDP growth rate	—	1.7%	6.2%	1.5%	4.6%	2.5%
Exports ($ mil.)	*19.4%*	590	708	883	997	1,200
Imports ($ mil.)	*18.5%*	837	1,065	1,240	1,569	1,650
Trade balance ($ mil.)	—	(248)	(357)	(357)	(572)	(450)
Current account ($ mil.)	—	(40)	(137)	30	(296)	(190)
Govt. budget bal. ($ mil.)	—	*(183)*	*(212)*	*(194)*	*(379)*	—
Consumer inflation	—	15.1%	6.7%	8.3%	14.3%	20.9%
Unemployment rate	—	—	—	18.9%	—	*18%*
Exchange rate with US$	—	5.48	5.49	5.49	5.75	7.20

Source: Economist Intelligence Unit and *The Reference Press*

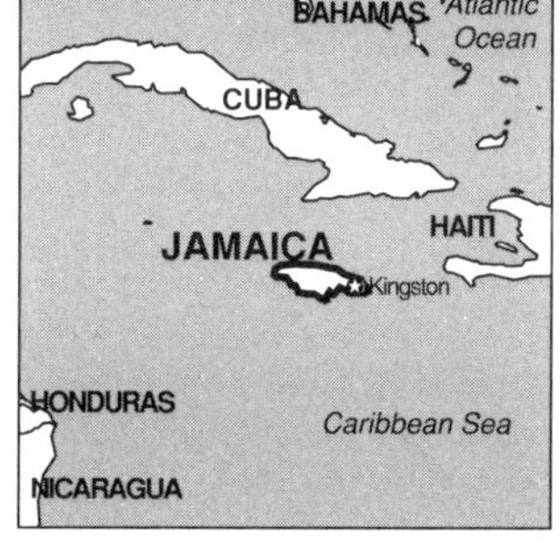

Area: 4,244 sq. mi. (10,991 sq. km)

Official name: Jamaica
Official language: English
Currency: 1 dollar = 100 cents
Fiscal year ends: March 31

WHO

Governor General: Hon. Edward Zacca (acting)
Prime Minister and Minister of Defense: Rt. Hon. Michael Manley, P.C., age 67
Deputy Prime Minister and Minister of Finance, Development, and Planning: Percival J. Patterson, QC
Minister of Foreign Affairs and Foreign Trade: David Coore, QC, age 65
Ambassador to US: Richard Bernal
US Ambassador to Jamaica: Glen A. Holden

WHERE

Executive HQ: Prime Minister, 1 Devon Rd., POB 272, Kingston, Jamaica
Embassy in US: Suite 355, 1850 K St. NW, Washington, DC 20006
Phone: 202-452-0660
Fax: 202-452-0081
US Embassy in Jamaica: Jamaica Mutual Life Center, 2 Oxford Rd., 3rd Fl., Kingston, Jamaica
Phone: 809-929-4850
Fax: 809-926-6743
Chamber of Commerce: Jamaica Chamber of Commerce, PO Box 172, East Parade, Kingston, Jamaica
Phone: 809-922-0150

Jamaica has 14 parishes and has diplomatic representatives in 31 countries.

Capital city: Kingston
Time change from EST: 0 hours
Avg. high/low temp: Jan. 86°F (30°C)/67°F (19°C)
July 90°F (32°C)/73°F (23°C)

Urbanization: 52%
Population density: 589/sq. mi. (227/sq. km)

Exports as % of Total		Imports as % of Total	
US	37	US	49
UK	18	UK	7
Canada	14	Canada	6
Netherlands	12	Mexico	5
Other countries	19	Other countries	33
Total	**100**	**Total**	**100**

WHAT

Origins of GDP	% of Total
Manufacturing	17
Distributive trades	16
Financial institutions	9
Transport & communications	8
Construction	8
Other	42
Total	**100**

1990 GDP per capita: $1,567
1990 year-end external debt: $5 billion
Literacy rate: 82%
UN Human Development Index: 76%
Human Freedom Index (0-40 scale): 25
Purchasing power as % of US: 14%
Capital city cost of living as % of DC: —
Defense as % of GNP: 1%
Education as % of GNP: —
Principal airline: Air Jamaica
Principal exchange: The Jamaica Stock Exchange

JAPAN

OVERVIEW

Despite a lack of any substantial natural resources and a late start in industrializing, Japan has the world's 2nd largest (after the US) capitalist economy.

By promoting national pride and emphasizing education and individual sacrifice for group goals, Japan has become one of the strongest economic powers on earth. The US played a critical role in Japan's success by benevolently occupying it after WWII, shouldering the cost of the military defense of Asia, and opening US markets to Japanese imports.

Japan's economy is an intricate partnership of government and business consisting of huge, interconnected corporations (known as *keiretsu*), small- and medium-sized companies supplying the large corporations, and a few (but decreasing number of) government companies. Japan has one of the world's most productive agriculture sectors and one of the largest fishing fleets (15% of the global catch).

Since WWII Japan has promoted economic growth above all else by protecting domestic markets, encouraging cartels, and aggressively promoting exports. International complaints of unfair trade practices and high domestic prices have led Japan to promote imports and open domestic markets to foreign goods. Japan has also encouraged consumerism in order to decrease a traditionally high savings rate, which funded much of its growth and made it the world's largest creditor.

Though Japan's economy remained strong in early 1991, the outlook was clouded by anti-Japanese sentiment in Europe and the US, tight credit, falling real estate prices, and stock market scandals.

WHEN

Chinese merchants introduced commerce to Japan's largely agricultural economy in the 5th century. From the 12th to the 19th century, the military overlord (*shogun*) ruled a feudal state composed of (in descending social order) lords (*daimyos*), samurai warriors, peasant farmers, artists, and merchants. Towns grew up around the *daimyos*' estates, with merchants providing goods and credit.

Except for some trading with the Spanish and Portuguese in the late 16th century and with the Dutch and English later, Japan had no substantial contacts with the West until the 19th century.

Modernization began during the isolationist Tokugawa shogunate (1603–1867) when a lively internal trade was aided by the shogunate's road-building program. Farmers (80% of the population) were heavily taxed, and the evolution from a rice-based, in-kind to a cash economy eroded their economic strength. In the 19th century some *daimyos* began illicitly trading with Westerners, acquiring technologies to start small foundries and shipyards.

US Commodore Matthew Perry's arrival in 1853 resulted in Japan's first foreign treaty. The *shogun*'s failure to repel the foreigners led to the 1868 "restoration" of the Meiji emperor, whose administrators were determined to modernize. *Daimyos*, deprived of their feudal holdings (but generously compensated for them), formed family-based businesses called *zaibatsu*.

The *zaibatsu* entered the textile industry and bought small government businesses on concessionary terms. In the 1880s the government provided capital for industry and promoted education. Peasants migrating to cities provided cheap labor.

Industrial development brought renewed militarism, which led Japan to fight and win wars with China for Korea (1894–95) and with Russia for Manchuria (1904). In WWI Japan sided with the Allies and prospered until the Great Depression. By the mid-1930s Japanese industry and military imperialism were expanding again. Japan entered WWII on the German side and surrendered after the US dropped atomic bombs on Hiroshima and Nagasaki.

At the end of WWII, 30% of Japanese were homeless, and industrial capacity was less than 1/3 its prewar level. Under US occupation Japan began to rebuild. US supply activity during the Korean War boosted the economy further. By 1955 industrial production had surpassed prewar levels. From the 1950s to the early 1970s, GNP grew 10% annually. Japan overtook West Germany in 1968 as the 2nd largest capitalist economy.

The 1973 oil embargo slowed growth, but, by 1979 when oil prices increased, Japan had begun converting its export economy from energy-dependent heavy industry to science-based industries.

In the 1980s Japan became the largest net exporter of goods and capital in the world.

HOW MUCH

	4-Year Growth	1986	1987	1988	1989	1990
Population (mil.)	*0.4%*	121.7	122.3	122.8	123.3	123.6
GDP ($ bil.)	*10.0%*	*1,999*	*2,424*	*2,915*	*2,889*	*2,932*
Real GDP growth rate	—	2.6%	4.3%	6.2%	4.7%	5.7%
Exports ($ mil.)	*8.0%*	205,600	224,600	259,800	269,700	280,200
Imports ($ mil.)	*17.7%*	112,800	128,200	164,800	192,700	216,300
Trade balance ($ mil.)	—	92,800	96,400	95,000	77,000	63,900
Current account ($ mil.)	—	85,800	87,000	79,600	57,200	35,700
Govt. budget bal. ($ mil.)	—	—	*0*	*0*	*0*	*0*
Consumer inflation	—	0.6%	0.1%	0.7%	2.3%	3.1%
Unemployment rate	—	—	2.8%	2.8%	2.3%	2.0%
Exchange rate with US$	—	168.0	144.6	128.2	138.0	144.6

Source: Economist Intelligence Unit and *The Reference Press*

Area: 145,856 sq. mi. (377,765 sq. km)

Official name:
Japan
Nippon (or *Nihon*)
Official language: Japanese
Currency: 1 yen (¥) = 100 sen
Fiscal year ends: March 31

WHO

Symbol of the State: Emperor Tsugu no Miya Akihito, age 58
Prime Minister: Toshiki Kaifu, age 60
Minister of Finance: Ryutaro Hashimoto, age 54
Minister of Foreign Affairs: Taro Nakayama, age 67
Ambassador to US: Ryohei Murata, age 67
US Ambassador to Japan: Michael H. Armacost

WHERE

Executive HQ: Prime Minister, 1-6-1, Nagata-cho, Chiyoda-ku, Tokyo 100, Japan
Embassy in US: 2520 Massachusetts Ave. NW, Washington, DC 20008
Phone: 202-939-6700
Fax: 202-265-9484
US Embassy in Japan: 10-1, Akasaka 1-chome, Minato-ku, Tokyo 107, Japan
Phone: 011-81-3-3224-5000
Fax: 011-81-3-3505-1862
Chamber of Commerce: International Chamber of Commerce, Tokyo Kaijo Bldg., 2-1 Marunouchi, 1-chome, Chiyoda-ku, Tokyo, Japan
Phone: 011-81-3-3213-8585
Fax: 011-81-3-3213-8589

Japan has 47 prefectures and has diplomatic representatives in 103 countries.

Capital city: Tokyo
Time change from EST: +14 hours
Avg. high/low temp: Jan. 47°F (8°C)/29°F (-2°C)
July 83°F (28°C)/70°F (21°C)

Urbanization: 77%
Population density: 847/sq. mi. (327/sq. km)

Exports as % of Total		Imports as % of Total	
US	34	US	23
Korea	6	Korea	6
Germany	6	Australia	6
Taiwan	6	China	5
Other countries	48	Other countries	60
Total	**100**	**Total**	**100**

WHAT

Origins of GDP	% of Total
Manufacturing	29
Banks, insurance & real estate	17
Wholesale & retail trade	13
Construction	9
Other	32
Total	**100**

1990 GDP per capita: $23,722
1990 year-end external debt: none
Literacy rate: 99%
UN Human Development Index: 99%
Human Freedom Index (0-40 scale): 32
Purchasing power as % of US: 72%
Capital city cost of living as % of DC: 195%
Defense as % of GNP: 1%
Education as % of GDP: 5%
Principal airlines: Japan Air Lines (JAL), Nippon Airways
Principal exchange: Tokyo Shouken Torihikijyo

JORDAN

OVERVIEW

Jordan's boundaries with Iraq, Syria, Israel, and Saudi Arabia are the result more of politics and history than of natural boundaries or national affinity. About 40% of Jordan's people are Palestinians, refugees or their descendants, who remain emotionally tied to areas now controlled by Israel.

Agriculture (11% of the land is arable) produces less than 9% of income and employs 20% of the people. Despite heavy investment in agricultural technology, including drip irrigation projects, Jordan remains a net importer of food. Chief crops include wheat, barley, citrus, vegetables, and fruits.

Natural resources include phosphate (3rd largest exporter, after Morocco and the US) and potash. Jordan dominates the East and South Asia phosphate market. Industries include phosphate fertilizers, cement, and textiles. Jordan possesses some oil but not enough to meet even its own needs.

Jordan was severely affected by the Gulf War. It was deluged with refugees, including Jordanians who had been working in other affected countries; lost one of its major trade partners (Iraq); and suffered ostracism from the rest of the Arab community for tilting toward Iraq.

King Hussein must try to balance the national interest, which favors Western alliance in exchange for aid and trade, and Palestinian interests, which have in the past destabilized his government in an effort to effect their own goals, the main one of which is an autonomous Palestinian homeland.

WHEN

Starting about 2000 BC Jordan was ruled first by Hittites and then by Egyptians, Israelites, Assyrians, Babylonians, Persians, Greeks, and Romans. Islam arrived in 630. Then the flourishing agricultural society declined, and nomadism dominated throughout the Ottoman era. In the late 19th century, government control and settlement increased somewhat, but Jordan remained a land of nomadic herders, farmers, and small towns.

In WWI the Allies weakened the Ottoman Empire by encouraging Arab nationalism. T. E. Lawrence (Lawrence of Arabia) worked closely with Sharif Hussein of Mecca, one of whose sons, Abdullah, was made king of Jordan by the British after the war; another son became king of Iraq. The British occupied the new Kingdom of Transjordan until the 1950s.

When the UN partitioned Palestine in 1947, creating Israel, Abdullah joined in the effort to destroy Israel. In the resulting war he annexed the West Bank, which the UN had intended to be part of a new Palestinian state that was to have been created concurrently with Israel. Abdullah proclaimed himself king of all Palestine. Jordan was flooded with refugees.

In the 1950s and 1960s, Jordan used foreign aid to develop agricultural irrigation and phosphate mining and used its custody of some of the holiest Islamic and Christian sites to develop tourism (its possession of the Wailing Wall complicated conflicts with Israel).

In 1967 Jordan joined another war against Israel, losing the West Bank (which produced 40% of GDP) and gaining more refugees. Jordan continued to pay the salaries of West Bank employees and teachers and to fund development projects until 1989.

Much of the loss was offset by aid from the Arab oil states, which helped Jordan pay for oil and funded economic development. Another source of revenue was remittances from Jordanians working abroad. During 1970–71, King Hussein (who had succeeded to the throne in 1952) expelled Palestinian partisans who had used Jordan as a base for attacking Israel. Jordan played only a limited role in the 1973 Yom Kippur War with Israel.

From 1976 to 1980 the economy grew 10% annually. In 1981 aid and remittances totaled almost $2.5 billion. The 1980s decline in oil prices and rise in interest rates brought a decline in aid and remittances, a rise in loan payments, and dwindling foreign reserves. Currency value fell, boosting import costs and fueling inflation. By 1989 the budget deficit was 20% of GDP. Economic growth turned negative.

After decades of balancing Western and Palestinian interests, King Hussein had to choose sides when Iraq invaded Kuwait; he seemed to choose Iraq (supported by many Palestinians). In September 1990 Saudi Arabia cut off oil to Jordan, expelled diplomats and guest workers, and started a trade embargo. During the Gulf War, Jordan took in one million refugees, a burden increased by declining aid. Since the war Hussein has tried to mend relations with the victors, and in July 1991 he lifted martial law imposed in 1967.

HOW MUCH

	4-Year Growth	1986	1987	1988	1989	1990
Population (mil.)	*5.7%*	2.8	2.9	3.0	3.1	3.5
GDP ($ bil.)	*(11.7%)*	*5.8*	*6.1*	*5.9*	*4.5*	*3.5*
Real GDP growth rate	—	2.1%	3.4%	(2.1%)	(3.9%)	(8.2%)
Exports ($ mil.)	*5.3%*	732	932	1,016	1,110	900
Imports ($ mil.)	*(1.8%)*	2,422	2,696	2,716	2,399	2,250
Trade balance ($ mil.)	—	(1,690)	(1,764)	(1,700)	(1,289)	(1,350)
Current account ($ mil.)	—	(40)	(352)	(294)	(82)	(600)
Govt. budget bal. ($ mil.)	—	*(438)*	*(585)*	*(550)*	*(241)*	*(143)*
Consumer inflation	—	—	(0.2%)	6.6%	25.8%	16.1%
Unemployment rate	—	—	—	—	—	20.0%
Exchange rate with US$	—	0.35	0.34	0.37	0.57	0.66

Source: Economist Intelligence Unit and *The Reference Press*

Area: 34,443 sq. mi. (89,206 sq. km)

Official name:
Hashemite Kingdom of Jordan
Al Mamlaka al Urduniya al Hashemiyah
Official language: Arabic
Currency: 1 dinar (JD) = 1,000 fils
Fiscal year ends: December 31

WHO

Monarch: King Hussein ibn Talal al-Hashimi, age 56
Crown Prince: Prince Hassan (brother of King Hussein), age 44
Prime Minister and Defense Minister: Taher Masri
Finance Minister: Basel Jardaneh
Minister of Foreign Affairs: Abdullah Nsour
Ambassador to US: Hussein A. Hammami
US Ambassador to Jordan: Roger G. Harrison

WHERE

Executive HQ: King, Royal Palace, Amman, Jordan
Embassy in US: 3504 International Dr. NW, Washington, DC 20008
Phone: 202-966-2664
Fax: 202-966-3110
US Embassy in Jordan: PO Box 354, Jabel Amman, Amman, Jordan
Phone: 011-962-6-644-371
Fax: 011-962-6-659-720
Chamber of Commerce: Federation of Jordanian Chambers of Commerce, PO Box 7029, Amman, Jordan
Phone: 011-962-6-665-492

Jordan has 8 governates and has diplomatic representatives in 39 countries.

Capital city: Amman
Time change from EST: +7 hours
Avg. high/low temp: Jan. 54°F (12°C)/39°F (4°C)
July 89°F (32°C)/65°F (18°C)

Urbanization: 67%
Population density: 102/sq. mi. (39/sq. km)

Exports as % of Total		Imports as % of Total	
Iraq	23	Iraq	17
India	18	US	14
Saudi Arabia	9	Germany	6
Indonesia	5	UK	6
Other countries	45	Other countries	57
Total	**100**	**Total**	**100**

WHAT

Origins of GDP	% of Total
Government	19
Finance & other services	18
Trade, restaurants & hotels	15
Transport & communications	13
Manufacturing	13
Mining & quarrying	7
Agriculture	6
Other	9
Total	**100**

1990 GDP per capita: $1,007
1990 year-end external debt: $9 billion
Literacy rate: 75%
UN Human Development Index: 61%
Human Freedom Index (0-40 scale): —
Purchasing power as % of US: 18%
Capital city cost of living as % of DC: 83%
Defense as % of GNP: 16%
Education as % of GNP: 7%
Principal airline: Royal Jordanian
Principal exchange: Amman Financial Market

KENYA

OVERVIEW

Kenya's population of approximately 25 million (50% under 14) is growing more than 5% per year, one of the world's fastest rates. This fact affects all sectors of Kenya's economy.

Agriculture accounts for about 30% of GDP and employs 70% of the work force. Kenya produces coffee, tea, and cut flowers for export, and food crops for domestic consumption. Yet population growth is beginning to outpace production, and farm size is beginning to decline because of subdivision by inheritance. Landlessness and settlement of land unsuitable for farming are growing problems. Kenya is also becoming a producer of illicit drugs for domestic use and a transit point in the international drug trade.

Mineral resources, including gold, limestone, diatomite, and magnesite, are not fully exploited. Small-scale industry is being developed, primarily to produce such current imports as plastics, furniture, batteries, textiles, soaps, and cigarettes. The government has recently begun export incentive programs. Though lacking petroleum Kenya refines imported crude oil and produces cement.

Tourism in Kenya's game parks is an important segment of the economy and the #1 source of foreign exchange. However, tourism is being hurt by lack of government resources, poaching (Kenya was a leader in the drive to ban the ivory trade worldwide), and crime against tourists.

With an estimated unemployment rate of 30% and an anticipated doubling of Kenya's current 7-million-person labor force by the turn of the century, Kenya cannot expect its economy to improve soon.

WHEN

Kenya's Lake Turkana was home to some of the oldest known ancestors of *Homo sapiens* 2.5 million years ago. Kenya's inhabitants were part of the Roman trading world, and Islamic traders reached Kenya in the 8th century.

The Portuguese arrived in 1498, challenging the Arab trade monopoly in ivory, gold, and coral. In the 17th century the area came under the rule of Oman and then became part of the Sultanate of Zanzibar. Slave trade joined that of the traditional goods.

British attempts to end the slave trade in 1823 led to an increase in their influence in the area throughout the century. Under the pressure of German colonial rivalry after 1878, the British East Africa Company secured a 50-year lease from the Sultan of Zanzibar for most of present-day Kenya. European powers set the boundaries of colonial East Africa in 1885, without regard to tribal settlement.

In 1895 a railway line opened from Lake Victoria to the chief port, Mombasa. Facilitated by the railroad, British settlers moved into Kenya in large numbers after 1900, appropriating the best upland agricultural areas for large coffee plantations and relegating the natives to the poorer land. Traders and merchants arrived from India as well.

In the 25 years before WWII, the native population doubled, overtaxing the poorer farmlands. Increasingly restrictive laws were enacted to control the African majority. This led in the 1950s to nearly a decade of bloody terror and counterterror during the Mau-Mau rebellion, culminating in anarchy in 1957. Most of the white population fled, and the British government granted Africans representation in the local legislature. Independence came in 1963.

In the 1960s intertribal rivalry was gradually brought under control by President Jomo Kenyatta. GDP grew 6.6% annually from 1963 to 1973. Kenya became relatively prosperous, with coffee and tea cash crops. Agriculture was stimulated by distribution of plantations to small farmers, and a thriving tourist industry centered on Kenya's game parks.

With no oil resources Kenya's economy suffered under oil price increases in the 1970s. Starting in 1982 semidrought conditions inhibited production of food and cash crops.

In 1986, with coffee prices high, energy prices low, and the drought in abeyance, Kenya's economy boomed. With a small balance of payment deficit, the government was able to undertake economic reform, especially in agricultural marketing, and recognize the need to increase industry based on its natural products. It also tried to cut government spending and to stay out of the business sector.

Since then, however, coffee prices have dropped and tourism has declined. Bright spots in agricultural diversification were Kenya's entry into the European and US cut-flower markets and its decision to export tropical fruits, but both were threatened by renewed drought in 1991.

HOW MUCH

	4-Year Growth	1986	1987	1988	1989	1990
Population (mil.)	*5.5%*	21.2	22.9	23.9	24.9	*26.3*
GDP ($ bil.)	—	*6.3*	*6.8*	*7.2*	*7.1*	—
Real GDP growth rate	—	5.6%	4.9%	5.2%	5.0%	3.5%
Exports ($ mil.)	*(0.3%)*	1,216	960	1,073	991	1,200
Imports ($ mil.)	*10.4%*	1,649	1,740	1,989	2,177	2,450
Trade balance ($ mil.)	—	(433)	(780)	(916)	(1,186)	(1,250)
Current account ($ mil.)	—	(39)	(497)	(454)	(587)	(800)
Govt. budget bal. ($ mil.)	—	*(264)*	*(531)*	*(297)*	*(263)*	*(407)*
Consumer inflation	—	4.0%	5.1%	8.3%	9.8%	12.5%
Unemployment rate	—	—	—	—	13.0%	—
Exchange rate with US$	—	16.23	16.45	17.75	20.57	22.92

Source: Economist Intelligence Unit and *The Reference Press*

Area: 224,960 sq. mi. (582,646 sq. km)

Official name:
Republic of Kenya
Jamhuri ya Kenya
Official language: English
Currency: 1 shilling (Ksh) = 100 cents
Fiscal year ends: June 30

WHO

President: Daniel Toroitich arap Moi, age 67
Vice-President and Minister for Finance: George Saitoti
Minister for Foreign Affairs: Wilson Ndolo Ayah
Ambassador to US and Mexico: Denis D. Afande
US Ambassador to Kenya: Smith Hempstone, Jr.

WHERE

Executive HQ: President's Office, POB 30510, Harambee House, Harambee Ave., Nairobi, Kenya
Embassy in US: 2249 R St. NW, Washington, DC 20008
Phone: 202-387-6101
Fax: 202-462-3829
US Embassy in Kenya: PO Box 30137, Moi/Haile Selassie Ave., Nairobi, Kenya
Phone: 011-254-2-333834
Fax: 011-254-2-340838
Chamber of Commerce: National Chamber of Commerce & Industry, PO Box 47024, Ufanisi House, Haile Selassie Ave., Nairobi, Kenya

Kenya has 41 rural districts (joined to form 7 rural provinces) and the Nairobi Area and has diplomatic representatives in 34 countries.

Capital city: Nairobi
Time change from EST: +7 hours
Avg. high/low temp: Jan. 77°F (25°C)/54°F (12°C)
July 69°F (21°C)/51°F (11°C)

Urbanization: 23%
Population density: 116/sq. mi. (45/sq. km)

Exports as % of Total		Imports as % of Total	
UK	20	UK	16
Germany	9	UAE	11
Uganda	7	Japan	11
Other countries	64	Other countries	62
Total	**100**	**Total**	**100**

WHAT

Origins of GDP	% of Total
Agriculture, forestry & fishing	31
Government services	14
Manufacturing	12
Trade, restaurants & hotels	11
Transport, storage & communications	7
Other	25
Total	**100**

1989 GDP per capita: $286
1989 year-end external debt: $6 billion
Literacy rate: 59%
UN Human Development Index: 40%
Human Freedom Index (0-40 scale): 8
Purchasing power as % of US: 5%
Capital city cost of living as % of DC: 64%
Defense as % of GNP: 1%
Education as % of GNP: 6%
Principal airline: Kenya Airways
Principal exchange: Nairobi Stock Exchange

KOREA

OVERVIEW

Korea is the only nation still split by the Cold War. The Republic of Korea (South Korea) occupies the southern part of the Korean peninsula. It has better agricultural lands but lacks the abundant mineral deposits of the north. It also has greater human resources, with 42 million people to North Korea's 22 million.

With an expansionist, export-driven market-share strategy, the ROK is now a major producer of electronics, textiles, cars, and ships. It is one of the world's fastest-growing countries (GDP grew at 11.5% in 1988, slowing to a still-high 8.9% in 1990), with a mixed economy that includes government planning as well as free-market private enterprise. South Korean business is characterized by R&D, cutthroat competitiveness, and diversified private business combines called *chaebols*. Among the largest *chaebols* are Samsung, Hyundai, Lucky-Goldstar, and Daewoo.

As the ROK has prospered, workers have demanded higher wages. After much labor unrest in the 1980s, wages rose nearly 50% between 1987 and 1990. This has brought higher inflation, 7.1% in 1988 and 8.6% in 1990. As purchasing power has grown, domestic demand has grown with it, leading to supply imbalances and swiftly rising prices, especially in the construction sector, where residential construction prices have increased.

Government attempts to maintain high savings levels and a favorable trade balance by discouraging the purchase of "luxury" foreign goods became a diplomatic and economic problem with the US and the EC. In July 1991 this policy was reversed. Korea is becoming a developed country, though domestic expansion is checked by near-full employment. Korean business is starting to invest overseas, particularly in the US, Canada, and the EC.

WHEN

Korea was united as a nation in the 10th century and came under Chinese control in the 19th century. In 1894 China lost a war to Japan over Korea, but Japan did not gain full control until 1910 when it annexed Korea.

Japanese rule was harsh; workers were taken as forced laborers to Japan, where their names and language were suppressed. Korea supplied Japan with the food and natural resources it lacked. The Japanese also established military bases and developed industry and hydroelectric power in the north.

In 1945, with the Japanese near surrender in WWII, the Soviet Union declared war and occupied northern Korea to the 38th parallel, installing a Communist government. In 1948 the UN sponsored elections in the south.

In 1950 northern forces nearly overran the south before ROK and US forces responded. When UN/US forces counterattacked, the Chinese intervened. Peace talks lasted from 1951 to 1953, when the current armed truce was agreed upon. The war devastated Korea and created countless refugees, and its settlement formally divided Korea into an industrial, resource-rich north and an agricultural south.

In the 1950s US aid to the south helped develop light industries and agriculture, leading to modest prosperity. Growth was slow through the 1950s, with high inflation and zero growth by 1960. Nominally a republic, South Korea was governed by authoritarian, sometimes military, leaders. With Soviet and Chinese aid, North Korea developed heavy industry and collectivized agriculture.

In 1962 the ROK began to develop heavy industry, privately owned but guided and fostered by government policy, incentives, and import controls. For the next 20 years, GDP growth averaged 8.5% per year.

In the 1970s low wages kept costs down while the auto and electronics industries grew by seizing market share with low prices.

In the 1980s South Korean workers struck for higher wages, hiking costs and disrupting production. A series of scandals in the upper management of the *chaebols* alienated the public. The stock market fell, inflation increased, productivity lagged, and the value of currency soared. The country became a "dumper" on the world market, selling products for less abroad than at home while keeping its own markets closed. By 1990 the labor unrest and management scandals had calmed, and the economy was back on track, but the increasing standard of living of its workers forced industry to compete with less-developed countries' lower labor costs.

In 1991 North and South Korea announced their first commercial ties and their plan to seek separate UN membership. That same year the government advised the *chaebols* that they would have to select 3 core businesses each and that non-Koreans would be allowed to own stock in Korean companies beginning in 1992.

HOW MUCH

	4-Year Growth	1986	1987	1988	1989	1990
Population (mil.)	*1.0%*	41.2	41.6	42.0	42.4	42.8
GDP ($ bil.)	*21.2%*	*106*	*132*	*175*	*212*	228
Real GDP growth rate	—	12.4%	11.8%	11.5%	6.1%	8.9%
Exports ($ mil.)	*16.7%*	34,700	47,300	60,700	62,400	64,400
Imports ($ mil.)	*22.0%*	31,600	41,000	51,800	61,500	70,100
Trade balance ($ mil.)	—	3,100	6,300	8,900	900	(5,700)
Current account ($ mil.)	—	4,700	9,900	14,200	5,100	(2,100)
Govt. budget bal. ($ mil.)	—	*1,087*	*2,035*	*2,297*	—	—
Consumer inflation	—	2.8%	3.0%	7.1%	5.7%	8.6%
Unemployment rate	—	—	—	2.5%	*2.6%*	*2.4%*
Exchange rate with US$	—	881.5	822.6	731.5	671.5	707.6

Source: Economist Intelligence Unit and *The Reference Press*

Area: 38,315 sq. mi. (99,237 sq. km)

Official name:
Republic of Korea
Han Kook
Official language: Korean
Currency: 1 won (W) = 100 jeon
Fiscal year ends: December 31

WHO

President of the Republic: Roh Tae-woo, age 59
Prime Minister: Chung Won Shik
Deputy Prime Minister: Choi Kag Kyu
Finance Minister: Chunk Yung Euy, age 54
Minister of Foreign Affairs: Lee Sang Ock
Ambassador to US: Hyun Hong Choo
US Ambassador to Korea: Donald P. Gregg

WHERE

Executive HQ: Office of the President, The Blue House, Sejong-No, Chongno-Ku, Seoul, Korea
Embassy in US: 2370 Massachusetts Ave. NW, Washington, DC 20008
Phone: 202-939-5600
Fax: 202-387-4695
US Embassy in Korea: 82 Sejong-Ro, Chongro-ku, Seoul, Korea
Phone: 011-82-2-732-2601
Fax: 011-82-2-738-8845
Chamber of Commerce: The Korea Chamber of Commerce and Industry, CPO Box 25, 45, 4-ka, Namdaemun-ro, Chung-ku, Seoul, Korea
Phone: 011-82-2-757-0757

Korea has 9 provinces and 6 special cities and has diplomatic representatives in 126 countries.

Capital city: Seoul
Time change from EST: +14 hours
Avg. high/low temp: Jan. 32°F (0°C)/15°F (-9°C)
July 84°F (29°C)/70°F (21°C)

Urbanization: 71%
Population density: 1,117/sq. mi. (431/sq. km)

Exports as % of Total		Imports as % of Total	
US	35	Japan	28
Japan	20	US	26
Hong Kong	6	Germany	4
Germany	4	Australia	4
Other countries	35	Other countries	38
Total	**100**	**Total**	**100**

WHAT

Origins of GDP	% of Total
Manufacturing	31
Financial & business services	14
Trade, restaurants & hotels	12
Agriculture, forestry & fishing	10
Construction	10
Government services	7
Transport, storage & communications	7
Other	9
Total	**100**

1990 GDP per capita: $5,336
1989 year-end external debt: $29 billion
Literacy rate: 95%
UN Human Development Index: 88%
Human Freedom Index (0-40 scale): 14
Purchasing power as % of US: 24%
Capital city cost of living as % of DC: 114%
Defense as % of GNP: 5%
Education as % of GNP: 4%
Principal airline: Korean Air Lines (KAL)
Principal exchange: Korea Stock Exchange

KUWAIT

OVERVIEW

Until the Iraqi invasion, Kuwait was one of the Middle East's wealthiest nations, with some of the largest oil reserves in the world. It boasted an impressive array of social services and a free-market economy and was a major source of aid to other Arab countries, including Iraq. Kuwaitis were a minority in their country, employing over one million foreign workers.

The war destroyed much of Kuwait's infrastructure (destruction estimated at $25 billion, Iraqi looting at $20 billion). Rebuilding will take years and cost billions. Fortunately, Kuwait has about $80 billion invested overseas through the Kuwaiti Investment Office (down from $100 billion in 1989) that it can use for the task.

The worst problem is the oil wells torched by the Iraqis. Though some fires have been extinguished and the wells returned to production, Kuwait's income will be reduced by over $6 billion annually until the fires are put out, and the smoke will continue to damage the ecological health of the region and the physical health of Kuwaitis and other downwind residents.

The discontent of the Kuwaiti people with the slow reestablishment of civil authority and their reluctance to resume the pre-war monarchical political status have already created new challenges for the country.

WHEN

Kuwait City was founded in the early 18th century by Arab tribesmen, who built an economy on pearling, trading, fishing, and herding. Though nominally part of the Ottoman Empire, it was ruled as an emirate by the Sabah family after 1756. In the 1770s the British diverted their mail service from nearby Basra to Kuwait. Ties between the Sabahs and Britain developed, and in 1899 the sheik signed a protection agreement with the British in exchange for an annual stipend. In 1914 Kuwait became a British protectorate.

Though oil was discovered in the 1930s, exports did not begin until after WWII, and Kuwait did not become a major exporter until the 1950s. Despite vast sums squandered by the Sabah family, the amount of money in relation to population (100,000 in the 1950s) was enough to provide comprehensive welfare benefits for all citizens, including medical care and education.

Kuwait's modernization was so swift that Kuwait could not provide all the labor and expertise necessary for development, and many foreigners from impoverished Middle Eastern and subcontinental nations were brought in to provide the administrative, skilled, and manual labor required.

Upon expiration of the British protection treaty in 1961, Iraq claimed Kuwait, arguing that a 1913 agreement with Turkey, which Iraq had not ratified, was inapplicable. British and UN action guaranteed Kuwait's borders.

In the 1960s and 1970s, Kuwait's wealth multiplied, and a modern city and free-market business center replaced the old mud-built trading town. Revenues grew too high for the domestic economy to absorb, and Kuwait embarked on an overseas investment binge.

In the 1980s oil revenues fell because of decreased demand. The economy suffered as government revenues declined. The local unofficial stock exchange (operating out of a parking garage) collapsed in 1982, weakening the banking system because unsecured loans had been used for investment.

A member of OPEC, Kuwait had agreed to abide by the cartel's production quotas. But as oil revenues dropped, Kuwait increased production to cure the shortfall in funds. In July 1990 Iraq's president Saddam Hussein demanded that Kuwait reduce production to its quota, repay revenues Iraq had lost due to the oil glut, and write off loans granted during Iraq's war with Iran. Kuwait refused. On August 2nd, Iraq invaded Kuwait, raising Iraqi control to 20% of world oil reserves.

World reaction was swift; the UN imposed an embargo on all Iraqi imports and a boycott of all Iraqi exports. News of atrocities and looting leaked out. When the UN's January 15, 1991, deadline for Iraqi withdrawal passed without compliance, UN/US forces began intensive air raids that were succeeded by a blitzkrieg that liberated Kuwait in 4 days.

Kuwait was shattered; desalinating plants, generators, and refineries had been destroyed and most wells set afire. The euphoria of liberation faded as the emir delayed his return to Kuwait and the repair of the service infrastructure was delayed. Among US companies contending for reconstruction contracts are Bechtel, CSX, and Dresser. In July 1991 Kuwait resumed oil exports during a period of low oil prices.

HOW MUCH

	4-Year Growth	1986	1987	1988	1989	1990
Population (mil.)	*4.1%*	1.79	1.87	1.96	2.05	2.10
GDP ($ bil.)	*(7.0%)*	*18*	*22*	*20*	*23*	*13*
Real GDP growth rate	—	8.5%	(4.0%)	3.5%	7.5%	11.0%
Exports ($ mil.)	*(2.3%)*	7,210	8,270	7,760	11,490	6,580
Imports ($ mil.)	*(13.0%)*	5,690	5,500	6,140	6,300	3,260
Trade balance ($ mil.)	—	1,520	2,770	1,620	5,190	3,320
Current account ($ mil.)	—	5,380	4,370	4,420	9,320	4,550
Govt. budget bal. ($mil.)	—	*(3,510)*	*(4,667)*	*(2,792)*	*(2,952)*	*(993)*
Consumer inflation	—	1.0%	0.6%	1.5%	3.4%	2.0%
Unemployment rate	—	—	—	—	—	—
Exchange rate with US$	—	0.292	0.279	0.279	0.294	0.292

Source: Economist Intelligence Unit and *The Reference Press*

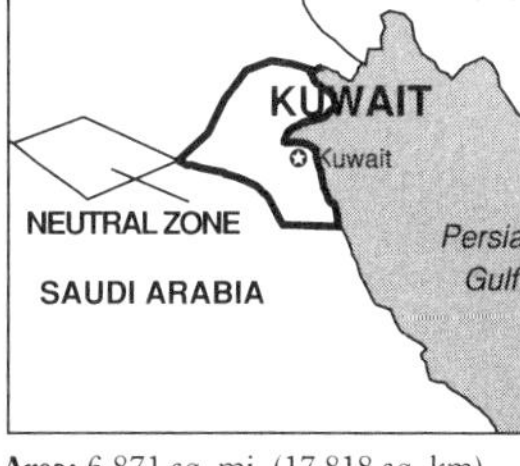

Area: 6,871 sq. mi. (17,818 sq. km)

Official name:
State of Kuwait
Dowlat al Kuwait
Official language: Arabic
Currency: 1 dinar (KD) = 1,000 fils
Fiscal year ends: June 30

WHO

Emir: His Highness Sheik Jabir al-Ahmad al-Jabir al-Sabah, age 65
Crown Prince and Prime Minister: HRH Sheik Saad Al-Abdulla Al-Salem Al-Sabah, age 67
Deputy Prime Minister and Minister of Foreign Affairs: Sheik Salem Sabah Al-Salem Al-Sabah
Minister of Finance: Nasir Abdulla Al-Rodhan
Ambassador to US: Sheik Saud Nasir al-Sabah
US Ambassador to Kuwait: Skip Gnehm

WHERE

Executive HQ: Emir of Kuwait, PO Box 799, Safat, Kuwait City, Kuwait
Embassy in US: 2940 Tilden St. NW, Washington, DC 20008
Phone: 202-966-0702
Fax: 202-966-0517
US Embassy in Kuwait: PO Box 77 Safat, 13001 Safat, Kuwait City, Kuwait
Phone: 011-965-242-4151
Chamber of Commerce: Kuwait Chamber of Commerce and Industry, PO Box 775, Ali-al-Salem St., 13008 Safat, Kuwait City, Kuwait
Phone: 011-965-243-3854

Kuwait has 4 governorates and has diplomatic representatives in 42 countries.

Capital city: Kuwait City
Time change from EST: +8 hours
Avg. high/low temp: Jan. 61°F (16°C)/49°F (9°C)
July 103°F (39°C)/86°F (30°C)

Urbanization: 95%
Population density: 306/sq. mi. (118/sq. km)

Exports as % of Total		Imports as % of Total	
Japan	19	US	15
Netherlands	9	Japan	11
US	8	Germany	8
Pakistan	6	UK	6
Other countries	58	Other countries	60
Total	**100**	**Total**	**100**

WHAT

Origins of GDP	% of Total
Hydrocarbons sector	41
Manufacturing	14
Domestic trade	7
Transport & communications	4
Financial institutions & insurance	2
Other	32
Total	**100**

1990 GDP per capita: $6,279
1989 year-end external debt: none
Literacy rate: 71%
UN Human Development Index: 83%
Human Freedom Index (0-40 scale): 8
Purchasing power as % of US: 79%
Capital city cost of living as % of DC: 100%
Defense as % of GNP: 7%
Education as % of GNP: 5%
Principal airline: Kuwait Airways
Principal exchange: Kuwait Stock Exchange

LIBYA

OVERVIEW

As a primary sponsor of terrorism, Libya, under the leadership of Muammar al-Qaddafi, was a disruptive force on the international scene for most of the 1970s and 1980s. Since 1986 it seems to have entered a new era of accommodation with its neighbors and the world. It is concentrating on economic development to improve the lot of its people.

Though self-sufficient in fruits and vegetables, Libya still imports 75% of its food, because only about 1% of its land (chiefly along the coast and at scattered desert oases) is arable. Much of the country is covered by the Sahara Desert, and there are no rivers for irrigation. Currently underway is a project to exploit Saharan aquifers to expand agricultural capacity. Traditional agricultural produce includes dates, fruits, barley, and wheat. Former colonial master Italy is still its largest trading partner.

Libya's chief source of wealth is oil (Libya is among the world's 10 largest exporters). During the boom years of the 1960s and 1970s, Libya prospered, but dependence upon oil led to a precipitous drop in revenues in the 1980s when world oil prices plummeted.

Accordingly, Libya's government has attempted to diversify the economy by exploiting other mineral resources — such as iron ore, gypsum, and sulfur — and expanding industry beyond traditional crafts into oil refining, steel production, and light industries.

In these efforts Libya has been handicapped by lack of educated personnel, international boycotts and embargoes (now being relaxed), and a decline in available funds.

WHEN

In the 13th century BC, Phoenician traders established Carthage on the coast of North Africa. Dominance of the area then passed to Greece (which called all of non-Egyptian North Africa "Libya"), Rome, the Vandals, and by the 4th century, the Byzantines.

Islam arrived in the 7th century. After the 13th century, North African Islam fragmented, and the Ottoman Turks (arriving in the 16th century) failed to unify it.

The lives of the people changed little over the centuries. They were poor farmers and herders, scratching out a living along the coast and at desert oases, or herding sheep, goats, and camels in the more arid regions and trading between the coast and the oases.

In the early 20th century, Italian settlers provoked a conflict that allowed Italy to declare Libya a protectorate in 1911.

After defeat in WWII Italy gave up its claim to Libya. Negotiations for freedom were conducted between the UN and local leaders (dominated by the Emir of Cyrenaica). In 1951 Libya became the first nation to gain independence under UN auspices, as a constitutional monarchy under the emir, known as King Idris.

The country remained poor (1950 per capita GDP: $40) until oil was discovered in 1959. Libya soon became one of the wealthiest nations in Africa, but the wealth was unevenly distributed. In 1969 a group of army officers, led by Muammar al-Qaddafi, overthrew the king and declared a Socialist state.

Qaddafi nationalized foreign oil company holdings (e.g., Occidental Petroleum) but allowed the former owners to continue to operate the wells and sell their oil. He closed foreign military bases (British and US) and expelled foreigners to curb their cultural influences.

To achieve his political ends, Qaddafi directed terrorism against his Libyan political enemies abroad and supporters of Israel. Yet, during the 1973 oil embargo, Libya continued to ship oil to the US. In the 1970s and 1980s, in search of Arab unity, Qaddafi attempted unions with several neighbors but was rebuffed, and a 1976 invasion of Chad proved financially draining and, ultimately, unsuccessful.

By 1980 per capita GDP had reached $11,000. But direct oil revenues fell from over $22 billion in 1980 to $6 billion in 1988. During the 1980s, as OPEC restricted oil production, Libya drew on its reserves for cash. Another financial blow was the US boycott of Libyan oil (1982) and all goods (1986).

Other expenses included military spending and large public works projects, such as the Man-Made River project, a pipeline to bring water from Saharan aquifers to the coast, for expansion of agriculture.

The US boycott still applies, much to the sorrow of US oil companies with potentially lucrative leases from the Libyan government. Since the US bombing of Tripoli in 1986, Qaddafi has tried to reconcile with the Arab community and the world at large. Libya was neutral in the Gulf War and even condemned the Iraqi missle attacks on Israel.

HOW MUCH

	4-Year Growth	1986	1987	1988	1989	1990
Population (mil.)	2.7%	3.93	4.08	4.23	4.30	4.38
GDP ($ bil.)	*6.2%*	*21*	*25*	*21*	*22*	*27*
Real GDP growth rate	—	—	—	—	—	—
Exports ($ mil.)	*17.3%*	5,810	5,830	5,640	7,750	11,000
Imports ($ mil.)	*15.9%*	4,430	5,390	5,750	5,500	8,000
Trade balance ($ mil.)	—	1,380	440	(110)	2,250	3,000
Current account ($ mil.)	—	(160)	(1,050)	(1,820)	1,280	1,000
Govt. budget bal. ($ mil.)	—	*(1,069)*	*(762)*	*(391)*	*(1,455)*	*(1,193)*
Consumer inflation	—	—	—	—	—	—
Unemployment rate	—	—	—	—	—	—
Exchange rate with US$	—	0.31	0.27	0.29	0.29	0.27

Source: Economist Intelligence Unit and *The Reference Press*

Area: 679,358 sq. mi. (1,759,540 sq. km)

Official name:
Socialist People's Libyan Arab Jamahiriya
Al-Jamahiriya Al-Arabiya Al-Libiya Al-Shabiya Al-Ishtirakiya Al-Uzma
Official language: Arabic
Currency: 1 dinar (LD) = 1,000 dirham
Fiscal year ends: December 31

WHO

Revolutionary Leader: Col. Muammar Abu Minyar al-Qaddafi, age 49
Chairman of the General People's Committee (Premier): 'Umar Mustafa al-Muntasir
Secretary of the General People's Congress: Muftah al-Usta' Umar
Minister of Foreign Affairs: Jadallah Azzuz al-Talhi

WHERE

Diplomatic relations with US: The US suspended all embassy activities in Tripoli on May 2, 1980.
Representation of US in Libya: US Interests Section (under protection of Belgium), Belgium Embassy, Tower 4, That Al-Imad Complex, PO Box 91650, Tripoli, Libya
Phone: 011-218-21-33660
Chamber of Commerce: Tripolitana Chamber of Commerce, Industry and Agriculture, PO Box 2321, Sharia Al-Jamhouria, Tripoli, Libya
Phone: 011-218-21-32755

Libya has 46 municipalities and has diplomatic representatives in 70 countries.

Capital city: Tripoli
Time change from EST: +6 hours
Avg. high/low temp: Jan. 61°F (16°C)/47°F (8°C)
July 85°F (29°C)/71°F (22°C)

Urbanization: 69%
Population density: 6/sq. mi. (2/sq. km)

Exports as % of Total		Imports as % of Total	
Italy	37	Italy	22
Germany	20	Germany	14
Spain	9	UK	8
France	6	France	7
Other countries	28	Other countries	49
Total	**100**	**Total**	**100**

WHAT

Origins of GDP	% of Total
Services	33
Mining, petroleum & natural gas	30
Construction	12
Manufacturing & public utilities	8
Trade, restaurants & hotels	6
Transport & communications	6
Agriculture, forestry & fishing	5
Total	**100**

1990 GDP per capita: $6,088
1989 year-end external debt: $5 billion
Literacy rate: 50-60%
UN Human Development Index: 67%
Human Freedom Index (0-40 scale): 1
Purchasing power as % of US: —
Capital city cost of living as % of DC: —
Defense as % of GNP: 11%
Education as % of GNP: —
Principal airline: Libyan Arab

MALAYSIA

OVERVIEW

Malaysia consists of land at the tip of the Malay peninsula and the states of Sarawak and Sabah on the island of Borneo. It is sparsely populated, largely rural, and overwhelmingly young. Per capita GDP is high for an Asian agricultural nation. Malaysia's economy has boomed in recent years, with GDP growing up to 11% annually.

Offshore petroleum and natural gas, tin, copper, bauxite, and coal make Malaysia one of Asia's most minerally endowed nations. It also produces rubber (world's largest producer), tropical oils, and timber. Agriculture was the largest part of GDP until 1987. As an exporter of commodities, Malaysia is vulnerable to world market cycles. As the largest producer of palm oil, it suffered when US food processors stopped using tropical oils. It is also vulnerable to environmentalists' efforts to preserve rain forests, as sale of hardwoods from its Borneo states is a major industry.

Malaysia creates manufacturing jobs through foreign investment incentives. Government restrictions on financial institutions limit the growth of financial services. Despite an active effort to sell off state-owned companies, the government is still a central force in the economy. Tourism is encouraged.

Malaysia faces political and economic challenges balancing the rights and interests of its ethnic and religious groups. Only 47% of the population is Malay (*bumiputras*, "sons of the soil"); 42% is Chinese and subcontinental. Since 1970 it has been formal government policy under the New Economic Plan (NEP) to redistribute wealth to *bumiputras*.

WHEN

In 1400 the Islamic Malacca sultanate was established on the Malay peninsula. Portuguese explorers arrived in 1511. In the 1600s the Dutch were the dominant trading power.

During the late 1700s the British East India Company acquired several coastal sites (including Singapore island, 1819), which became the Straits Settlements (1826) and were transferred to crown control (1867).

In 1840 tin deposits were found on the west coast. The ensuing "tin rush" brought an influx of Chinese laborers, whose cultural differences from the Malays threatened social stability. Between 1874 and 1914 Britain sought to dominate local government through treaties in which local rulers ceded control to a British Resident advisor. In 1878 native rulers ceded North Borneo to the British North Borneo Company. The Sultan of Brunei made Englishman James Brooke, Raja of Sarawak in 1841; Brooke family rule lasted until 1941.

Malaya became the largest tin producer in the world, and rubber trees, brought from Brazil, made it the world's #1 rubber producer. Europeans developed plantations, importing Chinese and Indian laborers.

In the early 20th century, there was little anticolonialism, but a rivalry grew between the urban, commercial Chinese and Indians, and the rural, agricultural Malays. By 1931, 39% of the population was Chinese and 45% Malay. While the Chinese and Indians prospered in trade, the British tried to keep the Malays from changing their traditional agricultural way of life.

The Japanese invaded in 1942, brutalizing the Chinese, who formed a resistance movement. The British returned after WWII and in 1946 took control of North Borneo and Sarawak. The Chinese launched an unsuccessful rebellion with communist overtones.

The Malayan peninsular states became independent in 1957; they joined North Borneo (renamed Sabah) and Singapore in the Federation of Malaysia in 1963. Singapore was expelled in 1965 because of Malay fears of Chinese mastery.

In 1960 the government promoted palm cultivation (for oil) and manufacturing. The first products were import substitutes. In the 1970s Malaysia emphasized exports, especially rubber, palm oil, timber, and electronics. It also began producing crude oil, for itself and for export during the 1970s.

Malaysia's GNP growth has been steady, averaging 7% from 1961 to 1976 and then 8.5% through 1980. After a downturn in the global recession of the early 1980s, GNP again attained the levels of the late 1970s.

In the 1980s US, Japanese, and Taiwanese manufacturers, faced with rising labor costs at home, relocated plants to Malaysia, which became the world's 3rd largest producer (after the US and Japan) and #1 exporter of silicon chips.

In 1991 the government unveiled NEP's replacement, The Second Outline Perspective Plan, which relies more on private enterprise than on government planning to achieve economic progress.

HOW MUCH

	4-Year Growth	1986	1987	1988	1989	1990
Population (mil.)	*2.5%*	16.1	16.5	16.9	17.4	17.8
GDP ($ bil.)	*11.5%*	*28*	*32*	*34*	*38*	*43*
Real GDP growth rate	—	1.2%	5.4%	8.9%	8.8%	9.4%
Exports ($ mil.)	*21.1%*	13,500	18,000	20,100	24,900	29,000
Imports ($ mil.)	*27.1%*	10,200	12,000	14,800	21,000	26,600
Trade balance ($ mil.)	—	3,300	6,000	5,300	3,900	2,400
Current account ($ mil.)	—	(100)	2,600	1,800	(200)	(1,200)
Govt. budget bal. ($ mil.)	—	(2,887)	(2,471)	(1,435)	(1,836)	*(2,365)*
Consumer inflation	—	0.6%	0.8%	2.5%	2.8%	3.5%
Unemployment rate	—	8.3%	8.2%	8.1%	7.9%	*5.5%*
Exchange rate with US$	—	2.60	2.49	2.71	2.70	2.70

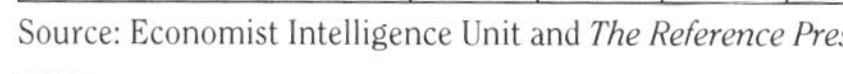
Source: Economist Intelligence Unit and *The Reference Press*

Area: 127,317 sq. mi. (329,759 sq. km)

Official name: Malaysia
Official language: Bahasa Malaysia
Currency: 1 ringgit (M$) = 100 sen
Fiscal year ends: December 31

WHO

Supreme Head of State (Yang di-Pertuan Agong): HM Sultan Azlan Muhibbuddin Shah ibni Almarhum Sultan Yussuf Izzuddin Ghafarullahu-Iahu Shah
Prime Minister and Minister of Home Affairs: Dato Seri Mahathir Mohamad, age 66
Finance Minister: Anwar Ibrahim
Minister of Foreign Affairs: Datuk Abdullah Ahmad Badawi
Ambassador to US: Dato Abdul Majid Mohamad
US Ambassador to Malaysia: Paul M. Cleveland

WHERE

Executive HQ: Prime Minister's Dept., Jalan Dato' Onn, 50502 Kuala Lumpur, Malaysia
Embassy in US: 2401 Massachusetts Ave. NW, Washington, DC 20008
Phone: 202-328-2700
Fax: 202-483-7661
US Embassy in Malaysia: PO Box 10035, 376 Jalan Tun Razak, 50400 Kuala Lumpur, Malaysia
Phone: 011-60-3-248-9011
Fax: 011-60-3-242-2207
Chamber of Commerce: Malaysian International Chamber of Commerce and Industry, 8th Floor, Wisma Damansara, Jalan Semantan, PO Box 10192, 50706 Kuala Lumpur, Malaysia
Phone: 011-60-3-254-2117
Fax: 011-60-3-255-4946

Malaysia has 13 states and 2 federal territories and has diplomatic representatives in 54 countries.

Capital city: Kuala Lumpur
Time change from EST: +13 hours
Avg. high/low temp: Jan. 90°F (32°C)/72°F (22°C)
July 90°F (32°C)/73°F (23°C)

Urbanization: 42%
Population density: 140/sq. mi. (54/sq. km)

Exports as % of Total		Imports as % of Total	
Singapore	20	Japan	24
US	19	US	17
Japan	16	Singapore	14
Other countries	45	Other countries	45
Total	**100**	**Total**	**100**

WHAT

Origins of GDP	% of Total
Manufacturing	27
Agriculture	19
Wholesale, retail trade & hotels	11
Other	43
Total	**100**

1990 GDP per capita: $2,393
1990 year-end external debt: $14 billion
Literacy rate: 65%
UN Human Development Index: 80%
Human Freedom Index (0-40 scale): 9
Purchasing power as % of US: 22%
Capital city cost of living as % of DC: 77%
Defense as % of GNP: 4%
Education as % of GNP: 7%
Principal airline: MAS (Malaysian Airline System)
Principal exchange: The Kuala Lumpur Stock Exchange

MEXICO

OVERVIEW

Mexico is the largest Spanish-speaking country in the world. Mexico City is the world's largest (with nearly 20 million inhabitants) and most polluted city.

Among the world's top 5 oil producers, Mexico also mines silver, sulfur, lead, and zinc. Coffee, cotton, and vegetables, 2/3 of which go to the US, are major export crops. The manufacturing sector generates over 1/2 of export revenue and 1/5 of annual GDP. *Maquiladora* plants along the US border provide low-cost labor for many US manufacturers.

Economic restructuring (begun in 1988) has been the catalyst for improvement in the Mexican economy. From 1987 to 1990 inflation decreased from over 130% to under 30% annually; foreign debt fell from $107 billion to $93 billion. Business confidence has returned since trade practices were liberalized, marginal tax rates were reduced (from 60% in 1986 to 35%), and public sector corruption is being seriously addressed.

Poverty, environmental pollution, and population growth, which is straining job-creation capacity, remain problems. Illegal emigration to the US, while providing jobs for many, adversely affects US–Mexico relations.

Since Mexico began talks with the US (joined by Canada in 1991) on a free trade agreement, US and foreign business investment, especially from Asia, has vastly increased. Higher oil prices following Iraq's invasion of Kuwait and increased oil production earned Mexico about $2.5 billion in 1990. Nevertheless, in 1991 Mexico felt the effects of the general economic slowdown in the US. Mexico's potential has attracted US businesses (Wal-Mart's first foreign investment will be there) and investors (Telmex, Mexico's telephone monopoly, has an avid Wall Street following).

WHEN

Mexico has been home to nomadic tribes for 12,000 years. One tribe, the Olmecs, developed a counting system over 2,700 years ago. The Mayans (who flourished from 100 to 1500 in the Yucatán peninsula) built the first cities in the Americas, the largest reaching a population of 60,000. They were skilled road builders and seafarers and had a thriving internal trade in cotton, furs, honey, jade, salt, and wax.

In the 15th century the Aztecs built the last and greatest pre-Columbian empire. Though warlike they were skilled in medicine and the arts. When Spanish explorer Hernando Cortez arrived in 1519, he and his men were thought to be gods. In 1521 he conquered the Aztecs, destroyed their capital, and plundered their wealth. The Aztecs were forced to work as serfs. Spanish colonialism lasted 300 years.

Mexico declared independence from Spain in 1810, but it was 14 years before it was officially named and recognized. Mexico then included California, Arizona, New Mexico, Texas, and parts of Colorado and Utah. A Texas revolt against General Santa Anna (1836) led to the Battle of the Alamo at San Antonio. Captured later that year, Santa Anna recognized Texan independence in exchange for his freedom. Most of the remaining territories north of the Rio Grande — 1/2 of Mexico's area — were ceded to the US in 1848 for $15 million and the cancellation of debt after the war with the US (1846–48).

A civil war in the late 1850s nearly bankrupted Mexico, prompting European creditors to install a French-sponsored monarchy, which was overthrown in 1867. Years of unrest ended in 1876 when General Porfirio Díaz took control and ruled for 35 years. He permitted foreign investment to encourage railway and mining expansion, monetary stability, and oil exploration. However, starving peasants led by revolutionaries Pancho Villa and Emiliano Zapata revolted in 1910. After years of chaos, a 1917 constitution was the impetus for much-needed land reform and the nationalization of the oil industry.

Since 1946 Mexico has enjoyed political stability. The discovery of significant oil deposits during the 1970s led to a government spending spree. Government jobs were fabricated to ease unemployment and foreign debt blossomed, as did corruption.

La crisis was triggered when oil prices declined in the early 1980s, unemployment exploded, the peso was devalued by nearly 50% (1982), and capital fled. During Miguel de la Madrid's presidency (1982–88), inflation rose to over 100% and foreign debt reached $107 billion, leading to an unprecedented bridge loan for $3.5 billion from the US in 1988.

President Carlos Salinas de Gortari, inaugurated in 1988, began taking steps to control the economy. These measures reduced inflation and debt but created economic hardship that is only now being relieved.

HOW MUCH

	4-Year Growth	1986	1987	1988	1989	1990
Population (mil.)	*1.6%*	75.8	77.2	78.8	80.5	81.1
GDP ($ bil.)	*16.3%*	*130*	*141*	*173*	*210*	*238*
Real GDP growth rate	—	(3.6%)	1.6%	1.4%	3.1%	3.9%
Exports ($ mil.)	*13.8%*	16,000	20,700	20,600	22,800	26,800
Imports ($ mil.)	*27.2%*	11,400	12,200	18,900	23,400	29,800
Trade balance ($ mil.)	—	4,600	8,500	1,700	(600)	(3,000)
Current account ($ mil.)	—	(1,700)	3,900	(2,400)	(5,400)	(5,500)
Govt. budget bal. ($ mil.)	—	*(17,010)*	*(19,028)*	*(17,748)*	*(8,974)*	*1,796*
Consumer inflation	—	86.2%	131.8%	114.2%	20.0%	26.7%
Unemployment rate	—	—	—	18.5%	—	13.5%
Exchange rate with US$	—	611.8	1,378.2	2,273.1	2,461.5	2,842.0

Source: Economist Intelligence Unit and *The Reference Press*

Area: 756,198 sq. mi. (1,958,201 sq. km)

Official name:
The United Mexican States
Estados Unidos Mexicanos
Official language: Spanish
Currency: 1 peso = 100 centavos
Fiscal year ends: December 31

WHO

President: Carlos Salinas de Gortari, age 43
Minister of Finance and Public Credit: Pedro Aspe Armella, age 41
Minister of Foreign Relations: Fernando Solana Morales, age 60
Ambassador to US: Gustavo Petricioli
US Ambassador to Mexico: John D. Negroponte

WHERE

Executive HQ: President, Residencia Oficial, Los Pinos, Mexico D.F., Mexico
Embassy in US: 1911 Pennsylvania Ave. NW, Washington, DC 20006
Phone: 202-728-1600
Fax: 202-728-1659
US Embassy in Mexico: Paseo de la Reforma 305, 06500 Mexico D.F., Mexico
Phone: 011-52-5-211-0042
Fax: 011-52-5-511-9980
Chamber of Commerce: Confederación de Cámaras Nacionales de Comercio, Servicios y Turismo, Balderas 144, 2 y 3 Piso, Apartado 133 bis, Centro Cuauhtémoc, 06079 Mexico D.F., Mexico
Phone: 011-52-5-709-1559
Fax: 011-52-5-709-1152

Mexico has 31 states and a federal district and has diplomatic representatives in 63 countries.

Capital city: Mexico City
Time change from EST: -1 hour
Avg. high/low temp: Jan. 66°F (19°C)/42°F (6°C)
July 73°F (23°C)/53°F (12°C)

Urbanization: 72%
Population density: 107/sq. mi. (41/sq. km)

Exports as % of Total		Imports as % of Total	
US	69	US	68
Spain	7	Japan	5
Japan	6	Germany	4
France	4	France	2
Other countries	14	Other countries	21
Total	**100**	**Total**	**100**

WHAT

Origins of GDP	% of Total
Commerce & hotels	28
Manufacturing	25
Agriculture, forestry & fishing	9
Transport & communications	7
Other	31
Total	**100**

1990 GDP per capita: $2,932
1990 year-end external debt: $93 billion
Literacy rate: 88%
UN Human Development Index: 84%
Human Freedom Index (0-40 scale): 15
Purchasing power as % of US: 26%
Capital city cost of living as % of DC: 69%
Defense as % of GNP: 1%
Education as % of GNP: 3%
Principal airlines: Aeromexico, Mexicana
Principal exchange: Bolsa Mexicana de Valores, SA de CV

THE NETHERLANDS

OVERVIEW

The Netherlands (popularly known as Holland, after one of its provinces) is located on the North Sea at the mouths of the Rhine, Meuse, and Scheldt rivers, a position that has determined much of its history and its technological, social, and economic development.

Much of the country's swampy, below-sea-level land was wrested from the sea through drainage projects that left the Netherlands crisscrossed with canals. Because of its location and its canals, the Netherlands became a nation of traders, and trade is still vital, because, apart from having the world's largest producing natural gas field (representing 1/2 of Europe's reserves), the country is largely without natural resources. Half of the GNP is derived from trade, and 30% of all EC shipping passes through Dutch ports. The country has a large balance-of-payments surplus.

The Netherlands is heavily industrialized under private ownership. Industry produces chemicals, petroleum products, and metals. Government is not involved in business management but exerts control through a variety of social welfare regulations in pay, vacation, medical benefits, etc. Business's share of these costs reduces profit margins to only 2–3%. Government accounts for 15% of all employment and is the only sector in which jobs are increasing; it runs a perennial budget deficit.

Though politically stable, the Netherlands faces many problems in the 1990s. Unemployment is high. A declining birthrate will make the welfare system harder to support, and labor shortages are developing. Although it is the most densely populated nation in Europe, with a severe urban housing shortage, environmental activism may block further attempts to reclaim land from the sea.

WHEN

Since the 15th century, windmills have been used to pump water from diked areas in the Netherlands. Towns growing up along natural and man-made waterways became major trade centers within Europe.

In the late 15th century, Holland passed into the hands of the Hapsburgs, who ruled Spain. Spanish attempts to control trade and religion incited the Protestant Dutch to a rebellion. In 1595, depleted by its wars with England and France, Spain withdrew but continued to wage war and claim sovereignty until 1648.

In the 17th century the Dutch expanded their trade, influence, and power and became the premier international power of the century. They controlled territory in India, Ceylon, China, and Indonesia; monopolized trade with Japan; and established presences in South Africa and South America. Englishman Henry Hudson was working for the Dutch when he discovered what is now Manhattan. Holland became an important center of mapmaking and world trade. The Dutch imported the first tulips from Turkey, setting off tulipmania, in which vast sums were paid for single bulbs before the market crashed in 1639.

The consequence of this power was war with Britain (in Ceylon and North America) and France (in Europe). Constant warfare was too much for a nation with few resources and a small population, and Holland declined during the 18th century, finally coming under the rule of Napoleon.

In 1815 the Kingdom of the United Netherlands was created. Trade remained important, especially with the kingdom's remaining colony in Indonesia, but in the 19th century industrialization began slowly, accompanied by strong trade unionism and socialist ferment.

Though successfully neutral in WWI, the Netherlands was occupied by Germany in WWII. By war's end its largest port, Rotterdam, was in ruins and vast areas of the nation flooded. With Marshall Plan aid, Holland expanded its industry, repaired and improved Rotterdam, and undertook large land-reclamation projects. However, it spent as much as it received in aid in an unsuccessful attempt to maintain an unwilling Indonesia as a colony. All Dutch holdings there were expropriated in 1957.

In the boom years of the 1950s and 1960s, the Netherlands prospered, became a founding member of the EC, adopted generous social programs at home, and contributed the highest level of international development aid in the world (1.5% of GNP). However, the lack of native resources and the comprehensiveness of its social benefits package proved to be liabilities in the 1970s and 1980s, as per capita income fell during the worldwide boom years of the 1980s, from 8th in the world in 1980 to 12th in 1985.

HOW MUCH

	4-Year Growth	1986	1987	1988	1989	1990
Population (mil.)	*0.7%*	14.6	14.7	14.8	14.8	15.0
GDP ($ bil.)	*12.1%*	*175*	*212*	*228*	*222*	*276*
Real GDP growth rate	—	2.0%	1.1%	2.9%	3.5%	3.4%
Exports ($ mil.)	*13.0%*	80,600	92,600	102,900	107,800	131,400
Imports ($ mil.)	*13.7%*	75,400	90,600	99,000	104,200	125,900
Trade balance ($ mil.)	—	5,200	2,000	3,900	3,600	5,500
Current account ($ mil.)	—	4,800	3,200	5,100	7,800	9,500
Govt. budget bal. ($ mil.)	—	—	*(7,309)*	*(8,545)*	*(11,126)*	—
Consumer inflation	—	0.1%	(0.7%)	0.8%	1.1%	2.5%
Unemployment rate	—	13.2%	12.7%	12.4%	7.3%	—
Exchange rate with US$	—	2.45	2.03	1.98	2.12	1.82

Source: Economist Intelligence Unit and *The Reference Press*

Area: 16,464 sq. mi. (41,473 sq. km)

Official name:
Kingdom of the Netherlands
Koninkrijk der Nederlanden
Official language: Dutch
Currency: 1 florin (Fl) = 100 cents
Fiscal year ends: December 31

WHO

Monarch: Queen Beatrix Wilhelmina Armgard, age 53
Heir Apparent: Crown Prince Willem Alexander
Prime Minister and Minister of General Affairs: Ruud Lubbers, age 52
Deputy Prime Minister and Finance Minister: Wim Kok, age 53
Minister of Foreign Affairs: Hans van den Broek
Ambassador to US: Johan H. Meesman
US Ambassador to the Netherlands: C. Howard Wilkins, Jr.

WHERE

Executive HQ: Prime Minister, Binnenhof 20, The Hague 2513 AA, The Netherlands
Embassy in US: 4200 Linnean Ave. NW, Washington, DC 20008
Phone: 202-244-5300
Fax: 202-362-3430
US Embassy in the Netherlands: Lange Voorhout 102, The Hague, The Netherlands
Phone: 011-31-70-362-4911
Fax: 011-31-70-361-4688
Chamber of Commerce: International Chamber of Commerce, Prinses Beatrixlaan 5, The Hague, The Netherlands
Phone: 011-31-70-383-646

The Netherlands has 12 provinces and has diplomatic representatives in 176 countries.

Capital city: The Hague
Time change from EST: +6 hours
Mean temperature: January 37°F (8°C)
July 61°F (16°C)

Urbanization: 89%
Population density: 908/sq. mi. (360/sq. km)

Exports as % of Total		Imports as % of Total	
Germany	28	Germany	26
Other Benelux	15	Other Benelux	14
France	11	UK	8
UK	10	US	8
Other countries	36	Other countries	44
Total	**100**	**Total**	**100**

WHAT

Origins of GDP	% of Total
Services	66
Mining, manufacturing & utilities	27
Construction	6
Agriculture, forestry & fishing	5
Imputed bank service charges	(4)
Total	**100**

1990 GDP per capita: $18,479
1990 year-end external debt: none
UN Human Development Index: 98%
Human Freedom Index (0-40 scale): 37
Purchasing power as % of US: 68%
Amsterdam cost of living as % of DC: 119%
Defense as % of GNP: 3%
Education as % of GNP: 16%
Principal airline: KLM (Royal Dutch)
Principal exchange: The Amsterdam Stock Exchange

NEW ZEALAND

OVERVIEW

New Zealand consists of 2 main islands and several small islands 1,200 miles southeast of Australia. Its population, 84% urban, is composed primarily of people of European descent (86%) and Maoris (9%), descendants of the original inhabitants. Until air travel became available, New Zealand was one of the world's most isolated nations.

With 53% of its land in pasture, New Zealand produces and exports mainly dairy products, red meat (world's #4 exporter), and wool (world's #2 exporter).

As imports, especially oil, have become more expensive, New Zealand has been trying to increase self-sufficiency. Since the 1960s deposits of iron sands, coal, and natural gas have been found.

Economic diversification has reduced agriculture's share of exports to 60%; manufactured goods, wood, and engineering products make up the other 40%. Enterprise is mostly private, with strict government rules on working conditions. Though the government controls major public utilities, it recently sold its telecommunications monopoly to Ameritech and Bell Atlantic.

After decades of dealing with high inflation, static productivity (lowest GDP growth rate of all developed nations), and heavy regulation, the government has begun to seek foreign investment and to reduce the high level of social benefits to the middle class, which some argued had made them complacent and lacking in the work ethic necessary to remain prosperous. Continuing problems include dependence on trade and tensions caused by Maori activists.

WHEN

Polynesian Maoris came to New Zealand about 1000 and evolved into the agricultural/hunting society Europeans found in the 1600s.

Dutch navigator Abel Tasman sighted and named, but did not land on, New Zealand. Captain James Cook explored, mapped, and claimed the islands for England on 3 voyages starting in 1769. For several decades Europeans hunted seals and whales in New Zealand's waters and established logging settlements.

Increasing British settlement led to an 1840 treaty between Great Britain and the Maoris allowing white settlement, while guaranteeing native rights to the land. Systematic colonization began, and differing interpretations of the treaty led to armed confrontations.

Early products were wool and gold. In the 1880s the use of refrigerated ships allowed expansion of New Zealand's stock industry, which became a prime meat supplier for the UK. Economic problems, plus the entry of working class immigrants, led to an early (1890s) welfare system covering labor conditions, hours, and pensions.

New Zealanders supported the British in WWI, and the survivors came home to a prosperous country and full employment. During the Great Depression income fell 20% and unemployment rose to 12%, leading to labor unrest. Price supports were enacted and, to stimulate demand for workers, hours were shortened. More welfare measures started as well, financed by income taxes. By WWII New Zealand was prosperous again.

After WWII industries nationalized during wartime were privatized and price supports removed. Prices rose and, with them, labor unrest and inflation. In the 1950s meat and dairy prices fell, eroding foreign exchange reserves. Increases in sin taxes (e.g., on liquor) spawned antigovernment feeling.

Government's proper role in the economy remained subject to debate during the 1960s but was overshadowed by the issue of New Zealand's role in the Vietnam War.

The 1970s rise in oil prices was a blow to New Zealand. Not only was most of its energy derived from imports, but rising oil prices increased the cost of shipping. The government formulated plans to reduce energy imports and find local substitutes. Natural gas and coal were discovered, and more use was made of geothermal and hydroelectric power.

In the 1980s, amid persistent inflation and rising unemployment (10% by 1989), emphasis was placed on the private sector and on government decontrol, including removal of agricultural price supports. This was unpopular with labor, but the economy improved.

As the UK turned toward its EC partners, its percentage of New Zealand's trade fell from 60% in 1950 to 9% by 1986. New Zealand found new trading partners in the US and Japan, and in 1982 made an open market agreement with Australia (currently its largest trading partner). By the 1990s, however, with the wool and dairy products markets in a slump, New Zealand's economy was in recession.

HOW MUCH

	4-Year Growth	1986	1987	1988	1989	1990
Population (mil.)	*0.7%*	3.29	3.31	3.33	3.34	3.38
GDP ($ bil.)	*15.5%*	*23*	*32*	*39*	*39*	*42*
Real GDP growth rate	—	(0.1%)	(1.2%)	2.3%	(0.1%)	2.3%
Exports ($ mil.)	*12.8%*	5,870	7,190	8,870	8,770	9,510
Imports ($ mil.)	*11.7%*	6,090	7,240	7,380	8,710	9,490
Trade balance ($ mil.)	—	(220)	(50)	1,490	60	20
Current account ($ mil.)	—	(1,770)	(1,880)	(590)	(1,280)	(1,100)
Govt. budget bal. ($ mil.)	—	*(725)*	*(1,108)*	*(740)*	*(802)*	*(540)*
Consumer inflation	—	13.2%	15.8%	6.4%	5.7%	6.1%
Unemployment rate	—	—	—	—	—	7.3%
Exchange rate with US$	—	1.91	1.69	1.52	1.67	1.68

Source: Economist Intelligence Unit and *The Reference Press*

Area: 103,886 sq. mi. (269,063 sq. km)

Official name: New Zealand
Official languages: English, Maori
Currency: 1 dollar (NZ$) = 100 cents
Fiscal year ends: June 30

WHO

Governor General: H.E. Dame Catherine Tizard, GCMG, DBE, age 60
Prime Minister: Rt. Hon. Jim Bolger, age 56, NZ$147,000 pay in 1989
Deputy Prime Minister, Minister of External Relations and Trade, and Minister of Foreign Affairs: Hon. Don McKinnon, age 52
Finance Minister: Ruth Richardson, age 40, NZ$103,000 pay in 1989
Ambassador to US: Denis McLean
US Ambassador to New Zealand: Della M. Newman

WHERE

Executive HQ: Prime Minister, Executive Wing, Parliament Bldgs., Wellington, New Zealand
Embassy in US: 37 Observatory Circle NW, Washington, DC 20008
Phone: 202-328-4800
Fax: 202-667-5227
US Embassy in New Zealand: PO Box 1190, 29 Fitzherbert Terr., Thorndon, Wellington, New Zealand
Phone: 011-64-4-722-068
Fax: 011-64-4-712-380
Chamber of Commerce: New Zealand Chamber of Commerce, PO Box 1071, Federation Hse, 7th Fl., 95–99 Molesworth St., Wellington, New Zealand
Phone: 011-64-4-723-376

New Zealand has 14 cities, 59 districts, and 14 regions and has diplomatic representatives in 52 countries.

Capital city: Wellington
Time change from EST: +17 hours
Avg. high/low temp: Jan. 69°F (21°C)/56°F (13°C)
July 53°F (12°C)/42°F (6°C)

Urbanization: 84%
Population density: 32/sq. mi. (13/sq. km)

Exports as % of Total		Imports as % of Total	
Australia	19	Australia	21
Japan	17	Japan	18
US	13	US	17
Other countries	51	Other countries	44
Total	**100**	**Total**	**100**

WHAT

Origins of GDP	% of Total
Manufacturing	21
Trade	18
Finance, business, etc.	16
Other	45
Total	**100**

1990 GDP per capita: $12,292
1990 year-end external debt: $17 billion
Literacy rate: 99%
UN Human Development Index: 96%
Human Freedom Index (0-40 scale): 36
Purchasing power as % of US: 61%
Capital city cost of living as % of DC: 90%
Defense as % of GNP: 2%
Education as % of GNP: 5%
Principal airline: Air New Zealand
Principal exchange: New Zealand Stock Exchange

NIGERIA

OVERVIEW

Nigeria is Africa's 14th largest country in land area but has the largest population on the continent. Its population consists of over 250 ethnic groups and grows about 3.6% annually.

Agricultural output has fallen steeply since independence, and Nigeria can no longer feed itself, though more than 1/2 its people work the land. Products include cocoa, peanuts, palm oil, rubber, corn, rice, and yams.

Mineral resources include petroleum (over 95% of exports), natural gas, coal, tin, and iron ore. Nigeria is among the world's 5 largest oil exporters and is the largest producer in Africa. Industries process and manufacture natural resources, textiles, shoes, food products, and building materials for local consumption.

However, factories operate at less than 1/2 their capacity.

Despite stringent financial austerity measures, inflation remains high (15% in 1990, down from a brief high of 41% in 1989).

Major foreign investors include Cadbury Schweppes, Nestlé, and Unilever. While the government recently liberalized foreign investment rules and identified 90 companies for privatization, the difficulties of doing business in Nigeria (political and social instability, tangled bureaucracy, inadequate foreign exchange, and poor communications facilities) are likely to dissuade many potential foreign investors. Even so, by the end of 1990, 1/2 of all targeted companies had been privatized.

Official name:
Federal Republic of Nigeria
Official language: English
Currency: 1 naira (N) = 100 kobo
Fiscal year ends: December 31

WHO

President and Commander in Chief of the Armed Forces: Maj. Gen. Ibrahim Badamisi Babangida, age 50
Chief of General Staff: Rear Adm. Augustus Aikhomu, age 52
Minister of Finance and Economic Development: Alhaji Abuballa Alhaji
Minister of External Affairs: Maj. Gen. Ike O. S. Nwachu Kwu (Rtd.)
Ambassador to US: Zubair Mahmud Kazaure
US Ambassador to Nigeria: Lannon Walker

WHEN

From the 11th to 19th centuries, what is now Nigeria was home to a succession of kingdoms that participated in trans-Saharan caravan trade. As Europeans began to establish trading posts on the Atlantic coast after 1472, the powerful Yoruba and Benin empires were approaching their zeniths. Until the Atlantic slave trade ended in the early 19th century, west coast African tribes supplied captives from tribal wars to Arabs and Europeans for overseas transport.

In the mid-19th century, in hopes of finding mineral wealth, the British began to penetrate the interior (until then unknown to Europeans), founding the Lagos colony in 1862. British influence expanded with the Royal Niger Company, chartered in 1886, which made contact with interior tribes.

In 1900 the entire territory came under Colonial Office administration, which finally outlawed internal slavery. Native revolts delayed full control until 1914. Between WWI and WWII the British expanded tin mining and built roads and schools in the south, sowing seeds of future sectional rivalry.

Petroleum was discovered in the late 1950s, and Nigeria embarked on independence (1960) as a fairly prosperous, advanced nation. But Nigeria was a patchwork of mutually distrustful ethnic groups.

By 1965 rivalry between the Hausas in the north (a large part of the army) and the Ibos in the south (civil servants and technocrats) led to civil disturbances and, in 1967, civil war when the Ibos unsuccessfully tried to break away as Biafra. Agriculture was devastated, resulting in widespread famine.

The civil war ended as the 1970s oil crisis began. Nigeria, an OPEC member, recovered, investing in capital projects and imports financed by loans on anticipated revenues. Agriculture recovered but then languished (in the early 1970s, Nigeria was a net food exporter; now it cannot feed itself). Urban migration of unskilled poor burdened the cities. Corruption was rife. Yet Nigeria reached the peak of prosperity in 1980 when oil sales rose.

In the 1980s the oil boom went bust. Revenues plummeted, but spending continued, depleting foreign exchange reserves and diminishing Nigeria's ability to service its debt. Payments were rescheduled in 1983.

A military coup in 1983 brought a regime that took strong remedial measures, expelling foreign workers to open up jobs for Nigerians and severely limiting imports. The impoverishing effects of these measures on the people brought a breakdown of law and order. Armed robbery and theft became endemic; drug smuggling to the US grew, and educated Nigerians left in droves.

In 1990 the rise in oil prices during the Gulf crisis brought in $2.1 billion used to create a foreign currency stabilization fund. Emphasis is now being placed on reviving agriculture (including a new cotton industry), exploiting other mineral resources (including coal and iron), and developing industry for domestic needs.

In a surprise move in April 1991, Nigeria announced that it was considering lifting its sanctions against South Africa because of positive developments toward the dissolution of apartheid.

WHERE

Executive HQ: President, Dodan Barracks, Lagos, Nigeria
Embassy in US: 2201 M St. NW, Washington, DC 20037
Phone: 202-822-1500
Fax: 202-775-1385
US Embassy in Nigeria: PO Box 554, 2 Eleke Crescent, Lagos, Nigeria
Phone: 011-234-1-610097
Fax: 011-234-1-635397
Chamber of Commerce: Nigerian Association of Chambers of Commerce, PO Box 12816, 15A Ikorodu, Maryland, Lagos, Nigeria
Phone: 011-234-1-635397

Nigeria has 21 states and a Federal Capital Territory and has diplomatic representatives in 75 countries.

Capital city: Lagos/Abuja
Time change from EST: +6 hours
Avg. high/low (Lagos) temp:
Jan. 88°F (31°C)/74°F (23°C)
July 83°F (28°C)/74°F (23°C)

Urbanization: 35%
Population density: 306/sq. mi. (118/sq. km)

Exports as % of Total		Imports as % of Total	
US	46	UK	13
Spain	11	Germany	11
Germany	6	US	10
Other countries	37	Other countries	66
Total	**100**	**Total**	**100**

WHAT

Origins of GDP	% of Total
Agriculture	31
Trade	17
Petroleum	13
Manufacturing	10
Other	29
Total	**100**

1990 GDP per capita: $211
1990 year-end external debt: $33 billion
Literacy rate: 42%
UN Human Development Index: 24%
Human Freedom Index (0-40 scale): 13
Purchasing power as % of US: 7%
Lagos cost of living as % of DC: 69%
Defense as % of GNP: 1%
Education as % of GNP: 1%
Principal airline: Nigeria Airways
Principal exchange: The Nigerian Stock Exchange

HOW MUCH

	4-Year Growth	1986	1987	1988	1989	1990
Population (mil.)	*3.6%*	98	101	105	109	113
GDP ($ bil.)	—	*45*	*28*	*30*	*22*	*24*
Real GDP growth rate	—	3.2%	1.8%	4.1%	5.3%	5.2%
Exports ($ mil.)	*21.2%*	6,020	7,550	6,900	8,140	13,000
Imports ($ mil.)	*17.3%*	3,700	4,100	4,270	5,290	7,000
Trade balance ($ mil.)	—	2,320	3,450	2,630	2,850	6,000
Current account ($ mil.)	—	370	(70)	(190)	(140)	3,000
Govt. budget bal. ($ mil.)	—	*(4,703)*	*(1,446)*	*(2,680)*	*(2,072)*	*(1,783)*
Consumer inflation	—	5.4%	10.2%	38.2%	40.9%	15.0%
Unemployment rate	—	—	—	5.3%	4.0%	—
Exchange rate with US$	—	1.76	4.02	4.54	7.37	8.04

Source: Economist Intelligence Unit and *The Reference Press*

Area: 356,669 sq. mi. (923,773 sq. km)

PAKISTAN

OVERVIEW

Pakistan's mostly Muslim population is the world's 8th largest.

Agriculture is the most important sector of the economy; it contributes 26% of GDP and supports 53% of the workforce. Crops include cotton (the #1 export), grains (in which Pakistan is generally self-sufficient), and sugar cane. Millennia of farming have left great areas deforested and eroded. Pakistan has the world's largest irrigation system, without which most land would not be arable.

Mineral resources include some petroleum and natural gas; low-grade coal and iron deposits; and unknown amounts of copper, manganese, bauxite, and phosphates.

Manufacturing, primarily privately owned, concentrates on consumer goods for internal consumption, textiles, food processing, fertilizer, and cement. Most exports are commodities rather than manufactured goods. Pakistan runs a chronic trade deficit.

Periodic fighting with India since independence in 1947 necessitates heavy defense spending and exacerbates trade imbalances. The Afghan war (1979–88) brought further expenditures for defense and for aid to over 2 million refugees.

Though literacy rates are low (about 26%), Pakistan's economy cannot support a large percentage of its most-educated citizens, many of whom work abroad, often in Arab oil-producing states. Their remittances (which were disrupted by the Gulf War) normally add significantly to foreign exchange reserves.

WHEN

Pakistan's Indus Valley is the cradle of subcontinental civilization, with agricultural and trading cities dating to the 3rd millennium BC. It was frequently invaded by numerous powers, including Alexander the Great (327 BC). In the 7th century Arabs introduced Islam, which soon became the major religion. In the 1500s the Islamic Moguls dominated the subcontinent, building great cities and temples and fostering a sophisticated trading and finance system.

When the British took over the Indian subcontinent in the 18th century, they considered the area that would become Pakistan economically unpromising and left it largely undeveloped. In the 19th century it served as a buffer, protecting what is now India from Russian expansionism.

After WWII, fearful of Hindu domination, Muslims demanded a separate state. Pakistan, the Land of the Pure, was carved from India in 1947, leading to massive migrations and widespread violence. Pakistan was a geographically divided nation, with a western and an eastern wing 1,000 miles apart. The eastern wing broke away in 1971 as Bangladesh.

At independence Pakistan lacked basic infrastructure. It had one large port city, Karachi; no industry; poor communication and transportation facilities; hordes of impoverished refugees; no civil service or commercial class; and no capital.

In the 1950s, with Western aid and profits from sales of jute during the Korean War, Pakistan stabilized agriculture, built communications and transport networks, and began industrializing.

In the early 1960s Pakistan was a model of economic development. But in 1965 an indecisive war with India (over long-disputed Kashmir) and a series of bad harvests ended its progress. Deteriorating economic conditions led to riots and toppled the government.

The new government of Zulfigar Ali Bhutto (1971–77) nationalized banks and industry, thereby damaging the economy. Little social progress was made because Bhutto's backers were of the land-owning class.

In 1977 General Mohammad Zia Ul-Haq seized power and hanged Bhutto. Zia instituted Islamic law, the *Shari'a*; moved slowly to reprivatize; and encouraged new investment. From 1977 to 1988 annual growth averaged 6%. The economic performance of agriculture, the country's largest sector, improved because of better infrastructure; higher, more consistent yields; and better irrigation. Pakistan's industrial growth has been primarily in the consumer-goods sector, especially processed food and textiles. The government offers incentive programs for private ownership.

Benazir Bhutto, daughter of Zulfigar Ali Bhutto, became prime minister in 1988 and continued privatization by partially denationalizing heavy industry. Small-scale manufacturing creates most industrial jobs. In 1990 Bhutto was ousted from power amid charges of corruption in her administration.

To speed privatization, the new government has relaxed restrictions on foreign investment in business and the stock market.

HOW MUCH

	4-Year Growth	1986	1987	1988	1989	1990
Population (mil.)	*3.1%*	99.2	102.4	105.4	108.6	112.0
GDP ($ bil.)	*6.8%*	*31*	*33*	*38*	*38*	*40*
Real GDP growth rate	—	6.4%	5.8%	6.2%	4.8%	5.2%
Exports ($ mil.)	*14.3%*	2,940	3,500	4,360	4,630	5,010
Imports ($ mil.)	*6.0%*	5,520	5,400	6,300	7,090	6,960
Trade balance ($ mil.)	—	(2,580)	(1,900)	(1,940)	(2,460)	(1,950)
Current account ($ mil.)	—	(1,240)	(720)	(1,680)	(1,930)	(1,700)
Govt. budget bal. ($ mil.)	—	—	—	—	*(123)*	*231*
Consumer inflation	—	4.8%	3.9%	6.3%	10.4%	6.0%
Unemployment rate	—	—	3.1%	3.1%	3.1%	3.1%
Exchange rate with US$	—	16.65	17.40	18.00	20.54	21.71

Source: Economist Intelligence Unit and *The Reference Press*

Area: 310,527 sq. mi. (803,943 sq. km)

Official name: Islamic Republic of Pakistan
Official language: English
Currency: 1 rupee (PR) = 100 paise
Fiscal year ends: June 30

WHO

President: Ghulam Ishaq Khan, age 76
Prime Minister: Mohammad Nawaz Sharif, age 43
Minister of Finance: Sartaj Aziz
Acting Foreign Minister and Secretary General: Akram Zaki
Ambassador to US: Najmuddin A. Shaikh
US Ambassador to Pakistan: (Ambassador designate) Nicholas Platt

WHERE

Executive HQ: President, Awan-e-Sadr, Constitution Ave., Islamabad, Pakistan
Embassy in US: 2315 Massachusetts Ave. NW, Washington, DC 20008
Phone: 202-939-6200
Fax: 202-387-0484
US Embassy in Pakistan: PO Box 1048, Dipl. Enclave, Ramna 5, Islamabad, Pakistan
Phone: 011-92-51-826161
Fax: 011-92-51-822004
Chamber of Commerce: Federation of Pakistan Chambers of Commerce and Industry, St. 28, Block 5, Shahrea Firdousi, Clifton, Karachi 6, Pakistan
Phone: 011-92-21-534621

Pakistan has 4 provinces, Northern Areas, and Tribal Areas and has diplomatic representatives in 72 countries.

Capital city: Islamabad
Time change from EST: +10 hours
Avg. high/low temp: Jan. 61°F (16°C)/36°F (2°C)
July: 97°F (36°C)/77°F (25°C)

Urbanization: 32%
Population density: 361/sq. mi. (139/sq. km)

Exports as % of Total		Imports as % of Total	
Japan	12	US	16
US	12	Japan	14
Germany	6	Kuwait	8
UK	6	Germany	7
Other countries	64	Other countries	55
Total	**100**	**Total**	**100**

WHAT

Origins of GDP	% of Total
Agriculture	26
Services	20
Mining & manufacturing	18
Wholesale & retail trade	17
Other	19
Total	**100**

1990 GDP per capita: $359
1990 year-end external debt: $15 billion
Literacy rate: 26%
UN Human Development Index: 31%
Human Freedom Index (0-40 scale): 5
Purchasing power as % of US: 9%
Karachi cost of living as % of DC: 64%
Defense as % of GNP: 7%
Education as % of GNP: 2%
Principal airline: PIA (Pakistan International Airlines)
Principal exchange: The Karachi Stock Exchange (Guarantee) Limited

PHILIPPINES

OVERVIEW

The Philippines consists of over 7,100 islands north of Borneo in the Pacific Ocean, but most of its people live on just 11 islands, of which Luzon and Mindanao are the largest.

Though endowed with a variety of mineral resources, the Philippines lacks the infrastructure to develop its copper, chromite, and nickel deposits. Oil was found in 1977, but production meets only 4% of energy needs.

Agriculture is the main economic sector; farmers grow coconuts (#1 exporter of coconut products), rice, maize, sugar cane, bananas, and pineapples. Yields are rising, but at too high a cost for some producers. Farmland clearance and uncontrolled logging have caused deforestation of tropical woods.

Under President Ferdinand Marcos (1966 to 1986), many industries were nationalized; they are now being privatized. Industry contributes about 1/3 of GDP, but President Corazón Aquino (elected in 1986) is trying to enlarge this sector, which includes textiles, electronics assembly, processed foods, wood products, ceramics, and handicrafts.

Decades of corruption and misgovernment have left the nation impoverished (among Asian free-market economies only Indonesia has a lower per capita GDP), with high unemployment (11.4% in 1989, underemployment around 30%), increasing inflation (12.7% in 1990), and declining investment rates. There is, however, a substantial underground economy.

WHEN

When Magellan landed (and died) in the Philippines in 1521, the islands were already part of a Pan-Asian trading culture. The Spanish founded Manila in 1571 as a transshipment point for trade between China and Mexico. Spanish settlers developed sugar-cane, banana, coconut, and coffee plantations.

Until the 19th century, trade was allowed only within the Spanish empire; thereafter, British and American trading companies and banks moved in. The Philippines' importance to Spain increased after most of its American colonies were lost in the 1820s. In 1898, with Spain and the US at war, the Philippines declared independence but was occupied by the US. At the end of the war, Spain ceded the country to the US for $20 million.

The US bought a nation in which most of the land was held by a minority of wealthy landowners. There was little trade or industry.

In 1935 the Philippines became a US commonwealth. WWII delayed plans for independence, and harsh Japanese occupation was a major setback. The Philippines became independent in 1946.

After WWII the US gave massive amounts of aid, helped put down a Communist rebellion, and infused money into the economy through its Clark and Subic Bay military installations. Though a US-style government was established, the entrenched, land-owning families who controlled agriculture, trade, and industry remained powerful. Migrants from the countryside flooded the cities. Lack of communications and transport links between islands remained a problem.

Dependence on agricultural products made the Philippine economy vulnerable to market cycles. Agricultural methods remained backward, including indiscriminate timber cutting and slash-and-burn techniques. Industrialization efforts emphasized import substitutes rather than world market products.

Despite these problems, the nation carried on democratically (if corruptly) until President Marcos took advantage of civil disorder and Communist agitation to declare martial law in 1972. Though Marcos announced reforms, money and power remained in the hands of the wealthy, especially Marcos's cronies and family (most infamously his wife, Imelda).

The 1983 assassination of political opponent Benigno Aquino led to Marcos's downfall and flight to the US in 1986. When the extent of the Marcos looting became known, legal action was taken against Imelda in the US (Ferdinand died in 1989). She was acquitted of all charges.

President Aquino (widow of Benigno) has tried to make some progress in land reform, diversification of the economy, and privatization of government-owned industries but has been hampered by frequent coup attempts, Islamic and Communist insurrection, natural disasters, and the vastness of the country's problems. In 1991 Mount Pinatubo erupted, causing widespread damage to area farmland, and destroying Clark Air Base and damaging Subic Bay Naval Station. US abandonment of Clark will not only decrease the lease payments to the government, but cost the local economy a large percentage of its trade.

HOW MUCH

	4-Year Growth	1986	1987	1988	1989	1990
Population (mil.)	*2.6%*	56.0	57.4	58.7	60.1	61.5
GDP ($ bil.)	*10.9%*	*31*	*34*	*39*	*44*	*46*
Real GNP growth rate	—	1.9%	5.8%	6.7%	5.7%	3.1%
Exports ($ mil.)	*14.0%*	4,842	5,720	7,074	7,821	8,185
Imports ($ mil.)	*24.5%*	5,044	6,737	8,159	10,419	12,128
Trade balance ($ mil.)	—	(202)	(1,017)	(1,085)	(2,598)	(3,943)
Current account ($ mil.)	—	950	(440)	(390)	(1,470)	(2,640)
Govt. budget bal. ($ mil.)	—	*(1,530)*	*(895)*	*(1,047)*	*(948)*	*(2,057)*
Consumer inflation	—	0.8%	3.8%	8.7%	10.6%	12.7%
Unemployment rate	—	11.1%	9.1%	8.3%	11.4%	—
Exchange rate with US$	—	20.39	20.57	21.10	21.74	24.31

Source: Economist Intelligence Unit and *The Reference Press*

CHINA
TAIWAN
Hong Kong
VIETNAM
PHILIPPINES
LAOS
Manila
Pacific Ocean
CAMBODIA
South China Sea
BRUNEI
MALAYSIA
INDONESIA

Area: 117,187 sq. mi. (300,439 sq. km)

Official name:
Republic of the Philippines
Republika ng Pilipinas
Official languages: English, Pilipino
Currency: 1 peso (P) = 100 sentimos or centavos
Fiscal year ends: December 31

WHO

President: Corazón Aquino, age 58
Vice-President: Salvador H. Laurel, age 63
Finance Secretary: Jesus Estanislao
Foreign Affairs Secretary: Raul Manglapus, age 73
Ambassador to US: Emmanuel Pelaez
US Ambassador to Philippines: Nicholas Platt

WHERE

Executive HQ: President, Malacañang Palace Compound, 5P Laurel St., San Miguel, Manila, Philippines
Embassy in US: 1617 Massachusetts Ave. NW, Washington, DC 20036
Phone: 202-483-1414
Fax: 202-328-7614
US Embassy in the Philippines: 1201 Roxas Blvd., Manila, Philippines
Phone: 011-63-2-521-7116
Chamber of Commerce: Philippine Chamber of Commerce, ODC International Plaza, 7th Fl., 219 Salcedo St., Legaspi Village, Makati, Manila, Philippines
Phone: 011-63-2-817-6981

The Philippines has 73 provinces and 61 chartered cities and has diplomatic representatives in 49 countries.

Capital city: Manila
Time change from EST: +13 hours
Avg. high/low temp: Jan. 86°F (30°C)/69°F (21°C)
July 88°F (31°C)/75°F (24°C)

Urbanization: 42%
Population density: 525/sq. mi. (205/sq. km)

Exports	as % of Total	Imports	as % of Total
US	38	Japan	20
Japan	20	US	19
Germany	4	Taiwan	7
UK	4	Singapore	5
Other countries	34	Other countries	49
Total	**100**	**Total**	**100**

WHAT

Origins of GDP	% of Total
Agriculture, forestry & fishing	27
Manufacturing	25
Government & services	19
Commerce	16
Transport & communications	5
Construction	5
Utilities	2
Mining	1
Total	**100**

1990 GDP per capita: $756
1990 year-end external debt: $27 billion
Literacy rate: 88%
UN Human Development Index: 61%
Human Freedom Index (0-40 scale): 10
Purchasing power as % of US: 11%
Capital city cost of living as % of DC: 57%
Defense as % of GNP: 2%
Education as % of GNP: 2%
Principal airline: Philippine Air Line (PAL)
Principal exchange: Manila Stock Exchange

POLAND

OVERVIEW

Poland is the largest nation in Eastern Europe in area and population. Mineral resources include coal, copper, natural gas, silver, and lead. Poland is usually agriculturally self-sufficient; it exports meat. Industries include coal mining, shipbuilding, chemicals, and autos.

In 1990 economic reform began with wage freezes and price increases. Central planning was jettisoned and industrial subsidies ended. The now free-floating zloty became convertible at about 9,500 per dollar (from 430 in 1988).

Poland is hampered by its inefficient industry and low-quality goods. In addition, oil, previously bartered or purchased from the USSR at low prices, must now be paid for with hard currency at world prices.

By September 1990 unemployment had risen to 1.5 million, living standards had dropped 30%, and emigration was up. Environmental cleanup necessitated by industrialization will be a further drain on an overburdened economy. Though generally supportive, the people have protested declining conditions and gone on strikes. Plans to privatize industry are under way. Such foreign companies as Coca-Cola, Asea Brown Boveri, Fiat, and Reliance Electric are all investing in Poland.

In the December 1990 presidential elections, Solidarity leader Lech Walesa won a resounding victory. But Poland has yet to hold a fully democratic parliamentary election and is hampered by outdated election laws.

WHEN

Poland was settled by the *Slavic Polanie*, the "plains people." In the 14th century towns grew as German craftsmen and artisans and Jewish merchants settled in Poland. The country became a dominant power in Europe and controlled important trade routes.

Poland reached its zenith in the 15th century. After the 16th century Poland went into eclipse. Its overland trade routes fell into disuse as ocean trade routes were opened. In 1795 Russia, Prussia, and Austria partitioned Poland into oblivion. Gaining independence in 1918, Poland was a backward land of subsistence agriculture, with a few centers of urban high culture.

Six million Poles died in WWII, half of them Jews. Soviet forces took control of Poland and set up a Communist government in 1944, forcing Poland to reject Marshall Plan aid and begin a process of Stalinist, state-controlled industrialization. But the process was never completed. Agricultural production remained 75% private, and there were many small private businesses and tradespeople.

Poland was restive under communism; workers rioted during the 1950s and 1960s. In 1970 they brought down a government over price rises. The new government raised real wages, provided better distribution of food and consumer goods, and modernized industry — mostly on Western credit.

But the inefficient, centralized economic structure remained, and, by the late 1970s, Poland was groaning under its Western debt. Austerity measures, followed by strikes (including the Gdansk shipyard strike that brought Lech Walesa and Solidarity to international attention), led again to the government's downfall and the recognition of free unions. But the turmoil went on; the Communist party installed General Wojciech Jaruzelski as leader.

When Solidarity suggested a referendum on Communist rule, martial law was imposed and Walesa was imprisoned. For several years Poland inched slowly toward independence from the USSR and toward freedom and capitalism. State power retreated before popular discontent and the power of the Catholic Church, which supported the movement.

With the economy lurching to a halt in the late 1980s, the government began a program of free-market reforms. Prices and inflation rose, sparking more strikes. Faced with near collapse in 1988, the government offered Solidarity supporters a chance to participate in government if they would repudiate Solidarity. But they refused, forcing the government eventually to legalize Solidarity.

In 1989, with a hard-currency debt of $39 billion and inflation of 40% to 60% per month, the government agreed to hold legislative elections. Despite rules that gave the Communist party an edge, the Communists lost and peacefully transferred authority. The new government proceeded to establish a free-market economy. Debt is Poland's worst problem, and various relief plans, from debt forgiveness (in 1991 the US said it would forgive 70% of Poland's debt) to a debt-for-nature swap, are in the works.

HOW MUCH

	4-Year Growth	1986	1987	1988	1989	1990
Population (mil.)	*0.3%*	37.6	37.8	37.9	38.0	38.2
NMP ($ bil.)	—	*61*	*53*	*58*	*73*	*66*
Real NMP growth rate	—	4.9%	1.9%	4.9%	(0.2%)	(13.0%)
Exports ($ mil.)	—	5,600	6,400	8,000	8,900	11,900
Imports ($ mil.)	—	4,700	5,400	6,900	7,400	8,100
Trade balance ($ mil.)	—	900	1,000	1,100	1,500	3,800
Current account ($ mil.)	—	(800)	(100)	(300)	(1,600)	1,400
Govt. budget bal. ($ mil.)	—	*(307)*	*(463)*	*182*	*(2,640)*	—
Consumer inflation	—	17.7%	26.0%	60.0%	251.0%	585.0%
Unemployment rate	—	—	—	—	—	4.5%
Exchange rate with US$	—	175.3	265.1	430.6	1439.2	9,500.0

Source: Economist Intelligence Unit and *The Reference Press*

Area: 120,628 sq. mi. (312,683 sq. km)

Official name:
Republic of Poland
Rzeczpospolita Polska
Official language: Polish
Currency: 1 zloty (Zl) = 100 groszy
Fiscal year ends: December 31

WHO

President: Lech Walesa, age 48, Zl11,000,000 pay
Prime Minister: Jan Krzysztof Bielecki, age 40
Deputy Prime Minister and Minister of Finance: Leszek Balcerowicz, age 44
Minister of Foreign Affairs: Krzysztof Skubiszewski, age 65
Ambassador to US: Kazimierz Dziewanowski, age 61
US Ambassador to Poland: Thomas Simons

WHERE

Executive HQ: President, Aleje Ujazdowskie 1/3, 00-583 Warsaw, Poland
Embassy in US: 2640 16th St. NW, Washington, DC 20009
Phone: 202-234-3800
Fax: 202-328-6271
US Embassy in Poland: Aleje Ujazdowskie 29/31, Warsaw, Poland
Phone: 011-48-22-283041
Chamber of Commerce: Polish Chamber of Commerce, Ulitsa Trevacka 4, PL-00-074 Warsaw, Poland
Phone: 011-48-22-260221

Poland has 49 provinces and has diplomatic representatives in 119 countries.

Capital city: Warsaw
Time change from EST: +6 hours
Avg. high/low temp: Jan. 32°F (0°C)/22°F (-6°C)
July 75°F (24°C)/58°F (15°C)

Urbanization: 62%
Population density: 315/sq. mi. (122/sq. km)

Exports as % of Total		Imports as % of Total	
USSR	25	Germany	20
Germany	18	USSR	18
UK	7	Austria	6
Czechoslovakia	6	Czechoslovakia	6
Other countries	44	Other countries	50
Total	**100**	**Total**	**100**

WHAT

Origins of Net Material Product	% of Total
Mining, manufacturing & utilities	48
Agriculture, forestry & fishing	13
Construction	12
Other	27
Total	**100**

1990 NMP per capita: $1,724
1990 year-end external debt: $47 billion
Literacy rate: 98%
UN Human Development Index: 86%
Human Freedom Index (0-40 scale): 10
Purchasing power as % of US: 25%
Capital city cost of living as % of DC: 41%
Defense as % of GNP: 3%
Education as % of GNP: 4%
Principal airline: Polish-LOT (Polskie Linie Lotnicze)
Principal exchange: The Warsaw Stock Exchange

PORTUGAL

OVERVIEW

Sharing the Iberian Peninsula with Spain, Portugal is divided in 2 by the Tagus River. In the north the countryside is cool, mountainous, and distinctive for its small family holdings. In the south the land is flatter, drier, and divided into larger, formerly hereditary landholdings called *latifundios*. Farming methods are less efficient than in the rest of Western Europe, and an attempt under the Marxists at collectivization made matters worse.

Major products include port wine, named after the 2nd largest city, Oporto; cork; wood products; processed fish (Portugal's fishing fleet is the oldest in Europe); olive oil; and clothing and shoes. Mineral resources include coal, tin, copper, and uranium. Portugal's rivers provide hydroelectric power. Tourism is increasingly important, now contributing over 5% of GDP, the highest in the EC.

Portugal's industrial sector is small, consisting largely of labor-intensive enterprises; its heavy industry is antiquated and inefficient. The nation had to make considerable concessions on protective measures to join the EC, in return for which it receives considerable aid from the Community.

Colonial wars in Africa and disastrous economic Marxist experiments in the 1970s created a recession, accompanied by inflation, in the early 1980s. But, by the late 1980s, the economy was growing again, averaging 4.6% annually between 1988 and 1990. Inflation is the highest in the EC, at nearly 15%. Unemployment is approximately 4% but would be much higher without emigration to the EC and the US, Portugal's 2 largest trading partners. Remittances from overseas workers play a significant part in the economy.

WHEN

Portugal emerged as a country separate from Spain in the 12th century. Isolated from the Mediterranean, it turned to the Atlantic. Prince Henry the Navigator (1394–1460) sponsored exploration of the African coast, and the Portuguese reached the Middle East and Asia, gaining advantage in the Asian trade. Portuguese explorers under Magellan completed the first global circumnavigation in 1522.

In the 15th and 16th centuries, Portugal settled territories in Asia, Africa, and South America. After dynastic disputes Spain ruled Portugal from 1580 to 1640. Portugal was pulled into costly Spanish wars with England and the Netherlands, leading to the loss of several colonies, including Ceylon in the 1650s.

Portugal's principal remaining colony, Brazil, produced sugar, coffee, gold, gems, and minerals. Like Spain, Portugal did not use its colonial wealth to develop the home country, and, from the 17th to the 19th centuries, it continually fell farther behind the rest of Western Europe. In 1822 Brazil declared independence. Portugal spent the 19th century in turmoil at home, administering its colonies in Africa, which included Mozambique, Guinea-Bissau, and Angola.

In 1910 the monarchy was toppled, leading to 16 years of unrest and an army takeover. In 1928, with the economy in ruins, economist Antonio Salazar became finance minister, and in 1932 he became prime minister, a post he held until 1968. Salazar established a fascist state, protecting industries and controlling wages, prices, and unions.

Heavily dependent on its colonies for trade, Portugal began a series of wars in the 1960s to keep its colonies, especially those in Africa. In 1974 Marxist officers seized power, freed the colonies, and established a Socialist state.

Decolonization brought over a million colonials, many destitute, to a Portugal ill-prepared to accommodate them. The Marxists nationalized 60% of the antiquated and inefficient economy, including banks, heavy industry, and agriculture, causing enormous debt, a bloated bureaucracy, and rampant inflation.

Since 1976 successive reforms have shifted the state from socialism to free enterprise. Experiments in privatization (in which 49% of the equity in key industries is sold) have proven promising, and the government is opening the country to foreign investment. Disruption from the influx of colonials has subsided.

Portugal joined the EC in 1986 and has received much developmental aid. Its per capita GDP has grown quickly but has far to go to reach parity with the rest of the EC. It has the lowest literacy and the highest infant mortality rates in Western Europe.

In 1989 and 1991 Portugal actively privatized state-owned companies by taking them public on local stock markets. Foreigners have been active buyers and their ownership now represents over 12% of the total market capitalization.

HOW MUCH

	4-Year Growth	1986	1987	1988	1989	1990
Population (mil.)	*0.7%*	10.2	10.3	10.3	10.5	10.5
GDP ($ bil.)	*18.9%*	*30*	*37*	*42*	*45*	*60*
Real GDP growth rate	—	4.1%	5.1%	4.0%	5.4%	4.4%
Exports ($ mil.)	*22.5%*	7,235	9,304	10,986	12,800	16,305
Imports ($ mil.)	*26.6%*	9,649	13,948	17,849	19,070	24,823
Trade balance ($ mil.)	—	(2,414)	(4,644)	(6,863)	(6,270)	(8,518)
Current account ($ mil.)	—	1,150	444	(1,064)	139	(61)
Govt. budget bal. ($ mil.)	—	—	*(2,690)*	*(2,854)*	*(1,937)*	*(4,453)*
Consumer inflation	—	11.7%	9.4%	9.7%	12.6%	13.4%
Unemployment rate	—	8.5%	7.1%	5.7%	5.0%	4.7%
Exchange rate with US$	—	149.6	140.9	144.0	157.5	142.6

Source: Economist Intelligence Unit and *The Reference Press*

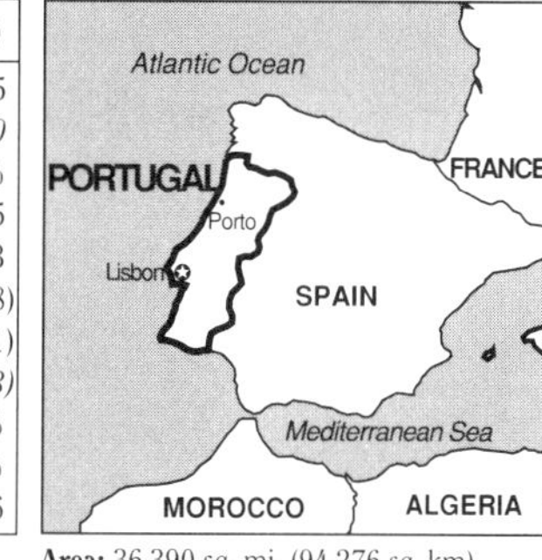

Area: 36,390 sq. mi. (94,276 sq. km)

Official name:
Republic of Portugal
República Portuguesa
Official language: Portuguese
Currency: 1 escudo (Esc) = 100 centavos
Fiscal year ends: December 31

WHO

President of the Portuguese Republic: Mario Alberto Soares, age 67
Prime Minister: Anibal Cavaco Silva, age 52
Minister of Finance: Miguel Beleza, age 41
Minister of Foreign Affairs: Joao de Deus Pinheiro, age 46
Ambassador to US: (Ambassador Nominate) Francisco Knopfli
US Ambassador to Portugal: Everett Ellis Briggs

WHERE

Executive HQ: President, Presidencia Da Republica, Palacio De Belem, Lisbon, Portugal
Embassy in US: 2125 Kalorama Rd. NW, Washington, DC 20008
Phone: 202-328-8610
Fax: 202-462-3726
US Embassy in Portugal: Avenida das Forcas Armadas, 1600 Lisbon, Portugal
Phone: 011-351-1-726-6600
Fax: 011-351-1-726-9109
Chamber of Commerce: International Chamber of Commerce, Rua Portas Sto. Antao 89-2, 1100 Lisbon, Portugal
Phone: 011-351-1-363-304

Portugal has 18 districts, 2 autonomous regions, and one dependency.

Capital city: Lisbon
Time change from EST: +5 hours
Avg. high/low temp: Jan. 57°F (14°C)/46°F (8°C)
July: 81°F (27°C)/63°F (17°C)

Urbanization: 33%
Population density: 289/sq. mi. (112/sq. km)

Exports as % of Total		Imports as % of Total	
Germany	17	Spain	14
France	16	Germany	14
Spain	13	France	12
UK	12	Italy	10
Other countries	42	Other countries	50
Total	**100**	**Total**	**100**

WHAT

Origins of GDP	% of Total
Services	56
Manufacturing & mining	28
Construction	6
Agriculture, forestry & fishing	6
Electricity, gas & water	4
Total	**100**

1990 GDP per capita: $5,654
1990 year-end external debt: $20 billion
Literacy rate: 83%
UN Human Development Index: 88%
Human Freedom Index (0-40 scale): 30
Purchasing power as % of US: 34%
Capital city cost of living as % of DC: 94%
Defense as % of GNP: 2%
Education as % of GNP: 5%
Principal airline: TAP-Air Portugal
Principal exchanges: Bolsa de Valores de Lisboa, Bolsa de Valores do Porto

SAUDI ARABIA

OVERVIEW

Saudi Arabia controls Islam's holiest places, Mecca and Medina, and thus plays an important role in world Islam.

Influential as the crucial "swing producer" in OPEC (compensating for other members' departures from quotas), Saudi Arabia gained more clout by subsidizing anti-Iraq Arab nations in the Gulf War. War-related payments are a great burden: $20 billion in 1990 and $13.6 billion in the first quarter of 1991.

With the world's largest oil reserves and a small domestic market, Saudi Arabia is the world's largest oil exporter. Lacking a large educated population, Saudi Arabia imports foreign workers (now 60% of the work force).

The government is the primary instrument of development, and the royal house of Saud, under King Fahd, dominates political life and controls the kingdom's vast wealth. He conducts business in accordance with Islamic law, the *Shari'a*, which differs from standard international financial practice in, among other things, prohibiting payment of interest.

With few natural agricultural areas, Saudi Arabia relies on a heavily irrigated, heavily subsidized agricultural sector that produces wheat, barley, fruits, vegetables, and meats. The country has recently become not only self-sufficient in food, but a net exporter.

Mineral resources include gold (estimated reserves: 20 million tons), copper, zinc, and iron ore. Industrial products include refined petroleum, steel, chemicals, plastics, and fertilizers, and the government operates the Arab world's largest airline, Saudia.

WHEN

The coasts and oases of the Arabian peninsula have been inhabited from earliest times; settlers traded with the ancient empires. Starting in the 7th century, the message of the prophet Mohammed spread from Mecca through the peninsula and beyond. Arabia was nominally ruled by various caliphates, including the Ottomans, but never united politically. The area was controlled by tribal sheiks.

One of these tribal sheiks was Ibn Saud of Riyadh. In 1902 he began to conquer the peninsula. In WWI he refrained from supporting the Turks for a $25,000 annual stipend from Britain. By 1932 Ibn Saud was king of a new country, Saudi Arabia.

Until American geologists discovered Saudi oil reserves in 1938, Saudi Arabia's income came from pilgrims traveling to Mecca. WWII halted the pilgrimages and delayed oil production, leaving the country near collapse.

The discovery of oil had little impact on most of the Saudi people's traditional lives of herding, farming, or trading. The Sauds treated the oil wealth as family treasure.

Ibn Saud died in 1952 and was succeeded by a son who had no financial aptitude and whose policies brought crisis. In 1958 another son, Faisal, took over the purse strings and then in 1964 deposed his half brother to become king. Faisal divided state funds from family funds and instituted budgets for education, health care, and transportation.

In the 1960s spending focused on developing infrastructure and education. In the 1970s the government heavily subsidized agriculture. OPEC (of which Saudi Arabia was a leading member) began to feel its power, first raising prices, and then in 1973 declaring an embargo on the US and making across-the-board production cuts. Money poured in.

The Saudis diversified into refining oil and into producing secondary products such as chemicals, steel, and aluminum. They planned and built new industrial cities, such as Jubail and Yanbu (completed in the 1980s), as centers of oil products and metals production.

Also in the 1970s and 1980s, Saudi Arabia became a world financial power, joining the World Bank and IMF, dominating Arab and Islamic aid organizations, and becoming one of the world's largest aid donors.

By 1982 Saudi foreign assets had reached $150 billion. But the boom fizzled out. The oil glut brought reductions in oil production from 3.5 billion barrels in 1981 to 1.1 billion in 1985. Revenues dropped, pushing the economy into the red.

Fearing entanglement in the Iran/Iraq war, Saudi Arabia continued to arm itself (36% of expenditures) and to pursue development. In 1990 Iraq invaded Kuwait and threatened Saudi Arabia. Though heavily armed, Saudi Arabia lacked the manpower to combat Iraq's larger army and appealed to the US and UN for help. Largely intact despite some missile attacks, Saudi Arabia now faces expenses related to deployment of foreign forces in the region as well as aid to Kuwait and other Arab nations. It also faces social disruption caused by the influx of foreigners.

HOW MUCH

	4-Year Growth	1986	1987	1988	1989	1990
Population (mil.)	*2.8%*	11.2	12.0	12.0	12.3	12.5
GDP ($ bil.)	*6.7%*	*73*	*74*	*76*	*83*	*95*
Real GDP growth rate	—	5.6%	(1.4%)	7.6%	0.2%	8.7%
Exports ($ mil.)	*24.2%*	20,180	23,200	23,740	27,740	48,060
Imports ($ mil.)	*2.2%*	19,110	20,110	21,780	21,150	20,810
Trade balance ($ mil.)	—	1,070	3,090	1,960	6,590	27,250
Current account ($ mil.)	—	(11,800)	(9,770)	(6,770)	(8,500)	(2,500)
Govt. budget bal. ($ mil.)	—	*0*	*(14,077)*	*(9,586)*	*(6,685)*	*(6,676)*
Consumer inflation	—	(3.0%)	(0.9%)	1.0%	1.1%	—
Unemployment rate	—	—	—	—	—	—
Exchange rate with US$	—	3.70	3.75	3.75	3.75	3.75

Source: Economist Intelligence Unit and *The Reference Press*

Area: 829,008 sq. mi. (2,149,690 sq. km)

Official name:
Kingdom of Saudi Arabia
al-Mamlaka al-'Arabiya as-Sa'udiya
Official language: Arabic
Currency: 1 riyal (SR) = 20 qursh, 100 halala
Fiscal year ends: December 31

WHO

King and Prime Minister and Supreme Commander of the Armed Forces: King Fahd bin 'Abd al-'Aziz Al Sa'ud, Custodian of the Two Holy Mosques, age 68
Crown Prince, Deputy Prime Minister, and Commander of the National Guard: H.R.H. Prince 'Abdallah bin 'Abd al-'Aziz Al Sa'ud (half brother to the king), age 67
Minister of Finance and National Economy: Muhammad al-Ali Aba'l Khail, age 56
Minister of Foreign Affairs: H.R.H. Prince Saud al-Faisal bin 'Abd al-'Aziz Al Sa'ud, age 51
Ambassador to US: H.R.H. Prince Bandar bin Sultan, age 42
US Ambassador to Saudi Arabia: Charles W. Freeman, Jr.

WHERE

Executive HQ: King and Prime Minister, Royal Court, Riyadh, Saudi Arabia
Embassy in US: 601 New Hampshire Ave. NW, Washington, DC 20037
Phone: 202-342-3800
Fax: 202-944-5983
US Embassy in Saudi Arabia: Collector Rd. M, Riyadh Diplomatic Qtr., Riyadh, Saudi Arabia
Phone: 011-966-1-488-3800
Fax: 011-966-1-488-3278
Chamber of Commerce: Council of Saudi Arabian Chambers of Commerce, PO Box 16683, Riyadh 11474, Saudi Arabia
Phone: 011-966-1-405-3200

Saudi Arabia has 14 provinces and has diplomatic representatives in 64 countries.

Capital city: Riyadh
Time change from EST: +8 hours
Avg. high/low temp: Jan. 70°F (21°C)/46°F (8°C)
July 107°F (42°C)/78°F (26°C)

Urbanization: 76%
Population density: 15/sq. mi. (6/sq. km)

Exports as % of Total		Imports as % of Total	
US	22	UK	17
Japan	20	US	15
Singapore	7	Japan	12
Other countries	51	Other countries	56
Total	**100**	**Total**	**100**

WHAT

Origins of GDP	% of Total
Services	30
Oil & gas, mining	24
Other	46
Total	**100**

1990 GDP per capita: $7,590
1990 year-end external debt: none
Literacy rate: 52%
UN Human Development Index: 70%
Human Freedom Index (0-40 scale): 6
Purchasing power as % of US: 47%
Capital city cost of living as % of DC: 86%
Defense as % of GNP: 17%
Principal airline: Saudia (Saudi Arabian Airlines)

SINGAPORE

OVERVIEW

Singapore ("City of the Lion" in Sanskrit) is a tiny island at the tip of the Malay peninsula whose only resources are its 2.7 million people (primarily of Chinese descent) and its harbor.

Under the leadership of Lee Kuan Yew from 1959 to 1991, Singapore became a leading economic power in Asia, producing petroleum products, petrochemicals, pharmaceuticals, rubber, electronics, and textiles and acting as a transportation and financial hub for Asia. About 650 multinational corporations have offices there.

The government directs economic development through tax and credit regulations. Though Lee and his successor believe in free markets, wages are controlled, and personal freedom, especially of the press, is curtailed.

Singapore's economy has had high average growth rates and relatively low inflation, and the government budget runs at a large surplus (projected to be 5% of GDP in 1991). In the late 1980s annual GDP growth reached 11.1% before slowing to 8.3% in 1990. With stern controls inflation remained relatively low even during slowdowns in 1985 and 1987; it is rising now but was still under 5% in 1990.

Because of its advanced state of development, Singapore was removed in 1988 from the US Generalized System of Preferences list and therefore became ineligible for special benefits and responsible for full membership fees in international organizations.

New Prime Minister Goh Chok Tong is continuing his predecessor's policies.

WHEN

Singapore was founded in 1824 by Sir Stamford Raffles of the East India Company on land granted by a Malay sultan 5 years earlier. The company ran Singapore and areas on the Malay peninsula under a *laissez-faire* trade and immigration policy, attracting many Chinese laborers. In 1867 Singapore became a UK colony.

Singapore's importance as a port was secured by the opening of the Suez Canal in 1869 and by Britain's growing control of the Malay peninsula (called Malaya) from 1874 until 1914. In the 20th century demand grew for the region's tin and rubber, which are processed in and shipped from Singapore.

The Depression led to restrictions on immigration by men but not women, changing the nature of the population from transients to permanent resident families.

Despite British fortifications the Japanese overran Singapore in 1941. After WWII the British prepared Malaya for independence, retaining Singapore as a colony for military reasons. Singapore and Malaya were deemed too culturally and religiously diverse to unite successfully. This was proven true when, following independence in 1959, they united in a 1963 federation, from which Singapore was ejected in 1965, largely because of Malay fears of Chinese domination.

Singapore's economy developed in planned stages, though ownership remained private and the market remained free. Singapore was a shipping and warehousing point for goods originating elsewhere until WWII. In the 1950s and early 1960s, with high unemployment and a large, impoverished population, the government promoted growth of labor-intensive industries (clothing and goods assembly) while launching educational, housing, and birth-control programs. Between 1956 and 1960, annual growth averaged 5.4%.

After 1968, with the economy stabilized, the government emphasized large-scale manufacturing and processing enterprises. Between 1968 and 1974, GDP grew 12% annually. The 1971 pullout of British forces was expected to be a severe economic blow, as the military had accounted for 20% of GDP; but the government mitigated its effects by encouraging foreign investment in construction of refineries and chemical plants. By 1973 Singapore's petroleum refining capacity had risen to become the 3rd largest in the world. GDP growth decreased during the oil crisis of the 1970s.

In 1979, partly because of protectionism worldwide, the government began steering the economy toward high-value-added, high-tech, capital-intensive enterprises. In the 1980s it offered more tax incentives and technical, financial, and marketing assistance to businesses, especially small- to medium-sized ones. New industries began, including aerospace, biotechnology, and computing.

Similar encouragement was given to the service sector, leading to growth in financial and banking services and tourism.

The successful birth-control campaigns of the 1960s caused labor shortages (unemployment is less than 2%), and labor is often imported. This may lead to further ethnic tensions between the Chinese majority and guest workers of other backgrounds.

HOW MUCH

	4-Year Growth	1986	1987	1988	1989	1990
Population (mil.)	*0.9%*	2.59	2.61	2.65	2.68	2.71
GDP ($ bil.)	*18.1%*	*18*	*20*	*25*	*29*	*35*
Real GDP growth rate	—	1.8%	9.4%	11.1%	9.2%	8.3%
Exports ($ mil.)	*23.7%*	22,500	28,600	39,300	44,700	52,600
Imports ($ mil.)	*24.1%*	25,500	32,400	43,900	49,700	60,500
Trade balance ($ mil.)	—	(3,000)	(3,800)	(4,600)	(5,000)	(7,900)
Current account ($ mil.)	—	320	220	1,260	2,550	2,350
Govt. budget bal. ($ mil.)	—	*2,151*	*950*	*3,271*	*4,014*	—
Consumer inflation	—	(1.4%)	0.5%	1.5%	2.4%	3.4%
Unemployment rate	—	6.5%	—	3.3%	2.2%	*1.7%*
Exchange rate with US$	—	2.18	2.11	2.01	1.95	1.81

Source: Economist Intelligence Unit and *The Reference Press*

Area: 239 sq. mi. (620 sq. km)

Official name: Republic of Singapore
Official languages: Chinese, English, Malay, Tamil
Currency: 1 dollar (S$) = 100 cents
Fiscal year ends: March 31

WHO

President: Wee Kim Wee, age 76
Prime Minister: Goh Chok Tong
Minister of Finance: Richard Hu Tsu Tau
Minister of Foreign Affairs: Wong Kan Seng
Ambassador to US: S. R. Nathan
US Ambassador to Singapore: Robert D. Orr

WHERE

Executive HQ: President, Istana, Orchard Rd., Singapore 0922
Embassy in US: 1824 R St. NW, Washington, DC 20009
Phone: 202-667-7555
Fax: 202-265-7915
US Embassy in Singapore: 30 Hill St., Singapore 0617
Phone: 011-65-338-0251
Fax: 011-65-338-4550
Chamber of Commerce: Singapore Federation of Chambers of Commerce & Industry, 03–01 Chinese Chamber of Commerce Bldg., Hill St., Singapore 0617
Phone: 011-65-338-9761
Fax: 011-65-339-5630

Singapore has diplomatic representatives in 22 countries.

Capital city: Singapore
Time change from EST: +13 hours
Avg. high/low temp: Jan. 86°F (30°C)/73°F (23°C)
July 88°F (31°C)/75°F (24°C)

Urbanization: 100%
Population density: 11,339/sq. mi. (4,371/sq. km)

Exports as % of Total		Imports as % of Total	
US	22	Japan	20
Malaysia	14	US	16
Japan	9	Malaysia	14
Thailand	7	Saudi Arabia	5
Other countries	48	Other countries	45
Total	**100**	**Total**	**100**

WHAT

Origins of GDP	% of Total
Financial & business services	33
Manufacturing	29
Commerce	17
Transport & communications	13
Construction	6
Utilities	2
Total	**100**

1990 GDP per capita: $12,783
1990 year-end external debt: none
Literacy rate: 87%
UN Human Development Index: 88%
Human Freedom Index (0-40 scale): 11
Purchasing power as % of US: 73%
Capital city cost of living as % of DC: 105%
Defense as % of GNP: 6%
Education as % of GDP: 6%
Principal airline: Singapore International Airways (SIA)
Principal exchange: Stock Exchange of Singapore Limited

SOUTH AFRICA

OVERVIEW

Although South Africa is Africa's most developed country, the maldistribution of resources caused by its separatist racial policies (known as apartheid) places South Africa firmly in the Third World in terms of the lifestyle and prospects of most of its black population.

South Africa has some of the world's richest deposits of diamonds and gold (world's largest producer of each), platinum, chrome, uranium, nickel, and iron ore. With little oil and natural gas, it relies on coal for energy.

South Africa is one of the few net food exporters on the continent, producing wheat, corn, wine grapes, and sugar cane.

The economy has been hard hit by years of sanctions and plagued by declining production. Because of the UN boycotts of the 1970s and 1980s, foreign investment has fled, and export industries (with the exception of armaments) are underdeveloped. Economic growth lags behind the growth in the work force, and unemployment for blacks is about 27%.

Real annual economic growth fell to 2% or less in the 1980s and was negative in 1990. Gold prices have been low for several years, and the Gulf War depressed them further.

In 1991, after South Africa scrapped the last official apartheid law, US president George Bush indicated he wanted to lift economic sanctions against South Africa, and the Olympic committee reinstated the country after 30 years.

WHEN

In 1486 Portuguese navigator Bartholomeu Dias rounded the Cape of Good Hope; later, in 1652, the Dutch East India Company established a supply station there. Built on imported slave labor, farming grew quickly, and Dutch settlers moved inland, fighting the Bantus who were also moving into the area.

In 1795 the British took over Cape Town. In the 1850s Dutch farmers (Boers, also known as Afrikaaners) moved northeast to establish the Orange Free State and the Transvaal republics. Around this time Indians came to work the sugar plantations. In 1870 diamonds were found at Kimberley, and in 1886 gold was discovered in the Transvaal, sparking massive European immigration and investment. British efforts to gain control of the gold fields led to wars with the Boers in 1880 and 1899. In 1902 the Boers were defeated. In 1910 the Orange Free State and the Transvaal joined with the Cape and Natal Colonies to become the Union of South Africa.

The gold and diamond finds focused the economy on mining. Cecil Rhodes created De Beers Consolidated Mines, which has controlled world diamond trade ever since.

In 1912 the government outlawed black land ownership in white areas, and the African National Congress (ANC) was formed. Between WWI and WWII the black population exploded; whites made little provision for education or health care for the blacks and excluded them from government. Other nonwhite people, Asians and "coloreds," were also discriminated against, but to a lesser extent.

After WWII the Boers regained control of the country and enacted more restrictive laws against blacks (the apartheid system). As South Africa's economy boomed, blacks were pushed onto the economic periphery. They were segregated into black "townships" and had inferior education and separate pay scales and career tracks.

Resistance to apartheid brought violence and suppression, including the 1964 imprisonment of Nelson Mandela. In the 1960s and 1970s, South Africa was divided into "homelands" to which people were assigned on the basis of race and tribe. The whites, with 13% of the population, took 87% of the land, leaving blacks an isolated 13% and reducing them to migrant laborers in a foreign land.

International opposition to apartheid brought trade embargoes. Foreign companies were pressured to divest their holdings or abide by the 1977 "Sullivan Principles" for equality in the workplace. The economy suffered and many blacks lost their jobs.

Protests against apartheid by white South Africans were growing, not only because of apartheid's injustice, but also because of the recognition that there were simply too few whites to prevail in the long run. Since the mid-1980s, intermarriage prohibitions, pass laws, and residency restrictions have been relaxed. Nelson Mandela was released from prison, and the ANC was legalized in 1990, paving the way for negotiations.

By 1991 some European countries had relaxed sanctions, and even Nigeria was considering doing so. South Africa's decision to formally abolish the legal basis of apartheid (many *de facto* elements remain) is diminishing the country's isolation.

HOW MUCH

	4-Year Growth	1986	1987	1988	1989	1990
Population (mil.)	*2.3%*	28.2	28.9	29.6	30.2	30.9
GDP ($ bil.)	*13.1%*	*62*	*81*	*86*	*89*	*101*
Real GDP growth rate	—	0.2%	2.1%	4.1%	2.1%	(0.9%)
Exports ($ mil.)	*6.3%*	18,000	21,400	22,400	22,200	23,400
Imports ($ mil.)	*10.7%*	11,200	14,100	17,100	16,900	17,000
Trade balance ($ mil.)	—	6,800	7,300	5,300	5,300	6,400
Current account ($ mil.)	—	3,150	3,020	1,300	1,560	2,240
Govt. budget bal. ($ mil.)	—	*(559)*	*(1,788)*	*(322)*	*(203)*	—
Consumer inflation	—	18.6%	16.1%	12.9%	14.7%	14.4%
Unemployment rate	—	16.4%	15.4%	13.2%	10.7%	—
Exchange rate with US$	—	2.28	2.04	2.27	2.62	2.59

Source: Economist Intelligence Unit and *The Reference Press*

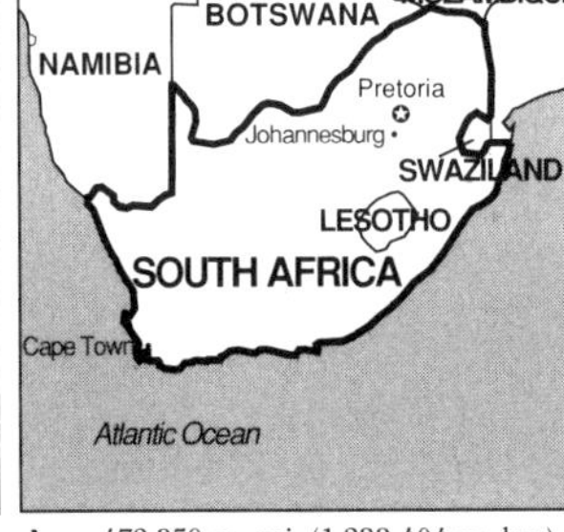

Area: 472,359 sq. mi. (1,233,404 sq. km)

Official name:
Republic of South Africa
Republiek van Suid-Afrika
Official languages: Afrikaans, English
Currency: 1 rand (R) = 100 cents
Fiscal year ends: March 31

WHO

President: Frederik Willem de Klerk, age 55
Minister of Finance: Barend du Plessis, age 51
Minister of Foreign Affairs: Roelof F. "Pik" Botha, age 59
Ambassador to US: Harry H. Schwarz, age 67
US Ambassador to South Africa: William L. Swing

WHERE

Executive HQ: President, Private Bag X1000, Pretoria 0001, South Africa
Embassy in US: 3051 Massachusetts Ave. NW, Washington, DC 20008
Phone: 202-232-4400
Fax: 202-265-1607
US Embassy in South Africa: Thibault House, 225 Pretorius St., Pretoria 0001, South Africa
Phone: 011-27-12-28-4266
Fax: 011-27-12-28-4266, ext. 259
Chamber of Commerce: Association of Chambers of Commerce of South Africa, Private Bag 34, Auckland Park 2092, South Africa
Phone: 011-27-11-726-5309
Fax: 011-27-11-726-8421

South Africa has 4 provinces and has diplomatic representatives in 52 countries.

Capital city: Pretoria
Time change from EST: +7 hours
Avg. high/low temp: Jan. 81°F (27°C)/60°F (16°C)
July 66°F (19°C)/37°F (3°C)

Urbanization: 58%
Population density: 65/sq. mi. (25/sq. km)

Exports as % of Total		Imports as % of Total	
Italy	11	Germany	20
Japan	8	Japan	10
US	7	UK	10
Germany	7	US	10
Other countries	67	Other countries	50
Total	**100**	**Total**	**100**

WHAT

Origins of GDP	% of Total
Services	27
Manufacturing	24
Financial services	14
Public administration	14
Mining & quarrying	12
Agriculture, forestry & fishing	6
Construction	3
Total	**100**

1990 GDP per capita: $3,284
1990 year-end external debt: $20 billion
Literacy rate: 99% (whites), 50% (blacks, est.)
UN Human Development Index: 77%
Human Freedom Index (0-40 scale): 3
Purchasing power as % of US: 28%
Johannesburg cost of living as % of DC: 74%
Defense as % of GNP: 4%
Education as % of GNP: —
Principal airline: South African Airways
Principal exchange: The Johannesburg Stock Exchange

SPAIN

OVERVIEW

After centuries of isolation, Spain has begun integrating itself into Europe in the last 15 years. Guided by King Juan Carlos, Spain has moved from fascism to democracy, from a controlled economy to a free market, and from outcast to full member of the EC.

Spain's efforts to join Europe include converting its railroads to the European standard gauge, building roads to accommodate increased auto traffic, and tunneling through the Pyrenees mountains to France.

Among the poorest nations in the EC, with a GNP 75% of the EC average, Spain had the highest GDP growth rate from 1986 to 1989 — 5%. In 1989 a tight monetary policy was instituted to fight inflation and a rising trade deficit, slowing growth to under 4% by 1990.

Even though Spain has 1/3 of the EC's arable land, Spanish agriculture is less efficient than the EC average because of archaic land ownership patterns and lack of mechanization.

Spain has actively sought foreign investment while partially divesting key industries, such as auto manufacturing and oil processing, from government ownership. Tourism, one of Spain's strongest industries (8–10% of GNP and 40% of foreign currency income), declined 5% in 1990.

Though dependent on imported oil for over 60% of its energy needs, Spain uses 30% less oil per capita than the EC average and is improving its hydroelectric and nuclear power generation capacity.

Spain still faces difficulties, however, in building a modern infrastructure to foster economic growth. Research investment is under 1% of GNP, and technical educational resources are limited.

Official name:
Spanish State
España
Official language: Spanish
Currency: 1 peseta (Pta) = 100 centimos
Fiscal year ends: December 31

WHO

Chief of State, Commander in Chief of the Armed Forces: King Juan Carlos de Borbón y Borbón I, age 53
President of the Government (Prime Minister): Felipe González Márquez, age 49
Vice-President of the Government: Narcis Serra Serra, age 48
Minister of Finance and Commerce: Carlos Solchaga Catalán, age 47
Minister of Foreign Affairs: Francisco Fernández Ordóñez, age 61
Ambassador to US: Jaime de Ojeda y Eiseley
US Ambassador to Spain: Joseph Zappala

WHEN

In the 8th century the Moors conquered Spain, bringing access to an Islamic free market that reached from India to the Atlantic. In 1492 the last Moors were driven out. The triumphant rulers, Ferdinand and Isabella, financed the voyage of Christopher Columbus, who, seeking Asia, found the New World — a source of raw materials and a new market for European goods. His discovery would transform the economic structure of the world.

By 1500 Spain owned the Netherlands, much of South and Central America, and the Philippines. Incalculable wealth in precious metals went to Spain, where it paid for wars and goods Spain could not make. Wars and lack of industrialization took their toll, and by 1588 (when England defeated Spain's Armada) Spain was in decline.

In the 17th and 18th centuries, Spain lost its European possessions. In the 1820s Spain's New World colonies revolted, depriving it of a captive market. It lost its Pacific and remaining Caribbean colonies in the Spanish-American War of 1898.

By 1900 lack of a trading and manufacturing base had impeded growth of a middle class, government was antiquated and unresponsive, and Marxism was on the rise. Anarchy led to a military coup in 1923.

In 1931 the king fled, and a new government attacked traditional powers, including the Catholic Church and the army, and nationalized key industries. In 1936 General Francisco Franco seized power. The resulting civil war devastated the country.

Though officially neutral in WWII, Franco sympathized with Germany. The Allies isolated Spain in a boycott lasting until 1950 and withheld Marshall Plan aid.

After the boycott was lifted, industrial production doubled, and prices rose, inciting protests. An economic restructuring in 1959 devalued the peseta, diminished economic controls, and set the economy toward capitalism, though government continued to control key industries and puppet unions. In the 1960s industrialization brought 3 million migrants from the countryside, and poverty drove 2 million people from Spain.

From 1965 to 1975 economic growth averaged 7% annually. Though educated by Franco (who died in 1975), King Juan Carlos moved to democratize Spain. In the 1970s worker unrest forced a loosening of wage controls, resulting in an inflation rate of 14% by 1981. An austerity program reduced inflation to 6% by 1986. Trade with the EC increased to 60% of all trade (Spain has little trade with its former colonies). Unemployment, though declining, remains high — 16%. The underground economy accounts for up to 20% of GNP and 30% of the work force.

After 5 years of EC membership, Spain has become a champion of the EC's poorer members, opposing environmental and labor laws that have a disproportionate impact on poor economies.

WHERE

Executive HQ: President, Palacio De La Moncloa, 28071 Madrid, Spain
Embassy in US: 2700 15th St. NW, Washington, DC 20009
Phone: 202-265-0190
Fax: 202-332-5451
US Embassy in Spain: Serrano 75, 28006 Madrid, Spain
Phone: 011-34-1-577-4000
Fax: 011-34-1-577-5735
Chamber of Commerce: Cámara Oficial de Comercio e Industria de Madrid, Huertas 13, 28012 Madrid, Spain
Phone: 011-34-1-429-3193

Spain has 17 autonomous communities and has diplomatic representatives in 154 countries.

Capital city: Madrid
Time change from EST: +6 hours
Avg. high/low temp: Jan. 47°F (9°C)/35°F (2°C)
July 87°F (31°C)/63°F (17°C)

Urbanization: 78%
Population density: 202/sq. mi. (78/sq. km)

Exports as % of Total		Imports as % of Total	
France	21	Germany	17
Germany	14	France	15
Italy	11	Italy	10
UK	9	US	8
Other	45	Other	50
Total	**100**	**Total**	**100**

WHAT

Origins of GDP	% of Total
Services	57
Manufacturing, mining & utilities	29
Construction	9
Agriculture, forestry & fishing	5
Total	**100**

1990 GDP per capita: $12,467
1990 year-end external debt: $44 billion
Literacy rate: 93%
UN Development Index: 95%
Human Freedom Index (0-40 scale): 26
Purchasing power as % of US: 46%
Capital city cost of living as % of DC: 133%
Defense as % of GNP: 2%
Education as % of GNP: 3%
Principal airline: Iberia
Principal exchange: Bolsa de Madrid

HOW MUCH

	4-Year Growth	1986	1987	1988	1989	1990
Population (mil.)	*0.4%*	38.7	38.8	39.0	39.2	39.4
GDP ($ bil.)	*21.2%*	*228*	*289*	*343*	*379*	*492*
Real GDP growth rate	—	3.3%	5.5%	5.2%	5.2%	3.6%
Exports ($ mil.)	*19.5%*	27,190	34,190	40,340	44,410	55,370
Imports ($ mil.)	*25.7%*	35,060	49,110	60,530	71,450	87,480
Trade balance ($ mil.)	—	(7,870)	(14,920)	(20,190)	(27,040)	(32,110)
Current account ($ mil.)	—	3,970	(230)	(3,780)	(11,640)	(15,720)
Govt. budget bal. ($ mil.)	—	*(12,020)*	*(10,543)*	*(10,172)*	*(8,150)*	*(9,840)*
Consumer inflation	—	8.8%	5.2%	4.8%	6.9%	6.7%
Unemployment rate	—	21.5%	20.6%	19.5%	17.3%	*16%*
Exchange rate with US$	—	140.1	123.5	116.5	118.4	101.9

Source: Economist Intelligence Unit and *The Reference Press*

Area: 194,884 sq. mi. (504,750 sq. km)

SRI LANKA

OVERVIEW

Sri Lanka (known as Ceylon until 1972) is a teardrop-shaped island off the southern tip of India. Its major ethnic groups include the Sinhalese (74% of the population, Buddhists) and the Tamils (about 18%, Hindus). Strife between these groups has blighted the nation's economy and politics since 1983.

Sri Lanka is noted for its high rate of literacy and good public health, despite its position as one of the world's 36 poorest nations.

Agriculture is Sri Lanka's most important sector, accounting for 25% of GDP and 46% of the work force. Products include tea (world's largest exporter and 3rd largest producer [after China and India]), coconut products, rubber, sugar, and rice.

Though possessing few mineral resources (limestone, graphite, mineral sands) and no petroleum or natural gas, Sri Lanka is rich in precious and semiprecious stones, including sapphires, tourmalines, and garnets.

Sri Lanka has also become a center for textile manufacture because of its highly literate and low-wage-scale work force. Small-scale machinery manufacture and cement and chemical production are also important.

Sri Lanka's problems include high foreign debt, loss of remittances from expatriates during the Gulf War, and low levels of foreign investment. But the country is addressing its problems. To avoid using up foreign currency reserves on oil imports, Sri Lanka has developed hydroelectric generation, which now accounts for 85% of electricity used. The government has been privatizing its industries and has liberalized foreign investment rules. This drew foreign investment to Colombo's stock market (70% of total investment in the market), driving its value up over 100% in 1990.

WHEN

In the 5th century BC, Indian settlers migrated to Sri Lanka. Their descendants established a kingdom that lasted 1,000 years, noted for its sophisticated farming and irrigation methods. It was known to the Romans as Taprobane and to the Arabs as Serendip. Subsequent waves of settlers included the Hindu Tamils from southern India.

The Portuguese arrived in 1505 and were succeeded by the Dutch in 1658 and the British in 1796. The British established a plantation economy, producing first coffee, tea, sugar, indigo, and opium and, later, rubber and coconut, with Tamil laborers. Ceylon became the world's largest tea exporter.

The late 19th and early 20th centuries saw protest against British rule. Nationalist ferment in the 1920s produced labor troubles and forced the British to institute a local representative government. Independence was granted in 1948.

By the mid-1950s, the economy had faltered because of world commodity price fluctuations; cash crops were cultivated at the expense of staples, which then had to be imported. Ethnic divisions were a problem. In the late 1960s a program for self-sufficiency in food benefited the economy. But rising inflation, falling commodity prices, and high unemployment of educated young people proved intractable problems.

In the 1970s the government nationalized the plantations, eventually bringing 60% of tea, 30% of rubber, and 10% of coconut acreage under government control. Simultaneously, production fell. The economy worsened.

In 1977 a new government sought to return the country to a market economy through investment incentives, land reform, and tourism promotion. By the early 1980s foreigners had invested in clothing manufacture and tourism had begun to thrive.

In 1983 ethnic rivalries turned violent, discouraging foreign investors and tourists; massacres and strikes paralyzed the economy. Insurgent Tamils took over large areas of the country, inhibiting domestic movement of goods and people. In 1987 Indian peacekeeping troops arrived to help pacify the Tamils. At first the Tamils welcomed them but later joined the Sinhalese in reviling them.

The civil war led to higher unemployment (20% unemployed in 1989, more underemployed), school and university closures, and reduced government expenditures. The drain of maintaining the army increased the national deficit. However, 1990 showed signs of economic improvement as the country brought in a record tea crop and increased its gem exports 33%.

Though Indian troops withdrew in 1990, relations between India and Sri Lanka were further complicated by the 1991 murder of Rajiv Gandhi, apparently by Sri Lankan Tamil terrorists.

HOW MUCH

	4-Year Growth	1986	1987	1988	1989	1990
Population (mil.)	*1.4%*	16.1	16.4	16.6	16.8	17.0
GDP ($ bil.)	*5.7%*	*6.4*	*6.7*	*7.0*	*7.0*	*8.0*
Real GDP growth rate	—	4.3%	1.5%	2.7%	2.3%	6.3%
Exports ($ mil.)	*13.0%*	1,216	1,397	1,475	1,558	1,984
Imports ($ mil.)	*8.4%*	1,947	2,055	2,238	2,226	2,689
Trade balance ($ mil.)	—	(731)	(658)	(763)	(668)	(705)
Current account ($ mil.)	—	(417)	(326)	(395)	(265)	(304)
Govt. budget bal. ($ mil.)	—	*(650)*	*(578)*	*(886)*	*(793)*	*(544)*
Consumer inflation	—	8.0%	7.7%	14.0%	11.5%	21.5%
Unemployment rate	—	—	—	—	20.0%	—
Exchange rate with US$	—	28.02	29.45	31.81	36.05	40.06

Source: Economist Intelligence Unit and *The Reference Press*

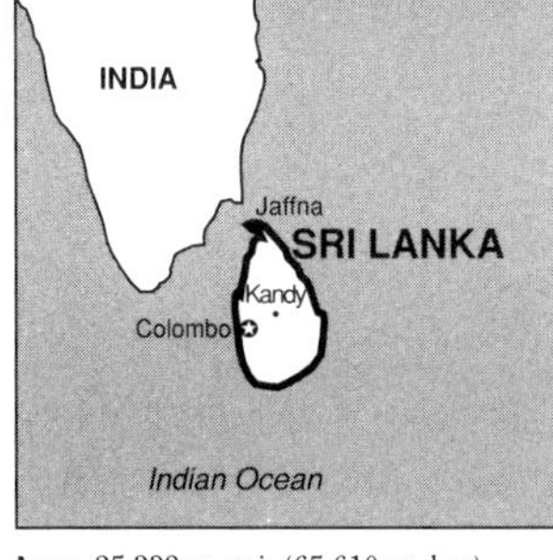

Area: 25,332 sq. mi. (65,610 sq. km)

Official name:
Democratic Socialist Republic of Sri Lanka
Ceylon
Official language: Sinhala
Currency: 1 rupee (SLRs) = 100 cents
Fiscal year ends: December 31

WHO

President: Ranasinghe Premadasa
Prime Minister and Minister of Finance: Dingri Banda Wijetunge
Minister of Foreign Affairs: Harold Herat
Ambassador to US: W. Susanta De Alwis
US Ambassador to Sri Lanka: Marion V. Creekmore, Jr.

WHERE

Executive HQ: Office of the President, Presidential Secretariate, Colombo 1, Sri Lanka
Embassy in US: 2148 Wyoming Ave. NW, Washington, DC 20008
Phone: 202-483-4025
Fax: 202-232-7181
US Embassy in Sri Lanka: PO Box 106, 210 Galle Rd., Colombo 3, Sri Lanka
Phone: 011-94-1-548007
Fax: 011-94-1-449070
Chamber of Commerce: National Chamber of Commerce, PO Box 1375, YMBA Bldg., 2nd Fl., Colombo 1, Sri Lanka
Phone: 011-94-1-25271
Fax: 011-94-1-448363

Sri Lanka has 24 districts and 8 provinces and has diplomatic representatives in 36 countries.

Capital city: Colombo
Time change from EST: +10.5 hours
Avg. high/low temp: Jan. 86°F (30°C)/72°F (22°C)
July 85°F (29°C)/77°F (25°C)

Urbanization: 21%
Population density: 671/sq. mi. (259/sq. km)

Exports as % of Total		Imports as % of Total	
US	26	Japan	12
Germany	6	US	6
Japan	6	UK	6
UK	6	Taiwan	5
Other countries	56	Other countries	71
Total	**100**	**Total**	**100**

WHAT

Origins of GDP	% of Total
Agriculture, forestry & fishing	26
Trade	20
Mining, quarrying & manufacturing	18
Banking & other services	17
Transport & utilities	11
Construction	8
Total	**100**

1990 GDP per capita: $470
1990 year-end external debt: $6 billion
Literacy rate: 87%
UN Human Development Index: 67%
Human Freedom Index (0-40 scale): 11
Purchasing power as % of US: 12%
Capital city cost of living as % of DC: —
Defense as % of GNP: 6%
Education as % of GNP: 2%
Principal airline: Air Lanka
Principal exchange: Colombo Stock Exchange

SWEDEN

OVERVIEW

Located at the northern edge of Europe, Sweden has the largest economy in Scandinavia.

Though rich in iron ore, timber, and water (with which it generates hydroelectric power) and also possessing copper, zinc, lead, and silver deposits, Sweden lacks fossil fuel sources. Its agricultural sector is small but efficient, and Sweden is almost agriculturally self-sufficient. Principal crops include dairy products, sugar beets, grains, and potatoes.

Sweden maintains a policy of armed neutrality, refusing to make political or defensive alliances. Most of its defense expenditures are at home, where 80% of its weapons and 100% of its aircraft are manufactured. It also sells arms in the global market, and such sales account for 2% of its exports.

Sweden is well known for its welfare programs. What is less well known is that these programs do nothing to redistribute wealth, which remains largely in the hands of a small percentage of the population.

Income tax rates have been as high as 72% (1989), and, during the 1980s global boom, as much as 91% of increases in business profits went to pay taxes. Tax reform has been introduced, but planned cuts are offset by the broadened application of the value-added tax and an increase in gasoline taxes.

After years of refusing to join the EC, Sweden, facing a recession at home and flight of capital to the EC, indicated its desire to become a member. In May 1991, in preparation for EC application, Sweden linked its currency to the ECU (European Currency Unit).

WHEN

Although there was trade in Baltic amber during the Roman era, the most impressive contact between Scandinavia and the rest of Europe came in the 9th century, when the Norsemen pillaged coasts from Ireland to Russia, seriously injuring European economic and social development. Bold, skilled seamen, the Norsemen had settled Greenland and explored North America by 1000. In subsequent centuries Sweden extended its reach into Russia, where it traded its furs for precious metals.

During the 17th century Sweden ruled Finland, Baltic coastal areas in Russia, Germany, Denmark, and much of Norway (dominating Baltic trade). It also established a colony in southeast Pennsylvania, which was seized by the Dutch in 1655.

In the 18th century Sweden's influence faded as constant warfare took its toll. It lost its Russian, German, and Baltic possessions. In the 19th century a modern free-market economy evolved as the countryside went from a village to private-farm economy, the cities industrialized (steel, metal, and wood products), and the strength of the still-influential trade guilds waned. Emigration, principally to North America, became a vital safety valve on population pressure. By 1900 over 20% of native Swedes had emigrated.

In WWI and WWII, Sweden remained neutral, continuing to sell high-grade steel and steel products, such as ball bearings. It began to develop its welfare structure following WWI. After WWII, Sweden declined to join NATO and the EC (citing its neutrality). It did, however, join with Finland, Denmark, Norway, and Iceland in the Nordic Council (1954) to form a single labor market.

Untouched by war and receiving Marshall Plan benefits, Sweden prospered as the rest of Europe struggled to rebuild. Auto, chemical, machinery, and metals production were especially important. As Sweden's wealth grew, so did its social programs, becoming ever more comprehensive and expensive. During the boom years of the 1950s and 1960s, an expanding economy supported the cost. In the 1970s the rising cost of oil stopped economic growth. Social welfare programs began to prove a disincentive to work, boosting absenteeism to nearly a month per year.

The general world prosperity and increased fiscal discipline of the 1980s revived the economy. The government removed subsidies to failing companies and focused aid on R&D (at 2.9%, the world's highest GDP share). Though Sweden's system has an enviable record, it has structural difficulties. The welfare programs cost 60% of GDP, and supporting them in a time of slowing growth is a severe burden; yet modifying them is politically risky, since actual disposable income of Swedish workers is currently lower than that of the poorest EC nations.

Fearing exclusion from the EC, Swedish companies began investing in it. This investment may cause a significant shift from domestic to foreign production. In 1991 economic woes brought disenchantment with the ruling Social Democratic Party.

HOW MUCH

	4-Year Growth	1986	1987	1988	1989	1990
Population (mil.)	*0.9%*	8.4	8.4	8.5	8.5	8.6
GDP ($ bil.)	*14.4%*	*133*	*161*	*182*	*189*	*228*
Real GDP growth rate	—	2.3%	2.9%	2.3%	2.1%	0.3%
Exports ($ mil.)	*11.4%*	37,230	44,390	49,760	51,550	57,400
Imports ($ mil.)	*13.7%*	32,670	40,670	45,780	49,020	54,600
Trade balance ($ mil.)	—	4,560	3,720	3,980	2,530	2,800
Current account ($ mil.)	—	100	(1,100)	(700)	(3,000)	(5,500)
Govt. budget bal. ($ mil.)	—	*(6,573)*	*(2,391)*	*(673)*	*2,807*	*578*
Consumer inflation	—	4.2%	4.2%	5.8%	6.5%	10.5%
Unemployment rate	—	2.2%	1.9%	1.6%	1.4%	1.5%
Exchange rate with US$	—	7.12	6.34	6.13	6.45	5.91

Source: Economist Intelligence Unit and *The Reference Press*

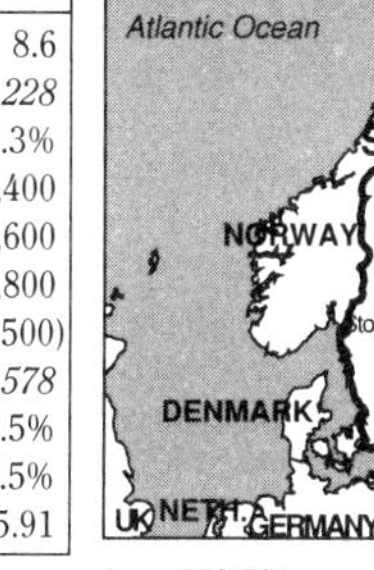

Area: 173,731 sq. mi. (449,964 sq. km)

Official name:
Kingdom of Sweden
Konungariket Sverige
Official language: Swedish
Currency: 1 krona (SEK) = 100 ore
Fiscal year ends: June 30

WHO

Monarch: King Carl XVI Gustaf, age 46
Heir Apparent: Crown Princess Victoria Ingrid Alice Désirée, Duchess of Västergötland, daughter of king, age 14
Head of Government and Prime Minister: Ingvar Carlsson, age 57
Minister of Finance: Allan Larson, age 53
Minister of Foreign Affairs: Sten Andersson
Ambassador to US: Anders Thunborg
US Ambassador to Sweden: Charles E. Redman

WHERE

Executive HQ: Prime Minister, Rosenbad 4, 10333 Stockholm, Sweden
Embassy in US: 600 New Hampshire Ave. NW, Suite 1200, Washington, DC 20037
Phone: 202-944-5600
Fax: 202-342-1319
US Embassy in Sweden: Strandvägen 101, S-11527 Stockholm, Sweden
Phone: 011-46-8-783-5300
Fax: 011-46-8-661-1964
Chamber of Commerce: Swedish Chamber of Commerce/Exportradet, PO Box 5513, S-11485 Stockholm, Sweden
Phone: 011-46-8-783-8500
Fax: 011-46-8-662-9093

Sweden has 24 counties and has diplomatic representatives in 85 countries.

Capital city: Stockholm
Time change from EST: +6 hours
Avg. high/low temp: Jan. 30°F (-1°C)/23°F (-5°C)
July 71°F (22°C)/57°F (14°C)

Urbanization: 84%
Population density: 50/sq. mi. (19/sq. km)

Exports as % of Total		Imports as % of Total	
Germany	13	Germany	20
UK	11	US	8
US	9	UK	8
Norway	8	Denmark	7
Other countries	59	Other countries	57
Total	**100**	**Total**	**100**

WHAT

Origins of GDP	% of Total
Manufacturing	32
Financial services	17
Retail & catering	16
Construction	10
Other	25
Total	**100**

1990 GDP per capita: $26,561
1990 year-end external debt: $14 billion
Literacy rate: 99%
UN Human Development Index: 98%
Human Freedom Index (0-40 scale): 38
Purchasing power as % of US: 77%
Capital city cost of living as % of DC: 163%
Defense as % of GNP: 3%
Education as % of GDP: 8%
Principal airlines: AB Aerotransport, Scandinavian Airlines System
Principal exchange: Stockholms Fondbörs

SWITZERLAND

OVERVIEW

Small, landlocked Switzerland, celebrating its 700th birthday in 1991, is one of the world's great economic powers. Despite lacking natural resources and arable land (70% of the country is covered by mountains), it has the world's highest GDP per capita. The Swiss economy is based on private enterprise and hard work (workers' average of 44.5 hours per week is the highest in the OECD). Wages have been steady and there have been few strikes.

Though bordered by frequently warring nations, Switzerland has maintained an armed neutrality since the early 19th century. Its various national groups coexist peacefully.

Because its small home market cannot absorb the business output of its companies (Swiss food giant Nestlé gets only 2% of sales domestically), Switzerland derives 1/2 of GNP from foreign trade in goods or services. Over 70% of Switzerland's foreign trade is with the EC (of which it is not a member), and Switzerland is positioning itself to compete in the post-1992 unified European market.

Though a high 50% of all workers work in industry, only 1/3 of GNP is generated by industry; the service sector (of which banking is the most prominent segment) generates 2/3. Nevertheless, Switzerland is a leading chemical and pharmaceuticals exporter and produces 15% of the world's textile machinery and 13% of all precision instruments. In recent years its traditional watchmaking and textile industries have been under pressure from low-price Asian competition, though Switzerland still has 85% of the world market for luxury watches.

Switzerland is beginning to experience social problems similar to those of other European nations; it now has the highest per capita rate of drug abuse in Europe.

Though not a UN member, Switzerland participates in many UN organizations and takes an active part in world diplomacy.

WHEN

Switzerland's role as a transit point through Europe began when the Romans opened mountain passes for supply operations in 47. The land became part of the Holy Roman Empire under Charlemagne. As more Alpine passes were opened, trade between Italy and northern Europe increased. Switzerland's original 3 cantons gained semi-autonomy from the Hapsburgs in 1291; more cantons were added and total independence came in 1648. Since Switzerland had few resources besides timber and water, its first great export was its people, disciplined mercenary soldiers.

During the Reformation Switzerland became a refuge for French Protestants, whose banking, trading, and manufacturing skills, including watchmaking, became Swiss specialties in the 17th century.

Switzerland's importance decreased as Europe's increasing Atlantic orientation and the turmoil of frequent wars cut trans-Alpine trade. Despite its reputation in banking and mechanics, Switzerland remained generally poor. In the 18th century Switzerland's scenic beauty began to bring tourists.

In the 19th century tourism (and traditional crafts such as woodcarving and weaving), watchmaking, and cheese production were important components of the economy. Banking brought capital, which led to industrialization and the development of precision tools and mechanical equipment production.

With industrialization Switzerland's central location again became important. The country was an early railroad center, and Basel became a prime port on the Rhine River.

Though neutral in WWI, Switzerland suffered from decreased trade. In 1923 it formed a customs union with Liechtenstein. Neutral again in WWII, it continued to trade, somewhat under duress, with Italy and Germany.

After WWII, with its industry untouched, Switzerland boomed. Tourism increased as skiing became popular. The tiny Swiss population was absorbed in its precision tool, machinery, chemical, and pharmaceutical industries, and foreign workers were imported. Government involvement in private business was minimal and supports rare except in protected industries such as watchmaking and textiles. Swiss banking is noted for stability and discretion (secret accounts were instituted in 1934 to help Jews hide money from the Nazis), though new rules have relaxed the secrecy.

Switzerland was relatively unscathed by the oil crises of the 1970s and the worldwide recession of the early 1980s. Though the Swiss franc has held its value, inflation grew to 5.4% in 1990. Unemployment is negligible, but growth will be restrained by limits on hiring new foreign workers. Swiss companies are entering joint ventures and buying companies in EC countries to assure access to those markets after 1992.

HOW MUCH

	4-Year Growth	1986	1987	1988	1989	1990
Population (mil.)	*0.4%*	6.57	6.60	6.62	6.64	6.67
GDP ($ bil.)	*13.9%*	*135*	*171*	*184*	*177*	*228*
Real GDP growth rate	—	2.8%	2.0%	3.0%	3.5%	2.6%
Exports ($ mil.)	*14.3%*	37,200	45,300	50,700	51,400	63,500
Imports ($ mil.)	*13.8%*	40,900	50,500	56,400	58,100	68,500
Trade balance ($ mil.)	—	(3,700)	(5,200)	(5,700)	(6,700)	(5,000)
Current account ($ mil.)	—	6,700	7,200	8,300	7,500	9,700
Govt. budget bal. ($ mil.)	—	*519*	*231*	*301*	*(257)*	—
Consumer inflation	—	0.8%	1.4%	1.9%	3.2%	5.4%
Unemployment rate	—	0.8%	0.8%	0.7%	0.6%	*0.6%*
Exchange rate with US$	—	1.80	1.49	1.46	1.64	1.39

Source: Economist Intelligence Unit and *The Reference Press*

Area: 15,941 sq. mi. (41,288 sq. km)

Official name:
Swiss Confederation
Suisse, Schweiz, Svizzea, Svizzera
Official languages: French, German, Italian, Romansch
Currency: 1 franc (SF) = 100 centimes or rappen
Fiscal year ends: December 31

WHO

President of the Confederation: Flavio Cotti, age 52, SF280,000 pay
Vice-President and Minister of Foreign Affairs: René Felber, age 58, SF280,000 pay
Finance Minister: Otto Stich, age 64, SF280,000 pay
Ambassador to US: Edouard Brunner, age 59
US Ambassador to Switzerland: Joseph B. Gildenhorn

WHERE

Executive HQ: President, 3003 Bern, Switzerland
Embassy in US: 2900 Cathedral Ave. NW, Washington, DC 20008
Phone: 202-745-7900
Fax: 202-387-2564
US Embassy in Switzerland: Jubilaeumstrasse 93, 3005 Bern, Switzerland
Phone: 011-41-31-437-011
Fax: 011-41-31-437-344
Chamber of Commerce: Swiss Federation of Commerce & Industry, Börsenstrasse 26, CH-8022 Zürich, Switzerland
Phone: 011-41-1-221-2707

Switzerland has 26 cantons and has diplomatic representatives in 160 countries.

Capital city: Bern
Time change from EST: +6 hours
Mean temperature: January 32°F (0°C)
July 65°F (19°C)

Urbanization: 61%
Population density: 418/sq. mi. (162/sq. km)

Exports as % of Total		Imports as % of Total	
Germany	22	Germany	34
France	10	France	11
Italy	9	Italy	11
US	8	US	6
Other countries	51	Other countries	38
Total	**100**	**Total**	**100**

WHAT

Origins of GDP	% of Total
Private consumption	61
Fixed investment	30
Government consumption	14
Stockbuilding	3
Adjustments	(8)
Total	**100**

1990 GDP per capita: $34,159
1990 year-end external debt: none
Literacy rate: 100%
UN Human Development Index: 98%
Human Freedom Index (0-40 scale): 34
Purchasing power as % of US: 87%
Zurich cost of living as % of DC: 158%
Defense as % of GNP: 2%
Education as % of GNP: 5%
Principal airline: Swissair
Principal exchange: Effektenbörsenverein Zürich

TAIWAN

OVERVIEW

Taiwan consists of Taiwan island, Quemoy, the Pescadores Islands, and several islets off the east coast of China. Its only natural resources are timber, a little petroleum, marble, and enough coal to last about 50 years. Only 25% of the land is cultivated; intensive farm methods have made Taiwan self-sufficient in rice.

The government promotes private ownership of business and an open market but invests in such strategic industries as petroleum refining, steel, shipbuilding, and banking.

Taiwan has the world's 2nd largest dollar reserves (after Japan) and a chronic trade surplus with the US. It is also a large manufacturer of textiles and electronics.

Prosperity has caused its own problems. Higher wages brought consumerism, creating demand for imports and fueling inflation.

Taiwan's unemployment rate (1.7%) limits business growth. Nevertheless, Taiwan is increasing public works spending (it has allocated $300 billion to upgrade infrastructure over the next 6 years), restructuring taxes, and changing regulations on banking and insurance to attract international investment.

Taiwan's relations with mainland China remain unresolved. Though trade (over 2,500 Taiwanese businesses operate in China, generating $4 billion in trade in 1990) and travel have increased, there are no formal relations between the nations. In 1991 President Lee Teng-hui decreed the end of the Communist rebellion on the mainland, in effect abandoning Taiwan's claim to government of both territories, though not recognizing the People's Republic of China.

WHEN

Chinese settlers came to Taiwan (Terraced Bay) in the 7th century; in 1206 Taiwan became a protectorate of China. In 1590 the Portuguese (the first Westerners to see Taiwan) called it *Ilha Formosa* (Beautiful Island). In 1624 the Dutch used it as a base for China trade but were driven out by the Chinese in the 1660s.

China ceded Taiwan to Japan in 1895, after the Sino-Japanese War. Japan built transportation routes, hydroelectric and thermal generators, irrigation projects, and research facilities and established schools.

In 1945 Taiwan was returned to China under Chiang Kai-shek's Nationalist Government. After the Chinese civil war, Taiwan, with US support, assumed China's places in international organizations. The US gave massive aid to Taiwan in the 1950s and 1960s.

The Nationalists redistributed large land holdings to tenant farmers, paying landlords with stock and commodities certificates, which many used as capital for new businesses. This brought jobs to an impoverished population swollen by refugees from China. Land reform led to better agricultural performance. Tenant farmers became owners and used new agricultural methods that yielded up to 3 crops per year.

At first, Taiwan fostered fledgling industries (chemicals and textiles) with protective taxes and duties. By 1954 protectionism and an import-substitution policy had hurt industry, as inventories rose and plants went idle.

In 1958 the government began encouraging businesses to pursue export markets.

By 1965 industry overtook agriculture as the largest contributor to income. From 1960 to 1973 GNP rose over 300%. By the mid-1960s domestic savings provided capital, reducing the need for foreign aid and investors.

High economic growth was accompanied by high population growth and low unemployment (less than 2% since 1964). In the 1970s the emphasis of new industrial development changed from light to heavy and to high-tech industries (steel, automotive, electronics).

In 1971 the UN recognized the People's Republic of China; in 1979 the US severed official (but not unofficial) diplomatic relations with Taiwan. Despite this, Taiwan's economy prospered on the strength of its low-cost, high-quality exports.

In the 1980s Taiwan became an international economic power, repealing protectionist laws, allowing Taiwanese to take money abroad for investment, and revaluing its currency. Banking regulations were modified so Taiwanese banks could open branches abroad. Unions were legalized. Because of Taiwan's chronic trade surplus and high rate of savings, Taiwanese investors turned to their stock market, making it more active than Hong Kong's and Singapore's combined. In addition, industry began to emphasize R&D to develop innovative new products, rather than simply using technologies developed by other nations.

In 1991 Taiwan for the first time permitted foreigners to invest in its stock market.

HOW MUCH

	4-Year Growth	1986	1987	1988	1989	1990
Population (mil.)	*0.9%*	19.5	19.7	19.9	20.1	20.2
GDP ($ bil.)	*19.7%*	*77*	*100*	*122*	*144*	*157*
Real GDP growth rate	—	11.6%	12.3%	7.3%	7.6%	5.2%
Exports ($ mil.)	*14.0%*	39,800	53,600	60,600	66,200	67,200
Imports ($ mil.)	*22.6%*	24,200	35,000	49,700	52,200	54,700
Trade balance ($ mil.)	—	15,600	18,600	10,900	14,000	12,500
Current account ($ mil.)	—	16,200	18,000	10,200	11,400	10,900
Govt. budget bal. ($ mil.)	—	*94*	*1,435*	*3,522*	*4,672*	—
Consumer inflation	—	0.7%	0.5%	1.3%	4.4%	4.1%
Unemployment rate	—	2.7%	2.0%	1.7%	1.6%	1.7%
Exchange rate with US$	—	37.84	31.85	28.59	27.15	26.67

Source: Economist Intelligence Unit and *The Reference Press*

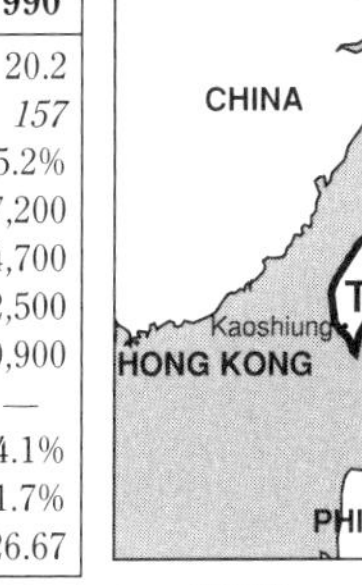

Area: 13,885 sq. mi. (35,981 sq. km)

Official name: Republic of China
Official language: Mandarin Chinese
Currency: 1 dollar (NT$) = 100 cents
Fiscal year ends: June 30

WHO

President: Lee Teng-hui, age 68
Prime Minister: Hau Pei-tsun, age 73
Vice-President: Li Yuan Zu
Vice–Prime Minister: Shih Chi-yang, age 56
Finance Minister: Wang Chien-shien
Minister of Foreign Affairs: Frederick Chien

WHERE

Executive HQ: President, Chiehshou Hall, Chungking Rd., Taipei 100, Taiwan
Diplomatic Relations with US: The US broke off diplomatic relations with Taiwan on January 1, 1979, after establishing diplomatic relations with the government of the People's Republic of China. US–Taiwan relations are maintained through the following organizations, which were established in 1979 and given diplomatic status in October of 1980.
Co-ordination Council for North American Affairs in the US: 5161 River Rd. NW, Washington, DC 20016
Phone: 202-895-1800
American Institute in Taiwan: 7 Ln. 134 Hsin Yi Rd., Section 3, Taipei, Taiwan
Phone: 011-886-2-709-2000
Fax: 011-886-2-702-7675
Chamber of Commerce: General Chamber of Commerce of R.O.C., 6/F, 390 Fu Hsing South Rd., Section 1, Taipei, Taiwan
Phone: 011-886-2-701-2671
Fax: 011-886-2-754-2107

Taiwan has one province, 2 special municipalities, and several offshore islands and has representation in 61 countries.

Capital city: Taipei
Time change from EST: +13 hours
Avg. high/low temp: Jan. 66°F (19°C)/54°F (12°C)
July 92°F (33°C)/76°F (24°C)

Urbanization: —
Population density: 1,455/sq. mi. (561/sq. km)

Exports as % of Total		Imports as % of Total	
US	32	Japan	29
Hong Kong	13	US	23
Japan	12	Germany	5
Germany	5	Australia	3
Other countries	38	Other countries	40
Total	**100**	**Total**	**100**

WHAT

Origins of GDP	% of Total
Manufacturing	35
Banking & insurance	19
Wholesale & retail trade	15
Other	31
Total	**100**

1990 GDP per capita: $7,796
1990 year-end external debt: $1 billion
Literacy rate: 92%
Capital city cost of living as % of DC: 129%
Defense as % of GNP: 7%
Education as % of GNP: —
Principal airline: China Airlines, Far Eastern Air Transport
Principal exchange: Taiwan Stock Exchange

THAILAND

OVERVIEW

Formerly known as Siam, Thailand lies in the central Indochina peninsula. The country has long been considered the "rice bowl" of Asia. Agriculture employs nearly 2/3 of the labor force and accounts for 17% of GDP. Rice, tapioca, and sugar cane are the principal crops. Thailand is one of the world's most important gem and jewelry exporters and is now the leading producer of sub-carat cut diamonds.

Thailand had one of the world's fastest growing economies (10%) in 1990, and the manufacturing sector has seen spectacular growth in the last 5 years. Of late the government has emphasized manufacturing diversification and the promotion of electronic exports. Support infrastructure has been unable to keep up with growth: water and electricity are in short supply, communications facilities are strained, and a shortage of skilled workers promotes corporate poaching. Political activists have begun to protest industrial waste dumping and the depletion of the forests.

The growing wealth of the cities does not flow to the countryside, where 75% of the population resides. Nearly 25% of the population lives below the poverty line. Unemployment is 6% and inflation has only moderately increased, from 3% in 1988 to 7% in 1990. Wage increases and higher interest rates may slow growth.

A bloodless military coup in early 1991 was prompted by concern over the government's abuse of power and its corruption in conjunction with the infrastructure programs. Political instability (17 coups or attempted coups since 1932) may adversely affect tourism and foreign investment in the near term.

WHEN

The Thais established their kingdom in the 13th century and began trading with the Portuguese, Chinese, and Indians in the 16th century. In the 17th century the Dutch and French attempted to control the kingdom but failed. European colonialism threatened in the late 19th century, as the country was bordered on the west by British Burma and on the east by French Laos, Cambodia, and Vietnam. But Siam became the only country in the area to avoid colonization, through its monarch's entry into strong commercial alliances with its trading partners, granting them extraterritorial rights. In the late 19th century, the Chakkri dynasty (1767 to present) abolished the feudal system and modernized the country, using American and European advisors.

By the early 20th century, Bangkok had become a major trading center, and the country's forests were already well known for their coveted teak wood. Both Britain and France gave up their extraterritorial rights during WWI (1917). The international rice market collapsed during the Great Depression; this collapse, coupled with an emerging pro-Western ideology, caused a revolution in 1932 that changed the absolute monarchy to a constitutional monarchy.

The name Thailand was formally adopted in 1939. Japan occupied Thailand during WWII. The emerging communist threat from mainland China in 1949 prompted Thailand to become a strong ally and major economic aid recipient of the US. Economic growth in the 1950s was high, largely because of US loans, grants, and direct investments.

GDP growth in the 1960s averaged nearly 7% annually but slowed in the 1970s because agricultural commodity prices fell. Seeking economic growth through industrial diversification, Thailand launched an aggressive program to lure foreign investment and joint ventures through a series of incentive programs.

GDP has grown about 11.5% annually the last 4 years, thanks to a strong increase in exports by the subsidiaries of foreign-owned electronics companies. Thailand also became less dependent on the US as a major trading partner, with Korea, Taiwan, and Japan absorbing a significant share of Thai exports by 1989. A balance-of-payment surplus of $1.6 billion existed in 1988 as a result of tourism and investment in the Thai Stock Exchange. The economic boom of the late 1980s came amidst warnings from advisors to spread investments throughout the region and to address the widening disparity of wealth in the country. Nearly 75% of all money in the Thai banks belongs to the residents of Bangkok.

In late 1990 and early 1991, the economy experienced a 34% drop in tourism, owing primarily to the Persian Gulf crisis. Contracts awarded to solve Thailand's pressing pollution problem in Bangkok, to expand the rail and road systems, and to construct a new container port are awaiting junta leader General Suchinda Krapayoon's review.

HOW MUCH

	4-Year Growth	1986	1987	1988	1989	1990
Population (mil.)	*1.7%*	53.0	54.0	55.0	55.9	56.8
GDP ($ bil.)	*18.2%*	*42*	*49*	*60*	*70*	*82*
Real GDP growth rate	—	4.9%	9.5%	13.2%	12.2%	10.0%
Exports ($ mil.)	*28.0%*	8,800	11,600	15,800	19,800	23,600
Imports ($ mil.)	*37.1%*	9,200	13,000	20,300	25,800	32,500
Trade balance ($ mil.)	—	(400)	(1,400)	(4,500)	(6,000)	(8,900)
Current account ($ mil.)	—	200	(400)	(1,700)	(2,500)	(6,200)
Govt. budget bal. ($ mil.)	—	*(1,298)*	*(345)*	*1,427*	*2,542*	—
Consumer inflation	—	1.8%	2.5%	3.8%	5.4%	6.0%
Unemployment rate	—	3.0%	2.8%	2.5%	2.4%	—
Exchange rate with US$	—	26.30	25.72	25.29	25.70	25.58

Source: Economist Intelligence Unit and *The Reference Press*

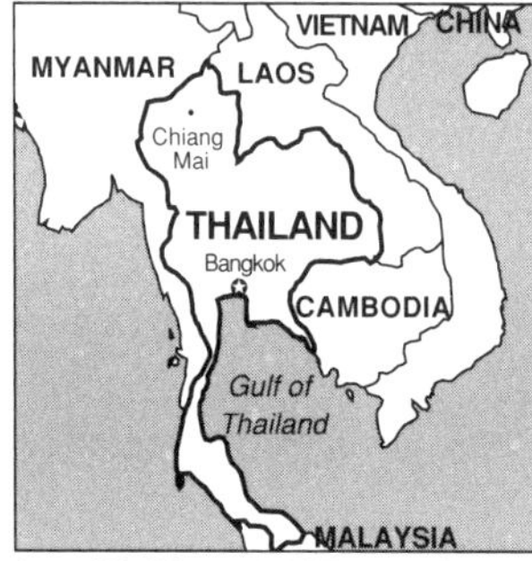

Area: 198,114 sq. mi. (513,115 sq. km)

Official name:
Kingdom of Thailand
Prathes Thai
Official language: Thai
Currency: 1 baht (Bt)= 100 satang
Fiscal year ends: September 30

WHO

Monarch: King Bhumibol Adulyadej, age 64
Caretaker Prime Minister, Commander of the Armed Forces: Gen. Sunthorn Kongsompong
Army Chief: Gen. Suchinda Krapayoon
Minister of Foreign Affairs: Arsa Sarasin, age 55
Minister of Finance: Suthee Singhasaneh, age 63
Ambassador to US: M.L. Birabhongse Kasemsri, age 56
US Ambassador to Thailand: Daniel A. O'Donohue

WHERE

Executive HQ: Office of the Prime Minister, Government House Thanon Nakhon Pathom, Bangkok 10300, Thailand
Embassy in US: 2300 Kalorama Rd. NW, Washington, DC 20008
Phone: 202-483-7200
Fax: 202-234-4498
US Embassy in Thailand: 95 Wireless Rd., Bangkok, Thailand
Phone: 011-66-2-252-5040
Fax: 011-66-2-254-2990
Chamber of Commerce: The Thai Chamber of Commerce, 150 Ratchabophit Rd., Bangkok 10200, Thailand
Phone: 011-66-2-225-0086
Fax: 011-66-2-225-3372

Thailand has 74 provinces and has diplomatic representatives in 52 countries.

Capital city: Bangkok
Time change from EST: +12 hours
Avg. high/low temp: Jan. 89°F (32°C)/68°F (20°C)
July 90°F (32°C)/76°F (24°C)

Urbanization: 22%
Population density: 287/sq. mi. (111/sq. km)

Exports as % of Total		Imports as % of Total	
US	22	Japan	30
Japan	17	US	11
Singapore	7	Singapore	8
Other countries	54	Other countries	51
Total	**100**	**Total**	**100**

WHAT

Origins of GDP	% of Total
Manufacturing	25
Agriculture, forestry, fishing & mining	19
Public administration	17
Wholesale & retail trade	15
Other	24
Total	**100**

1990 GDP per capita: $1,460
1989 year-end external debt: $17 billion
Literacy rate: 89%
UN Human Development Index: 71%
Human Freedom Index (0-40 scale): 14
Purchasing power as % of US: 17%
Capital city cost of living as % of DC: 78%
Defense as % of GNP: 4%
Education as % of GNP: 4%
Principal airline: Thai Airways International
Principal exchange: Securities Exchange of Thailand

TURKEY

OVERVIEW

Turkey is a study in contrasts. Straddling Asia and Europe, it is a secular country with a mostly Muslim population. A NATO member and an EC associate member, it has close political and economic ties with the West yet enjoys cordial relations with most Arab states and with Iran (a main trading partner), the USSR (with which trade is expanding), and Israel.

While the products of Turkey's rich agricultural land still account for 18% of GDP and 50% of employment, during the 1980s Turkey enjoyed unprecedented industrial and service-sector growth under the leadership of Turgut Özal (deputy prime minister 1980–82, prime minister 1983–89, president 1989–present). Rapid industrial growth resulted in high inflation (40% to 75% during the 1980s), inadequate housing, and strains on infrastructure.

Turkey encourages foreign investment, has many export incentive programs, continues to privatize its once heavily state-owned businesses by selling shares on Istanbul's nascent stock market, and has an excellent loan repayment history. With its low prices and 4,471 miles of coastline on the Black, Aegean, and Mediterranean Seas, Turkey has become a popular European tourist spot. Over 4 million tourists spend over $2 billion there annually.

Turkey has several large industrial groups (e.g., The Koç Group, Eczacibasi Holding, and Sabanci Holding), whose owners are in *Forbes*'s list of the world's billionaires.

The single most important economic issue for the Turks is gaining admission to the EC as a full member, a prospect made difficult by its continued occupation of Cyprus, complaints about its human-rights record, and the traditional enmity of EC member Greece. Turkey sided with the US in the Gulf War, cutting off Iraq's oil pipeline after the attack on Kuwait.

WHEN

Asia Minor (which comprises most of modern Turkey) has been home to 12 major civilizations, including the Hittites, Greeks, Romans, Byzantines, and Ottomans. Its position at the crossroad of Europe and Asia has made it an important trading center through the ages. Perhaps the single most important economic concept of all time — money — was invented there by the Lydians (of King Croesus fame) in the 7th century BC.

The Turks appeared in eastern Asia Minor in 1071, defeating the Byzantines at Manzikert. They eventually conquered Constantinople in 1453 and established an Ottoman reign that at its zenith reached from the Caspian Sea to the gates of Vienna.

After the defeat of the Ottomans (who sided with Germany) in WWI, the Allies began to dismantle the Ottoman Empire. Led by a young army officer, Mustafa Kemal (later known as Atatürk — Father of the Turks), the Turks repelled European occupation and negotiated a treaty with the Allies that created the borders of modern Turkey. The Republic of Turkey was created in 1923 with Atatürk as president.

Atatürk transformed Turkey from a backward remnant of an empire into a modern secular nation. From 1923 to 1926 agricultural output almost doubled. Though industrial activity grew almost 10% annually during the 1920s, the Great Depression devastated the still primarily agricultural economy by destroying export markets. In response, in 1935 Atatürk introduced *etatism* — state management and ownership of a large portion of the economy. Economic health improved, but WWII, in which Turkey remained neutral, brought another downturn.

During the post-WWII boom, the economy began to grow again. But state control of industry, a tangled bureaucracy, rapid expansion of the economy, heavy foreign debt, and a persistent trade deficit remained problems. These, along with violent political strife between the left and right, caused periodic economic and political crises. In 1960, 1971, and 1980, the Turkish military seized power to restore order, in each case voluntarily returning the government to civilian rule.

Under Turgut Özal, Turkey has enjoyed unparalleled economic growth as a result of his 1983 economic liberalization. However, not all his efforts (which have brought high inflation and unemployment) have been successful or popular. Turkey also faces problems caused by Islamic fundamentalism, migration of thousands of ethnic Turks from Bulgaria, and loss of a $7-billion-per-year trade relationship with Iraq. Though Turkey's stance in the Gulf War enhanced its prestige, the immigration of Iraqi Kurds drew attention to Turkey's own problems with the Kurds. In addition the war hit Turkey's tourist industry hard.

Foreign confidence in Turkey's future is shown by the plans of GM, Peugeot, and Toyota to build plants there.

HOW MUCH

	4-Year Growth	1986	1987	1988	1989	1990
Population (mil.)	*2.6%*	51.6	52.8	54.2	55.4	57.2
GNP ($ bil.)	*16.9%*	*58*	*68*	*71*	*80*	*109*
Real GNP growth rate	—	8.1%	7.5%	3.6%	1.6%	9.2%
Exports ($ mil.)	*14.8%*	7,460	10,190	11,660	11,630	12,940
Imports ($ mil.)	*18.8%*	11,200	14,280	14,340	15,760	22,300
Trade balance ($ mil.)	—	(3,740)	(4,090)	(2,680)	(4,130)	(9,360)
Current account ($ mil.)	—	(1,470)	(810)	1,600	970	(2,320)
Govt. budget bal. ($ mil.)	—	*(2,085)*	*(2,884)*	*(2,806)*	*(4,002)*	*(4,405)*
Consumer inflation	—	34.6%	38.9%	75.4%	63.3%	60.3%
Unemployment rate	—	10.5%	9.5%	9.8%	10.2%	10.4%
Exchange rate with US$	—	674.5	857.2	1,422	2,122	2,607

Source: Economist Intelligence Unit and *The Reference Press*

Area: 300,947 sq. mi. (779,452 sq. km)

Official name:
Republic of Turkey
Türkiye Cumhuriyeti
Official language: Turkish
Currency: 1 lira (TL) = 100 kurus
Fiscal year ends: December 31

WHO

President: Turgut Özal, age 64
Prime Minister: Mesut Yilmaz, age 44
Deputy Prime Minister and Minister of State: Ekrem Pakdemirli, age 52
Minister of Finance and Customs: Adnan Kahveci, age 42
Minister of Foreign Affairs: Safa Giray, age 60
Ambassador to US: Nüzhet Kandemir, age 57
US Ambassador to Turkey: Morton I. Abramowitz

WHERE

Executive HQ: Prime Minister, Basbakanlik, Bakanliklar, Ankara, Turkey
Embassy in US: 1714 Massachusetts Ave. NW, Washington, DC 20036
Phone: 202-659-8200
Fax: 202-659-0744
US Embassy in Turkey: Atatürk Bulvari 110, Ankara, Turkey
Phone: 011-90-4-126-5470
Fax: 011-90-4-167-0057
Chamber of Commerce: Association of Turkish Chambers of Commerce and Industry, Atatürk Bulvari 149/A, Kat:4, Bakanliklar, Ankara, Turkey
Phone: 011-90-41-117-7700

Turkey has 71 provinces and has diplomatic representatives in 145 countries.

Capital city: Ankara
Time change from EST: +7 hours
Avg. high/low temp: Jan. 39°F (4°C)/24°F (-4°C)
July 86°F (30°C)/59°F (15°C)

Urbanization: 48%
Population density: 190/sq. mi. (73/sq. km)

Exports as % of Total		Imports as % of Total	
Germany	24	Germany	16
Italy	9	US	10
US	8	Italy	8
UK	6	Japan	5
Other countries	53	Other countries	61
Total	**100**	**Total**	**100**

WHAT

Origins of GDP	% of Total
Services	49
Industry	29
Agriculture, forestry & fishing	18
Construction	4
Total	**100**

1990 GNP per capita: $1,906
1990 year-end external debt: $43 billion
Literacy rate: 89%
UN Human Development Index: 70%
Human Freedom Index (0-40 scale): 7
Purchasing power as % of US: 22%
Istanbul cost of living as % of DC: 95%
Defense as % of GDP: 3%
Education as % of GNP: 2%
Principal airline: Turk Hava Yollari (THY)
Principal exchange: Istanbul Menkul Klymeter Borsasi

UNITED KINGDOM

OVERVIEW

Great Britain consists of the kingdoms of England and Scotland and the principality of Wales. Together with Northern Ireland they constitute the United Kingdom (UK). Once controlling over 50 countries with 20% of the earth's land area and 25% of its population, the UK has given up what was the largest empire ever. Yet it is still the 6th largest capitalist economy in the world.

The UK has close trading ties with Europe, particularly Germany and France (its #1 and #3 trading partners), and with the US (its #2 trading partner), in which UK investors are the single largest group of foreign investors.

The UK's economic strength has traditionally lain in the industrial sector, particularly in machinery, steel, and automobiles. However, since WWII the UK has increasingly become a service economy, with approximately 60% of its GNP and work force in that sector. London is an important financial center, boasting the world's largest insurance market. The UK is one of the most efficient and mechanized agricultural producers in the world, providing approximately 60% of its food with less than 3% of its work force. It is also among the world's 10 largest petroleum producers.

A close military and economic ally of the US for over 100 years, the UK has been schizophrenic in its relationship with Europe. Twice rejected for EC membership (finally granted in 1973), the UK has, despite occasional lapses into nationalistic isolationism, moved into a closer economic relationship with Europe.

The UK experienced a moderate to severe economic recession in the early 1990s.

Official name: United Kingdom of Great Britain and Northern Ireland
Official languages: English, Welsh
Currency: 1 pound (£) = 100 pence (p)
Fiscal year ends: March 31

WHO

Monarch: Queen Elizabeth II Alexandra Mary, age 65, £5,090,000 pay
Prime Minister and First Lord of the Treasury and Minister for Civil Service: Rt. Hon. John Major MP, age 48, £66,851 pay
Lord Chancellor: Rt. Hon. The Lord Mackay of Clashfern, QC, age 64, £91,500 pay
Chancellor of the Exchequer: Rt. Hon. Norman Lamont, age 49, £55,221 pay
Secretary of State for Foreign and Commonwealth Affairs: Rt. Hon. Douglas Hurd, CBE, MP, age 61, £55,221 pay
Ambassador to US: Sir Robin Renwick KCMG
US Ambassador to UK: Raymond Seitz

WHEN

Britannia (as the Romans called it) became part of the Roman Empire in 43. After Roman withdrawal in 410, economic contact with Europe diminished. In 1066 William the Conqueror's successful invasion from France reinvolved England with Europe.

In the 14th century wool and cloth trade with Europe developed. In order to expand trade, England built a navy that defeated Spain's Armada in 1588 and became the world's dominant sea power. Naval power allowed England to establish its empire in the New World and to follow the spice trade to the Far East.

In the late 18th century, Great Britain (which had included Wales since 1536 and Scotland since 1707) began the Industrial Revolution, introducing mass production of goods to the world. Britain's lead in industrialization resulted from its bountiful natural resources, legislation that deprived the peasantry of their hereditary agricultural holdings (driving them into the cities in search of work), the free exchange of scientific and other ideas produced by emerging democratic institutions, and the application of this knowledge to improving production methods.

Despite the loss of its US colonies, by 1815 the United Kingdom (Ireland had been annexed in 1801) was the world's foremost economic power. Colonies provided raw materials for its industries and markets for its products.

WWI brought territorial gains, but aging industrial infrastructure and European advances diminished the UK's industrial lead. The newly industrialized US had also replaced Britain as the world's dominant economic force. Ireland gained its freedom in 1922 (except for Northern Ireland, which remained a part of the UK). Canada, Australia, and New Zealand became autonomous, forming the Commonwealth in 1926.

The Great Depression hurt the UK, which after WWII was unable to maintain its colonies. Deprived of its captive markets, devastated by the war, and beset by problems with organized labor, the UK suffered a more slow-growing economy than other European nations for the next 25 years. The creation of an expansive welfare state and the nationalization of industries by intermittent Labour governments led to government deficit spending and an inefficient economy. Between 1950 and 1970 the UK's per capita income dropped from the highest in Europe to one of the lowest. Inflation, unemployment, and labor unrest plagued the economy in the 1970s.

In 1979 Prime Minister Margaret Thatcher (1979–90) froze spending to cut inflation, privatized much of British industry, broke the back of the unions, and returned Britain to a prosperity it had not seen in years. During her tenure the UK experienced the highest economic growth of any major industrialized country. Inflation and unemployment were reduced. In 1990 the UK's economy slowed, and, in a dispute over economic integration with Europe, Thatcher resigned. She was succeeded by the less abrasive John Major.

WHERE

Executive HQ: Prime Minister, 10 Downing St., London SW1A 2AA, UK
Embassy in US: 3100 Massachusetts Ave. NW, Washington, DC 20008
Phone: 202-462-1340
Fax: 202-898-4255
US Embassy in the UK: 24-32 Grosvenor Sq., London W1A 1AE, UK
Phone: 011-44-71-499-9000
Fax: 011-44-71-409-1637
Chamber of Commerce: Association of British Chambers of Commerce, Sovereign House, 212 Shaftesbury Ave., London WC2H 8EW, UK
Phone: 011-44-71-240-5831
Fax: 011-44-71-379-6331

England and Wales have 53 counties. Scotland has 9 regions and Northern Ireland has 26 districts.

Capital city: London
Time change from EST: +5 hours
Avg. high/low temp: Jan. 43°F (6°C)/36°F (2°C)
July 71°F (22°C)/56°F (14°C)

Urbanization: 92%
Population density: 607/sq. mi. (234/sq. km)

Exports as % of Total		Imports as % of Total	
Germany	13	Germany	16
Benelux	13	US	11
US	13	France	9
Other countries	61	Other countries	64
Total	**100**	**Total**	**100**

WHAT

Origins of GDP	% of Total
Manufacturing	24
Services	34
Other	42
Total	**100**

1990 GDP per capita: $16,980
1988 year-end external debt: $50 billion
Literacy rate: 99%
UN Human Development Index: 97%
Human Freedom Index (0-40 scale): 32
Purchasing power as % of US: 66%
Capital city cost of living as % of DC: 145%
Defense as % of GNP: 5%
Education as % of GNP: 5%
Principal airline: British Airways
Principal exchange: International Stock Exchange

HOW MUCH

	4-Year Growth	1986	1987	1988	1989	1990
Population (mil.)	*0.2%*	56.8	56.9	57.1	57.1	57.2
GDP ($ bil.)	*5.1%*	*564*	*691*	*834*	*834*	*971*
Real GDP growth rate	—	3.6%	4.4%	4.2%	1.7%	0.5%
Exports ($ mil.)	*14.7%*	106,800	130,900	145,000	153,400	184,900
Imports ($ mil.)	*15.6%*	125,700	154,100	189,400	197,900	224,500
Trade balance ($ mil.)	—	(18,900)	(23,200)	(44,400)	(44,500)	(39,600)
Current account ($ mil.)	—	(100)	(7,200)	(26,900)	(31,300)	(22,800)
Govt. budget bal. ($ mil.)	—	*(3,256)*	*(8,034)*	*2,221*	*14,707*	—
Consumer inflation	—	3.4%	4.2%	4.9%	7.8%	9.5%
Unemployment rate	—	11.8%	10.6%	8.4%	6.3%	5.9%
Exchange rate with US$	—	0.68	0.61	0.56	0.61	0.56

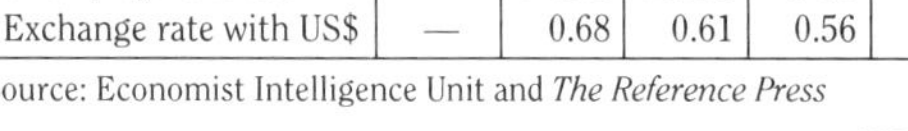
Source: Economist Intelligence Unit and *The Reference Press*

Area: 94,251 sq. mi. (244,111 sq. km)

UNITED STATES

OVERVIEW

The US is the most economically and militarily powerful nation on earth. Its role as a leader in ensuring world peace and economic prosperity has led commentators to call the current era a "Pax Americana."

Endowed with rich farmland capable of feeding the nation several times over, minerals of almost every kind in abundance, vast forests and fisheries, and a commercial infrastructure unrivaled in the world, the US dominates the world economy. Most currencies are measured by their exchange rate with the US dollar, many international commodities (e.g., oil) are priced only in US dollars, and the US remains the world's single largest truly unified market.

Its adherence to principles of free trade, its democratic political institutions, and its minimal regulation of industry make the US an archetypal capitalist nation. While the US has fallen behind Japan and Europe in some industries (notably steel and consumer electronics), its knowledge-based economy makes it a leader in computers, software design, financial services, medicine/biotechnology, and innovations in retailing. Its higher education system is the envy of the world.

Despite its prosperity, it faces numerous challenges, including dependence on foreign oil (45% imported), government overspending, a faltering primary and secondary education system, a large underclass in danger of permanent exclusion from the country's affluence, and a health care system with costs that are spiraling out of control.

The US is a nation of immigrants, and ongoing immigration (particularly from Latin America and Asia) is continually renewing the nation's economic and cultural vigor.

WHEN

In 1617 Jamestown (founded 1607) began shipping tobacco to England. Tobacco required intensive cultivation, so African slaves were imported starting in 1620. In 1621 religious dissidents landed at Cape Cod and established a society of farmers, merchants, and small manufacturers. In the 17th and 18th centuries, the colonies exported raw materials and developed manufacturing and trade. After the American Revolution (1775–81), in which the US won independence from Britain, settlement expanded westward. This coincided with the development of new technologies (canal excavation and steam power) that facilitated agricultural and mining products transport.

Disagreement over slavery led to the Civil War (1861–65), which cost 620,000 lives and over $25 billion; war ruined the South's economy and strengthened the North's.

Western settlement was aided by railroads, which received grants of land that they gave or sold to settlers. Immigration exploded. Besides farmers, new immigrants included urbanites seeking industrial work.

By 1880 the US led the world in food exports (thanks to innovations in farm machinery) and in railroad and telegraph mileage. More people worked in industry than in farming. Over 10% of the population was foreign born. In the 1890s the US expanded, annexing Hawaii and taking the Philippines, Cuba, and Puerto Rico from Spain.

After WWI the US became the world's greatest industrial power because of the modernity of its industrial plant and its lack of war damage. In the 1920s US prosperity seemed unbounded. However, the 1929 stock market crash, caused by inflated stock values and unrestrained margin trading, tripped the US into depression and brought protectionist legislation. Bank failures, industrial contraction, and bankrupt farms threw 16 million out of work. Despite public works and welfare projects, the US did not recover until WWII.

After WWII the US became the major economic force in the world. In the late 1960s attempts to fund the Vietnam War without new taxes brought inflation. In the 1970s Europe and Japan boasted newer industrial plants than the US and proved very competitive. The oil shocks of the 1970s upset the oil, auto, and housing industries. Stagflation set in. Unemployment reached 11% in 1982.

In the 1980s conservation and more efficient energy use slowed the growth of the demand for oil. Starting in 1983, the US enjoyed its longest postwar economic boom. However, the number of poor increased, and S&L degregulation brought abuses.

In 1990, as the US faced staggering costs for resolution of the S&L crisis, recession slowed the economy. By 1991 some banks and insurance companies seemed likely to follow S&Ls into failure, but the economy appeared to recover as consumer confidence rose and the housing market improved, and the US enjoyed renewed world prestige following its military success in the Gulf War.

HOW MUCH

	4-Year Growth	1986	1987	1988	1989	1990
Population (mil.)	*1.0%*	241.6	243.9	246.3	248.8	251.0
GNP ($ bil.)	*6.6%*	*4,238*	*4,516*	*4,881*	*5,201*	*5,465*
Real GNP growth rate	—	2.7%	3.5%	4.5%	2.5%	1.0%
Exports ($ mil.)	*14.8%*	227,200	254,100	322,400	363,900	394,100
Imports ($ mil.)	*7.8%*	382,300	424,400	459,500	492,900	516,700
Trade balance ($ mil.)	—	(155,100)	(170,300)	(137,100)	(129,000)	(122,600)
Current account ($ mil.)	—	(145,400)	(162,200)	(128,900)	(110,000)	(99,300)
Govt. budget bal. ($ mil.)	—	*(221,200)*	*(149,700)*	*(155,200)*	*(152,000)*	*(123,800)*
Consumer inflation	—	1.9%	3.7%	4.1%	4.9%	5.4%
Unemployment rate	—	6.9%	6.1%	5.4%	5.2%	5.5%

Source: Economist Intelligence Unit and *The Reference Press*

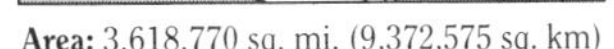

Area: 3,618,770 sq. mi. (9,372,575 sq. km)

Official name: United States of America
Official language: English
Currency: 1 dollar ($) = 100 cents
Fiscal year ends: September 30

WHO

President: George Herbert Walker Bush, age 67, $200,000 pay
Vice President: J. Danforth Quayle, age 44, $115,000 pay
Secretary of State: James Addison Baker III, age 61, $99,500 pay
Secretary of the Treasury: Nicholas F. Brady, age 61, $99,500 pay

WHERE

Executive HQ: President, 1600 Pennsylvania Ave. NW, Washington, DC 20510
Phone: 202-456-1414
Fax: 202-456-2883
Chamber of Commerce: Chamber of Commerce of the United States, 1615 H St. NW, Washington, DC 20062-4902
Phone: 202-659-6000
Fax: 202-463-5836

The US has 50 states, one federal district, 2 commonwealths, and 15 other dependent areas and has diplomatic representatives in 157 countries.

Capital city: Washington, DC
Time change from EST: 0 hours
Avg. high/low temp: Jan. 42°F (6°C)/27°F (-3°C)
July 87°F (31°C)/68°F (20°C)

Urbanization: 74%
Population density: 69/sq. mi. (27/sq. km)

Exports as % of Total		Imports as % of Total	
Canada	22	Japan	20
Japan	12	Canada	19
Mexico	7	Mexico	6
UK	6	Germany	5
Germany	5	Taiwan	5
South Korea	4	South Korea	4
Other countries	44	Other countries	41
Total	**100**	**Total**	**100**

WHAT

Origins of GNP	% of Total
Manufacturing	22
Services	16
Finance, insurance & real estate	14
Government & its enterprises	11
Retail trade	9
Transport & utilities	9
Wholesale trade	7
Construction	4
Mining	3
Communications	3
Agriculture, forestry & fishing	2
Total	**100**

1990 GNP per capita: $21,773
1990 year-end external debt: $393 billion
Literacy rate: 99%
UN Human Development Index: 98%
Human Freedom Index (0-40 scale): 33
Purchasing power as % of US: 100%
Capital city cost of living as % of DC: 100%
Defense as % of GNP: 6%
Education as % of GNP: 7%
Principal exchange: New York Stock Exchange

USSR

OVERVIEW

Although the USSR is the world's largest nation in area, with vast resources in minerals, precious metals and stones, and carbon fuels, its Communist system prevented the country from achieving its economic potential.

After becoming general secretary in 1985, Mikhail Gorbachev instituted the policies of *glasnost* (openness) and *perestroika* (restructuring). He relaxed control of the press, allowed elections, and started economic reform.

Economic reform meant giving up central control, creating profit-driven management, increasing production of consumer goods, instituting a market economy, and making the ruble convertible. Managements, bureaucracies, and the workers themselves often opposed these measures.

Independence movements and ethnic strife arose in the republics. There were food shortages, and strikes, formerly banned, broke out.

In 1990 national income declined 3% and inflation increased fivefold to 35%. In August 1991, on the eve of the signing of a new Union Treaty granting the republics more autonomy, Communist and military hardliners tried to overthrow Gorbachev but were foiled by popular opposition led by Boris Yeltsin. The coup attempt accelerated the changes it was meant to stop: the move to a market economy, disenfranchisement of the Communist Party, and the disintegration of the USSR, as the republics, led by the Baltics and the Ukraine, began declaring independence.

Official name:
Union of Soviet Socialist Republics
Soyuz Sovyetskikh Sotsialisticheskikh Respublik
Official language: Russian
Currency: 1 ruble (Rb) = 100 kopecks
Fiscal year ends: December 31

WHO

President: Mikhail Sergeyevich Gorbachev, age 60, 48,000 rubles pay (1989)
Executive President of the Russian Federation: Boris Nikolayevich Yeltsin, age 60
Chairman of the Committee on the National Economy: Ivan Silayev
Foreign Minister: Boris Pankin
Chargé d'Affaires to US: Sergey B. Chetverikov
US Ambassador to USSR: Robert Strauss

WHEN

Russia arose in the 9th century under the Viking king Rurik. In 1472 Ivan the Great married a niece of the last Byzantine emperor and took the title Tsar (Caesar). As Russia expanded, the tsars rewarded their followers with gifts of land and peasants, expanding serfdom, Russia's economic basis.

Peter Romanov (The Great) became tsar in 1682. He westernized Russia through sponsorship of trade and of metal, arms, and textile manufacturing. In 1762 Catherine the Great, a German princess, ascended the throne. She oversaw the absorption of part of Poland and the advances toward the Black Sea. In 1812 Napoleon invaded Russia but weather and hunger forced him to retreat, which decimated his army and led to his downfall. The serfs were freed in 1861 by an act in which the state paid the landowners for land and serfs, and the peasants, through a "commune," repaid the state. Many communes blocked peasants from moving, causing overpopulation, poverty, and hunger. In the 1870s Alexander II began a policy of political liberalization and industrialization, particularly railroad building. His son Alexander III continued the program through tariffs and foreign investment incentives.

In 1894, when Nicholas II became tsar, the economy was booming. But a global recession in 1899 and a 1904 war with Japan disrupted the economy. Revolt in 1905 forced Nicholas to make peace with Japan and cede some of his power to a representative body, the *Duma*.

In March 1917 a revolt by moderates forced Nicholas to abdicate. In November the Communists under V. I. Lenin seized power. Civil war followed; the victors collectivized large land holdings and started massive industrial development. Lenin died in 1924, and Joseph Stalin continued these policies, forcibly collectivizing peasant holdings and launching bloody political and social purges. Millions of people died or were imprisoned.

In 1941 Germany invaded the USSR. Over 20 million died. When the Germans withdrew, the Red Army pursued them to Berlin, forcibly communizing the "liberated nations." Stalin's purges continued until his death in 1953.

After WWII, crash industrialization continued, and the USSR experienced unprecedented prosperity. But consumer goods remained expensive and in short supply. By the late 1970s the state could no longer shield the people from their relative poverty, nor tell them when it would end. Dissent increased.

Since Gorbachev took office in 1985, promising economic and political reforms, the economy has decayed, and the nation has been increasingly threatened by disintegration as the individual republics seek independence or autonomy and control of their own economic resources. In 1991 in the first free election in Russian history, Boris Yeltsin was elected president of the Russian republic (the largest and richest). Gorbachev sought aid from the US and European nations. The nation was offered an associate membership in the IMF.

The August coup, led by Gorbachev's own cabinet, compromised Gorbachev's ability to govern, and Yeltsin's influence grew.

WHERE

Executive HQ: President of the USSR, Office of the Chairman, The Kremlin, Moscow, USSR
Embassy in US: 1125 16th St. NW, Washington, DC 20036
Phone: 202-628-7551
US Embassy in the USSR: Ulitsa Chaykovskogo 19/21/23, Moscow, USSR
Phone: 011-7-096-252-2451
Chamber of Commerce: USSR Chamber of Commerce & Industry, Ulitsa Kuibysheva 6, 101000 Moscow, USSR
Phone: 011-7-095-221-0811
Fax: 011-7-095-411-126

The USSR has 15 union republics, 20 autonomous republics, 6 krays, 123 oblasts, 8 autonomous oblasts, and 10 autonomous okrugs.

Capital city: Moscow
Time change from EST: +8 hours
Avg. high/low temp: Jan. 15°F (-9°C)/3°F (-16°C)
July 73°F (23°C)/55°F (13°C)
Urbanization: 66%
Population density: 34/sq. mi. (13/sq. km)

Exports as % of Total		Imports as % of Total	
Germany	14	Germany	16
Czechoslovakia	10	Poland	11
Poland	9	Bulgaria	11
Bulgaria	9	Czechoslovakia	11
Other countries	58	Other countries	51
Total	**100**	**Total**	**100**

WHAT

Origins of NMP	% of Total
Mining & manufacturing	43
Agriculture, forestry & fishing	23
Wholesale & retail trade	15
Construction	13
Transport, storage & communications	6
Total	**100**

1990 NMP per capita: $3,851
1990 year-end external debt: $60 billion
Literacy rate: 99%
UN Human Development Index: 91%
Human Freedom Index (0-40 scale): 3
Purchasing power as % of US: —
Capital city cost of living as % of DC: 88%
Defense as % of GNP: 16%
Education as % of GNP: 7%
Principal airline: Aeroflot
Principal exchange: Moscow Commodities Exchange

HOW MUCH

	4-Year Growth	1986	1987	1988	1989	1990
Population (mil.)	*0.7%*	281.7	284.5	286.7	288.8	290.1
NMP ($ bil.)	*8.1%*	*819*	*934*	*1,013*	*1,020*	*1,117*
Real NMP growth rate	—	1.6%	2.1%	4.3%	5.2%	(0.6%)
Exports ($ mil.)	*12.5%*	18,700	22,600	24,000	25,700	30,000
Imports ($ mil.)	*11.4%*	22,600	22,200	26,700	32,200	34,800
Trade balance ($ mil.)	—	(3,900)	400	(2,700)	(6,500)	(4,800)
Current account ($ mil.)	—	(1,000)	1,500	(1,500)	(4,500)	(5,000)
Govt. budget bal. ($ mil.)	—	*(64,723)*	*(83,732)*	*(131,915)*	—	—
Consumer inflation	—	—	—	—	—	—
Unemployment rate	—	—	—	—	3.0%	—
Exchange rate with US$	—	0.70	0.63	0.61	0.64	0.58

Source: Economist Intelligence Unit and *The Reference Press*

Area: 8,599,228 sq. mi. (22,402,200 sq. km)

VENEZUELA

OVERVIEW

Venezuela is among the world's 5 largest oil producers. A founding member of OPEC, Venezuela derives nearly 80% of its export revenue from oil. It is the only OPEC member to export much of its oil as refined products. Despite the oil industry's importance, PDVSA, the state-owned oil company, provides fewer than 50,000 jobs — representing less than 1% of the work force (compared to almost 170,000 provided by Mexico's Pemex). Aluminum, gold, nickel, and iron are also exported.

Venezuela has the highest GDP per capita in South America. However, wealth is distributed unevenly, with nearly 1/3 of the people living in poverty. Job seekers have migrated to the cities, straining urban resources.

Venezuela must import nearly 1/2 its food, though great strides were made in the 1980s in placing more land into production. The chief crops are cereals (in production of which it is self sufficient), fruits, sugar, and coffee.

A $1-per-barrel change in oil prices means a $600 million variation in annual export revenues. The oil gluts of the early 1980s and the unknown long-term effects of the Gulf War on oil prices have hobbled long-range planning. External uncertainties have been amplified by government mismanagement, long-standing traditions of corruption, and the failure to properly invest oil revenue.

Shortly after taking office in early 1989, President Carlos Pérez introduced an economic reform package designed to curb the country's 84.5% annual inflation and to encourage direct foreign investment. The government is privatizing its businesses and reducing or removing subsidies from state-owned enterprises; inflation was halved in 1990. However, Venezuela must still meet the challenges posed by high long-term debt, static economic growth, and high population growth.

WHEN

Spanish conquistador Alonso de Ojeda named Venezuela in 1499 after observing native villages built on poles over Lake Maricaibo. The villages reminded him of Venice, so he called the country Venezuela (Little Venice).

The Spaniards used natives and imported Africans as serfs and slaves to grow sugar cane and indigo. Venezuela became a Caribbean commercial center and a hub for the export of coffee and cocoa to Europe. Its thriving agricultural economy was a rarity in a Spanish empire more interested in mineral wealth.

In 1819 Simón Bolívar led the fight for the independence of Gran Colombia (Colombia, Venezuela, Ecuador, and Panama) from Spain. In 1830 Venezuela became a separate republic. Constant civil unrest and little economic development during the next 80 years kept the country overwhelmingly agrarian.

During the regime of dictator Juan Vincente Gómez (1908–35), the discovery of oil brought new wealth from contracts with Dutch, British, and American companies. Gómez established sound fiscal programs, and the national debt was paid off. Oil wealth led the government to neglect development of other economic sectors and to bloat its payroll with patronage jobs. President Rómulo Betancourt (1959–65) introduced social reforms and modernized the government. President Carlos Pérez (first term, 1974–79) nationalized the iron mines (1975) and oil companies (1976). Venezuela compensated all parties involved, though not to everyone's satisfaction.

With the OPEC oil price increase in 1973, Venezuela was awash in money, expanding industry and loaning funds to developing nations. This glut of money brought its own problems as imports rose 200% from 1974 to 1979, and luxuries abounded among the upper class. Inflation rose to nearly 20% and the standard of living of the poor actually declined. Administrative excesses, mismanagement, and inefficiencies were widespread.

With the fall of world oil prices in 1980, Venezuela's fortunes declined. This, coupled with the world recession, prompted then-president Luis Herrera Campíns (1979–84) to institute strict currency control that effectively devalued the currency. GDP fell by 4% in 1980 and continued to slide until 1985, when the government started easing controls on credit and foreign exchange.

Reelected in 1988, President Pérez commenced a series of reforms partially dictated by the IMF (which included raising the pump price of gasoline to $.25 per gallon). Real GDP fell by 8.3% in 1989 but turned positive again in 1990.

Increased oil revenues resulting from the Gulf War stimulated the economy in late 1990 and early 1991. The government intends to raise more money by privatizing several holdings, particularly in telecommunications.

HOW MUCH

	4-Year Growth	1986	1987	1988	1989	1990
Population (mil.)	*2.7%*	17.8	18.3	18.8	19.3	19.8
GDP ($ bil.)	*(5.5%)*	*60*	*48*	*60*	*44*	*48*
Real GDP growth rate	—	6.5%	3.6%	5.8%	(8.3%)	4.4%
Exports ($ mil.)	*19.8%*	8,540	10,440	10,080	12,990	17,590
Imports ($ mil.)	*(3.7%)*	7,870	8,870	12,080	7,130	6,770
Trade balance ($ mil.)	—	670	1,570	(2,000)	5,860	10,820
Current account ($ mil.)	—	(2,250)	(1,390)	(5,810)	2,500	7,390
Govt. budget bal. ($ mil.)	—	—	*(2,161)*	*(5,180)*	*(482)*	*(1,825)*
Consumer inflation	—	11.6%	28.1%	29.5%	84.5%	40.7%
Unemployment rate	—	10.3%	8.5%	6.9%	9.6%	14.0%
Exchange rate with US$	—	8.1	14.5	14.5	34.7	46.9

Source: Economist Intelligence Unit and *The Reference Press*

Area: 352,143 sq. mi. (912,050 sq. km)

Official name:
Republic of Venezuela
República de Venezuela
Official language: Spanish
Currency: 1 bolívar (B) = 100 centimos
Fiscal year ends: December 31

WHO

President: Carlos Andrés Perez, age 69
Finance Minister: Roberto Pocaterra
Foreign Minister: Armando Duran
Ambassador to US: Simon Alberto Consalvi
US Ambassador to Venezuela: Michael M. Skol

WHERE

Executive HQ: President, Office of the President, Caracas, Venezuela
Embassy in US: 1099 30th St. NW, Washington, DC 20007
Phone: 202-342-2214
Fax: 202-342-6820
US Embassy in Venezuela: PO Box 62291, Avenida Francisco de Miranda and Avenida Principal de la Floresta, Caracas 1060-A, Venezuela
Phone: 011-58-2-285-3111
Fax: 011-58-2-285-0336
Chamber of Commerce: Fedecámaras, Apartado 2568, Avenida El Empalme, Edificio Fedecámaras, Piso 5, Caracas 1010, Venezuela
Fax: 011-58-2-721-494

Venezuela has 20 states, and 4 federally controlled areas and has diplomatic representatives in 69 countries.

Capital city: Caracas
Time change from EST: +1 hour
Avg. high/low temp: Jan 75°F (24°C)/56°F (13°C)
July 78°F (26°C)/61°F (16°C)

Urbanization: 84%
Population density: 56/sq. mi. (22/sq. km)

Exports as % of Total		Imports as % of Total	
US	51	US	44
Germany	4	Germany	8
Japan	4	Italy	7
Cuba	4	Japan	4
Other countries	37	Other countries	37
Total	**100**	**Total**	**100**

WHAT

Origins of GDP	% of Total
Government & other services	27
Oil (crude, gas & refining)	23
Commerce	18
Manufacturing	16
Agriculture	6
Other	10
Total	**100**

1990 GDP per capita: $2,434
1990 year-end external debt: $33 billion
Literacy rate: 88%
UN Human Development Index: 85%
Human Freedom Index (0-40 scale): 29
Purchasing power as % of US: 24%
Capital city cost of living as % of DC: 56%
Defense as % of GDP: 1%
Education as % of GNP: 5%
Principal airline: Viasa (Venezolana Internacional de Aviación)
Principal exchange: Bolsa de Valores de Caracas

YUGOSLAVIA

OVERVIEW

Six republics and 2 autonomous provinces make up Yugoslavia. Natural resources include coal, copper, bauxite, iron ore, petroleum, and natural gas. Yugoslavia is agriculturally self-sufficient, exporting corn in bountiful years.

Yugoslavia never developed a centrally planned economy but practiced a gentle brand of decentralized communism that permitted small, worker-owned enterprises. Despite its capitalistic orientation, Yugoslavia's economy is in a shambles. Reckless borrowing for ill-considered capital projects raised foreign debt to unmanageable proportions and made austerity measures necessary.

Yugoslavia has been trying to participate in the democratization that swept Eastern Europe in 1989 but is hampered by its federal system. Slovenia and Croatia elected non-Communist governments and sought a loose free-market confederation, while the poorer republics remained Communist and wanted more central control. The poorer areas opposed discontinuation of price subsidies, and the richer areas felt they were not getting their fair share of government largesse.

In 1991 Slovenia and Croatia declared independence; Slovenia claims the right to control its external borders, while Serbia is attempting to impose a strong central government. Violence in Croatia is increasing. Civil unrest and ethnic divisiveness in Yugoslavia may turn into full-fledged civil war.

The economy has shrunk over 40% in the last 1 1/2 years. Tourism has declined because of the violence, and Hungary and Albania are protesting the treatment of ethnic minorities.

WHEN

The areas that are now Yugoslavia have spent most of recorded history ruled by Romans, Byzantines, Ottomans, and Austrians. In 1878, as the Turks receded from Europe, the Croats, Slovenians, and Bosnia-Herzegovinians were placed under Austrian control by European powers. Serbia and Montenegro were recognized as independent kingdoms.

The boundaries fixed did not correspond to ethnic distributions, nor were the groups happy with Austrian rule. In 1914 a Serbian nationalist assassinated the heir to the throne of Austria-Hungary, triggering WWI.

In 1918 these groups united as the Kingdom of the Serbs, Croats, and Slovenes (renamed Yugoslavia in 1929 in an effort to foster unity). Beyond some textile manufacture, modest coal, iron, and copper mining, and agricultural produce processing, no significant industry existed as of the 1920s, and the economy remained largely agricultural.

Yugoslavia sided with the Axis in WWII but, after a coup, was invaded. Following the war Nazi-resistance leader and Communist Marshal Josip Broz Tito began to collectivize farms and issued the first 5-year plan for rapid industrialization and electrification.

Relations with the USSR soured over terms for Yugoslavian–Soviet joint ventures. In 1948 Stalin declared Yugoslavia an Eastern bloc pariah, forcing it to turn to the West for aid and trading relations.

Under Yugoslavian communism, enterprises were owned by society as a whole rather than by the state, and workers had a high degree of control over production. Collectivization of agriculture was halted, leaving 85% of farms in private hands. Economic power was decentralized among the republics.

Postwar industrialization was centered in the north, near transit points into Europe, while the south remained largely agricultural. Economic disparities grew between the regions, inflaming ethnic rivalries.

In the 1970s Yugoslavia prospered relative to the Eastern bloc, receiving hard currency not only from foreign trade but also from tourism. Because of its Western orientation, Yugoslavia suffered from the West's boom–bust business cycles and was especially hard hit by oil price fluctuations. It borrowed heavily, owing nearly $20 billion by 1979.

Tito died in 1980, reopening the door to ethnic bickering. In 1982 Yugoslavia sought relief from debts it owed 600 banks in 16 countries and from IMF and World Bank obligations. In 1983 it instituted an economic stabilization program, seeking to reduce its debt-service ratio and increase trade, but it was again forced to reschedule its debts in 1988. Inflation reached 2,500% in 1989 but was reduced to less than 10% the following year, largely as the result of the decision to make the currency freely convertible.

The 1990s began with foreign investment declining and unemployment rising. Violence broke out as the Serbian-controlled national army clashed with local militias. A July 1991 agreement provided for a 3-month delay in secessionist actions.

HOW MUCH

	4-Year Growth	1986	1987	1988	1989	1990
Population (mil.)	*0.5%*	23.3	23.4	23.5	23.7	23.8
GSP ($ bil.)	*(10.8%)*	*550*	*704*	*594*	*688*	*348*
Real GSP growth rate	—	3.5%	(1.1%)	(1.7%)	0.8%	(6.0%)
Exports ($ mil.)	*11.7%*	7,250	8,520	9,620	10,520	11,300
Imports ($ mil.)	*11.4%*	9,740	9,590	10,200	11,970	15,000
Trade balance ($ mil.)	—	(2,490)	(1,070)	(580)	(1,450)	(3,700)
Current account ($ mil.)	—	1,100	1,250	2,490	2,010	(1,000)
Govt. budget bal. ($ mil.)	—	*165*	*136*	*176*	—	—
Consumer inflation	—	88%	118%	194%	1,240%	588%
Unemployment rate	—	11.7%	11.4%	11.9%	—	—
Exchange rate with US$	—	0.04	0.07	0.25	2.88	11.34

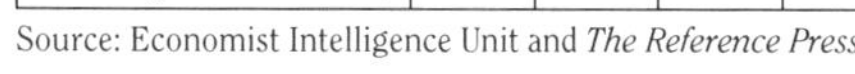
Source: Economist Intelligence Unit and *The Reference Press*

AUSTRIA
HUNGARY
ROMANIA
Belgrade
YUGOSLAVIA
BULGARIA
Adriatic Sea
ITALY
ALBANIA
GREECE

Area: 99,000 sq. mi. (255,804 sq. km)

Official name:
Socialist Federal Republic of Yugoslavia
Socijalistička Federativna Republika Jugoslavija
Official languages: Macedonian, Serbo-Croatian, Slovenian
Currency: 1 dinar (YuD) = 100 paras
Fiscal year ends: December 31

WHO

President: Borisav Jović, age 63
Prime Minister: Ante Marković, age 67
Deputy Prime Minister and Secretary for Finance: Branko Zekan, age 52
Secretary for Foreign Affairs: Budimir Lončar, age 67
Ambassador to US: Dzevad Mujezinovic
US Ambassador to Yugoslavia: Warren Zimmermann

WHERE

Executive HQ: President, Office of the President, Yugoslavia
Embassy in US: 2410 California St. NW, Washington, DC 20008
Phone: 202-462-6566
Fax: 202-797-9663
US Embassy in Yugoslavia: American Embassy, Box 5070, Belgrade, Yugoslavia
Phone: 011-38-11-645-655
Fax: 011-38-11-645-221
Chamber of Commerce: Yugoslav Chamber of Commerce, Privredna Momora Jugoslavije, Terazije 23, Belgrade, Yugoslavia
Phone: 011-38-11-339-461

Yugoslavia has 6 republics and 2 autonomous provinces.

Capital city: Belgrade
Time change from EST: +6 hours
Avg. high/low temp: Jan. 37°F (3°C)/26°F (-3°C)
July 83°F (28°C)/62°F (17°C)

Urbanization: 49%
Population density: 240/sq. mi. (93/sq. km)

Exports as % of Total		Imports as % of Total	
USSR	22	Germany	17
Italy	15	USSR	15
Germany	12	Italy	11
US	5	US	5
Other countries	46	Other countries	52
Total	**100**	**Total**	**100**

WHAT

Origins of GSP	% of Total
Mining & manufacturing	42
Agriculture, forestry & fishing	15
Transport & communications	7
Construction	7
Other	29
Total	**100**

1990 GSP per capita: $14,635
1990 year-end external debt: $17 billion
Literacy rate: 90%
UN Human Development Index: 89%
Human Freedom Index (0-40 scale): 8
Purchasing power as % of US: 29%
Capital city cost of living as % of DC: 100%
Defense as % of GNP: 4%
Education as % of GNP: 4%
Principal airline: Jugoslovenski Aero Transport
Principal exchange: Yugoslav Capital Market Beograd

ZIMBABWE

OVERVIEW

Zimbabwe possesses one of the best combinations of climate, soil, and abundant resources in Africa, as well as an industrial infrastructure and a modern transportation system. It has one of the highest literacy rates in Africa.

While agriculture employs 74% of the labor force and accounts for 40% of exports, it contributes just 13% of GDP. Only 7% of the land is arable. Export products include tobacco, cotton, coffee, and sugar. Agricultural performance has lagged because of recurrent dry spells since 1982.

Zimbabwe's mines produce gold, chromium, nickel, copper, iron, and coal (of which there are vast reserves). Though this sector accounts for 8% of GDP and employment, it contributes 40% of exports.

Manufacturing is primarily based on processing agricultural products but also includes steel, cement, and consumer goods for local use.

After a promising start at independence in 1980, Zimbabwe has run into difficulties. The Socialist government instituted controls on wages, prices, and investment, distorting the internal market and interfering with export growth. Unemployment is estimated at nearly 1 million, and job creation is slow; this will be a problem in coming years for a population with annual growth of nearly 3%. Recurrent political corruption scandals have shaken the faith of the people in government. However, the natural endowments of the country are so great that, properly managed, they could make recovery possible.

WHEN

Zimbabwe takes its name from the 3rd-century stone ruins of Dzimbahwe that are the sole pre-European architectural remains of sub-Saharan Africa. Natives of the area had contact with coastal trading centers but remained mostly undisturbed by Europeans until the mid-19th century.

David Livingstone's exploration of Victoria Falls in the mid-1850s brought the first record of the region. European settlement began in 1859. The discovery of gold and a desire to encircle the Boers of South Africa prompted the British government in 1889 to commission Cecil Rhodes's British South Africa Company to explore territory north of the Transvaal. Rhodes had secured mineral rights to the area from local tribal chiefs in 1888. The territory was named Rhodesia in 1895.

During the 1890s native uprisings prevented settlement but were subdued, and the company began developing gold mining, agriculture, transportation, and communications.

In the early 20th century, mining (primarily of gold and chromium) and agriculture (tobacco and corn) were the chief economic activities. As the white population grew, settlers demanded more land. This led in 1931 to new laws setting aside disproportionately large areas of the best land for white settlers.

After WWII the white population of Rhodesia nearly doubled through immigration. In 1953 Rhodesia joined an economic federation with British protectorates Nyasaland and Northern Rhodesia that broke up in 1963 at the behest of the latter two states.

In 1965, continuing its decades of resistance to majority rule, Rhodesia under Ian Smith declared itself independent from the UK. This led to 15 years of economic sanctions and civil war. Ironically, the sanctions improved and diversified Rhodesia's economy, forcing it to produce its own steel and machinery. Though dependent upon imported oil (supplied by South Africa during the embargo), the country had coal that made it nearly self-sufficient in energy for electrical and industrial uses.

In the mid-1970s Smith sought peace. Negotiations led to an independent Zimbabwe under rebel leader Robert Mugabe in 1980.

The new regime did not retaliate against whites but retained their expertise in administration. Free of sanctions, the economy took off, growing 20% during 1980–81. However, political unrest led to white flight, and droughts and lower demand for minerals hit the economy. Despite rallies in 1985, 1986, and 1988, Zimbabwe's economy declined and brought unemployment, falling wages, shortages of goods, high inflation, and deterioration in transport.

In 1989 President Mugabe proposed reforms to make the economy more responsive to market forces and to relax wage and price controls, but little has actually been done. Pressure for increased land redistribution has left the country torn between gratifying popular desires and maintaining the agricultural efficiency of large farms.

HOW MUCH

	4-Year Growth	1986	1987	1988	1989	1990
Population (mil.)	*2.7%*	8.4	8.6	8.9	9.1	9.4
GDP ($ bil.)	*4.8%*	*4.4*	*5.0*	*5.4*	*5.3*	*5.3*
Real GDP growth rate	—	2.2%	(0.5%)	7.3%	4.5%	1.9%
Exports ($ mil.)	*5.5%*	1,303	1,428	1,589	1,581	1,615
Imports ($ mil.)	*7.3%*	1,133	1,209	1,193	1,335	1,500
Trade balance ($ mil.)	—	170	219	396	246	115
Current account ($ mil.)	—	7	48	42	(120)	(300)
Govt. budget bal. ($ mil.)	—	*(305)*	*(461)*	*(284)*	*(527)*	*(404)*
Consumer inflation	—	14.6%	12.8%	7.5%	12.8%	20.0%
Unemployment rate	—	—	—	30.0%	—	—
Exchange rate with US$	—	1.67	1.66	1.80	2.11	2.45

Source: Economist Intelligence Unit and *The Reference Press*

Area: 150,872 sq. mi. (390,759 sq. km)

Official name: Zimbabwe
Official language: English
Currency: 1 dollar (Z$) = 100 cents
Fiscal year ends: June 30

WHO

Executive President: Robert Gabriel Mugabe, age 67
Vice-President: Simon Vengai Muzenda
Vice-President: Joshua M. Nkomo, age 74
Senior Minister of Finance, Economic Planning and Development in the President's Office: Dr. Bernard Chidzero, age 64
Minister of Foreign Affairs: Dr. Nathan Marwirakuw Shamuyarira, age 61
Ambassador to US: Stanislaus Garikai Chigwedere
US Chargé to Zimbabwe: Donald Patterson

WHERE

Executive HQ: President, Private Bag 7700, Causeway, Harare, Zimbabwe
Embassy in US: 1608 New Hampshire Ave. NW, Washington, DC 20009
Phone: 202-332-7100
Fax: 202-483-9326
US Embassy in Zimbabwe: PO Box 3340, 172 Herbert Chitapo Ave., Harare, Zimbabwe
Phone: 011-263-4-794-521
Fax: 011-263-4-796-488
Chamber of Commerce: Associated Chamber of Commerce of Zimbabwe, PO Box 1934, Equity House, Rezende St., Harare, Zimbabwe
Phone: 011-263-4-708-611

Zimbabwe has 8 provinces and has diplomatic representatives in 28 countries.

Capital city: Harare
Time change from EST: +7 hours
Avg. high/low temp: Jan. 78°F (26°C)/60°F (16°C)
July 70°F (21°C)/44°F (7°C)

Urbanization: 27%
Population density: 62/sq. mi. (24/sq. km)

Exports	as % of Total	Imports	as % of Total
UK	13	South Africa	21
Germany	10	UK	12
South Africa	10	US	9
US	7	Germany	9
Other countries	60	Other countries	49
Total	**100**	**Total**	**100**

WHAT

Origins of GDP	% of Total
Manufacturing	26
Transport & distribution	19
Agriculture	13
Mining	8
Public administration	8
Construction	2
Other	24
Total	**100**

1990 GDP per capita: $568
1989 year-end external debt: $3 billion
Literacy rate: 74%
UN Human Development Index: 41%
Human Freedom Index (0-40 scale): 8
Purchasing power as % of US: 10%
Capital city cost of living as % of DC: 53%
Defense as % of GNP: 8%
Education as % of GNP: 9%
Principal airline: Air Zimbabwe

The Company Profiles

ABB ASEA BROWN BOVERI LTD.

OVERVIEW

Operating 1,300 companies worldwide, Asea Brown Boveri (ABB) is the 2nd largest company based in Switzerland (after Nestlé). It is the world's foremost electrical engineering company, holding a commanding lead in its core businesses, electric power production and transmission equipment. These businesses include power plant construction and instrumentation, as well as cable and transformer production. ABB is also a world leader in the design and production of mass-transit systems equipment, high-speed trains, robotics, and manufacturing process control systems.

It is impossible to buy stock directly in ABB since the company is equally owned by Sweden's ASEA and Switzerland's BBC Brown Boveri, which are listed separately on several world stock exchanges. ASEA, controlled by the wealthy Wallenberg family, is the largest company in Sweden in terms of market value and has a substantial stake in Electrolux. Even so, ABB generates 87% of ASEA's earnings. BBC Brown Boveri ranks as one of Switzerland's leading companies (in terms of market value) and has 5 major subsidiaries in addition to its holdings in ABB.

NASDAQ symbols:
ASEAY (ASEA, ADR)
BBCZ (BBC Brown Boveri, ADR)
Fiscal year ends: December 31

Hoover's Rating **B+**

WHO

Co-Chairman: Fritz Leutwiler, age 67
Co-Chairman: Curt Nicolin, age 70
President and CEO: Percy Barnevik, age 50
Deputy CEO: Thomas Gasser, age 58
EVP Finance: Lars Thunell, age 43
Personnel Manager: Arne Olsson
Auditors: KPMG Klynveld Peat Marwick Goerdeler SA
Employees: 215,154

WHEN

Asea Brown Boveri was formed in 1988 when 2 competitive giants, ASEA of Sweden and BBC Brown Boveri of Switzerland, combined their electrical engineering and equipment businesses. Percy Barnevik, head of ASEA, became CEO of the new Zurich-based company.

Ludwig Fredholm had founded ASEA in Stockholm in 1883 as Electriska Aktiebolaget to manufacture engineer Jonas Wenstrom's electric dynamo. In 1890 he merged his company with Wenstrom's brother's company to form Allmänna Svenska Electriska Aktiebolaget (ASEA), which became a pioneer in industrial electrification. Ailing from the mismanagement of Gustaf de Laval (in control from 1896 to 1903), ASEA turned to J. Sigfrid Edstrom (former manager of Gothenburg Tramways Company), who remained in power until WWII. Under Edstrom the company participated in its first railway electrification project and in the 1920s and 1930s provided locomotives and other equipment for Sweden's national railway. ASEA became one of Sweden's largest electric equipment manufacturers by buying its rival, Elektromekano, in 1933; it entered the US market in 1947, while continuing to expand at home and abroad. In 1962 ASEA bought 20% of electric appliance maker Electrolux and formed Scandinavian Glasfiber with Owens-Corning Fiberglas (US). ASEA formed the nuclear power venture ASEA-ATOM with the Swedish government in 1968, buying full control of the venture in 1982.

BBC Brown Boveri had been formed as a partnership, Brown, Boveri, and Company, by Charles Brown and Walter Boveri in Baden, Switzerland, in 1891 to produce electrical generation equipment. It produced the first steam turbines in Europe (1900). BBC established companies in Germany (1893), France (1894), and Italy (1903) to produce and distribute its steam and gas turbine equipment. After WWII the company diversified into nuclear power generating equipment. Electrical machinery production expanded with the purchase of Maschinenfabrik Oerlikon (1967), a Swiss company that manufactured electrical equipment in France and Spain. In the US BBC formed a joint venture with Gould to produce electrical equipment in 1979.

In an unusual form of merger, both ASEA and BBC withheld certain assets, such as ASEA's holdings in Electrolux, from the combination, and each company continues as a separate entity, sharing ownership in the new company 50-50. Asea Brown Boveri formed 2 joint ventures with Westinghouse in 1988, one to produce turbines and generators, the other to manufacture electrical transmission and distribution equipment. In 1989 ABB bought Westinghouse's half of the transmission and distribution joint venture. The company has been restructuring to strengthen its power generation business and exploit opportunities in mass transit, electronics, and manufacturing and environmental control systems for the paper and food processing industries.

Recent acquisitions, including America's Combustion Engineering (1989) and the robotics business of Cincinnati Milacron (1990), have enhanced the company's industry automation and environmental control systems segments. In 1990 ABB formed ABB Henschel, a German-based transportation venture with Thyssen.

WHERE

HQ: PO Box 8131, CH-8050 Zurich, Switzerland
Phone: 011-41-1-317-71-11
Fax: 011-41-1-317-73-21
US HQ: Asea Brown Boveri, Inc., 900 Long Ridge Rd., Stamford, CT 06902-1194
US Phone: 203-329-8771
US Fax: 203-328-2263

ABB operates through 1,300 companies worldwide.

	1990 Sales	
	$ mil.	% of total
Western Europe	15,231	57
North America	5,483	21
Asia & Australasia	3,984	15
Other	1,990	7
Total	**26,688**	**100**

WHAT

	1990 Sales		1990 Operating Income	
	$ mil.	% of total	$ mil.	% of total
Power plants	4,653	15	242	13
Power transmission	5,287	18	421	23
Power distribution	3,073	10	199	11
Industry	4,022	13	123	7
Transportation	1,309	4	22	1
Environmental control	3,684	12	168	9
Financial services	1,092	4	175	9
Other	7,126	24	514	27
Adjustments	(3,558)	—	(74)	—
Total	**26,688**	**100**	**1,790**	**100**

Major Product Lines

AC and DC drives
Antipollution systems
Electrical cables and capacitors
Indoor climate control systems
Locomotives
Low- and medium-voltage systems
Monitoring and control instrumentation
Motors
Power plant control systems
Power plants
Rail systems
Relays
Robotics
Satellite communications equipment
Signaling systems
Steel-making equipment
Switchgear
Transformers
Waste handling systems

KEY COMPETITORS

Alcatel Alsthom
Bechtel
Cooper Industries
Daimler-Benz
Duke Power
GEC
General Electric
Halliburton
Hitachi
Honeywell
Ingersoll-Rand
Johnson Controls
McDermott
Mitsubishi
Reliance Electric
Rolls-Royce
Siemens
Square D
Toshiba
Westinghouse

HOW MUCH

	2-Year Growth	1981	1982	1983	1984	1985	1986	1987	1988	1989	1990
Sales ($ mil.)	22.3%	—	—	—	—	—	—	—	17,832	20,560	26,688
Net income ($ mil.)	23.6%	—	—	—	—	—	—	—	386	589	590
Income as % of sales	—	—	—	—	—	—	—	—	2.2%	2.9%	2.2%
Employees	12.7%	—	—	—	—	—	—	—	169,459	189,493	215,154

1990 Year-end:
Debt ratio: 39.0%
Return on equity: 14.5%
Cash (mil.): $4,975
Assets (mil.): $30,247
Current ratio: 1.29
Long-term debt (mil.): $2,712

Net Income ($ mil.) 1988–90

DHS/DABU

ACCOR SA

OVERVIEW

While Accor is not a name that most US travelers would recognize, the Paris-based company is a leading hotel and restaurant operator. Its 1990 acquisition of Motel 6 moved Accor from the 8th largest to the 2nd largest hotelier in the world (after Bass's Holiday Inns), with 159,877 rooms. Each of its hotel chains is unique, from the 4-star luxury of Sofitel International to the no-frills, low-cost rooms of Formule 1. The company's original full-service chain, Novotel, is #1 in Europe.

Accor's restaurant chains include wine bars (L'Écluse) and steakhouses (Le Bœuf Jardinier, Courte-Paille). In France L'Arche and Caféroute are the leading fast-food chains; Lenôtre is the leading bakery and caterer. Pizza del Arte is the leading Italian restaurant in both France and Spain. The company also provides catering for airlines and institutions, such as hospitals and schools, and offers service vouchers (coupons for services such as child care, gasoline, and meals) in 12 countries in Europe and the Americas.

In recent years Accor has expanded at a phenomenal rate, opening an average of one hotel or restaurant every day. Currently, about 34% of hotel sales and 54% of restaurant sales are generated outside of France.

WHEN

Gérard Pélisson and Paul Dubrule built their first hotel near the city of Lille in 1967, pioneering the development of 3-star hotels in France. Previously, most French hotels were either quaint old inns or very expensive luxury hotels inside cities. Pélisson and Debrule's Novotel neatly filled the niche in between. The pair went on to open the first 2-star Ibis in 1973 and bought the Mercure chain in 1975. Novotel had grown to become the #1 hotel chain in Europe, operating 184 hotels from Europe and Africa to South America and the Far East by 1979, when it opened its first US hotel in Minneapolis.

Dubrule and Pélisson married their growing hotel business to Jacques Borel International, forming Accor in 1983. Founder Jacques Borel had started out with one restaurant in 1957 and was Europe's #1 restaurateur by 1975, when he took over Belgium's Sofitel luxury hotels. Losses in the hotel game compelled Borel to sell Sofitel to Dubrule and Pélisson in 1980, placing them among the world's top 10 hotel operators — a list traditionally dominated by American chains. The 2 picked up the rest of Borel's empire in 1983, launching the newborn Accor into the restaurant business.

Accor started offering package vacation tours in 1984, after buying a majority stake in Africatours (the largest tour operator to Africa), then expanded its offerings to the South Pacific, Asia, and the Americas by buying Ted Cook's Islands in the Sun (1986), Asietours (1987), and Americatours (1987).

The company opened its first budget hotels (Formule 1) in France in 1985, offering bare accommodations at an affordable price. Accor started marketing Paquet cruises aboard the Mermoz cruise ship in 1986. The experimental Hotelia chain, offering senior citizens hotel service with in-house medical care, opened in 1987. That same year Accor opened the Parthenon chain of residential hotels in Brazil.

In 1988 the company and several partners opened Cipal-Parc Astérix, a theme park located 20 miles north of Paris, based on a cartoon character living in Gaul. That same year Accor lost out to British bookmaker Cyril Stein in a bidding war for Hilton International but in 1990 spent $1.3 billion to buy Dallas-based budget hotel chain Motel 6. Accor had been a minor player in the US for more than a decade, but with the purchase of Motel 6 it finally achieved a significant North American presence. Also in 1990 Accor joined Société Générale de Belgique to buy 26.7% of Belgium's Wagon-Lits, owner of about 300 hotels in Europe, Thailand, and Indonesia.

HOW MUCH

$=FF5.08 (Dec. 31, 1990)	8-Year Growth	1981	1982	1983	1984	1985	1986	1987	1988	1989	1990
Sales (FF mil.)	27.1%	—	2,019	5,887	6,755	8,053	9,558	11,121	12,337	14,311	13,776
Net income (FF mil.)	28.8%	—	105	117	142	178	232	334	469	606	795
Income as % of sales	—	—	5.2%	2.0%	2.1%	2.2%	2.4%	3.0%	3.8%	4.2%	5.8%
Earnings per share (FF)	12.1%	—	*16*	*13*	*16*	*19*	*21*	*24*	*29*	*35*	*40*
Stock price – high (FF)	—	—	—	226	244	300	593	573	594	910	1,065
Stock price – low (FF)	—	—	—	126	202	235	285	280	272	567	644
Stock price – close (FF)	—	—	—	—	238	285	478	316	594	906	679
P/E – high	—	—	—	17	15	16	28	24	20	26	26
P/E – low	—	—	—	10	13	12	13	12	9	16	16
Dividends per share (FF)	19.9%	—	3.52	4.20	4.90	5.80	6.50	8.50	10.50	12.50	15.00
Book value per share (FF)	23.6%	—	74	75	90	116	144	230	313	299	404

1990 Year-end:
Debt ratio: 34.8%
Return on equity: 11.5%
Cash (mil.): FF2,645
Long-term debt (mil.): FF4,537
No. of shares (mil.): 21
Dividends:
1990 average yield: 2.2%
1990 payout: 37.2%
Market value (mil.): $2,807
Sales (mil.): $2,712

Stock Price History High/Low 1983–90

1,200
1,000
800
600
400
200
0

Principal exchange: Paris Bourse
Fiscal year ends: December 31

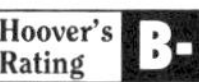

WHO

Co-Chairman: Paul Dubrule
Co-Chairman: Gérard Pélisson
VP Finance and Administration: Michel Baillon
Director Corporate Human Resources: Volker Büring
Auditors: Frinault Fiduciaire
Employees: 81,686

WHERE

HQ: 2, rue de la Mare-Neuve, 91021 Évry Cedex, France
Phone: 011-33-1-60-87-43-20
Fax: 011-33-1-60-77-04-58
US HQ: Accor North America Corp., 2 Overhill Rd., Suite 420, Scarsdale, NY 10583-5325
US Phone: 914-725-5055
US Fax: 914-725-5640

Accor operates 1,421 hotels and 3,112 restaurants in 62 countries.

	1990 Sales	
	FF mil.	% of total
France	8,399	57
Other Europe	4,802	32
North America	291	2
South America	1,092	7
Other countries	267	2
Adjustments	(1,075)	—
Total	**13,776**	**100**

WHAT

	1990 Sales	
	FF mil.	% of total
Hotels	7,840	53
Restaurants	4,947	33
Service vouchers	545	4
Other	1,519	10
Adjustments	(1,075)	—
Total	**13,776**	**100**

Hotel Chains
Formule 1
Hotelia
Ibis
Marine Hotel
Mercure
Motel 6
Novotel
PanSea
Parthenon
Sofitel
Thalassa International
Urbis

Restaurants
B & J Burger
Caféroute
Césario
Courte-Paille
L'Arche
Le Bœuf Jardinier
L'Écluse
Lenôtre
Meda's
Pizza del Arte

Other Activities
Airline and airport catering (Actair)
Business centers (Atria)
Cruises (Croisières Paquet)
Institutional catering
International hotel reservations (Résinter)
Package tours (Africatours, Asietours, Americatours, Episodes, Pacifica Travel, Ted Cook's Islands in the Sun)
Theme park (Cipal-Parc Astérix)
Wholesale food and equipment suppliers (Scapa, Devimco)

KEY COMPETITORS

American Express	Greyhound Dial	Ogden
ARA	Helmsley	Owens-Illinois
Bally	Hilton	PepsiCo
Bass	Hyatt	Rank
Canadian Pacific	ITT	Sysco
Carlson	Loews	Trammell Crow
Edward J. DeBartolo	Marriott	TW Holdings
General Mills	McDonald's	Walt Disney
Grand Metropolitan	Nestlé	Wendy's

AIRBUS INDUSTRIE

OVERVIEW

1990 was a landmark year at Airbus Industrie. The European jet maker turned a profit for the first time. No one outside the company knows how much money that represents, but sources estimate between $100 million and $150 million on $4.6 billion in sales.

Airbus functions as a coordinating and marketing body, handling the sales and service of all Airbus planes, which are financed, designed, and built by the consortium's members, Aerospatiale of France, Deutsche Airbus of Germany, British Aerospace, and Construcciones Aeronauticas SA (CASA) of Spain. Associate members Fokker (the Netherlands) and Belairbus (Belgium) take part in some, but not all, Airbus projects. Airbus also receives subsidies in the form of launch aid from member governments, totaling some $13.5 billion over the past 2 decades.

With 6 different airliners, Airbus is the world's 2nd largest jet maker after Boeing. It is steadily gaining market share (primarily from McDonnell Douglas), up from 16% of the aircraft sold in 1988 to 35% in 1990. Based on its $71.5 billion backlog, Airbus projects $7.4 billion in sales and continued profits for 1991, but, with the volatile state of the airline industry, it could face turbulence ahead.

WHEN

By the 1970s, 3 US companies — Boeing, Lockheed, and McDonnell Douglas — dominated the market for commercial jets. The British and French were discussing an alliance to build a competing jet as early as 1965, but political infighting crushed the spirit of cooperation. Finally, in 1969 the French and West Germans (the British having dropped out) committed to build the Airbus A300. Airbus Industrie was born in France in 1970 as a Groupement d'Intérêt Économique (grouping of economic interest), with no operating capital of its own. The money to launch the A300 came from Airbus's partners, Aerospatiale and Deutsche Airbus. CASA joined in 1971.

In 1974 Airbus moved from Paris to new headquarters at Blagnac (near Toulouse) to be closer to final assembly lines. The A300 entered service with Air France (1974), but Airbus had trouble selling it outside of member countries. In 1975 Bernard Lathière took over as chief executive and hired former American Airlines president George Warde to help him market the A300 in the US.

In 1978 Warde's and Lathière's efforts paid off when Eastern Air Lines decided to buy the A300. Airbus launched the A310, a smaller, more fuel-efficient version of the A300 (1978), and by 1980 it had surpassed McDonnell Douglas and Lockheed, trailing only Boeing among the world's commercial jet makers.

The UK joined the consortium in 1979. With the 1984 launch of the A320, Airbus pioneered the computer-operated "fly-by-wire" flight control system that has become standard equipment on today's commercial jets. Orders poured in for the A320, making it the fastest-selling jetliner in history.

In 1985 Lathière and Roger Béteille, the chief engineer credited as the father of Airbus, retired. Piloted by Jean Pierson, Airbus continued to gain popularity among the world's airlines but drew criticism from US jet makers, who accused the highly subsidized consortium of undercutting competitors by pricing its planes 15% to 25% lower.

In 1987 Airbus launched the A330 and A340. Designed to carry large numbers of passengers, these airliners represented Airbus's solution to global airport undercapacity. Delivery is expected in 1992 and 1993.

In 1989 Airbus launched the A321, a stretched version of the A320, expected off Toulouse assembly lines in 1994. Airbus's 1991 decision to develop its first jumbo jet (and compete head-to-head with Boeing's 747) sparked fresh controversy between the consortium and its US competitors. The US government petitioned the General Agreement on Tariffs and Trade (GATT) to limit Airbus subsidies, claiming that government launch aid gave Airbus an unfair advantage. Airbus is working to limit its dependence on government money, and in 1991 it floated its first international bond issue to help finance the A321.

Also in 1991 Airbus received 2 of its biggest orders to date — a $2 billion order to refit Kuwait Airways and a $6 billion order from Federal Express.

HOW MUCH

	6-Year Growth	1981	1982	1983	1984	1985	1986	1987	1988	1989	1990
Sales ($ mil.)	—	—	—	—	—	—	—	—	—	5,000	4,600
Aircraft orders	50.3%	—	—	—	35	92	170	114	167	421	404
Aircraft deliveries	12.1%	—	—	—	48	42	29	32	61	105	95
Order backlog	42.7%	—	—	—	123	152	288	370	476	774	1,038
Cumulative customers	12.4%	—	—	—	50	55	60	71	74	87	101
Cumulative operators	7.5%	—	—	—	44	46	51	55	64	70	68

1990 Year-end:
Orders value (bil.): $27
Market share: 35%

Aircraft Deliveries 1984–90

European consortium
Fiscal year ends: December 31

WHO

Supervisory Board Chairman: Hans Friderichs
Executive Board Chairman and Managing Director: Jean Pierson, age 50
COO: Heribert Flosdorff
Financial Director: Ian Massey, age 40
VP Human Relations: J. Baniere
Employees: 1,400

WHERE

HQ: 1 Rond Point Maurice Bellonte, 31707 Blagnac Cedex, France
Phone: 011-33-61-93-34-33
Fax: 011-33-61-93-49-55
US HQ: Airbus Industrie of North America, Inc., 593 Herndon Pkwy., Suite 300, Herndon, VA 22070
US Phone: 703-834-3400
US Fax: 703-834-3340

Airbus Industrie sells and services aircraft worldwide. About 90% of its employees are at Toulouse, with the rest situated mainly at maintenance facilities of Airbus operators.

	1990 New Aircraft Orders	
	No.	% of total
Member countries	66	17
Other Europe	179	44
Asia-Pacific	57	14
US	102	25
Total	**404**	**100**

WHAT

			1990 New Aircraft Orders	
Airbus Aircraft	Seats	Range	Orders	% of total
Wide-body				
A300	267	medium/long	31	8
A310	218	medium/long	40	10
A330	335	medium/long	25	6
A340	262-295	long	8	2
Standard-body				
A320	150	short/medium	183	45
A321	186	short/medium	117	29
Total			**404**	**100**

	Cumulative Orders	
	No.	% of total
Widebody	895	53
Standard-body	795	47
Total	**1,690**	**100**

Airbus Industrie Partners
Aerospatiale SA (37.9%, France)
British Aerospace PLC (20%, UK)
Construcciones Aeronauticas SA (CASA, 4.2%, Spain)
Deutsche Airbus (37.9%, Germany)

Associate Members
Belairbus (Belgium)
Fokker (the Netherlands)

Subsidiaries
Aeroformation (training for Airbus customers)
Airbus Industrie of North America, Inc.

KEY COMPETITORS

Boeing
McDonnell Douglas

ALCAN ALUMINIUM LTD.

OVERVIEW

Montreal-based Alcan is North America's largest producer of primary aluminum. The company's vertically integrated operations include mining and processing bauxite (an aluminum-bearing ore); refining bauxite into alumina; generating electricity for smelting aluminum; smelting, recycling, fabricating, marketing, and distributing aluminum; and producing and selling industrial chemicals.

The company derives approximately 80% of its sales from aluminum in ingot and fabricated form. Fabricated aluminum products (plate, sheet, foil, and extruded shapes) generate 65% of sales; Alcan sold slightly less than 1.5 million tons in 1990.

With major operations in Canada, the US, the UK, and Brazil, Alcan operates a global network of facilities that help to provide and process its raw materials.

Faced in 1990 with sluggish demand and low prices, Alcan plans to cut $200 million in costs, pare inventories, and trim capital expenditures. Despite the slump, the first decline in Western aluminum consumption in 8 years, Alcan increased its shipments, gaining market share in Europe and Asia.

WHEN

In 1900 the Aluminum Company of America (Alcoa) established its first Canadian smelter at Shawinigan Falls, Quebec. In 1928 Alcoa organized its Canadian and all other foreign operations as a separate company (mandated by a US antitrust divestment order), which took the name Aluminium Limited (name changed to Alcan in 1966). Alcan retained close ties with Alcoa (the Mellon and Davis families held stock in both companies) and appointed Edward K. Davis (the brother of former Alcoa chairman Arthur Vining Davis) as its first president. At the time of its formation, Alcan existed primarily as a smelter for raw bauxite that came from a company-owned mine in British Guiana (which would become Guyana).

After narrowly surviving the Great Depression years of the early 1930s, Alcan established a global sales force and a number of overseas plants in Europe, Australia, India, China, and Japan. The company profited tremendously from WWII, when the need for aluminum made it the world's largest smelter. At the end of the war, Alcan was 5 times larger than it had been in 1937.

In 1950 US courts, ruling on an earlier antitrust suit, ordered the Mellon and Davis families to end their joint ownership of Alcoa and Alcan. Both families opted to stay with Alcoa and sold most of their stock in Alcan. In 1954 Alcan opened its giant Kitimat-Kemano power complex in British Columbia.

During the 1960s and 1970s, the company (which had previously supplied aluminum to other companies for fabrication) started fabricating and distributing it themselves. In 1961 the company started fabricating products in the US in Oswego, New York.

In 1971 Alcan had to readjust its supply strategy when Guyana nationalized its raw resources. Six years later Jamaica (another major provider of bauxite) acquired 70% of all of Alcan's mining and refining assets, which resulted in the formation of a joint venture (Jamalcan).

In 1979 David Culver became CEO of the company (the first non–Davis family member to hold the position) and led Alcan through an early 1980s recession with a massive cost-cutting campaign. In 1988 the company achieved record profits ($931 million). In 1989 Alcan commissioned the world's largest aluminum beverage can recycling plant in Berea, Kentucky.

In 1990 Alcan's earnings were helped by the sale of its 24% ownership of a Spanish aluminum company and from one-time transactions related to its 45% participation in Nippon Light Metal Company of Japan. During the 1990s Alcan will work with Jaguar to produce an energy-saving aluminum automobile.

HOW MUCH

	9-Year Growth	1981	1982	1983	1984	1985	1986	1987	1988	1989	1990
Sales ($ mil.)	6.5%	4,978	4,644	5,208	5,467	5,718	5,956	6,797	8,529	8,839	8,757
Net income ($ mil.)	8.3%	264	(58)	58	216	(216)	218	433	931	835	543
Income as % of sales	—	5.3%	(1.2%)	1.1%	4.0%	(3.8%)	3.7%	6.4%	10.9%	9.4%	6.2%
Earnings per share ($)	5.5%	1.44	(0.31)	0.28	0.98	(0.96)	0.97	1.68	3.85	3.58	2.33
Stock price – high ($)	—	17.78	12.61	18.50	18.33	13.89	15.39	25.25	22.25	25.13	24.50
Stock price – low ($)	—	8.72	7.06	11.44	10.44	10.11	12.28	12.61	15.67	20.17	16.63
Stock price – close ($)	7.4%	10.22	12.39	17.67	12.78	12.89	12.56	17.92	21.75	22.88	19.50
P/E – high	—	12	—	65	19	—	16	15	6	7	11
P/E – low	—	6	—	40	11	—	13	8	4	6	7
Dividends per share ($)	3.8%	0.80	0.60	0.40	0.53	0.49	0.36	0.39	0.59	1.12	1.12
Book value per share ($)	5.1%	14.15	13.10	12.83	13.08	12.23	13.18	15.04	18.06	20.30	22.19

1990 Year-end:
Debt ratio: 25.8%
Return on equity: 11.0%
Cash (mil.): $200
Current ratio: 1.57
Long-term debt (mil.): $1,796
Number of shares (mil.): 223
Dividends:
1990 average yield: 5.7%
1990 payout: 48.1%
Market value (mil.): $4,342

Stock Price History High/Low 1981–90

30
25
20
15
10
5
0

NYSE symbol: AL
Fiscal year ends: December 31

WHO

Chairman and CEO: David Morton, age 61, $814,802 pay
President and COO: Jacques Bougie, age 43, $520,287 pay
VP and CFO: Allan A. Hodgson, age 53, $366,163 pay
VP Personnel: Owen M. Ness, age 60, $240,820 pay
VP Corporate Affairs: Michael C. d'E. Miller, age 62
VP, Chief Legal Officer, and Secretary: P.K. Pal, age 55
Auditors: Price Waterhouse
Employees: 55,000

WHERE

HQ: 1188 Sherbrooke St. West, Montreal, Quebec H3A 3G2, Canada
Phone: 514-848-8000
Fax: 514-848-8115

The company produces alumina in 9 countries and has bauxite holdings in 8, smelting operations in 7, and fabricating plants in 18.

	1990 Sales		1990 Net Income	
	$ mil.	% of total	$ mil.	% of total
Canada	1,171	13	29	5
US	2,876	33	83	15
Latin America	537	6	(12)	(2)
Europe	3,169	36	78	15
Pacific	922	11	264	49
All other	82	1	96	18
Adjustments	—	—	5	—
Total	**8,757**	**100**	**543**	**100**

WHAT

	1990 Sales	
	$ mil.	% of total
Fabricated products	5,711	65
Ingot products	1,439	16
Other products	1,303	15
Other revenues	304	4
Total	**8,757**	**100**

Products

Aluminum
Alumina
Bauxite
Cable and wire
Electrical wire
Rivets
Welding wire
Zippers
Cathode blocks
Containers
Extruded shapes
Airplane components
Automotive bumpers
Doors
Truck chassis
Windows
Foil
Ingot
Packaging
Petroleum coke
Plate
Sheet
Wire

Chemicals
Aluminum fluoride
Cryolite

KEY COMPETITORS

Alcoa
AMAX
Inco
Mitsui
Norsk Hydro
Peter Kiewit Sons'
Reynolds Metals
RTZ
Thyssen

ALCATEL ALSTHOM

OVERVIEW

Paris-based Alcatel Alsthom (renamed from Compagnie Générale d'Electricité in 1991) is one of France's largest industrial concerns. It is the namesake of its 2 biggest subsidiaries, Alcatel (which surpassed AT&T in 1989 to become the world's #1 manufacturer of telecommunications equipment, systems, and cables) and GEC Alsthom (the world's #2 manufacturer of power systems and equipment [after America's General Electric] and a leading builder of ships and rail equipment).

Other Alcatel Alsthom affiliates are among the leaders in their fields. Framatome is Europe's #1 maker of pressurized water reactors; Compagnie Européenne d'Accumulateurs (Ceac) is France's largest and Europe's 2nd largest lead-acid battery maker; and Saft is a leading maker of alkaline and industrial batteries. Alcatel Alsthom is also involved in electrical engineering and ranks as one of the world's 50 largest industrial companies.

In a concerted effort to maintain world leadership and profitability, Alcatel Alsthom is pursuing a program of acquisitions and seeking alliances with foreign partners who share in its core business fields, such as Britain's General Electric Company (GEC).

OTC symbol: ACALY (ADR)
Fiscal year ends: December 31

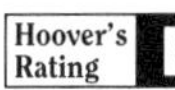

WHO

Chairman and CEO: Pierre Suard
President and COO: Francois de Laage de Meux
EVP: Philippe Dargenton
EVP and CFO: André Wettstein
EVP Industrial and International Affairs: Bernard Pierre
VP Human Resources: Pierre Bollache
Auditors: Acer-Cabinet Payer et Associés; Société Frinault-Fiduciaire
Employees: 205,500

WHEN

In 1898 Pierre Azaria combined his electric generating company with 3 others to form Compagnie Générale d'Electricité (CGE). As one of Europe's pioneer electric power and manufacturing companies, CGE expanded operations in France and abroad through acquisitions. By WWII CGE was making light bulbs and batteries, in addition to power generating equipment. After the French government nationalized electric utilities in 1946, CGE diversified into the production of telecommunications equipment, consumer appliances, and electronics.

In 1969 Thomson-Brandt (French electronics manufacturer, later renamed Thomson) transferred its heavy equipment maker, Alsthom, to CGE in exchange for CGE's data processing and appliance businesses. In 1976 Alsthom acquired Les Chantiers de l'Atlantique, the French shipbuilding giant.

In the meantime CGE expanded its telecommunications business by buying Alcatel. Founded in 1879, Alcatel was a French communications pioneer that went on to introduce digital switching exchanges (1970). CGE combined its existing telecommunications division, CIT, with Alcatel to form CIT Alcatel.

The Mitterrand government nationalized CGE in 1982. Soon afterward the company traded its defense and consumer electronics units for Thomson's communications businesses, making CGE the 5th largest telephone equipment manufacturer in the world (1983). Later, CGE combined Alcatel with ITT's phone equipment operations, forming Alcatel NV. The newly formed Brussels-based company (55.6% owned by CGE, 37% by ITT, and 7.4% by French and Belgian partners) started off as the world's 2nd largest telecommunications enterprise after AT&T.

In 1987 CGE's chairman, Pierre Suard, supervised the government's sale of CGE to the public for $1.9 billion. Later that year the company bought Sir James Goldsmith's 51% stake in Paris-based Générale Occidentale, which included France's 2nd largest book publisher, Groupe de la Cité.

In 1989 CGE and GEC combined their power systems and engineering businesses to create GEC Alsthom NV (equally owned by CGE and GEC). In 1990 (pending EC approval) CGE agreed to take over Fiat's telecommunications businesses (Telettra) and to buy a 3% stake in Fiat. Fiat, in turn, plans to buy 6% of CGE. After the company adopted its current name in 1991, its Alcatel unit bought Rockwell International's transmission equipment division, greatly enhancing Alcatel's presence in the US telecommunications market.

WHERE

HQ: Alcatel Alsthom Compagnie Générale d'Electricité, 54, rue La Boétie, 75008 Paris, France
Phone: 011-33-1-42-56-15-61
Fax: 011-33-1-40-76-14-00
US HQ: Alcatel North America Inc., 2512 Penny Rd., Claremont, NC 28610
US Phone: 704-459-9787
US Fax: 704-459-9312

Alcatel Alsthom has operations in more than 100 countries.

	1990 Sales	
	FF mil.	% of total
France	53,896	37
Germany	15,227	11
Other Europe	43,560	30
Other countries	31,370	22
Total	**144,053**	**100**

WHAT

	1990 Sales	
	FF mil.	% of total
Telecommunications	92,583	64
Energy & transportation	21,996	15
Electrical engineering	14,951	10
Batteries	5,151	4
Other	9,372	7
Total	**144,053**	**100**

Major Subsidiaries and Affiliates

Alcatel NV (70%, telecommunications systems, the Netherlands)
Cegelec (76.6%, electrical engineering, France)
Compagnie Européenne d'Accumulateurs (98.4%, lead-acid batteries, France)
Electro Banque (76.3%, financial services, France)
Framatome (45%, nuclear plants, France)
GEC Alsthom NV (50%, power plants and electrical equipment, the Netherlands)
Chantiers de l'Atlantique (ships, France)
Générale Occidentale (53.6%, publishing and media, France)
Saft (72.9%, alkaline batteries, France)
Sogelerg (99.1%, engineering, France)

HOW MUCH

$=FF5.08 (Dec. 31, 1990)	9-Year Growth	1981	1982	1983	1984	1985	1986	1987	1988	1989	1990
Sales (FF mil.)	10.8%	56,659	65,788	62,464	74,146	71,942	80,903	127,461	127,958	143,897	144,053
Net income (FF mil.)	32.2%	586	638	662	797	1,185	1,721	3,388	4,152	6,955	7,230
Income as % of sales	—	1.0%	1.0%	1.1%	1.1%	1.6%	2.1%	2.7%	3.2%	4.8%	5.0%
Earnings per share (FF)	—	—	—	—	10.98	14.12	20.20	27.80	32.20	40.66	48.95
Stock price – high (FF)	—	—	—	—	—	—	—	347	430	538	652
Stock price – low (FF)	—	—	—	—	—	—	—	206	182	368	460
Stock price – close (FF)	—	—	—	—	—	—	—	215	403	538	541
P/E – high	—	—	—	—	—	—	—	12	13	13	13
P/E – low	—	—	—	—	—	—	—	7	6	9	9
Dividends per share (FF)	—	—	—	—	3.37	4.40	6.67	7.50	9.00	11.00	12.50
Book value per share (FF)	—	—	—	—	198	208	224	235	257	276	317

1990 Year-end:
Debt ratio: 34.5%
Return on equity: 16.5%
Cash (bil.): FF34
Long-term debt (bil.): FF18
No. of shares (mil.): 108
Dividends:
1990 average yield: 2.3%
1990 payout: 25.5%
Market value (mil.): $11,502
Sales (mil.): $28,346

Stock Price History High/Low 1987–90
700 600 500 400 300 200 100 0

KEY COMPETITORS

ABB	General Electric
AT&T	GTE
BCE	Hachette
Bechtel	Hitachi
Centel	NEC
Cooper Industries	Philips
Dresser	Rolls-Royce
Emerson	Siemens
Ericsson	Toshiba
Fujitsu	Square D
GEC	Westinghouse

Other communications, rail equipment, electrical engineering, nuclear power, and battery companies

ALLIANZ AG HOLDING

OVERVIEW

Munich-based Allianz has long since outgrown the German insurance market; it's twice the size of its nearest domestic competitor. Prevented from meaningful expansion in Germany — by government regulation and its own success at grabbing market share — Allianz grew into Europe's largest insurance company. Premiums from foreign sources grew from 12% to 40% of its total between 1980 and 1989.

Along with its sizable investments in the bluest chips of German industry (Daimler-Benz, Thyssen), Allianz owns 25% of Münchener Rückversicherung, the world's largest reinsurance company, and in 1991 accumulated a 23% stake in Dresdner Bank, Germany's 2nd largest bank.

In the US it is acquiring Fireman's Fund, a former American Express unit, which specializes in property/casualty insurance. Fireman's Fund, with its $3.4 billion in premiums, ranks 15th among the world's insurance companies.

Principal exchange: Frankfurt
Fiscal year ends: December 31

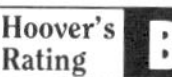

WHO

Chairman: Wolfgang Schieren
Member of the Board of Management, Business Administration: Jan Boetius
Member of the Board of Management, Finance: Friedrich Schiefer
Auditors: KPMG Deutsche Treuhand-Gesellschaft Aktiengesellschaft Wirtschaftsprüfungsgesellschaft
Employees: 43,117

WHEN

In 1890, the same year Carl Thieme founded the company in Germany, Allianz participated in the creation of the Calamity Association of Accident Insurance Companies, a consortium of German, Austrian, Swiss, and Russian firms to insure world commerce. Thieme also established Allianz offices in the UK (1893), Switzerland (1897), and the Netherlands (1898). Thieme's successor, Paul von der Nahmer, expanded Allianz into Scandinavia, the Balkans, the US, Italy, and France. After WWI Allianz returned to foreign markets.

After the German defeat in WWII, the victors seized Allianz's foreign holdings, except for a stake in Spain's Plus Ultra. In the 1950s Allianz repurchased lost holdings in Italian and Austrian companies.

Allianz saturated the German market and began a full-scale return to the international arena in the late 1950s and 1960s. Wolfgang Schieren took the CEO desk in 1971 and immediately began a decades-long program of creating and buying foreign enterprises. Allianz established a subsidiary in Britain (1973), bought a Brazilian company (1974), and, in a major step, plunged into the US, forming Los Angeles–based Allianz Insurance Company (1977). In 1979 the company added Fidelity Union Life Insurance of Dallas and North American Life and Casualty of Minneapolis.

In 1981 Allianz launched a takeover (which turned hostile) of the UK's Eagle Star insurance company. Allianz managed to gain more than 28% of the firm. Negotiations continued more than 2 years until Britain's B.A.T entered the fray as a white knight. After a 1983 bidding joust, Allianz withdrew.

Allianz consoled itself by going shopping, paying DM1.14 billion to win control of Riunione Adriatica di Sicurtà (RAS), Italy's 2nd largest insurance company, in 1984. Then the company returned to the UK to buy Cornhill (on its 3rd try) in 1986. In 1989 Allianz served as a white knight itself when it purchased the insurance holdings of French giant Compagnie de Navigation Mixte (CNM).

Also in 1989 Allianz acquired 49% of Hungária Biztosító, getting its foot in the rapidly opening Eastern European door. In 1990 it stormed into what once was East Germany to win control of Deutsche Versicherung AG.

And that was before it blew out the 100 candles on its birthday cake. Allianz came shopping in the US for its big 1990 present — Fireman's Fund Insurance Company — purchased from Fund American for a net $1.1 billion. Allianz paid Fund American, the American Express spin-off, $3.3 billion, and Fund American turned around and paid $2.2 billion for Fireman's Fund noninsurance assets.

WHERE

HQ: Königinstrasse 28, Postfach 44 01 24, D-8000 Munich 44, Germany
Phone: 011-49-89-3-8000
Fax: 011-49-89-34-9941
US HQ: Allianz Insurance Co., 6435 Wilshire Blvd., Los Angeles, CA 90048
US Phone: 213-658-5000
US Fax: 213-852-8366

Allianz operates 158 companies in 31 countries.

	1989 Premiums Written	
	DM mil.	% of total
Germany	19,115	60
Other EC	7,932	25
Other Europe	1,778	6
Americas	2,811	8
Other countries	197	1
Total	**31,833**	**100**

WHAT

	1989 Premiums Written	
	DM mil.	% of total
Property/casualty	19,425	61
Life/health	12,408	39
Total	**31,833**	**100**

Selected Major Subsidiaries

Adriatic Insurance Co. of Canada
Allianz Insurance Co. (US)
Allianz International Insurance Co. Ltd. (UK)
Allianz Lebensversicherungs-AG (Germany)
Allianz Management, Inc. (US)
Allianz Underwriters Insurance Co. (US)
Allianz Versicherungs-AG (Germany)
American Ambassador Casualty Co. (US)
The Canadian Commerce Insurance Co.
Canadian Home Assurance Co.
Cornhill Insurance PLC (UK)
Fidelity Union Life Insurance Co. (US)
Fireman's Fund Insurance Co. (US)
Jefferson Insurance Co. of N.Y. (US)
Münchener Rückversicherungs-Gesellschaft AG (25%)
North American Life and Casualty Co. (US)
Rhin et Moselle Assurances Françaises Compagnie Générale d'Assurances et de Réassurances SA (France)
Riunione Adriatica di Sicurtà SpA (Italy)
Trafalgar Insurance Co. of Canada

HOW MUCH

$=DM1.49 (Dec. 31, 1990)	9-Year Growth	1981	1982	1983	1984	1985	1986	1987	1988	1989[1]	1990
Assets (DM mil.)	—	14,720	16,188	18,155	20,049	23,162	26,053	29,503	33,127	133,273	—
Net income (DM mil.)	—	175	241	302	290	304	359	325	502	941	—
Income as % of assets	—	1.2%	1.5%	1.7%	1.4%	1.3%	1.4%	1.2%	1.5%	0.7%	—
Earnings per share (DM)	—	18	25	26	25	22	20	22	33	63	—
Stock price – high (DM)	—	427	469	746	980	1,772	2,457	1,976	1,895	2,440	2,963
Stock price – low (DM)	—	363	359	415	620	736	1,017	927	1,035	1,673	1,938
Stock price – close (DM)	25.7%	367	450	708	823	1,772	1,959	1,144	1,870	2,440	2,870
P/E – high	—	24	19	29	40	82	120	91	57	39	—
P/E – low	—	20	15	16	25	34	50	43	31	27	—
Dividends per share (DM)[2]	6.6%	8.6	8.6	8.6	9.4	10.3	10.3	12.0	12.0	12.0	16.0
Book value per share (DM)	—	204	226	240	255	300	284	384	301	548	—

1989 Year-end:
Equity as % of assets: 9.1%
Cash (mil.): DM723
No. of shares (mil.): 15
Dividends:
1989 payout: 19.0%
Sales (mil.): $22,423
Assets (mil.): $89,445
1990 Year-end:
Dividends:
1990 average yield: 0.6%
Market value (mil.): $28,893

Stock Price History High/Low 1981–90

3,000 / 2,500 / 2,000 / 1,500 / 1,000 / 500 / 0

[1]Worldwide results — not available for previous years [2]Not including rights offerings

KEY COMPETITORS

Aetna
AIG
B.A.T
Crédit Lyonnais
CS Holding
Deutsche Bank
Equitable
General Re
Lloyd's of London
MassMutual
MetLife
New York Life
Prudential
State Farm
Tokio Marine & Fire
Travelers
USF&G

Other international insurance companies

ALLIED-LYONS PLC

OVERVIEW

London-based Allied-Lyons is one of the largest beverage and food concerns in the world, with operations in beer, retailing, wines, spirits, and food.

Allied-Lyons's Beer and Retailing division produces several beer brands including Tetley Bitter (the UK's #1 draught ale), Skol, and Ansells. The company also operates a network of about 7,500 public houses (inns, restaurants, pubs, and wine shops) across the UK.

Allied-Lyons's Wines and Spirits segment benefited greatly from the 1986 acquisition of Hiram Walker, which added such brands as Kahlua and Canadian Club to the company's already-impressive brand list. Its 1990 acquisition of Whitbread's liquor business brought the company a long-sought-after premium white liquor brand, Beefeater Gin.

Stressing a strategy of increased concentration in the Foods sector, Allied-Lyons has built a strong range of consumer brands including Tetley (the world's #2 tea). The company also operates Baskin-Robbins (the world's leading ice cream store franchise, with 3,500 outlets in 43 countries), Dunkin' Donuts (the international donut leader, with 1,850 stores worldwide), and Mister Donut (550 stores in the US and Canada).

WHEN

Allied-Lyons was formed through the merger of 3 regional breweries. The oldest of these was an Essex brewing facility created by Edward Ind to provide beer for an inn he had bought in 1799. Ind's brewery merged with the Coope Brewery in 1845 and the combined Ind Coope Brewery established a commanding position in southern England's beer market.

Central England was the realm of Joseph Ansell, a hops merchant who opened his own brewery in 1881. The Ansell Brewery's ale became popular in metropolitan Birmingham and the rural Midlands.

Joshua Tetley entered the business in 1822 by purchasing a Leeds brewery that had been founded by William Sykes. Tetley's beers gained a following in northern England.

Up until the mid–20th century, the 3 breweries operated within their geographic spheres. As the industry consolidated and distribution channels expanded nationally, it became increasingly difficult for regional breweries to compete. Tetley was the first of the 3 to combine operations with another brewery, merging with Walker Cain in 1960.

In 1961 the 3 combined as Ind Coope Tetley Ansell Limited, taking the name Allied Breweries in 1963. In 1968 the greatly strengthened brewing operation purchased SVPW, a wine and spirits company that had also been formed through a 1961 triple merger of Showerings (founded in 1953), Vine Products (founded in 1905), and Whiteways (founded in 1903).

Allied established its Skol lager in 1974. In 1978 the company took its first step into food with the £60 million purchase of J. Lyons and Company, which included the Baskin-Robbins ice cream chain and several food brands. The company assumed its present name in 1981.

In 1982 Sir Derrick Holden-Brown, an ex–naval officer and the head of Allied's brewing operations, assumed the helm of the company and led it through an unsuccessful takeover attempt by Elders IXL (1985). He later engaged in a successful battle with the Reichmann family of Canada over control of Hiram Walker (founded in 1848), a major Canadian distilling, oil, and gas concern. Allied-Lyons walked away with Hiram Walker's liquor division, for which it paid C$2.64 billion.

The company entered the Japanese market in 1988 through a joint venture with Suntory. In 1989 Allied-Lyons acquired Dunkin' Donuts and the following year bought Whitbread's spirits division and Mister Donut. In 1991 the company purchased 24% of Lanson champagne and announced a huge foreign exchange loss of around $285 million which led to the finance director's resignation.

HOW MUCH

£=$1.93 (Dec. 31, 1990)	9-Year Growth	1981	1982	1983	1984	1985	1986	1987	1988	1989	1990
Sales (£ mil.)	8.8%	2,398	2,643	2,851	3,175	3,302	3,615	4,236	4,504	4,731	5,133
Net income (£ mil.)	16.0%	82	90	122	111	197	193	293	347	385	313
Income as % of sales	—	3.4%	3.4%	4.3%	3.5%	6.0%	5.3%	6.9%	7.7%	8.1%	6.1%
Earnings per share (p)	11.7%	*14*	*14*	*19*	*20*	*26*	*34*	*38*	*44*	*48*	*38*
Stock price – high (p)	—	80	149	153	178	306	363	471	494	578	520
Stock price – low (p)	—	62	66	129	138	153	252	290	320	427	408
Stock price – close (p)	23.6%	71	136	138	160	267	322	346	438	496	477
P/E – high	—	6	11	8	9	12	11	12	11	12	14
P/E – low	—	4	5	7	7	6	7	8	7	9	11
Dividends per share (p)	14.4%	5.6	6.1	6.8	7.5	9.5	11.4	13.0	15.0	17.0	18.8
Book value per share (p)	8.4%	147	152	186	196	271	240	250	395	331	303

1990 Year-end:
Debt ratio: 35.9%
Return on equity: 10.5%
Cash (mil.): £108
Long-term debt (mil.): £1,603
No. of shares (mil.): 865
Dividends:
1990 average yield: 3.9%
1990 payout: 49.5%
Market value (mil.): $7,963
Sales (mil.): $9,907

Stock Price History High/Low 1981–90

600
500
400
300
200
100
0

OTC symbol: ALLY (ADR)
Fiscal year ends: First Saturday in March

WHO

Chairman: Sir Derrick Holden-Brown, age 68, £223,720 pay
VC: Richard Martin, age 58
CEO: Tony Hales, age 42
Head of Finance: Anthony Trigg
Auditors: KPMG Peat Marwick McLintock
Employees: 83,000

WHERE

HQ: 24 Portland Place, London W1N 4BB, UK
Phone: 011-44-71-323-9000
Fax: 011-44-71-323-1742
No. Am. HQ: Hiram Walker Allied Vintners Ltd., PO Box 2518, Windsor, Ontario N8Y 4S5, Canada
No. Am. Phone: 519-254-5171
No. Am. Fax: 519-971-5710

	1990 Sales	
	£ mil.	% of total
UK	3,259	64
Other Europe	653	13
Canada	174	3
US	980	19
Other countries	67	1
Total	**5,133**	**100**

WHAT

	1990 Sales		1990 Operating Income	
	£ mil.	% of total	£ mil.	% of total
Beer & retail	1,954	37	259	32
Wines & spirits	1,975	38	403	50
Food	1,288	25	141	18
Adjustments	(84)	—	(147)	—
Total	**5,133**	**100**	**656**	**100**

Beer
Alloa's
Ansells Bitter and Mild
Double Diamond
Ind Coope Burton Ale
John Bull Bitter
Oranjeboom
Skol Lager
Tetley Bitter

Food
Bustelo (coffee)
Lyons (food and tea)
Maryland Cookies
Southern Tea
Tetley (tea)

Franchises
Baskin-Robbins 31
Caffé Classico
Dunkin' Donuts
Mister Donut

Selected Spirits
Ambassador
Ballantine's
Beefeater
Canadian Club
Courvoisier
Denaka
Frangelico
Hiram Walker
Irish Mist
Kahlua
Lamb's
Laphroaig
Maker's Mark
Teacher's
Tia Maria

Selected Wines
Black Tower
Callaway
Château Latour
Clos du Bois
Cockburn's
Harveys
Kendermann

KEY COMPETITORS

American Brands
Bass
Bond
Brown-Forman
BSN
Carlsberg
Foster's Brewing
Gallo
GrandMet
Guinness
Heineken
John Labatt
Kirin
LVMH
Nestlé
PepsiCo
Philip Morris
RJR Nabisco
San Miguel
Sara Lee
Seagram
Stroh
TLC Beatrice
Unilever

ANGLO AMERICAN CORPORATION

OVERVIEW

Anglo American is the lead company in the largest industrial and finance group in South Africa. The company is also a world leader in gold and platinum production.

The international furor over South Africa's racial policies has both helped and harmed Anglo American. While some business has shied away from the controversy, Anglo American has been able to buy assets of foreign firms exiting South Africa. Anglo American's associate, De Beers, has, in a way, joined that exodus by creating Switzerland-based De Beers Centenary to hold its foreign diamond interests. While De Beers controls 80% of the world's diamond production, no more than 10% of that output comes from South Africa.

Anglo American controls its international empire of companies through minority stakes, holding companies, and a wilderness of cross-holdings of stock. The company bristles at charges that it controls too much of the value of the Johannesburg Stock Exchange. The figure is no more than 30%, the company sniffs. An example of the company's labyrinthine holdings is Centenary, which owns 21% of Minorco, Anglo American's foreign investment company, and in turn is 9.5% owned by De Beers, 23.4% owned by Anglo American Investment Trust, and 6% by Anglo American.

WHEN

In 1905 the Oppenheimers, a German family with major interest in the Premier Diamond Mining Company of South Africa, acquired control of Consolidated Mines Selection, one of the smaller South African gold mining companies, and used it to buy up some of the richest gold-producing land in South Africa by 1917. The family formed Anglo American that year to raise money from J. P. Morgan and other US banking and mining interests for mine development. The name was chosen to disguise the company's German background during WWI and because the original suggestion, African American, was rejected by the US investors.

Under chairman Ernest Oppenheimer, Anglo American acquired diamond fields in German Southwest Africa (now Namibia) in 1920, and the company broke the De Beers hegemony in diamond production. De Beers Consolidated Mines had been formed by Cecil Rhodes in 1888 with the financial help of England's powerful Rothschild family and had since extended its control over the South African diamond industry.

De Beers had been able to reap large profits because of its monopoly position and cheap black labor, and had diversified into cattle ranching, agriculture, wine production, coal, railroads, explosives, and other basic industries. The diamond monopoly was reestablished, however, in 1929 when Anglo American took control of De Beers.

After WWII Anglo American and De Beers extended control over the gold industry, becoming the largest producers in South Africa by 1958. The companies were also major world producers of coal, uranium, and copper. In the 1960s and 1970s, Anglo American expanded through mergers and cross-holdings in industrial and financial companies.

The Oppenheimers, who still hold an 8% stake in Anglo American, have long supported moderate opposition politicians and black labor unions, but in 1987, when black unions went on strike, Anglo American dismissed 60,000 workers, and 7 men died in the ensuing violence.

Minorco, the company's 39%-owned overseas arm, sold its interest in Consolidated Gold Fields for a net gain of $645 million (1989) and bought US-based Freeport-McMoRan Gold Company (1990, name changed to Independence Mining). Minorco — whose US holdings already included 56% of Inspiration Resources and 49% of Adobe Resources — later created Minorco (U.S.A.) Inc. to oversee North American investments.

Anglo American faced difficulties in late 1990 and 1991. Sluggish demand hurt performance of diamond and gold mining operations.

HOW MUCH

$=R2.56 (Dec. 31, 1990)	9-Year Growth	1981	1982	1983	1984	1985	1986	1987	1988	1989	1990
Attributable earnings (R mil.)	12.4%	527	503	507	556	601	806	1,031	1,037	1,254	1,507
Earnings per share (R)	12.1%	2.34	2.23	2.23	2.44	2.64	3.53	4.51	4.53	5.45	6.51
Stock price – high (R)	—	18.45	20.00	30.50	26.65	39.75	74.00	95.50	66.00	116.25	147.75
Stock price – low (R)	—	14.40	8.90	17.50	19.75	22.00	37.00	51.50	44.10	62.75	89.50
Stock price – close (R)	21.6%	16.30	20.00	20.00	23.00	39.75	65.85	55.50	61.00	108.00	95.00
P/E – high	—	8	9	14	11	15	21	21	15	21	23
P/E – low	—	6	4	8	8	8	10	11	10	12	14
Dividends per share (R)	12.8%	1.10	1.10	1.10	1.20	1.35	1.80	2.25	2.25	2.70	3.25
Book value per share (R)	22.2%	26.97	20.81	33.71	42.38	46.91	70.71	105.39	85.36	124.10	163.39

1990 Year-end:
Debt ratio: 3.7%
Return on equity: 4.5%
Cash (mil.): R1,545
Long-term debt (mil.): R1,446
No. of shares (mil.): 231
Dividends:
1990 average yield: 3.4%
1990 payout: 49.9%
Market value (mil.): $8,572
Earnings (mil.): $589

Stock Price History High/Low 1981–90

160 140 120 100 80 60 40 20 0

OTC symbol: ANGLY (ADR)
Fiscal year ends: March 31

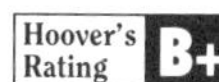

WHO

Chairman: Julian Ogilvie Thompson, age 56
Deputy Chairman: Nicholas F. Oppenheimer, age 45
Deputy Chairman: W. G. Boustred, age 65
Director of Financial Management and Consulting Services and Banking and Insurance: M. W. King, age 53
Manager Manpower Resources: J. F. Drysdale
Auditors: KPMG Aiken & Peat; Pim Goldby
Employees: 2,000

WHERE

HQ: 44 Main St., Johannesburg 2001, South Africa
Phone: 011-27-11-638-9111
Fax: 011-27-11-638-3221
US HQ: Minorco (U.S.A.) Inc., 5251 DTC Pkwy., Suite 700, Englewood, CO 80111
US Phone: 303-889-0700
US Fax: 303-889-0707

Anglo American operates worldwide.

WHAT

	1990 Equity Accounted Earnings	
	R mil.	% of total
Diamonds	889	28
Mining finance	649	21
Industry & commerce	563	18
Gold & uranium	373	12
Platinum & other mining	302	10
Banking, insurance & property	180	6
Coal	132	4
Prospecting	(181)	(6)
Other	223	7
Total	**3,130**	**100**

Affiliates

Anglo American Coal Corp. (51%, coal mining and export)
Anglo American Corp. of South America (40%, mining and other investments in South America)
Anglo American Farms (100%; grain, produce, meat, and wine production)
Anglo American Industrial Corp. (45%; steel, autos, paper, and chemicals)
Anglo American Investment Trust (52%) and Anglo American Gold Investment Co. (49%, investments in diamond and metals mining)
Anglo American Properties (66%, real estate property management)
De Beers Consolidated Mines (32.6%, diamond mining and marketing)
First National Bank Holding (22.5%, banking and related services)
Johannesburg Consolidated Investment Co. (40%, holding company for mining finance)
Minorco (39%, Luxembourg-based holding company, owns 30% of Engelhard Corporation [US] and 36% of Charter Consolidated [UK])

KEY COMPETITORS

AMAX
ASARCO
Broken Hill
Cyprus Minerals
FMC
Hanson
Inco
Phelps Dodge
RTZ
Thyssen
World mining firms

ARTHUR ANDERSEN & CO.

OVERVIEW

Arthur Andersen & Co. is the 4th largest accounting firm in the world. The firm is increasing its international presence — its representation grew from 54 countries in 1989 to 66 in 1990 — and decreasing its reliance on the US, where it reaped 55% of its 1990 revenues, down from 59% the year before. Arthur Andersen is taking a variety of routes to international growth — mergers, acquisitions, joint ventures, and the addition of new offices. The company has begun operations throughout Eastern Europe.

The partnership is, according to *CPA Personnel Report,* the most productive of the Big 6 accounting firms. An Arthur Andersen & Co. partner generates more than $1.8 million in annual revenue.

The company is completing its first year within a new structure. Arthur Andersen & Co. is 2 distinct units: Arthur Andersen provides auditing, business advisory services, tax services, and corporate specialty services; Andersen Consulting provides systems integration and technology consulting. These units are coordinated by a Swiss entity, Arthur Andersen & Co., S.C. The new structure is designed to remove conflicts of interest between auditing and consulting.

WHEN

Arthur Andersen, an orphan of Norwegian parents, worked in the Chicago office of Price Waterhouse in 1907. In 1908 at 23, after becoming the youngest CPA in Illinois, he began teaching accounting at Northwestern University. Following a brief period in 1911 as controller at Schlitz Brewing, Andersen became head of the accounting department at Northwestern. In 1913 at age 28, he formed a public accounting firm, Andersen, DeLany & Company, with Clarence DeLany.

Establishment of the Federal Reserve and implementation of the federal income tax in 1913 aided the firm's early growth by increasing the demand for accounting services. The company gained large clients, including ITT, Briggs & Stratton, Colgate-Palmolive, and Parker Pen, during the period between 1913 and 1920. In 1915 it opened a branch office in Milwaukee. After DeLany's departure in 1918, the firm adopted its present name.

Andersen grew rapidly during the 1920s and added, to its list of services, financial investigations, which formed the basis for its future strength in management consulting. The firm opened 6 offices in the 1920s, including ones in New York (1921), Kansas City (1923), and Los Angeles (1926).

When Samuel Insull's empire collapsed in 1932, Andersen was appointed the bankers' representative and guarded the assets during the refinancing. During the post-Depression period, Andersen opened additional offices in Boston and Houston (1937) and in Atlanta and Minneapolis (1940).

Arthur Andersen's presence dominated the firm during his life. Upon his death in 1947, the firm found new leadership in Leonard Spacek. During Spacek's tenure, which continued until 1963, the firm opened 18 new US offices and began a period of foreign expansion with the establishment of a Mexico City office, followed by 25 more in other countries. Over the same period (1947–63) revenues increased from $6.5 million to $51 million.

Andersen has been an innovator among the major accounting firms. The company opened Andersen University, its Center for Professional Education, in the early 1970s on a campus in St. Charles, Illinois, and provided the first worldwide annual report in 1973. To broaden its scope, it transferred its headquarters to Geneva in 1977.

During the 1970s Andersen increased its consulting business, which accounted for 21% of revenues by 1979; by 1988 consulting fees made up 40% of revenues, making Andersen the world's largest consulting firm. Tension between the consultants and the auditors eventually forced a 1989 restructuring, which established Arthur Andersen and Andersen Consulting as distinct entities.

A rash of megamergers among the then–Big 8 accounting firms led Andersen and Price Waterhouse to flirt briefly with a merger (1989), but discussions broke down over legal and stylistic issues. In 1990 revenues per partner from the consulting operations were nearly $2.6 million, compared to $1.4 million for the tax and auditing arm.

HOW MUCH

	9-Year Growth	1981	1982	1983	1984	1985	1986	1987	1988	1989	1990
Revenues ($ mil.)	17.5%	973	1,124	1,238	1,388	1,574	1,924	2,316	2,820	3,382	4,160
No. of countries	4.9%	43	42	45	45	49	50	49	49	54	66
No. of offices	7.5%	156	157	168	176	215	219	226	231	243	299
No. of partners	6.7%	1,274	1,388	1,477	1,528	1,630	1,847	1,957	2,016	2,134	2,292
No. of employees	11.7%	20,157	22,397	22,815	24,852	28,172	34,270	37,688	43,902	49,280	54,509

1990 revenues per partner: $1,815,000

Revenues ($ mil.) 1981–90

4,500 4,000 3,500 3,000 2,500 2,000 1,500 1,000 500 0

International partnership
Fiscal year ends: August 31

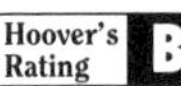

WHO

Chairman: Gerard Van Kemmel
Managing Partner and Chief Executive: Lawrence A. Weinbach, age 51
Managing Partner, Arthur Andersen: Richard L. Measelle
Managing Partner, Andersen Consulting: George T. Shaheen
CFO: John D. Lewis
Human Resources: Paul C. Wilson
Employees: 56,801

WHERE

HQ: Arthur Andersen & Co., Société Coopérative, 18, quai Général-Guisan, 1211 Geneva 3, Switzerland
Phone: 011-41-22-214444
Fax: 011-41-22-214418
US HQ: 59 W. Washington St., Chicago, IL 60602-3094
US Phone: 312-580-0069
US Fax: 312-507-6748

Arthur Andersen & Co. maintains 299 offices in 66 countries.

	1990 Revenues	
	$ mil.	% of total
US	2,282	55
Europe, India, Africa & Middle East	1,359	33
Asia/Pacific	309	7
Other Americas	210	5
Total	**4,160**	**100**

WHAT

	1990 Revenues	
	$ mil.	% of total
Arthur Andersen	2,284	55
Andersen Consulting	1,876	45
Total	**4,160**	**100**

Major Services and Operating Units

Arthur Andersen
Auditing and business advisory
Corporate specialty services
Tax services

Andersen Consulting
Application software products
Change management services
Integration services
Strategic services
Technology services

Center for Professional Education
Client services training
In-house technical training
Management training

Representative Clients

Bond
Cadbury Schweppes
Electrolux
Fiat
Hachette
John Labatt
Olivetti

KEY COMPETITORS

Coopers & Lybrand
Deloitte & Touche
Ernst & Young
KPMG
Marsh & McLennan
McKinsey & Co.
Price Waterhouse
Other consulting firms

BARCLAYS PLC

OVERVIEW

Barclays PLC, through its Barclays Bank PLC operating subsidiary, is the largest of the Big 4 London Clearing Banks (National Westminster, Lloyds, and Midland are the other 3), as well as the largest UK bank (in assets).

Barclays is restructuring into 3 divisions — Banking, Markets and Investment Banking, and Finance — and expects the process to be complete in 1991. Barclays hopes to increase its foreign contribution to profits to 40%. In the meantime Barclays Bank is cutting costs by trimming 1,800 employees and shuttering more than 100 of its 2,600 offices in Britain.

Barclays provides a wide array of banking services, from its Barclaycard (a Visa affiliate) to complex currency transactions to investment banking through Barclays de Zoete Wedd (BZW). After combining with BankAmerica's travelers check unit, Barclays is the world's largest issuer of Visa travelers checks.

NYSE symbol: BCS (ADR)
Fiscal year ends: December 31

WHO

Chairman and CEO: Sir John Quinton, age 61, £404,067 pay
VC and Managing Director: Andrew Robert Fowell Buxton, age 51
Finance Director: Peter A. Wood, age 48
Auditors: Price Waterhouse
Employees: 115,300

WHERE

HQ: Johnson Smirke Building, 4 Royal Mint Court, London EC3N 4HJ, UK
Phone: 011-44-71-930-3131
Fax: 011-44-71-930-0079
US HQ: Barclay's Bank of New York, N.A., 75 Wall St., New York, NY 10265
US Phone: 212-412-4000
US Fax: 212-797-3018

Barclays operates in 74 countries.

	1990 Assets	
	$ mil.	% of total
UK	165,349	63
Foreign, UK-based	17,487	6
Other Europe	29,548	11
US	30,147	13
Other countries	17,800	7
Adjustments	(201)	—
Total	**260,130**	**100**

WHEN

The eagle that is the symbol of Barclays first spread its wings in 1736 when James Barclay joined a family goldsmithing and banking firm under the sign of a black spread eagle. As other family members joined the London enterprise, it became known as Barclays, Bevan & Tritton (1782).

In the late 19th century, British banking underwent a legislative overhaul, and, as a defensive measure, 20 banks combined to ward off takeovers (1896). The new firm was known as Barclay & Co.

The bank then began to take over other banks. It bought 17 private banks in its first 20 years, including the Colonial Bank, chartered in 1836 to serve the West Indies and British Guiana. The bank renamed itself Barclays Bank Ltd. in 1917. It weathered the Great Depression as the 2nd largest of the Big 5 London Clearing Banks, after Midland Bank.

Barclays was poised to take advantage of international economic expansion after WWII, and by the late 1950s it had surpassed Midland Bank as the largest London Clearing Bank. Its large branch network was linked by computer (1959), and it introduced the Barclaycard in conjunction with Bank of America's BankAmericard (1966).

In 1968, 3 big London Clearing Banks — Barclays, Martins, and Lloyds — proposed to merge, but the UK's Monopolies Commission barred the combination, fearing an unreasonable reduction of competition. Barclays shifted its aim and bought Martins without any governmental objection.

Barclays entered the US consumer finance market in 1980 when it acquired American Credit. That same year the bank's North American unit, BarclaysAmerican, added 138 finance offices purchased from Beneficial, and Barclays's New York bank added 31 branches with a $26.5 million purchase from Bankers Trust (1982).

During the 1980s London Clearing Banks faced increased challenges from invading overseas banks, from local building and loans, and from overheated financial markets. After a 1984 act of Parliament, Barclays restructured itself as the holding company for Barclays Bank PLC, its chief operating subsidiary.

To prepare for the "Big Bang" of British financial deregulation in 1986, Barclays formed Barclays de Zoete Wedd through a merger of its merchant bank with 2 other London financial firms.

To rid itself of unprofitable lines of business in an era of sagging profits, Barclays sold its California banking operation (to Wells Fargo, 1988), and its US consumer finance outfit (to Primerica's Commercial Credit, 1989), returning to its strengths as a corporate and investment bank. In 1990, as it prepared for the 1992 removal of European trade barriers, it purchased Merck, Finck & Co., a private German bank, and L'Européenne de Banque, a Paris bank.

WHAT

	1990 Assets	
	$ mil.	% of total
Advances & other accounts	188,656	72
Cash & short-term funds	43,172	17
Items in course of collection	2,607	1
Investments	4,628	2
Trading assets of securities business	15,868	6
Interests in associated undertakings and trade investments	562	—
Property and equipment	4,839	2
Adjustments	(202)	—
Total	**260,130**	**100**

Major Subsidiaries

Barclays Bank Australia Ltd.
Barclays Bank Finance Co. (Jersey) Ltd.
Barclays Bank of Botswana Ltd. (80.4%)
Barclays Bank of Canada
Barclays Bank of New York N.A. (99.9%, US)
Barclays Bank of Zimbabwe
Barclays Bank SA (France)
Barclays Bank SAE (89.4%, Spain)
Barclays de Zoete Wedd Holdings Ltd. (UK)
Barclays Finance Company (Guernsey) Ltd. (UK)
Barclays Financial Services Italia SpA (Italy)
Barclays Financial Services Ltd. (UK)
Barclays Mercantile Business Finance Ltd. (UK)
BarclaysAmericanCorporation
L'Européenne de Banque (France)
Mercantile Credit Co. Ltd. (UK)
Merck, Finck & Co. (Germany)

HOW MUCH

Stock prices are for ADRs ADR = 4 shares	9-Year Growth	1981	1982	1983	1984	1985	1986	1987	1988	1989	1990
Assets ($ mil.)	12.1%	93,360	95,536	94,241	85,255	94,204	117,086	165,564	189,250	206,036	260,130
Net income ($ mil.)	(1.0%)	826	532	420	337	646	908	349	1,604	730	754
Income as % of sales	—	0.9%	0.6%	0.4%	0.4%	0.7%	0.8%	0.2%	0.8%	0.4%	0.3%
Earnings per share ($)	(15.1%)	8.34	4.46	3.51	2.81	2.87	3.76	1.39	4.54	1.86	1.91
Stock price – high ($)	—	—	—	—	—	—	22.14	30.36	26.79	26.43	30.75
Stock price – low ($)	—	—	—	—	—	—	18.93	20.71	18.84	19.11	22.00
Stock price – close ($)	—	—	—	—	—	—	21.96	24.11	20.89	26.43	28.25
P/E – high	—	—	—	—	—	—	6	22	6	14	16
P/E – low	—	—	—	—	—	—	5	15	4	10	12
Dividends per share ($)	—	0.00	0.00	0.00	0.00	0.00	0.54	1.40	1.57	1.51	1.98
Book value per share ($)	—	—	—	11.76	9.93	15.78	18.17	23.34	24.05	22.15	26.29

1990 Year-end:
Equity as % of assets: 4.5%
Return on equity: 7.9%
Cash (mil.): $45,780
No. of shares (mil.): 397
Dividends:
1990 average yield: 7.0%
1990 payout: 103.6%
Market value (mil.): $11,209
Assets (mil.): $260,130
Sales (mil.): $31,327

Stock Price History High/Low 1986–90

35
30
25
20
15
10
5
0

KEY COMPETITORS

H. F. Ahmanson
Bank of New York
BankAmerica
Bankers Trust
Canadian Imperial
Chase Manhattan
Citicorp
Crédit Lyonnais
CS Holding
Dai-Ichi Kangyo
Deutsche Bank
First Chicago
HSBC
Industrial Bank of Japan
J.P. Morgan
Royal Bank
Union Bank of Switzerland
Other money-center banks
Securities underwriting firms

BASF AG

OVERVIEW

Well-known to US consumers for its recording tapes, BASF is one of the world's largest chemical manufacturers. BASF operates in 6 lines of business: raw materials and energy, chemicals, agricultural chemicals, plastics, dyestuffs and finishing products, and consumer products.

BASF is headquartered within its immense facility in Ludwigshafen and derives approximately 1/3 of its sales from Germany and 1/3 from the rest of Europe. Since 1978 BASF has rapidly increased its US presence through a series of acquisitions. Parsippany, New Jersey–based BASF Corporation ($5.4 billion in 1990 sales) is the group's North American arm.

The parent company is spending over $1 billion annually on R&D. The company holds 7,600 patents and patent applications in Germany, 44,500 in other countries. BASF is building a biotech research center in the Boston area.

BASF pretax profits nosedived 37% in 1990. The company blamed a weak US economy, a weak dollar, and higher costs.

Principal exchange: Frankfurt
Fiscal year ends: December 31

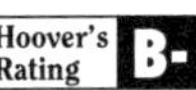

WHO

Chairman of the Supervisory Board: Hans Albers
Chairman of the Board of Executive Directors: Jürgen Strube, age 51
Principal Financial Officer: Max Dietrich Kley
Chairman, President, and CEO, BASF Corp. (US): J. Dieter Stein
Human Resources, BASF AG: Peter Eisenlohr
Auditors: Schitag Schwäbische Treuhand-Aktiengesellschaft; Deloitte Haskins + Sells GmbH
Employees: 134,647

WHEN

Originally known as Badische Anilin & Soda-Fabrik, BASF was founded in Mannheim, Germany, by jeweler Frederick Englehorn in 1861. Unable to find enough land for expansion in Mannheim, BASF moved to nearby Ludwigshafen in 1865. The company was a pioneer in coal tar dyes, developing a very successful synthetic indigo in 1897. BASF's synthetic dyes rapidly replaced more expensive, inconvenient organic dyes.

BASF scientist Fritz Haber synthesized ammonia in 1909, paving the way for the company's entry into nitrogenous fertilizers in 1913. Haber received a Nobel prize in 1919 but later was charged with war crimes for his work with poison gases. BASF continued to grow and concentrated its production at a sprawling manufacturing complex in Ludwigshafen.

Managed by Carl Bosch, another Nobel prize winner, BASF entered into the I.G. Farben cartel with Bayer, Hoechst, and others in 1925, creating a German chemical colossus. Within the cartel BASF developed polystyrene, PVC, and magnetic tape in the 1930s. Part of the Nazi war machine, I.G. Farben manufactured synthetic rubber, using labor from the Auschwitz concentration camp during WWII.

After the war I.G. Farben was dismantled, and in 1952 BASF regained its independence and began rebuilding its war-ravaged factories. Strong postwar domestic demand for basic chemicals aided BASF's recovery. In the late 1950s BASF began joint ventures abroad, including one in the US with Dow Chemical in 1958 (BASF bought out Dow's 1/2 in 1978). The company moved away from coal-based products and into petrochemicals, even acquiring German oil and gas producer Wintershall (1969), and became a leading plastic and synthetic fiber manufacturer.

Acquisitions figured prominently in BASF's global expansion and diversification into related businesses. In the US the company purchased Wyandotte Chemicals (1969); Chemetron (pigments, 1979); Fritzsche, Dodge & Olcott (flavors, fragrances; 1980; sold 1990 to Roche); and Inmont (paint, ink; 1985), among others. Despite its acquisitions and new product releases, BASF remains largely dependent on sales of basic chemicals.

In 1990 BASF's North American unit, BASF Corporation, and its partner, Fuji Photo Film USA, completed a Massachusetts plant for making as many as 90 million computer diskettes a year. That, along with its 1991 purchase of Agfa-Gevaert AG's magnetic media business, made BASF the world's 3rd largest supplier of magnetic media. Canadian operations were combined into a new organization, BASF Canada, to work more closely with US interests (1991).

WHERE

HQ: D-6700 Ludwigshafen, Germany
Phone: 011-49-621-601
Fax: 011-49-621-604-2525
US HQ: BASF Corporation, 8 Campus Dr., Parsippany, NJ 07054
US Phone: 201-397-2700
US Fax: 201-397-2737

BASF manufactures products in 35 countries and sells them in 160 countries.

	1990 Sales	
	DM mil.	% of total
West Germany	15,963	34
Other Europe	15,387	33
North America	9,383	20
Asia, Africa & Australia	3,818	8
Latin America	2,072	5
Total	**46,623**	**100**

WHAT

	1990 Sales	
	DM mil.	% of total
Chemicals	8,653	19
Consumer products	9,648	21
Dyestuffs & finishing products	8,182	17
Plastics	8,162	17
Raw materials & energy	6,973	15
Agricultural chemicals	5,005	11
Total	**46,623**	**100**

Chemicals
Basic and industrial chemicals
Colorants and dyes
Fertilizers
Fibers
Flavors and fragrances
Herbicides
Intermediates

Consumer Products
Antifreeze (Zerex)
Audio- and videotapes
Carpet fibers (Zeftron)
Coatings and paints
Computer diskettes
Pharmaceuticals (Knoll)
Printing inks and plates

Other Products
Coal
Feed additives
Oil and gas (Wintershall)
Plastics
Potash

HOW MUCH

$=DM1.49 (Dec. 31, 1990)	9-Year Growth	1981	1982	1983	1984	1985	1986	1987	1988	1989	1990
Sales (DM mil.)	4.7%	30,865	32,486	35,111	40,400	44,377	40,471	40,238	43,868	47,617	46,623
Net income (DM mil.)	13.1%	367	275	517	895	998	910	1,051	1,410	2,015	1,107
Income as % of sales	—	1.2%	0.8%	1.5%	2.2%	2.2%	2.2%	2.6%	3.2%	4.2%	2.4%
Earnings per share (DM)	8.9%	9	7	12	20	19	17	19	25	35	19
Stock price – high (DM)	—	149	138	176	186	275	332	347	287	315	324
Stock price – low (DM)	—	114	109	118	147	177	239	237	223	256	184
Stock price – close (DM)	4.7%	137	125	176	186	271	276	256	280	300	207
P/E – high	—	17	20	15	9	14	20	18	11	9	17
P/E – low	—	13	16	10	7	9	14	12	9	7	9
Dividends per share (DM)[1]	8.0%	7.0	7.0	5.0	7.0	9.0	10.0	10.0	10.0	12.0	14.0
Book value per share (DM)	4.2%	173	174	180	194	207	217	214	219	243	250

1990 Year-end:
Debt ratio: 14.8%
Return on equity: 7.9%
Cash (mil.): DM5,963
Long-term debt (mil.): DM2,469
No. of shares (mil.): 57
Dividends:
1990 average yield: 6.8%
1990 payout: 72.2%
Market value (mil.): $7,919
Sales (mil.): $31,291

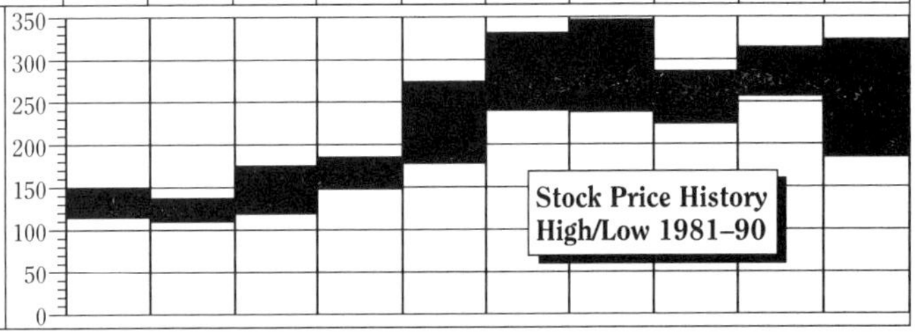

Stock Price History High/Low 1981–90
(scale: 0, 50, 100, 150, 200, 250, 300, 350)

[1] Not including rights offerings

KEY COMPETITORS

Allied-Signal
American Cyanamid
Bayer
Ciba-Geigy
Dow Chemical
Du Pont
Eastman Kodak
Formosa Plastics
Fuji Photo
FMC
W. R. Grace
Hercules
Hoechst
Imperial Chemical
3M
Monsanto
Polaroid
Rhône-Poulenc
Sony
Union Carbide
Oil companies
Other chemical and drug companies

BASS PLC

OVERVIEW

Bass is Britain's leading brewer; a large operator of pubs and restaurants in the UK; the owner of Holiday Inns; and, through its interests in Britvic Soft Drinks Ltd., a major UK soft drink bottler. The company's Carling Black Label, Britain's bestselling beer, is sold in over 36 countries. Bass enjoys extraordinary worker loyalty and a reputation for a strong corporate culture.

Since 1969 the company has diversified into hotels and leisure-related businesses. It has used proceeds from sales of existing, appreciated hotel properties, like its Crest Hotels (sale completed 1990), to lower acquisition-related debt.

Bass's 1990 acquisition of Holiday Inns made it the largest global hotel operator, with over 320,000 rooms worldwide.

NYSE symbol: BAS (ADR)
Fiscal year ends: September 30

WHO

Chairman and CEO: Ian M. G. Prosser, £415,717 pay
Financial Director: Philip Bowman, age 38
Director of Human Resources: P. R. Probert
Auditors: Ernst & Young
Employees: 98,345

WHERE

HQ: 66 Chiltern St., London W1M 1PR, UK
Phone: 011-44-71-486-4440
Fax: 011-44-71-486-7190
US HQ: Holiday Inn Worldwide, 1100 Ashwood Parkway, Suite 200, Atlanta, GA 30338
US Phone: 404-551-3500
US Fax: 404-390-0123

Bass runs 13 breweries and over 4,000 pubs in the UK, and owns, manages, or franchises more than 1,600 hotels in 48 countries.

	1990 Sales		1990 Operating Income	
	£ mil.	% of total	£ mil.	% of total
UK	3,826	86	525	83
Other Europe	219	5	26	4
North America	381	8	72	12
Other countries	35	1	8	1
Adjustments	—	—	(20)	—
Total	**4,461**	**100**	**611**	**100**

WHAT

	1990 Sales		1990 Operating Income	
	£ mil.	% of total	£ mil.	% of total
Brewing	929	21	177	28
Hotels & restaurants	774	17	127	20
Leisure	994	22	64	10
Soft drinks	413	9	43	7
Pub retailing	1,089	25	216	34
Other activities	262	6	4	1
Adjustments	—	—	(20)	—
Total	**4,461**	**100**	**611**	**100**

Beer Brands (UK)
Barbican (nonalcoholic)
Bass
Carling Black Label
Draught Bass
Lamot
Stones
Tennent's
Worthington

Hotels and Restaurants
Holiday Inns
Osprey
Toby Hotels
Toby Restaurants

Soft Drink Bottling (UK)
Britvic
Canada Dry
Pepsi
7-Up
Tango

Leisure
Betting (Coral Racing)
Bingo game promotion on US Indian reservations (British American Bingo)
Juke-box and game-machine rental services for pubs and other outlets

Other
Augustus Barnett (retail liquor)
Bass Developments (property)
Chateau Lascombes (wines)
Delta Biotechnology Ltd. (81%)
Westbay Distributors (20%)

WHEN

In 1777 William Bass decided to switch from transporting beer to brewing it in Burton-on-Trent in England. Burton's pure water supply allowed Bass to brew lighter ales than were being produced in London. In 1827, when Bass's grandson Michael took charge, the company produced 10,000 barrels. In 1876 Bass became the first company to gain trademark protection (for its red triangle) under the British Trademark Registration Act of 1875. By the time of Michael Bass's death in 1884, the 145-acre Bass brewery was the largest ale and bitter brewery in the world.

Most British brewers employed the tied-house system (where breweries controlled and supplied beer to their own pubs), which limited distribution but assured them of a market for their beer. Bass instead opted for the free-trade system, selling its beer through distributors and relying for expansion on consumers' growing demand for Bass beer. The temperance movement and WWI hurt all brewers, and consumers increasingly turned to movies and other diversions instead of spending evenings at the local pub. The tied-house pubs responded by upgrading and improving their facilities to lure customers back, and Bass's sales suffered when the pubs serving its beer failed to follow suit. During the 1920s the company acquired several breweries, including rival Worthington & Company in 1926.

When Sir James Grigg, age 70, took over in 1959, he began looking for a merger partner. Bass merged with efficient regional brewer Mitchells & Butler in 1961. Under Sir Alan Walker the company merged with Charrington United (Carling Black Label lager, pubs; 1967) to form a nationwide network of breweries and pubs. By 1970 Bass's British market share approached 25%. Led by lager, sales boomed.

When growth slowed in the 1980s, Bass sold its less profitable pubs and diversified. The rapid growth of the company's Crest Hotel chain (started in 1969) was augmented by the acquisition of Coral Leisure (hotels, gambling; 1980). Bass acquired Horizon Travel (packaged holidays) in 1987. The company bought the Holiday Inn chain in a series of steps beginning in 1987 and ending in 1990 with the $2.23 billion purchase of all North American Holiday Inns.

Named after the Bing Crosby/Fred Astaire movie, Holiday Inns had been founded in Memphis in 1952 by Kemmons Wilson. Franchises rapidly emerged along US highways, creating one of the world's largest lodging chains. The company bought Harrah's (casinos, 1979) and Granada Royale Hometel (later renamed Embassy Suites, 1984) and started Homewood Suites (1988), all of which were spun off to the company's shareholders as Promus Companies when Bass bought the Holiday Inn chain.

In 1990 the company sold Alex Lichine wines, began a $1 billion renovation of the Holiday Inn chain, and announced that it would dispose of over 3,000 pubs to placate government regulators.

HOW MUCH

£=$1.93 (Dec. 31, 1990)	9-Year Growth	1981	1982	1983	1984	1985	1986	1987	1988	1989	1990
Sales (£ mil.)	11.2%	1,713	1,861	1,988	2,252	2,411	2,710	3,213	3,734	4,036	4,461
Net income (£ mil.)[1]	19.0%	98	95	113	144	165	199	244	307	382	470
Income as % of sales	—	5.7%	5.1%	5.7%	6.2%	6.8%	7.3%	9.0%	8.2%	9.5%	10.5%
Earnings per share (p)	17.7%	31	29	35	44	50	60	72	88	108	134
Stock price – high (p)	—	251	302	346	483	692	840	1,050	867	1,155	1,128
Stock price – low (p)	—	182	196	287	300	472	625	579	733	793	895
Stock price – close (p)	19.8%	207	300	308	483	660	737	819	797	1,053	1,053
P/E – high	—	8	10	10	11	14	14	15	10	11	8
P/E – low	—	6	7	8	7	9	10	8	8	7	7
Dividends per share (p)	14.6%	9.5	10.1	11.4	12.9	14.7	17.0	19.5	23.5	28.2	32.4
Book value per share (p)	11.3%	317	334	354	381	419	438	721	733	792	828

1990 Year-end:
Debt ratio: 53.2%
Return on equity: 16.5%
Cash (mil.): £69
Long-term debt (mil.): £1,555
No. of shares (mil.): 351
Dividends:
1990 average yield: 3.1%
1990 payout: 24.2%
Market value (mil.): $7,133
Sales (mil.): $8,610

Stock Price History High/Low 1981–90
1,200
1,000
800
600
400
200
0

[1] Including extraordinary items

KEY COMPETITORS

Accor
Adolph Coors
Allied-Lyons
Anheuser-Busch
Bally
Bond
BSN
Cadbury Schweppes
Canadian Pacific
Carlsberg
Carlson
Coca-Cola
Dr Pepper/7Up
Edward J. DeBartolo
Foster's Brewing
Grand Metropolitan
Guinness
Heineken
Helmsley
Hilton
Hyatt
John Labatt
Kirin
LVMH
Marriott
Rank
San Miguel
Stroh
Trammell Crow

B.A.T INDUSTRIES PLC

OVERVIEW

Selling over 300 cigarette brands in 160 countries, B.A.T is the leader in cigarette sales outside the US. Major US brands include Kool and Capri. The company owns 40% of Imasco, the dominant Canadian cigarette manufacturer and operator of Shoppers Drug Mart (Canada's largest drugstore chain) and US-based Hardee's. Through its Allied Dunbar (UK) and Farmers Group (US) units, B.A.T is the #1 insurance company in England and #6 in the US.

In 1990 the company completed a restructuring in which it divested its retailing and paper holdings to concentrate exclusively on its tobacco and financial services operations. During the 1990s B.A.T hopes to increase its presence in Asia and such emerging Eastern European markets as Hungary, where the company is laying the foundation for a joint venture with Pecs, Hungary's leading tobacco producer.

WHEN

The British-American Tobacco Company was created to end a cigarette price war in Britain between Imperial Tobacco (UK) and American Tobacco. James Buchanan Duke, creator of American Tobacco and owner of exclusive rights to the best cigarette manufacturing technology of the times, had set his sights on the British market after attaining a 90% share in the US. After a year of vicious price cutting in Britain, Imperial counterattacked in America. The companies called a truce and created a cartel in 1902. The deal granted Imperial the British market, American the US market, and jointly owned British-American the rest of the world, with rights to the brand names of its founders.

With Duke in control, British-American began spreading throughout the world. He had his greatest early success in China, where a massive billboard campaign in 1907 and the distribution of millions of free samples in 1909 generated annual sales of 25 billion cigarettes by 1920. When the Communist Revolution ended British-American's operations in China, the company lost over 25% of its sales.

A 1911 US antitrust action forced American to sell its interest in British-American and opened the US market to the company. The company purchased an American cigarette manufacturer, Brown & Williamson, in 1927 and continued to grow through geographical expansion until the 1960s. Modest diversification efforts in the 1960s included packaging, paper, and cosmetics. The 1902 agreement was terminated in Britain in 1972 with the advent of the EC. British-American's subsequent attempts to penetrate the British market proved unsuccessful, and it withdrew from the market in 1984.

As public concern over smoking mounted, British-American acquired nontobacco businesses and changed its name to B.A.T Industries in 1976. The company bought food retailers in the early 1970s but sold them in the 1980s.

The acquisitions of retailers Saks (1973), Argos (UK, 1979), Marshall Field (1982), and numerous others significantly diversified the company's sales base. B.A.T then developed a taste for insurance companies, acquiring Eagle Star (UK, 1984), Allied Dunbar (UK, 1985), and Farmers Group (US, 1988).

Responding to a 1989 hostile takeover bid from Sir James Goldsmith, B.A.T announced a restructuring plan calling for the spinoff of its British retailers and the sale of all other retail and paper operations, leaving the company with tobacco and financial services. In 1990, after California insurance regulators blocked Goldsmith's attempt to force B.A.T to sell Farmers Group to Axa-Midi (France), Goldsmith abandoned his bid. Meanwhile, B.A.T sold Marshall Field to Minneapolis-based Dayton Hudson for just over $1 billion and Saks to Investcorp, an Arabian partnership, for $1.5 billion. That same year B.A.T spun off its Wiggins Teape Appleton paper operations.

HOW MUCH

Stock prices are for ADRs ADR = 1 share	9-Year Growth	1981	1982	1983	1984	1985	1986	1987	1988	1989	1990
Sales ($ mil.)	—	17,409	18,313	11,574	11,798	12,926	13,580	14,409	14,508	15,281	20,552
Net income ($ mil.)	(0.2%)	695	735	794	908	974	1,176	1,484	1,716	1,892	685
Income as % of sales	—	4.0%	4.0%	6.9%	7.7%	7.5%	8.7%	10.3%	11.8%	12.4%	3.3%
Earnings per share ($)	(0.4%)	0.48	0.51	0.55	0.62	0.66	0.79	1.00	1.14	1.24	0.46
Stock price – high ($)	—	1.84	2.72	2.75	4.25	4.63	7.00	11.56	8.81	15.25	13.88
Stock price – low ($)	—	1.50	1.63	2.00	2.50	3.56	4.19	6.69	6.75	8.00	9.56
Stock price – close ($)	23.6%	1.63	2.47	2.63	4.13	4.50	6.81	8.25	8.06	13.31	10.94
P/E – high	—	4	5	5	7	7	9	12	8	12	30
P/E – low	—	3	3	4	4	5	5	7	6	6	21
Dividends per share ($)	38.8%	0.13	0.12	0.13	0.14	0.19	0.24	0.33	0.41	0.66	2.56
Book value per share ($)	2.9%	2.92	3.03	3.15	3.37	3.59	4.15	4.97	4.28	4.97	3.76

1990 Year-end:
Debt ratio: 40.4%
Return on equity: 10.5%
Cash (mil.): $1,641
Assets (mil.): $48,153
Long-term debt (mil.): $3,761
No. of shares (mil.): 1,473
Dividends:
1990 average yield: 23.4%
1990 payout: —
Market value (mil.): $16,113

Stock Price History High/Low 1981–90

ASE symbol: BTI (ADR)
Fiscal year ends: December 31

Hoover's Rating **C**

WHO

Chairman: Sir Patrick Sheehy, age 60, £521,676 pay
Deputy Chairman: Brian P. Garraway, age 59
Senior Finance and Personnel Director: Martin F. Broughton, age 43
Chairman and CEO, Eagle Star Holdings: Michael A. Butt, age 48
Auditors: Coopers & Lybrand Deloitte
Employees: 217,373

WHERE

HQ: Windsor House, 50 Victoria St., London SW1H 0NL, UK
Phone: 011-44-71-222-7979
Fax: 011-44-71-222-0122
US HQ: BAT Capital Corp., 1600 Summer St., Stamford, CT 06905-5125
US Phone: 203-961-0660
US Fax: 203-964-0418

B.A.T has operations in over 80 countries.

	1990 Sales		1990 Operating Income	
	$ mil.	% of total	$ mil.	% of total
UK	6,964	28	(264)	(14)
Europe	5,814	23	168	9
North America	4,451	18	1,439	76
Other countries	7,550	31	555	29
Adjustments	(4,227)	—	54	—
Total	**20,552**	**100**	**1,952**	**100**

WHAT

	1990 Sales		1990 Operating Income	
	$ mil.	% of total	$ mil.	% of total
Tobacco & trading	7,251	35	1,628	69
General insurance & financial services	4,441	22	181	8
Life insurance	4,823	23	451	19
Disposed businesses	4,200	20	83	4
Adjustments	(163)	—	(391)	—
Total	**20,552**	**100**	**1,952**	**100**

Cigarettes (Non-US Markets)
Belmont
Benson & Hedges
HB
Hollywood
Kent
Lucky Strike
Pall Mall
Plaza
State Express 555

Cigarettes (US Markets)
Barclay
Belair
Capri
Kool
Raleigh
Richland
Viceroy

Major Subsidiaries and Affiliates
Allied Dunbar (insurance, UK)
BAT Cigarettenfabriken (tobacco, West Germany)
British-American Tobacco (UK)
Brown & Williamson Tobacco Corp. (US)
Eagle Star (insurance, UK)
Farmers Group, Inc. (insurance, US)
Imasco (40%; financial services, retailing, and tobacco; Canada)
Investor Guaranty Life (insurance, US)
Ohio State Life (insurance, US)
Souza Cruz (75%, tobacco, Brazil)
WD & HO Wills (67%, tobacco, Australia)

KEY COMPETITORS

Allianz	Imasco	RJR Nabisco
American Brands	Loews	Tokio Marine and Fire
Hanson	Philip Morris	Insurance companies

BAYER AG

OVERVIEW

Bayer is one of the world's largest chemical producers, vying for the top spot with fellow German firms BASF and Hoechst. A diversified, research-driven firm, Bayer manufactures chemicals, plastics, pesticides, herbicides, coatings, drugs, photographic equipment, and consumer products. Better-known US brands include Alka-Seltzer and One-A-Day vitamins.

In WWI the company lost US rights to Bayer aspirin, now owned by Kodak's Sterling Drug unit. In 70 countries Bayer owns the trademark to Aspirin, the world's #1 pain reliever.

Almost 60% of Bayer's sales are outside of Germany. The company has steadily added North American operations such as Mobay, Miles, and Agfa (the product of a merger of Agfa-Gevaert, Matrix Corporation, and Compugraphic). With the 1990 acquisition of the Polysar rubber division of Nova Corporation of Alberta, Bayer emerged as a world leader in the synthetic rubber market.

WHEN

Founded in Wuppertal-Barmen by Friedrich Bayer in 1863, Bayer was among the pioneers of the modern German chemical industry. The company's prolific research labs fueled Bayer's growth beyond its original synthetic dye business, leading to the introduction of such breakthrough compounds as Antinonin (first synthetic pesticide, 1892), aspirin (1899), and synthetic rubber (1915).

Bayer's German heritage figured prominently in its history. During WWI under Carl Duisberg, Bayer is said to have been the source of the first poison gas used by Germany. The US seized Bayer's American operations and trademark rights in 1917, selling them to Sterling Drug (US) in 1918.

Duisberg's desire to eliminate competition led to the merger of Bayer, BASF, Hoechst, and other German chemical concerns into the I.G. Farben Trust in 1925. Photography businesses of Bayer and the other I.G. Farben firms were combined, named Agfa, and folded into the trust. Between the wars Bayer's labs developed a treatment for African sleeping sickness (Germanin, 1921) and the first sulfa drug (Prontosil, 1935), while pioneering in the development of polyurethanes.

The outbreak of WWII found I.G. Farben solidly and profitably in the Nazi camp. The company took over chemical plants of Nazi-occupied countries and established factories near Auschwitz to take advantage of slave labor. I.G. Farben produced the deadly gas used in concentration camps. Twelve I.G. Farben executives were sentenced for war crimes at Nuremberg in 1948. At the end of the war, Bayer lost its 50% interest in Winthrop Laboratories (US) and Bayer of Canada, again to Sterling Drug. The Potsdam Agreement (1945) called for the breakup of I.G. Farben, and in 1951 Bayer emerged as an independent company consisting of many of its original operations, as well as Agfa.

After quickly rebuilding in Germany, Bayer entered into a US joint venture with Monsanto (Mobay, 1954) and later bought Monsanto's share (1967). Rapid postwar economic expansion in Germany and an expanding US economy bolstered Bayer's businesses. In the 1960s Bayer's labs continued to broaden the company's offerings in dyes, plastics, and polyurethanes, and the company built production facilities internationally. Agfa merged with Gevaert (photography, Belgium) in 1964. Bayer retained 60% ownership in Agfa-Gevaert.

Bayer acquired Cutter Labs (drugs, US, 1974), Metzeler (rubber, Germany, 1974), Miles Labs (Alka-Seltzer, Flintstones, One-A-Day vitamins; US; 1978), the rest of Agfa-Gevaert (1981), and Compugraphic and Matrix (electronic imaging, US, 1989). A weak world economy and a strong German mark combined to deflate Bayer pretax profits 18% in 1990.

HOW MUCH

$=DM1.49 (Dec. 31, 1990)	9-Year Growth	1981	1982	1983	1984	1985	1986	1987	1988	1989	1990
Sales (DM mil.)	2.4%	33,742	34,834	37,336	43,032	45,926	38,284	37,143	40,468	43,299	41,643
Net income (DM mil.)	15.7%	506	143	756	1,339	1,259	1,322	1,498	1,855	2,083	1,881
Income as % of sales	—	1.5%	0.4%	2.0%	3.1%	2.7%	3.5%	4.0%	4.6%	4.8%	4.5%
Earnings per share (DM)	4.2%	*20*	*3*	*15*	*26*	*27*	*24*	*24*	*29*	*33*	*29*
Stock price – high (DM)	—	140	207	176	193	276	350	377	311	322	334
Stock price – low (DM)	—	108	104	112	152	185	263	247	237	275	195
Stock price – close (DM)	7.3%	115	114	176	193	276	317	264	307	316	216
P/E – high	—	7	69	12	7	10	15	16	11	10	12
P/E – low	—	5	35	7	6	7	11	10	8	8	7
Dividends per share (DM)[1]	7.1%	7.0	7.0	4.0	7.0	9.0	10.0	10.0	11.0	12.0	13.0
Book value per share (DM)	6.1%	144	139	143	161	191	214	219	233	244	246

1990 Year-end:
Debt ratio: 10.6%
Return on equity: 11.8%
Cash (bil.): DM3.2
Long-term debt (bil.): DM1.9
No. of shares (mil.): 64
Dividends:
1990 average yield: 6.0%
1990 payout: 44.8%
Market value (mil.): $9,263
Sales (mil.): $27,948

Stock Price History High/Low 1981–90

400 350 300 250 200 150 100 50 0

[1]Not including rights offerings

Principal exchange: Frankfurt
Fiscal year ends: December 31

Hoover's Rating **B**

WHO

Chairman: Hermann J. Strenger, age 62
VC: Hermann Wunderlich
Chairman of the Committee of the Board for Finance: Helmut Loehr
Chairman of the Committee of the Board for Human Resources: Klaus Kleine-Weischede
Auditors: Treuhand-Vereinigung Aktiengesellschaft, Wirtschaftsprüfungsgesellschaft und Steuerberatungsgesellschaft
Employees: 171,000

WHERE

HQ: 5090 Leverkusen, Bayerwerk, Germany
Phone: 011-49-2174-301
Fax: 011-49-214-307-894
US HQ: Bayer USA Inc., One Mellon Center, 500 Grant St., Pittsburgh, PA 15219-2502
US Phone: 412-394-5500
US Fax: 412-394-5578

Bayer operates in more than 180 countries.

	1990 Sales		1990 Operating Income	
Point of Origin	**DM mil.**	**% of total**	**DM mil.**	**% of total**
Germany	17,436	42	1,676	47
Other Europe	10,644	26	822	23
North America	8,053	19	597	17
Asia	2,994	7	314	9
Latin America	1,892	5	97	3
Africa	624	1	46	1
Total	**41,643**	**100**	**3,552**	**100**

WHAT

	1990 Sales		1990 Operating Income	
	DM mil.	**% of total**	**DM mil.**	**% of total**
Industrial products	8,134	20	744	21
Health care	8,007	19	1,561	44
Polymers	7,239	17	130	4
Imaging products	7,211	17	390	11
Organic products	5,837	14	324	9
Agrochemicals	5,215	13	403	11
Total	**41,643**	**100**	**3,552**	**100**

Products
Agricultural chemicals
Dyes
Flavors and food additives
Medical imaging systems
Pharmaceuticals
Photographic films and lab equipment (Agfa)
Plastics
Polyurethanes
Rubber
Synthetic fibers
Typesetting and graphics equipment (Agfa, Compugraphic)
Veterinary products (Cutter, Diamond Scientific, Haver)

US Consumer Brands
Alka-Seltzer (antacid)
Bactine (antiseptic)
Cutter (insect repellent)
Domeboro (astringent)
Flintstones (vitamins)
One-A-Day (vitamins)
S.O.S. (soap pads)
Tuffy (scouring pads)

KEY COMPETITORS

American Home Products
BASF
Becton, Dickinson
Bristol-Myers Squibb
Ciba-Geigy
Dow Chemical
Du Pont
Eastman Kodak
Fuji Photo
General Electric
Hercules
Hoechst
Imperial Chemical
IFF
3M
Polaroid
Rhône-Poulenc
Roche
Siemens
SmithKline Beecham
Other chemical, drug, and household goods companies

BAYERISCHE MOTOREN WERKE AG

OVERVIEW

With 1% of the world's auto market, BMW is not an industry giant, but it has been consistently profitable. Its pricey, high-end cars (10% of the luxury segment) appeal to a specific market: in 1989 US BMW car buyers averaged $130,000 in annual income. BMW also builds high-end motorcycles and resumed aircraft engine development in 1990 in a joint venture with Rolls-Royce.

The Quandt family controls 60% of BMW, allowing the company to make large, long-term investments in automotive technology.

Export-dependent BMW is experiencing softness in foreign markets due to slowing economies and a new US tax on luxury cars, but German sales remain strong. Japanese nameplates such as Lexus (Toyota) and Infiniti (Nissan) are expected to challenge BMW in Europe in the 1990s. Despite the disdain for Japanese automakers expressed by Chairman Eberhard von Kuenheim, the company is taking the threat seriously and hopes that its recently launched, lower-priced models will win over entry-level luxury car buyers.

WHEN

Traces of BMW's origin may be found in its logo: a rotating propeller in blue and white, the colors of Bavaria. In 1913 Karl Rapp opened an aircraft engine design shop near a Munich airfield. Rapp named his organization Bayerische Motoren Werke (BMW) in 1917. Following WWI, the Treaty of Versailles brought German aircraft production to a halt and BMW was forced to make railway brakes.

After BMW was permitted to resume aircraft engine production, sales took off and grew through the 1930s. BMW introduced its first motorcycle, the R32, in 1923. A very successful product, the R32 held world speed records from 1929 to 1937. BMW entered automaking in 1928 by buying struggling Fahrzeugwerke Eisenach, a company making a small car under license from Austin (UK).

Beginning in 1933 BMW launched a successful series of larger and sportier cars. Hitler forced BMW to build aircraft engines for the Luftwaffe in the 1930s and stopped all auto and motorcycle production in 1941. BMW leader Josef Popp resisted and was forced to resign. In support of the Nazis, BMW operated plants in occupied countries, developed the world's first production jet engine, and built rockets.

With its factories dismantled following WWII, BMW survived by making kitchen and garden equipment. In 1948 the company introduced a one-cylinder motorcycle built from dealer-supplied parts. Cheap transportation was in demand in postwar Germany and the motorcycle sold well. BMW autos launched in the 1950s, too large and expensive for postwar Germany, sold poorly. Motorcycle sales began to decline and, in the late 1950s, BMW barely escaped extinction by launching the modestly successful Isetta, a 7 1/2-foot-long "bubble car."

In 1959 Herbert Quandt bailed out BMW by buying control of it for $1 million. Quandt's BMW concentrated on sports sedans, releasing the first of the "New Range" of BMWs in 1961. Success of the niche strategy enabled BMW to expand production by purchasing ailing automaker Hans Glas in 1966.

In the 1970s BMW's European exports soared, and the company set up its own distribution subsidiary in the US. The release of the larger 5 Series cars placed BMW more squarely in competition with Mercedes-Benz.

Rapid auto export growth continued in the 1980s, particularly in the US, Asia, and Australia, but motorcycle sales fell victim to Japanese competition and slackening demand for motorcycles as basic transportation in industrialized countries. The launch of the luxury 7 Series autos in 1986 intensified the BMW-Mercedes rivalry. US sales have dropped since 1986 as the DM appreciated and Japanese offerings lured auto shoppers from BMW showrooms.

HOW MUCH

$=DM1.49 (Dec. 31, 1990)	9-Year Growth	1981	1982	1983	1984	1985	1986	1987	1988	1989	1990
Sales (DM mil.)	12.3%	9,545	11,620	14,026	16,484	18,078	17,515	19,460	24,467	26,515	27,178
Net income (DM mil.)[1]	—	145	200	288	330	300	338	375	447	557	691
Income as % of sales	—	1.5%	1.7%	2.1%	2.0%	1.7%	1.9%	1.9%	1.8%	2.1%	2.5%
Earnings per share (DM)	—	—	—	—	—	—	—	—	30	36	44
Stock price – high (DM)	—	201	228	437	453	603	645	787	554	640	658
Stock price – low (DM)	—	144	176	222	291	351	473	383	429	496	379
Stock price – close (DM)	8.3%	191	228	437	372	570	584	447	525	567	393
P/E – high	—	—	—	—	—	—	—	—	18	18	15
P/E – low	—	—	—	—	—	—	—	—	14	14	9
Dividends per share (DM)[2]	2.5%	10.0	9.0	10.0	12.0	12.5	12.5	12.5	12.5	12.5	12.5
Book value per share (DM)	—	—	—	—	—	—	—	—	323	349	370

1990 Year-end:
Debt ratio: 99.6%
Return on equity: 12.2%
Cash (mil.): DM4,344
Long-term debt (mil.): DM1,500
No. of shares (mil.): 15
Dividends:
1990 average yield: 3.2%
1990 payout: 28.4%
Market value (mil.): $3,956
Sales (mil.): $18,240

Stock Price History High/Low 1981–90

800, 700, 600, 500, 400, 300, 200, 100, 0

[1] Foreign subsidiaries not consolidated 1981–87 [2] Not including rights issues

Principal exchange: Frankfurt
Fiscal year ends: December 31

WHO

Chairman, Supervisory Board: Hans Graf von der Goltz

Chairman, Board of Management: Eberhard von Kuenheim, age 61

President and CEO, BMW of North America, Inc.: Karl Gerlinger, age 52

Auditors: KPMG Deutsche Treuhand-Gesellschaft

Employees: 70,948

WHERE

HQ: POB 40 02 40, Petuelring 130, D-8000 Munich 40, Germany

Phone: 011-49-89-38-95-0

Fax: 011-49-89-3-59-36-22

US HQ: BMW of North America, Inc., PO Box 1227, Westwood, NJ 07675-1227

US Phone: 201-307-4000

US Fax: 201-307-4004 (Corporate Comm.)

BMW operates 10 plants in Germany, Austria, and South Africa.

	1990 Sales	
	DM mil.	% of total
Germany	10,453	38
Other Europe	8,572	32
Other countries	8,153	30
Total	**27,178**	**100**

WHAT

	1990 Sales	
	DM mil.	% of total
Automobiles	20,886	77
Motorcycles	384	1
Leasing	1,925	7
Other	3,983	15
Total	**27,178**	**100**

Vehicle Models (US Markets)

Automobiles
- 318i
- 318is
- 325i
- 525i
- 535i
- 735i
- 735iL
- 750iL
- 850i
- M3
- M5

Motorcycles
- K1
- K75
- K100
- R100

Other

BMW Fahrzeugtechnik GmbH (special-purpose tools)
BMW Motoren Gesellschaft m.b.H. (engines)
BMW Rolls-Royce GmbH (50.5%, aircraft engines)
Kontron GmbH (scientific electronic equipment)

KEY COMPETITORS

Chrysler
Daewoo
Daimler-Benz
Fiat
Ford
General Motors
Harley-Davidson
Honda
Hyundai
Isuzu
Mazda
Mitsubishi
Nissan
Peugeot
Renault
Saab-Scania
Suzuki
Toyota
Volkswagen
Volvo
Yamaha

BCE INC.

OVERVIEW

Montreal-based BCE is the holding company that includes Bell Canada, the largest telephone company in Canada. BCE is the largest private employer in Canada and the most widely held Canadian stock. Bell Canada and its sister BCE phone companies reach out and touch more than 2/3 of Canada's population, but local phone companies' monopoly of long distance service is being challenged by Unitel, a company that has applied to regulators for permission to compete, hoping to do for Canadian long distance what MCI did for the US. Unitel is a joint venture of Rogers Communications and Canadian Pacific.

BCE owns 53.1% of Northern Telecom, North America's 2nd largest telecommunications manufacturer after AT&T. Northern Telecom and Bell Canada own Bell-Northern Research, the largest Canadian R&D organization. Other BCE subsidiaries offer mobile telephone service, design and develop advanced telecommunications equipment, publish directories, and perform telecommunications consulting in a number of foreign countries.

BCE also owns Montreal Trustco Inc., one of Canada's oldest and most prestigious financial institutions. The company believes the financial services industry's growing reliance on telecommunications creates a logical link. BCE is untangling itself from an unsuccessful foray into real estate (BCE Development, investment written off in 1989) and short-lived diversification into energy (TransCanada PipeLines, sale of BCE's stake began in 1990).

WHEN

Bell Telephone Company of Canada traces its history to Alexander Graham Bell's father, who took his son's invention north. Bell of Canada was created by Parliament in 1880 to consolidate several smaller companies. Bell interests in the US originally owned part of the company, but AT&T, successor to the Bell companies, severed all ties in 1975. Bell Canada performed its role as a regional provider of telephone service for many years, and mergers with smaller telephone exchanges beginning in 1954 increased its presence in Canada.

Bell acquired a 90% interest in Northern Electric (small equipment, 1957) from AT&T's Western Electric, completing the buyout in 1964. As Canada's telecommunications needs grew and the technology became more complex, Bell branched out into related areas, including investment in a satellite joint venture (Telesat, 1970) and the formation of Bell Northern Research (1971) to direct R&D. Tele-Direct, established in 1971, consolidated the company's directory publishing operations. Bell reduced its ownership in Northern Electric to 69% (1975) and changed the manufacturer's name to Northern Telecom (1976). Also in 1976 Bell formed Bell Canada International to provide international telecommunications consulting.

In response to proposed legislation that would have calculated manufacturing profits in phone rate formulas, Bell Canada in 1983 created Bell Canada Enterprises (renamed BCE Inc., 1988) to act as a parent company and to separate unregulated businesses from the local regulated telephone carriers.

BCE bought 42% of TransCanada PipeLines (natural gas transmission, 1983, later increased to 49%) and branched into real estate with the purchase of 68% of Daon Development (1985, renamed BCE Development). CEO Raymond Cyr reversed course when the real estate operation hemorrhaged money. BCE took a $440 million loss when it wrote off its investment (1989).

BCE spun off its holdings in Encor, an oil-and-gas firm; sold 1/2 its stake in TransCanada to underwriters (1990); and issued warrants to sell the other 1/2. In late 1990 Northern Telecom announced its purchase of the UK's STC, the world's 12th largest telecommunications equipment manufacturer.

HOW MUCH

	9-Year Growth	1981	1982	1983	1984	1985	1986	1987	1988	1989	1990
Sales ($ mil.)	10.9%	6,230	6,838	7,135	8,008	9,479	10,116	11,267	12,788	14,406	15,832
Net income ($ mil.)	8.8%	464	506	599	712	751	743	836	744	1,037	988
Income as % of sales	—	7.5%	7.4%	8.4%	8.9%	7.9%	7.3%	7.4%	5.8%	7.2%	6.2%
Earnings per share ($)	2.4%	2.44	2.46	2.71	2.97	2.95	2.74	2.96	2.59	3.38	3.02
Stock price – high ($)	—	17.13	19.75	27.13	27.13	33.00	30.00	33.38	32.63	39.38	40.00
Stock price – low ($)	—	14.13	13.25	18.13	22.38	26.00	24.88	23.50	28.13	30.50	30.25
Stock price – close ($)	8.5%	16.38	19.75	27.00	26.88	30.13	27.00	28.50	31.25	39.25	34.13
P/E – high	—	7	8	10	9	11	11	11	13	12	13
P/E – low	—	6	5	7	8	9	9	8	11	9	10
Dividends per share ($)	3.9%	1.54	1.61	1.71	1.70	1.66	1.70	1.82	2.00	2.10	2.16
Book value per share ($)	5.0%	18.33	18.43	19.84	20.48	21.24	22.90	25.34	27.09	27.30	28.47

1990 Year-end:
Debt ratio: 52.5%
Return on equity: 10.8%
Cash (mil.): $1,151
Assets (mil.): $36,180
Long-term debt (bil.): $10.8
No. of shares (mil.): 305
Dividends:
1990 average yield: 6.3%
1990 payout: 71.7%
Market value (mil.): $10,422

Stock Price History High/Low 1981–90

NYSE symbol: BCE
Fiscal year ends: December 31

WHO

Chairman and CEO: Joseph Victor Raymond Cyr, age 57, C$1,331,100 pay
President and COO: L. R. "Red" Wilson, age 50, C$131,000 pay (for 2 months of 1990)
VP and Comptroller: Donald R. Newman, age 63
Director of Personnel: Ginette Seguin
Auditors: Deloitte & Touche
Employees: 119,000

WHERE

HQ: 2000 McGill College Ave., Suite 2100, Montreal, Quebec H3A 3H7, Canada
Phone: 514-499-7000
Fax: 514-499-7098 (Investor Relations)

BCE provides local phone service to most of Canada and sells equipment and services worldwide.

	1990 Sales		1990 Operating Income	
	$ mil.	% of total	$ mil.	% of total
Canada	11,173	70	2,720	71
US	4,247	27	1,117	29
Other countries	412	3	1	—
Adjustments	—	—	(161)	—
Total	**15,832**	**100**	**3,677**	**100**

WHAT

	1990 Sales		1990 Operating Income	
	$ mil.	% of total	$ mil.	% of total
Telecommunications services	7,297	46	1,875	71
Telecommunications equip.	6,765	43	675	26
Financial services	1,357	8	53	2
Other operations	413	3	34	1
Adjustments	—	—	1,040	—
Total	**15,832**	**100**	**3,677**	**100**

Subsidiaries and Affiliates

BCE Mobile Communications Inc. (69.7%)
BCE Telecom International Inc. (global telecommunications consulting)
Bell Canada, other carriers
- Maritime Telegraph and Telephone Co. and the Island Telephone Co. Ltd. (33.8%)
- The New Brunswick Telephone Co. Ltd. (31.4%)
- Newfoundland Telephone Co. Ltd. (55.7%)
- Northern Telephone Ltd. (99.9%)
- Northwestel Inc.
- Télébec Ltée

Bell Canada International (telecomm. consulting)
Bell-Northern Research Ltd. (systems research and development)
Memotec Data, Inc. (31.5%, overseas telecommunications and computers, Teleglobe Canada)
Montreal Trustco, Inc. (commercial and individual banking)
Northern Telecom (53.1%, telecommunications equipment)
Quebecor Inc. (21.6%, publishing)
STC (100% owned by Northern Telecom, communications)
Tele-Direct (Publications) Inc. (directories)
Videotron Corporation Ltd. (30%, cable TV, UK)

KEY COMPETITORS

Alcatel Alsthom
AT&T
British Telecom
Cable & Wireless
Campeau
Canadian Imperial
Canadian Pacific
Ericsson
Fujitsu
GTE
Imasco
Motorola
NEC
Oki
Philips
Royal Bank
Siemens

BERTELSMANN AG

OVERVIEW

Based in Gütersloh, Germany, Bertelsmann is the world's largest media company. It owns US publishers Bantam Books, Doubleday Publishing, and Dell Publishing, which together form one of the world's largest English-language trade book publishing groups. Gruner + Jahr (Europe's #1 publisher) publishes magazines in Germany (*Stern*, *Brigitte*), France (*Prima*), Italy (*Viva*), the UK (*best*), Spain (*Mia*), and the US (*Parents*, *ym*). Other activities include reference book and map publishing, paper production, and printing. Bertelsmann is also the world's largest book club operator, with more than 20 million members.

Bertelsmann's record labels include RCA and Arista in the US, BMG Ariola in Europe, and BMG Victor in Japan. The company is increasingly moving into TV broadcasting in Germany, owning a stake in RTL plus network and in the new pay TV channel Premiere.

With a solid balance sheet and low debt (compared to other media giants), Bertelsmann is poised to expand across the US and Europe, especially in eastern Germany, where the company plans to invest DM1 billion over the next 3 or 4 years. Although the company's stock is not publicly traded, nonvoting shares, known as profit-sharing certificates, are available on German exchanges. More than 40% are owned by Bertelsmann's employees. Chairman Reinhard Mohn, who has been with the company since WWII, controls all of its voting shares; he announced in 1988 that he will leave his fortune to charity.

WHEN

Carl Bertelsmann founded the publishing company that bears his name in Gütersloh, Germany, in 1835. One of his first books (a hymnal) was successful enough to allow the company to grow despite the poverty and low literacy in Germany at the time. Bertelsmann continued to thrive primarily as a publisher of religious books until WWII, when the Nazis shut it down.

Reinhard Mohn, whose grandfather had married Bertelsmann's granddaughter, was captured by the Allies while fighting for the Germans. He spent the remainder of the war in a Kansas POW camp, returning to Germany to find that Bertelsmann's Gütersloh plant had been destroyed. Mohn rebuilt the plant and was back in the publishing business by 1948.

Bertelsmann started Lesering, Germany's first book club, in 1950, followed by a record club in the late 1950s. The company bought Germany's UFA (TV and film production, 1964) and 25% of Gruner + Jahr (publisher of *Stern* and *Der Spiegel*, 1969; raised to a controlling interest, 1973). In the US, Bertelsmann bought 51% of Bantam Books in 1977 (and the remaining stock in 1981) and Arista Records in 1979, using these companies in 1980 to launch its US club, American Circle, which folded after 4 years of losses.

In 1981 Mark Wössner succeeded Mohn as CEO. Under Wössner, Bertelsmann increased its presence in the US music and publishing markets in 1986, when it bought RCA Records and control of Doubleday. Founded in 1897 by Frank Doubleday, Doubleday had grown to become one of America's largest publishers, mainly through its strength in hardbacks, Dell paperbacks, and book clubs. The company also owned the New York Mets, which the family, descendants of baseball inventor Abner Doubleday, had bought in 1980. Bertelsmann did not get the Mets when it bought Doubleday, and it was criticized for paying too much for Doubleday's publishing businesses, whose reputation had been soiled in the early 1980s by the poor quality of its books.

Bertelsmann did not enjoy as much success as hoped with its US operations. The book clubs that had once provided Doubleday with 35% of its profits lost thousands of members, prompting Bertelsmann to state that it would develop new activities in the US through joint ventures rather than large acquisitions. In 1990 Bertelsmann sold Doubleday Book Shops to B. Dalton and shut down its UK book club, Leisure Circle, leaving a near monopoly in that market to another Bertelsmann affiliate, Book Club Associates. That same year Gruner + Jahr, in partnership with Robert Maxwell, agreed to buy East Berlin magazine and newspaper publisher Berliner Verlag; Bertelsmann bought eastern Germany's largest book printer, Pössneck.

In 1991 Bertelsmann announced a possible record company venture with MCA (owned by Japan's Matsushita). The company now distributes MCA records outside the US.

HOW MUCH

$=DM1.49 (Dec. 31, 1990)	9-Year Growth	1981	1982	1983	1984	1985	1986	1987	1988	1989	1990
Sales (DM mil.)	10.1%	5,588	6,036	6,218	6,716	7,441	7,602	9,160	11,299	12,483	13,313
Net income (DM mil.)	26.2%	63	105	159	289	337	329	207	362	402	510
Income as % of sales	—	1.1%	1.7%	2.6%	4.3%	4.5%	4.3%	2.3%	3.2%	3.2%	3.8%
Employees	4.2%	30,110	29,527	30,948	31,639	31,835	31,593	42,013	41,961	43,702	43,509

1990 Year-end:
Debt ratio: 22.7%
Return on equity: 25.4%
Cash (mil.): DM161
Current ratio: 1.10
Long-term debt (mil.): DM544
Sales ($ mil.): $8,935

Net Income (DM mil.) 1981–90

Private company
Fiscal year ends: June 30

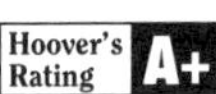

WHO

Chairman: Reinhard Mohn, age 71
President and CEO: Mark Wössner, age 53
CFO: Siegfried Luther
Head of Central Personnel: George Türnau
Auditors: KPMG TREUVERKEHR Aktiengesellschaft, Wirtschaftsprüfungsgesellschaft
Employees: 43,509

WHERE

HQ: Carl-Bertelsmann-Strasse 270, Postfach 55 55, D-4830 Gütersloh 100, Germany
Phone: 011-49-52-41-80-0
Fax: 011-49-52-41-7-51-66
US HQ: Bertelsmann, Inc., 666 Fifth Ave., New York, NY 10103
US Phone: 212-391-0143
US Fax: 212-391-1874

	1990 Sales	
	DM mil.	% of total
Germany	4,355	33
Other countries	8,958	67
Total	**13,313**	**100**

WHAT

	1990 Sales	
	DM mil.	% of total
Book & record clubs	3,126	22
Publishing	1,527	11
Printing & manufacturing	2,654	18
Music & video	3,391	24
Electronic media	570	4
Gruner + Jahr	3,100	21
Adjustments	(1,055)	—
Total	**13,313**	**100**

Book and Record Clubs
Bertelsmann Club (Ger.)
Book Club Associates (50%, UK)
Doubleday Book & Music Clubs (US; 49%, Canada)

Publishing
Bantam Doubleday Dell
European Law Press
Transworld Publishers

Printing and Manufacturing
Belser Offsetdruck
Bertelsmann Printing & Manufacturing (US)
Cartiere del Garda (paper manufacturing, Italy)

Music and Video
Arista Records
BMG Ariola
BMG Music Publishing
BMG Victor
BMG Video
RCA Records/BMG Classics
UFA Video

Electronic Media
Premiere
Radio Hamburg (29.2%)
RTL plus (39%, TV)
Ufa Filmproduktion

Gruner + Jahr Magazines
best (UK)
Brigitte (Germany)
Der Spiegel (24.9%, Germany)
Estar Viva (Spain)
Femme Actuelle (France)
Geo (France, Germany, Spain)
Mia (Spain)
Parents (US)
Prima (France, UK)
Stern (Germany)
ym (*Young Miss*, US)

Gruner + Jahr Newspapers
Berliner Zeitung
Berliner Zeitung am Abend
Chemnitzer Morgenpost
Dresdner Morgenpost
Hamburger Morgenpost

KEY COMPETITORS

Advance Publications
Capital Cities/ABC
Commerce Clearing House
R. R. Donnelley
Hachette
Hearst
Knight-Ridder
Matsushita
Maxwell
McGraw-Hill
News Corp.
Paramount
Pearson
Philips
Reader's Digest
Reed
Sony
Thomson Corp.
Time Warner

BOND CORPORATION HOLDINGS LTD.

OVERVIEW

The sun is setting on Bond Corporation, the crumbling Australian conglomerate that was once a force in brewing, media, energy, and real estate. Under former kingpin Alan Bond, the 1983 America's Cup winner who held 58% of its shares, the company accumulated a $10 billion debt. It now finds itself at the mercy of its many creditors.

Bond has been forced to shed assets in an attempt to stay alive. Recent disposals include its Australian brewing operations (Castlemaine Perkins, Tooheys, and Swan), its energy interests (petroleum, minerals, and coal mining), and its interest in a Chilean phone company, among others.

Bond's brewing operations once ranked #6 in the world but now are primarily limited to the US, where it produces such noted beers as Colt 45, Lone Star, Old Style, and Iron City, all through its G. Heileman subsidiary, which filed for bankruptcy in 1991.

The company has recently been trying to appease its creditors with a shares-for-debt scheme to dodge impending liquidation.

WHEN

In 1951 the family of 13-year-old Alan Bond emigrated from Britain to Australia. The following year Bond dropped out of school and went to work as a sign painter in Fremantle. With a few hundred dollars borrowed from his relatives, Bond invested in land and by age 21 had earned his first million in real estate.

In 1959 Bond formed Progress Development Organisation and gradually acquired interests in 14 other companies. In 1969 Bond incorporated his holdings as West Australian Land Holdings (name changed to Bond Corporation Holdings in 1974).

In 1982 Bond made his first foray into brewing when he acquired the Swan Brewery Company of Perth, after it had asked his help in fending off a takeover attempt. Bond became a major sports figure the next year when he won the America's Cup with his yacht, the *Australia II*.

In 1985 Bond expanded his beer holdings by purchasing Castlemaine Tooheys, a Brisbane brewer. The purchase, combined with Swan, gave Bond control of about 42% of the Australian beer market and set the company squarely against Carlton and United Breweries, Australia's other major brewer (now owned by Foster's Brewing). With a fair segment of the Australian market secured, Bond turned his attention to the US, buying Pittsburgh Brewing (Iron City beer) in 1986.

In 1987 the company launched its most ambitious acquisition attempt, against Wisconsin-based Heileman, then the US's 4th largest brewer. Heileman had been founded as the City Brewery in 1853 by Gottlieb Heileman and John Gund. After Heileman's death his wife Johanna took charge of the brewery and introduced Heileman's popular Old Style beer in 1902. Heileman remained a predominantly local brewer until 1959, when it launched a 21-year buying spree in which it purchased 13 regional breweries across the US.

Bond maintained its rapid-fire acquisition pace in 1988 with the purchases of Australia's Bell Group, New York's St. Moritz hotel, and a stake in British Satellite Broadcasting. The combined purchases ballooned the company's debt to around $10 billion.

Following a horrendous year in 1989 in which he lost A$814 million, Bond entered the 1990s under fire from his creditors (the company was even put into receivership for a couple of months) and stepped down as chairman to facilitate a needed restructuring. In 1991 Heileman filed for bankruptcy. That same year Heileman came under fire when it announced the launching of a high-alcohol malt liquor (PowerMaster) aimed at low-income, inner-city blacks. Amidst severe criticism, the company abandoned the project.

HOW MUCH

$=A$1.29 (Dec. 31, 1990)	9-Year Growth	1981	1982	1983	1984	1985	1986	1987	1988	1989	1990[1]
Sales (A$ mil.)	—	279	244	309	365	518	1,601	2,282	5,009	8,482	9,480
Net income (A$ mil.)	—	11	4	7	9	20	103	161	274	(980)	(1,066)
Income as % of sales	—	3.9%	1.6%	2.3%	2.5%	3.9%	6.4%	7.1%	5.5%	(11.6%)	(11.2%)
Earnings per share (A$)	—	—	0.02	0.02	(0.07)	(0.03)	0.17	0.25	0.65	(2.32)	(2.52)
Stock price – high (A$)	—	1.60	1.04	0.56	0.66	1.17	2.16	2.05	2.30	1.85	—
Stock price – low (A$)	—	0.81	0.34	0.07	0.44	0.37	0.60	0.97	1.25	0.13	—
Stock price – close (A$)	—	1.02	0.38	0.51	0.45	0.70	1.53	1.25	1.85	0.13	—
P/E – high	—	—	52	28	—	—	13	8	4	—	—
P/E – low	—	—	17	4	—	—	4	4	2	—	—
Dividends per share (A$)	(100%)	2.51	2.51	2.51	2.50	4.03	5.29	7.64	0.14	0.08	0.00
Book value per share (A$)	—	2.97	3.00	3.44	3.43	1.77	1.83	1.77	2.11	(0.27)	(3.05)

1990 Year-end:
Return on equity: —
Cash (mil.): A$44
Current ratio: 0.14
Long-term debt (mil.): A$172
No. of shares (mil.): 423
Dividends:
1990 average yield: —
1990 payout: —
Market value (mil.): —
Sales (mil.): $7,349[1]

Note: Stock delisted in 1990 [1] 15-month period

Trading suspended
Fiscal year ends: First Friday in October

WHO

Chairman: Peter Lucas
Executive Director: Zoltan Merszei
Executive Director: Kim McGrath
Executive Director: James Rawlings
Chief Executive Finance & Administration: Antony Oates
Auditors: Arthur Andersen & Co.
Employees: 23,000

WHERE

HQ: Level 43, R&I Bank Tower, 108 St. George's Terrace, Perth, Western Australia, 6000, Australia
Phone: 011-61-9-324-6000
Fax: 011-61-9-324-6081
US HQ: 135 East 57th St., 31st Floor, New York, NY 10022
US Phone: 212-223-4202
US Fax: 212-599-6095

	1990 Sales	
	A$ mil.	% of total
Australia	6,925	73
US	1,688	18
Other	867	9
Total	**9,480**	**100**

WHAT

	1990 Sales	
	A$ mil.	% of total
International brewing	1,441	15
Property	977	11
Print media	308	3
Unallocated	6,754	71
Total	**9,480**	**100**

US Beer Brands
Black Label
Blatz
Champale
Christian Schmidt
Colt 45
Henry Weinhard's
Iron City
Jacob Schmidt
Lone Star
Mickeys Malt Liquor
Old Style
Rainier
Special Export

Associated Companies
Airship Industries Ltd. (48%)
The Bell Group Ltd. (75%)
Bond Finance (Europe) Ltd. (50%)
Bridgefoot Investments Ltd. (36%)
Community Newspapers (1985) Ltd. (36%)
G. Heileman Brewing Company, Inc. (US)
Kona Kai Resort (US)
Limgold Property Ltd. (50%)
Parich Ltd. (50%, property development)
Pittsburgh Brewing Company (US)
Pulpit Property Ltd. (50%)
Seabrook Corporation Ltd. (50%, property development)

KEY COMPETITORS

Adolph Coors
Allied-Lyons
Anheuser-Busch
Bass
BSN
Carlsberg
Foster's Brewing
Guinness
Heineken
John Labatt
Kirin
Philip Morris
San Miguel
Stroh

BRIDGESTONE CORPORATION

OVERVIEW

Bridgestone, the world's #3 tire maker after Michelin and Goodyear, is #1 in Japan and #3 in the US. The company is also Japan's largest bicycle manufacturer and makes sporting goods, lithium batteries, weighing systems, and various rubber products. Bridgestone operates 1,550 MasterCare auto service centers in North America through its Bridgestone/Firestone subsidiary. The company houses one of the world's largest private collections of Impressionist art in its Tokyo museum.

Bridgestone President Akira Yeiri (who has never had a driver's license) has installed new management at money-losing Bridgestone/Firestone. The 1988 Firestone acquisition has proven costly for Bridgestone, and not simply because of industry-wide overcapacity and price-cutting. After failing to survey Firestone's plants prior to the purchase, Bridgestone is spending more than anticipated on upgrading its factories. Bridgestone is still mulling the consolidation of Bridgestone and Firestone sales organizations in the US.

Business is better in Asia, where Bridgestone is dominant, but competition in Japan is expected to intensify when Michelin begins Japanese production in late 1991.

Principal exchange: Tokyo
Fiscal year ends: December 31

WHO

President: Akira Yeiri, age 63
EVP Bridgestone/Firestone Operations: Yoichiro Kaizaki
EVP Finance Bridgestone/Firestone, Inc.: Kenzo Matsuo
Director, Human Resources Divison: Hisamitsu Koshio
Auditors: Asahi Shinwa & Co.
Employees: 95,276

WHEN

In 1906 on the southern Japanese island of Kyushu, Shojiro Ishibashi and his brother, Tokujiro, assumed control of their family's clothing business. They focused on making *tabi*, traditional Japanese footwear, and in 1923 they began working with rubber for soles. In 1931 Shojiro Ishibashi formed Bridgestone (Ishibashi means "stone bridge" in Japanese) to make tires. In the 1930s Bridgestone began producing auto tires, airplane tires, and golf balls. The company followed the Japanese military to occupied territories and built plants there. Ishibashi moved Bridgestone's headquarters to Tokyo in 1937.

Although Bridgestone lost all of its overseas factories in WWII, the Japanese plants escaped damage. The company began making bicycles (1946) and signed a technical assistance pact with Goodyear (1951), enabling Bridgestone to import badly needed technology. In the 1950s and 1960s, Bridgestone started making nylon tires and radials and again set up facilities overseas, mostly in Asia. The company benefited from the rapid growth in Japanese auto sales in the 1970s. Shojiro Ishibashi died at age 87 in 1976.

In 1983 Bridgestone bought a plant in LaVergne, Tennessee, from the venerable US tire maker Firestone. Harvey Firestone had founded his tire business in 1900 and expanded with the auto industry in the US. In the 1920s he leased one million acres in Liberia for rubber plantations and established a chain of auto supply and service outlets. After WWII Firestone started making synthetic rubber and automotive components, expanded overseas, and acquired US tire producers Dayton Tire & Rubber and Seiberling. In the 1980s Firestone chairman John Nevin sought to maximize shareholder return by cutting costs, closing plants, lowering capital spending, and focusing on retail operations.

Bridgestone had strong sales to Japanese carmakers but little US retail exposure to the more lucrative aftermarket and no US production capacity prior to the purchase of the Firestone plant. In 1988 Bridgestone topped a bid by Pirelli and bought the rest of Firestone for $2.6 billion, valuing the tire maker at a lofty 26 times earnings. Simultaneously, General Motors announced that Firestone would be dropped as a supplier. Bridgestone/Firestone has compensated for the 10% loss in volume by selling more tires through mass-market retailers. It also began selling tires to GM's Saturn Corporation in 1990.

Civil war in Liberia forced Bridgestone/Firestone to temporarily abandon its huge Liberian rubber plantation in 1990.

WHERE

HQ: Ishibashi, 10-1, Kyobashi 1-chome, Chuo-ku, Tokyo 104, Japan
Phone: 011-81-3-3567-0111
Fax: 011-81-3-3535-2553
US HQ: Bridgestone/Firestone, Inc., One Bridgestone Park, PO Box 140991, Nashville, TN 37214-0991
US Phone: 615-391-0088
US Fax: 615-872-2621

Bridgestone has manufacturing facilities on 6 continents and sells its products worldwide. US manufacturing plants are located in LaVergne and Morrison, TN; Decatur, IL; Wilson, NC; Des Moines, IA; Oklahoma City, OK; and Russellville, AR.

	1990 Sales	
	¥ bil.	% of total
Japan	759	43
Other countries	1,025	57
Total	**1,784**	**100**

WHAT

	1990 Sales	
	¥ bil.	% of total
Tire operations	1,291	72
Other products	493	28
Total	**1,784**	**100**

Products
Batteries
Bicycles (Bridgestone)
Ceramic foam
Fitness facilities
Golf and tennis equip.
Industrial rubber prods.
- Belts and hoses
- Inflatable rubber dams
- Marine products
- Multirubber bearings
- Rubber crawlers
- Vibration-isolating and noise-insulating materials

Waterproofing materials
Polyurethane foam products
Roofing and flooring materials
Steel fiber for concrete reinforcement
Tires (Bridgestone, Firestone)
Tire tubes
Water tanks
Weighing systems
Wheels

Retailing
MasterCare auto service centers

KEY COMPETITORS

Bally
Brunswick
Goodyear
Kmart
Michelin
Montgomery Ward
Peugeot
Pirelli
Premark
Sears
Sumitomo
Whitman

HOW MUCH

$=¥135 (Dec. 31, 1990)	9-Year Growth	1981	1982	1983	1984	1985	1986	1987	1988	1989	1990
Sales (¥ bil.)	10.5%	724	712	762	802	864	793	820	1,191	1,689	1,784
Net income (¥ bil.)	(13.0%)	16	13	19	16	21	21	36	40	10	5
Income as % of sales	—	2.2%	1.8%	2.5%	2.0%	2.4%	2.6%	4.4%	3.4%	0.6%	0.3%
Earnings per share (¥)	(13.9%)	23	20	28	24	32	30	54	59	13	6
Stock price – high (¥)	—	473	411	530	544	484	646	1,318	1,436	2,070	1,740
Stock price – low (¥)	—	352	330	360	421	412	421	545	1,036	1,330	985
Stock price – close (¥)	12.0%	356	405	530	426	431	599	1,045	1,360	1,690	990
P/E – high	—	21	21	19	23	15	22	24	24	159	—
P/E – low	—	15	17	13	18	13	14	10	18	10	—
Dividends per share (¥)	7.6%	7.51	8.26	8.26	8.26	8.26	8.26	8.26	10.00	12.00	14.50
Book value per share (¥)	5.8%	343	360	381	394	417	440	482	527	574	571

1990 Year-end:
Debt ratio: 29.1%
Return on equity: 1.0%
Cash (bil.): ¥84
Long-term debt (bil.): ¥181
No. of shares (mil.): 771
Dividends:
- 1990 average yield: 1.5%
- 1990 payout: 241.7%

Market value (mil.): $5,654
Sales (mil.): $13,215

Stock Price History High/Low 1981–90

2,500 / 2,000 / 1,500 / 1,000 / 500 / 0

BRITISH AIRWAYS PLC

NYSE symbol: BAB (ADR)
Fiscal year ends: March 31

OVERVIEW

British Airways, the world's 9th largest airline, carried over 25 million passengers in 1990 — more than any other European airline. At the heart of its route system is London's Heathrow Airport (one of the world's busiest), which provides about 70% of BA's passenger traffic.

Since US giants American and United are replacing TWA and Pan Am at Heathrow, BA may face stiffer competition on its home turf. A small British competitor, Virgin Atlantic Airways, has also gained important landing rights at Heathrow. In return BA has won expanded service to US cities and more freedom to form alliances with US airlines (its 2-year-old alliance with United ended when United gained service to Heathrow).

Early in 1990 the slump in air travel and uncertainty over the outcome of the Gulf War forced BA to implement cost-cutting measures, including staff and flight reductions. In the long term BA plans to capitalize on growing traffic to Eastern Europe by forming Air Russia with the Soviet Union's Aeroflot and establishing its own yet-unnamed Berlin-based airline. BA's Super Shuttle now offers commuters frequent flights from Heathrow to 4 UK cities, and Caledonian Airways provides charters for vacation tours.

WHEN

British Airways was born as Imperial Airways in 1924, when the British government merged 4 private airlines to form a stronger, subsidized airline to link the British Empire. Of the original 4, British Marine Air Navigation operated between Southampton, Guernsey, and northwestern France, while Daimler Airway, Handley Page Transport, and Instone Air Line connected London with Paris, Brussels, Berlin, and Cologne.

Imperial pioneered air routes from London to India (1929); Cape Town (1932); Singapore (1933); and, with Qantas Empire Airways, to Australia (1934). European service remained virtually unchanged, and private UK airlines emerged to fill this gap. Three of these (Hillman's Airways, Spartan Air Lines, and United Airways) merged in 1935 to form British Airways, which shared European service with Imperial until 1939, when the 2 were combined to form state-owned British Overseas Airways Corporation (BOAC).

After WWII BOAC continued as the UK's international airline, but another state-owned company, British European Airways (BEA), took over domestic and European routes. Private airlines survived primarily as charters. The government later combined BOAC and BEA to form British Airways (1972).

BA and Air France jointly pioneered supersonic passenger service (the Concorde) in 1976. A public relations victory rather than a financial success, the Concorde contributed to soaring costs, which left BA with a loss of $337 million in 1982. Former Avis president Colin Marshall became CEO in 1983, reduced manpower, sold planes, and pared the airline's route network, building BA into one of the world's most profitable airlines, despite the Concorde's high operating costs.

In 1987, the year the British government sold it to the public, BA bought its chief British competitor, British Caledonian. BCal had begun as a charter airline (Airwork, 1928) that merged with 7 other private operators in 1960 to form British United Airways (BUA). Caledonian Airways (founded in Prestwick, Scotland; 1961) bought BUA in 1970, adopting the name British Caledonian Airways in 1971. BCal was flying to Europe, Africa, Asia, and the US by 1987.

In 1988 BA gained a foothold in the US through an agreement with Chicago-based United Airlines and bought 11% of Covia Partnership, owner of United's Apollo computer reservation system. A 1989 deal with KLM to buy into Belgium's Sabena World Airlines collapsed in 1991, but BA and Sabena resumed talks later that year.

HOW MUCH

Stock prices are for ADRs ADR = 10 shares	9-Year Growth	1981	1982	1983	1984	1985	1986	1987	1988	1989	1990
Sales ($ mil.)	25.3%	1,046	1,384	1,719	2,168	2,036	4,511	5,215	7,086	7,174	7,973
Net income ($ mil.)	—	(75)	(337)	60	185	120	280	238	285	295	405
Income as % of sales	—	(7.2%)	(24.3%)	3.5%	8.5%	5.9%	6.2%	4.6%	4.0%	4.1%	5.1%
Earnings per share ($)	—	—	—	—	—	—	—	3.29	3.96	4.10	5.14
Stock price – high ($)	—	—	—	—	—	—	—	37.50	32.50	37.75	39.38
Stock price – low ($)	—	—	—	—	—	—	—	16.13	24.75	27.88	25.00
Stock price – close ($)	—	—	—	—	—	—	—	28.00	29.38	37.63	27.50
P/E – high	—	—	—	—	—	—	—	11	8	9	8
P/E – low	—	—	—	—	—	—	—	5	6	7	5
Dividends per share ($)	—	—	—	—	—	—	—	0.00	1.44	1.65	1.89
Book value per share ($)	—	—	—	—	—	—	—	13.50	16.58	17.52	20.86

1990 Year-end:
Debt ratio: 53.0%
Return on equity: 26.8%
Cash (mil.): $547
Current ratio: 0.71
Long-term debt (mil.): $1,693
No. of shares (mil.): 72
Dividends:
1990 average yield: 6.9%
1990 payout: 36.8%
Market value (mil.): $1,982

Stock Price History High/Low 1987–90

40 35 30 25 20 15 10 5 0

WHO

Chairman: Lord King of Wartnaby, age 72, £515,818 pay
Deputy Chairman: Sir Michael Angus
Deputy Chairman and CEO: Sir Colin Marshall, age 56
CFO: Derek Stevens, age 51
Secretary and Legal Director and Director of Human Resources: Robert Ayling, age 43
Auditors: Ernst & Young
Employees: 52,054

WHERE

HQ: Speedbird House, Heathrow Airport, Hounslow, Middlesex TW6 2JA, UK
Phone: 011-44-81-759-5511
Fax: 011-44-81-562-9930
US HQ: 75-20 Astoria Blvd., Jackson Heights, NY 11370
US Phone: 718-397-4000
US Fax: 718-397-4364
Reservations: 800-247-9297

British Airways serves 164 cities in 75 countries.

	1990 Sales		1990 Operating Income	
	$ mil.	% of total	$ mil.	% of total
Europe	3,007	38	5	1
The Americas	2,668	34	410	65
Africa	587	7	86	13
Other countries	1,711	21	132	21
Total	**7,973**	**100**	**633**	**100**

WHAT

	1990 Sales		1990 Operating Income	
	$ mil.	% of total	$ mil.	% of total
Airline operations	7,770	97	662	105
Package holidays	162	2	(13)	(2)
Other	41	1	(16)	(3)
Total	**7,973**	**100**	**633**	**100**

Major Subsidiaries and Affiliates
Alta Holidays Ltd. (51%, package holidays)
British Airways Capital Ltd. (89%, airline finance)
British Airways Engine Overhaul Ltd.
British Airways Holidays Ltd. (package holidays)
Caledonian Airways Ltd. (charters)
Overseas Air Travel Ltd. (package holidays)
Speedbird Insurance Co. Ltd.
The AirPlus Company Ltd. (25%, charge card services)

Computer Reservation Systems
Galileo (24%)
Covia Partnership (11%)

Flight Equipment	No.	Orders
BA & Caledonian		
Airbus A320	8	2
Boeing 737	47	37
Boeing 747	47	13
Boeing 757	36	3
Boeing 767	4	13
Concorde	7	—
DC-10	8	—
Lockheed TriStar	17	—
Other	50	—
Total	**224**	**58**

KEY COMPETITORS

AMR	Lufthansa	Singapore Airlines
Delta	NWA	Swire Pacific
JAL	Qantas	UAL
KLM	SAS	USAir

THE BRITISH PETROLEUM COMPANY PLC

OVERVIEW

British Petroleum (BP) is the UK's largest company and the world's 4th largest international oil company after Exxon, Royal Dutch/Shell, and Mobil. About 35% of the company's holdings are in the US.

The company leads the US and UK in oil production, deriving most of its output from holdings in Alaska and the North Sea. BP is a world leader in petrochemicals and animal feeds and owns 50% of the Trans Alaska Pipeline System. BP sells its gasoline through 19,400 service stations worldwide. The company's green and yellow logo will be increasingly evident in the US as BP America, formerly the Standard Oil Company of Ohio (SOHIO), gives its 7,400 US service stations the BP look as part of a network-wide refurbishing.

Since assuming the chairmanship in 1990, Robert Horton has shifted focus to British Petroleum's core businesses, emphasized marketing and refining, and expanded operations in Asia and Eastern Europe.

WHEN

After negotiating an extensive oil concession with the Grand Vizier in Persia, English adventurer William Knox D'Arcy began exploration in 1901. In 1908, with additional capital from Burmah Oil, D'Arcy's company became the first to strike oil in the Middle East. D'Arcy and Burmah Oil formed Anglo-Persian Oil Company in 1909 to exploit the enormous find. At Winston Churchill's urging, the British government purchased a 51% interest in cash-hungry Anglo-Persian in 1914.

Anglo-Persian had interests in the first major oil discoveries in Iraq (1927) and Kuwait (1938). In 1928, facing a potential oil glut, the company and its major competitors entered into a secret "As Is" agreement, fixing world production and prices for 2 decades.

While other oil companies were negotiating "50-50" deals with producer nations, Chairman Sir William Fraser refused to renegotiate the company's more lucrative concession with Iran. In 1951 its Iranian assets were seized. Following the 1953 coup that installed the Shah, an international consortium resumed business under a concession in which the company was allowed a 40% interest. In 1954 the company changed its name to British Petroleum. The Khomeini regime severed Iranian ties to foreign oil companies in 1979.

BP made major strikes in Prudhoe Bay, Alaska, in 1969 and in the North Sea in 1970. In 1970 BP swapped its Alaskan reserves for an eventual 55% interest in SOHIO. From 1979 to 1981 SOHIO invested its huge Alaskan oil profits in exploration and nonoil acquisitions, including Kennecott Copper (1981). Declining oil and copper prices in the mid-1980s, in addition to a large interest in a $1.7 billion dry hole in the Beaufort Sea, led to disappointing earnings. In 1986 BP named Robert Horton CEO of SOHIO. Horton ("the hatchet") cut overhead and sold poorly performing units.

Britain acquired an additional 20.15% of BP in 1975, then reduced its holdings through public offerings in 1977 and 1979, finally selling its remaining shares in 1987.

Under the direction of Sir Peter Walters from 1981 to 1990, BP purchased Purina Mills (1986); the remaining shares of SOHIO (1987); and Britoil (1988), a large North Sea oil and gas producer. BP sold most of its minerals businesses, including Kennecott, to RTZ and $1.3 billion in oil properties to Oryx in 1989. In the same year, under pressure from the UK, the Kuwaiti government reduced its holdings in BP from 21.6% to 9.9% of common stock.

Horton, promoted to BP's chairmanship in 1990, streamlined the company, cutting corporate staff from 2,500 to fewer than 400. Horton also pushed BP into exploring for new sources of oil as its Alaskan and North Sea fields passed their primes. In 1991 BP also agreed to buy Petromed, Spain's 3rd largest oil refiner and marketer.

HOW MUCH

	9-Year Growth	1981	1982	1983	1984	1985	1986	1987	1988	1989	1990
Sales ($ mil.)	2.1%	49,192	47,524	47,122	50,830	53,281	39,941	45,228	46,141	48,611	59,140
Net income ($ mil.)	4.3%	2,047	1,160	1,257	1,878	2,077	1,201	2,281	2,154	2,860	3,000
Income as % of sales	—	4.2%	2.4%	2.7%	3.7%	3.9%	3.0%	5.0%	4.7%	5.9%	5.1%
Earnings per share ($)	3.6%	4.88	2.56	2.76	4.12	4.54	2.62	4.92	4.32	6.24	6.72
Stock price – high ($)	—	39.63	23.75	27.25	30.00	35.13	43.75	80.38	63.75	65.88	86.25
Stock price – low ($)	—	17.88	17.50	18.00	21.75	21.38	30.13	43.25	48.25	53.63	59.63
Stock price – close ($)	13.9%	23.75	18.88	23.63	22.63	32.38	43.50	55.88	53.75	65.38	76.88
P/E – high	—	8	9	10	7	8	17	16	15	11	13
P/E – low	—	4	7	7	5	5	12	9	11	9	9
Dividends per share ($)	7.8%	2.33	2.01	1.83	2.07	2.37	2.87	3.41	3.86	4.99	4.56
Book value per share ($)	4.3%	32.44	30.80	30.66	29.32	31.39	32.19	40.67	41.00	39.02	47.44

1990 Year-end:
Debt ratio: 32.1%
Return on equity: 15.5%
Cash (mil.): $1,199
Current ratio: 1.08
Long-term debt (bil.): $10.1
No. of shares (mil.): 447
Dividends:
1990 average yield: 5.9%
1990 payout: 67.9%
Market value (mil.): $34,367

Stock Price History High/Low 1981–90

90 80 70 60 50 40 30 20 10 0

NYSE symbol: BP (ADR)
Fiscal year ends: December 31

WHO

Chairman and CEO: Robert B. Horton, age 51, £537,302 pay
Deputy Chairman and COO: David A. G. Simon, age 51
CFO: Steve Ahearne
Head of Human Resources for Strategy: Syd Robertson
Chairman, BP America: James H. Ross, age 52
Auditors: Ernst & Young
Employees: 118,050

WHERE

HQ: Britannic House, 1 Finsbury Circus, London EC2M 7BA, UK
Phone: 011-44-71-496-5027
Fax: 011-44-71-496-5033 (Investor Relations)
US HQ: BP America Inc., 200 Public Sq., Cleveland, OH 44114-2375
US Phone: 216-586-4141
US Fax: 216-586-8066 (Investor Relations)

BP holds oil and gas interests in 20 countries. The company's markets are worldwide.

	1990 Sales		1990 Net Income	
	$ mil.	% of total	$ mil.	% of total
UK	21,854	33	727	14
Other Europe	18,067	28	1,022	19
US	18,620	29	2,631	50
Other countries	6,559	10	922	17
Adjustments	(5,960)	—	(2,302)	—
Total	**59,140**	**100**	**3,000**	**100**

WHAT

	1990 Sales		1990 Operating Income	
	$ mil.	% of total	$ mil.	% of total
Nutrition	4,801	7	86	2
Refining & marketing	43,005	63	1,527	29
Exploration & production	14,028	21	3,734	70
Chemicals	5,664	8	231	4
Other & corporate	698	1	(276)	(5)
Adjustments	(9,056)	—	(942)	—
Total	**59,140**	**100**	**4,360**	**100**

Products and Services
Animal feeds
Chemicals and plastics
Crude oil and natural gas
Fueling services for the transportation industry
Petroleum refining and marketing
Service stations, convenience stores

KEY COMPETITORS

Amoco	Pennzoil
Ashland	Petrofina
Atlantic Richfield	Petrobrás
Broken Hill	PDVSA
Chevron	Pemex
Coastal	Phillips Petroleum
Du Pont	Royal Dutch/Shell
Elf Aquitaine	Sun
Exxon	Texaco
Imperial Oil	Unocal
Mobil	USX
Norsk Hydro	Animal feed producers
Occidental	Chemical and mining companies
Oryx	

BRITISH TELECOMMUNICATIONS PLC

OVERVIEW

British Telecom, the most valuable and most profitable of UK companies, operates one of the world's largest telecommunications networks. In the UK, where it derives 97% of its sales, it is the main provider of local and long distance telephone service. It has rung up 25 million residential and business telephone lines. Its only competitor — fledgling, Cable & Wireless–owned Mercury Communications — has fewer than 150,000.

British Telecom, 47.9% owned by Her Majesty's government, has been restructuring for the past year and has cut almost 9,000 employees from a payroll widely believed to be overinflated from the years British Telecom was a government agency. Under restructuring begun in 1991, British Telecom has formed 2 new divisions, Personal Communications and Business Communications, to focus on customers. A Worldwide Networks Division is to combine its international networks, and a Special Business Division oversees the company's other businesses. British Telecom owns US-based BT Tymnet, a data communications network, and a 20% stake in McCaw Cellular, the US's largest cellular phone firm.

NYSE symbol: BTY (ADR)
Fiscal year ends: March 31

WHO

Chairman: Iain D. T. Vallance, age 48, £374,152 pay
Group Director and Secretary: Malcolm Argent, age 56
Managing Director, British Telecom UK: Michael Bett, age 56
Managing Director, British Telecom International: Anthony J. Booth, age 52
Group Finance Director: Barry D. Romeril, age 47
Head of Personnel and Quality: Millie Banerjee
Auditors: Coopers & Lybrand Deloitte
Employees: 245,665

WHEN

When BT phones home, the Queen answers.

That's because telecommunications and the British government have been on the line together for more than a century. In 1879 the government granted the British Post Office an exclusive right to operate telegraph systems. When private companies tried to offer telephone service, the government objected, arguing in court that its telegraph monopoly was imperiled. The courts agreed, and the Post Office was empowered to license private telephone companies, collect a 10% royalty, and operate its own systems.

The National Telephone Company, a private firm, emerged as the leading telephone outfit, competing with the Post Office. When the company's license expired in 1911, the Post Office took over National Telephone's system and became the monopoly telephone company.

In 1936 the phone system introduced its familiar red "public call offices" (known as "phone booths" in the US). The kiosks were designed by Sir Giles Gilbert Scott for the jubilee of King George V.

Under a 1981 law, telecommunication activities were split from the Post Office and placed under a new British Telecom Corporation. The government also allowed for the first time a competitor — Mercury Communications, formed in 1981 in a joint effort by Cable and Wireless, British Petroleum, and Barclays Merchant Bank. (C&W bought out BP and Barclays in 1984.) Within a year the Thatcher government called for the privatization of BT.

The Telecommunications Act of 1984 set up the sale of a majority stake in British Telecom to the public later that year. After a $20 million publicity campaign, British Telecom became a publicly traded company in the largest UK stock offering in history. The Telecommunications Act set up an Office of Telecommunications (OFTEL) to regulate British Telecom and tied rates the company could charge to inflation. To become a multinational communications concern, British Telecom went shopping in North America. It bought control of Mitel (Canada, phone equipment maker, 1986), ITT Dialcom (US, electronic mail service, 1986), and 20% of McCaw (US, cellular telephone, 1989).

In 1990 the British government opened the UK to more phone competition. The company faces challenges from cable companies (many owned by US regional Bell operating companies), from cellular service providers, and from other large corporations with excess capacity on private networks. In 1991, amid complaints about its large profits and rumors that the government would privatize more of BT, British Telecom spent more than $106 million to change its corporate image — altering both its logo and its quality of service.

WHERE

HQ: British Telecom Centre, 81 Newgate St., London EC1A 7AJ, UK
Phone: 011-44-71-356-4008
Fax: 011-44-71-356-6583
US HQ: 100 Park Ave., New York, NY 10017
US Phone: 212-297-2711
US Fax: 212-297-2713

British Telecom offers telephone service and equipment in the UK and internationally.

WHAT

	1990 Sales		1990 Operating Income	
	$ mil.	% of total	$ mil.	% of total
BT UK	17,497	71	4,380	72
BT International	4,524	18	1,478	24
Comm. systems	2,624	11	243	4
Other activities	—	—	(2)	—
Adjustments	(1,246)	—	(53)	—
Total	**23,399**	**100**	**6,046**	**100**

Major Subsidiaries and Affiliates

Belize Telecommunications Ltd. (25%, telecommunications services)
BT & D Technologies Ltd. (40%, optoelectronic devices)
BT Consumer Electronics Ltd. (telecommunications equipment)
BT (Marine) Ltd. (cable ship operator)
BT Tymnet Inc. (digital data communications)
BT (Worldwide) Ltd. (international networks)
British Telecom (CBP) Ltd. (specialized telecommunications equipment)
CTG, Inc. (telephone systems)
Fulcrum Communications Ltd. (telecommunications equipment)
Gibraltar Telecommunications International Ltd. (50%, telecommunications services)
Marshalls Finance Ltd. (30%, financial services)
McCaw Cellular Communications, Inc. (20%, mobile cellular telephone systems)
Mitel Corp. (51%, telecommunications equipment)
Phonepoint Ltd. (50%, mobile cellular telephone systems)
Telecom Securicor/Cellular Radio Ltd. (mobile cellular telephone systems)
Telecom Security Ltd. (alarm services)
Yellow Pages Sales Ltd. (advertising sales)

KEY COMPETITORS

AT&T
BCE
Cable & Wireless
Ericsson
Hutchison Whampoa
MCI
United Telecom
Cellular telephone firms
Regional Bell operating companies
Telecommunications equipment makers

HOW MUCH

Stock prices are for ADRs ADR = 10 shares	6-Year Growth	1981	1982	1983	1984	1985	1986	1987	1988	1989	1990
Sales ($ mil.)	19.0%	—	—	—	8,251	9,490	12,329	15,173	17,314	17,160	23,399
Net income ($ mil.)	15.8%	—	—	—	1,188	1,172	1,568	2,116	2,473	2,427	2,867
Income as % of sales	—	—	—	—	14.4%	12.4%	12.7%	13.9%	14.3%	14.1%	12.3%
Earnings per share ($)	—	—	—	—	—	1.87	2.46	3.36	4.01	4.02	4.75
Stock price – high ($)	—	—	—	—	12.38	30.38	44.00	55.63	47.75	52.00	57.88
Stock price – low ($)	—	—	—	—	9.50	12.00	24.63	31.50	37.75	39.25	40.75
Stock price – close ($)	29.2%	—	—	—	12.38	28.00	32.63	42.13	45.88	50.50	57.50
P/E – high	—	—	—	—	—	16	18	17	12	13	12
P/E – low	—	—	—	—	—	6	10	9	9	10	9
Dividends per share ($)	—	—	—	—	0.00	0.00	1.41	1.63	2.04	2.29	2.33
Book value per share ($)	—	—	—	—	—	12.21	15.59	18.90	22.34	22.73	28.97

1990 Year-end:
Debt ratio: 31.9%
Return on equity: 18.4%
Cash (mil.): $1,239
Current ratio: 0.74
Long-term debt (mil.): $8,208
No. of shares (mil.): 605
Dividends:
1990 average yield: 4.1%
1990 payout: 49.1%
Market value (mil.): $34,789

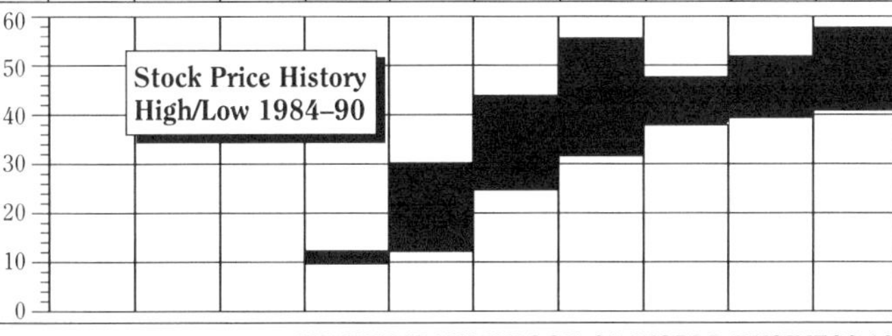

THE BROKEN HILL PROPRIETARY COMPANY LTD.

OVERVIEW

Broken Hill Proprietary (BHP), Australia's largest public company, is an international resources concern with primary operations in steel, minerals, and petroleum.

With an annual production of 6.2 million metric tons, BHP generates over 80% of Australia's steel requirements. Twenty-two percent of steel revenues come from sales outside the country. BHP is a world leader in high-value-added steel products, including coated steels.

The company's Minerals Group is one of the largest and most successful global mining operations. Most of the production comes from the BHP-Utah Minerals International group, which mines coal, iron ore, manganese, gold, copper, and other minerals, primarily in Australia and the US. The company also operates the mammoth Chilean Escondida copper project, of which it owns 57.5%.

BHP Petroleum explores for, produces, refines, and markets oil and natural gas. The company is drilling in Argentina, Egypt, and India. BHP is buying Denver-based Hamilton Oil, with reserves in the British North Sea, Europe, Malaysia, Chile, and West Africa.

NYSE symbol: BHP (ADR)
Fiscal year ends: May 31

Hoover's Rating 

WHO

Chairman: Sir Arvi Parbo, age 65
Deputy Chairman, Managing Director, and CEO: Brian T. Loton, age 62
Executive General Manager Finance: G. E. Heeley, age 56
Group General Manager Management, Manpower & Organization: C. D. Houser
Auditors: Ernst & Young; Arthur Andersen & Co.
Employees: 52,000

WHEN

In 1883 Charles Rasp, a boundary rider for the Mt. Gipps sheep station, discovered a massive lode of silver, lead, and zinc in the Broken Hill outcrop in New South Wales, Australia. The Broken Hill Proprietary Company was incorporated in 1885 to mine the ore, and 2 years later the company discovered iron ore deposits in southern Australia. By the early 1890s BHP was paying over £1 million a year in dividends.

Until 1915 the company mined, smelted, and refined iron ore, lead, silver, and zinc. That year BHP began producing steel at its Newcastle, Australia, plant. Aided by the steel demand caused by WWI, BHP soon became the largest steel producer in Australia and opened its own coal and iron ore mines to provide the necessary raw materials. By purchasing Australian Iron and Steel (1935) and a number of other steel companies, BHP had gained a virtual monopoly on the Australian steel industry by 1939. The company closed its exhausted Broken Hill mine in 1939.

In 1940 BHP established an operation to build deep-sea ships at Whyalla and later established its own fleet. During WWII the company produced munitions and led the syndicate that created Commonwealth Aircraft, a Melbourne-based manufacturer of fighters and training planes.

During the 1960s the company entered a partnership with Esso Standard Oil (Australia), subsidiary of Standard Oil of New Jersey, to explore for offshore oil and gas. In 1965 BHP and its partner found large quantities of natural gas and 2 years later discovered oil in the Bass Strait. The resulting Bass Strait oil and gas field soon supplied 70% of the nation's petroleum. In the 1960s and 1970s, BHP started mining iron ore, manganese, and coal for export. In 1969 the company became joint owner of John Lysaght Ltd., a steel products manufacturer, and in 1979 became 100% owner.

In 1984 BHP bought Utah International's overseas assets from General Electric for $700 million; the acquisition allowed BHP to expand its mining operations in the US, South Africa, Canada, Chile, and Brazil. The company underwent a major reorganization between 1983 and 1987 to adapt to its new role as a global company. Acquisitions during the late 1980s included Energy Reserves Group (petroleum, 1985), Monsanto Oil (1986), Gulf Energy Development (1988), Aquila Steel (1988), and Hawaii-based Pacific Resources (crude oil, 1989). In 1990 BHP bought the remaining 70% interest (it owned 30%) in Mount Goldsworthy (iron ore).

As part of a 1988 capital restructuring, BHP and Elders IXL (later Foster's Brewing) created Beswick Proprietary to hold BHP stock. Beswick owned 21.4% in 1990.

WHERE

HQ: BHP House, 140 William St., Melbourne, Victoria 3000, Australia
Phone: 011-61-3-609-3333
Fax: 011-61-3-609-3015
US HQ: 550 California St., San Francisco, CA 94104
US Phone: 415-774-2030
US Fax: 415-397-8178

The company operates in more than 26 countries.

	1990 Sales		1990 Net Income	
	$ mil.	% of total	$ mil.	% of total
Australia	7,417	69	737	83
North America	2,414	22	94	10
Other countries	1,010	9	63	7
Adjustments	(537)	—	(47)	—
Total	**10,304**	**100**	**847**	**100**

WHAT

	1990 Sales		1990 Operating Income	
	$ mil.	% of total	$ mil.	% of total
Steel	4,520	42	431	34
Petroleum	3,379	31	304	24
Minerals	2,584	24	407	32
Other	264	3	121	10
Adjustments	(443)	—	248	—
Total	**10,304**	**100**	**1,511**	**100**

Products

Steel	Minerals	Petroleum
Bar	Alumina	Crude oil
Coated products	Coal	Ethane
Coke	Copper concentrate	Liquefied natural gas
Iron ore	Ferro alloys	Liquefied petroleum gas
Plate	Gold	Natural gas
Rail products	Ilmenite	
Rod	Iron ore	
Rolled strip	Lead	
Slab	Manganese	
Structural products	Molybdenum	
Wire products	Nickel	
	Zinc	

HOW MUCH

	7-Year Growth	1981	1982	1983	1984	1985	1986	1987	1988	1989	1990
Sales ($ mil.)	14.6%	—	—	3,973	4,848	4,710	6,078	6,240	7,877	7,887	10,304
Net income ($ mil.)	21.6%	—	—	216	559	499	706	584	754	779	847
Income as % of sales	—	—	—	5.4%	11.5%	10.6%	11.6%	9.4%	9.6%	9.9%	8.2%
Earnings per share ($)	21.1%	—	—	0.61	1.39	0.61	1.70	1.37	1.84	2.20	2.33
Stock price – high ($)	—	—	—	11.92	12.48	15.78	19.32	29.55	25.91	32.38	37.63
Stock price – low ($)	—	—	—	5.03	8.70	8.28	13.26	15.00	16.36	20.34	26.38
Stock price – close ($)	14.9%	—	—	11.81	9.26	14.99	17.61	18.64	21.93	29.38	31.25
P/E – high	—	—	—	20	9	26	11	22	14	15	16
P/E – low	—	—	—	8	6	14	8	11	9	9	11
Dividends per share ($)	23.6%	—	—	0.32	0.70	0.46	0.74	1.66	0.87	0.81	1.41
Book value per share ($)	6.0%	—	—	10.50	11.59	4.80	11.32	12.38	10.85	13.94	15.79

1990 Year-end:
Debt ratio: 45.6%
Return on equity: 15.7%
Cash (mil.): $726
Current ratio: 1.21
Long-term debt (mil.): $4,905
No. of shares (mil.): 370
Dividends:
1990 average yield: 4.5%
1990 payout: 60.3%
Market value (mil.): $11,575

Stock Price History High/Low 1983–90

KEY COMPETITORS

Amoco	Du Pont	Norsk Hydro
Anglo American	Elf Aquitaine	Pennzoil
ASARCO	Exxon	Phelps Dodge
Ashland	Friedrich Krupp	Phillips Petroleum
Atlantic Richfield	Hanson	Royal Dutch/Shell
Bethlehem Steel	Inco	RTZ
British Petroleum	Inland Steel	Sun
Chevron	IRI	Texaco
Coastal	LTV	Thyssen
Cyprus Minerals	Mobil	Unocal
	Nippon Steel	USX

BSN GROUPE

OVERVIEW

Twenty years of acquisitions have transformed French glassmaker BSN into one of Europe's largest food and beverage concerns. Although sales are concentrated in Europe, particularly in France, BSN products are sold worldwide. Such brands as Dannon and Evian have made the company #1 in the world in fresh dairy products and mineral water. In Europe, BSN is the largest biscuit and condiment producer and #2 in pasta, beer, and bottle sales.

Under the leadership of Antoine Riboud, BSN has aggressively expanded in Europe in anticipation of 1992 market integration. Riboud has achieved his goal of establishing #1 or #2 positions throughout Europe in all major BSN markets. The company has increased its hold on Eastern Europe with the 1991 purchases of several dairy companies and a joint venture with Nestlé to privatize a Czechoslovak biscuit and chocolate company. BSN has also expanded its presence in Asia.

Riboud, now 72, has been the visionary and driving force behind BSN. He says that he intends to lead the company until he is 80.

WHEN

In 1965 Antoine Riboud replaced his uncle as chairman of family-run Souchon-Neuvesel, a Lyon-based glass bottle maker. Befitting a man whose brothers were Jean, then chairman of Schlumberger, and Marc, an internationally recognized photographer, Antoine quickly made his mark on the company. Riboud's first move was to merge (1966) with Boussois, a major French flat-glass manufacturer, creating BSN. In an audacious attempt to expand the company's glass business, he made a bid in 1968 for Saint-Gobain, a diversified French glass manufacturer 3 times BSN's size. The attempt failed.

Undaunted, Riboud enlarged BSN's glass business and filled the company's bottles by acquiring well-established beverage and food concerns. In 1970 BSN purchased Brasseries Kronenbourg (France's largest brewer), Societe Européenne de Brasseries (beer, France), and Evian (mineral water, France). The 1972 acquisition of Glaverbel (Belgium) gave BSN 50% of Europe's flat-glass market. A 1973 merger with Gervais Danone (yogurt, cheese, Panzani pasta; France) put BSN into pan-European brand-name food products for the first time and raised sales to $1.7 billion.

In the 1970s increasing energy costs depressed flat-glass earnings. BSN elected to divest its flat-glass businesses, selling the last of them in 1982. In 1978 and 1979 the company acquired interests in brewers in Belgium, Spain, and Italy. BSN bought Dannon, the leading US yogurt maker, in 1981. The company became a major player in the French champagne industry, taking over Pommery and Lanson in 1984. BSN established a strong presence in the Italian pasta market by purchasing majority ownership of Ponte (1985) and a minority interest in Agnesi (1986).

In 1986 BSN purchased Generale Biscuit, the 3rd largest biscuit company in the world. In 1989 the company bought RJR Nabisco's European cookie and snack food business for $2.5 billion, quickly selling Walkers Crisps and Smiths Crisps (snack foods) to PepsiCo for $1.35 billion to help finance the acquisition.

In a series of acquisitions starting in 1986, BSN took over the largest mineral water companies in Italy and Spain, several European pasta makers, Sonnen-Bassermann (grocery products, West Germany, 1987), HP Foods (UK, 1988), Lea & Perrins (US, 1988), La Familia (Spain, 1989), Birkel (Germany, 1990), and the rest of Agnesi (Italy, 1990), and made a bid for W & R Jacob (Ireland, 1991). The company has been active in strategic alliances, taking a 20% stake in Birra Peroni (beer, Italy, 1988), a 50% interest in Alken-Maes (beer, Belgium, 1988), and a 50% interest in Guangzhou Dairy (yogurt, China, 1989).

BSN divested its US cookie business in 1990 and the following year sold its Pommery and Lanson champagne brands to LVMH.

HOW MUCH

$=FF5.08 (Dec. 31, 1990)	9-Year Growth	1981	1982	1983	1984	1985	1986	1987	1988	1989	1990
Sales (FF mil.)	11.9%	19,256	21,890	24,889	27,293	28,475	33,623	37,156	42,177	48,669	52,897
Net income (FF mil.)	24.0%	446	574	741	755	798	1,081	1,550	2,186	2,698	3,091
Income as % of sales	—	2.3%	2.6%	3.0%	2.8%	2.8%	3.2%	4.2%	5.2%	5.5%	5.8%
Earnings per share (FF)	14.2%	16	20	21	20	21	27	34	42	50	53
Stock price – high (FF)	—	125	156	273	289	276	475	542	650	780	908
Stock price – low (FF)	—	78	114	131	235	197	272	371	376	608	685
Stock price – close (FF)	22.0%	119	144	268	240	275	435	434	648	774	710
P/E – high	—	8	8	13	14	13	18	16	16	16	17
P/E – low	—	5	6	6	12	9	10	11	9	12	13
Dividends per share (FF)	12.5%	4.50	5.00	5.20	5.50	6.00	7.00	8.50	10.00	11.50	13.00
Book value per share (FF)	11.6%	151	172	171	189	196	221	267	303	351	407

1990 Year-end:
Debt ratio: 39.0%
Return on equity: 14.0%
Cash (mil.): FF1,835
Long-term debt (mil.): FF14,327
No. of shares (mil.): 55
Dividends:
1990 average yield: 1.8%
1990 payout: 24.5%
Market value (mil.): $7,687
Sales (mil.): $10,413

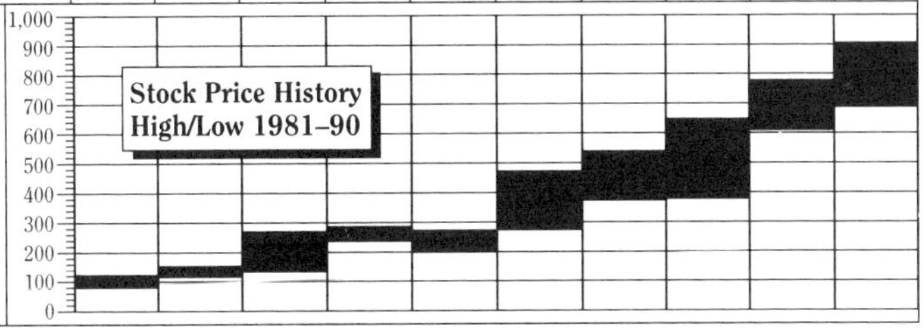

Stock Price History
High/Low 1981–90
1,000
900
800
700
600
500
400
300
200
100
0

OTC symbol: BSNOY (ADR)
Fiscal year ends: December 31

Hoover's Rating **B**

WHO

Chairman: Antoine Riboud, age 72
VC and President: Georges Lecallier
SVP Finance: Christian Laubie
SVP Human Resources: Antoine Martin
Auditors: Petiteau Scacchi et Associés (Price Waterhouse)
Employees: 45,932

WHERE

HQ: 7, rue de Téhéran, 75008 Paris, France
Phone: 011-33-1-44-35-20-20
Fax: 011-33-1-42-25-67-16
US HQ: The Dannon Company, 1111 Westchester Ave., White Plains, NY 10604
US Phone: 914-697-9700
US Fax: 914-934-2805

	1990 Sales		1990 Operating Income	
	FF mil.	% of total	FF mil.	% of total
France	33,294	63	4,053	71
Other Europe	15,454	29	1,238	22
Outside Europe	4,149	8	126	2
Unallocated	—	—	258	5
Total	**52,897**	**100**	**5,675**	**100**

WHAT

	1990 Sales		1990 Operating Income	
	FF mil.	% of total	FF mil.	% of total
Dairy	13,264	25	962	17
Grocery	10,603	20	1,032	18
Biscuits	12,766	23	1,223	21
Beer	6,598	12	843	15
Champagne, mineral water	4,963	9	866	15
Containers	5,877	11	720	13
Unallocated	—	—	29	1
Adjustments	(1,174)	—	—	—
Total	**52,897**	**100**	**5,675**	**100**

Major Brand Names

Dairy Products
Dannon
Danone
Galbani
Gervais

Grocery Products
Amora (condiments)
Birkel (pasta)
Blédina (baby food)
HP (sauces)
Lea & Perrins (Worcestershire sauce)
Liebig (soup)
Panzani (pasta)
Ponte (pasta)
Sonnen-Bassermann (prepared food)

Biscuits
L'Alsacienne
Britannia
Jacob's
LU
Saiwa
Vandamme

Beer
Kanterbräu
Kronenbourg
Maes
Mahou
Peroni
Tourtel

Mineral Water
Badoit
Evian
Ferrarelle
Font Vella
Sangemini

KEY COMPETITORS

Adolph Coors
Allied-Lyons
Anheuser-Busch
Bass
Cadbury Schweppes
Campbell Soup
Carlsberg
Foster's Brewing
General Mills
Grand Metropolitan
Guinness
Heineken
Heinz
Kirin
Nestlé
PepsiCo
Philip Morris
Ralston Purina
RJR Nabisco
Seagram
Source Perrier
TLC Beatrice
Unilever
Whitman
Other food companies

CABLE AND WIRELESS PLC

OVERVIEW

London-based Cable and Wireless is a leading provider of telecommunications services. The company operates in 37 countries. Its Asia and Pacific unit, which includes control of the lucrative Hong Kong phone system, accounts for almost 2/3 of its operating income.

Its Mercury Communications unit was, until recent British government action, the only challenger to British Telecom's dominance of UK phone service. Mercury competes in business and residential services (still less than 1% of total lines), in international long distance (14% market share), and in pay phones.

C&W is finishing its Global Digital Highway, undersea fiber optic cable that carries data and voice to and from Japan, Hong Kong, the US, and the UK. The company has the world's largest commercial fleet of cableships. C&W, along with Motorola and Telefónica de España, is developing Mercury Personal Communications Network for UK debut in 1992. It is a cellular-like system that permits calls to small, personal phones carried anywhere.

NYSE symbol: CWP (ADR)
Fiscal year ends: March 31

WHO

Chairman and CEO: Lord Young of Graffham
Director of Finance: Rod Olsen
Director of Personnel: Leigh Lewis
Auditors: KPMG Peat Marwick McLintock
Employees: 37,680

WHEN

In 1872 Britisher John Pender began Eastern Telegraph with financial assistance from his wife, Emma. By Pender's death in 1896, Eastern and associated companies owned one of every 3 miles of telegraph cable on the planet.

As the new century began, the scope of telecommunications expanded to include wireless radio communications promoted by, among others, inventor Guglielmo Marconi, head of the UK's Marconi Wireless Telegraph. After WWI, telecommunications grew in importance, and, partly to counter a threat from a new, US-based company called ITT, UK companies including Marconi Wireless and Eastern Telegraph combined to form Cable and Wireless in 1929.

As with the British Empire, the sun never set on Cable and Wireless, because it provided telegraph and telephone services in Britain's far-flung colonies. In 1947, after WWII, the company was nationalized by Clement Attlee's Labor government, and since the 1950s the company has lost some franchises in former British colonies or has seen local governments strip it of its monopolies.

In 1981 the Thatcher government began the process, completed in 1985, to return Cable and Wireless to private ownership. The government persuaded Eric Sharp (later Sir Eric Sharp and, still later, the Lord Sharp of Grimsdyke, Kt. CBE), a former Monsanto executive, to delay his retirement to lead C&W.

Lead he did. Over the next decade, as demand for telephone-based services swelled, profits grew at an annual rate of 27%. Sharp cut management layers and decentralized as the company began building its Global Digital Highway, an international fiber optic network.

In 1982 C&W joined British Petroleum and Barclays Merchant Bank to form Mercury Communications, the government-mandated competitor to giant British Telecom. C&W bought out BP and Barclays in 1984. Mercury made inroads into business-based services and in 1985 won the right to interconnect with British Telecom. Lord Sharp retired in 1990, and in 1991, after a review of telecommunications policy, the British government opened the field to more competitors. Mercury chose to concentrate on business customers rather than tackle BT's hold on local phone service.

Overseas, C&W bought control of Hong Kong's internal telephone system (1984). The move will give C&W, which already connects Hong Kong to the world, a leg up on the Chinese market once Hong Kong comes under communist control in 1997. C&W sold 20% of Hong Kong Telecom to an investment arm of the Chinese government (1990). C&W, C. Itoh, Toyota, and Pacific Telesis formed a Japan-based consortium called International Digital Communications. The Japanese government picked IDC to compete against KDD, Japan's former overseas communications monopoly.

WHERE

HQ: New Mercury House, 26 Red Lion Square, London WC1R 4UQ, UK
Phone: 011-44-71-315-4000
Fax: 011-44-71-315-5000
US HQ: Cable & Wireless Communications Inc., 1919 Gallows Rd., Vienna, VA 22182
US Phone: 703-790-5300
US Fax: 703-556-9687

Cable and Wireless PLC concentrates in 4 regions: the United Kingdom and Europe, Asia and the Pacific, the Western Hemisphere, and the Middle East.

	1990 Sales		1990 Operating Income	
	£ mil.	% of total	£ mil.	% of total
UK & Europe	586	25	84	14
Asia & Pacific	1,154	49	378	64
Western Hemisphere	553	24	115	20
Other countries	51	2	14	2
Adjustments	(28)	—	(28)	—
Total	**2,316**	**100**	**563**	**100**

WHAT

	1990 Sales	
	£ mil.	% of total
International telephone services	1,060	46
Domestic telephone services	470	20
Equipment sales & rental	308	13
Cableships & contracts	112	5
Other telecommunications services	366	16
Total	**2,316**	**100**

Major Subsidiaries and Affiliates

Barbados Telephone Co. Ltd.
Cable & Wireless Communications, Inc. (US)
Cable and Wireless (Far East) Ltd.
Cable and Wireless (Marine) Ltd.
Companhia de Telecomunicacoes de Macau (51%)
Dhivehi Raajjeyge Gulhun Private Ltd. (51%, Maldives)
Eastern Telecommunications Philippines, Inc. (40%)
Grenada Telecommunications Ltd. (70%)
Hong Kong Telecommunications Ltd. (58.5%)
Huaying Nanhai Oil Telecommunication Service Co. Ltd. (49%, China)
INTELSAT (4.7%)
International Digital Communications (16.18%, Japan)
Mercury Communications Ltd. (UK)
Mercury Personal Communications Network Ltd. (60%)
Merrac Ltd. (50%, UK)
Pacific Telecom Cable Inc. (20%, US)
Telecommunications of Jamaica Ltd. (79%)
Telephone Rentals PLC (UK)
Yemen International Telecommunications (65%)

KEY COMPETITORS

AT&T
BCE
British Telecom
Ericsson
GTE
Hutchison Whampoa
MCI
Cellular telephone firms
Regional Bell operating companies

HOW MUCH

£=$1.93 (Dec. 31, 1990)	9-Year Growth	1981	1982	1983	1984	1985	1986	1987	1988	1989	1990
Sales (£ mil.)	25.8%	293	352	403	673	1,106	1,154	1,201	1,244	1,534	2,316
Net income (£ mil.)	26.7%	39	45	98	113	144	180	224	245	285	328
Income as % of sales	—	13.3%	12.8%	24.2%	16.8%	13.0%	15.6%	18.7%	19.7%	18.6%	14.2%
Earnings per share (p)	24.1%	4	5	11	13	16	19	22	24	28	31
Stock price – high (p)	—	70	118	170	222	326	369	512	409	614	595
Stock price – low (p)	—	62	68	72	134	222	277	266	312	365	390
Stock price – close (p)	22.8%	70	112	137	221	298	329	331	377	554	446
P/E – high	—	16	23	16	18	21	19	23	17	22	19
P/E – low	—	14	13	7	11	14	14	12	13	13	12
Dividends per share (p)	24.6%	1.4	2.0	2.6	3.2	3.9	4.8	5.6	6.7	8.0	10.0
Book value per share (p)	19.7%	41	46	58	53	69	96	105	111	132	207

1990 Year-end:
Debt ratio: 20.7%
Return on equity: 18.5%
Cash (mil.): £936
Long-term debt (mil.): £578
No. of shares (mil.): 1,067
Dividends:
1990 average yield: 2.2%
1990 payout: 31.9%
Market value (mil.): $9,185
Sales (mil.): $4,470

Stock Price History
High/Low 1981–90

700
600
500
400
300
200
100
0

CADBURY SCHWEPPES PLC

OVERVIEW

Cadbury Schweppes is a major international soft drink and candy maker, producing over 7 billion liters of beverages and 450,000 tons of confectionery in 1990.

Cadbury Schweppes is #1 in the UK candy market. Its Wakefield, Great Britain, soft drink bottling plant is the largest in Europe. The company owns bottling facilities in many countries but uses 800 independent bottlers in the US. Popular US brands include Orange Crush, Canada Dry, and Schweppes.

Cadbury Schweppes is expanding globally through acquisitions and international partnerships. Cadbury's US candy brands (Mounds, Almond Joy) are produced and marketed under license by Hershey. The company owns Crush International and 51% of highly successful UK bottler Coca-Cola Schweppes.

NASDAQ symbol: CADBY (ADR)
Fiscal year ends: Saturday nearest December 31

WHO

Chairman: Sir Graham Day, age 57, £113,946 pay
CEO: N. Dominic Cadbury, age 50
Group Finance Director: David Jinks, age 55
Group Human Resources Director: G. R. Dale
Auditors: Arthur Andersen & Co.; Coopers & Lybrand Deloitte
Employees: 35,653

WHEN

Cadbury Schweppes is the product of a 1969 merger of 2 seasoned British firms. The world's first soft drink maker, Schweppes originated in 1783 in London, where Swiss national Jacob Schweppe first sold his artificial mineral water. Schweppe returned to Switzerland in 1799, but the company continued its British operations, introducing a lemonade in 1835 and tonic water (containing antimalarial quinine) and ginger ale in the 1870s. Beginning in the 1880s Schweppes expanded worldwide, particularly in British colonies. In the 1960s the company diversified into food products, acquiring, among others, Chivers (marmalade), Typhoo (tea), and Kenco (coffee).

John Cadbury began making cocoa in Birmingham, England, in 1831 and by 1841 was producing 15 varieties of chocolates. The Cadbury Dairy Milk bar, launched in 1905, became Britain's best-selling candy bar. In 1918 Cadbury bought British candy producer Fry. Cadbury established dominant market positions in the UK, Australia, South Africa, and India in the early 1900s.

Under the direction of Dominic Cadbury, Cadbury Schweppes acquired Peter Paul (Mounds, Almond Joy) in 1978. At the same time Schweppes was increasing beverage sales on the Continent and in the Far East. The company's flagging share of the British chocolate market revived with the 1982 introduction of the Wispa bar. In 1982 Cadbury Schweppes entered the US applesauce and juice market when the company acquired Duffy-Mott.

Through 1984 Cadbury Schweppes's businesses appeared to thrive, but by 1985 British candy demand had stopped growing. US candy distributor stockpiling had accounted for much of Cadbury's perceived growth in sales. Schweppes tonic was losing share at home and in the US. The US Wispa introduction was a failure. Apple juice was found to be a low-margin business. Dominic Cadbury invoked what Cadbury Schweppes executives call "the R word" — restructuring.

In 1986 Cadbury Schweppes sold its noncandy, nonbeverage businesses; consolidated divisions; eliminated layers of management; and purchased Canada Dry, rights to Sunkist soda, and 34% of Dr Pepper (now 8.5% of Dr Pepper/Seven-Up). The company entered into a joint venture with Coca-Cola in 1987, creating a $1 billion UK bottling enterprise. In 1989 Cadbury Schweppes purchased the Orange Crush and Hires brands from Procter & Gamble. Facing Mars's and Hershey's combined 70% share of US candy bar sales, Cadbury signed a $300 million licensing agreement with Hershey, ending direct involvement in the US candy market in 1988. In 1990 the company acquired candy makers Trebor and Bassett and combined all of its UK candy operations under the Trebor Bassett name.

Also in 1990 Cadbury Schweppes purchased the noncola soft drink operations of Source Perrier. Late in 1990 General Cinema sold most of its 3-year-old 17% stake in Cadbury Schweppes.

WHERE

HQ: 1-4 Connaught Place, London W2 2EX, UK
Phone: 011-44-71-262-1212
Fax: 011-44-71-706-0530
US HQ: Cadbury Schweppes Inc., High Ridge Park, PO Box 3800, Stamford, CT 06905
US Phone: 203-329-0911
US Fax: 203-968-7854 (Communications and Public Affairs)

Cadbury Schweppes products are sold in more than 110 countries worldwide.

	1990 Sales		1990 Operating Income	
	$ mil.	% of total	$ mil.	% of total
UK	2,846	47	286	44
Other Europe	1,230	20	131	20
Pacific Rim	956	16	113	18
Americas	778	13	84	13
Other countries	257	4	30	5
Adjustments	2	—	—	—
Total	**6,069**	**100**	**644**	**100**

WHAT

	1990 Sales		1990 Operating Income	
	$ mil.	% of total	$ mil.	% of total
Confectionery	2,551	42	314	49
Beverages	3,516	58	330	51
Adjustments	2	—	—	—
Total	**6,069**	**100**	**644**	**100**

Major Brand Names

US Markets
Soft drinks
- Canada Dry
- Crush
- Hires
- Schweppes
- Sun-drop
- Sunkist

Other products
- Clamato (mixer)
- Holland House (cocktail mixes, cooking wines)
- Mott's (apple products)
- Mr & Mrs "T" (cocktail mixes)
- Red Cheek (apple juice)
- Rose's (grenadine, lime juice)

Non-US Markets
Soft drinks
- Bali
- Coca-Cola (UK bottling, 51%)
- Gini
- Oasis
- Schweppes
- Solo
- Trina

Confectionery
- Beechnut
- Cadbury
- Fry's
- Jamesons
- Pascall
- Poulain
- Trebor
- Wispa

Other (Canada)
- Ocean Spray
- Welch's

HOW MUCH

Stock prices are for ADRs ADR = 10 shares	7-Year Growth	1981	1982	1983	1984	1985	1986	1987	1988	1989	1990
Sales ($ mil.)	13.6%	—	—	2,479	2,340	2,715	2,736	3,846	4,307	4,591	6,069
Net income ($ mil.)	21.6%	—	—	88	84	69	113	206	254	262	346
Income as % of sales	—	—	—	3.6%	3.6%	2.5%	4.1%	5.4%	5.9%	5.7%	5.7%
Earnings per share ($)	13.8%	—	—	1.97	1.81	1.35	1.94	3.41	4.17	3.99	*4.88*
Stock price – high ($)	—	—	—	—	19.88	26.13	29.50	47.63	77.25	80.25	67.13
Stock price – low ($)	—	—	—	—	16.75	17.50	20.63	27.75	41.00	52.00	50.13
Stock price – close ($)	—	—	—	—	18.88	23.00	27.75	42.75	61.13	56.13	61.25
P/E – high	—	—	—	—	11	19	15	14	19	20	14
P/E – low	—	—	—	—	9	13	11	8	10	13	10
Dividends per share ($)	61.5%	—	—	0.09	0.09	1.09	1.26	1.59	2.03	2.00	2.58
Book value per share ($)	7.3%	—	—	12.95	11.82	13.03	12.22	15.04	14.51	13.84	21.22

1990 Year-end:
Debt ratio: 34.7%
Return on equity: 27.8%
Cash (mil.): $348
Current ratio: 1.10
Long-term debt (mil.): $787
No. of shares (mil.): 70
Dividends:
- 1990 average yield: 4.2%
- 1990 payout: 52.8%

Market value (mil.): $4,272

Stock Price History High/Low 1984–90

90 80 70 60 50 40 30 20 10 0

KEY COMPETITORS

Bass	Heineken	Philip Morris
Berkshire Hathaway	Heinz	RJR Nabisco
BSN	Kirin	Sara Lee
Campbell Soup	Mars	Seagram
Coca-Cola	Nestlé	TLC Beatrice
Dr Pepper/7Up	PepsiCo	Whitman

CAMPEAU CORPORATION

OVERVIEW

Toronto-based Campeau Corporation, once one of the largest companies in Canada, has crashed. Created by flamboyant real estate tycoon Robert Campeau, the empire at its height consisted of Federated and Allied department stores, Ralphs supermarkets (California), and various real estate holdings.

Through the junk bond–financed purchases of Allied Stores in 1986 and Federated Department Stores in 1988, Campeau acquired some of the most prestigious names in retailing: Lazarus, Abraham & Straus, Burdines, Jordan Marsh, Rich's/Goldsmith's, The Bon Marché, and Bloomingdale's. But now the company is paying the piper.

Poor earnings from the stores, combined with enormous debt service, resulted in huge losses for Campeau. Consequently, Federated and Allied both filed for bankruptcy in 1990 (the largest retailing bankruptcy ever, with $8.2 billion in creditor claims).

A proposed reorganization filed in US bankruptcy court in April 1991 would strip Campeau of its interests in Allied and Federated (which will combine to form a single, publicly held corporation under the name Federated Department Stores). Accordingly, the company is no longer including the US units in its financial statements.

WHEN

Robert Campeau began his career as a housing developer in Ottawa, Canada, after WWII. He moved slowly into commercial and retail real estate development and in 1968 combined his businesses to form Campeau Corporation. In 1969 he sold a majority interest in the company to raise capital but quickly regretted the move and borrowed $38 million to regain a controlling stake.

In 1986 Campeau launched a successful hostile assault on Allied Stores Corporation, then the 6th largest department store operator in the US. Allied Stores had been founded in 1928 as Hahn Department Stores through the merger of 22 chains stretching from Jordan Marsh in Boston to The Bon Marché in Seattle to Maas Brothers in Tampa. Campeau bought Allied for $3.6 billion and sold 17 of its chains, including Ann Taylor, Brooks Brothers, Bonwit Teller, and Joske's, for $2.2 billion in order to reduce acquisition debt. Allied retained 4 chains: The Bon Marché, Maas Brothers, Stern's, and Jordan Marsh.

Although still reeling from the Allied purchase, Campeau set his sights on Federated Department Stores, which was 3 times Allied's size. After a white knight bid by May Department Stores failed to materialize, Campeau captured Federated for $6.5 billion in mostly borrowed money. The transaction would be remembered as one of the most overpriced LBOs of the 1980s.

Federated had been formed in 1929 by 4 families who together owned Lazarus of Columbus, Shillito of Cincinnati, Bloomingdale's of New York, Abraham & Straus of Brooklyn, and Filene's of Boston. Federated had grown throughout its history to include some of the best-known department store chains in the US. Campeau sold the Bullock's/Bullock's-Wilshire and I. Magnin divisions to R. H. Macy and also sold Filene's, Gold Circle, Foley's, MainStreet, and The Children's Place. The company kept only Abraham & Straus, Bloomingdale's, Burdines, Lazarus, and Rich's, which included Goldsmith's.

By 1989 Campeau had combined the headquarters operations of the 2 department store chains to increase efficiency, but the subsidiaries continued to lose money. Federated and Allied Stores filed for bankruptcy in 1990. Later in 1990 the board removed Campeau from his position as chairman and CEO. In 1991 the company began a real estate restructuring, selling 6 properties that comprised 37% of its rentable footage.

HOW MUCH

	7-Year Growth	1981	1982	1983	1984	1985	1986	1987	1988[1]	1989	1990[2]
Sales ($ mil.)	6.0%	—	—	146	160	156	1,012	3,659	8,848	10,660	220
Net income ($ mil.)	—	—	—	17	21	24	62	(203)	(34)	(1,636)	(428)
Income as % of sales	—	—	—	11.6%	13.1%	15.4%	6.1%	(5.5%)	(0.4%)	(15.3%)	—
Earnings per share ($)	—	—	—	—	—	—	1.43	(5.21)	(1.04)	(37.25)	(9.90)
Stock price – high ($)	—	—	—	—	—	—	—	14.25	20.63	18.63	3.38
Stock price – low ($)	—	—	—	—	—	—	—	9.75	11.75	2.75	0.75
Stock price – close ($)	—	—	—	—	—	—	—	14.13	13.38	3.00	1.75
P/E – high	—	—	—	—	—	—	—	—	—	—	—
P/E – low	—	—	—	—	—	—	—	—	—	—	—
Dividends per share ($)	—	—	—	—	—	—	0.08	0.09	0.24	0.17	0.00
Book value per share ($)	—	—	—	—	—	—	3.65	(0.16)	(0.29)	(39.88)	(50.91)

1990 Year-end:
Debt ratio: —
Return on equity: —
Cash (mil.): $11
Current ratio: 0.03
Long-term debt (mil.): $524
No. of shares (mil.): 44
Dividends:
1990 average yield: 0.0%
1990 payout: —
Market value (mil.): $77

Stock Price History High/Low 1987–90

25 20 15 10 5 0

[1] 13-month period [2] US subsidiaries not consolidated in 1990

Principal exchange: Montreal
Fiscal year ends: January 31

WHO

Chairman, President, and CEO: Stanley H. Hartt
SVP Finance and Treasurer: David W. Beirnes
SVP, General Counsel and Secretary: William I. Kennedy
SVP Real Estate: Randy Scharfe
Auditors: Peat Marwick Thorne
Employees: 540

WHERE

HQ: 40 King St. West, Suite 5800, Toronto, Ontario M5H 3Y8, Canada
Phone: 416-868-6460
Fax: 416-594-1888 (Public Relations)

Real estate sales and rent revenues are derived from Canada.

	No. of Properties as of Jan. 31, 1991	Sq. Ft.	% of Total
Ottawa	8	2,791,000	26
Toronto	3	2,398,000	23
Oshawa	2	1,064,000	10
London	1	798,000	8
Montreal	1	572,000	5
Other Canada	5	2,925,000	28
Total	**20**	**10,548,000**	**100**

WHAT

	1990 Sales $ mil.	% of total
Real estate rental	162	74
Sale of land	58	26
Total	**220**	**100**

Shopping Centers (Ontario)
Intercity Shopping Centre
Kanata Town Centre
London Galleria
New Sudbury Shopping Centre
Oshawa Shopping Centre

Office Complexes (Ontario)
Journal Towers
Oshawa Executive Tower
Pinecrest
Place de Ville
Scotia Plaza (50%)

Business Parks (Ontario)
Bell Northern
Brewer Hunt II
Bristol Myers
Dashwood Building

KEY COMPETITORS

BCE
Canadian Pacific
Canadian Imperial

CANADIAN IMPERIAL BANK OF COMMERCE

OVERVIEW

Canadian Imperial Bank of Commerce is Canada's 2nd largest bank, after Royal Bank of Canada, and among the 10 largest banks in North America.

The bank is organized into 5 strategic business units. CIBC's Individual Bank is responsible for many of the retail bank functions in 1,561 branches ranging from the Yukon to the West Indies.

CIBC also offers banking services to consumers in grocery store kiosks, on a personal computer network, and from a mobile van. The Corporate Bank serves commercial customers from Corporate Banking Centres on 5 continents.

The Investment Bank offers treasury products, capital management, investment management, and, through its majority stake in Wood Gundy, investment banking. The Administrative Bank is the unit for support and corporate functions, and the CIBC Development Corporation shepherds the bank's real estate properties.

With coast-to-coast branches to diffuse risk and with conservative lending habits, CIBC and other Canadian banks have been spared much of the upheaval that has beset the US industry. CIBC stockholders have approved a recapitalization, and the bank has reportedly been shopping for US acquisitions.

WHEN

Canadian Imperial Bank of Commerce started because another bank didn't. In 1858 a charter was granted to an entity called the Bank of Canada, but its investors could not raise enough money to open the bank. William McMaster, a Toronto financier, bought the charter in 1866 and persuaded the provincial legislature to amend the name to Canadian Bank of Commerce because the previous name was too close to another, soon-to-be-defunct bank.

Canadian Bank of Commerce opened in 1867, acquired the Gore Bank of Hamilton (1870), and expanded within 7 years to 24 branches in Ontario and to offices in Montreal and New York. Led by Edmund Walker, the bank spread west of the Great Lakes with the opening of a Winnipeg branch (1893) and joined the Gold Rush with branches in Dawson City, Yukon Territory, and Skagway, Alaska, in 1898. A Dawson City employee, Robert W. Service, was later heralded as the Poet of the Yukon.

As the new century began, the bank's acquisitions spanned the breadth of Canada, from the Bank of British Columbia (1901) to the Halifax Banking Company (1903) and the Merchants Bank of Prince Edward Island (1906).

After more acquisitions in the 1920s, Canadian Bank of Commerce's assets peaked in 1929, then plunged during the Depression. The bank recovered during WWII.

In 1961 Canadian Bank of Commerce merged with Imperial Bank of Canada to become Canadian Imperial Bank of Commerce. Imperial Bank had been founded in 1875 by Henry Stark Howland, a former Canadian Bank of Commerce VP. Imperial went west to Calgary and Edmonton and became known as The Mining Bank. In 1956 Imperial purchased Barclays Bank (Canada). At the time of the merger with Canadian Bank of Commerce, Imperial boasted assets of more than $1 billion (about 1/3 the assets of Canadian Bank of Commerce) and 343 branches.

As the 1980s began, CIBC ran into trouble with bad debts from 2 big customers, Dome Petroleum and tractor manufacturer Massey-Ferguson. CIBC also wrote down $451 million in loans to less-developed countries (1987).

CIBC acquired control of an investment banking firm (Wood Gundy, 1988), added the retail brokerage business of Merrill Lynch Canada Inc. (1990), purchased a media-loan-heavy portfolio from doomed Bank of New England (1990), and won the right to underwrite stocks in the US (1991).

HOW MUCH

$=C$1.16 (Dec. 31, 1990)	9-Year Growth	1981	1982	1983	1984	1985	1986	1987	1988	1989	1990
Assets (C$ mil.)	6.3%	65,698	68,436	68,112	68,118	75,834	80,841	88,375	94,688	100,213	114,196
Net income (C$ mil.)	9.9%	343	199	144	248	334	311	432	591	450	802
Income as % of assets	—	0.5%	0.3%	0.2%	0.4%	0.4%	0.4%	0.5%	0.6%	0.4%	0.7%
Earnings per share (C$)	(0.4%)	4.19	1.99	0.99	2.02	2.64	2.05	2.74	3.34	2.28	4.03
Stock price – high (C$)	—	16.06	15.81	19.88	16.19	19.81	22.00	23.63	25.88	32.50	33.63
Stock price – low (C$)	—	12.50	8.13	12.56	11.13	13.31	16.75	15.75	16.88	22.75	21.63
Stock price – close (C$)	5.1%	14.25	12.56	15.38	13.44	19.56	19.13	17.88	25.13	31.63	22.25
P/E – high	—	4	8	20	8	8	11	9	8	14	8
P/E – low	—	3	4	13	6	5	8	6	5	10	5
Dividends per share (C$)	3.7%	0.95	1.04	1.04	1.04	1.04	1.08	1.08	1.14	1.24	1.32
Book value per share (C$)	2.1%	22.33	22.93	22.91	23.59	23.88	23.16	21.12	23.35	24.31	26.90

1990 Year-end:
Equity as % of assets: 5.1%
Return on equity: 15.8%
Cash (mil.): C$6,751
No. of shares (mil.): 179
Dividends:
1990 average yield: 4.8%
1990 payout: 32.8%
Market value (mil.): $3,983
Assets (mil.): $98,448
Sales (mil.): $11,211

Stock Price History High/Low 1981–90

35
30
25
20
15
10
5
0

Principal exchange: Toronto
Fiscal year ends: October 31

WHO

Chairman and CEO: R. Donald Fullerton
EVP and CFO, Administrative Bank: J. C. Doran
EVP Human Resources, Administrative Bank: J. E. Ellsworth
Auditors: Peat Marwick Thorne; Price Waterhouse
Employees: 48,500

WHERE

HQ: Commerce Court, Toronto, Ontario M5L 1A2, Canada
Phone: 416-980-2211
Fax: 416-980-5026 (Investor Relations)
US HQ: Canadian Imperial Holdings Inc., 425 Lexington Ave., New York, NY 10017
US Phone: 212-856-4000
US Fax: 212-856-4178

CIBC operates in Canada and 23 other countries.

	1990 Sales	
	C$ mil.	% of total
Canada	10,084	77
US	1,071	8
Europe	1,169	9
Asia & Pacific	500	4
Other countries	268	2
Adjustments	(87)	—
Total	**13,005**	**100**

WHAT

	1990 Sales	
	C$ mil.	% of total
Canadian mortgage loans	2,598	20
Canadian personal loans	2,111	16
Canadian business loans	3,022	23
Other loans	2,304	17
Securities	1,198	9
Deposits with banks	484	4
Commissions on securities transactions	226	2
Foreign exchange & trading	236	2
Other	913	7
Adjustments	(87)	—
Total	**13,005**	**100**

Major Subsidiaries and Affiliates
Canadian Imperial Bank of Commerce (California)
Canadian Imperial Bank of Commerce (New York)
CEF Investment Management Ltd.
Chargex Ltd./Chargex Ltée (25%)
CIBC Asset Trading Inc.
CIBC Investment Management Corp. (51%)
CIBC Mortgage Corp.
CIBC Securities Inc.
CIBC Trust Co.
CIBC Venture Capital Corp.
The CIBC Wood Gundy Corp. (71.9%)
Edifice Dorchester-Commerce Inc.
Export Finance Corp. of Canada Ltd. (25.7%)
McKinnon Properties Ltd.
Stornoway Investment Ltd.

KEY COMPETITORS

Bank of New York
BankAmerica
Bankers Trust
Barclays
BCE
Chase Manhattan
Citicorp
Crédit Lyonnais
CS Holding
Dai-Ichi Kangyo
Deutsche Bank
HSBC
Imasco
Industrial Bank of Japan
Royal Bank
Union Bank of Switzerland
Other money-center banks
Securities underwriting firms

CANADIAN PACIFIC LTD.

OVERVIEW

Canada's 2nd largest public company (after BCE), Canadian Pacific (CP) operates businesses in transportation, hotels and real estate, forest products, energy, communications, and manufacturing.

CP operates a 20,100-mile railway (the 7th largest in North America), which includes Canada's CP Rail and 2 US railways, Soo Line and Delaware & Hudson, giving the company access to Canadian and eastern and midwestern US industrial centers. It also owns 20% of school bus operator Laidlaw (which owns 34% of Attwoods, Canada's leading waste management firm, and 29.4% of ADT, the world's largest security services company).

CP operates Canada's leading hotel chain and is one of the world's largest newsprint and pulp producers. The company's energy subsidiary, PanCanadian Petroleum, benefited from higher oil prices in 1990 and recently announced plans to sell its US oil and gas businesses (about 2.6% of sales).

CP's earnings declined in 1990 as a result of weak newsprint markets, the strong Canadian dollar, and the North American economic recession.

NYSE symbol: CP
Fiscal year ends: December 31

WHO

Chairman and CEO: William W. Stinson, age 57, C$1,181,895 pay
President and COO: James F. Hankinson, age 47, C$763,390 pay
EVP; Chairman, President, and CEO, CP Rail: I. B. Scott, age 61, C$532,962 pay
VP Finance and Accounting and CFO: W. R. Fatt
VP Personnel and Administration: K. S. Benson
Auditors: Price Waterhouse
Employees: 72,200

WHEN

Realizing that Canada's future depended upon a railway linking the populous east with the western frontiers, bankers George Stephen and R. B. Angus joined James J. Hill (future president of Great Northern Railway) to found Canadian Pacific Railway Company (CP Rail) in 1881, with Stephen as president.

With a 25-million-acre government land grant, the railroad was planned in 2 sections: one extending from Lake Nipissing to Lake Superior and the other crossing the Canadian prairies and mountains from Winnipeg to Kamloops Lake in British Columbia. William Cornelius Van Horne, CP Rail's general manager, started construction on the prairies in 1882, reached the summit of the Rockies in 1883, and saw the railroad completed at Eagle Pass in 1885, nearly 6 years ahead of schedule.

In 1886 a CP Rail passenger train made the first trans-Canadian rail crossing from Montreal to Port Moody — the world's longest scheduled train trip — in 139 hours. That same year CP Rail chartered ships to carry tea and silk from the Far East to the Canadian west coast, thereby laying the foundation for CP steamship services (later CP Ships). Hotel and telegraph services (later Canadian Pacific Hotels and Unitel Communications) also developed along with the railroad, providing comfort and convenience for CP Rail's passengers and employees.

CP Rail expanded by buying smaller railroads during the late 1800s and early 1900s. It gained a major competitor in 1917 when the Canadian government combined several railroads to form Canadian National Railways (CN). In 1942 Canadian Pacific united 10 local airlines to form Canadian Pacific Air Lines, which pioneered a polar route from Vancouver to Amsterdam in 1955. CP Rail and CN became all-freight railroads in 1979 by handing over passenger services to government-operated VIA Rail Canada.

When William Stinson became CEO in 1985, Canadian Pacific was operating a wide range of businesses, including Canadian Pacific Air Lines, the Minneapolis-based Soo Line Railroad, a hotel chain (Canadian Pacific Hotels), oil wells (PanCanadian Petroleum), and pulp and paper manufacturing (Canadian Pacific Forest Products). Stinson refocused the company on its most profitable businesses while selling those more cyclical in nature, including the airline (to Pacific Western Airlines, 1987). In 1988 the company bought 12% of Laidlaw (upped to 20% in 1989). In 1990 CP Hotels spent $62.6 million for 80% of Doubletree Hotels Corporation, the US-based operator of 59 Doubletree and Compri hotels. CP Rail bought the Delaware & Hudson Railway in 1991, adding 1,500 miles of track to its system.

WHERE

HQ: 910 Peel St., PO Box 6042, Station A, Montreal, Quebec H3C 3E4, Canada
Phone: 514-395-5151
Fax: 514-395-7306 (Investor Relations)

Canadian Pacific has operations throughout Canada, the US, and Europe.

	1990 Sales		1990 Net Income	
	$ mil.	% of total	$ mil.	% of total
Canada	6,775	75	248	89
US	1,689	19	(13)	(5)
Other countries	584	6	43	16
Adjustments	—	—	28	—
Total	**9,048**	**100**	**306**	**100**

WHAT

	1990 Sales		1990 Operating Income	
	$ mil.	% of total	$ mil.	% of total
Transportation	3,598	39	328	37
Forest products	1,993	21	13	1
Oil & gas, coal	1,165	12	365	41
Real estate, hotels	724	8	153	17
Manufacturing	1,445	16	42	5
Telecomms. & other	360	4	(10)	(1)
Adjustments	(237)	—	(14)	—
Total	**9,048**	**100**	**877**	**100**

Major Subsidiaries and Affiliated Companies

Canadian Pacific Forest Products Ltd. (80%)
Canadian Pacific Hotels Corp.
CP Rail System
CP Ships
CP Trucks
Delaware & Hudson Railway Co.
Fording Coal Ltd.
Laidlaw (20%)
Marathon Realty Co. Ltd.
PanCanadian Petroleum Ltd. (87%)
Soo Line Corp.
United Dominion Industries Ltd. (55%, manufacturing)
Unitel Communications Holdings, Inc. (60%)

KEY COMPETITORS

Accor
Alcatel Alsthom
American President
AT&T
Ashland
Bass
BCE
Boise Cascade
Browning-Ferris
Burlington Northern
Campeau
Carlson
Champion International
Chevron
Chicago and North Western
Consolidated Freightways
Consolidated Rail
CSX
Elf Aquitaine
Exxon
Federal Express
Fletcher Challenge
Georgia-Pacific
GTE
Halliburton
Hyatt
Imperial Oil
International Paper
ITT
James River
Kimberly-Clark
Loews
Marriott
Mead
Mobil
Nestlé
Norfolk Southern
Roadway
Schlumberger
Scott
Sun
Texaco
Union Pacific
UPS
Waste Management
Weyerhaeuser
Yellow Freight

HOW MUCH

	9-Year Growth	1981	1982	1983	1984	1985	1986	1987	1988	1989	1990
Sales ($ mil.)	(1.5%)	10,399	9,991	10,258	11,079	10,754	9,058	8,978	9,314	9,517	9,048
Net income ($ mil.)	(3.2%)	409	153	115	285	176	136	489	629	574	306
Income as % of sales	—	3.9%	1.5%	1.1%	2.6%	1.6%	1.5%	5.4%	6.8%	6.0%	3.4%
Earnings per share ($)	(7.3%)	1.90	0.70	0.53	1.32	0.79	0.46	1.62	2.03	1.80	0.96
Stock price – high ($)	—	14.75	11.75	14.29	14.33	15.75	14.63	22.88	20.13	24.38	22.88
Stock price – low ($)	—	10.33	6.42	9.50	9.38	11.63	10.00	12.75	15.88	18.00	14.88
Stock price – close ($)	4.2%	11.71	9.67	13.46	12.67	13.50	12.88	15.88	18.50	22.25	17.00
P/E – high	—	8	17	27	11	20	32	14	10	14	24
P/E – low	—	5	9	18	7	15	22	8	8	10	16
Dividends per share ($)	4.5%	0.53	0.44	0.38	0.36	0.35	0.35	0.41	0.56	0.71	0.79
Book value per share ($)	3.7%	15.28	14.98	15.05	15.84	14.76	13.98	16.37	19.28	21.12	21.16

1990 Year-end:
Debt ratio: 37.0%
Return on equity: 4.5%
Cash (mil.): $732
Current ratio: 0.98
Long-term debt (mil.): $3,969
No. of shares (mil.): 318
Dividends:
1990 average yield: 4.6%
1990 payout: 82.5%
Market value (mil.): $5,409

25 20 15 10 5 0

Stock Price History High/Low 1981–90

CANON INC.

OVERVIEW

Canon is a global leader in office equipment, supplying businesses with products ranging from electronic desktop calculators to the Navigator, a compact workstation integrating the features of a telephone, fax machine, word processor, and personal computer. The Tokyo-based company leads the world in the manufacture of copying machines, with about 40% of its business derived from copier sales. It's a leading maker of laser printers and the world's #1 supplier of laser "engines" to other printer makers. Canon is also benefiting from increased sales of Bubble Jet printers, which it recently developed as cheap, quality alternatives to dot-matrix printers.

Canon's long-standing reputation as a premier camera maker got a boost in 1990, when the company regained its leadership position from Minolta as the world's #1 maker of 35mm single-lens reflex cameras. Canon trails only Sony in the camcorder market, holding a 7.5% market share, and continues to stretch its capabilities in the field of optics, producing precision products such as retinal cameras. Canon is also the world's 5th largest producer of semiconductor manufacturing equipment.

NASDAQ symbol: CANNY (ADR)
Fiscal year ends: December 31

WHO

Chairman: Ryuzaburo Kaku, age 64
President: Keizo Yamaji
Senior General Manager Finance and Accounting: Keishi Fukuda
Auditors: KPMG Peat Marwick
Employees: 54,381

WHERE

HQ: 7-1, Nishi-Shinjuku 2-chome, Shinjuku-ku, Tokyo 163, Japan
Phone: 011-81-3-3348-2121
Fax: 011-81-3-3349-8287
US HQ: Canon U.S.A., Inc., One Canon Plaza, Lake Success, NY 11042-1113
US Phone: 516-488-6700
US Fax: 516-488-3623

Canon's products are sold in over 130 countries.

	1990 Sales	
	$ mil.	**% of total**
Japan	3,769	30
North America	3,820	30
Europe	4,272	33
Other countries	939	7
Total	**12,800**	**100**

WHEN

Dr. Takeshi Mitarai and a friend, Saburo Uchida, formed Seiki Kogaku Kenkyusho (Precision Optical Research Laboratory) in Tokyo in 1933 to build Japan's first 35mm camera. The camera was introduced in 1935 under the brand name Kwanon (after the Buddhist goddess of mercy) and later renamed Canon. In response to the military buildup before WWII, the company diversified into building X-ray machines for the Japanese military.

After WWII the company sold its Canon brand cameras to US GIs stationed in Japan and later adopted the name Canon Camera Company as the brand name gained popularity (1947). Canon diversified into business equipment in the 1960s, introducing the first 10-key electronic calculator (1964) and a plain-paper photocopier, independent of Xerox's patented technology (1968). Canon dropped "Camera Company" from its name in 1969.

In 1972 Canon invented the "liquid dry" system of copying, using plain paper and liquid developer, but failed to produce any new cameras in the interim and was surpassed by Minolta and Pentax as Japan's leading camera exporter. Sales were sluggish through the early 1970s, and Canon had to suspend its dividend in 1975 for the first time since WWII.

At that time Canon's managing director, Ryuzaburo Kaku, convinced Mitarai that the company's problems stemmed from indecisive leadership and weak marketing practices. Kaku turned Canon around, unleashing the electronic AE-1 in a media blitz that included the first-ever TV commercials for any 35mm camera (1976). With almost every feature (except focus) automated, the AE-1 made 35mm cameras accessible to even the clumsiest camera buff. Its success catapulted Canon past Minolta as the world's #1 camera maker. Kaku became president in 1977.

In 1979 Canon introduced the highly successful NP-200 (NP for New Process), the first copier to utilize a dry developer. As the plain-paper copier market matured in the early 1980s, Canon shifted to making other automated office machines, including laser printers and fax machines.

Minolta again replaced Canon as the world's #1 camera maker in 1985, when it introduced the fully automated Maxxum 7000. Then in 1986 Canon's earnings took a nose dive. Relying on exports for about 70% of its business, the company was crippled by the rising value of the yen. But Canon came back in 1987, introducing the EOS (electronic optical system) autofocus camera that returned the company to preeminence in 1990.

Canon spent $100 million in 1989 for 16.7% of Apple cofounder Steve Jobs's latest computer company NeXT.

WHAT

	1990 Sales	
	$ mil.	**% of total**
Business machines		
Copiers	5,082	40
Computer peripherals	2,574	20
Business systems	2,434	19
Cameras	1,856	14
Optical & other products	854	7
Total	**12,800**	**100**

Business Machines
Bubble Jet printers
Calculators
Copiers
Data storage and retrieval systems
Desktop publishing systems
Electronic typewriters
Fax machines
Japanese word processors
Laser printers
Microcomputers
Scanners

Cameras and Accessories
Cameras
Still video systems
Video camcorders

Optical Products
Broadcast lenses
Electronic components
Medical equipment
Semiconductor production equipment

KEY COMPETITORS

Casio	Hitachi	Pioneer
Eastman Kodak	IBM	Pitney Bowes
Fuji Photo	Matsushita	Polaroid
Fujitsu	Minolta	Sharp
GEC	NEC	Sony
Harris	Oki	Toshiba
Hewlett-Packard	Philips	Xerox

Other imaging and office automation companies

HOW MUCH

Stock prices are for ADRs ADR = 10 shares	9-Year Growth	1981	1982	1983	1984	1985	1986	1987	1988	1989	1990
Sales ($ mil.)	22.0%	2,137	2,460	2,833	3,308	4,779	5,523	7,941	8,778	9,381	12,800
Net income ($ mil.)	21.5%	79	95	123	140	185	67	108	294	266	455
Income as % of sales	—	3.7%	3.9%	4.3%	4.2%	3.9%	1.2%	1.4%	3.4%	2.8%	3.6%
Earnings per share ($)	—	0.81	0.83	0.97	1.06	1.34	0.52	0.80	2.04	1.71	2.89
Stock price – high ($)	—	26.38	18.86	26.68	26.98	27.16	34.20	44.55	56.93	69.50	66.00
Stock price – low ($)	—	12.49	8.25	15.90	16.60	16.59	23.75	21.02	32.95	48.86	45.13
Stock price – close ($)	14.3%	14.13	18.69	26.38	23.98	25.57	28.52	32.84	54.77	64.00	47.00
P/E – high	—	33	23	27	25	20	66	56	28	41	23
P/E – low	—	15	10	16	16	12	46	26	16	29	16
Dividends per share ($)	11.9%	0.16	0.16	0.21	0.20	0.29	0.38	0.34	0.21	0.63	0.45
Book value per share ($)	15.8%	8.18	8.58	9.55	9.95	13.43	16.46	22.93	24.53	26.17	30.63

1990 Year-end:
Debt ratio: 29.9%
Return on equity: 9.4%
Cash (mil.): $3,792
Current ratio: 1.51
Long-term debt (mil.): $1,947
No. of shares (mil.): 747
Dividends:
1990 average yield: 1.0%
1990 payout: 15.6%
Market value (mil.): $7,019

Stock Price History High/Low 1981–90

CARLSBERG AS

OVERVIEW

Copenhagen-based Carlsberg is one of the largest brewers in the EC. Although brewing is its primary business (71% of revenues), the company has 86 subsidiaries (most of which are outside Denmark) engaged in everything from glass art objects to biotechnology.

The company's famous beers, sold primarily under the Carlsberg and Tuborg labels, control about 3/4 of Denmark's beer market and are distributed in more than 130 countries, although they are strongest in Europe. The English are so fond of the beers that they consume more than the Danes. In addition to Carlsberg's many overseas breweries, the company maintains licensing agreements with such industry leaders as Labatt and Anheuser-Busch. Altogether about 71% (by volume) of Carlsberg's beer sales are outside Denmark.

Although the company is traded on the Copenhagen exchange, 51% is owned by the Carlsberg Foundation, a charitable organization that supports the social sciences and the humanities. The Foundation oversees the administration of the Frederiksborg Museum of Natural History and the Carlsberg Laboratory (an important research facility) and, through a subsidiary, acquires art for Danish museums and institutions.

Principal exchange: Copenhagen
Fiscal year ends: September 30

WHO

Chairman, Supervisory Board: Kristof Glamann
President and Group CEO: Poul Svanholm
VP Finances: Jesper Bærnholdt
VP Personnel: Kurt Israelsen
Auditors: Revisionsfirmaet C. Jespersen and Jens Langkilde Larsen
Employees: 12,192

WHERE

HQ: 100 Vesterfælledvej, DK-1799 Copenhagen V, Denmark
Phone: 011-45-31-21-12-21
Fax: 011-45-31-29-35-07
US HQ: Carlsberg Brand Team, Anheuser-Busch, Inc., One Busch Place, St. Louis, MO 63118-1852
US Phone: 314-577-2000
US Fax: 314-577-9749

The company's beer is exported to 130 countries.

WHEN

The modern Carlsberg AS stems from the amalgamation of 2 proud Danish brewing concerns. The first of these was founded in Copenhagen by Captain J. C. Jacobsen, whose father had worked as a brewery hand before acquiring a small brewery of his own in 1826. Jacobsen inherited the brewery in 1835. Determined to introduce a higher degree of technical skill to Danish brewing, Jacobsen studied extensively, even testing modern brewing methods in his mother's washtub. In 1847 he opened the Carlsberg Brewery (named for his son Carl) and in 1876 established the Carlsberg Foundation to conduct scientific research and oversee brewery operations.

Carl Jacobsen, who fell into disagreement with his father over brewery operations, opened a new brewery adjacent to his father's in 1881. Both men, operating under the motto *Laboremus pro patria* (Let us work for our country), bestowed rich gifts upon their beloved city, including a church, an art museum (the Glyptothek), renovation of a royal castle, and the famous statue of the Little Mermaid in Copenhagen Harbor. Both father and son willed their breweries to the Foundation.

Tuborg, the 2nd great Danish brewing enterprise, was founded as Tuborgs Fabrikker in 1873 by a group of Danish businessmen who wanted to establish a major industrial project (including a brewery, a glass factory, and a sulphuric acid works) on a piece of land around Tuborg Harbor. Philip Heyman headed the group and in 1880 spun off all operations but the brewery.

Carlsberg and Tuborg became Denmark's 2 leading brewers. After WWII both launched an intense marketing plan to carry their beers outside Denmark. In the period between 1958 and 1972, they tripled exports and established breweries in Europe and Asia.

Indeed, the intense drive of both brewers to establish markets in foreign countries greatly influenced their decision to merge. In 1970 the 2 companies joined as United Breweries.

During the 1980s the company diversified, forming Carlsberg Biotechnology in 1983 to extend elements of its research into other areas. It also strengthened its position in North America through licenses with Anheuser-Busch (1985) and John Labatt (1988). United Breweries reverted to the old Carlsberg name in 1987.

In 1991 Guinness made a $47 million bid for Unión Cervecera, a Spanish brewer in which Carlsberg has a 60% interest. If the bid goes through, Carlsberg will acquire 10% of Guinness's Spanish brewer Cruzcampo.

WHAT

	1990 Sales	
	DK mil.	% of total
Denmark brewing	3,430	33
Non-Danish brewing	4,043	38
Other	3,009	29
Total	**10,482**	**100**

Beverages
Budweiser (under license)
Carlsberg
Elephant Beer
Fine Festival
Gamle Carlsberg
Gron Tuborg
Hannen Alt
Julebryg C 47
KB Juleol
KB Paskeol
Kongens Bryg
Let Pilsner
Lys Tuborg
Oro
Paskebryg
Pilsner Hof
Porter
Rod Tuborg
Skol
Sort Guld
Splügen
Tuborg
Tuborg Gold
Tuborg Julebryg
Victoria

Brewing Subsidiaries and Affiliates
Carlsberg Brewery Hong Kong Ltd. (50%)
Carlsberg Brewery Ltd. (UK)
Carlsberg Brewery Malaysia Berhad (25%)
Carlsberg France SA
Carlsberg Malawi Brewery Ltd. (49%)
Carlsberg Marketing (Singapore) Pte. Ltd. (50%)
Danbrew Ltd. AS (brewing consultants, Denmark)
Fredericia Bryggeri AS (Denmark)
Hannen Brauerei GmbH (97%, Germany)
Industrie Poretti SpA (50%, Italy)
Unión Cervecera, SA (60%, Spain)
Wiibroes Bryggeri AS (brewing consultants, Denmark)

Selected Non-brewing Subsidiaries
AS Kjøbenhavns Sommer-Tivoli (44%, amusement parks)
AS Rynkeby Mosteri (fruit processing, Denmark)
Royal Copenhagen AS (80%; porcelain, Georg Jensen silverware, Holmegaard glass; Denmark)
Vingaarden AS (81%, wine and spirits, Denmark)

HOW MUCH

$=DK5.78 (Dec. 31, 1990)	9-Year Growth	1981	1982	1983	1984	1985	1986	1987	1988	1989	1990
Sales (DK mil.)	7.7%	5,391	6,310	7,717	7,836	8,599	9,076	9,122	10,002	10,215	10,482
Net income (DK mil.)[1]	14.6%	225	273	304	369	348	415	485	566	618	768
Income as % of sales	—	4.2%	4.3%	3.9%	4.7%	4.0%	4.6%	5.3%	5.7%	6.0%	7.3%
Earnings per share (DK)	10.0%	28	34	38	47	37	41	50	48	53	66
Stock price – high (DK)	—	—	—	—	—	—	—	—	1,036	1,330	1,375
Stock price – low (DK)	—	—	—	—	—	—	—	—	611	863	1,200
Stock price – close (DK)	—	—	—	—	—	—	—	—	927	1,330	1,250
P/E – high	—	—	—	—	—	—	—	—	22	25	21
P/E – low	—	—	—	—	—	—	—	—	13	16	18
Dividends per share (DK)[2]	8.9%	6.94	8.68	8.68	10.42	10.42	12.50	12.50	12.50	12.50	15.00
Book value per share (DK)	—	—	236	235	282	281	326	369	353	408	436

1990 Year-end:
Debt ratio: 21.5%
Return on equity: 15.6%
Cash (mil.): DK995
Long-term debt (mil.): DK1,429
No. of shares (mil.): 12
Dividends:
1990 average yield: 1.2%
1990 payout: 22.7%
Market value (mil.): $2,595
Sales (mil.): $1,813

Stock Price History High/Low 1988–90

[1] Including extraordinary items [2] "A" shares

KEY COMPETITORS

Adolph Coors
Allied-Lyons
Bass
Bond
Brown-Forman
BSN
Colgate-Palmolive
Corning
Foster's Brewing
Guinness
Heineken
Kirin
Pearson
Philip Morris
San Miguel
Stroh

CASIO COMPUTER CO., LTD.

OVERVIEW

With approximately 30% of the world calculator market, Casio is battling with Sharp for supremacy. The long-simmering rivalry has flared up as both seek to satisfy burgeoning demand for electronic diaries (hand-held devices that retain such information as addresses and telephone numbers and perform scheduling functions). Casio is trying to take the lead by taking a low-price approach and making the most of its integrated circuit card technology for data storage.

Casio dominates the digital watch market, with a share of over 70%. As the market for digital watches has matured, Casio has broadened its line of analog watches. Other Casio products include pocket televisions, electronic musical keyboards and other instruments, PCs, printers, and cash registers.

Casio has grown through innovation and creation of new markets. The company's R&D is principally focused on liquid crystal display technology and miniaturization of electronic circuitry. Although Casio derives most of its sales from overseas markets, most of its products are first launched in gadget-mad Japan.

WHEN

In 1942 Tadao Kashio started a Tokyo-based machine shop and called it Kashio Manufacturing. His brother, Toshio, later joined him. After reading about a 1946 computing contest in which an abacus bested an electric calculator, Toshio, an inventor, wrote a note to himself: "Abacus is human ability, calculator is technology." Toshio stumbled upon his note in 1950 and was inspired to begin development of a calculator. The remaining Kashio brothers — Yukio, a mechanical engineer, and Kazuo, who took over the sales function — joined the company in the 1950s.

The Kashio brothers incorporated in 1957 as Casio, an Anglicization of the family name. In the same year Casio launched its first product, an electric calculator featuring an innovative floating decimal point display. It was the first Japanese-built electric calculator. Casio took advantage of new transistor technology to create electronic calculators and in 1965 introduced the first electronic desktop calculator with memory. The company began exports to the US in 1970.

In the 1970s Casio fought in the fierce "calculator war," from which only Casio and Sharp emerged as significant Japanese survivors. Casio's strategy of putting lots of new functions on a proliferation of small models and selling them at rock-bottom prices worked not only with calculators, but with digital watches as well. The company introduced its first digital watch in 1974 and went on to dominate the market. Critical to both product lines was Casio's development of technology in liquid crystal displays and integrated circuit design and fabrication.

Casio continued to introduce new products, branching into electronic music synthesizers (1980), pocket TVs (1982), and thin, card calculators (1983). In the mid-1980s a rising yen and stiff price competition at the low end of the calculator market from developing Asian nations slammed Casio. The company responded by beefing up R&D spending and releasing more sophisticated calculators designed for such specialized users as architects and insurance agents. To help offset the effects of the heightened value of the yen, Casio moved manufacturing offshore to Taiwan, Hong Kong, Korea, and, in 1990, San Diego, California, and Tijuana, Mexico.

In 1988 Casio trailed Sharp into the Japanese market for electronic diaries by 6 months and remains a distant but solid #2. In 1990 Casio established Casio Electronic Devices to exploit the company's technology through the sales of components, principally liquid crystal displays and chip-on-film (tiny electronic circuit) products.

HOW MUCH

$=¥135 (Dec. 31, 1990)	9-Year Growth	1981[1]	1982[1]	1983[1]	1984	1985	1986	1987	1988[2]	1989	1990
Sales (¥ bil.)	7.6%	157	151	161	204	239	267	237	248	271	305
Net income (¥ bil.)	5.6%	5	5	6	8	8	5	4	5	7	8
Income as % of sales	—	2.9%	3.4%	3.5%	3.9%	3.4%	1.9%	1.5%	1.9%	2.4%	2.5%
Earnings per share (¥)	1.2%	*25*	*28*	*28*	*38*	*38*	*22*	*15*	*20*	*27*	*28*
Stock price – high (¥)	—	720	766	1,229	1,488	1,630	1,603	1,510	1,650	1,600	1,740
Stock price – low (¥)	—	403	392	631	803	1,147	1,124	810	1,100	1,300	905
Stock price – close (¥)	9.1%	438	709	1,066	1,385	1,541	1,381	1,140	1,350	1,520	963
P/E – high	—	28	27	44	39	43	75	101	83	60	62
P/E – low	—	16	14	23	21	31	52	54	55	49	32
Dividends per share (¥)	7.1%	6.72	7.40	8.12	8.93	9.84	10.77	11.91	12.50	12.50	12.50
Book value per share (¥)	10.0%	232	258	301	341	375	433	460	472	523	546

1990 Year-end:
Debt ratio: 38.7%
Return on equity: 5.3%
Cash (bil.): ¥126
Long-term debt (bil.): ¥92
No. of shares (mil.): 267
Dividends:
1990 average yield: 1.3%
1990 payout: 44.3%
Market value (mil.): $1,901
Sales (mil.): $2,259

Stock Price History High/Low 1981–90

[1] Unconsolidated data [2] Accounting change

Principal exchange: Tokyo
Fiscal year ends: March 31

WHO

Chairman: Toshio Kashio, age 68
President: Kazuo Kashio, age 64
Senior Managing Director: Yukio Kashio, age 62
Senior Managing Director: Toshio Kohzai
President, Casio, Inc. (US): John J. McDonald
Auditors: Asahi Shinwa & Co.
Employees: 3,757

WHERE

HQ: Casio Keisanki Kabushiki Kaisha, Shinjuku-Sumitomo Bldg., 2-6-1, Nishi-Shinjuku, Shinjuku-ku, Tokyo 163, Japan
Phone: 011-81-3-3347-4811
Fax: 011-81-3-3347-4650
US HQ: Casio, Inc., 570 Mount Pleasant Ave., Dover, NJ 07801-1620
US Phone: 201-361-5400
US Fax: 201-361-3819

Casio conducts operations in the US, Canada, the UK, Germany, the Netherlands, Taiwan, South Korea, Hong Kong, and Mexico, as well as Japan. The company sells its products in over 140 countries.

	1990 Sales	
	¥ bil.	% of total
Japan	119	39
Other countries	186	61
Total	**305**	**100**

WHAT

	1990 Sales	
	¥ bil.	% of total
Electronic calculators	123	40
Electronic timepieces	72	24
Electronic musical instruments	39	13
Electronic office equip. & other	71	23
Total	**305**	**100**

Products

Electronic Calculators
Digital diaries
Pocket computers
Scientific calculators

Electronic Timepieces
Digital/analog combination watches
Digital watches
Waterproof watches

Electronic Musical Instruments
Guitars
Keyboards

Electronic Office Equipment and Other
Cash registers
Integrated business systems
Mini-TVs
Office computers

KEY COMPETITORS

Canon
Fujitsu
Hewlett-Packard
NCR
Sharp
Sony
Texas Instruments
Toshiba
Yamaha

CIBA-GEIGY LTD.

OVERVIEW

Basel, Switzerland, arguably the chemical and pharmaceutical capital of the world, is the home base of Swiss powerhouse Ciba-Geigy, Switzerland's largest chemical company (5th in Europe) and the world's 6th largest producer of pharmaceuticals and 2nd largest producer of agrochemicals.

Truly an international company, Ciba-Geigy sells almost all of its products outside Switzerland and maintains production facilities throughout the world. Aside from a host of prescription brands, the company produces such recognizable consumer products as Acutrim diet aids and Sunkist vitamins.

Since the merger of Ciba and Geigy in 1970, the company has been continually on the defensive because of a series of negative events, such as a 1978 incident in which the company's diarrhea drug was linked to the deaths of more than 1,000 people in Japan. Other events causing public outcry include an incident in which the company paid 6 Egyptian boys to stand barefoot in a field that was being sprayed with Galecron insecticide to test its effects on humans (1976) and, more recently, the company's dumping of toxic waste in New Jersey (1985) and an herbicide spill into the Rhine (1986).

WHEN

Johann Geigy began selling organic merchandise (spices, natural dyes, etc.) in Basel in 1758. Successive generations of Geigys continued to produce his products and were still doing so when synthetic dyes were invented a century later. Geigy's family began producing the new dyes in 1859.

Geigy, however, was not the only Basel company to exploit the new technology. Alexander Clavel joined the synthetic dye trade at about the same time, forming the Gesellschaft für Chemische Industrie im Basle (later shortened to Ciba). By the turn of the century, Ciba was Switzerland's largest chemical firm.

When the powerful German chemical cartel fell during WWI, the Swiss were quick to fill the gap. After the war the German cartel was reestablished as I. G. Farben. Forced to compete with the Germans, Ciba, Geigy, and Sandoz (another Basel company) combined to form their own cartel, the Basel AG in 1918. Sharing profits, technology, and markets, Basel AG was soon outperforming its German competitors. The cartel used its profits to diversify into pharmaceuticals and other chemicals and also gained a foothold in the US.

In 1929 the German and Swiss cartels merged and later accepted the French and British as well. This so-called Quadrapartite Cartel lasted until 1939 when it was shattered by WWII, leaving only the Basel AG intact. That same year Paul Müller, a scientist at Geigy, invented DDT, for which he was awarded a Nobel Prize. After the war the companies of the Basel AG decided that they no longer needed the protection of the cartel and voluntarily dissolved it in 1951.

Ciba and Geigy continued to diversify. During the 1950s Geigy expanded rapidly, finding new markets in agricultural chemicals. By 1967 it had passed Ciba in sales. Faced again with competition from foreign companies as well as from its Swiss peers, Ciba and Geigy merged in 1970 after intense negotiations with US antitrust authorities.

After the company consolidated its joint holdings, it bought Airwick Industries in 1974 (sold in 1985). In 1986 Ciba-Geigy entered a joint venture with Chiron Corporation to produce and market a new line of genetically engineered vaccines. The following year the company completed the purchase of California-based Spectra-Physics (laser systems) but sold it in 1990 to Pharos (part of Nobel Industries). In 1988 Ciba-Geigy sold its Ilford segment (photographic products) to International Paper.

HOW MUCH

$=SF1.27 (Dec. 31, 1990)	9-Year Growth	1981	1982	1983	1984	1985	1986	1987	1988	1989	1990
Sales (SF mil.)	4.2%	13,599	13,808	14,741	17,474	18,221	15,955	15,764	17,647	20,608	19,703
Net income (SF mil.)	7.9%	521	622	776	1,187	1,472	1,161	1,100	1,325	1,557	1,033
Income as % of sales	—	3.8%	4.5%	5.3%	6.8%	8.1%	7.3%	7.0%	7.5%	7.6%	5.2%
Earnings per share (SF)	7.5%	97	116	145	221	274	216	205	245	286	186
Stock price – high (SF)[1]	—	1,320	1,640	2,475	2,560	3,900	4,550	4,220	3,575	4,720	3,820
Stock price – low (SF)[1]	—	970	1,165	1,605	2,085	2,470	3,775	2,440	2,400	2,670	2,270
Stock price – close (SF)[1]	7.6%	1,280	1,640	2,435	2,470	3,830	3,870	2,700	2,645	3,740	2,470
P/E – high	—	14	13	17	12	14	21	21	15	17	21
P/E – low	—	10	10	11	9	9	17	12	10	9	12
Dividends per share (SF)	10.2%	25.00	28.00	31.00	35.00	38.00	38.00	38.00	50.00	65.00	60.00
Book value per share (SF)	3.6%	2,028	2,151	2,250	2,592	2,606	2,685	2,645	2,847	2,980	2,776

1990 Year-end:
Debt ratio: 6.3%
Return on equity: 6.4%
Cash (mil.): SF3,711
Long-term debt (mil.): SF990
No. of shares (mil.): 5
Dividends:
1990 average yield: 2.4%
1990 payout: 32.3%
Market value (mil.): $10,288
Sales (mil.): $15,514

Stock Price History High/Low 1981–90

5,000 / 4,500 / 4,000 / 3,500 / 3,000 / 2,500 / 2,000 / 1,500 / 1,000 / 500 / 0

[1] Bearer shares

Principal exchange: Zurich
Fiscal year ends: December 31

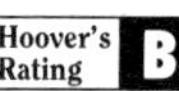

WHO

Chairman, Executive Committee: Heini Lippuner
Chairman and Managing Director: Alex Krauer
Deputy Chairman: Albert Bodmer
Senior Financial Officer: H. P. Schaer
Senior Personnel Officer: H. Kindler
Auditors: Swiss Auditing and Fiduciary Co.
Employees: 94,141

WHERE

HQ: CH-4002, Basel, Switzerland
Phone: 011-41-61-696-28-64
Fax: 011-41-61-696-43-54
US HQ: Ciba-Geigy Corporation, 444 Saw Mill River Rd., Ardsley, NY 10502
US Phone: 914-479-5000
US Fax: 914-478-1201

The company operates in 60 countries worldwide.

	1990 Sales	
	SF mil.	% of total
Europe	8,866	45
North America	6,108	31
Latin America	1,379	7
Asia	2,365	12
Other countries	985	5
Total	**19,703**	**100**

WHAT

	1990 Sales	
	SF mil.	% of total
Dyestuffs & Chemicals	2,657	14
Pharmaceuticals	6,365	32
Agricultural	4,128	21
Additives	1,884	10
Plastics	1,777	9
Pigments	882	4
Other	2,010	10
Total	**19,703**	**100**

Agricultural Products
Fungicides
Growth regulators
Herbicides
Hybrid seeds
Pesticides
Veterinary drugs

Ciba Vision Group
Contact lenses
Lens care products

US Consumer Brands
Acutrim (diet aid)
Doan's pills (analgesic)
Eucalyptamint (analgesic)
Fiberall (laxative)
Nupercainal (ointment)
Privine (nasal spray)
Sunkist vitamins

Dyestuffs and Chemicals
Dyeing auxiliaries
Dyes
Finishing agents
Proofing agents

Pharmaceuticals
Antibiotics
Anticold drugs
Antirheumatics
Cardiovascular drugs
Dermatological drugs
Neurotropic drugs
Psychotropic drugs

Plastics and Additives
Adhesives
Epoxy resins
Hardeners
Lacquers
Pigments
Plasticizers

US Subsidiaries and Affiliates
The Biocine Company
Ciba-Corning Diagnostics Corp.
Cord Laboratories
Geneva Generics Inc.
Ohaus Corp.

KEY COMPETITORS

BASF	Glaxo	Procter & Gamble
Bayer	Hoechst	Rhône-Poulenc
Brystol-Myers Squibb	Imperial Chemical	Roche
Dow Chemical	Johnson & Johnson	Sandoz
Du Pont	Monsanto	SmithKline Beecham
	Nobel	

Other agricultural, chemical, and pharmaceutical companies

COOPERS & LYBRAND

OVERVIEW

Coopers & Lybrand is the 5th largest of the Big 6 accounting firms. CEO Peter Scanlon has stepped down, unable to complete another term before reaching the firm's retirement age. Successor Eugene Freedman will reach retirement after a 3-year term.

While Coopers & Lybrand sat out the accounting mergers of the 1980s, it has become the unexpected beneficiary as the refuge for partners defecting from other international mergers. Since the 1989 merger of Deloitte Haskins & Sells and Touche Ross & Company, Coopers & Lybrand units have attracted disaffected DH&S partnerships in the Netherlands, Austria, and Belgium. In the UK, Coopers & Lybrand (leader in management consulting) joined with the former UK branch of Deloitte Haskins & Sells (the leader in international tax advice and corporate finance) to form Coopers & Lybrand Deloitte, the largest accounting firm in that nation.

The company aggressively uses technology, including expert systems (sophisticated computer programs that use large, specialized databases to analyze client problems). Coopers has joined IBM to offer computer consulting targeted to consumer goods companies, health care firms, and pharmaceutical concerns.

WHEN

Coopers & Lybrand, the product of a 1957 trans-Atlantic merger, literally wrote the book on auditing. Lybrand, Ross Bros. & Montgomery, as the US ancestor was known, had been formed in 1898 by 4 partners — William M. Lybrand, T. Edward Ross, Adam A. Ross, and Robert H. Montgomery. In 1912 Montgomery wrote *Montgomery's Auditing*, termed by many as the "Bible" of the accounting profession. The book is now in its 11th edition.

In the early years the accounting firm grew slowly, and the Ross brothers' sister served as secretary, typist, and bookkeeper. In 1902 the company opened a New York office at 25 Broad Street. Other offices across the country followed — Pittsburgh (1908), Chicago (1909), and Boston (1915). WWI focused attention on Washington, DC, and the Lybrand firm opened an office there (1919) and then branched out to the new auto capital of Detroit (1920), to Seattle (1920), and to Baltimore (1924). A merger with the firm of Klink, Bean & Company gave the firm a window on California (1924), and another merger drove the firm into Dallas (1930), with an offshoot office in Houston a year later.

In Europe the Lybrand firm established offices in Berlin (1924, closed in 1938 as WWII loomed), Paris (1926), and London (1929). During the same period the UK firm of Cooper Brothers was also expanding in Europe.

Cooper Brothers had begun in 1854 when William Cooper, the oldest son of a Quaker banker, formed his accountancy at 13 George Street in London. He was quickly joined by his brothers, Arthur, Francis, and Ernest. The firm's name of Cooper Brothers & Company was adopted in 1861. After WWI Cooper Brothers branched out to Liverpool (1920), Brussels (1921), New York (1926), and Paris (1930). After WWII Cooper Brothers acquired 3 venerable firms — Alfred Tongue & Company; Aspell Dunn & Company; and Rattray Brothers, Alexander & France.

In 1957 Coopers & Lybrand was formed by the amalgamation of the international accounting firms, and by 1973 the affiliated partnerships had gravitated toward the Coopers & Lybrand name. In the 1960s the company branched out to employee benefits consulting and introduced a new auditing method that included evaluating clients' systems of internal control. During the 1970s Coopers focused on integrating computer technology into the auditing process.

While some of its sisters in the then–Big 8 were pairing off in the 1980s, Coopers & Lybrand sat out the mergers. As a result it dropped from the top of the Big 8 to 5th in the Big 6. That was the least of its problems, though, as it faced charges from federal regulators relating to its 1986 audit of failed Silverado Banking, Savings & Loan, the Denver-based thrift made famous by its association with presidential son Neil Bush.

In the first such action against a Big 6 firm, the Office of Thrift Supervision accused Coopers & Lybrand of understating potential losses. In 1990 Coopers & Lybrand, without admitting to guilt, agreed to accept penalties that included banning one partner from audits of banks or thrifts.

HOW MUCH

	9-Year Growth	1981	1982	1983	1984	1985	1986	1987	1988	1989	1990
Worldwide revenues ($ mil.)	12.8%	998	1,066	1,100	1,250	1,375	1,695	1,998	2,398	3,000	4,100
No. of offices[1]	—	—	—	93	94	95	96	99	100	100	99
No. of partners	—	—	—	890	915	987	1,054	1,110	1,270	1,333	1,301
No. of employees	—	—	—	10,673	11,586	9,530	13,409	14,270	15,400	16,625	16,145

1990 revenues per partner: $1,076,095

[1] US offices

International association of partnerships

Fiscal year ends: September 30

WHO

Chairman and CEO: Peter R. Scanlon, age 60; Eugene M. Freedman, age 59 (effective Oct. 1, 1991)

Deputy Chairman for Operations: Stephen W. McKessy

CFO: Frank Scalia

Director of Personnel Management: Robert McDowell

Employees: 16,145

WHERE

HQ: 1251 Ave. of the Americas, New York, NY 10020

Phone: 212-536-2000

Fax: 212-642-7328

Coopers & Lybrand operates more than 95 offices in the US and 600 offices in 104 countries.

	1990 Revenues $ mil.	% of total
US	1,400	34
Foreign	2,700	66
Total	**4,100**	**100**

WHAT

Services

Accounting and Auditing
Computer audit services
Corporate financial planning
Financial audits, reviews, and compilations
Internal audit assistance
Management accounting systems
SEC services

Actuarial, Benefits, and Compensation Consulting
Defined benefit programs
Executive compensation
Group health and welfare services
Insurance/risk management

Business Investigation
Business reorganization
Litigation and claims

Government Contracting
Negotiations consulting
Standards compliance

International Trade
Business planning
Regulations compliance

Management Consulting
Business planning
Information systems
Productivity

Mergers and Acquisitions
Business planning
Corporate finance advice
Target identification
Valuation

Tax
International taxation
Financial planning
State and local tax services

Representative Clients

B.A.T
British Telecom
Cadbury Schweppes
Fletcher Challenge
Glaxo
Humana
Ito-Yokado
Johnson & Johnson
Maxwell
Pearson
Peugeot
RTZ
Telmex
Unilever

KEY COMPETITORS

Arthur Andersen
Deloitte & Touche
Ernst & Young
KPMG
Marsh & McLennan
McKinsey & Co.
Price Waterhouse
Other consulting firms

CRÉDIT LYONNAIS

OVERVIEW

State-owned Crédit Lyonnais is France's 3rd largest banking concern, after Crédit Agricole and Banque National de Paris, and among the top 10 in the world.

Crédit Lyonnais is following an aggressive growth plan designed to double 1988 net profit by 1992. But that aggressiveness backfired when the bank became mired in the American movie industry. Through its Dutch branch, it financed Italian Giancarlo Parretti's bid for MGM/UA. When the studio foundered, the bank took control, jettisoned its own Dutch executives, and swapped suits with Parretti. The bank's financial exposure in Hollywood may exceed $2 billion.

Undaunted, Crédit Lyonnais, through its 68%-owned Altus Finance, offered 54 cents on the dollar for failed Executive Life's $5 billion junk bond portfolio. The bank owns 20% of what used to be the J. C. Penney Building in midtown Manhattan. When Penney moved out, the bank moved in and renamed it the Crédit Lyonnais Building.

In France, Crédit Lyonnais is a universal bank, providing both retail and commercial banking. Modeling its growth after Deutsche Bank, it has amassed a $5 billion portfolio of blue-chip securities to seal relationships with French companies. Its own nonvoting shares (18.55% of capital) are publicly held.

WHEN

Henri Germain, son of a prosperous Lyons family, had been, at times, a lawyer, stockbroker, mine manager, and silk merchant. In 1863, with the support of local businessmen and Swiss bankers, he launched Crédit Lyonnais. The bank added branches in Paris and Marseille in 1865 and, as the widower Germain remarried into a Paris family and took a seat in Parliament, the bank shifted its emphasis toward the capital.

In the early 1870s, during war with Germany and the civil war that followed, some assets were also moved to London for safety, creating the bank's first foreign branch. In the late 19th and early 20th centuries, Crédit Lyonnais expanded overseas, with branches from Moscow to Jerusalem, from Madrid to Bombay. The bank became the world's largest.

Germain died in 1905. Crédit Lyonnais fell from its perch during WWI. By 1929 the bank returned to its #1 ranking in France, but the Great Depression forced Crédit Lyonnais to cut 18% of its staff in the face of a 20% drop in profits.

During WWII, the bank used a 32-car train to evacuate 500 tons of stocks, securities, and bonds for safekeeping. After the war, the French government nationalized the bank, and Crédit Lyonnais pushed into international markets. In South America, it helped form Banco Francês e Brasileiro in Brazil and other entities in Peru and Venezuela.

In 1970 Crédit Lyonnais formed a consortium with Commerzbank (then Germany's 4th largest bank) and Banco di Roma (then Italy's 3rd largest) to offer medium-term Eurocurrency loans. Spain's Banco Hispano Americano joined the consortium in 1973.

Crédit Lyonnais endured a costly strike (1972), the assassination of its president on the steps of its Paris headquarters (by a labor movement fanatic in 1977), and a series of leaders during the changes of French governments in the 1980s. Bank president Jean-Maxime Lévêque guided Crédit Lyonnais into dealing in securities, and Clinvest, the bank's investment arm, was created in 1987. Lévêque ran afoul of French officials by preaching privatization for the bank. Jean-Yves Haberer, formerly head of the Paribas merchant bank, succeeded Lévêque in 1988 and expanded the bank's holdings in French companies. In 1990, to raise capital, the bank took control of Thomson-CSF's finance operations and gave the state-owned electronics giant a stake in the bank.

HOW MUCH

$=FF5.08 (Dec. 31, 1990)	7-Year Growth	1981	1982	1983	1984	1985[1]	1986	1987	1988	1989	1990
Assets (FF bil.)	10.3%	—	—	736	868	831	837	899	1,084	1,220	1,463
Net income (FF bil.)	21.9%	—	—	1	1	1	2	2	2	3	4
Income as % of assets	—	—	—	0.1%	0.1%	0.1%	0.2%	0.2%	0.2%	0.2%	0.3%
Earnings per share (FF)	—	—	—	—	—	61	70	85	79	118	111
Stock price – high (FF)	—	—	—	—	—	—	—	—	—	763	898
Stock price – low (FF)	—	—	—	—	—	—	—	—	—	477	501
Stock price – close (FF)	—	—	—	—	—	—	—	—	—	708	561
P/E – high	—	—	—	—	—	—	—	—	—	6	8
P/E – low	—	—	—	—	—	—	—	—	—	4	5
Dividends per share (FF)[2]	—	—	—	—	—	—	—	—	15.00	19.00	23.00
Book value per share (FF)	—	—	—	—	—	—	—	—	—	—	—

1990 Year-end:
Equity as % of assets: 4.3%
Return on equity: 8.3%
Cash (mil.): FF17,524
No. of shares (mil.): 35
Dividends:
1990 average yield: 4.1%
1990 payout: 20.7%
Assets (mil.): $287,992
Sales (mil.): $8,037
Market value (mil.): $3,865

Note: All data presented for nonvoting shares [1] Accounting change [2] Not including rights issues

State-owned company
Fiscal year ends: December 31

WHO

Chairman and CEO: Jean-Yves Haberer
General Manager: Bernard Thiolon
Senior Manager, Corporate Finance and Services Division: Claude Rubinowicz
Senior Manager, Personnel Division: Joseph Musseau
Auditors: Pavie & Associes (Coopers & Lybrand); HSD Castel Jacquet (Ernst & Young)
Employees: 68,486

WHERE

HQ: 19, Boulevard des Italiens, 75002 Paris, France
Phone: 011-33-1-42-95-70-00
Fax: 011-33-1-42-95-59-02
US HQ: 1301 Ave. of the Americas, New York, NY 10019
US Phone: 212-261-7000
US Fax: 212-459-3170

Crédit Lyonnais operates 1,200 offices in 70 countries.

	1990 Assets	
	FF bil.	% of total
France	930	63
Other Europe	366	25
Other countries	170	12
Adjustments	(3)	—
Total	**1,463**	**100**

WHAT

	1990 Assets	
	FF bil.	% of total
Cash & cash equivalents	18	1
Loans to financial institutions	312	21
Treasury bills & other bills	130	9
Loans to customers	634	43
Receivables	198	14
Securities investments	86	6
Other	85	6
Total	**1,463**	**100**

Selected Subsidiaries and Affiliates
Altus Finance (68%)
Arnault et Associés (29.5%, computer services)
Banco Comercial Español (97.8%, Spain)
Banco Continental (88.3%, Chile)
Banco Francês e Brasileiro SA (53.9%, Brazil)
Banque Internationale de Gestion et de Trésorerie SA (57.3%)
Clinvest (investment banking)
Crédit Lyonnais Europe SA (holding company)
Crédit Lyonnais North America
International Moscow Bank (12%)
Société Rhodanienne Mobilère et Immobilière (investments)
Union de Banques Arabes et Françaises (40%)
Union des Assurances Fédérales (insurance)
Woodchester Group (44.9%, Ireland)

KEY COMPETITORS

Allianz
Bank of New York
Bankers Trust
Barclays
Canadian Imperial
Chase Manhattan
Chemical Banking
Citicorp
CS Holding
Dai-Ichi Kangyo
Deutsche Bank
HSBC
Industrial Bank of Japan
J.P. Morgan
Royal Bank
Tokio Marine and Fire
Union Bank of Switzerland
Securities underwriting firms
Other money-center banks

CS HOLDING

OVERVIEW

CS Holding is the parent company for Credit Suisse, Switzerland's 3rd largest bank (after Union Bank of Switzerland and Swiss Bank Corporation). Of late CS Holding has been buffeted by bad news from another subsidiary, its 64.2%-owned CS First Boston investment banking arm, which lost $587 million in 1990.

To raise money after a near–$1 billion recapitalization of CS First Boston, CS Holding is selling as much as 20% of the centerpiece Swiss bank to the public. Analysts see the move as an abrupt turnaround from the 1989 restructuring that Chairman Rainer Gut hoped would create a global commercial and investment banking network.

CS Holding remains more than solvent, though. It owns 53.8% of Leu Holding, which includes Bank Leu, the 5th largest Swiss bank; 99.6% of Fides Group, a leader in the trust business and management consulting; and 41.8% of Electrowatt, a group of power companies, manufacturers, and engineering service firms. CS Holding has launched CS Life, which offers insurance products.

WHEN

Shortly after the creation of the Swiss federal government, Alfred Escher opened the doors of Credit Suisse (CS) in Zurich in 1856. Initially CS operated more as a venture capital company than as a lender. The bank helped start Swiss railroads and other industries while opening banks in Italy and Switzerland, including Swiss Bank Corporation. In 1867 CS suffered the only annual deficit in its history when a cotton price collapse following the American Civil War led to losses on cotton import financing.

CS shifted to conventional commercial banking in 1867 and sold most of its stock holdings. By 1871 CS was Switzerland's largest bank. Rapid Swiss industrialization buoyed the bank's business. In 1895 CS helped create a hydroelectric business, the predecessor of Swiss utility Electrowatt.

CS's foreign activity expanded rapidly in the 1920s. During the Great Depression a run on banks forced CS to sell assets at a loss and dip into its undisclosed reserves (profits from past years hidden on its balance sheet).

Swiss neutrality helped CS survive WWII, and the bank's international business took off as Switzerland emerged as a major banking center in the postwar period. Foreign exchange dealing and gold trading became important activities to CS. The bank purchased Valcambi (gold ingots and coins, 1966), Crédit Foncier Suisse (mortgage financing, 1976), and Alliance Credit (consumer credit, 1976).

In 1978 the bank formed a joint venture with US investment bank First Boston. CS owned 60% of the new, London-based entity called Crédit Suissé-First Boston (CSFB) and took a minority stake in First Boston in the bargain. CSFB almost immediately became the largest Eurobond issuer.

Following management disputes, CS created a new holding company — CS First Boston — to own First Boston, CSFB, and CS First Boston Pacific, based in Tokyo. CS Holding took a 44.5% interest in the new company.

To restructure its commercial and investment banking activities, CS Holding, created as a sister entity to the bank in 1982, became the parent company of Credit Suisse and other operations in 1989.

First Boston continued to bleed red ink from wounds suffered from making $1 billion in bad loans on mergers and acquisitions. In 1990 CS Holding injected $300 million in equity and shifted $470 million in bad loans off First Boston's books. CS Holding took control of CS First Boston and, after Federal Reserve approval, became the first foreign bank to own a major Wall Street investment bank. Also in 1990 CS Holding gained control of 235-year-old Bank Leu (Switzerland).

HOW MUCH

$=SF1.27 (Dec. 31, 1990)	9-Year Growth	1981	1982	1983	1984	1985	1986	1987	1988	1989[1]	1990
Assets (SF mil.)	—	73,579	73,497	77,268	84,028	88,662	103,741	107,240	113,383	—	—
Net income (SF mil.)	—	276	303	352	417	507	566	550	634	861	192
Income as % of assets	—	0.4%	0.4%	0.5%	0.5%	0.6%	0.5%	0.5%	0.6%	—	—
Earnings per share (SF)[2]	—	*90*	*101*	*115*	*132*	*154*	*161*	*153*	*165*	*207*	*45*
Stock price – high (SF)[2]	—	2,379	2,033	2,033	2,098	3,255	3,555	3,491	2,664	2,935	2,740
Stock price – low (SF)[2]	—	1,609	1,351	1,685	1,795	2,045	2,818	2,114	1,986	2,233	1,475
Stock price – close (SF)[2]	(1.4%)	1,694	1,676	2,033	2,045	3,255	3,455	2,214	2,455	2,665	1,490
P/E – high	—	26	20	18	16	21	22	23	16	14	61
P/E – low	—	18	13	15	14	13	18	14	12	11	33
Dividends per share (SF)[2,3]	4.6%	73.64	68.09	70.41	79.18	83.59	88.00	91.90	91.90	91.90	110.00
Book value per share (SF)[2]	—	1,476	1,599	1,626	1,651	1,695	1,800	1,841	1,948	2,065	1,804

1990 Year-end:
Equity as % of assets: —
Return on equity: 2.3%
No. of shares (mil.): 4
Dividends:
1990 average yield: 7.4%
1990 payout: —
Market value (mil.): $4,693

Stock Price History High/Low 1981–90

Note: 1980-88 results for Credit Suisse only [1] Reorganization, accounting change [2] Bearer shares [3] Not including rights offerings

Principal exchange: Zurich
Fiscal year ends: March 31

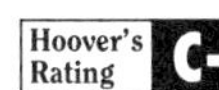

WHO

Chairman: Rainer E. Gut, age 58
Senior Executive: Peter W. Bachmann
Senior Executive: Max C. Roesle
Auditors: KPMG Klynveld Peat Marwick Goerdeler SA
Employees: 44,153

WHERE

HQ: Talacker 42, PO Box 669, CH-8021 Zurich, Switzerland
Phone: 011-41-1-212-1616
Fax: 011-41-1-333-2587
US HQ: CS First Boston, Inc., Park Ave. Plaza, 55 E. 52nd St., New York, NY 10005
US Phone: 212-909-2000
US Fax: 212-308-9151

CS Holding operates worldwide.

WHAT

	1990 Assets SF mil.	% of total
Investments		
Credit Suisse	8,710	73
Leu Holding Ltd.	826	7
CS First Boston	423	4
Electrowatt	681	6
Fides Holding	91	1
CS Life	31	—
Securities	551	5
Long-term loans	501	4
Liquid assets	28	—
Loans & receivables	20	—
Other	34	—
Adjustments	72	—
Total	**11,968**	**100**

Major Holdings

Credit Suisse (99.9%, universal banking)

CS First Boston, Inc. (64.2%, investment banking, US-based)
CS First Boston Pacific, Inc.
Financière Crédit Suisse-First Boston
The First Boston Corp.

CS Life (life insurance)

Electrowatt Ltd. (41.8%; utility, manufacturing, engineering services)

Fides Holding (99.6%; trust business, management consulting)

Leu Holding Ltd. (53.8%, financial service)
Bank Hofmann Ltd. (asset management)
Bank Leu Ltd. (full-service banking)
Clariden Bank

KEY COMPETITORS

American Express
Bank of New York
Bankers Trust
Barclays
Bear Stearns
Canadian Imperial
Chase Manhattan
Chemical Banking
Citicorp
Crédit Lyonnais
Dai-Ichi Kangyo
Deutsche Bank
Goldman Sachs
HSBC
Industrial Bank of Japan
Merrill Lynch
J.P. Morgan
Morgan Stanley
Nomura
Royal Bank
Salomon
Union Bank of Switzerland
Other banks and investment banking companies

DAEWOO GROUP

OVERVIEW

Kim Woo-Choong, chairman of Daewoo (Korean for "Great Universe"), has not taken a vacation in over 30 years and is unlikely to take one soon. Athough in 1988 and 1989 Daewoo Corporation remained profitable, Daewoo Group posted collective losses. Kim has cleaned house and taken a hands-on approach to managing the *chaebol* (industrial group), Korea's 4th largest. Kim is now trying to build the Daewoo brand name instead of producing goods for resale under other manufacturers' marks.

Chronically unprofitable Daewoo Shipbuilding threatened to topple all 24 cross-held Daewoo companies before a 1989 government bailout. After personally managing the unit for 18 months, Kim expects a profit in 1991. The company has started building minicars under license from Suzuki.

Other group units make heavy equipment and electronic goods. Daewoo Securities is Korea's largest brokerage firm. Daewoo Corporation, the lead company and trading and construction arm of the *chaebol*, has seen slower growth in recent years as labor problems, higher wage rates, and appreciation of the Korean currency have hurt exports.

WHEN

The Korean character for "risk" combines the characters for crisis and chance, both of which have figured prominently in Kim Woo-Choong's high-rolling career. In 1967 Kim and To Dae Do put together their names and $18,000 (much of it borrowed) to create Daewoo, a textile exporting company. Soon Kim bought out To and used low-cost Korean labor to turn Daewoo into a profitable clothing maker, garnering Sears, J.C. Penney, and Montgomery Ward as accounts. As the Korean economy took off, Daewoo entered construction.

In 1976 Korean President Park Chung Hee asked Kim to take over a government-owned machinery plant that had been unprofitable for 37 years. Kim accepted, lived in the plant for 9 months, and turned the business around. Since then the business, now known as Daewoo Heavy Industries, has been consistently profitable.

At the same time, most Korean construction firms were following the flow of oil money to the Middle East. To avoid competition, Kim sought riskier construction contracts and landed $2 billion worth in Libya. Kim eliminated political and economic risk by requiring Libya to pay in advance.

In the late 1970s Daewoo came to the rescue of 2 more state-owned enterprises. President Park asked Kim to take over the government's 50% share of faltering GM Korea. Kim renamed the automaker Daewoo Motor Company and turned it into Korea's 3rd largest car producer. However, the Great Universe acquired a black hole when Park announced Daewoo's takeover of a partially built, debt-ridden shipyard while Kim was out of the country. Out of patriotism Kim spent $500 million to build a state-of-the-art shipyard, but it remained unprofitable.

In the 1980s Kim inked a string of big export deals exchanging low-cost goods for technology. Daewoo Motor began making the Pontiac LeMans in 1986. Daewoo companies now build forklifts for Caterpillar; telephone equipment for Northern Telecom; and aerospace components for Boeing, Lockheed, General Dynamics, Daimler-Benz, and United Technologies.

Daewoo entered electronics and continued to buy ailing companies. In the mid-1980s the group bought foundering custom chipmaker ZyMOS (US), and Daewoo began making PCs for Leading Edge, a red-hot, US-based PC marketer. Sales at Leading Edge faded and the company went bankrupt. Daewoo bought it in 1989 and is attempting to revive the brand.

In 1991 the *chaebol* announced plans to make auto parts in the US as part of a production globalization program.

HOW MUCH

$=Won714 (Dec. 31, 1990)	5-Year Growth	1981	1982	1983	1984	1985	1986	1987	1988	1989	1990
Sales (Won bil.)	6.8%	—	—	—	—	3,779	4,215	4,453	4,729	4,790	5,246
Net income (Won bil.)[1]	9.3%	—	—	—	—	34	35	34	32	215	53
Income as % of sales	—	—	—	—	—	0.9%	0.8%	0.8%	0.7%	4.5%	1.0%
Earnings per share (Won)[1]	—	—	—	—	—	—	*1,083*	*876*	*628*	*3,474*	*783*
Stock price – high (Won)	—	—	—	—	—	—	—	10,574	25,749	27,773	25,023
Stock price – low (Won)	—	—	—	—	—	—	—	6,332	10,169	19,946	13,048
Stock price – close (Won)	—	—	—	—	—	—	7,622	9,941	25,587	23,028	19,400
P/E – high	—	—	—	—	—	—	—	12	41	8	32
P/E – low	—	—	—	—	—	—	—	7	16	6	17
Dividends per share (Won)[2]	—	—	—	—	—	—	—	375	375	495	45
Book value per share (Won)	—	—	—	—	—	—	—	—	—	14,476	14,918

1990 Year-end:
Debt ratio: 41.1%
Return on equity: 5.3%
Cash (bil.): Won104
Long-term debt (bil.): Won707
No. of shares (mil.): 68
Dividends:
1990 average yield: 0.2%
1990 payout: 5.7%
Market value (mil.): $1,848
Sales (mil.): $7,347

Stock Price History High/Low 1987–90

30,000
25,000
20,000
15,000
10,000
5,000
0

[1] Includes extraordinary items [2] Not including rights offerings

Principal exchange: Seoul
Fiscal year ends: December 31

WHO

Chairman: Kim Woo-Choong
Chairman: Kim Joon-Sung
Finance Director: Nam Sang-Woo
Auditors: KPMG San Tong & Co.
Employees: 14,286

WHERE

HQ: Daewoo Corporation, 541, 5-GA, Namdaemunno, Chung-Gu, Seoul, Korea
Phone: 011-82-2-759-2114
Fax: 011-82-2-753-9489
US HQ: Daewoo International (America) Corp., 100 Daewoo Place, Carlstadt, NJ 07072
US Phone: 201-935-8700
US Fax: 201-935-6491

Daewoo Corporation trades in over 130 countries through more than 70 offices and subsidiaries.

	1990 Exports % of total
Europe	31
North America	29
Asia	23
Middle East	9
Central & South America	5
Other countries	3
Total	**100**

WHAT

	1990 Exports % of total
Electric & electronics	28
Ships	17
Textiles	15
Steel & metal	13
Vehicles	10
Chemicals & building materials	6
Other	11
Total	**100**

Group Companies
Daewoo Automotive Components Ltd.
Daewoo Capital Management Co., Ltd.
Daewoo Carrier Corporation
Daewoo Corporation
Daewoo Electric Motor Industries Ltd.
Daewoo Electronic Components Co., Ltd.
Daewoo Electronics Co., Ltd.
Daewoo Heavy Industries, Ltd.
Daewoo Information Systems Co., Ltd.
Daewoo Motor Co., Ltd.
Daewoo Precision Industries Ltd.
Daewoo Research Institute
Daewoo Securities Co., Ltd.
Daewoo Shipbuilding & Heavy Machinery Ltd.
Daewoo-Sikorsky Aerospace, Ltd.
Daewoo Telecom Co., Ltd.
Daewoo ZyMOS Technology Ltd.
Dongwoo Development Co., Ltd.
Koram Plastics Co., Ltd.
Keangnam Enterprises, Ltd.
Kyungnam Metal Co., Ltd.
Orion Electric Co., Ltd.
Orion Electric Components Co., Ltd.
Shina Shipbuilding Co., Ltd.

KEY COMPETITORS

Hyundai
Lucky-Goldstar
Samsung

Other electric, electronics, ship building, textile, steel and auto companies

Information presented for Daewoo Corporation only

THE DAI-ICHI KANGYO BANK, LTD.

OVERVIEW

Dai-Ichi Kangyo Bank (DKB) is the world's largest bank and the oldest bank in Japan. DKB is the premier source of yen-denominated financing. The lead company of Sankin-kai, Japan's largest industrial group, DKB concentrates its business in Japan, where the bank gathers deposits through the country's largest branch network. DKB owns 60% of New York–based CIT Group, a commercial lending company.

Reacting to international agreements on bank capital adequacy (capital-to-assets ratio) standards, DKB raised new equity capital and shifted emphasis from size to profitability. The company expanded its horizons by allying with the UK's Hill Samuel Investment Management to provide investment advice and asset management. In Japan DKB teamed with Johnan Shinkin Bank in the first such agreement between a major bank and a credit association.

Principal exchange: Tokyo
Fiscal year ends: March 31

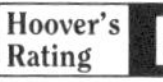

WHO

Chairman: Ichiro Nakamura, age 66
President: Kuniji Miyazaki, age 60
General Manager, International Financial Division: Tomoaki Tanaka
General Manager, Personnel Division: Yoshiharu Mani
Auditors: Century Audit Corporation
Employees: 18,466

WHEN

When established in 1873, Dai-Ichi Kokuritsu (First National) Bank was the first to be organized under the Japanese National Bank Act of 1872. As such, Dai-Ichi was authorized to issue currency until the Bank of Japan took over that role in 1883. Founder Eiichi Shibusawa's beliefs in ethical business behavior and positive work attitudes have had a lasting effect on Japanese management practices. Wanting widespread ownership of the bank rather than the common *zaibatsu* (family-controlled conglomerate) affiliation, Shibusawa issued stock in Dai-Ichi. After a series of acquisitions between 1912 and 1964, Dai-Ichi merged with Nippon Kangyo Bank in 1971 to create Japan's largest bank, Dai-Ichi Kangyo.

The Japanese government had established Nippon Kangyo in 1897 as a financing institution for farmers and industry. From 1921 to 1944 Nippon Kangyo consolidated its operations with several similar organizations. The bank suffered terrible losses on its real estate–backed loan portfolio in WWII but emerged as a full-service commercial bank in 1950.

A merger agreement calling for a strict balance of power between Dai-Ichi and Kangyo executives created a bureaucratic morass and institutionalized a culture clash between the two banks. Although merger-induced inertia slowed DKB's expansion overseas, the bank's size and Japan's rapid economic expansion enabled it to prosper.

Like other Japanese banks DKB benefited from the low cost of funds that resulted from the extraordinarily high Japanese savings rate (2 to 3 times the US rate). As government policies discouraged foreign investment and encouraged domestic savings, banks became the principal conduit of investment capital for Japan.

Although DKB still considers itself to be different from its *keiretsu*-affiliated brethren, the bank organized the Sankin-kai (3rd Friday group), leaders from 47 major Japanese firms, in 1978. The Sankin-kai meets regularly, as do the leaders of former *zaibatsu* groups.

In the 1970s and 1980s, DKB chose internal growth over acquisitions and called itself "the bank with heart," using pink heart emblems in its retail banking advertisements. Measured in assets DKB became the world's largest privately owned bank in 1984, although the massive Japanese Post Office savings operation remained the world's biggest bank.

Japanese financial deregulation of the 1980s introduced foreign competition and facilitated the use of debt securities in place of bank loans. DKB has tried to offset lower profitability in lending to large corporations by emphasizing consumer credit and bolstering its US and middle market business with the 1989 purchase of 60% of the CIT Group from Manufacturers Hanover for $1.28 billion. New Jersey-based CIT engages in asset-based financing, including leasing, factoring (purchasing receivables from companies at a discount, then collecting them), and LBO funding.

WHERE

HQ: 1-5, Uchisaiwaicho 1-chome, Chiyoda-ku, Tokyo 100, Japan
Phone: 011-81-3-3596-1111
Fax: 011-81-3-3596-2539
US HQ: One World Trade Center, Suite 4911, New York, NY 10048
US Phone: 212-466-5200
US Fax: 212-524-0579

Dai-Ichi Kangyo has 380 branches in Japan and operates in 41 cities in 28 countries.

	1990 Sales % of total
Japan	63
Other Asia & Oceania	10
Europe	16
The Americas	11
Total	**100**

WHAT

	1990 Assets ¥ bil.	% of total
Loans and bills discounted	34,661	50
Cash & due from banks	16,259	24
Securities	6,894	10
Customers' liabilities for acceptances and guarantees	4,624	7
Call loans	1,322	2
Foreign exchanges	740	1
Money held in trust	335	—
Trading account securities	114	—
Commercial paper and other debt	3	—
Other	3,813	6
Total	**68,765**	**100**

Major Subsidiaries and Associates
Chekiang First Bank
CIT Group (60%)
Century Research Center Corp. (data management)
Dai-Ichi Kangin Factoring Co., Ltd.
Dai-Ichi Kangin Housing Center, Ltd. (home loan guarantee services)
Dai-Ichi Kangyo Bank Nederland
Dai-Ichi Kangyo Bank (Schweiz)
Dai-Ichi Kangyo Investment Management Co., Ltd.
DKB Computer Service Ltd. (software, data processing)
Heart Finance Co., Ltd. (consumer finance)
Housing Loan Service Co., Ltd. (home loans)
The Japan Lottery Marketing Co., Ltd.
The MasterCard Japan, Ltd. (credit cards)
Nippon O.C.R. Ltd. (data processing)
Tokyo Leasing Co., Ltd.
Union Credit Co., Ltd. (credit cards)

HOW MUCH

$=¥135 (Dec. 31, 1990)	9-Year Growth	1981	1982	1983	1984	1985	1986	1987	1988	1989	1990
Assets (¥ bil.)	14.6%	20,198	24,639	26,342	29,365	33,173	36,890	42,330	47,073	54,778	68,765
Net income (¥ bil.)	20.0%	28	36	38	57	59	63	102	152	199	145
Income as % of assets	—	0.1%	0.1%	0.1%	0.2%	0.2%	0.2%	0.2%	0.3%	0.4%	0.2%
Earnings per share (¥)	18.6%	11	14	15	22	23	25	40	59	75	51
Stock price – high (¥)	—	470	458	460	1,291	1,791	1,825	3,223	3,400	3,750	3,180
Stock price – low (¥)	—	304	439	453	456	1,244	1,367	1,796	2,590	3,120	1,600
Stock price – close (¥)	17.1%	470	458	460	1,291	1,527	1,777	2,730	3,380	3,160	1,950
P/E – high	—	42	33	31	59	78	73	81	58	50	62
P/E – low	—	28	31	30	21	54	55	45	44	42	31
Dividends per share (¥)	9.2%	3.85	4.71	5.18	5.66	6.13	6.60	6.80	7.50	7.50	8.50
Book value per share (¥)	17.4%	151	168	178	195	247	276	309	406	542	640

1990 Year-end:
Equity as % of assets: 2.7%
Return on equity: 8.6%
Cash (bil.): ¥16,594
No. of shares (mil.): 2,916
Dividends:
1990 average yield: 0.4%
1990 payout: 16.7%
Market value (mil.): $42,120
Assets (mil.): $516,778
Sales (mil.): $31,380

Stock Price History High/Low 1981–90

4,000 · 3,500 · 3,000 · 2,500 · 2,000 · 1,500 · 1,000 · 500 · 0

KEY COMPETITORS

Barclays
Canadian Imperial
Chase Manhattan
Citicorp
Crédit Lyonnais
CS Holding
Deutsche Bank
HSBC
Industrial Bank of Japan
Royal Bank
Union Bank of Switzerland
Other money-center banks

DAIMLER-BENZ AG

OVERVIEW

Stuttgart-based Daimler-Benz is Germany's largest company and the world's #1 heavy-truck maker. The company depends on cars and trucks for most of its sales and profits. Mercedes raised prices of its S Class luxury cars by 20% in 1991, maintaining its high price strategy. In 1990 robust car sales in Germany and East Asia offset weakness elsewhere. US sales were off in 1991. The company's Freightliner truck unit is phasing out the Mercedes-Benz truck brand name in the US.

Units acquired in Chairman Edzard Reuter's attempt to build an integrated high-tech company have performed poorly. Deutsche Aerospace (DASA), an Airbus partner and Daimler-Benz's defense and aviation division, suffered a 43% plunge in orders in 1990 as East-West relations warmed. Both DASA and AEG, Daimler's electrical equipment unit, posted losses in 1990. Highly publicized talks between Daimler-Benz and Mitsubishi companies, initiated in 1990, have not yet yielded significant collaborative projects.

Deutsche Bank, Mercedes-Benz AG Holding, and the Kuwait Investment Office own 28%, 25.2%, and 14% of Daimler-Benz, respectively.

WHEN

Daimler-Benz is the product of a merger (1926) between companies started by German automobile pioneers Gottlieb Daimler and Karl Benz. Daimler and Wilhelm Maybach had set up an engine workshop near Stuttgart in 1882. In the 1880s they created the first motorcycle and sold their engines to French automakers. In 1890 they incorporated as Daimler Engine. Austro-Hungarian Emil Jellinek arranged to buy 36 racing cars from Daimler in 1900, with the understanding that they would be named after his daughter Mercedes. The cars won a race in 1901, and Daimler registered the Mercedes mark the next year.

Benz & Companies was established in Mannheim in 1883 and by 1886 had patented a 3-wheeled car. Despite crashing into a brick wall in the first public demonstration of his car, Benz enjoyed quick success, and by 1899 his company was the world's #1 automaker.

Ford's Model T and WWI hurt both Daimler and Benz, and the companies merged in 1926. Daimler-Benz recovered in the 1930s as Germany began building *autobahns* (highways). The company's factories turned out military vehicles and airplane engines during WWII, but most were destroyed by bombing.

In the 1950s Germany's postwar recovery led to strong demand for cars and trucks. Daimler-Benz bought Auto Union (Audi) in 1958 (sold to Volkswagen in 1966). Daimler-Benz acquisitions in the 1960s strengthened its positions in truck and engine markets.

Mercedes sales expanded worldwide in the 1970s. The high-quality luxury car appealed to the growing high end of the car market. The oil crisis spared Mercedes, partly because of the wealth of its car customers.

Fearing increased Japanese competition in the luxury car market, then vice-chairman Reuter sought to diversify and acquire technology to make "intelligent" cars. In 1985 Daimler-Benz bought 65.6% of Dornier, all of MTU, and 56% of AEG, all West German firms.

Chairman since 1987, Reuter engineered the acquisition of Messerschmitt-Bölkow-Blohm (defense, aerospace) in 1989. In 1990 he established an aircraft engine alliance with United Technologies (US). In 1991 Daimler-Benz agreed to buy 10% of Metallgesellschaft (metals, Germany) and an indirect stake in Cap Gemini Sogeti (computer services, France), and DASA joined a European commuter jet consortium. In the same year, in a stunning shift from its "made in Germany" mindset, Mercedes announced it would consider exporting Mexican-built cars to the US.

HOW MUCH

$=DM1.49 (Dec. 31, 1990)	9-Year Growth	1981	1982	1983	1984	1985	1986	1987	1988	1989	1990
Sales (DM mil.)[1]	9.9%	36,661	38,905	40,005	43,505	52,409	65,498	67,475	73,495	76,392	85,500
Net income (DM mil.)	21.0%	304	944	1,034	1,145	1,735	1,805	1,787	1,675	1,700	1,684
Income as % of sales	—	0.8%	2.4%	2.6%	2.6%	3.3%	2.8%	2.6%	2.3%	2.2%	2.0%
Earnings per share (DM)[1]	20.0%	7	23	25	27	41	43	42	40	36	36
Stock price – high (DM)	—	240	290	524	517	1,041	1,256	1,220	772	831	955
Stock price – low (DM)	—	169	202	277	417	481	896	575	527	626	550
Stock price – close (DM)	11.4%	209	290	481	480	1,009	1,233	575	737	828	554
P/E – high	—	34	13	21	19	25	29	29	19	23	27
P/E – low	—	24	9	11	15	12	21	14	13	17	15
Dividends per share (DM)[2]	5.6%	7.3	7.4	8.5	8.5	8.5	11.8	12.0	12.0	12.0	12.0
Book value per share (DM)	10.8%	145	159	178	200	225	233	210	241	348	364

1990 Year-end:
Debt ratio: 27.7%
Return on equity: 10.1%
Cash (mil.): DM8,940
Long-term debt (mil.): DM6,552
No. of shares (mil.): 47
Dividends:
1990 average yield: 2.2%
1990 payout: 33.3%
Market value (mil.): $17,475
Sales (mil.): $57,383

[1] 1989 results include minority interests [2] Not including rights offerings

Principal exchange: Frankfurt
Fiscal year ends: December 31

WHO

Chairman, Board of Management: Edzard Reuter
Deputy Chairman, Board of Management: Dr. Werner Niefer
Board of Management – Finance and Materials: Dr. Gerhard Liener
Board of Management (Deputy Member) – Personnel: Dr. Hans-Wolfgang Hirschbrunn
Auditors: KPMG Deutsche Treuhand-Gesellschaft Aktiengesellschaft Wirtschaftsprüfungsgesellschaft
Employees: 376,785

WHERE

HQ: Postfach 80 02 30, D-7000 Stuttgart 80, Germany
Phone: 011-49-7-11-1-79-22-87
Fax: 011-49-7-11-1-79-41-16
US HQ: Mercedes-Benz of North America, Inc., One Mercedes Dr., PO Box 350, Montvale, NJ 07645-0350
US Phone: 201-573-0600
US Fax: 201-573-0117

Daimler-Benz has plants in Germany, Argentina, Brazil, South Africa, Spain, and the US.

	1990 Sales	
	DM mil.	% of total
Germany	36,674	43
Other EC	18,876	22
Non-EC Europe	5,288	6
North America	12,820	15
Latin America	3,160	4
Other regions	8,682	10
Total	**85,500**	**100**

WHAT

	1990 Sales	
	DM mil.	% of total
Mercedes-Benz	57,872	68
AEG	12,721	15
Deutsche Aerospace	12,168	14
Other	2,739	3
Total	**85,500**	**100**

Corporate Units and Divisions
AEG (80%, electrical equipment and transit)
Deutsche Aerospace (93%)
- Dornier (58%, aviation, space, defense)
- Messerschmitt-Bölkow-Blohm (65%, aircraft)
- Motoren- und Turbinen-Union (propulsion systems)
- Telefunken Systemtechnik (defense electronics)

Mercedes-Benz
- Commercial Vehicle Division
- Passenger Car Division

Daimler-Benz InterServices (software, insurance, financial services, trading, marketing services)

KEY COMPETITORS

BMW	Hyundai	Renault
Chrysler	Isuzu	Saab-Scania
Dial	Mazda	Tata
Fiat	Navistar	Toyota
Ford	Nissan	Volkswagen
General Motors	PACCAR	Volvo
Honda	Peugeot	

Other aerospace companies, defense contractors, and electrical equipment manufacturers

DELOITTE & TOUCHE

OVERVIEW

Deloitte & Touche is #3 of the Big 6 accounting firms. A year after the 1989 merger of Deloitte Haskins & Sells with Touche Ross & Company, Deloitte & Touche proclaimed itself the #1 auditor of US- and Canadian-based companies with sales of more than $500 million.

The company specializes in retail (Macy's, Toys "R" Us), utilities (13 of the 36 electric and gas companies included in the *Fortune* 50 Utilities), health care (Mayo Clinic), brokerage (Bear Stearns), insurance (Metropolitan Life), and manufacturing (General Motors). As with its 5 major competitors, Deloitte & Touche offers a range of services, including auditing, management consulting, tax advice, and mergers-and-acquisitions support.

Its overseas operations — handled under the umbrella of DRT International — are positioning the company for expansion in the Pacific Rim, in a unified Western Europe, and in a newly market-driven Eastern Europe. DRT stands for "Deloitte Ross Tohmatsu." Tohmatsu & Company, Japan's largest auditor, came under the DRT banner as a part of Touche Ross. In the Soviet Union, DRT has a joint venture with Inaudit, the state-run accounting and auditing group.

WHEN

In 1845 — 3 years after the UK initiated an income tax — William Welch Deloitte opened his accounting office in London. Deloitte was the grandson of a Count de Loitte, who fled France during the Reign of Terror (1793–94), abandoned his title, and made a living as a French teacher.

In the early years of his accountancy, William Deloitte, a former staff member of the Official Assignee in Bankruptcy of the City of London, solicited business from bankrupts. During the 1850s and 1860s, Parliament established general rules for forming limited liability companies, and the rules required companies to hire accountants. Deloitte performed accounting for the Great Western Railway and, later, for telegraph companies.

As the firm grew, Deloitte added partners, among them John Griffiths (1869). Griffiths visited the US in 1888, and in 1890 the Deloitte firm opened a branch on Wall Street. Branches followed in Cincinnati (1905), Chicago (1912), Montreal (1912), Boston (1930), and Los Angeles (1945). In 1952, the Deloitte firm formed an alliance with the accounting firm of Haskins & Sells. Haskins & Sells operated 34 US offices.

Deloitte developed a reputation as a thorough, and therefore expensive, firm. By the late 1970s a partner proclaimed to *Fortune*, "We want to be the Cadillac, not the Ford, of the profession." But Deloitte Haskins & Sells, as it had become known, began to lose its conservatism as competition for auditing contracts and for management consulting clients became more intense. When government regulators nudged the profession to drop restrictions on advertising, Deloitte Haskins & Sells was the first Big 8 firm with aggressive ads extolling its virtues as an advisor.

In 1984, in a move that foreshadowed the merger mania to come, Deloitte Haskins & Sells tried to merge with Price Waterhouse. British partners in Price Waterhouse objected to the deal, and it was dropped.

The Big 8 accounting firms became the Big 6 in 1989. Ernst & Whinney merged with Arthur Young to become Ernst & Young, and Deloitte Haskins & Sells teamed up with Touche Ross & Company to form Deloitte & Touche. Touche Ross had been founded in New York in 1947. Premerger Touche Ross earned a reputation as the hard-charging, bare-knuckled bad boy of the Big 8. Touche Ross had run into controversy for its role in junk-bond deals that turned sour during the 1980s.

In 1990 DRT International was formed as an umbrella for the Deloitte & Touche organization around the world. That same year the UK arm of Spicer and Oppenheim was merged into the DRT organization. Faced with reduced business during the 1990 economic downturn, Deloitte announced that it was cutting its number of partners by 5%.

HOW MUCH

	9-Year Growth	1981	1982	1983	1984	1985	1986	1987	1988	1989	1990
Worldwide revenues ($ mil.)											
Deloitte Haskins & Sells	10.7%	800	852	894	940	953	1,188	1,500	1,920	3,700	3,760
Touche Ross	10.7%	704	800	845	904	973	1,151	1,450	1,840		
No. of offices[1,2]	—	—	—	183	185	192	205	195	196	—	110
No. of partners[1]	—	—	—	1,585	1,614	1,619	1,600	1,590	1,600	—	1,670
No. of employees[1]	—	—	—	14,463	16,009	17,253	17,521	18,252	19,276	—	18,800

1990 revenues per partner: $2,514,970

[1] Combined Deloitte Haskins & Sells, Touche Ross [2] US offices

International partnership
Fiscal year ends: First Saturday in June

WHO

Chairman and CEO: J. Michael Cook
Managing Partner: Edward A. Kangas
CFO: Jerry W. Kolb
Recruitment/College Relations: Lester M. Sussman
Employees: 18,800

WHERE

HQ: 10 Westport Rd., PO Box 820, Wilton, CT 06897-0820
Phone: 203-761-3179
Fax: 203-834-2231

Deloitte & Touche operates 110 offices in the US and has offices in 100 countries.

WHAT

	1990 Revenues % of total
Accounting & auditing	56
Tax	24
Management consulting	20
Total	**100**

Services
Accounting and auditing
Management consulting
Mergers and acquisitions consulting
Tax advice, planning

Representative Clients

Bank of New York	Merrill Lynch
BASF	MetLife
Bayer USA	Mitsubishi
Bear Stearns	Mitsui
Boeing	Monsanto
Bridgestone	New York Times
Chrysler	Nissan Motor (USA)
Dow Chemical	PPG
Equitable	Procter & Gamble
General Motors	Prudential
Great A&P	Macy
Honeywell	Rockwell
KKR	Sears
Litton Industries	Sumitomo Corp. of America
Loews	Toshiba America
Mayo Clinic	Toys "R" Us

Affiliated Firms
Actuarial, Benefits, and Compensation Group (consultation on employee pay and benefits)
Braxton Associates (strategic planning)
Deloitte & Touche Valuation Group (business valuations)
Douglass Group of Deloitte & Touche (health care facility planning and strategy)
DRT Eastern Europe
DRT International
DRT Systems Ltd. (computer consulting)
Garr Consulting Group (consulting to retail and wholesale industries)
Polaris Consulting Services (database, systems development)
Tohmatsu & Co. (auditing, Japan)

KEY COMPETITORS

Arthur Andersen	Marsh & McLennan
Coopers & Lybrand	McKinsey & Co.
Ernst & Young	Price Waterhouse
KPMG	Other consulting firms

DENTSU INC.

OVERVIEW

With 25% of Japan's gross billings, Dentsu is the country's dominant advertising agency and the world's #5 advertising group. Dentsu also engages in TV programming, TV ratings services, and market research and event planning, and owns 2.5% of Japan's largest private-sector TV broadcaster, Tokyo Broadcasting. The agency's clients include the ruling Liberal-Democratic Party and all of Japan's major automakers. Having competing clients is common in Japan, where independently managed accounts reduce fears of conflict of interest. The Kyodo and Jiji news agencies own 28.3% and 20.1% of Dentsu, respectively.

To enhance its overseas presence, Dentsu has joined with Young & Rubicam to create an international advertising network. The US arm of the partnership has been known as Lord, Dentsu & Partners since the 1991 merger with Lord Einstein O'Neill & Partners.

Recently T. Boone Pickens complained that Dentsu wielded its power to interfere with his attempt to place Japanese advertisements charging Toyota and other Dentsu clients with collusive behavior. Pickens claimed that, when the advertisements were published, none of the companies was mentioned. Dentsu vigorously denies abuse of its power.

WHEN

Sino-Japanese war correspondent Hoshiro Mitsunaga wanted to set up a Japanese wire service for faster reporting from the front lines. In 1901 he founded 2 companies: Telegraphic Service Company and Japan Advertising Ltd. Mitsunaga's wire service allowed newspapers to pay their bills with advertising space, which was resold through his advertising agency. In 1907 he merged the companies. The company later became known as Dentsu, a contraction of part of the old name, Nihon Denpo-Tsushin Sha (Japan Telegraphic Communication Company). After gaining Japanese rights to the United Press wire in 1908, Dentsu was able to extract favorable advertising rates from its clients.

In 1936 the Japanese government seized and consolidated all news services into Domei, a propaganda machine under its control, and awarded Domei 1/2 of Dentsu's stock. The government forced the consolidation of all Japanese advertising agencies into 12 entities in 1943. Due to the efforts of future Dentsu president Hideo Yoshida, Dentsu controlled 4 of the agencies.

During the postwar occupation of Japan, Domei was dismantled and Dentsu stock was transferred to the Kyodo and Jiji news agencies. Yoshida became president in 1947 and oversaw the hiring of executives previously purged from their companies by occupation forces, and of numerous sons of politicians and business leaders. In this manner Dentsu gained invaluable business connections and established its successful formula of emphasizing personal connections and building loyalty.

Yoshida's Dentsu essentially created the Japanese TV broadcasting industry by investing in start-up broadcasters. Gratitude of the broadcasters translated into preferential treatment for Dentsu and led to the agency's dominance of Japanese TV advertising through decades of explosive growth.

In 1973 Dentsu became the world's largest advertising agency. But, by the early 1980s, growth had slowed in parallel with Japan's economy, upon which Dentsu remained dependent. Having failed to follow its clients as they expanded overseas, Dentsu derived only 1% of its revenue from foreign advertising in 1980. To expand abroad, the agency teamed with Young & Rubicam (US) in 1981 to form DYR. In 1986 foreign billings still amounted to only 7% of revenues, and the next year Saatchi & Saatchi passed Dentsu as the world's #1 advertising group. In the same year Eurocom, a French agency, joined the Young & Rubicam/Dentsu partnership — renamed HDM Worldwide after Havas (Eurocom's parent), Dentsu, and Marsteller (a Y&R agency) — and brought with it hopes for significant expansion in Europe.

In the late 1980s a domestic consumption boom lifted Dentsu's revenue, but the agency continued to struggle abroad as Eurocom pulled out of HDM Worldwide in 1990. Newly named Dentsu, Young & Rubicam Partnerships reorganized to focus on North America, Asia, and Australia.

HOW MUCH

	9-Year Growth	1981	1982	1983	1984	1985	1986	1987	1988	1989	1990
Sales ($ mil.)	14.6%	341	377	373	470	472	524	755	1,055	1,274	1,166
Net income ($ mil.)	16.1%	25	21	22	24	27	30	38	62	102	96
Income as % of sales	—	7.3%	5.6%	5.9%	5.1%	5.7%	5.7%	5.0%	5.9%	8.0%	8.2%
Earnings per share ($)	10.1%	87.81	73.23	78.49	87.20	86.27	65.22	82.64	135.53	221.85	208.73
Dividends per share ($)	6.3%	3.64	3.37	3.20	3.48	3.27	3.62	5.00	6.06	7.81	6.33
Book value per share ($)	11.2%	593	769	707	935	882	710	1,055	1,403	1,658	1,541
Employees	0.7%	5,533	5,600	5,662	5,749	5,752	5,803	5,759	5,844	5,867	5,896

1990 Year-end:
Debt ratio: 7.4%
Return on equity: 13.0%
Cash (mil.): $340
Current ratio: 1.21
Long-term debt (mil.): $57
No. of shares (thou.): 461
Dividends:
1990 average yield: —
1990 payout: 3.0%
Market value (mil.): —

Net Income ($ mil.) 1981–90

Private company
Fiscal year ends: March 31

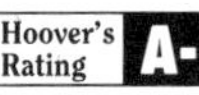

WHO

President and CEO: Gohei Kogure, age 67
Managing Director – Finance and Accounting Division: Hiroyuki Shigemasa
Managing Director – Personnel Division: Fumio Suzuki
Auditors: KPMG Peat Marwick
Employees: 5,893

WHERE

HQ: 1-11-10 Tsukiji, Chuo-ku, Tokyo 104, Japan
Phone: 011-81-3-3544-5111
Fax: 011-81-3-3545-9953 (Public Relations)
US HQ: 30th Floor, Grace Bldg., 1114 Ave. of the Americas, New York, NY 10036
US Phone: 212-869-8318
US Fax: 212-719-5028

Dentsu has 28 branch offices in Japan and 5 overseas offices. Dentsu, Young & Rubicam Partnerships operates in Asia, Australia, and North America.

WHAT

	1990 Billings	
	$ mil.	% of total
Newspaper advertising	1,606	20
Magazine advertising	328	4
Radio advertising	227	3
TV advertising	2,987	36
Sales promotion	1,289	16
Other businesses	1,699	21
Total	**8,136**	**100**

Advertising
DCA Advertising
Dentsu
Dentsu, Young & Rubicam Partnerships
Lord, Dentsu & Partners

Sales Promotion
Expositions
New product launches
Trade shows

Other Business Divisions
Convention Business (organizing conventions)
Corporate Identity (corporate image enhancement)
Dentsu Actis (printing and premium production)
Dentsu Cotec (typesetting and engraving)
Dentsu Institute for Human Studies (think tank)
Dentsu Kosan (real estate)
Dentsu Research (market research)
Information Services International (joint venture with General Electric, data processing and software)
Marketing (consulting services)
New Electronics Media (business TV network; database services)
Project Planning & Development (corporate sponsorship of cultural events)
Public Relations (consulting services)
Sports & Culture Business (corporate sponsorship of sporting events)
Urban Development (planning and promotion services for municipalities)

Representative Advertising Clients

Hitachi	Mitsubishi	Reebok
Honda	Nestlé	Suzuki
Kirin	Nippon Steel	Toshiba
Matsushita	Nissan	Toyota
Mazda	Philip Morris	UAL

KEY COMPETITORS

Carlson
Saatchi & Saatchi

DEUTSCHE BANK AG

OVERVIEW

Deutsche Bank is the largest bank in Germany, 18th largest in the world, and a leading Euromarket underwriter. Deutsche is active in commercial, retail, and investment banking and operates more than 1,800 offices internationally. With 200,000 corporate customers, it bankrolls 20% of German foreign trade.

German banking regulations have allowed Deutsche to accumulate large equity interests in its clients, including 28% of Daimler-Benz. The equity holdings are included on the bank's balance sheet at cost and give Deutsche considerable influence in German commerce. Under Germany's law of *Depotstimmrecht*, the bank may also wield the votes of other shareholders at annual meetings, giving it power beyond its own substantial holdings.

Deutsche is acquiring leading corporate banking firms in European markets in anticipation of 1992, when trade barriers drop. The bank has been quick to establish 240 branches in what once was East Germany, where it quickly racked up DM12 billion in deposits, and offices in Poland and Hungary.

Principal exchange: Frankfurt
Fiscal year ends: December 31

WHO

Spokesman of the Board of Managing Directors: Hilmar Kopper, age 56
Member of the Board of Managing Directors for Treasury: Ulrich Cartellieri
Member of the Board of Managing Directors for Personnel: Ulrich Weiss, age 55
Auditors: KPMG Treuverkehr Aktiengesellschaft Wirtschaftsprüfungsgesellschaft
Employees: 68,552

WHEN

In 1870, concurrent with German unification, Deutsche Bank opened its doors in Berlin under the leadership of Georg von Siemens. He quickly opened branches in Bremen and Hamburg and, with an eye on foreign trade, established branches overseas, the first in London (1873). The bank's foreign business allowed it to survive a German financial crisis (1873–75) and buy other German banks, greatly increasing its size and importance.

In the late 1800s Deutsche helped finance the electrification of Germany and the construction of railroads, including the Baghdad Railway (Ottoman Empire) and the Northern Pacific Railway (US). Von Siemens managed the bank until his death in 1901.

In the face of extreme economic difficulty plaguing Germany following its defeat in WWI, Deutsche merged with its largest competitor, Disconto-Gesellschaft, and survived the Depression. By purchasing government debt, Deutsche and other German banks helped finance the Nazi war machine. In 1945 Allied authorities split the bank's West German operations into 10 separate institutions, closed its East German branches, and stripped it of its overseas operations. Deutsche Bank was reassembled from its West German parts in 1957.

Led by Hermann Abs, Deutsche rapidly regained international prominence. After concentrating on commercial banking for a relatively small group of West German companies in the 1940s and 1950s, the bank began offering a wide array of retail banking services in the 1960s. Between 1957 and 1970 the bank expanded from 345 to 1,100 branches. Eurochecks (personal checks accepted throughout Western Europe), conceived at Deutsche, were launched in 1969 to combat US bank credit cards. In the 1960s and 1970s, Deutsche helped finance the West German export boom and became a major Euromarket dealer. The bank again expanded overseas.

Until the 1987 stock market crash, Deutsche was active in public stock offerings, including Flick (industrial group, 1985). In the 1980s Deutsche diversified and bought banks, including Bank of America's Italian subsidiary (1986) and the large UK merchant bank, Morgan Grenfell (1989).

Deutsche Bank leader Alfred Herrhausen, a symbol of German big business, was murdered by terrorists in 1989. Successor Hilmar Kopper continued foreign expansion and in 1991 presided over a restructuring that centralized management and bolstered service to private and midsized customers. Also in 1991, officials of the Frankfurt stock exchange investigated some Deutsche Bank executives for insider rules violations, but the bank said its own investigation turned up no violations.

WHERE

HQ: Taunusanlage 12, PO Box 100601, D-6000 Frankfurt am Main, Germany
Phone: 011-49-69-71500
Fax: 011-49-69-7150-4225
US HQ: Deutsche Bank AG, New York Branch, 31 W. 52nd St., New York, NY 10019
US Phone: 212-474-8000
US Fax: 212-355-5655

The Deutsche Bank Group has 1,856 offices throughout the world. Affiliated companies are located in 17 countries and Hong Kong.

WHAT

	1990 Sales	
	DM mil.	% of total
Interest	24,690	63
Investments and securities	2,271	6
Mortgage bank interest	4,725	12
Commissions	3,838	10
Leasing business	1,997	5
Life insurance business	141	—
Other	1,459	4
Total	**39,121**	**100**

Major Subsidiaries and Affiliates

BAI Leasing SpA (Italy)
Bain & Company Ltd. (50%, investment banking, Australia)
Banca d'America e d'Italia SpA (98.6%, commercial banking, Italy)
Banco Comercial Transatlántico, SA (96.9%, commercial banking, Spain)
Banco de Montevideo (95.4%, commercial banking, Uruguay)
DB Capital Markets (Asia) Ltd. (54.5%; investment banking; Hong Kong, Japan)
Europäische Hypothekenbank SA (mortgage banking, Luxembourg)
Frankfurter Hypothekenbank AG (93.8%, mortgage banking, Germany)
H. Albert de Bary & Co. NV (commercial banking, Netherlands)
Lübecker Hypothekenbank AG (mortgage banking, Germany)
McLean McCarthy Ltd. (investment banking, Canada)
Deutsche Bank de Investimento, SA (investment banking, Portugal)
Morgan Grenfell Group PLC (investment banking, UK)
P.T. Euras Buana Leasing Indonesia (60%)
Schiffshypothekenbank zu Lübeck AG (mortgage banking, Germany)

KEY COMPETITORS

Allianz
Barclays
Canadian Imperial
Chase Manhattan
Citicorp
Crédit Lyonnais
CS Holding
Dai-Ichi Kangyo
HSBC
Industrial Bank of Japan
Royal Bank
Union Bank of Switzerland
Other US money-center banks

HOW MUCH

$=DM1.49 (Dec. 31, 1990)	9-Year Growth	1981	1982	1983	1984[2]	1985	1986	1987	1988	1989	1990
Assets (DM bil.)	8.5%	192	199	210	232	237	257	268	305	344	400
Net income (DM mil.)	11.1%	397	328	635	662	854	1,056	658	1,183	1,315	1,025
Income as % of assets	—	0.2%	0.2%	0.3%	0.3%	0.4%	0.4%	0.2%	0.4%	0.4%	0.3%
Earnings per share (DM)	4.1%	*16*	*12*	*23*	*23*	*27*	*33*	*19*	*33*	*33*	*23*
Stock price – high (DM)	—	297	288	352	385	935	920	817	569	843	850
Stock price – low (DM)	—	261	245	259	302	384	724	387	357	502	554
Stock price – close (DM)	9.5%	263	274	349	383	925	822	388	563	843	597
P/E – high	—	19	24	15	17	35	28	43	17	26	37
P/E – low	—	16	20	11	13	14	22	20	11	15	24
Dividends per share (DM)[1]	3.8%	10.0	10.0	11.0	12.0	12.0	12.0	12.0	12.0	12.0	14.0
Book value per share (DM)	4.2%	244	243	253	266	281	281	299	318	353	353

1990 Year-end:
Equity as % of assets: 4.0%
Return on equity: 6.5%
Cash (mil.): DM6,540
No. of shares (mil.): 44
Dividends:
1990 average yield: 2.3%
1990 payout: 60.9%
Market value (mil.): $17,630
Assets (mil.): $268,456
Sales (mil.): $8,520

Stock Price History High/Low 1981–90

1,000
900
800
700
600
500
400
300
200
100
0

[1] Not including rights offerings [2] Accounting change

AB ELECTROLUX

OVERVIEW

Electrolux is a global producer of appliances marketed under established brand names in the US and Europe. The Swedish company is the European market leader in white goods (washers, dryers, refrigerators, etc.) and, through its Cleveland-based White Consolidated subsidiary, is #3 in the US, after Whirlpool and GE. Electrolux is the world's largest producer of vacuum cleaners, industrial laundry equipment, and chainsaws, and Europe's leader in food service equipment and seat belts. Other activities include aluminum smelting and gardening equipment production.

Well-known US brands include Tappan, Kelvinator, Frigidaire, and Eureka. Electrolux Corporation, an unrelated company, owns the US rights to the Electrolux mark.

Experiencing weakness in its major markets and start-up problems at new plants, Electrolux suffered a 71% drop in 1990 earnings. The company has eased its acquisition pace and is unloading companies unrelated to its core appliance business. Electrolux is cutting jobs and trying to achieve economies of scale through further integration of its 600 operating companies.

WHEN

In 1910 Swedish salesman Axel Wenner-Gren saw an American-made vacuum cleaner in a Vienna store window and envisioned selling the cleaners door-to-door, a technique he had learned in the US. In 1912 he worked with fledgling Swedish vacuum cleaner makers AB Lux and Elektromekaniska to improve their existing designs. In 1919 the 2 companies merged to form Electrolux. When the board of the new company balked at Wenner-Gren's suggestion to mass-produce vacuum cleaners, he guaranteed Electrolux's sales through his own sales company.

In the 1920s the company used the "Every home — an Electrolux home" slogan as Wenner-Gren drove his sales force on and launched new sales companies in Europe, the US, and South America. Company lore has him paying a sales call on the pope in competition with 4 other vacuum cleaner salesmen. After the others had swept their preassigned portions of the carpet, Wenner-Gren pushed his Electrolux over the area cleaned by the competition, dumped out a large pile of dust, and won the order. He scored another publicity coup by securing the blessing of Pope Pius XI to vacuum the Vatican, gratis, for a year. By the end of the 1920s, Electrolux had purchased most of Wenner-Gren's sales companies (excluding Electrolux US) and had gambled on refrigerator technology and won.

By buying vacuum cleaner maker Volta (Sweden, 1934), Electrolux gained retail distribution.

Despite the loss of East European subsidiaries in WWII, the company did well until the 1960s, when Electrolux backed an unpopular refrigeration technology. In 1964 Swedish electrical equipment giant ASEA, controlled by Marcus Wallenberg, bought a large stake in Electrolux. In 1967 Wallenberg installed Hans Werthén as chairman. Werthén slashed overhead and sold the company's minority stake in Electrolux US to Consolidated Foods (the US Electrolux business was taken private in 1987). He also bought troubled appliance makers, updated their plants, and gained global component manufacturing efficiencies.

Since 1970 Electrolux has acquired over 300 companies, including National Union Electric (Eureka vacuum cleaners, US, 1974), Tappan (appliances, US, 1979), Gränges (metals, Sweden, 1981), Zanussi (appliances, industrial products; Italy; 1984), White Consolidated (appliances, industrial products; US; 1986), and the garden products division of Roper (US, 1988).

In 1990 Electrolux put its commercial cleaning services group up for sale. In 1991 it bought Lehel, Hungary's leading refrigerator maker.

OTC symbol: ELUXY (ADR)
Fiscal year ends: December 31

WHO

Chairman and CEO: Anders Scharp, age 57
President: Leif Johansson, age 40
SEVP and CFO: Lennart Ribohn, age 48
Auditors: Ernst & Young AB
Employees: 150,892

WHERE

HQ: Lilla Essingen, S-105 45 Stockholm, Sweden
Phone: 011-46-8-738-6000
Fax: 011-46-8656-4478
US HQ: White Consolidated Industries, 11770 Berea Rd., Cleveland, OH 44111-1688
US Phone: 216-252-3700
US Fax: 216-252-8073

Electrolux conducts operations in approximately 40 countries.

	1990 Sales	
	SEK mil.	% of total
Sweden	12,090	15
Germany	7,829	9
UK	7,316	9
Other European countries	26,730	32
US	20,189	24
Canada	2,344	3
Asia	3,157	4
Other regions	2,779	4
Total	**82,434**	**100**

WHAT

	1990 Sales		1990 Operating Income	
	SEK mil.	% of total	SEK mil.	% of total
Household appliances	44,890	54	1,194	37
Commercial appliances	8,699	11	645	20
Outdoor products	8,680	11	661	20
Industrial products	15,822	19	490	15
Commercial services	4,343	5	258	8
Total	**82,434**	**100**	**3,248**	**100**

Appliance Brands

Outside US
- Arthur Martin (France)
- Electrolux
- Faure
- Husqvarna (Scandinavia)
- Zanussi

US
- Eureka
- Frigidaire
- Gibson
- Kelvinator
- Poulan
- Tappan
- Viking
- Weed Eater
- White-Westinghouse

Other Products
- Agricultural equipment
- Aluminum
- Chainsaws
- Commercial cleaning equipment
- Commercial refrigeration
- Food service equipment
- Home cabinetry
- Industrial laundry equipment
- Lawn-care equipment
- Material handling equipment
- Seat belts and other safety equipment

KEY COMPETITORS

Allied-Signal	Masco	Siemens
Berkshire Hathaway	Maytag	Textron
Black & Decker	Premark	Thomson SA
Deere	Raytheon	Toshiba
GEC	Robert Bosch	TRW
General Electric	Sharp	Whirlpool

HOW MUCH

$=SEK5.63 (Dec. 31, 1990)	9-Year Growth	1981	1982	1983	1984	1985	1986	1987	1988	1989	1990
Sales (SEK mil.)	13.4%	26,595	31,661	32,146	34,547	39,688	53,090	67,430	73,960	84,919	82,434
Net income (SEK mil.)	(0.1%)	750	304	1,036	1,418	1,997	1,790	2,116	2,375	2,582	741
Income as % of sales	—	2.8%	1.0%	3.2%	4.1%	5.0%	3.4%	3.1%	3.2%	3.0%	0.9%
Earnings per share (SEK)	(4.4%)	15.10	5.90	19.80	25.90	30.50	25.60	28.80	32.30	35.20	10.10
Stock price – high (SEK)	—	68	59	130	144	195	344	342	301	380	311
Stock price – low (SEK)	—	8	41	58	108	123	194	189	192	240	124
Stock price – close (SEK)	12.8%	110	59	119	121	194	311	193	293	280	162
P/E – high	—	5	10	7	6	6	13	12	9	11	31
P/E – low	—	3	7	3	4	4	8	7	6	7	12
Dividends per share (SEK)	14.3%	3.75	4.00	4.50	5.50	6.50	7.50	8.75	10.00	11.50	12.50
Book value per share (SEK)	11.5%	85	92	98	115	131	161	164	203	232	226

1990 Year-end:
Debt ratio: 48.5%
Return on equity: 4.4%
Cash (mil.): SEK2,288
Long-term debt (bil.): SEK16
No. of shares (mil.): 73
Dividends:
1990 average yield: 7.7%
1990 payout: 123.8%
Market value (mil.): $2,101
Sales (mil.): $14,642

Stock Price History High/Low 1981–90

400 – 350 – 300 – 250 – 200 – 150 – 100 – 50 – 0

SOCIÉTÉ NATIONALE ELF AQUITAINE

OVERVIEW

Paris-based Société Nationale Elf Aquitaine is the world's 8th largest petroleum company. It is 53.9% owned by the French government (the rest is publicly traded), but its scope is international. It explores for oil from Alaska to Angola.

The Elf Aquitaine group of companies is divided into 3 major segments: hydrocarbons, chemicals, and health and hygiene products.

The hydrocarbons group drills for and refines petroleum, then transports and markets petroleum products. Elf Aquitaine's recently restructured chemical unit, Atochem, is the 5th largest chemical company in Europe. Elf Aquitaine's US holdings — which comprise 25% of Elf's assets — include Texasgulf, a mineral company, and Atochem North America, the result of a 1989 consolidation of 3 US-based chemical subsidiaries.

Sanofi, the pharmaceutical and personal products arm that is 62% controlled by Elf Aquitaine, is allying with Eastman Kodak's Sterling Drug to extend its reach into North America. Sanofi also owns 49.9% of Nina Ricci, a manufacturer of perfumes (Van Cleef & Arpels, Oscar de la Renta, and Perry Ellis).

WHEN

Just before the outbreak of WWII, the French government formed Régie Autonome des Pétroles (RAP) to exploit the discovery of natural gas in Saint Marcet in southwest France. During the war the Vichy government created a publicly traded company in which the government held a majority interest. Called Société Nationale des Pétroles d'Aquitaine (SNPA) in honor of the French region, the company's mandate was to find oil. After the war De Gaulle set up the Bureau de Recherches de Pétrole (BRP) to hold RAP and the government's majority stake in SNPA.

SNPA struck a large gas field in Lacq (1951), and BRP invested in subsidiaries that discovered oil and gas in Algeria (1956), Gabon (1956), and the Congo (1957). In 1966 the government creations were consolidated under Entreprise de Recherches et d'Activités Pétrolières (ERAP) led by Pierre Guillaumat. ERAP oversaw the government's SNPA stake, but SNPA remained separate because of its size and private shareholders.

ERAP launched the Elf tradename to consolidate 7 trademarks in 1967. Company legend holds that the name, with no meaning in French, was generated by a computer. SNPA continued to sell under the Aquitaine banner. A small US subsidiary, Elf Petroleum Corp., began oil and gas exploration and production in 1967. SNPA invested in petrochemicals with the formation of ATO, Aquitaine Total Organico (1969).

The French companies lost production from nationalized Algerian fields (1971) but gained gas from the Frigg discovery in the North Sea. SNPA launched Sanofi in 1973 to oversee pharmaceuticals and cosmetics manufacturing.

In 1976 Elf-ERAP and SNPA merged into Société Nationale Elf Aquitaine (SNEA), with the French government initially controlling 70% of the new entity. The company expanded abroad, buying the US–based M&T Chemicals (1977) and Texasgulf, a mining company that produced sulfur and other chemicals (1981).

As the French government grappled with the nation's fractured chemical industry in 1983, Atochem was created from the pieces and placed under Elf Aquitaine. Elf Aquitaine added to its chemical holdings with the $1.05 billion purchase of Philadelphia-based Pennwalt (1989), part of a vigorous company-wide acquisition program that included 25% of Enterprise Oil (UK, 1988); Racon (chemicals, US, 1989); Parfums Stern from Avon (perfumes, US, 1989); and Continental Flavors & Fragrances (US, 1989). In 1991 the company pursued more acquisitions — by paying $1.35 billion for Occidental's North Sea holdings and by taking a larger stake in CEPSA, a Spanish refining and marketing company.

HOW MUCH

$=FF5.08 (Dec. 31, 1990)	9-Year Growth	1981	1982	1983	1984	1985	1986	1987	1988	1989	1990
Sales (FF mil.)	6.3%	109,543	120,690	142,166	184,665	189,542	127,911	135,088	135,638	159,710	189,065
Net income (FF mil.)	12.5%	3,687	3,527	3,723	6,493	5,250	4,279	4,149	7,205	7,218	10,625
Income as % of sales	—	3.4%	2.9%	2.6%	3.5%	2.8%	3.3%	3.1%	5.3%	4.5%	5.6%
Earnings per share (FF)	8.6%	21	20	21	34	26	22	21	36	33	44
Stock price – high (FF)	—	—	84	102	139	126	189	200	195	278	365
Stock price – low (FF)	—	—	47	56	86	89	98	106	110	193	255
Stock price – close (FF)	—	—	51	86	109	101	158	118	195	258	284
P/E – high	—	—	4	5	4	5	9	10	5	8	8
P/E – low	—	—	2	3	3	3	4	5	3	6	6
Dividends per share (FF)	8.0%	5.25	5.25	5.25	6.00	6.75	6.75	6.75	7.50	10.00	10.50
Book value per share (FF)	6.8%	173	118	200	217	242	253	266	292	305	312

1990 Year-end:
Debt ratio: 23.6%
Return on equity: 14.3%
Cash (mil.): FF23,251
Long-term debt (mil.): FF23,661
No. of shares (mil.): 245
Dividends:
1990 average yield: 3.7%
1990 payout: 23.9%
Market value (mil.): $13,697
Sales (mil.): $37,218

Stock Price History High/Low 1981–90

400
350
300
250
200
150
100
50
0

NYSE symbol: ELF (ADR)
Fiscal year ends: December 31

Hoover's Rating **B-**

WHO

Chairman, President, and CEO: Loïk Le Floch-Prigent
SVP and CFO: Philippe Hustache
SVP Finance and Strategy, Hydrocarbons Division: Marc Cossé
Auditors: Ernst & Young
Employees: 90,000

WHERE

HQ: Tour Elf, Cedex 45, 92078 Paris La Défense, France
Phone: 011-33-1-47-44-45-46
Fax: 011-33-1-47-44-69-46
US HQ: Elf Aquitaine, Inc., 280 Park Ave., 36th Floor, New York, NY 10017
US Phone: 212-922-3000
US Fax: 212-922-3001

Elf Aquitaine operates worldwide.

	1990 Sales		1990 Operating Income	
	FF mil.	% of total	FF mil.	% of total
France	141,918	70	7,401	36
Other Europe	22,085	11	4,798	23
North America	21,512	10	721	4
Other countries	18,357	9	7,511	37
Adjustments	(14,807)	—	40	—
Total	**189,065**	**100**	**20,471**	**100**

WHAT

	1990 Sales		1990 Operating Income	
	FF mil.	% of total	FF mil.	% of total
Exploration & production	42,239	21	11,766	57
Refining & marketing	87,174	43	1,359	7
Chemicals	55,922	27	5,730	28
Health/hygiene	18,553	9	1,576	8
Adjustments	(14,823)	—	40	—
Total	**189,065**	**100**	**20,471**	**100**

Major Subsidiaries and Affiliates
Atochem North America, Inc. (chemicals)
Atochem SA (99%, basic and specialty chemicals)
Elf Aquitaine, Inc. (North American holding company)
Elf Aquitaine Norge AS (North Sea production)
Elf Aquitaine UK (Holdings) PLC
Elf Asphalt, Inc. (US)
Elf Congo SA (75%, exploration and production)
Elf Exploration, Inc. (US)
Elf Gabon SA (57%, exploration and production)
Elf Trading, Inc. (crude oil and refined products trading, US)
Sanofi SA (62%; health, bioactivities, and perfume)
Texasgulf (85%, minerals, US)
Tg Soda Ash, Inc. (US)

KEY COMPETITORS

Amoco	Mobil	Royal Dutch/Shell
Ashland	Norsk Hydro	Sun
Atlantic Richfield	Occidental	Texaco
British Petroleum	Oryx	Unocal
Broken Hill	Pennzoil	USX
Canadian Pacific	Petrofina	Cosmetics companies
Chevron	Petrobrás	Pharmaceutical companies
Coastal	PDVSA	Other major oil companies
Du Pont	Pemex	
Exxon	Phillips Petroleum	
Imperial Oil		

LM ERICSSON TELEPHONE COMPANY

OVERVIEW

LM Ericsson Telephone is the 6th largest world telecommunications equipment supplier, 3rd largest in Europe (after Alcatel and Siemens). Ericsson is divided into 6 areas: Public Telecommunications, Radio Communications, Business Communications, Cable and Network, Components, and Defense Systems.

From its Swedish base (where it is controlled by 2 banks and the Wallenberg family), Ericsson is a canny exporter of both its traditional and its cellular technology. Its AXE switching system is used in 78 countries. In the US a joint venture with GE won a lucrative contract to upgrade equipment for McCaw Cellular, the nation's largest operator.

Ericsson enjoys a 40% world market share in cellular switching and transmitting equipment. Its R&D effort concentrates on its Personal Communications Network (PCN). Scheduled for debut in 1991, PCN offers personal, minicellular phones within large companies or institutions.

NASDAQ symbol: ERICY (ADR)
Fiscal year ends: December 31

Hoover's Rating **A+**

WHO

Chairman: Björn Svedberg, age 53
President and CEO: Lars Ramqvist
EVP and CFO: Carl Wilhelm Ros, age 49
SVP Corporate Human Resources and Organization: Britt Reigo
Auditors: Price Waterhouse
Employees: 70,238

WHEN

Lars Magnus Ericsson opened a shop to repair telegraph equipment in Stockholm in 1876, the same year American Alexander Graham Bell applied for a US patent on the telephone. Within 2 years Ericsson began making telephones, and his firm grew rapidly as it supplied equipment, first to Swedish telephone companies and later to other European companies. In 1885 Ericsson crafted a combination receiver-speaker in one handset.

Early in the 20th century, Lars Magnus Ericsson retired, and the company branched out overseas. It joined a consortium to operate the Mexican telephone system (1905), won a contract for phone modernization in Bangkok (1908), and built a factory in Paris (1911). Its Russian holdings were nationalized in 1918.

In 1918 Ericsson and SAT, the Stockholm telephone company, merged under the Ericsson banner. The company adopted its present name, Telefonaktiebolaget LM Ericsson, in 1926. In 1930 financier Ivar Kreuger, known as the Match King because his Swedish Match Company was the centerpiece of his international financial empire, won control of Ericsson. But the Match King's plans fizzled. Kreuger commited suicide in 1932, and Sosthenes Behn's ITT, one of Kreuger's creditors, won controlling interest in Ericsson.

After WWII the company's holdings in Mexico were nationalized. When ITT began to diversify in 1960, it sold its interest in Ericsson to the Wallenbergs, the first family of Swedish industry. In 1975 Ericsson introduced its computer-controlled exchange, called the AXE. Buoyed by AXE's success the company launched, with US partner ARCO, development of the "office of the future" in the early 1980s. It diversified into computer making and the office furniture business.

Ericsson's timing was off: AT&T's breakup and British Telecom's privatization were 2 of the highlights of a telecommunications revolution in the early 1980s. The demand for office automation never materialized, Ericsson profits plunged, and ARCO cashed in (1985). Electrolux chairman Hans Werthén was recruited to split his time between the companies and pull Ericsson out of its nosedive.

Ericsson shed its computer business (to Nokia Oy Corporation of Finland, 1988) and focused on telephone equipment. An Ericsson joint venture edged out larger rivals AT&T and Siemens in bidding for CGCT, a phone equipment maker with 16% of the French market (1987). Under then-EVP Lars Ramqvist, Ericsson dusted off its aging AXE system for use in the burgeoning cellular market. The concentration paid off, and Ericsson won a cellular contract with Japanese giant NTT and purchased half of Britain's Orbitel, the equipment manufacturer for Racal Telecom. Ericsson posted record earnings in fiscal 1991.

WHERE

HQ: Telefonaktiebolaget LM Ericsson, S-126 25, Stockholm, Sweden
Phone: 011-46-8-719-0000
Fax: 011-46-8-719-1976 (Investor Relations)
US HQ: Ericsson Corp., 100 Park Ave., Suite 2705, New York, NY 10017
US Phone: 212-685-4030
US Fax: 212-683-2631

Ericsson operates worldwide.

	% of 1990 Sales
Sweden	12
Other Europe	47
North America	13
Latin America	12
Asia, Australia & Africa	16
Total	**100**

WHAT

	1990 Sales		1990 Operating Income	
	$ mil.	% of total	$ mil.	% of total
Public Telecomm.	3,577	45	675	67
Radio Comm.	2,026	25	157	15
Business Comm.	838	11	26	3
Cable & Network	1,136	14	103	10
Components	103	1	45	4
Defense Systems	308	4	6	1
Adjustments	194	—	(1)	—
Total	**8,182**	**100**	**1,011**	**100**

Public Telecommunications
Telephone exchanges and operations
Transmission equipment

Radio Communications
Mobile data systems, telephones, and cellular systems
Personal paging systems and mobile radio

Business Communications
Data networks
MD 110 and other subscriber exchanges (call processing equipment)
Telephone instruments

Cable and Network
Network construction
Power, specialty, and telecommunications cable

Components

Defense Systems
Avionics
Microwave and satellite communications
Mobile defense systems

KEY COMPETITORS

Alcatel Alsthom
AT&T
BCE
British Telecom
Cable & Wireless
Fujitsu
GTE
NEC
Oki
Siemens
Cellular telephone firms
Regional Bell operating companies

HOW MUCH

	9-Year Growth	1981	1982	1983	1984	1985	1986	1987	1988	1989	1990[1]
Sales ($ mil.)	11.6%	3,037	2,761	3,220	3,297	4,337	4,731	5,653	5,179	6,437	8,182
Net income ($ mil.)	25.6%	78	49	64	49	111	84	127	214	297	605
Income as % of sales	—	2.6%	1.8%	2.0%	1.5%	2.5%	1.8%	2.2%	4.1%	4.6%	7.4%
Earnings per share ($)	20.1%	0.48	0.30	0.36	0.27	0.60	0.44	0.66	1.12	1.48	2.49
Stock price – high ($)	—	5.67	9.40	12.80	9.68	7.00	8.45	9.50	11.88	28.80	47.58
Stock price – low ($)	—	3.20	4.27	8.95	5.40	4.65	5.53	5.05	5.33	11.73	25.85
Stock price – close ($)	22.7%	5.10	9.30	10.00	5.75	5.93	6.23	5.30	11.83	28.73	32.25
P/E – high	—	12	31	36	36	12	19	14	11	19	19
P/E – low	—	7	14	25	20	8	13	8	5	8	10
Dividends per share ($)	8.5%	0.22	0.22	0.20	0.22	0.20	0.25	0.28	0.30	0.31	0.46
Book value per share ($)	15.0%	4.07	3.33	4.21	3.95	4.93	5.67	6.76	7.36	8.67	14.27

1990 Year-end:
Debt ratio: 14.3%
Return on equity: 17.4%
Cash (mil.): $1,186
Current ratio: 1.74
Long-term debt (mil.): $488
No. of shares (mil.): 206
Dividends:
1990 average yield: 1.4%
1990 payout: 18.5%
Market value (mil.): $6,635

Stock Price History High/Low 1981–90

[1] Accounting change

ERNST & YOUNG

OVERVIEW

With annual revenues exceeding $5 billion worldwide, Ernst & Young is 2nd in US accounting firm revenues, after Arthur Andersen, and 2nd in the world, after KPMG.

Ernst & Young apparently subscribes to the theory that 2 heads are better than one, because it has 2 CEOs — William Gladstone and Ray Groves — a legacy of the 1989 merger of Ernst & Whinney and Arthur Young. Says Groves, "We concluded that, at least in the early going, it's a 2-person job."

Accounting firm pairings are the logical result of the mergers and consolidations conducted in other industries during the 1980s; big accounting firms compete for fewer big clients. As accounting firms use auditing services to attract more lucrative consulting jobs, critics contend that auditing quality suffers, and several big firms — including Ernst & Young — are being called to account by angry regulators and shareholders of clients in the troubled thrift industry.

WHEN

While the 1494 publication in Venice of Luca Pacioli's *Summa di Arithmetica* — the first published work dealing with double-entry bookkeeping — boosted the accounting profession, it really wasn't until the Industrial Revolution in the UK that accountants developed their craft.

Frederick Whinney joined the UK firm of Harding & Pullein in 1849. R. P. Harding reputedly had been a hatmaker whose business ended up in court. The ledgers he produced were so well kept that an official advised him to take up accounting.

Whinney's name was added to the firm in 1859, and later his sons also became partners. The firm's name changed to Whinney, Smith & Whinney (1894). The name became the longest-lived of the firm's many incarnations, not yielding until 1965.

After WWII, Whinney, Smith & Whinney formed an alliance with the American firm of Ernst & Ernst. Ernst & Ernst had been founded in Cleveland in 1903 by brothers Alwin and Theodore Ernst. The alliance, which recognized that the accountants' business clients were getting larger and more international in orientation, provided that each firm would operate in the other's behalf within their respective markets.

In 1965 the Whinney firm merged with Brown, Fleming & Murray to become Whinney Murray. The merger also included the fledgling computer department — the harbinger of electronic accounting systems — set up by Brown, Fleming & Murray to serve British Petroleum. Whinney Murray also formed joint ventures with other accounting firms to provide consulting services.

In 1979 Whinney Murray and Turquands Barton Mayhew — itself the product of a merger that began with a cricket match — united with Ernst & Ernst to form Ernst & Whinney, a firm with an international scope.

Ernst & Whinney, a merger melting pot, was by no means finished with its combinations. Having grown to the world's 4th largest accounting firm by 1989, it merged with the 5th largest, Arthur Young. Arthur Young had taken its name from the Scottish immigrant who had founded a partnership with C. U. Stuart in Chicago in 1894. When Stuart withdrew, Young took brother Stanley as a partner. Arthur Young — the firm — was long known as the "old reliable" of the accounting giants. In 1984 the spotlight shone on it as then–vice-presidential candidate Geraldine Ferraro chose the firm to sort out her tax troubles.

The new firm of Ernst & Young, for a time the world's largest accounting company, faced a rocky start, though. At the end of 1990, it was forced to defend itself from rumors of collapse, just as 2nd-tier firms Laventhol & Horwath and Spicer & Oppenheim filed for bankruptcy and disbanded, respectively. In 1991 Ernst & Young planned to cut 150 partners from the rolls, either through retirement or dismissal. The firm also faced legal problems. A suit against Ernst & Young by the FDIC sought $841 million on 6 separate claims. The claims arose out of audits performed by its predecessor firms on troubled savings and loans. Ernst & Young steadfastly denied the FDIC allegations. The firm was also under fire in California, where it eventually settled with a state agency that had threatened to revoke its license (1990).

HOW MUCH

	9-Year Growth	1981	1982	1983	1984	1985	1986	1987	1988	1989	1990
Worldwide revenues ($ mil.)											
Arthur Young	12.8%	880	955	1,003	1,060	1,160	1,427	1,702	2,053	4,300	5,006
Ernst & Whinney	12.8%	807	887	972	1,028	1,185	1,492	1,778	2,191		
No. of offices[1,2]	—	—	—	200	203	206	265	212	210	124	125
No. of partners	—	—	—	1,650	1,735	2,139	1,925	2,039	2,109	2,000	2,025
No. of employees[1]	—	—	—	17,912	19,335	20,657	21,837	21,864	25,440	—	22,702

1990 revenues per partner: $2,472,099

Worldwide Revenues ($ mil.) 1981–90

6,000
5,000
4,000
3,000
2,000
1,000
0

[1] Combined Ernst & Whinney, Arthur Young [2] US offices

International partnership
Fiscal year ends: September 30

WHO

Co-CEO: William L. Gladstone
Co-CEO: Ray J. Groves
Chief Financial Partner: Stephen Key
VC Human Resources: Paul Ostling
Employees: 65,000

WHERE

HQ: 277 Park Ave., 32nd Fl., New York, NY 10127
Phone: 212-773-3000
Fax: 212-773-2821

Ernst & Young operates in more than 100 countries.

	1990 Revenues	
	$ mil.	% of total
US	2,239	45
Foreign	2,767	55
Total	**5,006**	**100**

WHAT

	1990 Revenues
	% of total
Accounting & auditing	53
Tax	25
Management consulting	22
Total	**100**

Services

Accounting and Auditing
- Compliance services
- Financial statement examination
- Management assistance

Tax Planning
- Compensation planning
- Compliance assistance
- Corporate tax planning
- International tax planning
- Merger and acquisition assistance
- Personal financial planning
- Return preparation

Management Consulting
- Financial management
- Human resources consulting
- Information systems
- Operations enhancement
- Strategic planning

Representative Clients

American Airlines
American Express
Apple Computer
BankAmerica
British Airways
British Petroleum
Coca-Cola
Eli Lilly
Hanson
Lloyd's of London
LVMH
Martin Marietta
McDonald's
Mobil
Pirelli
Renault
Thorn EMI
Time Warner
Unisys

KEY COMPETITORS

Arthur Andersen
Coopers & Lybrand
Deloitte & Touche
KPMG
Marsh & McLennan
McKinsey & Co.
Price Waterhouse
Other consulting firms

FIAT SPA

OVERVIEW

Fiat is Italy's biggest private-sector company. The company, 40% controlled by the Agnelli family, is a fully integrated automobile manufacturer and diversified industrial giant. Fiat is #2, after Volkswagen, in European auto sales and #6 worldwide, with an economy-oriented model lineup. In Italy Fiat's commanding lead in auto sales is eroding as foreign models, the Ford Fiesta in particular, gain market share. Fiat's response, the launch of a new Uno model, is not expected until 1993. With most of its auto sales in Europe's most protected markets, Fiat is expected to suffer from Japanese competition as the EC frees trade. The company is preparing to fight back by investing $4.3 billion in new Italian auto plants. Fiat is already among the most efficient automakers in Europe.

Fiat periodically considers mergers and joint ventures with foreign automakers but ended talks concerning cooperative ventures with Chrysler in 1990.

WHEN

Ex–cavalry officer Giovanni Agnelli founded Fabbrica Italiana di Automobili Torino (Fiat) in 1899. The Turin-based automaker soon expanded into trucks (1903), railcars (1906), aviation (1908), and tractors (1918). Protected by high import tariffs, Fiat became Italy's dominant auto company. Between WWI and WWII Fiat reduced its dependence on foreign suppliers by manufacturing its own parts.

Mussolini's WWII modernization drive boosted Fiat's fortunes, but bombing damaged many of its plants. With US support Fiat rebuilt its facilities and survived weak postwar domestic demand by exporting and by building plants abroad. In 1950 Fiat licensed its know-how to Spain's SEAT, a state-owned automaker. As growth resumed in Italy, Fiat began making steel and construction equipment.

When the EC forced Italy to lower import tariffs in 1961, Fiat lost market share and responded with a new mid-range car and an import-bashing campaign in its *La Stampa* newspaper. Fiat's domestic woes were offset by success abroad. In 1965 Fiat agreed to build a USSR plant to produce 600,000 cars annually.

In 1966 Giovanni Agnelli II, the founder's grandson, became Fiat's chairman. Under Agnelli, Fiat bought high-end Italian carmakers Lancia and Ferrari (1969) and diversified into biotechnology and telecommunications. Allis Chalmers and Fiat merged their earthmoving equipment businesses in 1973.

Labor strife and the oil crisis hurt Fiat in the 1970s. By 1979, 27 executives had been wounded by the Red Brigade. Needing cash, Fiat sold a 10% interest to Libya in 1976.

In 1980 Cesare Romiti became managing director. Dubbed "Il duro" (the hard one), Romiti announced the elimination of 23,000 jobs. After a 5-week strike, 40,000 workers marched in support of management, crushing the strike and union influence at Fiat.

In the 1980s factory automation improved Fiat's productivity. The Uno, a small car, was an instant success in 1983. The company ended its chronically unprofitable Fiat auto sales operations in the US (1983).

Merger talks with Ford collapsed in 1985, but Fiat's truck operations and Ford's British truck business were combined in 1986. In the same year Libya sold its holdings and Fiat outbid Ford for Alfa Romeo, whose dealers accounted for 50% of Fiat's domestic sales. In 1988 Chrysler agreed to sell Alfas in the US.

In 1989 and 1990 Fiat agreed to help build over 1 million cars annually in the USSR and Poland. In 1990 Fiat and Alcatel Alsthom announced plans to swap stock and to merge their car battery and Italian telecommunication equipment units. The next year Fiat and Ford merged their farm and construction equipment businesses.

HOW MUCH

$=L1,125 (Dec. 31, 1990)	9-Year Growth	1981	1982	1983	1984	1985[1]	1986	1987	1988	1989	1990
Sales (L bil.)	12.2%	20,312	20,619	21,985	23,813	27,594	29,873	39,644	45,512	52,019	57,209
Net income (L bil.)	37.8%	90	137	253	627	1,326	2,162	2,373	3,026	3,306	1,613
Income as % of sales	—	0.4%	0.7%	1.2%	2.6%	4.8%	7.2%	6.0%	6.6%	6.4%	2.8%
Earnings per share (L)	30.7%	64	98	180	298	630	924	1,014	1,293	1,433	713
Stock price – high (L)	—	1,255	959	1,627	2,224	5,750	15,865	16,503	10,455	12,189	11,320
Stock price – low (L)	—	673	711	786	1,611	1,986	6,280	7,965	7,602	9,021	5,169
Stock price – close (L)	23.8%	786	808	1,627	2,067	5,721	13,817	8,220	9,813	11,131	5,361
P/E – high	—	20	10	9	7	9	17	16	8	9	16
P/E – low	—	11	7	4	5	3	7	8	6	6	7
Dividends per share (L)[2]	22.4%	60	67	77	87	106	144	212	270	320	370
Book value per share (L)	16.6%	1,704	2,328	2,425	3,000	3,468	4,282	4,877	5,790	6,781	6,805

1990 Year-end:
Debt ratio: 44.1%
Return on equity: 10.5%
Cash (bil.): L10,170
Long-term debt (bil.): L12,123
No. of shares (mil.): 2,262
Dividends:
1990 average yield: 6.9%
1990 payout: 51.9%
Market value (mil.): $10,779
Sales (mil.): $50,852

Stock Price History High/Low 1981–90

[1]Accounting change [2]Not including rights offerings

NYSE symbol: FIA (ADR)
Fiscal year ends: December 31

WHO

Chairman: Giovanni Agnelli, age 70
VC: Umberto Agnelli
Managing Director: Cesare Romiti, age 68
EVP Financing and Accounting: Francesco Paolo Mattioli, age 50
President, Fiat USA, Inc.: Vittorio Vellano
Auditors: Arthur Andersen & Co.
Employees: 303,238

WHERE

HQ: Fiat S.p.A., Corso Marconi 10-20, 10125 Turin, Italy
Phone: 011-39-11-65651
US HQ: Fiat USA, Inc., 375 Park Ave., New York, NY 10152
US Phone: 212-355-2600
US Fax: 212-688-2848

Fiat operates in Italy and 58 other countries.

	1990 Sales		1990 Operating Income	
	L bil.	% of total	L bil.	% of total
Italy	39,483	69	1,725	80
Other Europe	15,315	27	442	20
Other countries	2,411	4	(38)	—
Total	**57,209**	**100**	**2,129**	**100**

WHAT

	1990 Sales		1990 Operating Income	
	L bil.	% of total	L bil.	% of total
Automobiles	27,224	48	907	43
Commercial vehicles	7,225	13	106	5
Farm & construction equipment	2,432	4	(84)	(4)
Other automotive	4,139	7	182	8
Other industrial	8,862	15	1,018	48
Services	7,327	13	—	—
Total	**57,209**	**100**	**2,129**	**100**

Brand Names

Automobiles
Alfa Romeo
Ferrari
Fiat
Innocenti
Lancia-Autobianchi

Commercial Vehicles
Iveco (heavy trucks)

Farm and Construction Equipment
Agrifull
Fiat
Fiatallis
Fiat Hitachi
Hesston
Laverda
Woods

Selected Major Group Companies

Comau Finanziaria SpA (factory automation)
Editrice La Stampa SpA
FiatGeotech SpA (farm and constuction equipment)
Fiatimpresit SpA (engineering)
Fidis SpA (financial services)
Gilardini SpA (industrial components)
Magneti Marelli SpA (automotive components)
Snia BPD SpA (diversified industrial)
Teksid SpA (metallurgical products)
Toro Assicurazioni SpA (insurance)

KEY COMPETITORS

BMW	Honda	Peugeot
Caterpillar	Hyundai	Renault
Chrysler	Ingersoll-Rand	Saab-Scania
Daimler-Benz	Mazda	Suzuki
Deere	Mitsubishi	Tenneco
Dresser	Navistar	Toyota
Ford	Nissan	Volkswagen
General Motors	PACCAR	Volvo

FLETCHER CHALLENGE LTD.

OVERVIEW

New Zealand's largest public company, Fletcher Challenge, has businesses in forest products, construction, agriculture, and petroleum, providing about 10% of New Zealand's total exports. In a country where 9 of the 10 largest companies have gone bankrupt in the last decade, Fletchers (as it is known) has survived. Its success is the result of acquisitions, which have catapulted it from a domestic operation in 1981 to a worldwide enterprise, with more than 53% of 1990 sales overseas.

Fletcher Challenge is the world's 6th largest forest products company. In the US it is one of the West Coast's leading builders (Wright Schuchart, Dinwiddie Construction). At home the company is a major gas producer and building materials supplier. Its subsidiaries provide New Zealand with newsprint (Tasman Pulp and Paper); rural services, such as wool brokerage and financing (Wrightson, Rural Bank); and petroleum exploration and products (Petrocorp, Synfuel, Petralgas).

The company plans to continue its international expansion. However, at the heart of its $17.6 billion mountain of assets is $4.6 billion of debt, brought on by the same expansion that thrust Fletcher Challenge onto the global stage.

WHEN

Three companies came together in 1981 to create Fletcher Challenge. The oldest, Challenge Corporation, was a Dunedin-based livestock partnership founded in 1861 by John Wright and Robert Robertson. Christened Wright Stephenson & Co. (1868), the firm expanded throughout New Zealand, opening its first overseas office (London) in 1906.

In the coming decades Wright Stephenson diversified into fertilizers (1920), breeding stock (1922), motor cars (1927), electrical appliances (1937), land development (1945), and bicycle and lawn mower manufacturing (1962). Under the chairmanship of Ronald Trotter, the company merged with NMA Company of New Zealand to form Challenge Corporation in 1972. Another New Zealand livestock broker, NMA (founded in 1864) had grown to become a major meat and seafood exporter.

The 2nd building block of Fletcher Challenge was founded in Dunedin as a construction company in 1909 by Scottish immigrant James Fletcher. James's brothers William and Andrew later joined the company, named Fletcher Construction Company in 1919. Up through the 1930s the company bought several suppliers, such as marble quarries and brickworks, and in 1939 started producing wood-based building materials. The company was reorganized as Fletcher Holdings in 1940. James's son (also James) ran the company from 1942 to 1980.

Tasman Pulp and Paper Company (the 3rd branch of Fletcher Challenge) was formed in 1952 and originally owned by the public, Fletcher, and the New Zealand government. The government sold its stake in 1979, and, after a shuffling of stock, Fletcher emerged with 56% of Tasman, and Challenge with 28%. The marriage of these 3 companies in 1981 created an entity that generated about $2 billion in sales (equal to about 8% of New Zealand's total GNP) in its first year.

With Trotter as CEO and Hugh Fletcher (the founder's grandson) as COO, Fletcher Challenge moved into the Canadian paper business, buying the Canadian forest products operations of San Francisco–based Crown Zellerbach Corporation (renamed Crown Forest Industries) in 1983 and a majority stake in British Columbia Forest Products in 1987. At home Fletcher Challenge bought Petrocorp from the government (oil and gas, 1988) and the government-owned Rural Bank (financial services, 1989). The company has projected a sharp drop in earnings for 1991, resulting from weak markets in its core industries.

HOW MUCH

$=NZ$1.70 (Dec. 31, 1990)	8-Year Growth	1981	1982	1983	1984	1985	1986	1987	1988	1989	1990
Sales (NZ$ mil.)	25.5%	—	1,978	2,172	3,238	4,184	3,986	5,399	8,188	10,461	12,204
Net income (NZ$ mil.)[1]	28.3%	—	90	45	131	181	241	255	532	653	662
Income as % of sales	—	—	4.6%	2.1%	4.0%	4.3%	6.0%	4.7%	6.5%	6.2%	5.4%
Earnings per share (NZ$)[1]	16.1%	—	*0.17*	*0.09*	*0.24*	*0.30*	*0.36*	*0.46*	*0.56*	*0.60*	*0.56*
Stock price – high (NZ$)[2]	—	—	1.18	1.15	1.72	2.20	3.73	6.20	7.60	5.40	5.68
Stock price – low (NZ$)[2]	—	—	0.82	0.69	1.08	1.23	1.79	3.54	3.85	4.16	3.92
Stock price – close (NZ$)	—	—	—	—	—	—	—	—	—	—	—
P/E – high[2]	—	—	7	13	7	7	10	13	14	9	10
P/E – low[2]	—	—	5	8	5	4	5	8	7	7	7
Dividends per share (NZ$)	18.4%	—	0.07	0.08	0.10	0.13	0.17	0.21	0.24	0.26	0.27
Book value per share (NZ$)[3]	12.8%	—	1.40	1.50	1.55	1.65	1.90	2.83	3.01	3.39	3.68

1990 Year-end:
Debt ratio: 62.6%
Return on equity: 14.2%
Cash (mil.): NZ$689
Long-term debt (mil.): NZ$7,797
No. of shares (mil.): 1,151
Dividends:
1990 average yield: —
1990 payout: 48.2%
Market value (mil.): $2,141
Sales (mil.): $7,179

Stock Price History High/Low 1982–90

[1] Includes extraordinary items [2] Fiscal year basis [3] Excluding intangibles

OTC symbol: FLCAY (ADR)
Fiscal year ends: June 30

WHO

Chairman: Sir Ronald Trotter, age 62
CEO: Hugh A. Fletcher, age 42
CFO: David G. Sadler, age 59
Employee Relations Director: John B. Hart
Auditors: Coopers & Lybrand; KPMG Peat Marwick
Employees: 40,000

WHERE

HQ: Fletcher Challenge House, 810 Great South Rd., Penrose, Auckland, New Zealand
Phone: 011-64-9-590-000
Fax: 011-64-9-525-0559
No. Am. HQ: Fletcher Challenge Finance Canada Inc., Suite 1908, 20 Queen St. West, (PO Box 61), Toronto, Ontario M5H 3R3, Canada
No. Am. Phone: 416-340-0944
No. Am. Fax: 416-340-0948

Fletcher Challenge has operations in New Zealand, Australia, Brazil, Canada, Chile, the UK, and the US. Its products are sold in more than 50 countries.

WHAT

	1990 Sales		1990 Net Income	
	NZ$ mil.	% of total	NZ$ mil.	% of total
Pulp & paper	3,410	26	195	27
Building materials & construction	8,145	61	211	29
Rural services	1,044	8	161	22
Energy	725	5	157	22
Adjustments	(1,120)	—	(62)	—
Total	**12,204**	**100**	**662**	**100**

Pulp and Paper
Bleached softwood kraft
Lightweight coated paper
Market pulp
Newsprint
Woodfree papers

Building Materials and Construction
Cement
Commercial construction
Engineering
Gypsum-based products
House building
Lumber
Property development and management
Steel production
Wood paneling

Rural Services
Financial services
Insurance
Livestock
Real estate
Seeds
Wool brokerage

Energy
Gas pipelines
Petrochemicals
Petroleum products
Synthetic fuels

KEY COMPETITORS

Boise Cascade
Canadian Pacific
Champion International
Georgia-Pacific
International Paper
James River
Kimberly-Clark
Manville
Mead
Owens-Corning
PPG
Scott
USG
Weyerhaeuser
Other natural resource companies

FORMOSA PLASTICS GROUP

OVERVIEW

Formosa Plastics Group, Taiwan's largest private-sector industrial concern, is the empire of chairman and founder Yung-ching Wang. With a personal fortune estimated by *Forbes* at over $1.2 billion, Wang is widely recognized as Taiwan's wealthiest man; he made most of his money in PVC plastic. Formosa Plastics leads the world in production of PVC and is America's #1 maker of PVC pipe.

The company owes its success to the foresight of Chairman Wang, who developed it as a vertically integrated PVC producer. Nothing is wasted; for instance, Wang formed Formosa Chemicals & Fibre in 1965 to produce rayon from discarded limbs in his logging yards. Formosa Plastics now makes all 4 man-made textile fibers: acrylic, nylon, polyester, and rayon.

The company is now faced with increased pressure from environmentalists, which has slowed its expansion on both sides of the Pacific. In the US, local groups have labeled Formosa Plastics an "environmental outlaw" for allegedly poisoning soil and groundwater near its unfinished ethylene plant at Point Comfort, Texas.

WHEN

In 1932 Yung-ching Wang borrowed $200 from his father, a Taiwanese tea merchant, to buy a rice mill near the town of Jiayi. The mill was destroyed by Allied bombs in 1944, but Wang went on to make a fortune in timber and founded Formosa Plastics, a small PVC plant, in 1954. He bought the technology from the Japanese and jokes that, when he formed the company, he didn't even know what the P in PVC stood for.

At first Wang had trouble finding buyers for his PVC resins, but in 1958 he set up his own PVC resin processor, Nan Ya Plastics. He formed Formosa Chemicals & Fibre to make rayon backing for PVC leather (1965). For the next 15 years, the company continued to grow exclusively as a Taiwanese enterprise.

Between 1980 and 1988 Wang bought 14 US PVC-related manufacturers, including Imperial Chemical's Baton Rouge vinyl chloride monomer plant (1981), Stauffer Chemical's Delaware City PVC plant (1981), and Manville Corporation's PVC businesses (1983). He started building a PVC plant in Point Comfort, Texas, in 1981, cutting construction costs up to 40% by importing equipment from Taiwan.

When the PVC market reached saturation in the mid-1980s, Wang built plants in Taiwan to make chemicals for semiconductors. Nan Ya enlisted the help of Hewlett-Packard to build a plant capable of producing printed circuit boards and the necessary chemicals.

Wang bought several Texas-based oil and gas properties, including 218 producing wells, a gas processing plant, and a pipeline company from Alcoa in 1988. He continued to expand PVC operations but, faced with stricter pollution controls in Taiwan, announced his intention to build an ethylene plant in Point Comfort (1988). Construction was delayed in 1990, when the EPA began investigating allegations that Formosa Plastics had contaminated groundwater near the plant. Wang then turned to mainland China, where there are no pollution controls, planning to build an ethylene complex there (1990). Taiwan balked at the proposal, suggesting that Formosa Plastics should build at home instead. But rather than accept his homeland's environmental constraints (or perhaps to leverage negotiations with the Taiwanese government), Wang sought Chinese approval of the multi-billion-dollar project, planning to control it through a Hong Kong subsidiary to circumvent a Taiwanese law against direct investment in the mainland. The Chinese government rejected the plan in 1991, but the delay won Wang the support of Prime Minister Pei-tsun Hau. The company now plans to build its plant in Mailiao, a town on Taiwan's southeast coast.

HOW MUCH

$=NT$26.6 (Dec. 31, 1990)	9-Year Growth	1981	1982	1983	1984	1985	1986	1987	1988	1989	1990
Sales (NT$ mil.)	6.9%	16,269	16,871	19,222	23,747	24,832	27,973	30,274	33,302	30,426	29,578
Net income (NT$ mil.)	22.5%	583	804	1,104	1,577	1,562	2,469	3,017	3,809	3,181	3,627
Income as % of sales	—	3.6%	4.8%	5.7%	6.6%	6.3%	8.8%	10.0%	11.4%	10.5%	12.3%
Earnings per share (NT$)	22.5%	0.45	0.62	0.85	1.21	1.20	1.90	2.32	2.94	2.45	2.79
Stock price – high (NT$)	—	5.7	4.9	12.3	15.2	15.8	22.0	66.6	126.1	86.0	117.0
Stock price – low (NT$)	—	4.4	4.4	4.6	8.7	9.3	15.5	20.3	34.0	55.2	29.0
Stock price – close (NT$)	27.4%	4.5	4.6	10.7	12.8	15.7	20.2	35.0	60.8	74.8	39.7
P/E – high	—	13	8	14	13	13	12	29	43	35	42
P/E – low	—	10	7	5	7	8	8	9	12	23	10
Dividends per share (NT$)	—	—	—	—	—	—	0.49	0.64	0.75	0.90	1.10
Book value per share (NT$)	—	—	—	—	—	—	—	—	—	15.18	17.05

1990 Year-end:
Debt ratio: 0.0%
Return on equity: 17.3%
Cash (mil.): —
Long-term debt (mil.): 0
No. of shares (mil.): 1,298
Dividends:
1990 average yield: 2.8%
1990 payout: 39.4%
Market value (mil.): $1,937
Sales (mil.): $1,112

Stock Price History High/Low 1981–90

140 120 100 80 60 40 20 0

Note: Financial information provided for Formosa Plastics Corp. only

Principal exchange: Taiwan
Fiscal year ends: December 31

Hoover's Rating 

WHO

Chairman: Yung-ching Wang, age 74
President: Yung-tsai Wang
EVP: C. S. Wang
Employees: 43,065

WHERE

HQ: 201 Tun Hwa North Rd., Taipei, Taiwan, Republic of China
Phone: 011-886-2-712-2211
Fax: 011-886-2-712-9211
US HQ: Formosa Plastics Corp., U.S.A., 9 Peach Tree Hill Rd., Livingston, NJ 07039
US Phone: 201-992-2090
US Fax: 201-992-9627

Formosa Plastics has plants in Taiwan and the US.

WHAT

	1990 Sales		1990 Pretax Income	
	NT$ mil.	% of total	NT$ mil.	% of total
Formosa Plastics	29,578	18	4,074	25
Nan Ya Plastics	55,170	34	4,680	28
Formosa Chemicals & Fibre	27,472	17	4,228	26
Other	49,759	31	3,460	21
Total	**161,979**	**100**	**16,442**	**100**

Formosa Plastics Corp.
Acrylic fibers
Bulky yarns
Calcium carbonate
Carbon fiber
Carpet and carpet yarn
Caustic soda
Knitted cloth
Liquid chlorine
Machinery and gear products
PVC resins
Quicklime
Rubber products

Nan Ya Plastics Corp.
Copper-clad laminate
Dyed and finished fabric
Epoxy resin
Floor and wall coverings
Plasticizer
Polyester
Polyurethane leather
Printed circuit boards
PVC products
Rigid, wrap, and BOPP films

Formosa Chemicals & Fibre Corp.
Acrylic jersey and bulky yarn
Anhydrous sodium sulphate
Detergent
Dodecyl benzene sulphonic acid
Knitted cloth
Nylon
Rayon
Sulphuric products

Other Affiliated Companies
Formosa Hydrocarbons Co., Inc. (gas processing, US)
Formosa Plastics Corp., U.S.A. (PVC products)
Formosa Taffeta Co., Ltd. (nylon cloth and taffeta)
J-M Manufacturing Co., Inc. (PVC pipe, US)
Lavaca Pipeline Co. (gas transmission pipeline, US)
Nan Ya Plastics Corp., U.S.A. (plastic products marketing)
Neumin Production Co. (Natural gas exploration and production, US)
Sunrise Plywood Co., Ltd. (furniture)
Tah Shin Spinning Corp. (yarn)
Tai Shih Textile Industry Corp. (yarns)
Tairay (polyester filler)
Weng Fung Industrial Co., Ltd. (PVC products)
Yung Chia Chemical Industries Corp. (polypropylene)

KEY COMPETITORS

BASF
Bayer
Du Pont
Georgia-Pacific
Hercules
Masco
Milliken
Nobel
Rhône-Poulenc
Union Carbide

Chemical, forest products, building materials, and textile companies

FOSTER'S BREWING GROUP LTD.

OVERVIEW

Formerly Elders IXL, multi-billion-dollar Australian conglomerate Foster's Brewing is the world's 5th largest beer producer, with additional operations in agriproducts and finance.

Through its breweries Foster's has established itself as a major player in 3 geographic areas: Australasia, Europe, and North America. Carlton, the company's Australian brewer, holds about 50% of the domestic market and produces Foster's Lager, the country's #1 domestic and export beer. Courage, the company's UK brewer, will become Britain's #2 beer producer (after Bass) following its 1991 purchase of Grand Metropolitan's brewing operations. In North America, Foster's has established a 50/50 joint venture with Molson, giving the partnership a 52% share of the Canadian market.

As part of its 1990 restructuring, the company announced its intentions to sell its nonbrewing assets. Subsequently, large parts of its agribusiness, finance, and other operations have been sold, while others are still on the block.

WHEN

In 1839 Scotsman Alexander Lang Elder arrived at what would become Port Adelaide, Australia, and founded Elder Smith Goldsborough, a trading company to serve local farmers. Over the next 140 years, his enterprise grew into one of Australia's largest commodities trading and farm services companies, although it did not achieve international notoriety until the early 1980s when it became a takeover target for Robert Holmes à Court, then reputed to be Australia's richest man.

For help, Elder Smith turned to John Elliott, managing director of Henry Jones (IXL), a Tasmanian jam and food company. (The name *IXL* was coined around the turn of the century by the company's semiliterate founder to mean "I excel.") Elliott suggested that Elder Smith take over Henry Jones (IXL) to thwart Holmes à Court, and the 2 companies were joined as Elders IXL in 1981. Elliott and his management group assumed control of the new company. In 1982 Elders acquired Wood Hall Trust, a British trading operation.

In 1983 Carlton and United Breweries (CUB), which owned 49% of Elders, was also threatened by a takeover, requiring Elder's immediate attention. CUB had been founded near Melbourne in 1888 by brothers W. M. and R. R. Foster. The company had first exported its Foster's Lager in 1901 to serve Australian forces fighting the Boer War, and in 1907 had joined with 6 other breweries. By 1986 the lager was sold in 80 countries.

Within 2 days Elliott raised over $720 million and captured more than half of the brewery (full ownership in 1984), instantly making Elders one of Australia's largest companies.

Following a failed attempt to acquire Britain's Allied-Lyons, the company purchased Courage Breweries (UK) for $3.5 billion (Australia's largest overseas takeover) in 1986, and in 1987 acquired Carling O'Keefe Breweries (Canada) for $413 million. (Carling joined with Molson Breweries in a 50/50 joint venture in 1989.) At the same time the company greatly expanded its banking and other operations.

In 1989 Elliott and other Elders executives created Harlin Holdings and launched a $4.4 billion management takeover that netted Harlin around 50% of Elders. (The group now owns about 36% of Foster's.) In 1990 Elliott stepped down as CEO and became non-executive deputy chairman. Under Elliott's replacement, Peter Bartels, the company launched a major restructuring in which it changed its name to Foster's Brewing Group and put all of its nonbrewing assets up for sale.

In 1991 Foster's acquired the brewing interests of Grand Metropolitan in exchange for Foster's 50% interest in Courage Pubs. The purchase makes the company a legitimate contender to surpass Bass as the #1 British brewer.

HOW MUCH

$=A$1.29 (Dec. 31, 1990)	9-Year Growth	1981	1982	1983	1984	1985	1986	1987	1988	1989	1990
Sales (A$ mil.)	22.4%	2,500	2,800	3,700	5,582	6,995	7,659	10,560	15,350	17,647	15,406
Net income (A$ mil.)	16.6%	34	58	63	68	112	179	263	449	615	135
Income as % of sales	—	1.4%	2.1%	1.7%	1.2%	1.6%	2.3%	2.5%	2.9%	3.5%	0.9%
Earnings per share (A$)	—	—	0.09	0.08	0.09	0.14	0.21	0.21	0.24	0.29	0.07
Stock price – high (A$)	—	1.19	1.10	1.13	1.33	1.54	3.20	4.23	2.59	2.73	2.42
Stock price – low (A$)	—	0.71	0.61	0.63	0.88	1.07	1.25	1.78	1.84	2.13	1.10
Stock price – close (A$)	3.4%	1.10	0.75	1.09	1.16	1.44	2.81	1.81	2.38	2.16	1.49
P/E – high	—	—	12	14	15	11	15	20	11	9	35
P/E – low	—	—	7	8	10	8	6	8	8	7	16
Dividends per share (A$)	—	—	0.04	0.04	0.05	0.07	0.08	0.10	0.15	0.18	0.20
Book value per share (A$)	—	—	0.59	0.63	0.51	0.69	0.85	1.35	1.65	1.83	1.19

1990 Year-end:
Debt ratio: 50.3%
Return on equity: 4.6%
Cash (mil.): A$754
Long-term debt (mil.): A$2,693
No. of shares (mil.): 2,233
Dividends:
1990 average yield: 13.4%
1990 payout: —
Market value (mil.): $2,579
Sales (mil.): $11,943

Stock Price History High/Low 1981–90

Principal exchange: Sydney
Fiscal year ends: June 30

WHO

Chairman: Neil R. Clark
CEO: Peter T. Bartels
Deputy Chairman: John D. Elliott
Executive Director Treasury: Robert Elstone
Executive Director Personnel: Barry K. Russell
Auditors: Price Waterhouse
Employees: 33,702

WHERE

HQ: One Garden St., South Yarra, Victoria, 3141, Australia
Phone: 011-61-3-828-2424
Fax: 011-61-3-828-2556
No. Am. HQ: Foster's Brewing Group, 175 Bloor St. East, North Tower, Suite 114, Toronto, Ontario M4W 3R8, Canada
No. Am. Phone: 416-921-0055
No. Am. Fax: 416-921-5357

The company's primary offices are in Australia, Canada, Hong Kong, New Zealand, and the UK.

	1990 Sales		1990 Operating Income	
	$ mil.	% of total	$ mil.	% of total
Australasia/ Pacific	10,419	68	159	66
Europe	2,356	15	49	20
North America	2,417	16	(48)	(20)
Asia	205	1	64	27
Other regions	9	—	16	7
Adjustments	—	—	43	—
Total	**15,406**	**100**	**283**	**100**

WHAT

	1990 Sales		1990 Operating Income	
	$ mil.	% of total	$ mil.	% of total
Brewing	5,209	34	550	89
Agribusiness	8,577	56	33	5
Finance	570	4	25	4
Resources	40	—	40	6
Other	1,010	6	(29)	(4)
Adjustments	—	—	(336)	—
Total	**15,406**	**100**	**283**	**100**

Brewing Group
Carlton and United Breweries (Australia)
Carlton Draught
Crown Lager
Foster's Lager
Foster's Light
Redback
Victoria Bitter
Courage Limited (UK)
Courage Best Bitter
Hofmeister Lager
John Smith's Yorkshire Bitter
Kronenbourg 1664
Miller Lite
Molson Breweries (50%, Canada)
Foster's Lager
Molson Canadian
Molson Export
Molson Golden
O'Keefe Ale
Old Vienna

Agribusiness Group
Agricultural processing and trading
Brewing materials
Meat
Wool

Finance Group
Investment management
Property finance and development
Stockbroking
Treasury services
Trustee services

KEY COMPETITORS

Adolph Coors
Allied-Lyons
Anheuser-Busch
Bass
Bond
BSN
Carlsberg
Guinness
Heineken
John Labatt
Kirin
Philip Morris
San Miguel
Stroh
Agriculture companies
Finance companies

FRIEDRICH KRUPP GMBH

OVERVIEW

Located in Germany's Ruhr area, Friedrich Krupp is an industrial dynasty of almost mythic proportions. Generations of German schoolchildren were raised on stories of the stout company that armed the deadly war machines of Otto von Bismarck, Kaiser Wilhelm, and Adolf Hitler. Hitler himself once proudly wrote that Germany's youth were *hart wie Kruppstahl* (hard as Krupp steel).

Since WWII, when Krupp was dismantled by the Allies, the company has rebuilt and turned its attention to more peaceful ends. Today Krupp produces a wide range of steel and industrial products and facilities, everything from excavating equipment to navigation systems to cement plants.

Nevertheless, the company, which was once Germany's industrial leader, has fallen severely from the glory days of its past. No longer controlled by the Krupp family (a foundation owns 75% of its stock), the company has shed operations in an attempt to reverse years of slow decline. Even the government of Iran, which after the 1979 revolution confiscated the 25% of Krupp previously purchased by the Shah, is vainly looking for buyers.

WHEN

Penniless Arndt Krupp arrived in Essen around 1587 and began working as a merchant. Using his profits to buy extensive land holdings at bargain prices from victims of the bubonic plague, Krupp was soon one of the city's richest men.

Krupp's son Anton was equally successful, fortuitously entering the gun trade just in time for the Thirty Years' War. Indeed, Krupp fortunes seemed blessed for several generations, until 1811 when Friedrich Krupp, a 6th generation family member, opened a steel factory. The enterprise was a failure, and in 1826 Krupp died, leaving the near-bankrupt factory in the hands of his 14-year-old son Alfred.

Alfred turned the operation around, introducing steel products for the railroad (including the nonwelded, seamless railroad wheel that he had invented) and, at the first World's Fair in 1851, unveiling Krupp's powerful steel cannon (which was far superior to older bronze models).

When Otto von Bismarck assumed power in Prussia, he used Krupp weapons to defeat the French in the Franco-Prussian War. The "Cannon King," as Alfred became known, died in 1887, leaving what was now the world's largest industrial company in the hands of his son Fritz, a bumbling eccentric who killed himself following a sexual scandal in 1902.

Alfred's granddaughter Bertha (the namesake for Germany's Big Bertha guns) and her new husband, Gustav von Bohlen und Halbach (later Gustav Krupp), picked up the reins and armed the Kaiser for WWI.

The Treaty of Versailles momentarily shut down the company, but Gustav Krupp was back in time to build U-boats, tanks, battleships, and other weapons for his newest idol, Adolf Hitler. In 1943 the ailing Gustav was replaced by his son Alfried, who was convicted at the 1948 Nuremburg trials for using slave laborers during the war.

Alfried was released from prison in 1951 and quickly rebuilt Krupp into Germany's largest steel and machine conglomerate. In 1967 he passed control of the company to a private foundation and died later that year, ending the long era of Krupp leadership.

Berthold Beitz followed Alfried as chairman and greatly expanded Krupp's overseas presence (in 1974 he orchestrated the sale of 25% of the company to the Shah of Iran), although the company's fortunes began a slow decline in the early 1970s due largely to management quarrels, a stubborn insistence on holding on to unprofitable divisions, and the faltering state of the global steel market.

After weathering a strike by steelworkers in 1987 and rejecting a takeover bid by Thyssen in 1988, Krupp ousted Beitz and initiated a major restructuring in which loss-producing divisions (including shipbuilding) were spun off. Also in 1988 the company's trading divison (Krupp Lonrho) was formed when a German subsidary of Lonrho acquired a stake in Krupp Handel.

In 1990 the company purchased Nevada-based Precision Rolled Products (high-performance products, primarily for aircraft) and Press- und Stanzwerk (auto parts, Liechtenstein).

HOW MUCH

\$=DM1.49 (Dec. 31, 1990)	9-Year Growth	1981	1982	1983	1984	1985	1986	1987	1988	1989	1990
Sales (DM mil.)	0.5%	14,838	16,720	17,273	18,239	18,479	15,847	14,105	14,737	17,684	15,570
Net income (DM mil.)[1]	—	—	680	66	579	358	338	252	209	338	272
Income as % of sales	—	—	4.1%	0.4%	3.2%	1.9%	2.1%	1.8%	1.4%	1.9%	1.7%
Employees	—	—	78,201	69,291	66,320	67,402	68,043	65,205	63,391	60,767	59,044

Net Income (DM mil.) 1982–90

[1] Estimated 1982–84

Private company
Fiscal year ends: December 31

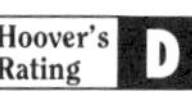

WHO

Chairman: Gerhard Cromme
Deputy Chairman: Gerhard Neipp
Head of Corporate Financing: Klaus Hübner
Head of Corporate Personnel: Jochen Voss
Auditors: Treuhand-Vereinigung Aktiengesellschaft
Employees: 59,044

WHERE

HQ: Altendorfer Strasse 103, PO Box 10 22 52, D-4300 Essen 1, Germany
Phone: 011-49-201-188-24-28
Fax: 011-49-201-188-41-00
US HQ: Krupp Industries Inc., 1370-T Washington Pike, Bridgeville, PA 15017
US Phone: 412-257-5680
US Fax: 412-221-7684

The Krupp group consists of 86 German and 118 foreign subsidiaries.

	1990 Sales	
	DM mil.	% of total
Germany	7,796	50
Other Europe	4,740	30
America	1,623	10
Africa	243	2
Asia	1,059	7
Other countries	109	1
Total	**15,570**	**100**

WHAT

	1990 Sales	
	DM mil.	% of total
Mechanical Engineering	3,478	21
Plantmaking	1,976	12
Electronics	704	4
Steel	7,872	47
Trading	1,926	12
Other	714	4
Adjustments	(1,100)	—
Total	**15,570**	**100**

Electronics
Marine surveying systems
Navigation systems
Production control systems
Radio transmission control systems
Ship handling systems
Training simulators
TV transmission control systems

Mechanical Engineering
Diesel engines
Industrial machinery
Locomotives
Medical/dental equipment

Plantmaking
Chemical processing
Coal conversion
Metals technology
Raw material extraction and processing
Steel production

Steel
Bar
Drop forgings
Power metallurgy
Pressing
Specialty steel
Strip

Trading
Agricultural supplies
Fuels
Industrial development projects
Inland waterway shipping
Ocean shipping
Steel export

KEY COMPETITORS

Bechtel
Bethlehem Steel
Broken Hill
Cargill
Caterpillar
Cummins Engine
Fiat
FMC
General Signal
Hyundai
Ingersoll-Rand
Inland Steel
IRI
LTV
Mitsubishi
Navistar
Nippon Steel
Raytheon
USX

FUJI PHOTO FILM CO., LTD.

OVERVIEW

Fuji Photo Film is Japan's leading manufacturer of photographic film and paper, with 73% of the Japanese market for color film. It trails Eastman Kodak in the US and in Europe, making it the world's #2 producer.

Fuji's push into the US over the last 7 years has occurred at Kodak's expense. Before, Kodak owned the US market, with a 90% share. Fuji has been chipping away at the Rochester film giant (since 1982 its US market share has increased by 7 points to 12%) by developing and introducing new products before Kodak can act. In Europe, Fuji has doubled its market share to 20% since 1980.

At the same time, Kodak is putting pressure on Fuji in Japan, where Kodak's share of the amateur market has been growing steadily by 1% per year since 1984 (to 15% in 1990).

Fuji continues to innovate, recently developing the first film to mimic color as it is perceived by the human eye. Disposable cameras (another Fuji first) generate nearly 10% of Fuji's color film revenues. The company also makes high-performance videotapes and other magnetic storage products and offers electronic imaging equipment for printing, graphic design, and medical diagnostic applications.

WHEN

Mokichi Morita, president of Japan's leading celluloid maker (Dainippon Celluloid Company, founded in 1919), decided to start making motion picture film in the early 1930s. Movies were becoming popular in Japan, but there was no domestic film supplier. Working with a grant from the government, Dainippon Celluloid established Fuji Photo Film, an independent company, in 1934 in Minami Ashigara Village, near Mount Fuji. At first the company had trouble gaining acceptance in Japan as a quality film producer but, with the help of German emulsion specialist Dr. Emill Mauerhoff, overcame its product deficiencies, producing black-and-white photographic film (1936) and the first Japanese-made color film (1948). In the meantime Fuji added 35mm photographic film, 16mm motion picture film, and X-ray film to its product line.

By the early 1940s Fuji was operating 4 factories and a research laboratory in Japan. Its first overseas office, in Brazil, opened in 1955, followed by offices in the US in 1958 and Europe in 1964.

Fuji continued to expand its product line, adding magnetic tape in 1960. In 1962 the company joined Rank Xerox of the UK (an affiliate of America's Xerox and the UK's Rank Organisation) to form Fuji Xerox, a Japanese-based joint venture to sell copiers. In the US Fuji operated as a private label film supplier and did not market its products under its own brand name until 1972.

International marketing VP Minoru Ohnishi became Fuji's president in 1980. Ohnishi's succession marked a new direction for the company; at 55 he was Fuji's youngest president, chosen over more senior officers. Ohnishi worked to decrease Fuji's dependence on Japanese film sales by building sales in the US and pumping money into the production of videotapes, floppy disks, and medical diagnostic equipment.

In 1987 Fuji introduced Fujicolor Quicksnap, the world's first 35mm disposable camera. Quicksnap users simply used up the preloaded roll of film, then took the camera to the developer, getting their pictures (sans camera) in return.

In 1989 Fuji formed a joint 3.5-inch floppy disk manufacturing venture with BASF's US subsidiary and bought Olin Hunt's photographic division (photographic chemicals, now Fuji Hunt Photographic Chemicals). Also that year the company joined Du Pont to buy UK imaging company Crosfield Electronics, forming a joint venture, Du Pont & Fuji Film Electronic Imaging. In 1990 Fuji created FUJIFILM Microdevices, a Japanese subsidiary, to produce image processing semiconductors.

HOW MUCH

	9-Year Growth	1981	1982	1983	1984	1985	1986	1987	1988	1989	1990
Sales ($ mil.)	15.4%	2,364	2,554	2,719	2,686	3,481	4,927	6,366	6,901	6,539	8,588
Net income ($ mil.)	14.0%	224	248	251	227	308	404	562	646	587	728
Income as % of sales	—	9.5%	9.7%	9.2%	8.5%	8.8%	8.2%	8.8%	9.4%	9.0%	8.5%
Earnings per share ($)	12.5%	1.09	1.12	1.12	0.98	1.34	1.75	2.45	2.79	2.52	3.12
Stock price – high ($)	—	13.30	13.74	17.15	16.12	17.15	39.15	55.89	56.51	64.32	60.34
Stock price – low ($)	—	6.50	7.31	10.64	9.71	10.02	15.70	27.27	38.33	39.15	42.27
Stock price – close ($)	20.6%	8.66	13.74	13.95	10.23	16.74	37.81	52.48	47.00	56.48	46.75
P/E – high	—	12	12	15	17	13	22	23	20	26	19
P/E – low	—	6	7	10	10	7	9	11	14	16	14
Dividends per share ($)	16.7%	0.05	0.04	0.06	0.07	0.09	0.12	0.14	0.16	0.15	0.18
Book value per share ($)	21.3%	5.58	6.49	7.43	7.90	10.37	16.09	21.76	24.89	24.77	31.65

1990 Year-end:
Debt ratio: 9.9%
Return on equity: 11.1%
Cash (mil.): $3,596
Current ratio: 2.13
Long-term debt (mil.): $809
No. of shares (mil.): 233
Dividends:
1990 average yield: 0.4%
1990 payout: 5.8%
Market value (mil.): $10,889

Stock Price History High/Low 1981–90

OTC symbol: FUJIY (ADR)
Fiscal year ends: October 20

Hoover's Rating **A**

WHO

President: Minoru Ohnishi, age 66
Senior Managing Director: Hirozo Ueda
Senior Managing Director: Juntaro Suzuki
CFO: Ryunichi Wakasugi
Personnel Manager: D. Takamatsu
Auditors: Price Waterhouse
Employees: 21,946

WHERE

HQ: Fuji Shashin Film Kabushiki Kaisha, 26-30, Nishiazabu 2-chome, Minato-ku, Tokyo 106, Japan
Phone: 011-81-3-3406-2755
Fax: 011-81-3-3406-2193
US HQ: Fuji Photo Film U.S.A., Inc., 555 Taxter Rd., Elmsford, NY 10523
US Phone: 914-789-8100
US Fax: 914-682-4955

Fuji has operations in North America, Europe, Brazil, and the Pacific Basin.

	1990 Sales	
	$ mil.	% of total
Japan	5,295	62
Other countries	3,293	38
Total	**8,588**	**100**

WHAT

	1990 Sales	
	$ mil.	% of total
Commercial products	3,385	40
Magnetic products	874	10
Consumer photographic products	4,329	50
Total	**8,588**	**100**

Consumer Photographic Products
Cameras
Electronic imaging equipment
Photographic films
Photographic paper

Magnetic Products
Audio tape
Floppy disks
Memory tape
Videotape

Commercial Products
Color scanners
Copiers
Data management systems
Graphic arts films
Medical imaging equipment
Microfilm products
Motion picture films
Printing plates
Specialized semiconductors
Thermal paper

Major Joint Ventures
B&F Microdisks (3.5-inch floppy disks, with BASF)
Du Pont & Fuji Film Electronic Imaging Ltd. (printing, with Du Pont)
Fuji Xerox Co., Ltd. (copiers, with Rank Xerox)

KEY COMPETITORS

BASF
Bayer
Canon
Du Pont
Eastman Kodak
GEC
Hewlett-Packard
Hitachi
IBM
Matsushita
3M
Minolta
Pitney Bowes
Polaroid
Sharp
Siemens
Sony
Toshiba
Xerox

FUJITSU LTD.

OVERVIEW

After IBM, Fujitsu is the world's 2nd largest computer maker. It is the #1 mainframe computer manufacturer in Japan, the only country in which IBM is not the leader. Amdahl and Siemens sell Fujitsu's IBM-plug-compatible mainframes in the US and Europe, respectively.

Fujitsu is also a world leader in DRAM production and continues in its original line of business — the manufacture of telecommunications equipment. The company is still related to its original parent, Fuji Electric, through cross-holdings of stock. Fujitsu owns controlling interests in Amdahl (49.5%) and the UK's International Computers Ltd. (ICL, 80%), and in Japanese companies Fanuc, Fujitsu General, and Fujitsu Business Systems.

In 1990 Fujitsu announced a new line of mainframes designed to compete with expected offerings from IBM and Hitachi and to reverse a recent decline in domestic market share. The company is trying to expand in the supercomputer and PC markets and is stepping up spending on semiconductor production and development. R&D spending reached 11.7% of sales in 1990.

OTC symbol: FJTSY (ADR)
Fiscal year ends: March 31

WHO

Chairman: Takuma Yamamoto, age 65
VC: Matami Yasufuku
President: Tadashi Sekizawa
EVP: Kazuo Watanabe
Auditors: Showa Ota & Co.
Employees: 115,012

WHERE

HQ: 6-1, Marunouchi 1-chome, Chiyoda-ku, Tokyo 100, Japan
Phone: 011-81-3-3216-3211
Fax: 011-81-3-3213-7174
US HQ: Fujitsu America, Inc., 3055 Orchard Dr., San Jose, CA 95134-2017
US Phone: 408-432-1300
US Fax: 408-432-1318

Fujitsu has plants in 29 countries.

	1990 Sales	
	¥ bil.	% of total
Japan	1,941	76
Other countries	609	24
Total	**2,550**	**100**

WHEN

In 1923 Siemens and Furukawa Electric created Fuji Electric to produce electrical equipment. Fuji spun off Fujitsu, its communications division, in 1935. Originally a manufacturer of telephone equipment, Fujitsu produced anti-aircraft weapons during WWII. After the war Fujitsu returned to telecommunications, becoming one of 4 major suppliers to state-owned monopoly Nippon Telegraph and Telephone and benefiting from Japan's rapid economic recovery in the 1950s and 1960s.

With encouragement from Japan's Ministry of International Trade and Industry (MITI), Fujitsu entered the data processing industry by developing the country's first commercial computer in 1954. Starting in 1959 MITI erected trade barriers to protect Japan's new computer industry. In the early 1960s MITI sponsored the production of mainframe computers, directing Fujitsu to develop the central processing unit. The company expanded into the related areas of semiconductor production and factory automation in the late 1960s. Fujitsu's factory automation business was spun off as Fujitsu Fanuc in 1972. Now called Fanuc, the company has become an important manufacturer of industrial robots.

In the 1970s Fujitsu sought to gain market share by making IBM-plug-compatible computers that provided superior value to buyers. The company bought 30% (since raised to 49.5%) of plug-compatible manufacturer Amdahl (1972) and gained badly needed technical information. In 1974 Fujitsu introduced its first plug-compatible computer and the following year began supplying Amdahl with OEM mainframe subassemblies. In 1979 Fujitsu passed IBM to become Japan's #1 computer manufacturer.

In Europe Fujitsu entered into computer marketing ventures with Siemens (1978) and ICL (1981). The company teamed with TRW (US) to sell point-of-sale systems in 1980, assuming full control of the operation in 1983. Fujitsu released its first supercomputer in 1982. The company dropped its 1986 bid for Fairchild Semiconductor when the US government expressed concern over foreign ownership of the chipmaker.

In 1985 IBM accused Fujitsu of stealing proprietary operating system software technology. Fujitsu objected, citing a secret 1983 agreement under which Fujitsu had paid IBM for software information. In 1988 an arbitrator awarded IBM $237 million. It also granted Fujitsu the right to inspect certain IBM software for 10 years for a relatively small annual fee of $25 million to $52 million.

In 1990 Fujitsu bought 80% of British mainframe maker ICL (from STC). In 1991 Fujitsu again found itself the target of a US company's patent infringement suit — this time by Texas Instruments on a chip patent.

WHAT

	1990 Sales	
	¥ bil.	% of total
Computers & data processing systems	1,690	66
Communications systems	394	16
Electronic devices	357	14
Other operations	109	4
Total	**2,550**	**100**

Computer and Data Processing Systems
FACT III (ATMs)
FAST Series (retail automation systems)
FENICS (value-added network [VAN] services)
FM R Series, FM TOWNS (personal computers)
Fujitsu S (engineering workstations)
K Series (small business computers)
M Series (mainframe computers)
MSP-EX (operating system)
SURE SYSTEM 2000 (fault-tolerant computers)
VP2000 (supercomputers)

Telecommunications Products
COINS (corporate information network systems)
FETEX Series (digital switching and PBX systems)
Integrated services digital network (ISDN) systems

Other Products
Car audio equipment
Electronic components
Semiconductors
Vehicle security systems

HOW MUCH

$ = ¥135 (Dec. 31, 1990)	9-Year Growth	1981	1982	1983	1984	1985	1986	1987	1988	1989	1990
Sales (¥ bil.)	17.8%	582	800	957	1,210	562	1,692	1,789	2,047	2,387	2,550
Net income (¥ bil.)	18.8%	18	32	48	67	89	39	21	42	70	87
Income as % of sales	—	3.2%	4.0%	5.0%	5.5%	5.7%	2.3%	1.2%	2.1%	2.9%	3.4%
Earnings per share (¥)	13.0%	15	24	33	44	55	24	13	24	37	45
Stock price – high (¥)	—	666	758	1,125	1,313	1,187	1,250	1,610	1,930	1,690	1,640
Stock price – low (¥)	—	323	409	635	884	793	819	700	1,160	1,400	936
Stock price – close (¥)	7.7%	503	718	1,010	1,136	1,000	1,060	1,110	1,510	1,510	980
P/E – high	—	44	32	34	30	22	53	120	82	46	36
P/E – low	—	22	17	19	20	15	35	52	48	38	21
Dividends per share (¥)	6.3%	4.5	4.5	5.1	5.9	7.6	7.4	8.0	8.0	9.0	9.0
Book value per share (¥)	16.0%	158	205	245	296	394	410	427	484	546	602

1990 Year-end:
Debt ratio: 23.5%
Return on equity: 7.8%
Cash (bil.): ¥329
Long-term debt (bil.): ¥334
No. of shares (mil.): 1,802
Dividends:
1990 average yield: 0.9%
1990 payout: 20.0%
Market value (mil.): $13,081
Sales (mil.): $18,889

Stock Price History High/Low 1981–90
2,000
1,800
1,600
1,400
1,200
1,000
800
600
400
200
0

KEY COMPETITORS

Alcatel Alsthom
AT&T
BCE
Canon
Casio
Compaq
Computer Associates
Control Data
Cray Research
Data General
DEC
Ericsson
GEC
GTE
Harris
Hewlett-Packard
Hitachi
Hyundai
IBM
Intel
ITT
Lucky-Goldstar
Machines Bull
Mitsubishi
Motorola
National Semiconductor
NCR
NEC
Oki
Philips
Prime
Siemens
Sun Microsystems
Tandem
Texas Instruments
Toshiba
Unisys
Wang
Electronics companies
Telecommunications manufacturers

THE GENERAL ELECTRIC COMPANY PLC

OVERVIEW

Although its name is similar, London-based General Electric Company is not related to America's GE. The 2 cooperate (through joint ownership of General Domestic Appliances) to make and sell Hotpoint, Creda, Cannon, and other home appliances, primarily in the UK; otherwise, GEC is separate from GE, actually predating it by 6 years.

But, like GE, GEC makes everything electrical, from Gilbarco gas pumps to nuclear power plants. It is the UK's largest and the world's 17th largest electronics company.

In the defense electronics sector, GEC produces Spearfish and Stingray torpedoes. The company's 1990 purchase of Ferranti International's defense operations put GEC in close competition with French rival Thomson-CSF as Europe's #1 defense electronics supplier. In 1991 GEC and Thomson-CSF formed a partnership to produce advanced radars.

GEC Alsthom, the joint venture between GEC and France's Alcatel Alsthom, is Europe's largest and the world's 2nd largest electrical engineering company. Gilbarco is the world's #1 maker of electronic fuel pumps. GEC also produces printing and graphics design equipment through its subsidiary, A. B. Dick Company, USA.

WHEN

Hugo Hirst and Gustav Byng went into the electrical equipment wholesale business in London in 1886. By 1889 their company, The General Electric Company, was manufacturing its own products, including bells, switches, and telephones. Before long GEC made light bulbs (1893) and commercial electric motors (1896). GEC became a pioneer in factory electrification and had expanded to Europe, India, South Africa, and the Pacific by the time it went public in 1900.

GEC formed Peel-Connor Telephone Works to install community telephone exchanges in 1910. Work on television receivers commenced in 1935, and GEC eventually branched into nuclear power, computers, and semiconductors. In 1961 GEC bought a small but profitable radio and TV business, Radio & Allied Industries. Former Radio & Allied manager Arnold Weinstock joined GEC as managing director in 1963, and under his leadership the company became the UK's leading electronics and electrical products supplier. Weinstock initiated GEC's hostile takeover of rival electrical equipment maker Associated Electrical Industries in 1967 and then merged GEC with English Electric, owner of radio and electronics pioneer Marconi Company, in 1968. In the US, GEC bought office equipment maker A. B. Dick Company of Chicago in 1979 and RCA's medical diagnostic equipment maker Picker International Holdings in 1981.

In 1985 GEC launched an unsuccessful takeover bid for British defense and telecommunications firm Plessey. The 2 companies formed a joint venture (GEC Plessey Telecommunications, 1988). Soon afterward GEC made another bid for Plessey, this time through GEC Siemens, a joint venture with German electronics giant Siemens (1988). GEC then found itself the target of a hostile takeover from Metsun, a company formed by Plessey and France's Thomson (1989). The Metsun offer fell apart in 1989, after GEC announced a joint venture with the US GE linking their appliance, medical equipment, and electrical products distribution businesses (General Domestic Appliances).

GEC Siemens won British government approval to buy Plessey in 1989. Since then GEC and Siemens have effectively divided Plessey's businesses. GEC entered a joint venture with Alcatel Alsthom of France (formerly CGE), combining their power generation, rail transportation, and electrical distribution businesses in 1989. In 1990 GEC bought the defense operations of British electronics company Ferranti International.

HOW MUCH

£=$1.93 (Dec. 31, 1990)	9-Year Growth	1981	1982	1983	1984	1985	1986	1987	1988	1989	1990
Sales (£ mil.)	9.5%	3,883	4,691	5,232	5,271	5,575	5,560	5,555	5,816	6,664	8,786
Net income (£ mil.)	7.1%	294	365	397	390	407	428	450	451	510	543
Income as % of sales	—	7.6%	7.8%	7.0%	7.4%	7.3%	7.7%	8.1%	7.8%	7.7%	6.2%
Earnings per share (p)	7.1%	11	13	14	14	15	16	16	17	19	20
Stock price – high (p)	—	167	252	250	238	220	224	251	191	281	245
Stock price – low (p)	—	115	144	172	160	150	160	148	143	187	170
Stock price – close (p)	0.6%	166	209	180	218	164	184	160	189	226	175
P/E – high	—	15	19	18	17	15	14	16	11	15	12
P/E – low	—	11	11	12	11	10	10	9	8	10	8
Dividends per share (p)	18.2%	2.1	2.6	3.0	3.5	4.0	4.3	5.3	6.5	7.8	9.3
Book value per share (p)	5.7%	53	65	76	82	89	98	109	102	112	87

1990 Year-end:
Debt ratio: 12.8%
Return on equity: 20.3%
Cash (mil.): £874
Long-term debt (mil.): £341
No. of shares (mil.): 2,670
Dividends:
1990 average yield: 5.3%
1990 payout: 45.8%
Market value (mil.): $9,018
Sales (mil.): $16,957

300
250
200
150
100
50
0

Stock Price History High/Low 1981–90

OTC symbol: GNELY (ADR)
Fiscal year ends: March 31

Hoover's Rating 

WHO

Chairman: The Rt. Hon. Lord Prior, PC, age 62, £113,000 pay
VC: Sir Ronald Grierson, age 68
Managing Director: Lord Weinstock, age 65
Group Finance Director: D. B. Newlands, age 43
Director Employee Relations: Sara Morrison, age 55
Auditors: Touche Ross & Co.
Employees: 107,435

WHERE

HQ: 1 Stanhope Gate, London W1A 1EH, UK
Phone: 011-44-71-493-8484
Fax: 011-44-71-493-1974
US HQ: A. B. Dick Company, USA, 5700 W. Touhy Ave., Chicago, IL 60648-4606
US Phone: 708-647-8800
US Fax: 708-647-0845

GEC has operations worldwide.

	1990 Sales		1990 Operating Income	
	£ mil.	% of total	£ mil.	% of total
UK	4,374	52	430	64
Other Europe	2,273	27	144	21
The Americas	1,465	17	62	9
Australasia	262	3	14	2
Asia	120	1	17	3
Africa	17	—	4	1
Adjustments	275	—	—	—
Total	**8,786**	**100**	**671**	**100**

WHAT

	1990 Sales		1990 Operating Income	
	£ mil.	% of total	£ mil.	% of total
Electronic systems	2,219	26	223	33
Power systems	2,606	31	130	19
Telecommunications	909	11	87	13
Consumer goods	276	3	21	3
Electronic metrology	501	6	49	7
Office equipment & printing	387	5	31	5
Medical equipment	447	5	25	4
Electronic components	336	4	16	2
Industrial apparatus	374	4	37	6
Distribution & trading	345	4	28	4
Other activities	111	1	24	4
Adjustments	275	—	—	—
Total	**8,786**	**100**	**671**	**100**

Major Subsidiaries and Associated Companies
A. B. Dick Company, USA (office equipment and printing)
Associated Electrical Industries Ltd.
Avery India Ltd. (39.9%, electronic metrology)
The English Electric Co., Ltd.
GEC Alsthom NV, Holland (50%, power systems)
GEC Thomson Airborne Radar (GTAR, 50%)
GEC-Elliot Automation Ltd. (electronics)
GEC-Marconi Ltd. (electronics)
General Domestic Appliances Ltd. (50%)
Cannon Industries Ltd.
Creda Ltd.
Hotpoint Ltd.
Redring Electric Ltd.
Xpelair Ltd.
Gilbarco Group (electronic measuring devices)
GPT Holdings Ltd. (60%, telecommunications)
Picker International Inc., USA (medical equipment)
The Plessey Company Ltd. (50%, electronics)

KEY COMPETITORS

Other electronics, power systems, industrial equipment, telecommunications, office equipment, and consumer appliance companies.

GLAXO HOLDINGS PLC

OVERVIEW

British pharmaceutical giant Glaxo Holdings is the largest drug producer in the UK and 2nd largest in the world after Merck. Zantac, its best-selling anti-ulcer drug, brings in about 1/2 of company sales and is the world's top-selling drug.

Glaxo is expanding primarily through internal product development. R&D expenditures are running at a hefty 14% of sales. Promising Glaxo drugs include Sumatriptan, a migraine headache medicine, and Salmeterol, a treatment for asthma.

A creative dealmaker, Glaxo recently swapped its over-the-counter version of Zantac for rights to a calcium channel blocker from Sandoz and agreed to sell 2 other heart drugs for Roche. By selling these drugs Glaxo is preparing its huge (9,500) sales force for future, internally developed cardiovascular medications.

WHEN

Englishman Joseph Nathan started an import-export business in New Zealand in 1873. While on a buying trip in London, one of his sons encountered a process for drying milk. Intrigued, Nathan obtained the rights and began producing powdered milk in New Zealand. The product was most successful in its application as a baby food, sold under the Glaxo name.

Nathan's son Alec was dispatched to London to oversee sales of the baby food in Britain. He published the *Glaxo Baby Book*, a guide to child care, introducing the "Builds Bonnie Babies" slogan and leading to the rapid acceptance of Glaxo baby foods in the early 1900s. The company expanded in Britain and, shortly after WWI, began distribution in India and South America.

In the 1920s Glaxo acquired a license to process vitamin D and launched vitamin D–fortified formulations. The company entered the pharmaceutical business with its 1927 introduction of Ostelin, a liquid vitamin D concentrate, and continued to grow globally in the 1930s, introducing Ostermilk (vitamin-fortified milk), a successful retail product.

Glaxo produced penicillin and anesthetics during WWII. After the war it stepped up penicillin production and isolated vitamin B_{12}. Following precipitous declines in antibiotic prices in the mid-1950s, Glaxo diversified, acquiring veterinary, medical instrument, and drug distribution firms.

Glaxo was the target of a hostile takeover attempt by Beecham in the 1970s. The company arranged a merger with drug manufacturer and retailer Boots to fend off Beecham's bid. The British Monopolies Commission quashed both transactions, claiming that increased size inhibited innovation.

Paul Girolami became CEO in 1980, as clinical trials of Zantac, an anti-ulcer drug, neared completion. At the time the company's sales in Nigeria exceeded those in the US. Armed with Zantac (deemed to have slightly fewer side effects than Tagamet, SmithKline's established blockbuster drug) Girolami mounted a marketing blitzkrieg on Tagamet's lucrative US market in 1983.

Negotiating the use of Hoffmann–La Roche's large, underutilized sales force, Girolami attained the US marketing clout he had lacked. The Zantac sales assault stunned a complacent SmithKline, wrenching away leadership in US anti-ulcer drug sales and establishing a 53% share while reducing Tagamet's to 29%. Zantac's great success made Glaxo the world's 2nd largest pharmaceutical company in 1988.

In the 1980s Glaxo shed its nondrug operations and completed a $350 million research facility in North Carolina (1988). Sir Paul Girolami turned over his post in 1989 to Glaxo's new CEO, American Ernest Mario.

In 1991 the company's monopoly on Zantac was jeopardized when its patent (not due to expire until 2002) for the drug was challenged in court by the Tabatznik generic pharmaceuticals group.

HOW MUCH

	9-Year Growth	1981	1982	1983	1984	1985	1986	1987	1988	1989	1990
Sales ($ mil.)	15.4%	1,371	1,503	1,575	1,629	1,850	2,189	2,808	3,521	3,984	4,966
Net income ($ mil.)	31.6%	117	140	177	229	366	613	800	976	1,066	1,380
Income as % of sales	—	8.5%	9.3%	11.2%	14.1%	19.8%	28.0%	28.5%	27.7%	26.8%	27.8%
Earnings per share ($)	31.0%	0.16	0.19	0.24	0.31	0.50	0.83	1.08	1.32	1.43	1.84
Stock price – high ($)	—	2.11	6.09	7.88	6.56	11.56	17.25	30.63	20.50	26.88	34.63
Stock price – low ($)	—	1.45	1.97	4.97	4.94	6.19	10.88	15.38	15.88	18.50	22.63
Stock price – close ($)	36.6%	1.98	5.09	5.00	6.31	11.06	15.38	18.25	19.25	26.00	32.75
P/E – high	—	13	32	33	21	23	21	28	16	19	19
P/E – low	—	9	10	21	16	13	13	14	12	13	12
Dividends per share ($)	31.4%	0.07	0.07	0.07	0.09	0.12	0.21	0.31	0.53	0.66	0.84
Book value per share ($)	21.6%	1.09	1.08	1.14	1.25	1.51	2.26	3.16	4.12	4.77	6.36

1990 Year-end:
Debt ratio: 1.3%
Return on equity: 33.1%
Cash (mil.): $2,736
Current ratio: 2.05
Long-term debt (mil.): $64
No. of shares (mil.): 747
Dividends:
1990 average yield: 2.6%
1990 payout: 45.6%
Market value (mil.): $24,468

NYSE symbol: GLX (ADR)
Fiscal year ends: June 30

WHO

Chairman: Sir Paul Girolami, age 64, £683,927 pay
CEO: Ernest Mario, age 52
Finance Director: John M. Hignett, age 56
Senior Personnel Officer: John Beal
Auditors: Coopers & Lybrand Deloitte
Employees: 31,327

WHERE

HQ: Clarges House, 6-12 Clarges St., London W1Y 8DH, UK
Phone: 011-44-71-493-4060
Fax: 011-44-71-493-4809
US HQ: Glaxo Inc., 5 Moore Dr., Research Triangle Park, NC 27709
US Phone: 919-248-2100
US Fax: 919-248-2381

Glaxo manufactures its products in 30 countries, principally the UK, Italy, and the US, and sells them in 150 countries.

	1990 Sales	
	$ mil.	% of total
UK	586	12
Other Europe	1,655	33
North America	2,145	43
Other countries	580	12
Total	**4,966**	**100**

WHAT

	1990 Sales	
	$ mil.	% of total
Anti-ulcerants	2,438	49
Respiratory drugs	1,187	24
Systemic antibiotics	837	17
Cardiovasculars	76	2
Dermatologicals	183	4
Other drugs	228	4
Animal health	5	—
Food	12	—
Total	**4,966**	**100**

Brand Names

Antibiotics
Ceftin/Zinnat
Ceporin
Fortaz/Fortum
Zinacef

Antirhinitics
Beconase
Flixonase

Anti-ulcerants
Zantac

Cardiovasculars
Trandate

Dermatologicals
Betnovate
Temovate/Dermovate

Respiratory Drugs
Beclovent/Becotide
Ventolin
Volmax

KEY COMPETITORS

Abbott Labs
American Cyanamid
American Home Products
Amgen
Bayer
Bristol-Myers Squibb
Ciba-Geigy
Eli Lilly
Genentech
Hoechst
Johnson & Johnson
Merck
Monsanto
Pfizer
Procter & Gamble
Rhône-Poulenc
Roche
Sandoz
Schering-Plough
SmithKline Beecham
Syntex
Upjohn
Warner-Lambert

GRAND METROPOLITAN PLC

OVERVIEW

Once a major hotel operator, Grand Metropolitan has evolved into an important international food, liquor, and retailing concern. Measured by case volume, its International Distillers and Vintners unit is the world's largest wine and spirits company, led by such brands as J&B, Smirnoff, Baileys, and Almaden. GrandMet owns Pearle, the world's largest eye-care retailer, and Burger King, the #2 hamburger chain. In the US the company's brands are leaders in refrigerated dough (Pillsbury), canned and frozen vegetables (Green Giant), and luxury ice cream (Häagen-Dazs).

GrandMet has been buying consumer goods and service companies whose products have international branding potential and complement each other. At recently acquired Pillsbury, GrandMet is trying to rebuild brand names and market shares by focusing resources on advertising and product development. The company views the upgrade of Burger King's operations and image as a long-term project.

WHEN

Maxwell Joseph dropped out of school in 1926 to work for a real estate agency in London. Five years later he set off on his own and began acquiring properties for resale. A weak British economy and WWII slowed his progress, but in 1946 he purchased a bomb-damaged hotel in London. Feeling that hotels were severely undervalued, he bought progressively larger and more prestigious hotels throughout the late 1950s and the 1960s, including the Mount Royal in London and the Hotel d'Angleterre in Copenhagen. Joseph's company, Grand Metropolitan, went public in 1961, just in advance of its acquisition of Grand Hotels (Mayfair) Ltd.

Diversification began in 1970 with the purchases of Express Dairy, Berni Inns (catering, restaurants), and Mecca (betting shops). In 1971, in what was the largest British takeover to date, GrandMet bought Truman Hanburg, a brewing concern, followed by Watney Mann in 1972. With Watney Mann's brewing operations came recently acquired International Distillers and Vintners, makers of J&B, Bombay Gin, and Baileys, as well as wine.

After pausing for a few years to sell unwanted assets and reduce debt, GrandMet returned to its acquisitive ways. Under the scrutiny of the English Monopolies Commission, the company looked overseas, taking over the Liggett Group, an American cigarette maker whose Paddington unit was the US distributor of J&B Scotch, GrandMet's #1 brand. In his last major acquisition before his death, newly knighted Sir Maxwell engineered the 1981 buyout of Intercontinental Hotels from Pan Am.

After Sir Maxwell, GrandMet shifted focus. It bought Pearle Health Services (Pearle Vision Centers, US) in 1985 and sold the last of the Liggett tobacco businesses in 1986.

Under the leadership of Allen Sheppard, GrandMet acquired Heublein in 1987, picking up such brands as Smirnoff, Lancers, and Cuervo, and creating the world's largest wine and spirits company. Sheppard again changed the emphasis of the company, disposing of the Intercontinental chain in 1988 for 52 times earnings and acquiring the food giant Pillsbury (Burger King, Häagen-Dazs, Green Giant) in a 1989 hostile takeover. In the same year GrandMet sold several businesses because of the limited international appeal of their brands.

In 1990 GrandMet's new Alpo brand cat food went from zero to $150 million in sales, capturing 9% of the US market.

In 1991 GrandMet finalized an agreement to sell its UK brewing operations (Webster's and Ruddles) to Foster's Brewing and to form a joint venture with Foster's to own the pubs. GrandMet will operate a number of the pubs.

HOW MUCH

£=$1.93 (Dec. 31, 1990)	9-Year Growth	1981	1982	1983	1984	1985	1986	1987	1988	1989	1990
Sales (£ mil.)	12.6%	3,221	3,849	4,469	5,075	5,590	5,291	5,706	6,029	9,298	9,394
Net income (£ mil.)[1]	25.6%	137	151	201	235	272	261	461	702	1,068	1,069
Income as % of sales	—	4.3%	3.9%	4.5%	4.6%	4.9%	4.9%	8.1%	11.6%	11.5%	11.4%
Earnings per share (p)	13.0%	21.3	22.8	27.8	32.4	28.3	31.4	38.1	46.9	55.6	64.1
Stock price – high (p)	—	228	336	366	360	405	482	605	521	658	681
Stock price – low (p)	—	138	171	297	270	277	332	348	418	425	514
Stock price – close (p)	15.3%	188	334	350	315	398	457	449	430	628	675
P/E – high	—	11	16	13	11	14	15	16	11	12	11
P/E – low	—	6	8	11	8	10	11	9	9	8	8
Dividends per share (p)[2]	11.9%	7.4	8.4	9.6	9.2	10.0	10.2	12.0	15.0	17.8	20.4
Book value per share (p)	—	—	—	—	—	—	—	—	—	—	—

1990 Year-end:
Debt ratio: 47.8%
Return on equity: 20.3%
Cash (mil.): £243
Long-term debt (mil.): £3,116
No. of shares (mil.): 992
Dividends:
1990 average yield: 3.0%
1990 payout: 31.8%
Market value (mil.): $12,923
Sales (mil.): $18,130

[1] Including extraordinary items [2] Not including rights issues

NYSE symbol: GRM (ADR)
Fiscal year ends: September 30

Hoover's Rating **B**

WHO

Chairman and Group CEO: Sir Allen J. G. Sheppard, age 58, £639,125 pay
Deputy Group CEO: Ian A. Martin, age 56
Group Finance Director: David P. Nash, age 50
Senior Personnel Officer: Howard Chandler
Auditors: KPMG Peat Marwick McLintock
Employees: 138,149

WHERE

HQ: 20 St. James Square, London SW1Y 4RR, UK
Phone: 011-44-71-321-6000
Fax: 011-44-71-321-6001
US HQ: Grand Metropolitan, Inc., 712 Fifth Ave., Suite 4600, New York, NY 10019-4102
US Phone: 212-554-9200
US Fax: 212-554-9243

	1990 Sales		1990 Operating Income	
	£ mil.	% of total	£ mil.	% of total
UK & Ireland	3,685	39	451	42
Other Europe	661	7	81	7
North America	4,753	51	496	46
Other countries	295	3	54	5
Total	**9,394**	**100**	**1,082**	**100**

WHAT

	1990 Sales		1990 Operating Income	
	£ mil.	% of total	£ mil.	% of total
Food	3,506	37	309	28
Drinks	3,000	32	473	44
Retailing	2,531	27	278	26
Other	357	4	22	2
Total	**9,394**	**100**	**1,082**	**100**

Major Brands

Food
Green Giant
Häagen-Dazs
Hungry Jack
Jeno's
Pillsbury
Totino's

Liquor
Absolut Vodka
Amaretto di Saronno
Baileys
Black Velvet
Bombay Gin
Cinzano
Cointreau
Gilbey's
Grand Marnier
Heublein
J&B
Jose Cuervo
Malibu
Metaxa
Popov
Sambuca Romana
Smirnoff

Pet Food
Alpo
Blue Mountain

Retailing
Burger King
Pearle Vision Centers
Peter Dominic (UK)
Texas State Optical
Wienerwald (Germany)

Wine
Almaden
Beaulieu Vineyards
Christian Brothers
Inglenook
Lancers
Le Piat d'Or

KEY COMPETITORS

Accor
Allied-Lyons
American Brands
Anheuser-Busch
Bass
Borden
Brown-Forman
BSN
Campbell Soup
ConAgra
CPC
Gallo
General Mills
Guinness
Heinz
Imasco
Jack Eckerd
LVMH
Mars
McDonald's
Nestlé
PepsiCo
Philip Morris
Procter & Gamble
Quaker Oats
Ralston Purina
RJR Nabisco
Sara Lee
Seagram
TW Holdings
Unilever
U.S. Shoe
Wendy's
Whitman

GUINNESS PLC

OVERVIEW

Although its name evokes images of dark, foamy stout, Guinness derives 80% of its operating profit from liquor sales. The company's beer and liquor brands include Guinness, Harp, Johnnie Walker (world's #1 scotch brand), Dewar's, I.W. Harper, Gordon's, and Tanqueray (best-selling imported gin in the US). Guinness has 37% of the world's scotch market. Facing a decline in worldwide hard liquor consumption, Guinness has successfully encouraged consumers to trade up to more expensive brands. Sales of Guinness's beer are concentrated in Europe, but they are growing rapidly in Southeast Asia.

With 82% of its profits coming from outside the UK, the company is increasing its presence internationally and is now the largest brewer in Spain, the 3rd largest imported beer distributor in the US, and the UK's largest exporter of branded consumer goods. Only Coca-Cola makes more profits from beverages than Guinness.

WHEN

Arthur Guinness leased a small brewery in Dublin in 1759. At the brewery Guinness made ales and porters, which were at first sold only in Dublin. In 1799 Guinness began specializing in porters. In 1821 Extra Superior Porter, later named stout, represented 4% of Guinness's sales. In 1840 it represented 82% of sales and was spreading across Ireland to England. Sales growth was greatest in Ireland, which still consumes over 50% of Guinness's stout.

In 1886, managed by the 3rd generation of Guinnesses, the company went public. For many years Guinness was content to focus on stout, slowly extending its reach internationally and advertising the product's legendary health benefits. In the 1950s managing director Hugh E. C. Beaver persuaded company executives to launch Harp, a lager, which today remains a leading brand in a highly fragmented British market. Beaver is also credited with conceiving of the remarkably successful *Guinness Book of World Records* in 1955.

In the 1970s Guinness embarked on an acquisition binge, buying more than 200 unrelated companies, with disappointing results. In 1981 Guinness appointed Ernest Saunders CEO. He disposed of over 140 companies in 2 years, slashed overhead, and spent heavily on successful advertising of Guinness Stout. In 1984 Saunders began his own shopping spree, buying British newsstands, health spas, 7-Elevens, and Arthur Bell & Sons scotch. With earnings ascending, Saunders involved Guinness in a takeover battle against Argyll Group for control of Distillers Company (Johnnie Walker, Gordon's, Tanqueray). He bought Distillers for £2.5 billion in 1986.

In the months following the Distillers acquisition, the SEC investigation of Ivan Boesky's illegal trading activities uncovered records linking Saunders to a bold stock manipulation scheme. Saunders was subsequently fired in 1987 and convicted on criminal charges in 1990.

Anthony Tennant, earlier passed over for the top job at Grand Metropolitan, became Guinness's chairman. He has focused Guinness on brewing, distilling, and controlling distribution, selling peripheral businesses and acquiring Schenley (Dewar's) in 1987.

In 1988 and 1989 Guinness bought 24.1% of French cognac, champagne, perfume, and leather goods maker LVMH Möet Hennessy Louis Vuitton. LVMH then raised its stake in Guinness from 12% to 24.1% in 1990, encouraging takeover speculation. In 1991 Guinness bought Spanish brewer Cruzcampo for over $900 million, the largest foreign investment in Spain's history. The acquisition brought the company control of about 22% of the Spanish beer market. Guinness stands to increase its Spanish market share to about 28% with a proposed bid to buy Unión Cervecera, 61% of which is owned by Carlsberg.

HOW MUCH

£=$1.93 (Dec. 31, 1990)	9-Year Growth	1981	1982	1983	1984	1985	1986[1]	1987	1988	1989	1990
Sales (£ mil.)	16.2%	906	1,043	872	924	1,188	3,252	2,818	2,776	3,076	3,511
Net income (£ mil.)	42.0%	23	23	30	38	54	230	257	325	440	541
Income as % of sales	—	2.5%	2.2%	3.4%	4.1%	4.5%	7.1%	9.1%	11.7%	14.3%	15.4%
Earnings per share (p)	22.5%	9.4	12.9	17.1	20.9	25.4	36.3	29.5	36.0	47.4	58.5
Stock price – high (p)	—	83	104	125	245	324	355	393	358	689	824
Stock price – low (p)	—	51	61	101	116	225	270	227	262	329	626
Stock price – close (p)	31.9%	63	103	116	244	320	313	291	334	686	763
P/E – high	—	9	8	7	12	13	—	15	10	15	14
P/E – low	—	5	5	6	6	9	—	9	7	7	11
Dividends per share (p)	16.1%	4.9	5.2	5.8	6.4	7.2	10.2	9.2	11.5	15.3	18.8
Book value per share (p)	11.9%	137	112	125	124	89	71	252	289	348	378

1990 Year-end:
Debt ratio: 20.7%
Return on equity: 15.5%
Cash (mil.): £513
Long-term debt (mil.): £878
No. of shares (mil.): 901
Dividends:
1990 average yield: 2.5%
1990 payout: 32.1%
Market value (mil.): $13,268
Sales (mil.): $6,776

Stock Price History High/Low 1981–90

900 800 700 600 500 400 300 200 100 0

[1] 15-month accounting period

OTC symbol: GURSY (ADR)
Fiscal year ends: December 31

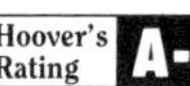

WHO

Chairman: Anthony J. Tennant, age 60, £615,000 pay
President: The Earl of Iveagh, age 53
Managing Director, Finance & Administration: Ian M. Duncan, age 59
Auditors: Price Waterhouse
Employees: 23,000

WHERE

HQ: 39 Portman Sq., London W1H 9HB, UK
Phone: 011-44-71-486-0288
Fax: 011-44-71-486-4968
US HQ: Guinness Import Company, Inc., 6 Landmark Sq., Stamford, CT 06901
US Phone: 203-359-7100
US Fax: 203-975-1820

Guinness has brewing interests in 36 countries and sells beer in more than 120 countries. The company's distilled products are sold in more than 200 countries.

	1990 Sales		1990 Operating Income	
	£ mil.	% of total	£ mil.	% of total
UK	1,164	33	148	18
Other Europe	969	27	202	24
North America	553	16	181	22
Asia/Pacific	561	16	171	20
Other countries	264	8	135	16
Total	**3,511**	**100**	**837**	**100**

WHAT

	1990 Sales		1990 Operating Income	
	£ mil.	% of total	£ mil.	% of total
Spirits	2,149	61	669	80
Brewing	1,299	37	160	19
Enterprises	63	2	8	1
Total	**3,511**	**100**	**837**	**100**

Beer
Alcázar
Anchor
Budweiser (Ireland)
Carlsberg (Ireland)
Estrella del Sur
Guinness
Harp
Kaliber
Keler
Lion

Liquor
Asbach Uralt (brandy)
Bell's
Buchanan's
Bundaberg
Dewar's
Dimple/Pinch
Gordon's
I.W. Harper
Johnnie Walker
Old Parr
Rebel Yell
Tanqueray
White Horse

Other
Champneys (health spa)
Gleneagles (hotels, Scotland)
Guinness Publishing
British Hit Albums
British Hit Singles
Guinness Book of World Records
Guinness Encyclopedia

Major Holdings
Bundaberg Distilling (50%, Australian rum)
Christian Dior (16.8%, France)
LVMH Moët Hennessy Louis Vuitton (24.1%, France)
Weinbrennerei Asbach & Company (67.5%, Germany)

KEY COMPETITORS

Allied-Lyons
American Brands
Anheuser-Busch
Bass
Bond
Brown-Forman
BSN
Carlsberg
Foster's Brewing
Grand Metropolitan
Heineken
John Labatt
Kirin
Philip Morris
San Miguel
Seagram
Stroh

HACHETTE SA

OVERVIEW

Since taking control in 1980, Jean-Luc Lagardère has transformed Hachette into the world's 5th largest media company by making large, debt-financed acquisitions. Hachette was already the largest publisher and printer in France; a movie producer; and the holder of a 49% interest in NMPP, France's newspaper and magazine distribution cooperative. By buying Diamandis Communications, Lagardère added US magazines, including *Woman's Day*, *Car & Driver*, and *Stereo Review*, to a strong roster of French periodicals, including *Elle*, *France Dimanche*, and *Télé 7 Jours*. Other recent buys included US and Spanish encyclopedia publishers.

Hachette's global expansion has been slowed by a heavy debt load, recession, and weakness in US magazine operations. *Woman's Day* lost advertisers after Hachette's failed attempt to sell it. Now the company intends to sell "nonstrategic" assets to reduce debt and buy more media properties. TV broadcasters and production companies are on the shopping list.

Matra, a Lagardère-controlled defense electronics firm, controls Société Marlis, which owns 51.3% of Hachette. In 1991 Hachette suspended dividend and trading rights on an 8.4% block of its stock thought to be controlled by Iraq through a Swiss holding company.

Principal exchange: Paris
Fiscal year ends: December 31

Hoover's Rating **C**

WHO

Chairman and CEO: Jean-Luc Lagardère, age 63
VC: Daniel Filipacchi, age 63
CEO: Jacques Lehn
SVP and CFO: Emmanuel Rault
Auditors: Guy Barbier et Autres (Arthur Andersen & Co.)
Employees: 30,000

WHERE

HQ: 83, avenue Marceau, F-75116 Paris, France
Phone: 011-33-1-40-69-16-00
Fax: 011-33-1-47-23-01-92
US HQ: Hachette Magazines, Inc., 1633 Broadway, New York, NY 10019
US Phone: 212-767-6000
US Fax: 212-767-5600

Hachette operates 300 companies in 40 countries.

	1990 Sales	
	FF mil.	% of total
France	15,051	50
Other countries	14,996	50
Total	**30,047**	**100**

WHEN

In 1826 schoolteacher Louis Hachette bought a small book-publishing and bookselling business in Paris. He published his first periodical, a journal for teachers, in 1827 and began buying rights to primary school texts in 1831. Business took off in 1833 when a law calling for free primary school education was enacted in France. Librarie Hachette received an enormous order from the Ministry of Public Education, including orders for 500,000 alphabet primers and 40,000 arithmetic books.

An 1851 visit to W.H. Smith in London convinced Hachette that rail passengers would buy books from stores in stations. The next year he began signing contracts with French railroads and soon had a virtual monopoly on bookselling in French train stations. In 1853 Hachette started the Bibliothèque de Chemins de Fer (Railway Library) series of books and travel guides. In 1862 Emile Zola began a 4-year stint in press relations with Hachette.

Louis Hachette died in 1864. Librarie Hachette launched its first women's magazine, *La Mode Practique*, in 1891. Around the turn of the century, Hachette bought France's leading newspaper distributors. The company then purchased Hetzel, Jules Verne's publisher, in 1914 and acquired major French printing and binding companies in 1920.

Following 4 years of management by German occupation forces during WWII, Hachette launched *Elle* (1945) and began publishing the Livre de Poche line of paperbacks (1953). The company acquired control of French publishers Grasset, Fayard, and Stock in the 1950s.

In the 1970s Hachette diversified with poor results. Société Marlis amassed 51.5% of Hachette in 1980. Under Lagardère, Hachette launched international spinoffs of its magazines, including a very successful US *Elle* (1985) in partnership with Rupert Murdoch.

In the late 1980s Hachette bought an interest in the #2 French radio station, Europe 1; helped start another, Europe 2; purchased the 2nd largest magazine distributor in the US, Curtis Circulation; and bought Spanish encyclopedia publisher Salvat. In 1988 alone Hachette spent over $1 billion on Grolier (encyclopedias) and Diamandis Communications and bought out Murdoch's share of *Elle*. The company launched *Elle Decor* in the US in 1989 and purchased 25% of a money-losing French TV network, La Cinq, in 1990.

The 1991 resignation of Peter Diamandis capped a series of departures of US managers, raising questions about Hachette's ability to manage across cultures. Undaunted, the company bought *Home* magazine in the same year.

WHAT

	1990 Sales	
	FF mil.	% of total
Books	6,882	23
Magazines & newspapers	10,204	34
Broadcast, film & display	2,087	7
Distribution services	10,744	36
Other	130	—
Total	**30,047**	**100**

Book Publishing
Fayard
Grasset
Grolier
Hachette
Jean-Claude Lattès
Le Chêne
Livre de Poche
Salvat
Stock

French Magazines
Dernières Nouvelles d'Alsace
Elle
France Dimanche
Ici-Paris
Le Journal de Mickey
Le Journal du Dimanche
Parents
Picsou Magazine
Première
Super Picsou Géant
Télé 7 Jeux
Télé 7 Jours

US Magazines
Car & Driver
Elle
Elle Decor
Popular Photography
Road & Track
Stereo Review
Woman's Day

Broadcasting, Film, and Display
Europe 1 Communication (TV, radio, film, billboards)
La Cinq (25%, TV network)

Distribution
Curtis Circulation Company (US)
Nouvelles Messageries de la Presse Parisienne (49%, France)
Payot Naville Distribution (49%, Switzerland)
Relais H (France)
W. E. Saarbach GmbH (Germany)

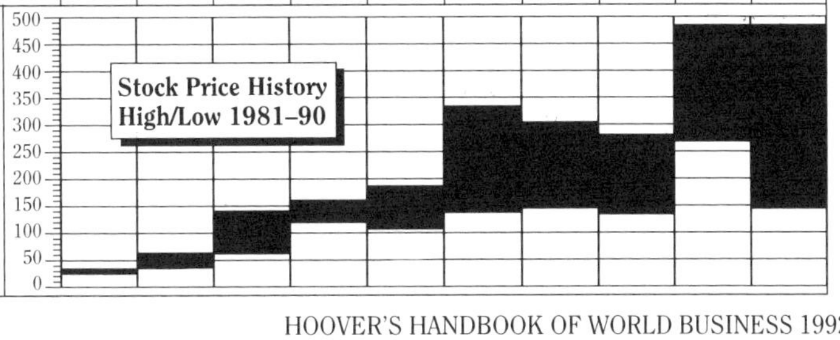

KEY COMPETITORS

Advance Publications
Alcatel Alsthom
Berkshire Hathaway
Bertelsmann
Hearst
Maxwell
New York Times
News Corp.
Paramount
Pearson
Reader's Digest
Reed

HOW MUCH

$=FF5.08 (Dec. 31, 1990)	9-Year Growth	1981	1982	1983	1984	1985	1986	1987	1988	1989	1990
Sales (FF mil.)	16.1%	7,863	8,675	9,042	10,706	11,575	14,729	17,208	24,404	28,946	30,047
Net income (FF mil.)	—	(10)	142	187	202	169	216	251	323	331	231
Income as % of sales	—	(0.1%)	1.6%	2.1%	1.9%	1.5%	1.5%	1.5%	1.3%	1.1%	0.8%
Earnings per share (FF)	—	(1)	7	10	10	9	11	13	17	17	12
Stock price – high (FF)	—	36	65	142	162	188	335	305	282	485	485
Stock price – low (FF)	—	23	34	61	118	106	136	144	133	267	143
Stock price – close (FF)	17.6%	35	61	140	150	133	265	151	168	410	150
P/E – high	—	—	9	15	16	22	30	24	17	29	41
P/E – low	—	—	5	6	11	12	12	11	8	16	12
Dividends per share (FF)	37.0%	0.23	0.23	1.00	1.50	1.68	1.91	2.23	2.73	3.30	3.90
Book value per share (FF)	—	—	67	81	91	94	105	99	113	129	129

1990 Year-end:
Debt ratio: 74.1%
Return on equity: 9.1%
Cash (mil.): FF3,527
Long-term debt (mil.): FF7,368
No. of shares (mil.): 20
Dividends:
1990 average yield: 2.6%
1990 payout: 33.3%
Market value (mil.): $591
Sales (mil.): $5,915

Stock Price History High/Low 1981–90

500
450
400
350
300
250
200
150
100
50
0

HANSON PLC

OVERVIEW

Hanson PLC is both a management company and a trader in companies. Lord Hanson manages the UK parent while Sir Gordon White directs Hanson Industries from his New York office without ever visiting operating units. Hanson is an amalgam of low-tech enterprises in such diverse businesses as chemicals, tobacco, housewares, building products, and mining. Gold Fields is the largest non–South African gold mining company, and Peabody is the largest US coal mining organization.

Hanson has grown by using bank debt to buy businesses with poor management or unrealized market value. Typically, Hanson quickly sells portions of purchased companies, slashes overhead and improves operations at remaining units, and sells them if and when the price is right.

Both Lord Hanson and Sir Gordon are approaching retirement age, leading to speculation about a final, spectacular takeover or total divestiture of Hanson holdings.

WHEN

In the 1950s and 1960s, James Hanson and Gordon White were British bon vivants. Hanson was once engaged to Audrey Hepburn and White enjoyed the company of Joan Collins. They are now better known as sharp businessmen. Their first venture, Hanson-White Greeting Cards, sold in 1963, was a success. When the buyer demanded £10,000 to sell back the Hanson-White name, White, showing typical frugality, refused. After merging Wiles Group, a public fertilizer company, with their family businesses, the two began seeking bank-financed acquisitions in 1964. The company became Hanson Trust in 1969.

From the beginning Hanson and White sought poorly managed companies in mature industries at low prices. Within 10 years Hanson Trust consisted of 24 companies in such businesses as brickmaking, aggregates, and construction equipment, with sales in excess of $120 million.

Tired of England's antibusiness attitudes, White formed a New York subsidiary, Hanson Industries, in 1973. Operating autonomously, he made his first American purchase in 1974, buying Seacoast (animal feed). Others followed, including Hygrade (Ball Park Franks, 1976), Interstate United (food service, 1978, sold in 1985 for over 3 times cost), McDonough (tools, shoes, 1981), and US Industries (conglomerate, 1984). Meanwhile, James Hanson bought British Ever Ready (batteries, UK, 1981) and Allders (retail, UK, 1983).

In bitterly fought hostile takeovers in 1986, Hanson acquired SCM (Smith-Corona office equipment, Glidden Paints, Durkee's Famous Foods, SCM Chemicals) and Imperial Group (cigarettes, Courage beer, food, hotels, restaurants). Within a year sales of a few SCM units (including Glidden and Durkee) generated $960 million in cash, $30 million more than Hanson had paid. Sales of nontobacco Imperial assets covered 65% of its cost.

In 1987 Hanson acquired Kaiser Cement for $250 million (later selling 6 plants for $283 million) and Kidde (security systems, fire protection, Jacuzzi) for $1.5 billion. In 1989 Hanson acquired Consolidated Gold Fields (UK) and, with it, 49% of Newmont Mining (gold, US). It sold Gold Fields's South African investments, Kidde fire protection, Allders, Hygrade, and Lea & Perrins, and sold 52% of Smith-Corona to the public.

The company acquired Peabody in 1990 from joint owners Boeing, Bechtel Investments, Eastern Enterprises, and Newmont. It also sold its 49% stake in Newmont Mining to companies controlled by Sir James Goldsmith, in exchange for Cavenham Industries (forest products); it intends to complete the swap in August 1991. In May 1991 Jacuzzi made an unsolicited offer to buy Eljer Industries (plumbing products), and Hanson bought 2.82% of Imperial Chemical (paints, coatings, explosives, and a valuable pharmaceutical division), sparking takeover rumors.

HOW MUCH

	4-Year Growth	1981	1982	1983	1984	1985	1986	1987	1988	1989	1990
Sales ($ mil.)	21.3%	—	—	—	—	—	6,196	10,975	12,507	11,302	13,401
Net income ($ mil.)	37.0%	—	—	—	—	—	517	939	1,143	1,313	1,819
Income as % of sales	—	—	—	—	—	—	8.3%	8.6%	9.1%	11.6%	13.6%
Earnings per share ($)	25.1%	—	—	—	—	—	0.76	1.15	1.34	1.49	1.86
Stock price – high ($)	—	—	—	—	—	—	11.81	16.00	14.63	19.88	21.88
Stock price – low ($)	—	—	—	—	—	—	10.03	9.00	10.88	14.00	17.00
Stock price – close ($)	14.4%	—	—	—	—	—	10.88	12.13	14.13	18.50	18.63
P/E – high	—	—	—	—	—	—	16	14	11	13	12
P/E – low	—	—	—	—	—	—	13	8	8	9	9
Dividends per share ($)	61.9%	—	—	—	—	—	0.15	0.38	0.57	0.85	1.03
Book value per share ($)	17.4%	—	—	—	—	—	2.91	3.97	4.84	2.15	5.53

1990 Year-end:
Debt ratio: 60.0%
Return on equity: 48.4%
Cash (mil.): $12,895
Current ratio: 2.13
Long-term debt (mil.): $7,977
No. of shares (mil.): 960
Dividends:
1990 average yield: 5.6%
1990 payout: 55.6%
Market value (mil.): $17,871

Stock Price History High/Low 1986–90

25
20
15
10
5
0

NYSE symbol: HAN (ADR)
Fiscal year ends: September 30

WHO

Chairman: Lord Hanson, age 69, £1,457,000 pay
Chairman, Hanson Industries: Sir Gordon White, age 68
VC: Derek N. Rosling, age 61
VC: Martin G. Taylor, age 56
VC, Hanson Industries: Edward D. Collins, age 67
President and COO, Hanson Industries: David H. Clarke, age 50
VP and CFO, Hanson Industries: William M. Landuyt, age 36
VP Human Resources, Hanson Industries: Donald W. Skelly
Auditors: Ernst & Young
Employees: 80,000

WHERE

HQ: 1 Grosvenor Place, London SW1X 7JH, UK
Phone: 011-44-71-245-1245
Fax: 011-44-71-235-3455
US HQ: Hanson Industries, 99 Wood Ave. South, Iselin, NJ 08830-2715
US Phone: 908-603-6600
US Fax: 908-603-6878

	1990 Sales		1990 Operating Income	
	$ mil.	% of total	$ mil.	% of total
UK	7,773	58	1,085	58
US	5,628	42	779	42
Adjustments	—	—	94	—
Total	**13,401**	**100**	**1,958**	**100**

WHAT

	1990 Sales		1990 Operating Income	
	$ mil.	% of total	$ mil.	% of total
Consumer goods	6,229	47	605	33
Building products	2,824	21	397	21
Industrial operns.	4,348	32	862	46
Adjustments	—	—	94	—
Total	**13,401**	**100**	**1,958**	**100**

US Consumer Brands
Ames (tools)
Bear (archery equipment)
Ertl (toys, model kits)
Farberware (cookware)
Frye (boots)
Jacuzzi (spas)
Spartus (clocks)
Tommy Armour (golf supplies)
Universal (fitness equipment)
Valley (pool tables, games)

Major US Companies
Carisbrook (textiles)
Cavenham (forest products)
Endicott Johnson (shoes)
Garden State Tanning (leather for autos)
Gold Fields Mining
GR Foods (49%)
Grove Worldwide (cranes)
Hanson Building Products
Hanson Housewares
Hanson Lighting
Hanson Office Products (furniture)
Hanson Recreation and Leisure
Kaiser Cement
Peabody (coal mining)
SCM Chemicals
Smith Corona (48%)
Weber Aircraft (aircraft interiors)

Major UK Companies
ARC (aggregates)
British Ever Ready (batteries)
Butterley Brick
Hanson Amalgamated Industries (construction, household products)
Imperial Tobacco
Lindustries (electrical and gas equipment, health products)
London Brick

Australian Company
Renison Goldfields (46%)

KEY COMPETITORS

Due to the broadly based and constantly shifting structure of Hanson PLC, the company faces many continually changing competitors.

HEINEKEN NV

OVERVIEW

With a 4.4% global market share, Amsterdam-based Heineken is the 3rd largest beer producer in the world (after Anheuser-Busch and Miller) and the largest in Europe. The company dominates the Dutch beer market with a 53% share. Family-operated and 50% family-owned Heineken sells its beer, soft drinks, spirits, and wine in 150 countries. Beer accounts for over 80% of sales.

Heineken's brewing operations are among the most respected in the world. The brewery's meticulous attention to quality and tradition has earned praise and demand for its Heineken, Amstel, and other beer brands. Since its introduction to the US in 1933, Heineken has continuously held the #1 import spot with an almost 25% market share.

The company produces beer globally in its own and associated breweries, as well as through licenses and partnerships with companies like Whitbread and Kirin. However, Heineken has refrained from establishing any breweries in the US to avoid domesticating the product's trendy foreign image, a mistake Miller Brewing made when it started producing Löwenbräu in Texas.

WHEN

Every Sunday morning, Gerard Heineken's mother was appalled by the crowds of drunken Dutchmen who had consumed too much gin the night before. Heineken, who wanted his mother's financial backing, insisted that drunkenness would decrease if people were drinking beer instead of gin. He also pointed out that there were no good beers in Holland. His strategy worked. In 1864 Heineken's mother put up the money for the 270-year-old De Hooiberg (The Haystack) brewery in Amsterdam.

Heineken quickly proved his aptitude in brewing and within 10 years had established a brewery in Rotterdam. He is also credited with launching the company's lucrative foreign trade by exporting beer first to France, then across Europe, and eventually to the Far East. During the 1880s and early 1890s, the company perfected the yeast strain (Heineken A-yeast) that it still uses in its beer today.

In 1914 Heineken passed the company down to his son, Dr. Henri Pierre Heineken. The younger Heineken decided to expand the company's operations to the US and made the voyage himself. While still at sea, Heineken met Leo van Munching, a bartender on the ship who displayed a remarkable knowledge of beer. Recognizing van Munching's talent, Heineken hired him as the company's US importer. Van Munching peddled the beers to upscale bars and restaurants.

Prohibition killed the US operations, although the company entered new markets elsewhere; after repeal, Heineken was the first foreign beer to reenter the US market.

After the war H. P. Heineken sent his son Alfred to learn the business under van Munching. While in New York, Alfred mastered the art of advertising and marketing and brought his new skills home with him in 1948. Meanwhile in the US, van Munching worked to create a national distribution system.

In 1968 Heineken bought the Amstel Brewery in Holland (founded in 1870). Two years later the company became a producer of stout through the acquisition of James J. Murphy in Cork, Ireland. Heineken also entered the soft drink and wine industries and in 1971 purchased the Bokma distillery in Holland.

Facing a consolidation of the European market, the company launched a campaign during the 1980s to expand its continental beer operations, purchasing breweries in France, Greece, Ireland, Italy, and Spain. During the 1980s the company was victimized by blackmail and extortion attempts and the kidnapping of Alfred Heineken. Alfred stepped down from day-to-day management in 1989, and in 1991 the company bought the Van Munching US import business and a majority interest in Hungarian brewer Komaromi Sorgyar.

HOW MUCH

$=Fl1.68 (Dec. 31, 1990)	9-Year Growth	1981	1982	1983	1984	1985	1986	1987	1988	1989	1990
Sales (Fl mil.)	9.5%	3,613	4,215	4,612	6,135	6,402	6,684	6,659	7,291	7,820	8,210
Net income (Fl mil.)	13.2%	120	153	198	229	265	285	287	291	325	366
Income as % of sales	—	3.3%	3.6%	4.3%	3.7%	4.1%	4.3%	4.3%	4.0%	4.2%	4.5%
Earnings per share (Fl)	13.1%	3.75	4.77	6.18	7.14	8.26	8.89	8.93	9.06	10.14	11.39
Stock price – high (Fl)	—	27	45	83	95	138	152	158	125	143	137
Stock price – low (Fl)	—	19	22	37	70	88	120	88	91	95	102
Stock price – close (Fl)	22.4%	22	41	82	88	138	142	100	114	127	136
P/E – high	—	7	9	13	13	17	17	18	14	14	12
P/E – low	—	5	5	6	10	11	13	10	10	9	9
Dividends per share (Fl)	9.2%	1.58	1.58	2.10	2.10	2.10	2.80	2.80	2.80	3.50	3.50
Book value per share (Fl)	7.9%	49.34	53.76	56.86	64.93	68.50	70.01	76.75	86.33	91.93	97.98

1990 Year-end:
Debt ratio: 17.7%
Return on equity: 12.0%
Cash (mil.): Fl693
Long-term debt (mil.): Fl674
No. of shares (mil.): 32
Dividends:
1990 average yield: 2.6%
1990 payout: 30.7%
Market value (mil.): $2,590
Sales (mil.): $4,887

Stock Price History High/Low 1981–90

160
140
120
100
80
60
40
20
0

OTC symbol: HINKY (ADR)
Fiscal year ends: December 31

WHO

Chairman, Supervisory Council: Alfred H. Heineken, age 68
Chairman, Executive Board: Gerard van Schaik
Corporate Financial Director: J. B. H. M. Beks
Director Corporate Human Resources: B. Sarphati
Auditors: KPMG Klynveld Kraayenhof & Company
Employees: 28,908

WHERE

HQ: 2e Weteringplantsoen 21, 1017 ZD, PO Box 28, 1000 AA Amsterdam, The Netherlands
Phone: 011-31-206-70-91-11
Fax: 011-31-206-26-35-03
US HQ: Van Munching & Co. Inc., 1270 Ave. of the Americas, New York, NY 10020-1798
US Phone: 212-265-2685
US Fax: 212-262-9498

The company sells its products in 150 countries.

	1990 Sales	
	Fl mil.	% of total
Europe	6,097	76
The Americas	929	12
Africa	442	5
Other countries	596	7
Adjustments	146	—
Total	**8,210**	**100**

WHAT

	1990 Sales	
	Fl mil.	% of total
Beer	6,760	82
Soft drinks	876	11
Spirits & wine	360	4
Other	214	3
Total	**8,210**	**100**

Beer
Adlerbrau
Aguila
Amstel
Amstel Light
Anchor
Bintang
Brand
Buckler
Dreher
Dry 100
George Killian's
Gulder
Heineken
Murphy
Mützig
Pelforth
Pélican
Primus
Ridder
Star
'33'
Tiger

Shandy (beer and lemonade)
Green Sands
Panach
Royal Club

Soft Drinks
Amigo
Pepsi-Cola (Netherlands)
Royal Club
Seven-Up (Netherlands)
Sisi
Sourcy

Spirits and Wine
Claeryn
Coebergh
Glenmark
Grand Monarque
Hartevelt
Henkes Jonge Jenever
Hoppe
Jägermeister
Jonge Bols
Joseph Guy

Selected Subsidiaries and Affiliates
Asia Pacific Breweries (43%, Singapore)
Athenian Brewery SA (99%, Greece)
Birra Dreher SpA (95%, Italy)
El Aguila SA (51%, Spain)
Guinness Anchor Berhad (11%, Malaysia)
Komaromi Sorgyar RT (50.3%, Hungary)
Sogebra SA (France)
South Pacific Brewery Ltd. (33%, New Guinea)

KEY COMPETITORS

Allied-Lyons
Anheuser-Busch
Bass
Bond
Brown-Forman
BSN
Cadbury Schweppes
Carlsberg
Coca-Cola
Foster's Brewing
Grand Metropolitan
Guinness
John Labatt
Philip Morris
San Miguel
Seagram
Stroh

HITACHI, LTD.

OVERVIEW

Hitachi, meaning "rising sun" in Japanese, is Japan's largest electronic and electrical engineering company. Besides being a major Japanese producer of industrial machinery, home electronics, and power systems, Hitachi is a world leader in semiconductors (3rd after NEC and Toshiba) and in IBM-plug-compatible mainframe computers. It has the 2nd largest R&D budget (6.1% of sales) in Japan (after NTT) and continues to invest substantial sums in semiconductor R&D and production facilities. Hitachi recently entered the HDTV race and set up an Eastern European business group.

Hitachi's factories have been managed as independent profit centers where sales activities have sometimes been treated as unnecessary expense. As a result Hitachi has a reputation as an excellent manufacturer but a less impressive marketer. The company is Japan's #2 VCR producer (after Matsushita), but, because most of Hitachi's VCRs are sold under other names (e.g., RCA), brand recognition is low.

WHEN

Namihei Odaira, an employee of Kuhara Mining in the Japanese coastal city of Hitachi, wanted to prove that Japan did not have to depend on foreigners for technology. In 1910 he began building 5-hp electric motors in Kuhara's engineering and repair shop. Japanese power companies were forced to buy Odaira's generators when WWI made imports scarce. Impressed, they reordered, and in 1920 Hitachi became an independent company.

During the 1920s acquisitions and growth turned Hitachi into a major manufacturer of electrical equipment and machinery. In the 1930s and 1940s, Hitachi developed vacuum tubes and light bulbs and produced radar and sonar for the Japanese war effort. Postwar occupation forces removed Odaira and closed 19 Hitachi plants. Reeling from the plant closures, war damage, and labor strife, Hitachi was saved from bankruptcy by American military contracts during the Korean War.

In the 1950s Hitachi was designated a supplier to Nippon Telegraph and Telephone (NTT), the state-owned communications monopoly. Japan's economic recovery led to strong demand for the company's communications and electrical equipment. Hitachi began mass-producing home appliances, radios, TVs, and transistors. The company spun off Hitachi Metals and Hitachi Cable in 1956 and Hitachi Chemical in 1963.

With the help of NTT, the Ministry of International Trade and Industry (MITI), and computer technology licensed from RCA, Hitachi produced its first computer in 1965. In the 1960s Hitachi began producing color TVs, built factories in Southeast Asia, and started manufacturing integrated circuits.

Hitachi launched an IBM-plug-compatible computer in 1974. The company sold its computers in the US through Itel until 1979, and afterwards through National Semiconductor's NAS (National Advanced Systems) unit. In the 1980s the company sold plug-compatibles in Europe through Olivetti (Italy) and BASF (Germany). In 1982 FBI agents caught Hitachi employees buying documents purportedly containing IBM software secrets. Hitachi settled a civil case with IBM for an estimated $300 to $500 million and $2 to $3 million per month for 8 years as compensation for the use of IBM's software technology.

In the late 1980s the rising Japanese yen hurt exports. Hitachi responded by focusing on burgeoning domestic markets and investing heavily in factory automation. In 1988 the company and Texas Instruments agreed to join in the costly development and production of 16 megabit DRAM. In 1989 Hitachi bought 80% of NAS, giving it direct control of its US distribution for the first time. That same year Hitachi and Motorola became embroiled in a patent dispute that nearly halted sales of the Motorola microprocessor used in Apple's Macintosh. The 2 companies settled out of court in 1990.

HOW MUCH

Stock prices are for ADRs ADR = 10 shares	9-Year Growth	1981	1982	1983	1984	1985	1986	1987	1988	1989	1990
Sales ($ mil.)	12.1%	15,996	15,411	16,432	19,410	20,053	29,473	34,633	39,801	48,496	44,797
Net income ($ mil.)	9.0%	615	571	627	743	841	884	705	1,094	1,406	1,335
Income as % of sales	—	3.8%	3.7%	3.8%	3.8%	4.2%	3.0%	2.0%	2.8%	2.9%	3.0%
Earnings per share ($)	6.9%	2.15	1.97	2.10	2.51	2.75	2.84	2.28	3.36	4.26	3.91
Stock price – high ($)	—	37.56	34.17	39.29	42.02	37.02	70.48	105.24	145.00	127.38	108.38
Stock price – low ($)	—	14.32	19.52	30.00	29.52	25.24	33.81	56.43	88.69	95.24	76.75
Stock price – close ($)	12.3%	28.81	34.05	34.29	32.74	36.90	65.71	86.43	122.86	100.48	82.00
P/E – high	—	17	17	19	17	13	25	46	43	30	28
P/E – low	—	7	10	14	12	9	12	25	26	22	20
Dividends per share ($)	10.9%	0.31	0.28	0.26	0.30	0.34	0.47	0.55	0.66	0.65	0.78
Book value per share ($)	13.0%	16.76	16.65	18.36	21.78	22.25	34.82	44.11	52.64	54.55	50.23

1990 Year-end:
Debt ratio: 25.7%
Return on equity: 7.5%
Cash (mil.): $13,788
Current ratio: 1.63
Long-term debt (mil.): $5,613
No. of shares (mil.): 323
Dividends:
1990 average yield: 0.9%
1990 payout: 19.8%
Market value (mil.): $26,457

Stock Price History High/Low 1981–90

NYSE symbol: HIT (ADR)
Fiscal year ends: March 31

Hoover's Rating **B**

WHO

President: Katsushige Mita, age 67
EVP: Shiro Kawada
EVP and CFO: Yasuo Miyauchi
Auditors: Peat Marwick Minato; Century Audit Corporation
Employees: 290,811

WHERE

HQ: Kabushiki Kaisha Hitachi Seisakusho, 6, Kanda-Surugadai 4-chome, Chiyoda-ku, Tokyo 101, Japan
Phone: 011-81-3-3258-1111
Fax: 011-81-3-3258-2375
US HQ: Hitachi America, Ltd., 50 Prospect Ave., Tarrytown, NY 10591-4698
US Phone: 914-332-5800
US Fax: 914-332-5834

Hitachi manufactures products in Japan and 10 other countries.

	1990 Sales $ mil.	% of total
Japan	34,305	77
Other countries	10,492	23
Total	**44,797**	**100**

WHAT

	1990 Sales $ mil.	% of total
Power systems & equipment	6,257	14
Consumer products	6,332	14
Information systems & electronic devices	14,671	33
Industrial machinery & plants	7,643	17
Wire, chemicals & other	9,894	22
Total	**44,797**	**100**

Product Lines
Auto parts
Computers
Copper, iron, and steel products
Electrical controls
Electrical wire and cable
Elevators and escalators
Generators
Heavy machinery
Household appliances
Industrial equipment
Locomotives
Magnetic tape products (Maxell)
Medical electronics
Power plants
Printed circuit boards
Robots
Semiconductors
Stereo/audio equipment
Synthetic resins
Telecommunications equipment
Turbines
Video equipment

KEY COMPETITORS

ABB
Alcatel Alsthom
Amdahl
AT&T
AMP
BASF
Caterpillar
Commodore
Compaq
Control Data
Cray Research
Cummins Engine
Data General
Deere
Digital Equipment
Dresser
Eaton
Emerson
Ericsson
Fiat
Fuji Photo
Fujitsu
GEC
General Electric
Harris
Hewlett-Packard
Hyundai
IBM
Ingersoll-Rand
Lucky-Goldstar
Machines Bull
3M
Mitsubishi
Motorola
NCR
NEC
Oki
Olivetti
Philips
Pioneer
Polaroid
Prime
Rolls-Royce
Samsung
Seagate
Sharp
Siemens
Sony
Sun Microsystems
Tenneco
Texas Instruments
Thomson SA
Toshiba
Unisys
Wang
Xerox
Zenith

HOECHST AG

OVERVIEW

Frankfurt am Main–based Hoechst (pronounced "herxt") is a diversified chemical producer, with substantial revenue from basic and agricultural chemicals, dyes, fibers, plastics, and pharmaceuticals. The company is one of the Big 3 German companies that lead the world in chemical sales; the other 2 are Bayer and BASF.

As with its German competitors, the company's pretax profits slumped — 11% — in early 1991, as it suffered from recession overseas, Persian Gulf uncertainty, and a strong deutsche mark. Hoechst does business in 120 countries and derives 3/4 of its revenue from outside Germany.

Chairman Wolfgang Hilger has shaken up the formerly staid Hoechst, steadily changing top management, defining corporate priorities, acquiring US chemical giant Celanese, and selling such nonstrategic units as Berger, Jenson & Nicholson paint company. R&D spending, 6% of sales in 1990, emphasizes pharmaceuticals and new specialty plastics, both high-margin businesses.

Principal exchange: Frankfurt
Fiscal year ends: December 31

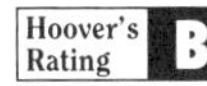
Hoover's Rating B

WHO

Chairman, Board of Management: Wolfgang Hilger, age 60
Deputy Chairman, Board of Management: Günter Metz
Managing Director of Finance and Accounts: Jürgen Dormann
Director of Personnel: Justus Miche
Auditors: Treuhand-Vereinigung Aktiengesellschaft
Employees: 172,890

WHEN

Chemist Eugene Lucius founded Hoechst in the German village of the same name in 1863 to make dyes. While successfully developing thousands of dyes, Hoechst chemists moved into the new field of pharmaceutical research, producing diphtheria vaccines and analgesics (1890s) and Salvarsan (syphilis cure, first man-made disease-specific medicine, 1910). In 1923 they isolated insulin. In the early 20th century, Hoechst acquired German dye and fertilizer producers.

In 1925 Hoechst joined with Bayer, BASF, and other German chemical firms to form the I.G. Farben cartel. The huge cartel was instrumental in supplying the Nazi war machine and was dismantled following WWII. Hoechst reemerged as an independent company in 1952, most of its plants having survived the war intact.

Expanding rapidly with the postwar boom in Germany, Hoechst moved into fibers, plastics, and petrochemicals in the 1950s. Most of the company's overseas expansion was accomplished by establishing foreign subsidiaries, until the 1970s when Hoechst acquired Berger, Jenson & Nicholson (Britain's largest paint producer), Hystron Fibers (US), and majority control of Roussel Uclaf (pharmaceuticals, perfume; France). The company enjoyed continued success in pharmaceuticals, particularly diuretics, diabetic medications, antibiotics, and polio vaccines.

In the 1980s Hoechst emphasized pharmaceuticals and US expansion. The company invested in genetic engineering, establishing a joint venture with Massachusetts General Hospital. Hoechst gave $70 million — the largest grant in history at the time — to have first crack at the product of biotechnical research at Harvard's teaching hospital.

The company acquired Celanese — then the US's 8th largest chemical company — for $2.8 billion (1987). New York–based Celanese had been founded in 1918 and through acquisitions had become a major diversified chemical company. The purchase gave Hoechst a major US presence in chemical production and marketing but countered the company's strategy of shifting away from low-margin commodity fibers and chemicals.

In 1990 the French government reduced its holdings in Roussel Uclaf to 1% when it gave 35% of the drug company, in which Hoechst owns a 54% stake, to Rhône-Poulenc. In 1991, after Hoechst posted disappointing 1990 results, Roussel Uclaf and Hoechst contemplated cutting costs by combining operations in some European countries where both have plants. Roussel Uclaf is best known for its abortion pill, RU-486.

WHERE

HQ: D-6230 Frankfurt am Main 80, Germany
Phone: 011-49-69-3050
Fax: 011-49-69-303-666
US HQ: Hoechst Celanese Corp., PO Box 2500, Route 202-206 North, Somerville, NJ 08876-1258
US Phone: 908-231-2000
US Fax: 908-231-3225

	1990 Sales		1990 Operating Profit	
	DM mil.	% of total	DM mil.	% of total
EC	31,845	66	2,152	68
Other Europe	1,266	3	85	3
North America	9,708	20	761	24
Latin America	1,861	4	13	—
Other countries	3,183	7	166	5
Adjustments	(3,001)	—	—	—
Total	**44,862**	**100**	**3,177**	**100**

WHAT

	1990 Sales		1990 Operating Profit	
	DM mil.	% of total	DM mil.	% of total
Chemicals & colors	10,658	24	730	23
Fibers & film	7,911	17	489	15
Polymers	7,657	17	606	19
Health	9,333	21	934	29
Technology	6,687	15	246	8
Agriculture	2,616	6	172	6
Total	**44,862**	**100**	**3,177**	**100**

Chemicals and Colors
Chemicals
Dyes
Surfactants

Fibers and Plastic Film
Fibers and fiber intermediates
Plastic films

Polymers
Engineering plastics
Paints and synthetic resins
Plastics and waxes

Health
Cosmetics
Pharmaceuticals

Engineering and Technology
Carbon products
Engineering ceramics
Industrial gases, welding technology
Information systems
Plant engineering

Agriculture
Herbicides
Pesticides

HOW MUCH

$=DM1.49 (Dec. 31, 1990)	9-Year Growth	1981	1982	1983	1984	1985	1986	1987	1988	1989	1990
Sales (DM mil.)	3.0%	34,435	34,986	37,189	41,457	42,722	33,231	36,956	40,964	45,898	44,862
Net income (DM mil.)	18.2%	349	253	735	1,077	1,200	1,216	1,378	1,824	1,929	1,573
Income as % of sales	—	1.0%	0.7%	2.0%	2.6%	2.8%	3.7%	3.7%	4.5%	4.2%	3.5%
Earnings per share (DM)	14.0%	*8*	*5*	*16*	*21*	*23*	*22*	*25*	*32*	*33*	*26*
Stock price – high (DM)	—	132	127	181	196	294	328	347	311	320	319
Stock price – low (DM)	—	111	104	109	156	183	239	227	237	259	177
Stock price – close (DM)	6.3%	121	113	181	191	294	269	251	305	291	210
P/E – high	—	17	25	11	9	13	15	14	10	10	12
P/E – low	—	14	21	7	7	8	11	9	7	8	7
Dividends per share (DM)[1]	7.1%	7.0	5.5	7.0	9.0	10.0	10.0	10.0	11.0	12.0	13.0
Book value per share (DM)	4.4%	134	130	139	157	158	190	155	179	196	198

1990 Year-end:
Debt ratio: 23.4%
Return on equity: 13.2%
Cash (mil.): DM2,641
Long-term debt (bil.): DM3.5
No. of shares (mil.): 58
Dividends:
1990 average yield: 6.2%
1990 payout: 50.0%
Market value (mil.): $8,174
Sales (mil.): $30,109

[1] Not including rights offering

KEY COMPETITORS

Allied-Signal
American Cyanamid
BASF
Bayer
Ciba-Geigy
Dow Chemical
Du Pont
FMC
W. R. Grace
Hercules
Imperial Chemical
Monsanto
Occidental
PPG
Rhône-Poulenc
Sherwin-Williams
Other chemical and pharmaceutical companies

HONDA MOTOR CO., LTD.

OVERVIEW

Honda is battling with Chrysler and Toyota for the #3 spot in US car sales, trying to maintain its #3 status in Japan, and establishing a European beachhead in partnership with Rover (UK). In each region Honda is attempting to create self-contained operating companies. A 4th regional unit is evolving in Asia. Honda is the world leader in motorcycle sales.

After a decade of solid growth in the US with an essentially unchanged Honda product line, sluggish sales forced the company to give incentives on its top-selling Accord in 1991. The company introduced 2 new Acura models in 1991 and is mulling a light truck entry in the North American market, where Honda's sales are concentrated.

Honda president Nobuhiko Kawamoto and 2 other top executives have taken direct control of Japanese auto operations and are reworking the company's vaunted "teamwork" approach to decision-making. Long hindered by a small dealer network and outmanned 4-to-1 by Toyota salespeople in a country in which door-to-door car sales are common, Honda is now seeing young car buyers shun its staid models in favor of its rivals' flashier cars. Honda is fighting back by launching inexpensive but stylish minicars.

WHEN

After 6 years as an apprentice at Art Shokai, a Tokyo auto service station, Soichiro Honda opened his own branch of the repair shop in Hamamatsu (1928). In addition to repairing autos, he raced cars and received a patent for metal spokes that replaced wood in wheels (1931). In a race in 1936, Honda set a long-standing Japanese speed record, then crashed at the finish line, but escaped critical injury.

In 1937 Honda started a company to manufacture piston rings. The Sino-Japanese War and WWII increased demand for piston rings, and the company mass-produced metal propellers for Japanese bombers, replacing handmade wooden ones. When bombs and an earthquake destroyed most of Honda's factory, he sold it to Toyota (1945) for nearly $800,000. He then installed a large drum of alcohol in his home, drank, and entertained friends.

In 1946 Honda established the Honda Technical Research Institute to motorize bicycles with small, war-surplus engines. This inexpensive form of transportation proved popular amid the scarcity of postwar Japan, and Honda soon began manufacturing engines.

The company was renamed Honda Motor in 1948 and began producing motorcycles. To allow himself to focus on engineering, Honda hired Takeo Fujisawa (1949) to take on management tasks. Honda's innovative overhead valve design made the Dream Type E (1951) motorcycle an immediate runaway success. Fujisawa enlisted 13,000 bicycle dealers to launch Honda's smaller F-type Cub (1952), which accounted for 70% of Japan's motorcycle production by the end of the year.

Funded by a public offering (1954) and heavy support from Mitsubishi Bank, Honda expanded capacity and began exporting in the 1950s. The versatile C100 Super Cub, released in 1958, became an international bestseller. American Honda Motor was formed in Los Angeles (1959), accompanied by the slogan "You meet the nicest people on a Honda," created to counter the stereotypical "biker" image. In the 1960s the company added overseas factories and began producing lightweight trucks, sports cars, and minicars.

In 1972, on the eve of the oil crisis, Honda introduced the economical Civic, emphasizing the US market and targeting Volkswagen buyers. Honda released the higher-priced Accord in 1976, as cumulative Civic sales passed one million. In 1982 Accord production started at Honda's Marysville, Ohio, plant, now a source of exports to Japan. Honda successfully launched the mid- to upscale Acura line in the US in 1986 and bought 20% of the Rover Group in 1990.

Soichiro Honda died in 1991.

HOW MUCH

Stock prices are for ADRs ADR = 2 shares	9-Year Growth	1981	1982	1983	1984	1985	1986	1987	1988	1989	1990
Sales ($ mil.)	13.2%	7,980	7,945	9,376	10,166	10,222	16,115	18,747	27,240	26,434	24,385
Net income ($ mil.)	1.8%	441	277	304	409	495	811	547	871	737	517
Income as % of sales	—	5.5%	3.5%	3.2%	4.0%	4.8%	5.0%	2.9%	3.2%	2.8%	2.1%
Earnings per share ($)	(0.4%)	1.10	0.68	0.71	0.89	1.07	1.65	1.12	1.73	1.49	1.06
Stock price – high ($)	—	10.59	7.95	9.75	12.05	12.75	17.78	25.75	37.55	34.95	26.00
Stock price – low ($)	—	4.50	4.32	6.58	8.30	9.60	11.00	15.60	20.10	24.50	18.50
Stock price – close ($)	13.0%	6.45	7.82	9.70	9.70	11.85	17.15	20.50	33.35	25.13	19.38
P/E – high	—	10	12	14	14	12	11	23	22	23	25
P/E – low	—	4	6	9	9	9	7	14	12	16	17
Dividends per share ($)	9.7%	0.08	0.08	0.07	0.10	0.09	0.13	0.16	0.20	0.20	0.19
Book value per share ($)	15.2%	3.97	3.96	5.15	5.58	6.29	9.40	10.75	13.50	14.41	14.20

1990 Year-end:
Debt ratio: 25.9%
Return on equity: 7.4%
Cash (mil.): $2,403
Current ratio: 1.16
Long-term debt (mil.): $2,403
No. of shares (mil.): 483
Dividends:
1990 average yield: 1.0%
1990 payout: 17.8%
Market value (mil.): $9,364

Stock Price History High/Low 1981–90

40
35
30
25
20
15
10
5
0

NYSE symbol: HMC (ADR)
Fiscal year ends: March 31

WHO

Chairman: Koichiro Yoshizawa, age 59
President: Nobuhiko Kawamoto, age 55
EVP: Shoichiro Irimajiri, age 51
EVP: Yoshihide Munekuni, age 52
Auditors: Peat Marwick Minato
Employees: 79,000

WHERE

HQ: Honda Giken Kogyo Kabushiki Kaisha, No. 1-1, 2-chome, Minami-Aoyama, Minato-ku, Tokyo 107, Japan
Phone: 011-81-3-3423-1111
Fax: 011-81-3-3423-0511
US HQ: Honda North America, Inc., 1290 Ave. of the Americas, Suite 3330, New York, NY 10104
US Phone: 212-765-3804
US Fax: 212-541-9855

Honda manufactures its products in 40 countries. Four of its 17 largest manufacturing plants are located in the US.

	1990 Sales	
	$ mil.	% of total
Japan	8,357	34
North America	11,744	48
Europe	2,577	11
Other regions	1,707	7
Total	**24,385**	**100**

WHAT

	1990 Sales	
	$ mil.	% of total
Automobiles	17,963	74
Motorcycles	2,202	9
Power products	729	3
Parts & other	3,491	14
Total	**24,385**	**100**

Automobile Models (US Markets)

Acura
- Integra
- Legend
- NSX
- Vigor

Honda
- Accord
- Civic
- CRX
- Prelude

Motorcycle Models (US Markets)
Elite (scooter)
Gold Wing
Hawk
Nighthawk

Power Products
All-terrain vehicles (ATVs)
General purpose engines
Lawn mowers
Lawn tractors
Outboard motors
Portable generators
Power tillers
Snow blowers
Water pumps

KEY COMPETITORS

BMW
Black & Decker
Brunswick
Caterpillar
Chrysler
Daewoo
Daimler-Benz
Deere
Fiat
Ford
General Motors
Harley-Davidson
Hyundai
Isuzu
Mazda
Mitsubishi
Nissan
Outboard Marine
Peugeot
Renault
Saab-Scania
Suzuki
Textron
Toyota
Volkswagen
Volvo
Yamaha

HSBC HOLDINGS PLC

OVERVIEW

HSBC Holdings is the newly created, nonresident, UK-domiciled parent company for Hongkong and Shanghai Banking Corporation, one of the 30 largest banking organizations in the world. The bank is known as a *gweilo* ("foreign devil") because it is controlled by non-Chinese. Its 1991 restructuring transplanted the company to the UK to lessen the impact of the 1997 transfer of Hong Kong to the Chinese government. With the restructuring the bank put its foreign holdings out of reach of the Chinese.

The bank is Hong Kong's most important financial institution, issuing about 80% of the colony's banknotes. In the US, HSBC's Marine Midland unit is one of the largest foreign-owned banks. The former money-center bank is retreating, becoming a northeastern regional bank after real estate loan losses.

In the UK the company's James Capel Group, a securities firm, has suffered losses. Hongkong and Shanghai Banking has called off plans to buy the rest of troubled, 14.7%-owned Midland Bank.

WHEN

Founded by Scotsman Thomas Sutherland and a group of businessmen, the Hongkong & Shanghai Bank opened its doors in Hong Kong in 1865. The bank initially financed and promoted British imperial trade in opium, silk, and tea in the East Asian region and quickly established a London office. Hongkong & Shanghai Bank created an international branch network emphasizing China and the Far East, where it claims to have been the first bank in Thailand (1888).

War repeatedly disrupted the bank's operations, but it managed to survive. When chief manager Sir Vandeleur Grayborn died in a Japanese POW camp during WWII, the bank temporarily relocated its headquarters to London. Following the Communist takeover, the bank withdrew from China, and by 1955 only a single Shanghai office remained. The bank played a key role in Hong Kong's explosive postwar growth by financing industrialists who fled there from China.

Hongkong & Shanghai Bank began expanding its Far East activities in the late 1950s and later executed a strategy of globalization. In 1959 the bank acquired the British Bank of the Middle East, founded in 1889, with branches throughout its namesake region. The bank acquired Mercantile Bank (India, Southeast Asia, 1959) and 61.5% of Hang Seng, Hong Kong's 2nd largest bank (1965). In 1978 the Saudi British Bank assumed control of the Saudi Arabian branches of British Bank of the Middle East. BBME retained a 40% interest in the Saudi bank and managed the new entity.

During the 1980s the bank purchased a controlling interest in Marine Midland Bank (US, 1980), 51% of primary treasury security dealer Carroll McEntee & McGinley (US, 1983), major London stockbroker James Capel & Co. (1986), most of the assets and liabilities of the Bank of British Columbia (1986), and the rest of Marine Midland (1987).

The bank established subsidiaries Wayfoong (mortgage and small business finance, Hong Kong, 1960), Wardley (investment banking, Hong Kong, 1972), Hongkong Bank of Canada (1981), and HongkongBank of Australia (1986). Hongkong & Shanghai Bank's 1981 bid for the Royal Bank of Scotland failed when the British government stopped the transaction, citing the bank's international, rather than Scottish, orientation.

Performance of some of the recent additions has been disappointing. In 1990 Marine Midland lost $296 million, HongkongBank of Australia lost $212 million, and the James Capel Group lost $56 million. Hong Kong and other operations were strong enough that the bank still posted a HK$3.1 billion ($398 million) profit, down 35% from 1989. Hongkong Bank of Canada, by acquiring Lloyds Bank Canada in 1990, became the largest foreign-owned bank there.

HOW MUCH

$=HK$7.80 (Dec. 31, 1990)	9-Year Growth	1981	1982	1983	1984	1985	1986	1987	1988	1989	1990
Assets (HK$ bil.)	16.3%	297	369	452	467	537	707	823	884	1,038	1,158
Net income (HK$ bil.)	4.3%	2	2	2	3	3	3	4	4	5	3
Income as % of assets	—	0.7%	0.6%	0.6%	0.6%	0.5%	0.4%	0.4%	0.5%	0.5%	0.3%
Earnings per share (HK$)	2.9%	0.37	0.42	0.44	0.46	0.48	0.54	0.60	0.68	0.75	0.48
Stock price – high (HK$)	—	4.77	3.89	3.49	3.95	4.30	6.08	7.29	6.24	6.91	7.00
Stock price – low (HK$)	—	2.92	2.30	1.25	2.59	3.75	4.11	4.85	4.87	4.50	4.52
Stock price – close (HK$)	3.4%	3.49	2.45	2.81	3.95	4.22	6.08	4.45	5.29	6.73	4.72
P/E – high	—	13	9	8	9	9	11	12	9	9	15
P/E – low	—	8	5	3	6	8	8	8	7	6	9
Dividends per share (HK$)	11.7%	0.14	0.18	0.20	0.22	0.23	0.25	0.27	0.29	0.33	0.38
Book value per share (HK$)	16.0%	2.17	2.39	3.41	3.64	3.81	4.62	5.29	5.66	8.24	8.28

1990 Year-end:
Equity as % of assets: 4.6%
Return on equity: 6.9%
Cash (mil.): HK$289,868
No. of shares (mil.): 6,464
Dividends:
1990 average yield: 8.1%
1990 payout: 79.2%
Market value (mil.): $3,912
Assets (mil.): $148,494
Sales (mil.): —

Stock Price History High/Low 1981–90

Principal exchange: Hong Kong
Fiscal year ends: December 31

WHO

Chairman: William Purves, age 60
Deputy Chairman: John M. Gray
Deputy Chairman: Li Ka-shing
Executive Director Banking: John R. H. Bond
Group Human Resources: J. C. S. Rankin
Auditors: KPMG Peat Marwick
Employees: 54,408

WHERE

HQ: 1 Queen's Rd. Central, Hong Kong
Phone: 011-852-822-1111
Fax: 011-852-810-1112
US HQ: HongkongBank, 140 Broadway, 4th Floor, New York, NY 10015
US Phone: 212-658-5100
US Fax: 212-658-5179

The company and its subsidiaries operate in more than 1,300 offices in 48 countries.

	1990 Assets	
	HK$ bil.	% of total
Asia-Pacific	606	52
Americas	295	25
Middle East	30	3
Europe	227	20
Total	**1,158**	**100**

WHAT

	1990 Assets	
	HK$ bil.	% of total
Cash & short-term funds	290	26
Bank placings maturing between 1 & 12 months	116	10
Trade bills & CDs	44	4
Investments	63	6
Other accounts	72	6
Fixed assets	38	3
Advances	501	45
Adjustments	34	—
Total	**1,158**	**100**

Principal Subsidiaries
The British Bank of the Middle East (UK)
Carlingford Insurance Co. Ltd. (Hong Kong)
Carroll McEntee & McGinley, Inc. (securities, US)
The Cyprus Popular Bank Ltd. (21.3%)
Equator Bank Ltd. (83.3%, Bahamas)
Fort Hall Ltd. (investment holding, Hong Kong)
Gibbs Hartley Cooper Ltd. (insurance brokerage, UK)
Hang Seng Bank Ltd. (61.5%, Hong Kong)
HKBG Holdings Ltd.
Hongkong and Shanghai Banking Corp. Ltd.
Hongkong Bank of Canada
Hongkong Egyptian Bank SAE (40%)
HongkongBank London Ltd.
HongkongBank of Australia Ltd.
HSBC Finance (Malaysia) Berhad
James Capel Group (stockbrokerage, UK)
Marine Midland Bank, N.A. (US)
MidAval Asia Pte. Ltd. (60%)
The Saudi British Bank (40%)
Wardley Ltd. (merchant banking, Hong Kong)
Wayfoong Finance Ltd. (Hong Kong)
World Finance International Ltd. (37.5%, Bermuda)

KEY COMPETITORS

Barclays
Canadian Imperial
Crédit Lyonnais
CS Holding
Dai-Ichi Kangyo
Deutsche Bank
Industrial Bank of Japan
Marsh & McLennan
Royal Bank
Union Bank of Switzerland
Other international money-center banks

HUDSON'S BAY COMPANY

OVERVIEW

Hudson's Bay Company (HBC) is Canada's largest department store operator and the oldest corporation in North America. This remarkable company's operations significantly shaped modern Canada.

Hudson's Bay's domain, which at its height encompassed almost 3 million square miles, has dwindled in recent years, and the company sustained significant losses in the 1980s. In an attempt to refocus, HBC has sold off its non–department store interests in an effort to bring the company back into the familiar retailing grounds that reflect its trading post past.

Today the company is controlled primarily by Canada's wealthy Thomson family. The Thomsons own 79% of HBC's common shares through the Woodbridge Company Limited.

HBC's range of department stores across Canada includes The Bay (its traditional department stores), Zellers (discount stores), and Fields (value-priced family stores). HBC announced in mid-1991 that it would close its Simpsons high fashion stores, converting some to Bays and selling the rest to Sears Canada.

HBC faces several challenges in 1991, including a deep recession and the exodus of Canadian shoppers to the US.

WHEN

In 1668 the British ketch *Nonsuch* reached the bay named for English explorer Henry Hudson. The ship returned to Britain the following year laden with furs, attracting the attention of King Charles II. In 1670 Charles granted a royal trading charter to a party of 18 men and appointed Prince Rupert, an ex-Royalist cavalry officer, as the company's first governor.

The company built a series of fortifications and engaged in a seesawing battle for control of the Bay with French warships until 1713 when the Treaty of Utrecht placed the Bay officially in British hands. From HBC's base at York Factory, company explorers began to penetrate Canada's vast interior. In 1774 Samuel Hearne established HBC's first inland post on the Saskatchewan River.

During the late 18th century, the Montreal-based North West Company, a rival fur-trading concern, arose to threaten HBC's fur-trading dominance. Both HBC and NWC organized increasing numbers of inland routes and forts, sparking frequent and often violent clashes between the competing traders.

In 1821 the 2 competitors ceased hostilities by merging under the HBC name, giving the company control over 173 posts throughout 3 million square miles of wilderness. In 1869 the company transferred possession of HBC-chartered land to the Canadian government.

By the turn of the century, HBC had transformed many posts into stores to serve growing Canadian cities. In 1929 the company formed the Hudson's Bay Oil and Gas Company. HBC acquired the Henry Morgan department store chain in 1960 and 5 years later changed its store name to The Bay. In 1970 the company finally moved its headquarters from London (most of the company's governors had never ventured into Canada) to Winnipeg and later to Toronto.

The company expanded its department store holdings in the late 1970s by purchasing Zellers, Fields, and Simpsons. In turn, newspaper magnate Kenneth Thomson bought 3/4 of HBC in 1979. During the 1980s the company became mired in debt from its prolific acquisitions. To trim the fat the company sold its oil and gas operations, its large fur houses (under pressure from animal rights activists), and, to the horror of many company veterans, 179 of its original northern province stores.

In 1990 the company spun off its Markborough real estate subsidiary to shareholders and purchased the Towers Bonimart chain of discount department stores that HBC will integrate into its Zellers chain. The company is currently trying specialty retailing, and in 1990 set up 6 test-market stores in such areas as lingerie and imported candy.

HOW MUCH

$=C$1.16 (Dec. 31, 1990)	9-Year Growth	1981	1982	1983	1984	1985	1986	1987	1988	1989	1990
Sales (C$ mil.)	2.0%	4,173	4,139	4,371	4,829	5,271	5,692	4,345	4,491	4,604	4,970
Net income (C$ mil.)	50.5%	4	(122)	(18)	(107)	(9)	33	13	37	144	158
Income as % of sales	—	0.1%	(2.9%)	(0.4%)	(2.2%)	(0.2%)	0.6%	0.3%	0.8%	3.1%	3.2%
Earnings per share (C$)	—	(0.34)	(5.63)	(1.63)	(5.40)	(1.23)	0.32	(0.51)	0.32	3.64	3.34
Stock price – high (C$)	—	30.63	23.00	25.38	24.00	26.63	33.00	26.50	25.13	37.38	23.75
Stock price – low (C$)	—	20.25	15.00	16.25	17.00	16.25	22.13	18.25	18.38	24.63	12.25
Stock price – close (C$)	(0.5%)	21.00	18.25	24.63	17.25	24.63	23.25	19.38	25.13	31.00	20.00
P/E – high	—	—	—	—	—	—	103	—	78	10	7
P/E – low	—	—	—	—	—	—	69	—	56	7	4
Dividends per share (C$)	(4.4%)	1.20	0.75	0.60	0.60	0.60	0.60	0.60	0.60	0.60	0.80
Book value per share (C$)	(6.0%)	44.58	38.00	39.36	33.28	30.49	28.40	16.33	14.41	21.09	25.53

1990 Year-end:
Debt ratio: 34.0%
Return on equity: 14.3%
Cash (mil.): C$19
Long-term debt (mil.): C$593
No. of shares (mil.): 45
Dividends:
1990 average yield: 4.0%
1990 payout: 24.0%
Market value (mil.): $776
Sales (mil.): $4,284

Stock Price History
High/Low 1981–90

Principal exchange: Toronto
Fiscal year ends: January 31

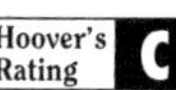

WHO

Governor: Donald S. McGiverin
President and COO: George J. Kosich
President, The Bay: N. R. Peter
President, Zellers Inc.: Paul S. Walters
President, Fields Stores: Janis R. Ostling
EVP and CFO: Gary J. Lukassen
VP Human Resources: David J. Crisp
Auditors: Peat Marwick Thorne
Employees: 55,000

WHERE

HQ: 401 Bay St., Toronto, Ontario M5H 2Y4, Canada
Phone: 416-861-611
Fax: 416-861-4517

	No. of Stores	Sq. Ft. Thou.
Alberta	84	3,723
British Columbia	119	4,213
Manitoba	12	1,598
New Brunswick	13	785
Newfoundland	5	258
Nova Scotia	19	1,549
Ontario	146	14,268
Prince Edward Island	4	255
Quebec	70	6,527
Saskatchewan	18	1,142
Total	**490**	**34,318**

WHAT

	1990 Sales		1990 Operating Income	
	C$ mil.	% of total	C$ mil.	% of total
The Bay	1,887	38	119	38
Fields	91	2	3	1
Simpsons	435	9	3	1
Zellers	2,330	47	200	63
Other	227	4	(8)	(3)
Total	**4,970**	**100**	**317**	**100**

	No. of Stores	Sq. Ft. Thou.
The Bay	79	12,380
Fields	132	969
Simpsons	14	2,881
Zellers	265	18,088
Total	**490**	**34,318**

Stores
The Bay (department stores)
Zellers Inc. (discount stores)
Fields Stores (discount family stores)

KEY COMPETITORS

Campeau
Costco
Imasco
Kmart
Marks and Spencer
Sears
Toys "R" Us
Woolworth

HUTCHISON WHAMPOA LTD.

OVERVIEW

Hutchison Whampoa is the first *hong* (colonial trading company) to pass from British to Chinese control. The company is a major property owner and container terminal operator in Hong Kong and is involved in retailing and telecommunications in the colony and abroad. Hutchison also owns large minority stakes in Hongkong Electric (utility) and Husky Oil, the largest independent integrated oil company in Canada.

Hong Kong tycoon Li Ka-shing controls 39.5% of Hutchison Whampoa stock through his Cheung Kong Holdings property company. Li, estimated by *Forbes* to be worth $2 billion, started a plastics manufacturing company and parlayed it into a real estate fortune.

Li has tried to foster good relations with the Chinese government, which in 1997 will take control of Hong Kong.

Hutchison is investing heavily in cellular telecommunications throughout Asia and is the largest cellular operator in Hong Kong and the UK. In September 1991 the company's 50%-owned Hutchvision unit will begin pan-Asian TV broadcasting via AsiaSat I, a satellite 1/3-owned by Hutchison with a broadcasting range encompassing 52% of the world's population.

Principal exchange: Hong Kong
Fiscal year ends: December 31

WHO

Chairman: Li Ka-shing, age 63
Deputy Chairman: George C. Magnus
Group Managing Director: Simon Murray, age 50
Auditors: Price Waterhouse

WHERE

HQ: Hutchison House, 22nd Fl., 10 Harcourt Rd., Hong Kong
Phone: 011-852-523-0161
Fax: 011-852-810-0705

	1990 Sales		1990 Operating Income	
	HK$ mil.	% of total	HK$ mil.	% of total
Hong Kong	13,359	84	2,919	83
Asia	1,621	10	514	15
Europe	924	6	26	1
North America	71	—	52	1
Total	**15,975**	**100**	**3,511**	**100**

WHAT

	1990 Sales		1990 Operating Income	
	HK$ mil.	% of total	HK$ mil.	% of total
Property	2,874	18	1,554	35
Container terminals	1,937	12	1,225	27
Retail & other services	9,831	62	1,021	23
Energy, finance & investment	1,333	8	656	15
Adjustments	—	—	(945)	—
Total	**15,975**	**100**	**3,511**	**100**

Property
Hongkong and Whampoa Dock Company, Ltd.
Hutchison Properties Ltd.
International City Holdings Ltd. (83%)
Kingsmill Properties Ltd.

Container Terminals
Hongkong International Terminals Ltd. (67%, shipping services)
Hongkong United Dockyards Ltd. (50%, ship repair and engineering)

Other Services
Hongkong Hilton Hotel
Hutchison China Trade Holdings Ltd. (Chinese investment and trade)
Procter & Gamble–Hutchison Limited (31%, manufacturing)
Sheraton Hong Kong Hotel & Towers (39%)
A.S. Watson & Co. Ltd. (Park'N Shop supermarkets, Watson's personal care stores, Fortress appliance stores, Watson's bottled water, Mountain Cream ice cream)

Energy, Finance, and Investment
Cluff Resources PLC (25%, mining, UK)
Hongkong Electric Holdings Ltd. (34.6%, utility)
Husky Oil Ltd. (43%, Canada)

Telecommunications
AsiaSat I (33%)
Hutchison Paging Ltd. (70%)
Hutchison Telecommunications Ltd.
Hutchison Telephone Co. Ltd. (70%)
Hutchvision, Ltd. (50%)

KEY COMPETITORS

British Telecom
Cable & Wireless
Jardine Matheson
Swire Pacific

WHEN

In 1977 Hong Kong companies Hutchison International and Hongkong and Whampoa Dock merged to form Hutchison Whampoa. Originally established in 1880 by John Hutchison, Hutchison International became a major Hong Kong consumer goods importer and wholesaler. Managed by Sir Douglas Clague, the company bought controlling interests in Hongkong and Whampoa Dock (dry docks) and A.S. Watson (drugstores, supermarkets, soft drinks) in the midst of a wild acquisition binge in the 1960s. The purchases were accomplished through a complex web of deals that fell apart in the mid-1970s. To save Hutchison International, the Hongkong & Shanghai Bank took a large stake in the company and replaced Clague with Australian turnaround specialist "Dollar" Bill Wyllie. Wyllie slashed expenses, sold 103 companies in 1976, and bought the rest of Hongkong and Whampoa Dock in 1977.

Hongkong and Whampoa Dock, the first registered company in Hong Kong, had been established in 1861. The company bought dry docks in Whampoa (port of Canton, China) following the kidnapping and disappearance of their owner, John Couper, during the 2nd Opium War. Hong Kong docks were first purchased in 1865. Hongkong and Whampoa Dock operated shipyards and shipping container terminals at the time of the merger with Hutchison.

Hutchison Whampoa's finances improved vastly under Wyllie. In a surprise move, Hongkong & Shanghai Bank sold its 22.8% stake in Hutchison to Li Ka-shing's Cheung Kong Holdings in 1979 at 50% of its estimated value. Bank chairman Michael Sandberg was thought to feel the need to increase the role of the Chinese in Hong Kong commerce in light of China's increasing scrutiny of the colony. Wyllie, believed to have been preparing his own bid for Hutchison, left in 1981.

In the 1980s Hutchison developed its former dockyard sites (now prime real estate). The company's International Terminals unit grew with Hong Kong's container traffic and became the world's largest privately owned container terminal operator. Following the appointment of former French foreign legionnaire Simon Murray as managing director in 1984, the company bought large minority stakes in Hongkong Electric (utility, 1985), Husky Oil (Canada, 1987), and Cluff Resources (gold and minerals mining, UK, 1987). The company also purchased Australian paging and UK mobile telephone units (1989).

In 1990 the *hong* sold its John D. Hutchison trading unit and in 1991 bought the UK's largest container port and the UK cellular telephone operations of Millicom.

HOW MUCH

$=HK$7.80 (Dec. 31, 1990)	9-Year Growth	1981	1982	1983	1984	1985	1986	1987	1988	1989	1990
Sales (HK$ mil.)	18.6%	3,444	3,717	4,361	5,215	5,466	7,529	10,524	12,875	17,685	15,975
Net income (HK$ mil.)	18.0%	791	952	1,171	1,029	1,194	1,630	1,864	2,340	3,031	3,519
Income as % of sales	—	23.0%	25.6%	26.9%	19.7%	21.8%	21.6%	17.7%	18.2%	17.1%	22.0%
Earnings per share (HK$)	15.0%	0.33	0.40	0.49	0.35	0.42	0.57	0.65	0.77	1.00	1.16
Stock price – high (HK$)	—	5.10	3.70	3.04	3.66	5.60	9.30	15.90	9.70	12.30	13.20
Stock price – low (HK$)	—	2.60	1.64	1.60	1.68	3.70	4.80	5.65	6.65	6.80	7.95
Stock price – close (HK$)	14.8%	3.50	1.89	2.90	3.64	5.50	9.25	7.05	8.60	8.80	12.10
P/E – high	—	15	9	6	10	13	16	24	13	12	11
P/E – low	—	8	4	3	5	9	8	9	9	7	7
Dividends per share (HK$)	26.2%	0.08	0.09	0.93	0.16	0.20	0.25	0.35	0.42	0.54	0.65
Book value per share (HK$)	20.6%	1.5	1.8	1.4	1.8	2.3	3.6	4.7	5.2	7.4	8.1

1990 Year-end:
Debt ratio: 32.6%
Return on equity: 17.4%
Cash (mil.): HK$11,651
Long-term debt (bil.): HK$12
No. of shares (mil.): 3,046
Dividends:
1990 average yield: 5.4%
1990 payout: 56.0%
Market value (mil.): $4,725
Sales (mil.): $2,048

Stock Price History High/Low 1981–90

HYUNDAI GROUP

OVERVIEW

Hyundai is pronounced "hi-un-dye" everywhere except in the US, where American marketers prefer a pronunciation rhyming with Sunday. Hyundai is a *chaebol* (industrial group) consisting of 27 affiliated companies, including Hyundai Corporation (trading), Hyundai Engineering and Construction, Hyundai Heavy Industries, Hyundai Motor, and Hyundai Electronics. The *chaebol* is Korea's 2nd largest after Samsung.

A buoyant domestic economy, strong postwar demand in the Middle East, and an export push into Eastern Europe have enabled Hyundai Motor to grow despite plummeting exports to the US. Hyundai's semiconductor business continues to struggle with technical and production problems in its quest to catch up technologically with global rivals. The *chaebol* is negotiating with the USSR for energy supplies and a chance to enter Soviet consumer and construction markets.

In 1991 the Korean government ordered each *chaebol* to focus on only 3 core businesses. Hyundai has chosen motor vehicles, electronics, and petrochemicals.

WHEN

At the end of WWII, elementary school dropout Chung Ju-Yung went into business repairing trucks for US occupation forces in South Korea. In 1947 Chung established Hyundai Engineering and Construction, the first Korean contractor to win overseas construction projects. Chung's Hyundai Motor, formed in 1967, originally assembled Fords.

Chung repeatedly gambled on new businesses. When Hyundai won a $1 billion contract in the 1970s to build a port in Jubail, Saudi Arabia, Chung saved money by importing Korean parts and not insuring the shipments, risking ruin. The gamble paid off, and Hyundai became a major factor in Middle East construction.

In the 1970s Chung enjoyed the support of the Park government, and his Hyundai enterprises multiplied. In 1973 he began building the world's largest shipyard (Hyundai Heavy Industries) despite having no experience in shipbuilding. He succeeded thanks to government backing, near-monopoly conditions, and an extremely hardworking Korean labor force. With help from 15% owner Mitsubishi Motors, Hyundai Motor built the first Korean automobile in 1975 — the popular Pony. Chung created Hyundai Corporation in 1976 and established the Ulsan Institute of Technology in 1977 to increase South Korea's pool of engineering talent.

The Hyundai *chaebol* continued to expand its scope in the 1980s, forming Hyundai Electronics Industries (1983) to produce semiconductors and microcomputer equipment despite a lack of experience in technology-based industries. Hyundai spent heavily on electronics but did not enjoy immediate success. In 1985 the company closed a plant in Santa Clara, California, when it found that Americans would not regularly work nights and weekends, as South Koreans will.

Hyundai took advantage of low labor costs to start an export drive in the 1980s, beginning shipments of the Pony to Canada (1984), where it became #4 in auto sales (1985). In the US the company introduced Blue Chip brand IBM-compatible PCs (1986) and, in the most successful imported car launch in US history, inexpensive Excel subcompacts (1986).

In the late 1980s Hyundai suffered from a slump in worldwide shipbuilding, strikes (1987, 1989), slow progress in its electronics ventures, and the narrowing of its cost advantage as South Korean wages doubled in 3 years and the country's currency appreciated. Hyundai's US-bound car exports plunged 57% between 1988 and 1990. Hyundai produced the first Korean-designed auto engine in 1991.

HOW MUCH

$=Won714 (Dec. 31, 1990)	9-Year Growth	1981	1982	1983	1984	1985	1986	1987	1988	1989	1990
Sales (Won bil.)	24.1%	908	1,057	1,547	1,550	2,853	3,876	5,254	5,622	5,703	6,328
Net income (Won bil.)	7.3%	3.5	4.2	5.4	3.2	4.5	4.9	3.7	8.6	4.6	6.6
Income as % of sales	—	0.4%	0.4%	0.3%	0.2%	0.2%	0.1%	0.1%	0.1%	0.1%	0.1%
Earnings per share (Won)	—	—	—	—	1,005	1,394	1,530	761	1,798	966	966
Stock price – high (Won)	—	—	—	—	—	13,190	16,350	21,900	30,300	35,200	30,000
Stock price – low (Won)	—	—	—	—	—	8,590	9,210	12,800	17,500	22,700	23,400
Stock price – close (Won)	—	—	—	—	—	—	13,500	20,290	30,300	26,600	25,500
P/E – high	—	—	—	—	—	9	11	29	16	36	31
P/E – low	—	—	—	—	—	6	6	17	10	23	24
Dividends per share (Won)[1]	—	—	—	—	—	500	500	500	500	500	500
Book value per share (Won)	—	—	—	—	—	9,220	10,024	9,380	11,046	11,557	12,381

1990 Year-end:
Debt ratio: 19.6%
Return on equity: 8.1%
Cash (mil.): Won2,395
Long-term debt (mil.): Won15,085
No. of shares (mil.): 5
Dividends:
1990 average yield: 2.0%
1990 payout: 51.8%
Market value (mil.): $179
Sales (mil.): $8,863

Stock Price History High/Low 1985–90

40,000
35,000
30,000
25,000
20,000
15,000
10,000
5,000
0

[1] Not including rights offerings

Principal exchange: Korea
Fiscal year ends: December 31

WHO

Group Chairman: Chung Se Yung
Chairman: Lee Choon Lim
President: Park Se Yong
Auditors: Young Wha Accounting Corp. (Ernst & Young)
Employees: 845

WHERE

HQ: Hyundai Corp., CPO Box 8943, 140-2, Kye-Dong, Chongro-Ku, Seoul, Korea
Phone: 011-82-2-746-1114
Fax: 011-82-2-741-2341
US HQ: Hyundai Corp. U.S.A., One Bridge Plaza North, Suite 600, Fort Lee, NJ 07024
US Phone: 201-346-2020
US Fax: 201-346-2098

The company maintains 48 trading offices in 33 countries.

	1990 Sales % of total
South Korea	35
Outside South Korea	65
Total	**100**

WHAT

	1990 Sales % of total
Machinery & transportation	30
Ships & industrial plants	21
Electronics & electrical equipment	32
Steel & metal	8
General merchandise	5
Resources & energy	4
Total	**100**

Major Affiliates
Aluminum of Korea, Ltd. (34.4%)
Dongsu Industrial Co., Ltd.
Hyundai Construction Equipment Industries Co., Ltd.
Hyundai Electronics Industries Co., Ltd.
Hyundai Engineering & Construction Co., Ltd.
Hyundai Heavy Industries Co., Ltd.
Hyundai Housing & Industrial Development Co., Ltd.
Hyundai Marine & Fire Insurance Co., Ltd.
Hyundai Merchant Marine Co., Ltd.
Hyundai Mipo Dockyard Co., Ltd.
Hyundai Motor Co.
Hyundai Motor Service Co. Ltd.
Hyundai Pipe Co., Ltd.
Hyundai Precision & Industry Co., Ltd.
Hyundai Robot Industry Co., Ltd.
Hyundai Securities Co., Ltd.
Hyundai Steel Tower Industries Co., Ltd.
Hyundai Wood Industries Co., Ltd.
Inchon Iron & Steel Co., Ltd.
KKBC International Ltd.

KEY COMPETITORS

Bethlehem Steel
Broken Hill
Caterpillar
Chrysler
Commodore
Compaq
Daewoo
Deere
Fiat
Ford
Fujitsu
General Motors
Hitachi
Honda
IBM
Inland Steel
Isuzu
LTV
Lucky-Goldstar
Mazda
Mitsubishi
Motorola
National Semiconductor
NEC
Nippon Steel
Nissan
Peugeot
Renault
Samsung
Siemens
Texas Instruments
Toyota
USX
Volkswagen
Volvo

Information presented for Hyundai Corporation only.

IMASCO LTD.

OVERVIEW

Headquartered in Montreal, Imasco is a major diversified company with formidable positions in tobacco, retailing, fast food, and finance. Forty percent of Imasco is still controlled by British giant B.A.T, which assisted in Imasco's formation in 1912.

Imasco's tobacco operations (Imperial) bring in 59% of its operating income and control 60% of the Canadian market. Its Player's and du Maurier cigarette brand lines are Canada's 2 top sellers. The division's future is clouded by ever-increasing taxes on and dropping consumption of cigarettes in Canada.

A major force in retail drugstores, Imasco's Shoppers Drug Mart/Pharmaprix is Canada's largest drugstore chain. Its 645 outlets command a 30% market share. Through its UCS group, Imasco controls 533 specialty stores (including hotel/airport stores, Canadian Woolco/Woolworth, and other stores).

In the US the company operates the Hardee's hamburger chain (3rd in the fast-food hamburger category) and Roy Rogers (a 480-restaurant East Coast chain currently being converted to the Hardee's format).

Imasco's banking arm consists of Canada Trust, Canada Trustco Mortgage, and Truscan Realty. Financial services range from lending to real estate brokerage to investment counseling.

Principal exchanges: Montreal, Toronto, Vancouver

Fiscal year ends: December 31

WHO

Chairman and CEO: Purdy Crawford, age 58
VC: Jean-Louis Mercier
President: Brian Levitt
EVP and CFO: Raymond E. Guyatt
SVP Human Resources, Hardee's: Edna Morris
VP Human Resources, Imperial Tobacco: Marius Dagneau
Auditors: Deloitte & Touche
Employees: 190,000

WHERE

HQ: 600 de Maisonneuve Blvd. West, 20th Floor, Montreal, Quebec H3A 3K7, Canada
Phone: 514-982-9111
Fax: 514-982-9369
US HQ: Imasco USA, Inc., 1233 Hardee's Blvd., Rocky Mount, NC 27804-2815
US Phone: 919-977-2000
US Fax: 919-977-4342

Imasco operates 645 Shoppers Drug Mart and 533 UCS Group stores in Canada. The company oversees 3,497 Hardee's restaurants in the US (about 2/3 of which are operated by licensees) and 45 overseas.

WHEN

The Imperial Tobacco Company of Canada was incorporated in 1912 with the assistance of B.A.T (which had been created by the joining of Imperial Tobacco and American Tobacco) to produce and market tobacco products across Canada. The company grew steadily, gradually absorbing many other tobacco operations, including several brands from British-American Tobacco (1921), General Cigar Company (1921, purchase completed in 1930), Tuckett Tobacco (1930), Imperial Tobacco of Newfoundland (1949), and Brown & Williamson Tobacco (1950).

During the 1960s the company took its first steps outside of tobacco with the purchases of 2 winemakers (Grower's Wine, 1964; Beau-Chatel Wines, 1966), Simtel (closed-circuit equipment, 1967), S&W Fine Foods (1969), and Pasquale Brothers (food, 1969), among other companies.

In 1969 tobacco industry veteran Paul Paré became CEO of Imperial. Seeking to expand beyond tobacco (as was the pattern with other tobacco companies), Paré set up Imasco in 1970 to be a holding company for Imperial's increasingly diversified operations. During the 1970s Imasco added several food and retail companies but had sold almost all of them by 1980.

After developing more rigid standards for potential acquisitions, Imasco again dived into the buying mode, this time finding a winner in 1979 with the Shoppers Drug Mart chain. The company also dipped into the US to buy fast-food franchiser Hardee's Food Systems (1981), and Burger Chef (from General Foods, 1982). Following a failed takeover attempt of the Canadian Tire Store chain, Imasco took its drugstore business south by purchasing the Mid-Atlantic Peoples Drug Stores (1984) and Rea and Derick (1984).

In 1986 Paré captured the Genstar Corporation (founded in 1951), owner of Canada Trustco Mortgage, Canada's largest trust company, for $2.6 billion (as well as assuming Genstar's massive debt). Genstar, which included Canada Trustco, was dissolved and its assets were placed under the control of Imasco Enterprises. Following the deal Paré retired in favor of Purdy Crawford, an ex–corporate attorney who had joined Imasco in 1985.

In 1990 Imasco bought the Roy Rogers chain of US restaurants (from Marriott, $365 million), sold Peoples Drug Store (to Melville Corporation, $325 million), and agreed to purchase a controlling interest in Rochester-based First Federal S&L.

WHAT

	1990 Sales		1990 Operating Income	
	C$ mil.	% of total	C$ mil.	% of total
Imperial Tobacco	2,708	18	367	59
Hardee's	4,834	32	69	11
Shoppers Drug Mart	2,844	18	80	13
UCS Group	315	2	9	1
Imasco Enterprises	4,573	30	102	16
Adjustments	(144)	—	—	—
Total	**15,130**	**100**	**627**	**100**

Cigarettes
Imperial Tobacco
du Maurier
du Maurier Extra Light
du Maurier Light
du Maurier Special
Matinée
Matinée Extra Mild
Matinée Slims
Matinée Special Mild
Player's Extra Light
Player's Filter
Player's Light
Player's Medium
Player's Plain

Restaurants
Fast Food Merchandisers
Hardee's
Roy Rogers

Financial
CT Financial Services Inc. (98%)
Canada Trust Company
Canada Trustco Mortgage Company
Truscan Realty

Retail Stores
Den for Men/Au Masculin
Shoppers Drug Mart/Pharmaprix
Tax and Duty Free
Woolco/Woolworth (Canada)

HOW MUCH

$=C$1.16 (Dec. 31, 1990)	9-Year Growth	1981	1982	1983	1984	1985	1986	1987	1988	1989	1990
Sales (C$ mil.)	17.2%	3,623	4,695	5,304	5,853	6,635	9,176	11,038	11,939	13,457	15,130
Net income (C$ mil.)	10.2%	123	152	185	222	262	226	283	314	366	295
Income as % of sales	—	3.4%	3.2%	3.5%	3.8%	3.9%	2.5%	2.6%	2.6%	2.7%	1.9%
Earnings per share (C$)	5.4%	1.40	1.72	1.81	2.19	2.40	1.92	2.24	2.51	2.87	2.25
Stock price – high (C$)	—	10.50	14.94	19.13	23.88	29.25	39.25	39.63	29.50	40.13	38.13
Stock price – low (C$)	—	7.44	9.00	14.38	15.94	22.75	25.00	23.25	23.63	27.75	25.88
Stock price – close (C$)	11.1%	10.50	14.94	17.63	23.75	27.88	32.13	25.88	28.00	37.50	27.13
P/E – high	—	8	9	11	11	12	20	18	12	14	17
P/E – low	—	5	5	8	7	9	13	10	9	10	12
Dividends per share (C$)	15.9%	0.34	0.39	0.48	0.59	0.72	0.84	0.96	1.04	1.12	1.28
Book value per share (C$)	15.0%	5.65	7.57	9.43	11.75	13.62	16.22	17.19	17.24	18.91	19.85

1990 Year-end:
Debt ratio: 46.7%
Return on equity: 11.6%
Cash (mil.): C$86
Long-term debt (mil.): C$2,072
No. of shares (mil.): 119
Dividends:
1990 average yield: 4.7%
1990 payout: 56.9%
Market value (mil.): $2,783
Sales (mil.): $13,043

Stock Price History High/Low 1981–90
45 40 35 30 25 20 15 10 5 0

KEY COMPETITORS

American Brands
American Stores
B.A.T
BCE
Canadian Imperial
General Mills
Grand Metropolitan
Hudson's Bay
Loews
McDonald's
Melville
PepsiCo
Philip Morris
Rite Aid
RJR Nabisco
Royal Bank
TW Holdings
Wendy's
Banks

IMPERIAL CHEMICAL INDUSTRIES PLC

OVERVIEW

Britain's entry in the big leagues of the world's chemical industry is Imperial Chemical Industries. ICI is the world's largest paintmaker and largest commercial explosives manufacturer.

After serving as a textbook example of how to go global in the mid-1980s, Britain's largest manufacturer turned a page in 1991 and was forced to prepare for a possible takeover defense. Corporate raider Lord Hanson bought 2.8% of ICI. The company had already begun restructuring in the face of slumping profits. It carved its 3 huge components into 7 more maneuverable divisions: materials, industrial chemicals, drugs, farm chemicals, paints, specialties, and explosives. ICI plans to withdraw from unprofitable enterprises; it wants to close its UK fertilizer business, and the company has shuttered a Brazilian plant. ICI has begun paring staff.

ICI wants UK regulators to keep Hanson at bay and frets that Hanson's short-term fixes for profitability threaten the long-term research required in the chemical industry. The big question is what piece or pieces of ICI Hanson would sell if a takeover were successful.

WHEN

Imperial Chemical Industries was created from the 1926 combination of 4 British chemical companies. The companies — Nobel Industries; Brunner, Mond and Company; United Alkali; and British Dyestuffs — joined in reaction to the German amalgamation that created I. G. Farben.

The most famed ICI predecessor, Nobel Industries, was created as the British arm of Alfred Nobel's explosives empire. Nobel mixed highly explosive, unstable nitroglycerin with porous clay to make dynamite. In 1886 Nobel created the London-based Nobel Dynamite Trust to embrace British and German interests. After Nobel's death in 1896, the empire began to unravel, and WWI severed the German and UK components of the Nobel firm. The British arm became Nobel Industries (1920).

ICI relied on the old Nobel alliance with the premier American chemical company, Du Pont. In 1929 ICI and Du Pont signed a patents-and-process agreement, sharing research information. ICI also muscled into consortia with I. G. Farben in 1931 and 1932.

ICI, as Britain's representative in the worldwide chemical industry, plunged into research. It recruited skilled chemists, engineers, and managers. It formed alliances with universities. Between 1933 and 1935 its Dyestuffs Group laboratory created 87 new products, and in 1935 its Alkali Group lab invented polyethylene.

After WWII the chummy club of cartels began to disband. The US government won antitrust sanctions against the Du Pont–ICI alliance (1952), and ICI faced new competition with the sundered components of I. G. Farben (Bayer, BASF, Hoechst). ICI added operations in Germany, the UK, and the US (a Bayonne, NJ, plant) in the 1960s, but fortunes declined until 1980, when ICI posted losses and cut its dividend for the first time.

The company turned to John Harvey-Jones in 1982. Harvey-Jones cut layers of decision-making, reorganized internationally along product lines, and added directors from outside the UK to the board. ICI also shifted production from bulk chemicals, such as soda and chlorine, to high-margin specialty chemicals (ICI calls them "effect chemicals"), such as pharmaceuticals and pesticides.

Harvey-Jones bought 100 companies from 1982 until his retirement in 1987. ICI expanded in the US market by purchasing Beatrice's chemical operations (1985, $750 million); Glidden paints (1986, $580 million); and Stauffer Chemicals (1987, $1.7 billion), of which it sold all but the agricultural chemicals operations. In 1990 ICI paid $310 million for the 50% of Tioxide (titanium oxide) that it didn't already own.

HOW MUCH

Stock prices are for ADRs ADR = 4 shares	9-Year Growth	1981	1982	1983	1984	1985	1986	1987	1988	1989	1990
Sales ($ mil.)	7.9%	12,603	11,905	11,988	11,475	15,444	15,001	20,800	21,058	21,074	24,909
Net income ($ mil.)	14.0%	368	235	576	701	795	888	1,421	1,586	1,488	1,191
Income as % of sales	—	2.9%	2.0%	4.8%	6.1%	5.1%	5.9%	6.8%	7.5%	7.1%	4.8%
Earnings per share ($)	11.8%	2.48	1.56	3.79	4.56	4.98	5.45	8.50	9.34	8.64	6.79
Stock price – high ($)	—	30.50	26.50	38.50	37.13	44.13	65.63	108.13	86.50	87.25	85.25
Stock price – low ($)	—	18.00	18.50	22.00	27.75	33.00	42.13	62.75	67.00	68.13	59.75
Stock price – close ($)	13.3%	21.50	22.00	37.50	34.00	44.00	63.00	82.00	72.88	74.25	66.00
P/E – high	—	12	17	10	8	9	12	13	9	10	13
P/E – low	—	7	12	6	6	7	8	7	7	8	9
Dividends per share ($)	14.5%	1.51	1.79	1.62	2.00	2.28	2.81	3.39	4.19	4.68	5.08
Book value per share ($)	3.3%	37.99	32.97	31.63	28.58	30.99	33.07	38.12	41.32	46.11	50.93

1990 Year-end:
Debt ratio: 26.3%
Return on equity: 14.0%
Cash (mil.): $1,091
Current ratio: 1.58
Long-term debt (bil.): $3.2
No. of shares (mil.): 177
Dividends:
1990 average yield: 7.7%
1990 payout: 74.8%
Market value (mil.): $11,682

Stock Price History High/Low 1981–90

0 20 40 60 80 100 120

NYSE symbol: ICI (ADR)
Fiscal year ends: December 31

Hoover's Rating **B**

WHO

Chairman: Sir Denys Henderson, age 58, £448,000 pay
Deputy Chairman and Group Personnel Director: Frank Whiteley, age 60
Group Finance Director and Group Information Services Director: C. M. Short, age 56
Auditors: KPMG Peat Marwick McLintock
Employees: 132,100

WHERE

HQ: Imperial Chemical House, Millbank, London SW1P 3JF, UK
Phone: 011-44-71-834-4444
Fax: 011-44-71-834-2042
US HQ: ICI American Holdings Inc., 645 Fifth Ave., New York, NY 10022
US Phone: 212-685-4030
US Fax: 212-213-0159

ICI markets its products worldwide.

	1990 Sales		1990 Operating Income	
	$ mil.	% of total	$ mil.	% of total
UK	11,823	40	569	29
Other Europe	6,083	20	303	16
Americas	7,046	24	737	38
Asia/Pacific	3,951	13	262	14
Other countries	778	3	56	3
Adjustments	(4,772)	—	(289)	—
Total	**24,909**	**100**	**1,638**	**100**

WHAT

	1990 Sales		1990 Operating Income	
	$ mil.	% of total	$ mil.	% of total
Pharmaceuticals	2,731	11	944	47
Consumer & spec.	7,596	29	214	11
Industrial	10,885	42	625	32
Agriculture	4,227	16	235	12
Other	384	2	(39)	(2)
Adjustments	(914)	—	(341)	—
Total	**24,909**	**100**	**1,638**	**100**

Products

Explosives
Blasting accessories
Commercial products

Farm Chemicals
Fertilizers
Herbicides
Pesticides (Ambush)

Industrial Chemicals
Chlorine derivatives
Salt
Soda ash

Specialties
Dyes
Lubricants
Packaging specialties (inks, coatings, adhesives)
Pigments
Polymer additives
Polyurethanes

Pharmaceuticals
Elavil (antidepressant)
Nolvadex (anticancer drug)
Tenormin (hypertension drug)
Zestril (ACE inhibitor)
Zoladex (prostate cancer treatment)

Materials
Engineering plastics
Polyester film (Melinex)
Resins

Paints
Decorative (Glidden)
High performance finishes

KEY COMPETITORS

Allied-Signal
American Cyanamid
BASF
Bayer
Ciba-Geigy
Dow Chemical
Du Pont
Hoechst
Norsk Hydro
PPG
Rhône-Poulenc
Sherwin-Williams
Union Carbide
USG
Other chemical and pharmaceutical companies

IMPERIAL OIL LTD.

ASE symbol: IMOA
Fiscal year ends: December 31

OVERVIEW

Imperial Oil, 69.7% owned by Exxon, is the largest oil company in Canada. Its efforts of late have been devoted to swallowing what was once Canada's 4th largest oil company, Texaco Canada.

Imperial concentrates on natural resources, petroleum products, and chemicals. Natural resources operations, conducted through subsidiary Esso Resources Canada, include drilling for oil and gas and mining heavy crude oil and bitumen. Esso Petroleum Canada makes 700 products at 7 refineries, then transports and markets them nationwide and in the US. Most of its crude oil supply comes from Canada, but Imperial imports from Venezuela and from Exxon's overseas holdings. Esso Chemical makes and sells petroleum-derived chemicals and fertilizers.

Since the Texaco Canada acquisition, Imperial has reduced its debt and satisfied Canadian regulators by selling assets such as Texaco Canada's refining and marketing properties. To cut payroll, Imperial is offering voluntary staff-reduction programs to employees.

WHEN

London, Ontario, boomed from the discovery of oil in the 1860s and 1870s, but the market for Canadian kerosene became saturated in 1880, and 16 refiners banded together to form the Imperial Oil Company.

The company refined sulfuric Canadian oil, nicknamed "skunk oil" for its powerful smell. Imperial faced tough competition from America's Standard Oil, which marketed kerosene made from lighter, less odorous Pennsylvania crude. Guided by American expatriate Jacob Englehart, Imperial built a better refinery and hired a chemist who developed a process to cleanse the crude of sulfur.

By the mid-1890s Imperial had expanded from coast to Canadian coast. Cash-starved from its expansion, the company turned to old nemesis Standard Oil, which bought controlling interest in Imperial in 1898.

After the turn of the century, Imperial began producing gasoline to serve the new automobiles. In 1907 an Imperial manager in Vancouver, to prevent the commotion when horseless carriages spooked workhorses at the warehouse where fuel was sold, opened the first Canadian service station. Imperial marketed its gasoline under the Esso banner borrowed from Standard Oil.

In 1920 an Imperial crew discovered oil at Norman Wells in the remote Northwest Territories. In 1924 a subsidiary sparked a new boom with a gas well discovery in the Turner Valley area northeast of Edmonton. Soon Imperial's luck ran as dry as the holes it was drilling; it came away empty from the next 133 consecutive wells. That string ended in 1947 when it struck oil in Alberta at the Leduc No. 1. To get the oil to market, Imperial invested in the Interprovincial Pipe Line from Alberta to Superior, Wisconsin. The pipeline, later extended to the Toronto area, was the longest crude oil pipeline in the non-Communist world.

In the 1970s, amid the OPEC-spawned oil crisis, Imperial continued to search for oil in northern Canada. It found crude on land near the Beaufort Sea (1970) and dipped its toes into the icy Beaufort, building a gravel island to serve as its drilling base (1972). In 1978 it formed its Esso Resources Canada Ltd. subsidiary to oversee natural resources production.

In 1989 Texaco, still reeling from the Pennzoil court battle and its brief flight into bankruptcy court, sold Texaco Canada to Imperial. Imperial paid C$5 billion and rechristened Texaco Canada McColl-Frontenac Inc., its name before Texaco's 1938 hostile takeover. To diminish debt and comply with regulators, Imperial agreed to sell some of Texaco Canada's refining and marketing assets in Atlantic Canada (C$115 million), its interests in Interhome Energy, Inc. (C$500 million), and Western Canada oil and gas properties (C$300 million).

WHO

Chairman and CEO: Arden R. Haynes, age 63, C$1,100,000 pay
President and COO: Robert B. Peterson, age 53, C$729,000 pay
SVP and CFO: Ronald A. Brenneman, age 44, C$563,000 pay
VP Human Resources: P. J. Levins
Auditors: Price Waterhouse
Employees: 15,200

WHERE

HQ: 111 St. Clair Ave. West, Toronto, Ontario M5W 1K3, Canada
Phone: 416-968-4111
Fax: 416-968-4272 (Investor Relations)

Exploration and Production: Western Provinces of Canada, Arctic Islands, Beaufort Sea/MacKenzie Delta, Northwest Territories, and offshore Atlantic
Refining and Marketing: 6 Canadian refineries, 4,300 retail outlets throughout Canada
Chemicals: Petrochemical and plastics plants in Ontario, Nova Scotia, and British Columbia; fertilizer complex in Alberta

WHAT

	1990 Sales		1990 Operating Income	
	$ mil.	% of total	$ mil.	% of total
Natural resources	708	7	705	100
Petroleum prods.	8,199	84	363	51
Chemicals	751	8	40	6
Corporate & other	78	1	(401)	57
Adjustments	63	—	—	—
Total	**9,673**	**100**	**707**	**100**

Selected Subsidiaries and Affiliates
Atlas Supply Co. of Canada Ltd.
Beaverhill Resources Ltd.
Byron Creek Collieries (1983) Ltd.
Cascade Fertilizers (1990) Ltd.
Chinchaga Resources Ltd.
Devon Estates Ltd.
Esso Chemical Alberta Ltd.
Esso Resources (1989) Ltd.
Esso Resources Canada Ltd.
Esso Resources Enterprises Ltd.
Esso Resources N.W.T. Ltd.
Esso Resources Ventures Ltd.
The Imperial Pipe Line Co. Ltd.
Maple Leaf Petroleum Ltd.
McColl-Frontenac Inc.
Metro Fuel Co. Ltd.
Mr. Lube Canada Inc.
Syncrude (25%)
Taglu Enterprises Ltd.
Winnipeg Pipe Line Co. Ltd.

KEY COMPETITORS

Amoco	Pennzoil
Ashland	Petrofina
Atlantic Richfield	Petrobrás
British Petroleum	PDVSA
Chevron	Pemex
Coastal	Phillips Petroleum
Du Pont	Royal Dutch/Shell
Elf Aquitaine	Sun
Mobil	Texaco
Norsk Hydro	Unocal
Occidental	USX

HOW MUCH

	9-Year Growth	1981	1982	1983	1984	1985	1986	1987	1988	1989	1990
Sales ($ mil.)	4.1%	6,742	6,877	7,171	6,395	6,197	5,057	5,816	5,957	8,642	9,673
Net income ($ mil.)	0.9%	392	235	267	404	489	319	551	420	394	425
Income as % of sales	—	5.8%	3.4%	3.7%	6.3%	7.9%	6.3%	9.5%	7.1%	4.6%	4.4%
Earnings per share ($)	(1.3%)	2.50	1.50	1.68	2.51	3.01	1.95	3.36	2.57	2.19	2.22
Stock price – high ($)	—	31.75	27.00	33.38	34.38	40.25	37.38	61.63	51.25	55.38	59.63
Stock price – low ($)	—	20.25	16.13	21.50	25.38	30.25	25.13	36.50	36.63	40.63	45.88
Stock price – close ($)	10.1%	21.38	23.25	29.75	32.00	36.50	37.13	43.50	41.88	55.13	50.63
P/E – high	—	13	18	20	14	13	19	18	20	25	27
P/E – low	—	8	11	13	10	10	13	11	14	19	21
Dividends per share ($)	3.1%	1.17	1.13	1.14	1.12	1.20	1.16	1.24	1.46	1.52	1.54
Book value per share ($)	4.9%	21.68	21.15	21.32	21.58	22.12	22.59	26.16	29.57	32.70	33.48

1990 Year-end:
Debt ratio: 25.3%
Return on equity: 6.7%
Cash (mil.): $2
Current ratio: 1.29
Long-term debt (mil.): $2,177
No. of shares (mil.): 192
Dividends:
1990 average yield: 3.0%
1990 payout: 69.3%
Market value (mil.): $9,708

Stock Price History High/Low 1981–90

INCO LTD.

OVERVIEW

Toronto-based Inco Limited is the leading miner of nickel, producing more than twice its nearest competitor. Nickel is a key component of stainless steel, and about 60% of all nickel finds its way into stainless steel products.

Inco's activities are divided into 2 major areas. Its primary metals operations produce nickel, copper, platinum-group metals, gold, silver, cobalt, sulfuric acid, and liquid sulfur dioxide. These operations include nickel production in Canada and Indonesia and refining in Canada and Wales. The company is spending $250 million to search for new ore as part of its strategy of expanding and modernizing its holdings.

Inco's 2nd focus is on metal alloys and engineered products. Inco Alloys International (IAI) runs plants in the US and the UK and produces nickel alloys for the aerospace, energy, and other major industries. Inco Engineered Products manufactures metal products in the UK, Belgium, and the US. Other, minor businesses range from the manufacture of mining equipment to venture capital funding.

NYSE symbol: N
Fiscal year ends: December 31

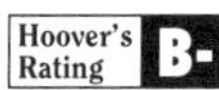

WHO

Chairman and CEO: Donald J. Phillips, age 61, $1,030,000 pay
VC: Walter Curlook, age 61
VC and CFO: Ian McDougall, age 60
President: Michael D. Sopko, age 52
EVP, General Counsel, and Secretary: Scott M. Hand, age 48
VP Human Resources: James D. Guiry, age 57
Auditors: Price Waterhouse
Employees: 19,387

WHEN

Hundreds of millions of years ago, a meteorite slammed into the earth, punching a hole that allowed molten, mineral-rich material to bubble up to the crust. The mineral treasures just below Canada's landscape were hidden until 1883 when a Canadian Pacific Railway blacksmith noticed copper and nickel deposits in an excavation in the Sudbury Basin.

Two companies — the Orford Nickel and Copper Company and the Canadian Copper Company — tried to exploit the ore but were confounded by the lack of a process to separate nickel, all but worthless at the time, and copper. In 1890 Orford, led by Robert Mearns Thompson, patented a process for separation, just as the US Navy was beginning to use a nickel-steel alloy for armaments.

Enter financier J. P. Morgan, father of the newly formed US Steel: with Morgan's assistance Orford and Canadian Copper combined with 5 smaller companies (Anglo-American Iron; American Nickel Works; Nickel Corporation, Limited; Vermillion Mining of Ontario; and Société Minière Caledonienne) in 1902 to form New Jersey–based International Nickel Company. The company in 1916 formed a Canadian subsidiary, International Nickel Company of Canada.

After WWI, sales plummeted 60% and International Nickel, under President Robert Crooks Stanley, cut costs. In a 1928 restructuring the Canadian subsidiary became the parent company, and in 1929 International Nickel bought Mond Nickel, a British refiner of nickel and copper ores. With the Mond deal International Nickel controlled the world's nickel output. In the 1950s it accounted for 85% of non-Communist production.

Oil crises and inflation decreased demand for metals and battered International Nickel in the 1970s and early 1980s. In 1974 International Nickel launched a successful takeover bid for ESB Ray-O-Vac, the world's largest maker of batteries, and in 1976 International Nickel shortened its name to Inco Ltd. The battery operations were sold in the early 1980s.

Inco continued to suffer from lack of demand for its metals until 1986. CEO Donald Phillips cut employees and invested heavily in techniques to boost productivity at Inco's mines and refineries. When demand — especially for stainless steel — began its upswing in the late 1980s and prices rose, Inco results went from dismal to delightful. Sales more than doubled from $1.8 billion in 1987 to $3.9 billion in 1989. Sales dropped to $3.1 billion in 1990 as nickel prices took a nosedive, from about $6 a pound to near $4.

Inco, which began prospecting the gold mining business in 1987, announced plans in 1990 to merge gold interests with TVX Mining to spin off a publicly traded, Inco-controlled company called TVX Gold.

WHERE

HQ: Royal Trust Tower, Toronto-Dominion Centre, Toronto, Ontario M5K 1N4, Canada
Phone: 416-361-7511
Fax: 416-361-7781
US HQ: One New York Plaza, New York, NY 10004-2078
US Phone: 212-612-5500
US Fax: 212-612-5770

Inco operates in Canada, the US, the UK, and 16 other countries.

	1990 Sales		1990 Operating Income	
	$ mil.	% of total	$ mil.	% of total
Canada	407	13	467	66
US	961	31	30	4
Europe	1,015	33	60	9
Other countries	725	23	148	21
Adjustments	—	—	(117)	—
Total	**3,108**	**100**	**588**	**100**

WHAT

	1990 Sales		1990 Operating Income	
	$ mil.	% of total	$ mil.	% of total
Primary metals	2,369	76	617	89
Alloys & engineered prods.	688	22	50	7
Other business	51	2	27	4
Adjustments	—	—	(106)	—
Total	**3,108**	**100**	**588**	**100**

Primary Metals
Cobalt
Copper
Gold
Liquid sulfur dioxide
Palladium
Platinum
Primary nickel
Rhodium
Silver
Sulfuric acid

Alloys and Engineered Products
Blades
Casings
Discs
Nickel alloys
Rings
Superalloy tubular products
Vanes
Welding products

Other Businesses
Corrosion testing (LaQue Center for Corrosion Technology, Inc.)
Lightweight aggregates (Western Aggregates, Inc.)
Metals reclamation (International Metals Reclamation Co., Inc.)
Mining equipment (Continuous Mining Systems Ltd.)
Venture capital (Inco Venture Capital Management)

KEY COMPETITORS

Alcan
AMAX
Anglo American
Broken Hill
Ingersoll-Rand
Inland Steel
Nippon Steel
RTZ
USX
Other mining companies

HOW MUCH

	9-Year Growth	1981	1982	1983	1984	1985	1986	1987	1988	1989	1990
Sales ($ mil.)	5.7%	1, 886	1,236	1,173	1,468	1,491	1,452	1,789	3,263	3,948	3,108
Net income ($ mil.)	40.7%	20	(204)	(235)	(77)	52	0	125	691	753	441
Income as % of sales	—	1.1%	(16.5%)	(20.0%)	(5.3%)	3.5%	0.0%	7.0%	21.2%	19.1%	14.2%
Earnings per share ($)	—	(0.10)	(2.82)	(2.69)	(1.02)	0.28	(0.16)	1.09	6.50	7.11	4.18
Stock price – high ($)	—	23.63	14.75	18.75	15.25	15.38	16.88	24.00	35.13	37.63	31.88
Stock price – low ($)	—	12.50	7.88	10.75	8.63	10.38	10.50	11.75	17.38	25.63	22.13
Stock price – close ($)	6.6%	14.25	11.75	14.63	12.38	13.25	11.75	22.00	25.88	26.88	25.38
P/E – high	—	—	—	—	—	55	—	22	5	5	8
P/E – low	—	—	—	—	—	37	—	11	3	4	5
Dividends per share ($)	6.0%	0.59	0.20	0.20	0.20	0.20	0.20	0.20	10.70	0.85	1.00
Book value per share ($)	(0.7%)	16.80	12.98	10.54	9.32	9.68	9.56	10.33	6.51	12.33	15.78

1990 Year-end:
Debt ratio: 34.2%
Return on equity: 29.7%
Cash (mil.): $70
Current ratio: 1.88
Long-term debt (mil.): $893
No. of shares (mil.): 104
Dividends:
1990 average yield: 3.9%
1990 payout: 23.9%
Market value (mil.): $2,650

Stock Price History High/Low 1981–90

40
35
30
25
20
15
10
5
0

THE INDUSTRIAL BANK OF JAPAN, LTD.

OVERVIEW

Industrial Bank of Japan is the 6th largest bank in the world and the largest of the 3 so-called long-term credit banks. Created as a government entity to advance Japanese interests by financing Japanese industry, now-private IBJ boasts that it does business with 90% of Japan's top 200 corporations. The bank often places its alumni executives at the highest levels of those companies, and IBJ has been described as an aristocrat among banks.

Its power in Japan is obscured by its relatively few locations. As a wholesale bank, barred from seeking public deposits, it has only 28 branches and a mere 5,500 employees. IBJ's profits dipped in 1990, because its traditional Japanese heavy-industry clients have stumbled. Standard & Poor's has stripped it of its triple-A rating.

The bank has turned to a robust growth plan overseas, though, where it is unfettered by Japanese legal restraints on combining banking, securities underwriting, and trust banking. In the US, it is an active player in mergers and acquisitions and has even endowed professorships at Harvard and Stanford.

WHEN

After Japan met the West in the 19th century, the Meiji Restoration replaced the old ways of the shogunate with a national imperative to modernize (1868). Prince Masayoshi Matsukata, the Meiji finance minister, shaped the country's modern banking system.
Out of Matsukata's plan came specialized, government-controlled banks designed to provide long-term financing for commerce.

Industrial Bank of Japan, its specialty the fledgling industries arising from the Meiji reforms, was formed in 1902. Almost immediately IBJ had to finance Japan's first war against a European power, Russia.

IBJ grew along with Japanese industry. Before WWII it helped finance Japanese incursions into China. During the war the Japanese government leaned more and more on the bank's financing of the war machine. In 1944, faced with imminent defeat, the government assigned 2,000 key companies to the top 4 banks of Japan. Then the government ordered the banks to grant the companies unlimited credit. After Japan was beaten, US occupiers attempted to "demilitarize" IBJ. One law forced IBJ to write down ¥7.5 billion in war-related loans. IBJ was nearly disbanded, but the Japanese government convinced the Americans to allow the bank to continue, its direct links with the government severed.

Once restored, IBJ, along with its sister long-term banks, prospered during Japan's resurgence in the 1950s and 1960s. In the 1960s IBJ helped create Nippon Steel through a merger. In 1971 the bank received permission to establish overseas branches.

In the 1980s IBJ fell prey to lower demand for loans, partly because of the oil shocks of the late 1970s and partly because wealthy Japanese clients could finance growth through abundant cash or through issuing bonds. But IBJ began to change in mid-decade by diversifying its activities. It expanded overseas with successful Eurobond issues, and in 1985 it bought J. Henry Schroder Bank & Trust, a New York–based merchant bank with $5.2 billion in assets, and renamed it IBJ Schroder Bank & Trust. It bought Aubrey G. Lanston & Co., a primary dealer (transacting business directly with the Federal Reserve Bank) in US Treasury securities (1986) and formed an American subsidiary, the Bridgeford Group (1990), to focus on mergers and acquisitions.

In 1991 new president Yoh Kurosawa declared that the bank intends to immerse itself in the securities and trust businesses. Anticipating deregulation of the domestic financial industry, IBJ has purchased stakes in 2 medium-sized securities firms, New Japan Securities and Wako Securities.

HOW MUCH

$=¥135 (Dec. 31, 1990)	9-Year Growth	1981	1982	1983	1984	1985	1986	1987	1988	1989	1990
Assets (¥ bil.)	13.8%	13,589	15,781	17,713	18,723	22,279	24,768	28,276	32,785	37,449	43,603
Net income (¥ bil.)	21.3%	15	40	41	42	44	49	55	75	94	83
Income as % of assets	—	0.1%	0.3%	0.2%	0.2%	0.2%	0.2%	0.2%	0.2%	0.2%	0.2%
Earnings per share (¥)	17.3%	*8*	*19*	*20*	*20*	*21*	*24*	*27*	*35*	*41*	*35*
Stock price – high (¥)	—	—	—	405	850	1,640	2,650	5,500	4,500	6,540	6,740
Stock price – low (¥)	—	—	—	397	400	844	1,000	2,480	2,520	4,010	2,090
Stock price – close (¥)	—	—	—	—	—	1,080	2,240	2,700	4,350	6,380	3,300
P/E – high	—	—	—	20	42	77	112	206	128	158	190
P/E – low	—	—	—	20	20	40	42	93	72	97	59
Dividends per share (¥)	6.1%	5.00	5.75	6.00	6.50	7.00	7.00	7.50	7.50	8.00	8.50
Book value per share (¥)	12.9%	172	167	181	196	210	226	246	361	485	513

1990 Year-end:
Equity as % of assets: 2.8%
Return on equity: 7.1%
Cash (bil.): ¥6,600
No. of shares (mil.): 2,351
Dividends:
1990 average yield: 0.3%
1990 payout: 24.0%
Market value (mil.): $57,469
Assets (mil.): $322,985
Sales (mil.): $21,453

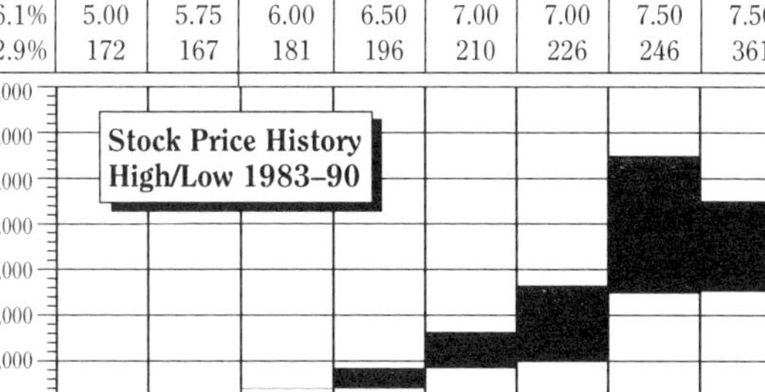

Note: Unconsolidated data

Principal exchange: Tokyo
Fiscal year ends: March 31

Hoover's Rating **B**

WHO

Chairman: Kaneo Nakamura, age 67
President: Yoh Kurosawa, age 65
Deputy President: Tatsuo Goda
Deputy President: Hideo Ishihara
Managing Director and General Manager of Personnel: Kazuhide Kashiwabara
Auditors: Chuo Shinko Audit Corporation
Employees: 5,500

WHERE

HQ: 3-3 Marunouchi 1-chome, Chiyoda-ku, Tokyo 100, Japan
Phone: 011-81-3-3214-1111
Fax: 011-81-3-3201-7643
US HQ: The Industrial Bank of Japan Trust Company, 245 Park Ave., New York, NY 10167
US Phone: 212-557-3500
US Fax: 212-692-9075

Industrial Bank of Japan operates 26 domestic branches, 9 overseas branches, 21 representative offices, and 1 agency. It also owns 12 major overseas subsidiaries.

WHAT

	1990 Assets ¥ bil.	% of total
Cash & due from banks	6,609	15
Trading account securities	85	—
Investment securities	6,977	16
Loans & bills discounted	23,017	53
Foreign exchanges	315	1
Other assets	2,297	5
Customers' liabilities for acceptances, guarantees	4,303	10
Total	**43,603**	**100**

Major Overseas Subsidiaries
Aubrey G. Lanston & Co. Inc. (US government securities)
Banque IBJ (France) SA
The Bridgeford Group, Inc. (mergers and acquisitions, US)
Execution Services Inc. (brokerage services, US)
IBJ Asia Ltd. (Hong Kong)
IBJ Australia Bank Ltd.
IBJ Futures Pte. Ltd. (futures trading, Singapore)
IBJ International Ltd. (UK)
IBJ Merchant Bank (Singapore) Ltd.
IBJ Schroder Bank & Trust Co. (98.3%, US)
"IBJ-CA Consult" Handels- und Investitionsberatungsgesellschaft mbH (Austria)
I.M.I.B.J. SpA (50%, financial consulting, Italy)
The Industrial Bank of Japan (Canada)
The Industrial Bank of Japan (Luxembourg) SA
The Industrial Bank of Japan (Switzerland) Ltd.
The Industrial Bank of Japan Trust Co. (US)
Industriebank von Japan (Deutschland) Aktiengesellschaft (83.3%)
P.T. Bumi Daya — IBJ Leasing (60%)
P.T. IBJ Indonesia Bank (85%)
Saehan Merchant Banking Corp. (Korea)

KEY COMPETITORS

Barclays
Canadian Imperial
Chase Manhattan
Chemical Banking
Citicorp
Crédit Lyonnais
CS Holding
Dai-Ichi Kangyo
Deutsche Bank
HSBC
J.P. Morgan
Royal Bank
Union Bank of Switzerland
Other money-center banks
Securities underwriting firms

IRI HOLDING

OVERVIEW

IRI is the government-owned holding company of Italy's largest industrial group. Through its *finanziarie* (2nd-tier holding companies), IRI controls over 500 companies engaged in widely varied enterprises, some of which are listed on the Milan Stock Exchange. In 1989 the IRI Group employed 2.5% of Italy's workforce and accounted for 3.1% of the country's exports of manufactured goods. The group has contributed significantly to economic growth in southern Italy.

IRI companies' 1989 share of Italian production was enormous: 89% in cast iron, 45% in steel, 62% in power plants, and 70% in shipbuilding. In the same year IRI's Italian market share was 32% in ice cream, 18% in frozen foods, and 14% in bank loans. About 60% of Italy's highways are operated by the group. IRI owns 84.9% of Alitalia (airline) and operates Italy's telephone and broadcasting systems.

As a state-owned organization, IRI remains subject to political influence, but it achieved an extra degree of autonomy after hard-nosed business decisions ended 12 consecutive years of losses in 1986. IRI is trying to globalize and is increasingly tapping private sources of capital by taking its subsidiary companies public.

WHEN

The Depression of the 1930s drove many major Italian enterprises to insolvency, in turn threatening their creditor banks. The Italian government established IRI as a temporary, Resolution Trust–style holding company in 1933 to rescue the banks and sell off their unwanted assets. IRI soon controlled many troubled businesses, including Alfa Romeo, 3 regional telephone companies (consolidated as STET), and 3 major Italian banks: Banca Commerciale Italiana, Credito Italiano, and Banco di Roma.

IRI established 2 more *finanziarie*, FINMARE (shipping) and FINSIDER (steel), and was given permanent status by the Mussolini regime in 1937. The Fascist state directed IRI to focus on businesses most useful to the military. In 1939 IRI built an aircraft engine plant near Naples.

IRI sustained heavy damage during WWII and experienced difficulty recovering from the war as pressure from labor and political groups limited the organization's ability to reduce employment. IRI began to emerge from its malaise with the construction of its Cornigliano steel mill, which had been started before the war but dismantled by the Nazis. Major expansion in steel production followed. In 1952 the government turned over control of RAI, the national broadcaster, to IRI.

In 1955 the government had trouble financing road construction and turned to IRI to raise money and build and operate *autostrade* (highways). Other government-inspired transactions of the 1950s included the purchases of a large bankrupt textile company, the rest of the regional telephone companies, and control of Alitalia. In 1957 IRI was instructed to help develop the economy of southern Italy. In the 1960s, when the government nationalized the electric utility operations of IRI unit SME, the *finanziaria* became a food processor instead.

In the early 1970s IRI was, in some quarters, considered to be a model state enterprise, but later in the decade heavy debt, surging interest rates, economic recession, Japanese competition in steel, and a load of failing companies forced on IRI by the government led to mounting losses. In 1982 economics professor Romano Prodi became president and began slashing payroll and selling businesses. He sold Alfa Romeo to Fiat in 1986 and sold shares of IRI companies to the public. In 1986 IRI returned to profitability.

IRI's SGS Microelettronica chipmaking unit merged with a Thomson CSF subsidiary in 1987. The next year the troubled FINSIDER steel unit began restructuring in an effort to trim losses while maintaining an Italian steel industry. In 1990 IRI announced that it would consider merging its 2 biggest banks to form Italy's largest banking group.

HOW MUCH

$=L1,125 (Dec. 31, 1990)	5-Year Growth	1981	1982	1983	1984	1985	1986	1987	1988	1989	1990
Sales (L bil.)[1]	4.1%	—	—	—	46,585	50,536	52,583	53,006	59,017	66,747	—
Net income (L bil.)[2]	—	—	—	—	(2,036)	(850)	367	247	1,263	1,606	1,100
Income as % of sales	—	—	—	—	(4.4%)	(1.7%)	0.7%	0.5%	2.1%	2.4%	—
Employees (thou.)											
Industrial	(2.2%)	—	—	—	443	420	408	361	358	363	—
Banking	(2.1%)	—	—	—	64	63	62	61	60	53	—
Total	—	—	525	516	506	483	470	422	418	416	—
Book value (L bil.)	3.5%	—	—	—	16,302	20,520	23,403	20,722	20,049	22,259	—

1989 Year-end:
Debt ratio: 55.4%
Return on equity: 8.7%
Cash (bil.): —
Long-term debt (bil.): L36,907
No. of shares (mil.): —
Dividends:
1990 average yield: —
1990 payout: —
Market value (mil.): $34,445[3]
Sales (mil.): $59,331

[1] Value of production [2] Preliminary results for 1990 [3] Market value of listed group companies using 1989 prices and exchange rates

Government-owned company
Fiscal year ends: December 31

Hoover's Rating **C-**

WHO

Chairman: Franco Nobili
VC: Pietro Armani
Central Manager, Finance Division: Renato Cassaro
Chairman, Board of Auditors: Domenico Tosato
Employees: 416,193

WHERE

HQ: Istituto per la Ricostruzione Industriale, Via Vittorio Veneto 89, 00187 Rome, Italy
Phone: 011-39-6-47271
Fax: 011-39-6-47272308
US HQ: Alitalia, 666 Fifth Ave., New York, NY 10103
US Phone: 212-903-3300
US Fax: 212-903-3331

Although the IRI Group holds interests in companies in 32 countries, most of its operations are in Italy.

	1989 Sales	
	L bil.	% of total
Italy	57,220	86
Other countries	9,527	14
Total	**66,747**	**100**

WHAT

	1989 Sales		1989 Net Income	
	L bil.	% of total	L bil.	% of total
ALITALIA	4,899	7	(217)	—
Banking	—	—	730	26
CEMENTIR	380	1	23	1
FINCANTIERI	2,221	3	(254)	—
FINMARE	1,771	3	16	1
FINMECCANICA	8,126	12	94	3
FINSIDER	2,615	4	(153)	—
FINSIEL	892	1	17	1
ILVA	10,760	15	208	7
ITALIMPIANTI	2,054	3	(47)	—
ITALSTAT	5,556	8	154	6
RAI	3,399	5	4	—
SOFIN	93	—	2	—
SME	4,836	7	98	4
STET	21,977	31	1,355	49
Other	353	—	53	2
Adjustments	(3,185)	—	(477)	—
Total	**66,747**	**100**	**1,606**	**100**

Major Group Holdings
ALITALIA (84.9%, aviation)
Banca Commerciale Italiana SpA (56.6%)
Banco di Roma SpA (87.5%)
CEMENTIR (51.2%, cement)
Compagnia Finanziamenti e Rifinanziamenti SpA
Credito Italiano SpA
FINCANTIERI (shipbuilding)
FINMARE (99.9%, shipping)
FINMECCANICA (high technology and mechanical engineering)
FINSIEL (83.3%, data processing)
ILVA-FINSIDER (steel)
ITALIMPIANTI (industrial engineering)
ITALSTAT (civil engineering)
RAI (99.6%, broadcasting)
SME (64.6%, food production and retailing)
SOFIN (tourism and environment)
STET (65.8%, telecommunications)

KEY COMPETITORS

IRI competes with many companies, from steelmakers to banks.

ISUZU MOTORS LTD.

OVERVIEW

Isuzu is a world leader in truck production and a renowned manufacturer of diesel engines. In Japan Isuzu ranks 2nd after Hino Motors in heavy- and medium-duty trucks, first in light trucks, and 8th in auto sales. In the US Isuzu is 10th in light trucks and holds a negligible auto market share. Sales have been soft in the US and Japan in 1991. The company projects losses through 1992.

General Motors owns 37.5% of Isuzu after selling a 2% stake in 1989. The companies are partners in truck production in the UK and Australia. Isuzu makes the GEO Storm and has announced that it will market GM cars in Japan. Despite huge US dealer inventory levels, Isuzu plans to raise US production of light trucks and is asking GM to sell them.

Isuzu expects growth in Southeast Asia and in 1990 announced a linkup with P.T. Gaya Motor to make pickup trucks in Indonesia. Isuzu already operates factories in Thailand, Malaysia, and Egypt.

WHEN

After collaborating on car and truck production for 21 years, Tokyo Ishikawajima Shipbuilding and Engineering and Tokyo Gas and Electric Industrial formed Tokyo Motors, Inc., in 1937. The partners, Japanese pioneers in automotive manufacturing, had begun by producing the A truck (1918) and the A9 car (1922) under licenses from Wolseley (UK). A lengthy study of diesel technology resulted in the 1937 introduction of the company's first air-cooled diesel motor.

Tokyo Motors produced its first truck under the Isuzu nameplate in 1938 and by 1943 was selling trucks powered by its own diesel engines, mostly to the Japanese military. The company spun off Hino Heavy Industries, predecessor of Hino Motors, in 1942.

The company renamed itself Isuzu (Japanese for "50 bells") in 1949. With generous public and private sector financing and truck orders from the US Army during the Korean War, Isuzu survived and established a reputation as a top diesel engine and truck producer. A pact with the Rootes Group (UK) enabled Isuzu to enter automaking. Beginning in 1953 Isuzu built Rootes's Hillman Minx in Japan. The company attempted to marry diesels with autos in 1961 when it introduced a diesel-powered car. A few years later the noisy auto was discontinued.

Despite its strong reputation as a truck builder, Isuzu suffered financially, and by the late 1960s its bankers were shopping the company around to more stable competitors. General Motors, after witnessing rapid Japanese progress in US and Asian auto markets, bought 34.2% of Isuzu in 1971. In the 1970s Isuzu launched the popular Gemini car and gained rapid entry into the US through GM, exporting vehicles including the Chevy Luv truck and Buick Opel.

In 1981, as exports to GM waned, Isuzu set up its own dealer network in the US. In the same year GM CEO Roger Smith told a stunned Isuzu chairman T. Okamoto that, as a foreign partner in auto production, Isuzu lacked the global scale GM sought and asked Okamoto for help in buying a piece of Honda. After Honda declined and GM settled for 5% of Suzuki, Isuzu extended its GM ties, building the GEO Storm and establishing joint production facilities in the UK and Australia.

Despite the widely noticed advertising campaign featuring a lying Joe Isuzu, the company suffered in the 1980s as it failed to retain a significant share of the US passenger car market. Post-1985 yen appreciation hurt exports. Subaru-Isuzu Automotive, a joint venture with Fuji Heavy Industries, started production in Lafayette, Indiana, in 1989. The factory was intended to save both companies money by halving the cost of investment, but faltering Subaru sales and inefficient operations have plagued the plant.

HOW MUCH

$=¥135 (Dec. 31, 1990)	9-Year Growth	1981[1]	1982[1]	1983	1984	1985	1986	1987	1988	1989	1990
Sales (¥ bil.)	8.5%	727	719	754	872	1,139	1,120	1,086	1,212	1,324	1,520
Net income (¥ bil.)[2]	—	9	6	(5)	(17)	17	12	7	7	17	(8)
Income as % of sales	—	1.2%	0.8%	(0.7%)	(2.0%)	1.4%	1.1%	0.6%	0.5%	1.3%	(0.5%)
Earnings per share (¥)[2]	—	10	7	(6)	(20)	18	(13)	7	7	16	(8)
Stock price – high (¥)	—	535	445	402	345	445	376	466	982	1,036	1,160
Stock price – low (¥)	—	190	257	289	240	291	282	280	345	782	445
Stock price – close (¥)	1.5%	444	390	336	329	350	315	380	881	975	506
P/E – high	—	52	62	—	—	24	—	65	150	63	—
P/E – low	—	19	36	—	—	16	—	39	53	48	—
Dividends per share (¥)	1.1%	4.55	4.55	4.55	0.00	0.00	0.00	0.00	4.55	4.55	5.00
Book value per share (¥)	4.2%	110	113	101	76	115	98	128	140	153	160

1990 Year-end:
Debt ratio: 56.2%
Return on equity: —
Cash (bil.): ¥140
Long-term debt (bil.): ¥211
No. of shares (mil.): 1,031
Dividends:
1990 average yield: 1.0%
1990 payout: —
Market value (mil.): $3,864
Sales (mil.): $11,259

Stock Price History High/Low 1981–90

1,200
1,000
800
600
400
200
0

[1] Unconsolidated data [2] Including extraordinary items

OTC symbol: ISUZY (ADR)
Fiscal year ends: October 31

WHO

Chairman: Joji Mizusawa
President: Kazuo Tobiyama, age 65
EVP: Kazuhira Seki
President, American Isuzu Motors Inc.: Kozo Sakaino
Auditors: Century Audit Corporation
Employees: 13,427

WHERE

HQ: 26-1, Minami-oi 6-chome, Shinagawa-ku, Tokyo 140, Japan
Phone: 011-81-3-5471-1285
Fax: 011-81-3-5471-1086
US HQ: American Isuzu Motors Inc., 13181 Crossroads Pkwy. North, 4th Fl., City of Industry, CA 91746
US Phone: 213-699-0500
US Fax: 213-723-2125

Isuzu's primary manufacturing plants are located in Japan, the US, the UK, and Thailand.

	1990 Sales ¥ bil.	1990 Sales % of total
Japan	611	51
Other countries	585	49
Adjustments	324	—
Total	**1,520**	**100**

WHAT

	1990 Sales ¥ bil.	1990 Sales % of total
Heavy- and medium-duty trucks	276	23
Light-duty trucks	401	34
Passenger cars	178	15
Engines, components & other	341	28
Adjustments	324	—
Total	**1,520**	**100**

Vehicle Models (US Markets)

- Amigo
- I-Mark
- Impulse
- Rodeo
- Stylus
- Trooper
- Trucks (various models)

Principal Subsidiaries and Affiliates

- American Isuzu Motors Inc.
- Automotive Foundry Co., Ltd. (Japan)
- Automotive Manufacturers (Malaysia) Sdn. Bhd.
- Convesco Vehicle Sales GmbH (Germany)
- Daikin Mfg. Co., Ltd. (Japan)
- General Motors Egypt S.A.E.
- I.K. Coach Co., Ltd. (buses, Japan)
- IBC Vehicles Ltd. (UK)
- Isuzu Motors America, Inc.
- Isuzu Motors Co. (Thailand) Ltd.
- Isuzu Motors Finance Co., Ltd. (Japan)
- Isuzu Truck of America, Inc.
- Isuzu–General Motors Australia Ltd.
- Jidosha Buhin Kogyo Co., Ltd. (Japan)
- P.T. Mesin Isuzu Indonesia
- Shatai Kogyo Co., Ltd. (Japan)
- Subaru-Isuzu Automotive Inc. (US)
- Zexel Corp. (Japan)

KEY COMPETITORS

- BMW
- Caterpillar
- Chrysler
- Cummins Engine
- Daewoo
- Daimler-Benz
- Dial
- Fiat
- General Motors
- Honda
- Hyundai
- Mazda
- Mitsubishi
- Navistar
- Nissan
- PACCAR
- Peugeot
- Renault
- Saab-Scania
- Suzuki
- Toyota
- Volkswagen
- Volvo

ITO-YOKADO CO., LTD.

OVERVIEW

Ito-Yokado is Japan's 2nd largest supermarket chain and a major player in virtually every sector of the Japanese retail industry, where it ranks 2nd in sales and 1st in earnings. Ito-Yokado's chains of Western-style, self-service stores (superstores, convenience stores, restaurants, department stores, supermarkets, and specialty stores) have helped to revolutionize retailing in Japan.

The company's founder, Masatoshi Ito, built his retail empire by imitation rather than innovation. Ito makes a yearly pilgrimage to the US, where he visits American stores for new ideas to bring back to Japan. Occasionally he brings back the stores as well. So far he has bought and successfully transported several franchises to his homeland, including 7-Eleven (which has become Japan's leading convenience store chain), Denny's (restaurants), Oshman's (sporting goods), and Robinson's (department stores).

Ironically, the company recently acquired control of Southland (owner of 7-Eleven), the Dallas-based company that was once Ito-Yokado's model. The deal gives the company a major presence in the US. Ito-Yokado has plans to streamline operations to make US 7-Elevens the models of Japanese efficiency.

NASDAQ symbol: IYCOY (ADR)
Fiscal year ends: Last day of February

WHO

President and CEO: Masatoshi Ito
EVP and Chief Administrative Officer: Toshifumi Suzuki
EVP and COO: Hyozo Morita
Managing Director, Finance: Tatsuhiro Sekie
Senior Managing Director, Corporate Personnel: Hiroei Masukawa
Auditors: Coopers & Lybrand
Employees: 31,110

WHEN

In the early 1940s Masatoshi Ito graduated from a commercial high school in Yokohama. After briefly working for Mitsubishi, he left to fight for Japan in 1944. After WWII the 21-year-old joined his mother and brother, who were operating a small family clothing shop (founded in 1913) in the Kitasenju district of Tokyo. The small enterprise grew into a respectable department store, which Ito took charge of following his brother's death in 1956. In 1958 the company was incorporated as Kabushiki Kaisha Yokado.

In 1961 Ito was invited to the US by National Cash Register (NCR), a company interested in replacing Japanese retailers' abacuses with cash registers. While in the US, Ito attended an NCR seminar on self-service retailing and visited such successful retailers as J. C. Penney, Sears, and Safeway.

Confident that US-style retailing could be transplanted across the Pacific, Ito quickly opened 2 superstores (low-priced food, clothing, and household products stores) in high-traffic areas of Tokyo. The superstores were highly successful, and by 1965 Ito had opened 6 more. That same year he changed the company's name to Ito-Yokado.

In 1972 the company launched Famil, a chain of family-style restaurants serving American, Japanese, and Chinese food. It followed this by opening several Denny's coffee-shop restaurants in Japan. Returning to the US in 1972 to meet with the Dallas-based Southland Corporation (7-Eleven convenience stores), Ito negotiated a royalty agreement and opened Japan's first 7-Eleven in 1974.

The new 7-Elevens in Japan quickly stole much of the market from the small mom-and-pop stores that had dominated Japanese retailing (Ito's 7-Elevens were small enough to avoid Japan's Large-Scale Retail Store Law, which was designed to protect the traditional mom-and-pop stores by establishing rigid guidelines for forming big stores). Ito capitalized on those shops that could not compete by letting them become 7-Eleven franchisees, thus sprouting stores all across Japan. In 1975 the company established its York Mart subsidiary to open a chain of supermarkets in areas that could not support superstores.

From visits to the US in the 1980s, Ito acquired the rights to establish Robinson's department stores (from Associated Dry Goods, now part of May Co., 1984) and Oshman's (sporting goods, 1985) in Japan. In 1989 the company bought 58 7-Elevens in Hawaii. The following year Ito purchased 70% of the struggling Southland Corporation for $430 million.

WHERE

HQ: 1-4 Shibakoen 4-chome, Minato-ku, Tokyo 105, Japan
Phone: 011-81-3-3459-2111
Fax: 011-81-3-3459-6873 (Investor Relations)
US HQ: One Union Square, 600 University St., Suite 2829, Seattle, WA 98101-1129
US Phone: 206-624-6682
US Fax: 206-624-6778

The company has 5,409 stores in Japan, 58 7-Elevens in Hawaii, and 7,223 7-Elevens in the US and Canada through its holdings in Southland.

7-Eleven Locations	No. of Stores
Japan	4,270
Hawaii	58
Continental US & Canada	7,223
Total	**11,551**

WHAT

	1990 Sales		1990 Operating Income	
	$ mil.	% of total	$ mil.	% of total
Superstores & other retailing	12,047	87	795	58
Convenience stores	1,040	7	513	37
Restaurants	780	6	70	5
Total	**13,867**	**100**	**1,378**	**100**

Stores and Restaurants	No.
7-Eleven (convenience stores)	11,551
Daikuma (discount stores)	17
Denny's (restaurants)	353
Famil (restaurants)	323
Ito-Yokado (superstores)	140
Mary Ann (women's wear)	66
Oshman's (sporting goods)	2
Robinson's (department stores)	2
Steps (men's wear)	29
York Mart (supermarkets)	42
Other superstores	5
Other	160
Total	**12,690**

Food Processing
Daily Foods
I.Y. Foods
Kanseien
Nihon Nosuisan
York Seika

Real Estate
Nittsu System Kaihatsu
Urawa Building
Y.R. Kaihatsu
Yokado

Service
Union Lease
York Keibi

Other
Southland Corporation (70%)

KEY COMPETITORS

Circle K
Hudson's Bay
Kroger
Marks and Spencer
Vendex
Specialty and discount stores
Oil company convenience stores

HOW MUCH

Stock prices are for ADRs ADR = 4 shares	9-Year Growth	1981	1982	1983	1984	1985	1986	1987	1988	1989	1990
Sales ($ mil.)	16.2%	3,592	3,930	4,239	4,067	6,674	8,374	10,718	12,007	11,170	13,867
Net income ($ mil.)	28.2%	56	63	91	99	177	227	340	406	392	524
Income as % of sales	—	1.6%	1.6%	2.1%	2.4%	2.7%	2.7%	3.2%	3.4%	3.5%	3.8%
Earnings per share ($)	26.3%	0.63	0.68	0.96	1.02	1.78	2.29	3.38	4.00	3.84	5.16
Stock price – high ($)	—	13.79	11.33	21.00	31.74	51.03	106.82	110.45	140.00	143.50	130.00
Stock price – low ($)	—	9.31	7.61	10.93	20.49	28.72	47.83	75.23	100.00	100.00	85.00
Stock price – close ($)	29.4%	10.23	11.18	20.58	30.52	49.79	92.27	108.64	130.46	131.00	103.88
P/E – high	—	22	17	22	31	29	47	33	35	37	25
P/E – low	—	15	11	11	20	16	21	22	25	26	16
Dividends per share ($)	13.9%	0.18	0.19	0.22	0.23	0.34	0.47	0.60	0.33	0.93	0.58
Book value per share ($)	21.3%	6.79	7.60	8.61	8.81	14.48	19.02	26.03	30.84	30.02	38.62

1990 Year-end:
Debt ratio: 13.6%
Return on equity: 15.0%
Cash (mil.): $2,147
Current ratio: 1.28
Long-term debt (mil.): $613
No. of shares (mil.): 101
Dividends:
1990 average yield: 0.6%
1990 payout: 18.0%
Market value (mil.): $10,445

Stock Price History
High/Low 1981–90

160
140
120
100
80
60
40
20
0

JAPAN AIRLINES COMPANY, LTD.

OVERVIEW

Japan Airlines (JAL) carries on a tradition as Japan's international flag carrier even though the government no longer holds an interest. In 1990 it ranked as the world's 2nd most profitable airline, after Singapore Airlines, and was rated among the world's top 3 for quality service by the *Zagat Airline Survey*.

As Asia's largest airline, JAL expects to benefit from continued economic growth in the Pacific Rim. Currently 10 million Japanese nationals travel overseas annually; this number is expected to double by the year 2000. To accommodate this growth, JAL has ordered $25 billion worth of new planes and is expanding facilities at both Tokyo International (Haneda) and New Tokyo International (Narita) airports. In 1991 the airline formed a new subsidiary, Japan Air Charter, which operates from less-congested regional airports. Construction of a new airport on Osaka Bay will also help JAL meet capacity requirements.

JAL owns at least 20% of more than 200 affiliates, in businesses ranging from airlines to publications. Two of the largest, Japan Asia Airways and Okinawa-based Southwest Air Lines, operate regional and commuter airline services. Another, Japan Airlines Development, manages 20 Nikko hotels worldwide. JAL also operates its own computer reservation system, AXESS.

WHEN

After WWII, foreign airlines, chiefly Northwest and Pan Am, provided air service to Japan, which was not allowed to form its own airline until the end of US occupation in 1951. That year a group of bankers, led by Seijiro Yanagito, founded Japanese Air Lines. The Allied Peace Treaty forbade the airline to use Japanese flight crews; therefore, in the early days, it leased pilots and equipment from Northwest. In 1953 the airline was reorganized as Japan Air Lines, with the government and the public owning equal shares. This company was a sort of revival of the prewar Nihon Koku Kabushiki Kaisha, or Japan Air Transport Company, the Japanese national airline created by the government in 1928 and dissolved by the Allies after Japan's defeat in 1945.

Under Yanagito, who ran the company until 1961, JAL expanded quickly, opening a transpacific route from Tokyo to San Francisco (1954) and extending regional service to Hong Kong (1955), Bangkok (1956), and Singapore (1958). The airline gained a foothold in Europe in 1961, after opening a polar route from Tokyo to London and Paris. Service from Tokyo to Moscow began in 1967. That year JAL formed Southwest Airlines (later Southwest Air Lines) to provide flights between the island of Japan and the Ryukyu Islands. Meanwhile, JAL adopted the crane, the symbol of good luck, as its official symbol (1965).

In 1974 JAL suspended flights to Taipei, mainstay of the Chinese anticommunist government, in favor of establishing service to Beijing and Shanghai. Japan Asia Airways, a new subsidiary, resumed flights to Taipei the next year. JAL ran into problems in the early 1980s, first in 1982, when a mentally unstable JAL pilot crashed his plane into Tokyo Bay, killing 24. Then in 1985 a JAL 747 crashed into a mountainside, killing all but 4 of the 524 on board. Termed the worst single-plane accident in aviation history, this disaster led to the resignation of most of JAL's top executives, including President Yasumoto Tagaki, who assumed full responsibility.

In 1987 the government sold its stake in the airline to the public. Since air transport was no longer nationalized, overseas routes were opened to JAL's long-time domestic competitor, All Nippon Airways (founded as Japan Helicopter and Aeroplane Transport, 1952). JAL also faces stiffer competition from foreign airlines, including United, which started direct service from Chicago to Tokyo in 1991.

HOW MUCH

$=¥135 (Dec. 31, 1990)	9-Year Growth	1981	1982	1983	1984	1985	1986	1987	1988	1989	1990
Sales (¥ bil.)	6.6%	705	777	811	830	923	925	876	972	1,092	1,255
Net income (¥ bil.)	21.4%	3	5	(9)	(3)	11	(4)	(8)	20	20	18
Income as % of sales	—	0.4%	0.7%	(1.1%)	(0.4%)	1.2%	(0.4%)	(0.9%)	2.0%	1.8%	1.4%
Earnings per share (¥)	19.0%	*2*	*4*	*(7)*	*(2)*	*7*	*(3)*	*(5)*	*13*	*13*	*11*
Stock price – high (¥)	—	230	220	226	530	882	1,247	1,824	1,534	1,903	1,940
Stock price – low (¥)	—	206	200	203	221	440	780	1,071	1,116	1,456	921
Stock price – close (¥)	19.6%	215	217	217	503	835	1,216	1,161	1,534	1,883	1,080
P/E – high	—	102	58	—	—	120	—	—	121	142	179
P/E – low	—	91	52	—	—	60	—	—	88	109	85
Dividends per share (¥)	3.3%	3.63	3.63	0.00	0.00	3.63	0.00	0.00	3.63	4.85	4.85
Book value per share (¥)	16.9%	60	63	81	78	95	93	88	101	167	245

1990 Year-end:
Debt ratio: 62.1%
Return on equity: 5.3%
Cash (bil.): ¥486
Long-term debt (bil.): ¥680
No. of shares (mil.): 1,694
Dividends:
1990 average yield: 0.4%
1990 payout: 44.8%
Market value (mil.): $13,552
Sales (mil.): $9,296

Stock Price History High/Low 1981–90

OTC symbol: JAPNY (ADR)
Fiscal year ends: March 31

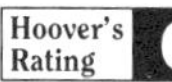

WHO

Chairman: Fumio Watanabe
President: Matsuo Toshimitsu
EVP: Mitsunari Kawano
SVP Accounting Financing and Revenue Accounting: Osamu Igarashi
Auditors: Showa Ota & Co.
Employees: 21,047

WHERE

HQ: Nippon Koku Kabushiki Kaisha, Tokyo Building, 7-3, Marunouchi 2-chome, Chiyoda-ku, Tokyo 100, Japan
Phone: 011-81-3-3284-2315
Fax: 011-81-3-3284-2316
US HQ: 655 5th Ave., New York, NY 10022-5303
US Phone: 212-310-1221
US Fax: 212-310-1230
Reservations: 800-525-3663

JAL serves 63 cities in 31 countries, including the major cities of Japan.

	1990 Sales	
	¥ bil.	% of total
Japan	274	22
Other countries	774	62
Other	207	16
Total	**1,255**	**100**

WHAT

	1990 Sales	
	¥ bil.	% of total
Passenger	860	69
Cargo	188	15
Other	207	16
Total	**1,255**	**100**

Major Airline Subsidiaries
Japan Air Charter (charter services)
Japan Asia Airways Co., Ltd. (regional services in Southeast Asia)
Southwest Air Lines Co., Ltd. (51%, commuter services)

Computer Reservation System
AXESS

Major Non-airline Subsidiaries
Airport Ground Service Co., Ltd. (87.5%, ground support services)
Hotel Nikko of New York, Inc. (hotels and restaurants)
JAL Trading Inc. (70.5%, insurance)
Japan Airlines Development Co., Ltd. (67.1%, hotel management)
Japan Creative Tours Co., Ltd. (75.1%, package tours)

Flight Equipment	No.	Orders
Boeing 747	66	30
Boeing 767	16	—
DC-10	16	—
MD-11	—	10
Total	**98**	**40**

KEY COMPETITORS

America West
AMR
British Airways
Continental Airlines
Delta
KLM
Lufthansa
NWA
Qantas
SAS
Singapore Airlines
Swire Pacific
UAL

JARDINE MATHESON HOLDINGS LTD.

OVERVIEW

Jardine Matheson is a holding company controlled by the Keswick family, descendants of one of the company's founders. Jardine's investments include prime Hong Kong real estate; Mandarin Oriental hotels, including The Oriental, Bangkok; Wellcome (Hong Kong and Taiwan) and Franklins (Australia) supermarkets; Pizza Hut restaurants in Hawaii; trading and shipping companies; car dealerships; and financial services and insurance companies.

In light of the UK's agreement to transfer control of Hong Kong to China in 1997, Jardine has a goal of reducing its Hong Kong assets to 50% of the company's total. In further anticipation of 1997, Jardine has reincorporated in Bermuda and moved its primary stock listing and regulatory center to London.

WHEN

Scotsmen William Jardine and James Matheson first met in Bombay in 1820. In 1832 they established Jardine, Matheson (Jardine) in Canton, the only city in which China, then a closed society, allowed foreigners to live. The trading company started shipping tea from China to Europe and smuggling opium from India to China. In 1839 Chinese authorities attempted to stop the drug trade, seizing 20,000 chests of opium, 7,000 of them Jardine's. Jardine persuaded Britain to send gunboats to China, precipitating the First Opium War. China lost and signed an 1842 treaty opening 5 ports and ceding Hong Kong to Britain.

Jardine moved its headquarters to Hong Kong and resumed trading in opium. The Second Opium War resulted in the opening of 11 more ports and the legalization of opium importation. Jardine flourished as China opened. The company left the politically dangerous opium business and entered brewing, silk trading, textiles, banking, insurance, and sugar; formed real estate company Hongkong Land (HKL); introduced steamships to China; and built the country's first railroad. In 1930 employment reached 113,000.

The Sino-Japanese war and WWII shut down Jardine. In 1941 Tony Keswick, a Jardine relative and the company's *taipan* (big boss), was shot and injured in Shanghai by a patriotic Japanese community leader. In 1945 Jardine reopened in Hong Kong with an airline, a brewery, textile mills, and real estate operations. Attempts to reestablish operations in China ended in 1954 after the Communist takeover. Proceeds from Jardine's 1961 public offering (oversubscribed 56 to one) were used to expand into shipping.

In 1973 Jardine bought Reunion Properties (real estate, Britain) and Theo H. Davies (trading, sugar, Hawaii). In the 1970s local competition and the diminishing need for Hong Kong trading companies hurt the company. By 1980 Jardine was a takeover target. *Taipan* David Newbigging erected a defense by arranging for extensive crossholdings of Jardine and HKL stock. The heavy debt incurred pushed Jardine to the brink of bankruptcy, forcing the company to sell Reunion.

Tony Keswick's son Simon succeeded Newbigging in 1983 and in the next 2 years sold numerous businesses to lower debt. He invested in Mercedes-Benz distributorships and fast-food franchises, turning Jardine around. In March 1984, as the UK and China negotiated the 1997 transfer of Hong Kong to Chinese control, Keswick announced the relocation of Jardine's legal headquarters to Bermuda. In a 1986 antitakeover transaction, the company created Jardine Strategic Holdings to hold interests in HKL and its spinoffs.

In 1987 Jardine aborted its acquisition of 20% of Bear Stearns (stock brokerage, US) following the 1987 stock market crash. This led to litigation that ended in March 1991 with Jardine's agreeing to pay a $60 million settlement to Bear Stearns.

HOW MUCH

$=HK$7.80 (Dec. 31, 1990)	9-Year Growth	1981	1982	1983	1984	1985	1986	1987	1988	1989	1990[1]
Sales (HK$ mil.)	—	9,266	11,240	10,644	8,881	10,497	10,416	12,720	14,817	15,058	47,069
Net income (HK$ mil.)	10.6%	723	708	139	80	157	499	785	1,113	1,577	1,792
Income as % of sales	—	7.8%	6.3%	1.3%	0.9%	1.5%	4.6%	6.2%	7.5%	10.5%	3.8%
Earnings per share (HK$)	10.3%	*1.36*	*1.26*	*0.20*	*0.13*	*0.30*	*0.90*	*1.47*	*2.04*	*2.95*	3.29
Stock price – high (HK$)	—	19.79	13.29	11.50	10.29	9.86	16.86	28.40	14.90	25.50	37.25
Stock price – low (HK$)	—	8.79	8.07	5.64	3.93	5.75	7.86	8.50	9.90	14.30	22.90
Stock price – close (HK$)	7.9%	14.36	9.29	8.00	6.21	9.79	16.07	10.30	14.60	24.40	28.50
P/E – high	—	15	11	58	79	33	19	19	7	9	11
P/E – low	—	6	6	28	30	19	9	6	5	5	7
Dividends per share (HK$)	7.7%	0.57	0.57	0.29	0.07	0.07	0.29	0.48	0.65	0.95	1.11
Book value per share (HK$)	6.4%	11.91	11.06	9.18	7.32	8.26	8.67	10.02	15.83	18.13	20.75

1990 Year-end:
Debt ratio: 29.2%
Return on equity: 16.9%
Cash (mil.): HK$7,631
Long-term debt (mil.): HK$5,445
No. of shares (mil.): 637
Dividends:
1990 average yield: 3.9%
1990 payout: 33.7%
Market value (mil.): $2,328
Sales (mil.): $6,034

Stock Price History High/Low 1981–90

40
35
30
25
20
15
10
5
0

[1] Accounting change

Principal exchange: London
Fiscal year ends: December 31

WHO

Chairman: Henry Keswick
Managing Director: Nigel Rich
Finance Director: P. J. Collins
Personnel: M. G. Barrow
Auditors: Price Waterhouse
Employees: 120,000

WHERE

HQ: Jardine House, 33-35 Reid St., Hamilton, Bermuda
Hong Kong HQ: Jardine Matheson Ltd., 48th Fl., Jardine House, GPO Box 70, Hong Kong
Phone: 011-852-843-8388
Fax: 011-852-845-9005
US HQ: Theo H. Davies & Co., Davies Pacific Center, 841 Bishop St., Suite 2300, Honolulu, HI 96802
US Phone: 808-531-8531
US Fax: 808-521-7352

Jardine companies operate in 30 states and territories, primarily in the Asia-Pacific region.

	1990 Sales		1990 Pretax Income	
	HK$ mil.	% of total	HK$ mil.	% of total
Hong Kong & China	14,949	32	2,438	56
Australasia	18,424	39	512	12
Europe & Middle East	7,788	17	440	10
North America	2,873	6	122	3
Northeast Asia	1,647	3	586	13
Southeast Asia	1,388	3	283	6
Total	**47,069**	**100**	**4,381**	**100**

WHAT

	1990 Sales		1990 Pretax Income	
	HK$ mil.	% of total	HK$ mil.	% of total
Marketing & distribution	38,789	83	2,132	48
Financial services	2,826	6	621	14
Eng. & constr.	2,972	6	213	5
Transport services	1,361	3	193	4
Property & hotels	1,121	2	1,260	29
Adjustments	—	—	(38)	—
Total	**47,069**	**100**	**4,381**	**100**

Major Subsidiaries and Affiliates

Jardine Fleming (50%)
- Corporate banking
- Investment management
- Stock brokerage

Jardine Insurance Brokers

Jardine Pacific
- Auto dealerships
- Construction
- Property
- Restaurants
- Shipping, security, and financial services
- Trading and distribution

Jardine Strategic (52%)
- Dairy Farm (supermarkets, restaurants, 46%)
- Hongkong Land (real estate, 32.7%)
- Jardine Matheson Holdings (35.5%)
- Mandarin Oriental (hotels, 49.9%)

KEY COMPETITORS

Accor	Hyundai	Samsung
American President	ITT	Swire Pacific
HSBC	Marriott	Financial services companies
Hutchison Whampoa	McDonald's	
Hyatt	Mitsubishi	

JOHN LABATT LTD.

OVERVIEW

John Labatt is Canada's 2nd largest brewer (after Molson), with additional operations in food, broadcasting, and entertainment. Stiff Canadian antitrust laws have prompted the company to expand its marketplace to encompass all of North America. Despite rumors that it might sell, Brascan, a holding company of the Toronto branch of Canada's Bronfman family, still owns 39% of Labatt.

The company's share of the Canadian market increased to over 42% in 1990 largely through the strength of its Labatt's Blue (Canada's favorite beer) and 37 other brands. In the international market Labatt produces such beers as Rolling Rock in the US (through its Latrobe subsidiary, the 9th largest US brewer and growing 16% annually) and Birra Moretti in Italy. Labatt also brews and sells the Budweiser and Michelob brands in Canada under license from Anheuser-Busch.

Labatt's food segment includes Johanna, Sealtest, and Light n' Lively (dairy); Five Roses (flour), and Everfresh (juices).

In the broadcast and entertainment industry, Labatt owns, among other things, 2 Cana dian sports networks and 45% of the Toronto Blue Jays and major interests in a US rock talent agency and a concert promotion company.

Principal exchange: Toronto
Fiscal year ends: April 30

WHO

Chairman: Peter N. T. Widdrington
President and CEO: Sidney M. Oland
VP Human Resources: Robert F. Dolan
VP Finance: Robert G. Vaux
Auditors: Ernst & Young
Employees: 16,500

WHERE

HQ: 451 Ridout St. North, PO Box 5870, Terminal A, London, Ontario N6A 5L3, Canada
Phone: 519-667-7500
Fax: 519-667-7589

Labatt's beer is exported to more than 20 countries.

	1990 Sales		1990 Operating Income	
	C$ mil.	% of total	C$ mil.	% of total
Canada, UK & Italy	3,372	64	240	91
US	1,902	36	24	9
Total	**5,274**	**100**	**264**	**100**

WHEN

John Labatt arrived in London, Ontario, from England in 1833. He started farming and gained a reputation for his malting barley, which he sold to a local innkeeper's brewery. Deciding to start brewing himself, Labatt teamed up with master brewer Samuel Eccles and bought a stake in the innkeeper's operation in 1847.

In the beginning the partners produced only 3 brands of beer (X, XX, XXX). In 1854 Labatt gained full control of the brewery. When the Great Western Railway came, he started shipping his products to nearby cities. Labatt died in 1866, leaving the brewery to his wife and son John II.

John II modernized the company, increased production, and expanded operations as far as the Northwest Territories. In 1911 the company was incorporated as John Labatt Limited. John II died in 1915, a year before Prohibition in Canada, which would bankrupt all but 15 of Ontario's 65 breweries. Labatt survived owing to a loophole in the law that allowed the production of alcohol for export purposes.

During the 1920s and 1930s, the company gained a reputation for generous treatment of employees by introducing vacation pay and insurance benefits at a time when they were quite rare.

After WWII Labatt went public and began a period of rapid expansion, beginning with the acquisition of Toronto-based Copland Brewing in 1946. Ten years later W. H. R. Jarvis became the first nonfamily president of the company.

In the 1960s Schlitz tried to acquire a 40% interest in Labatt but was blocked by US antitrust regulations. By 1965 the company had a brewing capacity of 1.3 million barrels. Shortly thereafter the company began diversifying into food. Throughout this period Brascan acquired increasing interest in Labatt.

In 1980 the company scored a major victory when it made a deal with Anheuser-Busch to brew Budweiser in Canada, where it immediately captured about 8% of the market. With its leadership in beer intact, Labatt went on a decade-long shopping spree, acquiring an interest in the Toronto Blue Jays and several food and entertainment companies. Because Canada's antitrust laws threatened to block further Canadian expansion, Labatt began purchasing US businesses, including Johanna Farms (dairy, 1985) and Latrobe Brewing (Rolling Rock beer, 1987).

In 1989 the company sold Catelli (foods) and purchased 77.5% ownership of Birra Moretti and Prinz Brau (Italy, brewing). In 1991 Labatt sold its US-based JL Foods division ($475 million in 1990 sales) to Heinz.

WHAT

	1990 Sales		1990 Operating Income	
	C$ mil.	% of total	C$ mil.	% of total
Brewing	1,920	36	174	66
Food	3,354	64	90	34
Total	**5,274**	**100**	**264**	**100**

Beer
Birra Moretti
Blue Light
Budweiser (Canada)
Carlsberg (Canada)
Carlsberg Light (Canada)
Club
Crystal
Guinness (Canada)
IPA (Canada)
John Labatt Classic
Keith's
Kokanee
Labatt's Blue
Labatt's Canadian Lager
Labatt's 50
Labatt's Lite
Labatt's Strong Canadian Lager
Légère
Lucky
Michelob (Canada)
Michelob Dry (Canada)
Oland Export
Rolling Rock
Rolling Rock Light
Schooner
Tuborg (Canada)
Twistshandy (Canada)

Broadcast and Entertainment
BCL Entertainment Corp. (45%)
Dome Productions
International Talent Group (50%)
Le Réseau des Sports (70%)
The Sports Network
Supercorp Entertainment (50%)
Toronto Blue Jays (45%)

Food
Ault Foods (dairy)
Everfresh (fruit juice and mineral water)
Johanna Dairies
Ogilvie Mills (flour and grain products)

Affiliates
Allelix Crop Technologies (30%)
Auscan Closures Canada and Company (50%)
Canada Malting (19.9%)
Catelli-Primo (46.4%, grocery products, Trinidad)
McGavin Foods (60%)

HOW MUCH

$=C$1.16 (Dec. 31, 1990)	9-Year Growth	1981	1982	1983	1984	1985	1986	1987	1988	1989	1990
Sales (C$ mil.)	15.0%	1,496	2,077	2,225	2,450	2,807	3,594	4,273	5,107	5,424	5,274
Net income (C$ mil.)	16.9%	41	54	69	67	82	102	125	141	135	169
Income as % of sales	—	2.8%	2.6%	3.1%	2.7%	2.9%	2.8%	2.9%	2.8%	2.5%	3.2%
Earnings per share (C$)	10.2%	0.74	0.91	1.13	1.26	1.18	1.38	1.55	1.68	1.60	1.78
Stock price – high (C$)	—	7.35	9.06	12.50	12.63	16.00	25.75	30.25	25.88	27.38	24.63
Stock price – low (C$)	—	5.81	6.00	9.00	8.57	10.88	13.63	21.13	20.63	21.25	18.75
Stock price – close (C$)	13.3%	6.81	9.06	11.94	10.88	15.38	23.88	22.75	21.50	24.50	21.00
P/E – high	—	10	6	11	10	14	19	20	15	17	14
P/E – low	—	8	7	8	7	9	10	14	12	13	11
Dividends per share (C$)	9.4%	0.33	0.36	0.39	0.44	0.47	0.50	0.55	0.62	0.69	0.73
Book value per share (C$)	14.2%	5.47	6.11	6.95	7.65	8.52	9.40	10.61	11.75	14.87	18.03

1990 Year-end:
Debt ratio: 28.4%
Return on equity: 10.8%
Cash (mil.): C$300
Long-term debt (mil.): C$544
No. of shares (mil.): 76
Dividends:
1990 average yield: 3.5%
1990 payout: 41.0%
Market value (mil.): $1,376
Sales (mil.): $4,547

Stock Price History High/Low 1981–90

35
30
25
20
15
10
5
0

KEY COMPETITORS

Adolph Coors
Allied-Lyons
Anheuser-Busch
Associated Milk Producers
Bass
Bond
Borden
BSN
Carlsberg
Coca-Cola
Foster's Brewing
Guinness
Heineken
Kirin
Philip Morris
Procter & Gamble
RJR Nabisco
San Miguel
Seagram
Source Perrier
Stroh
Whitman

Food companies
Broadcasting companies

KIRIN BREWERY COMPANY, LTD.

OVERVIEW

The mythical Kirin is a half-horse, half-dragon creature that is said to bring good fortune to those lucky enough to see it. Appropriately, it is the symbol of the Kirin Brewing company, Japan's oldest and largest brewery (with almost 50% of the Japanese market) and the 4th largest in the world. Including its soft drink operations, Kirin is the 2nd largest international beverage company after Coca-Cola.

A member of the Mitsubishi *keiretsu* (business group), which owns 19% of its stock, Kirin is a recognized leader in brewing technology, having brought the industry several major innovations including its *Amagi-Nijo* malting strain, now used in over half of the world's beer. The company has recently added several new beers to augment its internationally popular flagship Kirin Lager.

In addition to increasing sales volume in its beer segment, Kirin has implemented an active diversification program, in which the company is gaining a presence in everything from food to biotechnology (a natural extension of its brewing research).

Kirin has launched several joint ventures with Molson, San Miguel, Seagram, and Amgen and exchanged technologies with Heineken and Czech brewer Pilsner Urquell.

WHEN

American William Copeland came to Yokohama in 1864 and 5 years later established the Spring Valley Brewery, the first in Japan, to provide beer for the foreign nationals on the island. Lacking funds to continue the enterprise, Copeland closed the brewery in 1884. In 1885 a group of foreign and Japanese businessmen reopened it as Japan Brewery. The business created the Kirin label in 1888 and was soon turning a profit.

Initially, the company was predominantly operated by Americans and Europeans, but by 1907 the Japanese had filled the ranks and had adopted the Kirin name. During the early decades of the 20th century, the company expanded across Japan by establishing breweries and its own bottling plant.

Sales plummeted during WWII when the government set limits on brewing output. Nevertheless, Kirin established its R&D facilities, which are now a model for the industry.

After the war the US occupation forces inadvertently assisted Kirin when they split Dai Nippon Brewery (Kirin's primary competitor) into 2 companies (Asahi and Sapporo) while leaving Kirin intact. The company pressed its new advantage and established itself as Japan's leading brewer during the 1950s.

The company made rapid technological advances in the 1960s (the decade when beer overtook sake as the nation's favorite drink) when it developed superior strains of malting barley and learned new ways to control the fermentation process.

During the 1970s Kirin introduced several new soft drinks to the market and in 1972 branched into liquor through a joint venture (a scotch distillery) with Seagram (Kirin-Seagram). In 1976 Kirin established Kirin Australia to provide a steady supply of Australian malt to its breweries.

In the 1980s Kirin purchased several Coca-Cola bottling operations in New England and Japan. In 1988 the company entered the wine business by launching its Kirin Wine Club line and signed an agreement with Molson Companies to produce Kirin beer for the North American market. That same year the company created its information systems subsidiary.

In 1989 the company greatly expanded its beer line by introducing Kirin Fine Draft, Kirin Fine Pilsner, Kirin Malt Dry, and Kirin Cool. It also bought Napa Valley's Raymond Vineyards in 1989. Two more beers (Kirin Mild Lager and Kirin Ichibanshibori) were launched in 1990 and contributed to a 31.4% profit growth that same year.

HOW MUCH

$=¥135 (Dec. 31, 1990)	9-Year Growth	1981[1]	1982[1]	1983[1]	1984	1985	1986	1987	1988[2]	1989	1990
Sales (¥ bil.)	5.9%	856	985	1,042	1,141	1,226	1,290	1,302	1,314	1,257	1,428
Net income (¥ bil.)	9.3%	19	20	19	20	25	32	34	33	31	42
Income as % of sales	—	2.2%	2.0%	1.8%	1.8%	2.1%	2.5%	2.6%	2.5%	2.4%	3.0%
Earnings per share (¥)	—	—	—	*22*	*22*	*28*	*34*	*36*	*34*	*32*	*42*
Stock price – high (¥)	—	498	399	523	603	758	1,686	3,019	2,390	2,120	2,040
Stock price – low (¥)	—	352	316	365	481	514	692	1,504	1,571	1,750	1,230
Stock price – close (¥)	15.6%	392	381	504	529	715	1,571	1,829	1,940	2,040	1,440
P/E – high	—	—	—	24	27	27	49	84	70	67	48
P/E – low	—	—	—	17	22	19	20	42	46	55	29
Dividends per share (¥)	2.0%	6.68	7.14	7.14	7.14	7.14	7.14	9.05	7.14	7.50	8.00
Book value per share (¥)	11.1%	204	214	218	238	264	291	322	372	516	528

1990 Year-end:
Debt ratio: 25.1%
Return on equity: 8.1%
Cash (bil.): ¥447
Long-term debt (bil.): ¥177
No. of shares (mil.): 1,002
Dividends:
1990 average yield: 0.6%
1990 payout: 19.0%
Market value (mil.): $10,688
Sales (mil.): $10,578

Stock Price History High/Low 1981–90

[1] Unconsolidated data [2] 11-month period

NASDAQ symbol: KNBWY (ADR)
Fiscal year ends: December 31

Hoover's Rating **B+**

WHO

President: Hideyo Motoyama
EVP: Keizaburo Nakakuki
EVP: Yasushi Yamamoto
Senior Financial Officer, Managing Director: Ryo Ueda
Senior Personnel Officer, Managing Director: Keisaku Manabe
Auditors: Asahi Shinwa
Employees: 7,673

WHERE

HQ: 26-1 Jingumae 6-chome, Shibuya-ku, Tokyo 150, Japan
Phone: 011-81-3-3499-6111
Fax: 011-81-3-3499-6151
US HQ: Kirin USA, Inc., 600 3rd Ave., 21st Floor, New York, NY 10016
US Phone: 212-687-1865
US Fax: 212-286-8065

Kirin has overseas offices in New York, Los Angeles, San Francisco, Hong Kong, and Germany. Through its joint ventures the company's products are manufactured and sold in North America, Europe, and the Pacific Rim.

WHAT

	1990 Sales	
	¥ bil.	% of total
Beer	1,207	84
Soft drinks	128	9
Food	11	1
Other	82	6
Total	**1,428**	**100**

Beer
Kirin Cool
Kirin Dry
Kirin Fine Draft
Kirin Fine Malt
Kirin Fine Pilsner
Kirin Ichibanshibori Draft Beer
Kirin Lager Beer
Kirin Malt Dry
Kirin Mild Lager

Biomedical
Pharmaceuticals
Plant strains

Engineering
Bioengineering
Plant engineering

Food
Koiwai (dairy)

Information Systems
KIC Net

Services
Distribution
Health and leisure
Real estate
Restaurants
Beer Market (pubs)
Cafés Suavor (coffee shops)
Kirin City Pubs
Shakey's Pizza Parlors (Japan)

Other Beverages
Afternoon Tea
Cafés Suavor French Cafe (coffee)
Kirin Honey & Lemon
Kirin Jive Coffee
Kirin Lemon
Kirin Orange
Kirin Post Water
Kirin Tomato Juice
Kirin Vege Take
Tobiume

KEY COMPETITORS

Adolph Coors
Allied-Lyons
Anheuser-Busch
Bass
Bond
BSN
Cadbury Schweppes
Carlsberg
Dole
Dr Pepper/7Up
Foster's Brewing
Grand Metropolitan
Guinness
Heineken
John Labatt
LVMH
PepsiCo
Philip Morris
San Miguel
Seagram
Stroh
Food companies

KLM ROYAL DUTCH AIRLINES

OVERVIEW

Amsterdam-based Koninklijke Luchtvaart Maatschappij (known in English as KLM Royal Dutch Airlines) is the world's oldest international airline. The flag carrier of the Netherlands since its creation in 1919, KLM is now 38.2% owned by the Dutch government.

Because the demand for air service to Amsterdam is low in comparison with other world capitals, KLM has developed into one of the most international of airlines, flying to every continent except Antarctica. It offers European regional and commuter services through its NLM CityHopper, NetherLines, and KLM Helicopters subsidiaries. The company has also invested in US-based Northwest Airlines.

But losses at Northwest and laggard cost controls as KLM spread its wings around the world have crimped 1990 earnings. KLM also faces the problems of airport congestion and volatile fuel and insurance costs that are plaguing almost every international airline. The company reduced staff by about 12% and sold 75% of its Golden Tulip hotel management subsidiary to raise cash in 1990, but it wasn't enough to stem a fiscal 1991 loss of over $300 million — KLM's first full-year loss since 1975.

WHEN

Flight lieutenant Albert Plesman founded KLM in The Hague in 1919. A group of Dutch businessmen financed the venture, which had been granted the honorary title of Koninklijke or "royal" by Queen Wilhelmina.

Under Plesman's leadership KLM established service between Amsterdam and London (1920), Copenhagen (1920), Brussels (1922), and Paris (1923). The airline initiated the longest air route in the world (8,700 miles), from Amsterdam to Indonesia (1927), and extended its European network to Zurich (1928), Rome (1931), Prague (1935), Vienna (1936), and Oslo (1939). Hitler's occupation of Holland shut down KLM's European operations in 1940; Plesman was imprisoned by the Germans that year but was released in 1942.

After the war Plesman quickly reestablished commercial service, and by the mid-1950s KLM had expanded to Africa and the Americas. Service to Australia, first offered in 1938, was resumed in 1951. The company formed an aerial photography and survey subsidiary, KLM Aerocarto, in 1954, based on a department created by the airline in 1921. In 1957 KLM's stock began trading on the NYSE.

KLM formed KLM Helicopters to serve offshore drilling platforms in the North Sea in 1965. The airline established NLM Dutch Airlines to provide commuter services within the Netherlands in 1966, renaming it NLM CityHopper in 1976, after service had been expanded to adjoining countries.

Sergio Orlandini, KLM's president from 1973 to 1987, addressed the problems of overcapacity by converting the rear portions of KLM's 747s to cargo storage. In 1988 the company bought 40% of Transavia (Dutch charter airline) from Nedlloyd (Dutch shipping and energy concern).

KLM started looking for partners in the late 1980s to help it compete in key markets, particularly Europe and the US. The airline bought 10% of Covia Partnership, owner and operator of United Airlines's Apollo computer reservation system (1988), and invested in Wings Holdings, a company established to buy NWA (parent company of Northwest Airlines, 1989). It looked as though the US DOT would force KLM to reduce its investment in NWA from $400 million to $150 million, based on a law limiting foreign ownership of US airlines, but in 1991 Transportation Secretary Samuel Skinner decided to let KLM retain its 20% stake. Also in 1991 KLM raised its stake in Transavia by buying another 40% interest from Nedlloyd. At about the same time, a deal giving KLM and British Airways 20% each of Belgium's national airline, Sabena, fell apart.

HOW MUCH

	9-Year Growth	1981	1982	1983	1984	1985	1986	1987	1988	1989	1990
Sales ($ mil.)	8.7%	1,602	1,702	1,748	1,692	1,629	2,215	2,641	3,002	2,787	3,395
Net income ($ mil.)	37.2%	5	12	15	35	84	118	148	169	175	82
Income as % of sales	—	0.3%	0.7%	0.9%	2.1%	5.1%	5.3%	5.6%	5.6%	6.3%	2.4%
Earnings per share ($)	31.7%	0.13	0.32	0.39	0.74	1.57	2.32	2.91	3.20	3.31	1.55
Stock price – high ($)	—	11.15	11.45	12.75	14.80	20.38	23.88	27.75	21.63	26.50	26.00
Stock price – low ($)	—	5.23	5.90	9.40	9.40	12.75	17.50	13.25	15.00	19.88	11.00
Stock price – close ($)	4.9%	7.50	10.85	12.50	12.88	18.75	18.13	15.75	21.00	25.38	11.50
P/E – high	—	86	35	32	20	13	10	10	7	8	17
P/E – low	—	40	18	24	13	8	8	5	5	6	7
Dividends per share ($)	—	0.00	0.00	0.00	0.00	0.00	0.51	0.69	0.75	0.75	0.81
Book value per share ($)	8.8%	14.51	13.33	13.74	11.16	11.90	17.98	25.35	28.82	26.35	31.13

1990 Year-end:
Debt ratio: 63.8%
Return on equity: 5.4%
Cash (mil.): $757
Current ratio: 1.45
Long-term debt (mil.): $3,078
No. of shares (mil.): 53
Dividends:
1990 average yield: 7.1%
1990 payout: 52.5%
Market value (mil.): $607

Stock Price History High/Low 1981–90

NYSE symbol: KLM
Fiscal year ends: March 31

WHO

Chairman: M. Albrecht
President: Jan F. A. de Soet, age 64
SVP Finance and Holdings: P. C. W. Alberda van Ekenstein
SVP Personnel Division: C. van Woudenberg
Auditors: KPMG Klynveld Kraayenhof & Co.
Employees: 25,195

WHERE

HQ: Koninklijke Luchtvaart Maatschappij NV, Amsterdamseweg 55, Amstelveen, The Netherlands
Phone: 011-31-20-649-91-23
Fax: 011-31-20-641-28-72
US HQ: 565 Taxter Rd., Elmsford, NY 10523
US Phone: 914-784-2000
US Fax: 914-784-2103
Reservations: 800-777-5553

KLM serves 148 cities in 77 countries.

	1990 Sales	
	$ mil.	% of total
Europe & Africa	1,320	39
Near & Far East	852	26
Americas	1,187	35
Adjustments	36	—
Total	**3,395**	**100**

WHAT

	1990 Sales	
	$ mil.	% of total
Passengers & baggage	2,172	64
Freight	566	17
Mail	40	1
Charters	37	1
Other revenue	580	17
Total	**3,395**	**100**

Major Subsidiaries and Affiliates
Frans Maas Beheer (minority, trucking company)
Golden Tulip (25%, hotel management service)
KLM Aerocarto (60%, aerial photography and surveying)
KLM Helicopters (helicopter charters)
Martinair (minority, charters and freight)
NetherLines (regional airline)
NLM CityHopper (regional airline)
Polygon Insurance Co., Ltd. (33%)
Schreiner Aviation Group (33.3%, aviation services)
Service Q, General Service Co. (industrial cleaning)
Transavia Airlines (80%, charters and scheduled service)
Wings Holdings Inc. (20%, owns NWA Inc., parent of Northwest Airlines)

Computer Reservation Systems
Covia Partnership (10%; Apollo)
The Galileo Company, Ltd. (10.6%)

Flight Equipment	No.	Orders
Airbus A310	10	—
Boeing 737	16	10
Boeing 747	23	9
DC-10	5	—
MD-11	—	10
Other	25	19
Total*	**79**	**48**

* Does not include 3rd party leases.

KEY COMPETITORS

AMR	Lufthansa	Swire Pacific
British Airways	Qantas	TWA
Continental Airlines	SAS	UAL
Delta	Singapore Airlines	
JAL		

KOOR INDUSTRIES LTD.

OVERVIEW

CEO Benjamin Gaon is restructuring the operations and finances of Koor, Israel's largest industrial organization and a major employer and exporter. Products include military electronics, chemicals, steel, appliances, and processed foods sold under the Telma label. Technically bankrupt, Koor is getting concessions from its creditors and help from the Israeli government. The company is controlled by Hevrat Haovdim, the business arm of the Histadrut (General Federation of Labor), a large Israeli union. If a proposed restructuring is completed, the Histadrut's ownership will drop to 26% from 97%. The government owns a nonvoting interest in the company.

Gaon's turnaround efforts have begun to narrow losses, but Koor's Soltam defense and metals business continues to operate in the red. Gaon has cut employment to less than 2/3 of its peak level, leading to worker protests. Koor's close links to labor and the government have politicized the conglomerate and clouded decision making in the past. For example, in 1990, before rejecting takeover bids from the Belzberg family (Canada) and Shamrock Investment (US), management was reported to have favored Shamrock, the Finance Ministry apparently preferred the Belzberg offer, and the union rank and file were thought to want continued Israeli ownership.

WHEN

Koor Industries is an offshoot of Solol Boneh, a construction company established in 1924 in British Palestine by the Histadrut. Solel Boneh founded Koor as its manufacturing division in 1944 to provide employment for many of the Jews relocating to the area during and after WWII. Initially Koor made construction materials in Haifa. In 1951 the company took the first of many diversification steps by entering a telecommunications joint venture, Telrad.

An Arab attack on Israel quickly followed the nation's creation in 1948. Israel defeated its attackers, but the threat of future conflicts spurred the development of the country's defense industry. In 1952 Koor teamed with a Finnish firm to create Soltam, an Israeli artillery manufacturer.

Koor continued to expand and diversify through joint ventures, usually with foreign partners, creating a steel company in 1954 and Alliance Tire & Rubber in 1955. Koor and the Israeli government founded Tadiran, a defense electronics company, in 1962. In the next year Koor bought chemical maker Makhteshim. Koor purchased food processor Hamashbir Lata in 1970. The Sinai campaign (1956), Six-Day War (1967), and Yom Kippur War (1973) created opportunities for Tadiran, Soltam, and Telrad as Israeli defense spending increased. Koor and United Technologies set up a jet engine component venture in 1983.

With primary emphasis on employment, Koor never became very profitable. In 1983 Koor bought full control of Alliance Rubber & Tire after outside investors threatened to force the liquidation of the unprofitable company. Koor was hurt in the 1980s by a government anti-inflation program that cut subsidies and lowered trade barriers for foreign competitors. Despite the program, inflation rates outstripped the rate of devaluation of the shekel, further damaging Koor's international cost competitiveness. Koor received a temporary boost from Drexel Burnham Lambert junk bond king Michael Milken, who arranged a $105 million US debenture issue in 1986.

Koor posted its first loss (excluding tax credits) in 20 years in 1986 and losses widened in 1987. Gaon became CEO in 1988 and began restructuring the heavily indebted company. Alliance filed for bankruptcy, leading former Alliance workers to demonstrate against Koor. Bankers Trust filed suit for Koor's liquidation after Koor missed a payment on its debt. Gaon kept closing plants, but the company incurred a loss in 1988 and a record $303 million deficit in 1989. A debt-relief plan worked out with the government, Israeli banks, and foreign creditors in 1989 fell apart in 1990, and Koor suspended interest payments on its debts. Gaon agreed to put up Tadiran for sale and negotiated a new arrangement with creditors in 1991. Shortly afterward the Israeli government approved $100 million in loan guarantees to help bail out Koor.

HOW MUCH

$=NIS2.03 (Dec. 31, 1990)	5-Year Growth	1981	1982	1983	1984	1985	1986	1987	1988	1989	1990
Sales (NIS mil.)	(7.3%)	—	—	—	—	7,426	6,678	6,917	5,990	5,385	5,089
Net income (NIS mil.)	—	—	—	—	—	189	11	(643)	(529)	(700)	(99)
Income as % of sales	—	—	—	—	—	2.5%	0.2%	(9.3%)	(8.8%)	(13.0%)	(1.9%)
Earnings per share (NIS)	—	—	—	—	—	—	—	(15)	(12)	(16)	(2)
Stock price – close (NIS)	—	—	—	—	—	—	—	—	—	—	34
Dividends per share (NIS)	—	—	—	—	—	—	—	0.00	0.00	0.00	0.00

1990 Year-end:
Debt ratio: 103.2%
Return on equity: —
Cash (mil.): NIS120
Long-term debt (mil.): NIS1,310
No. of shares (mil.): 18
Dividends:
1990 average yield: 0.0%
1990 payout: 0.0%
Market value (mil.): $301
Sales (mil.): $2,507

Note: Historical figures are adjusted to December 1990 price levels.

Principal exchange: Tel Aviv
Fiscal year ends: December 31

WHO

Chairman: Eytan Sheshinski, age 56
CEO and President: Benjamin Gaon, age 56
SVP and CFO: Yehuda Milo, age 56
Head of Personnel and Administration: Savinoam Avivi, age 53
Auditors: Kesselman & Kesselman
Employees: 18,450

WHERE

HQ: Koor Bldg., 8 Shaul Hamelekh Blvd., Tel Aviv 61332, Israel
Phone: 011-972-3-5432222
Fax: 011-972-3-5432228
US HQ: Koor USA Inc., 245 Fifth Ave., New York, NY 10016-8728
US Phone: 212-561-7200
US Fax: 212-684-7653

Nearly all of Koor's operations are in Israel.

	1990 Export Sales	
	NIS mil.	% of total
North America	682	43
South America	162	10
Europe	560	35
Other regions	183	12
Total	**1,587**	**100**

WHAT

	1990 Sales		1990 Operating Income	
	NIS mil.	% of total	NIS mil.	% of total
Electronics	1,832	36	55	32
Building supplies	863	17	108	63
Metals	385	8	(40)	(23)
Chemicals	580	11	33	19
Food	751	15	18	10
Trading	454	9	—	—
Other	224	4	(2)	(1)
Total	**5,089**	**100**	**172**	**100**

Electronics
Tadiran Ltd. (97.5%; defense electronics, appliances, cable)
Telrad Telecommunication & Electronic Industries Ltd.

Building Supplies
Koor Ceramic Works Ltd.
Nesher Israel Cement Enterprises Ltd. (48.1%)
United Steel Mills Ltd.

Metals
Koor Metals Ltd. (structural engineering)
Middle East Tube Co. Ltd. (92.4%; steel pipes and tubes)
Soltam Ltd. (74%; ammunition, weapons, kitchenware)

Chemicals
Agan Chemical Manufacturers Ltd. (49.1%, herbicides)
Alliance Rubber & Tire Co. Ltd. (86%)
Makhteshim Chemical Works Ltd. (pesticides)

Food
Etz-Hazayith Ltd. (edible oil, detergent, soap)
Shemen Industries, Ltd. (78.6%; edible oil, animal feed, detergent, soap)
Mata Food Industries Ltd. (50%; margarine, powdered food)

Trading
Koor Trade Ltd.
Koor USA Inc.

KEY COMPETITORS

Defense electronics, food, armament, and chemical companies

KPMG

OVERVIEW

Klynveld Peat Marwick Goerdeler (KPMG) is the largest of the Big 6 accounting firms. KPMG is owned by its 6,300 partners.

The firm has focused recently on increased international coverage, major quality service initiatives, and development of industry specializations. In 1989 KPMG participated in successful mergers in Sweden (Bohlins Revisionsbyrå) and Germany (the Treuverkehr AG with affiliate Deutsche Treuhand), and the firm grew 30% in Europe. In 1990 European revenues (47% of total) surpassed those in the US (44%).

In the US new KPMG Peat Marwick chairman Jon Madonna (described by the *New York Times* as "a raven-haired man with an incandescent smile") came to office in 1990 with a mandate to increase partner pay, reportedly $25,000 to $50,000 a year below partners at competitors. After only a 3% increase in US revenues in 1990, Madonna announced that 265 partners would be cut from the payroll and that the firm would take an interdisciplinary approach to the industries it served, rather than divide its services along traditional audit, tax, and consulting lines.

WHEN

KPMG was formed in 1987 when Peat, Marwick, Mitchell, & Copartners joined KMG, an international federation of accounting firms. The combined firms immediately jumped into first place in worldwide revenues.

Peat Marwick traces its roots back to 1911. In that year William Peat, who had established a respected accounting practice in London, met James Marwick on a westbound crossing of the Atlantic. Marwick and fellow University of Glasgow alumnus S. Roger Mitchell had formed Marwick, Mitchell & Company in New York in 1897. Peat and Marwick agreed to join their firms, first under an agreement that terminated in 1919, and again in 1925 through a permanent merger to form Peat, Marwick, Mitchell, & Copartners.

In 1947 a partner named William Black became the senior partner, a position he held until 1965. Black guided the firm's 1950 merger with Barrow, Wade, Guthrie, the oldest and most prestigious US firm. Black also built up the firm's management consulting practice. Peat Marwick restructured its international practice as PMM&Co. (International) in 1972 and reformed as Peat Marwick International in 1978.

In 1979 a group of European accounting firms led by the Netherlands' top-ranked Klynveld Kraayenhoff and Germany's 2nd-ranked Deutsche Treuhand discussed the formation of an international federation of accounting firms to aid in serving multinational companies. At that time 2 American firms that had been founded around the turn of the century, Main Lafrentz and Hurdman Cranstoun, agreed to merge in order to combat the growing reach of the Big 8. The Europeans needed an American member for their federation to succeed and had encouraged the formation of the new firm, Main Hurdman & Cranstoun. By the end of 1979, Main Hurdman had joined the Europeans to form Klynveld Main Goerdeler (KMG), named after 2 of the member firms and the chairman of Deutsche Treuhand, Dr. Reinhard Goerdeler. Other members of the federation included C. Jespersen (Denmark), Thorne Riddel (Canada), Thomson McLintok (UK), and Fides Revision (Switzerland). KMG immediately became the one of the world's largest accounting firms, muscling into the ranks of the Anglo-American firms.

In 1987 Peat Marwick, then the 2nd largest firm, merged with KMG to form Klynveld Peat Marwick Goerdeler (KPMG). Through the merger KPMG lost 10% of its business due to the departure of competing companies that had formerly been clients of Peat Marwick or KMG; but the firm nevertheless jumped into the #1 position worldwide, exceeding 2nd-ranked Arthur Andersen in total revenues in 1987.

Larry Horner, chairman of the keystone US operation, stepped down in 1990 after younger partners, vexed by what they saw as top-heavy management, jockeyed for higher pay and more say in the firm. The partners turned to 47-year-old Jon Madonna, head of the firm's San Francisco office.

HOW MUCH

	9-Year Growth	1981	1982	1983	1984	1985	1986	1987	1988	1989	1990
Revenues ($ mil.)	20.8%	979	1,146	1,232	1,340	1,446	1,672	3,250	3,900	4,300	5,368
No. of countries	7.2%	66	71	79	82	89	88	115	94	117	123
No. of offices	—	—	—	—	328	335	342	620	637	700	800
No. of partners	14.0%	1,931	2,015	2,242	2,326	2,507	2,726	5,150	5,050	5,300	6,300
No. of employees	14.3%	23,149	25,492	27,033	27,746	29,864	32,183	60,000	63,700	68,000	77,300

1990 Revenues per partner: $852,063

Revenues ($ mil.) 1981–90

6,000
5,000
4,000
3,000
2,000
1,000
0

Note: Figures prior to 1987 are Peat Marwick only; 1987 through 1990 are total figures for post-merger KPMG Peat Marwick.

International association of partnerships

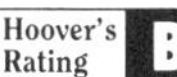

Fiscal year ends: September 30

WHO

Chairman: P. Jim Butler
Chairman, KPMG Peat Marwick: Jon C. Madonna, age 47
Administration and Finance Partner, KPMG Peat Marwick: Daniel Brennan, age 48
Human Resources Partner, KPMG Peat Marwick: Bernie Milano
Personnel: 77,300

WHERE

HQ: Klynveld Peat Marwick Goerdeler, PO Box 74111, 1070 BC Amsterdam, The Netherlands
Phone: 011-31-20-656-6700
Fax: 011-31-20-656-6777
US HQ: KPMG Peat Marwick, 767 Fifth Ave., New York, NY 10153-0002
US Phone: 212-909-5000
US Fax: 212-909-5088 (Communications)

KPMG maintains 800 offices in 123 countries.

	1990 Revenues	
	$ mil.	% of total
North & Latin America	2,373	44
Europe	2,503	47
Asia/Pacific	424	8
Other regions	68	1
Total	**5,368**	**100**

WHAT

	1990 Revenues	
	$ mil.	% of total
Auditing & accounting	2,707	50
Tax	1,032	19
Management consulting	786	15
Other	843	16
Total	**5,368**	**100**

Areas of Specialization

Banking and financial services
Food and agribusiness
Health care
High technology
Insurance
Manufacturing
Merchandising
Petroleum
Real estate
Transportation

Representative Clients

Aetna
Apple Computer
BMW
State of California
Citicorp
Daimler-Benz
Deutsche Bank
Grand Metropolitan
Heineken
Imperial Chemical
Motorola
Paine Webber
PepsiCo
Polaroid
Rolls-Royce
Saatchi & Saatchi
Siemens
Texaco
Thyssen
Union Carbide
United Nations
Volvo
Xerox

Affiliated Firms

Berger, Block, Kirschen, Schellekens & Co. (Belgium)
Century Audit Corp. (Japan)
KPMG Deutsche Treuhand (Germany)
KPMG Klynveld Kraayenhoff (Netherlands)
KPMG Peat Marwick (US)
KPMG Peat Marwick (UK)
KPMG Peat Marwick Thorne (Canada)

KEY COMPETITORS

Arthur Andersen
Coopers & Lybrand
Deloitte & Touche
Ernst & Young
Marsh & McLennan
McKinsey & Co.
Price Waterhouse
Other consulting firms

LLOYD'S OF LONDON

OVERVIEW

From its landmark building on Lime Street in London, Lloyd's provides a physical, legal, and operational framework for the insurance of risks. Although Lloyd's is best known and uniquely suited for insuring unusual items (Elizabeth Taylor's eyes, for example), most of its business is mundane. It is a major provider of marine insurance. During the 1991 Gulf War, Lloyd's opened its doors on a Sunday, for the first time in 303 years, in part to provide coverage for shipping in the turbulent area.

The financial elite joining Lloyd's as insurers are called "Names." Names pool their resources by joining syndicates formed by underwriters, insurance experts who negotiate deals with Lloyd's brokers.

Names' profits have been declining because of natural disasters in Europe and the US; increasing environmental and asbestos claims (Lloyd's insured the *Exxon Valdez*); and UK tax law changes. With profits slumping and risks rising, Names have abandoned Lloyd's like one of the sinking ships it insures; Names total fewer than 27,000 in 1991, down from a high of more than 32,000 in 1987.

Lloyd's is scrambling to catch up technologically. It has only recently abandoned its computer punch card system.

Insurance society
Fiscal year ends: December 31

WHO

Chairman: David Coleridge
Deputy Chairman and CEO: Alan Lord
Deputy Chairman: Alan Jackson
Deputy Chairman: John Greig
Head of Finance: John H. F. Gaynor
Head of Administration (Personnel): R. Woodford
Auditors: Ernst & Young
Employees: 2,147

WHERE

HQ: One Lime St., London EC3M 7HA, UK
Phone: 011-44-71-623-7100
Fax: 011-44-71-626-2389
US HQ: Lloyd's of London Press, Inc., 611 Broadway, Suite 308, New York, NY 10012
US Phone: 212-529-9500
US Fax: 212-529-9826

Lloyd's underwriters accept business from all over the world, about 75% from outside the UK.

WHEN

In the 2nd half of the 17th century, coffeehouses emerged in England as places to meet and do business. In 1688 Edward Lloyd opened Lloyd's Coffee House in London with an eye toward capturing a marine insurer clientele. Lloyd's provided brokers and individual underwriters with a central place to meet and agree to deals. Underwriters did not assume risks jointly; rather, each was liable for only his own portion of the deal. This enabled individuals to enter insurance syndicates knowing the maximum amount at risk.

Lloyd's reputation for consistently obtaining accurate shipping news made it the hub of London's maritime insurance industry. The coffeehouse pressed its advantage when it began publishing *Lloyd's List*, a shipping newspaper, in 1734.

Lloyd's attracted people who used insurance as a cover for gambling. In one instance customers "insured" the gender of the Chevalier d'Eon, a transvestite. Serious insurers persuaded a Lloyd's waiter to open the New Lloyd's Coffee House nearby in 1769. By 1774 the brokers and underwriters needed more space and moved to the Royal Exchange, taking Lloyd's out of coffeehouses for good.

In the 1800s Lloyd's began regulating its membership. Parliament passed the Lloyd's Act in 1871 to establish Lloyd's as an incorporated society. In the 1880s Lloyd's branched out into nonmarine insurance. By the turn of the century, Lloyd's was writing 50% of the world's nonlife insurance.

Prompt settlement of claims related to the 1906 San Francisco earthquake boosted Lloyd's image in the US. Underwriters profited from war risk insurance in WWI. After the war Lloyd's entered automobile, credit, and aviation insurance. In 1958 Lloyd's moved to its Lime Street headquarters. Hurricane Betsy hit the US Gulf Coast in 1965, inflicting severe losses on Lloyd's underwriters and sharply reducing their capacity to take on subsequent risks.

In 1981 and 1982 a syndicate managed by Outhwaite, an underwriter, wrote so-called run-off contracts (accepted future liabilities of old insurance contracts with claims still pending, in exchange for premium income) that exposed Outhwaite Names to US asbestos-related claims — some from the 1940s — and potential losses of $480 million. Numerous questions about the transactions have been raised, most concerning the disclosure Lloyd's requires when writing run-off policies.

Lloyd's grappled with reform in 1990. It lowered barriers that had kept syndicates from writing more than one type of insurance. It initiated an in-house reinsurance company, and in 1991 it dispatched a task force to guide Lloyd's into the late 1990s. The task force is even tackling the thorny issue of unlimited liability — the longstanding practice that risks all Names' personal wealth to satisfy claims.

WHAT

	1990 Operating Income	
	£ mil.	% of total
Entrance fees & subscriptions	88	51
Direct marketing recoveries	74	42
Other	12	7
Total	**174**	**100**

Subsidiaries and Affiliates
Additional Securities Ltd. (overseas insurance transactions, UK)
Brian Trodd Publishing House Ltd. (75.5%, publications, UK)
Lioncover Insurance Co. Ltd. (insurance, UK)
Lloyd's of London Press Ltd. (publications, UK)
Lloyd's of London Press (Far East) Ltd. (publications, Hong Kong)
Lloyd's of London Press (Germany) GmbH (publications, Germany)
Lloyd's of London Press, Inc. (publications, US)
Lloyd's Maritime Information Services, Ltd. (50%, operation of information services, UK)
LLP Video Ltd. (publications, UK)
Sharedealer Ltd. (asset management, UK)

Maritime and Legal Publications (Lloyd's of London Press Ltd.)
Legal textbooks and directories
Lloyd's Law Reports
Lloyd's List (insurance, transportation, freight, and other industrial news)
Lloyd's Loading List
Lloyd's Maritime and Commercial Law Quarterly
Lloyd's Monthly List of Laid up Vessels
Lloyd's Shipping Economist
Lloyd's Shipping Index
Lloyd's Voyage Record
Lloyd's Weekly Casualty Reports
Product Liability International

HOW MUCH

£=$1.93 (Dec. 31, 1990)	9-Year Growth	1981	1982	1983	1984	1985	1986	1987	1988	1989	1990
Total Names[1]	3.1%	20,145	21,601	23,438	26,050	28,597	30,936	32,413	31,329	28,770	26,568
New Names	(16.7%)	1,295	1,754	2,177	2,949	3,087	2,827	2,572	951	312	251
UK Names	2.4%	17,393	18,588	19,986	21,941	24,032	25,443	26,625	25,702	23,437	21,610
US Names	4.6%	1,370	1,470	1,694	2,011	2,401	2,620	2,614	2,421	2,259	2,055
Underwriting capacity (£ bil.)	11.7%	4.1	4.3	5.0	6.6	8.5	10.3	11.0	10.9	10.8	11.1
Net premiums (£ bil.)	—	—	2,892	2,570	2,959	3,056	3,712	4,195	3,713	—	—
Profit to Names (£ mil.)[2]	—	—	—	—	290	196	649	509	(510)	—	—

New Names 1981–90

3,500
3,000
2,500
2,000
1,500
1,000
500
0

[1] Participating Names only 1986–90 [2]Books are closed 3 years in arrears

Aetna
Allianz
AIG
CIGNA
Commerce Clearing House
General Re
ITT
Kemper
Maxwell
McGraw-Hill
Tokio Marine and Fire
Travelers
USF&G

L'ORÉAL SA

OVERVIEW

Paris-based L'Oréal is a giant in the world cosmetics industry. The company owns 12% of the world market and its share has risen one percentage point annually for the past several years. Once hidden in the shadows of such rivals as Revlon and Avon, L'Oréal has muscled its way into the #1 spot with an array of powerful brand names like Guy Laroche, Helena Rubenstein, Ralph Lauren, Lancôme, and Gloria Vanderbilt. The company is the world's largest producer of perfume and in many countries boasts a decisive lead in skin- and hair-care products.

Since the company's founding, research has played a primary role in its strategy. L'Oréal's ultramodern labs are staffed by over 1,000 scientists, a phenomenal number for the industry.

L'Oréal also has interests in pharmaceuticals (through its Synthélabo subsidiary, 64.2% owned) and publishing (49% interest in *Marie-Claire*), and interests in TV and motion picture companies.

Liliane Bettencourt, daughter of the company's founder and France's wealthiest individual, is L'Oréal's primary stockholder. Bettencourt controls 51% of Gesparel, the holding company that owns 56% of L'Oréal. The Swiss giant Nestlé controls the remaining shares of Gesparel.

WHEN

Parisian Eugène Schueller, a chemist by trade, developed the country's first synthetic hair dye in 1907. Schueller quickly found a market for his products with local hairdressers and in 1909 established L'Oréal to pursue his growing hair-products operations. The company's new name was a nonsensical word coined by Schueller because he liked the way it sounded.

L'Oréal expanded its line to include shampoos and soaps, all under the watchful direction of the energetic Schueller. Always the chemist, Schueller was known to taste hair creams to ensure that they were made with the exact chemical composition that he required. In the 1920s L'Oréal became the first French company in the industry to advertise on radio.

After WWII demand for L'Oréal's products intensified. When Schueller died in 1957, control of the company passed to his right-hand man, François Dalle. Dalle carried L'Oréal's hair care products into the consumer market and overseas, and sold the company's soap operations in 1961. The next year Dalle launched Elnett, L'Oréal's popular hairspray.

In 1963 the company went public, although Eugène Schueller's daughter, Liliane Betten–court, retained a majority interest. Diversification came in 1965 with the acquisition of Lancôme, a French maker of upscale cosmetics. Dalle followed the Lancôme purchase with a string of cosmetics acquisitions. L'Oréal entered the pharmaceutical business in 1973 by purchasing Synthélabo.

The company's interests became intertwined with those of the Swiss firm Nestlé in 1974, when Bettencourt traded nearly half of her L'Oreal stock for a 3% stake in Nestlé. Three years later the company bought a minority interest in the publisher of *Marie-Claire*.

During the 1980s L'Oréal vaulted from relative obscurity to become the world's leading cosmetics company, largely through such acquisitions as Metabio-Joullie (1980); Société d'Hygiene Dermatologique de Vichy (1980); and the cosmetics operations of Warner Communications (1984), which brought the company the Ralph Lauren and Gloria Vanderbilt brand names. In 1988 L'Oréal bought Laboratoires Pharmaceutiques Goupil (France's #1 toothpaste producer) and US beauty-products-maker Helena Rubinstein. In 1989 the company acquired a controlling interest in Laboratoires Pharmaceutiques Roche-Posay (skin care products) and the following year bought 47.5% of Jeanne Lanvin (perfumes).

In 1991 Jacques Corrèze, chairman of L'Oréal's US unit (Cosmair), resigned after stories surfaced linking him to pro-Nazi activities during WWII. He died 2 weeks later.

HOW MUCH

$=FF5.08 (Dec. 31, 1990)	9-Year Growth	1981	1982	1983	1984	1985	1986	1987	1988	1989	1990
Sales (FF mil.)	13.5%	9,686	10,882	13,564	15,804	16,430	18,130	20,095	24,445	27,170	30,360
Net income (FF mil.)	15.1%	517	550	663	729	775	898	1,090	1,315	1,542	1,828
Income as % of sales	—	5.3%	5.1%	4.9%	4.6%	4.7%	5.0%	5.4%	5.4%	5.7%	6.0%
Earnings per share (FF)	11.3%	11	12	14	15	17	14	18	21	25	29
Stock price – high (FF)	—	69	85	185	217	240	336	405	440	497	555
Stock price – low (FF)	—	49	59	83	175	185	234	207	230	392	420
Stock price – close (FF)	25.3%	62	81	184	187	238	320	254	440	497	471
P/E – high	—	6	7	13	14	14	23	22	21	20	19
P/E – low	—	4	5	6	11	11	16	11	11	16	14
Dividends per share (FF)	10.8%	2.38	2.57	2.96	2.82	3.00	3.30	3.70	5.00	6.00	6.00
Book value per share (FF)	12.3%	66	76	93	109	118	135	126	147	167	188

1990 Year-end:
Debt ratio: 11.6%
Return on equity: 16.3%
Cash (mil.): FF3,356
Long-term debt (mil.): FF1,430
No. of shares (mil.): 58
Dividends:
1990 average yield: 1.3%
1990 payout: 20.7%
Market value (mil.): $5,378
Sales (mil.): $5,976

Stock Price History High/Low 1981–90

600
500
400
300
200
100
0

OTC symbol: LORLY (ADR)
Fiscal year ends: December 31

WHO

Chairman and CEO: Lindsay Owen-Jones, 45
VC: André Bettencourt
Director and EVP: Marc Ladreit de Lacharrière
Financial and Legal Director: Pierre Castres Saint Martin
VP Personnel: Guy Landon
Auditors: Pierre Feuillet; Albert Pavie
Employees: 29,286

WHERE

HQ: 41 Rue Martre, 92117 Clichy, France
Phone: 011-33-1-47-56-70-00
Fax: 011-33-1-47-30-46-01
US HQ: Cosmair Inc., 575 Fifth Ave., New York, NY 10017
US Phone: 212-818-1500
US Fax: 212-984-4128

The company has operations in 25 countries.

	1990 Sales	
	FF mil.	% of total
France	10,867	36
Other countries	19,493	64
Total	**30,360**	**100**

WHAT

	1990 Sales	
	FF mil.	% of total
Consumer/salon	15,000	49
Perfumes/beauty	10,903	36
Other cosmetics	138	1
Synthélabo	3,326	11
Other	993	3
Total	**30,360**	**100**

Beauty Products
Ambre Solaire
Aquavital
Armani
Belle Color
Biotherm
Cacharel
Daniel Hechter
Elnett
Gemey
Gloria Vanderbilt
Guy Laroche
Helena Rubenstein
Jeanne Piaubert
Kérastase
L'Oréal
Lancôme
Lanvin
Loulou
Mennen
Paloma Picasso
Phas
Ralph Lauren
Studio Line
Synergie
Vichy
Vittel

Pharmaceuticals
Roche-Posay
Synthélabo (64.2%)

Publishing
Marie-Claire (49%)

TV and Film
Canal Plus (European TV, 7%)
Paravision (film, 92.5%)

Other
Artcurial (99%, art gallery)
Eurofinac (10%, communications & finance)
Orcofi (5.1%, luxury goods)

KEY COMPETITORS

Amway
Avon
Colgate-Palmolive
Estée Lauder
S.C. Johnson
LVMH
MacAndrews & Forbes
Procter & Gamble
Unilever
Pharmaceutical companies

THE LUCKY-GOLDSTAR GROUP

OVERVIEW

Consisting of 39 cross-held companies with sales of $22.8 billion in 1990, Lucky-Goldstar is Korea's 3rd largest *chaebol* (industrial group), after Samsung and Hyundai. It is involved principally in chemicals, electronics, financial services, and trading. The group's parent is Lucky, Ltd., Korea's largest chemical company. Lucky is merging with 3 other group chemical manufacturers at the urging of the Korean government. Goldstar is the *chaebol's* lead electronics company; it ranks 10th among global consumer electronics firms.

The debt-laden *chaebol* began reorganizing after Goldstar posted a sales decline in 1989. Facing quality and technical deficiencies, a slowdown in US spending on consumer electronics, intense price competition from Japanese manufacturers in Southeast Asia, and the disappearance of its cost advantage, Goldstar is stepping up R&D spending to improve in-house technological know-how and to develop more advanced, higher-margin products.

In 1991 Goldstar bought 5% of Zenith (US) and limited rights to Zenith's flat-screen and HDTV technology. With Zenith as a partner, Goldstar hopes to catch up technologically with Japanese rivals, rather than lag behind by 3 to 5 years as it has in the past.

WHEN

During WWII Koo In-Hwoi made tooth powder for Koreans to use in place of salt, then the common toothbrushing substance. Koo founded the Lucky Chemical Company in 1947 to make facial creams and, later, detergent, shampoo, and Lucky Toothpaste. The company soon became Korea's only plastics maker. Koo established a trading company (now known as Lucky-Goldstar International) in 1953.

Emulating Japanese exporters, Koo formed Goldstar Company in 1958 to make electric appliances. Goldstar initially made fans but later became the first company in Korea to make radios (1959), refrigerators (1965), televisions (1966), elevators and escalators (1968), and washing machines and air conditioners (1969). In 1967 Lucky collaborated with Caltex to build the Honam Oil Refinery, the first privately owned refinery in Korea.

Both Lucky and Goldstar benefited from the *chaebol's* cozy relationship with the government throughout the rule of Park Chung Hee (1962–79).

Koo died in 1969 and his eldest son, Koo Cha-Kyung, took control of the *chaebol* in 1970. Lucky Chemical changed its name to Lucky, Ltd., in 1974, began petrochemical production in 1977, entered a biotech venture with Chiron (US) in 1984, and built the world's largest single-unit petrochemical plant in Saudi Arabia in 1986.

In the 1970s and 1980s, Goldstar expanded rapidly as it established new electronics companies. Goldstar took advantage of cheap Korean labor to export private-label electronics items to customers, including J. C. Penney and Sears. In the late 1970s Goldstar began investing heavily in semiconductor production in an effort to fulfill its own requirements for chips and to thrust itself into the high-tech world. To head off protectionism Goldstar set up a television factory in Huntsville, Alabama, in 1982. Goldstar companies entered several ventures with more technically advanced partners, including AT&T, NEC, Hitachi, and Siemens, and set out to capture office automation and higher-end consumer electronics markets with Goldstar brand goods.

Although revenue from electronic products grew rapidly, archrival Samsung sprinted past Goldstar in sales and profit (1984), as duplication of effort among group units and an inefficient organizational structure slowed progress. Goldstar reorganized in 1987. In the late 1980s the company suffered from rising wage rates, Korean currency appreciation, and severe labor unrest, but sales and earnings rebounded in 1990.

HOW MUCH

$=Won714 (Dec. 31, 1990)	5-Year Growth	1981	1982	1983	1984	1985	1986	1987	1988	1989	1990
Sales (Won bil.)	21.4%	—	—	—	—	602	723	928	1,210	1,285	1,585
Net income (Won bil.)[1]	41.3%	—	—	—	—	11	16	29	64	64	62
Income as % of sales	—	—	—	—	—	1.8%	2.2%	3.1%	5.3%	5.0%	3.9%
Earnings per share (Won)	—	—	—	—	—	—	—	996	1,452	1,323	1,145
Stock price – high (Won)	—	—	—	—	—	—	—	14,463	22,545	27,300	27,900
Stock price – low (Won)	—	—	—	—	—	—	—	10,950	13,636	21,091	15,800
Stock price – close (Won)	—	—	—	—	—	—	—	13,223	22,454	27,300	19,300
P/E – high	—	—	—	—	—	—	—	15	16	21	24
P/E – low	—	—	—	—	—	—	—	11	9	16	14
Dividends per share (Won)[2]	—	—	—	—	—	—	—	496	545	682	750
Book value per share (Won)	—	—	—	—	—	—	—	7,018	8,703	10,461	11,872

1990 Year-end:
Debt ratio: —
Return on equity: 11.4%
Cash (bil.): —
Long-term debt (bil.): —
No. of shares (mil.): 54
Dividends:
1990 average yield: 3.9%
1990 payout: 58.9%
Market value (mil.): $1,460
Sales (mil.): $2,220

Stock Price History High/Low 1987–90

30,000
25,000
20,000
15,000
10,000
5,000
0

[1] Including extraordinary items [2] Not including rights offerings

Principal exchange: Korea
Fiscal year ends: December 31

WHO

Group Chairman: Koo Cha-Kyung, age 66
President, Lucky, Ltd. (Industrial & Consumer Products Sector): Choi Keun Sun
President, Lucky, Ltd. (Chemicals & Plastics Sector): Lee Joung Soung
Auditors: Samil Accounting Corporation
Employees: 100,000

WHERE

HQ: Lucky, Ltd., 20 Yoido-dong, Yongdungpo-gu, Seoul 150-721, Korea
Phone: 011-82-2-787-1114
Fax: 011-82-2-787-7038
US HQ: Lucky America, Inc., 1000 Sylvan Ave., Englewood Cliffs, NJ 07632
US Phone: 201-816-2300
US Fax: 201-816-0961

Lucky-Goldstar Group's 39 companies operate in more than 120 countries.

	1989 Sales % of total
South Korea	64
Other countries	35
Other income	1
Total	**100**

WHAT

	1989 Sales % of total
Electric & electronics	48
Petrochemicals	16
Chemicals & foodstuffs	12
Textiles	10
Machinery & metals	10
Others	4
Total	**100**

Principal Member Companies
Goldstar Cable Co., Ltd.
Goldstar Co., Ltd. (consumer electronics)
Goldstar Electric Co., Ltd. (specialty electronic components)
Goldstar Electron Co., Ltd. (semiconductors)
Goldstar Information & Communications, Ltd.
Goldstar Instrument & Electric Co., Ltd. (industrial electric equipment)
Goldstar Investment & Finance Corp.
Goldstar Precision Co., Ltd.
Goldstar Software, Ltd.
Goldstar Telecommunication Co., Ltd.
Goldstar-Alps Electronics Co., Ltd. (electronic components)
Hee Sung Co., Ltd. (retailing, real estate development, paper manufacturing, building maintenance services)
Honam Oil Refinery Co., Ltd. (joint venture with Caltex)
Kukje Electric Wire Co., Ltd.
LG Credit Card Co., Ltd.
Lucky, Ltd. (chemicals)
Lucky Development Co., Ltd.
Lucky Engineering Co., Ltd.
Lucky Insurance Co., Ltd.
Lucky Metals Corp.
Lucky Petrochemical Co., Ltd.
Lucky Securities Co., Ltd.
Lucky-Goldstar International Corp. (trading)
Pusan Investment & Finance Corp.
Yosu Energy Co., Ltd. (petroleum gas)

KEY COMPETITORS

Daewoo
Hyundai
Samsung
Other electronics and chemical companies

Information presented for Lucky, Ltd. only

DEUTSCHE LUFTHANSA AG

OVERVIEW

Lufthansa is the 51.6%-government-owned flag carrier of Germany. Noted for its on-time record rather than its charm, Lufthansa carried over 22 million passengers in 1990, ranking as the world's 12th largest airline.

Already the #1 Western European airline in Eastern Europe, Lufthansa has enhanced its presence in that region through Intercondor (an airline joint venture with former East German national airline Interflug), which began serving Eastern Europe late in 1990. The German government barred Lufthansa from buying a 26% stake in Interflug in 1990, on anticompetitive grounds, but Interflug's shutdown in 1991 will give Lufthansa dominance in Germany's skies.

After Federal Express, Lufthansa is the world's #2 air cargo transporter. It also owns the Penta hotel chain, 40% of Kempinski Hotels, and up to 50% of nearly 35 other travel-related companies, including Amadeus, the European computer reservation system.

Aircraft sales and other nonoperating gains allowed Lufthansa to report positive earnings in 1990, despite operating losses (caused primarily by high fuel costs). Jürgen Weber will take over as chairman in September 1991, when Heinz Ruhnau steps down.

WHEN

As a result of Dr. Kurt Weigelt's study, "Fusion in the Field of Air Traffic," the Weimar government created Deutsche Luft Hansa (DLH) in 1926 by merging 2 private German airlines, Deutscher Aero Lloyd (founded as Deutsche Luft Reederei in 1919) and Junkers Luftverkehr (formed in 1921 by aircraft manufacturer Junkers Flugzeugwerke).

With a core of routes emanating from Germany to Austria, Switzerland, England, Denmark, Sweden, Russia, and Hungary at the time of its founding, DLH went on to build Europe's most comprehensive air route network by 1931. The company served the USSR through Deruluft, an airline (formed in 1921 and dissolved in 1941) jointly owned by DLH and the Soviet government. In 1930 DLH and the Chinese government formed a subsidiary at Nanking called Eurasia Aviation Corporation to develop air transport in China.

DLH established the world's first regular transatlantic airmail service from Berlin to Buenos Aires in 1934 and went on to develop air transport throughout South America. The outbreak of WWII ended operations in Europe. The Chinese government seized Eurasia Aviation in 1941. In 1944 Dr. Klaus Bonhoeffer, head of DLH's legal department, led an unsuccessful coup against the Nazi leadership and was executed in 1945. Soon afterward all DLH operations ceased.

German airline service was not restored until 1954 when the Allies allowed the recapitalization of Deutsche Lufthansa. Starting with domestic routes (except to Berlin, which was reserved for Allied carriers), Lufthansa returned to London and Paris (1955), and then to South America (1956). In 1958 the airline made its first nonstop flight between Germany and New York and initiated service to Tokyo and Cairo. Lufthansa reported a $25,000 profit, its first ever, in 1963.

The airline opened a polar route from Frankfurt to Tokyo in 1964. Service behind the Iron Curtain resumed in 1966 when Lufthansa initiated flights to Prague. The stable West German economy helped Lufthansa maintain profitability through the 1970s, despite a world recession.

In 1988 Lufthansa bought 49% of Euro-Berlin France, a regional airline jointly owned by Air France, gaining, in a roundabout fashion, service to Berlin. The reunification of Germany in 1990 ended Allied control over Berlin air space, allowing Lufthansa, which had bought Pan Am's Berlin routes for about $150 million, to fly there under its own colors for the first time since the end of WWII.

HOW MUCH

$=DM1.49 (Dec. 31, 1990)	9-Year Growth	1981	1982	1983	1984	1985	1986	1987	1988	1989	1990
Sales (DM mil.)	7.8%	7,359	7,813	8,464	9,856	10,726	10,384	10,960	11,845	13,055	14,447
Net income (DM mil.)	7.9%	6	45	63	162	66	71	88	77	107	11
Income as % of sales	—	0.1%	0.6%	0.7%	1.6%	0.6%	0.7%	0.8%	0.7%	0.8%	0.1%
Earnings per share (DM)	2.5%	0.32	2.59	3.62	9.31	3.81	4.06	4.10	3.60	3.84	0.40
Stock price – high (DM)	—	79	91	151	183	419	312	216	163	219	235
Stock price – low (DM)	—	51	51	81	133	180	155	106	130	145	101
Stock price – close (DM)	8.7%	53	88	151	182	225	180	136	148	200	112
P/E – high	—	—	35	42	20	110	77	53	45	57	—
P/E – low	—	—	20	22	14	47	38	26	36	38	—
Dividends per share (DM)[1]	—	—	—	2.5	3.5	3.5	3.5	3.5	3.5	4.0	4.0
Book value per share (DM)	—	—	68	69	75	74	75	100	100	114	111

1990 Year-end:
Debt ratio: 49.1%
Return on equity: 0.4%
Cash (mil.): DM412
Long-term debt (mil.): DM3,000
No. of shares (mil.): 28
Dividends:
 1990 average yield: 3.6%
 1990 payout: —
Market value (mil.): $2,105
Sales (mil.): $9,696

Stock Price History High/Low 1981–90

450, 400, 350, 300, 250, 200, 150, 100, 50, 0

[1] Not including rights issues

Principal exchange: Frankfurt
Fiscal year ends: December 31

WHO

Chairman: Heinz Ruhnau, age 62
Deputy Chairman: Jürgen Weber, age 49
CFO: Klaus G. Schlede
Head of Personnel: Heiko Lange
Auditors: Treuarbeit Aktiengesellschaft Wirtschaftsprüfungsgesellschaft Steuerberatungsgesellschaft
Employees: 57,567

WHERE

HQ: 2-6 Von-Gablenz-Strasse, D-5000 Cologne 21, Germany
Phone: 011-49-221-8261
Fax: 011-49-69-696-6818 (Public Relations)
US HQ: Lufthansa German Airlines, 1640 Hempstead Turnpike, East Meadow, NY 11554
US Phone: 516-794-2020
US Fax: 516-794-7430
Reservations: 800-645-3880

Lufthansa serves 170 cities worldwide.

	1990 Sales	
	DM mil.	% of total
Germany	1,786	12
Other Europe	4,271	30
Africa & the Middle East	831	6
Asia/Pacific	2,496	17
North America	2,609	18
South America	553	4
Other	1,901	13
Total	**14,447**	**100**

WHAT

	1990 Sales	
	DM mil.	% of total
Passenger	10,124	70
Freight	2,373	17
Mail	198	1
Other activities	1,752	12
Total	**14,447**	**100**

Major Subsidiaries and Affiliates
Amadeus (25%, computer reservation system)
AMECO – Beijing Aircraft Maintenance and Engineering Corp. (40%)
Cargolux Airlines International SA (25%)
Condor Flugdienst GmbH (air charters)
Delvag Luftfahrtversicherungs-AG (insurance)
DLT Deutsche Luftverkehrs mbH (52%, regional airline)
EuroBerlin France SA (49%, regional airline)
German Cargo Services GmbH (charter air freight)
Lufthansa Commercial Holding GmbH
Lufthansa Hotel GmbH (Penta & Kempinski hotels)
Lufthansa Service GmbH (catering)

Flight Equipment	No.	Orders
Airbus A300 & A310	32	4
Airbus A320 & A321	17	37
Airbus A340	—	15
Boeing 727	14	—
Boeing 737	77	62
Boeing 747	33	8
Boeing 757 & 767	8	27
DC 8	5	—
DC 10	14	—
Others	20	18
Total	**220**	**171**

KEY COMPETITORS

AMR
British Airways
Continental Airlines
Delta
JAL
KLM
NWA
Qantas
SAS
Singapore Airlines
Swire Pacific
TWA
UAL
USAir

LVMH MOËT HENNESSY LOUIS VUITTON

OVERVIEW

If you have ever sipped Dom Pérignon, worn a Christian Dior perfume, or carried a Louis Vuitton suitcase, you have encountered LVMH Moët Hennessy Louis Vuitton. LVMH is the world's largest luxury goods empire, controlling such upper crust brand names as Givenchy, Moët & Chandon, and Hennessy.

The company's 4 primary segments (champagne and wines, cognac and spirits, luggage and leather goods, and perfumes and beauty products) epitomize the French tradition of luxury. LVMH leads the world in champagne production and export (its prestigious brands account for 1 of every 3 champagne bottles leaving France) and is also the largest global producer of cognacs, with brands that sell for upwards of $300 a bottle. LVMH sells over 1/3 of its luxury products and gets almost half of its profits from the Far East.

LVMH's luggage segment produces a wide range of suitcases, travel bags, trunks, briefcases, and other travel gear. Perfumes and beauty products are sold by the company's Christian Dior, Christian Lacroix, Givenchy, and RoC segments. Other operations include Delbard (rosebushes and fruit trees) and a number of specialty boutiques.

Among LVMH's largest shareholders is Guinness PLC, which owns 24% of the company. LVMH in turn owns 24% of Guinness.

OTC symbol: LVMHY (ADR)
Fiscal year ends: December 31

WHO

President and CEO: Bernard Arnault
Executive Board Member: Pierre Godé
Executive Board Member: Anthony Greener
Executive Board Member: Robert Léon
EVP and CFO: Patrick Houël
Senior Personnel Officer: Louis Dugas
Auditors: Ernst & Young
Employees: 13,732

WHERE

HQ: 30, avenue Hoche, 75008 Paris, France
Phone: 011-33-1-45-63-01-01
Fax: 011-33-1-45-61-46-95
US HQ: LVMH U.S. Corporation, 135 E. 57th St., New York, NY 10022
US Phone: 212-758-7200
US Fax: 212-758-2801

	1990 Sales		1990 Operating Income	
	FF mil.	% of total	FF mil.	% of total
France	6,673	34	2,584	45
Other Europe	3,421	17	113	2
US	2,592	13	179	3
Far East	6,916	35	2,770	49
Other countries	230	1	26	1
Total	**19,832**	**100**	**5,672**	**100**

WHEN

Louis Vuitton opened his first store in Paris in 1854 to sell luggage and trunks. In 1896 the company introduced the LV monogram fabric that is still used on most of its products. By the turn of the century, Louis Vuitton had stores in the US and England.

Throughout the 20th century the company operated primarily as a wholesaler, until 1977 when Henry Racamier, an ex–steel executive who had married into the Vuitton family, took charge. Under Racamier sales soared from $20 million to almost $1 billion within 10 years.

Concerned about being a takeover target, Racamier merged his company in 1987 with Moët Hennessy (a conglomerate that produced fine champagnes, cognacs, wines, and perfumes) and changed the company's name to LVMH Moët Hennessy Louis Vuitton. Moët Hennessy had been formed through the 1971 merger of Moët et Chandon (France's #1 champagne producer) and the Hennessy Cognac company. Perfume maker Christian Dior was acquired by Moët that same year.

Almost immediately, Racamier and Moët chairman Alain Chevalier found themselves in disagreement over the running of the company. To help consolidate his position within LVMH, Racamier invited outside investor Bernard Arnault to acquire stock in the company. Racamier expected a friendly and passive investor in Arnault but was quickly disillusioned. With the support of Guinness (a large shareholder of LVMH), Arnault managed to land a 43.5% controlling interest in LVMH. Chevalier stepped down, but former friend Racamier engaged Arnault in a battle for control of the company. After 18 months of legal fighting, with the courts usually favoring Arnault, Racamier left LVMH and set up Orcofi, a rival company that is in partnership with cosmetics giant L'Oréal. After the legal battle, Arnault weeded out LVMH's top executives and began consolidating his empire.

In 1988 Arnault acquired a 12.4% interest in Guinness (now 24%) and bought the Givenchy Couture Group. In 1989 Arnault shocked the fashion world by replacing Dior's French artistic director Marc Bohan with Gianfranco Ferré, an Italian designer.

In 1990 LVMH acquired Lanson champagne from BSN for $620 million and kept its vineyards and the Pommery brand. It sold the Lanson brand in 1991. That same year the company announced its intention to buy 49% of *Femme* magazine from Hachette.

WHAT

	1990 Sales		1990 Operating Income	
	FF mil.	% of total	FF mil.	% of total
Champagne & wine	5,147	26	1,340	24
Cognac & spirits	5,074	26	2,299	40
Luggage & leather	4,450	22	1,755	31
Perfume & beauty	4,654	23	462	8
Other	507	3	(184)	(3)
Total	**19,832**	**100**	**5,672**	**100**

Champagne and Wines
Blue Nun
Canard-Duchêne
Chandon
Dom Pérignon
Henriot
Mercier
Moët & Chandon
Petite Liquorelle
Pierlant
Rozes Port
Ruinart
Simi
Veuve Clicquot Ponsardin

Cognac and Spirits
Cognac Hine
Napoleon
Paradis
Raynal
Three Barrels
V.S.
V.S.O.P.
X.O.

Luggage and Leather Goods
Cuir Epi
Loewe
Louis Vuitton
Nomade

Perfumes and Beauty Products
Christian Dior
Diorella
Dioressence
Diorissimo
Eau Fraiche
Eau Sauvage
Eau Sauvage Extrême
Fahrenheit
Miss Dior
Poison
Christian Lacroix
C'est la Vie!
Givenchy
Eau de Givenchy
Givenchy Gentleman
Givenchy III
L'Interdit
Monsieur de Givenchy
Prisme Soleil
Xeryus
Ysatis
RoC
Kefrane
Keops
RoC

HOW MUCH

$=FF5.08 (Dec. 31, 1990)	9-Year Growth	1981	1982	1983[1]	1984	1985	1986	1987	1988	1989	1990
Sales (FF mil.)	18.9%	4,179	4,588	5,329	6,841	7,689	9,797	13,247	16,442	19,635	19,832
Net income (FF mil.)	28.9%	343	339	415	547	696	1,101	1,490	2,040	2,932	3,375
Income as % of sales	—	8.2%	7.4%	7.8%	8.0%	9.1%	11.2%	11.2%	12.4%	14.9%	17.0%
Earnings per share (FF)	18.4%	*54*	*53*	57	74	92	86	135	176	218	249
Stock price – high (FF)	—	440	574	987	1,338	1,674	2,325	2,542	3,456	5,540	5,450
Stock price – low (FF)	—	324	358	532	912	1,201	1,528	1,270	1,500	3,316	3,110
Stock price – close (FF)	27.3%	379	556	973	1,302	1,652	1,971	1,570	3,302	5,520	3,338
P/E – high	—	8	11	17	18	18	27	19	20	25	22
P/E – low	—	6	7	9	12	13	18	9	9	15	13
Dividends per share (FF)	22.8%	10.69	12.03	13.89	15.97	19.17	25.00	32.00	44.00	61.00	68.00
Book value per share (FF)	18.2%	269	316	380	449	485	531	681	835	1,073	1,214

1990 Year-end:
Debt ratio: 33.3%
Return on equity: 21.7%
Cash (mil.): FF6,875
Long-term debt (mil.): FF8,483
No. of shares (mil.): 14
Dividends:
1990 average yield: 2.0%
1990 payout: 27.4%
Market value (mil.): $9,199
Sales (mil.): $3,904

Stock Price History High/Low 1981–90
6,000
5,000
4,000
3,000
2,000
1,000
0

[1] Accounting change

KEY COMPETITORS

Allied-Lyons
Amway
Anheuser-Busch
Avon
Bass
Brown-Forman
Colgate-Palmolive
Estée Lauder
Gallo
Grand Metropolitan
Kirin
L'Oréal
MacAndrews & Forbes
Nestlé
Procter & Gamble
Seagram
Unilever

COMPAGNIE DES MACHINES BULL

OVERVIEW

Paris-based Compagnie des Machines Bull (commonly known as Groupe Bull) is the 3rd largest Europe-based computer maker (after Siemens-Nixdorf and Olivetti). The French government owns 93% of Bull, which has been kept afloat by subsidies since 1963.

Suffering from the same malady that affects other European computer makers — intense competition from the US and Japan — Bull has racked up losses exceeding $1.25 billion since 1989. Recent attempts by the government to inject cash into the ailing company have come under scrutiny from the EC, so Bull has embarked on a major cost-cutting restructuring effort.

Uniting Bull's 4 operating companies (Bull SA, Bull HN Information Systems, Bull International NV, and Zenith Data Systems) under one central authority is the challenge now facing chairman Francis Lorentz. In addition to moving the company away from its proprietary operating system to a UNIX-based open system, he laid off 5,000 workers and closed 7 of Bull's 13 plants in 1991. The reorganization of Bull HN was facilitated by NEC's 1991 decision to swap its 15% stake in the venture for a 4.7% stake in Bull itself. Bull also maintains a close working relationship with Honeywell (US), which owns 12.8% of Bull HN.

WHEN

Bull is named for Norwegian engineer Frederik Bull, who in 1919 invented a punch-card machine. Georges Vieillard, a French bank employee, bought the patents for Bull's machine in 1931. Vieillard, who wanted to develop a better adding machine, persuaded the owners of a punch-card supplier to finance his venture, and Compagnie des Machines Bull was incorporated in Paris in 1933.

Bull started competing with IBM in 1935, after unveiling a tabulator capable of printing up to 150 lines a minute. Bull went on to confound its American rival by pioneering the use of germanium diodes (instead of electron tubes) in its first mainframe computer, the Gamma 3 (introduced in 1952). But the battle of one-upmanship proved to be costly. Bull defaulted on a $4 million loan payment in 1964 and, faced with financial ruin, jumped at the chance when General Electric (US) offered to buy a 50% stake (later increased to 66%). The company (renamed Bull-GE) continued to lose money until 1969. It became Honeywell Bull in 1970, when GE sold its computer businesses to Honeywell.

In the meantime the French government had formed Compagnie Internationale pour l'Informatique (CII) to ensure the survival of the French computer industry (1966). In 1975 CII merged with Honeywell Bull to form CII-Honeywell Bull (CII-HB). Initially, Honeywell owned a 47% minority stake in the company, but in 1982 it accepted a gradual buyout offer from the French government. CII-HB then merged with 3 other French computer companies (Transac, Sems, and R2E) to form Groupe Bull in 1983.

Bull was on shaky financial ground in the early 1980s, posting sizable losses from 1981 through 1984, but it got back on track, at least temporarily, under the leadership of Jacques Stern. In 1987 Bull entered a US-based 3-way mainframe computer partnership (Honeywell Bull Inc.) with Honeywell and NEC. Originally owning 42.5% of the venture, Bull upped its share to 72.2% (reducing Honeywell's share from 42.5% to 12.8%) and renamed the venture Bull HN Information Systems. In 1989 Bull bought Zenith's computer businesses (Zenith Data Systems, a leading US laptop computer and IBM-clone maker).

In 1990 Francis Lorentz (named chairman in 1989) initiated a reorganization plan that he hopes will return Bull to profitability by 1992. Growing competition from American and Japanese computer makers had combined with reorganization costs to produce large losses in 1989 and 1990.

HOW MUCH

$=FF5.08 (Dec. 31, 1990)	9-Year Growth	1981	1982	1983	1984	1985	1986	1987	1988	1989	1990
Sales (FF mil.)	18.8%	7,347	8,134	11,639	13,596	16,109	17,796	18,701	31,546	32,721	34,580
Net income (FF mil.)	—	(449)	(1,351)	(625)	(489)	110	271	225	303	(267)	(6,790)
Income as % of sales	—	(6.1%)	(16.6%)	(5.4%)	(3.6%)	0.7%	1.5%	1.2%	1.0%	(0.8%)	(19.6%)
Earnings per share (FF)	—	—	(55)	(24)	(17)	3	8	6	8	(6)	(141)
Stock price – high (FF)	—	—	170	185	155	245	380	281	138	125	90
Stock price – low (FF)	—	0	95	135	125	130	200	79	70	75	31
Stock price – close (FF)	—	—	—	—	—	—	205	82	87	78	32
P/E – high	—	—	—	—	—	82	48	47	17	—	—
P/E – low	—	—	—	—	—	43	25	13	9	—	—
Dividends per share (FF)	0.0%	0.0	0.0	0.0	0.0	0.0	0.0	0.0	0.0	0.0	0.0
Book value per share (FF)	—	—	(2)	18	34	53	107	120	127	120	(22)

1990 Year-end:
Debt ratio: 112.1%
Return on equity: —
Cash (mil.): FF1,937
Long-term debt (mil.): FF9,778
No. of shares (mil.): 48
Dividends:
1990 average yield: 0.0%
1990 payout: —
Market value (mil.): $302
Sales (mil.): $6,807

Stock Price History High/Low 1982–90

400
350
300
250
200
150
100
50
0

Principal exchange: Paris
Fiscal year ends: December 31

WHO

Chairman and CEO: Francis Lorentz, age 49
Director Corporate Finance and Administration: Jean-Claude Buono
Director Marketing and Business Planning: Michel Bloch
Director Human Resources: Christian Briere de la Hosseraye
Auditors: Bernard Montagne, André Amic & Associés; Deloitte Ross Tohmatsu; Roger Marron
Employees: 44,476

WHERE

HQ: 121, avenue de Malakoff, 75764 Paris, Cedex 16, France
Phone: 011-33-1-45-02-90-90
Fax: 011-33-1-45-02-96-96
US Address: Bull HN Information Systems Inc., 300 Concord Rd., Billerica, MA 01821
US Phone: 508-294-6000
US Fax: 508-294-4470

Bull sells its products in more than 90 countries.

	1990 Sales		1990 Pretax Income	
	FF mil.	% of total	FF mil.	% of total
Western Europe	24,755	67	(1,545)	—
North America	9,548	26	(1,115)	—
Other countries	2,686	7	10	—
Adjustments	(2,409)	—	(4,818)	—
Total	**34,580**	**100**	**(7,468)**	**—**

WHAT

Major Product Lines
Application software
ATMs
Banking systems
Computer peripherals
Mainframes
Minicomputers
Office automation systems
PCs, portables, and laptops
Programming languages
Scientific minicomputers
Smart cards

Selected Subsidiaries and Affiliates
Bull Data Systems NV
Heath Company (computers, US)
Zenith Data Systems Corp. (portable and desktop computers, workstations, US)
Bull HN Information Systems Inc. (87.2%, US)
Bull International NV (Netherlands)
Bull SA (97.5%, France)
Bull Ingénierie, SA (53.6%, office automation, France)
Micro Card Technologies Inc. (90%, US)
Prologue SA (operating systems, France)
European Computer Industry Research Centre GmbH (33.3%, Germany)

KEY COMPETITORS

Amdahl	Hewlett-Packard	Prime
AT&T	Hitachi	Sharp
Apple	Hyundai	Siemens
Atari	Intergraph	Storage Technology
Commodore	IBM	Sun Microsystems
Compaq	Matsushita	Tandem
Control Data	NCR	Unisys
Data General	NEC	Wang
DEC	Olivetti	
Fujitsu	Philips	
Harris		

MARKS AND SPENCER PLC

OVERVIEW

Referred to as "Marks and Sparks" by its British patrons, Marks and Spencer is the UK's leading retailer and the most admired company in the UK, according to a survey by the *Economist*. The company's prosperity stems largely from the simplicity of its department stores. Marks & Spencer stores do not indulge in unnecessary merchandise displays; they provide no fitting rooms; and they offer only one brand, St Michael, which is Britain's best-seller.

The company's policy of offering high quality goods at a reasonable price draws 14 million customers to its stores every week, giving Marks and Spencer a 16% share of the UK's clothing market and 5% of its food market.

Despite its success in the UK, the company has had a difficult time exporting its stodgy style of retailing across the Atlantic, where shoppers are accustomed to more pizazz from their stores. Subsidiaries D'Allaird's (women's clothing) and Peoples (general merchandise) in Canada and Brooks Brothers (upscale clothing) in the US have yet to live up to Marks and Spencer's stunning UK retailing achievements.

Principal exchange: London
Fiscal year ends: March 31

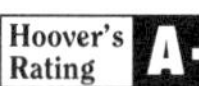

WHO

Chairman and CEO: Richard Greenbury
Deputy Chairman: Clinton Silver
Managing Director Finance: John Oates
Executive Directors of Personnel: David Sieff, Peter Salsbury
Auditors: Coopers & Lybrand Deloitte
Employees: 75,000

WHEN

Fleeing anti-Semitic persecution in Russian Poland, 19-year-old Michael Marks emigrated to England in 1882. Eventually settling in Leeds, Marks eked out a meager existence as a traveling peddler until 1884 when he opened a small stall at the town market.

Because he spoke little English, Marks laid out all of his merchandise and hung a sign that read "Don't Ask the Price, It's a Penny," unaware at the time that self-service and self-selection would eventually become the retailing standard. His methods were so successful that he had penny bazaars in 5 cities by 1890.

Rapid expansion, including a new warehouse and permanent store, continued during the 1890s. Finding himself unable to single-handedly run the growing operation, Marks established an equal partnership with Englishman Tom Spencer, a cashier for a local distributor, forming Marks and Spencer in 1894. By the turn of the century, the company had 36 branches.

Following the deaths of Spencer (1905) and Marks (1907), management of the company did not return to family hands until 1917 when Marks's 28-year-old son Simon became chairman. In 1914 the company bought the London Penny Bazaar, an imitator of its original penny store idea.

During the 1920s Marks and Spencer broke with time-honored British retailing tradition by eliminating wholesalers and establishing links directly with manufacturers, a strategy at which the company still excels today. In 1927 Marks and Spencer went public and the following year launched its famous St Michael brand.

The company quickly turned its attention to pruning unprofitable departments to concentrate only on goods that had a rapid turnover. By the middle of the 1930s, Marks and Spencer was Europe's largest textile retailer.

The company sustained severe losses during WWII, when approximately half of its stores were damaged. Marks and Spencer rebuilt and in 1965 Simon Marks's brother-in-law Israel Sieff became chairman.

During the early 1970s the company decided to expand to North America by purchasing 3 Canadian chains: Peoples (general merchandise), D'Allaird's (women's clothing), and Walker's (clothing shops, since converted to Marks & Spencer). For the next decade and a half, Marks and Spencer's Canadian operations struggled to turn a profit, slowly realizing that Canada did not accept British tastes in retailing.

In 1985 the company launched its long-overdue charge card. In 1988 Marks and Spencer entered the US retailing market by purchasing Kings Super Markets (New Jersey) and Brooks Brothers (upscale clothing stores).

WHERE

HQ: Michael House, 37-67 Baker St., London W1A 1DN, UK
Phone: 011-44-71-268-4174
Fax: 011-44-71-268-2675
US HQ: Marks and Spencer US Holdings Inc., 1120 Ave. of the Americas, 14th Floor, New York, NY 10036
US Phone: 212-382-1045
US Fax: 212-382-2649

	No. of Stores	Sq. Ft. Thou.
UK & Ireland	292	9,225
Other Europe	11	325
N. America & Hong Kong	376	3,895
Total	**679**	**13,445**

	1990 Sales		1990 Operating Income	
	£ mil.	% of total	£ mil.	% of total
UK & Ireland	4,845	86	598	96
Other Europe	121	2	15	2
N. America & Hong Kong	593	11	15	2
Export	49	1	—	—
Total	**5,608**	**100**	**628**	**100**

WHAT

	1990 Sales	
	£ mil.	% of total
Clothing	2,755	49
Homeware	652	12
Foods	2,120	38
Financial activities	81	1
Total	**5,608**	**100**

	No. of Stores
Brooks Brothers (clothing stores)	
US	52
Japan	30
D'Allaird's (Canadian clothing stores)	119
Kings Super Markets (US)	16
Marks & Spencer (department stores)	
UK & Ireland	292
Canada	76
France	8
Hong Kong	3
Belgium	2
Spain	1
Peoples (Canadian department stores)	80
Total owned	679
St Michael (franchise shops)	50
Total	**729**

HOW MUCH

£=$1.93 (Dec. 31, 1990)	9-Year Growth	1981	1982	1983	1984	1985	1986	1987	1988	1989	1990
Sales (£ mil.)	12.9%	1,879	2,209	2,517	2,869	3,208	3,735	4,221	4,577	5,122	5,608
Net income (£ mil.)	16.3%	100	121	135	166	181	222	276	323	343	390
Income as % of sales	—	5.3%	5.5%	5.4%	5.8%	5.6%	5.9%	6.5%	7.1%	6.7%	7.0%
Earnings per share (p)	16.0%	4	5	5	6	7	8	10	12	13	15
Stock price – high (p)	—	72	119	113	135	192	227	281	190	225	228
Stock price – low (p)	—	54	63	96	99	115	167	160	140	149	181
Stock price – close (p)	15.1%	63	111	108	120	176	180	183	154	201	223
P/E – high	—	19	26	22	21	28	27	27	16	17	16
P/E – low	—	14	14	19	16	17	20	15	11	12	12
Dividends per share (p)	14.4%	1.9	2.3	2.6	3.1	3.4	3.9	4.5	5.1	5.6	6.4
Book value per share (p)	6.5%	46	41	44	47	50	55	59	81	72	81

1990 Year-end:
Debt ratio: 14.0%
Return on equity: 19.0%
Cash (mil.): £276
Long-term debt (mil.): £355
No. of shares (mil.): 2,695
Dividends:
1990 average yield: 2.9%
1990 payout: 44.1%
Market value (mil.): $11,599
Sales (mil.): $10,823

Stock Price History
High/Low 1981–90

300
250
200
150
100
50
0

KEY COMPETITORS

Albertson's
American Stores
Carter Hawley Hale
Dayton Hudson
Great A&P
Hudson's Bay
Ito-Yokado
The Limited
Macy
May
Mercantile Stores
Montgomery Ward
Nordstrom
J. C. Penney
Sears
Vendex
Vons

MATSUSHITA ELECTRIC INDUSTRIAL CO., LTD.

OVERVIEW

Matsushita is the world's foremost consumer electronics manufacturer and the leader in VCR production. Much of the company's business is done through majority-owned, publicly held subsidiaries, such as Victor Company of Japan (JVC). Overseas sales provide 44% of the company's total revenues.

In addition to TVs, VCRs, appliances, and other consumer goods marketed under familiar brand names, including Panasonic, JVC, and Quasar, Matsushita makes fax and telecommunications equipment, semiconductors, PCs, and robots. The company is now shifting its emphasis to industrial electronics.

With its 1991 purchase of MCA, Matsushita gained access to a wide array of entertainment software. MCA produces and distributes film and music entertainment (Universal Pictures and MCA Records), publishes books (G. P. Putnam's Sons), and broadcasts cable TV (USA Network, 50%). MCA also owns Hollywood and Florida theme parks (Universal Studios) and 50% of Cineplex Odeon, one of the largest movie theater chains in North America.

NYSE symbol: MC (ADR)
Fiscal year ends: March 31

Hoover's Rating **B+**

WHO

Chairman: Masaharu Matsushita
President: Akio Tanii, age 63
EVP and Head of Financial and Accounting Administration: Masahiko Hirata
Head of Personnel Management and General Affairs: Hideo Takahashi
Auditors: KPMG Peat Marwick
Employees: 198,299

WHEN

Grade school dropout Konosuke Matsushita founded the company that bears his name in Osaka in 1918 to manufacture electrical sockets. The company grew by developing inexpensive lamps, batteries, radios, and motors in the 1920s and 1930s. During WWII the Japanese government ordered the company to build wood-laminate products for the military. Postwar occupation forces prevented Matsushita from working at his company for 4 years.

Matsushita returned just in time for Japan's postwar boom. Matsushita entered into a joint venture, Matsushita Electronics, with Philips (Netherlands) in 1952; it began producing televisions, refrigerators, and washing machines in 1953. Matsushita bought a majority stake in Victor Company of Japan (JVC, originally established by RCA Victor) in 1954. The 1959 opening of a subsidiary in New York began Matsushita's drive overseas.

By 1960 Matsushita had introduced vacuum cleaners, tape recorders, stereos, and color TVs. Marketed under the National, Panasonic, and Technics names, the company's products were usually not cutting edge but were always made efficiently in huge quantities and sold at low prices. Matsushita became Japan's largest home appliance maker in the 1960s and continued to broaden its product lines, introducing air conditioners, microwave ovens, stereo components, and VCRs in the 1960s and 1970s. JVC developed the VHS format for VCRs. In 1974 the company bought Motorola's US TV plants, adding Quasar to its brand-name roster.

Already a world leader in consumer electronics, Matsushita (under the management of Akio Tanii since 1986) has expanded its semiconductor, office and factory automation, automobile electronics, audiovisual, housing, and air conditioning product offerings. In 1991 Matsushita moved into the entertainment field by paying $6.6 billion for MCA (the largest single purchase of an American company by a Japanese company to date). MCA had been founded in 1924 by Jules Stern, a Chicago ophthalmologist who had worked his way through medical school by organizing bands to play one-night stands. By 1937, when the company moved to Hollywood, MCA was handling talent for radio, television, and motion pictures. The company bought Decca Records, which owned 87% of Universal Pictures, in 1961.

Once under Matsushita's ownership, MCA spun off its New York–area TV station to comply with FCC rules governing foreign ownership. Likewise, the Interior Department (disturbed by a Japanese company in a national park) pressured Matsushita to sell MCA's concession stands in Yosemite.

In 1991 Matsushita joined Philips as colicenser of Digital Compact Cassette (DCC) technology. DCC machines can play both conventional and digitally recorded tapes.

WHERE

HQ: Matsushita Denki Sangyo Kabushiki Kaisha, 1006, Oaza Kadoma, Kadoma City, Osaka, Japan
Phone: 011-81-6-908-1121
Fax: 011-81-6-906-1762
US HQ: Matsushita Electric Corp. of America, One Panasonic Way, Secaucus, NJ 07094-2917
US Phone: 201-348-7000
US Fax: 201-348-8378 (Personnel)

Matsushita operates 354 factories in 39 countries.

	1990 Sales	
	$ mil.	% of total
Japan	21,690	56
North America	6,698	18
Other countries	9,786	26
Total	**37,753**	**100**

WHAT

	1990 Sales	
	$ mil.	% of total
Home appliances	5,047	13
Electronic components	4,913	13
Batteries & kitchen-related products	1,963	5
Audio equipment	3,529	9
Communication & industrial equipment	8,647	23
Video equipment	10,051	27
Other products	3,603	10
Total	**37,753**	**100**

Consumer Brand Names
JVC
National
Panasonic
Quasar
Technics
Victor

Major Products
Audio products
Bar code readers
Batteries
Camcorders
Capacitors
CD-ROM drives
Computers
Copiers
Displays and CRTs
Fax machines
Home appliances
Industrial robots
Motors
Pagers
PCs
Point of sale systems
Semiconductors
Telephones
TVs
VCRs
Welding machines

Book Publishing
Grosset & Dunlap
Perigee Books
G.P. Putnam's Sons

Broadcasting
USA Network (50%)

Film Production and Distribution
Cinema International (49%)
MCA Home Video
MCA TV
United International Pictures (33%)
Universal Pay Television
Universal Pictures

Music
MCA
Universal Amphitheatre

KEY COMPETITORS

Other consumer and industrial electronics companies; computer, office equipment, and telecommunications equipment manufacturers; book publishers; film production and distribution companies; and cable TV broadcasters

HOW MUCH

Stock prices are for ADRs ADR = 10 shares	9-Year Growth	1981	1982	1983	1984	1985	1986	1987	1988	1989	1990
Sales ($ mil.)	11.9%	13,690	15,617	14,037	16,901	19,347	24,890	28,067	38,552	41,699	37,753
Net income ($ mil.)	10.9%	585	709	604	774	977	1,214	1,004	1,303	1,617	1,482
Income as % of sales	—	4.3%	4.5%	4.3%	4.6%	5.1%	4.9%	3.6%	3.4%	3.9%	3.9%
Earnings per share ($)	8.4%	3.31	3.85	3.26	4.17	5.16	6.31	*5.25*	6.41	7.57	6.81
Stock price – high ($)	—	64.94	53.46	74.57	76.73	64.29	129.05	186.43	219.05	198.10	166.00
Stock price – low ($)	—	30.70	31.17	40.91	49.35	46.19	57.14	88.81	159.29	153.75	115.50
Stock price – close ($)	10.8%	46.75	52.81	74.57	58.57	61.31	120.71	160.36	197.62	164.00	118.00
P/E – high	—	20	14	23	18	12	20	36	34	26	24
P/E – low	—	9	8	13	12	9	9	17	25	20	17
Dividends per share ($)	7.7%	0.35	0.33	0.34	0.45	0.34	0.46	0.62	0.72	0.92	0.68
Book value per share ($)	14.1%	29.53	32.24	30.65	37.15	40.83	54.27	70.86	101.38	111.04	96.77

1990 Year-end:
Debt ratio: 27.2%
Return on equity: 6.6%
Cash (mil.): $14,756
Current ratio: 1.77
Long-term debt (mil.): $7,529
No. of shares (mil.): 208
Dividends:
1990 average yield: 0.6%
1990 payout: 9.9%
Market value (mil.): $24,547

Stock Price History High/Low 1981–90
250
200
150
100
50
0

MAXWELL COMMUNICATION CORPORATION PLC

OVERVIEW

One of the world's top 10 media companies, London-based Maxwell Communication (named for its founder, Robert Maxwell) is facing an uncertain future. Since 1988 the company has used acquisitions (financed by heavy borrowing) to transform itself from primarily a UK-based printer to a publisher with about 70% of its assets in North America. Now, with debt exceeding $2.1 billion, the company is putting core assets on the block.

In 1991 Maxwell sold Pergamon Press (scientific journals). Also for sale is P.E. Collier (encyclopedias), and Maxwell plans to spin off major US assets (including publisher Macmillan, Official Airlines Guides, and language guide publisher Berlitz), which contribute about 90% of the company's operating profits. Other subsidiaries (currently not for sale) include Que (computer manuals) and Maxwell Online (databases).

Maxwell's stock is traded on several exchanges, but the Maxwell family and a private trust (Maxwell Foundation) control nearly 70% of its stock.

OTC symbol: MWCL (ADR)
Fiscal year ends: March 31

WHO

Chairman and CEO: Robert Maxwell, age 68, £300,000 pay
Deputy Chairman: Jean-Pierre Anselmini
Joint Managing Director: Ian Maxwell
Joint Managing Director: Kevin Maxwell
Finance Director: Basil Brookes
Group Human Resources Director: Robert B. Gregory
Auditors: Coopers & Lybrand Deloitte
Employees: 20,652

WHEN

In 1938, 15-year-old Jan Ludwig Hoch fled Czechoslovakia to avoid Nazi persecution. He fought for the French Resistance and, after the fall of France, served in the British army with distinction. He changed his identity several times in the interim, finally settling on the name Ian Robert Maxwell.

After WWII Maxwell started importing scientific journals from Germany for a London-based joint venture of German and British publishing interests. He bought the venture in 1951 and renamed it Pergamon Press. He took the company public in 1964, the same year he was elected to Parliament for the Labour party. In 1969 New York financier Saul Steinberg pulled out of a deal to buy Pergamon, claiming Maxwell had misrepresented its value. Maxwell was ousted from the board and blackballed by British authorities as being unfit to run a public company. The scandal cost him his parliamentary seat in 1970. In 1974 he redeemed himself by retaking control of Pergamon.

Maxwell bought British Printing & Communications Corporation (BPCC) in 1980 and entered the newspaper business in 1984 when he purchased Mirror Group, publisher of the *Daily Mirror*. Both companies were in financial straits when Maxwell bought them; he turned them around by wresting concessions (including huge staff cuts) from their unions. Maxwell sold BPCC in 1989.

Maxwell became America's largest media printer after buying Alco Gravure in 1988 (sold as part of Maxwell Graphics in 1990). With his purchase of Macmillan in 1988, Maxwell became a publisher of language instruction materials (*Berlitz*), encyclopedias (*Collier's*), and computer manuals (*Que*). Maxwell also became the publisher of *Official Airline Guides* after buying the company from Dun & Bradstreet in 1988. Acquisitions in 1989 included BRS (electronic information), Merrill Publishing (educational books), and the Prentice Hall tax and legal information business. That year Maxwell sold 44% of Berlitz to the public to raise cash.

In 1990 Maxwell launched a weekly pan-European newspaper, the *European*, and bought one of East Germany's biggest publishers, Berliner Verlag. His latest acquisition, the New York *Daily News*, marks Maxwell's first attempt at US newspaper publishing. After enduring a 5-month-long strike and losing about $1 million a month, Chicago's Tribune Company paid Maxwell $60 million to take the *Daily News* in 1991. The paper is now part of Robert Maxwell's 51%-owned Mirror Group (he sold 49% to the public in 1991).

Maxwell's companies were blacklisted by the Arab League in 1991 for doing business with Israel.

WHERE

HQ: Maxwell House, 8/10 Mew Fetter Ln., London EC4 1DU, UK
Phone: 011-44-71-353-0246
Fax: 011-44-71-353-3398
US HQ: 866 Third Ave., New York, NY 10022
Phone: 212-702-2000
Fax: 212-319-1216

	1990 Sales	
	£ mil.	**% of total**
UK	198	15
Other Europe	169	13
US & Canada	874	65
Other countries	97	7
Adjustments	(96)	—
Total	**1,242**	**100**

WHAT

	1990 Sales	
	£ mil.	**% of total**
Communications & publishing	858	64
Other	480	36
Adjustments	(96)	—
Total	**1,242**	**100**

Information Services and Electronic Publishing
The Aberdeen University Press Ltd. (reference and scientific books)
BRS Software Products
Marquis Who's Who (*Who's Who in America*)
Maxwell Online (patent research)
Nimbus Records, Inc. (75%, music on compact disc)
Official Airline Guides
ORAC, Ltd. (60%, chemical information services)
Prentice Hall Information Services (*Federal Taxes 2nd* and *Payroll Guide*)
Standard Rate & Data Service (*Circulation*)

Language Instruction
Berlitz (56%; language instruction, translation, travel publications)

Reference and Professional Publishing
Collier's and *Caxton's* encyclopedias
Macdonald paperbacks (Abacus, Cardinal, and Futura)
Macmillan/McGraw-Hill School Publishing Company (50%; joint venture with McGraw-Hill, Inc.; US)
Macmillan Publishing Company (US)
Charles Scribner's Sons
Que computer manuals
Maxwell Magazines & Exhibitions (business pubs.)

KEY COMPETITORS

Advance Publications
Berkshire Hathaway
Bertelsmann
Commerce Clearing House
R. R. Donnelley
Dow Jones
Dun & Bradstreet
Gannett
Hachette
Hearst
Knight-Ridder
Lloyd's of London
McGraw-Hill
Mead
News Corp.
New York Times
Paramount
Pearson
Reed
Thomson Corp.
Time Warner
Times Mirror

HOW MUCH

£=$1.93 (Dec. 31, 1990)	9-Year Growth	1981	1982	1983	1984	1985	1986	1987	1988	1989[1]	1990
Sales (£ mil.)	22.6%	198	193	231	267	265	462	884	—	1,390	1,242
Net income (£ mil.)	—	(14)	12	10	40	20	60	132	—	190	101
Income as % of sales	—	(7.1%)	6.2%	4.3%	15.0%	7.5%	13.0%	14.9%	—	13.7%	8.1%
Earnings per share (p)	39.5%	1	11	15	27	17	23	27	—	24	20
Stock price – high (p)	—	—	—	—	—	—	—	395	270	238	234
Stock price – low (p)	—	—	—	—	—	—	—	197	180	167	133
Stock price – close (p)	—	—	—	—	—	—	—	240	187	223	148
P/E – high	—	—	—	—	—	—	—	15	—	10	12
P/E – low	—	—	—	—	—	—	—	7	—	7	7
Dividends per share (p)	—	0.0	0.0	6.0	11.0	12.0	14.0	14.0	—	18.0	15.0
Book value per share (p)	—	—	—	—	—	—	—	163	—	158	149

1990 Year-end:
Debt ratio: 63.6%
Return on equity: 10.4%
Cash (mil.): £65
Long-term debt (mil.): £1,680
No. of shares (mil.): 646
Dividends:
1990 average yield: 10.1%
1990 payout: 75.0%
Market value (mil.): $1,845
Sales (mil.): $2,397

Stock Price History High/Low 1987–90

400 350 300 250 200 150 100 50 0

[1] 15-month period

MAZDA MOTOR CORPORATION

OVERVIEW

Mazda is putting the pedal to the metal. In the last 3 years, Japan's #4 carmaker established 2 new Japanese automobile product lines and sales networks, introduced several new models, and spent heavily on a 9-model factory under construction in Hiroshima. In the 1992 model year, Mazda plans 4 to 6 more introductions, possibly including a high-margin luxury model destined for the US.

Successful niche market entries, including the sporty Miata and MPV minivan, are boosting Mazda's Japanese and US revenue. However, smaller, less profitable 323 models continue to dominate Mazda's sales mix.

Not large in its industry — #11 worldwide — Mazda relies heavily on deals and partnerships with other carmakers in pursuing its global ambitions. Ford owns 23.9% of Mazda. Mazda sells Fords, Lancias, and Citroëns in Japan and builds Ford Probes (as well as 626s and MX-6s) in its Flat Rock, Michigan, plant.

Principal exchange: Tokyo
Fiscal year ends: March 31

WHO

Chairman: Kenichi Yamamoto
President: Norimasa Furuta, age 62
EVP: Yoshihiro Wada
Chairman, Mazda Motor Manufacturing (USA) Corp.: Osamu Nobuto
Auditors: Asahi Shinwa & Co.
Employees: 28,573

WHEN

Founded in 1920, Toyo Cork Kogyo initially produced cork in Hiroshima. Under President Jujiro Matsudo the company changed its name to Toyo Kogyo in 1927 and began producing machine tools in 1929. Impressed by Ford trucks used in post-earthquake relief efforts in 1923, Matsudo had the company produce a 3-wheel motorcycle/truck hybrid (1931).

In the 1930s Toyo Kogyo expanded truck production but, with the outbreak of the 2nd Sino-Japanese War, was forced to cut truck output and make rifles. The company built a prototype passenger car in 1940 but then focused on making weapons during WWII.

The August 1945 atom bomb explosion in Hiroshima killed more than 400 Toyo Kogyo workers, but the devastated company persevered, producing 10 trucks in December. Four years later the company was turning out 800 per month. The Korean War boosted demand for Toyo Kogyo's 3-wheel trucks in the early 1950s. The company finally introduced a 4-wheel model in 1958.

The company launched the first Mazda, a 2-seat minicar, in 1960 (Mazda is the name of the good deity in the ancient, dualistic Zoroastrian religion). In 1961 Toyo Kogyo licensed new, promising Wankel (rotary) engine technology from Audi. After a string of new model releases, Mazda became Japan's #3 automaker in 1964. The following year the company gained diesel technology in a licensing deal. In 1967 Toyo Kogyo introduced the first rotary engine Mazda, the Cosmo/110S, and followed with the Familia in 1968.

Exports to the US began in 1970 and the company grew rapidly, spending heavily on new production capacity. However, recession, high gas prices, and concern over the inefficiency of rotary engines led to a halt in growth and a massive inventory buildup in the mid-1970s. Sumitomo Bank stepped in to bail out Toyo Kogyo. The company shifted emphasis back to piston engines but managed to launch the popular rotary engine RX-7 in 1978.

Ford's need of small car expertise and Sumitomo's desire for a large partner for its client led to Ford's purchase of 25% of Toyo Kogyo in 1979. Toyo Kogyo's GLC/323 and 626 models, introduced in the early 1980s, were sold as Fords in Asia, the Middle East, and Latin America. Later in the 1980s the company provided parts for the Ford Festiva, began assembling the Ford Probe, started supplying parts for the new Ford Escort, and began importing Fords (1988).

The company changed its name to Mazda in 1984 and established a US plant in 1985. Profits recovered until appreciation of the yen began to hurt margins in 1986. Under Mazda president Norimasa Furuta, a 29-year MITI veteran, the company launched the hot-selling Miata and MPV in 1989 and the Ford-built Navajo in 1990.

WHERE

HQ: 3-1, Shinchi, Fuchu-cho, Aki-gun, Hiroshima 730-91, Japan
Phone: 011-81-82-282-1111
Fax: 011-81-82-287-5190
US HQ: Mazda Motor Manufacturing (USA) Corporation, 1 Mazda Dr., Flat Rock, MI 48134
US Phone: 313-782-7800
US Fax: 313-782-2189

Mazda operates 3 manufacturing plants in Japan and conducts assembly operations in 19 other countries, including the US. The company's vehicles are sold in over 120 countries.

	1990 Sales	
	No. of vehicles	% of total
Japan	551,198	41
North America	341,427	25
Europe	282,695	21
Other regions	181,875	13
Total	**1,357,195**	**100**

WHAT

	1990 Sales	
	No. of vehicles	% of total
Mazda 323	452,442	33
Mazda 626	237,885	18
Mazda Miata	66,709	5
Other passenger cars	283,850	21
Commercial vehicles	316,309	23
Total	**1,357,195**	**100**

Japanese Sales Networks
Autorama
AUTOZAM
EUNOS
Mazda
Mazda Auto

Passenger Car Models (US Markets)
323
626
929
Miata
MPV
MX-6
Navajo
Protegé
RX-7

Commercial Vehicle Models (US Markets)
B-Series pickup trucks

HOW MUCH

$=¥135 (Dec. 31, 1990)	9-Year Growth	1981[1]	1982[1]	1983	1984	1985	1986	1987[2]	1988	1989[3]	1990
Sales (¥ bil.)	8.4%	1,163	1,180	1,455	1,530	1,669	1,728	1,691	2,004	862	2,402
Net income (¥ bil.)	1.8%	20	25	27	35	40	15	5	10	7	23
Income as % of sales	—	1.7%	2.2%	1.9%	2.3%	2.4%	0.9%	0.3%	0.5%	0.8%	1.0%
Earnings per share (¥)	(1.1%)	*25*	*30*	*32*	*40*	*44*	*16*	*5*	*10*	*7*	*22*
Stock price – high (¥)	—	464	458	570	570	492	430	491	888	1,130	993
Stock price – low (¥)	—	281	278	379	420	385	361	354	385	736	500
Stock price – close (¥)	5.8%	341	440	566	435	390	372	395	745	1,010	568
P/E – high	—	19	15	18	14	11	27	106	86	—	44
P/E – low	—	11	9	12	11	9	23	76	37	—	22
Dividends per share (¥)	5.7%	4.55	5.50	6.50	7.00	7.50	7.50	7.50	7.50	7.50	7.50
Book value per share (¥)	8.4%	176	206	241	281	323	329	326	331	337	365

1990 Year-end:
Debt ratio: 33.8%
Return on equity: 6.4%
Cash (bil.): ¥215
Long-term debt (bil.): ¥200
No. of shares (mil.): 1,072
Dividends:
1990 average yield: 1.3%
1990 payout: 33.6%
Market value (mil.): $4,510
Sales (mil.): $17,793

Stock Price History High/Low 1981–90

1,200
1,000
800
600
400
200
0

[1] Unconsolidated data [2] Accounting change [3] 5-month period

KEY COMPETITORS

BMW
Chrysler
Daewoo
Daimler-Benz
Fiat
Ford
General Motors
Honda
Hyundai
Isuzu
Mitsubishi
Nissan
Peugeot
Renault
Saab-Scania
Suzuki
Toyota
Volkswagen
Volvo

MICHELIN

OVERVIEW

With the 1989 purchase of Uniroyal Goodrich, Michelin claimed the #1 position in the world tire market. The French tire maker has plants in Europe, the Americas, Africa, and Asia and produces natural rubber in Africa and Brazil. The Michelin family controls the company, permitting management to forfeit short-term profit in favor of long-term investment.

The Uniroyal acquisition saddled Michelin with a heavy debt load just as auto and tire markets began to weaken in the US and Europe. Facing worldwide tire-making overcapacity and rampant price cutting, the company has announced plans to reduce employment by 15-16,000 workers. Anticipated severance and retraining costs made up much of the large charge Michelin took against its 1990 earnings. The company is also slashing spending on plant modernization and R&D.

Locked in a 3-way struggle for dominance in world tire markets, Michelin executives express more respect for Bridgestone than Goodyear, citing the Japanese tire maker's R&D orientation and long-term perspective.

WHEN

After dabbling in the manufacture of rubber balls, Edouard Daubrée and Aristide Barbier formed a partnership in Clermont-Ferrand, France, in 1863 and entered the rubber business in earnest. Both founders died shortly afterward and the company struggled. In 1886 the Barbier family asked André Michelin, a successful businessman who had married into the family, to take over. Unable to devote full time to the venture, André persuaded his brother, Edouard, a Paris artist, to run the company, renamed Michelin in 1889.

In 1889 Edouard noticed the riding comfort afforded by air-filled tires. The tires were experimental, glued to the rims, and required several hours to replace. In 1891 Edouard made a bicycle tire with a detachable bolt that allowed replacement in 15 minutes.

The Michelin brothers promoted their removable tires by persuading cyclists to use them in long-distance races in which punctures were likely. The brothers demonstrated that pneumatic tires could work on cars in an auto race in 1895. In 1898 André commented that a stack of tires would look like a man if it had arms, a notion that led to "Bib," the Michelin Man. André also launched the Michelin Guide for auto tourists in 1900.

Michelin opened a sales office in London (1905) and began production in Italy (1906) and New Jersey (1908). It made airplanes during WWI. Michelin inventions included detachable rims and, consequently, spare tires (1906), tubeless tires (1930), treads (1934), and low-profile (squat, like today's) tires (1937). During the Great Depression Michelin closed the New Jersey plant and accepted a stake in Citroën, later converted into a minority interest in Peugeot, in lieu of payment for tires. André Michelin died in 1931, Edouard in 1940.

Michelin received a patent for radial tires in 1946. Expansion was largely confined to Europe in the 1950s. Michelin grew internationally in the 1960s, unchallenged in radials. In 1966 the company's US position was enhanced by Ford's decision to put Michelin radials on its 1968 Lincoln Continental Mark III and Sears's decision to sell Michelins.

Michelin enjoyed worldwide growth in radial sales in the 1970s. The company spent heavily on global expansion and started production in Greenville, South Carolina, in 1975. Michelin had become the #2 tire maker by 1980, but recession and expansion-related debt service induced losses of $1.5 billion between 1980 and 1984. Michelin rebounded and opened plants and sales companies in Asia. In 1989 the company paid $1.5 billion for Uniroyal Goodrich, the product of a merger of 2 US tire companies founded in the late 1800s.

HOW MUCH

$=FF5.08 (Dec. 31, 1990)	9-Year Growth	1981	1982	1983	1984	1985	1986	1987	1988	1989	1990
Sales (FF mil.)	7.2%	33,653	36,610	41,084	44,382	46,641	46,328	46,936	51,280	55,256	62,737
Net income (FF mil.)[1]	—	(290)	(4,165)	(2,145)	(2,242)	989	1,910	2,444	2,367	2,449	(4,811)
Income as % of sales	—	(0.9%)	(11.4%)	(5.2%)	(5.1%)	2.1%	4.1%	5.2%	4.6%	4.4%	(7.7%)
Earnings per share (FF)	—	*(9)*	*(101)*	*(52)*	*(55)*	*19*	*28*	*34*	*29*	*24*	*(45)*
Stock price – high (FF)	—	87	84	98	108	165	357	384	226	212	177
Stock price – low (FF)	—	61	58	71	73	74	173	169	136	152	58
Stock price – close (FF)	0.2%	62	63	80	75	165	255	178	197	168	63
P/E – high	—	—	—	—	—	9	13	11	8	9	—
P/E – low	—	—	—	—	—	4	6	5	5	6	—
Dividends per share (FF)	(3.6%)	3.35	1.68	0.00	0.00	0.00	1.80	2.00	2.20	2.25	2.40
Book value per share (FF)	(11.7%)	319	324	267	187	140	138	165	173	168	104

1990 Year-end:
Debt ratio: 75.8%
Return on equity: —
Cash (mil.): FF6,356
Long-term debt (mil.): FF34,636
No. of shares (mil.): 107
Dividends:
1990 average yield: 3.8%
1990 payout: —
Market value (mil.): $1,327
Sales (mil.): $12,350

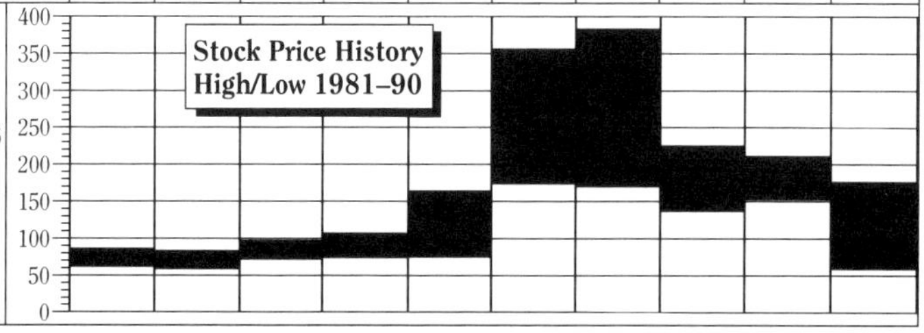

Note: All share data pertain to "B" shares [1]Including extraordinary items; including minority interests 1981–84

Principal exchange: Paris
Fiscal year ends: December 31

Hoover's Rating **C-**

WHO

Chairman, Managing Partner: François Michelin
Managing Partner: M. Edouard Michelin
Managing Partner: René Zingraff
Auditors: Paul-Carlos Mulquin and Gonzague Lauras, Compagnie Régionale de Paris
Employees: 140,826

WHERE

HQ: Compagnie Générale des Etablissements Michelin, 23 Place des Carmes, 63040 Clermont-Ferrand Cedex, France
Phone: 011-33-73-30-42-21
Fax: 011-33-73-30-22-02
US HQ: Michelin Tire Corp., PO Box 19001, Greenville, SC 29602-9001
US Phone: 803-458-5000
US Fax: 803-458-6359

Michelin operates 70 plants, primarily in Europe, and rubber plantations in Brazil, the Ivory Coast, and Nigeria. The company's products are sold in 140 countries.

	1990 Sales % of total
France	21
Western Europe, excluding France	42
Americas	31
Other countries	6
Total	**100**

WHAT

	1990 Sales % of total
Tires & wheels	98
General rubber goods, maps, guides & sundries	2
Total	**100**

Major Subsidiaries and Affiliates

Compagnie Financière Michelin (95%, holding company)
- Companhia Brasileira de Pneumaticos Michelin Industria e Comércio (Brazil)
- Nihon Michelin Tire Co. Ltd. (sales company, Japan)
- Michelin Aircraft Tire Corp. (96.3%, US)
- Michelin Tire Corp. (US)
- Michelin Tires (Canada) Ltd.
- Uniroyal Goodrich Tire Co. (US)

Manufacture Française des Pneumatiques Michelin (99%, French operations)
- Pneu Laurent (retreading)
- Pneumatiques Kléber (94.1%, tires)
- Société Wolber (bicycle tires)

Michelin Korea Tire Co. Ltd. (48%)

Other Shareholdings

American Synthetic Rubber Corp. (81.1%)
Peugeot SA (6.1%)
Société Générale (2.4%)

KEY COMPETITORS

Bridgestone
Goodyear
Pirelli
Sears
Sumitomo

MINOLTA CAMERA CO., LTD.

OVERVIEW

In the 63 years that Minolta has been making and selling cameras, the Tashima family has been running the Osaka-based company. It commands 25% of the world camera market but late in 1990 lost its edge against Canon in 35mm single-lens reflex (SLR) camera sales. Minolta also produces compact cameras; video equipment; and sensitive measuring instruments for use by professional photographers, scientists, and health care professionals.

Minolta's business machines include laser printers and fax machines. Its copiers offer features ranging from color reproduction to zoom lenses. In 1990 about 81% of office equipment sales (and 73% of camera sales) were generated overseas. Minolta is hoping to increase sales of office equipment in Eastern Europe. In 1991 it opened marketing subsidiaries in Czechoslovakia, Poland, and Romania.

What many people don't realize about Minolta is that it's the world's leading manufacturer of planetariums. The company started making planetariums in 1958; unfortunately, sales flattened in 1990 after a 4-year upswing resulting from the 1985 unveiling of Minolta's Infinium universal planetarium.

WHEN

Kazuo Tashima, aided by German trader Wilhelm Heilemann and optical engineer Wilhelm Neumann, founded the Japanese-German Camera Company (Nichi-Doku Shashinki Shoten) in Osaka in 1928 to make quality optical equipment, introducing the Nifcalette bellows camera in 1929. Heilemann and Neumann left the company in 1931.

In 1933 Tashima coined the name Minolta for his expanding line of cameras. Similar in sound to the Japanese expression for ripening rice fields (*minoru-ta*), Minolta also is an English acronym for *M*achinery and *In*struments Optica*l* by *Ta*shima.

In 1934 Tashima introduced the Minolta Vest, the camera that made Minolta a household word in Japan. Renamed Chiyoda Optics and Fine Engineering (Chiyoda Kogaku Seiko, 1937), the company made the first Japanese twin-lens camera in 1937 and during WWII made optical equipment such as binoculars and range finders for the Japanese military. Although its facilities were destroyed by Allied bombs in 1945, the company benefited from US postwar recovery loans.

The company expanded to the US and Europe in the 1950s and increased its presence in Southeast Asia in the 1960s. After astronaut John Glenn used a Minolta camera to take pictures from orbit in 1962, Tashima changed the company's name to Minolta Camera Company. In the meantime, the company diversified into office equipment, producing its first copier in the 1950s under license from the Van der Grinten company of the Netherlands.

Minolta introduced the best-selling SR-T 101 SLR camera in 1966, overtaking Nikon as America's SLR leader in 1973. In 1974 it started producing the successful EG 101 copier. By 1975 exports made up about 80% of sales.

However, the company ran into some trouble in the late 1970s, when Canon's automated AE-1 outsold the SR-T 101. Nearly a decade passed before Minolta was able to regain leadership in the SLR market by introducing the fully automated Maxxum 7000 in 1985.

In 1982 Tashima, who had directed Minolta for over 50 years, stepped into the chairmanship, allowing his son Hideo to replace him as president. The founder died in 1985.

In 1990 Minolta entered a joint venture, P. T. Mazda Indonesia Manufacturing, with Indo Mobil Group (30%) and Sumitomo Corporation (15%) to make and assemble Mazda car engines and body parts in Indonesia. Also in 1990 Minolta agreed to sell Polaroid-built "instant" cameras under the Minolta name.

Minolta reported a 41% drop in pretax profits in 1991, citing escalating R&D expenses and price competition as reasons for the decline.

HOW MUCH

$=¥135 (Dec. 31, 1990)	9-Year Growth	1981	1982	1983	1984	1985	1986	1987	1988	1989	1990
Sales (¥ bil.)	8.0%	174	194	193	214	245	309	309	291	306	347
Net income (¥ bil.)	(5.8%)	7	5	(1)	4	7	11	7	3	2	4
Income as % of sales	—	3.7%	2.6%	(0.4%)	2.0%	2.8%	3.6%	2.4%	0.9%	0.7%	1.1%
Earnings per share (¥)	(10.2%)	*36*	*23*	*(3)*	*20*	*31*	*46*	*30*	*10*	*7*	*14*
Stock price – high (¥)	5.1%	735	490	606	574	933	857	730	845	1,120	1,150
Stock price – low (¥)	2.9%	412	328	324	420	476	593	492	528	735	535
Stock price – close (¥)	2.7%	478	390	564	492	867	639	519	753	1,070	608
P/E – high	—	21	21	—	29	30	19	25	81	152	84
P/E – low	—	12	14	—	21	15	13	17	51	99	39
Dividends per share (¥)	3.0%	6.49	6.49	7.14	7.14	7.14	7.14	7.87	7.87	8.50	8.50
Book value per share (¥)	7.0%	225	243	232	244	248	334	361	363	386	414

1990 Year-end:
Debt ratio: 12.8%
Return on equity: 3.4%
Cash (bil.): ¥64
Long-term debt (bil.): ¥17
No. of shares (mil.): 279
Dividends:
1990 average yield: 1.4%
1990 payout: 62.4%
Market value (mil.): $1,257
Sales (mil.): $2,573

Principal exchange: Tokyo
Fiscal year ends: March 31

Hoover's Rating **B**

WHO

President: Hideo Tashima
EVP: Takayoshi Toshimitsu
Finance Director: Masamoto Nishizawa
Executive Director Personnel: Kenzo Nakai
Auditors: Showa Ota & Co.
Employees: 6,537

WHERE

HQ: 3-13, 2-chome, Azuchi-machi, Chuo-ku, Osaka 541, Japan
Phone: 011-81-6-271-2251
Fax: 011-81-6-266-1010
US HQ: Minolta Corporation (U.S.A.), 101 Williams Dr., Ramsey, NJ 07446-1293
US Phone: 201-825-4000
US Fax: 201-423-0590

Minolta operates facilities in Japan, Brazil, Germany, Malaysia, and the US. Minolta's products are sold worldwide.

	1990 Sales	
	¥ bil.	% of total
Japan	77	22
North America	126	36
Europe	121	35
Other countries	23	7
Total	**347**	**100**

WHAT

	1990 Sales	
	¥ bil.	% of total
Cameras	86	25
Interchangeable lenses	22	6
Camera accessories & other photographic equipment	41	12
Copiers	150	43
Microfilm equipment & other business machines	48	14
Total	**347**	**100**

Cameras and Accessories
Binoculars
Cameras
Color analyzers and sensors
Exposure meters
Glossmeters
Interchangeable lenses
Pulse oximeters
Thermometers
Video equipment

Business Machines
Copiers
Fax machines
Laser printers
Microfilm equipment
Word processors

Other Products
Planetariums

KEY COMPETITORS

Canon
Eastman Kodak
Fuji Photo
GEC
Harris
Hewlett-Packard
IBM
Matsushita
3M
NEC
Oki
Olivetti
Pitney Bowes
Polaroid
Sharp
Sony
Toshiba
Xerox

MITSUBISHI GROUP

OVERVIEW

Consisting of about 160 companies with interlocking ownership, the Mitsubishi Group is the largest *keiretsu* (industrial group) in Japan. Its 3 core companies are Mitsubishi Bank, Mitsubishi Corporation (trading), and Mitsubishi Heavy Industries (heavy machinery). Other important group companies include Mitsubishi Electric, known in the US for its large-screen Diamond Vision TVs (*mitsubishi* means "3 diamonds" in Japanese), and Mitsubishi Motors, which supplies Chrysler with such cars as the Dodge Stealth and Plymouth Laser.

Leaders of the 27 most important companies meet monthly in Tokyo to exchange information and discuss joint projects. Mitsubishi Corporation is Japan's #1 oil importer. A plethora of new models, including the Diamante, an economical luxury offering, has lifted Mitsubishi Motors's sales. Results at Mitsubishi Bank are better than at its less conservatively managed Japanese rivals.

Talks concerning cooperative ventures between Mitsubishi Group companies and Daimler-Benz in areas ranging from cars to rockets are progressing slowly.

WHEN

Yataro Iwasaki's close ties to the Japanese government ensured the early success of his shipping and trading company, Mitsubishi. Founded in 1870, Mitsubishi diversified into mining (1873), banking (1885), and shipbuilding (1887) and began its withdrawal from shipping in the 1880s. In the 1890s it invested in Japanese railroads and property.

In 1918 the Mitsubishi *zaibatsu* (family-run conglomerate) spun off Mitsubishi Trading, its purchasing, sales, and central management arm. By WWII the Mitsubishi *zaibatsu* had become a huge amalgam of divisions and public companies. During WWII the group made warplanes, ships, and explosives.

US postwar occupation forces ordered *zaibatsu* families to sell their stock and in 1946 split Mitsubishi into 139 separate entities. In 1954, after occupation ended, Mitsubishi Trading regrouped with the merger of 3 of its old trading companies and regained its position as the trading arm and lead firm in the Mitsubishi constellation of companies.

In 1954 Mitubishi Trading established Mitsubishi International (New York), a trading subsidiary that has become a leading exporter of US goods. In the 1960s and 1970s Mitsubishi Trading exploited Japan's increasing need for raw materials by importing minerals and fuels. Renamed Mitsubishi Corporation in 1971, the company was a leader of the Japanese government's export drive.

Mitsubishi Kasei, separated from its Asahi Glass (now the largest glassmaker in Japan) and Mitsubishi Rayon (fibers) divisions by Allied forces, grew to become Japan's largest chemical concern. Kirin is Japan's largest brewer. Mitsubishi Bank purchased the Bank of California in 1983. Mitsubishi Estate purchased 51% of the company that manages Rockefeller Center in 1989 and raised its interest to 80% in 1991. Mitsubishi Electric became one of Japan's leading electrical equipment and electronics manufacturers.

The 1964 merger of 3 Mitsubishi companies created Mitsubishi Heavy Industries, now Japan's leading producer of ships, power plants, heavy machinery, and aircraft. Chrysler bought 15% of Mitsubishi Motors (1971). Mitsubishi Motors and Chrysler formed Diamond-Star Motors to make cars in Illinois (1985).

In 1989 the group launched its own communications satellite, and Mitsubishi Corporation bought 74% of Pittsburg-based Aristech Chemical in 1990. In 1991 Mitsubishi Motors agreed to buy 1/3 of Netherlands-based Volvo BV and Mitsubishi Electric announced that it would sell IBM minis and mainframes under its own name in Japan.

HOW MUCH

$=¥135 (Dec. 31, 1990)	9-Year Growth	1981	1982	1983	1984	1985	1986	1987	1988	1989	1990
Sales (¥ bil.)	2.5%	14,834	15,635	15,683	15,815	17,221	17,095	12,660	13,365	15,644	18,523
Net income (¥ bil.)	3.2%	45	34	25	27	32	32	27	31	46	60
Income as % cf sales	—	0.3%	0.2%	0.2%	0.2%	0.2%	0.2%	0.2%	0.2%	0.3%	0.3%
Earnings per share (¥)	1.9%	32	24	18	19	23	23	18	20	29	38
Stock price – high (¥)	—	626	582	531	594	720	1,500	1,660	1,380	2,010	1,990
Stock price – low (¥)	—	455	427	455	500	510	582	941	959	1,350	1,120
Stock price – close (¥)	10.0%	582	495	494	555	624	990	989	1,330	2,010	1,370
P/E – high	—	20	24	30	31	31	65	92	69	69	52
P/E – low	—	14	18	25	26	22	25	36	48	47	29
Dividends per share (¥)	5.0%	5.79	6.06	6.36	6.36	6.68	7.00	7.00	7.00	7.00	9.00
Book value per share (¥)	5.7%	262	290	297	303	322	287	301	324	358	432

1990 Year-end:
Debt ratio: 84.2%
Return on equity: 9.6%
Cash (bil.): ¥3,862
Long-term debt (bil.): ¥3,606
No. of shares (mil.): 1,561
Dividends:
1990 average yield: 0.7%
1990 payout: 23.7%
Market value (mil.): $15,841
Sales (mil.): $137,207

Stock Price History High/Low 1981–90

2,500
2,000
1,500
1,000
500
0

Principal exchange: Tokyo
Fiscal year ends: March 31

WHO

Chairman: Yohei Mimura, age 74
President: Shinroku Morohashi
Auditors: Deloitte Ross Tohmatsu
Employees: 13,623

WHERE

HQ: Mitsubishi Shoji Kabushiki Kaisha, 6-3, Marunouchi 2-chome, Chiyoda-ku, Tokyo 100-86, Japan
Phone: 011-81-3-3210-2121
Fax: 011-81-3-3287-1312
US HQ: Mitsubishi International Corp., 520 Madison Ave., New York, NY 10022
US Phone: 212-605-2000
US Fax: 212-605-2597

Mitsubishi Corp. has 56 offices in Japan and 104 in other countries.

	1990 Sales		1990 Operating Income	
	¥ bil.	% of total	¥ bil.	% of total
Japan	15,138	82	101	81
North America	1,127	6	2	2
Europe	1,905	10	4	3
Other regions	353	2	17	14
Adjustments	—	—	2	—
Total	**18,523**	**100**	**126**	**100**

WHAT

	1990 Sales	
	¥ bil.	% of total
Metals	4,962	27
Machinery/information systems & services	4,801	26
Fuels	3,668	20
Foods	2,254	12
Chemicals	1,450	8
Textiles & general merchandise	1,388	7
Total	**18,523**	**100**

Major Affiliated Companies (% owned by group members)
Asahi Glass Co., Ltd. (28%)
Kirin Brewery (19%)
The Meiji Mutual Life Insurance Co. (100%)
Mitsubishi Aluminum Co., Ltd. (100%)
The Mitsubishi Bank, Ltd. (26%)
Mitsubishi Cable Industries, Ltd. (48%)
Mitsubishi Construction Co., Ltd. (100%)
Mitsubishi Electric Corp. (17%)
Mitsubishi Estate Co., Ltd. (25%)
Mitsubishi Gas Chemical Co., Inc. (24%)
Mitsubishi Heavy Industries, Ltd. (20%)
Mitsubishi Kakoki Kaisha, Ltd. (37%, chemical-processing equipment)
Mitsubishi Kasei Corp. (23%, chemicals)
Mitsubishi Materials Corp.
Mitsubishi Motors Corp. (55%)
Mitsubishi Oil Co., Ltd. (41%)
Mitsubishi Paper Mills, Ltd. (32%)
Mitsubishi Petrochemical Co., Ltd. (37%)
Mitsubishi Plastics Industries, Ltd. (57%)
Mitsubishi Rayon Co., Ltd. (25%)
Mitsubishi Steel Manufacturing Co., Ltd. (38%)
The Mitsubishi Trust and Banking Corp. (28%)
Mitsubishi Warehouse & Transportation Co., Ltd. (40%)
Nikon Corp. (27%, cameras)
Nippon Yusen Kabushiki Kaisha (25%, NYK Line, marine transportation)
The Tokio Marine and Fire Insurance Co., Ltd. (24%)

KEY COMPETITORS

Mitsui
Sumitomo

Information presented for Mitsubishi Corp. only.

MITSUI GROUP

OVERVIEW

In 1991 Mitsui was the world's 2nd largest company after Japanese rival C. Itoh. At the heart of the Mitsui *keiretsu* (industrial group) are Mitsui & Co., the group's trading arm, and The Mitsui Taiyo Kobe Bank, its financing arm. Another 511 cross-held companies with varying degrees of affiliation constitute the rest of the group. The *keiretsu*'s joint activities are coordinated by 77 Nimoku-kai (Second Thursday Conference) and Getsuyo-kai (Monday Conference) members at regular meetings.

Members include Mitsui Real Estate Development (#1 in Japan), Mitsui Mining (Japan's leading coal miner), Mitsui O.S.K. Lines (shipping), Mitsukoshi (department stores), Oji Paper (Japan's #1 paper firm), Mitsui Mutual Life Insurance, The Mitsui Trust and Banking Co., and Toshiba. Toyota is an observer.

Mitsui & Co. wrote off a large portion of its $1.4 billion investment in a war-ravaged petrochemical plant in Iran in 1990 and is actively seeking business in Eastern Europe.

WHEN

Defeated by the Japanese shogun Nobunaga, the Mitsui family fled Omi Province in 1568. Unemployed samurai Sokubei Mitsui opened a sake and soy sauce brewery at the urging of his wife, Shuho, who eventually took over management of the business. Shuho encouraged her sons to enter business and the youngest, Hachirobei, went to Edo (now Tokyo) and opened a dry goods store (Mitsukoshi's predecessor) in 1673. Breaking with Japanese retailing tradition, the store offered merchandise at fixed prices on a cash-and-carry basis.

In 1683 Hachirobei started a currency exchange that evolved into Mitsui Bank. The business received a big boost in 1691 when it became the Osaka government's official money changer. Hachirobei's bank introduced money orders to Japan and profited by securing up to 90 days' float on funds transfers between Osaka, Edo, and Kyoto. Before he died in 1694, Hachirobei created a nontraditional succession scheme to pass control of the business to all related families, not just to the eldest son's family.

In the mid-1800s the government ordered Mitsui to help finance its war with rebels. The family hired Rizaemon Minomura, an outsider with government links, who managed to protect Mitsui from increasing demands for cash. Minomura then made a timely switch of support to the victorious rebel side, and Mitsui became the bank of the Meiji government. The government's industrialization drive led Mitsui into paper, textiles, and a machinery business that was an antecedent of Toshiba. Minomura emphasized expansion in foreign trade and banking, formally creating Mitsui Bussan (now Mitsui & Co.) and Mitsui Bank in 1876. In the late 1800s the Mitsui *zaibatsu* (family-run conglomerate) profited from Japanese military activity, challenged Mitsubishi's shipping monopoly with its own line, and acquired coal mines. Four years after the 1932 assassination of Bussan leader Takuma Dan by right-wing terrorists, the Mitsui family withdrew from management.

Prior to WWII the group benefited from the Japanese military buildup and helped fund Toyota. After the war occupation forces split war-torn Mitsui into over 180 separate entities, but in 1950 27 leaders of former Mitsui companies formed the Getsuyo-kai and the group began gathering itself together again. The larger Nimoku-kai was established in 1961.

The group has expanded rapidly in petrochemicals and metals. Mitsui & Co. extended its overseas presence and bought 50% of AMAX's aluminum operations in 1974.

In 1990 Mitsui Bank and Taiyo Kobe Bank merged to form the world's 2nd largest bank after Dai-Ichi Kangyo. Analysts fear a lengthy 3-way corporate culture clash will ensue since differences between the Taiyo and Kobe banks, merged in 1973, are still being reconciled.

HOW MUCH

Stock prices are for ADRs ADR = 20 shares	9-Year Growth	1981	1982	1983	1984	1985	1986	1987	1988	1989	1990
Sales ($ mil.)	6.4%	70,797	62,834	65,981	71,958	70,152	101,638	97,115	127,337	126,131	123,537
Net income ($ mil.)	11.5%	87	5	28	39	40	66	104	187	303	230
Income as % of sales	—	0.1%	0.0%	0.0%	0.1%	0.1%	0.1%	0.1%	0.1%	0.2%	0.2%
Earnings per share ($)	8.1%	1.53	*0.09*	*0.51*	0.71	0.72	1.09	1.66	2.90	4.30	3.08
Stock price – high ($)	—	32.11	30.56	31.77	29.35	39.72	91.35	126.46	159.13	205.50	192.00
Stock price – low ($)	—	21.29	17.54	25.04	22.62	21.84	37.07	64.81	96.84	129.25	89.75
Stock price – close ($)	17.3%	27.36	30.56	27.36	24.05	35.75	64.32	105.95	157.00	192.75	115.00
P/E – high	—	21	346	62	42	55	83	76	55	48	62
P/E – low	—	14	199	49	32	30	34	39	33	30	29
Dividends per share ($)	5.1%	0.56	0.38	0.36	0.37	0.36	0.14	0.54	1.07	0.82	0.88
Book value per share ($)	10.8%	19.82	14.92	15.46	16.19	15.05	19.34	25.20	34.78	41.84	49.96

1990 Year-end:
Debt ratio: 79.9%
Return on equity: 6.7%
Cash (mil.): $19,569
Current ratio: 1.08
Long-term debt (mil.): $15,186
No. of shares (mil.): 77
Dividends:
1990 average yield: 0.8%
1990 payout: 28.5%
Market value (mil.): $8,799

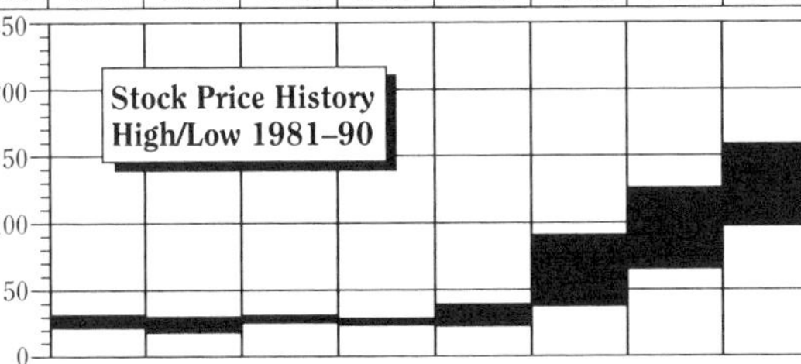

NASDAQ symbol: MITSY (ADR)
Fiscal year ends: March 31

WHO

Chairman: Koichiro Ejiri
VC: Kazuo Horino
President: Naohiko Kumagai
Senior Executive Managing Director, Finance and Accounting: Keiichi Sugita
Auditors: Deloitte Ross Tohmatsu
Employees: 11,656

WHERE

HQ: Mitsui Bussan Kabushiki Kaisha, 2-1, Ohtemachi 1-chome, Chiyoda-ku, Tokyo 100, Japan
Phone: 011-81-3-3285-1111
Fax: 011-81-3-3285-9800
US HQ: Mitsui & Co. (U.S.A.), Inc., 200 Park Ave., New York, NY 10166-0130
US Phone: 212-878-4000
US Fax: 212-878-4261

Mitsui & Co. has 220 trading offices worldwide.

	1990 Sales		1990 Operating Income	
	$ mil.	% of total	$ mil.	% of total
Japan	79,846	65	701	84
North America	22,267	18	53	7
Europe	16,234	13	28	3
Other regions	5,114	4	52	6
Adjustments	76	—	(15)	—
Total	**123,537**	**100**	**819**	**100**

WHAT

	1990 Sales	
	$ mil.	% of total
Iron & steel	13,570	11
Nonferrous metals	19,937	16
Machinery	23,861	19
Chemicals	11,753	10
Foodstuffs	14,101	11
Energy	25,721	21
Other	14,518	12
Adjustments	76	—
Total	**123,537**	**100**

Principal Mitsui Group Affiliates
Hokkaido Colliery & Steamship Co., Ltd.
The Japan Steel Works, Ltd.
Mitsui & Co., Ltd.
Mitsui Construction Co., Ltd.
Mitsui Engineering & Shipbuilding Co., Ltd.
Mitsui Mining & Smelting Co., Ltd.
Mitsui Mining Co., Ltd.
Mitsui Mutual Life Insurance Co.
Mitsui O.S.K. Lines, Ltd. (shipping)
Mitsui Petrochemical Industries, Ltd.
Mitsui Real Estate Development Co., Ltd.
The Mitsui Taiyo Kobe Bank, Ltd.
Mitsui Toatsu Chemicals, Inc.
The Mitsui Trust and Banking Co., Ltd.
The Mitsui Warehouse Co., Ltd.
Mitsukoshi Ltd. (department stores)
Nippon Flour Mills Co., Ltd.
Oji Paper Co., Ltd.
Onoda Cement Co., Ltd.
Sanki Engineering Co., Ltd.
Taisho Marine & Fire Insurance Co., Ltd.
Toray Industries, Inc. (fibers, plastics)
Toshiba Corp.
Toyota Motor Corp.

KEY COMPETITORS

Mitsubishi
Sumitomo

Information presented for Mitsui & Co., Ltd. only.

MOORE CORPORATION LTD.

OVERVIEW

Moore's US business-forms market share dropped from 30% in 1972 to 19% in 1990. Desktop publishing and competition from an increasing number of smaller printers have hurt the company's sales and margins. Moore's restructuring program has resulted in significant layoffs and plant closures. Is Moore in big trouble? Not really. The company remains the world's dominant business-forms manufacturer, sports an exceptionally strong balance sheet, and is solidly in the black.

The introduction of microcomputers and word processing software in the 1980s began to bite into the growth of Moore's forms business. In a time when the "paperless office" was the vision of the future, Moore management took the company into several computer-related fields. Today, Moore is involved in database management and publishing, mailing systems, and direct mail services. The company is searching for sizable information management niches to enter while driving down costs in its forms business.

WHEN

In 1879 UK-born printer Samuel J. Moore and political cartoonist Thomas Bengough met in Toronto. Moore joined Bengough in publishing a conservative political newsletter called the *Grip* and soon met John R. Carter, a salesclerk trying to sell an innovative means of creating sales records. To end salespeople's fumbling with separate sets of forms and loose sheets of messy carbon paper, Carter proposed binding together multiple sets of customer and store receipts with a single sheet of carbon paper to be inserted between the forms as needed. Moore bought the idea, hired Carter, patented the product, and in 1882 formed Grip Printing and Publishing Company to produce The Paragon Black Leaf Counter Check Book. The next year Grip built a salesbook factory in Niagara Falls, New York. The product was a great success.

Moore and his associates set up the Paragon Check Book Company, a new UK operation, in 1886. Lamson Store Service Company, seeing synergies with its own product line, acquired the UK unit in 1889. Lamson sold retail cash-handling systems utilizing hollow balls to carry currency down sloped tracks between salespeople and cashiers.

As the forms business grew, Moore bought Kidder Press, the maker of the printing presses he used (1899), and created box and forms maker F.N. Burt (1909). In 1925 Moore bought Gilman Fanfold, whose owner purportedly had invented fanfolded paper after observing pleated skirts, in vogue at the time. In the same year Moore's organization began selling inexpensive, single-use carbon paper to be bound into sets of business forms, eliminating any handling of carbon paper. The product quickly proved popular and led to the development of snap-apart forms. The US government's utilization of carbon copies resulted in their use as legal documents in business, ultimately boosting sales. In 1929 Moore began consolidating his businesses into Moore Corporation Limited. Moore died in 1948.

By WWII all large, modern organizations were hooked on forms. During the war US Army paper-pushers sent a transport plane on an emergency mission to pick up Moore forms. After WWII Moore grew globally, initiating a slow-motion acquisition of Lamson in 1964 (culminating in 1977) and establishing Toppan Moore (Japan), a joint venture with Toppan Printing. Increased computer usage accelerated demand for Moore's forms.

In the 1970s and 1980s Moore entered direct marketing, image processing, and database management. Failed diversification attempts included US computer supply retailing and microcomputer systems sales. In 1991 Toppan Moore began supplying United Parcel Service with portable terminals designed to collect package delivery information and replace forms.

HOW MUCH

	9-Year Growth	1981	1982	1983	1984	1985	1986	1987	1988	1989	1990
Sales ($ mil.)	4.4%	1,879	1,847	1,814	2,021	2,068	2,114	2,282	2,544	2,708	2,770
Net income ($ mil.)	0.5%	115	102	100	126	137	140	146	186	202	121
Income as % of sales	—	6.1%	5.5%	5.5%	6.2%	6.6%	6.6%	6.4%	7.3%	7.4%	4.4%
Earnings per share ($)	(0.7%)	1.35	1.19	1.16	1.36	1.53	1.54	1.59	2.00	2.14	1.27
Stock price – high ($)	—	12.88	13.83	17.17	15.25	21.88	27.63	26.75	26.63	33.75	30.25
Stock price – low ($)	—	9.58	8.50	13.63	11.58	14.88	18.63	16.50	19.00	24.88	21.63
Stock price – close ($)	8.4%	11.00	13.79	14.17	15.08	20.25	20.63	20.00	25.25	28.88	22.75
P/E – high	—	10	12	15	11	14	18	17	13	16	24
P/E – low	—	7	7	12	9	10	12	10	10	12	17
Dividends per share ($)	5.1%	0.60	0.67	0.67	0.67	0.71	0.72	0.74	0.78	0.88	0.94
Book value per share ($)	7.8%	8.15	8.39	8.79	8.97	10.09	11.01	12.69	13.89	15.27	16.05

1990 Year-end:
Debt ratio: 3.5%
Return on equity: 8.1%
Cash (mil.): $279
Current ratio: 2.88
Long-term debt (mil.): $56
No. of shares (mil.): 96
Dividends:
1990 average yield: 4.1%
1990 payout: 74.0%
Market value (mil.): $2,180

Stock Price History High/Low 1981–90

35 30 25 20 15 10 5 0

NYSE symbol: MCL
Fiscal year ends: December 31

Hoover's Rating 

WHO

Chairman, President, and CEO: M. Keith Goodrich, age 56, $600,455 pay
VC and CFO: Joseph B. McArthur, age 62, $314,798 pay
SVP and Chief Development Officer: Louis J. Rupnik, age 49, $351,676 pay
SVP; President and COO, North American Operations: John R. Anderluh, age 56, $371,134 pay
SVP; President and COO, Latin America and Pacific: James L. Saunders, age 61, $355,419 pay
Director Human Resources: Charles F. Canfield
Auditors: Price Waterhouse
Employees: 25,021

WHERE

HQ: 1 First Canadian Place, PO Box 78, Toronto, Ontario M5X 1G5, Canada
Phone: 416-364-2600
Fax: 416-364-1667
US HQ: Moore Business Forms, Inc., 1205 Milwaukee Ave., Glenview, IL 60025-2496
US Phone: 708-615-6000
US Fax: 708-615-7300

Moore operates 156 manufacturing plants, including 58 in the US, and does business in 53 countries.

	1990 Sales		1990 Operating Income	
	$ mil.	% of total	$ mil.	% of total
Canada	266	10	19	10
US	1,645	59	120	65
Europe	445	16	(25)	(13)
Other countries	414	15	70	38
Adjustments	—	—	50	—
Total	**2,770**	**100**	**234**	**100**

WHAT

	1990 Sales		1990 Operating Income	
	$ mil.	% of total	$ mil.	% of total
Business forms & products	2,390	86	217	97
Direct marketing services	147	5	—	—
Database services	125	5	10	4
Business communication services	108	4	(3)	(1)
Adjustments	—	—	10	—
Total	**2,770**	**100**	**234**	**100**

Business Forms and Products
Designing, printing, and distributing forms, labels, checks, and other business supplies

Direct Marketing Services
Managing direct-mail advertising campaigns

Database Services
Computerized listing databases for real estate professionals
Mapping, mass appraisal, and tax systems for municipalities

Business Communication Services
Designing, manufacturing, and mailing business communications (e.g., US census)
Response analysis for mailing projects
Telemarketing

KEY COMPETITORS

Deluxe
R. R. Donnelley
Dun & Bradstreet

NEC CORPORATION

OVERVIEW

NEC is a global supplier of computers, telecommunications, and semiconductors. Smaller operations include video products and on-line services. The company is the world leader in semiconductor production, 2nd to Fujitsu in Japanese computer revenue, and #1 in Japan in PC sales. Nippon Telegraph and Telephone (NTT) remains NEC's biggest customer. NEC is NTT's largest supplier.

NEC has sacrificed short-term profit in favor of sales volume and development of technology to realize its vision of integrated computers and communications. In response to sagging demand, NEC has cut production of 4-megabit DRAMs and is expanding its PC and ASIC product lines to reduce dependence on DRAMs. R&D spending (up 14% in 1990) remains high at 16% of sales.

NEC is realigning international production. In the past the company simply produced goods near the markets in which they were sold. NEC is trying to integrate production across borders to take advantage of global cost differentials and specialized factories.

NASDAQ symbol: NIPNY (ADR)
Fiscal year ends: March 31

WHO

Chairman: Kenzo Nakamura
President: Tadahiro Sekimoto
EVP and CFO: Kazuyoshi Akimoto
General Manager Personnel Relations: H. Akiyama
Auditors: Price Waterhouse
Employees: 114,599

WHERE

HQ: Nippon Denki Kabushiki Kaisha, 7-1, Shiba 5-chome, Minato-ku, Tokyo 108-01, Japan
Phone: 011-81-3-3454-1111
Fax: 011-81-3-3798-1519
US HQ: NEC America, Inc., 8 Old Sod Farm Rd., Melville, NY 11747
US Phone: 516-753-7000
US Fax: 516-753-7041

NEC operates worldwide.

	1990 Sales	
	$ mil.	% of total
Japan	16,152	74
North America	2,410	11
Asia	1,120	5
Other countries	2,117	10
Total	**21,799**	**100**

WHEN

A group of Japanese investors led by Kunihiko Iwadare formed Nippon Electric Company (NEC) in a joint venture with Western Electric (US) in 1899. Starting as an importer of telephone equipment, NEC soon became a manufacturer and major supplier to Japan's Communications Ministry. Western Electric sold its stake in NEC in 1925. ITT (US) began acquiring shares and owned 59% of NEC before selling its stake in the 1960s. NEC became affiliated with the Sumitomo *zaibatsu* (conglomerate) in the 1930s.

After Nippon Telegraph and Telephone (NTT) was formed in 1952, NEC became one of its 4 leading suppliers. The postwar need to repair Japan's telephone systems and the country's rapid economic recovery resulted in strong demand from NTT. In the 1950s and 1960s, NTT business represented over 50% of NEC's sales, despite overseas expansion, diversification into home appliances, and a computer alliance with Honeywell (US). In 1968 NTT began working with NEC, Hitachi, and Fujitsu to develop computers for use in telecommunications.

In the 1970s Honeywell's lagging position in computers hurt NEC; the company recovered through in-house development efforts and a mainframe venture with Toshiba. In 1977 CEO Koji Kobayashi articulated his vision of NEC's future as an integrator of computers and communications through semiconductor technology. Now generally accepted, Kobayashi's thoughts were revolutionary at the time.

A joint effort between the Japanese government and private industry to develop VLSI chips took place in NEC's labs in the 1970s. NEC invested heavily in R&D and capacity expansion and became the world's largest independent semiconductor manufacturer in 1985. The company produced the world's first prototype of a 4-megabit DRAM chip in 1986.

The company enjoyed great success in the Japanese PC market, garnering over 50% of the market in the 1980s despite a proprietary operating system. NEC's portable IBM clones were also well received internationally. NEC passed IBM to become Japan's #2 computer maker (after Fujitsu) in 1986 and entered into a mainframe computer partnership (now Bull HN Information Systems) with Honeywell and France's Machines Bull in 1987.

NEC has focused R&D spending on next-generation semiconductors (announcing joint development of advanced memory chips with AT&T in 1991), HDTVs, and supercomputers. The company swapped its 15% stake in Bull HN for about 5% of Machines Bull in 1991.

The company suffered embarrassment in 1991 when a 50.2%-owned affiliate (Japan Aviation Electronics Industry Company) admitted that it had illegally sold missile parts to Iran during the Iran-Iraq war.

WHAT

	1990 Sales	
	$ mil.	% of total
Communications systems & equipment	5,538	25
Computers & industrial electronic systems	9,536	44
Electron devices	3,835	17
Home electronics products	1,669	8
Other operations	1,221	6
Total	**21,799**	**100**

Communications Systems and Equipment
Direct broadcast satellite receiver systems
Fiber optic and radio transmission systems
Mobile and other telephones and facsimile equipment
Telecommunications systems

Computers and Industrial Electronics Systems
Automation systems for buildings
Computers (PCs to supercomputers) and peripheral equipment
Mail-processing systems
Robots and machine tools

Semiconductors and Electronic Components

Home Electronics Products
Home automation sys.
Kitchen appliances and air conditioners
TV sets, VCRs, and other video equipment

Other Operations
Electrical connectors
Measuring and testing systems
Subscription computer services

HOW MUCH

Stock prices are for ADRs ADR = 5 shares	9-Year Growth	1981	1982	1983	1984	1985	1986	1987	1988	1989	1990
Sales ($ mil.)	18.6%	4,711	4,872	6,013	7,830	8,998	13,116	16,779	21,893	23,179	21,799
Net income ($ mil.)	19.6%	99	109	138	198	267	153	103	205	412	497
Income as % of sales	—	2.1%	2.2%	2.3%	2.5%	3.0%	1.2%	0.6%	0.9%	1.8%	2.3%
Earnings per share ($)	15.2%	0.43	0.46	0.54	0.74	0.93	0.54	0.37	0.70	1.32	1.55
Stock price – high ($)	—	16.14	17.86	28.86	29.66	33.63	79.00	90.00	91.88	81.00	71.50
Stock price – low ($)	—	10.31	11.23	15.80	18.98	18.63	30.25	45.00	67.50	59.50	45.75
Stock price – close ($)	13.6%	15.05	17.86	28.41	24.25	32.88	63.88	73.50	78.50	65.50	47.50
P/E – high	—	37	39	54	40	36	146	243	131	61	46
P/E – low	—	24	25	29	26	20	56	122	96	45	30
Dividends per share ($)	11.9%	0.12	0.13	0.11	0.15	0.16	0.25	0.29	0.35	0.34	0.34
Book value per share ($)	19.6%	3.34	3.41	4.89	6.65	6.92	10.09	12.51	16.29	17.36	16.77

1990 Year-end:
Debt ratio: 42.2%
Return on equity: 9.1%
Cash (mil.): $2,745
Current ratio: 1.14
Long-term debt (mil.): $3,716
No. of shares (mil.): 304
Dividends:
1990 average yield: 0.7%
1990 payout: 21.7%
Market value (mil.): $14,436

Stock Price History High/Low 1981–90

KEY COMPETITORS

Alcatel Alsthom	Fujitsu	Oki
Amdahl	GEC	Olivetti
AT&T	Harris	Philips
AMP	Hewlett-Packard	Pioneer
Apple	Hitachi	Pitney Bowes
Atari	Honeywell	Raytheon
BCE	Intel	Sharp
Compaq	IBM	Siemens
Canon	Lucky-Goldstar	Tandy
Control Data	Machines Bull	Texas Instruments
Cray Research	Mitsubishi	Toshiba
Data General	Motorola	TRW
Ericsson	Nintendo	Unisys

NESTLÉ SA

OVERVIEW

Nestlé is the world's largest packaged food manufacturer, coffee roaster, and chocolate maker. The company's global candy aspirations have led to the purchase of several international chocolate businesses.

Nestlé is the largest company in Switzerland but derives less than 2% of its revenue from its home country. Major US product lines and brand names include drinks (Nescafé, Quik), chocolate and candy (Crunch, Toll House Morsels), culinary products (Contadina), dairy products (Carnation), and frozen foods (Lean Cuisine). The company operates 33 Stouffer's Hotels and owns 25% of French cosmetics giant L'Oréal.

To compete more effectively in the US, in 1991 Nestlé restructured its operations under newly formed Nestlé USA.

WHEN

In 1866 Americans Charles and George Page founded the Anglo-Swiss Condensed Milk Company in central Switzerland. Importing canned milk technology from the US, the brothers began production in 1867. In the same year, 120 miles away in Vevey, Switzerland, amid growing concern about infant mortality, Henri Nestlé tested his new concoction of concentrated milk, sugar, and cereal on a baby who refused his mother's milk. Six months later the healthy boy was still consuming the formula. Nestlé introduced his product, Farine Lactée, commercially in 1867.

By 1874 both firms were prospering, and Nestlé, age 61, was looking for a buyer. He sold his company, then doing business in 16 countries, to 3 local businessmen for one million francs in 1875. Nestlé and Anglo-Swiss built capacity to meet skyrocketing demand for their products until 1878, when Anglo-Swiss launched a milk-based infant food product. Nestlé's new owners responded by introducing a condensed milk product, beginning a battle that lasted until the companies merged in 1905 under the Nestlé name.

Aided by Swiss neutrality, Nestlé continued its worldwide expansion throughout WWI. In 1904 the company began selling chocolate under the Nestlé name. In 1929 Nestlé acquired Cailler, the first company to mass-produce chocolate bars, and Swiss General, inventor of milk chocolate.

Nestlé's 1920s investment in a Brazilian milk condensery paid an unexpected dividend when, in 1930, Brazilian coffee growers suggested that Nestlé develop a water-soluble "coffee cube." Nescafé instant coffee was released in 1938 and received a boost when the US Army distributed it to troops in WWII.

Nestlé continued its global expansion, entering new product categories through acquisition and internal product development. Major purchases included Alimenta (first dehydrated soup, seasonings; Switzerland; 1947); Crosse & Blackwell (packaged foods, marmalade; UK; 1960); Findus International (frozen foods, Sweden, 1962); Beringer Brothers (wine, US, 1971); Stouffer (hotels, restaurants, frozen foods; US; 1973); 25% of L'Oréal (perfumes, cosmetics, hair products; France; 1974); Libby, McNeill & Libby (canned foods, US, 1976); Beech-Nut (baby food, US, 1979, sold to Ralston Purina in 1989); Carnation (US, 1985); Hills Brothers and MJB (coffee, US, 1985); 52% of Vittel (mineral water, France, 1987); Buitoni (pasta, chocolate; Italy; 1988); and Rowntree (candy, UK, 1988). Among Nestlé's important product introductions were its Crunch bar (1938), Quik drink mix (1948), and Taster's Choice coffee (1966).

In 1990 Nestlé bought the Baby Ruth and Butterfinger brands from RJR Nabisco. In 1991 the company announced a joint venture with Coca-Cola to market concentrates for its coffee, tea, and chocolate beverages through Coca-Cola's 170-country distribution system.

HOW MUCH

$=SF1.27 (Dec. 31, 1990)	9-Year Growth	1981	1982	1983	1984	1985	1986	1987	1988	1989	1990
Sales (SF mil.)	5.9%	27,734	27,664	27,943	31,141	42,225	36,909	34,183	39,502	48,036	46,369
Net income (SF mil.)	10.0%	964	1,098	1,261	1,487	1,750	1,843	1,879	2,058	2,412	2,272
Income as % of sales	—	3.5%	4.0%	4.5%	4.8%	4.1%	5.0%	5.5%	5.2%	5.0%	4.9%
Earnings per share (SF)	8.2%	323	368	422	471	506	532	543	577	656	655
Stock price – high (SF)	—	3,125	3,688	4,801	5,499	9,034	9,697	11,244	8,863	8,930	9,240
Stock price – low (SF)	—	2,695	2,915	3,630	4,443	5,499	7,193	7,070	6,236	6,925	6,960
Stock price – close (SF)	9.8%	3,160	3,870	4,980	5,600	8,925	9,775	8,025	7,240	8,820	7,360
P/E – high	—	10	10	11	12	18	18	21	15	14	14
P/E – low	—	8	8	9	9	11	14	13	11	11	11
Dividends per share (SF)	8.5%	96.18	107.49	121.35	133.36	142.39	142.39	147.30	171.85	200.00	200.00
Book value per share (SF)	2.2%	3,004	3,379	3,728	4,168	3,370	4,564	4,600	3,193	3,793	3,644

1990 Year-end:
Debt ratio: 34.7%
Return on equity: 17.6%
Cash (mil.): SF5,528
Long-term debt (mil.): SF7,182
No. of shares (thou.): 3,705
Dividends:
1990 average yield: 2.7%
1990 payout: 30.5%
Market value (mil.): $21,471
Sales (mil.): $36,511

Stock Price History High/Low 1981–90

12,000
10,000
8,000
6,000
4,000
2,000
0

Note: All data pertain to bearer shares.

OTC symbol: NESAY (ADR)
Fiscal year ends: December 31

Hoover's Rating **B**

WHO

Chairman, CEO, and Managing Director of USA, Personnel, and Corporate Affairs: Helmut Maucher
General Manager Finance, Control, Legal, Taxes, Administration: Reto F. Domeniconi
Auditors: KPMG Peat Marwick McLintock
Employees: 199,021

WHERE

HQ: Ave. Nestlé 55, CH-1800 Vevey, Switzerland
Phone: 011-41-21-924-2111
Fax: 011-41-21-921-1885
US HQ: Nestlé USA Inc., 100 Manhattanville Rd., Purchase, NY 10577
US Phone: 914-251-3000
US Fax: 914-251-2961

Nestlé operates 423 factories worldwide.

	1990 Sales	
	SF mil.	% of total
Europe	22,567	49
North America	11,243	24
Latin America & Caribbean	5,054	11
Other countries	7,505	16
Total	**46,369**	**100**

WHAT

	1990 Sales	
	SF mil.	% of total
Drinks	10,928	24
Cereals/milks/dietetic	9,326	20
Chocolate & confectionery	7,427	16
Culinary products	5,914	13
Frozen foods & ice cream	4,678	10
Refrigerated products	4,138	9
Pet foods	2,080	4
Other	1,878	4
Total	**46,369**	**100**

Major Brand Names (US Markets)

Drinks
Beringer (wines)
Cain's (coffee)
Hills Bros. (coffee)
Kern's (nectars)
Milo
Nescafé
Nestea
Quik
Taster's Choice

Confections
After Eight
Baby Ruth
Beich
Butterfinger
Chunky
Crunch
DeMet's Turtles
KitKat
Oh Henry!
Perugina
Raisinets

Foods
Buitoni
Carnation
Chambourcy
Contadina
Crosse & Blackwell
Lean Cuisine
Libby
Stouffer's
Toll House

Drugs, Cosmetics
Alcon (optical goods)
L'Oréal (25%)

Hotels and Restaurants
Stouffer

Pet Foods
Chef's Blend
Fancy Feast
Friskies
Grand Gourmet
Mighty Dog

KEY COMPETITORS

Accor
Allied-Lyons
Borden
Bristol-Myers Squibb
BSN
Cadbury Schweppes
Campbell Soup
ConAgra
General Mills
Grand Metropolitan
Heinz
Hershey
Mars
Philip Morris
Procter & Gamble
Ralston Purina
RJR Nabisco
Sara Lee
TLC Beatrice
Unilever
Whitman

THE NEWS CORPORATION LTD.

OVERVIEW

Rupert Murdoch's Australia-based News Corporation is a global media giant. It publishes the *Times* (UK), the *San Antonio Express-News*, and the *Boston Herald* daily newspapers; *TV Guide*, one of the most widely circulated magazines in the US; and books (through its HarperCollins subsidiary). In the field of film and television, News Corporation owns Twentieth Century Fox (*Home Alone*, "L. A. Law"), Fox Broadcasting ("The Simpsons"), 50% of British Sky Broadcasting (UK), and 7 US television stations.

In Australia the company publishes 9 magazines and 101 newspapers, including the *Australian*, and is involved in book publishing, commercial printing, paper production, and sheep farming. Ansett Australia, one of Australia's 2 largest domestic airlines, is 50% owned by News Corporation. Ansett owns 20% of Phoenix-based America West Airlines.

Rather than dilute his family's 43.3% stake to pay for News Corporation's US acquisitions, Murdoch borrowed heavily, resulting in about $8 billion of debt by early 1991. To raise cash the company has recently sold over $1.3 billion of assets and is planning to part with more. Further acquisitions are on hold — at least for the time being.

WHEN

Rupert Murdoch started in the newspaper business in 1952 when he inherited 2 Adelaide, Australia, newspapers from his father. After launching the *Australian*, the country's first national daily, in 1964, Murdoch bought *News of the World*, a London Sunday paper, in 1968. In 1969 he bought London's *Sun*, which he transformed into a sensationalist tabloid, featuring lurid headlines and topless women. In the US Murdoch created the supermarket tabloid *Star* in 1974 and bought the *New York Post* in 1976, again using sensationalist tactics to boost circulation (one headline: "Headless Body Found in Topless Bar").

In 1981 Murdoch bought London's *Times* and a 40% stake in Collins Publishers, a family-run London book publisher. After buying the *Chicago Sun-Times* in 1983 (sold in 1986), Murdoch bought 13 US travel, hotel, and aviation trade magazines from Ziff-Davis and Twentieth Century Fox from Denver billionaire Marvin Davis in 1985. He became a US citizen to comply with FCC rules on broadcast ownership and in 1986 bought 6 Metromedia TV stations; Hong Kong's *South China Morning Post*; and Australia's #1 media company, the Herald & Weekly Times Group.

Murdoch launched Fox Broadcasting in 1986, the first new US TV network since 1948. In 1987 he bought US book publisher Harper & Row and 20% of the UK's Pearson media group (since reduced to 9.9%). In 1988 News Corporation paid $2.8 billion for Triangle Publications, publisher of *TV Guide*, the *Daily Racing Form*, and *Seventeen*, and bought religious publisher Zondervan. In 1989 it bought textbook publisher Scott, Foresman and the rest of Collins Publishers.

The company started Sky Television, a British satellite TV network, in 1989. After 18 months of intense competition, Sky joined forces with rival network British Satellite Broadcasting to form British Sky Broadcasting.

Murdoch bought 2 Hungarian dailies and 50% of Germany's Burda printing company in 1990. But after years of buying (and accumulating debt to do so), News Corporation is now putting assets on the block. In 1990 Murdoch parted with 49% of *South China Morning Post* and sold the *Star* to *Enquirer* publisher G.P. Group for $200 million and an 80% stake in the newly formed Enquirer/Star Group. In 1991 Murdoch agreed to sell the *Daily Racing Form* and his US magazine holdings (except *Mirabella* and *TV Guide*) to K-III Holdings, a partnership controlled by Kohlberg Kravis Roberts. News Corporation sold its stake in Enquirer/Star Group to the public in 1991. Its UK magazines are also for sale.

HOW MUCH

	4-Year Growth	1981	1982	1983	1984	1985	1986	1987	1988	1989	1990
Sales ($ mil.)	27.1%	—	—	—	—	—	2,575	3,503	4,355	6,397	6,720
Net income ($ mil.)	7.3%	—	—	—	—	—	163	241	336	403	216
Income as % of sales	—	—	—	—	—	—	6.3%	6.9%	7.7%	6.3%	3.2%
Earnings per share ($)	6.8%	—	—	—	—	—	1.20	1.68	2.17	2.57	1.56
Stock price – high ($)	—	—	—	—	—	—	—	35.75	21.88	27.13	23.38
Stock price – low ($)	—	—	—	—	—	—	—	12.25	14.88	16.63	6.63
Stock price – close ($)	—	—	—	—	—	—	—	16.88	16.50	22.25	7.88
P/E – high	—	—	—	—	—	—	—	21	10	11	15
P/E – low	—	—	—	—	—	—	—	7	7	6	4
Dividends per share ($)	25.7%	—	—	—	—	—	0.06	0.07	0.12	0.16	0.15
Book value per share ($)	57.3%	—	—	—	—	—	7.94	19.46	23.43	27.55	48.64

1990 Year-end:
Debt ratio: 52.5%
Return on equity: 4.1%
Cash (mil.): $126
Current ratio: 0.57
Long-term debt (mil.): $7,224
No. of shares (mil.): 134
Dividends:
1990 average yield: 1.9%
1990 payout: 9.8%
Market value (mil.): $1,057

NYSE symbol: NWS (ADR)
Fiscal year ends: June 30

WHO

Chairman: Richard H. Searby, age 59
Managing Director and CEO: Keith Rupert Murdoch, age 59
Finance Director: David F. DeVoe, age 43
Auditors: Pannell Kerr Forster
Employees: 38,400

WHERE

HQ: 2 Holt St., Sydney, NSW 2010, Australia
Phone: 011-61-2-288-3000
Fax: 011-61-2-288-2300
US HQ: News America Publishing Inc., 1211 Ave. of the Americas, New York, NY 10036-8703
US Phone: 212-852-7000
US Fax: 212-852-7145

News Corporation operates principally in the US, the UK, Australia, and the Pacific Basin.

	1990 Sales		1990 Operating Income	
	$ mil.	% of total	$ mil.	% of total
Australasia	1,606	24	326	31
US	3,781	56	613	59
UK	1,333	20	101	10
Adjustments	—	—	5	—
Total	**6,720**	**100**	**1,045**	**100**

WHAT

	1990 Sales		1990 Operating Income	
	$ mil.	% of total	$ mil.	% of total
Newspapers	2,313	34	499	48
Magazines	1,108	17	244	23
Film	970	15	84	8
TV	898	13	5	1
Comm. printing	396	6	44	4
Other	1,035	15	165	16
Adjustments	—	—	4	—
Total	**6,720**	**100**	**1,045**	**100**

Major Newspapers
The Australian
Boston Herald
News of the World (UK)
San Antonio Express-News
South China Morning Post (51%, Hong Kong)
The Sun (UK)
The Times (UK)

Major Magazines
Mirabella (US)
The Times Educational Supplement (UK)
TV Guide (US)
TV Week (Australia)

Film
CBS/FOX (50%, home video, US)
Twentieth Century Fox Film (US)

TV Broadcasting
British Sky Broadcasting (50%)
Fox Broadcasting (US)
KDAF-TV, Dallas/Fort Worth
KRIV-TV, Houston
KSTU-TV, Salt Lake City
KTTV-TV, Los Angeles
WFLD-TV, Chicago
WNYW-TV, New York
WTTG-TV, Washington

Book Publishing
HarperCollins
Golden Press (Australia)
Scott, Foresman (US)
Times Books (UK)
Zondervan Corp. (US)

Other
Ansett Transport Industries (50%, air transport, Australia)
Australian Newsprint Mills (50%)
Eric Bemrose (commercial printing, UK)
Etak (electronic maps, US)
Pearson PLC (9.9%)
Reuters (1.9%)

KEY COMPETITORS

Other publishers, printers, TV broadcasting companies, film production companies, and Australian domestic airlines

NINTENDO CO., LTD.

OVERVIEW

In the multibillion-dollar home video game industry, Kyoto-based Nintendo is the undisputed king of the mountain, controlling almost 90% of the Japanese market and over 80% of the US market. The company also manufactures playing cards, as it has done for over a century.

Nintendo has redefined and given new life to the home video game industry, which was given up for dead by many in the early 1980s. The company's Nintendo Entertainment System (NES) is now entrenched in 32% of American homes. Nintendo's mascot, an animated Italian plumber named Mario, has surpassed Mickey Mouse in popularity according to recent polls of US schoolchildren.

Cautious about complacency, the company has continually generated such innovative ideas as Game Boy (a hand-held game system), a phone line staffed by 200 game counselors, and the World of Nintendo (in-store boutiques selling the company's products).

Nintendo hopes to sustain its success by selling its new 16-bit Super Family Computer game system in the US while exporting the NES to the untapped European market.

WHEN

In 1889 members of Japan's Yamauchi family founded the Marufuku Company to produce and market *hanafuda* playing cards (traditional Japanese playing cards). For most of the next century, the company remained relatively constant in its focus, although it changed its name to the Nintendo Playing Card Company in 1951 (*nintendo* translates as "leave it to heaven") and took its current name in 1963.

In 1980 Nintendo, under the direction of President Hiroshi Yamauchi (with 11.4% ownership of the company he is now one of Japan's richest billionaires), broke new ground by introducing Game and Watch, hand-held, liquid crystal video games. That same year the company established its US subsidiary, Nintendo of America. Nintendo also diversified into coin-operated video games (which were very popular in the early 1980s), with titles that included the arcade classic Donkey Kong.

In what was undoubtedly its most lucrative product introduction, the company released Famicom, a technologically advanced home video game system, to the Japanese market in 1983. With its high-quality sound and graphics, Famicom was an astounding success, selling 15.2 million consoles and more than 183 million game cartridges in Japan alone.

In 1986 the company brought Famicom to the US, introducing it as the Nintendo Entertainment System. The NES introduction launched the renaissance of the US home video game industry, which had died in the early 1980s after the prosperous but brief glory years of California-based Atari.

To prevent a barrage of independently produced, low-quality software (which had contributed to Atari's demise), the company established a stringent licensing policy for NES software developers: they must gain Nintendo's approval on every game design; purchase the blank game cartridges from the company; agree not to manufacture the game for any of Nintendo's competitors; and bear the cost of development and marketing.

Naturally, such stringent policies did not endear the company to its competitors. Rivals Atari and Tengen filed antitrust suits (still pending) against Nintendo in the late 1980s.

Determined not to lose its privileged position in what has become a saturated market, the company released Game Boy in 1989 and in 1991 brought to the US its new 16-bit Super Family Computer game system which has much finer graphics and sound. That same year Nintendo signed a deal with Philips NV to develop a CD video game system. The company is currently thinking about introducing a cord that will enable users to link their NES units to a nationwide telephone network.

HOW MUCH

$=¥135 (Dec. 31, 1990)	9-Year Growth	1981	1982	1983	1984[1]	1985	1986	1987	1988	1989	1990[2]
Sales (¥ bil.)	29.8%	23	58	65	68	81	123	145	203	291	240
Net income (¥ bil.)	39.9%	2	8	12	9	10	17	25	30	34	33
Income as % of sales	—	7.0%	13.4%	18.0%	13.8%	12.1%	13.6%	17.4%	14.8%	11.8%	13.7%
Earnings per share (¥)	—	—	—	—	—	—	160	240	287	327	314
Stock price – high (¥)	—	—	—	2,843	3,207	3,182	7,475	6,969	6,333	17,300	34,300
Stock price – low (¥)	—	—	—	1,136	1,818	2,020	3,101	3,928	4,427	5,207	14,600
Stock price – close (¥)	—	—	—	1,959	2,434	3,187	6,263	4,595	6,333	15,000	18,900
P/E – high	—	—	—	—	—	—	47	29	22	53	109
P/E – low	—	—	—	—	—	—	19	16	15	16	47
Dividends per share (¥)	27.0%	3.50	4.20	8.80	15.00	15.00	20.00	24.00	27.00	33.00	30.00
Book value per share (¥)	—	—	—	—	—	477	733	948	1,206	1,499	1,809

1990 Year-end:
Debt ratio: 0.0%
Return on equity: 19.0%
Cash (bil.): ¥217
Long-term debt (bil.): ¥0
No. of shares (mil.): 105
Dividends:
1990 average yield: 0.2%
1990 payout: 9.6%
Market value (mil.): $14,700
Sales (mil.): $1,778

Stock Price History
High/Low 1983–90

35,000
30,000
25,000
20,000
15,000
10,000
5,000
0

[1] Unconsolidated data 1981–84 [2] Change in fiscal year; 7 months data

OTC symbol: NINTY (ADR)
Fiscal year ends: March 31

Hoover's Rating A+

WHO

President: Hiroshi Yamauchi, age 63
Senior Managing Director: Katsunori Tanimoto
Senior Managing Director: Tokio Sotani
Auditors: Chuo Shinko Audit Corporation
Employees: 730

WHERE

HQ: 60 Fukuine Kamitakamatsu-cho, Higashiyama-ku, Kyoto 605, Japan
Phone: 011-81-75-541-6111
Fax: 011-81-75-541-6127
US HQ: Nintendo of America Inc., 4820 150th Ave. NE, Redmond, WA 98052-9733
US Phone: 206-882-2040
US Fax: 206-882-3585

The company has offices in Canada, Germany, Japan, and the US.

	1990 Sales % of total
Japan	24
Overseas	76
Total	**100**

WHAT

	1990 Sales % of total
Leisure products	99
Other	1
Total	**100**

Game Consoles
Famicom/Nintendo Entertainment System
Game Boy
Super Family Computer

Games
Balloon Fight
Baseball
Clu Clu Land
Donkey Kong
Donkey Kong Jr.
Dragon Warrior
Duck Hunt
Excitebike
Golf
Gumshoe
Hogan's Alley
Ice Hockey
Kid Icarus
Kung Fu
Legend of Zelda
Mach Rider
Mario Bros.
Metroid
Mike Tyson's Punch-Out!
Pinball
Popeye
Pro Wrestling
Rad Racer
R.C. Pro Am
Soccer
Super Mario Bros.
Tennis
10-Yard Fight
Urban Champion
Volleyball
Wild Gunman
Wrecking Crew
Zelda II — The Adventure of Link

Miscellaneous
Coin-operated video games
Playing cards

Periodicals
Nintendo Power

KEY COMPETITORS

Atari
Commdore
Hasbro
Mattel
NEC

NIPPON STEEL CORPORATION

Principal exchange: Tokyo
Fiscal year ends: March 31

OVERVIEW

Japan's Nippon Steel is the world's 3rd largest steelmaker, after Italy's IRI and Germany's Thyssen. The company, of late, has been afflicted with the same maladies that once afflicted its US counterparts. Facing sluggish demand and competition from imports (in this case, Korean upstarts), Nippon Steel is decreasing its reliance on steel, shuttering plants and expanding into other lines of business.

The company's Engineering Divisions Group provides construction services on major projects including oil-and-gas pipelines, bridges, and skyscrapers. This group's Service Business Division includes interests in restaurants, in homes for the elderly, and in the newly opened Space World education/amusement park in Japan.

Nippon Steel's Electronics & Information Systems Division includes computer hardware, software, systems design, and telecommunications. Other areas of development for the company include new materials such as silicon wafers, gold-bonding wire, and spherical silica and aluminum powders for shielding materials. Its Biotechnology Business Division performs R&D in the US (on plants with Calgene Inc.) and in Japan (on rice seedlings with Japanese firms).

WHO

Chairman: Akira Miki
President: Hiroshi Saito
EVP: Kensuke Koga
EVP: Zensaku Yamamoto
EVP: Shuichi Kimura
EVP: Kazuo Sugiyama
EVP (Finance): Takashi Imai
Managing Director (Personnel): Takeshi Miyazaki
Auditors: Chuo Shinko Audit Corp.
Employees: 41,257

WHEN

Nippon Steel was forged in the first blast furnace in Japan, at Kamaishi, in 1857. Takato Oshima translated a Dutch manual to learn steelmaking technology.

In 1901 the Japanese government launched its Yawata Works on the island of Kyushu, and Japanese steelmaking again relied on Western teaching, this time in the form of foreign engineers who offered advice and counsel. Yawata grew and accounted for the bulk of Japanese steel production in the early years of the 20th century.

In the 1930s, as Japan prepared for war in the Pacific, the government merged the Yawata Works and other Japanese steelmakers into the giant Japan Iron & Steel combine. During postwar occupation, Japan Iron and Steel was ordered dissolved under the Excessive Economic Power Deconcentration Law of 1950. Yawata Iron & Steel and Fuji Iron & Steel emerged from the dissolution and, with the aid of Western training, the Japanese steel industry staggered to its feet . . . then took off running. In the late 1960s Fuji Steel bought Tokai Iron & Steel (1967), and Yawata Steel took over Yawata Steel Tube Company (1968).

Yawata and Fuji merged in 1970, over government objections, and became Nippon Steel, the largest steelmaker in the world. In the 1970s the Japanese steel industry was criticized in the US; American competitors complained that Japan was "dumping" low-cost exports. Nippon Steel aggressively courted China as another customer.

Nippon Steel began to diversify in the mid-1980s to wean itself from dependence on steel. It created a New Materials Projects Bureau in 1984 and retrained "redundant" steelworkers to make silicon wafers. It created an Electronics Division in 1986 and in 1988 began joint ventures with IBM Japan (small computers and software), with Hitachi (office workstations), and with C. Itoh (information systems for small- and medium-sized companies). It announced a $200 million investment in database-software-maker Oracle in 1991 and said it hoped to generate 20% of sales from electronics by 1995.

While the company plans to decrease its dependence on steel sales from 80% of total sales in 1989 to 60% by 1993, Nippon Steel has not given up on steel. It opened a cold-rolled steel plant in Indiana (1990). The plant is the result of a $525 million joint venture, called I/N Tek, with Inland Steel of the US. A similar venture with Inland, the $450 million I/N Kote, will churn out coated steel for the automotive industry.

WHERE

HQ: Shin Nippon Seitetsu Kabushiki Kaisha, 6-3 Otemachi 2-chome, Chiyoda-ku, Tokyo, 100-71, Japan
Phone: 011-81-3-3242-4111
Fax: 011-81-3-3275-5607
US HQ: Nippon Steel U.S.A., Inc., 345 Park Ave., 41st Floor, New York, NY 10154
US Phone: 212-486-7150
US Fax: 212-593-3049

Nippon Steel operates worldwide.

WHAT

Major Lines of Business

Steel
Cold-rolled stainless steel strip
Heavy and medium plates
Rails
Reinforcing bars
Stainless steel tubing
Wire rods

Titanium Products

Chemicals
Coal chemicals and petrochemicals
Coke
Oil products

Engineering and Construction
Major-project construction
Plant engineering
Service businesses (theme parks, restaurants)
Urban development

New Materials
Automotive industry materials
Electronics industry materials
Magnetic materials
Semiconductor materials

Electronics and Information/Communications
Computers
Data processing
Software development
Systems integration

HOW MUCH

$=¥135 (Dec. 31, 1990)	9-Year Growth	1981	1982	1983	1984	1985	1986	1987	1988	1989	1990
Sales (¥ bil.)	(2.1%)	3,113	3,102	2,725	2,660	2,860	2,685	2,178	2,147	2,385	2,573
Net income (¥ bil.)	3.5%	71	56	33	3	42	37	(13)	32	63	97
Income as % of sales	—	2.3%	1.8%	1.2%	0.1%	1.5%	1.4%	(0.6%)	1.5%	2.6%	3.8%
Earnings per share (¥)	3.2%	*11*	*9*	*5*	*0*	*6*	*6*	*(2)*	*5*	*9*	*14*
Stock price – high (¥)	—	236	185	177	188	209	276	454	969	984	795
Stock price – low (¥)	—	139	122	136	141	142	153	168	353	692	371
Stock price – close (¥)	10.7%	179	144	175	155	155	169	362	870	793	448
P/E – high	—	22	22	35	418	33	50	—	202	104	55
P/E – low	—	13	14	27	313	23	28	—	74	73	26
Dividends per share (¥)	2.0%	5.00	5.00	5.00	5.00	5.00	5.00	3.00	3.00	5.00	6.00
Book value per share (¥)	4.3%	86	88	89	91	93	93	89	91	95	126

1990 Year-end:
Debt ratio: 50.6%
Return on equity: 13.1%
Cash (bil.): ¥646
Long-term debt (bil.): ¥890
No. of shares (mil.): 6,888
Dividends:
1990 average yield: 1.3%
1990 payout: 41.4%
Market value (mil.): $22,858
Sales (mil.): $19,059

Stock Price History High/Low 1981–90

1,000
900
800
700
600
500
400
300
200
100
0

Note: All data unconsolidated

KEY COMPETITORS

Alcan
Anglo American
Bethlehem Steel
Broken Hill
Cargill
Friedrich Krupp
Hyundai
Inco
IRI
LTV
Mitsubishi
RTZ
Thyssen
USX
Biotechnology companies
Chemical companies
Computer companies

NIPPON TELEGRAPH AND TELEPHONE CORP.

OVERVIEW

Measured by stock market capitalization, Nippon Telegraph and Telephone (NTT) is the world's most valuable company. NTT, Japan's largest employer, provides domestic phone service in Japan.

The Japanese government owns 66.25% of the company's stock; Japanese citizens own the rest. The government is considering allowing foreigners to hold NTT stock and has delayed until 1995 proposals to break up the company to spur competition.

Telephone services contribute 78% of company sales. Other activities include data communications and videotex services. The company is also developing voice dialing and 2-way visual communications. NTT spent 4.1% of its revenues on R&D in 1990, more money than any other Japanese company.

NTT is forming alliances to join the club of international telecommunications giants. One outing links it with a Siemens-Corning joint venture and 3 domestic partners to develop a new fiber optic cable. Another, announced in 1991, would join NTT with British Telecom and Deutsche Bundespost Telekom to serve multinational corporations.

Principal exchange: Tokyo
Fiscal year ends: March 31

WHO

Chairman: Haruo Yamaguchi
President: Masashi Kojima
SEVP: Tomeo Kanbayashi
SEVP: Shozo Iwasaki
SEVP: Katsumi Iida
SEVP: Shigeo Sawada
EVP and CFO: Muneo Ohashi
Personnel: S. Shioda
Auditors: Price Waterhouse
Employees: 272,903

WHEN

The Japanese Ministry of Communications began telephone service in 1889 and operated as a monopoly after 1900. After WWII the ministry reorganized and, in 1952, formed Nippon Telegraph and Telephone Public Corporation (NTT). Regulated by the Ministry of Posts and Telecommunications, NTT was charged with rebuilding and running Japan's war-ravaged phone system. The ministry created a separate company (KDD) to handle international telephone service in 1953. NTT owns 10% of KDD.

Japanese authorities created NTT in the image of AT&T but prohibited NTT from manufacturing, preferring to encourage competition among equipment suppliers. NTT bought most of its equipment from favored Japanese vendors. Four companies benefited most from this arrangement: NEC (the most favored), Hitachi, Fujitsu, and Oki Electric.

NTT expanded rapidly during the 1960s as Japan's economy surged. In the late 1960s NTT was installing 3 million lines per year. In 1968 NTT enlisted Hitachi, Fujitsu, and NEC to design and build computers for NTT's use, subsidizing critical R&D for Japan's future computer giants.

By the 1970s NTT had become a large, bureaucratic utility, and public suspicions of inefficiency and corruption led to political pressure to reform. In the late 1970s US trade representatives called for NTT to purchase non-Japanese equipment and were stunned when NTT president Tokuji Akikusa told them that the only items it would consider buying overseas were telephone poles and mops.

Change came to NTT in the 1980s. The company entered into an agreement in 1981 to open procurement to US companies. NTT inaugurated a public fax network in 1981 and a videotex service in 1984. The company spent heavily in the 1980s on the nationwide installation of optical fiber for integrated systems digital networks (ISDN), capable of high-volume, high-speed data transmission.

In 1985 Japanese authorities began deregulating the telecommunications industry, opening NTT markets to competition (while maintaining price regulation) and selling NTT shares to the public. NTT became the world's most valuable public company at its initial public offering. The Japanese government sold additional NTT shares to the public in 1987 and again in 1988, at 130 times earnings.

Faced with increased competition and the constraints of regulation, NTT's new president, Masashi Kojima, complained in 1990 that earnings for the company would suffer through a 2- to 3-year slump. Another factor depressing earnings will be capital required to modernize its systems. In 1990 NTT selected AT&T, Motorola, and Ericsson to develop a digital mobile telephone system.

WHERE

HQ: Nippon Denshin Denwa Kabushiki Kaisha, 1-6, Uchisaiwaicho 1-chome, Chiyoda-ku, Tokyo 100, Japan
Phone: 011-81-3-3509-3101
Fax: 011-81-3-3509-4290
US HQ: NTT America, Inc., Room 2905, Pan American Bldg., 200 Park Ave., New York, NY 10166
US Phone: 212-867-1511
US Fax: 212-286-8970

NTT operates principally in Japan but provides telecommunications consulting worldwide.

WHAT

	1990 Sales	
	¥ bil.	% of total
Telephone services	4,723	78
Telegraph services	59	1
Leased circuit services	357	6
Data communications facility services	175	3
Terminal equipment sales	284	5
Other	424	7
Total	**6,022**	**100**

Services

Leased Circuit Services
High-speed digital circuit services
Satellite communications
Standard circuit services
Video and record communications

Data Communications Facility Services
ANSER (Automatic Answer Network System for Electrical Request) Response Service
Financial information systems
Public and private data communications facility services

Digital Data Exchange Services
Circuit-switching services
Packet-switching services

Other Telecommunications Services
Fax network services
Operator information services
Paging services
Telecommunications consulting
Terminal equipment sales
Videoconference services
Videotex services

KEY COMPETITORS

No companies in this book compete with NTT.

HOW MUCH

$=¥135 (Dec. 31, 1990)	9-Year Growth	1981	1982	1983	1984	1985	1986	1987	1988	1989	1990
Sales (¥ bil.)	4.6%	4,006	4,167	4,314	4,552	4,756	5,091	5,354	5,662	5,842	6,022
Net income (¥ bil.)	(4.3%)	388	356	370	384	328	186	193	267	264	261
Income as % of sales	—	9.7%	8.5%	8.6%	8.4%	6.9%	3.7%	3.6%	4.7%	4.5%	4.3%
Earnings per share (¥)	—	—	—	—	—	—	11,903	12,350	17,127	16,898	16,737
Stock price – high (¥ thou.)	—	—	—	—	—	—	—	3,180	2,530	1,930	1,470
Stock price – low (¥ thou.)	—	—	—	—	—	—	—	1,600	1,700	1,350	720
Stock price – close (¥ thou.)	—	—	—	—	—	—	—	2,160	1,810	1,470	985
P/E – high	—	—	—	—	—	—	—	257	148	114	88
P/E – low	—	—	—	—	—	—	—	130	99	80	43
Dividends per share (¥)	—	—	—	—	—	—	5,000	5,000	5,000	5,000	5,000
Book value per share (¥ thou.)	—	—	—	—	—	—	225	230	242	254	266

1990 Year-end:
Debt ratio: 48.2%
Return on equity: 6.4%
Cash (bil.): ¥777
Long-term debt (bil.): ¥3,859
No. of shares (mil.): 16
Dividends:
1990 average yield: 0.5%
1990 payout: 29.9%
Market value (mil.): $113,822
Sales (mil.): $44,459

Stock Price History High/Low 1987–90

3,500
3,000
2,500
2,000
1,500
1,000
500
0

NISSAN MOTOR CO., LTD.

OVERVIEW

Tokyo-based Nissan is the world's 4th largest automobile manufacturer. Sales are soft in Japan and the US, where Nissan ranks #2 and a distant #6, respectively. Profits are hurting from increased R&D spending, rising labor costs, and a lull in new products, although sales of Nissan's luxury Infiniti line are rising.

Operations outside Japan are important (47% of all units sold). US engineers designed the 240SX, Maxima, and Pathfinder, and overseas production accounts for over 22% of output.

In Europe, where Nissan leads all Japanese automakers, anticipated restrictions on sales of Japanese cars are expected to blunt the company's progress. Nissan is trying to take control of the distribution of its autos in France and the UK, where legal wrangling continues over the severance of the company's agreement with its import and distribution agent. Nissan is rapidly building production capacity in the US, Mexico, the UK, and Spain.

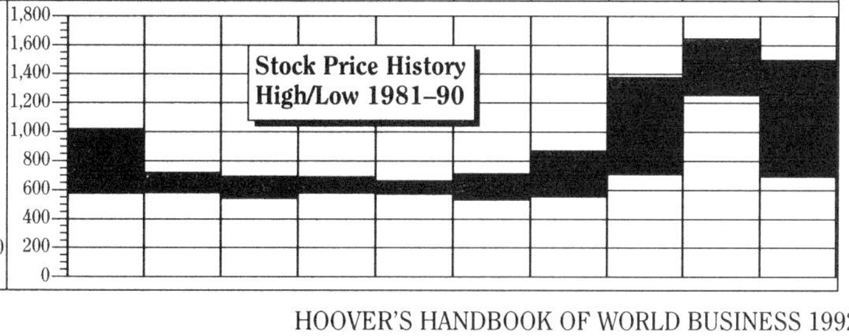

OTC symbol: NSANY (ADR)
Fiscal year ends: March 31

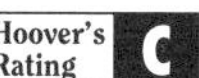

WHO

Chairman: Takashi Ishihara
President: Yutaka Kume
EVP Finance, Accounting and Personnel: Atsushi Muramatsu
Auditors: Showa Ota & Co.
Employees: 129,546

WHERE

HQ: Nissan Jidosha Kabushiki Kaisha, 17-1, Ginza 6-chome, Chuo-ku, Tokyo 104-23, Japan
Phone: 011-81-3-3543-5523
Fax: 011-81-3-3546-2669 (Corporate Communications)
US HQ: Nissan North America, Inc., 990 W. 190th St., Torrance, CA 90502
US Phone: 310-532-3111
US Fax: 310-719-5825 (Public Relations)

Nissan operates assembly and production plants in 21 countries and markets its products in more than 150 countries.

	1990 Unit Sales	
	No. of vehicles	% of total
Japan	1,373,171	47
North America	669,018	23
Europe	521,796	18
Middle East	56,599	2
Southeast Asia	70,926	2
Latin America & Caribbean	134,788	5
Oceania	95,549	3
Other regions	14,879	—
Total	**2,936,726**	**100**

WHEN

In 1911 US-trained Hashimoto Masujiro established Tokyo-based Kwaishinsha Motor Car Works to repair, import, and produce automobiles. Using DAT ("fast rabbit" in Japanese) as its logo, Kwaishinsha made its first car in 1913. Renamed DAT Motors in 1925 and suffering from a strong domestic preference for American cars, the company consolidated its operations with ailing Jitsuyo Motors in 1926. In 1931 DAT introduced the son of DAT, the Datsun minicar (*son* means damage or loss in Japanese, hence the change in spelling).

Tobata Casting, a cast iron and auto parts maker, acquired the Datsun production facilities in 1933. Tobata's Aikawa Yoshisuke believed that a niche existed for small cars that did not compete head-on with large US imports. Tobata's car operations were spun off as Nissan Motors in 1933. Aikawa imported US machinery and engineers in the 1930s. In 1936 he imported all the production equipment in a plant owned by financially troubled US carmaker Graham-Paige, creating Japan's first mass-producer of automobiles.

In WWII the Japanese government forced Nissan to build only trucks and airplane engines, leaving its dealers with little to sell. The resulting dealer defections gave Toyota a postwar advantage. During the occupation Nissan survived, in part, on US Army business.

A 1952 licensing agreement with Austin Motor (UK) put Nissan back in the car business. Adhering to US quality-control statistician William E. Deming's teachings, Nissan mass-produced reliable, inexpensive autos. A 40% import tax let Nissan compete in Japan despite higher costs than foreign makers.

Nissan elected to enter the US market in 1958 using the Datsun name and established Nissan Motor Corporation in Los Angeles in 1960. The company built an assembly plant in Mexico (1961) and introduced the popular Sunny in Japan (1966) and the 240Z in the US (1969). Exports rose during the 1960s as quality increased and unit costs declined as a result of just-in-time inventory management, factory automation, and higher volume.

In the 1970s Nissan expanded exports of fuel-efficient cars (e.g., Datsun B210), and diversified into rockets and motorboats.

In the 1980s the company built facilities worldwide, including a pickup truck plant in Tennessee and an R&D center in Michigan. The US name change from Datsun to Nissan confused customers and took 6 years (1981 to 1987) to complete. Nissan's high-end Infiniti line was launched in the US in 1989.

In a nonfinancial, face-saving way, Nissan (with the approval of Fuji's banker, the Industrial Bank of Japan) quietly took control of Fuji Heavy Industries, the troubled maker of Subaru autos, in 1990.

In 1991 Nissan roiled commodities markets with its announcement that it had developed a catalytic converter that would not use platinum.

WHAT

	1990 Sales	
	¥ bil.	% of total
Motor vehicles	4,393	78
Automotive parts & others	1,100	19
Production parts & components	49	1
Industrial machinery & marine equipment	52	1
Textile machinery	17	—
Aerospace equipment	34	1
Total	**5,645**	**100**

Automobile Models (US Markets)

Infiniti
- G20
- M30
- Q45

Nissan
- 4x2 (trucks)
- 4x4 (trucks)
- 240SX
- 300ZX
- Maxima
- Pathfinder (sport utility vehicle)
- Sentra
- Stanza

Industrial Machinery and Marine Equipment
- Automotive parts
- Forklifts
- Outboard motors
- Pleasure boats
- Trucks and tractors (Barrett)

Aerospace Equipment
- Rockets
- Satellite launch vehicles

Textile Machinery
- Jet looms

HOW MUCH

$ = ¥135 (Dec. 31, 1990)	9-Year Growth	1981	1982	1983	1984	1985	1986	1987	1988	1989	1990
Sales (¥ bil.)	5.0%	3,649	3,901	4,071	4,308	4,626	4,628	4,273	4,244	4,812	5,645
Net income (¥ bil.)	0.9%	107	102	105	74	82	36	20	65	115	116
Income as % of sales	—	2.9%	2.6%	2.6%	1.7%	1.8%	0.8%	0.5%	1.5%	2.4%	2.1%
Earnings per share (¥)	(2.0%)	*55*	*41*	*46*	*36*	*39*	*16*	*9*	*29*	*48*	*46*
Stock price – high (¥)	—	1,025	723	698	695	668	717	875	1,380	1,650	1,500
Stock price – low (¥)	—	572	576	538	575	569	529	550	705	1,250	690
Stock price – close (¥)	0.2%	690	690	686	625	570	550	725	1,200	1,470	700
P/E – high	—	19	18	15	19	17	45	97	48	34	33
P/E – low	—	10	14	12	16	15	33	61	24	26	15
Dividends per share (¥)	3.9%	9.92	10.74	11.57	12.73	12.73	14.00	14.00	14.00	14.00	14.00
Book value per share (¥)	4.9%	460	423	459	526	629	627	616	628	666	707

1990 Year-end:
Debt ratio: 33.4%
Return on equity: 6.7%
Cash (bil.): ¥104
Long-term debt (bil.): ¥888
No. of shares (mil.): 2,509
Dividends:
- 1990 average yield: 2.0%
- 1990 payout: 30.4%

Market value (mil.): $13,010
Sales (mil.): $41,815

Stock Price History High/Low 1981–90

(Chart axis: 0, 200, 400, 600, 800, 1,000, 1,200, 1,400, 1,600, 1,800)

KEY COMPETITORS

BMW	General Motors	Reebok
Brunswick	Honda	Renault
Caterpillar	Hyundai	Saab-Scania
Chrysler	Isuzu	Suzuki
Daimler-Benz	Mazda	Thiokol
Deere	Mitsubishi	Toyota
Fiat	Outboard Marine	Volkswagen
Ford	Peugeot	Volvo

NOBEL INDUSTRIES SWEDEN AB

Principal exchange: Stockholm
Fiscal year ends: December 31

OVERVIEW

Every year the Nobel Foundation announces winners of the prizes that bear the name of its founder and benefactor, Alfred Nobel — the same man who founded 2 of the companies that now form Nobel Industries.

Nobel Industries is a diversified defense, aerospace, and chemicals company, formerly controlled by industrialist Erik Penser (now mostly owned by the Swedish government since the financial collapse of Penser's empire in August 1991). It is Sweden's leading chemical company, and, with subsidiaries located worldwide, it manufactures and sells a surprising range of products, from the TRINITY air defense system to Finesse hair care products.

The company's Eka Nobel division specializes in the production of chemicals used in the pulp and paper industries, leading the world's production of sodium chlorate used for bleaching paper. Nobel Industries also makes pharmaceutical chemicals and chemical surfactants used in mineral processing and industrial cleaning. Another division makes adhesives, printing inks, lacquers, and paints.

Nobel Industries' defense and aerospace companies produce weapons (Bofors), lasers, and laser-based systems (Pharos). Related biotechnology subsidiaries have pioneered medical techniques, including dental replacement surgery.

WHEN

Remembered best for the annual prizes that bear his name, Alfred Nobel was also the inventor of dynamite. In 1863 Nobel invented the blasting cap, making it possible to control the detonation of nitroglycerin. He then persuaded Stockholm merchant J. W. Smitt to help him finance Nitroglycerin Ltd. to manufacture and sell the volatile fluid (1864). Nobel's ongoing quest to improve nitroglycerin led to the invention of dynamite in 1867. After dynamite, Nobel invented blasting gelatine (1875) and smokeless gunpowder (1887).

In 1894 Nobel bought the Swedish munitions factory A. B. Bofors-Gullspång, putting his assistant Ragnar Sohlman in charge. (Sohlman later became an executor of Nobel's controversial will, which left most of his estate to establish and fund the Nobel prizes.)

After Nobel's death in 1895, Bofors continued to produce munitions, gaining international recognition in the 1930s for its 40-mm anti-aircraft gun, used by the US and the UK during WWII. After the war Bofors made armaments primarily for the Swedish government, but, when that market faltered in the 1970s, it had to rely more on exports. In the meantime Nitroglycerin remained an explosives maker and in 1965 changed its name to Nitro Nobel.

In 1978 Swedish industrialist Marcus Wallenberg bought Nitro Nobel for his KemaNord chemical group, known afterward as KemaNobel.

Erik Penser started buying stakes in Bofors in the late 1970s and in KemaNobel in the early 1980s. By 1982 he controlled Bofors and in 1984 wrested control of KemaNobel from the Wallenbergs, bringing the 2 companies together as Nobel Industries. Penser named longtime friend Anders Carlberg CEO, and in 1986 Nobel Industries bought control of the Swedish defense electronics firm Pharos.

In the mid-1980s Bofors and KemaNobel were accused of illegally smuggling weapons to Iran and Iraq. Bofors was further embroiled in scandal in 1986, concerning its alleged payment of $60 million in kickbacks to middlemen in connection with a $1.3 billion howitzer sale to India. The charges were dropped in 1988.

In 1990 Nobel Industries bought some of Gillette's European personal care brands; Pharos bought Ciba-Geigy's California-based Spectra-Physics subsidiary (the world's #1 laser and laser systems manufacturer) and the UK's Continental Microwave.

HOW MUCH

$=SEK5.63 (Dec. 31, 1990)	9-Year Growth	1981	1982	1983	1984	1985[1]	1986	1987	1988	1989	1990
Sales (SEK mil.)	24.4%	3,710	4,157	4,375	7,039	10,889	11,535	13,920	21,328	22,088	26,399
Net income (SEK mil.)[2]	41.4%	46	62	18	5	83	474	459	654	939	1,037
Income as % of sales	—	1.2%	1.5%	0.4%	0.1%	0.8%	4.1%	3.3%	3.1%	4.3%	3.9%
Earnings per share (SEK)	22.7%	1.55	1.54	0.90	1.32	1.78	7.60	7.05	9.25	10.10	9.80
Stock price – high (SEK)	—	—	—	—	—	—	—	—	—	—	117
Stock price – low (SEK)	—	—	—	—	—	—	—	—	—	—	60
Stock price – close (SEK)	11.9%	21	19	29	32	32	79	72	144	91	58
P/E – high	—	—	—	—	—	—	—	—	—	—	12
P/E – low	—	—	—	—	—	—	—	—	—	—	6
Dividends per share (SEK)	14.3%	0.60	0.67	0.67	0.70	0.70	0.80	1.00	1.25	1.65	2.00
Book value per share (SEK)	15.9%	17	18	18	17	20	25	36	45	53	64

1990 Year-end:
Debt ratio: 57.7%
Return on equity: 16.8%
Cash (mil.): SEK4,322
Long-term debt (bil.): SEK8
No. of shares (mil.): 92
Dividends:
1990 average yield: 3.4%
1990 payout: 20.4%
Market value (mil.): $948
Sales (mil.): $4,689

Net Income (SEK mil.) 1981–90

1,200
1,000
800
600
400
200
0

Note: All per share data pertain to restricted shares only [1] Accounting change [2] Including extraordinary items 1981–84

WHO

Chairman: Erik Penser, age 49
President and CEO: Anders G. Carlberg, age 48
Head of Group Staff Finance and Control: Jan Kihlberg, age 54
Personnel Director: Willy Ekberg
Auditors: Öhrlings Reveko AB
Employees: 26,654

WHERE

HQ: Gustav Adolfs Torg 18, PO Box 16397, S-103 27 Stockholm, Sweden
Phone: 011-46-8-613-25-00
Fax: 011-46-8-20-12-05
US HQ: Nobel Industries USA, Inc., 595 Skippack Pike, Suite 300, Blue Bell, PA 19422
US Phone: 215-641-9330
US Fax: 215-641-9334

Nobel Industries is composed of more than 300 companies with operations in 34 countries.

	1990 Sales		1990 Operating Income	
	SEK mil.	% of total	SEK mil.	% of total
Sweden	15,703	53	890	50
Other Europe	11,103	37	627	35
North America	2,391	8	255	14
Other countries	578	2	26	1
Adjustments	(3,376)	—	—	—
Total	**26,399**	**100**	**1,798**	**100**

WHAT

	1990 Sales		1990 Operating Income	
	SEK mil.	% of total	SEK mil.	% of total
Biotechnology	817	3	103	8
Pulp & paper chems.	3,387	13	243	18
Pharma chems.	887	3	(26)	(2)
Consumer goods	2,190	8	188	14
Adhesives & paints	8,680	33	304	23
Plastics	922*	3	26*	2
Surface chem.	1,661	6	65	5
Ordnance	5,627	21	262	19
Pharos	2,548	10	181	13
Adjustments	(320)	—	(309)	—
Total	**26,399**	**100**	**1,037**	**100**

*9 months only

Major Consumer Brands
Aapri, Mont St Michel (personal care)
Finesse, Salon Selective, Silkience (hair care)
Licor del Polo, Sergio Tacchini (fragrance)

Major Group Companies
Berol Nobel AB (surface chemistry)
AB Bofors (defense electronics)
Casco Nobel AB (adhesives, paints)
Eka Nobel AB (bleaching and specialty chemicals for pulp and paper industries)
Extracto AB (gelatine-based chemicals)
Nobel Chemicals AB (pharmaceutical and fine chemicals)
Nobel Consumer Goods AB (personal care products)
Nobelpharma AB (dental implants)
Pharos AB (83.2%, laser-based systems, other high-tech operations)
Spectra-Physics Inc. (laser systems, bar-code scanners)

KEY COMPETITORS

Other defense contractors and chemical, consumer products, pulp and paper, pharmaceutical, and engineering companies

THE NOMURA SECURITIES COMPANY, LTD.

OVERVIEW

Nomura is the world's largest securities company. Aided by Japanese government restrictions on foreign investment houses and by a fixed commission system, Nomura has been one of the most consistently profitable of the world's giant financial services firms.

The leading Eurobond underwriter, Nomura has made significant progress overseas, but the firm's main business remains Japanese stock brokerage. The company, though, is reeling from a world-class scandal. In mid-1991 the Japanese government investigated allegations that Nomura improperly covered $114 million in stock losses by wealthy clients. Nomura was also being investigated for manipulating stock to aid a crime lord.

All of Japan's Big 4 securities firms have been singed by the flames of allegations, but Nomura, largest of the group, was the most badly burned. Chairman Setsuya Tabuchi and President Yoshihisa Tabuchi left the firm. The Tokyo market nosedived 500 points when the scandal was revealed.

The scandal was the latest in the brokerage firm's travails. After the Nikkei average of Tokyo stock prices fell 39% during fiscal 1990–91, Nomura profits declined sharply.

WHEN

Nomura Tokushichi started a currency exchange business in Osaka under the Nomura Shoten name in 1872. As money changing subsided with Japanese monetary reform, Nomura entered stock dealing. His business prospered and was taken over by his son, Tokushichi II, prior to the senior Nomura's death in 1907. In 1910 Tokushichi II formed Nomura's first syndicate to underwrite a portion of a government bond issue. As business grew, Nomura established the Osaka Nomura Bank (1918). The bond department became independent in 1925 and was named Nomura Securities.

The company opened a New York office (1927), entered stock brokerage (1938), and introduced its enormously successful stock investment trusts (1941).

Nomura rebuilt and aggressively expanded retail operations after WWII. The company encouraged stock market investing by promoting "million ryo [an old form of currency] savings chests," small boxes in which people were encouraged to save cash. When savings reached 5,000 yen, savers, usually women, would bring their boxes to Nomura and buy into investment trusts. Nomura distributed over one million chests in 10 years.

Nomura looked overseas for investment capital, helping to underwrite a US issue of Sony stock (1961) and opening a London office (1962). The company emerged as Japan's leading securities firm after a 1965 stock market crash left rival Yamaichi Securities near bankruptcy. When trade surpluses encouraged the Ministry of Finance to allow public ownership of foreign securities in 1971, Nomura began offering *samurai* (yen-denominated foreign) bonds. The company grew rapidly in the 1970s, ushering investment capital in and out of Japan and competing with bank lending by issuing corporate debt securities.

Nomura expanded worldwide in the 1970s and 1980s, attained NYSE membership (1981), secured a seat on the London Stock Exchange (1986), opened Nomura Bank International in London (1986), became the world leader in Eurobonds (1987), and paid $100 million for 20% of merger and acquisition advisor Wasserstein Perella (1988). Nomura pursued retail business aggressively, hosting Tupperware-style investment parties in Japan.

With a sudden drop in the Tokyo stock market in calendar year 1990, Nomura stock toppled 70% from its 1987 peak. The company saw its equity underwritings fall from 1,201 in FY 1990 to 12 in the first 6 months of 1991.

HOW MUCH

$=¥135 (Dec. 31, 1990)	9-Year Growth	1981	1982	1983	1984	1985	1986	1987	1988	1989[1]	1990
Sales (¥ bil.)	16.3%	308	268	367	437	590	942	1,073	960	585	1,201
Net income (¥ bil.)	20.9%	50	42	69	73	111	221	268	214	138	276
Income as % of sales	—	16.2%	15.7%	18.8%	16.7%	18.8%	23.5%	25.0%	22.3%	23.6%	23.0%
Earnings per share (¥)	19.7%	28	22	37	39	59	118	142	112	72	141
Stock price – high (¥)	—	637	551	690	853	1,287	3,612	5,816	4,185	4,100	3,430
Stock price – low (¥)	—	297	319	511	533	793	934	2,402	2,402	3,060	1,380
Stock price – close (¥)	15.1%	499	550	645	809	980	2,835	2,583	3,750	3,440	1,770
P/E – high	—	23	25	19	22	22	31	41	37	—	24
P/E – low	—	13	15	14	14	13	8	17	21	—	10
Dividends per share (¥)	11.4%	5.69	5.86	6.04	6.67	7.25	9.71	12.14	13.11	7.25	15.02
Book value per share (¥)	18.4%	208	214	239	274	325	412	582	685	816	953

1990 Year-end:
Debt ratio: —
Return on equity: 16.0%
Cash (bil.): ¥1,279
Long-term debt (bil.): —
No. of shares (mil.): 1,959
Dividends:
1990 average yield: 0.8%
1990 payout: 10.7%
Market value (mil.): $25,685
Sales (mil.): $8,896

Stock Price History High/Low 1981–90

6,000
5,000
4,000
3,000
2,000
1,000
0

[1] 6-month period

OTC symbol: NMRJY (ADR)
Fiscal year ends: March 31

Hoover's Rating **B**

WHO

Honorary Chairman: Yukio Aida
President and CEO: Hideo Sakamaki, age 56
Co-chairman, Nomura Securities International, Inc.: Max C. Chapman, Jr.
Auditors: Price Waterhouse
Employees: 15,000

WHERE

HQ: Nomura Shoken Kabushiki Kaisha, 1-9-1, Nihonbashi, Chuo-ku, Tokyo 103, Japan
Phone: 011-81-3-3211-1811
Fax: 011-81-3-3278-0420
US HQ: Nomura Securities International, Inc., The Continental Center, 180 Maiden Ln., New York, NY 10038
US Phone: 212-208-9300
US Fax: 212-509-8907

Nomura has 146 offices in Japan and 61 offices in 23 other countries.

	1990 Sales	
	¥ bil.	% of total
Japan	963	80
US	49	4
Europe	152	13
Other countries	37	3
Total	**1,201**	**100**

WHAT

	1990 Sales	
	¥ bil.	% of total
Commissions	489	41
Underwriting & distribution	277	23
Net gain on trading	141	12
Interest & dividends	287	24
Other	7	—
Total	**1,201**	**100**

Lines of Business

Securities
- Brokerage
- Dealing
- Distribution
- Underwriting

Financial consulting
- Asset management
- Banking
- Leveraged leasing
- Mergers and acquisitions
- Real estate

US Affiliates

Babcock & Brown, Inc.
Eastdil Realty, Inc.
Tudor/Nomura Global Trading Partners
Wasserstein Perella Group, Inc. (20%)

KEY COMPETITORS

American Express
Barclays
Bear Stearns
Canadian Imperial
Crédit Lyonnais
CS Holding
Dai-Ichi Kangyo
Deutsche Bank
Goldman Sachs
HSBC
Industrial Bank of Japan
Merrill Lynch
J.P. Morgan
Morgan Stanley
Primerica
Prudential
Royal Bank
Salomon
Sears
Travelers
Union Bank of Switzerland
Other brokerage and investment banking firms

NORSK HYDRO AS

OVERVIEW

Norsk Hydro, 51% owned by the Kingdom of Norway, is the world's largest producer of fertilizer and a leader in aluminum and magnesium production. It is the largest publicly traded industrial concern in Norway.

The company began as a producer and user of hydroelectric energy to manufacture fertilizer, and its agricultural operations still account for more than 40% of its revenues. But faced with declining demand in the late 1980s, Hydro closed or consolidated some plants. The company currently leans heavily on oil and gas, which provides almost 1/2 its profits. Hydro owns an interest in 2/3 of the wells drilled in the rich fields in the Norwegian North Sea and owns a piece of every major pipeline off the coast of Norway. It owns an interest in a Swedish refinery and sells gasoline in Norway, Denmark, and Sweden under the Hydro brand. Its petrochemical operations in Scandinavia and the UK produce ethylene, propylene, and PVC.

In the light metals arena, Hydro produces primary aluminum at 5 plants in Norway and operates 18 extrusion plants in 9 European countries and the US. Hydro is also a leading magnesium producer after developing a large Canadian facility. The company dabbles in other businesses ranging from salmon farming to roofing to insurance.

WHEN

Norwegian entrepreneurs Sam Eyde and Kristian Birkeland began Norsk Hydro-Elektrisk Kvaelstofaktieselskap (Norwegian Hydro-Electric Nitrogen Corporation) in 1905. The company used electricity generated from waterfalls to extract nitrogen from the air for the production of fertilizer. The company sold most of its output in Scandinavia.

After WWII the Norwegian government seized German holdings in Hydro and took a 48% stake in the company. Hydro grew to be the largest chemical firm in Scandinavia, and in 1965, when Norway granted licenses for offshore petroleum exploration, Hydro was a Norwegian concessionaire, in partnership with foreign companies on many fields.

In 1969 the Phillips Petroleum–operated drilling rig Ocean Viking struck oil in the giant Ekofisk field and spurred the boom in the North Sea. Norsk Hydro owned a stake in the well's production. The Norwegian government, struggling to forge its petroleum policy, increased its share of Hydro to 51% and created Statoil, a completely state-owned company, in 1972. Hydro's North Sea success continued with the Elf Aquitaine–operated Frigg discovery in 1971.

During much of the 1970s, Hydro focused on oil and gas development. Hydro had begun to branch out, with hydroelectric-powered aluminum processing at its KarmØy Works (1967) and with its fish-farming subsidiary Mowi (1969). Development of oil and gas added to the treasury and helped finance growth, often through acquisitions.

Hydro pushed into the European fertilizer market with the acquisition of NSM, a Dutch firm (1979); 75% of Supra of Sweden (1981); a British firm renamed Norsk Hydro Fertilizers Ltd. (1982); a West German company renamed Ruhr Stickstoff AG (1985); and 80% of the French manufacturer Cofaz (1986). In petrochemicals it purchased 2 British PVC makers (Vinatex Ltd, 1981; BIP Vinyls Ltd.'s PVC business, 1982) to form Norsk Hydro Polymers. Hydro added aluminum extrusion plants in Europe, and in 1986 the Hydro-controlled Hydro Aluminum merged with ÅSV, another Norwegian aluminum company. Hydro consolidated its aluminum holdings in 1988.

Hydro served as operator in the Oseberg field, which began production in 1988 and grew rapidly to become a major source of oil and gas. In 1990 Hydro bought 300 Danish gasoline stations from UNO-X, proposed to buy W. R. Grace's fertilizer interests in Trinidad, and planned another magnesium plant in Canada.

NYSE symbol: NHY (ADR)
Fiscal year ends: December 31

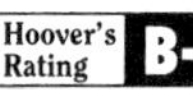

WHO

Chairman: Egil Abrahamsen
President: Egil Myklebust
CFO: Leiv L. Nergaard
Personnel and Organization: Hans Jørn Rønningen
Auditors: Forum Touche Ross ANS
Employees: 33,042

WHERE

HQ: Bygdøy allé 2, N-0240, Oslo 2, Norway
Phone: 011-47-2-43-21-00
Fax: 011-47-2-43-27-25
US HQ: Norsk Hydro Sales Corporation, 800 Third Ave., New York, NY 10022
US Phone: 212-688-6606
US Fax: 212-750-1252

Exploration and production: North Sea
Refining and marketing: Refining in Sweden; service stations in Scandinavia.
Chemicals and minerals: Major fertilizer plants in Norway, Sweden, the UK, France, and the Netherlands; petrochemicals produced in Norway, Sweden, and the UK.
Light metals: Aluminum in Norway, 9 other European nations, and the US; magnesium in Norway and Quebec.
Other: Salmon farming, roofing, insurance, and pharmaceuticals in Norway.

	1990 Sales		1990 Operating Income	
	$ mil.	% of total	$ mil.	% of total
Norway	4,077	39	926	80
Other Europe	4,668	45	249	22
Other countries	1,645	16	(27)	(2)
Adjustments	—	—	(37)	—
Total	**10,390**	**100**	**1,111**	**100**

WHAT

	1990 Sales		1990 Operating Income	
	$ mil.	% of total	$ mil.	% of total
Petrochemicals	792	8	172	15
Light metals	2,958	29	218	19
Agriculture	4,385	42	221	19
Oil & gas	1,904	18	564	49
Other	351	3	(26)	(2)
Adjustments	—	—	(38)	—
Total	**10,390**	**100**	**1,111**	**100**

Interests in North Sea Fields

Brae (2%)	Northeast Frigg (13.81%)
East Frigg (32.11%)	Oseberg (13.75%)
Ekofisk (6.7%)	Sleipner East (10%)
Forties (0.75%)	Snorre (8.27%)
Frigg (19.99%)	Troll (7.69%)
Gullfaks (9%)	Ula (1.81%)
Gyda (1.44%)	Veslefrikk (9%)
Heimdal (6.23%)	

HOW MUCH

Stock prices are for ADRs ADR = 1 share	5-Year Growth	1981	1982	1983	1984	1985	1986	1987	1988	1989	1990
Sales ($ mil.)	13.4%	—	—	—	—	5,530	7,687	8,764	9,142	10,049	10,390
Net income ($ mil.)	29.1%	—	—	—	—	97	(117)	70	315	228	348
Income as % of sales	—	—	—	—	—	1.8%	(1.5%)	0.8%	3.4%	2.3%	3.4%
Earnings per share ($)	24.4%	—	—	—	—	0.57	(0.69)	0.41	1.57	1.11	1.70
Stock price – high ($)	—	—	—	—	—	—	11.56	19.69	18.50	27.75	41.75
Stock price – low ($)	—	—	—	—	—	—	8.44	9.50	11.63	18.50	24.25
Stock price – close ($)	—	—	—	—	—	—	9.69	11.75	18.00	25.25	30.75
P/E – high	—	—	—	—	—	—	—	48	12	25	25
P/E – low	—	—	—	—	—	—	—	23	7	17	14
Dividends per share ($)	20.9%	—	—	—	—	0.24	0.38	0.34	0.48	0.52	0.62
Book value per share ($)	18.6%	—	—	—	—	3.12	2.83	3.45	5.15	5.67	7.33

1990 Year-end:
Debt ratio: 68.1%
Return on equity: 26.1%
Cash (mil.): $910
Current ratio: 1.13
Long-term debt (mil.): $3,207
No. of shares (mil.): 205
Dividends:
1990 average yield: 2.0%
1990 payout: 36.4%
Market value (mil.): $6,316

KEY COMPETITORS

Alcan	Elf Aquitaine	Pemex
Amoco	Exxon	Phillips Petroleum
British Petroleum	Mobil	Royal Dutch/Shell
Broken Hill	Occidental	Texaco
Cargill	Pennzoil	USX
Chevron	Petrofina	Aluminum makers
Coastal	Petrobrás	Chemical companies
Continental Grain	PDVSA	

OKI ELECTRIC INDUSTRY CO., LTD.

OVERVIEW

Oki Electric Industry, Japan's 10th largest electronics company, is a major global supplier of telecommunications systems, semiconductors, data processing systems, and printers. Most of its products are geared toward the corporate (rather than the consumer) marketplace; even so, many business-minded Americans are familiar with the company's cellular phones and Okidata line of dot matrix printers. It is no accident that Oki's headquarters is located in the Fuji Bank building in Tokyo — Fuji, one of Oki's largest shareholders, is also one of its biggest customers. Another of Oki's longstanding customers is Nippon Telephone & Telegraph (NTT).

Oki recently strengthened its position as one of the world's leading suppliers of computer systems and ATMs to the banking and financial sector by entering an agreement with Sun Microsystems (signed in 1989) that gives Oki access to Sun's financial software. In the long run Oki plans to increase R&D spending and personnel, particularly in its telecommunications businesses, to stay well positioned to meet its customers' changing needs. Current R&D expenditures stand at 6.3% of sales.

WHEN

Oki dates back to 1881, when engineer Kibataro Oki, formerly of Japan's Department of Industry, founded Meikosha Company in Tokyo. Originally formed to manufacture and sell telephones, Meikosha was soon also producing telegraphs, bells, and medical equipment. The company's main manufacturing plant adopted the name Oki Electric Plant in 1889; the marketing division began operating under the name Oki & Company in 1896.

In 1907, a year after the death of Kibataro Oki, the Oki groups were united as a limited partnership, divided again in 1912, then ultimately recombined in 1917 as Oki Electric Company. Oki continued to expand its product line to include automatic switching equipment (1926) and electric clocks (1929).

Oki produced communications equipment for the Japanese military during WWII but shifted back to civil production after the war, starting work on the teleprinter and adding consumer goods, such as portable stoves and irons. The company adopted its present name in 1949.

Oki entered the semiconductor and computer industries in the 1950s, joining Fujitsu, Hitachi, Toshiba, Nippon Electric Company, and Mitsubishi as one of Japan's Big 6 electronic makers by 1960. The company started developing its overseas business, particularly in Latin America, where it built communications networks in Honduras (1962) and Bolivia (1966) and radio networks in Brazil (1971).

Oki formed a computer software division in 1970 and started building PCs in 1981. The company continued as a major supplier of telecommunications equipment to the Japanese government until the mid-1970s, when the government increased purchases from other companies. The loss of government business eroded both sales and profits for Oki, resulting in a $7 million loss in 1978. Afterward, former NTT executive Masao Miyake took over as Oki's president, initiating a dramatic reorganization of the company into 15 highly focused and profitable business units.

Oki later consolidated its US operations, forming Oki America (1984). But a new financial crisis followed in the mid-1980s, when the bottom fell out of the semiconductor market, and earnings plummeted more than 110% between 1985 and 1986.

In 1987 Oki set up a division to provide oceanographic services (Oki Seataec). As a major provider of ATMs and bank computer systems, Oki enjoyed a ninefold increase in profits in 1989, sparked by growth in the Japanese financial industry. In 1990 Oki and Hewlett-Packard formed a joint venture in Puerto Rico to build printed circuit boards.

HOW MUCH

$=¥135 (Dec. 31, 1990)	9-Year Growth	1981	1982	1983	1984	1985	1986	1987	1988	1989	1990
Sales (¥ bil.)	12.8%	213	243	280	345	418	393	407	451	556	630
Net income (¥ bil.)	24.4%	5	4	3	9	9	(1)	2	4	36	38
Income as % of sales	—	2.5%	1.5%	0.9%	2.7%	2.2%	(0.2%)	0.5%	0.8%	6.5%	6.0%
Earnings per share (¥)	—	—	*9*	*6*	*20*	*19*	*(2)*	*4*	*6*	*28*	*28*
Stock price – high (¥)	—	453	438	780	894	719	835	879	1,153	1,260	1,260
Stock price – low (¥)	—	272	260	382	572	463	539	468	625	936	582
Stock price – close (¥)	8.8%	325	410	766	667	639	610	632	965	1200	695
P/E – high	—	—	50	128	44	37	—	207	178	45	45
P/E – low	—	—	30	63	28	24	—	110	96	33	21
Dividends per share (¥)	3.1%	4.54	4.54	4.76	4.76	5.71	5.71	2.86	5.72	6.00	6.00
Book value per share (¥)	14.4%	90	91	96	136	156	175	196	218	259	302

1990 Year-end:
Debt ratio: 51.7%
Return on equity: 10.0%
Cash (bil.): ¥157
Long-term debt (bil.): ¥181
No. of shares (mil.): 560
Dividends:
1990 average yield: 0.9%
1990 payout: 21.5%
Market value (mil.): $2,883
Sales (mil.): $4,667

Stock Price History High/Low 1981–90

1,400
1,200
1,000
800
600
400
200
0

Principal exchange: Tokyo
Fiscal year ends: March 31

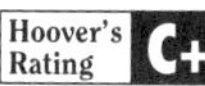

WHO

Chairman: Namio Hashimoto
President and CEO: Nobumitsu Kosugi
EVP: Yoshio Masuda
EVP: Masao Nogami
Auditors: Showa Ota & Co.
Employees: 19,331

WHERE

HQ: Oki Denki Kogyo, 7-12, Toranomon 1-chome, Minato-ku, Tokyo 105, Japan
Phone: 011-81-3-3501-3111
Fax: 011-81-3-3508-9465
US HQ: Oki America, Inc., Three University Plaza, Hackensack, NJ 07601
US Phone: 201-646-0011
US Fax: 201-646-9229

Oki has offices and plants in 15 countries. Its products are sold worldwide.

	1990 Sales	
	¥ bil.	% of total
Japan	436	69
Other countries	194	31
Total	**630**	**100**

WHAT

	1990 Sales	
	¥ bil.	% of total
Telecommunications systems	173	29
Information processing systems	288	47
Electronic devices	145	24
Adjustments	24	—
Total	**630**	**100**

Major Products

Telecommunications Systems
Switching systems (PBX, Telex)
Telephone sets (cellular, push-button)
Transmission systems (fax machines, radio equipment, fiber optics)

Information Processing Systems
Banking systems (ATMs)
Building management systems
Medical electronic systems
Minicomputers
Personal computers
Printers and other peripherals
Radar systems
Seismometric systems
Underwater acoustic systems
Water resource control systems

Electronic Devices
Memories
Microprocessors
Optoelectronic devices
Plasma display panel units
Printed circuit boards

KEY COMPETITORS

Alcatel Alsthom	IBM	Philips
AT&T	Matsushita	Pioneer
BCE	Minolta	Sharp
Canon	Mitsubishi	Siemens
Casio	NCR	Sony
Ericsson	NEC	Thorn EMI
Fujitsu	Olivetti	Toshiba
Hitachi		

Other communications, electronics, and computer cos.

ING. C. OLIVETTI & C., SPA

OVERVIEW

Italy's Olivetti is the 2nd largest Europe-based computer maker (after Germany's Siemens) and ranked among the world's top 10 computer companies in 1990. Olivetti sells Hitachi mainframes and, through joint ventures, makes copiers with Canon and fax machines with Sanyo. The company is strengthening ties with Digital Equipment through marketing and research agreements.

Stormy weather for the European computer industry has brought hard times to Olivetti, which has experienced an 83% drop in earnings since 1988. As its largest single shareholder (owning 43%), Chairman Carlo De Benedetti has a lot riding on Olivetti's recovery. He saved the company from bankruptcy when he first took office in 1978, but a reorganization of Olivetti into 4 cohesive business units (office equipment, computer and office automation systems, software and turnkey systems, and computer components and peripherals), ordered by De Benedetti in 1989, so far has failed to produce results. In a cost-cutting effort, Olivetti plans to cut 7,000 jobs in 1991 (on top of 3,000 in 1990) and has eliminated its dividend.

OTC symbol: OLIVY (ADR)
Fiscal year ends: December 31

WHO

Chairman and CEO: Carlo De Benedetti
Managing Director: Vittorio Cassoni
CFO: Angelo Fornasari
Director of Personnel: Paolo Ruzzini
Auditors: Arthur Andersen & Co.
Employees: 53,679

WHERE

HQ: Via Jervis 77, 10015 Ivrea, Italy
Phone: 011-39-125-522639
Fax: 011-39-125-523884
US HQ: Olivetti USA, Inc., 765 US Hwy. 202, Somerville, NJ 00876
US Phone: 908-526-8200
US Fax: 908-526-8405

Olivetti has operations in 33 countries. Its products are sold worldwide.

	1990 Sales	
	L bil.	% of total
Italy	3,312	36
Other Europe	4,056	45
North America	604	7
Latin America	271	3
Far East & Africa	794	9
Total	**9,037**	**100**

WHEN

Camillo Olivetti founded Olivetti in Ivrea in 1908 to produce the first Italian-made typewriter (introduced in 1911). The company later diversified into office furniture (1930), teleprinters (1938), and adding machines (1940). In 1933, a year after the company went public, Camillo's eldest son, Adriano, became general manager, leading Olivetti's diversification into computers, which resulted in Italy's first mainframe in 1959. That year Olivetti bought control of ailing US typewriter maker Underwood (founded by John Thomas Underwood, 1896), operating it as Olivetti Underwood until 1971, when it was restructured as Olivetti Corporation of America (OCA).

After Adriano's death in 1960, the Olivetti family sold most of its stake in the company to the Pirelli/Fiat syndicate in 1964. General Electric bought Olivetti's mainframe business that year. Because the company was slow to switch from mechanical to electric office equipment in the 1960s, earnings stagnated; Olivetti suspended its dividend in 1974.

Then in 1978 former Fiat executive Carlo De Benedetti invested $17 million in the company and, as CEO, slashed debt (and the payroll) while increasing R&D spending eight-fold between 1978 and 1984. Olivetti introduced its first electronic typewriter in 1978 and bought Swiss typewriter maker Hermes Precisa International in 1981.

OCA, in the meantime, had suffered through more than a decade of losses. De Benedetti hoped to end this by selling OCA to Dallas-based Docutel (ATMs) in exchange for a 46% stake in the ATM maker in 1982. When the strategy failed and losses continued, Olivetti bought the rest of Docutel and used it to establish Olivetti USA (1985).

Olivetti unveiled its first PC in 1982, only one year after IBM had pioneered the industry. In 1983 AT&T bought a 25% stake in Olivetti. Toshiba bought 20% of its Japanese operations in 1985. De Benedetti hoped this would increase Olivetti's US and Japanese market share. Unfortunately, sales in the US and Japan never met expectations, and AT&T later traded its stake in Olivetti to De Benedetti, in exchange for 18.6% of his holding company Compagnie Industriali Riunite (1989).

In the meantime Olivetti bought 80% of the UK's Acorn Computers Group (1985) and Volkswagen's ailing office-products maker, Triumph-Adler (1986). Olivetti boosted its stake in bank automation by buying Bunker Ramo (1986) and I.S.C. Systems Corporation (1989). The company considered buying a stake in bankrupt French computer maker SMT-Goupil in 1991, but when the French could not meet financial conditions Olivetti pulled out of the deal.

WHAT

	1990 Sales	
	L bil.	% of total
Olivetti Office	3,439	38
Olivetti Systems & Networks	4,682	52
Olivetti Information Services	479	5
Olivetti Technologies Group	432	5
Others	5	—
Total	**9,037**	**100**

	1990 Sales
	% of total
Typewriters & videotyping systems	12
PCs	33
Minicomputers & terminals	18
Printers	9
Telecommunications equipment	4
Software	13
Calculators & cash registers	3
Copiers	6
Office furniture	2
Total	**100**

Major Subsidiaries and Affiliates

Acorn Computers Group PLC (79.8%, UK)
Baltea SpA (office equipment and supplies, Italy)
Delphi SpA (55.3%, university research systems, Italy)
Elea SpA (software consultancy, Italy)
ISC-Bunker Ramo Corp. (automated banking equipment, US)
Olivetti-Canon Industriale SpA (50%, copiers, joint venture with Canon, Italy)
Olivetti Sanyo Industriale SpA (51%, fax machines, joint venture with Sanyo, Italy)
S.I.A.B. SA (51%, banking technology, France)
Syntax Sistemi Software SpA (information systems development, Italy)
TA Triumph-Adler AG (98.4%, office information systems, Germany)
Tecnost-Mael SpA (52.8%, turnkey systems, Italy)
Teknecomp SpA (35.9%, ancillary computer hardware, Italy)

KEY COMPETITORS

Other computer and office equipment companies

HOW MUCH

$=L1,125 (Dec. 31, 1990)	9-Year Growth	1981	1982	1983	1984	1985	1986	1987	1988	1989	1990
Sales (L bil.)	13.5%	2,888	3,341	3,736	4,578	6,141	7,317	7,376	8,407	9,031	9,037
Net income (L bil.)	—	—	103	295	356	504	566	402	356	203	60
Income as % of sales	—	—	3.1%	7.9%	7.8%	8.2%	7.7%	5.5%	4.2%	2.2%	0.7%
Earnings per share (L)	—	—	318	857	760	1,023	1,097	733	647	366	98
Stock price – high (L)	—	5,150	3,040	5,550	6,080	8,790	18,690	14,700	11,505	9,349	7,699
Stock price – low (L)	—	2,450	1,960	1,901	3,865	5,755	8,710	7,010	7,305	7,232	3,030
Stock price – close (L)	2.6%	2,549	1,960	3,874	5,875	8,780	13,650	7,480	9,000	7,395	3,220
P/E – high	—	—	10	6	8	9	17	20	18	26	79
P/E – low	—	—	6	2	5	6	8	10	11	20	31
Dividends per share (L)	—	0	200	200	240	275	320	340	340	340	270
Book value per share (L)	—	—	3,401	4,288	4,887	5,711	7,072	7,106	7,306	7,000	6,740

1990 Year-end:
Debt ratio: 56.0%
Return on equity: 1.4%
Cash (bil.): L4,932
Long-term debt (bil.): L4,441
No. of shares (mil.): 502
Dividends:
1990 average yield: 8.4%
1990 payout: —
Market value (mil.): $1,437
Sales (mil.): $8,033

Stock Price History High/Low 1981–90

20,000
18,000
16,000
14,000
12,000
10,000
8,000
6,000
4,000
2,000
0

DABU

PEARSON PLC

OVERVIEW

Pearson is primarily a publisher but has interests in such diverse businesses as wax museums (Madame Tussaud's), fine china (Royal Doulton), oil services (Camco), investment banking (Lazard Brothers), and satellite TV broadcasting (British Sky Broadcasting, 16%). Major publishing operations include the Financial Times, Addison-Wesley, Penguin, Longman, Federal Publications, and a 50% stake in the Economist (which provided economic data for the country profiles in this book).

The founder's heirs have managed the company since 1927 and control about 20% of the stock. Rupert Murdoch's News Corporation owns a 9.9% stake, and Pearson associate Lazard Frères controls another 8.9%. After merger plans with Dutch publisher Elsevier failed in 1990, Pearson sold its 22.2% stake in the Dutch company to reduce debt in 1991. Elsevier has followed suit, selling its 8.8% stake in Pearson.

Principal exchange: London
Fiscal year ends: December 31

WHO

Chairman and CEO: Viscount Michael Blakenham, age 53, £256,000 pay
Managing Director and COO: Frank Barlow, age 61
Finance Director: James Joll, age 54
Head of Personnel: Robert Head
Auditors: Coopers & Lybrand Deloitte
Employees: 29,410

WHEN

In 1844 Samuel Pearson became a partner in a small Yorkshire building firm. When he retired in 1879, his grandson, Weetman, took over, moving the company to London in 1884, 2 years after it had won its first London contract. The company enjoyed extraordinary success, winning numerous contracts, including one to build the first tunnel under New York's Hudson River and another to construct the main drainage system in Mexico City. By the 1890s the company (incorporated as S. Pearson & Son in 1897) was the world's largest contractor. Weetman Pearson was knighted in 1894 and later received the titles of baron (1910) and viscount (1917).

In 1901 Weetman Pearson missed a railroad connection in Laredo, Texas, and, during his 9-hour wait, heard about the nearby Spindletop oil gusher. Recalling reports of oil seepages in Mexico, he bought drilling rights on huge tracts of Mexican land. Pearson sank $25 million into his Mexican Eagle Oil Company. In turn, it made him a very wealthy man before he sold it to Shell Oil in 1919.

In 1919 Pearson, by then Lord Cowdray, restructured S. Pearson & Son as a holding company separate from the construction business. In the 1920s the company bought newspapers and a stake in Lazard Brothers, and engaged in oil exploration (including the startup and sale of US-based Amerada). Cowdray died in 1927 and, without him, so did the construction business. His heirs took over S. Pearson & Son and added unrelated businesses to a company that has since been called "a collection of rich men's toys."

In 1935 Pearson helped form British Airways (merged into British Overseas Airways Corporation, the predecessor of today's British Airways, in 1939). In 1957 Pearson bought control (it now owns all) of the *Financial Times* business newspaper and, with it, 50% of the *Economist* magazine. Pearson bought 54% of Château Latour (wine, 1963), 64% of Longman (1968), and, after going public in 1969, Penguin Books (1971), Royal Doulton (1971), Madame Tussaud's (1978), the rest of Longman (1982), and Camco (1987).

After a takeover scare in 1986, when Hong Kong's Hutchison Whampoa bought 4.9% of the company, Pearson's Lazard Frères affiliate bought a block of Pearson's stock to discourage the would-be suitor. Murdoch's News Corporation bought a 20% stake in Pearson in 1987, rekindling rumors of a takeover.

Murdoch never took control and has since reduced his stake to 9.9%. In the meantime Pearson has taken steps to improve profitability. In 1988 and 1989 it sold Château Latour and its oil production businesses and bought Addison-Wesley (publisher, US), *Les Echos* (financial newspaper, France), 22.2% of Elsevier (scientific publisher, the Netherlands), and TRW's Reda Pump (oil services, US). The company bought Cuisenaire (teaching materials, US) in 1990.

WHERE

HQ: Milbank Tower, London SW1P 4QZ, UK
Phone: 011-44-71-411-2000
Fax: 011-44-71-411-2390
US HQ: Pearson, Inc., One Rockefeller Plaza, New York, NY 10020
US Phone: 212-713-1919
US Fax: 212-247-4616

	1990 Sales		1990 Operating Income	
	£ mil.	% of total	£ mil.	% of total
UK	551	36	114	44
Other Europe	154	10	58	23
North America	582	38	40	16
Other countries	248	16	44	17
Total	**1,535**	**100**	**256**	**100**

WHAT

	1990 Sales		1990 Operating Income	
	£ mil.	% of total	£ mil.	% of total
Information & entertainment	1,045	68	157	63
Oil services	288	19	30	12
Fine china	202	13	23	9
Investment banking	—	—	38	16
Adjustments	—	—	8	—
Total	**1,535**	**100**	**256**	**100**

Major Periodicals
Canadian Financial Post (25%)
CFO
The Economist (50%)
Expansiòn
The Financial Times
Investor's Chronicle
Les Echos

Book Publishers
Addison-Wesley (textbooks)
Federal and Capitol Publications
Longman Group (study aids, textbooks)
Penguin

Entertainment
Alton Towers
British Sky Broadcasting (16%, satellite TV, UK)
Chessington World of Adventures
The London Planetarium
Madame Tussaud Scenerama Amsterdam
Madame Tussaud's
Pickwick (20%, music and video label)
Rock Circus (London)
Warwick Castle

Investment Banking
Lazard Brothers (50%, UK)
Lazard Frères (10%, US; 10%, France)

Oil Services
Camco (well completion equipment)
Hycalog (drill bits)
Reda (pumps for offshore wells)
Reed Tool (drill bits)

Fine China
Minton
Royal Albert
Royal Crown Derby
Royal Doulton

HOW MUCH

£=$1.93 (Dec. 31, 1990)	9-Year Growth	1981	1982	1983	1984	1985	1986	1987	1988	1989	1990
Sales (£ mil.)	9.1%	702	719	730	843	970	953	952	1,195	1,460	1,535
Net income (£ mil.)	17.4%	37	31	42	54	58	74	98	127	172	157
Income as % of sales	—	5.3%	4.3%	5.8%	6.4%	6.0%	7.8%	10.3%	10.6%	11.8%	10.2%
Earnings per share (p)	10.9%	23	17	23	29	30	37	47	56	67	59
Stock price – high (p)	—	121	146	205	295	433	617	1,013	796	829	806
Stock price – low (p)	—	93	101	135	202	288	393	525	620	620	598
Stock price – close (p)	22.6%	105	135	204	291	425	616	684	646	769	656
P/E – high	—	5	9	9	10	14	17	22	14	12	14
P/E – low	—	4	12	6	7	10	11	11	11	9	10
Dividends per share (p)	17.6%	5.0	5.6	5.6	7.0	8.5	10.0	12.0	15.0	18.0	21.5
Book value per share (p)	3.6%	190	172	179	211	198	216	246	192	250	262

1990 Year-end:
Debt ratio: 38.6%
Return on equity: 22.9%
Cash (mil.): £217
Long-term debt (mil.): £443
No. of shares (mil.): 271
Dividends:
1990 average yield: 3.3%
1990 payout: 36.8%
Market value (mil.): $3,431
Sales (mil.): $2,963

Stock Price History High/Low 1981–90

1,200
1,000
800
600
400
200
0

KEY COMPETITORS

Advance Publications	Dresser	Paramount
Baker Hughes	FMC	Rank
Bertelsmann	Goldman Sachs	Reed
Brown-Forman	Matsushita	Salomon
Carlsberg	Maxwell	Thomson Corp.
Corning	McGraw-Hill	Thorn EMI
Crédit Lyonnais	News Corp.	Time Warner
Dow Jones	Nomura	Investment bankers

PETROFINA SA

OVERVIEW

Petrofina is Belgium's largest industrial company. Its oil and gas production activities extend to 21 nations, but most of its supplies come from the US and from the North Sea. The company has been exploring prospects in Asia, notably in Thailand and Vietnam.

The company refines and markets its petroleum products under the Fina banner in Europe and the US. Its chemical component makes petrochemicals, oleochemicals, and paints (marketed in Europe principally through its Sigma Coatings subsidiary).

Petrofina is the center strand in a web of international financial companies. Belgian steel magnate Albert Frere and Canadian Paul Desmarais, Sr., control Pargesa, a Swiss holding company, which in turn controls Groupe Bruxelles Lambert (GBL), one of the big Belgian holding companies. GBL owns about 20% of Petrofina, and another Frere company owns 5%.

Petrofina oversees some 200 companies and is preparing for the unified European marketplace by grouping subsidiaries there under the umbrella of Fina Europe. Petrofina controls Dallas-based American Petrofina, Inc., a publicly traded integrated petroleum company in its own right, with more than $3 billion in sales and more than 3,177 retail outlets.

WHEN

In 1920 a defeated Germany surrendered its interests in Rumanian oil. Belgian financiers formed the Compagnie Financière Belge des Pétrole, and this financial organization, later known as Petrofina, acquired the properties and began building an integrated petroleum company. The company's main investor was the wealthiest financial group in Belgium, Société Générale de Belgique.

In the years between WWI and WWII, Petrofina added refining and transportation, and its service stations sprang up throughout Europe. In the 1940s Petrofina suffered 2 blows — first the invasion of Belgium by Hitler's armies, then the Communists' seizure of the Rumanian oilfields after the Iron Curtain dropped. To recover, Petrofina expanded abroad. In the 1950s Petrofina searched for crude oil in Africa and North America. American Petrofina, the company's main US subsidiary, was created in 1956. In 1971 the rich Norwegian North Sea field of Ekofisk began production, and Petrofina had a 30% stake in the field.

Petrofina flourished in the late 1970s and early 1980s, when its profits grew 15% a year. With those profits, Petrofina bought Britain's Charterhouse Petroleum (1985) and oil and gas interests of US-based Williams Companies (1986). American Petrofina elbowed into the higher echelon of US oil companies, paying $600 million for Tenneco's southwestern exploration and production properties (1988).

In 1982 steel magnate–financier Albert Frere led a group of investors who took control of Groupe Bruxelles Lambert (GBL), the 2nd largest holding company in Belgium. Frere-led GBL and Société Générale joined forces in 1987 to lay siege to Petrofina. They sought control of Imperial Continental Gas (UK) to add its 7.2% stake in Petrofina to their 18% holding. Société Générale, though, became the target of an unsuccessful hostile takeover by Italian Carlo De Benedetti; then, in 1990, GBL had to face the fall of New York securities firm Drexel Burnham Lambert, in which the Belgian group was a major investor.

The Belgian holding companies returned their attention to Petrofina. With the 1990 retirement of CEO Jean-Pierre Amory, Frere became Petrofina's chairman and Viscount Etienne Davignon, chairman of Société Générale, became deputy chairman. The board of directors was expanded to give half the seats to the 2 holding companies. Away from the board room, Petrofina in 1991 won an agreement with Russian authorities to search 20,000 square kilometers for oil.

HOW MUCH

$=BF30.9 (Dec. 31, 1990)	9-Year Growth	1981	1982	1983	1984	1985	1986	1987	1988	1989	1990
Sales (BF bil.)	2.2%	359	415	438	500	584	351	319	364	444	435
Net income (BF bil.)	8.0%	11	12	14	15	17	18	18	20	22	22
Income as % of sales	—	3.1%	2.9%	3.2%	3.0%	2.9%	5.1%	5.6%	5.6%	5.1%	5.3%
Earnings per share (BF)	6.3%	567	647	754	821	895	919	879	1,002	1,007	981
Stock price – high (BF)	—	3,907	3,832	4,545	6,785	6,864	9,073	12,841	14,250	13,928	12,350
Stock price – low (BF)	—	2,750	3,223	3,464	4,515	5,055	5,500	7,300	7,545	11,525	9,770
Stock price – close (BF)	12.2%	3,486	3,554	4,530	5,669	6,136	9,073	7,745	13,675	12,050	9,820
P/E – high	—	7	6	6	8	8	10	15	14	14	13
P/E – low	—	5	5	5	5	6	6	8	8	11	10
Dividends per share (BF)	8.7%	199	222	225	248	300	327	345	400	416	421
Book value per share (BF)	8.0%	2,918	3,199	3,624	3,988	4,903	5,682	6,121	5,871	6,625	5,827

1990 Year-end:
Debt ratio: 63.9%
Return on equity: 15.8%
Cash (bil.): BF14
Long-term debt (bil.): BF227
No. of shares (mil.): 22
Dividends:
1990 average yield: 4.3%
1990 payout: 42.9%
Market value (mil.): $6,992
Sales (mil.): $14,078

Stock Price History High/Low 1981–90

16,000 / 14,000 / 12,000 / 10,000 / 8,000 / 6,000 / 4,000 / 2,000 / 0

OTC symbol: PTRFY (ADR)
Fiscal year ends: December 31

WHO

Chairman: Albert Frere
Deputy Chairman: Viscount Etienne Davignon
CEO and Managing Director: François Cornelis, age 41
General Manager, Corporate Finance–Insurance: Michel-Marc Delcommune
VP Human Resources: José G. Rebelo
President and CEO, American Petrofina, Inc.: Ron W. Haddock , age 50
Auditors: Berger, Block, Kirschen, Schellekens & Co.; Tinnemans, Pourbaix, Vaes & Co.; Huybrechts, Verhaegen, Vlaminckx, Wodon, Fallon & Co.
Employees: 23,800

WHERE

HQ: 52, Rue de L'Industrie, B-1040 Brussels, Belgium
Phone: 011-32-2-233-91-11
Fax: 011-32-2-233-34-45
US HQ: American Petrofina, Inc., Fina Plaza, 8350 N. Central Expressway, Dallas, TX 75206
US Phone: 214-750-2400
US Fax: 214-750-2508

Petrofina operates in Africa, Asia, Australia, Europe, and the Americas.

WHAT

	1990 Sales		1990 Operating Income	
	BF bil.	% of total	BF bil.	% of total
Exploration & Production	55	9	20	47
Refining & Marketing	454	73	14	32
Chemicals & Paints	109	17	12	28
Others	6	1	(3)	(7)
Adjustments	(189)	—	—	—
Total	**435**	**100**	**43**	**100**

Selected Subsidiaries and Affiliates
American Petrofina, Inc. (86.3%)
Charterhouse Petroleum (UK)
Cosmar J - V (43.2%, styrene, US)
Fina Europe
Fina Exploration Gabon
Fina Exploration Tanzania
Fina France
Fina Italiana
Fina Petroleos de Angola (65.8%)
Lanfina Bitumen (UK)
Norske Fina (Norway)
Petrofina Exploration Australie
Petrofina U.K.
Sigma Coatings (paints)
U I C Insurance Co. Ltd. (66.7%, UK)

KEY COMPETITORS

Amoco	Mobil	PPG
Ashland	Norsk Hydro	Royal Dutch/Shell
Atlantic Richfield	Occidental	Sherwin-Williams
British Petroleum	Oryx	Sun
Chevron	Pennzoil	Texaco
Coastal	Petrobrás	Unocal
Du Pont	PDVSA	USX
Elf Aquitaine	Pemex	Chemical companies
Exxon	Phillips Petroleum	
Imperial Oil		

PETRÓLEO BRASILEIRO SA

OVERVIEW

Petrobrás, the 51%-state-controlled oil monopoly in Brazil, is the largest industrial company in South America and the 12th largest integrated petroleum company in the world. Even so, Brazil imports about 40% of the 1.2 million barrels of oil it uses each day.

Before the invasion of Kuwait, Brazil relied heavily on Saddam Hussein's Iraq, trading military weapons for oil. After the invasion spawned increases in crude prices, Petrobrás raised prices at the pump but, yielding to the government's anti-inflation program, still did not raise them enough to cover costs. The company lost $13 million a day. To ease dependence on imports, Petrobrás in 1990 announced a 5-year, $16.9 billion plan to boost oil production 50%, but the plan may be subject to change: during President Fernando Collor de Mello's first 18 months of power in Brazil, Petrobrás operated under 4 different government-appointed CEOs.

Some officials feel competition could also spur the company's productivity, and Petrobrás's constitution-granted monopoly may be reviewed once the Brazilian Congress has power to amend the constitution in 1993.

WHEN

"O petróleo e nosso!"

"The oil is ours!" proclaimed the nationalist slogan in 1953 Brazil, and Brazilian President Getulio Vargas approved a bill creating a state-run monopoly on petroleum discovery, development, refining, and transport. The same year that Petróleo Brasileiro SA — Petrobrás — was created, a team led by American geologist Walter Link reported that prospects of finding petroleum in Brazil were slim. The report outraged Brazilian nationalists, who saw it as a ploy for foreign exploitation.

Petrobrás proved it could find oil (one 1957 discovery prompted a week-long holiday for students), but Brazil continued to import crude oil and petroleum products. By 1973 Petrobrás produced about 10% of the nation's needs. When crude oil prices soared during the Arab oil embargo, the government, instead of encouraging exploration for domestic oil, launched Petrobrás into a program to promote alcohol fuels. Petrobrás was forced to raise its gasoline prices to make more costly gasohol attractive to consumers. A decision during the 1979 oil shock fixed the price of gasohol at 65% of gasoline, but, during the oil glut of the mid-1980s, Petrobrás's cost of making the alcohol fuel was twice that of gasoline.

In its search for oil, Petrobrás explored overseas. In 1980 it found an oilfield in Iraq, an important trading partner during the 1980s. Petrobrás drilled in Angola and, through a 1987 agreement with Texaco, in the Gulf of Mexico.

Domestically, Petrobrás plunged deeper into the thick Amazon jungle in 1986 to explore for oil. Since 1917, when petroleum exploration began in the region, only 229 wells had been drilled because of the remote and hostile environment. By 1990 Amazon wells helped boost Petrobrás's total production for the year to a record high.

Also in the mid-1980s, Petrobrás plunged into domestic production in the deepwater Campos basin off Rio de Janeiro state. Discoveries there, in the Marlim and Albacora fields, in 1988 more than tripled Brazil's oil reserves. As it exploited its offshore wealth, Petrobrás developed an international reputation for its deep-water expertise. A 1991 Campos discovery increased proven reserves almost 30%.

Brazilian economic woes in the late 1980s hurt Petrobrás. Forced by the government to restrain its price increases amid 1,765% annual inflation, the company suspended dividends for the first time in its history in 1989. Petrobrás cut its exploration budget to reduce costs. As part of Collor administration efforts to focus Petrobrás on oil and gas, the company's petrochemical arm, Petroquisa, was ordered in 1990 to spin off some subsidiaries, and Petrobrás's fertilizer unit, Petrofértil, was ordered privatized. Two Petrobrás units — Interbrás (trading) and Petromisa (mining) — were also to be liquidated.

In 1990 Petrobrás CEO Luis Octavio da Motta Veiga presented a 5-year, $16.9 billion plan to raise crude oil production to 71% of demand by 1995. After the Iraqi invasion of Kuwait, Brazil lost Iraq as a trading partner, and soaring import oil prices renewed pressures on Petrobrás. Motta Veiga, angry at the Brazilian government's constraints on the company's prices, resigned. His successor, Eduardo Teixeira, won a higher government post, and Alfeu Valença became president until he quit after 5 months in office.

HOW MUCH

	9-Year Growth	1981	1982	1983	1984	1985	1986	1987	1988	1989	1990
Gross oper. rev. ($ mil.)	2.0%	17,049	16,745	18,055	19,804	18,595	17,476	19,882	14,500	18,788	20,448
Net income ($ mil.)	(1.9%)	606	410	478	634	1,056	1,895	94	265	128	511
Income as % of sales	—	3.6%	2.4%	2.6%	3.2%	5.7%	10.8%	0.5%	1.8%	0.7%	2.5%

1990 Year-end:
Debt ratio: 51.0%
Return on equity: 7.2%
Cash (mil.): $668
Current ratio: 0.99
Long-term debt (mil.): $937
No. of shares (mil.): 584

Net Income ($ mil.) 1981–90

Principal exchange: Rio de Janeiro
Fiscal year ends: December 31

WHO

President: Ernesto Weber
Finance: Antonio Claudio P. da Silva
Human Resources: Ari Matos Cardoso
Auditors: Arthur Young Auditores Associados S/C
Employees: 55,569

WHERE

HQ: Av. República do Chile, 65, Rio de Janeiro, RJ - CEP 20035, Brazil
Phone: 011-55-21-534-4477
Fax: 011-55-21-534-1939
US HQ: Petrobrás America Inc., 10777 Westheimer, Suite 625, Houston, TX 77042
US Phone: 713-781-9798
US Fax: 713-781-9790

Petrobrás explores for and produces oil in Africa, Asia, Europe, and North and South America.

	1990 Oil Production	
	Bbls./day	% of total
Onshore	200,168	31
Offshore	453,462	69
Total	**653,630**	**100**

WHAT

	1990 Sales		1990 Net Income	
	$ mil.	% of total	$ mil.	% of total
Petrobrás	15,777	59	557	90
Petroquisa & subsidiaries	1,700	6	24	4
Distribuidora - BR	6,570	25	127	20
Braspetro & subsidiaries	1,753	7	8	1
Petrofértil & subsidiaries	716	3	(95)	(15)
Adjustments	(6,068)	—	(110)	—
Total	**20,448**	**100**	**511**	**100**

Subsidiaries and Affiliates

Petrobrás Química SA — Petroquisa (chemicals)
Companhia Nacional de Álcalis*
Petroquímica União SA
Companhia Petroquímica do Sul*
Petroflex Indústria e Comércio SA*

Petrobrás Distribuidora SA - BR (marketing)

Petrobrás Internacional SA — Braspetro (overseas exploration and production)
Braspetro Oil Services Co. — Brasoil
Brasoil UK Ltd.
Petrobrás Norge AS
Petrobrás America Inc.

Petrobrás Fertilizantes SA - Petrofértil (fertilizers)*

*Subject to privatization under Brazilian law

KEY COMPETITORS

Amoco	Elf Aquitaine	PDVSA
Ashland	Exxon	Pemex
Atlantic Richfield	Imperial Oil	Phillips Petroleum
British Petroleum	Mobil	Royal Dutch/Shell
Chevron	Norsk Hydro	Sun
Coastal	Occidental	Texaco
Du Pont	Oryx	Unocal
	Pennzoil	USX
	Petrofina	

PETRÓLEOS DE VENEZUELA, SA

OVERVIEW

Petróleos de Venezuela — also known as PDVSA (pronounced paydayVAYsuh) — is a state-owned oil monopoly with the flair of an international entrepreneur.

The 11th largest integrated petroleum company in the world in revenues, PDVSA has proven reserves of 59 billion barrels of oil, which ranks it 6th among the world's oil companies (larger than Royal Dutch/Shell, Exxon, and British Petroleum combined). It plans to spend $20 billion to double oil production to 4.2 million barrels a day by 1996. Financing that goal could include roles for foreign investors.

It supplies 11% of US crude oil imports and boasts major downstream holdings abroad, including refining joint ventures in Germany, Sweden, and the US. Through its wholly owned subsidiary CITGO (9,700 stations), the Venezuelan company accounts for 5% of US retail gasoline sales.

About $8 out of every $10 PDVSA makes goes to the Venezuelan government, but the company isn't mired in the usual politics of a state-run company. Its employees are not considered public employees, and at least 10% of its profits must be plowed back into corporate development.

WHEN

On invitation from dictator Juan Vincente Gómez, Royal Dutch/Shell explored for and produced oil in Venezuela just before WWI. After the war American companies, shying away from politically unstable Mexico, plunged into Venezuela. Standard Oil of Indiana (later Amoco) began Creole Petroleum in 1920 and sold it in 1928 to Standard of New Jersey (later Exxon). In 1928 Venezuela became the world's largest exporter of oil, a position it would hold until 1970 when Iran overtook the top spot.

In 1938 the Venezuelan government threatened nationalization of its oil industry. To avoid that fate, the large foreign oil companies, at the encouragement of their war-wary home governments, agreed to pay more taxes and royalties. Venezuela set a pattern for the rest of the world's oil-rich nations when, in 1945, it decreed that it was a 50% partner in all oil operations. In 1960 Venezuela, through Oil Minister Juan Pablo Pérez Alfonzo, was a guiding force in the creation of OPEC, and in 1961 the Venezuelan government created the Venezuelan Petroleum Corporation (CVP) to become an integrated petroleum concern. CVP was granted all unassigned petroleum reserves in the nation. By the early 1970s CVP produced about 2% of the nation's oil; units of international oil companies produced 70%.

In 1975 the first administration of President Carlos Andrés Pérez nationalized oil holdings, paid $1 billion for the assets of the oil companies, and created Petróleos de Venezuela (PDVSA) as the basket to hold its new properties. Instead of obliterating the oil companies, though, Venezuela formed stand-alone PDVSA subsidiaries similar to the old private structure. Shell operations became Maraven, Creole became Lagoven, and other smaller companies eventually combined into Corpoven. The oil companies operated their former possessions for a fee, and PDVSA took advantage of the expertise.

Free of debt and buoyed by high crude prices in the late 1970s and early 1980s, PDVSA went shopping, forming joint ventures (Ruhr Oel) with Germany's Veba Oel and with AB Nynäs Petroleum in Sweden.

In the US, PDVSA bought 50% of CITGO, the former refining and marketing arm of Cities Service Company, from Southland (1986) and Champlin Refining from Union Pacific (1989). Mobil outbid PDVSA for Tenneco refineries, and the Saudi Arabian oil company snatched a joint venture refining-and-marketing deal with Texaco, but, undiscouraged, PDVSA bought 1/2 interest in a Unocal refinery (1989) and purchased the remaining 1/2 of CITGO from flagging Southland (1990).

After the Gulf War of 1991, Venezuela pledged to support OPEC oil quotas while increasing its capacity. President Carlos Andrés Pérez appointed a special commission to review Venezuelan oil policy as the government opened some marginal fields and refining ventures to foreign investment.

HOW MUCH

$=B49.70 (Dec. 31, 1990)	9-Year Growth	1981	1982	1983	1984	1985	1986	1987	1988	1989	1990
Sales (B bil.)	33.9%	84	71	64	96	89	69	120	138	478	1,166
Net income (B bil.)	26.7%	14	11	8	16	11	9	22	15	95	120
Income as % of sales	—	16.9%	15.4%	11.9%	16.4%	12.5%	12.9%	18.2%	10.7%	19.9%	10.2%
Petroleum reserves (mil. bbls.)	—	20,150	24,581	25,845	28,034	29,326	55,521	58,084	58,504	59,041	—
Natural gas reserves (bcf)	—	48,185	53,938	55,350	58,810	61,175	92,557	100,252	100,958	105,653	—
Employees	2.3%	42,353	44,699	44,506	43,553	44,851	44,674	44,203	45,069	46,940	51,883

1989 Year-end:
Debt ratio: 26.4%
Return on equity: 42.8%
Cash (B mil.): B31,615
Current ratio: 1.87
Long-term debt (mil.): B6,019
1990 sales (mil.): $23,469

Net Income (B bil.) 1981–90

State-owned company
Fiscal year ends: December 31

WHO

President: Andrés Sosa Pietri
Coordinator Control and Finances: Carlos Patiño
Coordinator Organization and Human Resources: Nelson Olmedillo
Auditors: Espiñeira, Sheldon y Asociados
Employees: 46,940

WHERE

HQ: Edif. Petróleos de Venezuela, Torre Este, Av. Libertador, La Campiña, Apartado Postal 169, Caracas 1010-A, Venezuela
Phone: 011-58-2-708-4111
Fax: 011-58-2-708-4661
US HQ: Petróleos de Venezuela (USA) Corp., 499 Park Ave., 11th Floor, New York, NY 10022
US Phone: 212-339-7770
US Fax: 212-339-7725

PDVSA operates in Belgium, Colombia, Curaçao, Germany, Sweden, the US, and Venezuela.

	1989 Exports of Crude Oil	
	Thou. bbl./day	% of total
US	1,077	66
Central America/ Caribbean	235	14
Europe	205	13
South America	64	4
Other countries	36	2
Japan	7	1
Total	**1,624**	**100**

WHAT

	1989 Sales	
	B bil.	% of total
International sales of hydrocarbons	435	91
Domestic sales of hydrocarbons	32	7
Fertilizers, other petrochemicals	11	2
Total	**478**	**100**

Venezuelan Subsidiaries and Affiliates
Bariven (trading)
Bitúmenes Orinoco (bitumen)
Carbozulia (coal)
Corpoven (integrated petroleum)
Interven (foreign downstream investments)
Intevep (research and support)
Lagoven (integrated petroleum)
Maraven (integrated petroleum)
Palmaven (fertilizers)
Pequiven (petrochemicals)
Refinería Isla (Curaçao refinery)

Overseas Subsidiaries and Affiliates
BP Bitor Ltd. (50%, bitumen, UK)
Champlin Refining & Chemicals (US)
CITGO Petroleum Corp. (US)
Monómeros Colombo Venezolanos (47%, petrochemicals, Colombia)
Nynäs Petroleum (50%, Sweden)
Ruhr Oel GmbH (50%, refining, Germany)
Uno-Ven (50%, refining and marketing, US)

KEY COMPETITORS

Amoco	Exxon	Petrobrás
Ashland	Imperial Oil	Pemex
Atlantic Richfield	Mobil	Phillips Petroleum
British Petroleum	Norsk Hydro	Royal Dutch/Shell
Chevron	Occidental	Sun
Coastal	Oryx	Texaco
Du Pont	Pennzoil	Unocal
Elf Aquitaine	Petrofina	USX

PETRÓLEOS MEXICANOS

OVERVIEW

State-owned PEMEX — Petróleos Mexicanos — is the world's 14th largest petroleum company. It is also the tangible expression of Mexican nationalism and, some contend, unity. Recognizing that, Mexican President Carlos Salinas de Gortari has vowed that, while other state-owned businesses may be privatized during his reforms, PEMEX will remain free of foreign ownership.

PEMEX accounts for 7% of US oil imports — selling mostly to ARCO, Chevron, Exxon, and Royal Dutch/Shell. Other customers are Japan, Spain, and Israel. PEMEX, though, needs capital to find more oil lest it be forced to import while sitting atop some of the largest pools outside the Middle East. PEMEX investment in exploration dropped from $6 billion in 1981 to $1 billion in 1989 as the government used the difference to service Mexico's debt. Most of its annual earnings have been siphoned off to finance the government budget deficit, but PEMEX costcutting and borrowing are allowing the oil giant to come up with $2 billion a year for exploration.

WHEN

Histories of Mexico recount the nation's first oil business. Natives along the Tampico coast gathered asphalt from naturally occurring deposits and traded with the Aztecs.

Just after the turn of the century, Americans Edward Doheny and Charles Canfield struck oil near Tampico, but their success was eclipsed in 1910 by a nearby well drilled by British engineer Weetman Pearson, leader of the company that became Pearson PLC. The legendary Potrero del Llano No. 4 gushed a plume of crude 35 stories high into the air.

The discoveries opened an area of Mexico called the Golden Lane to development by foreign oil companies. President Porfirio Díaz had welcomed foreign ownership of Mexican resources, but revolution ousted Díaz, and the Constitution of 1917 proclaimed that natural resources, including oil, belonged to the nation. However, without legislation to enforce the provision, foreign oil companies continued to build Mexico into a leading world oil exporter. A 1925 act limited foreign companies' concessions.

During a bitter labor dispute in 1938, Mexican President Lázaro Cárdenas expropriated foreign oil holdings. It was the first-ever nationalization of oil holdings by a non-Communist state. Legislation following the Cárdenas order created Petróleos Mexicanos — PEMEX.

Without foreign capital and expertise, the new state-owned company struggled. Mexico became a net importer of petroleum and petroleum-based products in the early 1970s. For many Mexicans, though, PEMEX remained a symbol of pride, national identity, and economic independence, and that faith was rewarded in 1972 when a major oil discovery — on a scale with the Alaskan North Slope or North Sea — made PEMEX one of the world's top oil producers again.

The heady combination of ample domestic oil supplies and high world prices during the Iranian upheaval late in the 1970s fueled a boom and a government borrowing spree in Mexico. Between 1982 and 1985 PEMEX contributed more than 50% of government revenues. PEMEX profits serviced government debt, and corruption in the state-owned company was widespread.

When oil prices collapsed in 1985, Mexico cut investment in exploration, and production dropped. PEMEX also lowered investment in its oil refining and petrochemical facilities. To decrease its reliance on oil, Mexico began lowering trade barriers and encouraging manufacturing, even allowing foreigners stakes in some petrochemical processing, but not crude oil production. Oil made up 2/3 of Mexico's exports in 1985; it had dropped to 1/3 by 1990.

In 1989, in the first wave of President Salinas's reforms, police captured the leader of the 200,000-member PEMEX union after a violent gunbattle. He and 36 other leaders faced charges ranging from corruption to stockpiling weapons. Salinas has eliminated union sway over PEMEX contracts and cut the payroll to 150,000. Also in 1989 PEMEX created an export marketing arm called PMI, and in 1990 it renewed borrowing for the first time in 8 years to finance oil exploration.

The company also plans to invest $4 billion through 1996 to upgrade refineries and their products (PEMEX didn't make unleaded gasoline available until 1990). Under pressure to combat thick air pollution in Mexico City, the government closed a 58-year-old, 430-acre refinery in 1991.

HOW MUCH

$=2,948 pesos (Dec. 31, 1990)	9-Year Growth	1981	1982	1983	1984	1985	1986	1987	1988	1989	1990
Sales ($ mil.)	0.3%	18,804	14,853	16,140	19,405	20,381	11,033	13,130	13,060	15,258	19,330
Net income ($ mil.)	49.1%	41	14	(5)	7	6	4	3	571	320	1,486
Income as % of sales	—	0.22%	0.09%	(0.03%)	0.04%	0.03%	0.03%	0.02%	4.37%	2.10%	7.69%
Employees	2.8%	131,000	125,000	157,000	175,420	183,179	155,907	178,745	170,766	164,744	167,952

1990 Year-end:
Assets (mil.): $44,987
Oil & gas reserves (mil bbls. equiv.): 65,500
Service stations: 3,164

Net Income ($ mil.) 1981–90

1,600
1,400
1,200
1,000
800
600
400
200
0
-200

State-owned company
Fiscal year ends: December 31

WHO

General Director: Francisco Rojas Gutiérrez
Finance Director: Ernesto Marcos Giacoman
Administration Director: Cuauhtémoc Santa Ana Seuthe
Public Relations and Information Manager: Francisco Casanova Alvarez
Employees: 167,952

WHERE

HQ: Marina National No. 329, C.P. 11900 México, DF, Mexico
Phone: 011-52-5-250-2611
Fax: 011-52-5-531-6409 (Public Relations)
US HQ: 3600 S. Gessner, Suite 100, Houston, TX 77063
US Phone: 713-978-7974
US Fax: 713-978-5997

PEMEX operates throughout Mexico and maintains offices in Curaçao, the Netherlands, Spain, the US, and the UK.

WHAT

	1990 Sales	
	$ mil.	% of total
Domestic	8,571	44
Exports	8,975	47
Other	1,784	9
Total	**19,330**	**100**

Subsidiaries and Affiliates

Cloro de Tehuantepec, SA de CV (CLOROTEC, 20%, chlorine and other chemicals)
Compañía Mexicana de Exploraciones, SA (COMESA, exploration support)
Compañía Operadora de Estaciones de Servicio, SA de CV (CODESSA, service station operations)
Distribuidora de Gas de Querétaro, SA (DIGAQRO, 96%, natural gas distribution)
Distribuidora de Gas Natural del Estado de México, SA (DIGANAMEX, 51%, natural gas distribution)
Grupo PMI (international operations)
Instalaciones Inmobiliarias para Industrias, SA de CV (IIISA, construction)
Repsol, SA (5%, integrated petroleum company, Spain)
Tetraetilo de México, SA (TEMSA, 60%, petrochemicals)

KEY COMPETITORS

Amoco
Ashland
Atlantic Richfield
British Petroleum
Chevron
Coastal
Du Pont
Elf Aquitaine
Exxon
Imperial Oil
Mobil
Norsk Hydro
Occidental
Pennzoil
Petrofina
Petrobrás
PDVSA
Phillips Petroleum
Royal Dutch/Shell
Sun
Texaco
Unocal
USX

PEUGEOT SA

OVERVIEW

Peugeot's Jacques Calvet personifies the lion rampant emblem of France's #1 automaker. The tough, outspoken CEO has turned Peugeot profitable by cutting costs and modernizing plants while benefiting from France's protectionism and highway system expansion. Calvet scoffs at the automotive alliances currently in vogue but advocates US/European cooperation against the "Japanese threat."

Although it is the world's #6 automaker, the lion's share of Peugeot's business is in Europe, where the company's Peugeot, Citroën, and Talbot autos combined to take the #3 spot in sales with a 12.8% share in 1990. Peugeot is the leader in French bicycles and mopeds, and leads the world in diesel engine production.

In 1991, after 5 consecutive years of declining US sales, Peugeot announced it would withdraw from the US market. Peugeot's US sales had remained low despite excellent reviews of its models.

WHEN

In 1810 Jean-Frédéric and Jean-Pierre Peugeot made a foundry out of the family textile mill in the Alsace region of France and invented the cold-roll process for producing spring steel. The brothers expanded by making saws, watch springs, and other metal products. Bicycle production began in 1885 at the behest of avid cyclist Armand Peugeot, Jean-Pierre's grandson.

Armand turned his interest to automobiles and built Peugeot's first car, a steam-powered 3-wheeler, in 1889. A gas-fueled Peugeot tied for first place in the 1894 Paris-Rouen Trials, the earliest auto race on record. In the same year Peugeot built the world's first station wagon, followed by the world's first compact, the 600-pound "Le Bébé," in 1905.

Peugeot built auto factories throughout France, including one in Sochaux (1912) that remains the company's main factory. The company made the first diesel-powered passenger car in 1922. The 1929 introduction of the reliable 201 model was followed by a series of new Peugeots featuring such innovations as synchromesh gears (1936). Despite heavy war damage, Peugeot bounced back quickly after WWII and began expanding overseas.

In 1954 CEO Roland Peugeot rebuffed a board proposal to rapidly expand Peugeot to global scale and push the company into head-to-head competition with US automakers. However, "bigger is better" thinking resurfaced in 1976 when the French government persuaded Peugeot to merge with Citroën.

André Citroën had founded his company in 1915 and in 1919 had become the first in Europe to mass-produce cars. Citroën hit the skids during the Depression and in 1934 handed Michelin a large block of stock in lieu of payment for tires. Although Citroën never fully recovered financially, by 1976 the company's line ranged from limousines to the *deux chevaux* minicar (discontinued in 1990).

In 1978, determined to become the "GM of Europe," Peugeot bought Chrysler's aging European plants and withering nameplates, including Simca (France) and Rootes (UK). Peugeot changed the nameplates to Talbot but failed to halt their sales slide. Peugeot lost nearly $1.2 billion in the 5 years ending in 1984, the year in which Calvet took over as CEO.

Calvet cut 30,000 jobs and spent heavily on modernization. Aided by the strong launch of the 205 superminicar, he returned Peugeot to profitability in 1985 and by 1989 had halved its production break-even point.

In the 1980s Peugeot inked production deals with Renault (industrial vehicles, motors, gearboxes) and Fiat (light trucks), and Japanese marketing deals with partners Suzuki and Austin Rover (Peugeot), and Mazda (Citroën). In 1990 the company introduced a reasonably priced electric van. Peugeot plans high-volume production of the vehicle and hopes to introduce an electric car at a conventional car price in 1994.

HOW MUCH

$=FF5.08 (Dec. 31, 1990)	9-Year Growth	1981	1982	1983	1984	1985	1986	1987	1988	1989	1990
Sales (FF mil.)	9.2%	72,389	75,263	85,207	91,111	100,295	104,946	118,167	138,452	152,955	159,976
Net income (FF mil.)	—	(1,993)	(2,148)	(2,590)	(341)	314	2,269	4,916	8,848	10,301	9,258
Income as % of sales	—	(2.8%)	(2.9%)	(3.0%)	(0.4%)	0.3%	2.2%	4.2%	6.4%	6.7%	5.8%
Earnings per share (FF)	—	(79)	(86)	(104)	(14)	20	104	166	178	204	185
Stock price – high (FF)	—	89	98	113	129	254	626	839	700	979	919
Stock price – low (FF)	—	56	52	59	90	119	254	408	395	695	479
Stock price – close (FF)	22.2%	81	59	104	119	254	593	450	700	825	493
P/E – high	—	—	—	—	—	13	6	5	4	5	5
P/E – low	—	—	—	—	—	6	2	2	2	3	3
Dividends per share (FF)	—	0.00	0.00	0.00	0.00	0.00	0.00	5.00	8.50	14.00	16.00
Book value per share (FF)	9.8%	407	326	228	212	242	325	411	585	772	944

1990 Year-end:
Debt ratio: 11.0%
Return on equity: 21.6%
Cash (mil.): FF8,712
Long-term debt (mil.): FF5,851
No. of shares (mil.): 50
Dividends:
1990 average yield: 3.2%
1990 payout: 8.6%
Market value (mil.): $4,852
Sales (mil.): $31,491

Stock Price History High/Low 1981–90

Principal exchange: Paris
Fiscal year ends: December 31

WHO

Chairman and CEO: Jacques Calvet, age 59
General Manager: Pierre Peugeot
General Manager: Yves Rapilly
Director Group Finance: Yann Delabrière
Auditors: Societe Frinault-Fiduciaire; Befec Mulquin Associes; Coopers & Lybrand
Employees: 159,100

WHERE

HQ: 75, avenue de la Grande-Armée, 75116 Paris, France
Phone: 011-33-1-40-66-55-11
Fax: 011-33-1-40-66-41-85
US HQ: Peugeot Motors of America, Inc., One Peugeot Plaza, Lyndhurst, NJ 07071
US Phone: 201-935-8400
US Fax: 201-935-6425

Peugeot sells through 22,640 outlets in more than 150 markets worldwide.

	1990 Sales	
	FF mil.	% of total
France	74,363	46
Other countries	85,613	54
Total	**159,976**	**100**

WHAT

	1990 Sales		1990 Pretax Income	
	FF mil.	% of total	FF mil.	% of total
Peugeot	93,134	58	9,472	67
Citroën	59,441	37	2,108	15
Engineering & svcs.	7,121	5	1,501	11
Finance companies	—	—	989	7
Other	280	—	7	—
Total	**159,976**	**100**	**14,077**	**100**

Automobiles
Automobiles Citroën
Automobiles Peugeot
Citroën Hispania (Spain)
Peugeot-Talbot España (Spain)
Peugeot-Talbot Motor (UK)

Mechanical Engineering and Services
Engrénages et Réducteurs Citroën-Messian-Durand (63%, transmissions)
Equipements et Composants pour l'Industrie Automobile (72%, automobile components)
GEFCO (transportation services)
Peugeot Cycles
Peugeot Motocycles (74%)
Société de Constructions Mecaniques Panhard et Levassor (military vehicles)

Finance Companies
PSA Finance Holding
PSA International SA
Société de Crédit à l'Industrie Automobile

KEY COMPETITORS

BMW	Fiat	Navistar
Borg-Warner	Ford	Nissan
Bridgestone	General Motors	Renault
Caterpillar	Harley-Davidson	Saab-Scania
Chrysler	Honda	Suzuki
Cummins Engine	Hyundai	Toyota
Daewoo	Isuzu	Volkswagen
Daimler-Benz	Mazda	Volvo
	Mitsubishi	Yamaha

PHILIPS ELECTRONICS NV

NYSE symbol: PHG
Fiscal year ends: December 31

OVERVIEW

Philips is the world's 2nd largest consumer electronics company after Matsushita. The Dutch electronics giant also makes semiconductors, appliances, minicomputers, and PCs and is the world's largest light bulb maker. For inventing the digital audio technology used in CD players, Philips and Sony receive royalties on each one sold. Philips owns 79% of PolyGram (recordings), 35% of Matsushita Electronics (component venture with Matsushita), and 32% of Grundig (electronics, Germany).

Heavy losses in 1990 (brought on by overstaffing and losses in semiconductors and computers) has prompted chairman Jan Timmer to announce that Philips will lay off up to 55,000 workers by the end of 1991. The company is streamlining operations by closing or selling unprofitable businesses; Philips and Du Pont dissolved their optical disks partnership in 1990. Philips sold its 47% stake in Whirlpool International (appliance partnership) to Whirlpool in 1991 and plans to sell its ailing computer division to Digital Equipment. Philips is stepping up development of high-definition TV. Its semiconductor operations have been reorganized, and Philips is considering a related partnership with Matsushita.

WHEN

In 1891 Gerard Philips (later joined by brother Anton) founded Philips & Co. in Eindhoven, Holland. Surviving an industry shakeout, Philips prospered as a result of Gerard's engineering and Anton's foreign sales efforts and had become Europe's 3rd largest light bulb maker by 1900. The company adopted the name Philips' Gloeilampenfabrieken (light bulb factory) in 1912.

Dutch neutrality during WWI allowed Philips to expand and integrate into glass manufacturing (1915) and X-ray and radio tubes (1918). The company set up sales offices abroad, beginning in Belgium in 1919, and started building plants abroad to avoid trade barriers and tariffs in the 1930s.

During WWII Philips created US and British trusts to hold majority interests in North American Philips (NAP) and in Philips's British operations. The British businesses were repurchased by Philips in 1955, while NAP operated as an independent company until it was reacquired in 1987. After WWII Philips established hundreds of subsidiaries worldwide.

Philips started marketing televisions and appliances in the 1950s. The company acquired a stake in Matsushita Electronics through a technology-licensing agreement in 1952. With an established reputation for innovation, Philips invented audiocassette, VCR, and laser disc technology in the 1960s, but its ventures into computers and office equipment failed to match its success in consumer electronics.

Despite its development of new technologies, Philips was unable to maintain market share against an onslaught of inexpensive goods from Japan in the 1970s. NAP acquired Magnavox (consumer electronics, US) in 1974. Philips's 1970s acquisitions included Signetics (semiconductors, US, 1975) and a minority interest in Grundig (1979).

Philips introduced its Video 2000 VCR system in 1980, after previous VHS (Matsushita) and Beta (Sony) entries — too late to win a major share of the VCR market. In 1983 the company began licensing VHS technology from Matsushita.

NAP purchased GTE Television (Sylvania, US, 1981) and Westinghouse's lighting business (1983). Philips's successful PolyGram unit (formed in 1972) issued 20% of its stock to the public in 1989 and bought record companies A&M (US) and Island (UK) in 1990. Philips adopted its present name in 1991 and announced a partnership with Nintendo to develop CD-based video games. That year Philips and Matsushita agreed to jointly produce a new CD-quality audio cassette system which can play both conventional and digitally recorded tapes.

WHO

Chairman Board of Management and President: Jan D. Timmer, age 58
Director of Finance: C. A. M. Busch
Managing Director (Personnel), Philips International B.V.: J. D. de Leeuw
Auditors: KPMG Klynveld
Employees: 272,800

WHERE

HQ: Groenewoudseweg 1, 5621 BA Eindhoven, The Netherlands
Phone: 011-31-40-786022
Fax: 011-31-40-785486
US HQ: North American Philips Corp., 100 E. 42nd St., New York, NY 10017-5699
US Phone: 212-850-5000
US Fax: 212-850-7314

Philips has subsidiaries and affiliates in 59 countries.

	1990 Sales		1990 Operating Income	
	$ mil.	**% of total**	**$ mil.**	**% of total**
The Netherlands	2,134	7	487	37
Other Europe	17,980	54	843	65
US & Canada	6,998	21	(364)	(28)
Other countries	5,906	18	332	26
Adjustments	—	—	(51)	—
Total	**33,018**	**100**	**1,247**	**100**

WHAT

	1990 Sales		1990 Operating Income	
	$ mil.	**% of total**	**$ mil.**	**% of total**
Lighting	4,160	13	248	18
Prof. prods. & systems	7,732	23	11	1
Components	4,832	15	(7)	—
Consumer prods.	15,040	45	1,014	75
Miscellaneous	1,254	4	85	6
Adjustments	—	—	(104)	—
Total	**33,018**	**100**	**1,247**	**100**

Consumer Brands
Magnavox
Marantz
Norelco
Philco
Philips
Schick (electric shavers)
Sylvania

Major Products
Audio and video equip.
Bank automation sys.
Batteries
CD-ROMs
Lighting
Medical electronics
Semiconductors
Telecommunications prods.

Subsidiaries and Affiliates
Airpax (electronic components)
Bang and Olufsen A/S (25%, audio/video products)
Grundig (32%)
Matsushita Electronics (35%)
PolyGram (79%)
A&M
Island
Signetics

KEY COMPETITORS

Alcatel Alsthom	Machines Bull	Sharp
AT&T	Matsushita	Siemens
BCE	Maytag	Sony
Bertelsmann	3M	Thomson SA
Canon	Mitsubishi	Thorn EMI
Compaq	Motorola	Time Warner
Daewoo	NEC	Toshiba
Fujitsu	Oki	Walt Disney
GEC	Olivetti	Xerox
General Electric	Paramount	Yamaha
Hitachi	Pioneer	Zenith
Lucky-Goldstar	Samsung	

Other electronics, computer, semiconductor, lighting, music, and consumer products companies

HOW MUCH

	9-Year Growth	1981	1982	1983	1984	1985	1986	1987	1988	1989	1990
Sales ($ mil.)	7.5%	17,274	16,380	15,102	15,167	21,802	25,334	29,831	28,011	29,985	33,018
Net income ($ mil.)	—	131	165	212	314	356	441	458	265	415	(2,680)
Income as % of sales	—	0.8%	1.0%	1.4%	2.1%	1.6%	1.7%	1.5%	0.9%	1.4%	(8.1%)
Earnings per share ($)	—	0.65	0.83	1.03	1.40	*1.65*	*1.91*	*1.87*	*1.03*	*1.56*	*(9.41)*
Stock price – high ($)	—	8.47	9.77	17.73	17.38	22.50	25.88	27.38	17.75	25.25	25.00
Stock price – low ($)	—	6.25	7.27	9.55	12.05	14.25	18.63	13.75	12.63	16.38	11.00
Stock price – close ($)	5.3%	7.39	9.43	13.07	15.63	22.38	19.88	14.50	17.13	25.00	11.75
P/E – high	—	13	12	17	12	14	14	15	17	16	—
P/E – low	—	10	9	9	9	9	10	7	12	11	—
Dividends per share ($)	1.3%	0.65	0.63	0.57	0.53	0.62	0.83	1.00	1.04	0.96	0.73
Book value per share ($)	(1.6%)	25.67	23.94	21.37	22.43	25.89	31.39	34.39	31.79	32.00	22.24

1990 Year-end:
Debt ratio: 51.3%
Return on equity: —
Cash (mil.): $1,488
Current ratio: 1.35
Long-term debt (mil.): $6,966
No. of shares (mil.): 297
Dividends:
1990 average yield: 6.3%
1990 payout: —
Market value (mil.): $3,492

Stock Price History
High/Low 1981–90

PIONEER ELECTRONIC CORPORATION

OVERVIEW

The name Pioneer has been a symbol for audio quality and prestige since the 1960s. The company is one of Japan's leading audio equipment makers and a world leader in videodisc technology, with 1/2 of the world market for laser video and combination audio/video players (under the LaserDisc label) and 80% of the related disk (software) market. Traditionally, Pioneer specialized in consumer sound systems but since the 1970s has increased emphasis on video products, particularly the LaserDisc (LD) player. Concentration on LDs, rather than VCRs, cost Pioneer in the short run, but, after a slump in the mid-1980s, the company's earnings have taken off, increasing steadily since 1986. Pioneer is cautious about the future, however, predicting a slight drop in earnings for fiscal 1992, as the Japanese audiovisual market matures.

The Matsumoto family has controlled Pioneer since its founding in 1938, providing the stable leadership essential for a relatively small company ($3.2 billion in 1990 sales) to compete with electronics giants, such as Sony ($18.8 billion in 1990 sales).

NYSE symbol: PIO (ADR)
Fiscal year ends: March 31

WHO

President: Seiya Matsumoto
EVP: Kanya Matsumoto
General Manager Finance and Accounting: Masaaki Sono
Director and General Manager Personnel Division: Katsuhiro Abe
Auditors: Price Waterhouse
Employees: 13,898

WHERE

HQ: Pioneer Kabushiki Kaisha, 4-1, Meguro 1-chome, Meguro-ku, Tokyo 153, Japan
Phone: 011-81-3-3494-1111
Fax: 011-81-3-3495-4428
US HQ: Pioneer North America, Inc., 2265 E. 220th St., Long Beach, CA 90810-1720
US Phone: 310-835-6177
US Fax: 310-816-0402

Pioneer has plants in Japan, Europe, Mexico, Singapore, the US, and Taiwan. Its products are sold worldwide.

	1990 Sales	
	$ mil.	% of total
Japan	1,441	44
North America	751	23
Europe	832	26
Other countries	214	7
Total	**3,239**	**100**

WHAT

	1990 Sales	
	$ mil.	% of total
Audio products	1,134	35
Video products	968	30
Car electronics products	939	29
Other	198	6
Total	**3,239**	**100**

Major Products

Answering machines
Cable TV converters
Car navigation systems
Car stereos
Cassette players
CD players
CD/CDV/LD combination players
CD-ROM changers
CDVs
Color monitors
Cordless telephones
Digital audio players
Factory automation systems
Laser Karaoke (sing-along) systems
LD players
LD software
LD video jukebox systems
LD-ROMs
Multiscreen video systems
Optical memory disks
Precision motors
Satellite broadcast receivers
Semiconductors
Stereo components
Telecommunications systems
Televisions
VCRs
WORM optical memory disks

KEY COMPETITORS

Canon
Fujitsu
General Electric
Hitachi
Lucky-Goldstar
Matsushita
Mitsubishi
NEC
Oki
Philips
Samsung
Sharp
Sony
Tandy
Thomson SA
Toshiba
Yamaha
Zenith
Other electronics and telecommunications manufacturing companies

WHEN

Nozomu Matsumoto first listened to the high-fidelity sound of dynamic stereo speakers in 1932. For audio quality, nothing made in Japan could compare, so he founded Fukuin Shokai Denki Seisakusho (Gospel Electric Works) in Osaka to develop Japan's first hi-fi loudspeaker, introduced in 1937. Matsumoto designed the company's trademark — a tuning fork overlaying the symbol for ohm (unit for measuring electrical resistance) — and chose the brand name Pioneer to reflect the company's spirit. The company moved to Tokyo in 1938. Pioneer turntables and amplifiers appeared in 1955, followed by hi-fi receivers in 1958. The growing success of its products led the company to adopt the name Pioneer Electronic Corporation in 1961.

Pioneer went on to emerge as Japan's #1 audio equipment maker in the 1960s, introducing the world's first car stereo in 1963. Subsidiaries opened in the US and Europe in 1966, and the company's ADRs were listed on the NYSE in 1976.

Convinced that laser disc (LD) technology represented the audiovisual wave of the future, Pioneer started work on an LD video player in 1972, joining MCA in 1977 to form Universal Pioneer Corporation (UPC), which sold the first LD player to General Motors in 1979. Home LD players (under the LaserDisc name) appeared in the US in 1980 and in Japan in 1981. But consumers, particularly US consumers, wanted VCRs, not LD players. Demand for LDs remained sluggish through the early 1980s; so did Pioneer's earnings. The company lost money (about $12 million on $1.1 billion in sales) in 1982 but remained firm in its commitment to LD technology. A player for both LDs and CDs (compact discs) and the world's first car CD system appeared in 1984.

Pioneer used its LD know-how to branch into office automation, introducing the Write-Once Read-Many (WORM) optical memory disk in 1985, and added a combination CD/CDV/LD (CD-with-video) player to its LD product line in 1987. The company bought the IBM-MCA partnership, with over 1,400 laser-optical technology–related patents (Discovision Associates), and released the name laser disc for use by other manufacturers in 1989. LD players are now among the hottest consumer electronics products in the US and Japan.

Pioneer sold its interest in Warner-Pioneer (music software marketing) to its partner Warner (now Time Warner) in 1989. That same year Pioneer and US-based Trimble Navigation formed Pioneer Trimble to develop a computerized car navigation system. Based on the same type of satellite linkage used for aviation and marine navigation, the car navigation system can accurately determine the car's position anywhere in Japan.

HOW MUCH

Stock prices are for ADRs ADR = 2 shares	9-Year Growth	1981	1982	1983	1984	1985	1986	1987	1988	1989	1990
Sales ($ mil.)	10.1%	1,366	1,408	1,124	1,303	1,302	1,572	2,253	2,487	3,015	3,239
Net income ($ mil.)	8.3%	91	64	(12)	9	28	(16)	26	69	125	186
Income as % of sales	—	6.6%	4.5%	(1.0%)	0.7%	2.2%	(1.0%)	1.2%	2.8%	4.1%	5.8%
Earnings per share ($)	6.5%	0.63	0.41	(0.08)	0.06	0.18	(0.10)	0.16	0.41	0.75	1.11
Stock price – high ($)	—	11.80	7.70	12.16	12.35	11.05	13.84	20.00	27.27	39.38	43.38
Stock price – low ($)	—	6.10	3.76	6.76	7.04	5.58	6.61	9.19	18.92	21.14	26.50
Stock price – close ($)	18.8%	6.20	7.61	11.93	8.63	7.33	13.22	18.18	26.36	39.09	29.25
P/E – high	—	19	19	—	205	62	—	127	66	53	39
P/E – low	—	10	9	—	117	31	—	59	46	28	24
Dividends per share ($)	6.7%	0.11	0.12	0.07	0.08	0.08	0.05	0.06	0.13	0.15	0.19
Book value per share ($)	11.4%	3.89	4.21	3.43	3.76	3.73	4.34	6.15	6.81	8.06	10.26

1990 Year-end:
Debt ratio: 7.0%
Return on equity: 12.1%
Cash (mil.): $770
Current ratio: 2.17
Long-term debt (mil.): $139
No. of shares (mil.): 180
Dividends:
1990 average yield: 0.7%
1990 payout: 17.1%
Market value (mil.): $5,252

Stock Price History High/Low 1981–90

PIRELLI SPA

OVERVIEW

Pirelli SpA is the operating company at the core of the Pirelli group. The company is principally a manufacturer of tires and power transmission and telecommunications cables. Pirelli Tyre, 64% owned by Pirelli SpA, is #5 in an industry suffering from overcapacity and price cutting. Economic difficulties in Argentina and Brazil are hurting the group's substantial Latin American operations.

Pirelli & Company, a holding company in which the Pirelli family has a 5% interest, is at the top of the group, owning 38% of another holding company, Société Internationale Pirelli, which in turn owns 49% of Pirelli SpA and 12% of Pirelli Tyre. The group may spin off a portion of its cable business.

Pirelli has been trying to effect a merger between Continental AG (Germany), the world's #4 tire maker, and Pirelli Tyre since 1990. The Pirelli group would become a passive majority shareholder in a company that would command a 16% global tire market share. Horst Urban, Continental chairman and opponent to the merger, resigned in May 1991, under pressure from board members more amenable to the Pirelli proposal.

WHEN

After fighting for Italian unification with Garibaldi in the 1860s, Giovanni Battista Pirelli observed that France, not Italy, was providing rubber tubes for an Italian ship salvage attempt. The young patriot reacted by founding Pirelli & Co. in Milan in 1872 to manufacture rubber products. In 1879 Pirelli began making insulated cables for the rapidly growing telegraph industry and in 1890 started making bicycle tires. He introduced his first air-filled automobile tire in 1899.

Foreign expansion began in 1902 with a tire plant in Spain. In 1914 the company entered a British cable partnership with General Electric (UK). By 1929 Pirelli owned factories in Argentina, Brazil, and the UK. The company set up Société Internationale Pirelli (SIP) in Switzerland in 1937 and consolidated all non-Italian operations within it. After WWII the group expanded with the worldwide growth in auto sales and began production in Turkey and Greece in 1962.

By the early 1970s Michelin's steel-belted radial tires had put other manufacturers on the defensive. Pirelli's entry into radials backfired when it became apparent that the tires wore out too quickly. In 1971 the company joined with UK tiremaker Dunlop through a stock swap. Although the firms managed to engage in joint R&D, they never consolidated production. Soon after the deal was announced, Pirelli's Italian businesses incurred huge losses. A 1973 car crash knocked company chairman Leopoldo Pirelli out of action for 7 months. Although the Italian operations survived, the 2 companies parted ways in 1981 after bickering over accounting methods.

In 1982 Pirelli SpA, the Italian operating company, and SIP became holding companies by transferring their operating units into jointly owned Pirelli Société Générale (Switzerland). Heavy spending on R&D and new equipment bolstered the newly unified tire business, and the 1986 purchase of Metzeler Kautschuk (Germany) made Pirelli the world's #2 motorcycle tire maker. In the same year the group transferred its tire units to Pirelli Tyre Holding, a Dutch subsidiary, for tax reasons.

Pirelli SpA became an operating company again in 1988 when it bought SIP's Pirelli Société Générale holdings. In the same year Pirelli Tyre, seeking a US presence, launched a hostile bid for Firestone. Outbid by Bridgestone, Pirelli settled for much smaller Armstrong Tire. In 1989 Pirelli sold 23.6% of Pirelli Tyre to the public to reduce debt from the Armstrong acquisition. In 1990 Pirelli inked a deal with American Superconductor Corporation (of which it now owns 25.9%) to codevelop superconductor power cables.

HOW MUCH

$=L1,125 (Dec. 31, 1990)	9-Year Growth	1981	1982	1983	1984	1985	1986	1987[1]	1988	1989	1990
Sales (L bil.)	—	—	—	—	—	—	—	7,251	9,120	10,342	10,139
Net income (L bil.)[2]	27.2%	16	26	19	33	48	51	97	224	239	139
Income as % of sales	—	—	—	—	—	—	—	1.3%	2.5%	2.3%	1.4%
Earnings per share (L)	—	—	—	—	—	—	—	—	267	282	140
Stock price – high (L)	—	2,491	1,436	1,500	1,795	3,383	5,918	5,227	3,055	4,054	3,125
Stock price – low (L)	—	1,123	1,045	1,066	1,290	1,751	3,064	2,609	1,700	2,760	1,505
Stock price – close (L)	4.6%	1,155	1,078	1,346	1,785	3,177	4,132	2,609	2,932	2,985	1,735
P/E – high	—	—	—	—	—	—	—	—	11	14	22
P/E – low	—	—	—	—	—	—	—	—	6	10	11
Dividends per share (L)[3]	6.9%	55	73	82	82	82	82	91	91	100	100
Book value per share (L)	—	—	—	—	—	—	—	—	—	—	—

1990 Year-end:
Debt ratio: 40.6%
Return on equity: 4.6%
Cash (bil.): L1,390
Long-term debt (bil.): L2,131
No. of shares (mil.): 998
Dividends:
1990 average yield: 5.8%
1990 payout: 71.4%
Market value (mil.): $1,539
Sales (mil.): $9,012

Stock Price History High/Low 1981–90

[1] Pro forma, reorganization, fiscal year change [2] Unconsolidated 1981–86 [3] Not including rights issues

Principal exchange: Milan
Fiscal year ends: December 31

WHO

Chairman: Leopoldo Pirelli, age 66
VC: Filiberto Pittini
Managing Director: Gianbattista De Giorgi
General Manager, Finance and Administration: Andrea Travelli
Auditors: Ernst & Young
Employees: 68,703

WHERE

HQ: Piazzale Cadorna, 5, 20123 Milan, Italy
Phone: 011-39-2-8535-4215 (Public Relations)
Fax: 011-39-2-8535-4029 (Public Relations)
US HQ: Pirelli Armstrong Tire Corporation, 500 Sargent Dr., New Haven, CT 06536-0201
US Phone: 203-784-2200
US Fax: 203-784-2579 (Communications)

Pirelli companies operate 146 factories, mostly in Europe and the Americas.

	1990 Sales	
	L bil.	% of total
Italy	2,483	24
Other Europe	4,271	42
North America	1,474	15
Central & South America	1,476	15
Other regions	435	4
Total	**10,139**	**100**

WHAT

	1990 Sales	
	L bil.	% of total
Cables	4,315	42
Tires	4,037	40
Diversified products	1,519	15
Other	268	3
Total	**10,139**	**100**

Pirelli Cavi SpA
Building wires
Enameled wires
Power cables
Special cables
Telecommunications cables

Pirelli Tyre Holding NV (64%)
Car tires
Farm machinery tires
Industrial and commercial vehicle tires
Motorcycle tires
Steel cord

Pirelli Prodotti Diversificati SpA
Antivibration systems
Automotive profiles
Bedding
Conveyor belts
Industrial and automotive belts and hoses
Power transmission belts
Protective fabrics
Sports and leisure products

KEY COMPETITORS

Bridgestone
Cooper Industries
Corning
Goodyear
Michelin
Phelps Dodge
Sears
Siemens
Sumitomo

PRICE WATERHOUSE

OVERVIEW

For decades London-based Price Waterhouse was one of the top 3 accounting firms in the US and the world. The firm earned a reputation as the "Rolls-Royce" of auditors, primarily because of its impressive list of blue-chip clients, but slow growth and recent mergers among accounting firms have placed Price Waterhouse last among the US Big 6.

Price Waterhouse has responded to these changes by developing a 3-part strategy. First, the firm is focusing on improving its client service. The 2nd part of the strategy is to improve the recruitment and training of young college graduates. The final part of the strategy is to concentrate on selected types of clients; Price Waterhouse is focusing on multinational companies, financial institutions, and information technology services.

As Price Waterhouse grapples with growth issues, it also finds itself ensnared in the BCCI banking collapse. Regulators around the world are investigating fraud at BCCI, already convicted of money laundering and revealed as the owner of Washington's largest bank. BCCI may be missing billions. Price Waterhouse's British unit gave the intrigue-laden international bank a favorable audit report in 1990 while privately apprising the bank of irregularities. Price Waterhouse defended its actions, saying its report conformed to British standards.

WHEN

In 1860 S. H. Price and Edwin Waterhouse, both chartered accountants, founded Price Waterhouse in England. The firm quickly attracted several important accounts and a group of prestigious partners that included 4 Knights of the British Empire. Aided by the explosive industrial growth of Britain and the rest of the world, Price Waterhouse expanded rapidly (as did the accounting industry as a whole) and by the late 1900s had established itself as the most prestigious accounting firm, providing its services in accounting, auditing, and business consulting.

By the 1890s the firm's dealings in America had grown sufficiently to warrant permanent representation, so Lewis Jones and William Caesar were sent to open offices in New York City and Chicago. In 1902 United States Steel chose the firm as its auditors.

Through the next several decades, Price Waterhouse's London office initiated tremendous expansion into other countries. By the 1930s, 57 Price Waterhouse offices boasting 2,500 employees operated globally. The growth of Price Waterhouse in New York was largely due to the Herculean efforts of partner Joseph Sterrett, and Price Waterhouse, along with other accounting firms, benefited from SEC audit requirements. The firm's reputation was enhanced further in 1935 when it was chosen to handle the Academy Awards balloting (which it still does today), and its prestige attracted several important clients, notably large oil and steel interests.

During WWII Price Waterhouse recruited women with college experience to fill its depleted ranks for the duration; some remained with the firm after the end of the hostilities.

While Price Waterhouse tried to coordinate and expand its international offices after the war, the firm lost its dominance in the 1960s, although by 1970 it still retained 100 of the *Fortune* 500 as clients. The company came to be viewed as the most traditional and formal of the major firms. Price Waterhouse tried to show more aggressiveness in the 1980s.

In 1989 the firm announced plans to merge with Arthur Andersen, but the 2 managements were unable to agree on terms and style and the merger was called off. When the deal fell through, the firm expanded internationally, merging with Swiss firm Revisuisse and opening a Budapest office (1989).

As the 1990s began, legal wrangling vexed Price Waterhouse. In addition to the BCCI affair, an ex-employee sued, claiming the firm had unfairly denied her a partnership. When the then-employee had asked how to earn a promotion, a male supervisor suggested she dress "more femininely," wear makeup, and get her hair done. Price Waterhouse denied discrimination, but a court ordered that the ex-employee be made a partner and receive back pay.

HOW MUCH

	9-Year Growth	1981	1982	1983	1984	1985	1986	1987	1988	1989	1990
Worldwide revenues ($ mil.)	14.6%	850	946	1,013	1,082	1,170	1,411	1,691	2,097	2,468	2,900
US revenues ($ mil.)	13.2%	392	458	502	568	645	742	848	960	1,098	1,200
No. of offices[1]	—	—	—	84	90	99	111	112	115	—	115
No. of partners	—	—	—	587	623	662	704	805	870	900	920
No. of employees	—	—	—	8,499	9,018	10,374	10,937	—	12,150	13,000	13,000

1990 revenues per partner: $3,152,174

Worldwide Revenues ($ mil.) 1981–90

[1] US offices

International association of partnerships
Fiscal year ends: June 30

Hoover's Rating C+

WHO

Chairman – Europe: Ian Brindle
Chairman – US: Shaun F. O'Malley
CFO: Thomas H. Chamberlain
National Director, Human Resources: Richard P. Kearns
Employees: 46,406

WHERE

HQ: Southwark Towers, 32 London Bridge St., London SE1 9SY, UK
Phone: 011-44-71-939-3000
Fax: 011-44-71-378-0647
US HQ: 1251 Ave. of the Americas, New York, NY 10020
US Phone: 212-819-5000
US Fax: 212-790-6620

Price Waterhouse maintains 450 offices in 110 countries.

	1990 Revenues	
	$ mil.	% of total
US	1,200	41
Foreign	1,700	59
Total	**2,900**	**100**

WHAT

	1990 Revenues
	% of total
Auditing & accounting	52
Tax	24
Management consulting	22
Total	**100**

Services
Audit and Business Advisory Services
Employee Benefits Services
Government Services
Industry Services
International Business Development Services
International Trade Services
Inventory Services
Investment Management and Securities Operations Consulting
Litigation and Reorganization Consulting
Management Consulting Services
Merger and Acquisition Services
Partnership Services
Personal Financial Services
Tax Services
Valuation Services

Representative Clients
Anheuser-Busch
Barclays
Barnett Banks
Baxter
Campbell Soup
Canadian Pacific
Chase Manhattan
Chemical Banking
CIGNA
Compaq
Du Pont
Ericsson
Exxon
Fuji Photo
Gannett
W. R. Grace
Guinness
Imperial Oil
IBM
K mart
NEC
NIKE
NTT
Nomura
Phelps Dodge
Scott
Shell
Telefónica
Warner-Lambert
Washington Post

KEY COMPETITORS

Arthur Andersen
Coopers & Lybrand
Deloitte & Touche
Ernst & Young
KPMG
Marsh & McLennan
McKinsey & Co.
Other consulting firms

QANTAS AIRWAYS LTD.

OVERVIEW

Qantas, the official airline of Australia, has a stylized kangaroo on its tail and a koala bear as a spokesman. It is the world's 2nd oldest international airline and ranks among the top 5 in customer satisfaction.

Although currently state-owned, Qantas plans to sell 49% of its stock to the public. The Australian government hasn't hammered out the details of the offering, but, with Qantas flying through financial turbulence, the deficit-burdened government simply cannot foot the bill. Qantas's earnings for 1990, weakened by the domestic pilot strike (1989) and fleet expansion, tumbled 93% from an all-time high in 1989. Qantas has proposed layoffs (3,651 jobs) and aircraft sales in 1991 to cut costs.

Most of Qantas's flights serve Pacific destinations, but the airline also flies to the Middle East, Europe, and North America, offering Jetabout, Creative, and other brand-name package tours to many of its destinations (through its QH Tours subsidiary). Fantasia, Qantas's computer reservation system, is affiliated with AMR's SABRE. Qantas is barred by the government from flying domestic routes in Australia, but it may get around the prohibition by buying a stake in Ansett Australia (one of Australia's leading domestic airlines).

WHEN

Ex-WWI pilots W. Hudson Fysh and Paul J. McGinness and stockman Fergus McMaster founded Queensland and Northern Territory Aerial Services (Qantas) in 1920 to link, via airline service, Darwin in the Northern Territory with the railheads in Queensland. In 1922 Qantas started carrying airmail over a 577-mile route between Charleville and Cloncurry, and by 1930 it had blanketed northeastern Australia with air routes stretching from Darwin and Brisbane to the Coral Sea. Qantas moved its headquarters to Brisbane from Longreach (1930) and then to Sydney (1938).

In 1934 Qantas and Imperial Airways (predecessor of British Airways) formed Qantas Empire Airways to fly the last leg of a London to Australia mail route (Singapore to Brisbane via Darwin) — the so-called Kangaroo route. Qantas bought the British share of Qantas Empire in 1947 and was nationalized, making it the official airline from Down Under.

By 1950 the airline had extended service to almost every major city in the Pacific Rim. Qantas inaugurated the Wallaby route across the Indian Ocean to Johannesburg (1952) and opened the Southern Cross route, previously operated by British Commonwealth Pacific Airlines, across the Pacific to San Francisco and Vancouver via Honolulu (1954).

In 1958 Qantas offered the world's first complete round-the-world service. (Pan Am had started a similar service in 1957 but was barred by the US government from crossing North America.)

Qantas bought Fiji Airways in 1958 (renamed Air Pacific, 1971; nationalized by the Fijian government, 1978) and a 29% stake in Malayan Airways in 1959. The company added several European destinations in the 1960s, including Frankfurt (1966) and Amsterdam (1967), and adopted its present name in 1967.

Tourism to Australia boomed in the 1970s. Initially, the surge of competition from foreign (especially US) airlines hurt Qantas, contributing to its 2nd loss since 1924 ($4 million, 1971). But in 1973 annual boardings jumped 28% to exceed one million. Qantas's passengers flew about 4,217 miles per journey — the longest average trip length of any airline.

Qantas bought 20% of Fiji's national airline, Air Pacific (1987, later reduced to 10%), Australia-Asia Airlines (1989), and 19.9% of Air New Zealand (1990). Australia-Asia is now negotiating to provide direct service between Australia and Taiwan. Under the management of Chairman William Dix (formerly of Ford Motor Company) and CEO John Ward, Qantas enjoyed its most profitable year ever in 1989, but a strike by domestic pilots paralyzed Australia's tourist industry that year, bashing Qantas's earnings for fiscal 1990, even though its pilots were not involved.

HOW MUCH

$=A$1.29 (Dec. 31, 1990)	9-Year Growth	1981	1982	1983	1984	1985	1986	1987	1988[1]	1989	1990
Sales (A$ mil.)	15.1%	1,019	1,111	1,251	1,375	1.576	1,914	2,297	3,510	3,266	3,606
Net income (A$ mil.)	—	(17)	2	(72)	59	148	23	64	173	177	12
Income as % of sales	—	(1.6%)	0.2%	(5.8%)	4.3%	9.4%	1.2%	2.8%	4.9%	5.4%	0.3%
Passengers (thou.)	9.4%	1,887	1,986	2,167	2,115	2,450	2,587	3,021	4,329	4,001	4,233
Available seat km (mil.)	6.5%	23,618	23,328	24,932	24,779	26,553	28,641	32,095	45,502	39,222	41,469
Rev. passenger km (mil.)	6.6%	15,282	14,590	14,993	14,584	16,716	17,613	21,009	29,464	26,546	27,097
Passenger load factor	—	64.7%	62.8%	60.9%	60.0%	64.2%	63.3%	67.3%	69.7%	70,2%	69.1%
Size of fleet	6.4%	24	24	24	21	23	24	30	32	40	42
Employees	2.9%	13,500	12,980	12,364	11,358	11,710	12,501	13,711	14,759	15,397	17,401

1990 Year-end:
Debt ratio: 67.0%
Return on equity: 1.3%
Cash (mil.): A$63
Current ratio: 0.77
Long-term debt (mil.): A$1,874
Sales (mil.): $2,795

Net Income 1981–90

200
150
100
50
0
-50
-100

[1] 15-month accounting period

Government owned
Fiscal year ends: June 30

WHO

Chairman: William L. Dix
CEO: John F. Ward, age 44
CFO: L. A. Olsen
General Manager Human Resources: H. J. Fellows
General Manager Passenger Sales and Marketing: I. W. McNicol
Auditors: M. J. Jacobs, Acting Auditor-General
Employees: 17,997

WHERE

HQ: Qantas International Centre, International Square, Sydney, NSW 2000, Australia
Phone: 011-61-2-236-3636
Fax: 011-61-2-236-3339
US HQ: 360 Post St., San Francisco, CA 94108
US Phone: 415-445-1400
US Fax: 415-981-1152
Reservations: 800-227-4500

Qantas serves 48 cities in 25 countries.

	1990 Sales	
	A$ mil.	% of total
Australia	1,605	45
Other countries	2,001	55
Total	**3,606**	**100**

WHAT

	1990 Sales	
	A$ mil.	% of total
Passengers, freight, mail & tours	3,144	87
Charters	128	4
Other sources	334	9
Total	**3,606**	**100**

Major Subsidiaries and Affiliates
Air New Zealand Ltd. (19.9%)
Air Pacific (10%, Fiji)
Australia-Asia Airlines Ltd.
Gateway Passenger Services LP
Jupiter Air (Australia) Pty. Ltd. (49%)
Pacific Air Travel Ltd. (UK)
Qantas Flight Catering Holdings Ltd.
Qantas Information Technology Ltd.
QH Tours Ltd.
- Creative Vacations, Inc.
- Holidays Ltd.
- Jetabout Holidays Ltd.
- Sun Tours Ltd.
- Viva! Holidays Ltd.

Computer Reservation System
Fantasia

Flight Equipment	No.	Orders
Boeing 747	30	9
Boeing 767	12	7
Total	**42**	**16**

KEY COMPETITORS

AMR	Lufthansa
British Airways	NWA
Continental Airlines	SAS
Delta	Singapore Airlines
JAL	Swire Pacific
KLM	UAL

THE RANK ORGANISATION PLC

OVERVIEW

Once a powerful motion picture production and distribution company, Rank is now a leisure-related conglomerate and passive investor in Rank Xerox. No longer the growth company it was in the 1960s, 49%-owned Rank Xerox nevertheless has accounted for about 1/2 of Rank's earnings in recent years. The unit owns exclusive rights to produce and market Xerox products outside North America.

Rank provides various travel services and operates holiday facilities, hotels, casinos, bingo parlors, and restaurants, mostly in the UK, where paid vacations average 4 to 5 weeks per year. The company also offers video and film services and products, operates theaters, finances movies, and owns a 50% interest in the Universal Studios theme park in Orlando, Florida. Other US businesses include 5 Hard Rock Cafes and the Kingston Plantation resort development in Myrtle Beach, South Carolina.

Rank would like to see its Universal Studios investment develop into the Rank Xerox of the 1990s, but initial attendance levels have been disappointing.

WHEN

Joseph Arthur Rank, millionaire son of a founder of UK food giant Ranks Hovis McDougall, entered moviemaking in 1934 by cofounding British National Films to produce religious movies. Rank quickly shifted emphasis. In 1935 he helped establish Pinewood Studios and General Film Distributors which, following Rank's purchase of a stake in US-based Universal Pictures, became Universal's UK distributor.

Taking advantage of a depressed UK film industry, Rank bought 2 large studios, Denham (1938) and Amalgamated (1939). In 1941 Rank bought control of the Odeon and Gaumont-British theater chains, creating a huge, fully integrated film business.

In 1947 the British government slapped stiff tariffs on foreign films. When US filmmakers responded by cutting off movies to the UK, Rank's companies rushed into the void, quickly producing as many movies as possible for UK distribution. The government rescinded the tariff the next year, and the UK was flooded with backlogged US films. Rank's companies reeled from the US onslaught.

The Rank empire suffered in the 1950s as television and other alternate entertainment forms flourished. But in 1956 the company's fortunes reversed when Rank chairman Sir John Davis struck a deal with the Haloid Company, now known as Xerox. In exchange for financing, Rank would receive about 1/3 of the profits of Rank Xerox. IBM and Gestetner had previously rejected the Haloid offer.

For 2 decades Rank Xerox registered better than 30% sales growth, and, after J. Arthur Rank's death in 1972, its profits dwarfed those of Rank's operating units. Davis and his successors pumped the ever-increasing cash torrent into a diverse and perennially underperforming group of businesses, including bingo parlors, hotels, dance halls, and TV, appliance, and furniture manufacturing. The pitiful results of the diversification effort were exposed in the late 1970s as Rank Xerox's earnings receded under intensified competition in the copier market, particulary from Canon and Ricoh.

Disgruntled institutional investors installed Michael Gifford as chief executive in 1983. Gifford immediately began trimming overhead and dumping businesses, at one point at a rate of 1 1/2 per day. By focusing the company on selected leisure- and entertainment-related sectors, Gifford greatly enhanced the profitability of Rank's operating businesses. At the same time Rank Xerox's earnings improved through cost cutting, the elimination of unprofitable retail and computer operations, and success with new, document-related products.

In 1988 Rank joined with MCA, now a part of Matsushita, to create the Universal Studios theme park. Rank absorbed Mecca Leisure Group's bingo parlors, casinos, hotels, and clubs in a 1990 acquisition.

HOW MUCH

£=$1.93 (Dec. 31, 1990)	9-Year Growth	1981	1982	1983	1984	1985	1986	1987	1988	1989	1990
Sales (£ mil.)	8.9%	621	682	743	725	631	718	668	824	1,093	1,333
Net income (£ mil.)	15.8%	53	27	30	57	69	95	126	157	180	198
Income as % of sales	—	8.5%	4.0%	4.0%	7.8%	10.9%	13.2%	18.9%	19.0%	16.5%	14.8%
Earnings per share (p)	12.1%	25	13	14	27	33	44	56	70	80	70
Stock price – high (p)	—	209	193	188	282	467	569	798	723	1,032	845
Stock price – low (p)	—	126	98	100	176	276	406	467	533	696	493
Stock price – close (p)	14.7%	176	102	179	282	420	509	533	712	829	603
P/E – high	—	8	15	14	11	14	13	14	10	13	12
P/E – low	—	5	8	7	7	8	9	8	8	9	7
Dividends per share (p)	12.9%	10.4	7.7	9.7	11.6	14.5	17.4	21.0	25.3	29.0	31.0
Book value per share (p)	5.8%	271	255	253	252	252	252	273	376	429	449

1990 Year-end:
Debt ratio: 33.6%
Return on equity: 16.0%
Cash (mil.): £213
Long-term debt (mil.): £699
No. of shares (mil.): 308
Dividends:
1990 average yield: 5.1%
1990 payout: 44.2%
Market value (mil.): $3,584
Sales (mil.): $2,573

Stock Price History
High/Low 1981–90

1,200
1,000
800
600
400
200
0

OTC symbol: RANKY (ADR)
Fiscal year ends: October 31

Hoover's Rating **B-**

WHO

Chairman: Sir Patrick Meaney, age 65, £178,000 pay
Managing Director and Chief Executive: Michael B. Gifford, age 55
Finance Director: Nigel V. Turnbull, age 48
Auditors: KPMG Peat Marwick McLintock
Employees: 47,816

WHERE

HQ: 6 Connaught Place, London W2 2EZ, UK
Phone: 011-44-71-706-1111
Fax: 011-44-71-262-9886
US HQ: Rank America Inc., 5 Concourse Pkwy., Suite 2400, Atlanta, GA 30328-5350
US Phone: 404-392-9029
US Fax: 404-392-0585

	1990 Sales		1990 Operating Income	
	£ mil.	% of total	£ mil.	% of total
UK	910	68	130	81
Other Europe	40	3	3	2
US	315	24	13	8
Rest of the world	37	3	6	4
Discont. & other	31	2	9	5
Total	**1,333**	**100**	**161**	**100**

WHAT

	1990 Sales		1990 Operating Income	
	£ mil.	% of total	£ mil.	% of total
Film & TV	527	40	37	23
Holidays & hotels	438	33	74	46
Recreation	227	17	36	22
Leisure	110	8	5	3
Discont. & other	31	2	9	6
Total	**1,333**	**100**	**161**	**100**

Principal Subsidiaries

Copiers
Rank Xerox Ltd. (48.8%)

Film and TV
Pinewood Studios Ltd. (film production)
Rank California Inc. (Deluxe film labs)
Rank Cintel Ltd. (broadcasting equipment)
Rank Theatres Ltd. (Odeon cinemas, UK)

Holidays and Hotels
Butlin's Ltd. (Holiday World Centres, UK)
Mecca Leisure Holidays Ltd. (Warner Holiday Centres, UK)
Rank Hotels Ltd. (29 hotels in the UK and US)

Recreation
Associated Leisure Ltd. (gaming machines, UK)
County Clubs Ltd; Grosvenor Clubs Ltd. (casinos, UK)
Mecca Leisure Ltd.; Top Rank Ltd. (social and bingo clubs, UK)

Leisure
Hard Rock International PLC (15 Hard Rock Cafes)
Mecca Leisure Catering Ltd. (Prima Pasta and Sweeney Todd restaurants, UK)
Pizza Piazza Ltd. (restaurants, UK)
Rank Development Inc. (Kingston Plantation resort, Myrtle Beach, SC)
Rank Orlando, Inc. (owns 50% of Universal Studios Florida partnership)

KEY COMPETITORS

Accor	Eastman Kodak	Pearson
Anheuser-Busch	Matsushita	Sony
Bass	Paramount	Walt Disney

THE RED CROSS

OVERVIEW

The International Red Cross and Red Crescent Movement is an international humanitarian effort to alleviate human suffering. The organization consists of 3 major components: the International Committee of the Red Cross (ICRC), the Red Cross's founding body, which is based in Geneva; the League of Red Cross and Red Crescent Societies, a federation of the national societies; and the 149 recognized national Red Cross and Red Crescent societies.

Completely neutral in its orientation, the Red Cross and Red Crescent Movement operates under the principles established by the Geneva Conventions. The Movement indiscriminately provides aid to victims of international conflicts and internal disturbances, often under fire from parties who disregard the Red Cross and Red Crescent emblems.

In 1990 the Red Cross/Red Crescent distributed over 40,000 tons of food and material in 43 countries, visited prisoners of war (as well as civilian internees and security detainees) in 1,327 locations in 42 countries, and through its Central Tracing Agency forwarded 985,237 messages and registered 74,119 tracing enquiries on missing persons worldwide.

In 1991 the American Red Cross, under President Elizabeth Dole, announced a 2 1/2-year reorganization of its US blood supply system, in which a centralized computer network will be installed to provide more efficient monitoring and record-keeping capabilities.

WHEN

In 1859 Jean-Henri Dunant, a Swiss businessman who was traveling in northern Italy, witnessed the aftermath of the battle of Solferino, one of the century's bloodiest battles, in which more than 40,000 French, Italian, and Austrian troops were killed or wounded. Horrified by the countless wounded men left on the battlefield (as was the custom of the day), Dunant began organizing relief efforts in a nearby village.

Three years later Dunant published a pamphlet, *Un Souvenir de Solferino,* in which he called for the formation of international volunteer societies to aid wounded soldiers. In 1863 the Societe d'Utilite Publique (a public welfare organization) in Geneva set up a 5-person committee (which included Dunant) to explore his proposal. The 5 men formed the International Committee of the Red Cross (ICRC) and called a conference that was attended by delegates of 16 countries. The conference resulted in the formation of national Red Cross societies across Europe. A red cross on a white background (the reverse of the Swiss flag) was chosen as the organization's symbol.

In 1864 the ICRC principles were codified into international law through the Geneva Convention (the first of 4), which was initially signed by 12 nations. The ICRC's first major relief effort occurred during the Franco-Prussian War (1870), when the organization cared for 510,000 sick and wounded. The ICRC continued to draw new member nations during the latter half of the 19th century. By 1900 national Red Cross societies existed in almost 30 countries.

The American Red Cross was founded in 1881 by Clara Barton, who had become famous for her aid to soldiers on both sides in the US Civil War (1861–65) and had subsequently assisted the International Red Cross in the Franco-Prussian War. Barton's contribution to the International Red Cross Movement was her expansion of Red Cross aid to victims of natural disasters (fires, floods, etc.).

During WWI Red Cross workers from several nations served beside the armed forces on the battlefields of Europe. The horrors of WWI led the ICRC to recommend bans on chemical and biological weapons and to extend protection to prisoners of war. In 1919 Henry P. Davison, chairman of the Red Cross War Council, led the formation of the League of Red Cross Societies to establish a peacetime program of international assistance and development.

The International Red Cross mobilized massive relief efforts during WWII and again served beside the armed forces. Since then the Red Cross and Red Crescent (national organizations in Muslim countries) have developed humanitarian programs while providing assistance in hundreds of international conflicts, natural disasters, and areas of political turmoil. In 1977 the most recent additions to the Geneva Convention were adopted. Today the ICRC's 149 member societies are active worldwide, providing assistance to victims of everything from natural disasters in the Philippines to the Gulf War in the Middle East.

HOW MUCH

$=SF1.27 (Dec. 31, 1990)	9-Year Growth	1981	1982	1983	1984	1985	1986	1987	1988	1989	1990
Income (SF mil.)	—	—	—	224	305	475	248	264	349	389	388
Total assets (SF mil.)	11.5%	53	64	92	116	94	108	111	114	125	141

Total Assets (SF mil.) 1981–90

Nonprofit organization
Fiscal year ends: December 31

WHO

President of the ICRC: Cornelio Sommaruga
Director General: Guy Deluz
Director of Operations: Jean De Courten
Director of Doctrine, Law, and Relations with the Movement: Yves Sandoz
Chairman, American Red Cross: George F. Moody
President, American Red Cross: Elizabeth Dole
VP Finance and CFO, American Red Cross: John D. Campbell
Auditors: ATAG Fiduciaire Générale SA
Employees: 5,940

WHERE

HQ: International Committee of the Red Cross, 19 Avenue de la Paix, CH-1202 Geneva, Switzerland
Phone: 011-41-22-734-60-01
Fax: 011-41-22-733-20-57
US HQ: American Red Cross, 17th and D Sts. NW, Washington, DC 20006
US Phone: 202-737-8300
US Fax: 202-347-1794

The ICRC maintains 46 global delegations in Africa, Asia, Europe, North America, Latin America, and the Middle East. There are 149 national Red Cross and Red Crescent societies worldwide.

	1990 Expenditures	
	SF mil.	% of total
Africa	132	34
Asia & the Pacific	69	18
Middle East & North Africa	52	13
Latin America	21	5
Europe & North America	10	3
General activities	104	27
Total	**388**	**100**

WHAT

	1990 Sources of Income	
	SF mil.	% of total
Governments	268	69
Supranational organizations	65	17
National societies	14	4
Public sources	4	1
Private sources	8	2
Financial income	4	1
Participation from field budgets	17	4
Other	8	2
Total	**388**	**100**

Activities
Aid to prisoners of war and security detainees
Blood donations and tissue transplants
Health education
Medical and material relief to victims of war and disaster
Refugee aid
Tracing of victims of armed conflicts

Basic Principles
Humanity
Impartiality
Independence
Neutrality
Unity
Universality
Voluntary Service

REED INTERNATIONAL PLC

OVERVIEW

CEO Peter Davis has turned Reed into the UK's largest publishing and information company and Europe's 3rd biggest print media publisher, after Bertelsmann and Hachette. Reed publishes magazines, books, regional newspapers, CD-ROMs, on-line databases, and travel guides, mostly in English; it also runs trade shows. Davis has generally avoided more risky entertainment-oriented media.

Reed is Europe's largest business-to-business publisher and, in the UK, publishes over 130 regional newspapers and such consumer magazines as *TV Times*, *Woman's Own*, and *Country Life*. Reed's Cahners Publishing unit is the #1 business and trade magazine publisher in the US, with titles including *Datamation*, *Variety*, *Electronic Business*, and *Publishers Weekly*. Butterworth (UK) and Martindale-Hubbell (US) are legal publishers. Reed's periodicals are suffering from recession-related weakness in advertising income.

Reed's electronically published products include library references, legal databases, and travel-related publications and services. American Airlines has agreed to promote and distribute Reed's Jaguar on-line hotel advertising and booking service through its SABRE reservation system.

OTC symbol: RENEY (ADR)
Fiscal year ends: March 31

WHO

Chairman and CEO: Peter J. Davis, age 49, £307,524 pay

Deputy CEO; CEO, Reed International Books Ltd.: Ian A. N. Irvine, age 54

Deputy CEO; Chairman and CEO, Reed Publishing (USA) Inc.: Ronald G. Segel, age 55

Finance Director: Nigel J. Stapleton, age 44

Auditors: Price Waterhouse

Employees: 19,000

WHEN

Named after the man who founded the company as a newsprint manufacturer in 1894, Albert E. Reed & Co. went public in 1903. For the next 60 years, Reed grew by purchasing UK pulp and paper mills. In the 1930s Reed began making packaging materials; in 1954 it expanded into building products. Reed bought a 25% stake in New Zealand's Tasman Pulp and Paper in 1955 and expanded its paper operations to Canada and Australia in 1960 and to Norway in 1962.

Reed Chairman Sir Don Ryder radically altered the company in the 1960s and 1970s. Ryder pursued a vision of a company engaged not only in paper production, but also in the manufacture of paper-based and paper-related products. Through a rapid succession of acquisitions, Reed began making paints, wallpaper, and interior-decorating and do-it-yourself household products.

In 1970 Reed bought International Publishing Corporation, a UK publisher with extensive holdings including *Woman* and *Woman's Own* magazines, Mirror Group Newspapers, and 29% of Cahners Publishing. Reed continued to buy building products companies and to expand its paper operations. Reed bought the rest of Cahners in 1977.

By 1978 Reed was in trouble, as Ryder's strategy proved flawed. Efficient integration had been stymied by Reed's geographic breadth and its difficulty in coordinating its many companies as they experienced independent business cycles. A heavy acquisition-related debt load, poor labor relations at Mirror Newspapers, and global recession worsened matters. Strapped for cash, Reed quickly dumped most of its Australian businesses.

Reed sold the Mirror Group Newspapers to Robert Maxwell in 1984 and disposed of its building and decorating products divisions in 1986. Under Davis, Reed then sold its paint and do-it-yourself companies in 1987.

Davis decided to get out of the capital-intensive paper business and focus on publishing. Reed bought Octopus Publishing, then the UK's 2nd largest book publisher, in 1987. The 1988 sale of the company's paper and packaging operations created a large acquisition fund, allowing Reed to buy the UK's *TV Times* (1989), News Corporation's Travel Information Group (electronic and printed guides, 1989), Martindale-Hubbell (legal publications, 1990), *Variety* magazine (1990), and numerous smaller businesses.

In 1991 Reed's Cahners unit bought *Broadcasting* magazine. In the same year Reed declined to add to its $300 million investment in British Sky Broadcasting, dropping its ownership from 10.5% to 3.7%.

WHERE

HQ: Reed House, 6 Chesterfield Gardens, London W1A 1EJ, UK
Phone: 011-44-71-499-4020
Fax: 011-44-71-491-8212
US HQ: Reed Publishing (USA) Inc., 275 Washington St., Newton, MA 02158
US Phone: 617-964-3030
US Fax: 617-558-4667

Reed's operations are concentrated in the UK, the US, and Australasia.

	1990 Sales	
	£ mil.	% of total
UK	805	51
US	540	34
Other countries	233	15
Total	**1,578**	**100**

WHAT

	1990 Sales		1990 Operating Income	
	£ mil.	% of total	£ mil.	% of total
Eur. business pub.	333	21	67	24
US business pub.	464	29	80	29
Books	357	23	65	23
Consumer pub.	424	27	65	24
Total	**1,578**	**100**	**277**	**100**

Principal Subsidiaries

IPC Magazines Ltd. (European magazines, e.g., *TV Times*, *Marie Claire*)
Reed Business Publishing Ltd. (specialty business magazines, e.g., *Computer Weekly*)
The Reed Exhibition Companies Ltd. (trade show production and management)
Reed International Books Ltd.
R.R. Bowker (bibliographic directories, e.g., *Books in Print*, *Ulrich's International Periodicals Directory*)
Martindale-Hubbell (law directories)
Reed Publishing (USA) Inc.
Cahners Business Newspapers (4 business newspapers, e.g., *Variety*)
Cahners Magazines (59 business and 11 consumer magazines, e.g., *Electronic Business*, *Datamation*, *Modern Bride*, *Publishers Weekly*)
Reed Regional Newspapers Ltd. (130 UK newspapers)
Reed Telepublishing Ltd. (publishing and database services for the travel industry)

Related Companies and Investments

Book Club Associates (50%)
BSB Holdings Ltd. (3.7%)

HOW MUCH

£=$1.93 (Dec. 31, 1990)	9-Year Growth	1981	1982	1983	1984	1985	1986	1987	1988	1989	1990
Sales (£ mil.)	0.7%	1,480	1,699	1,809	2,043	2,115	1,931	1,950	2,011	1,555	1,578
Net income (£ mil.)	21.0%	38	54	40	68	64	95	127	172	190	211
Income as % of sales	—	2.6%	3.2%	2.2%	3.3%	3.0%	4.9%	6.5%	8.6%	12.2%	13.4%
Earnings per share (p)	18.2%	9	12	8	14	13	20	27	33	35	38
Stock price – high (p)	—	72	83	94	136	185	308	633	471	471	475
Stock price – low (p)	—	45	58	58	94	133	163	299	332	345	328
Stock price – close (p)	22.5%	61	60	94	136	172	303	394	370	444	378
P/E – high	—	8	7	11	9	14	15	24	14	14	12
P/E – low	—	5	5	7	7	10	8	11	10	10	9
Dividends per share (p)	17.6%	3.3	3.5	3.5	4.1	4.6	5.6	8.0	10.0	12.0	14.0
Book value per share (p)	10.3%	103	110	117	130	136	132	145	180	267	248

1990 Year-end:
Debt ratio: 31.3%
Return on equity: 14.8%
Cash (mil.): £427
Long-term debt (mil.): £624
No. of shares (mil.): 553
Dividends:
1990 average yield: 3.7%
1990 payout: 36.6%
Market value (mil.): $4,034
Sales (mil.): $3,046

Stock Price History
High/Low 1981–90

700
600
500
400
300
200
100
0

KEY COMPETITORS

Advance Publications
Bertelsmann
Commerce Clearing House
Dun & Bradstreet
Maxwell
McGraw-Hill
News Corp.
Pearson
Thomson Corp.

RENAULT

OVERVIEW

French government–controlled Renault is Europe's #6 carmaker. Renault and Volvo have agreed to cooperate in automotive product development and production and have sealed their relationship with an exchange of stock in each other's car, truck, and parent companies. This transaction netted Renault over $1 billion in new capital.

In 1990 Renault's truck division, the world's #3 truck builder after Daimler-Benz and Volvo, bought full control of US-based, money-losing Mack Trucks. Renault plans to keep Mack's sizable US distribution system independent from Volvo GM, but hopes to provide Mack with components developed by the Volvo/Renault alliance in the future.

Selling most of its cars in France and other protected markets (e.g., Spain), Renault is vulnerable to the opening of European markets to Japanese cars. Company chairman Ramond Lévy has advocated large government subsidies to finance European automakers as they restructure to compete with Japanese rivals.

Sluggish demand for cars in Renault's major European markets resulted in lower earnings in 1990 and a company forecast for poor results in 1991.

WHEN

In the Paris suburb of Billancourt in 1898, 21-year-old Louis Renault assembled a motorized vehicle with a transmission box of his own design. Louis and his brothers, Marcel and Fernand, established Renault Frères and produced the world's first sedan in 1899. Marcel died in a racing accident (1903) and Fernand left the business (1908), leaving Louis in sole possession of the company. He renamed it La Société Louis Renault in 1908.

Taxis soon became Renault's best-selling products. In 1914 a fleet of 600 Paris taxis shuttled French troops to fight the Germans in the Battle of the Marne. Renault also contributed to the war effort by building light tanks and airplane engines.

Between the wars Renault became increasingly self-sufficient, producing its own components and building foundries. The company expanded into trucks and tractors and became a major aircraft engine maker. Renault sustained heavy damage in WWII, but Louis Renault operated the remaining Paris facilities for the Germans during their occupation of France. After the liberation of Paris, he was accused of collaboration with the enemy and died in prison, awaiting trial, in 1944. The De Gaulle government nationalized Renault in 1945 and gave it its present name.

Worldwide economic growth aided Renault's postwar comeback in France and abroad. The company achieved its greatest success in high-volume, low-cost cars such as the 4 CV in the late 1940s and 1950s, the Renault 4 in the 1960s and 1970s, and the Renault 5 in the 1970s and 1980s.

In 1979 Renault acquired 46% of American Motors Corporation (AMC), expecting the purchase to help the company gain US market share. In the early 1980s AMC fared poorly, and Renault sales suffered from a worldwide slump in auto sales, an aging product line, and stiff competition from Japanese carmakers in the US. Decreasing sales revealed the company's unwieldy bureaucracy, low productivity, and above-average payscales. In 1984 Renault lost over $1.5 billion.

Georges Besse took over management of Renault in 1985, trimmed employment by 20,000, and tried to reinstill the profit motive in the government-owned firm. When Besse was assassinated by terrorists in 1986, Raymond Lévy assumed his role and continued his policies, laying off 30,000 more workers and pulling out of the US by selling AMC to Chrysler (1987). Renault returned to profitability, aided by a booming car market and strong protectionist policies against Japanese carmakers in France, Italy, and Spain.

Renault and Volvo agreed to extensive cross-ownership and cooperation in international auto and truck operations in 1990.

After being forced by the EC to return $1 billion in subsidies in 1990, Renault was allowed to keep a fresh government infusion of $800 million the next year.

HOW MUCH

$=FF5.08 (Dec. 31, 1990)	9-Year Growth	1981	1982	1983	1984	1985	1986	1987	1988	1989	1990
Sales (FF mil.)	7.9%	82,574	97,126	101,714	106,911	111,382	122,317	147,510	161,438	174,477	163,620
Net income (FF mil.)	—	(579)	(1,420)	(1,803)	(12,721)	(10,897)	(5,874)	3,256	8,834	9,289	1,210
Income as % of sales	—	(0.7%)	(1.5%)	(1.8%)	(11.9%)	(9.8%)	(4.8%)	2.2%	5.5%	5.3%	0.7%
Personnel[1]	(4.5%)	103,613	103,759	102,528	98,153	86,122	79,191	75,911	71,898	70,720	68,713
Capital contributions by French govt. (FF mil.)	—	1,725	2,745	2,745	4,661	3,030	8,030	0	12,028	0	(6,000)
Book value (FF mil.)	4.8%	11,203	10,699	10,164	(234)	(9,450)	(11,433)	(7,811)	14,012	22,466	17,014

1990 Year-end:
Debt ratio: 48.6%
Return on equity: 6.1%
Cash (mil.): FF3,673
Current ratio: 0.68
Long-term debt (mil.): FF16,068
No. of shares (mil.): —
Dividends:
1990 average yield: —
1990 payout: —
Sales (mil.): $32,209

Net Income (FF mil.) 1981–90

10,000
5,000
0
-5,000
-10,000
-15,000

[1] Parent company only

Government-owned company
Fiscal year ends: December 31

WHO

Chairman and CEO: Raymond H. Lévy, age 64
COO: Louis Schweitzer
CFO: Christian Dor
SVP Human Resources: Georges Bouverot
Auditors: BDA; Michel Poisson; HSD Castel Jacquet, Ernst & Young International
Employees: 157,378

WHERE

HQ: Régie Nationale des Usines Renault, 34, quai du Point-du-Jour, 92109 Boulogne Billancourt Cedex, France
Phone: 011-33-1-46-09-15-30
Fax: 011-33-1-46-09-66-01
US HQ.: Mack Trucks, Inc., 2100 Mack Blvd., Allentown, PA 18105
US Phone: 215-439-3011
US Fax: 215-439-3308

Renault does business in more than 100 countries.

	1990 Sales	
	FF mil.	% of total
France	83,549	51
Other EC	56,861	35
Other Western Europe	3,649	2
Eastern Europe	1,844	1
Africa	4,074	3
North & South America	10,204	6
Asia & Pacific	3,439	2
Total	**163,620**	**100**

WHAT

	1990 Sales		1990 Pretax Income	
	FF mil.	% of total	FF mil.	% of total
Automobiles	129,230	79	2,116	71
Industrial vehicles	29,011	18	(1615)	—
Other industrial products	5,379	3	181	6
Financial services	—	—	698	23
Total	**163,620**	**100**	**1,380**	**100**

US Subsidiary
Mack Trucks, Inc.

Joint Venture Partners
Daf (small utility vehicles)
Matra (auto production)
Peugeot (motors, vehicle assembly)
Toyota (4x4 vehicles)
Volvo (autos & trucks)

Automobiles
Renault Clio
Renault Express
Renault Trafic
Renault 5 & Superfive
Renault 19 Chamade
Renault 21
Renault 25

Cross-Holdings of Renault & Volvo	% owned by Renault	% owned by Volvo
Renault (parent company and auto division)	—	20
Renault (truck division)	55	45
Volvo (parent company)	6	—
Volvo (auto division)	25	75
Volvo (truck division)	45	5

KEY COMPETITORS

BMW	Honda	PACCAR
Chrysler	Hyundai	Peugeot
Daewoo	Isuzu	Saab-Scania
Daimler-Benz	Mazda	Suzuki
Fiat	Mitsubishi	Toyota
Ford	Navistar	Volkswagen
General Motors	Nissan	

REUTERS HOLDINGS PLC

OVERVIEW

With 200,852 terminals installed in 128 countries, Reuters is the world's leading distributor of computerized information. In addition to its well-known general news wire, Reuters offers on-line access to business news stories and market data. The company's bestseller is Money 2000, which provides subscribers with the latest money market quotations and the ability to trade with other participants over terminals. Dealing 2000 offers similar services to currency traders.

Reuters's Instinet, an electronic, off-exchange stock trading system, continues to attract an increasing volume of institutional business. Globex, an international after-hours futures exchange, is under development with the Chicago Board of Trade and the Chicago Mercantile Exchange. With the Chicago Board of Options Exchange, the ASE, and the Cincinnati Stock Exchange, Reuters is developing an after-hours stock and option trading system.

Reuters is cutting costs as problems at financial institutions have led to a decline in orders. In addition, the company has delayed the release of its potentially lucrative Dealing 2000-2, which features automated matching of bid and asked currency prices.

Newspaper publishers owning Reuters stock since the 1940s collectively control a "Founders Share" enabling them to veto any transaction deemed to threaten Reuters's independence as a news source. Major shareholders include the Abu Dhabi Investment Authority (7.3%) and the Daily Mail Trust (6.8%).

WHEN

Paul Julius Reuter, a former Berlin bookseller, noticed delays in the flow of financial information between Paris and Berlin caused by a gap in a new telegraph system. In 1850, using carrier pigeons to bridge the gap between Aachen, Germany, and Brussels, Belgium, Reuter created a business that was successful until the telegraph system was completed.

Moving to London in 1851, just as the first cable under the English Channel was completed, Reuter began transmitting stock quotes between Paris and London and selling the information to financial institutions. He soon set up overseas agencies and broadened coverage to include general news sold to newspapers. The Duke of Saxe-Coburg-Gotha (Germany) conferred the title of baron upon Reuter in 1871.

Reuter ceded management to his son, Herbert, in 1878. The baron died in 1899. Herbert made a financially disastrous decision to establish Reuters Bank (1913) and committed suicide in 1915. Under successor Roderick Jones, Reuters sold the bank (1917) and started using radio technology (1923) and teleprinters (1927). In 1941 Reuters again faced ruin as its far-flung correspondent network strained company finances. Winston Churchill saw the advantage of having a news gathering and disseminating organization based in London and persuaded British newspapers to buy Reuters. In 1947 Australian and New Zealand news publishers also bought in.

In 1964, responding to technical developments in the US, Reuters gained the non-US rights to Ultronic Systems Corporation's Stockmaster, an electronic stock price reporting system that eliminated the need to pore over ticker tapes for current quotes. In 1973, shortly after currency exchange rates began to float freely, Reuters launched its Monitor electronic marketplace, electronically collecting and distributing real-time foreign exchange quotations entered into the system by market participants themselves. Monitor Dealing, introduced in 1981, enabled dealers to trade currencies on-line.

With computer-based businesses dominating its general news services, Reuters went public in 1984. Since then the company acquired Rich, Inc. (trading room systems, US, 1985) and Instinet (US, 1987), and introduced a host of upgraded and new on-line financial news and quotation services.

HOW MUCH

Stock prices are for ADRs ADR = 3 shares	7-Year Growth	1981	1982	1983	1984	1985	1986	1987	1988	1989	1990
Sales ($ mil.)	33.4%	—	—	352	363	629	921	1,635	1,814	1,916	2,640
Net income ($ mil.)	36.6%	—	—	45	48	79	119	205	241	292	399
Income as % of sales	—	—	—	12.9%	13.2%	12.5%	12.9%	12.6%	13.3%	15.2%	15.1%
Earnings per share ($)	—	—	—	—	0.38	0.58	0.87	1.47	1.74	2.11	2.86
Stock price – high ($)	—	—	—	—	10.63	16.38	25.50	45.69	31.25	53.63	71.13
Stock price – low ($)	—	—	—	—	8.44	9.94	15.06	20.25	22.88	28.13	32.13
Stock price – close ($)	—	—	—	—	10.13	16.19	24.94	27.69	28.38	49.63	40.50
P/E – high	—	—	—	—	28	28	29	31	18	25	25
P/E – low	—	—	—	—	22	17	17	14	13	13	11
Dividends per share ($)	—	—	—	—	0.05	0.15	0.24	0.41	0.56	0.64	0.95
Book value per share ($)	—	—	—	—	1.29	1.93	1.93	2.93	3.63	4.75	7.61

1990 Year-end:
Debt ratio: 3.4%
Return on equity: 46.3%
Cash (mil.): $491
Current ratio: 1.19
Long-term debt (mil.): $37
No. of shares (mil.): 140
Dividends:
1990 average yield: 2.3%
1990 payout: 33.2%
Market value (mil.): $5,656

NASDAQ symbol: RTRSY (ADR)
Fiscal year ends: December 31

Hoover's Rating A+

WHO

Chairman: Sir Christopher Anthony Hogg, age 54, £38,000 pay
CEO: Peter James Denton Job, age 49
Editor-in-Chief: Mark Wood, age 39
Finance Director: Robert Oscar Rowley, age 41
Auditors: Price Waterhouse
Employees: 10,810

WHERE

HQ: 85 Fleet St., London EC4P 4AJ, UK
Phone: 011-44-71-250-1122
Fax: 011-44-71-510-4064 (Corp. Relations)
US HQ: Reuters America Inc., 1700 Broadway, New York, NY 10019
US Phone: 212-603-3300
US Fax: 212-912-7394

Reuters has 952 journalists in 115 offices in 74 countries.

	1990 Sales	
	$ mil.	% of total
UK & Ireland	463	17
Continental Europe	1,088	41
Middle East & Africa	135	5
Asia/Pacific	524	20
Americas	451	17
Adjustments	(21)	—
Total	**2,640**	**100**

WHAT

	1990 Sales	
	$ mil.	% of total
Information products	2,082	79
Transaction products	384	14
Media products	174	7
Total	**2,640**	**100**

Information Products
Commodities 2000
Energy 2000
Equities 2000
Monitor Capital Markets Service
Reuter Benchmark Daily Oil Report
Reuter Country Reports
Reuter Textline (business database)
Triarch 2000 (trading room systems)

Transaction Products
Dealing 2000
Instinet
Reuter Monitor Dealing Service

Media Products
Reuter Business Report
Reuters Media News
Reuters News Pictures Service
Visnews (51%, international TV news agency)

KEY COMPETITORS

ADP
Citicorp
Control Data
Dow Jones
Dun & Bradstreet
H & R Block
Knight-Ridder
McGraw-Hill
Mead
NYSE

RHÔNE-POULENC SA

NYSE symbol: RPU (ADR)
Fiscal year ends: December 31

OVERVIEW

Rhône-Poulenc, the largest chemical company in France and 8th largest in the world, is controlled by the French government. Major business segments include Organic and Inorganic Intermediates (raw chemicals), Specialty Chemicals, Fibers and Polymers, Health, and Agricultural Chemicals.

Rhône-Poulenc owns 66.7% of Rhône-Poulenc Rorer, the product of a merger of its drug business with US-based Rorer. The company is catching its breath after a frenzy of acquisitions designed to muscle into the global arena. The company plans to sell off some pieces of its acquisitions to reduce debt.

As a nationalized company, Rhône-Poulenc cannot issue common stock to the public to raise capital. Instead, it has issued unusual, stock-like securities, including nonvoting preferred investment certificates (CIPs), paying the same dividend as common shares owned by the government, plus 5 francs annually. The company has also issued capital equity notes (interest-bearing securities with no maturity date).

WHEN

The product of a merger between Société Chimique des Usines du Rhône and Poulenc Frères, Rhône-Poulenc has continued to expand through mergers and acquisitions.

Etienne Poulenc, a pharmacist, had bought a Parisian apothecary in 1858. Poulenc began making pharmaceuticals and collaborated with drug company Comptoir des Textiles Artificielles (CTA).

Société Chimique des Usines du Rhône began producing dyes in Lyon in 1895. In 1919 Usines du Rhône launched Rhodia, a Brazilian arm that made perfumes for the famed carnival, then grew to Brazil's largest chemical company. Faced with German competition in Europe, Usines du Rhône switched to making specialty chemicals, then merged with CTA (1922) and with Poulenc (1928).

Rhône-Poulenc developed new drugs, including antibiotics and antihistamines, and increased fiber production. Growth resumed after WWII, and the company acquired Theraplix (drugs, France, 1956), 50% of Institut Mérieux (drugs, France, 1968), and Progil and Pechiney–St. Gobain (basic and agricultural chemicals, France, 1969). By 1970 Rhône-Poulenc dominated the French chemical industry and was the 3rd largest chemical company in Europe.

In the 1970s protectionist tariff lowering exposed Rhône-Poulenc to international competition at home. By licensing the US marketing rights of Thorazine, a tranquilizer, to SmithKline, the company failed to capitalize on the drug's success. Between 1980 and 1982 Rhône-Poulenc lost over FF3.1 billion. In 1982 the Mitterrand government nationalized the company.

The government turned to 39-year-old Loïk Le Floch-Prigent. Le Floch changed managers, eliminated poorly performing units, cut the payroll, and returned Rhône-Poulenc to profitability. In 1986 Jean-René Fourtou took over from Le Floch. Fourtou sold 20 businesses and bought more than 30, including Union Carbide's agricultural chemical operations (1986) and Stauffer's industrial chemical business (1987). In 1989 he acquired RTZ's chemical operations and a specialty chemical unit of GAF. Institut Mérieux bought Connaught BioSciences (vaccines, Canada, 1989).

In 1990 Rhône-Poulenc merged its drug businesses with Rorer (pharmaceuticals, US). Also in 1990 the French government transferred to Rhône-Poulenc 35% of Roussel-Uclaf, France's 3rd largest drug producer. Hoechst is 54% owner of Roussel.

Government tinkering with the Brazilian economy hurt Rhône-Poulenc's subsidiary there in 1990, and the cost of acquisitions also cut into the company's 1990 profits. Rhône-Poulenc formed a new unit for US specialty chemical operations in 1991.

HOW MUCH

$=FF5.08 (Dec. 31, 1990)	9-Year Growth	1981	1982	1983	1984	1985	1986	1987	1988	1989	1990
Sales (FF mil.)	10.7%	31,515	37,196	43,117	51,207	56,102	52,694	56,160	65,334	73,068	78,810
Net income (FF mil.)	—	(335)	(844)	98	1,755	2,058	1,912	2,193	2,878	3,016	1,097
Income as % of sales	—	(1.1%)	(2.3%)	—	3.4%	3.7%	3.6%	3.9%	4.4%	4.1%	1.4%
Earnings per share (FF)	—	(15)	(26)	2	51	55	47	45	62	61	20
Stock price – high (FF)	—	—	—	—	—	—	—	471	540	618	486
Stock price – low (FF)	—	—	—	—	—	—	—	280	254	449	191
Stock price – close (FF)	—	—	—	—	—	—	—	340	520	460	236
P/E – high	—	—	—	—	—	—	—	—	—	—	24
P/E – low	—	—	—	—	—	—	—	—	—	—	10
Dividends per share (FF)	—	—	—	—	—	—	—	14.66	16.50	20.00	22.50
Book value per share (FF)	—	—	—	—	—	—	—	—	—	—	—

1990 Year-end:
Debt ratio: 53.7%
Return on equity: 6.0%
Cash (mil.): FF4,581
Long-term debt (mil.): FF21,166
No. of shares (mil.): 52
Dividends:
1990 average yield: 9.5%
1990 payout: 112.5%
Market value (mil.): $2,416
Sales (mil.): $15,514

Stock Price History High/Low 1987–90
700
600
500
400
300
200
100
0

WHO

Chairman and CEO: Jean-René Fourtou, age 51
President; Chairman and CEO, Rhône-Poulenc Chimie: Jean-Marc Bruel, age 54
Group Chief Financial Officer: Jean-Pierre Tirouflet, age 40
Group SVP Human Resources: René Penisson
Auditors: Coopers & Lybrand
Employees: 91,571

WHERE

HQ: 25, quai Paul Doumer, 92408 Courbevoie Cedex, France
Phone: 011-33-1-47-68-12-34
Fax: 011-33-1-47-68-16-00
US HQ: Rhône-Poulenc Inc., 125 Black Horse Ln., Monmouth Junction, NJ 08852
US Phone: 908-297-0100
US Fax: 908-297-1597

Rhône-Poulenc operates more than 200 production and research facilities, principally in France, Austria, Brazil, Germany, Spain, Switzerland, the UK, and the US.

	1990 Sales		1990 Operating Income	
	FF mil.	% of total	FF mil.	% of total
France	41,053	44	2,342	44
Other Europe	27,714	29	1,682	31
North America	16,697	18	1,472	27
Brazil	4,953	5	(229)	(4)
Other countries	3,598	4	90	2
Adjustments	(15,205)	—	61	—
Total	**78,810**	**100**	**5,418**	**100**

WHAT

	1990 Sales		1990 Operating Income	
	FF mil.	% of total	FF mil.	% of total
Intermediates	18,040	22	1,573	29
Specialty Chemicals	14,086	17	(63)	(1)
Fibers & Polymers	14,132	17	340	6
Health	23,869	29	2,465	46
Agro	10,168	13	1,321	24
Other	1,383	2	(235)	(4)
Adjustments	(2,868)	—	17	—
Total	**78,810**	**100**	**5,418**	**100**

Chemicals
Agricultural chemicals
Chemical and organic intermediates
Coatings
Industrial chemicals
Metals and minerals
Specialty chemicals

Health
Animal feed supplements
Pharmaceuticals
Vaccines and human proteins
Veterinary pharmaceuticals

Fibers
Industrial fibers and yarns
Nylon
Polyester

KEY COMPETITORS

American Cyanamid
BASF
Bayer
Ciba-Geigy
Dow Chemical
Du Pont
Eastman Kodak
FMC
Formosa Plastics
W. R. Grace
Hercules
Hoechst
Imperial Chemical
Monsanto
Sandoz
Union Carbide
Pharmaceutical companies
Other chemical companies

ROBERT BOSCH GMBH

OVERVIEW

Robert Bosch is the world's #1 electronic automobile equipment manufacturer and owns 6% of #2, Nippondenso (Japan). The company is the inventor and leading producer of fuel injection and antilock braking systems. The company's Blaupunkt unit is a major car audio manufacturer, and 50%-owned Bosch-Siemens Hausgeräte is a European appliance leader. Bosch continues to invest heavily in product development to maintain its reputation for innovation and quality, employing 13,483 R&D personnel.

Bosch is 90% owned by the Robert Bosch Foundation, a charitable organization whose shares have no voting rights. Control of the business rests with Robert Bosch Industrietreuhand, a partnership effectively controlled by the company's chief executive.

Rising labor costs in Germany, home of 2/3 of the company's work force, have increased costs of Bosch products. The company is moving production to lower-cost locations, including the new German states (formerly East Germany).

WHEN

Self-taught electrical engineer Robert Bosch opened a Stuttgart workshop in 1886 and, in the next year, produced the world's first alternator for a stationary engine. In 1897 his company produced the world's first automobile alternator, beginning a series of electrical automotive product launches, including spark plugs (1902), starters (1912), and regulators (1913). Bosch believed in treating employees well and shortened their workday to 8 hours (extraordinary for 1906).

US operations started in 1909 were confiscated in WWI as part of a trade embargo against Germany. Bosch survived the German depression of the 1920s, introduced power tools (1928) and appliances (1933), and bought Blaupunkt (car radios, 1933). Growth in German industrial and military demand for the company's products continued from the 1930s until WWII. Robert Bosch died in 1942, leaving 90% of his company to charity.

Bosch suffered severe damage in WWII, and its US operations were again confiscated. The company rebuilt its plants and enjoyed growing demand for its appliances and automotive products as postwar incomes increased worldwide. In 1963 Hans Merkle took control at Bosch. Because Merkle believed fuel efficiency and pollution control would be important issues in the future, Bosch invested large sums to develop electronic automotive components that raised gas mileage and lowered emissions. Bosch made the world's first electronic fuel injection system in 1967, equipping Volkswagen Beetles to satisfy California's new, stringent emission standards. In the same year Bosch and Siemens (West Germany) formed Bosch-Siemens Hausgeräte, an appliance manufacturer.

The oil crisis of the 1970s increased awareness of fuel efficiency, benefiting sales of Bosch's electronic fuel injection systems. In 1974 Bosch reentered the US, buying a plant in Charleston, South Carolina, to make fuel injection systems. That same year Bosch launched the first electronic ignition. The company introduced the first antilock braking system (ABS) in 1978.

A 1984 strike against Bosch in Germany disrupted automobile production throughout Europe and resulted in 38.5-hour workweeks for Bosch employees. By the end of the 1980s, electronic fuel injection was found in most new cars, and ABS was standard in most luxury cars. Bosch had a 50% share of each market. In the late 1980s the company developed a technology for multiplexing (employing one wire to replace many by using semiconductor controllers) in automobiles, established it as an industry standard, and licensed it to chipmakers Intel (US), Philips (Netherlands), and Motorola (US). Throughout the 1980s and into the 1990s, Bosch has acquired various telecommunications companies, including equipment and systems manufacturers.

In 1990 Bosch bought Airflow, a US-based automotive fan manufacturer. A proposed merger between Bosch and Varta Batteries (a German starter battery manufacturer) came under EC Commission scrutiny in 1991 on antitrust grounds.

HOW MUCH

$=DM1.49 (Dec. 31, 1990)	9-Year Growth	1981	1982	1983	1984	1985	1986	1987	1988	1989	1990
Sales (DM mil.)	10.5%	12,950	13,812	16,126	18,373	21,223	23,807	25,365	27,675	30,588	31,824
Net income (DM mil.)[1]	—	181	181	242	446	402	454	825	554	626	560
Income as % of sales	—	1.4%	1.3%	1.5%	2.4%	2.0%	1.9%	3.3%	2.0%	2.0%	1.8%
R&D expense (DM mil.)	12.9%	681	753	883	977	1,097	1,262	1,425	1,640	1,803	2,030
Equity (DM mil.)	—	2,888	3,228	3,725	4,377	4,664	5,177	5,623	6,174	6,668	7,050
Employees (thou.)	5.1%	116	112	128	132	140	158	161	166	175	180

1990 Year-end:
Debt ratio: 23.4%
Return on equity: 8.2%
Cash (mil.):DM5,290
Long-term debt (mil.): DM2,156
Sales (mil.): $21,358

Net income (DM mil.) 1981–90

900 800 700 600 500 400 300 200 100 0

[1] Includes minority interests

Private company
Fiscal year ends: December 31

WHO

Chairman, CEO, and CFO: Marcus Bierich, age 64
Director of Personnel: Günter Bensinger
Auditors: Schitag, Schwäbische Treuhand-Aktiengesellschaft
Employees: 179,636

WHERE

HQ: Robert Bosch Platz 1, Postfach 10 60 50, D-7000 Stuttgart 10, Germany
Phone: 011-49-711-811-0
Fax: 011-49-711-811-6630
US HQ: Robert Bosch Corp., 2800 S. 25th Ave., Broadview, IL 60153-4594
US Phone: 708-865-5200
US Fax: 708-865-5203

Bosch has 110 plants operating in 18 countries and sales and service operations in 130 countries.

	1990 Sales	
	DM mil.	% of total
Europe	26,493	83
The Americas	3,390	11
Asia, Africa, Australia	1,941	6
Total	**31,824**	**100**

WHAT

	1990 Sales	
	DM mil.	% of total
Automotive equipment	16,070	50
Communications technology	7,240	23
Consumer goods	6,417	20
Capital goods	2,097	7
Total	**31,824**	**100**

Automotive Equipment
Antilock braking systems
Electronic fuel injection systems
Lighting technology
Safety systems
Semiconductors and electronic controls
Starters and alternators

Communications Technology
Broadcast TV systems (50%, BTS)
Entertainment electronics and mobile communications (Blaupunkt-Werke)
Medical electronics
Telecommunications equipment (Telenorma, ANT Nachrichtentechnik, Teldix)

Consumer Goods
Heating technology (Junkers)
Household appliances (50%, Bosch-Siemens Hausgeräte)
Power tools

Capital Goods
Factory automation and machine tools (Weldun International)
Hydraulics and pneumatics (Racine Fluid Power)
Magnetic and sintered-metal parts (50%, BT Magnet-Technologie, joint venture with TDK)
Packaging machinery

KEY COMPETITORS

Allied-Signal	Eaton	ITT
AT&T	Electrolux	Litton Industries
Black & Decker	Emerson	Motorola
Borg-Warner	Fiat	Stanley Works
Chrysler	Ford	Thomson SA
Cooper Industries	GEC	Whirlpool
Dana	General Motors	

ROCHE GROUP

OVERVIEW

Roche is a leading pharmaceutical producer, the world's #1 vitamin maker, and the #2 fragrance supplier. The company's Rocephin is the US's most widely used antibiotic.

Once largely dependent on its drug Valium, the company has sought new drugs by investing in R&D (14.9% in 1990), buying several companies, and entering into biotechnology partnerships, one of which involves its licensing of the Polymerase Chain Reaction (PCR) technology of Cetus, which will allow for much better and faster medical diagnostics.

Roche also owns 60% of Genentech, the California-based genetic engineering firm. The company is providing Genentech with much-needed funding in exchange for access to a potentially prolific product pipeline. Roche has an option to buy the rest of Genentech at escalating prices in the future.

Roche was created in 1989 as a holding company for F. Hoffman–La Roche and Sapac, which had been separate but linked companies. The founder's descendants control Roche through their voting stock.

Primary exchange: Zurich
Fiscal year ends: December 31

WHO

Chairman and CEO: Fritz Gerber, age 61
COO: Armin M. Kessler
Managing Director Finance and Accounting: Henri B. Meier
Managing Director Personnel, Law, and Logistics: Guido Richterich
Auditors: Price Waterhouse, ATAG Allgemeine Treuhand AG (Ernst & Young International)
Employees: 52,685

WHEN

Backed by his family's wealth, Fritz Hoffmann–La Roche began making pharmaceuticals in a small lab in Basel, Switzerland, in 1894. At the time drug compounds were mixed at pharmacies, resulting in a lack of uniformity. Hoffmann was not a chemist but was committed to the concept of standardization of pharmaceutical content and packaging. He recognized the potential for mass-produced, branded drugs.

Immediately prior to WWI, after years of financial difficulty, Hoffmann was selling Thiocal (cough medicine), Digalen (digitalis extract), and other products on 4 continents under the Roche name. During WWI the presence of a Roche factory in nearby Grenzach, Germany, engendered Allied speculation that the company was supporting the German war effort. Concurrently, the Germans suspected the company of supplying the French and began a boycott. The Bolsheviks seized Roche's St. Petersburg facility. Devastated by the war, in 1919 Hoffmann–La Roche sold shares outside the family for the first time.

Between the wars Roche expanded its scope, synthesizing vitamins C, A, and E, and eventually became the world's leading vitamin manufacturer. As volume grew, the company built plants and research centers internationally, including a facility in Nutley, New Jersey (1928). Expecting war, Hoffmann–La Roche had split in 2 in 1926, transferring its more distant operations into Sapac, a holding company.

Roche continued to develop successful drugs, including blockbuster tranquilizers Librium (1960) and Valium (1963). Valium was the world's best-selling drug until 1981, when SmithKline's Tagamet took the lead.

In the 1970s Roche was accused by several governments of Librium and Valium price gouging. After years of legal proceedings, Roche agreed to price restraints. In 1976 the company was found guilty of vitamin price fixing. In the same year a dioxin cloud escaped from a company-owned factory in Italy, killing tens of thousands of animals and forcing the evacuation of hundreds of families. Roche was criticized for its failure to respond quickly and accept the magnitude of the accident.

Valium went off patent in the US in 1985, and Roche's sales suffered for a few years. The company was able to maintain its large US sales force by agreeing in 1982 to sell Glaxo's Zantac. In 1990 Roche sold its plant protection segment and bought 60% of Genentech (a leading US biotechnology firm) and Fritzsche, Dodge & Olcott (a US flavorings company) from BASF. In 1991 Roche agreed to buy Sara Lee's European consumer-medicine business (Nicholas), which includes the Aspro (pain reliever) and Rennie (antacid) brands.

WHERE

HQ: POB CH-4002, Basel, Switzerland
Phone: 011-41-61-271122
Fax: 011-41-61-6918012
US HQ: Hoffmann–La Roche, Inc., 340 Kingsland St., Nutley, NJ 07110-1199
US Phone: 201-235-5000
US Fax: 201-235-7606

The company has operations in 51 countries.

	1990 Sales	
	SF mil.	% of total
Switzerland	365	4
Other Europe	3,689	38
North America	3,443	36
Latin America	714	7
Asia	1,127	12
Other countries	332	3
Total	**9,670**	**100**

WHAT

	1990 Sales	
	SF mil.	% of total
Pharmaceuticals	4,806	50
Vitamins & fine chemicals	2,399	25
Diagnostics	1,312	13
Fragrances & flavors	1,068	11
Instruments	30	—
Other	55	1
Total	**9,670**	**100**

Pharmaceuticals
Anti-infectives
- Fansimef
- Globocef
- Lariam
- Loceryl
- Quinodis
- Rocephin

Cardiovascular
- Inhibace

Central nervous system
- Anexate
- Aurorix
- Dormicum
- Madopar
- Valium

Dermatology
- Roaccutane
- Tigason

Oncology and virology
- Neupogen (Europe)
- Proleukin (Europe)
- Roferon-A

Rheumatology and metabolic disorders
- Rocaltrol
- Tilcotil

Vitamins and Fine Chemicals
Animal feeds
Animal health products
Vitamins

Diagnostics
Drug abuse testing
Reagents and analytical systems

Fragrances and Flavors
Consumer and industrial goods
Flavorings
Perfumes (Givaudan)

Other
Home care centers
Liquid crystal displays

KEY COMPETITORS

Agricultural chemical companies
Fragrance and flavorings companies
Pharmaceutical companies

HOW MUCH

$=SF1.27 (Dec. 31, 1990)	9-Year Growth	1981	1982	1983	1984	1985	1986	1987	1988	1989	1990
Sales (SF mil.)	4.0%	6,775	7,103	7,510	8,267	8,940	7,822	7,705	8,690	9,814	9,670
Net income (SF mil.)	15.8%	253	281	328	380	452	416	482	642	852	948
Income as % of sales	—	3.7%	4.0%	4.4%	4.6%	5.1%	5.3%	6.3%	7.4%	8.7%	9.8%
Earnings per share (SF)	15.5%	63	70	82	95	113	104	120	160	206	230
Stock price – high (SF)[1]	—	1,750	1,570	2,198	2,255	2,385	2,820	3,105	2,590	4,245	4,555
Stock price – low (SF)[1]	—	1,220	1,075	1,445	1,700	1,670	1,890	1,680	1,775	2,545	3,240
Stock price – close (SF)[1]	12.8%	1,275	1,560	2,170	1,700	2,385	2,250	1,840	2,545	3,590	3,780
P/E – high	—	28	22	27	24	21	27	26	16	21	20
P/E – low	—	19	15	18	18	15	18	14	11	16	14
Dividends per share (SF)	7.4%	20.00	20.46	20.90	21.82	24.50	25.70	25.70	26.40	30.50	38.00
Book value per share (SF)	7.2%	1,714	1,764	1,825	1,898	1,986	2,078	2,174	2,516	2,814	3,206

1990 Year-end:
Debt ratio: 21.9%
Return on equity: 7.6%
Cash (mil.): SF11,091
Long-term debt (mil.): SF3,720
No. of shares (mil.): 4
Dividends:
1990 average yield: 1.0%
1990 payout: 16.5%
Market value (mil.): $12,292
Sales (mil.): $7,614

Stock Price History High/Low 1981–90
5,000
4,500
4,000
3,500
3,000
2,500
2,000
1,500
1,000
500
0

[1] Participation certificates

ROLLS-ROYCE PLC

OVERVIEW

Rolls-Royce is a name traditionally associated with quality engineering. Two companies (descendants of the original company founded by Charles Rolls and Frederick Royce) now bear that famous name: one, a luxury car maker, and the other, Rolls-Royce plc.

Rolls-Royce plc is one of the big 3 jet engine makers (along with General Electric and United Technologies's Pratt & Whitney), with 22% of the world market share for commercial engines. Its engines range from the reliable Spey, which has powered civil and military jets since 1964, to the Trent, the world's most powerful turbofan. Rolls-Royce industrial engines, produced in part by subsidiary Northern Engineering Industries (NEI), drive electric and nuclear power plants, nuclear submarines, and oil and gas pumping units. NEI companies also build power plants, mining and drilling equipment, cranes, and bridges.

Rolls-Royce conducts about 72% of its business abroad, making it one of the UK's biggest exporters. However, with military orders down and the airline industry deferring some deliveries, Rolls-Royce is tightening its belt, instituting a mandatory 6-month pay freeze and cutting some 6,000 jobs by the end of 1991.

Principal exchange: London
Fiscal year ends: December 31

WHO

Chairman: Lord Tombs of Brailes, age 66, £180,064 pay
Chief Executive and Deputy Chairman: Sir Ralph Robins, age 58
Finance Director: Peter Macfarlane, age 52
Director Personnel: D'Arcy T. N. Payne
Auditors: KMPG Peat Marwick McLintock
Employees: 64,200

WHERE

HQ: 65 Buckingham Gate, London SW1E 6AT, UK
Phone: 011-44-71-222-9020
Fax: 011-44-71-233-1733
US HQ: Rolls-Royce Inc., 11911 Freedom Dr., Reston, VA 22090-5602
US Phone: 703-318-9023
US Fax: 703-709-6086

Rolls-Royce has operations in Australia, Brazil, Canada, Saudi Arabia, South Africa, the US, the UK, and Zimbabwe.

	1990 Sales	
	£ mil.	% of total
UK	1,047	28
Other Europe	609	17
North America	1,306	36
Asia	374	10
Africa	193	5
Other countries	141	4
Total	**3,670**	**100**

WHEN

In 1906 automobile and aviation enthusiast Charles S. Rolls and engineer Frederick H. Royce unveiled the Silver Ghost, an automobile that soon earned their newly founded company, Rolls-Royce Ltd., a reputation as the maker of the best car in the world.

A year after Rolls's death in 1910, Royce (an inveterate workaholic) suffered a breakdown. He continued to design Rolls-Royce engines from his home, but management of the company fell to Claude Johnson, who remained chief executive until 1926.

During WWI the company started making aircraft engines but afterward returned primarily to making cars, buying Bentley Motor Company in 1931. Development of aircraft engines continued on a more limited basis, and in 1933 Rolls-Royce introduced the Merlin, which powered the Spitfire, Hurricane, and Mustang fighters of WWII.

Under Ernest Hives (chief executive from 1936 to 1957), Rolls-Royce assumed production of the Whittle turbojet engine in 1941. Renamed the Welland, this engine powered the Gloster Meteor, the only Allied jet fighter in active service during WWII. The Avon turbojet powered the world's first commercial jet airliner, de Havilland's Comet.

Hives's successor, Sir Denning Pearson, realized that Rolls-Royce had to break into the lucrative US airliner market to stay alive. The company bought its main British competitor, Bristol-Siddley Engines, in 1966, acquiring with it the contract to build the engine for the Anglo-French Concorde. But US engine makers General Electric and Pratt & Whitney kept Rolls-Royce out of the US market until 1966, when the company won the contract to build the engine for Boeing's 747. Lockheed ordered the company's RB211 for its TriStar in 1968, but Rolls-Royce underestimated the project's technical and financial challenges and entered bankruptcy in 1971. The British government stepped in and nationalized the aerospace division, spinning off the automobile division to the public. The RB211 entered service on the TriStar in 1972. Later versions now power Boeing's 747, 757, and 767.

The government sold Rolls-Royce (aerospace) to the public in 1986. In the meantime (1983) Rolls-Royce created International Aero Engines with United Technologies and 3 other concerns to build the V2500 engine, which entered service on the Airbus 320 in 1989. That year, in its first move outside the aerospace field, the company bought Northern Engineering Industries.

Rolls-Royce joined forces with Germany's BMW to form BMW Rolls-Royce, an aircraft engine–making venture, in 1990.

WHAT

	1990 Sales		1990 Pretax Income	
	£ mil.	% of total	£ mil.	% of total
Aircraft engines	2,340	64	124	53
Power engineering	976	26	82	35
General engineering	354	10	27	12
Total	**3,670**	**100**	**233**	**100**

Engines

Civil Aircraft
FJ44
Olympus 593
RB211-524
RB211-535
Tay
Trent
V2500

Military Aircraft
Adour
EJ200
Pegasus
RB199
Spey
Viper

Helicopter
Gem
Gnome
MTR 390
RTM322

Industrial
Avon
RB211

Engineering

Power
Industrial power plants
Marine engines
Nuclear power plants
Power station equipment

General
Aircraft refuelers
Bridges
Cranes
Locomotives
Marine equipment
Mining equipment
Robotic systems
Tanker trucks

HOW MUCH

£=$1.93 (Dec. 31, 1990)	9-Year Growth	1981	1982	1983	1984	1985	1986	1987	1988	1989	1990
Sales (£ mil.)	10.9%	1,443	1,493	1,331	1,409	1,601	1,802	2,059	1,973	2,962	3,670
Net income (£ mil.)	33.1%	14	(96)	(119)	77	120	123	141	174	196	184
Income as % of sales	—	1.0%	(6.4%)	(8.9%)	5.5%	7.5%	6.8%	6.8%	8.8%	6.6%	5.0%
Earnings per share (p)	—	—	—	—	—	—	19	19	22	22	19
Stock price – high (p)	—	—	—	—	—	—	—	240	148	203	233
Stock price – low (p)	—	—	—	—	—	—	—	96	108	132	149
Stock price – close (p)	—	—	—	—	—	—	—	119	132	183	161
P/E – high	—	—	—	—	—	—	—	13	7	9	12
P/E – low	—	—	—	—	—	—	—	5	5	6	8
Dividends per share (p)	—	—	—	—	—	—	—	5.3	6.3	7.0	7.3
Book value per share (p)	1.6%	105	81	50	51	64	83	107	118	117	121

1990 Year-end:
Debt ratio: 12.2%
Return on equity: 16.1%
Cash (mil.): £1,319
Long-term debt (mil.): £161
No. of shares (mil.): 960
Dividends:
 1990 average yield: 4.5%
 1990 payout: 38.0%
Market value (mil.): $2,983
Sales (mil.): $7,083

Stock Price History High/Low 1987–90

250
200
150
100
50
0

KEY COMPETITORS

ABB
Alcatel Alsthom
Bechtel
Cooper Industries
Dresser
Duke Power
GEC
General Electric
Halliburton
Hitachi
McDermott
Mitsubishi
Peter Kiewit Sons'
Reliance Electric
RTZ
Siemens
Square D
Thyssen
Toshiba
United Technologies
Westinghouse

ROYAL BANK OF CANADA

OVERVIEW

Royal Bank is the largest bank in Canada and one of the 10 largest in North America, even though it barely makes the Top 50 worldwide. The Royal and 4 other banks — Canadian Imperial Bank of Commerce, Bank of Montreal, Bank of Nova Scotia, and Toronto Dominion — hold 82.5% of Canada's bank assets. Royal Bank of Canada is the nation's largest bank credit card issuer, with 25% of the market.

Royal Bank of Canada hopes to export its experience in high-tech, coast-to-coast banking south — as the US drops barriers to interstate banking. Its computers already handle 64 million transactions a month, and more than 1/3 of its loans are to Americans. It operates offices in 10 US cities. "The Royal," as it's called, claims it trades more foreign currency in the US than any other foreign bank.

The Royal's cross-border strategy is guided by CEO Allan Taylor, who did a 15-year stint with the bank's international division (including an assignment in New York City). Taylor is an outspoken advocate of North American free trade.

WHEN

Royal Bank has always had a southern exposure, ever since its creation as Merchants Bank in 1864. As the bank opened its doors in Halifax, the port city was bustling with trade spawned by the US Civil War raging below the border.

After its incorporation in 1869 as Merchants Bank of Halifax, it added branches in other cities of eastern Canada. In 1882 Merchants opened a branch in Bermuda, turning south before it headed west. The gold strikes in Canada and Alaska in the late 1890s spurred Merchants to establish branches in western Canada.

At the same time, Merchants pushed into New York and — even farther south — into Cuba in 1899. Its success in Cuba led it to purchase 2 Cuban banks, Banco de Oriente (1903) and Banco del Comercio (1904).

The bank was on the move in other ways. To avoid confusion with another bank, it changed its name in 1901 to Royal Bank of Canada and transferred its headquarters from Halifax to Montreal in 1907.

Royal Bank continued to acquire banks: Union Bank of Halifax (1910), Traders Bank of Canada (1912), Bank of British Honduras (1912), Quebec Bank (1917), and Northern Crown Bank (1918). Its largest acquisition was Union Bank of Canada (1925).

The bank stumbled, along with the rest of the economy, during the Great Depression but recovered its strength as war broke out in Europe in 1939. After WWII Royal Bank aggressively financed expansion of Canadian oil-and-gas and minerals industries.

When Castro seized power in Cuba, Royal Bank tried to operate its branches under communist rule but sold its assets to Banco Nacional de Cuba in 1960. In the late 1970s and early 1980s, the Royal aggressively grew overseas, with units in Britain (1979), West Germany (1980), Puerto Rico (1980), and the Bahamas (1980). Under CEO Rowland Frazee, the bank also beefed up its New York subsidiary, Royal Bank and Trust Company.

As Canada relaxed regulation on its banks, Royal Bank acquired Dominion Securities in 1987, after the Black Monday crash had deflated the price by an estimated $100 million. Allan Taylor, who started with the bank as a 16-year-old clerk and rose to the CEO post in 1986, turned the bank's gaze south again for expansion.

"We're looking covetously at the US," Taylor acknowledged in a 1989 interview with *American Banker*. Royal Bank is believed to be looking for more US holdings, possibly a retail bank. In 1991 the US Federal Reserve approved its brokerage arm, RBC Dominion, for participation in stock underwriting, but, on the other side of the world, Saudi Arabia blacklisted Royal Bank for limiting activities in the region after Iraq invaded Kuwait.

HOW MUCH

$=C$1.16 (Dec. 31, 1990)	9-Year Growth	1981	1982	1983	1984	1985	1986	1987	1988	1989	1990
Assets (C$ mil.)	4.4%	85,359	88,456	84,682	88,003	96,017	99,607	102,170	110,054	114,660	125,938
Net income (C$ mil.)	8.6%	458	182	313	352	454	452	512	712	529	965
Income as % of assets	—	0.5%	0.2%	0.4%	0.4%	0.5%	0.5%	0.5%	0.6%	0.5%	0.8%
Earnings per share (C$)	0.9%	2.73	0.89	1.50	1.50	1.82	1.73	1.81	2.42	1.63	2.96
Stock price – high (C$)	—	16.13	13.75	18.00	17.69	16.19	17.63	19.44	18.25	24.38	25.69
Stock price – low (C$)	—	12.06	9.00	11.75	12.44	13.75	13.75	12.81	13.06	16.88	19.75
Stock price – close (C$)	5.4%	12.88	11.75	15.88	14.19	15.75	16.63	13.88	18.00	24.25	20.75
P/E – high	—	6	15	12	12	9	10	11	8	15	9
P/E – low	—	4	10	8	8	8	8	7	5	10	7
Dividends per share (C$)	3.5%	0.85	1.00	1.00	1.00	1.00	1.00	1.01	1.04	1.10	1.16
Book value per share (C$)	1.8%	15.40	14.91	15.03	15.43	16.55	17.07	14.20	15.58	16.16	18.10

1990 Year-end:
Equity as % of assets: 2.3%
Return on equity: 17.5%
Cash (mil.): C$8,763
No. of shares (mil.): 293
Dividends:
1990 average yield: 5.1%
1990 payout: 39.2%
Market value (mil.): $6,080
Assets (mil.): $108,567
Sales (mil.): $14,628

Stock Price History High/Low 1981–90

30
25
20
15
10
5
0

Principal exchange: Toronto
Fiscal year ends: October 31

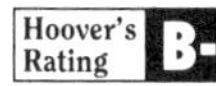

WHO

Chairman and CEO: Allan R. Taylor
President and COO: John E. Cleghorn
EVP and CFO: J. E. Bolduc
EVP Corporate Human Resources: W. J. McCartney
Auditors: Deloitte & Touche; Price Waterhouse
Employees: 56,889

WHERE

HQ: 1 Place Ville Marie, PO Box 6001, Montreal, Quebec H3C 3A9, Canada
Phone: 514-874-2110
Fax: 514-874-7197
US HQ: Financial Square, 23rd Floor, New York, NY 10005
US Phone: 212-428-6200
US Fax: 212-968-1293

Royal Bank of Canada operates 1,617 branches in Canada and 125 business units in 32 other nations.

	1990 Assets	
	C$ mil.	% of total
Canada	85,158	67
US	8,076	6
Europe, Middle East & Africa	9,383	7
Latin America & Caribbean	5,387	4
Asia Pacific	3,351	2
Nonearning	16,595	14
Adjustments	(2,012)	—
Total	**125,938**	**100**

WHAT

	1990 Assets	
	C$ mil.	% of total
Cash & Bank of Canada deposits	1,240	1
Deposits with other banks & loans	100,217	80
Securities	9,449	8
Customers' liabilities	10,369	8
Land, buildings & equipment	1,800	1
Other	2,863	2
Total	**125,938**	**100**

Major Subsidiaries and Affiliates
Chargex Ltd. (25%)
R.B.C. Holdings (Bahamas) Ltd.
RBC Dominion Securities Corp. (69%, US)
RBC Dominion Securities Ltd. (69%)
RBC Finance B.V.
RBC Holdings (USA) Inc.
Royal Bank Leasing Inc.
Royal Bank Mortgage Corp.
Royal Bank Realty Inc.
The Royal Bank of Canada Holdings (U.K.) Ltd.

KEY COMPETITORS

H. F. Ahmanson
Bank of New York
BankAmerica
Bankers Trust
Barclays
BCE
Canadian Imperial
Chase Manhattan
Citicorp
Crédit Lyonnais
CS Holding
Dai-Ichi Kangyo
Deutsche Bank
First Chicago
HSBC
Imasco
Industrial Bank of Japan
J.P. Morgan
Union Bank of Switzerland
Other money center banks
Securities underwriting firms

ROYAL DUTCH/SHELL GROUP OF COMPANIES

OVERVIEW

The Royal Dutch/Shell Group handles 6% of the world's oil and gas. It made more money in 1990 than any other company and surged past Exxon to become the world's largest oil concern. Its Houston-based Shell Oil unit alone ranks 14th in the *Fortune* 500.

Each of the 900 operating units is owned 60% by Royal Dutch Petroleum (the Netherlands) and 40% by Shell Transport and Trading (UK). Group leadership alternates between the 2 parent companies, which maintain headquarters in The Hague and London.

The well-known scallop shell logo adorns the world's largest tanker fleet and stands over 50,000 gas stations around the globe. A truly international organization, Shell tries to adopt the local character of each of the 100+ countries in which it operates.

Even though it boasts 9.5 billion barrels of oil reserves, Shell has been stockpiling potential hydrocarbon-producing properties and owns 400 million acres in more than 50 countries. Its nearly $9 billion in cash gives it the clout to deal for even more acreage.

WHEN

In 1870 Marcus Samuel inherited an interest in his father's London-based company, a trading business specializing in seashells from the Far East. Samuel expanded the business and, after securing a contract for Russian oil, began selling oil products in the Far East.

Standard Oil engaged in severe price-cutting to defend its Asian markets. Samuel secretly prepared his response and in 1892 unveiled the first of a fleet of tankers, all named after seashells. Specially designed to transport kerosene in bulk (Standard's was in cans), the ships pumped their cargo into storage tanks he had built at key ports. Samuel's transportation cost advantage allowed him to compete with Standard while competitors went bankrupt. Rejecting acquisition overtures from Standard, Samuel created Shell Transport and Trading in 1897.

Concurrently, a Dutchman, Aeilko Zijlker, struck oil in Sumatra and formed Royal Dutch in 1890 to exploit the oil field. Young Henri Deterding joined the firm in 1896 and established a Far Eastern sales organization.

Deterding became president of Royal Dutch in 1900 amid the battle for Asian market dominance. In 1903 Deterding, Samuel, and the Rothschilds created Asiatic Petroleum, an oil marketing alliance in the Far East. In 1907, when Shell's non-Asian business was eroding, Deterding engineered a merger between Royal Dutch and Shell. The deal stipulated 60% control of the combined companies by Royal Dutch shareholders, 40% by owners of Shell Transport and Trading stock.

Following the 1911 breakup of Standard Oil, Deterding entered the American market, building refineries and buying producers in the US. Shell products were available in every state by 1929. Royal Dutch joined the 1928 "As Is" cartel that fixed prices for most of 2 decades. Disturbed by Deterding's pro-Nazi sentiments, Shell management persuaded him to step down in 1936.

In its post-Deterding years, Shell profited from worldwide growth in consumption of oil-based products. It acquired 100% of its subsidiary Shell Oil (US) in 1985, but shareholders sued, complaining that the US arm's assets were undervalued in the deal. A judge awarded the shareholders $110 million (1990).

With the Persian Gulf crisis in 1990, the Royal Dutch/Shell Group saw net income drop 9%, but, as postwar inventories swelled, pump prices fell more slowly than crude prices. That led to a 71% surge in the first quarter of 1991. The US subsidiary, however, saw a 39% drop in profits. Houston-based Shell Oil was hurt by an explosion-crippled Louisiana refinery. To combat sluggishness Shell put a refinery in Los Angeles on the block and announced its first-ever layoff of 10–15% of its US force.

NYSE symbols: RD (Royal Dutch); SC (Shell) (ADR)

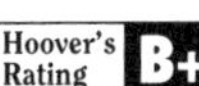

Fiscal year ends: December 31

WHO

Group Chairman; President, Royal Dutch: L. C. van Wachem, age 60
Group VC; Chairman, Shell Transport: Sir Peter Holmes, age 59, £529,360 pay
President and CEO, Shell Oil Co. (US): Frank H. Richardson
Group Treasurer: M. Harvey
Coordinator, Group Human Resources and Organization: E. van Mourik Broekman
Auditors: KPMG Klynveld (the Netherlands); Ernst & Young (UK); Price Waterhouse (US)
Employees: 137,000

WHERE

HQ: Royal Dutch Petroleum Company (N.V. Koninklijke Nederlandsche Petroleum Maatschappij), 30 Carel van Bylandtlaan, 2596 HR The Hague, The Netherlands
Phone: 011-31-70-377-4540
Fax: 011-31-70-377-4848
HQ: The "Shell" Transport and Trading Company, PLC, Shell Centre, London SE1 7NA, UK
Phone: 011-44-71-934-3856
Fax: 011-44-71-934-8060
US HQ: Shell Oil Company, One Shell Plaza, PO Box 2463, Houston, TX 77252
US Phone: 713-241-6161
US Fax: 713-241-6781 (Communications)

Royal Dutch/Shell operates in over 100 nations.

	1990 Sales		1990 Net Income	
	$ mil.	% of total	$ mil.	% of total
Europe	55,790	52	3,138	42
US	24,046	23	812	11
Other Eastern Hemisphere	15,170	14	2,875	38
Other Western Hemisphere	11,473	11	674	9
Adjustments	—	—	(966)	—
Total	**106,479**	**100**	**6,533**	**100**

WHAT

	1990 Sales		1990 Operating Income	
	$ mil.	% of total	$ mil.	% of total
Exploration & production	19,015	16	8,150	61
Refining, transport & marketing	87,063	71	3,821	29
Chemicals	12,230	10	1,120	8
Coal, metals & other	3,709	3	262	2
Adjustments	(15,538)	—	(483)	—
Total	**106,479**	**100**	**12,870**	**100**

KEY COMPETITORS

Amoco	Imperial Oil	Phillips Petroleum
Ashland	Mobil	Sun
Atlantic Richfield	Norsk Hydro	Texaco
British Petroleum	Occidental	Unocal
Broken Hill	Oryx	USX
Chevron	Pennzoil	Chemical companies
Coastal	Petrofina	Mining companies
Du Pont	Petrobrás	
Elf Aquitaine	PDVSA	
Exxon	Pemex	

HOW MUCH

	9-Year Growth	1981	1982	1983	1984	1985	1986	1987	1988	1989	1990
Sales ($ mil.)	3.6%	77,550	83,785	80,417	84,790	81,562	64,761	78,312	78,394	85,412	106,479
Net income ($ mil.)	12.9%	2,197	3,488	4,155	4,883	3,877	3,714	4,740	5,234	6,539	6,533
Income as % of sales	—	—	4.2%	5.2%	5.8%	4.8%	5.7%	6.1%	6.7%	7.7%	6.1%
Earnings per share ($)	7.4%	4.10	3.97	4.80	5.57	4.57	4.33	5.66	6.27	7.58	7.78
Stock price – high ($)	—	24.69	18.56	25.06	27.31	32.56	48.00	70.50	62.13	77.63	87.00
Stock price – low ($)	—	13.50	14.06	16.75	20.63	24.19	29.88	47.19	52.19	56.88	70.50
Stock price – close ($)	18.3%	17.44	17.31	22.50	24.69	31.50	47.75	55.94	57.00	77.50	78.63
P/E – high	—	6	5	5	5	7	11	12	10	10	11
P/E – low	—	3	4	4	4	5	7	8	8	8	9
Dividends per share ($)	14.0%	1.31	1.46	1.41	1.44	1.65	2.64	3.16	3.62	3.36	4.25
Book value per share ($)	8.8%	28.29	30.56	31.82	33.08	37.77	41.42	48.08	50.67	53.58	60.43

1990 Year-end:
Debt ratio: 7.7%
Return on equity: 12.9%
Cash (mil.): $8,513
Current ratio: 1.22
Long-term debt (mil.): $4,482
No. of shares (mil.): 536
Dividends:
1990 average yield: 5.4%
1990 payout: 54.7%
Market value (mil.): $42,149

Stock Price History High/Low 1981–90

Note: Sales, net income, and cash are stated for Group. All other figures are presented for Royal Dutch only.

THE RTZ CORPORATION PLC

OVERVIEW

RTZ presides over the world's largest mining operation from its London headquarters. Much of its profits comes from North America, where its US Borax mines more than 1/2 of the world's borates and where its Kennecott operations contribute the bulk of RTZ's copper, silver, and gold output. RTZ contributes 7% of the world's copper production and is the world's leading producer of talc.

In line with its strategy of being a low-cost producer with a diverse geographic base, RTZ owns pieces of the Escondida copper project (Chile), the Argyle diamond mine (Australia), and 2 gold mines (Brazil).

In Africa RTZ operates the Rössing Uranium mine (Namibia) and a gold mine (Zimbabwe). Its CRA affiliate gives the company a strong foothold on the Pacific Rim, with Australian iron mines and coal projects. RTZ Pillar provides building and engineering services and is the leading UK manufacturer of electrical products.

NYSE symbol: RTZ (ADR)
Fiscal year ends: December 31

WHO

Chairman: Sir Derek Birkin, age 61
CEO: Robert P. Wilson, age 47
Deputy CEO: Ian C. Strachan, age 47
Finance Director: Chris R. H. Bull
Mining Director: Leon Davis
Auditors: Coopers & Lybrand Deloitte
Employees: 73,612

WHERE

HQ: 6 St. James's Square, London SW1Y 4LD, UK
Phone: 011-44-71-930-2399
Fax: 011-44-71-930-3249
US HQ: Kennecott Corporation, PO Box 11248, Salt Lake City, UT 84147
US Phone: 801-322-7000
US Fax: 801-322-8181

RTZ operates worldwide.

	1990 Sales		1990 Net Income	
	£ mil.	% of total	£ mil.	% of total
UK	1,091	21	18	3
Other Europe	360	7	40	7
US	1,317	25	239	44
Australia & New Zealand	910	18	136	25
Canada	856	17	57	11
Africa	535	10	52	9
Other countries	113	2	6	1
Adjustments	(104)	—	(41)	—
Total	**5,078**	**100**	**507**	**100**

WHEN

RTZ was formed as Rio Tinto-Zinc Corporation, the result of the 1962 merger of the Rio Tinto Company and Consolidated Zinc. Rio Tinto, a British company, had begun mining in Spain in 1873. It sold most of its Spanish holdings in 1954 and branched out to Australia, southern Africa, and Canada. Consolidated Zinc had been founded as The Zinc Corporation in 1905 around the mineral-rich Broken Hill area of Australia. After The Zinc Corporation combined with New Broken Hill Consolidated and Imperial Smelting, the company discovered the world's largest deposit of bauxite (1955).

The product of the 1962 merger, Rio Tinto-Zinc, acquired US Borax in 1968. US Borax, with its 20 Mule Team trademark, had been built on one of the few great boron deposits. Boron use in cleansers became widespread in the late 19th century. Early miners in California's Death Valley used 20-mule teams to haul huge wagons to meet the demand.

A 1927 discovery in the Mojave Desert led to development of another huge boron mine. Before its purchase by RTZ, US Borax leaned heavily on its Western roots. Its detergent products sponsored *Death Valley Days*, an Old West TV series hosted for a time by White House–bound Ronald Reagan. Until its Turkish mine was nationalized, RTZ controlled the world's boron supply. RTZ sold US Borax's consumer products to Greyhound (later Dial Corporation) in 1988.

RTZ added a huge copper mine at Bougainville in Papua New Guinea (1969). The company suffered through a slump in metals prices in the early 1980s, but in 1985 Derek Birkin was named CEO. He solidified RTZ's minerals business with the $3.7 billion purchase of BP Minerals from British Petroleum in 1989. Among the booty from the BP purchase was Utah-based Kennecott Corporation.

Kennecott had taken its name from Robert Kennicott (a typographical error had altered the company's spelling), who had died in Alaska while trying to blaze the trail for an intercontinental telegraph line. In 1901 Alaskan prospectors in the area named for Kennicott convinced Stephen Birch of the potential for copper mining. Birch returned to New York, enlisted backing from the Guggenheims and J. P. Morgan, and built a railroad to haul the ore. Kennecott Copper joined railroad and mine operations in 1915.

Kennecott consolidated its hold on the Braden copper mine in Chile (1925) and on the Utah Copper Company (1936) and other US mining properties. Utah holdings include the Bingham Canyon copper mine, the world's largest open-pit facility. In 1981 British Petroleum–controlled SOHIO bought Kennecott, and in 1989, the first year RTZ owned it, Kennecott was the largest single contributor to RTZ's bottom line. RTZ sold its chemicals business in 1989 and entered the 1990s with almost 30% of its assets in the US.

WHAT

	1990 Sales		1990 Net Income	
	£ mil.	% of total	£ mil.	% of total
Traded metals	1,659	32	268	50
Other mined products	673	13	101	19
Industrial minerals	955	18	169	31
Explor. & develop.	—	—	(40)	(7)
Related industries	1,895	37	41	7
Adjustments	(104)	—	(32)	—
Total	**5,078**	**100**	**507**	**100**

Mining and Metals
Aluminum
Coal
Copper
Gold
Iron ore
Lead
Molybdenum
Silver
Uranium
Zinc

Industrial Minerals
Borax
Diamonds
High-purity iron and steel
Kaolin
Rutile
Silica sands
Talc
Titanium dioxide feedstock
Zircon

Related Industries
Aircraft engine overhaul
Building products
Electrical products
Engineering services
Metals distribution

US Subsidiaries
Commonwealth Aluminum Corp. (32.8%)
Kennecott Corp.
US Borax & Chemical Corp.
US Silica

HOW MUCH

£=$1.93 (Dec. 31, 1990)	9-Year Growth	1981	1982	1983	1984	1985	1986	1987	1988	1989	1990
Sales (£ mil.)	7.9%	2,563	3,146	3,730	4,602	4,647	4,345	4,527	4,928	6,156	5,078
Net income (£ mil.)	17.9%	115	128	199	230	286	244	284	425	588	507
Income as % of sales	—	4.5%	4.1%	5.3%	5.0%	6.2%	5.6%	6.3%	8.6%	9.6%	10.0%
Earnings per share (p)	12.8%	17	19	27	29	36	31	36	53	63	51
Stock price – high (p)	—	253	189	269	284	274	316	580	464	590	605
Stock price – low (p)	—	149	138	175	200	203	205	259	315	404	392
Stock price – close (p)	11.0%	177	182	238	237	207	282	350	421	581	451
P/E – high	—	15	10	10	10	8	10	16	9	9	12
P/E – low	—	9	7	6	7	6	7	7	6	6	8
Dividends per share (p)	13.2%	6.4	6.4	7.2	8.0	8.8	9.4	11.5	15.0	18.5	19.5
Book value per share (p)	3.5%	187	194	207	224	191	209	207	259	259	254

1990 Year-end:
Debt ratio: 35.5%
Return on equity: 20.0%
Cash (mil.): £876
Long-term debt (mil.): £1,379
No. of shares (mil.): 987
Dividends:
1990 average yield: 4.3%
1990 payout: 37.9%
Market value (mil.): $8,591
Sales (mil.): $9,801

Stock Price History High/Low 1981–90

700
600
500
400
300
200
100
0

KEY COMPETITORS

Alcan	Cyprus Minerals	Phelps Dodge
Alcoa	FMC	Reynolds Metals
AMAX	General Electric	Rolls-Royce
Anglo American	GTE	Thyssen
ASARCO	Hanson	United Technologies
Broken Hill	JWP	

SAAB-SCANIA AB

OVERVIEW

In the largest LBO in Swedish history, companies controlled by Swedish industrialist Peter Wallenberg are buying the shares of Saab-Scania they do not already own. The target company is a global truck and bus manufacturer (Scania), Sweden's largest importer of passenger cars (Volkswagen, Audi, Porsche), and an important aircraft and armaments producer. Saab-Scania and General Motors each own 50% of Saab Automobile.

In 1990 Saab-Scania experienced cost overruns in its Gripen fighter aircraft program and wrote off its remaining equity in Saab Automobile. After posting losses of over $800 million in 1990, Saab Automobile closed its 18-month-old Malmö, Sweden, factory, which featured waterfalls, scenic views, and car assembly without production lines. The automaker, Europe's 16th largest, has posted sales declines since 1987 and suffers from poor productivity.

WHEN

In 1937 companies controlled by Axel Wenner-Gren, head of Electrolux, created Svenska Aeroplan AB (Saab) in response to the Swedish government's need for a producer of military aircraft. The government intended for Saab to cooperate with an aircraft manufacturer controlled by Marcus Wallenberg (Peter's father), but intercompany feuding slowed progress. Wallenberg joined the Saab board in 1939 when the government orchestrated Saab's acquisition of his enterprise. The first Saab-designed plane flew in 1940.

Swedish neutrality in WWII lessened the need for weaponry and, as the war's end approached, Saab management began planning to produce small cars.

The basic styling of Saab autos remained unchanged from their introduction in 1947 until their redesign in 1967. In that period the cars became popular in Sweden but failed to catch on in the large US market. Saab benefited from massive Swedish rearmament in the 1960s and began building satellites, missiles, and computers. Wallenberg engineered the acquisition of Swedish truckmaker Scania in 1969.

Hilding Hessler and Anton Svensson took over management of the Masinfabriks AB Scania, a Swedish bicycle factory, in 1901. Hessler and Svensson used the company's experience in making a moped-like vehicle to begin production of autos (1901) and trucks (1902). Following the 1911 merger with Swedish truck rival and railcar maker Vabis, Scania-Vabis entered bus production (1911) and exited the auto business in the 1920s.

Trucks dominated Scania-Vabis's output until WWII, when the company built tanks and other military vehicles. Scania-Vabis enjoyed strong postwar demand for trucks and buses, and the 1948 appointment of the company as the Swedish Volkswagen importer enabled it to recruit a national dealer network. Exports boomed through the 1960s.

Soon after the merger Saab-Scania acquired arms makers Malmö Flygindustri and Nordarmatur. The recession of the mid-1970s took its toll on the auto and computer segments, while détente dimmed prospects for the aerospace division. The company considered a merger with Volvo in 1977. After rejecting the idea, Saab-Scania began withdrawing from computers and finally scored a success in the US in the late 1970s with upscale autos.

In the 1980s Saab-Scania introduced a popular line of trucks, began developing commuter aircraft, and introduced the Saab 9000 series of cars. Seeking a prestigious European nameplate, General Motors bought 50% of Saab's passenger car business for $600 million in 1989. In 1990 Swedish property developer Sven Olof Johansson acquired a 22% voting interest in Saab-Scania. Peter Wallenberg bought back the stock at a hefty premium and in 1991 launched a takeover bid to defend his empire.

HOW MUCH

$=SEK5.63 (Dec. 31, 1990)	9-Year Growth	1981	1982	1983	1984	1985	1986	1987	1988	1989	1990[3]
Sales (SEK mil.)	6.7%	16,188	18,726	20,773	25,956	31,840	35,222	41,403	42,488	44,905	29,035
Net income (SEK mil.)[1]	—	398	471	379	682	695	1,306	1,446	1,562	1,009	353
Income as % of sales	—	2.5%	2.5%	1.8%	2.6%	2.2%	3.7%	3.5%	3.7%	2.2%	1.2%
Earnings per share (SEK)	7.2%	11.25	13.65	16.70	20.65	20.80	27.75	30.80	28.05	15.55	21.10
Stock price – high (SEK)[2]	—	—	—	—	—	—	—	295	218	273	288
Stock price – low (SEK)[2]	—	—	—	—	—	—	—	141	151	195	125
Stock price – close (SEK)[2]	—	—	—	—	—	—	—	152	208	252	140
P/E – high	—	—	—	—	—	—	—	10	8	18	14
P/E – low	—	—	—	—	—	—	—	5	5	13	6
Dividends per share (SEK)	12.9%	2.60	2.92	3.57	3.57	5.00	5.71	6.75	7.75	7.75	7.75
Book value per share (SEK)	16.2%	38	43	46	51	57	70	99	114	123	146

1990 Year-end:
Debt ratio: 24.5%
Return on equity: 15.7%
Cash (mil.): SEK9,420
Long-term debt (mil.): SEK3,220
No. of shares (mil.): 68
Dividends:
1990 average yield: 5.5%
1990 payout: 36.7%
Market value (mil.): $1,691
Sales (mil.): $5,157

Stock Price History High/Low 1987–90

300 250 200 150 100 50 0

[1] Including extraordinary items, after appropriations to/from reserves [2] Unrestricted "B" shares [3] Passenger Auto Division excluded from 1990 sales

Principal exchange: Stockholm
Fiscal year ends: December 31

Hoover's Rating 

WHO

Chairman: Anders Scharp, age 57
President and CEO: Georg Karnsund, age 58
EVP Corporate Finance: Sivert Nordgren, age 52
Auditors: Svensson, Erikson & Tjus Revisionsbyrå
Employees: 29,388

WHERE

HQ: S-581 88 Linköping, Sweden
Phone: 011-46-13-18-00-00
Fax: 011-46-13-18-18-02
US HQ: Saab Cars USA, Inc., Saab Dr., PO Box 697, Orange, CT 06477
US Phone: 203-795-5671
US Fax: 203-799-8396

The company has production sites in 14 nations

	1990 Sales	
	SEK mil.	% of total
Sweden	10,237	35
Other Europe	12,207	42
North America	1,698	6
Latin America	2,921	10
Other countries	1,972	7
Total	**29,035**	**100**

WHAT

	1990 Sales		1990 Pretax Income	
	SEK mil.	% of total	SEK mil.	% of total
Scania Division	22,892	79	2,902	—
Saab Aircraft Division	4,322	15	111	—
Saab-Scania Combitech	1,821	6	204	—
50% of losses of Saab Automobile	—	—	(2,320)	—
Corporate & other	—	—	(34)	—
Total	**29,035**	**100**	**863**	**—**

Operating Divisions

Scania Division
Buses
Industrial and marine engines
Marketing of Volkswagen/Audi vehicles in Sweden
Trucks

Saab Aircraft Division
Aircraft components
Commercial and military aircraft

Operating Subsidiary

Saab-Scania Combitech AB
Automotive electronics
Computers and systems for space vehicles
Defense systems
Industrial electronics

Associated Company

Saab Automobile AB (50% owned)

KEY COMPETITORS

BMW	Mazda	Suzuki
Chrysler	Mitsubishi	Tata
Daimler-Benz	Navistar	Thomson SA
Fiat	Nissan	Toyota
Ford	PACCAR	Volkswagen
General Motors	Peugeot	Volvo
Honda	Renault	Other auto, defense, and aerospace companies
Hyundai	Robert Bosch	
Isuzu	Siemens	

SAATCHI & SAATCHI COMPANY PLC

OVERVIEW

London-based Saatchi & Saatchi, once the world's largest advertising group, managed to cling to the #2 spot in 1990 despite a decline in sales and poor financial results.

Founding brothers Charles and Maurice Saatchi rose to fame with such campaigns as "Labour isn't working" for the Conservative party and ads for the Health Council with a pregnant man asking "Would you be more careful if it was you that got pregnant?"

In the late 1970s Saatchi began buying a host of disparate advertising and consulting firms. By 1989 high debt and lower-than-hoped profits from consulting businesses caused losses. Since 1990 new management under Robert Louis-Dreyfus (nicknamed "Jaws") has laid off personnel, sold most of the consulting firms, and successfully restructured the company's finances.

Despite having caused most of the firm's problems, both Saatchis remain on the board; they now own only about 1% of the firm. Louis-Dreyfus (recently fined by the SEC for giving inside information on his former firm to a friend who traded on it) has recessed himself from day-to-day management to strategize and appointed Charles Scott (formerly the Finance Director) as COO, with all operating units reporting to him.

With most of Saatchi's consulting components sold and some of its advertising units on the block, Louis-Dreyfus led a recapitalization in early 1991 that converted preferred shares to common, raised £60 million, diluted existing shareholders by 84%, and left British financier Jacob Rothschild and a group including the Tisch family as the largest shareholders, with 12% and 6% interests, respectively. The firm must still grapple with an industry-wide slump stemming from the 1990-91 recession in the US and UK and the loss of several major clients.

WHEN

In 1947 Nathan Saatchi, a prosperous Jewish merchant, emigrated from Iraq to London with his wife and 3 sons, David, Charles, and Maurice. Charles left school at 17 and held a series of jobs before becoming a junior copywriter at an advertising agency. Feeling creatively confined he opened his own consultancy in 1967. Younger brother Maurice finished university and went to work for a publisher that wrote about the advertising industry.

By 1970 Charles wanted to start his own ad agency and recruited the financially oriented Maurice. The agency opened in 1971 with a flashy campaign of self-promotion. It prospered, and in 1973, showing a profit of £90,000, it began to make acquisitions; one of the first failed when its liabilities turned out higher — and assets lower — than expected. Despite this setback and an industry recession, profits rose steadily. In 1975 the Saatchis completed the takeover of the much larger, publicly held Compton UK Partners, rising from 13th to 5th in size in the UK. Acquisitions and internal growth made Saatchi & Saatchi the largest agency in the UK by 1979.

In 1982 the Saatchis set their sights on another much larger firm — Compton Advertising in New York. Its acquistion made Saatchi & Saatchi the 9th largest agency in the world. In 1985 the Saatchis acquired the Hay Group, a US consulting firm, for $125 million and the Howard Marlboro sales promotion company for $414 million. In 1986 the firm bought Backer Spielvogel for $56 million and Ted Bates Worldwide for $450 million, vaulting the Saatchis to #1 in the world. The Bates acquisition caused several key clients with over $250 million in billings to withdraw because of perceived client conflicts among the agencies now part of Saatchi.

In 1987 Saatchi tried unsuccessfully to buy 2 UK banks, but by the end of the year high debt and the lower-than-expected profitability of many of the consulting groups acquired by the Saatchis caused financial problems from which the agency has yet to recover.

HOW MUCH

Stock prices are for ADRs ADR = 3 shares	7-Year Growth	1981	1982	1983	1984	1985	1986	1987	1988	1989	1990
Sales ($ mil.)	38.9%	—	—	152	181	425	642	1,257	1,458	1,572	1,514
Net income ($ mil.)	5.4%	—	—	9	14	34	63	123	142	(30)	13
Income as % of sales	—	—	—	1.0%	1.3%	1.8%	2.1%	1.9%	2.2%	(0.4%)	0.9%
Earnings per share ($)	—	—	—	0.63	0.88	1.42	1.61	2.14	2.26	(1.12)	(0.86)
Stock price – high ($)	—	—	—	12.31	18.42	26.81	33.38	34.38	25.25	22.50	13.75
Stock price – low ($)	—	—	—	11.81	12.09	15.68	18.38	16.50	17.00	11.25	1.63
Stock price – close ($)	(22.9%)	—	—	12.31	17.79	26.81	24.28	23.25	17.88	12.75	2.00
P/E – high	—	—	—	20	21	19	21	16	11	—	—
P/E – low	—	—	—	19	14	11	11	8	8	—	—
Dividends per share ($)	—	—	—	0.00	0.17	1.01	2.37	0.87	1.21	1.06	0.11
Book value per share ($)	—	—	—	4.00	4.87	9.20	(0.34)	(1.85)	(5.70)	(11.11)	(16.79)

1990 Year-end:
Debt ratio: —
Return on equity: 6.2%
Cash (mil.): $211
Current ratio: 0.99
Long-term debt (mil.): $454
No. of shares (mil.): 53
Dividends:
1990 average yield: 5.3%
1990 payout: —
Market value (mil.): $107

Stock Price History High/Low 1983–90

0 5 10 15 20 25 30 35

NYSE symbol: SAA (ADR)
Fiscal year ends: December 31

WHO

Chairman: Maurice Saatchi, age 45, £437,500 pay
Deputy Chairman: Jeremy T. Sinclair, age 44
CEO: Robert L. M. Louis-Dreyfus, age 45, £500,000 pay
COO: Charles T. Scott, age 42
Finance Director: Wendy Smyth, age 37
Auditors: KPMG Peat Marwick McLintock
Employees: 13,300

WHERE

HQ: 83/89 Whitfield St., London W1A 4XA, UK
Phone: 011-44-71-436-4000
Fax: 011-44-71-436-1998
US HQ: Saatchi & Saatchi Advertising, 375 Hudson St., New York, NY 10014
US Phone: 212-463-2000
US Fax: 212-463-9855

The company has 100 subsidiaries operating in 30 countries and affiliates in 25 additional countries.

	1990 Sales		1990 Operating Income	
	$ mil.	% of total	$ mil.	% of total
UK	279	19	14	11
US	745	49	63	53
Other Europe	362	24	38	32
Other countries	128	8	5	4
Total	**1,514**	**100**	**120**	**100**

WHAT

	1990 Sales		1990 Operating Income	
	$ mil.	% of total	$ mil.	% of total
Communications	1,476	97	118	98
Consulting	38	3	2	2
Total	**1,514**	**100**	**120**	**100**

Major Services and Operating Units

Advertising
AC&R (US)
Backer Spielvogel Bates Worldwide
Campbell-Mithun-Esty Inc. (US)
Conill Advertising Inc. (US)
Hall Harrison Cowley (UK)
KHBB (UK)
Klemtner Advertising Inc. (US)
Saatchi & Saatchi Advertising Worldwide

Consulting
Litigation Sciences Inc. (US)
MSL International (UK) Ltd.

Direct Marketing
Kobs & Draft Worldwide

Media Services
Zenith Media Worldwide

Public Relations
Rowland Worldwide

Commmunications Services
Howard Marlboro Group (in-store marketing)
HP:ICM (face-to-face communications)
National Research Group (market research)
Siegel & Gale (corporate identity and design)
Yankelovich Clancy Shulman (market research)

Representative Advertising Clients

Alcatel Alsthom	Ericsson	Johnson & Johnson
Allied Lyons	Gallo	Mars
B.A.T	General Mills	3M
British Airways	Grand Metropolitan	Philip Morris
British Telecom	Hewlett-Packard	Procter & Gamble
Carlsberg	Hyundai	Toyota
Deutsche Bank		

KEY COMPETITORS

Dentsu
Young & Rubicam

SAMSUNG GROUP

OVERVIEW

Consisting of 29 publicly and privately owned firms with 1990 sales of $35.6 billion, Samsung is South Korea's leading *chaebol* (industrial group). The Lee family controls the group through interlocking ownership of the component companies. Samsung Company is the lead company of the *chaebol* and a major Korean import/export organization. Samsung Electronics is Korea's #1 semiconductor manufacturer. Other activities include electronics, shipbuilding, and food processing. Samsung management is highly regarded.

Samsung continues to emulate Japanese business strategies and corporate structures. The group is maintaining a high-volume orientation and long-term view while shifting its consumer product mix toward more sophisticated, higher-profit items. Samsung Electronics is reducing its dependence on exports to the US by increasing trade with Europe.

Samsung will focus on electronics, chemicals, and heavy machinery to comply with the South Korean government's wishes that each *chaebol* specialize in only 3 businesses.

WHEN

Japan-educated Lee Byung-Chull began operating a rice mill in Korea, then under Japanese rule (1936). By 1938 Lee had begun trading in dried fish and had incorporated as Samsung (Korean for "Three Stars"). WWII did not inflict widespread destruction on Korea, and, by the end of the war, Samsung had established transportation and real estate businesses.

The Korean War destroyed nearly all Samsung assets. Using the profits from a surviving brewery and importing goods for UN personnel, Lee reconstructed Samsung in South Korea. In 1953 he formed highly profitable Cheil Sugar Company, the only South Korean sugar refiner at the time. Later Samsung established Cheil Wool Textile (1954) and entered banking and insurance.

When a 1961 coup brought Park Chung Hee to power in South Korea, Lee, well known for his wealth and ties to the former government, was accused of illegal profiteering, and a 1966 smuggling scandal involving one of Lee's sons led to another investigation. The government dropped the charges when Lee agreed to give it an immense fertilizer plant he was building. Despite the setback Samsung continued to grow and diversify in the 1960s, expanding into paper, department stores, and newspaper publishing, and establishing Samsung Electronics with help from Sanyo in 1969. Samsung Electronics grew rapidly as a result of the South Korean government's export drive and low wage rates. The company gained engineering know-how by disassembling Western-designed electronic goods and producing inexpensive, private-label, black-and-white televisions and, later, color televisions, VCRs, and microwave ovens for General Electric, J. C. Penney, Sears, and others.

In concert with the government's industrialization push, the *chaebol* formed Samsung Shipbuilding (1974), Samsung Petrochemical (1977), and Samsung Precision Industries (aircraft engines and maintenance, 1977). Exports and a higher domestic standard of living helped group sales to reach $3 billion in 1979. Samsung entered broadcasting, but, following the assassination of President Park, the new Chun regime took over all Samsung's broadcast properties.

In the 1980s Samsung began exporting electronic goods under its own name in an effort to increase margins. Success in low-end products encouraged Samsung to export upmarket items.

When Lee died in 1987, his son, Lee Kun-Hee, assumed control of Samsung. The new chairman has cut costs, tightened inventory control, and decentralized management. After years of importing technology and spending freely on R&D, in 1990 Samsung became a world leader in 4-megabit chip production.

HOW MUCH

$=Won 714 (Dec. 31, 1990)	7-Year Growth	1981	1982	1983	1984	1985	1986	1987	1988	1989	1990
Sales (Won bil.)	21.5%	—	—	2,029	2,568	3,802	4,275	5,670	6,811	7,613	7,952
Net income (Won bil.)	7.2%	—	—	8	7	6	7	8	11	11	13
Income as % of sales	—	—	—	0.4%	0.3%	0.2%	0.2%	0.1%	0.2%	0.1%	0.2%
Earnings per share (Won)	—	—	—	—	—	1,220	1,079	1,321	1,467	1,069	1,083
Stock price – high (Won)	—	—	—	—	—	9,170	15,480	18,700	32,400	36,300	29,900
Stock price – low (Won)	—	—	—	—	—	6,650	6,800	10,000	16,900	23,400	22,300
Stock price – close (Won)	—	—	—	—	—	—	11,450	18,100	32,400	32,400	24,800
P/E – high	—	—	—	—	—	8	14	14	22	34	28
P/E – low	—	—	—	—	—	5	6	8	12	22	21
Dividends per share (Won)[1]	—	—	—	—	—	—	500	500	600	600	600
Book value per share (Won)	—	—	—	—	—	—	11,720	13,294	13,966	14,711	16,239

1990 Year-end:
Debt ratio: 16.2%
Return on equity: 7.0%
Cash (bil.): Won 22
Long-term debt (bil.): Won 36
No. of shares (mil.): 12
Dividends:
1990 average yield: 2.4%
1990 payout: 55.4%
Market value (mil.): $403
Sales (mil.): $11,137

[1] Not including rights issues

Principal exchange: Seoul
Fiscal year ends: December 31

Hoover's Rating **B+**

WHO

Chairman: Lee Kun-Hee
Chairman, Samsung Co., Ltd.: Shin Hyon Hwak
Corporate Executive Counsellor: Song Sae Chang
President: Rhee Pil Gon
Auditors: Samil Accounting Corp.
Employees: 180,000 (1989)

WHERE

HQ: 26th Fl., Samsung Main Bldg., 250, 2-ka, Taepyung-ro, Ching-gu, Seoul, Korea
Phone: 011-82-2-751-2114
Fax: 011-82-2-751-2083 (Public Affairs)
US HQ: Samsung America Inc., One Executive Dr., Fort Lee, NJ 07024
US Phone: 201-592-7900
US Fax: 201-592-1444

The Samsung Group's principal companies operate 229 overseas branch offices in 54 countries.

Samsung Company	1990 Sales	
	Won bil.	% of total
Korea	3,180	40
Other countries	4,760	60
Adjustments	12	—
Total	**7,952**	**100**

WHAT

	1989 Group Sales	
	Won bil.	% of total
Trade	7,613	33
Service	5,777	25
Electronics	5,240	23
Heavy industries & chemicals	2,164	9
Food processing & textiles	1,512	6
Culture & social welfare	630	3
Precision products	340	1
Total	**23,276**	**100**

Principal Samsung Group Affiliates

Trade
Samsung Co., Ltd.

Service
Ankuk Fire & Marine Insurance Co., Ltd.
Hotel Shilla Co., Ltd.
Samsung Life Insurance Co., Ltd.
Samsung Winners Card Co., Ltd.
Shinsegae Department Store Co., Ltd.

Electronics
Samsung Corning Co., Ltd.
Samsung Electro-mechanics Co., Ltd.
Samsung Electron Devices Co., Ltd.
Samsung Electronics Co., Ltd.

Heavy Industries and Chemicals
Chonju Paper Manufacturing Co., Ltd.
Samsung Construction Co., Ltd.
Samsung Engineering Co., Ltd.
Samsung Petrochemical Co., Ltd.
Samsung Shipbuilding & Heavy Industries Co., Ltd.

Food Processing and Textiles
Cheil Foods & Chemicals Inc.
Cheil Industries Inc.
Cheil Synthetics Inc.

Culture and Social Welfare
The Joong-ang Daily News
Joong-ang Development Co., Ltd.

Precision Products
Samsung Aerospace Industries Ltd.
Samsung Watch Co., Ltd.

KEY COMPETITORS

Daewoo
Hyundai
Lucky-Goldstar
Other electronics and chemical companies

Information presented for Samsung Co., Ltd. only (unconsolidated)

SAN MIGUEL CORPORATION

OVERVIEW

Based in Manila, San Miguel is the Philippines' largest and most diversified company. With its subsidiaries the company generates approximately 4% of the country's GNP.

Although known primarily for its beer, San Miguel produces a wide range of products including soft drinks, packaging materials, livestock, animal feeds, dairy foods, and agribusiness products. The company also owns 45% of Nestlé's Philippines operation and recently swapped 13.5% of its stock for SHK Hong Kong Industries, which owns minority interests in leading Hong Kong industries.

San Miguel beer dominates the national market, where it enjoys a virtual monopoly, although competition is stiffening in the wake of Carlsberg's recent entry into the Philippines. With its brewing and Coca-Cola bottling operations, the company derives 68% of its sales from beverages.

Outside the Philippines San Miguel beer has successfully penetrated markets throughout the Pacific Rim and beyond, including China, Vietnam, and, most recently, Nepal, Tibet, and Bhutan.

WHEN

In 1890 Don Enrique Barretto y de Ycaza opened La Fabrica de Cerveza de San Miguel brewery in the San Miguel district of Manila. Don Pedro Pablo Roxas joined Don Enrique and, to ensure European-style brewing, hired German Ludwig Kiene as technical director. In 1895 the company's beer won its first prize at the Philippines Regional Exposition.

By 1900 San Miguel was outselling imported brands 5 to 1. Upon Don Pedro Roxas's death in 1913, the company became a corporation. By WWI San Miguel was selling beer in Hong Kong, Shanghai, and Guam.

Andrés Soriano y Roxas joined San Miguel in 1918 and in the 1920s diversified by establishing the Royal Soft Drinks Plant (1922), the Magnolia Ice Cream Plant (1925), and the first non-US national Coca-Cola bottling and distribution franchise (1927).

Following the devastation of WWII, the company rebuilt and embarked on a major expansion effort adding a 2nd brewery; 3 new soft drink facilities; a power plant; a poultry and livestock feeds plant; and factories to produce glass, carbon dioxide, and cartons.

In the 1960s the company changed its name to San Miguel Corporation. After the death of Don Andrés in 1964, his son Andrés Soriano, Jr., assumed the presidency. He modernized and decentralized operations into product segments. San Miguel continued to diversify in the 1970s.

A family feud erupted in 1983 when members of the 2 families controlling San Miguel (the Sorianos and their cousins, the Zobels) engaged in a proxy fight over control of the company. Enrique Zobel realized that he could not win the struggle and sold all of his shares (about 20% of San Miguel) to Eduardo Cojuangco, a Ferdinand Marcos crony and president of United Coconut Planters Bank. Upon Soriano's death in 1984, Cojuangco became chairman, thus securing the company under Marcos's sphere of influence.

During the 1986 election, Cojuangco ordered all of the company's employees to vote for Marcos. When Aquino won, her government seized assets associated with Marcos and his followers, including Cojuangco's share of San Miguel. Cojuangco fled the country with Marcos, and Andrés Soriano III became CEO.

In 1989 Cojuangco returned to the Philippines. Two years later the Supreme Court effectively returned to Cojuangco his stake in San Miguel, prompting Cojuangco to announce his intentions to reclaim his position as chairman and CEO. Also in 1991 the company set up a joint venture with Yamamaura Glass (Japan) to manufacture containers for the Philippine market.

HOW MUCH

$=P27.20 (Dec. 31, 1990)	9-Year Growth	1981	1982	1983	1984	1985	1986	1987	1988	1989	1990
Sales (P mil.)	26.6%	5,240	5,484	6,461	10,369	10,992	12,225	16,014	30,866	36,713	43,815
Net income (P mil.)	22.8%	283	311	404	422	364	1,111	1,758	2,052	2,431	1,796
Income as % of sales	—	5.4%	5.7%	6.3%	4.1%	3.3%	9.1%	11.0%	6.6%	6.6%	4.1%
Earnings per share (P)	22.5%	0.51	0.56	0.72	0.75	0.65	1.99	3.14	3.67	4.31	3.17
Stock price – high (P)[1]	—	8.30	6.93	11.36	8.33	5.40	36.30	67.83	76.00	141.00	82.00
Stock price – low (P)[1]	—	6.74	4.77	5.96	3.60	3.63	4.17	32.83	47.83	68.50	28.50
Stock price – close (P)[1]	17.8%	6.85	5.96	8.52	3.75	4.83	35.22	47.83	73.00	78.00	30.00
P/E – high	—	16	12	16	11	8	18	22	21	33	26
P/E – low	—	13	9	8	5	6	2	10	13	16	9
Dividends per share (P)	13.8%	0.25	0.26	0.28	0.26	0.26	0.29	0.48	0.70	0.78	0.80
Book value per share (P)	17.3%	5.48	5.77	6.21	6.70	8.06	9.78	12.84	15.84	19.98	23.06

1990 Year-end:
Debt ratio: 39.7%
Return on equity: 14.7%
Cash (mil.): P4,745
Long-term debt (mil.): P8,610
No. of shares (mil.): 566
Dividends:
1990 average yield: 2.7%
1990 payout: 25.2%
Market value (mil.): $624
Sales (mil.): $1,611

Note: Unconsolidated data 1981–87 [1] Class "A" shares.

Principal exchange: Manila
Fiscal year ends: December 31

Hoover's Rating **B**

WHO

Chairman and CEO: Andrés Soriano III
VC: Benigno P. Toda, Jr.
President and COO: Francisco C. Eizmendi, Jr.
SVP, CFO, and Treasurer: Delfin C. Gonzalez, Jr.
SVP, Division Manager Human Resources: José B. Lugay
Auditors: Joaquin Cunanan & Co. (Price Waterhouse)
Employees: 35,694

WHERE

HQ: 40 San Miguel Ave., Mandaluyong, Metropolitan Manila, Philippines
Phone: 011-63-2-722-3000
Fax: 011-63-2-631-6117

San Miguel exports primarily to Australia, China, Hong Kong, Japan, Kuwait, New Zealand, Singapore, Taiwan, the US, and Vietnam.

WHAT

	1990 Sales % of total
Beverages	68
Food & Agribusiness	21
Packaging	11
Total	**100**

Beer
Gold Eagle
Lagerlite
Red Horse
San Miguel Cerveza Negra
San Miguel NAB (non-alcoholic beer)
San Miguel Pale Pilsen
San Miguel Super Dry Beer

Soft Drinks
Coca-Cola (Philippines)
Diet Coca-Cola (Philippines)
Royal Ginger Ale
Royal Rootbeer
Royal Soda Water
Royal Tonic Water
Royal Tru-Orange
Sprite (Philippines)

Wine and Spirits
Añejo Rum
Ginebra San Miguel

Packaging
Applied color labels
Closures
Corrugated carton boxes
Fuji seal shrink labels
Glass containers
Glass molds
Metal lithography
Paper and paperboard
Plastic crates
Polybags and films

Feeds and Livestock
B-Meg feed products
Magnolia poultry products
Monterey Farms products

Foods
Butter
Cheese products
Customized specialty products
Food preparations and supplements
Juices and drinks (Hi-C, Dole, and Nestea)
Magnolia frozen desserts and snacks
Margarine
Milk and milk products

Agribusiness
Coconut oil
Copra
Shrimp

Investments
Banking
Commodities
Insurance brokerage
Real estate

KEY COMPETITORS

Allied-Lyons
Anheuser-Busch
Bass
Beatrice
Bond
Borden
BSN
Carlsberg
Foster's Brewing
Guinness
Heineken
John Labatt
Kirin
Nestlé
PepsiCo
Philip Morris
Source Perrier
Stroh
TLC Beatrice

SANDOZ LTD.

OVERVIEW

Swiss pharmaceutical and chemical giant Sandoz, one of the country's "Big Three" drug companies, shares its Basel home with competitors Ciba-Geigy and Roche and, like them, does the majority of its business outside the country.

Through a strategy of focused diversification, Sandoz has established itself as a power in 6 different industries: pharmaceuticals, chemicals, nutrition, seeds, agrochemicals, and construction/environmental products. The company's pharmaceutical segment, the world's 9th largest, produces a wide range of prescription drugs to treat everything from cardiovascular disease to mental illness.

The chemicals division produces dyes, plastics, and chemicals for industrial use. The nutrition division produces dietetic and specialty foods, including Ovaltine (chocolate-flavored drinks) and the Wasa line of crispbreads.

Sandoz's seeds segment, the 2nd largest in the world, produces a full line of vegetable, flower, and grain seeds. The related agrochemicals division makes a full line of herbicides, fungicides, and other biological pest control products.

WHEN

In 1886 Alfred Kern and Edouard Sandoz established Kern und Sandoz to manufacture synthetic dyes in Basel. Kern died in 1893, and 2 years later the enterprise became a limited company with Sandoz as chairman.

The company expanded rapidly by introducing new dyes and gaining access to overseas markets. After weathering several difficult years at the beginning of the 20th century, Sandoz grew through the end of WWI, when Germany's capitulation opened up the world chemical industry. To better compete in the world market, Sandoz joined with Basel neighbors Ciba and Geigy (which combined in 1970 to become Ciba-Geigy) to form the Basel AG cartel.

In the 1920s, a lean decade for the Swiss cartel, the company diversified into chemicals needed by the paper, textile, leather, and agricultural industries. Sandoz also established a pharmaceuticals division under Dr. Arthur Stoll, who created a way to commercially develop ergotamine, an alkaloid that would provide the basis for many of the company's pharmaceuticals.

During WWII Sandoz bought a Swiss coal mine to provide fuel for its operations, allowing the company to run unhindered during the war. After WWII Sandoz established operations in important global markets, went its own way when the Basel AG was dissolved in 1951, and by 1964 had annual sales of SF1 billion. During the postwar period the company's pharmaceutical division made significant inroads in developing psychoactive drugs, including an experimental drug called Delysid (commonly known as LSD).

In 1967 Sandoz entered the nutrition field by purchasing the Berne-based WANDER group of companies (dietetic products). In 1976 the company diversified into seeds, buying Minneapolis-based Northrup, King & Company and later Zaadunie B. V. (a Netherlands seed company, 1980). During the 1980s the company continued its rapid diversification, adding the WASA Group (Swedish crispbread, 1982) and buying Master Builders from Martin Marietta (construction chemicals, 1985).

Catastrophe marred the company's 100th anniversary in 1986 when a warehouse fire spilled tons of chemicals into the Rhine, killing hundreds of thousands of fish and contaminating the water all the way to the North Sea. In 1990 the company won FDA approval to market Clozaril, a drug used for treating schizophrenia, in the US. The company's controversial marketing ploy of requiring expensive blood monitoring of patients taking Clozaril was discontinued in 1991.

HOW MUCH

\$=SF1.27 (Dec. 31, 1990)	9-Year Growth	1981	1982	1983	1984	1985	1986	1987	1988	1989	1990
Sales (SF mil.)	8.9%	5,766	6,053	6,546	7,434	8,453	8,361	8,979	10,151	12,497	12,367
Net income (SF mil.)	17.5%	227	273	320	411	529	541	627	761	958	967
Income as % of sales	—	3.9%	4.5%	4.9%	5.5%	6.3%	6.5%	7.0%	7.5%	7.7%	7.2%
Earnings per share (SF)	14.5%	206	247	285	365	442	401	453	549	691	698
Stock price – high (SF)[1]	—	4,625	4,600	7,650	7,600	10,950	13,000	15,800	12,925	13,500	12,400
Stock price – low (SF)[1]	—	3,350	3,850	4,500	6,450	7,000	9,900	9,800	9,100	9,600	8,500
Stock price – close (SF)[1]	9.1%	4,100	4,525	7,300	7,000	10,950	11,000	11,800	9,575	11,525	9,000
P/E – high	—	22	19	27	21	25	32	35	24	20	18
P/E – low	—	16	16	16	18	16	25	22	17	14	12
Dividends per share (SF)	9.7%	65.00	72.50	80.00	90.00	100.00	105.00	110.00	120.00	150.00	150.00
Book value per share (SF)	5.5%	3,104	3,289	3,402	3,711	3,849	3,330	4,040	4,127	4,507	5,038

1990 Year-end:
Debt ratio: 8.3%
Return on equity: 14.6%
Cash (mil.): SF1,451
Long-term debt (mil.): SF663
No. of shares (thou.): 1,386
Dividends:
1990 average yield: 1.7%
1990 payout: 21.5%
Market value (mil.): \$9,822
Sales (mil.): \$10,525

Stock Price History High/Low 1981–90

16,000 14,000 12,000 10,000 8,000 6,000 4,000 2,000 0

[1] Bearer shares

Principal exchanges: Basel, Zurich, Geneva

Fiscal year ends: December 31

WHO

Chairman and CEO: Marc Moret
VC: Hans Letsch
VC: Pierre Languetin
Senior Financial Officer: Victor Bischoff
Senior Personnel Officer: Franz Joerg Juengling
Auditors: Swiss Auditing and Fiduciary Company
Employees: 52,640

WHERE

HQ: CH-4002, Lichtstrasse 35, Basel, Switzerland
Phone: 011-41-61-324-11-11
Fax: 011-41-61-324-80-01
US HQ: Sandoz Corp., 608 Fifth Ave., New York, NY 10020
US Phone: 212-307-1122
US Fax: 212-246-0185

The company has operations in 54 countries.

	1990 Sales	
	SF mil.	% of total
Europe	5,689	46
US & Canada	3,587	29
Asia	2,102	17
Latin America	618	5
Africa & Australia	371	3
Total	**12,367**	**100**

WHAT

	1990 Sales	
	SF mil.	% of total
Chemicals	2,226	18
Pharmaceuticals	5,689	46
Agro	1,113	9
Seeds	989	8
Nutrition	1,361	11
Construction & environment	989	8
Total	**12,367**	**100**

MBT Holding Ltd.
Concrete admixtures
Construction products
Environmental engineering and consulting

Sandoz Agro Ltd.
Fungicides
Herbicides
Insecticides

Sandoz Chemicals Ltd.
Anticorrosion chemicals
Leather
Paper
Pigments/additives
Textile chemicals
Textile dyes

Sandoz Nutrition Ltd.
Baked goods
Dietetic foods
Malt and cocoa products
Sports foods
Weight reduction products

Sandoz Pharma Ltd.
Clozaril (antischizophrenic)
Dynacirc (antihypertensive)
Lamisil (antifungal)
Miacalcic (calcitonin)
Pamelor (antidepressant)
Sandimmun (immunosuppressant)
Sandoglobulin (gammaglobulin)
Sandostatin (gastrointestinal)
Visken (cardiovascular)
Zaditen (asthma and allergy)

Sandoz Seeds Ltd.
Corn
Flowers
Forestry plants
Horticulture seeds
Industrial seeds
Oil seeds
Sorghum
Vegetables

KEY COMPETITORS

Agriculture companies
Chemical companies
Food companies
Pharmaceutical companies

SCANDINAVIAN AIRLINES SYSTEM

OVERVIEW

The Scandinavian Airlines System, or SAS, is an airline consortium, representing Denmark, Norway, and Sweden. It is owned by Det Danske Luftfartselskab (Danish Airlines, DDL), Det Norske Luftfartselskap (Norwegian Airlines, DNL), and AB Aerotransport (Swedish Airlines, ABA), which are, in turn, equally owned by their respective governments and the public.

Ranked 12th in the world in terms of 1990 sales, SAS is building a reputation as "The Businessman's Airline," offering quality worldwide service geared toward the frequent business traveler. SAS is developing a worldwide network of gateway cities and has affiliated itself with airlines that have traditionally served those cities; for instance, a marketing agreement with Thai Airways International brings passengers into the SAS network at Bangkok.

SAS offers regional airline service through SAS Commuter. It is one of 4 owners of the European computer reservation system Amadeus and operates Europe's largest airline catering service (the world's 3rd largest). SAS offers vacation tour packages and charters (Scanair and Spanair), operates its own hotel chains (SAS International Hotels and Sunwing), and owns an interest in Inter-Continental Hotels.

WHEN

Although SAS wasn't established until after WWII, the national airlines of Sweden (ABA), Norway (DNL), and Denmark (DDL) first met in 1938 to negotiate joint service to New York. The plan was delayed by the war but kept alive in Sweden, where banker Marcus Wallenberg founded Svensk Interkontinental Luftrafik (SILA), a private airline that later replaced ABA as Sweden's international carrier (1943). With SILA's financial backing, the yet-to-be-formed SAS obtained the necessary landing concessions to open a Stockholm–New York air route (1945). SAS was formed in 1946, with DDL and DNL each owning 2/7 and SILA/ABA owning 3/7.

After opening service to South America (Buenos Aires, 1946), Southeast Asia (Bangkok, 1949), and Africa (Johannesburg, 1953), SAS inaugurated the world's first commercial polar route, from Copenhagen to Los Angeles, in 1954. SAS bought 50% of the Swedish domestic airline Linjeflyg in 1957 (sold in 1990) and later formed the charter airline Scanair (1961) and the Danish domestic airline Danair (through a joint venture, 1971).

Deregulation of America's airlines (1978) signaled the demise of protectionist attitudes that had traditionally shielded the world's airlines from competition. SAS, born and raised in such a protected environment (and burdened by rising fuel costs), seemed ill-equipped to adapt, reporting its first loss in 18 years in 1980. Jan Carlzon, former head of Linjeflyg, became SAS's president in 1981. By targeting businessmen as the airline's most stable market and substituting an economy-rate business class for first-class service on European flights, Carlzon had turned SAS's losses into profits by the end of 1982.

Carlzon's latest strategy has been to ally SAS with other airlines through marketing and ownership agreements. Although SAS lost a bid for British Caledonian to British Airways in 1988, it went on to buy about 25% of Airlines of Britain Holdings, gaining a foothold at London's Heathrow airport. Another purchase in 1988 brought SAS nearly 10% of Continental Airlines Holdings (raised to 16.8% in 1990). In 1989 SAS signed agreements with Swissair, Finnair, All Nippon Airways, LanChile, and Canadian Airlines International, providing route coordination and hub-sharing, and bought 40% of Saison Overseas Holdings, owner of the Inter-Continental Hotels chain. Continental Airlines's 1990 bankruptcy filing prompted SAS to write down its 16.8% interest in that airline by SEK780 million. To cut costs, SAS plans to lay off up to 16% of its work force by year-end 1992.

HOW MUCH

$=SEK5.63 (Dec. 31, 1990)	9-Year Growth	1981	1982	1983	1984	1985	1986	1987[1]	1988	1989	1990
Sales (SEK mil.)	13.5%	10,172	12,807	15,973	18,005	19,790	21,585	24,288	27,556	28,786	31,883
Pretax income (SEK mil.)	—	(102)	291	497	829	892	1,322	1,445	3,262	1,977	(65)
Income as % of sales	—	(1.0%)	2.3%	3.1%	4.6%	4.5%	6.1%	5.9%	11.8%	6.9%	(0.2%)
Passengers (thou.)	6.6%	8,413	8,861	9,222	10,066	10,735	11,708	12,662	13,341	14,005	14,962
Available seat km (mil.)	4.1%	17,761	17,118	17,037	17,395	17,818	18,849	19,019	20,941	23,320	25,475
Rev. passenger km (mil.)	4.8%	10,817	10,879	11,159	11,681	11,966	12,471	13,207	14,027	15,229	16,493
Passenger load factor	—	60.9%	63.6%	65.5%	67.2%	67.2%	66.2%	69.4%	67.0%	65.3%	64.7%
Size of fleet	5.0%	85	86	86	85	87	104	102	109	119	132
Employees	6.0%	24,160	25,368	26,657	28,526	29,730	31,770	34,900	36,150	39,060	40,830

1990 Year-end:
Debt ratio: 60.4%
Cash (mil.): SEK11,388
Current ratio: 1.39
Long-term debt (mil.): SEK16,938
Sales (mil.): $5,663

Pretax Income (SEK mil.) 1981–90

[1] 15-month accounting year

Consortium
Fiscal year ends: December 31

WHO

Chairman: Tage Andersen, age 64
President and CEO: Jan Carlzon, age 50
Deputy President: Helge Lindberg
SVP and CFO: Anders Claesson
EVP and COO, SAS Airline: Kjell Fredheim
VP Staff Relations, SAS Airline: Karl Miiro
Auditors: KPMG; DRT International
Employees: 40,830

WHERE

HQ: S-161 87 Stockholm, Sweden
Phone: 011-46-8-797-00-00
Fax: 011-46-8-85-82-87
US HQ: Scandinavian Airlines System of North America, Inc., 9 Polito Ave., Lyndhurst, NJ 07071
US Phone: 201-896-3600
US Fax: 201-896-3725
Reservations: 800-221-2350

SAS serves 85 cities worldwide.

WHAT

	1990 Sales	
	SEK mil.	% of total
Airline activities		
Passengers	16,476	49
Freight & mail	1,356	4
Other	4,567	13
Non-airline activities	11,612	34
Adjustments	(2,128)	—
Total	**31,883**	**100**

SAS Consortium
SAS Airline (global airline services)
SAS Commuter (regional airline services)
SAS Trading (travel-related retail sales, wholesale trade, and media production)
SAS Finance (financial services)

Major Subsidiaries and Affiliates
Airlines of Britain Holdings PLC (ABH), Derby (24.9%, owns British Midland, Loganair, and Manx Airlines)
Danair A/S, Copenhagen (57%, Danish airline)
Diners Club Nordic A/S (charge card)
Grønlandsfly A/S, Godthåb (37.5%, Greenland's domestic airline)
LanChile S.A. (35%, South American airline)
Polygon Insurance Co. Ltd., Guernsey (33%)
SAS International Hotels A/S
Saison Holdings B.V. (40%, owns Inter-Continental Hotels)
SAS Leisure AB (travel-related services)
Scanair, Sweden (air charters)
Spanair S.A., Madrid (49%, air charters)
Sunwing (hotel chain)
SAS Service Partner A/S (food services)

Computer Reservation System
Amadeus (25%)

Flight Equipment	No.	Orders
Boeing 767	12	6
DC-10	4	—
DC-9	57	—
MD-80 derivatives	39	34
Fokker 50	20	2
Total	**132**	**42**

KEY COMPETITORS

AMR	Lufthansa	Swire Pacific
British Airways	NWA	TWA
Delta	Pan Am	UAL
JAL	Qantas	Hotels and caterers
KLM	Singapore Airlines	

THE SEAGRAM COMPANY LTD.

OVERVIEW

Montreal-based Seagram is a leading producer and distributor of spirits, wine, wine coolers, fruit juices, and soft drinks, with such widely recognized names as 7 Crown, Crown Royal, and V.O. whiskeys, and Chivas Regal scotch, Myers's rum, Martell cognac, and Tropicana fruit juices. In addition, the company owns approximately 24.5% of Du Pont, which accounts for over 70% of Seagram's earnings. Although Seagram is headquartered in Quebec, 45% of its sales come from the US.

Seagram's wine operations (with an inventory of approximately 50 million gallons) produce and market over 250 brands and control 42% of the US cooler market. Tropicana, which is produced by the company's fruit juice segment, is the leading nonconcentrate orange juice in the US.

The Bronfman family (descendants of Sam Bronfman, the company's founder) collectively own approximately 38% of the total outstanding shares.

NYSE symbol: VO
Fiscal year ends: January 31

Hoover's Rating **A-**

WHO

Chairman and CEO: Edgar M. Bronfman, age 61, $1,688,215 pay
Co-Chairman: Charles R. Bronfman, age 59, $895,000 pay
President and COO: Edgar Bronfman, Jr., age 35, $1,180,176 pay
EVP Finance: Richard K. Goeltz, age 48
VP Human Resources: Jeananne K. Hauswald
Auditors: Price Waterhouse
Employees: 17,700

WHEN

In 1916 Sam Bronfman bought the Bonaventure Liquor Store Company in Montreal and started selling liquor by mail order (the only legal way during Canadian Prohibition, which lasted from 1918 until the early 1920s). In 1924, with the help of his brother Allan, Bronfman opened the first family distillery in neighboring La Salle and took the name Distillers Corporation Limited. Bronfman, later known as "Mr. Sam," purchased the larger Joseph E. Seagram & Sons in 1928, went public, and changed his company name to Distillers Corporation–Seagrams Limited.

During the 1920s Bronfman established a lucrative bootlegging operation that smuggled whiskey by land and sea into the "dry" United States. The company may have accounted for half of the illegal liquor crossing the border.

In 1928 Bronfman, expecting the end of Prohibition in the US, began stockpiling whiskey. When Prohibition ended in 1933, Bronfman had the world's largest supply of aged rye and sour mash whiskeys. To further meet US demand, he also purchased 3 US distilleries in quick succession in the 1930s.

Bootlegging had given whiskey a harsh image, which Bronfman sought to change by introducing his smooth, blended Seagram's 7 Crown in 1934. In 1939, after blending over 600 whiskey samples, Bronfman created Crown Royal in honor of the visit of King George VI and Queen Elizabeth to Canada.

During the 1940s Seagram expanded its liquor line. In 1942 the company formed a partnership with Fromm and Sichel to buy Paul Masson (sold in 1987) and shortly thereafter purchased distilleries in the West Indies that would later produce the Captain Morgan and Myers's brand rums. After WWII it acquired Mumm and Perrier-Jouët (champagne), Barton & Guestier and Augier Frères (wine), and Chivas Brothers (scotch).

Edgar Bronfman succeeded his father as company president in 1957, expanding the company's wine and spirits lines substantially.

Beginning in the late 1950s the Bronfman family accumulated substantial cash and diversified into everything from Israeli supermarkets to Texas gas fields. The company adopted its present name in 1975 and in 1980 acquired a major interest in Du Pont when Du Pont bought Seagram's interest in Conoco. Seagram introduced its Golden Wine Cooler in 1986 and in 1988 acquired Martell SA (cognac) and Tropicana (fruit juices). In 1989 the company bought American Natural Beverages (Soho Natural Soda, put up for sale in 1991).

In 1990 Seagram completed the purchase of Premium beverages (Seagram's mixers) and in 1991 realigned its businesses into spirits and nonspirits groups (they had previously been organized geographically). That same year Tropicana edged out Coca-Cola's Minute Maid for the #1 spot in the US orange juice market, with a 22.5% share.

WHERE

HQ: 1430 Peel St., Montreal, Quebec H3A 1S9, Canada
Phone: 514-849-5271
Fax: 514-933-5390 (Public Relations)

Seagram sells its products in over 150 countries.

	1990 Sales		1990 Operating Income	
	$ mil.	% of total	$ mil.	% of total
Canada	185	3	117	17
Europe	2,312	38	418	59
US	2,779	45	67	9
Other countries	851	14	106	15
Adjustments	(1,096)	—	—	—
Total	**5,031**	**100**	**708**	**100**

WHAT

	1990 Sales		1990 Operating Income	
	$ mil.	% of total	$ mil.	% of total
Spirits & wines	4,847	79	612	85
Fruit juices, coolers & mixers	1,280	21	110	15
Adjustments	(1,096)	—	(14)	—
Total	**5,031**	**100**	**708**	**100**

Major Brand Names and Agencies

Whiskeys
Blender's Pride (Latin America)
Boston Club (Japan)
Calvert Extra
Chivas Regal
Crown Royal
Four Roses
Glen Grant
Glenlivet
Kessler
Lord Calvert
Passport
Robert Brown (Japan)
Royal Salute
Seagram's "83"
Seagram's Five Star
Seagram's 7 Crown
Seagram's V.O.

Other Spirits
Boodles (gin)
Cacique (rum)
Captain Morgan (rum)
Janneau (armagnacs)
Leroux (cordials)
Martell (cognacs)
Montilla (rum)
Myers's (rum)
Seagram's Extra Dry (gin)
Wolfschmidt (vodka)

Wines and Champagnes
Barton & Guestier
Charles Krug Winery
Heidsieck-Monopole
Matheus Müller
C.K. Mondavi
Monterey Vineyard
Mumm
Mumm Cuvée Napa
Perrier-Jouët
Saltram
Sandeman
Seagram's Wine Coolers
Sterling

Fruit Juices and Mixers
Seagram's Mixers
Tropicana

HOW MUCH

	9-Year Growth	1981	1982	1983	1984	1985	1986	1987	1988	1989	1990
Sales ($ mil.)	12.2%	1,790	1,916	1,781	2,006	2,114	2,412	2,799	3,935	4,508	5,031
Net income ($ mil.)	9.6%	330	279	318	384	319	423	521	589	711	756
Income as % of sales	—	18.5%	14.6%	17.8%	19.1%	15.1%	17.6%	18.6%	15.0%	15.8%	15.0%
Earnings per share ($)	11.0%	3.14	2.95	3.53	4.05	3.34	4.30	5.26	6.12	7.37	8.03
Stock price – high ($)	—	20.50	24.92	40.00	40.38	48.75	65.13	82.38	61.88	91.50	94.00
Stock price – low ($)	—	15.08	14.54	24.04	30.00	37.38	42.75	49.00	50.00	60.25	72.25
Stock price – close ($)	18.4%	19.21	24.58	36.25	40.25	48.00	60.75	54.50	61.38	91.50	88.00
P/E – high	—	7	8	11	10	15	15	16	10	12	12
P/E – low	—	5	5	7	7	11	10	9	8	8	9
Dividends per share ($)	17.3%	0.44	0.60	0.68	0.80	0.80	0.95	1.05	1.18	1.40	1.85
Book value per share ($)	10.1%	26.59	27.94	30.96	33.50	37.31	41.42	47.03	50.65	56.12	63.49

1990 Year-end:
Debt ratio: 25.5%
Return on equity: 13.4%
Cash (mil.): $131
Current ratio: 1.27
Long-term debt (mil.): $2,038
No. of shares (mil.): 94
Dividends:
1990 average yield: 2.1%
1990 payout: 23.0%
Market value (mil.): $8,249

Stock Price History High/Low 1981–90

KEY COMPETITORS

Allied-Lyons
American Brands
Anheuser-Busch
Brown-Forman
BSN
Cadbury Schweppes
Coca-Cola
Gallo
Grand Metropolitan
Guinness
Kirin
LVMH
PepsiCo
Procter & Gamble

SHARP CORPORATION

OVERVIEW

Headquartered in Osaka, Sharp is an electronics powerhouse producing a wide range of products, including audio and video equipment, electronic diaries, computers, fax machines (#1 in the US), and electronic components.

Although not as large as such rivals as Hitachi and Matsushita, Sharp has muscled its way into global domination in several markets, including electroluminescent displays, liquid crystal displays (LCDs), laser diodes, and manufacturer-programmable memory chips.

Since its development of the mechanical pencil in 1915, Sharp has developed a reputation for consistent innovation and has pioneered such important electronic inventions as desktop calculators, LCD calculators, high-definition LCD TVs, and color fax machines. In 1991 the company spent approximately ¥90 billion (6.7% of sales) on R&D.

Sharp, which experienced its best year ever in 1990, is investing heavily in the future. Demand for its LCD technology products is expected to skyrocket in the coming decade, as LCDs continue to displace the older cathode-ray tubes used in TVs and computer monitors. Already the leading producer of flat-panel computer screens, the company announced in 1991 that it would begin producing some of the screens in the US.

WHEN

In 1912 Tokuji Hayakawa established a metal works in Tokyo to manufacture a type of belt buckle he had designed. Three years later he invented the first mechanical pencil, which he named the Ever-Sharp. The pencil was a commercial success and would eventually become the namesake of the company.

In 1923 an earthquake leveled much of Tokyo, including Hayakawa's business. Undaunted, Hayakawa moved to Osaka, built a new facility (which he financed by selling the rights to his pencil), and in 1925 introduced Japan's first crystal radio sets. Four years later he introduced a vacuum tube radio. In 1935 the company was incorporated.

After WWII the company developed an experimental TV, which it started to mass-produce in 1953 when Japan aired its first television broadcasts. Likewise Sharp was ready with color TVs when Japan initiated color broadcasts in 1960. During the 1960s the company saw tremendous growth and innovation, launching mass-produced microwave ovens (1962); mass-produced solar cells (1963); the first electronic, desktop all-transistor-diode calculator (1964); and the first gallium arsenide light emitting diode (LED, 1969). The company opened its first US office in 1962.

In 1970 Sharp built a factory to manufacture its own microchips and continued to produce innovative electronic products, such as the first electronic calculator with a liquid crystal display (1973), solar-powered calculators (1976), and the first credit-card-sized calculator (1979).

In the early 1980s the company began producing VCRs and in 1984 released its color copier. That same year Sharp introduced a fax machine and concentrated its marketing efforts toward small businesses (while its competitors were scrambling for large corporate accounts). The strategy paid off handsomely. By 1989 the explosion of fax machines in the low end of the market had propelled Sharp to the #1 spot in the US.

By the late 1980s Sharp was ready to blitz the market with a new line of creative products, including a high-definition LCD color TV (1987), a notebook-sized personal computer (1988), a refrigerator with a door that opens both ways (1989), and an LCD projector capable of projecting TV or video pictures onto a large screen (1989). In 1990 the company released the first desktop color fax machine.

HOW MUCH

$=¥135 (Dec. 31, 1990)	9-Year Growth	1981[1]	1982	1983	1984	1985	1986	1987	1988	1989	1990
Sales (¥ bil.)	11.6%	501	732	898	1,017	1,167	1,149	1,038	1,078	1,238	1,345
Net income (¥ bil.)	11.0%	16	29	30	38	40	36	21	20	29	42
Income as % of sales	—	3.3%	4.0%	3.3%	3.7%	3.4%	3.1%	2.0%	1.9%	2.4%	3.1%
Earnings per share (¥)	—	—	*38*	*39*	*48*	*49*	*44*	*25*	*23*	*31*	*42*
Stock price – high (¥)	—	902	1,080	1,348	1,286	1,027	1,071	1,223	1,350	1,880	1,980
Stock price – low (¥)	—	576	549	946	866	656	723	728	901	1,110	1,070
Stock price – close (¥)	5.2%	737	1,045	1,250	982	817	982	921	1,120	1,860	1,160
P/E – high	—	—	28	35	27	21	24	49	58	61	48
P/E – low	—	—	14	25	18	13	17	29	38	36	26
Dividends per share (¥)	5.7%	6.70	7.37	8.48	8.93	9.82	9.82	9.82	11.00	11.00	11.00
Book value per share (¥)	12.8%	220	290	330	379	437	462	473	526	563	650

1990 Year-end:
Debt ratio: 26.6%
Return on equity: 6.8%
Cash (bil.): ¥715
Long-term debt (bil.): ¥248
No. of shares (mil.): 1,054
Dividends:
1990 average yield: 0.9%
1990 payout: 26.5%
Market value (mil.): $9,057
Sales (mil.): $9,963

Stock Price History High/Low 1981–90

[1] Unconsolidated data

OTC symbol: SHCAY (ADR)
Fiscal year ends: March 31

WHO

President: Haruo Tsuji
SEVP: Taizo Katsura
SEVP: Atsushi Asada
Auditors: Arthur Andersen & Co.
Employees: 34,017

WHERE

HQ: 22-22 Nagaike-cho, Abeno-ku, Osaka 545, Japan
Phone: 011-81-6-621-1221
Fax: 011-81-6-628-1667
US HQ: Sharp Electronics Corporation, Sharp Plaza, Mahwah, NJ 07430-2135
US Phone: 201-529-8200
US Fax: 201-529-8413

The company operates 33 manufacturing facilities in 26 countries.

	1990 Sales % of total
Japan	50
Overseas	50
Total	**100**

WHAT

	1990 Sales ¥ bil.	% of total
Electronic equipment	377	28
Audio equipment	134	10
Consumer electronics	229	17
Information equipment & electronic parts	605	45
Total	**1,345**	**100**

Products
Air conditioning equipment
Answering systems
Calculators
Camcorders
Cash registers
Cassette recorders
Computers
Copiers
Electronic diaries
Fax machines
Heaters
Home appliances
Integrated circuits
Medical equipment
Optoelectric products
Printers
Projectors
Stereos
Tape decks
Telephones
TVs
Typewriters
VCRs
Video projectors
Videotapes
Watches

KEY COMPETITORS

Canon
Casio
Compaq
Electrolux
Fuji Photo
Fujitsu
GEC
General Electric
Harris
Hitachi
Hyundai
Lucky-Goldstar
Machines Bull
Matsushita
Maytag
Minolta
Mitsubishi
Motorola
NEC
Oki
Olivetti
Philips
Pioneer
Premark
Raytheon
Samsung
Siemens
Sony
Thomson SA
Thorn EMI
Toshiba
Whirlpool
Xerox
Yamaha
Zenith

SIEMENS AG

OVERVIEW

Munich-based Siemens is Germany's 3rd largest public company (after Daimler-Benz and Volkswagen) and is the European leader in electronics. Since joining forces with Nixdorf (to form 78%-owned Siemens Nixdorf) in 1990, it has become the 2nd largest computer company in Europe after IBM. Other businesses include Siemens Plessey (defense electronics), Osram (lighting), 50% of Rolm (telecommunications), 50% of Bosch-Siemens Hausgeräte (appliances), and 6.8% of Fuji Electric (electric machinery).

The company's goal is to focus on business areas in which it can attain leadership. It is investing heavily in semiconductor technology to catch up with chip-making competitors, and in 1990 Siemens announced joint development of 64-megabit DRAM with IBM. Siemens is building a strong market position in eastern Germany by investing over DM1 billion in local production facilities.

Despite spending heavily on R&D (11% of sales) and acquisitions, Siemens still has over $12 billion in cash.

WHEN

In 1847 Werner von Siemens, an electrical engineer, teamed with a craftsman, Johann Halske, to make telegraphs as Siemens & Halske in Germany. Although Halske left the firm 20 years later, the company name was not shortened to Siemens until 1966. The firm's first major project linked Berlin and Frankfurt with the first long-distance telegraph system in Europe (1848). Siemens continued to string telegraph wires across Europe and in 1870 completed the 6,600-mile India Line running from London to Calcutta. The company manufactured the first transatlantic cable, which connected Ireland to the US in 1874.

Siemens built Europe's first electric power transmission system (1876), the world's first electrified railway (1879), and one of the first elevators (1880). As a result of Werner von Siemens's discussions with Thomas Edison (1881), the company received a license to manufacture incandescent lights. Disagreement between the 2 inventors contributed to the different electrical voltage standards employed by North America (110 volts) and Europe (220 volts). In 1896 the company patented the world's first X-ray tube and completed the first European subway, in Budapest.

Despite losses in WWI the company rebounded, forming Osram, a German light bulb cartel, with AEG and Auer (1919) and entering into a venture with Furukawa Electric called Fuji Electric (1923). Siemens developed radios and traffic lights in the 1920s and began production of electron microscopes in 1939.

Siemens suffered heavy losses in WWII but staged a quick recovery, developing silicates for semiconductors, data processing equipment, and the world's first implantable pacemaker in the 1950s. Siemens formed joint ventures with Bosch (Bosch-Siemens Hausgeräte, appliances, 1967) and AEG (Kraftwerk Union, nuclear power, 1969), among others. The company profited from Germany's protectionist telecommunications policies, but its computer ventures with RCA and Philips in the 1960s and 1970s were disappointing.

In 1981 Karlheinz Kaske became the company's first CEO from outside the Siemens family. Under his direction Siemens entered into joint ventures with Philips (DRAM), Intel (computers), and Advanced Micro Devices (telecommunication chips) and bought Bendix Electronics (US, 1988), Rolm (PBXs, US, 1989), and the telecommunications businesses of Plessey (UK, 1989). In 1990 Siemens and ailing German computer maker Nixdorf combined their computer businesses, forming Siemens Nixdorf. That year Siemens became North America's 3rd largest telecommunications supplier by combining its US telecommunications businesses with Stromberg-Carlson (unit of GEC Plessey Telecommunications, UK).

HOW MUCH

$=DM1.49 (Dec. 31, 1990)	9-Year Growth	1981	1982	1983	1984	1985	1986	1987	1988	1989	1990
Sales (DM mil.)	6.9%	34,561	40,106	39,471	45,819	54,616	47,023	51,431	59,374	61,128	63,185
Net income (DM mil.)	14.7%	449	662	743	1,049	1,502	1,455	1,217	1,317	1,473	1,547
Income as % of sales	—	1.3%	1.7%	1.9%	2.3%	2.8%	3.1%	2.4%	2.2%	4.7%	2.4%
Earnings per share (DM)	11.8%	*11*	*17*	*17*	*24*	*32*	*31*	*25*	*27*	*30*	*30*
Stock price – high (DM)	—	297	288	352	385	935	920	790	569	843	816
Stock price – low (DM)	—	251	245	259	302	384	724	387	357	502	512
Stock price – close (DM)	9.3%	263	274	349	383	925	822	388	563	843	585
P/E – high	—	27	17	21	16	29	30	32	21	28	27
P/E – low	—	23	14	15	13	12	23	15	13	17	17
Dividends per share (DM)[1]	5.1%	8.0	8.0	8.0	8.0	10.0	12.0	12.0	11.0	11.0	13.0
Book value per share (DM)	4.3%	221	241	244	263	280	317	324	344	358	322

1990 Year-end:
Debt ratio: 8.8%
Return on equity: 1.7%
Cash (mil.): DM19,347
Long-term debt (mil.): DM1,588
No. of shares (mil.): 51
Dividends:
1990 average yield: 2.2%
1990 payout: 41.7%
Market value (mil.): $20,023
Sales (mil.): $42,406

[1] Not including rights offering

OTC symbol: SMAWY (ADR)
Fiscal year ends: September 30

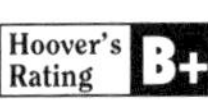

WHO

Chairman: Heribald Närger
President and CEO: Karlheinz Kaske
Corporate Finance: Karl-Hermann Baumann
Corporate Personnel: Gerhard Kühne
Auditors: KPMG Deutsche Treuhand-Gesellschaft AG; Wirtschaftsprüfungsgesellschaft
Employees: 373,000

WHERE

HQ: Siemens AG Wittelsbacherplatz 2, D-8000 Munich 2, Germany
Phone: 011-49-89-234-0
Fax: 011-49-89-234-4242
US HQ: Siemens Corp., 1301 Ave. of the Americas, New York, NY 10019
US Phone: 212-258-4000
US Fax: 212-258-4370

Siemens has operations worldwide.

	1990 Sales	
	DM mil.	% of total
Germany	44,504	58
Other Europe	19,532	26
North America	7,543	10
Other countries	4,870	6
Adjustments	(13,264)	—
Total	**63,185**	**100**

WHAT

	1990 Sales	
	DM mil.	% of total
Power generation	5,812	8
Power trans. & distrib.	4,950	7
Industrial & building systems	7,577	11
Drives & standard products	6,279	9
Automation	5,548	8
Data & information systems	7,690	11
Communications systems	13,891	19
Defense electronics	1,073	1
Transportation systems	1,158	1
Automotive systems	1,819	2
Medical engineering	6,580	9
Semiconductors	1,983	3
Other products & services	7,658	11
Adjustments	(8,833)	—
Total	**63,185**	**100**

Major Product Areas and Subsidiaries
Appliances (50%, Bosch-Siemens Hausgeräte, joint venture with Robert Bosch)
Automotive electronics
Defense electronics (Siemens Plessey)
Electrical motors and automation
Electronic components and semiconductors
Fiber optics (50%, Siecor, joint venture with Corning)
Imaging (Linotype-Hell)
Information processing (78%, Siemens Nixdorf)
Lighting (Osram)
Medical instrumentation
Nuclear and non-nuclear power (KWU)
Power transmission
Telecommunications

KEY COMPETITORS

ABB
Alcatel Alsthom
Amdahl
AT&T
Bayer
BCE
Cooper Industries
Eastman Kodak
Ericsson
Fujitsu
GEC
General Electric
Hitachi
IBM
Matsushita
NEC
Oki
Philips
Rolls-Royce
Samsung
Sharp
Thomson SA
Toshiba

SINGAPORE AIRLINES LTD.

OVERVIEW

Singapore Airlines (SIA), the 54% state-owned flag carrier of Singapore, is the most modern and best run airline in the world's fastest growing travel market — Asia and the Pacific. It is the world's 5th largest airline in international passenger traffic and has achieved profitability paralleled by none. Given rave reviews by passengers and travel agents alike, SIA is rated by the *Zagat Airline Survey* as the world's #1 airline for customer service. First-class passengers are treated to freshly cooked meals and Dom Pérignon, and the airline is famous for its sarong-clad and gracious Singapore Girls.

The airline battles soaring fuel costs with one of the industry's youngest and most fuel-efficient fleets. Its planes average about 5 years of age, and to keep its fleet young, SIA placed an $8.6 billion order for new planes in 1990. The company participates in the Abacus computer reservation system (which it owns with 5 other Asian airlines) and employs 1 in every 79 workers in Singapore, making it the city-state's biggest private employer.

WHEN

Singapore Airlines was formed as Malayan Airways in 1937 but did not begin scheduled service until 1947, when it was revived by the Mansfield & Co. shipping line to link Singapore with other Malayan cities. The airline added service to Vietnam and the Indonesian islands of Sumatra and Java by 1951, opening routes to Borneo, Brunei, Thailand, and Burma by 1958.

Meanwhile, British Overseas Airways Corporation (BOAC, predecessor of British Airways) bought 10% of Malayan (1948), raising its stake to 30% in 1959. That year Australia's flag carrier, Qantas, bought 30% of Malayan. In 1962 the governments of Singapore, Malaya, Sarawak, and Sabah merged to form Malaysia, sparking Malayan to change its name to Malaysian Airways. Singapore then seceded from the federation (1965) but joined Malaysia to buy control of the airline from BOAC and Qantas (1966), changing its name to Malaysia-Singapore Airlines (1967).

The airline extended service to Melbourne, Bombay, Rome, and London (1971) and then to Osaka, Athens, Zurich, and Frankfurt (1972). But disagreements about the company's direction and objectives led Malaysia and Singapore to dissolve it in 1972 in favor of 2 separate national airlines. The company's routes were divided, with the domestic network going to the Malaysian Airline System and international routes going to Singapore Airlines (SIA). Joe Pillay (part of Singapore's Ministry of Finance) became SIA's first chairman. Ownership was divided chiefly between the government (82%) and the airline's employees (17%).

By 1974 SIA was serving 25 cities in 20 countries, adding flights to Auckland and Paris in 1976, Tehran and Copenhagen in 1977, and San Francisco, its first US destination, in 1978. The airline was famous for its quality service by the mid-1970s, and its glamorous hostesses, known as Singapore Girls, attracted about 3 million passengers a year.

In 1985 the government reduced its holding in SIA to 63% and currently maintains a 54% stake through Temasek Holdings. SIA joined Cathay Pacific and Thai International in 1988 to form Abacus, a computer reservation system for Asia- and Pacific-based carriers, and formed an alliance with Delta Air Lines and Swissair in 1989, creating a coordinated route network of 288 cities in 82 countries. Each partner offered the others strength in a major world market: Delta in the US, Swissair in Europe, and SIA in the Pacific. In addition, Delta bought a 2.8% stake in SIA; SIA reciprocated, buying 4.7% of Delta in 1990. Swissair and SIA came to a similar agreement in 1991, with SIA buying 2.8% of Swissair and Swissair buying 0.6% of SIA.

HOW MUCH

$=S$1.74 (Dec. 31, 1990)	8-Year Growth	1981	1982	1983	1984	1985	1986	1987	1988	1989	1990
Sales (S$ mil.)	8.2%	—	2,707	2,814	2,943	3,166	3,175	3,483	4,011	4,566	5,093
Net income (S$ mil.)	44.8%	—	62	79	116	180	285	451	603	985	1,201
Income as % of sales	—	—	2.3%	2.8%	3.9%	5.7%	9.0%	12.9%	15.0%	21.6%	23.6%
Earnings per share (S$)	—	—	—	0.22	0.29	0.36	0.50	0.73	0.97	1.59	1.92
Stock price – high (S$)[1]	—	—	—	—	—	—	9.90	15.00	15.00	21.90	21.80
Stock price – low (S$)[1]	—	—	—	—	—	—	5.65	7.95	10.10	13.60	11.50
Stock price – close (S$)[1]	—	—	—	—	—	—	9.20	9.95	14.70	20.30	13.10
P/E – high	—	—	—	—	—	—	20	21	15	14	11
P/E – low	—	—	—	—	—	—	11	11	10	9	6
Dividends per share (S$)	43.0%	—	2.00	3.96	5.24	5.36	10.00	12.50	15.00	22.50	35.00
Book value per share (S$)	20.9%	—	1.89	2.10	2.28	2.95	3.66	4.30	5.18	6.61	8.63

1990 Year-end:
Debt ratio: 8.6%
Return on equity: 25.2%
Cash (mil.): S$1,934
Long-term debt (mil.): S$518
No. of shares (mil.): 637
Dividends:
1990 average yield: 2.7%
1990 payout: 18.2%
Market value (mil.): $4,796
Sales (mil.): $2,927

Stock Price History High/Low 1986–90

25
20
15
10
5
0

[1] Foreign shares

Principal exchange: Singapore
Fiscal year ends: March 31

WHO

Chairman: J. Y. Pillay
Managing Director: Cheong Choong Kong
Director of Finance: Tan Hui Boon
Director of Personnel: Anthony Syn Chung Wah
Auditors: Ernst & Young
Employees: 19,867

WHERE

HQ: Airline House, Airline Rd., Singapore 1781
Phone: 011-65-542-3333
Fax: 011-65-545-5034
US HQ: 8350 Wilshire Blvd., Beverly Hills, CA 90211-2381
US Phone: 213-934-8833
US Fax: 213-934-4482
Reservations: 800-421-3133

Singapore Airlines serves 57 cities in 37 countries.

	1990 Sales	
	S$ mil.	% of total
Asia	1,519	30
Europe	1,435	28
The Americas	1,023	20
Southwest Pacific	647	13
Other operations	486	9
Adjustment	(17)	—
Total	**5,093**	**100**

WHAT

	1990 Sales	
	S$ mil.	% of total
Airline operations		
Passenger	3,644	72
Cargo	899	18
Mail	41	1
Baggage	23	—
Nonscheduled services	13	—
Other airline operations	111	2
Non-airline operations	362	7
Total	**5,093**	**100**

Major Subsidiaries and Affiliates
SIA Properties (Pte.) Ltd. (real estate)
Singapore Airport Terminal Services Group
Singapore Engine Overhaul Center Pte. Ltd.
Singapore Flying College Pte. Ltd. (pilot training)
Singapore Jamco Pte. Ltd. (51%, aircraft cabin equipment manufacturing)
Tradewinds Pte. Ltd. (regional airline services and tour packages)

Computer Reservation System
Abacus (with 5 partners)

Flight Equipment	No.	Orders
A310	12	3
Boeing 747	26	24
Boeing 757	2	—
MD-11	—	5
Total	**40**	**32**

KEY COMPETITORS

AMR
British Airways
Continental Airlines
Delta
JAL
KLM
Lufthansa
NWA
Qantas
SAS
Swire Pacific
UAL

SMITHKLINE BEECHAM PLC

OVERVIEW

The product of a 1989 merger between Beecham and SmithKline Beckman, UK-based SmithKline Beecham is a major health care company, selling goods and services in 130 countries.

SmithKline Beecham sells such products as Tagamet, an antiulcer drug with sales over $1 billion, and Augmentin, an antibiotic. Over-the-counter drugs and consumer products known in the US include Contac, Tums, Geritol, Sucrets, and Aquafresh.

The merger created one of the world's largest pharmaceutical sales forces (6,000 representatives). To keep its sales force busy, SmithKline Beecham wants to gain approval for 2 of its drugs annually, a very aggressive rate by industry standards, and plans to increase penetration of Asian and Eastern European markets. Sales of the lucrative Tagamet declined 6% in 1990, and market share slipped from 30% to 26%; the patent on Tagamet expires in 1994.

NYSE symbol: SBE (ADR)
Fiscal year ends: December 31

WHO

Chairman: Henry Wendt, age 57, $1,160,325 pay
President and CEO: Robert P. Bauman, age 60, $2,177,876 pay
VP and CFO: Hugh R. Collum, age 50, $740,889 pay
Group Personnel Director: Peter Jackson
Auditors: Price Waterhouse; Coopers & Lybrand Deloitte
Employees: 54,100

WHEN

Thomas Beecham established an apothecary in England in 1847 and began newspaper advertising for Beecham's Pills, a laxative, in 1859. He believed in the efficacy of advertising. At one point in the late 1800s, 14,000 newspapers carried advertisements for Beecham's Pills. Sales soared in the UK and the US, where pill production had begun in 1888, and the company's pill output surpassed one million per day in the early 1900s.

In 1924 land developer Philip Hill purchased the Beecham estate and, with it, the pill business. He registered the enterprise as Beecham's Pills Ltd. in 1928 and began acquiring other consumer product lines, including Macleans (toothpaste, US, 1938), Eno Fruit Salt (laxatives, UK, 1938), and Brylcreem (men's hair care, UK, 1939).

Beecham's 1940s and 1950s investment in pharmaceutical R&D paid off in 1959, when it introduced the world's first partly synthetic penicillin, and in 1961, with the development of the first broad-spectrum antibiotic. Beecham's Amoxil became the most prescribed antibiotic in the US, and a derivative (Augmentin, 1985) is building on its success.

Beecham sought consumer goods companies with strong positions in markets outside the UK, acquiring Massengill (drugs, personal products; US, 1971), Calgon (bath products, US, 1977), Jovan (fragrances, US, 1979), Bovril (foods, UK, 1980; sold 1990), J.B. Williams (Aqua Velva, Sominex, Geritol; US, 1982), DAP (caulk, US, 1983; sold 1987 to USG), Germaine Monteil (Yardley, cosmetics; UK, 1984; sold 1990), and Norcliff Thayer (Tums, medications; US, 1985).

After years of lackluster earnings, Beecham changed strategy and CEOs in 1986, selling several of its smaller businesses and assigning American Robert Bauman the task of restructuring the company. Bauman sold nondrug companies between 1987 and 1990 and merged Beecham with troubled SmithKline Beckman in 1989.

Having started in 1830 as a small Philadelphia apothecary, SmithKline became a major pharmaceutical company, developing the Benzedrine Inhaler (1936), Dexedrine (1944), and Tagamet (1976) and marketing Thorazine (1954) in the US. SmithKline's Contac cold medicine was a hit, but Tagamet, an antiulcer drug, transformed the company, becoming the world's best-selling drug in 1981. Led by CEO Henry Wendt since 1976, SmithKline diversified and invested heavily in R&D. Poor diversification results, low R&D productivity, and underestimation of Glaxo's Zantac, a Tagamet competitor, reversed the company's fortunes.

In 1991 SmithKline Beecham gained approval to market Seroxat, its new antidepressant, in the UK, and filed suit against Glaxo, alleging that its new antinausea drug Zofran infringed a SmithKline Beecham patent.

WHERE

HQ: SB House, Great West Rd., Brentford, Middlesex TW8 9BD, UK
Phone: 011-44-81-560-5151
Fax: 011-44-81-847-0830
US HQ: SmithKline Beecham Corporation, One Franklin Plaza, Philadelphia, PA 19102-1225
US Phone: 215-751-4000
US Fax: 215-751-7655

SmithKline Beecham operates worldwide.

	1990 Sales		1990 Operating Income	
	$ mil.	% of total	$ mil.	% of total
UK	1,545	16	177	10
Other Europe	2,757	29	526	29
US	3,871	41	895	49
Other countries	1,313	14	210	12
Adjustments	(291)	—	58	—
Total	**9,195**	**100**	**1,866**	**100**

WHAT

	1990 Sales		1990 Operating Income	
	$ mil.	% of total	$ mil.	% of total
Pharmaceuticals	4,584	50	1,188	64
Consumer brands	2,588	28	401	21
Animal health	592	6	116	6
Clinical labs	916	10	104	6
Discontinued operations	507	6	56	3
Adjustments	8	—	1	—
Total	**9,195**	**100**	**1,866**	**100**

Brand Names (US Markets)

Prescription Drugs
Amoxil (antibiotic)
Augmentin (antibiotic)
Calcitonin (osteoporosis drug)
Compazine (nausea drug)
Dyazide (blood pressure drug)
Eminase (blood clot dissolver)
Ornade (cold treatment)
Relifex (arthritis drug)
Stelazine (antidepressant)
Tagamet (ulcer drug)
Thorazine (anxiety drug)
Timentin (antibiotic)

Consumer Products
Aquafresh
Brylcreem
Contac
Ecotrin
Geritol
Horlicks (malted milk products)
Massengill
N'ice
Oxy (acne treatment)
Sominex
Sucrets
Tums
Vivarin

HOW MUCH

Stock prices are for ADRs* ADR = 5 shares	4-Year Growth	1981	1982	1983	1984	1985	1986	1987	1988	1989	1990
Sales ($ mil.)	20.3%	—	—	—	—	—	4,395	4,688	4,233	7,906	9,195
Net income ($ mil.)	33.7%	—	—	—	—	—	329	453	509	769	1,050
Income as % of sales	—	—	—	—	—	—	7.5%	9.7%	12.0%	9.7%	11.4%
Earnings per share ($)	45.7%	—	—	—	—	—	0.88	1.20	1.34	2.95	3.96
Stock price – high ($)	—	—	—	—	—	—	13.75	19.50	18.25	44.88	53.25
Stock price – low ($)	—	—	—	—	—	—	9.00	11.63	15.00	16.75	33.75
Stock price – close ($)	41.3%	—	—	—	—	—	13.25	16.38	16.75	43.13	52.75
P/E – high	—	—	—	—	—	—	16	16	14	15	13
P/E – low	—	—	—	—	—	—	10	10	11	6	9
Dividends per share ($)	36.6%	—	—	—	—	—	0.46	0.60	0.69	0.83	1.60
Book value per share ($)	15.7%	—	—	—	—	—	5.39	7.45	5.62	(1.93)	2.72

1990 Year-end:
Debt ratio: 47.7%
Return on equity: —
Cash (mil.): $1,492
Current ratio: 1.00
Long-term debt (mil.): $658
No. of shares (mil.): 265
Dividends:
1990 average yield: 3.0%
1990 payout: 40.3%
Market value (mil.): $13,992

Stock Price History High/Low 1986–90

60
50
40
30
20
10
0

*Prices are for equity unit ADRs

KEY COMPETITORS

Abbott Labs
American Cyanamid
American Home Products
Amgen
Bayer
Bristol-Myers Squibb
Ciba-Geigy
Colgate-Palmolive
Corning
Eli Lilly
Genentech
Glaxo
Hoechst
Johnson & Johnson
MacAndrews & Forbes
Merck
Monsanto
Pfizer
Procter & Gamble
Rhône-Poulenc
Roche
Sandoz
Schering-Plough
Syntex
Unilever
Upjohn
Warner-Lambert

SONY CORPORATION

OVERVIEW

The name Sony is derived from *sonus*, the Latin word for sound, symbolic of the company's early successes and Chairman Akio Morita's affinity for music. Sony is a world leader in consumer electronics, video technology, recordings, and films, generating about 70% of its sales outside of Japan. It owns 52.5% of audio equipment manufacturer Aiwa.

Spending over $1 billion on R&D, Sony has traditionally sold innovative products at high prices rather than compete on price with commodity products. However, after consistently losing market leadership to price- and cost-cutting rivals, Sony has become more price conscious. The company has also moved into less intensely competitive industrial markets.

Sony recently combined its entertainment businesses (including CBS Records and Columbia Pictures) into US-based Sony Software, which will develop and market entertainment software in formats suitable for Sony's new hardware technologies, such as high-definition television and 8mm video.

Chairman Morita tarnished his sterling US image by contributing to an America-bashing book in 1989. He has withdrawn his contribution from the 1991 English language version.

NYSE symbol: SNE (ADR)
Fiscal year ends: March 31

Hoover's Rating **A-**

WHO

Chairman: Akio Morita, age 70
President and CEO: Norio Ohga
Deputy President: Masaaki Morita
Deputy President: Nobuo Kanoi
Deputy President (Finance): Ken Iwaki
Deputy President (Personnel): Tsunao Hashimoto
Auditors: Price Waterhouse
Employees: 95,600

WHEN

Akio Morita, Masaru Ibuka, and Tamon Maeda, Ibuka's father-in-law, established Tokyo Telecommunications Engineering in 1946 with funding from Morita's father's sake business. Determined to innovate and create new markets, the company produced the first Japanese tape recorder (1950).

In 1953 Morita paid Western Electric (US) $25,000 for transistor technology licenses — a move that sparked a consumer electronics revolution in Japan. His company launched one of the world's first transistor radios in 1955, followed by the first Sony-trademarked product, a pocket-sized radio, in 1957. The company changed its name to Sony in 1958. It introduced the first transistor TV (1959) and the first solid-state video tape recorder (1961). Sony preempted the competition, becoming a leader in these newly emerging markets.

Morita moved to New York in 1960 to oversee US expansion. Sony launched the first home video recorder (1964), solid-state condenser microphone (1965), and integrated circuit–based radio (1966). Sony's 1968 introduction of the Trinitron color TV tube began another decade of explosive growth. Its Betamax VCR (1976) was defeated in the marketplace by products employing rival Matsushita's VHS technology. The Walkman (1979), in all its forms, was another Sony success.

By 1980 Sony faced an appreciating yen and intense price and quality competition, especially from developing Far Eastern countries. The company began to use its technology base to diversify outside consumer electronics, and it began to move production to other countries to reduce the effects of currency fluctuations. In the 1980s Sony introduced Japan's first 32-bit workstation and became a major producer of semiconductors, audio/video chips and components, and floppy disk drives. The company remained active in the consumer market, introducing the Watchman and an 8mm camcorder, developing CD technology with Philips, and becoming the market leader in CD players. Sony made large investments in digital audiotape (DAT) technology and high-definition television.

Sony acquired CBS Records from CBS for $2 billion in 1988 and Columbia Pictures from Coca-Cola in 1989 for $4.9 billion. The purchases made Sony a major force in the rapidly growing entertainment industry and gave the company control of a large library of films, television programs, and recordings. In 1991 the company signed superstar Michael Jackson to a new record and film contract (the biggest ever in the industry). Sony had its best year ever in fiscal 1991, with sales up nearly 26% and profits up nearly 14%.

WHERE

HQ: 7-35, Kitashinagawa 6-chome, Shinagawa-ku, Tokyo 141, Japan
Phone: 011-81-3-3448-2111
Fax: 011-81-3-3448-2244
US HQ: Sony Corp. of America, Sony Dr., Park Ridge, NJ 07656
US Phone: 201-930-6440
US Fax: 201-358-4058

Sony operates worldwide.

	1990 Sales	
	$ mil.	% of total
Japan	5,538	30
US	5,464	30
Europe	4,557	25
Other countries	2,785	15
Adjustments	416	—
Total	**18,760**	**100**

WHAT

	1990 Sales	
	$ mil.	% of total
Video equipment & TVs	7,581	41
Audio equipment	4,600	25
Records	2,900	16
Movies	589	3
Other products	2,674	15
Adjustments	416	—
Total	**18,760**	**100**

Consumer Brands
Betamax
Data Discman
Discman
Mini Disc
Sony
Trinitron
Walkman
Watchman

Consumer Products
Audio systems
Audiotapes
Camcorders
Car video systems
CD players
Prerecorded music
Still-image video cameras
TVs & VCRs
Videodisc players
Videotapes

Commercial/Industrial Products
Airborne audio/visual systems
Batteries
Commercial display systems
Computer disks and drives
Digital position readout sys.
Optical disks and laserdiscs
PCs and workstations
Semiconductors
Sputtering equipment

Entertainment
Sony Pictures Entertainment (formerly Columbia Pictures)
Sony Music (formerly CBS Records)

HOW MUCH

Stock prices are for ADRs ADR = 1 share	9-Year Growth	1981	1982	1983	1984	1985	1986	1987	1988	1989	1990
Sales ($ mil.)	17.9%	4,266	4,863	4,578	4,804	5,211	6,788	8,309	11,655	16,678	18,760
Net income ($ mil.)	8.1%	325	307	186	127	292	344	259	294	549	655
Income as % of sales	—	7.6%	6.3%	4.1%	2.7%	5.6%	5.1%	3.1%	2.5%	3.3%	3.5%
Earnings per share ($)	2.9%	1.51	1.34	0.81	0.55	1.18	1.38	1.04	1.15	1.82	1.95
Stock price – high ($)	—	26.13	18.00	16.75	17.38	21.38	23.50	40.25	58.50	65.75	61.50
Stock price – low ($)	—	14.50	11.00	12.63	12.75	13.50	18.13	18.25	35.38	49.75	40.25
Stock price – close ($)	10.5%	17.50	15.25	15.63	14.00	20.38	20.50	37.75	57.88	60.50	43.00
P/E – high	—	17	13	21	32	18	17	39	51	36	32
P/E – low	—	10	8	16	23	11	13	18	31	27	21
Dividends per share ($)	10.2%	0.14	0.15	0.18	0.18	0.18	0.20	0.28	0.33	0.34	0.34
Book value per share ($)	16.1%	7.15	8.47	8.36	8.85	9.58	12.23	16.19	21.79	24.44	27.44

1990 Year-end:
Debt ratio: 31.1%
Return on equity: 7.5%
Cash (mil.): $4,388
Current ratio: 1.10
Long-term debt (mil.): $4,114
No. of shares (mil.): 332
Dividends:
1990 average yield: 0.8%
1990 payout: 17.4%
Market value (mil.): $14,273

KEY COMPETITORS

BASF
Bertelsmann
Canon
Daewoo
Fuji Photo
Fujitsu
Hitachi
Lucky-Goldstar
Matsushita
3M
Motorola
NEC
Oki
Olivetti
Paramount
Philips
Pioneer
Polaroid
Rank
Samsung
Sharp
Thomson SA
Thorn EMI
Time Warner
Toshiba
Walt Disney
Zenith

SOURCE PERRIER, SA

OVERVIEW

Touted as "earth's first soft drink," Perrier is the 2nd largest global producer of bottled water (after BSN). The source of the company's water is the spring at Vergèze, France, where almost 500,000 gallons of naturally carbonated water flow through the limestone every day.

Perrier, which dominated the industry in the 1980s, is not the only water brand the company has on the market. It also owns such names as Arrowhead, Calistoga, and Poland Spring in the US, and Vichy, Volvic and Contrex in France.

Aside from water Perrier produces a wide range of dairy products under such names as Roquefort (Perrier is the #1 global producer of Roquefort cheese) and Sorrento (Italian cheeses).

In light of 1990's benzene contamination recall, Perrier's reputation as the "champagne of bottled waters" has been severely tarnished. Despite a massive advertising campaign and a new label declaring *"nouvelle production,"* Perrier lost the #1 imported bottled water spot in the US to BSN's Evian in 1990.

WHEN

For over 100 million years, naturally carbonated water has been bubbling up from the ground at what is now Vergèze, France. For centuries the spring served as a source of public pleasure for everyone from the Romans to modern Frenchmen. The fun ended in 1841 when Alphonse Granier bought the property.

Granier recognized the commercial possibilities of the water and in 1863 built a health spa at Vergèze. Granier could not turn a profit, and in 1888 the property was auctioned to Louis Rouviere.

Rouviere hired Louis Perrier, a medical doctor with expertise in hydrotherapy, to serve as a consultant. Perrier acquired the spring in 1898 and started to bottle the water, claiming it had medicinal value. Perrier was also unable to make money and sold the spring to Englishman A. W. St. John Harmsworth (who renamed it La Source Perrier).

Under Harmsworth's leadership the company was revitalized. He closed the spa and began selling Perrier water (in a green bottle that he had designed) to clubs and restaurants across Europe. By the 1930s the company was selling almost 20 million bottles annually.

After WWII the company fell back into Gallic hands when Frenchman Gustave Leven bought it in 1947. During the next decades Leven operated Perrier essentially as a one-person operation, and expanded and diversified by acquiring several dairy operations and other water companies.

Leven's greatest accomplishment was his US advertising blitz during the late 1970s, which established Perrier as the primary brand in the growing US mineral water market. In 1987 the company purchased Beatrice's Arrowhead bottled water division. That same year Perrier sold 48% of its US operations, reportedly to friends of Leven.

Catastrophe came in 1990 when minute traces of the carcinogen benzene were found in Perrier's water, sparking a US and later worldwide recall of 160 million bottles. Later that year, Perrier sold its noncola soft drink operations to Cadbury Schweppes.

Following the benzene incident, Jacques Vincent, who headed investment group Exor SA (Perrier's largest shareholder, with 35% of its stock), wrested control of the company away from Leven (whose family owns 18% of the company) and proclaimed himself chairman. Vincent narrowed the company's focus to concentrate primarily on water and Roquefort cheese. In 1990 the FDA insisted that Perrier drop the "naturally sparkling" from its labels as the company began artificially carbonating some of its water.

In 1991 the company sold its unprofitable Valmont and Jean-Jacques cheese subsidiaries to Besnier, a French dairy company.

HOW MUCH

$=FF5.08 (Dec. 31, 1990)	9-Year Growth	1981	1982	1983	1984	1985	1986[1]	1987	1988	1989	1990
Sales (FF mil.)	21.1%	2,434	2,841	3,240	4,109	10,825	12,452	11,519	15,148	16,672	13,628
Net income (FF mil.)[2]	18.2%	80	117	173	196	241	262	570	1,027	266	359
Income as % of sales	—	3.3%	4.1%	5.3%	4.8%	2.2%	2.1%	4.9%	6.8%	1.6%	2.7%
Earnings per share (FF)	—	*11*	*16*	*24*	*27*	*34*	*29*	*63*	*114*	*30*	—
Stock price – high (FF)	—	187	228	460	574	563	845	927	1,479	2,036	1,875
Stock price – low (FF)	—	126	146	200	462	417	470	490	481	1,479	1,034
Stock price – close (FF)	24.8%	149	200	453	489	470	780	490	1,479	1,875	1,095
P/E – high	—	17	14	19	21	17	—	15	13	68	—
P/E – low	—	11	9	8	17	12	—	8	4	49	—
Dividends per share (FF)	—	6.08	6.06	9.45	12.00	13.50	14.50	16.00	20.00	20.00	—
Book value per share (FF)	—	69.10	100.00	116.20	129.70	130.10	109.90	143.50	254.70	255.60	—

1990 Year-end:
Debt ratio: —
Return on equity: —
Cash (mil.): —
Long-term debt (mil.): —
No. of shares (mil.): 9
Dividends:
1990 average yield: —
1990 payout: —
Market value (mil.): $1,940
Sales (mil.): $2,683

[1] Fiscal year change, 15 months of data [2] Including extraordinary items

Principal exchange: Paris
Fiscal year ends: December 31

Hoover's Rating **B**

WHO

Honorary President: Gustave Leven
Chairman, President and General Director: Jacques Vincent
VC: Thierry Chéreau, age 44
President, Perrier Group (US): Ron Davis
Auditors: Michel Jouan, Groupe Guy Gendrot "3G"; Bernard Montagne, André Amic et Associés
Employees: 16,781

WHERE

HQ: 30310 Vergèze, France
Phone: 011-33-66-87-62-00
Fax: 011-33-66-35-04-58
US HQ: The Perrier Group, 777 W. Putnam Ave., Greenwich, CT 06830
US Phone: 203-531-4100
US Fax: 203-863-0297

The company has overseas subsidiaries in Canada, Hong Kong, Japan, Spain, the UK, the US, and the West Indies.

WHAT

	1990 Sales	
	FF mil.	% of total
Water	8,699	56
Dairy products	5,076	33
Other	1,622	11
Adjustments	(1,769)	—
Total	**13,628**	**100**

Major Subsidiaries

Amalthea Cheese Corporation (56%, US)
Buxton Mineral Water Co. (UK)
Chateauneuf-les-Bains SA
Compagnie Française de Boissons Gazeuses
Eau Minerale de Plancoet
France St.-Yorre
Freenex Corporation (55%, US)
G.I.E. Perrier Export
Immobilière de la Distribution
Imprimerie Wallon
The Perrier Group (52.1%, US)
American Landmark Springs
Arrowhead Water Corp.
Calistoga Mineral Company
Grand Specialties
Great Bear Spring Company
Great Spring Waters of America
Great Water of France
Poland Spring Corp.
Zephyrhills Corporation
Perrier UK Ltd.
San Pellegrino (35%, Italy)
Société Generale De Grandes Sources d'Eaux Minerales Françaises
Société Commerciale des Eaux Minerales du Bassin de Vichy Saint-Yorre
SOMYCEL
Soveper NV
Sucos Refrigerantes Aguas Minerais Industria E Comercia

KEY COMPETITORS

Beatrice
Borden
BSN
John Labatt
Philip Morris
San Miguel
TLC Beatrice

SUMITOMO GROUP

OVERVIEW

The Sumitomo group is one of Japan's leading *keiretsu* (industrial groups). Group companies are affiliated by a web of cross-ownership. Leaders from the most important firms confer in monthly meetings.

Sumitomo Corporation, the *keiretsu*'s sourcing, sales, and general trading arm, has diverse international operations and in 1990 was the world's largest publicly held company (since surpassed by C. Itoh & Mitsui). The company recorded staggering sales growth in that year as gold trading operations benefited from the popularity of new gold savings accounts in Japan. Sumitomo Bank is central to the group and in 1990 was the world's 3rd largest and Japan's most profitable bank. Other affiliates include NEC, Asahi Breweries, Sumitomo Chemical, Sumitomo Electric Industries, and Sumitomo Metal Industries.

Sumitomo Bank Chairman Ichiro Isoda resigned in 1990 in an illegal loan scandal. The quality of the bank's huge loan portfolio is in question. The bank has sent senior managers to rescue Itoman & Co., a textile trader whose real estate deals soured. Itoman is thought to owe Sumitomo over $1 billion.

WHEN

Around 1630 Masatomo Sumitomo, a Buddhist priest from the Kyoto area, opened a medicine shop/bookstore following the dissolution of his sect. His descendants have preserved his writings on business ethics and consider him the spiritual founder of the Sumitomo group. The technological founder of the group was Riemon Soga, Sumitomo's brother-in-law, who researched and duplicated a Western copper smelting technique, enabling him to build a prosperous copper company. After Soga died in 1636, his son, Tomomochi, married Sumitomo's daughter and became the head of the Sumitomo family.

Tomomochi combined the families' businesses and moved to Osaka, where Sumitomo became Japan's dominant copper company. By 1693 the family had turned an old, dilapidated copper mine into one of Japan's top producers.

The family had earlier been tipped off to Besshi, a promising copper mining site. Besshi turned out to be a tremendous producer for over a century, but by the mid-1800s output had dropped. In the 1860s the government demanded funds from Sumitomo to quell a rebellion. Victorious rebels took over the family's businesses until Saihei Hirose, general manager of Besshi, convinced them that Sumitomo had been forced to contribute to the old regime.

Amid financial problems Hirose mortgaged the family's assets to modernize the mine, imported French technology, and bought ships for copper transport. Production soared and the grateful family appointed Hirose Director General in 1878. His nephew, Teigo Iba, created Sumitomo Bank from existing family operations in 1895.

A copper wire business, founded in 1897, evolved into Sumitomo Electric and Sumitomo Metal Industries. The family formed Sumitomo Chemical in 1913 and in 1925 entered life insurance and established Sumitomo Trust.

Sumitomo managed Nippon Electric Company (NEC) from 1932 until occupation forces split the *zaibatsu* into numerous independent pieces following WWII. Employees of the old Sumitomo holding company migrated to a real estate and trading company, today's Sumitomo Corporation. Sumitomo companies regrouped, but much more loosely, in the 1950s. Sumitomo Corporation grew rapidly in concert with Japan's economic expansion and moved aggressively overseas.

Sumitomo Rubber bought control of Dunlop tire operations in Japan, the US, Canada, the UK, France, and Germany in the mid-1980s. Sumitomo Bank bought 12.5% of Goldman Sachs in 1986.

HOW MUCH

$=¥135 (Dec. 31, 1990)	9-Year Growth	1981	1982	1983	1984[1]	1985	1986	1987	1988	1989	1990
Sales (¥ bil.)	9.8%	9,763	11,009	11,433	11,782	13,310	14,410	13,077	13,891	14,842	22,598
Net income (¥ bil.)	9.9%	21	29	23	28	34	29	28	29	35	50
Income as % of sales	—	0.2%	0.3%	0.2%	0.2%	0.3%	0.2%	0.2%	0.2%	0.2%	0.2%
Earnings per share (¥)	6.9%	*27*	*38*	*23*	*40*	*46*	*36*	*34*	*34*	*40*	*50*
Stock price – high (¥)	—	410	401	422	541	719	1,118	1,173	1,155	1,760	1,770
Stock price – low (¥)	—	273	322	336	362	476	596	764	773	1,127	948
Stock price – close (¥)	11.0%	399	372	393	520	628	886	806	1,136	1,750	1,020
P/E – high	—	15	10	18	14	16	31	34	34	44	36
P/E – low	—	10	8	14	9	10	17	22	23	28	19
Dividends per share (¥)	5.9%	4.77	5.01	5.51	5.51	5.79	5.79	6.36	6.36	8.18	8.00
Book value per share (¥)	11.1%	233	264	285	282	333	338	359	397	507	602

1990 Year-end:
Debt ratio: 61.3%
Return on equity: 9.0%
Cash (bil.): ¥2,076
Long-term debt (bil.): ¥1,009
No. of shares (mil.): 1,060
Dividends:
  1990 average yield: 0.8%
  1990 payout: 16.1%
Market value (mil.): $8,009
Sales (mil.): $167,393

Stock Price History
High/Low 1981–90

1,800
1,600
1,400
1,200
1,000
800
600
400
200
0

[1] Accounting change

Principal exchange: Tokyo
Fiscal year ends: March 31

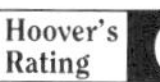

WHO

Chairman: Tadashi Itoh
President: Tomiichi Akiyama
EVP Personnel, Treasury & Accounting: Akitoshi Oshima
President, Sumitomo Corp. of America: Kenji Miyahara
Auditors: Asahi Shinwa & Co.
Employees: 8,630

WHERE

HQ: 2-2, Hitotsubashi 1-chome, Chiyoda-ku, Tokyo 100, Japan
Phone: 011-81-3-3217-5000
Fax: 011-81-3-3217-5128 (Corporate Communications)
US HQ: Sumitomo Corp. of America, 345 Park Ave., 13th Fl., New York, NY 10154-0042
US Phone: 212-207-0700
US Fax: 212-207-0456

Sumitomo Corporation conducts operations in 87 countries.

	1990 Sales	
	¥ bil.	% of total
Japan	8,284	37
Import	5,307	23
Export	4,622	21
Offshore	4,385	19
Total	**22,598**	**100**

WHAT

	1990 Sales	
	¥ bil.	% of total
Metals	11,873	52
Machinery	5,176	23
Chemicals & fuels	2,546	11
Foodstuffs	1,064	5
Textiles	449	2
General products, construction & real estate	1,490	7
Total	**22,598**	**100**

Principal Sumitomo Group Affiliates
Asahi Breweries, Ltd.
NEC Corp.
Nippon Sheet Glass Co., Ltd.
Sumitomo Aluminum Smelting Co., Ltd.
Sumitomo Bakelite Co., Ltd.
The Sumitomo Bank, Ltd.
Sumitomo Cement Co., Ltd.
Sumitomo Chemical Co., Ltd.
Sumitomo Coal Mining Co., Ltd.
Sumitomo Construction Co., Ltd.
Sumitomo Corp.
Sumitomo Electric Industries, Ltd.
Sumitomo Forestry Co., Ltd.
Sumitomo Heavy Industries, Ltd.
Sumitomo Life Insurance Co.
Sumitomo Light Metal Industries, Ltd.
The Sumitomo Marine & Fire Insurance Co., Ltd.
Sumitomo Metal Industries, Ltd.
Sumitomo Metal Mining Co., Ltd.
Sumitomo Realty & Development Co., Ltd.
Sumitomo Rubber Industries, Ltd.
The Sumitomo Trust & Banking Co., Ltd.
The Sumitomo Warehouse Co., Ltd.

KEY COMPETITORS

Mitsubishi
Mitsui

Information presented for Sumitomo Corp. only

SUZUKI MOTOR CORPORATION

OVERVIEW

Perhaps best known in the US for its motorcycles, Suzuki is chiefly a minicar manufacturer. Suzuki has been #1 in minicars for 17 years in Japan, where cumulative unit volume of the Alto series, launched in 1979, has surpassed 2 million. Suzuki is Japan's #3 motorcycle manufacturer, after Honda and Yamaha, but mopeds make up 80% of the volume. Other products include subcompact cars, sport-utility vehicles, marine engines, and electric wheelchairs. Suzuki plans to diversify into medical equipment.

Suzuki has grown internationally through joint ventures. General Motors, owner of 3.5% of Suzuki, sells Suzuki cars as GEO Metros and Trackers. Mazda sells minicars built from Suzuki parts. Foreign vehicle assembly partnerships are principally located in Asia, Europe, and Latin America. A Hungarian partnership plans to begin car production in 1992.

Suzuki of America has not recovered from a disastrous sales slide stemming from safety questions about the 4-wheel-drive Samurai.

WHEN

In 1909 Michio Suzuki started Suzuki Loom Works in Hamamatsu, Japan. The company went public in 1920 and continued producing weaving equipment until, as WWII neared, it began manufacturing war-related products.

Following the war Suzuki moved its headquarters to the Shizuoka prefecture (1947) and turned its attention to the development of inexpensive motor vehicles. Suzuki first introduced a 36cc engine designed for motorizing bicycles in 1952. The company changed its name to Suzuki Motor in 1954, the same year Suzuki launched its first motorcycle. The unveiling of the 360cc Suzulight in 1955 marked the company's entry into minicars and was followed by the Suzumoped in 1958, a delivery van in 1959, and the Suzulight Carry FB small truck in 1961.

Suzuki's triumph in the 1962 50cc-class Isle of Man TT motorcycle race initiated a long string of racing successes that propelled the Suzuki name to international prominence. The company expanded and established its first overseas plant in Thailand in 1967.

In the 1970s Suzuki accommodated market demand for motorcycles with large engines. Recession in the mid-1970s and the decreasing popularity of low-powered vehicles in increasingly affluent Japan hurt the company's domestic sales. The Japanese minicar industry produced 2/3 fewer cars in 1974 than in 1970. Suzuki responded by pushing overseas, beginning auto exports in 1974 and greatly expanding foreign distribution. In 1975 the company started motorcycle production in Taiwan, Thailand, and Indonesia.

Throughout the 1980s Suzuki boosted capacity internationally through joint ventures. In 1988 the company agreed to handle Japanese distribution of Peugeot cars. In Japan motorcycle sales peaked in 1982 but enjoyed a modest rebound in the late 1980s.

Suzuki's relationship with General Motors began in 1981 when it sold a 5.2% stake to the US auto giant. Suzuki began producing Swift subcompacts in 1983 and sold them through GM as the Chevy Sprint and, later, the GEO Metro. In 1986 Suzuki and GM of Canada jointly formed CAMI Automotive to produce vehicles, including Sprints, Metros, and GEO Trackers (Suzuki Sidekicks), in Ontario. Production began in 1989.

Although sales through GM increased through 1990, US efforts with the Suzuki nameplate faltered shortly after the company formed its US subsidiary in Brea, California, in 1986. A 1988 *Consumer Reports* claim that the Samurai was prone to rolling over devastated US sales. The next year the company's top US executives quit, apparently questioning Suzuki's commitment to the US market.

HOW MUCH

$=¥135 (Dec. 31, 1990)	9-Year Growth	1981[1]	1982	1983	1984	1985	1986	1987	1988	1989	1990
Sales (¥ bil.)	8.9%	458	598	604	634	677	822	870	900	961	983
Net income (¥ bil.)	1.7%	5	7	1	6	8	6	10	11	7	6
Income as % of sales	—	1.0%	1.1%	0.2%	0.9%	1.2%	0.7%	1.1%	1.2%	0.7%	0.6%
Earnings per share (¥)	—	—	—	—	*20*	*28*	*21*	*32*	*35*	*17*	*14*
Stock price – high (¥)	—	875	646	565	540	635	778	705	829	1,010	1,040
Stock price – low (¥)	—	276	443	450	400	475	470	500	586	700	520
Stock price – close (¥)	0.4%	583	520	475	527	502	529	590	725	990	605
P/E – high	—	—	—	—	27	23	38	22	24	58	75
P/E – low	—	—	—	—	20	17	23	15	17	40	38
Dividends per share (¥)	3.3%	5.24	5.71	6.19	6.50	6.50	6.50	6.50	6.50	6.50	7.00
Book value per share (¥)	5.6%	286	270	270	304	325	345	367	407	453	466

1990 Year-end:
Debt ratio: 28.8%
Return on equity: 3.0%
Cash (bil.): ¥142
Long-term debt (bil.): ¥77
No. of shares (mil.): 408
Dividends:
1990 average yield: 1.2%
1990 payout: 50.7%
Market value (mil.): $1,828
Sales (mil.): $7,281

Stock Price History High/Low 1981–90

1,200
1,000
800
600
400
200
0

[1] Unconsolidated data

Principal exchange: **Tokyo**
Fiscal year ends: March 31

WHO

Chairman: Seiichi Inagawa
President: Osamu Suzuki
VP: Hisao Uchiyama
Chairman and President, American Suzuki Motor Corp.: Kenji Shimizu
Auditors: Satoru Imamura
Employees: 13,561

WHERE

HQ: Hamamatsu-Nishi, PO Box 1, 432-91, Hamamatsu, Japan
Phone: 011-81-534-40-2111
Fax: 011-81-534-56-2109
US HQ: American Suzuki Motor Corp., 3251 E. Imperial Hwy., Brea, CA 92621
US Phone: 714-996-7040
US Fax: 714-970-6005

Suzuki operates 50 plants in 27 countries and sells its products in 159 countries. American Suzuki oversees 305 dealerships in 49 states.

	1990 Sales	
	¥ bil.	% of total
Japan	435	52
Other countries	409	48
Adjustments	139	—
Total	**983**	**100**

WHAT

	1990 Sales	
	¥ bil.	% of total
Automobiles	596	71
Motorcycles	129	15
Parts	87	10
Outboard motors & other products	32	4
Adjustments	139	—
Total	**983**	**100**

Products

Cars and Sport-Utility Vehicles (US Markets)
GEO Metro, GEO Tracker (sold by General Motors Corp.)
Suzuki Samurai
Suzuki Sidekick
Suzuki Swift

Other Products
General-purpose engines
Generators
Looms
Outboard motors
Prefabricated houses
Water pumps

Other Vehicles
Motorcycles
Motorized wheelchairs
Motor scooters

Principal Overseas Assembly Affliates

Cami Automotive Inc. (joint venture with General Motors of Canada Ltd.)
Land Rover Santana SA (Spain)
Maruti Udyog Ltd. (India)
Pak Suzuki Motor Co., Ltd. (Pakistan)

KEY COMPETITORS

BMW
Brunswick
Chrysler
Fiat
Ford
General Motors
Harley-Davidson
Honda
Hyundai
Isuzu
Mazda
Mitsubishi
Nissan
Outboard Marine
Peugeot
Renault
Saab-Scania
Toyota
Volkswagen
Volvo
Yamaha

SWIRE PACIFIC LTD.

OVERVIEW

Swire Pacific is 49% controlled by London-based Swire Group. A 51.8% stake in Cathay Pacific Airways, the Hong Kong flag carrier, generates the bulk of the company's earnings. Swire Pacific is beginning to manage, rather than sell, its developed Hong Kong real estate, penalizing earnings over the short term. It also owns property in Hawaii and Florida. Other activities include aircraft and shipping services; Coca-Cola bottling in Hong Kong, China, Taiwan, and the US; insurance; trading; and manufacturing.

Cathay Pacific has profited greatly from treaties protecting its Far Eastern routes; it serves other regions on a limited basis only. Taiwanese through-traffic accounts for a large portion of revenue because direct flights between Taiwan and mainland China are prohibited.

Swire Pacific has expressed confidence in the 1997 transfer of Hong Kong to mainland control and has announced its intention to remain based in Hong Kong. Since Cathay Pacific's routes are nontransferable, the company has little choice but to stay.

WHEN

John Swire began a Liverpool trading company in 1816. By the time of his death in 1847, the company, named John Swire & Sons, derived a large share of its business from the import of raw cotton from the US. Swire's son, John, redirected the company's focus to tea and textile trading in China when the US Civil War disrupted cotton shipments. Unhappy with his Far Eastern agents, Swire traveled to Shanghai and in 1866 formed a partnership with a customer, Richard Butterfield. The partnership, called Butterfield & Swire, took Taikoo ("great and ancient") as a Chinese name. Although Butterfield lasted only 2 years as a partner, the name survived.

By 1868 Butterfield & Swire had established offices in New York and in Yokohama, where business subsequently benefited from the industrialization of Japan. In 1870 Butterfield & Swire opened an office in Hong Kong. Then John Swire & Sons entered the related field of shipping, creating China Navigation Company in 1872 to transport goods along the Yangtze River. The shipping line was serving all major Pacific Rim ports by the late 1880s. The Hong Kong–based Tai-Koo Sugar Refinery began operations in 1884.

The 3rd John Swire took over in 1898 and built the Taikoo Dockyard in Hong Kong and other shipping-related facilities in China. The Japanese attack on China in 1937 and invasion of Hong Kong in 1941 halted the Swires' Far Eastern business. WWII devastated their operations and, soon after, China nationalized the group's Chinese assets. Butterfield & Swire rebuilt in Hong Kong and in 1948 bought control of Cathay Pacific, a new Hong Kong airline with 6 DC-3s.

In the 1950s and 1960s, the Swires expanded the airline and established airport and aircraft service companies. Swire Pacific, the successor to Butterfield & Swire and holding company for most of the family's Hong Kong interests excluding China Navigation, went public in 1959. Swire Pacific picked up the Coca-Cola bottling franchise for hot, humid Hong Kong in 1965. The 5th generation of Swires, John and Adrian, rose to the top of the Swire Group in 1968. The Taikoo Dockyard merged its business with Hongkong & Whampoa Dockyard in 1972, and Swire Pacific began redeveloping the old site.

By the 1980s Cathay Pacific had become a large, profitable airline. Cathay Pacific went public (oversubscribed 55-to-1) in 1986, and in 1987 the Chinese government bought 12.5%. Swire Pacific and Cathay Pacific deepened their links to China in 1990 when they purchased 35% of Hong Kong's Dragonair and gave it Cathay Pacific's Shanghai and Beijing routes. Dragonair is 38% owned by the Chinese government and emphasizes mainland routes.

HOW MUCH

$=HK$7.80 (Dec. 31, 1990)	9-Year Growth	1981	1982	1983	1984	1985	1986	1987	1988	1989	1990
Sales (HK$ mil.)	18.2%	6,944	7,955	10,120	11,997	13,692	16,604	20,166	25,108	27,676	31,175
Net income (HK$ mil.)	14.4%	728	601	837	1,049	1,226	1,785	2,396	2,002	3,083	2,450
Income as % of sales	—	10.5%	7.6%	8.3%	8.7%	9.0%	10.8%	11.9%	8.0%	11.1%	7.9%
Earnings per share (HK$)	12.6%	0.53	0.43	0.59	0.68	0.81	1.16	1.54	1.90	1.94	1.54
Stock price – high (HK$)	—	5.13	3.18	4.34	5.38	8.47	16.92	28.90	19.30	23.20	22.40
Stock price – low (HK$)	—	2.45	1.63	2.06	3.26	5.13	8.25	12.20	14.80	13.20	14.10
Stock price – close (HK$)	20.1%	2.85	2.10	3.69	5.38	8.47	16.58	15.30	19.00	15.70	14.80
P/E – high	—	10	7	7	8	10	15	19	10	12	15
P/E – low	—	5	4	3	5	6	7	8	8	7	9
Dividends per share (HK$)	17.3%	0.19	0.19	0.26	0.32	0.39	0.52	0.62	0.76	0.80	0.80
Book value per share (HK$)	19.9%	3.54	3.11	2.80	2.83	4.01	5.78	9.51	14.44	17.06	18.07

1990 Year-end:
Debt ratio: 36.7%
Return on equity: 8.8%
Cash (mil.): HK$4,121
Long-term debt (bil.): HK$17
No. of shares (mil.): 1,588
Dividends:
1990 average yield: 5.4%
1990 payout: 51.9%
Market value (mil.): $3,013
Sales (mil.): $3,997

Stock Price History High/Low 1981–90

30
25
20
15
10
5
0

Note: Per share data presented for "A" shares only

Principal exchange: Hong Kong
Fiscal year ends: December 31

WHO

Chairman: David A. Gledhill
Deputy Chairman: Peter D. A. Sutch
Finance Director: Peter A. Johansen
Auditors: Price Waterhouse
Employees: 28,000

WHERE

HQ: 4th Floor, Swire House, 9 Connaught Rd., Central, Hong Kong
Phone: 011-852-840-8888
Fax: 011-852-810-6563
US HQ: John Swire & Sons, Inc., PO Box 140, Milford, DE 19963
US Phone: 302-422-7536
US Fax: 302-422-6311

Swire Pacific's activities are concentrated in Hong Kong.

WHAT

	1990 Sales		1990 Operating Income	
	HK$ mil.	% of total	HK$ mil.	% of total
Aviation	21,419	66	3,924	77
Properties	1,678	5	894	17
Offshore oil & shipping svcs.	352	1	12	—
Industries	4,929	15	211	4
Trading	4,296	13	88	2
Insurance	68	—	7	—
Adjustments	(1,567)	—	(218)	—
Total	**31,175**	**100**	**4,918**	**100**

Principal Subsidiaries and Affiliates
Carroll Reed International Ltd. (70%, Carroll Reed clothing and retail outlets in US)
Cathay Pacific Airways Ltd. (51.8%)
Continental Can Hong Kong Ltd. (40%, aluminum beverage cans)
The Eagle's Eye International Ltd. (Eagle's Eye sportswear, sold in US)
Hong Kong Aircraft Engineering Company Ltd. (44.1%)
Hong Kong Dragon Airlines Ltd. (Dragonair) (28.6%)
ICI Swire Paints Ltd. (40%)
Swire & Maclaine Ltd. (exporting)
Swire BFI Waste Services Ltd. (50%)
Swire Bottlers Ltd. (bottling and distributing Coca-Cola in Hong Kong)
Swire Marketing Ltd. (franchisee for Kentucky Fried Chicken in Hong Kong)
Swire Pacific Holdings Inc. (Coca-Cola bottling in 10 western US states)
Tai-Koo Sugar Ltd.

Other Products
Audio- and videocassettes
Semiconductors

Other Services
Computer marketing
Electrical and mechanical contracting
Exporting and retailing garments
Importing and marketing medical and household consumer goods in Hong Kong
Importing and marketing Reebok shoes in Hong Kong
Life, property/casualty, and aviation insurance
Marketing Chrysler, Jaguar, and Volvo cars in Korea and Taiwan
Marketing Motorola cellular telephones in Taiwan
Real estate development and investment
Shipping support services

KEY COMPETITORS

Hutchison Whampoa
Jardine Matheson
Airlines serving Asia

TATA GROUP

OVERVIEW

Consisting of 80 public and private Indian companies, the Tata Group generates yearly sales of over $4 billion. Tata is one of the Big 2 family business empires in India, a distinction shared with the Birla Group. Tata Iron and Steel and Tata Engineering and Locomotive are the 2 largest publicly held Indian industrial companies. Tata activities include power generation; the manufacture of trucks, packaged foods, soap, cosmetics, chemicals, tea, and textiles; and the management of the Taj Hotel chain. Tata enjoys an excellent reputation as an employer.

India's recent economic liberalization offers Tata opportunities for expansion but also introduces competition where little existed before. Tata is expanding in petrochemicals and computer hardware and software. In 1990 Tata Tea bought 52.4% of India's Consolidated Coffee. Tata Industries has evolved into the group's new-venture arm.

In 1991 Tata Sons chairman J. R. D. Tata stepped down in favor of his nephew, Ratan Tata. As 80% of Tata Sons, the group's lead company, has been given to charitable trusts and the company itself has had little legal or financial leverage over its sister companies since 1970, J. R. D. kept the group intact by force of personal loyalty. Ratan's challenge is to hold the group together in the future.

WHEN

Jamsetji Tata, a Parsee (Zoroastrian) from Bombay, started a textile trading company in 1868. He began manufacturing textiles, then embarked on a mission to industrialize India. A fervent nationalist, Tata did not subscribe to the popular opinion that such a feat was impossible. Before his death in 1904, Tata had built the Taj Mahal Hotel in Bombay and set in motion plans to create a hydroelectric power plant, a forum for technical education and research in India, and a steel mill (and worker town) to supply rapidly expanding railroads.

Jamsetji's son, Dorabji, carried out the plans. Tata Hydro-Electric Power went on-line in 1910. The next year saw the creation of the Indian Institute of Science at Bangalore. Dorabji found a jungle site for the steel mill, renamed the area Jamshedpur after his father, and established Tata Iron and Steel in 1907, financed entirely by Indians. Doubtful that Indians could make steel rail, the British chairman of the Railway Board said he would "undertake to eat every pound of steel rail" Tata made. Dorabji would later comment on the man's probable indigestion after the mill shipped 1,500 miles of rail to British troops in Mesopotamia during WWI.

The steel company struggled after the war until British colonial powers enacted protective duties. After WWII and Indian independence, the government built a state-owned steel industry but allowed Tata's mills to operate through a grandfathering provision. Inefficient government operations led to high fixed prices for steel, and Tata profited.

Six years after Dorabji's death in 1932, the son of his cousin, 34-year-old J. R. D. Tata, took over the family empire. India's first licensed pilot, J. R. D. had started Tata Airlines, later nationalized as part of Air India. He started Tata Chemicals in 1939. Tata Engineering and Locomotive, founded in 1945 to make steam locomotives, entered truck production in 1954 by collaborating with Daimler-Benz. With help from Volkart Brothers, a Swiss firm, the Tata Group started the Voltas manufacturing conglomerate in 1954. In 1962 Tata teamed with James Finlay of Scotland to create Tata-Finlay, now Tata Tea and 100% Indian-owned since 1982.

Until recently India's socialist government and unwieldy bureaucracy hampered Tata. The group was reluctant to pay bribes for licenses to enter new fields, and red tape and trade restrictions discouraged international expansion. A 1970 antitrust law ended the "managing agency" system through which Tata Sons held interests in subsidiary companies, and Tata Industries managed them for a fee. The companies are now managed independently. Economic reform of the 1980s has allowed Tata to resume aggressive expansion.

HOW MUCH

$=Rs18.20 (Dec. 31, 1990)	9-Year Growth	1981	1982	1983	1984	1985	1986	1987	1988	1989	1990
Tata Iron and Steel:											
Sales (Rs mil.)	17.0%	5,209	7,074	7,982	8,895	11,050	12,855	14,164	15,268	18,618	21,356
Net income (Rs mil.)	21.1%	265	477	449	200	847	871	584	922	1,543	1,485
Income as % of sales	—	5.1%	6.7%	5.6%	2.2%	7.7%	6.8%	4.1%	6.0%	8.3%	7.0%
Tata Engineering and Locomotive:											
Sales (Rs mil.)	13.9%	6,096	7,924	8,532	8,345	9,121	10,008	11,725	13,755	16,764	19,691
Net income (Rs mil.)	24.6%	177	337	250	193	231	162	29	270	633	1,280
Income as % of sales	—	2.9%	4.3%	2.9%	2.3%	2.5%	1.6%	0.2%	2.0%	3.8%	6.5%

1990 Year-end:
Group assets (bil.): Rs65
(mil.): $3,555
Group sales (bil.): Rs80
(mil.): $4,374
Tata Iron and Steel
Sales (mil.): $1,173
Tata Engineering and Locomotive
Sales (mil.): $1,082

Tata Iron & Steel Net Income (Rs mil.) 1981–90

1,600
1,400
1,200
1,000
800
600
400
200
0

Principal exchange: Bombay
Fiscal year ends: March 31

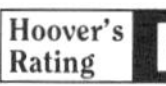

WHO

Chairman, Tata Sons Ltd.: Ratan Tata, age 53
Chairman and Managing Director, The Tata Iron and Steel Co., Ltd.: Russi H. Mody, age 72, Rs305,754 pay
Auditors, The Tata Iron and Steel Co. Ltd.: A.F. Ferguson & Co.; S.B. Billimoria & Co.
Employees: 248,000

WHERE

HQ: Tata Sons Ltd., Bombay House, 24, Homi Mody St., Bombay 400 001, India
Phone: 011-91-22-204-9131
Fax: 011-91-22-204-8187
US HQ: 101 Park Ave., New York, NY 10178
US Phone: 212-557-8131
US Fax: 212-557-7987

The Tata Group's 80 companies are located principally in India. Overseas trading and manufacturing enterprises are located in the UK, the US, Switzerland, the Netherlands, Singapore, and Hong Kong.

WHAT

Principal Member Companies
The Andhra Valley Power Supply Co. Ltd.
The Indian Hotels Co. Ltd. (Taj Group) (33 hotels in India and 49% of 20 hotels in other countries, including New York's Lexington Hotel, Chicago's Executive House, and 5 hotels in Washington, DC)
Tata Chemicals Ltd.
The Tata Engineering and Locomotive Co. Ltd. (TELCO) (commercial vehicles)
The Tata Hydro-Electric Power Supply Co. Ltd.
Tata Industries Ltd.
  Hitech Drilling Services India Ltd. (oil drilling joint venture with Schlumberger)
  Tata Finance Ltd. (commercial and industrial equipment financing)
  Tata Honeywell Ltd. (manufacturing joint venture with Honeywell)
  Tata Industrial Finance Corp. Ltd. (banking joint venture with American Express)
  Tata Keltron Ltd. (manufacturing telephones in collaboration with Siemens)
  Tata Telecom Ltd. (manufacturing PBXs in collaboration with Oki)
The Tata Iron and Steel Co. Ltd.
  Ipitata Sponge Iron Ltd.
  Special Steels Ltd. (wire products)
  Tata Refractories Ltd.
  Tata Timken Ltd. (manufacturing joint venture with The Timken Co.)
  Tata-Robins-Fraser Ltd. (heavy equipment manufacturing)
  The Tinplate Co. of India Ltd.
The Tata Oil Mills Co. Ltd.
The Tata Power Co. Ltd.
Tata Sons Ltd.
  Tata Consultancy Services (computer systems/software and management consulting; R&D for outside clients)
  Tata Consulting Engineers
  Tata Economic Consultancy Services
  Tata Financial Services
Tata Tea Ltd.
Tata Unisys Ltd. (manufacturing and marketing joint venture with Unisys)
Voltas Ltd. (consumer and industrial products)

KEY COMPETITORS

India's protectionist policies shield Tata companies from most non-Indian competition in their home market.

TELEFÓNICA DE ESPAÑA, SA

OVERVIEW

Spanish telephone monopoly Telefónica is Spain's largest company. The government of Spain and state-owned Banco de España together own 33% of Telefónica.

Telefónica has invested heavily to satisfy the booming domestic demand for telephone service resulting from Spain's rapid economic development. The company has cut its backlog of phone orders from more than 500,000 to 312,507. Its investment in physical plant has cut into its net income, down 25% in the first quarter of 1991 from the same period in 1990.

The company will be further challenged by increased demand relating to the 1992 Barcelona Olympics.

To expand globally Telefónica has acquired stakes in South American telephone networks and has flirted with buying the Puerto Rican phone system. The European Community Commission has ordered France's Alcatel to buy out Telefónica's 21.1% stake in equipment-maker Alcatel Standard Eléctrica if Alcatel buys Fiat's telecommunications arm. The order hopes to preserve competition in Spain.

WHEN

When a 1923 military coup brought General Miguel Primo de Rivera to power in Spain, the government-run telephone system was a shambles. Over 1/2 of the country's 90,000 lines did not work. With little cash in the government coffers, Primo de Rivera sought foreign assistance in running the Spanish telephone network. Several European telephone equipment manufacturers expressed interest, as did US-based telephone service company International Telephone and Telegraph (ITT).

Supported financially by National City Bank (now Citicorp), ITT bought 3 private Spanish telephone companies, later combining them to form Compañía Telefónica Nacional de España (Telefónica). After placing several influential Spaniards on Telefónica's board and getting help from the US ambassador to Spain, the ITT unit gained the telephone concession in 1924. ITT retained a controlling interest in Telefónica, and the government agreed not to try to reclaim the system for 20 years.

ITT purchased AT&T's European telephone equipment businesses and began operating a Spanish manufacturing subsidiary, the predecessor of Alcatel Standard Eléctrica. Modernization and expansion of the telephone network quickly followed.

When Franco came to power in 1939, he was thought to want to reward his German backers with the telephone franchise. US State Department pressure helped prevent expropriation, but Franco froze Telefónica's earnings and assets. ITT tried to sell Telefónica to German buyers in 1941 but backed out of the deal when the State Department objected. When the ITT franchise expired in 1945, the government bought ITT's share of Telefónica. Telefónica grew with the Spanish economy, introducing long-distance direct dialing in 1960, satellite communications in 1967, and international direct dialing in 1971.

In the 1980s Telefónica joined in several electronics and telecommunications partnerships with such companies as AT&T, Fiat, Fujitsu, and Electronic Data Systems. Spain's 1986 entry into the EC led to an explosion in demand for telephone services. Telefónica was unprepared, and complaints rose.

In 1990 Telefónica purchased a minority stake in Compañía de Teléfonos de Chile from Australian Alan Bond. In the same year a Telefónica-led consortium that included Citicorp won a bid to manage (with 60% control) the southern 1/2 of Argentina's formerly state-run telephone system.

Telefónica and AT&T agreed in 1991 to develop private international networks and, as part of a proposed fiber optic network, to construct a transatlantic cable, called the Columbus II, to link the US, Mexico, the Caribbean, Spain, and Italy.

HOW MUCH

Stock prices are for ADRs ADR = 3 shares	4-Year Growth	1981	1982	1983	1984	1985	1986	1987	1988	1989	1990
Sales ($ mil.)	24.7%	—	—	—	—	—	3,688	4,955	5,406	6,495	8,904
Net income ($ mil.)	22.0%	—	—	—	—	—	357	488	555	629	792
Income as % of sales	—	—	—	—	—	—	9.7%	9.8%	10.3%	9.7%	8.9%
Earnings per share ($)	17.8%	—	—	—	—	—	1.33	1.76	1.87	2.04	2.56
Stock price – high ($)	—	—	—	—	—	—	—	29.50	26.25	27.88	29.38
Stock price – low ($)	—	—	—	—	—	—	—	16.00	21.38	22.63	22.13
Stock price – close ($)	—	—	—	—	—	—	—	22.38	23.63	24.63	26.38
P/E – high	—	—	—	—	—	—	—	17	14	14	11
P/E – low	—	—	—	—	—	—	—	9	11	11	9
Dividends per share ($)	—	—	—	—	—	—	0.00	0.70	1.39	1.40	1.61
Book value per share ($)	9.5%	—	—	—	—	—	30.45	39.17	36.40	38.26	43.76

1990 Year-end:
Debt ratio: 41.6%
Return on equity: 6.3%
Cash (mil.): $27
Current ratio: 32.5%
Long-term debt (mil.): $9,646
No. of shares (mil.): 309
Dividends:
1990 average yield: 6.1%
1990 payout: 62.9%
Market value (mil.): $8,151

NYSE symbol: TEF (ADR)
Fiscal year ends: December 31

WHO

Chairman: Cándido Velázquez-Gaztelu Ruiz, age 55
Managing Director and CEO: Germán Ancochea Soto, age 47
Deputy General Manager Finance and Budgetary Control: Francisco Mochón Morcillo
Deputy General Manager Personnel Management: Oscar Maraver Sánchez-Valdepeñas
Auditors: Price Waterhouse Auditores, SA; Audiberia, SA
Employees: 74,827

WHERE

HQ: Gran Vía, 28, 28013 Madrid, Spain
Phone: 011-34-1-584-7010 (Financial Department)
Fax: 011-34-1-584-7582
US HQ: Telefónica – USA, Inc., 535 Madison Ave., 35th Floor, New York, NY 10022
US Phone: 212-221-5991
US Fax: 212-759-3084

Telefónica's domestic telephone network extends throughout mainland Spain and to the Balearic and Canary Islands and the North African cities of Ceuta and Melilla.

WHAT

	1990 Sales	
	$ mil.	% of total
Subscriber service charges	2,163	25
Domestic data transmission	915	10
Domestic automatic services	3,911	44
Trunk calls through operator	17	—
International services	1,189	13
Mobile land & maritime services	91	1
Directories & yearbooks	89	1
Connection fees & other	529	6
Total	**8,904**	**100**

Subsidiaries, Affiliates, and Investments
Amper SA (15.3%, electronic components)
ATT Microelectrónica, SA (20%, integrated circuits)
ENTEL (20%, telecommunications, Chile)
Fujitsu España, SA (40%, data processing)
Hispasat SA (25%, telecommunications satellite)
Industria Electrónica de Comunicaciones, SA (30%, portable and mobile communications equipment)
Sistemas e Instalaciones de Telecomunicación, SA (SINTEL, cable and installation)
Sistemas Técnicos de Loterías del Estado, SA (31.75%, lottery systems)
Telefónica Internacional de España, SA (telecommunications services and equipment export)
Torre de Collserola, SA (35%, communication towers)

KEY COMPETITORS

Alcatel Alsthom
Cellular telephone companies
Regional Bell operating companies

TELÉFONOS DE MÉXICO, SA DE CV

OVERVIEW

Teléfonos de México (Telmex), the monopoly telephone service in Mexico, has climbed to the top of some Wall Street buy lists. Telmex's stock has done well, rising 40-fold between 1986 and mid-1991. One analyst describes it as "the fastest growing telecommunications company in the world."

The government sold 51% of voting control of Telmex to a consortium of Southwestern Bell, France Télécom, and Mexico's Grupo Carso in 1990. After a 1991 stock offering, the government owned about 15% of Telmex. With fewer than 10 telephones per 100 people, way below Southwestern Bell's penetration of 40 per 100 in the US, Mexico wants to increase the number of lines 12% a year for 5 years.

Telmex owns one Mexican cellular telephone franchise and faces 8 competitors, including BellSouth, McCaw, Britain's Racal, and Bell Canada. Other Telmex subsidiaries provide construction, real estate, and telephone directory services.

WHEN

Mexican Telephone & Telegraph, backed by Boston interests allied with AT&T, received a government concession to operate in Mexico City in 1903. A similar concession was granted to a Swedish consortium, including equipment-maker Ericsson and the company operating Stockholm's phone system, in 1905. The consortium's interests were consolidated in Empresa de Teléfonos Ericsson in 1909. Mexico's phone system remained fragmented, though, because individual states could set up their own systems.

In 1915 Mexican Telephone and Telegraph was nationalized. The company languished after WWI, but the Ericsson enterprise thrived. In 1925 ITT's Sosthenes Behn won the concession to operate Mexican Telephone and Telegraph, and ITT quickly expanded the company's Mexico City operations nationwide. ITT linked the Mexican system to AT&T in the US and to other ITT operations in Latin America. In 1932 ITT won control of Ericsson and its subsidiaries. After WWII Telmex was created with the amalgamation of Mexican Telephone and the Ericsson subsidiary. Mexican investors bought Telmex in 1953, and the government closely regulated the company, then bought control of Telmex in 1972.

Mexico's phone service grew slowly while Telmex was part of the government. But the telecommunications revolution of the 1980s began to transform the once-sleepy monopoly. As early as 1982 Telmex engineers developed a plan to reconfigure Mexico City's often frustrating phone system.

Telmex, along with the rest of Mexico City, suffered devastation from 1985 earthquakes. The quakes affected more than 55,000 Telmex lines and severed long distance phone service. Damage to Telmex facilities exceeded $25 million. The quakes, though, did offer the Mexican phone company the chance to rebuild and modernize. Telmex's capacity in the capital jumped 70% over its prequake network and included features such as 20 fiber optic routes and digital microwave systems.

Harvard-educated Mexican President Carlos Salinas announced in 1989 that Telmex would join the list of government entities to be privatized. In late 1990, after seeking bids from rival investment groups, the government awarded 51% voting control (20.4% of equity) of Telmex to a consortium that included Southwestern Bell, France Télécom, and Grupo Carso. Southwestern Bell and France Télécom each took 5% of equity and Grupo Carso controlled 10.4% of equity. Grupo Carso, run by financier Carlos Slim, includes retailing, mining, manufacturing, and tobacco interests. Southwestern Bell, one of the regional operating companies split from AT&T in 1984, serves Mexico's neighbor, Texas. State-run France Télécom is expected to bring skills in digital technology to modernize Telmex.

HOW MUCH

Stock prices are for "A" ADRs ADR = 1 share	4-Year Growth	1981	1982	1983	1984	1985	1986	1987	1988	1989	1990
Sales ($ mil.)[1]	22.4%	—	—	—	—	—	1,709	1,963	2,096	2,660	3,838
Net income ($ mil.)[1]	14.3%	—	—	—	—	—	658	699	601	889	1,122
Income as % of sales	—	—	—	—	—	—	38.5%	35.6%	28.7%	33.4%	29.2%
Earnings per share ($)[2]	53.1%	—	—	—	—	—	0.02	0.03	0.09	0.06	0.11
Stock price – high ($)[3]	—	—	—	0.17	0.12	0.07	0.04	0.24	0.14	0.36	0.77
Stock price – low ($)[3]	—	—	—	0.06	0.05	0.03	0.01	0.03	0.06	0.10	0.36
Stock price – close ($)[3]	—	—	—	—	—	—	—	—	—	—	0.68
P/E – high	—	—	—	—	—	—	2	8	2	6	7
P/E – low	—	—	—	—	—	—	1	1	1	2	3
Dividends per share ($)	(14.1%)	—	—	—	—	—	0.0046	0.0026	0.0021	0.0019	0.0025
Book value per share ($)	—	—	—	—	—	—	—	0.33	0.40	0.50	0.50

1990 Year-end:
Debt ratio: 26.4%
Return on equity: 22.0%
Cash (mil.): $1,093
Current ratio: 2.75
Long-term debt (mil.): $1,895
No. of shares (mil.): 10,561
Dividends:
1990 average yield: 0.4%
1990 payout: 2.3%
Market value (mil.): $7,181

Stock Price History High/Low 1983–90

0.8 0.7 0.6 0.5 0.4 0.3 0.2 0.1 0

[1] Inflation-adjusted to December 1990 price levels [2] Including extraordinary item in 1988 [3] "A" share ADR=1/20th TMX ADR

NYSE symbol: TMX (ADR)
NASDAQ symbol: TFONY
Fiscal year ends: December 31

Hoover's Rating **A**

WHO

Chairman: Carlos Slim Helú
General Manager and CEO: Juan Antonio Pérez Simón
Finance and Administration: Carlos Casasús López Hermosa
Corporate Labor Relations and Legal Affairs: Francisco Sánchez Garcia
Auditors: Coopers & Lybrand
Employees: 65,195

WHERE

HQ: Parque Via 190, Colonia Cuauhtémoc, 06599 México, DF, Mexico
Phone: 011-52-5-222-5915
Fax: 011-52-5-566-5825

Telmex operates throughout Mexico. Almost 50% of the country's phone lines are concentrated in Mexico City, Monterrey, and Guadalajara. Telmex also owns a nationwide cellular franchise, with networks operating in Mexico City, Baja California, Guadalajara, Monterrey, Tijuana, and other cities.

WHAT

	1990 Sales	
	$ mil.	% of total
International long distance	1,115	29
Domestic long distance	1,364	36
Local service	1,213	31
Other	146	4
Total	**3,838**	**100**

Telephone Services
800 services (Lada 800)
Local service
National/international long distance
Pay phones (Ladatel)

Telephone Support Services (SERCOTEL)

Telephone Group
Cellular telephone services (national)
Telephone services in Baja California

Physical Plant Group
Building leasing, construction, maintenance, and support services
Civil engineering

Advertising Group
Phone directory production

Construction Group
Construction of physical plant
Equipment installation

Service Group
Administrative services
Equipment leasing
Equipment manufacture
Heating and air conditioning maintenance
Planning and evaluation

KEY COMPETITORS

AT&T
BellSouth
Centel
GTE
McCaw
Cellular telephone firms

THOMSON SA

OVERVIEW

French government–owned Thomson is the world's 4th largest consumer electronics company, and its 60%-owned, publicly traded Thomson-CSF subsidiary is the world's 2nd largest defense electronics firm (after GM Hughes). The company leads in US TV sales and is 2nd to Philips in Europe. US consumer brands include RCA and General Electric (consumer electronics only).

In 1991 EC regulations against state aid forced the French government to suspend plans to infuse Thomson with FF2 billion. The company took a $365 million write-off that year to consolidate its US and European consumer electronics businesses. The write-off should boost 1991 profits, reflecting favorably on chairman Alain Gomez, who comes up for reappointment in 1992.

Gomez continues his policy of acquisitions to strengthen Thomson's core businesses — consumer and defense electronics. The company is investing heavily in the development of high-definition TV (HDTV) in both the US and Europe and is pursuing a partner for its chipmaking business (SGS-Thomson), possibly Philips (Netherlands) or Siemens (Germany).

WHEN

In 1893, after buying patents from US-based Thomson-Houston Electric (predecessor of General Electric), a group of French businessmen created Compagnie Française Thomson-Houston (CFTH) to make power generation equipment. CFTH soon diversified into electric railways and light bulbs, and, through acquisitions in the 1920s and 1930s, started making appliances, radios, broadcast and X-ray equipment, and electrical cable. The company created Alsthom in 1928 to take over its electrical equipment manufacturing businesses.

CFTH's consumer businesses prospered after WWII. In 1966 the company merged with Hotchkiss-Brandt (appliances, defense electronics, automobiles, and postal equipment) to form Thomson-Brandt. In 1968 Thomson-Brandt formed Thomson-CSF by merging its professional electronics businesses with Compagnie Générale de Telegraphie Sans Fil (electronics, communications).

In 1969 Thomson-Brandt transferred Alsthom to Compagnie Générale d'Electricité (CGE, now Alcatel Alsthom). In exchange CGE ceded the French appliance and data processing markets to Thomson-Brandt. In the 1970s the company continued acquiring and diversifying, but profits began to erode as "les barons," Thomson senior executives, established fiefdoms, and financial controls broke down. In 1982 the Mitterrand government nationalized the technically bankrupt company; Alain Gomez was chosen to run it.

Gomez soon discovered that the sprawling company had no treasury function. He hired Jean-François Henin as treasurer, cut costs and staffing, and focused Thomson-Brandt on consumer electronics and Thomson-CSF on defense electronics, fields in which he felt the company could compete globally.

In 1983 Gomez formed Thomson SA as a holding company for the firm's operating units and swapped the company's civil telecommunications business for CGE's military and consumer electronics units. Thomson-CSF bought most of the assets of America's Mostek (semiconductors, 1986) and merged its chipmaking businesses with Italy's SGS Microelettronica (semiconductors, 1987) to create chipmaker SGS-Thomson. Gomez traded Thomson's medical division and $800 million for General Electric's GE and RCA consumer electronics businesses in 1987. Thomson-CSF and Aerospatiale formed Sextant Avionique, a joint flight electronics venture, in 1988. Thomson bought Ferguson (consumer electronics, UK, 1988); SGS bought Inmos (microprocessors, UK, 1989).

In 1990 Thomson-CSF bought 50% of Ferranti's (UK) sonar business and Philips's defense businesses. Philips and Thomson also agreed to a $3.6 billion effort to develop HDTV (EC Eureka), which got a boost in 1991 when the EC approved about $100 million in state support for HDTV research. Although talks with British Aerospace regarding a joint missile venture reached an impasse in 1991, Thomson-CSF joined GEC-Marconi (UK) to jointly produce advanced radars. In 1991 Thomson bought 50% of Pilkington Optronics (laser and optical guidance systems, UK).

HOW MUCH

$=FF5.08 (Dec. 31, 1990)	9-Year Growth	1981	1982	1983	1984	1985	1986	1987	1988	1989	1990
Sales (FF mil.)	6.2%	43,657	47,031	49,448	57,895	59,883	62,650	60,182	74,834	76,663	75,228
Net income (FF mil.)	—	—	(895)	(1,073)	(21)	126	882	1,063	1,197	497	(2,474)
Income as % of sales	—	—	(1.9%)	(2.2%)	0.0%	0.2%	1.4%	1.8%	1.6%	0.6%	(3.3%)
Earnings per share (FF)	—	—	(112)	(105)	(2)	9	51	56	63	24	(93)
Dividends per share (FF)	(100%)	7.87	0.00	0.00	0.00	0.00	0.00	8.44	7.20	0.00	0.00
Book value per share (FF)	(5.3%)	490	337	196	275	291	366	335	421	425	299

1990 Year-end:
Debt ratio: 78.5%
Return on equity: —
Cash (mil.): FF7,061
Long-term debt (mil.): FF29,021
No. of shares (mil.): 27
Dividends:
1990 average yield: —
1990 payout: —
Sales (mil.): $14,809

2,000
1,000
0
-1,000
-2,000
-3,000

Net Income (FF mil.) 1982–90

Government-owned company
Fiscal year ends: December 31

WHO

Chairman and CEO: Alain Gomez, age 52
SVP Finance: Alain Hagelauer
Director of Human Resources: Martine Bidegain
Auditors: Guy Barbier et Associés; Arthur Andersen & Co.
Employees: 105,500

WHERE

HQ: Cedex 67, 92045 Paris La Défense, France
Phone: 011-33-1-49-07-80-00
Fax: 011-33-1-49-07-83-00
US HQ: Thomson-CSF, 2231 Crystal Dr., Suite 814, Arlington, VA 22202-3739
US Phone: 703-486-0780
US Fax: 703-486-2646

Thomson has facilities in more than 50 countries.

	1990 Sales	
	FF mil.	% of total
France	22,318	30
Other Europe	18,861	25
Latin America	819	1
North America	18,085	24
Middle East	9,850	13
Far East	2,422	3
Africa	937	1
Other countries	1,936	3
Total	**75,228**	**100**

WHAT

	1990 Sales
	% of total
Consumer electronics	44
Defense & professsional electronics	49
Home appliances	7
Total	**100**

Consumer Brands	Major Consumer Products
Brandt	Camcorders
Ferguson	CD players
General Electric	Dishwashers
Nordmende	Microwave ovens
RCA	Radios
Saba	Refrigerators and freezers
Sauter	Stereo equipment
Telefunken	Stoves
Thermor	TVs and VCRs
Thomson	Washers and dryers
Vedette	

Subsidiaries
Thomson Consumer Electronics
Thomson-CSF (60%, defense and professional electronics)
Thomson Electroménager (home appliances)

Joint Ventures
Altus Finance (financial services, with Crédit Lyonnais)
GEC Thomson Airborne Radar (GTAR, advanced radars, with GEC-Marconi)
Sextant Avionique (flight electronics, with Aerospatiale)
SGS-Thomson Microelectronics (semiconductors, with IRI/Finmeccanica)

KEY COMPETITORS

Daimler-Benz	NEC	Sharp
EG&G	Nobel	Siemens
Electrolux	Philips	Sony
GEC	Pioneer	Thorn EMI
General Dynamics	Raytheon	Toshiba
Lucky-Goldstar	Robert Bosch	Whirlpool
Maytag	Rockwell	Yamaha
Matsushita	Samsung	Zenith

THE THOMSON CORPORATION

OVERVIEW

Thomson is a $5 billion media giant. In the US and Canada, Thomson leads in number of daily newspapers published. In the UK it is #1 in regional newspapers, package tours (Thomson Tour Operations), charter airlines (Britannia Airways), and travel agencies (Lunn Poly). Although registered in Canada, the company maintains executive offices in New York, reflecting its large and increasing stake in US specialty publishing. Recession in the US and UK has hurt advertising linage and holiday travel.

Thomson's small-town newspapers are cash cows. The company is using the cash to buy leading publishers in lucrative niches. Better known titles are *Jane's Defence Weekly*, *Physicians' Desk Reference*, *American Banker*, and *Federal Tax Coordinator*. Thomson is also increasing its sales of database products.

Expense control is rigorously enforced at Thomson. The company's billionaire chairman, Lord Kenneth Thomson, travels economy class despite controlling 68.4% of Thomson stock.

WHEN

After failing at farming and auto parts distribution, Roy Thomson left Toronto for the hinterlands of Ontario and started a radio station in 1930. He began selling advertising and never stopped. Thomson entered the newspaper business when he bought the *Timmons Press*, a newspaper serving a gold mining town, in 1934. Frugal and bottom-line oriented, Thomson started a profitable series of acquisitions of small-town newspapers.

Thomson made his first acquisition outside Ontario in 1949 and his first US purchase in 1952. In the 1950s Thomson Newspapers became the leader in number of newspapers published in Canada and began rapid expansion in the US. In 1953 Thomson personally bought the *Scotsman*, an Edinburgh-based newspaper, and moved to Scotland. When the UK opened the airways to commercial TV broadcasting, Thomson started Scottish Television Ltd. (1957) and merged it with the UK's Kemsley Newspapers, publisher of rural newspapers and the *Sunday Times*, to create International Thomson Organisation in 1959.

In the 1960s and 1970s, International Thomson entered holiday travel services and oil and gas production and bought the *Times* of London (1967). Meanwhile, in North America, the number of Thomson Newspaper's US dailies surpassed its Canadian total. Queen Elizabeth II conferred the title of Lord Thomson of Fleet upon Thomson, by this time a British subject, in 1970. J. Paul Getty invited International Thomson into a North Sea oil drilling venture in 1971. In 1973 the consortium struck oil. By the time of Lord Thomson's death in 1976, oil accounted for the bulk of International Thomson's profits. Lord Kenneth Thomson, Roy's son, took over control of the family empire.

International Thomson management, foreseeing the ultimate depletion of its oil wells, began buying publishers in an effort to subsititute publishing profits for oil earnings. After selling the *Times* to News Corporation in 1981, International Thomson hunted for leading specialty publishers with subscription-based, rather than advertising-based, profitability that lessened their vulnerability to recession. Purchases included *American Banker* and *Bond Buyer* (financial publications, 1983), Gale Research (library reference, 1985), South-Western Publishing (textbooks, 1986), Associated Book Publishers (legal, textbooks, 1987), Lawyers Co-operative Publishing (1989), and several on-line information providers. The company added tour and charter airline operator Horizon Travel in 1988 and completed the sale of its oil and gas holdings a year later.

In 1989 Thomson Newspapers and International Thomson merged to form The Thomson Corporation.

HOW MUCH

$=C$1.16 (Dec. 31, 1990)	5-Year Growth	1981	1982	1983	1984	1985[1]	1986[1]	1987[1]	1988[1]	1989	1990
Sales ($ mil.)	15.3%	—	—	—	—	2,634	3,946	3,940	4,726	5,112	5,364
Net income ($ mil.)	13.1%	—	—	—	—	208	258	304	380	420	385
Income as % of sales	—	—	—	—	—	7.9%	6.5%	7.7%	8.0%	8.2%	7.2%
Earnings per share ($)	5.3%	—	—	—	—	0.54	0.53	0.66	0.80	0.78	0.70
Stock price – high (C$)[2]	—	—	—	—	—	14.45	19.31	20.81	17.96	20.00	17.00
Stock price – low (C$)[2]	—	—	—	—	—	9.96	13.17	13.55	15.12	15.75	13.00
Stock price – close (C$)[2]	3.6%	—	—	—	—	14.22	18.04	16.54	16.43	16.63	17.00
P/E – high	—	—	—	—	—	—	—	—	—	—	—
P/E – low	—	—	—	—	—	—	—	—	—	—	—
Dividends per share ($)	—	—	—	—	—	—	—	—	—	0.21	0.44
Book value per share ($)	—	—	—	—	—	—	—	—	—	—	—

1990 Year-end:
Debt ratio: 30.5%
Return on equity: 5.2%
Cash (mil.): $442
Current ratio: 1.10
Long-term debt (mil.): $1,430
No. of shares (mil.): —
Dividends:
1990 average yield: —
1990 payout: 62.9%
Market value (mil.): $8,000

Stock Price History High/Low 1985–90

[1] Pro forma [2] Adjusted prices of Thomson Newspapers, Ltd. common stock prior to 1989

Principal exchange: Toronto
Fiscal year ends: December 31

WHO

Chairman: Kenneth R. Thomson, age 68
Deputy Chairman: John A. Tory
President: W. Michael Brown, age 56
EVP and CFO: Nigel R. Harrison
VP and Director of Human Resources, Thomson Newspapers: Allan R. Weir
Auditors: Price Waterhouse
Employees: 44,800

WHERE

HQ: Toronto Dominion Bank Tower, Suite 2706, PO Box 24, Toronto-Dominion Centre, Toronto, Ontario M5K 1A1, Canada
Phone: 416-360-8700
Fax: 416-360-8812
US HQ: 245 Park Ave., New York, NY 10167
US Phone: 212-309-8700
US Fax: 212-309-8708

	1990 Sales		1990 Operating Income	
	$ mil.	% of total	$ mil.	% of total
UK	2,684	50	166	23
US	1,954	36	426	59
Canada	577	11	116	16
Other countries	149	3	18	2
Total	**5,364**	**100**	**726**	**100**

WHAT

	1990 Sales		1990 Operating Income	
	$ mil.	% of total	$ mil.	% of total
Newspapers	1,158	22	282	39
Info./publishing	2,315	43	372	51
Travel	1,891	35	72	10
Total	**5,364**	**100**	**726**	**100**

Newspapers
40 daily and 30 weekly newspapers in Canada, including the *Globe and Mail* (Toronto)
123 daily and 40 weekly small-town newspapers in the US

Information/Publishing
Bancroft-Whitney (law, US)
Callaghan & Company (law, US)
The Carswell Company (law, Canada)
Clark Boardman Company (law, US)
Compu-Mark (trademark databases)
Richard De Boo Publishers (law, Canada)
Derwent Publications (patents)
Gale Research (reference books, US)
International Thomson Professional Information (law)
Jane's Information Group (defense, UK)
Lawyers Cooperative Publishing (US)
Mitchell auto mechanics' guides
Physicians' Desk Reference
The Research Institute of America (law)
St. James Press (business reference books)
Thomson & Thomson (intellectual property)
Thomson Regional Newpapers (UK)
Van Nostrand Reinhold (reference books, US)
Warren, Gorham & Lamont (US)

Travel
Britannia Airways (UK)
Lunn Poly (travel agencies, UK)
Thomson Tour Operations (UK)

KEY COMPETITORS

American Express
Bertelsmann
Carlson
Commerce Clearing House
Cox
Dow Jones
Dun & Bradstreet
Gannett
McGraw-Hill
Maxwell
News Corp.
Paramount
Pearson
Reed
E.W. Scripps

THORN EMI PLC

OVERVIEW

London-based Thorn EMI is a leader in the areas of music, lighting, electronics, TV and appliance rental shops, music retail stores, and TV broadcasting (Thames). International sales account for 61% of company profits.

Thorn EMI's music segment, which controls such powerful record labels as Capitol, EMI, and Chrysalis (50%), maintains an impressive roster of musicians, including Paul McCartney, M. C. Hammer, and recent Grammy-winner Bonnie Raitt.

The company's lighting operations produce everything from fluorescent lamps to custom lighting systems, such as the one for the shark tank at the Sydney Aquarium. In the area of electronics, Thorn produces a diverse line of products ranging from railway passenger ticketing devices to security and defense systems.

Thorn's rental shops (such as Radio Rentals and Rent-A-Center), which currently number more than 2,200 units globally, hold the #1 rental shop spot in each of the 19 countries in which they operate. The company's HMV record stores unit, which controls about 12% of the UK market, in 1990 opened the largest music store in the US in New York City.

WHEN

Jules Thorn founded the Electrical Lamp Service Company in London in 1928 to distribute electric lamps that he had imported from other parts of Europe. For the next several years, he acquired various radio and lamp companies, which he combined under the Thorn Electrical Industries name in 1936.

After WWII Thorn diversified into appliances, electronics, and TV manufacturing. By the early 1960s the company was Britain's largest radio and TV maker and later that decade became the largest global TV rental company by acquiring Robinson Radio Rentals.

Diversification continued in the 1970s as Thorn picked up a host of small companies. In 1979 the company swallowed its biggest fish, electronics and entertainment concern Electric & Musical Industries (EMI). EMI had been established in 1931 as a successor to a 19th-century gramophone producer. EMI gradually expanded its operations to produce everything from radar systems during WWII to the first television system for the BBC. In 1954 the company acquired Capitol Records in the US and became a major force in the entertainment industry, signing such major artists as the Beatles in the 1960s and Pink Floyd in the 1970s. In 1972 EMI released its new scanning X-ray, which won global market leadership until it lost its technological edge and competitors' models made it obsolete. By the late 1970s the company was struggling and agreed to be purchased by Thorn for £165 million in 1979.

For the next several years, each of the constituent companies operated in isolation from the others with little focus or direction. In 1984 the company bought 76.1% of UK-based INMOS (DRAM products, sold in 1989). Colin Southgate became CEO of Thorn in 1985 and refocused the company into 4 business sectors (music, technology, rental and retail, and lighting), selling all that did not fit.

In 1987 the company strengthened its rental operations by purchasing US-based Rent-A-Center for $594 million. Two years later Thorn acquired 50% of Chrysalis Records, which brought the company such popular artists as Pat Benatar and Jethro Tull.

In 1990 Thorn EMI acquired Filmtrax (music publishing, UK) and the 50% that it did not already own of SBK Record Productions, whose artists include Wilson Phillips and Vanilla Ice.

In 1991 the company sold its European light bulb operations to General Electric for $138 million. Also in 1991 the company received approval from the British government to proceed with its announced intention to buy control of broadcasting company Thames Television (Thorn already holds 58.9% of Thames).

HOW MUCH

£=$1.93 (Dec. 31, 1990)	9-Year Growth	1981	1982	1983	1984	1985	1986	1987	1988	1989	1990
Sales (£ mil.)	5.8%	2,229	2,436	2,716	2,821	3,240	3,317	3,203	3,054	3,291	3,716
Net income (£ mil.)	14.5%	60	71	66	88	65	61	100	138	182	204
Income as % of sales	—	2.7%	2.9%	2.4%	3.1%	2.0%	1.9%	3.1%	4.5%	5.5%	5.5%
Earnings per share (p)	8.6%	*34*	*37*	*35*	*47*	*30*	*27*	*44*	*53*	*64*	*71*
Stock price – high (p)	—	503	485	648	700	484	528	830	674	896	824
Stock price – low (p)	—	282	375	416	375	300	377	436	533	625	570
Stock price – close (p)	4.4%	458	433	647	464	401	469	553	625	777	677
P/E – high	—	15	13	19	15	16	20	19	13	14	12
P/E – low	—	8	10	12	8	10	14	10	10	10	8
Dividends per share (p)	8.3%	14.6	14.6	15.8	17.5	17.5	17.5	18.5	22.0	27.0	30.0
Book value per share (p)	(3.2%)	288	306	304	323	262	241	260	210	190	214

1990 Year-end:
Debt ratio: 34.0%
Return on equity: 35.0%
Cash (mil.): £129
Long-term debt (mil.): £319
No. of shares (mil.): 290
Dividends:
1990 average yield: 4.4%
1990 payout: 42.4%
Market value (mil.): $3,789
Sales (mil.): $7,172

OTC symbol: THOEY (ADR)
Fiscal year ends: March 31

Hoover's Rating **B+**

WHO

Chairman and CEO: Colin Southgate, age 52, £401,923 pay
Group Finance Director: Michael Metcalf, age 39
Director Personnel & Industrial Relations: J. B. Richards
Auditors: Ernst & Young
Employees: 57,932

WHERE

HQ: 4 Tenterden St., Hanover Square, London W1A 2AY, UK
Phone: 011-44-71-355-4848
Fax: 011-44-71-355-1308
US HQ: Capitol Industries–EMI, 1750 N. Vine St., Hollywood, CA 90028
US Phone: 213-462-6252
US Fax: 213-467-6550

Thorn EMI has operations in 38 countries.

	1990 Sales		1990 Operating Income	
	£ mil.	% of total	£ mil.	% of total
UK	1,790	48	142	39
Other Europe	995	27	128	35
North America	670	18	60	16
Other countries	261	7	35	10
Total	**3,716**	**100**	**365**	**100**

WHAT

	1990 Sales		1990 Operating Income	
	£ mil.	% of total	£ mil.	% of total
Rental/Retail	1,481	40	178	49
Technology	600	16	54	15
Music	1,028	28	99	27
Lighting	574	15	33	9
Disc. operations	33	1	1	—
Total	**3,716**	**100**	**365**	**100**

Lighting
Commercial lighting
Industrial lighting
Scientific lighting

Music and Broadcasting
Capitol
Chrysalis (50%, UK)
EMI
EMI Tunes (formerly Filmtrax, UK)
SBK Records (US)
Terwright Records (50%, US)
Thames Television (58.9%, UK)
Toshiba-EMI (50%, Japan)

Rental and Retail
Atlantis (electrical superstores, UK)
DER, Focus, Multibroadcast (rental shops, UK)
FONA (electrical retailing, Denmark)
HMV (global music retailing)
Radio Rentals (rental shops, Australia)
Rent-A-Center (US)
Rumbelows (electrical retailing, UK)
Skala TV (rental shops, Belgium)
Visea TV (rental shops, France)

Technology
Software and systems
Currency exchange support systems
Electronic funds transfer systems
Electronic point-of-sale systems
Fire and security systems
Passenger ticketing systems
Personal comm. networks (33.3%, Unitel, UK)
Radar systems
Reservation systems
Weapons and defense systems

Other
Babcock Thorn (35%, dock management, UK)
SGS-Thomson Microelectronics NV (10%)

KEY COMPETITORS

Electronics, rental, semiconductor, lighting, music, retail, and consumer products companies

THYSSEN AG

OVERVIEW

Thyssen — pronounced "TISS-in" — is the world's 2nd largest steel company, after Italy's IRI. In addition to steel the company has profitable operations in components and manufactured products, trading and support services, and specialty steel products.

Its steel operations, praised for their efficiency, focus on customer response: Thyssen Stahl works closely with auto manufacturers to fashion laser-welding technology for steel sheets. Its capital goods operations include shipbuilding at its Blohm + Voss yards and railway systems at Thyssen Henschel. Its Budd Company, with sales of more than $1.5 billion, makes auto parts in the US. Thyssen is casting about for joint ventures to take advantage of the reunification of Germany.

Thyssen Handelsunion is responsible for trading in metals in 70 countries. Services include recycling, coal trading, and transportation. Specialty steel operations (Thyssen Edelstahl-werke) produce stainless steel, bars, and wire products.

WHEN

August Thyssen founded a puddling and rolling mill near Mulheim on the Ruhr in 1871. Thyssen specialized in winning control of small factories and mines and, by WWI, was Germany's largest iron and steel company.

When August Thyssen died in 1926, son Fritz headed the company as it was amalgamated into a trust, similar to the I. G. Farben chemical cartel. Called Vereinigte Stahlwerke, the trust assembled Germany's coal and steel producers under one structure. Fritz Thyssen was an early, ardent supporter of the Nazis, but he bucked the party and fled to France at the beginning of WWII. His brother, Heinrich, escaped to Switzerland (Heinrich's son, Baron Heinrich Thyssen-Bornemisza, used his piece of the family fortune to build a world-renowned art collection). When Germany conquered France in 1940, Fritz Thyssen was imprisoned in an insane asylum and, later, a concentration camp. When the Allies liberated France, Thyssen was arrested as a war criminal (1945). He was acquitted, and he and his wife moved to Argentina.

The Thyssen steel operation was carved up during the Allied occupation; it began anew in 1953, with its Bruckhausen complex as its only asset. As the German economy revived, Thyssen prospered and returned to its leadership in the steel industry.

Thyssen moved to diversify. In 1973 it purchased manufacturing giant Rheinstahl AG (later renamed Thyssen Industrie). Rheinstahl included everything from shipyards to Henschel locomotives, and integrating Rheinstahl's components proved difficult. Flamboyant CEO Dieter Spethmann (nicknamed Sun King of the Ruhr) rose to the challenge. Thyssen's shipyards retooled and began making offshore oil rigs just as the energy crises of the 1970s boosted demand. Thyssen also plunged into specialty steel markets and created Thyssen Handelsunion to wholesale other manufacturers' metal products.

In 1978 Thyssen bought American automotive-components-maker Budd in its first overseas outing. Budd's railcar manufacturing operations proved a drag on profits. In 1985 Thyssen spun off Budd's railway car operations as Transit America.

Demand for steel dropped in the early 1980s, and European steelmakers cut work forces until demand for steel returned late in the decade. In the meantime Thyssen's trading activity grew until it was the largest single contributor to sales in the late 1980s.

As Spethmann prepared to step down from the chairmanship, he received one vindication in 1989. The German government approved building track between Düsseldorf and Cologne/Bonn for Thyssen Henschel's high-speed train. The futuristic train, a Spethmann pet project, uses magnetic levitation to cut friction.

HOW MUCH

$=DM1.49 (Dec. 31, 1990)	9-Year Growth	1981	1982	1983	1984	1985	1986	1987	1988	1989	1990
Sales (DM mil.)	2.8%	28,167	30,610	28,368	32,430	34,784	31,997	28,132	29,220	34,249	36,186
Net income (DM mil.)	—	(68)	(66)	(550)	181	472	370	270	680	825	690
Income as % of sales	—	(0.2%)	(0.2%)	(1.9%)	0.6%	1.4%	1.2%	1.0%	2.3%	2.4%	1.9%
Earnings per share (DM)	—	(2.61)	(2.54)	(21.15)	6.96	15.08	11.82	8.62	21.72	26.35	22.04
Stock price – high (DM)	—	77	92	88	95	181	198	142	196	272	335
Stock price – low (DM)	—	58	65	66	65	86	122	98	98	189	178
Stock price – close (DM)	11.6%	69	70	66	82	170	124	105	191	272	185
P/E – high	—	—	—	—	14	12	17	16	9	10	15
P/E – low	—	—	—	—	10	6	10	11	5	7	8
Dividends per share (DM)	20.9%	2.0	2.0	0.0	0.0	5.0	5.0	5.0	7.5	10.0	11.0
Book value per share (DM)	3.8%	109	106	86	91	104	109	111	129	145	152

1990 Year-end:
Debt ratio: 27.2%
Return on equity: 14.8%
Cash (mil.): DM1,096
Long-term debt (mil.): DM1,763
No. of shares (mil.): 31
Dividends:
1990 average yield: 5.9%
1990 payout: 49.9%
Market value (mil.): $3,849
Sales (mil.): $24,285

Stock Price History High/Low 1981–90

350 300 250 200 150 100 50 0

Principal exchange: Frankfurt
Fiscal year ends: September 30

WHO

Chairman Supervisory Board: Günter Vogelsang
Chairman Board of Management: Dieter Spethmann, age 65
CFO: Heinz-Gerd Stein
Chief Personnel Officer: Hans Gert Woelke
Auditors: KPMG Deutsche Treuhand-Gesellschaft Dr. Rätsch & Co. GmbH
Employees: 152,078

WHERE

HQ: Kaiser-Wilhelm-Strasse 100, PO Box 11 95 61, D-4100 Duisburg 11, Germany
Phone: 011-49-2-03-52-1
Fax: 011-49-2-03-52-2-51-02
US HQ: The Budd Company, 3155 W. Big Beaver Rd., Troy, MI 48084-3002
US Phone: 313-643-3500
US Fax: 313-643-3593

	1990 Sales	
	DM mil.	% of total
Germany	19,114	53
Other Western Europe	8,893	24
Eastern Europe	923	3
North America	4,385	12
Latin America	624	2
Other countries	2,247	6
Total	**36,186**	**100**

WHAT

	1990 Sales	
	DM mil.	% of total
Capital goods & manufactured products	11,489	25
Trading & services	14,566	31
Specialty steel	4,464	9
Steel	10,552	23
Other	5,520	12
Adjustments	(10,405)	—
Total	**36,186**	**100**

Capital Goods and Manufactured Products
Automotive components
Defense technology
Mining
Railway systems
Shipbuilding

Specialty Steel
Bars and wire rod
Bright steel
Flat products
Precision strip

Steel
Flat products
Hot rolled wide strip
Long products (wire rod)
Semi-finished products

Trading and Services
Construction products
Fuels
Logistics
Maintenance
Project management
Recycling

Major Subsidiaries and Affiliates
Blohm + Voss (74.1%, shipbuilding, Germany)
The Budd Co. (auto components, US)
Otto Wolff (steel processing, trading, Germany)
Rasselstein (tin, Germany)
Thyssen Edelstahlwerke AG (specialty steel, Germany)
Thyssen Handelsunion AG (trading, Germany)
Thyssen Industrie AG (90%, manufacturing, Germany)
Thyssen Stahl (steel, Germany)

KEY COMPETITORS

Alcan
AMAX
Anglo American
Bechtel
Broken Hill
Cargill
Hyundai
Inland Steel
IRI
Nippon Steel
Rolls-Royce
RTZ
USX
Automotive components manufacturers
Shipbuilders
Trainmakers

TOKIO MARINE AND FIRE

OVERVIEW

Tokio Marine and Fire, Japan's largest nonlife insurance company, is the world's largest property and casualty insurance company. Japan's property and casualty insurance market is 2nd largest in the world, after the US.

Through a domestic network of 529 offices, the company provides marine, fire and casualty, and auto insurance. Assets at year-end 1990 totaled almost $60 billion. Tokio is one of the Mitsubishi Group, a network of Japanese companies that work closely together. Mitsubishi companies own 21.2% of Tokio.

Tokio has subsidiaries and affiliates in 40 countries and territories, serving Japanese businesses worldwide. In 1990 it established a subsidiary in London to oversee operations that it expects will grow with the 1992 integration of European markets.

Tokio Marine Asset Management New York and Tokio Marine Capital Research (London) provide investment consulting. Tokio also owns 10% of Delaware Management Holdings, an investment advisory firm; and, to expand its role in Japan's asset-backed securities market, has bought 9.9% of Financial Security Assurance Holdings, formerly a wholly owned subsidiary of Denver-based U S West.

WHEN

Japan's first insurance company was founded with 11 employees in 1879 to insure cargo. The following year Tokio Marine and Fire began operations in London, Paris, and New York. During the 1880s the company began writing hull insurance and working through insurers in Marseilles, Liverpool, and Brussels.

In the late 1800s and early 1900s, the firm developed its foreign markets by appointing agents. Willis, Faber & Company, a London insurance broker, served as Tokio's agent in placing ship cargo and hull reinsurance. Tokio profited in marine insurance during the Russo-Japanese War (1904–05) and became one of the world's leading marine insurers. Tokio selected Appleton & Cox (New York) as the agent to develop its US operation.

The company began underwriting fire insurance in 1914 as a step toward becoming a full nonlife insurance company. In the period prior to WWII Tokio broadened its foreign operations through Cornhill Insurance of the UK and Assicurazioni Generali of Italy.

Tokio reorganized in 1944 by merging with Mitsubishi Marine Insurance and Meiji Fire Insurance. In 1956 Tokio resumed its overseas operation, disrupted by WWII, 4 years after the end of the US occupation of Japan. The company became affiliated with Mitsubishi, one of the largest business groups in Japan. Other financial organizations in the group are Mitsubishi Trust & Banking (Japan's largest trust company), Mitsubishi Bank (Japan's 4th largest), and Meiji Mutual Life.

In 1980 Tokio bought Houston General Insurance (Fort Worth), a commercial property and casualty insurer, and established a property and casualty company in Malaysia. The company formed Tokio Reinsurance in Switzerland in 1982.

Tokio registered 3 million ADRs, each representing 5 shares of common stock, with the SEC in 1987. The company undertook the public securities offering to increase ownership of its shares in the US and to increase operating funds.

In the late 1980s Tokio continued its foreign expansion by acquiring a 10% interest in Sark Sigorta T.A.S., a Turkish insurance company. It also opened offices in Madrid (1988), Istanbul (1990), Milan (1990), and Santiago (1990). In 1989 the company paid $42 million for a 10% interest in Delaware Management Holdings, a Philadelphia-based investment counseling firm.

After restructuring of the corporation in 1990, Tokio formed 7 regional headquarters and added branches. Also in 1990 the company began a program to adapt to consumer needs, focusing on insurance written for individuals.

HOW MUCH

$=¥135 (Dec. 31, 1990)	9-Year Growth	1981	1982	1983	1984	1985	1986	1987	1988	1989	1990
Assets (¥ bil.)	17.0%	1,868	2,008	2,258	2,798	3,786	3,833	5,263	6,241	7,676	7,650
Net income (¥ bil.)	6.3%	48	41	32	32	36	44	48	60	93	83
Income as % of assets	—	2.6%	2.0%	1.4%	1.1%	1.0%	1.1%	0.9%	1.0%	1.2%	1.1%
Earnings per share (¥)	5.4%	33	28	22	23	24	29	32	39	60	53
Stock price – high (¥)	—	681	477	541	678	961	1,777	2,665	2,267	2,286	2,130
Stock price – low (¥)	—	410	363	408	465	635	749	1,442	1,405	1,867	946
Stock price – close (¥)	12.6%	455	426	481	626	786	1,571	1,442	2,152	2,076	1,320
P/E – high	—	12	17	25	29	40	61	83	58	38	40
P/E – low	—	12	13	19	20	26	26	45	36	31	18
Dividends per share (¥)	8.3%	3.46	1.08	4.99	5.44	5.44	5.89	5.89	6.35	7.12	7.12
Book value per share (¥)	—	—	—	—	—	—	—	—	—	—	—

1990 Year-end:
Equity as % of assets: 33.4%
Return on equity: 3.1%
Cash (bil.): ¥195
No. of shares (mil.): 1,471
Dividends:
1990 average yield: 0.5%
1990 payout: 13.4%
Market value (mil.): $14,383
Assets (mil.): $56,667
Sales (mil.): $7,165

Stock Price History High/Low 1981–90

3,000
2,500
2,000
1,500
1,000
500
0

OTC symbol: TKIOY (ADR)
Fiscal year ends: March 31

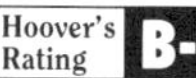

WHO

Chairman: Haruo Takeda
President: Shunji Kono
Managing Director and General Manager of Financial Planning Dept.: Norihiko Tokunaga
Director and General Manager of Personnel Planning Dept.: Katsuhiko Shibue
Auditors: KPMG Peat Marwick
Employees: 12,000

WHERE

HQ: The Tokio Marine and Fire Insurance Co., Ltd., Tokio Kaijo Kasai Hoken Kabushiki Kaisha, 2-1, Marunouchi 1-chome, Chiyoda-ku, Tokyo 100, Japan
Phone: 011-81-3-3212-6211
Fax: 011-81-3-3214-3944
US HQ: Tokio Marine Management, Inc., 101 Park Ave., New York, NY 10178-0095
US Phone: 212-297-6600
US Fax: 212-986-6815 (Investor Relations)

Tokio operates 75 branches and 454 subbranches in Japan and offices in the US and 39 other countries and territories.

WHAT

	1990 Net Premiums Written	
	¥ mil.	% of total
Hull	21,380	2
Cargo & transit	55,752	6
Fire & allied lines	126,812	14
Noncompulsory auto	380,973	41
Personal accident	118,393	13
Compulsory auto	102,635	11
Other	118,670	13
Total	**924,615**	**100**

Key Subsidiaries and Affiliates
América Latina Companhia de Seguros (São Paulo)
The Arab International Insurance Co. (Cairo)
First Insurance Co. of Hawaii, Ltd.
Houston General Insurance Co. (Fort Worth)
Jerneh Insurance Corp. Sendirian Berhad (Kuala Lumpur)
The Koryo Fire & Marine Insurance Co., Ltd. (Seoul)
La Rural del Paraguay SA Paraguaya de Seguros
Pan-Malayan Insurance Corp. (Manila)
P.T. Asuransi Jayasraya (Jakarta)
Sri Muang Insurance Co., Ltd. (Bangkok)
Tokio Marine Asset Management New York Co., Ltd. (New York)
Tokio Marine Capital Research Ltd. (UK)
Tokio Marine & Fire Insurance Co. (UK) Ltd.
Tokio Marine and Fire Insurance Co. (Singapore) Pte. Ltd.
Tokio Marine de Venezuela, CA
Tokio Marine Internacional, SA (Mexico City)
Tokio Marine International Fund (Bahama) Co., Ltd.
Tokio Marine International Fund (Luxembourg) SA
Tokio Marine Management, Inc. (New York)
Tokio Marine Management (Australasia) Pty. Ltd. (Sydney)
Tokio Marine Property Ltd. (UK)
Tokio Marine Realty Co., Ltd. (New York)
Tokio Re (New York)
Trans Pacific Insurance Co. (New York)
The Wuphoon Insurance Co. Ltd. (Hong Kong)

KEY COMPETITORS

AIG	General Re	MetLife
Allianz	ITT	Prudential
B.A.T	Kemper	State Farm
CIGNA	Lloyd's of London	Asset mgmt. firms

THE TOKYO ELECTRIC POWER COMPANY, INC.

Principal exchange: Tokyo
Fiscal year ends: March 31

OVERVIEW

Tokyo Electric Power Company (TEPCO) is the world's largest investor-owned electric utility. The company serves Japan's Kanto area, a 15,000-square-mile region in and around Tokyo. In 1989 TEPCO supplied over 22 million customers with about 205 billion kilowatt-hours of electricity — about 1/3 of Japan's total consumption.

To meet Japan's rising demand for electricity, TEPCO utilizes a mixture of fuel sources, including nuclear power (28%) and liquefied natural gas (LNG, 31%). The company imports much of its LNG (12 million tons in 1989), making it the world's #1 LNG customer. TEPCO's LNG suppliers include Australia, Indonesia, Malaysia, Abu Dhabi, Brunei, and the US.

Since the company also relies heavily on nuclear power, TEPCO is working to improve the safety and reliability of its nuclear plants. It has 12 existing reactors, and construction is underway on 3 new plants, with 2 others in planning stages. The company also promotes energy conservation by traditional and more unusual methods, such as tapping methane from sewage and capturing heat from rivers.

WHO

Chairman and CEO: Gaishi Hiraiwa
President: Shoh Nasu
EVP: Mizuo Iwasa
EVP: Yuzo Fujii
EVP: Shige-etsu Miyahara
EVP: Toshiyuki Kondo
EVP: Susumu Yoda
Auditors: Showa Ota & Co.
Employees: 39,404

WHEN

TEPCO traces its heritage to Tokyo Electric Lighting, Japan's first electric utility, formed in 1883. It switched on Japan's first power plant in 1887, a 25-kilowatt fossil fuel generator that supplied many businesses and factories with electric power for the first time. Fossil fuels continued as the primary source of electricity in Japan until 1912, when long-distance transmission techniques became more efficient, making hydroelectric power a cheaper source of energy.

In 1938 the Japanese government nationalized electric utilities, despite strong objections from Yasuzaemon Matsunaga, a leader in Japan's utility industry and former president of the Japan Electric Association. After WWII Matsunaga championed public ownership of Japan's electric utilities, helping to establish in 1951 the current system of 9 regional companies, each with a service monopoly. Of these, Tokyo Electric Power, which took over utilities operating in Tokyo and the surrounding districts, was the largest. It was listed on the Tokyo exchange in 1951. Kazutaka Kikawada became TEPCO's president in 1961. Regulation of Japan's electric utilities has been entrusted to the Ministry of International Trade and Industry (MITI) since 1965.

Fossil fuels made a comeback in Japan in the postwar era, since those plants could be built more economically than hydroelectric plants. When the Arab oil embargo of the 1970s highlighted Japan's dependence on foreign oil as a fuel source, TEPCO responded by increasing its use of nuclear and LNG energy supplies. In 1977 the company formed the Energy Conservation Center to promote conservation and conservation-related legislation and the following year opened an office in Washington, DC, to exchange data with the US government and utility industry.

The company then joined Toshiba, Texaco, SCEcorp, GE, and others to build a coal gasification plant in California's Mojave Desert, intending to use coal gasification technology to further shrink its dependence on foreign oil (1982). In 1984 TEPCO announced that it would build its first coal-burning generator since the oil crisis.

Since then TEPCO has set up Tokyo Telecommunication Network Company (a partnership that provides industrial and public telecommunications services, 1986) and TEPCO Cable TV (1989).

A 22.3% rate reduction contributed to a sharp drop in the company's 1990 earnings when the value of the yen declined, making oil more costly. By 1999 TEPCO plans to have reduced its dependence on LNG and oil imports by increasing its reliance on nuclear energy (to 40% of total volume) and coal (to 5% of total volume).

WHERE

HQ: Tokyo Denryoku Kabushiki Kaisha, 1-3, Uchisaiwai-cho, 1-chome, Chiyoda-ku, Tokyo 100, Japan
Phone: 011-81-3-3501-8111
Fax: 011-81-3-3591-4609
US HQ: 1901 L St. NW, Suite 720, Washington, DC 20036
US Phone: 202-457-0790
US Fax: 202-457-0810

Tokyo Electric Power conducts business solely in Japan but operates liaison offices in London and Washington, DC.

Generating Facilities

Hydroelectric
Azumi
Imaichi
Midono
Okukiyotsu
Shimogoh
Shin-Takasegawa
Shinanogawa
Tamahara
Yagisawa

Nuclear
Fukushima I & II
Kashiwazaki Kariwa

Fossil Fuel
Anegasaki
Chiba
Futtsu
Goi
Higashi Ohgishima
Hirono
Kashima
Kawasaki
Minami Yokohama
Ooi
Shin Tokyo
Shinagawa
Sodegaura
Yokohama
Yokosuka

WHAT

	1990 Sales	
	¥ bil.	% of total
Residential	1,382	34
Commercial & industrial	2,569	63
Other	136	3
Total	**4,087**	**100**

	1990 Fuel Sources
	% of total
LNG	31
Nuclear	28
Oil	26
Hydroelectric	9
Coal	2
Other	4
Total	**100**

Major Nonutility Activities
Cable TV (TEPCO Cable TV)
Telecommunications systems and services (Tokyo Telecommunication Network Co.)

HOW MUCH

$=¥135 (Dec. 31, 1990)	9-Year Growth	1981	1982	1983	1984	1985	1986	1987	1988	1989	1990
Sales (¥ bil.)	3.0%	3,135	3,339	3,484	3,712	3,915	4,189	3,906	3,940	3,938	4,087
Net income (¥ bil.)	(6.1%)	144	108	111	122	85	130	190	138	123	82
Income as % of sales	—	4.6%	3.2%	3.2%	3.3%	2.2%	3.1%	4.9%	3.5%	3.1%	2.0%
Earnings per share (¥)	(8.3%)	121	48	81	91	84	97	142	103	89	56
Stock price – high (¥)	—	966	949	1,165	1,805	2,844	8,299	9,235	7,210	7,716	6,150
Stock price – low (¥)	—	776	772	926	1,010	1,388	2,611	4,706	4,780	5,451	2,510
Stock price – close (¥)	16.8%	903	942	1,145	1,728	2,766	7,745	5,049	6,912	6,069	3,650
P/E – high	—	8	20	14	20	34	86	65	70	86	111
P/E – low	—	6	16	11	11	16	27	33	46	61	45
Dividends per share (¥)	0.1%	48.51	48.51	48.51	48.51	48.51	48.51	49.00	49.00	49.00	49.00
Book value per share (¥)	4.9%	676	635	721	764	800	848	941	995	1,035	1,042

1990 Year-end:
Debt ratio: 82.2%
Return on equity: 5.3%
Cash (bil.): ¥127
Long-term debt (bil.): ¥6,330
No. of shares (mil.): 1,313
Dividends:
1990 average yield: 1.3%
1990 payout: 88.2%
Market value (mil.): $35,500
Sales (mil.): $30,274

Stock Price History High/Low 1981–90

10,000 9,000 8,000 7,000 6,000 5,000 4,000 3,000 2,000 1,000 0

TOSHIBA CORPORATION

OVERVIEW

Toshiba makes a full range of electrical and electronic products, from nuclear power plants to color TVs. It is often referred to as the General Electric of Japan and is that nation's 5th largest industrial company. Toshiba trails Hitachi and Matsushita in the Japanese electronics industry but is the world's leading producer of the DRAM memory chip. Its popular laptop computers have earned it 40% of the worldwide market. Toshiba is also a leader in medical electronics, with the lion's share of the ultrasound equipment market.

Toshiba has been working with AT&T since 1982 to improve its own telecommunications capabilities. The company also has developed partnerships with VISA International (SuperSmart credit card), Alcatel (telecommunications), Siemens (semiconductors), Motorola (semiconductors), United Technologies (fuel cells), Cummins Engine (ceramic components), and Olivetti (computers). Toshiba plans to focus more on its nuclear power operations and recently completed a joint nuclear power project with General Electric to develop an advanced boiling water reactor.

WHEN

Two Japanese electrical equipment manufacturers came together in 1939 to create Toshiba. The older company was founded in 1875 by Hisashige Tanaka, the so-called Edison of Japan, as Tanaka Seizo-sha, Japan's first telegraph equipment manufacturer. In the 1890s the company started making heavier electrical equipment, such as transformers and electric motors, adopting the name Shibaura Seisakusho Works in 1893. Shibaura Seisakusho went on to pioneer the manufacture of hydroelectric generators (1894) and X-ray tubes (1915) in Japan.

The other half of Toshiba, Hakunetsusha & Company, was founded by Dr. Ichisuke Fujioka and Shoichi Miyoshi as Japan's first incandescent lamp maker (1890). Renamed Tokyo Electric Company (1899), the company invented the coiled filament light bulb (1921) and the internally frosted glass light bulb (1925). It produced Japan's first radio receiver and cathode ray tube in 1924. In 1939 it merged with Shibaura Seisakusho to form Tokyo Shibaura Electric Company (Toshiba).

Toshiba was the first company in Japan to make fluorescent lamps (1940), radar (1942), and broadcasting equipment (1952). Production of black-and-white TVs began in 1949, the same year the company was listed on the Tokyo and Osaka exchanges. Toshiba produced Japan's first digital computer (1954); even so, through the 1970s it was considered an also-ran, trailing other Japanese *keiretsu* (business groups) in size, market share, sales skills, and brand recognition. Part of the problem was a traditional and bureaucratic management that impeded technological innovation.

Then in 1980 electrical engineer Shoichi Saba became president. Saba invested heavily in Toshiba's telecommunications, semiconductor, and computer segments. As a result the company became the first in the world to produce the powerful 1-megabit DRAM chip (1985). In 1986 Toshiba unveiled the popular T3100 laptop computer. In the meantime Saba (named chairman in 1986) pushed Toshiba into joint ventures with Siemens (1985) and Motorola (1986), to exchange microcomputer and memory-chip technology.

But in 1987 Toshiba incurred the wrath of the US government. A subsidiary (Toshiba Machine) sold submarine sound-deadening equipment to the USSR, resulting in threats of US sanctions and a precipitous decline in US sales and its stock price. Chairman Saba and President Sugichiro Watari resigned in shame.

With Joichi Aoi now at the helm, Toshiba has recovered from the scandal and hopes to stay #1 in memory chips with its introduction of 4-megabit DRAM (1991) and 16-megabit DRAM (1992).

HOW MUCH

$=¥135 (Dec. 31, 1990)	9-Year Growth	1981	1982	1983	1984	1985	1986	1987	1988	1989	1990
Sales (¥ bil.)	4.0%	3,000	2,344	2,401	2,707	3,343	3,373	3,308	3,572	3,801	4,252
Net income (¥ bil.)	11.3%	50	44	38	59	86	59	34	61	119	132
Income as % of sales	—	1.7%	1.9%	1.6%	2.2%	2.6%	1.8%	1.0%	1.7%	3.1%	3.1%
Earnings per share (¥)	7.6%	22	17	15	22	32	22	13	21	39	42
Stock price – high (¥)	—	504	378	422	491	438	853	852	1,240	1,500	1,310
Stock price – low (¥)	—	203	246	281	365	329	318	551	560	1,020	680
Stock price – close (¥)	7.6%	364	355	422	420	370	350	580	1,010	1,270	706
P/E – high	—	23	22	29	22	14	28	68	60	39	31
P/E – low	—	9	14	19	16	10	14	44	27	26	16
Dividends per share (¥)	4.6%	6.67	6.67	6.67	7.50	8.00	8.00	8.00	8.00	8.00	10.00
Book value per share (¥)	12.2%	121	154	162	177	205	212	217	244	286	342

1990 Year-end:
Debt ratio: 45.7%
Return on equity: 13.2%
Cash (bil.): ¥1,208
Long-term debt (bil.): ¥915
No. of shares (mil.): 3,173
Dividends:
  1990 average yield: 1.4%
  1990 payout: 24.0%
Market value (mil.): $16,594
Sales (mil.): $31,496

Stock Price History High/Low 1981–90

Principal exchange: Tokyo
Fiscal year ends: March 31

WHO

President and CEO: Joichi Aoi, age 65
SEVP: Kinichi Kadono
SEVP: Fumio Sato
SEVP and Financial Office Director: Osamu Iemura
SEVP: Tsuyoshi Kawanishi
VP and Personnel Resources Director: Terunori Aiga
Auditors: Price Waterhouse
Employees: 142,000

WHERE

HQ: 1-1, Shibaura 1-chome, Minato-ku, Tokyo 105, Japan
Phone: 011-81-3-3457-2104
Fax: 011-81-3-3456-4776
US HQ: Toshiba America, Inc., 375 Park Ave., Suite 1705, New York, NY 10152
US Phone: 212-308-2040
US Fax: 212-838-1179

Toshiba has operations worldwide.

	1990 Sales	
	¥ bil.	% of total
Japan	2,908	69
North America	562	13
Europe	357	8
Asia & other regions	425	10
Total	**4,252**	**100**

WHAT

	1990 Sales	
	¥ bil.	% of total
Information & communication systems, electronic devices	2,149	50
Heavy electrical apparatus	797	19
Consumer products & other	1,306	31
Total	**4,252**	**100**

Major Products
Cellular telephones
Color TV and picture tubes
Computers and peripherals
Control and automation systems
Electron tubes
Elevators and escalators
Home audio and video systems
Household appliances
Industrial electrical equipment
Industrial robots
Lighting equipment and light bulbs
Locomotives and railway equipment
Medical diagnostic imaging systems
Nuclear power plants
Office equipment
Power plant systems
Prefabricated housing
Printed circuit boards
Radar and air traffic control systems
Radio and TV broadcasting systems
Satellite communication systems
Semiconductors and semiconductor lasers
Telecommunications systems
VCRs
Workstations

KEY COMPETITORS

ABB
Alcatel Alsthom
AT&T
Canon
Casio
Compaq
Cooper Industries
Electrolux
Emerson
Fuji Photo
Fujitsu
GEC
General Electric
General Signal
Hitachi
Honeywell
IBM
Ingersoll-Rand
Matsushita
Minolta
NEC
Nobel
Oki
Philips
Pioneer
Reliance Electric
Rolls-Royce
Sharp
Siemens
Sony
Square D
Thomson SA
Thorn EMI
Westinghouse
Yamaha
Zenith

TOYOTA MOTOR CORPORATION

OVERVIEW

With a market share of over 40%, Toyota is Japan's #1 carmaker, its largest industrial concern, and its most profitable listed company. Ranked 3rd after General Motors and Ford in world auto sales, Toyota is expanding globally. In the US, #5 Toyota is challenging Chrysler and Honda for the #3 position in car sales.

Despite slowing sales growth in Japan and slumping US sales, Toyota is investing in new, more efficient factories to cope with a Japanese labor shortage and to be ready to compete for increased market share when auto sales rebound, a typical company strategy. The company's luxury Lexus autos are already built with 1/6 the labor content of comparable Mercedes models.

Toyota's European expansion may be slowed by an EC Commission decision to hold Japanese auto imports to 1990 levels until the year 2000. Sales of cars built in Toyota's UK plant (set to start up in 1992) may face further EC limits.

Toyota is associated with the Mitsui *keiretsu* and owns stakes in a number of related companies, including Daihatsu, Hino Motors (trucks), and Nippondenso (electronic auto parts). Many of the companies provide parts to Toyota.

WHEN

In 1926 Sakichi Toyoda established the Toyoda Automatic Loom Works in central Japan to produce a loom he had invented. Prior to his death in 1930, he sold the rights to his invention and gave the proceeds to his son, Kiichiro Toyoda, to begin an auto business. In 1933 Kiichiro opened an automotive department within the loom works and began copying US engine designs. When protectionist legislation (1936) improved prospects for Japanese automakers, Kiichiro split off the car department, took it public (1937), and, for clarity in spoken Japanese, changed its name to Toyota.

As Toyota began car production, the Japanese government forbade passenger vehicle manufacturing (1939) and forced the company to make trucks for the military.

The company suffered financial problems in the 5 years after WWII. In 1950 Toyota restructured by organizing Toyota Motor Sales, its marketing arm, as a separate company.

Toyota's postwar commitment to R&D, modernization, quality, and the Kanban system of synchronized parts delivery paid off with the successful introductions of the 4-wheel-drive Land Cruiser (1951); full-sized Crown (1955), sold mostly as a taxi; and the small, mass-market Corona (1957). Toyota Motor Sales doubled the number of Toyota franchises in 1957 but kept rivalry low by forcing dealers to specialize in segments of the Toyota line. In 1961 the sales company opened driving schools to broaden its market in increasingly prosperous Japan.

Toyota Motor Sales, U.S.A., launched the Toyopet Crown in the US in 1957. The small engine failed to bring the car up a hill to the showroom. After suspending exports to the US and studying the market, Toyota introduced the successful Corona (1965) and the Corolla subcompact (1968), now the best-selling car of all time. By 1970 Toyota was the 4th largest automaker in the world.

With efficient manufacturing systems and reliable products, Toyota continued to expand rapidly abroad through the 1970s and 1980s. In 1975 Toyota displaced Volkswagen as the #1 importer of autos into the US. After the oil crisis caused a shift in demand for fuel-efficient cars, Toyota developed systems for quickly retooling factories.

Toyota recombined with Toyota Motor Sales in 1982. US auto production began in 1984 with NUMMI, a joint venture with General Motors, and was augmented by output from Toyota Motor Manufacturing (Georgetown, KY) in 1988. Toyota successfully launched its Lexus line in the US in 1989.

In 1991 US automakers accused Toyota of dumping Previa minivans in the US.

HOW MUCH

$=¥135 (Dec. 31, 1990)	9-Year Growth	1981	1982	1983	1984	1985	1986	1987	1988	1989	1990
Sales (¥ bil.)	13.0%	3,056	3,850	5,324	5,909	6,770	6,646	6,675	7,216	8,021	9,193
Net income (¥ bil.)	14.2%	133	142	228	295	406	346	261	311	346	441
Income as % of sales	—	4.4%	3.7%	4.3%	5.0%	6.0%	5.2%	3.9%	4.3%	4.3%	4.8%
Earnings per share (¥)	11.8%	*46*	*48*	*71*	*91*	*125*	*107*	*79*	*93*	*100*	*126*
Stock price – high (¥)	—	1,020	829	1,129	1,144	1,084	1,938	2,020	2,498	2,673	2,382
Stock price – low (¥)	—	447	600	710	897	825	932	1,122	1,468	2,086	1,660
Stock price – close (¥)	11.1%	680	823	1,122	958	1,006	1,814	1,517	2,095	2,309	1,750
P/E – high	—	22	17	16	13	9	18	26	27	27	19
P/E – low	—	10	13	10	10	7	9	14	16	21	13
Dividends per share (¥)	8.0%	8.65	9.09	11.22	12.35	14.73	15.25	15.25	15.25	16.08	17.27
Book value per share (¥)	14.1%	385	444	585	694	816	884	941	1,016	1,124	1,258

1990 Year-end:
Debt ratio: 22.4%
Return on equity: 10.0%
Cash (bil.): ¥1,362
Long-term debt (bil.): ¥1,221
No. of shares (mil.): 3,061
Dividends:
1990 average yield: 1.0%
1990 payout: 13.7%
Market value (mil.): $43,648
Sales (mil.): $68,096

Stock Price History High/Low 1981–90

3,000
2,500
2,000
1,500
1,000
500
0

OTC symbol: TOYOY (ADR)
Fiscal year ends: June 30

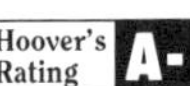

WHO

Chairman: Eiji Toyoda
President: Shoichiro Toyoda
President, Toyota Motor Sales, U.S.A., Inc.: Yukiyasu Togo, age 66
Auditors: Itoh Audit Corporation
Employees: 96,849

WHERE

HQ: Toyota Jidosha Kabushiki Kaisha, 1, Toyota-cho, Toyota City, Aichi Prefecture 471, Japan
Phone: 011-81-565-28-2121
Fax: 011-81-565-23-5741 (Administration)
US HQ: Toyota Motor Sales, U.S.A., Inc., 19001 S. Western Ave., Torrance, CA 90509
US Phone: 310-618-4000
US Fax: 310-618-7800

Toyota operates approximately 50 manufacturing plants in 24 countries.

	1990 Sales	
	¥ bil.	% of total
Japan	5,400	59
Other countries	3,793	41
Total	**9,193**	**100**

WHAT

	1990 Sales	
	¥ bil.	% of total
Motor vehicles	6,800	74
Replacement parts & service	740	8
Industrial vehicles	141	2
Leasing, financial services, housing & other	1,512	16
Total	**9,193**	**100**

Automobile Models (US Markets)

Toyota
- Camry
- Celica
- Corolla
- Cressida
- 4x2 (trucks)
- 4x4 (trucks)
- 4Runner (sport utility vehicle)
- Land Cruiser
- MR2
- Paseo
- Previa (minivans)
- Supra
- Tercel

Lexus
- ES250
- LS400
- SC400

Other Products and Services
Automobile financing and rental
Cellular car telephone service
Factory automation equipment
Forklifts
Prefabricated houses

KEY COMPETITORS

BMW
Caterpillar
Chrysler
Daewoo
Daimler-Benz
Fiat
Ford
General Motors
Honda
Hyundai
Isuzu
Mazda
Mitsubishi
Nissan
Peugeot
Renault
Saab-Scania
Suzuki
Volkswagen
Volvo

UNILEVER

OVERVIEW

Unilever is one of the world's largest packaged consumer goods companies, with a host of internationally recognized products, including Lipton, all, Dove, Vaseline, and Q-Tips. The Anglo-Dutch giant recently expanded its presence in the cosmetics industry through acquisitions and lessened its European sales concentration. Major product groups include margarine and oils, soap and detergents, frozen foods, food and drinks, personal care products, specialty chemicals, and agribusiness.

The group is owned by 2 parent companies, Unilever PLC (UK) and Unilever NV (Netherlands), whose boards of directors are identical. An equalization agreement provides for shareholders of both firms to be treated as nearly the same as if they held shares in a single company.

In 1990 Unilever implemented a restructuring of its European operations to prepare for the common market. The company had previously operated on national levels.

WHEN

After sharpening his sales skills in the family wholesale grocery business in England, William Hesketh Lever formed a new company in 1885 with his brother, James. Lever Brothers introduced Sunlight, the world's first packaged, branded laundry soap. A proponent of large-scale advertising, Lever launched the product with a campaign that queried, "Why does a woman look old sooner than a man?" The answer: because she is aged by the "washday evil" of laundering without Sunlight soap. Sunlight was a success in Britain, and within 15 years Lever was selling soap in Europe, Australia, South Africa, and the US.

From 1906 through 1915 Lever acquired several soap companies in Britain, Australia, and South Africa, and dominated those markets. Needing vegetable oil to make soap, Lever established plantations and trading companies around the world. Lever's United Africa Company was Africa's largest enterprise in the 20 years following its formation in 1929. During WWI the company began using its vegetable oil to make margarine.

Rival Dutch buttermakers Jurgens and Van den Berghs were pioneers in margarine production. In 1927 they created the Margarine Union, a cartel that owned the European market. The Margarine Union and Lever Brothers merged in 1930 but for tax reasons formed 2 separate entities: Unilever PLC in London and Unilever NV in Rotterdam.

Despite the Depression, WWII, and efforts of archrival Procter & Gamble, Unilever expanded, acquiring American companies Thomas J. Lipton (1937) and Pepsodent (1944). However, Unilever's domination of the US market ended with P&G's 1946 introduction of the first synthetic detergent, Tide. Backed by massive advertising, Tide quickly became America's leading detergent in the first of many marketing battles lost by Unilever's Lever Brothers subsidiary to P&G in the US.

Outside America, Unilever was more successful. Its businesses benefited from the postwar boom in Europe, increasing acceptance of margarine, new detergent technologies, and increasing use of personal care products.

Although internal product development fueled some of its growth, acquisitions (recently running at the rate of one per week) have played a major role in shaping Unilever. Major acquisitions included Birds Eye Foods of the UK (1957) and, in the US, Good Humor (1961), National Starch (1978), Lawry's Foods (1979), Ragú (1986), Chesebrough-Pond's (1987), Calvin Klein Cosmetics (1989), and Fabergé/Elizabeth Arden (1989).

In 1990 Unilever's Lipton unit posted its first loss in 38 years, prompting the company to close 2 US plants and reduce its personnel by about 15%. Undeterred, Unilever is said to be looking to acquire a large US food company to complement its European food operations.

NYSE symbols: UL (Unilever PLC [ADR]); UN (Unilever NV)

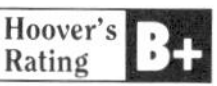

Fiscal year ends: December 31

WHO

Chairmen: Sir Michael Angus, age 60, £586,116 pay (Unilever PLC); Floris A. Maljers, age 57 (Unilever NV)

Financial Director: C. Miller Smith, age 51

Personnel Director: M. G. Heron, age 56

Auditors: Coopers & Lybrand Deloitte (Unilever PLC); Coopers & Lybrand Dijker Van Dien (Unilever NV)

Employees: 304,000

WHERE

HQ: Unilever PLC, Unilever House, Blackfriars, London EC4P 4BQ, UK; Unilever NV, Burgemeester s'Jacobplein 1, 3015 CA, Rotterdam, The Netherlands

US HQ: Unilever United States, Inc., 390 Park Ave., New York, NY 10022-4698

US Phone: 212-888-1260

US Fax: 212-906-4411

	1990 Sales		1990 Operating Income	
	$ mil.	% of total	$ mil.	% of total
Europe	24,169	61	2,193	60
North America	8,247	21	647	18
Other countries	7,204	18	810	22
Total	**39,620**	**100**	**3,650**	**100**

WHAT

	1990 Sales		1990 Operating Income	
	$ mil.	% of total	$ mil.	% of total
Food products	19,510	49	1,823	50
Specialty chemicals	3,080	8	397	11
Detergents	8,452	21	651	18
Personal products	4,725	12	483	13
Other	3,853	10	296	8
Total	**39,620**	**100**	**3,650**	**100**

Major Brand Names

Personal Products
Aim
Axe
Close Up
Cutex
Denim
Impulse
Mentadent
Pepsodent
Pond's
Q-Tips
Rexona
Signal
Sunsilk
Vaseline

Cosmetics/Perfume
Aziza
Calvin Klein
Elizabeth Arden
Fabergé

Soap/Laundry
all
Comfort
Dove
Jif/Cif
Lever 2000
Lifebuoy
Lux
Omo
Shield
Snuggle
Sunlight
Surf
Vim
Wisk

Foods
Becel
Boursin
Country Crock
Du darfst
Flora
Fruit d'Or
Good Humor
Imperial
Lawry's
Lipton
Mrs. Butterworth's
Popsicle
Promise
Ragú
Rama
Salada
Stork
Wishbone

Other
A&W (Canada)
Agribusiness
Chemicals
Medical products
Packaging
UAC Group (power applications, textiles, and brewing)

KEY COMPETITORS

Allied-Lyons
Amway
Avon
BSN
Campbell Soup
Clorox
Colgate-Palmolive
Estée Lauder
Grand Metropolitan
Nestlé
S. C. Johnson
L'Oréal
LVMH
MacAndrews & Forbes
Nestlé
Philip Morris
Procter & Gamble
RJR Nabisco
Sara Lee
SmithKline Beecham
TLC Beatrice

HOW MUCH

	9-Year Growth	1981	1982	1983	1984	1985	1986	1987	1988	1989	1990
Sales ($ mil.)	—	—	21,383	19,470	18,795	24,257	25,428	31,036	30,980	34,434	39,620
Net income ($ mil.)	—	—	610	559	583	748	982	1,413	1,510	1,687	1,980
Income as % of sales	—	—	2.9%	2.9%	3.1%	3.1%	3.9%	4.6%	4.9%	4.9%	5.0%
Earnings per share ($)[1]	8.6%	1.66	1.27	1.08	1.23	1.91	1.75	2.53	3.00	2.98	3.48
Stock price – high ($)	—	9.80	10.80	10.40	11.10	16.10	26.40	47.50	38.00	47.75	54.75
Stock price – low ($)	—	7.90	8.20	8.60	9.00	9.60	15.20	25.70	29.25	33.00	40.50
Stock price – close ($)	21.2%	9.45	9.60	10.40	10.15	16.10	26.40	35.25	33.00	47.75	53.25
P/E – high	—	6	9	10	9	8	15	19	13	16	16
P/E – low	—	5	6	8	7	5	9	10	10	11	12
Dividends per share ($)	17.0%	0.39	0.45	0.44	0.40	0.48	0.70	1.00	0.85	1.59	1.58
Book value per share ($)	0.9%	11.96	11.16	10.83	9.75	12.19	12.96	12.10	12.53	10.33	12.99

1990 Year-end:
Debt ratio: 37.9%
Return on equity: 29.7%
Cash (mil.): $1,609
Current ratio: 1.31
Long-term debt (mil.): $3,383
No. of shares (mil.): 201
Dividends:
1990 average yield: 3.0%
1990 payout: 45.4%
Market value (mil.): $25,184

Stock Price History High/Low 1981–90

60
50
40
30
20
10
0

[1] All share data are for Unilever PLC only

UNION BANK OF SWITZERLAND

OVERVIEW

Union Bank of Switzerland is the largest of the Big 3 banks of Switzerland (Swiss Bank Corporation and Credit Suisse are the other 2) and the 33rd largest bank in the world.

Switzerland has long enjoyed a reputation as a banking center, and the 3 largest financial institutions also garner as much as 80% of the commissions on stocks and bonds traded in Zurich. Swiss banks' reputation for discretion, sometimes obscured during the noisy globalization of financial markets, remains intact: after the Iraqi invasion of Kuwait, nervous and wealthy individuals from the Persian Gulf area deposited $450 million to UBS's safekeeping.

UBS wants to become a global financial powerhouse and, with a healthy capital base at home, is concentrating on international wholesale banking. UBS's second home is in London, where its UBS Phillips & Drew investment arm is headquartered. UBS Securities, infused with $160 million in capital in the late 1980s, is the New York branch of the underwriting family.

UBS is acquiring Chase Manhattan's asset management unit, which handles $30 billion in holdings. The move confirms the Swiss bank's world-class role in serving institutional investors.

WHEN

Prominent businessmen in Winterthur, Switzerland, formed the Bank of Winterthur in 1862 with an initial stock equity of 5 million Swiss francs. The bank catered to trading interests, operated a warehouse, and financed railroads.

In 1912 the Bank of Winterthur merged with the Bank of Toggenburg, formed in 1863, to create Schweizerische Bankgesellschaft — the Union Bank of Switzerland.

The bank expanded its reach in Switzerland through acquisition of smaller banks and by adding branches. Its assets nosed close to the SF1 billion mark but plunged — along with those of the rest of the world — during the Great Depression. With the acquisition of Eidgenössische Bank of Zurich after the end of WWII, UBS assets at last climbed over the SF1 billion mark.

UBS continued to build its business in Switzerland through acquisitions in the 1950s. In 1962 it could point to 81 branch offices. It purchased Interhandel, a cash-rich Swiss financial concern (1967) and 4 savings banks (1968). Although it had opened a New York office for representation in 1946, UBS's first full-fledged foreign branch was opened in London in 1967. In the 1970s it created securities underwriting subsidiaries abroad.

International financial markets became supercharged in the 1980s, and UBS, which started slowly, resolved to catch up quickly. As London prepared for the Big Bang of financial deregulation in 1986, UBS purchased Phillips & Drew, a brokerage house. Other international efforts in the late 1980s included purchasing a German bank (Deutsche Länderbank, 1986), opening a Tokyo office for Phillips & Drew (1986), and creating an Australian merchant-bank subsidiary (UBS Australia Ltd., 1987).

Lack of sophisticated electronic accounting systems at Phillips & Drew sparked losses on top of a £48 million loss in the 1987 stock market crash. Between 1987 and 1989, UBS lost £115 million on Phillips & Drew, merged Phillips & Drew with UBS Securities in London, and set a 5-year goal of turning UBS Phillips & Drew into a leading European investment bank as well as a profitable securities broker.

As the market for lending for highly leveraged transactions (HLTs) collapsed in 1990, UBS's North American operations turned contrarian and went looking for deals. The bank underwrote the $313 million purchase of Great Northern Nekoosa by Georgia-Pacific.

HOW MUCH

$=SF1.27 (Dec. 31, 1990)	9-Year Growth	1981	1982	1983	1984	1985	1986	1987	1988	1989	1990
Assets (SF mil.)	10.7%	93,738	106,353	115,142	131,031	139,453	152,167	160,416	166,583	216,430	233,983
Net income (SF mil.)	10.0%	382	438	506	584	692	776	753	778	989	897
Income as % of assets	—	0.4%	0.4%	0.4%	0.4%	0.5%	0.5%	0.5%	0.5%	0.5%	0.4%
Earnings per share (SF)	—	—	—	—	—	176.70	191.40	179.00	183.60	226.60	193.60
Stock price – high (SF)[1]	—	3,714	3,310	3,600	3,650	5,250	6,070	6,120	3,490	4,180	4,180
Stock price – low (SF)[1]	—	2,514	2,680	3,140	3,150	3,580	4,850	2,975	2,820	2,980	2,580
Stock price – close (SF)[1]	(0.3%)	2,809	3,280	3,600	3,580	5,180	6,000	3,020	3,200	4,100	2,730
P/E – high	—	—	—	—	—	30	32	34	19	18	22
P/E – low	—	—	—	—	—	20	25	17	15	13	13
Dividends per share (SF)[2]	4.5%	90.90	100.00	110.00	115.00	120.00	160.00	120.00	120.00	135.00	135.00
Book value per share (SF)	—	1,609	1,795	1,796	1,869	1,966	2,109	2,315	2,149	3,708	3,699

1990 Year-end:
Equity as % of assets: 9.5%
Return on equity: 5.8%
Cash (mil.): SF4,630
No. of shares (mil.): 5.58
Dividends:
1990 average yield: 4.9%
1990 payout: 69.7%
Market value (mil.): $11,995
Assets (mil.): $184,239
Sales (mil.): $3,677

Stock Price History High/Low 1981–90

7,000
6,000
5,000
4,000
3,000
2,000
1,000
0

Note: Unconsolidated data 1981–88 [1] Bearer shares [2] Not including rights issue

Principal exchange: Zurich
Fiscal year ends: December 31

WHO

Chairman: Nikolaus Senn
VC: Gustav Tobler
President: Robert Studer
EVP, Financial Division: Stephan Haeringer
EVP, Financial Division: U. Grete
SVP Personnel Policy: B. Stotz
Auditors: ATAG Bank Auditing
Employees: 27,470

WHERE

HQ: Bahnhofstrasse 45, 8021 Zurich, Switzerland
Phone: 011-41-1-234-1111
Fax: 011-41-1-234-3415 (Investor Relations)
US HQ: 299 Park Ave., New York, NY 10171
US Phone: 212-715-3000
US Fax: 212-715-3285

UBS operates 266 branches and 22 agencies in Switzerland and 43 business offices elsewhere.

	1990 Assets	
	SF mil.	% of total
Switzerland/ Liechtenstein	102,611	44
OECD countries	111,939	48
Eastern Europe	1,009	—
Developing countries	6,626	3
Other countries	11,798	5
Total	**233,983**	**100**

WHAT

	1990 Assets	
	SF mil.	% of total
Cash, clearing & postal checking accounts	2,052	1
Balances due from banks	65,598	28
Bills and money market paper	2,578	1
Customer loans	122,328	53
Securities	22,604	10
Participations	682	—
Tangibles	5,590	2
Other	12,551	5
Total	**233,983**	**100**

Major Swiss Subsidiaries and Affiliates
Bank Aufina
Bank Cantrade Ltd. (85%)
BDL Banco di Lugano
HYPOSWISS (99.6%)
Orca Bank Ltd.
PBZ Privatbank Zurich (99.9%)
Saudi-Swiss Bank (51%)

Major Foreign Subsidiaries and Affiliates
UBS Australia Ltd.
UBS Phillips & Drew Ltd. (UK)
UBS Phillips & Drew International Ltd. (Japan)
UBS Securities Inc. (US)
Union Bank of Switzerland (Canada)
Union Bank of Switzerland (Germany) AG
Union Bank of Switzerland (Trust and Banking) Ltd. (Japan)

KEY COMPETITORS

Barclays
Canadian Imperial
Crédit Lyonnais
CS Holding
Dai-Ichi Kangyo
Deutsche Bank
HSBC
Industrial Bank of Japan
Royal Bank
Other money-center banks
Securities underwriting firms

VENDEX INTERNATIONAL NV

OVERVIEW

Amsterdam-based Vendex International is the Netherlands' largest retailing concern. The company's many European stores include supermarkets, department stores, clothing boutiques, discount showrooms, photography and electronic shops, and specialty stores. Vendex also provides a wide variety of unrelated services, including insurance and temporary-help services.

Aside from its strong position in Europe, Vendex has constructed a formidable, though largely silent, presence in the US, through its ownership of 50% of B. Dalton (bookstores); 78% of Mr. Goodbuys (home centers); 50% of Software, Etc.; and, until recently, 25.2% of Dillard's (department stores), which the company sold in 1991.

Although Vendex was a steady retailer for many years, dark clouds began to appear on its horizon in the late 1980s. The company's income plummeted 68% between 1987 and 1990, and its market share started to crumble as Vendex lost touch with fickle consumer tastes. Lumbering beneath its high debt, the company announced a reorganization beginning in 1989 to spin off its nonretail segments (e.g., natural resources and travel) while strengthening its core retail operations.

Vendex has announced that it will go public with a stock offering no later than 1992.

Private company
Fiscal year ends: January 31

Hoover's Rating 

WHO

Chairman Supervisory Board: D. de Bruyne
VC Supervisory Board: Anton C. R. Dreesmann, age 68
Chairman Board of Management: J. M. Hessels
Auditors: KPMG Klynveld Kraayenhof & Co.
Employees: 89,100

WHERE

HQ: PO Box 7997, 1008 AD Amsterdam
De Klencke 6, 1083 HH Amsterdam
The Netherlands
Phone: 011-31-20-5490500
Fax: 011-31-20-6461954
US HQ: Vendamerica Inc., 104 Field Point Rd., Greenwich, CT 06830
US Phone: 203-629-4676
US Fax: 203-629-2273

	1990 Sales	
	Fl mil.	% of total
Netherlands	11,900	65
Other Europe	2,800	15
Outside Europe	3,700	20
Total	**18,400**	**100**

WHEN

In 1974 Anton Dreesmann, a doctor of economics and law and professor at the University of Amsterdam, assumed the leadership of Vroom & Dreesmann, a private Dutch department store company that his grandfather had founded over a century earlier.

Wanting to diversify from department stores, Dreesmann started an explosive expansion streak in the late 1970s, branching into commercial banking, temporary-help services, catering operations, office-cleaning services, and other retail operations, including photography and optical shops, a chain of jewelry stores, and electronics shops.

As the economy of the Netherlands became increasingly socialist in the late 1970s, Dreesmann began to look for expansion opportunities overseas, particularly in the US, Brazil, and Japan. He established Vendamerica, a US subsidiary to monitor retailing events in the US, and in 1978 met with William Dillard, founder of Dillard's department stores. Dreesmann paid $24 million for over one million shares of nonvoting stock and took a place on Dillard's board of directors.

In 1980 the company established a mail-order division and made a bid for 50% of the retailing operations of W. R. Grace, but the 2 companies were unable to come to terms. That same year Dreesmann bought 3% of UNY, a leading Japanese retailer (superstores and a variety of smaller stores). In 1985 the company incorporated as Vendex International (although the Dreesmann family retained full control).

In 1987 Vendex strengthened its US retailing presence by purchasing a 50% stake in B. Dalton (bookstores) and a 32% share of Barnes & Noble's College Book Stores, both in partnership with Barnes & Noble CEO Leonard Riggio. At the same time the company continued to expand its European holdings by buying everything from a Dutch travel agency to a Belgian furniture store chain.

With its eyes focused on expansion in the late 1980s, Vendex failed to recognize changing trends in retailing at home, and profits began to fall, all at a time when Dreesmann was falling victim to recurring strokes. In 1988 Dreesmann suffered a brain hemorrhage and appointed Arie Van der Zwan (another economics professor) as his successor. Van der Zwan attacked Vendex's problems by laying off 18% of its department store employees and upgrading the stores. Dreesmann, whose employees affectionately know him as "Uncle Anton," could not tolerate the layoffs and returned to sack Van der Zwan. In 1990 he launched his own reorganization despite his failing health. Aside from shedding money-losing operations, the company placed particular emphasis on revamping the Vroom & Dreesmann department store chain to return it to profitability.

In 1991 Vendex sold its stake in Dillard's for almost $1 billion and announced an almost complete withdrawal from Brazil in response to that country's rampant economic crisis. The company's Brazilian presence is now limited to a minority interest in Mappin, the company that acquired many of Vendex's Brazil-based department stores. In the US Vendex's Mr. Goodbuys unit filed for Chapter 11 protection that same year.

WHAT

	1990 Sales	
	Fl mil.	% of total
Retail	6,898	37
Services	2,566	14
Participations in Netherlands	1,734	9
Participations abroad	2,863	16
Other	4,339	24
Total	**18,400**	**100**

European Stores
Basismarkt (grocery stores)
Best-sellers (showroom retailing)
Claudia Sträter (women's clothing)
Dagmarkt (supermarkets)
Dixons (photography and electronics)
Edah (supermarkets)
Edi (supermarkets)
Hunkemöller (clothing)
Kien (clothing)
Kijkshop (showroom retailing)
Konmar (hypermarkets)
Kreymborg (clothing)
Lederland (leather furniture)
Luigi Lucardi (jewelry)
Perry Sport (sporting goods)
Pet's Place (pet products)
Siebel (jewelry)
Stoutenbeek Wooncentrum (furniture)
Superdoe (home centers)
Torro (supermarkets)
Vedelectric (electric products and appliances)
Vroom & Dreesmann (department stores)

US Stores
Barnes & Noble College Bookstores, Inc. (32%)
Barnes & Noble, Inc. (50%, bookstores)
Mr. Goodbuys (78%, home centers)
Software, Etc. (50%)

Services
Financial services
Insurance
Mail-order services
Maintenance services
Temporary-help services

Joint Venture
Elsevier-Vendex Film (50%, film financing)

KEY COMPETITORS

Home Depot
Ito-Yokado
Kmart
Lowe's
Marks and Spencer

HOW MUCH

$=Fl1.68 (Dec. 31, 1990)	9-Year Growth	1981	1982	1983	1984	1985	1986	1987	1988	1989	1990
Sales (Fl mil.)	7.4%	9,700	10,700	11,800	14,010	14,990	15,900	16,800	17,500	17,900	18,400
Net income (Fl mil.)	(0.7%)	96	125	190	236	265	302	226	172	96	90
Income as % of sales	—	1.0%	1.2%	1.6%	1.7%	1.8%	1.9%	1.3%	1.0%	0.5%	0.5%

1990 Year-end:
Debt ratio: 53.8%
Return on equity: 5.3%
Cash (mil.): Fl76
Current ratio: 1.05
Long-term debt (mil.): Fl1,872
Assets (mil.): Fl6,431
Sales (mil.): $10,952

Net Income (Fl mil.) 1981–90

VOLKSWAGEN AG

OVERVIEW

Volkswagen is the world's 5th largest automaker and #1 in Europe. Surging demand through the first half of 1991 in unified Germany led to months-long waiting periods for VWs and resulted in a wide lead over Fiat in European sales. Volkswagen hopes that its 1990 deal to buy control of Czechoslovakian carmaker SKODA will help solidify its lead. SKODA and SEAT (Sociedad Española de Automóviles de Turismo) are Volkswagen's low-end nameplates. Mid-range Volkswagens and upscale Audis round out the company's offerings.

Chairman Carl Hahn admits to "enormous risk" in Volkswagen's $20 billion planned expansion in Czechoslovakia; Spain; China; eastern Germany; and Mexico, where Beetles are still produced at the country's largest plant. The company and Ford have agreed to jointly produce minivans in Portugal. The automakers are also partners in Autolatina, South America's leading car maker.

Despite *fahrvergnügen*, Volkswagen's US market share remains below 2%. US Audi sales have never recovered from a mid-1980s sudden-acceleration scare.

OTC symbol: VLKAY (ADR)
Fiscal year ends: December 31

WHO

Chairman of the Board of Management: Carl H. Hahn, age 64
Member of the Board of Management for Controlling and Finance: Dieter Ullsperger, age 45
Member of the Board of Management for Human Resources: Martin Posth, age 47
Auditors: Treuarbeit Aktiengesellschaft; Wollert-Elmendorff Deutsche Industrie-Treuhand
Employees: 268,744

WHEN

Since the early 1920s automotive engineer Ferdinand Porsche, whose son founded the Porsche car company, had wanted to make a small car for the masses. He found no financial backers for his idea until he met Adolf Hitler in 1934. Hitler formed the Gesellschaft zur Vorbereitung des Volkswagens (Company for the Development of People's Cars) in 1937 and built a factory and worker housing in Wolfsburg, Germany.

A German government agency instituted a savings plan in which workers regularly set aside small sums with the expectation of receiving a car in 3 years. During WWII, however, the plant produced military vehicles, and no cars were ever delivered.

Following WWII, British occupation forces oversaw the reconstruction of the bomb-damaged plant and initial production of the odd-looking "people's car" (1945). The British appointed Heinz Nordhoff, a tough but inspirational leader, to manage Volkswagen (1948) and turned the company over to the German government (1949).

In the 1950s Volkswagen launched the Microbus and built plants internationally. Although US sales began slowly, by the end of the decade acceptance of the unpretentious car had increased. Advertising carved VW's niche in the US, coining the name "Beetle" and featuring humorous slogans such as "ugly is only skin deep" and "think small."

In 1960 Volkswagen stock was sold to the German public. A year later the company settled with 87,000 participants in Hitler's savings plan. Volkswagen purchased Auto Union GmbH (Audi) in 1966 from Daimler-Benz. In the 1960s the Beetle became a counterculture symbol and US sales took off. By the time of Nordhoff's death in 1968, the VW Beetle had become the world's best-selling car.

In the 1970s the outdated Beetle was discontinued in every country except Mexico. Volkswagen lost heavily during the model-changeover period, although its Brazilian unit was highly profitable. New models sold well in the late 1970s. Volkswagen opened America's first foreign-owned auto plant in Westmoreland, Pennsylvania, in 1978 (closed 1988).

Volkswagen agreed to several international deals in the 1980s, including a car venture in China (1984), the purchase of 75% of SEAT (Spain, 1986), and the merger of its suddenly faltering Brazilian unit with Ford's ailing Argentinian operations to form Autolatina (1987). In 1990 Volkswagen agreed to build China's largest auto plant and committed over $6 billion to buy and modernize SKODA. The next year Toyota agreed to begin selling Volkswagens and Audis in Japan in 1992.

WHERE

HQ: Postfach, W-3180 Wolfsburg 1, Germany
Phone: 011-49-53-61-92-44-88
Fax: 011-49-53-61-92-82-82
US HQ: Volkswagen of America, Inc., 888 W. Big Beaver Rd., Troy, MI 48007-3951
US Phone: 313-362-6000
US Fax: 313-362-6047

	1990 Sales	
	DM mil.	% of total
Germany	26,929	40
Other Europe	26,680	39
North America	5,243	8
Latin America	5,595	8
Other countries	3,614	5
Total	**68,061**	**100**

WHAT

	1990 Sales
	% of total
Vehicles	78
Parts	9
Other	13
Total	**100**

Vehicles

Makes and Models (US Markets)
Audi
80/90
100/200
Coupe Quattro
V8 Quattro
Volkswagen
Corrado
Golf
Jetta
Passat

Other Makes (Foreign Markets)
SEAT
SKODA

Subsidiaries

Manufacturing
AUDI AG (Germany, 99%)
Autolatina Argentina SA (51%)
Autolatina Brasil SA (43%)
Shanghai-Volkswagen Automotive Co. Ltd. (50%, China)
Sociedad Española de Automóviles de Turismo, SA (SEAT) (99%, Spain)
TAS Tvornica Automobila Sarajevo GmbH (50%, Yug.)
Volkswagen Bruxelles SA (Belgium)
Volkswagen de Mexico, SA de C.V.
Volkswagen of Nigeria Ltd. (40%)
Volkswagen of South Africa (Pty.) Ltd.

Automobile Rental
Europcar International SA (50%)

HOW MUCH

$=DM1.49 (Dec. 31, 1990)	9-Year Growth	1981	1982	1983	1984	1985	1986[1]	1987	1988	1989	1990
Sales (DM mil.)	6.7%	37,878	37,434	40,089	45,671	52,502	52,794	54,635	59,221	65,352	68,061
Net income (DM mil.)	18.8%	224	(233)	(130)	245	665	621	598	738	984	1,054
Income as % of sales	—	0.6%	(0.6%)	(0.3%)	0.5%	1.3%	1.2%	1.1%	1.2%	1.5%	1.5%
Earnings per share (DM)	15.1%	*9*	*(10)*	*(5)*	*10*	*28*	*21*	*20*	*25*	*33*	*32*
Stock price – high (DM)	—	180	153	237	232	498	684	430	348	546	643
Stock price – low (DM)	—	120	126	141	163	189	424	218	202	308	332
Stock price – close (DM)	11.0%	132	150	228	205	498	427	225	348	540	337
P/E – high	—	20	—	—	23	18	33	22	14	17	20
P/E – low	—	13	—	—	16	7	20	11	8	9	10
Dividends per share (DM)	3.6%	8	5	0	0	5	10	10	10	10	11
Book value per share (DM)	—	—	—	—	—	—	—	—	—	—	—

1990 Year-end:
Debt ratio: 23.2%
Return on equity: 8.0%
Cash (mil.): DM14,606
Long-term debt (mil.): DM4,867
No. of shares (mil.): 33
Dividends:
1990 average yield: 3.3%
1990 payout: 25.0%
Market value (mil.): $7,464
Sales (mil.): $45,679

Stock Price History High/Low 1981–90

700 600 500 400 300 200 100 0

[1]Accounting change

KEY COMPETITORS

BMW
Chrysler
Daewoo
Daimler-Benz
Fiat
Ford
General Motors
Honda
Hyundai
Isuzu
Mazda
Mitsubishi
Nissan
Peugeot
Renault
Saab-Scania
Suzuki
Toyota
Volvo

AB VOLVO

OVERVIEW

In 1990 Volvo posted a loss for the first time in nearly 60 years. Sweden's largest company is aggressively restructuring, cutting capacity and jobs amid slack car and truck demand in its major markets: the US, the UK, and Sweden. Volvo hopes to bring Swedish worker productivity up to levels achieved at its Belgian plant, but is committed to locate future production "where it is the most profitable."

Through its financial and operating alliance with Renault and through Volvo Car BV, jointly owned with the Dutch government and new investor Mitsubishi Motors, Volvo aims to reap large savings by sharing R&D costs, plants, and components with its partners. Volvo anticipates no savings from the Renault link-up until the latter half of the 1990s.

Volvo owns 26% of Park Ridge, parent of Hertz Corporation, and 39.5% of Procordia, a Swedish food and drug holding company. Other non-automotive products include marine and aircraft engines.

NASDAQ symbol: VOLVY (ADR)
Fiscal year ends: December 31

WHO

Chairman: Pehr G. Gyllenhammar, age 56
President and CEO: Christer Zetterberg, age 50
VP and Treasurer: Hakan Johansson
VP, Working Life Development (Personnel): Lars Cambert
President, Volvo North America Corp.: Albert R. Dowden
Auditors: Ragne Billing and Nils Brehmer
Employees: 68,797

WHEN

Swedish ball bearing manufacturer SKF formed Volvo as a subsidiary in 1915. Volvo began assembling cars (1926), trucks (1928), and bus chassis (1932) in Göteborg, Sweden. The 1931 purchase of an engine maker marked Volvo's move beyond assembly and into manufacturing. In 1935 Volvo became an independent company led by Assar Gabrielsson, a businessman, and Gustaf Larson, who attended to technical matters.

In the 1940s Volvo acquired automotive component manufacturers and began farm tractor production. Truck sales were particularly strong, aided by the company's innovations in diesel engines and axles. In 1949 cumulative vehicle output exceeded 100,000 units, 80% of which were sold in Sweden.

Volvo's acquisition of Bolinder-Munktell (farm machinery, diesel engines; Sweden; 1950) gave the company a major position in the Swedish tractor market. Later in the 1950s Volvo introduced the first turbocharged diesel truck engines, windshield defrosters, and windshield washers. Sales of its PV444 automobile advanced to 100,000 in 1956 as car production outstripped truck and bus output. European and North American sales helped Volvo export nearly 50% of its output in 1959.

Exports soared in the 1960s as Volvo's reputation for durability spread and the highly acclaimed model 144 was launched (1966). Volvo began building production facilities internationally, the first in Belgium (1962).

In 1971, 36-year-old Pehr Gyllenhammar took over as Volvo's CEO. Under his direction the company tried to provide more humane work conditions and opened an experimental plant in Kalmar (1974). Aware that Volvo was too small to compete for long in its global markets, Gyllenhammar diversified and enlarged the company's business.

In 1981 Volvo bought Beijerinvest (energy, industrial products, food, finance, trading; Sweden) and White Motors's truck division (US), and in 1986 formed a North American truck venture with General Motors. A 1984 joint venture agreement with Clark Equipment (US) created the world's 3rd largest construction equipment company. Volvo acquired Leyland Bus (UK) in 1988. Throughout the 1980s Volvo steadily increased its holdings in Pharmacia (drugs, biotechnology; Sweden), Custos (investments, Sweden), and Park Ridge, among others. In 1990 the company consolidated its food and drug units with state-controlled holding company Procordia.

In 1990 Volvo was embarrassed by a faked ad in which a truck was shown running over a series of cars, crushing all but a Volvo.

In the largest industrial undertaking in Swedish history, Volvo spent over $2 billion to modernize its plants and develop the 800 series of performance-oriented family sedans, introduced in 1991. In the same year the company and Renault swapped stock and allied their car and truck units.

WHERE

HQ: S-405 08 Göteborg, Sweden
Phone: 011-46-31-59-00-00
Fax: 011-46-31-54-79-59 (Volvo Car Corp.)
US HQ: Volvo North America Corporation, 535 Madison Ave., New York, NY 10022
US Phone: 212-754-3300
US Fax: 212-418-7435

	1990 Sales	
	$ mil.	% of total
Sweden	2,539	17
Other Europe	6,490	44
North America	3,810	26
Other countries	1,926	13
Total	**14,765**	**100**

WHAT

	1990 Sales		1990 Operating Income	
	$ mil.	% of total	$ mil.	% of total
Cars	6,999	47	(152)	(62)
Engines	517	4	12	5
Aerospace	422	3	8	3
Food	803	5	66	27
Trucks	4,277	29	250	101
Buses	697	5	12	5
Other operations	1,050	7	53	21
Adjustments	—	—	(148)	—
Total	**14,765**	**100**	**101**	**100**

Products

Aerospace
- Aircraft engines
- Rocket and aircraft components

Buses
- Leyland Bus
- Steyr Bus
- Volvo

Cars (North American markets)
- 240 Series
- 740 Series
- 940 Series
- Coupe

Marine and industrial engines
- Volvo Penta

Trucks
- Volvo
- WHITEGMC

Major Associated Companies

AB Catena (49.3%, auto dealerships)
AB Custos (24.2%, investments)
Investment AB Cardo (47%, investments)
Park Ridge Corporation (Hertz, 26%)
Procordia AB (42.7%; food, pharmaceuticals)
Protorp Förvaltnings AB (36.2%, investments)
Saga Petroleum AS (20%)

HOW MUCH

Stock prices are for ADRs ADR = 1 share	7-Year Growth	1981	1982	1983	1984	1985	1986	1987	1988	1989	1990
Sales ($ mil.)	2.8%	—	—	12,160	9,689	11,378	12,474	15,965	15,762	14,657	14,765
Net income ($ mil.)	—	—	—	25	174	336	378	568	543	827	(181)
Income as % of sales	—	—	—	0.2%	1.8%	3.0%	3.0%	3.6%	3.4%	5.6%	(1.2%)
Earnings per share ($)	—	—	—	0.33	2.25	4.33	4.87	7.32	7.00	10.65	(2.33)
Stock price – high ($)	—	—	—	—	—	41.75	61.50	68.25	64.25	81.13	74.88
Stock price – low ($)	—	—	—	—	—	24.38	40.50	38.38	46.75	60.75	35.50
Stock price – close ($)	—	—	—	—	—	41.00	50.13	47.25	63.00	72.13	37.25
P/E – high	—	—	—	—	—	10	13	9	9	8	—
P/E – low	—	—	—	—	—	6	8	5	7	6	—
Dividends per share ($)	—	—	—	—	0.62	0.60	1.17	1.46	1.76	2.16	2.56
Book value per share ($)	32.1%	—	—	11.47	10.55	14.96	19.35	27.27	31.17	40.65	80.72

1990 Year-end:
Debt ratio: 15.6%
Return on equity: —
Cash (mil.): $3,121
Current ratio: 1.09
Long-term debt (mil.): $1,159
No. of shares (mil.): 78
Dividends:
- 1990 average yield: 6.9%
- 1990 payout: —

Market value (mil.): $2,891

Stock Price History High/Low 1985–90

KEY COMPETITORS

Avis	Ford	Nissan
BMW	General Motors	Outboard Marine
Brunswick	Honda	PACCAR
Chrysler	Hyundai	Peugeot
Cummins Engine	Isuzu	Saab-Scania
Daewoo	Mazda	Toyota
Daimler-Benz	Mitsubishi	Volkswagen
Fiat	Navistar	Yamaha

YAMAHA CORPORATION

OVERVIEW

Whenever you play a piano, ride a motorcycle, or take a bath, you could be using a product made by Yamaha. Best known for its world-class pianos, Yamaha is the world's #1 manufacturer of musical instruments. It also makes stereo sets, bathtubs, tennis racquets, and microchips. Its affiliate, Yamaha Motor (32% owned), is the world's 2nd largest motorcycle maker (after Honda).

So why would a company that outfits marching bands outfit outboard motors too? For Yamaha it's been a matter of survival. The market for musical instruments is mature, and the company has had to come up with some creative solutions to flattening sales. Yamaha usually builds new businesses with knowledge and technology gained from the old (i.e., the skills acquired in making pianos can be applied to making furniture or kitchen cabinets).

Yamaha operates about 10,000 music schools in Japan through the Yamaha Music Foundation, established by chairman Gen'ichi Kawakami. Three generations of the Kawakami family have managed the company since the 1920s.

WHEN

Torakusu Yamaha, a Japanese watchmaker and medical equipment repairman, tinkered with his first reed organ in 1885. Captivated, he decided to build one, completing it in 1887. He established Yamaha Organ Manufacturing Company in 1889 to manufacture reed organs and, as production intensified, incorporated the company as Nippon Gakki (Japan Musical Instruments) in 1897. Nippon Gakki began producing upright pianos in 1900 and grand pianos in 1902.

In 1920 the company diversified into the production of wooden airplane propellers (based on woodworking skills used in making pianos) and soon had added pipe organs (1932) and guitars (1946) to its line of musical instruments. Gen'ichi Kawakami, whose father had managed the company since 1927, took over in 1950. He moved the company into motorcycle production in 1954, transferring the motorcycle business to Yamaha Motor, a separate but affiliated company, in 1955.

Kawakami established the Yamaha Music School System in 1954. Under his leadership Nippon Gakki became the world's largest producer of musical instruments, developing Japan's first electronic organ, the Electone, in 1959. Kawakami spearheaded the company's move into wind instruments (1965), stereos (1968), and microchips (1971). By 1982 musicians in the Americas, Europe, and Asia could buy Yamaha brand products locally.

Yamaha Motor also diversified, starting with motorboats and outboard motors in 1960. By 1980 the company had added yachts (1965), automobile engines (1966), snowmobiles (1968), golf carts (1975), and all-terrain vehicles (1979). Motorcycle production continued to grow, and in 1982 Yamaha Motor claimed (prematurely) that it would surpass Honda as the world's #1 motorcycle maker. Honda responded with aggressive product introductions and price slashing that sent Yamaha Motor into red ink.

The combination of fiscal woes at Yamaha Motors and a maturing musical instrument market resulted in losses at Nippon Gakki in 1984. The company has remained competitive through clever diversification, particularly into customized chips for CD players. In 1983 the company introduced the revolutionary DX-7 portable keyboard — a powerful synthesizer cheap enough to appeal to a mass market. Under the leadership of Kawakami's son, Hiroshi, Nippon Gakki adopted the name Yamaha Corporation in 1987. The company is now emphasizing exports of electronic instruments (a facility opened in China in 1989) and the mass production of integrated circuits.

HOW MUCH

$=¥135 (Dec. 31, 1990)	9-Year Growth	1981[1]	1982[1]	1983[1]	1984	1985	1986[2]	1987	1988	1989	1990
Sales (¥ bil.)	4.7%	330	346	335	407	426	413	436	467	487	499
Net income (¥ bil.)	(1.3%)	7	6	3	(12)	6	9	11	8	4	6
Income as % of sales	—	2.1%	1.6%	0.9%	(2.8%)	1.3%	2.2%	2.5%	1.8%	0.8%	1.2%
Earnings per share (¥)	(1.4%)	36	29	17	(61)	30	48	56	46	19	32
Stock price – high (¥)	—	736	512	481	1,120	1,719	1,974	1,960	2,460	2,390	2,200
Stock price – low (¥)	—	417	417	408	412	701	949	1,070	1,500	1,630	1,340
Stock price – close (¥)	14.4%	503	426	444	945	1,265	1,357	1,670	1,860	2,080	1,690
P/E – high	—	20	18	29	—	58	41	35	54	124	69
P/E – low	—	11	14	25	—	24	20	19	33	85	42
Dividends per share (¥)	4.3%	6.87	6.87	6.87	6.87	6.87	7.91	8.70	10.00	10.00	10.00
Book value per share (¥)	7.1%	409	431	440	535	558	655	692	734	757	813

1990 Year-end:
Debt ratio: 26.0%
Return on equity: 4.3%
Cash (bil.): ¥74
Long-term debt (mil.): ¥51,246
No. of shares (mil.): 193
Dividends:
1990 average yield: 0.6%
1990 payout: 31.2%
Market value (mil.): $2,410
Sales (mil.): $3,694

Stock Price History High/Low 1981–90

2,500 / 2,000 / 1,500 / 1,000 / 500 / 0

[1] Parent company only [2] 11-month period

Principal exchange: Tokyo
Fiscal year ends: March 31

Hoover's Rating B+

WHO

Chairman: Gen'ichi Kawakami
President: Hiroshi Kawakami
EVP: Seisuke Ueshima
Managing Director: Teruo Hiyoshi
Managing Director: Keiji Kinbara
Managing Director: Tetsuo Koyama
Managing Director: Toshiji Oda
Auditor: Masazumi Miyake
Employees: 12,423

WHERE

HQ: 10-1, Nakazawa-cho, Hamamatsu, Shizuoka Pref. 430, Japan
Phone: 011-81-534-60-2141
Fax: 011-81-534-64-8554
US HQ: Yamaha Corporation of America, 6600 Orangethorpe Ave., Buena Park, CA 90620
US Phone: 714-522-9011
US Fax: 714-670-0108

	1990 Sales % of total
Japan	68
Other countries	32
Total	**100**

WHAT

	1990 Sales ¥ bil.	1990 Sales % of total
Pianos	85	17
Electones	39	8
Digital musical instruments	113	23
Other musical instruments	60	12
Audio products	51	10
Furniture & household products	44	9
Sporting goods	28	6
Metal products & LSIs	34	7
Recreation	23	4
Other	22	4
Total	**499**	**100**

Yamaha Corporation

Major Products and Services

Bathroom fixtures
Car audio equipment
CD players
Computer-related equipment
Decorative doors
Furniture
Hotel and golf course mgmt.
LD players
Music schools
Music scores
Musical instruments
Piano tuning
Records
Semiconductor-related materials
Semiconductors
Sporting goods
Sportswear
Stereo systems
Water heaters

Yamaha Motor

Major Products

Air conditioners
All-terrain vehicles
Boats
Golf carts
Marine and automobile engines
Motorcycles
Snowmobiles

KEY COMPETITORS

BMW
Brunswick
Casio
General Electric
Harley-Davidson
Honda
Hyundai
MacAndrews & Forbes
Matsushita
Mitsubishi
NEC
Nissan
Outboard Marine
Peugeot
Philips
Pioneer
Reebok
Samsung
Sharp
Sony
Suzuki
Tandy
Thomson SA
Toshiba
Volvo
Zenith

The Indexes

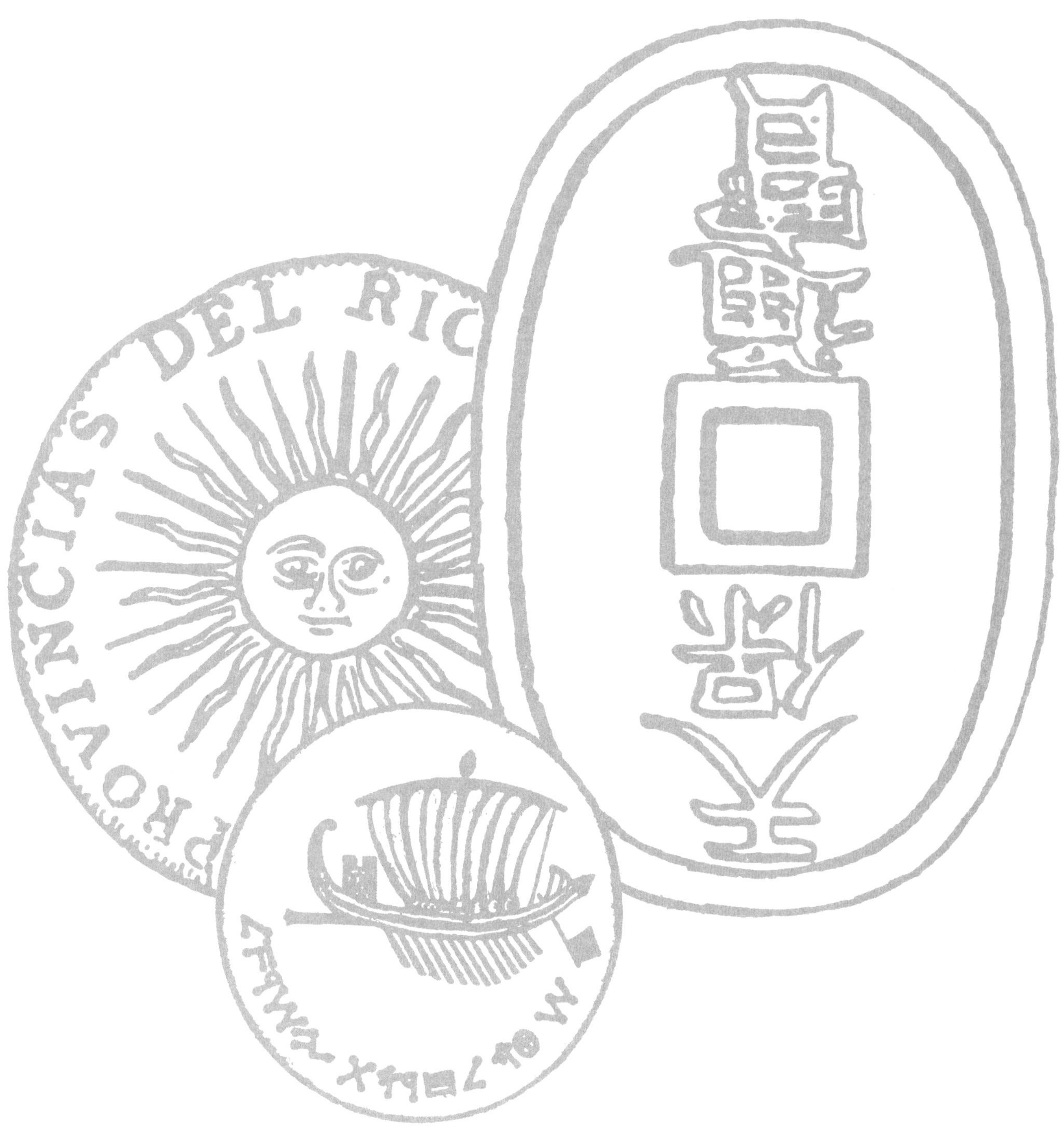

INDEX OF PROFILES BY INDUSTRY

INDEX OF PROFILES BY HEADQUARTERS LOCATION

Note: Page numbers in boldface indicate the company's or country's profile. Lightface page numbers indicate references to other profiles.

A

C

D

E

H

J

K

L

N

O

P

Q

R

S

U

V

W

X

Y

Z

The Economist
Intelligence Unit

From the People Who Brought You The Key Indicators for Countries Profiled in This Book—

The Best is Yet to Come!

In case you didn't notice, we're the source that supplied the statistics for the one-page country profiles you see throughout this book. We're **The Economist Intelligence Unit— EIU** for short.

But there's a whole lot more to know about these countries than latest GNP and trade statistics. The emergence of a single market in Europe, the shift toward a free market system in Eastern Europe, the growing competition from the newly industrialized countries of Asia and the scramble for market shares in the wake of global deregulation are a few of the critical developments shaping today's business climate and corporate strategies. To help you keep pace with these seismic changes, **EIU**, a division of **Business International (BI)**, provides the full range of information you need through our organized system of country reports and forecasts, weekly newsletters, reference services, conferences and custom research and consulting.

What Sets Us Apart

- **Global Reach—**The **EIU/BI** global network spans 75 countries with regional headquarters in London, New York and Hong Kong, and major offices in Frankfurt, Madrid, Melbourne, Mexico City, Paris, Rome, Sao Paulo, Singapore and Tokyo.

- **Corporate Contact—** Our client base consists of over 1,000 of the world's leading companies and banks. We maintain close and frequent contact with CEOs and senior corporate executives, top banking officers and leading government officials worldwide to give us a strong and objective understanding of today's ever-changing operating environment.

- **In-House Resources—** Our staff includes 300 full-time consultants, analysts and researchers, with expertise in all areas of international business, including finance, strategic planning, development, human resources, operations and systems., marketing and specific industries. They are located in virtually every major country of the world and have extensive business and finance libraries and advanced telecommunications and computer technology.

To receive further information about our publications or research and consulting capabilities, please contact the Marketing Department in our New York office at 212-460-0600 (telephone) or 212-995-8837 (fax).

New York
Business International
215 Park Ave. South
New York, NY10003
USA

London
Business International Ltd
40 Duke Street
London W1A 1DW
England

Hong Kong
Business International
10th floor, Luk Kwok Centre
72 Gloucester Road, Wanchai
Hong Kong

A member of The Economist Group

If you find this book useful,
you need

Hoover's Handbook of American Business 1992

Only $24.95

- ★ **500 one-page profiles of America's largest and most influential companies**
  - Over 400 major US public companies
  - Top young growth companies, from Adobe and Amgen to Blockbuster and L.A. Gear
  - Over 50 key private companies, including Cargill, Hallmark, and Mars
  - More than 20 nonprofits, from AFL-CIO to United Way
  - Companies from aerospace to textiles, microchips to shampoo, accounting to oil
- ★ An overview of the business world, with a look at its rapidly changing nature
- ★ Lists of the biggest companies by industry and location
- ★ Our ratings of each company's strength, from A+ to F
- ★ Our pick of the top 10 American companies for the 1990s
- ★ Completely indexed by industry, headquarters location, people, companies, and brand names, with over 11,000 entries

Available November 1991 at your favorite bookstore

or

Call 800-486-8666 to order

or

Use the reader response card in the back of this book.

I want to order the indicated quantities of:

Publications:

Hoover's Handbook of World Business 1992

_______ $21.95 plus $3.00 shipping and handling

Hoover's Handbook of American Business 1992 (available November 1991)

_______ $24.95 plus $3.00 shipping and handling

Hoover's Handbook 1991: Profiles of Over 500 Major Corporations

_______ $19.95 plus $3.00 shipping and handling

Future Editions:

Please enter my standing order for future copies of:

_______ ***Hoover's Handbook of World Business***

_______ ***Hoover's Handbook of American Business***

I understand that I am entitled to a 5% discount on all standing orders and will receive them as soon as they are published. Bill my credit card on shipment. If I am not satisfied, I may return any book received on standing order for a full refund.

Mailing Labels:

_______ Names and US headquarters addresses of companies listed in both *Hoover's Handbooks* (800 total) — $35.00 per set plus $3.00 shipping and handling

Electronic Book:

_______ Sony Data Discman Electronic Book disc version of *Hoover's Handbook* — $39.95 plus $3.00 shipping and handling (available November 1991)

❑ Send me information about future *Hoover's Handbooks*.

❑ I have the following suggestions for future editions:

❑ I bought *Hoover's Handbook* at _______

Name _______ Telephone No. (_______) _______

Affiliation _______ Title _______

Street Address _______

City _______ State _______ Zip _______

❑ MasterCard ❑ Visa ❑ American Express Account No. _______

Signature _______ Expiration Date _______

To order call 800-486-8666 or fax us at: 512-454-9401

The Reference Press, Inc. • 6448 Hwy. 290 East, Suite E-104, Austin, Texas 78723 • 512-454-7778

I want to order the indicated quantities of:

Publications:

Hoover's Handbook of World Business 1992

_______ $21.95 plus $3.00 shipping and handling

Hoover's Handbook of American Business 1992 (available November 1991)

_______ $24.95 plus $3.00 shipping and handling

Hoover's Handbook 1991: Profiles of Over 500 Major Corporations

_______ $19.95 plus $3.00 shipping and handling

Future Editions:

Please enter my standing order for future copies of:

_______ ***Hoover's Handbook of World Business***

_______ ***Hoover's Handbook of American Business***

I understand that I am entitled to a 5% discount on all standing orders and will receive them as soon as they are published. Bill my credit card on shipment. If I am not satisfied, I may return any book received on standing order for a full refund.

Mailing Labels:

_______ Names and US headquarters addresses of companies listed in both *Hoover's Handbooks* (800 total) — $35.00 per set plus $3.00 shipping and handling

Electronic Book:

_______ Sony Data Discman Electronic Book disc version of *Hoover's Handbook* — $39.95 plus $3.00 shipping and handling (available November 1991)

❑ Send me information about future *Hoover's Handbooks*.

❑ I have the following suggestions for future editions:

❑ I bought *Hoover's Handbook* at _______

Name _______ Telephone No. (_______) _______

Affiliation _______ Title _______

Street Address _______

City _______ State _______ Zip _______

❑ MasterCard ❑ Visa ❑ American Express Account No. _______

Signature _______ Expiration Date _______

To order call 800-486-8666 or fax us at: 512-454-9401

The Reference Press, Inc. • 6448 Hwy. 290 East, Suite E-104, Austin, Texas 78723 • 512-454-7778

Please tape this edge before mailing.

BUSINESS REPLY MAIL

FIRST-CLASS MAIL PERMIT NO. 7641 AUSTIN, TEXAS

POSTAGE WILL BE PAID BY ADDRESSEE

THE REFERENCE PRESS INC
6448 HWY 290 E STE E 104
AUSTIN TX 78723-9828

Please tape this edge before mailing.

BUSINESS REPLY MAIL

FIRST-CLASS MAIL PERMIT NO. 7641 AUSTIN, TEXAS

POSTAGE WILL BE PAID BY ADDRESSEE

THE REFERENCE PRESS INC
6448 HWY 290 E STE E 104
AUSTIN TX 78723-9828

I want to order the indicated quantities of:

Publications:

Hoover's Handbook of World Business 1992
_______ $21.95 plus $3.00 shipping and handling

Hoover's Handbook of American Business 1992 (available November 1991)
_______ $24.95 plus $3.00 shipping and handling

Hoover's Handbook 1991: Profiles of Over 500 Major Corporations
_______ $19.95 plus $3.00 shipping and handling

Future Editions:

Please enter my standing order for future copies of:
_______ ***Hoover's Handbook of World Business***
_______ ***Hoover's Handbook of American Business***

I understand that I am entitled to a 5% discount on all standing orders and will receive them as soon as they are published. Bill my credit card on shipment. If I am not satisfied, I may return any book received on standing order for a full refund.

Mailing Labels:

_______ Names and US headquarters addresses of companies listed in both *Hoover's Handbooks* (800 total) — $35.00 per set plus $3.00 shipping and handling

Electronic Book:

_______ Sony Data Discman Electronic Book disc version of *Hoover's Handbook* — $39.95 plus $3.00 shipping and handling (available November 1991)

❑ Send me information about future *Hoover's Handbooks*.

❑ I have the following suggestions for future editions:

❑ I bought *Hoover's Handbook* at _______

Name _______ Telephone No. (_______) _______

Affiliation _______ Title _______

Street Address _______

City _______ State _______ Zip _______

❑ MasterCard ❑ Visa ❑ American Express Account No. _______

Signature _______ Expiration Date _______

To order call 800-486-8666 or fax us at: 512-454-9401

The Reference Press, Inc. • 6448 Hwy. 290 East, Suite E-104, Austin, Texas 78723 • 512-454-7778

I want to order the indicated quantities of:

Publications:

Hoover's Handbook of World Business 1992
_______ $21.95 plus $3.00 shipping and handling

Hoover's Handbook of American Business 1992 (available November 1991)
_______ $24.95 plus $3.00 shipping and handling

Hoover's Handbook 1991: Profiles of Over 500 Major Corporations
_______ $19.95 plus $3.00 shipping and handling

Future Editions:

Please enter my standing order for future copies of:
_______ ***Hoover's Handbook of World Business***
_______ ***Hoover's Handbook of American Business***

I understand that I am entitled to a 5% discount on all standing orders and will receive them as soon as they are published. Bill my credit card on shipment. If I am not satisfied, I may return any book received on standing order for a full refund.

Mailing Labels:

_______ Names and US headquarters addresses of companies listed in both *Hoover's Handbooks* (800 total) — $35.00 per set plus $3.00 shipping and handling

Electronic Book:

_______ Sony Data Discman Electronic Book disc version of *Hoover's Handbook* — $39.95 plus $3.00 shipping and handling (available November 1991)

❑ Send me information about future *Hoover's Handbooks*.

❑ I have the following suggestions for future editions:

❑ I bought *Hoover's Handbook* at _______

Name _______ Telephone No. (_______) _______

Affiliation _______ Title _______

Street Address _______

City _______ State _______ Zip _______

❑ MasterCard ❑ Visa ❑ American Express Account No. _______

Signature _______ Expiration Date _______

To order call 800-486-8666 or fax us at: 512-454-9401

The Reference Press, Inc. • 6448 Hwy. 290 East, Suite E-104, Austin, Texas 78723 • 512-454-7778

Please tape this edge before mailing.

NO POSTAGE
NECESSARY
IF MAILED
IN THE
UNITED STATES

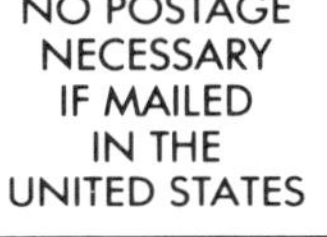

BUSINESS REPLY MAIL

FIRST-CLASS MAIL PERMIT NO. 7641 AUSTIN, TEXAS

POSTAGE WILL BE PAID BY ADDRESSEE

THE REFERENCE PRESS INC
6448 HWY 290 E STE E 104
AUSTIN TX 78723-9828

Please tape this edge before mailing.

NO POSTAGE
NECESSARY
IF MAILED
IN THE
UNITED STATES

BUSINESS REPLY MAIL

FIRST-CLASS MAIL PERMIT NO. 7641 AUSTIN, TEXAS

POSTAGE WILL BE PAID BY ADDRESSEE

THE REFERENCE PRESS INC
6448 HWY 290 E STE E 104
AUSTIN TX 78723-9828